THE AMERICAN FAMILY

REFLECTING A CHANGING NATION

ISSN 1534-164X

THE AMERICAN FAMILY

REFLECTING A CHANGING NATION

Cynthia Becker

INFORMATION PLUS® REFERENCE SERIES
Formerly published by Information Plus, Wylie, Texas

GALE®

THOMSON

GALE

Detroit • New York • San Diego • San Francisco • Cleveland • New Haven, Conn. • Waterville, Maine • London • Munich

The American Family: Reflecting a Changing Nation

Cynthia Becker

Project Editors
Kathleen J. Edgar and Ellice Engdahl

Editorial
Paula Cutcher-Jackson, Dana Ferguson, Debra Kirby, Prindle LaBarge, Charles B. Montney, Heather Price

Permissions
Debra Freitas

Product Design
Cynthia Baldwin

Composition and Electronic Prepress
Evi Seoud

Manufacturing
Keith Helmling

LIBRARY OF CONGRESS CATALOGING-IN-PUBLICATION DATA

ISBN 0-7876-5103-6 (set)
ISBN 0-7876-6068-X
ISSN 1534-164X

Printed in the United States of America
10 9 8 7 6 5 4 3 2 1

TABLE OF CONTENTS

Drawing a general profile of the American family is a daunting task, especially given the wide variety of living arrangements in the United States. But this chapter does just that by tracing trends in the number of births, divorces, and married-couple, single-parent, and same-sex households.

The shape of the American family has been drastically altered by three significant trends: a declining fertility rate; an increase in the number of births among young, unmarried women; and a growing desire by women—especially working women—to put off having children until later in life. These and other trends, such as the changing family roles of men and women, are discussed here.

This chapter presents an overview of the U.S. child population. Some of the topics discussed include trends in the age, racial, and ethnic composition of America's children; different types of living arrangements, such as one- and two-parent households and grandparent-maintained families; adoption and foster care; and the numerous challenges posed by child care, including cost and availability.

American children face a lot of challenges today. This chapter explores some of those challenges, including poverty, lack of health insurance, teen sexuality, pregnancy, substance abuse, divorce, and school violence.

This chapter analyzes the issues of employment, income, and poverty, as they pertain to the American family. Some of the topics explored here include the increasing number of wives and mothers in the work force; the wage gap between men and women; trends in U.S. household income; and the disturbing rise in the number of homeless families.

The American family has undergone numerous changes since the 1950s. Many of these changes are discussed here, including the "suburban flight" that began in the late 1940s and continues today; the increasing racial and ethnic diversity of the suburbs; and single-parent and same-sex adoptions.

Using results from various polls, this chapter analyzes Americans' feelings on a variety of family-related issues, including strengthening the family, moral values, work demands, economic and financial pressures, religion, and family-life and technology.

PREFACE

The American Family: Reflecting a Changing Nation is the latest volume in the ever-growing *Information Plus Reference Series*. Previously published by the Information Plus Company of Wylie, Texas, the *Information Plus Reference Series* (and its companion set, the *Information Plus Compact Series*) became a Gale Group product when Gale and Information Plus merged in early 2000. Those of you familiar with the series as published by Information Plus will notice a few changes. Gale has adopted a new layout and style that we hope you will find easy to use. Other improvements include greatly expanded indexes in each book, and more descriptive tables of contents.

While some changes have been made to the design, the purpose of the *Information Plus Reference Series* remains the same. Each volume of the series presents the latest facts on a topic of pressing concern in modern American life. These topics include today's most controversial and most studied social issues: abortion, capital punishment, care for the elderly, crime, family issues, health care, the environment, immigration, minorities, social welfare, women, youth, and many more. Although written especially for the high school and undergraduate student, this series is an excellent resource for anyone in need of factual information on current affairs.

By presenting the facts, it is Gale's intention to provide its readers with everything they need to reach an informed opinion on current issues. To that end, there is a particular emphasis in this series on the presentation of scientific studies, surveys, and statistics. These data are generally presented in the form of tables, charts, and other graphics placed within the text of each book. Every graphic is directly referred to and carefully explained in the text. The source of each graphic is presented within the graphic itself. The data used in these graphics are drawn from the most reputable and reliable sources, in particular from the various branches of the U.S. government and from major independent polling organizations.

Every effort was made to secure the most recent information available. The reader should bear in mind that many major studies take years to conduct, and that additional years often pass before the data from these studies are made available to the public. Therefore, in many cases the most recent information available in 2003 dated from 2000 or 2001. Older statistics are sometimes presented as well, if they are of particular interest and no more-recent information exists.

Although statistics are a major focus of the *Information Plus Reference Series* they are by no means its only content. Each book also presents the widely held positions and important ideas that shape how the book's subject is discussed in the United States. These positions are explained in detail and, where possible, in the words of those who support them. Some of the other material to be found in these books includes: historical background; descriptions of major events related to the subject; relevant laws and court cases; and examples of how these issues play out in American life. Some books also feature primary documents, or have pro and con debate sections giving the words and opinions of prominent Americans on both sides of a controversial topic. All material is presented in an even-handed and unbiased manner; the reader will never be encouraged to accept one view of an issue over another.

HOW TO USE THIS BOOK

Throughout history, the family has been seen as the basic social and economic unit of American life. Most people would agree that it continues to hold this status today. However, exactly what constitutes a family changed dramatically over the last half of the twentieth century. Some people believe that these changes have been for the worse, and conflict has arisen about different people's opinions concerning what makes a "good" family. This book presents the latest information available on

America's families. Trends in American family size and structure are explored, and their effects examined. The significant racial and ethnic differences in family structure are also presented. Many theories explain these trends and differences; some of the most widely accepted are discussed. This includes coverage of such controversial topics as unwed mothers, same-sex couples, the roles of fathers and mothers in child care, and other issues.

The American Family: Reflecting a Changing Nation consists of seven chapters and three appendices. Each chapter covers a major issue related to families in the United States; for a summary of the information covered in each chapter, please see the synopses provided in the Table of Contents at the front of the book. Chapters generally begin with an overview of the basic facts and background information on the chapter's topic, then proceed to examine sub-topics of particular interest. For example, Chapter 2: Women, Men, and the Family begins by listing some of the major changes that occurred since the 1950s in the roles that men and women play in family life. It then moves on to examine these changes in detail, starting with the decline in the overall fertility rate and changes concerning the age women were most likely to have children. Differences between the fertility rates of women of varying races and ethnicities are discussed. Moving on, the chapter examines the increasing number of women who work outside the home, and the impact this has had on families. Next comes a discussion of the roles women have played as caregivers, and how these roles have changed in recent years. This is followed by a similar examination of the care-giving roles of men and the future of fatherhood. The chapter concludes with sections on never-married men and women, and domestic violence in the United States. Special coverage is given to artificial reproduction and the issues associated with it. Readers can find their way through a chapter by looking for the section and sub-section headings, which are clearly set off from the text. Or, they can refer to the book's extensive index, if they already know what they are looking for.

Statistical Information

The tables and figures featured throughout *The American Family: Reflecting a Changing Nation* will be of particular use to the reader in learning about this topic. These tables and figures represent an extensive collection of the most recent and valuable statistics on American families—for example the graphics in this book cover: the number of married couples in America, the poverty rate of various types of families, the number of multigenerational households in the United States, and the opinions of Americans on families as key to the future. Gale believes that making this information available to the reader is the most important way in which we fulfill the goal of this book: to help readers understand the topic of family life in America and reach their own conclusions about controversial issues related to it.

Each table or figure has a unique identifier appearing above it, for ease of identification and reference. Titles for the tables and figures explain their purpose. At the end of each table or figure, the original source of the data is provided.

In order to help readers understand these often complicated statistics, all tables and figures are explained in the text. References in the text direct the reader to the relevant statistics. Furthermore, the contents of all tables and figures are fully indexed. Please see the opening section of the index at the back of this volume for a description of how to find tables and figures within it.

In addition to the main body text and images, *The American Family: Reflecting a Changing Nation* has three appendices. The first is the Important Names and Addresses directory. Here the reader will find contact information for a number of government and private organizations that can provide further information on aspects of families. The second appendix is the Resources section, which can also assist the reader in conducting his or her own research. In this section, the author and editors of *The American Family: Reflecting a Changing Nation* describe some of the sources that were most useful during the compilation of this book. The final appendix is the index. It has been greatly expanded from previous editions, and should make it even easier to find specific topics in this book.

ADVISORY BOARD CONTRIBUTIONS

The staff of Information Plus would like to extend their heartfelt appreciation to the Information Plus Advisory Board. This dedicated group of media professionals provides feedback on the series on an ongoing basis. Their comments allow the editorial staff who work on the project to make the series better and more user-friendly. Our top priorities are to produce the highest-quality and most useful books possible, and the Advisory Board's contributions to this process are invaluable.

The members of the Information Plus Advisory Board are:

- Kathleen R. Bonn, Librarian, Newbury Park High School, Newbury Park, California
- Madelyn Garner, Librarian, San Jacinto College—North Campus, Houston, Texas
- Anne Oxenrider, Media Specialist, Dundee High School, Dundee, Michigan
- Charles R. Rodgers, Director of Libraries, Pasco-Hernando Community College, Dade City, Florida
- James N. Zitzelsberger, Library Media Department Chairman, Oshkosh West High School, Oshkosh, Wisconsin

COMMENTS AND SUGGESTIONS

The editors of the *Information Plus Reference Series* welcome your feedback on *The American Family: Reflecting a Changing Nation*. Please direct all correspondence to:

Editors
Information Plus Reference Series
27500 Drake Rd.
Farmington Hills, MI, 48331-3535

ACKNOWLEDGMENTS

The editors wish to thank the copyright holders of material included in this volume and the permissions managers of many book and magazine publishing companies for assisting us in securing reproduction rights. We are also grateful to the staffs of the Detroit Public Library, the Library of Congress, the University of Detroit Mercy Library, Wayne State University Purdy/Kresge Library Complex, and the University of Michigan Libraries for making their resources available to us.

Following is a list of the copyright holders who have granted us permission to reproduce material in The American Family: Reflecting a Changing Nation. *Every effort has been made to trace copyright, but if omissions have been made, please let us know.*

For more detailed source citations, please see the sources listed under each individual table and figure.

Alabama Center for Health Statistics: Table 1.8

American Bar Association. Reprinted by permission. All rights reserved.: Figure 4.21

American Council on Education and University of California at Los Angeles Higher Education Research Institute. Reprinted by permission.: Table 7.14

Annie E. Casey Foundation. Reprinted by permission.: Table 6.2

Centers for Disease Control and Prevention: Figure 1.6, Table 4.2

Child Trends DataBank. Reprinted by permission.: Figure 3.12, Figure 3.13, Table 3.14, Figure 4.4, Figure 4.5, Figure 4.6, Table 4.4

Children's Defense Fund. Reprinted by permission.: Table 3.1

Compensation and Working Conditions Online, Bureau of Labor Statistics: Table 3.15

Current Population Reports, U.S. Census Bureau: Figure 1.5, Figure 1.7, Table 1.5, Table 1.6, Table 1.9, Figure 2.13, Figure 2.14, Figure 2.15, Figure 2.16, Figure 2.17, Table 2.4, Figure 3.1, Figure 3.2, Figure 3.3, Table 3.4, Figure 4.1, Figure 4.2, Figure 4.3, Table 4.1, Figure 5.3, Figure 5.4, Figure 5.5, Figure 5.6, Figure 5.7, Figure 5.8, Figure 5.9, Figure 5.10, Figure 5.11, Figure 5.12, Figure 5.13, Table 5.2, Table 5.3, Table 5.4, Table 5.5, Table 5.6, Table 5.7, Figure 6.2, Figure 6.3, Figure 6.4, Figure 6.5, Figure 6.6, Figure 6.7, Table 6.1, Table 6.3, Table 6.4, Table 6.5

National PTA. Reprinted by permission.: Figure 7.6, Figure 7.7, Figure 7.8, Figure 7.9

National Vital Statistics Reports, Centers for Disease Control and Prevention: Figure 1.4, Figure 1.8, Figure 1.9, Table 1.4, Figure 2.1, Figure 2.2, Figure 2.3, Figure 2.4, Figure 2.5, Figure 2.6, Figure 2.7, Figure 2.8, Figure 2.9, Table 2.1, Table 2.2, Figure 4.7, Table 4.3

Pew Internet & American Life Project. Reprinted by permission.: Figure 7.12, Table 7.7, Table 7.8, Table 7.9, Table 7.10, Table 7.11, Table 7.12, Table 7.13

Pew Research Center for the People and the Press. Reprinted by permission.: Table 4.5, Table 4.6, Figure 7.10, Table 7.2, Table 7.3, Table 7.4, Table 7.15

Urban Institute, Justice Policy Center. Reprinted by permission.: Figure 4.16, Figure 4.17, Figure 4.18, Figure 4.19, Figure 4.20, Table 4.7

U.S. Census Bureau: Figure 1.1, Figure 1.2, Figure 1.3, Figure 1.10, Figure 1.11, Table 1.1, Table 1.2, Table 1.3, Table 1.7, Table 1.10, Table 2.3, Table 3.2, Table 3.3, Figure 5.1, Figure 5.2, Figure 5.14, Figure 5.15, Figure 5.16, Figure 5.17, Figure 5.18, Figure 5.19, Figure 5.20, Figure 5.21, Figure 5.22, Figure 5.23, Table 5.8, Table 5.9, Table 5.10, Table 5.11, Table 5.12, Table 5.13, Table 5.14, Figure 6.1, Figure 6.8, Figure 6.9, Table 6.6, Table 6.7, Table 6.8

U.S. Department of Agriculture, Center for Nutrition Policy and Promotion: Table 3.16, Table 3.17, Table 3.18

U.S. Department of Education, National Center for Education Statistics, and U.S. Department of Justice, Bureau of Justice Statistics: Figure 4.9, Figure 4.10, Figure 4.11, Figure 4.12, Figure 4.13, Figure 4.14, Figure 4.15, Figure 7.11

U.S. Department of Health and Human Services, Administration for Children and Families, Administration on Children, Youth, and Families, Children's Bureau: Figure 3.4, Figure 3.5, Figure 3.6, Figure 3.7, Figure 3.8, Figure 3.9, Figure 3.10, Figure 3.11, Table 3.6, Table 3.7, Table 3.8, Table 3.9, Table 3.10, Table 3.11, Table 3.12, Table 3.13

U.S. Department of Health and Human Services, Maternal and Child Health Bureau: Figure 4.8

U.S. Department of Health and Human Services/University of Michigan: Table 7.5, Table 7.6

U.S. Department of Labor, Bureau of Labor Statistics: Figure 2.10, Figure 2.11, Figure 2.12

U.S. Department of Labor, Women's Bureau: Table 5.1

U.S. Department of State: Table 3.5

Wirthlin Worldwide. Reprinted by permission.: Figure 7.1, Figure 7.2, Figure 7.3, Figure 7.4, Figure 7.5, Table 7.1

CHAPTER 1
AMERICA'S FAMILIES

In virtually all cultures, the family is considered the basic societal unit. Because the U.S. Census Bureau provides the most comprehensive statistics available on families in America, this book uses its terms and definitions as they concern the American family.

To understand the Census Bureau's definition of the family, one must first understand its terminology describing the wide variety of living arrangements in the United States. In gathering its statistics, the Census Bureau starts with the American household—a single housing unit occupied by a person or group of people. Group quarters, such as correctional institutions and nursing homes, are not counted as households.

The "householder" is the person in whose name the housing unit is owned, being purchased, or rented. A "family household" consists of a householder and one or more people who are related to the householder by birth, marriage, or adoption. A "nonfamily household" consists of a person living alone or living only with nonrelatives, such as boarders or roommates.

Family households are further divided into the traditional family maintained by a "married couple" and "other families" maintained by a male or female householder with no spouse present. These might include a single parent living with a child or children, siblings sharing a home, and any combination of relatives other than the householder's spouse.

POPULATION

In Census 2000, 281.4 million people were counted in the United States, a 13.2 percent increase from the 1990 census. This population growth of 32.7 million people between 1990 and 2000 represented the largest census-to-census increase in American history. The previous record increase was 28 million between 1950 and 1960, a gain fueled primarily by the post-World War II baby boom

FIGURE 1.1

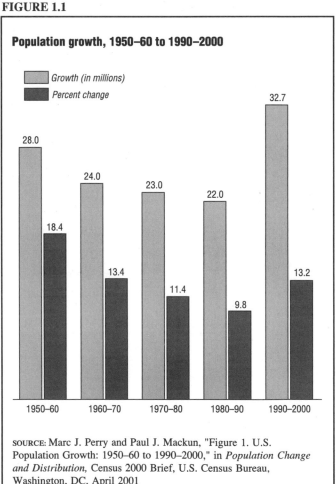

Population growth, 1950–60 to 1990–2000

SOURCE: Marc J. Perry and Paul J. Mackun, "Figure 1. U.S. Population Growth: 1950–60 to 1990–2000," in *Population Change and Distribution*, Census 2000 Brief, U.S. Census Bureau, Washington, DC, April 2001

(1946 to 1964). Total decennial population growth declined steadily in the three decades following the 1950s peak before rising again in the 1990s. (See Figure 1.1.)

HOUSEHOLDS

Census 2000 counted 104.7 million households in the United States. About 72 million were family households

TABLE 1.1

Households by type and selected characteristics, March 2000

(In thousands, except average size)

Characteristic	All households	Family households				Nonfamily households		
		Total	Married couple	Other families		Total	Male householder	Female householder
				Male householder	Female householder			
All households	104,705	72,025	55,311	4,028	12,687	32,680	14,641	18,039
Age of householder								
15 to 24 years old	5,860	3,353	1,450	560	1,342	2,507	1,286	1,221
25 to 34 years old	18,627	13,007	9,390	886	2,732	5,620	3,448	2,172
35 to 44 years old	23,955	18,706	14,104	1,102	3,499	5,250	3,261	1,989
45 to 54 years old	20,927	15,803	12,792	713	2,299	5,123	2,583	2,541
55 to 64 years old	13,592	9,569	8,138	351	1,080	4,023	1,533	2,490
65 years old and over	21,744	11,587	9,437	416	1,735	10,157	2,530	7,626
Race and ethnicity of householder								
White	87,671	60,251	48,790	3,081	8,380	27,420	12,204	15,215
Non-Hispanic	78,819	53,066	43,865	2,468	6,732	25,753	11,278	14,475
Black	12,849	8,664	4,144	706	3,814	4,185	1,876	2,309
Asian and Pacific Islander	3,337	2,506	1,996	179	331	831	432	399
Hispanic (of any race)	9,319	7,561	5,133	658	1,769	1,758	974	783
Presence of related children under 18								
No related children	67,350	34,670	28,919	1,826	3,924	32,680	14,641	18,039
With related children	37,355	37,355	26,392	2,202	8,762	(X)	(X)	(X)
One related child under 18	15,493	15,493	9,897	1,321	4,275	(X)	(X)	(X)
Two related children under 18	14,020	14,020	10,567	644	2,809	(X)	(X)	(X)
Three related children under 18	5,510	5,510	4,238	185	1,087	(X)	(X)	(X)
Four or more related children under 18	2,332	2,332	1,690	52	591	(X)	(X)	(X)
Presence of own children under 18								
No own children	70,100	37,420	30,062	2,242	5,116	32,680	14,641	18,039
With own children	34,605	34,605	25,248	1,786	7,571	(X)	(X)	(X)
With own children under 1	2,939	2,939	2,264	174	501	(X)	(X)	(X)
With own children under 3	8,786	8,786	6,784	441	1,561	(X)	(X)	(X)
With own children under 6	14,986	14,986	11,393	706	2,887	(X)	(X)	(X)
With own children under 12	25,885	25,885	19,082	1,235	5,568	(X)	(X)	(X)
Size of households								
1 person	26,724	(X)	(X)	(X)	(X)	26,724	11,181	15,543
2 people	34,666	29,834	22,899	1,730	5,206	4,832	2,607	2,225
3 people	17,152	16,405	11,213	1,106	4,086	746	570	177
4 people	15,309	15,064	12,455	682	1,927	245	179	66
5 people	6,981	6,894	5,723	307	864	87	70	17
6 people	2,445	2,413	1,916	130	366	32	26	6
7 or more	1,428	1,415	1,105	73	237	13	8	5
Average size	2.62	3.24	3.26	3.16	3.17	1.25	1.34	1.17

X Not applicable.

Note: Data are not shown separately for the American Indian and Alaska Native population because of the small sample size in the Current Population Survey in March 2000.

SOURCE: Jason Fields and Lynne M. Casper, "Table 1. Households by Type and Selected Characteristics: March 2000," in *America's Families and Living Arrangements: March 2000,* Current Population Reports, U.S. Census Bureau, Washington, DC, June 2001

and 32.6 million were nonfamily households. (See Table 1.1.) Family households have traditionally accounted for the majority of all households. However, nonfamily households are becoming increasingly more common. In 1940, the 31.5 million family households represented 90 percent of the total of 34.9 million households. By 1970 the number of households had nearly doubled to 63.4 million, but only 80 percent, or 51.5 million, were family households. By 2000, families made up barely 69 percent of all households. (See Table 1.2.)

The most noticeable trend since the 1970s is the decline in the traditional family—a married couple with children. The proportion of married-couple-with-own-children households decreased from 40.3 percent of all households in 1970 to 24.1 percent in 2000. Married couples without children remained relatively stable at 30.3 percent of all households in 1970 and 28.7 percent in 2000. Other families, those in which the householder has relatives or children but no spouse present, increased from 10.6 percent of all households in 1970 to 16 percent in 2000. (See Figure 1.2.)

Family Structure Changing

The structure of the American family has continued to evolve since World War II. The uncertainty of the war drove many young couples to rush into marriage. At the war's end, returning soldiers married in record numbers and promptly began families. The "American Dream" became the security of a family in which the father earned a good living and the mother kept house and lovingly cared for the children. Couples generally started families immediately, and women bore more children and spaced

TABLE 1.2

Households by type, 1940–2000

(Numbers in thousands)

| Year | Total households | Family households | | | | Nonfamily households | | |
| | | Total | Married couples | Other family | | Total | Other family | |
				Male householder	Female householder		Male householder	Female householder
2000	104,705	72,025	55,311	4,028	2,687	32,680	14,641	18,039
1999	103,874	71,535	54,770	3,976	12,789	32,339	14,368	17,971
1998	102,528	70,880	54,317	3,911	12,652	31,648	14,133	17,516
1997	101,018	70,241	53,604	3,847	12,790	30,777	13,707	17,070
1996	99,627	69,594	53,567	3,513	12,514	30,033	13,348	16,685
1995	98,990	69,305	53,858	3,226	12,220	29,686	13,190	16,496
1994	97,107	68,490	53,171	2,913	12,406	28,617	12,462	16,155
1993[1]	96,426	68,216	53,090	3,065	12,061	28,210	12,297	15,914
1993	96,391	68,144	53,171	3,026	11,947	28,247	12,254	15,993
1992	95,669	67,173	52,457	3,025	11,692	28,496	12,428	16,068
1991	94,312	66,322	52,147	2,907	11,268	27,990	12,150	15,840
1990	93,347	66,090	52,317	2,884	10,890	27,257	11,606	15,651
1989	92,830	65,837	52,100	2,847	10,890	26,994	11,874	15,120
1988[2]	91,124	65,204	51,675	2,834	10,696	25,919	11,282	14,637
1988	91,066	65,133	51,809	2,715	10,608	25,933	11,310	14,624
1987	89,479	64,491	51,537	2,510	10,445	24,988	10,652	14,336
1986	88,458	63,558	50,933	2,414	10,211	24,900	10,648	14,252
1985	86,789	62,706	50,350	2,228	10,129	24,082	10,114	13,968
1984[3]	85,290	62,015	50,081	2,038	9,896	23,276	9,689	13,587
1984	85,407	61,997	50,090	2,030	9,878	23,410	9,752	13,658
1983	83,918	61,393	49,908	2,016	9,469	22,525	9,514	13,011
1982	83,527	61,019	49,630	1,986	9,403	22,508	9,457	13,051
1981	82,368	60,309	49,294	1,933	9,082	22,059	9,279	12,780
1980[4]	80,776	59,550	49,112	1,733	8,705	21,226	8,807	12,419
1980	79,108	58,426	48,180	1,706	8,540	20,682	8,594	12,088
1979	77,330	57,498	47,662	1,616	8,220	19,831	8,064	11,767
1978	76,030	56,958	47,357	1,564	8,037	19,071	7,811	11,261
1977	74,142	56,472	47,471	1,461	7,540	17,669	6,971	10,698
1976	72,867	56,056	47,297	1,424	7,335	16,811	6,548	10,263
1975	71,120	55,563	46,951	1,485	7,127	15,557	5,912	9,645
1974	69,859	54,917	46,787	1,421	6,709	14,942	5,654	9,288
1973	68,251	54,264	46,297	1,432	6,535	13,986	5,129	8,858
1972	66,676	53,163	45,724	1,331	6,108	13,513	4,839	8,674
1971	64,778	52,102	44,928	1,254	5,920	12,676	4,403	8,273
1970	63,401	51,456	44,728	1,228	5,500	11,945	4,063	7,882
1969	62,214	50,729	44,086	1,221	5,422	11,485	3,890	7,595
1968	60,813	50,012	43,507	1,195	5,310	10,801	3,658	7,143
1967	59,236	49,086	42,743	1,190	5,153	10,150	3,419	6,731
1966	58,406	48,399	42,263	1,163	4,973	10,007	3,299	6,708
1965	57,436	47,838	41,689	1,167	4,982	9,598	3,277	6,321
1964	56,149	47,381	41,341	1,204	4,836	8,768	2,965	5,803
1963	55,270	46,872	40,888	1,295	4,689	8,398	2,838	5,560
1962	54,764	46,262	40,404	1,268	4,590	8,502	2,932	5,570
1961	53,557	45,383	39,620	1,199	4,564	8,174	2,779	5,395
1960	52,799	44,905	39,254	1,228	4,422	7,895	2,716	5,179
1959	51,435	43,971	38,410	1,285	4,276	7,464	2,449	5,015
1958	50,474	43,426	37,911	1,278	4,237	7,047	2,329	4,718
1957	49,673	43,262	37,718	1,241	4,304	6,411	2,038	4,374
1956	48,902	42,593	37,047	1,408	4,138	6,309	2,058	4,250
1955	47,874	41,732	36,251	1,328	4,153	6,142	2,059	4,083
1954	46,962	40,998	35,926	1,315	3,757	5,964	1,925	4,039
1953	46,385	40,540	35,577	1,206	3,757	5,845	1,902	3,943
1952	45,538	40,235	35,164	1,119	3,952	5,303	1,757	3,546
1951	44,673	39,502	34,391	1,154	3,957	5,171	1,732	3,439
1950	43,554	38,838	34,075	1,169	3,594	4,716	1,668	3,048
1949	42,182	38,080	33,257	1,197	3,626	4,102	1,308	2,794
1948	40,532	36,629	31,900	1,020	3,709	3,903	1,198	2,705
1947	39,107	34,964	30,612	1,129	3,223	4,143	1,388	2,755
1940[5]	34,949	31,491	26,571	1,510	3,410	3,458	1,599	1,859

[1]Revised using population controls based on the 1990 census.
[2]Data based on 1988 revised processing.
[3]Incorporates Hispanic-origin population controls.
[4]Revised using population controls based on the 1980 census.
[5]Based on 1940 census.

SOURCE: "Households By Type: 1940–Present," U.S. Census Bureau, Washington, DC, June 2001 [Online] http://www.census.gov/population/socdemo/hh-fam /tabHH-1.txt [accessed December 2, 2002]

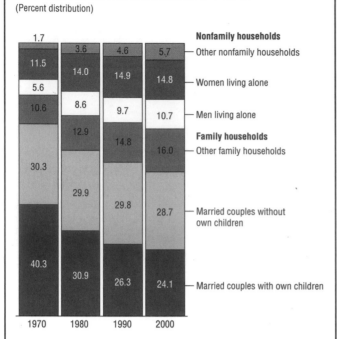

Households by type: selected years, 1970–2000
(Percent distribution)

SOURCE: Jason Fields and Lynne M. Casper, "Figure 1. Households by Type: Selected Years, 1970 to 2000," in *America's Families and Living Arrangements: March 2000,* Current Population Reports, U.S. Census Bureau, Washington, DC, June 2001

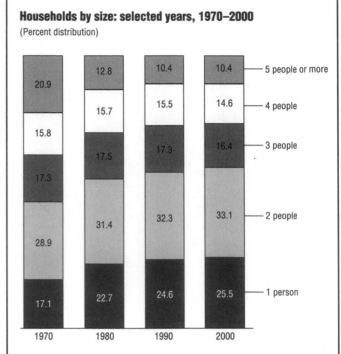

Households by size: selected years, 1970–2000
(Percent distribution)

SOURCE: Jason Fields and Lynne M. Casper, "Figure 2. Households by Size: Selected Years, 1970 to 2000," in *America's Families and Living Arrangements: March 2000,* Current Population Reports, U.S. Census Bureau, Washington, DC, June 2001

them closer together than in previous generations. The 77 million children born during the years 1946–1964, the single largest generation in U.S. history, came to be known as the baby boom generation.

Attitudes toward divorce began to relax as couples who rushed to marry during the war years went their separate ways. Divorces continued to increase in the 1950s and 1960s. The children of these divorced couples experienced new challenges brought on by the breakup of their families. They grew up questioning the value of marriage and launched a sexual revolution in which living together without being married became common. Birth rates slowed as men and women delayed marriage and having children. The number of cohabiting couples continued to grow in the 1970s and 1980s, and young men and women further delayed marriage and having children. Women found careers and put off childbearing even into their 40s. By the 1990s, the definition of "family" broadened to include married couples, cohabiting couples, same-sex couples, and single persons, any of whom might have children of their own, as well as stepchildren and adopted children. Once considered odd or eccentric, people who chose to live alone became more common.

Nonfamily Households

As traditional families declined, nonfamily households increased. The majority of this growth was due to more people living alone. In 1970, persons living alone represented 17.1 percent of all households. In 2000, single persons accounted for 25.5 percent of households. Women represented 67 percent of one-person households in 1970, but by 2000 only 58 percent of one-person householders were female. Householders who live with nonrelatives make up the other growing nonfamily household type. In 1970, they accounted for 1.7 percent of all households, but by 2000 they represented 5.7 percent. (See Figure 1.2.)

HOUSEHOLD SIZE

Households have decreased in size. Between 1970 and 2000, households with five or more people decreased from 20.9 percent to 10.4 percent of all households. As the number of people per household declined, one- and two-person households increased from 46 percent in 1970 to 58.6 percent in 2000. (See Figure 1.3.) The average number of people per household declined from 3.14 in 1970 to 2.62 in 2000. (See Table 1.3.)

Women Having Fewer Children

Changes in rates of fertility, marriage, divorce, and mortality have all contributed to declines in the size of American households. The number of women of childbearing age increased substantially from the mid-1960s until the early 1980s as the baby boom generation matured.

TABLE 1.3

Households by size: 1960 to present

(Numbers in thousands)

Year	All households	One person	Two persons	Three persons	Four persons	Five persons	Six persons	Seven or more persons	Persons per household
2000	104,705	26,724	34,666	17,172	15,309	6,981	2,115	1,131	2.02
1999	103,874	26,606	34,262	17,386	15,030	6,962	2,367	1,261	2.61
1998	102,528	26,327	32,965	17,331	15,358	7,048	2,232	1,267	2.62
1997	101,018	25,402	32,736	17,065	15,396	6,774	2,311	1,334	2.64
1996	99,627	24,900	32,526	16,724	15,118	6,631	2,357	1,372	2.65
1995	98,990	24,732	31,834	16,827	15,321	6,616	2,279	1,382	2.65
1994	97,107	23,611	31,211	16,898	15,073	6,749	2,186	1,379	2.67
1993ʳ	96,426	23,558	31,041	16,964	14,997	6,404	2,217	1,244	2.66
1993	96,391	23,642	31,175	16,895	14,926	6,357	2,180	1,215	2.63
1992	95,669	23,974	30,734	16,398	14,710	6,389	2,126	1,338	2.62
1991	94,312	23,590	30,181	16,082	14,556	6,206	2,237	1,459	2.63
1990	93,347	22,999	30,114	16,128	14,456	6,213	2,143	1,295	2.63
1989	92,830	22,708	29,976	16,276	14,550	6,232	2,003	1,084	2.62
1988	91,066	21,889	29,295	16,163	14,143	6,081	2,176	1,320	2.64
1987	89,479	21,128	28,602	16,159	13,984	6,162	2,176	1,268	2.66
1986	88,458	21,178	27,732	16,088	13,774	6,276	2,138	1,272	2.67
1985	86,789	20,602	27,389	15,465	13,631	6,108	2,299	1,296	2.69
1984	85,407	19,954	26,890	15,134	13,593	6,070	2,372	1,394	2.71
1983	83,918	19,250	26,439	14,793	13,303	6,105	2,460	1,568	2.73
1982	83,527	19,354	26,486	14,617	12,868	6,103	2,480	1,619	2.72
1981	82,368	18,936	25,787	14,569	12,768	6,117	2,549	1,643	2.73
1980	80,776	18,296	25,327	14,130	12,666	6,059	2,519	1,778	2.76
1979	77,330	17,201	23,928	13,392	12,274	6,187	2,573	1,774	2.78
1978	76,030	16,715	23,334	13,040	11,955	6,356	2,723	1,906	2.81
1977	74,142	15,532	22,775	12,794	11,630	6,285	2,864	2,263	2.86
1976	72,867	14,983	22,321	12,520	11,407	6,268	3,001	2,367	2.89
1975	71,120	13,939	21,753	12,384	11,103	6,399	3,059	2,484	2.94
1974	69,859	13,368	21,495	11,913	10,900	6,469	3,063	2,651	2.97
1973	68,251	12,635	20,632	11,804	10,739	6,426	3,245	2,769	3.01
1972	66,676	12,189	19,482	11,542	10,679	6,431	3,374	2,979	3.06
1971	64,778	11,446	18,892	11,071	10,059	6,640	3,435	3,234	3.11
1970	63,401	10,851	18,333	10,949	9,991	6,548	3,534	3,195	3.14
1969	62,214	10,401	18,034	10,769	9,778	6,387	3,557	3,288	3.21
1968	60,813	9,802	17,377	10,577	9,623	6,319	3,627	3,488	3.00
1967	59,236	9,200	16,770	10,403	9,559	6,276	3,491	3,550	3.30
1966	58,406	9,093	16,679	9,993	9,465	6,257	3,465	3,465	3.32
1965	57,436	8,631	16,119	10,263	9,269	6,313	3,327	3,514	3.32
1964	56,149	7,821	15,622	10,034	9,565	6,328	3,373	3,405	3.34
1963	55,270	7,501	15,279	9,989	9,445	6,240	3,473	3,342	3.33
1962	54,764	7,473	15,461	10,077	9,347	6,016	3,368	3,022	3.32
1961	53,557	7,112	15,185	9,780	9,390	6,052	3,085	2,953	3.38
1960	52,799	6,917	14,678	9,979	9,293	6,072	3,010	2,851	3.35

ʳRevised based on population from the decennial census for that year.

SOURCE: "Table HH-4. Households by Size: 1960 to Present," U.S. Census Bureau, Washington, DC, June 2001 [Online] http://landview.census.gov/population/socdemo/hh-fam/tabHH-4.xls [accessed December 3, 2002]

However, the fertility rate—the number of live births per thousand women ages 15–44—has remained significantly lower than it was before World War II. The high fertility rate of 118 births per thousand women in 1960 plummeted to 65 in 1997. The fertility rate has risen only slightly since that time to 66.1 in 1999 and 67.6 in 2000. In 2001, the fertility rate dipped to 67.0. (See Table 1.4.)

In its study "Fertility of American Women," the Census Bureau reports that in 1900 the average woman gave birth to four children. The average dropped to 2.2 births per woman during the Great Depression of the 1930s, then rose to a post-World War II peak of 3.7 births per woman in 1957. The introduction of birth-control pills and intrauterine devices in the early 1960s drove the average down to a low of 1.8 births per woman by the mid-1970s. As of 2003,

the average had remained at a little under two births per woman for the previous 25 years. (See Figure 1.4.)

The Census Bureau compared women nearing the end of their childbearing years in 1976 and in 1998. Only 9.6 percent of these women in 1976 had given birth to only one child, while 17.3 percent of women in 1998 had only one child. By contrast, 35.9 percent of women in 1976 had four or more children, compared to 9.6 percent of women in 1998. Of never-married women, 15.8 percent had two or more children in 1976, compared to 22.3 percent in 1998. (See Table 1.5.)

More women are choosing to remain childless than in past generations. In 1976, about 10 percent of women completed their childbearing years never having a child.

TABLE 1.4

Provisional vital statistics for the United States, 2001

	December				January–December				
	Number		Rate		Number		Rate		
Item	2001	2000	2001	2000	2001	2000	2001	2000	1999
Live births	327,000	339,000	13.8	14.5	4,028,000	4,063,000	14.5	14.8	14.6
Fertility rate	[1]	[1]	64.0	66.5	[1]	[1]	67.0	67.6	66.1
Deaths	210,000	205,000	8.9	8.8	2,419,000	2,408,000	8.7	8.8	8.8
Infant deaths	2,400	2,200	7.1	6.4	27,600	27,200	6.9	6.7	7.1
Natural increase	117,000	134,000	4.9	5.7	1,609,000	1,655,000	5.8	6.0	5.8
Marriages	153,000	152,000	6.4	6.5	2,327,000	2,329,000	8.4	8.5	8.6
Divorces[3]	[2]	[2]	[2]	[2]	[2]	[2]	4.0	4.2	4.1
Population base (in millions)	[1]	[1]	278.8	276.2	[1]	[1]	277.7	275.1	272.9

[1]Category not applicable.
[2]Data not available.
[3]Divorce rates exclude data for California, Colorado, Indiana, and Louisiana. Populations for these rates also exclude these states.

SOURCE: "Table 1. Provisional Vital Statistics for the United States for 2001," *Births, Marriages, Divorces, and Deaths: Provisional Data for 2001*, National Vital Statistics Reports, Vol. 50, No. 14, Centers for Disease Control and Prevention, National Center for Health Statistics, Hyattsville, MD, September 2002

FIGURE 1.4

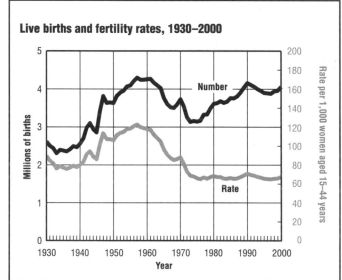

Live births and fertility rates, 1930–2000

Note: Beginning with 1959, trend lines are based on registered live births; trend lines for 1930–59 are based on live births adjusted for underregistration.

SOURCE: J.A. Martin, B.E. Hamilton, S.J. Ventura, F. Menacker, and M.M. Park, "Figure 1. Live births and fertility rates: United States, 1930–2000," in *Births: Final Data for 2000*, National Vital Statistics Reports, Vol. 50, No. 5, Centers for Disease Control and Prevention, National Center for Health Statistics, Hyattsville, MD, February 2002

TABLE 1.5

Fertility indicators among different generations, women 40–44 years old, June 1976 and June 1998

(Numbers in thousands)

Characteristic	1976	1998
All women	5,684	11,113
Children ever born (percent)	100.0	100.0
None	10.2	19.0
One	9.6	17.3
Two	21.7	35.8
Three	22.7	18.2
Four or more	35.9	9.6
Children ever born per 1,000 women	3,091	1,877
Never-married women	228	1,118
Children ever born (percent)	100.0	100.0
None	75.5	66.8
One	8.7	10.9
Two or more	15.8	22.3
Children ever born per 1,000 women	724	758

SOURCE: Amara Bachu and Martin O'Connell, "Table B. Fertility Indicators Among Different Generations, Women 40 to 44 Years Old: June 1976 and June 1998," in *Fertility of American Women,* Current Population Reports, P20-526, U.S. Census Bureau, Washington, DC, September 2000

Currently, 19 percent of women in their early forties remain childless. (See Figure 1.5.)

Young Adults Delaying Marriage

Beginning in the mid-1960s, an increasing proportion of women and men postponed marriage. Between 1965 and 1998, the percent of women between ages 20 and 24 years who were unmarried more than doubled, from 33 to 73 percent. Among women age 25–29 years, the percent unmarried tripled in the same period, rising from 13 to 45

percent. (See Figure 1.6.) In 1970, the average age of men at first marriage was 23.2 and of women, 20.8. By 2000, men's age at first marriage had increased to 26.8 and women's to 25.1. (See Figure 1.7.)

While young adults are delaying marriage, the number of married teenagers grew nearly 50 percent in the 1990s. In 1950, 9.5 percent of teens age 15–19 were married. A steady decline took teen marriages to a low of 3.4 percent of all teens in 1990. In 2000, 4.5 percent of 15- to 19-year-olds were married. In a November 9, 2002, Associated Press article, David Popenoe of the National Marriage Project at Rutgers University said, "There's been a slight trend toward conservatism among teens, less premarital sex,

FIGURE 1.5

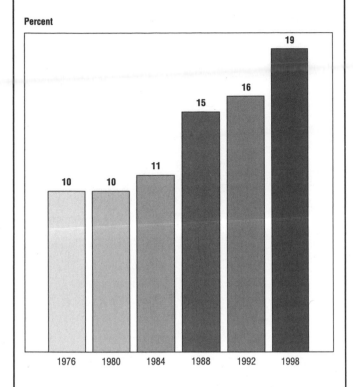

Childlessness among women 40–44 years old, selected years 1976–98

Percent

SOURCE: Amara Bachu and Martin O'Connell, "Figure 1. Childlessness Among Women 40 to 44 Years Old: Selected Years, June 1976 to June 1998," in *Fertility of American Women,* Current Population Reports, P20-526, U.S. Census Bureau, Washington, DC, September 2000

TABLE 1.6

Living arrangements of younger and older adults, March 2000
(In thousands)

	Number		Percent	
Characteristic	Men	Women	Men	Women
YOUNGER ADULTS				
18 to 34 years old				
Total	31,854	32,464	100.0	100.0
Living alone	2,830	2,156	8.9	6.6
Married spouse present	10,603	13,298	33.3	41.0
Not married spouse present - child of householder	9,737	6,661	30.6	20.5
None of the above	8,684	10,349	27.3	31.9
18 to 24 years old				
Total	13,291	13,242	100.0	100.0
Living alone	551	588	4.1	4.4
Married spouse present	1,305	2,332	9.8	17.6
Not married spouse present - child of householder	7,497	5,629	56.4	42.5
None of the above	3,938	4,693	29.6	35.4
25 to 34 years old				
Total	18,563	19,222	100.0	100.0
Living alone	2,279	1,568	12.3	8.2
Married spouse present	9,298	10,966	50.1	57.0
Not married spouse present - child of householder	2,240	1,032	12.1	5.4
None of the above	4,746	5,656	25.6	29.4
OLDER ADULTS				
65 years old and over				
Total	13,886	18,735	100.0	100.0
Living alone	2,355	7,427	17.0	39.6
Married spouse present	10,084	7,743	72.6	41.3
None of the above	1,447	3,565	10.4	19.0
65 to 74 years old				
Total	8,049	9,747	100.0	100.0
Living alone	1,108	2,983	13.8	30.6
Married spouse present	6,170	5,156	76.7	52.9
None of the above	771	1,608	9.6	16.5
75 years old and over				
Total	5,837	8,988	100.0	100.0
Living alone	1,247	4,444	21.4	49.4
Married spouse present	3,914	2,587	67.1	28.8
None of the above	676	1,957	11.6	21.8

SOURCE: Jason Fields and Lynne M. Casper, "Table 6. Living Arrangements of Younger and Older Adults: March 2000," in *America's Families and Living Arrangements: March 2000,* Current Population Reports, U.S. Census Bureau, Washington, DC, June 2001

more fear of disease." Some researchers attribute the rise in teen marriages to immigrants from countries where teen marriage is common. The National Center for Health Statistics found that nearly half of marriages in which the bride is 18 or younger end in separation or divorce within 10 years. The rate is cut in half for brides 25 and older.

Adult Children Living with Parents

Delays in marriage may increase the number of one-person households or increase the size of family households when adult children continue living with their parents. In 2000, 56 percent of men age 18 to 24 lived at home with one or both parents; 43 percent of women lived with one or both parents. Both men and women in this age group were more likely to cohabit, live with roommates, or live with people other than spouses than live alone. Thirty percent of men and 35 percent of women in this age group lived with others who were neither spouses nor parents. (See Table 1.6.)

Married Couples Had Fewer Children

Married couples contributed to the decreasing household size by having fewer children. From 1960 to the mid-1970s, the birth rate for married women fell more than 40 percent. After leveling off, the birth rate for married women gradually declined through the mid-1990s. (See Figure 1.8.) In 2000, only 46 percent of married-couple family groups included any own children under age 18, while 61 percent of other family groups included own children under 18. (See Table 1.7.)

Single-Parent Households Increased

According to the Census Bureau's report "America's Families and Living Arrangements 2000," single-mother households increased from 12 percent of family households in 1970 to 26 percent in 2000. In the same period, single-father households grew from 1 percent to 5 percent of all family households. The sharp rise in birth rates among unmarried women between the mid-1970s and mid-1990s raised the proportion of children living with a single parent. (See Figure 1.9.)

FIGURE 1.6

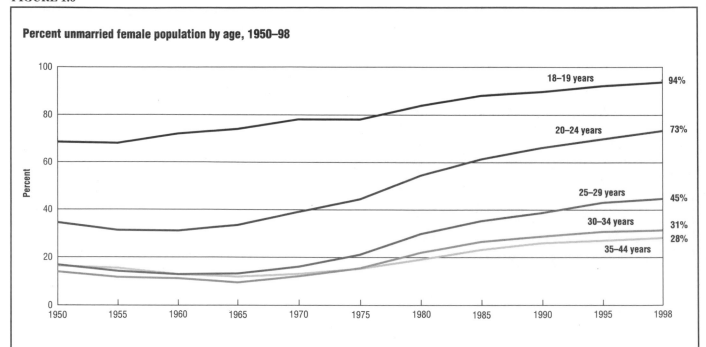

Percent unmarried female population by age, 1950–98

Note: Compiled from data published by the U.S. Census Bureau.

SOURCE: Stephanie J. Ventura and Christine A. Bachrach, "Figure 5. Percent unmarried, female population by age: United States, 1950–98," in "Nonmarital Childbearing in the United States, 1940–99," *National Vital Statistics Reports,* vol. 48, no. 16, October 18, 2000

FIGURE 1.7

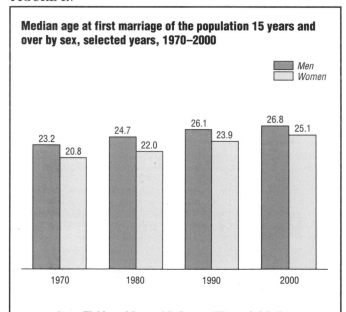

Median age at first marriage of the population 15 years and over by sex, selected years, 1970–2000

SOURCE: Jason Fields and Lynne M. Casper, "Figure 3. Median Age at First Marriage of the Population 15 Years and Over by Sex: Selected Years, 1970 to 2000," in *America's Families and Living Arrangements: March 2000,* Current Population Reports, U.S. Census Bureau, Washington, DC, June 2001

Divorces Continue

Divorce rates soared in the 1970s, reaching a peak of 5.3 divorces per thousand population in about 1979, then began a slow decline through the 1990s to 4.1 per thousand

in 1999 and 2000. (See Table 1.8.) Increases in divorce may reduce the size of households when one household separates into two smaller ones. Remarriage by divorced persons, however, may bring stepchildren into the new household or create larger families. It should be noted that stepchildren are counted as "own children" by the Census Bureau.

Americans Live Longer

Improvements in health and health care may have mixed effects on average household size. Longer-lived couples tend to increase the number of two-person households. Surviving spouses add to the number of one-person households. In 2000, 72.6 percent of men and 41.3 percent of women age 65 and older lived with a spouse. In this age group, 17 percent of men and 39.6 percent of women lived alone. (See Table 1.6.)

The cumulative effect of these trends is a reduction in the average size of households.

UNMARRIED PARTNERS

In 2000, 3.8 million households were classified as unmarried-partner households, representing 3.7 percent of all households in the United States. According to the Census Bureau, these figures may underrepresent the true number of cohabiting couples. Some couples may be reluctant to classify themselves as cohabiting and may instead describe themselves as roommates or friends. Children under 18 years resided in 40.9 percent of unmarried-

FIGURE 1.8

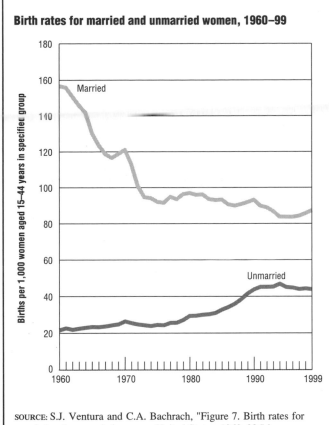

Birth rates for married and unmarried women, 1960–99

SOURCE: S.J. Ventura and C.A. Bachrach, "Figure 7. Birth rates for married and unmarried women: United States, 1960–99," in *Nonmarital Childbearing in the United States, 1940–99,* National Vital Statistics Reports, Vol. 48, No. 16, Centers for Disease Control and Prevention, National Center for Health Statistics, Hyattsville, MD, October 2000

TABLE 1.7

Family groups by type and selected characteristics of the family, March 2000

(In thousands)

Characteristic	Total	Married couple	Other family groups Total	Male	Female
All family groups	75,579	56,497	19,083	4,286	14,797
Family type					
Family household	72,025	55,311	16,715	4,028	12,687
Related subfamily	2,983	1,149	1,834	201	1,633
Unrelated subfamily	571	37	534	57	477
Size of family group					
1 person	(X)	(X)	(X)	(X)	(X)
2 people	33,749	23,794	9,955	2,529	7,426
3 people	16,909	11,497	5,412	1,016	4,396
4 people	14,800	12,640	2,160	446	1,714
5 people	6,622	5,668	954	168	786
6 or more	3,498	2,897	601	126	475
Number of own children under 18					
No own children	38,084	30,726	7,358	2,242	5,116
1 child	16,221	9,682	6,539	1,300	5,239
2 children	13,949	10,452	3,497	543	2,954
3 children	5,235	4,076	1,159	146	1,013
4 or more children	2,091	1,561	530	55	475
Presence of own children under 18					
No own children	38,084	30,726	7,358	2,242	5,116
With own children	37,496	25,771	11,725	2,044	9,681
With own children under 1	3,370	2,350	1,020	196	824
With own children under 3	9,832	7,002	2,830	511	2,319
With own children under 6	16,645	11,711	4,934	819	4,115
With own children under 12	28,297	19,519	8,778	1,441	7,337
Family income					
Under $10,000	5,426	1,505	3,921	393	3,528
$10,000-$14,999	3,919	1,817	2,102	320	1,782
$15,000-$19,999	4,706	2,675	2,031	341	1,690
$20,000-$24,999	4,694	3,008	1,686	304	1,382
$25,000-$29,999	4,606	3,060	1,546	365	1,181
$30,000-$39,999	8,702	6,323	2,379	638	1,741
$40,000-$49,999	7,835	6,147	1,688	476	1,212
$50,000-$74,999	15,495	13,238	2,257	788	1,469
$75,000 and over	20,198	18,723	1,475	663	812
Metropolitan residence					
Metropolitan	60,461	44,580	15,881	3,564	12,317
In central cities	20,803	13,532	7,271	1,501	5,770
Outside central cities	39,658	31,048	8,610	2,063	6,547
Nonmetropolitan	15,119	11,917	3,202	722	2,480
Tenure					
Owns/buying	56,029	46,280	9,749	2,505	7,244
Rents	18,562	9,561	9,001	1,707	7,294
Occupies without payment	987	655	332	74	258

X Not applicable.

SOURCE: Jason Fields and Lynne M. Casper, "Table 2. Family Groups by Type and Selected Characteristics of the Family: March 2000," in *America's Families and Living Arrangements: March 2000,* Current Population Reports, U.S. Census Bureau, Washington, DC, June 2001

partner households, while 45.6 percent of married-couple households had children under age 18. (See Table 1.9.)

Unmarried partners tend to be younger than married couples. Thirty-seven percent of male and 33.2 percent of female unmarried partners were in the 25–34 age range in Census 2000, compared to 16.5 percent of male and 19.4 percent of female married partners. More unmarried partners held jobs than married partners. Eighty-three percent of male and 75.7 percent of female unmarried partners were employed, compared to 75.9 percent of male and 60.3 percent of female married partners. (See Table 1.9.)

LESBIAN AND GAY PARENTS

The sexual revolution of the 1960s, which changed society's attitudes about male and female relationships, also spearheaded the "coming out" of lesbians and gays. The modern gay-rights movement traces its beginning to New York City in the late 1960s. Previously, lesbians and gays had kept a low profile within their communities. Reflecting changing societal attitudes toward lesbian and gay partners, the *New York Times* announced in August 2002 that it would include reports of same-sex commit-

ment ceremonies and some formal registrations of lesbian and gay partnerships in its Sunday Style section along with reports of opposite-sex engagements and weddings.

The Lambda Legal Defense and Education Fund, an advocacy organization supporting the civil rights of lesbians and gays, seeks to have same-sex couples included in the popular definition of family. It claims there are between 6 and 10 million same-sex parents in the United States who are the mothers and fathers of an estimated 6 to 14 million children. The American Association of

FIGURE 1.9

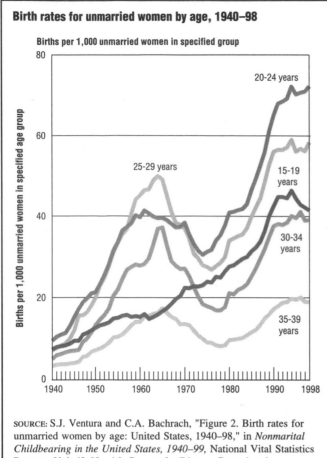

Birth rates for unmarried women by age, 1940–98

Births per 1,000 unmarried women in specified group

SOURCE: S.J. Ventura and C.A. Bachrach, "Figure 2. Birth rates for unmarried women by age: United States, 1940–98," in *Nonmarital Childbearing in the United States, 1940–99,* National Vital Statistics Reports, Vol. 48, No. 16, Centers for Disease Control and Prevention, National Center for Health Statistics, Hyattsville, MD, October 2000

Single People estimates that 1.6 percent of households consist of same-sex partners. Census 2000 data reports 594,391 self-identified same-sex-partner households, representing 10.8 percent of unmarried-partner households and 0.6 percent of all households. (See Table 1.10.) Reluctance on the part of many same-sex partners to self-identify may prevent accurate demographic analysis of families headed by lesbian and gay parents.

IMMIGRATION

Between 1991 and 1998, the number of immigrants arriving in the United States reached its highest level since the 1901–1910 period. (See Figure 1.10.) In February 2002, the Census Bureau announced that 1 out of every 10 U.S. residents was foreign-born or a first-generation resident. Twenty-one percent of the nation's population under age 25 in 2000 was either foreign born or first generation, up from only 7 percent in 1970. Foreign-born families, with an average of 3.72 family members, were slightly larger than the average native-born families, with 3.1 family members. Of foreign-born married couples, 16.1 percent had three or more children, compared to 10 percent of native-born married couples. (See Figure 1.11.)

TABLE 1.8

Divorce rates, 1945–2000

YEAR	U.S. RATE[1]
1945	3.5
1946	4.3
1947	3.4
1948	2.8
1949	2.7
1950	2.6
1951	2.5
1952	2.5
1953	2.5
1954	2.4
1955	2.3
1956	2.3
1957	2.2
1958	2.1
1959	2.2
1960	2.2
1961	2.3
1962	2.2
1963	2.3
1964	2.4
1965	2.5
1966	2.5
1967	2.6
1968	2.9
1969	3.2
1970	3.5
1971	3.7
1972	4.0
1973	4.3
1974	4.6
1975	4.8
1976	5.0
1977	5.0
1978	5.1
1979	5.3
1980	5.2
1981	5.3
1982	5.0
1983	4.9
1984	5.0
1985	5.0
1986	4.8
1987	4.8
1988	4.7
1989	4.7
1990	4.7
1991	4.7[2]
1992	4.8[2]
1993	4.6[2]
1994	4.6[2]
1995	4.4[2]
1996	4.3[2]
1997	4.3[2]
1998	4.2[2]
1999	4.1[2]
2000	4.1[2]

[1]Rate is per 1,000 population.
[2]Provisional data.

SOURCE: Adapted from "Divorces and Divorce Rates Alabama and the United States: 1945–2000," Alabama Center for Health Statistics, Montgomery, AL, 2000 [Online] http://ph.state.al.us/chs/healthstatistics/Tables/2000/aveTAB71.htm [accessed December 2, 2002]

MULTIGENERATIONAL FAMILIES

Census 2000 recorded 3.9 million American households, or 4 percent of all households, composed of three or more generations living together. Since 1990, the number of multigenerational families increased approximately

TABLE 1.9

Characteristics of unmarried partners and married spouses by sex, March 2000

(In thousands)

Characteristic	Number				Percent			
	Unmarried partners		Married spouses		Unmarried partners		Married spouses	
	Men	Women	Men	Women	Men	Women	Men	Women
Total	3,822	3,822	55,107	50,497	100.0	100.0	100.0	100.0
Age								
15 to 24 years old	597	937	1,321	2,386	15.6	24.5	2.3	4.2
25 to 34 years old	1,413	1,269	9,296	10,964	37.0	33.2	16.5	19.4
35 years old and over	1,811	1,616	45,881	43,146	47.4	42.3	81.2	76.4
Race and Hispanic origin								
White	3,127	3,147	49,668	49,581	81.8	82.3	87.9	87.8
Non-Hispanic	2,710	2,742	44,350	44,142	70.9	71.7	78.5	78.1
Black	562	498	4,294	4,097	14.7	13.0	7.6	7.3
Asian and Pacific Islander	63	105	2,118	2,393	1.6	2.7	3.7	4.2
Hispanic (of any race)	453	433	5,550	5,671	11.9	11.3	9.8	10.0
Education								
Less than high school	683	599	8,314	7,160	17.9	15.7	14.7	12.7
High school graduate	1,441	1,357	17,506	19,950	37.7	35.5	31.0	35.3
Some college	996	1,223	14,002	14,968	26.1	32.0	24.8	26.5
College graduate	702	643	16,674	14,419	18.4	16.8	29.5	25.5
Labor force status								
Employed	3,179	2,894	42,854	34,067	83.2	75.7	75.9	60.3
Unemployed	187	178	992	961	4.9	4.7	1.8	1.7
Not in labor force	453	747	12,650	21,468	11.9	19.5	22.4	38.0
Personal earnings								
Without earnings	402	642	11,353	19,368	10.5	16.8	20.1	34.3
With earnings	3,419	3,178	45,144	37,132	89.5	83.2	79.9	65.7
Under $5,000 or loss	184	373	1,874	4,683	4.8	9.8	3.3	8.3
$5,000 to $9,999	286	395	1,665	4,183	7.5	10.3	2.9	7.4
$10,000 to $14,999	360	445	2,401	4,497	9.4	11.6	4.2	8.0
$15,000 to $19,999	410	441	3,101	4,427	10.7	11.5	5.5	7.8
$20,000 to $24,999	401	397	3,561	4,249	10.5	10.4	6.3	7.5
$25,000 to $29,999	336	315	3,595	3,429	8.8	8.2	6.4	6.1
$30,000 to $39,999	548	405	7,492	4,954	14.3	10.6	13.3	8.8
$40,000 to $49,999	337	201	6,096	2,976	8.8	5.3	10.8	5.3
$50,000 to $74,999	370	137	8,703	2,683	9.7	3.6	15.4	4.7
$75,000 and over	187	69	6,656	1,051	4.9	1.8	11.8	1.9
Presence of children								
With children[1]	1,563	1,563	25,771	25,771	40.9	40.9	45.6	45.6

[1]May be own children of either partner or both partners. Excludes ever married children under 18 years.

Note: Data are not shown separately for the American Indian and Alaska Native population because of the small sample size in the Current Population Survey in March 2000.

SOURCE: Jason Fields and Lynne M. Casper, "Table 7. Characteristics of Unmarried Partners and Married Spouses by Sex: March 2000," in *America's Families and Living Arrangements: March 2000*, Current Population Reports, U.S. Census Bureau, Washington, DC, June 2001

60 percent. In 2000 there were 2.6 million multigenerational families that included the householder, his or her children, and his or her grandchildren. Nearly 1.3 million multigenerational families included the householder, his or her children, and his or her parents. Another 78,000 households, about 2 percent of all multigenerational family households, consisted of four generations.

The Census Bureau reported that multigenerational families may be most common in areas where recent immigrants live with relatives, housing shortages or high costs force families to share living space, and teenage birth rates are high. As older adults live longer, the need for family caregiving also creates multigenerational households.

TABLE 1.10

Unmarried-partner households, by sex of partners, 2000

	United States
Total:	105,480,101
Unmarried-partner households:	5,475,768
Male householder and male partner	301,026
Male householder and female partner	2,615,119
Female householder and female partner	293,365
Female householder and male partner	2,266,258
All other households	100,004,333

SOURCE: "PCT14. Unmarried Partner Households by Sex of Partners," in *American FactFinder*, Census 2000 Summary File 1, U.S. Census Bureau, Washington, DC [Online] http://factfinder.census.gov/servlet/BasicFactsServlet [accessed December 4, 2002]

FIGURE 1.10

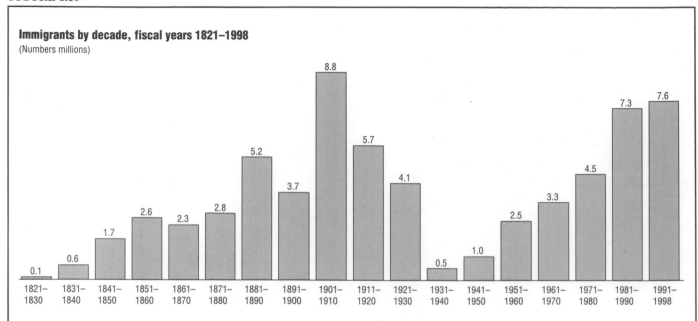

Immigrants by decade, fiscal years 1821–1998
(Numbers millions)

Decade	Millions
1821–1830	0.1
1831–1840	0.6
1841–1850	1.7
1851–1860	2.6
1861–1870	2.3
1871–1880	2.8
1881–1890	5.2
1891–1900	3.7
1901–1910	8.8
1911–1920	5.7
1921–1930	4.1
1931–1940	0.5
1941–1950	1.0
1951–1960	2.5
1961–1970	3.3
1971–1980	4.5
1981–1990	7.3
1991–1998	7.6

SOURCE: "Figure 1-2. Immigrants to the United States by Decade: Fiscal Years, 1821–1998," in *Profile of Foreign-Born Population in the United States: 2000,* U.S. Census Bureau, Washington, DC, December 2001

FIGURE 1.11

Families by type, nativity of householder, and number of related children, 2000

Percent distribution of families by number of related children under 18 years old

	Households (in millions)	None	1	2	3 or more	Average family size
Total families	72.0	48.3	21.5	19.4	10.9	3.17
Native householder	63.0	49.5	21.2	19.0	10.3	3.10
Foreign-born householder	9.0	39.2	23.7	22.0	15.2	3.72
Married-couple family	55.3	52.3	17.9	19.1	10.7	3.24
Native householder	48.5	54.2	17.3	18.5	10.0	3.15
Foreign-born householder	6.8	38.7	22.1	23.2	16.1	3.85
Male householder, no wife present	4.0	46.2	32.3	15.7	5.8	2.79
Native householder	3.3	44.4	34.1	15.9	5.6	2.69
Foreign-born householder	0.7	54.3	24.4	14.5	6.9	3.25
Female householder, no husband present	12.7	31.1	33.7	22.0	13.1	3.01
Native householder	11.2	30.8	34.1	22.2	12.9	2.97
Foreign-born householder	1.5	34.2	30.7	20.2	14.9	3.35

Note: Civilian noninstitutional population plus Armed Forces living off post or with their families on post.

SOURCE: "Figure 12-1. Families by Type, Nativity of Householder, and Number of Related Children: 2000," in *Profile of Foreign-Born Population in the United States: 2000,* U.S. Census Bureau, Washington, DC, December 2001

CHAPTER 2
WOMEN, MEN, AND THE FAMILY

CHILDBEARING

Beginning around the early 1960s, three growing trends—a lower fertility rate, women (especially working women) delaying childbearing, and the increase in the number of births among young unmarried women—greatly changed the composition of the American family.

The turn of the new century in 2000 marked a new high point in birth trends. According to the U.S. Department of Health and Human Services, Division of Vital Statistics, the number of U.S. births increased 3 percent for the year 2000, marking the third consecutive increase following a 7 percent decline from 1990 to 1997. The crude birth rate also rose slightly to 14.7 births per 1,000 total population in 2000. The fertility rate, which relates births to the number of women of childbearing age, was up 2 percent for 2000. These numbers dropped slightly in 2001.

Decline in the Teen Birth Rate

Birth rates have shifted significantly by age groups. Teenage birth rates have dropped continuously since 1991. For the 15- to 19-year-old age group, the birth rate reached a record low of 48.5 per 1,000 in 2000, reversing a trend that had resulted in a 24 percent increase in teen births from 1986 to 1991. This decline in first births applies to teenagers of all races and to those of Hispanic origin. The most dramatic change is the 31 percent decline from 1991 to 2000 in the birth rate for African American teenagers, to an historic low rate of 81.9. (See Table 2.1.)

An important trend in addition to the decline in teenage pregnancy rates is the decline in second births to teenagers. At its peak in the early 1990s, for every 1,000 women age 15–19 who had given birth to a child, 220 gave birth to a second child while still a teenager. This trend dropped dramatically to about 173 second births per thousand. The rate of second births to black, Native American, and Asian or Pacific Islander teens has been consistently higher than for white teens, but the difference greatly diminished after about 1995. (See Figure 2.1.)

While the birth rate for women age 20–24 increased slightly in 2000, the birth rate for women age 25–29 reached 121.4, its highest level since 1971. Birth rates for women in their 20s, the principal childbearing ages, have been relatively stable for the past 20 years. For women in their 30s, the birth rate rose 5 percent in 2000, continuing a steady rise since the mid-1970s. As of 2000, the birth rate for women age 40–44 had more than doubled in the previous 20 years. (See Figure 2.2.)

Extending the Childbearing Years

Before the 1960s, when larger families were more common, it was not unusual for a woman to continue having babies well into her 30s or even her 40s. However, as families became smaller, it became more common to have the typical two or three children during the first years of marriage when the woman was generally in her 20s. While most women still give birth while in their 20s, a significant proportion now wait until their 30s. The difference between women in the 1950s and women in the 1990s who had children in their 30s was that the former were generally having their third and fourth child, while the latter were typically having their first or second.

Historically, ages 15 to 44 were considered the childbearing years for record-keeping purposes. However, women are having babies beyond these years. The 0.5 birth rate for women age 45–49 in 2000 was the highest in three decades. In part, this reflects the increasing number of women in this age group but also a greater likelihood of giving birth at a later age. According to the Bureau of Vital Statistics, there were 255 births in 2000 to women age 50–54, a substantial increase over 174 births reported for this age group in 1999. Birth data for women age 50 and older has only recently become available.

TABLE 2.1

Birth rates for teenagers 15–19 years by selected characteristics, 1991–2000

[Rates are live births per 1,000 women in specified group]

Year and age	Total[1]	Non-Hispanic		American Indian[2]	Asian or Pacific Islander[2]	Hispanic[3]
		White	Black			
15–19 years						
2000	48.5	32.5	81.9	67.8	21.6	94.4
1999	49.6	34.0	83.7	67.8	22.3	93.4
1991[4]	62.1	43.4	118.9	85.0	27.4	106.7
Percent change, 1991–2000.	−22	−25	−31	−20	−21	−12
Percent change, 1999–2000	−2	−4	−2	0	−3	1
15–17 years						
2000	27.4	15.8	52.0	39.6	11.5	60.0
1999	28.7	17.1	53.7	41.4	12.3	61.3
1991[4]	38.7	23.6	86.7	52.7	16.1	70.6
Percent change, 1991–2000	−29	−33	−40	−25	−29	−15
Percent change, 1999–2000	−5	−8	−3	−4	−7	−2
18–19 years						
2000	79.2	56.8	125.1	113.1	37.0	143.6
1999	80.3	58.9	126.8	110.6	38.0	139.4
1991	94.4	70.5	163.1	134.3	43.1	158.5
Percent change, 1991–2000	−16	−19	−23	−16	−14	−9
Percent change, 1999–2000	−1	−4	−1	2	−3	3

[1]Includes origin not stated.
[2]Includes persons of Hispanic and non-Hispanic origin.
[3]Persons of Hispanic origin may be of any race.

SOURCE: J.A. Martin, B.E. Hamilton, S.J. Ventura, F. Menacker, and M.M. Park, "Table A. Birth rates for teenagers 15-19 years by age, race, and Hispanic origin of mother: United States, 1991, 1999, and 2000, and percent change, 1991-2000 and 1999-2000," in *Births, Final Data for 2000,* National Vital Statistics Report, Vol 50, No 5, Centers for Disease Control and Prevention, February 2002

The rise in birth rates for women in their late 30s and older for the last 20 years has been linked to several factors, including the availability and use of fertility-enhancing therapies. Women in this age group have sought fertility treatment in steadily increasing numbers since 1982, according to the National Survey of Family Growth. For 2000, 103 of the 255 births to women age 50 to 54 years were multiple deliveries, an outcome associated with infertility therapy.

In 2000, there were 4,058,814 live births in the United States. Of these, 118,916 were twin deliveries (2.9 percent) and 7,325 were "higher order multiple deliveries," or more than twins (0.2 percent). Black non-Hispanic women had the highest rate of twin births, 33.4 per 1,000 live births. White non-Hispanic women had 32.2 twins per 1,000 births. Hispanic women had a significantly lower incidence of twins, with only 20.2 twin births per 1,000 live births. White women, however, were three times as likely as black or Hispanic women to deliver more than two infants. White non-Hispanic women had 246.3 "higher order multiple births" per 100,000 live births, compared to 83.7 for black non-Hispanic women and 80.8 for

Hispanic women. While the rate of "higher order births" for white women increased dramatically past age 40, black women over 40 had so few that the Census Bureau could not reliably calculate a rate. This may suggest that white women in this age group are more likely to seek fertility treatments. (See Table 2.2.)

Fertility Rates

The fertility rate—the number of live births per 1,000 women of reproductive age (15 to 44)—peaked in the late 1950s and began a steady decline into the mid-1970s. While the overall fertility rate has remained relatively flat for the past 25 years, fertility rates for women over age 30 have shown dramatic increases. Since the mid-1970s, birth rates for women in the 30–34 age group increased steadily from 52.3 per 1,000 in 1975 to 94.1 in 2000. Even more dramatic, the rate for women in the 35–39 age group more than doubled, rising from 19.0 per 1,000 in 1978 to 40.4 in 2000. The fertility rate also more than doubled for women in the 40–44 age group—and in a much shorter time period. In just 19 years, the fertility rate for this age group rose from a 1981 low of 3.8 to 7.9 in 2000. By contrast, since the early 1990s, the fertility rates for women under age 19 have decreased. (See Figure 2.2.)

Nonmarital Childbearing

Prior to the 1970s, the typical pregnant, unmarried female either got married or gave the child up for adoption. Some women had abortions. However it was handled, the pregnancy was often cloaked in great secrecy. An unmarried pregnant woman often left home during the pregnancy to stay with a relative or in a home for unwed mothers while her family made some excuse for her absence. The infant was given up for adoption and never openly discussed. Few women risked the social stigma of raising a child alone, at least without concocting a story of a husband who abandoned the woman or met an untimely death. The period 1960–1964 was the peak for choosing marriage. During that time, 60 percent of women who were unmarried at the time of conception married before the births of their babies. Immediately prior to and immediately following those years, about 54 percent of pregnant women wed before giving birth. The dramatic change occurred in the late 1970s, when the women's liberation movement that had begun a decade earlier gained momentum. Between 1975 and 1979, just 32 percent of unmarried, pregnant women chose marriage. Over the next two decades, the number dropped to 23 percent. (See Figure 2.3.)

Births to women who are unmarried but cohabiting with a partner increased from 29 percent in the 1980s to 39 percent in the 1990s. The greatest increase occurred among non-Hispanic white women, from 33 percent in the 1980s to 50 percent in the 1990s. (See Figure 2.4.)

Women Who Marry Before Giving Birth

Trends in Premarital Childbirth, a study completed by the Census Bureau in 1999, revealed that in the late 1960s, 67 percent of unmarried, pregnant white women married before giving birth, compared to 26 percent of black women. By the 1980s, only 39 percent of white women and 7 percent of black women who were unmarried and pregnant chose to marry before giving birth. The number of white women choosing marriage continued to drop to 29 percent in the 1990s, while the trend changed slightly for black women, increasing to 10 percent. Unmarried, pregnant Hispanic women, who in 1965 married at a rate of 37 percent, by the 1990s nearly matched white women, with a marriage rate of 26 percent. In 1999, 40 percent of nonmarital births were to white women, 32 percent to black women, and 25 percent to Hispanic women. (See Figure 2.5.)

Births to unmarried women have increased over the past two decades in most industrialized nations. While the U.S. rate jumped from 18 to 33 percent, more dramatic increases were seen in Norway (15 to 49 percent), France (11 to 40 percent), and Ireland (5 to 28 percent). Iceland

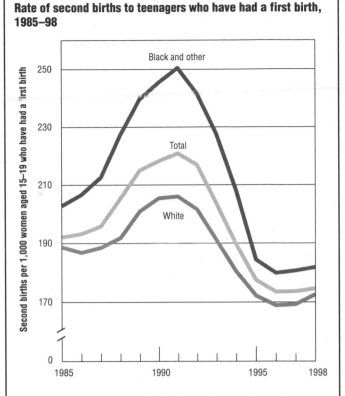

FIGURE 2.1

Rate of second births to teenagers who have had a first birth, 1985–98

Note: Data for "Black and other" include American Indian and Asian or Pacific Islander teenagers; in 1998, 88 percent of "all other" teenage mothers were black.

SOURCE: S.J. Ventura and C.A. Bachrach, "Figure 12. Rate of second births to teenagers who have had a first birth: United States, 1985–98," in *Nonmarital Childbearing in the United States, 1940–99*, National Vital Statistics Reports, Vol. 48, No. 16, Centers for Disease Control and Prevention, National Center for Health Statistics, Hyattsville, MD, October 2000

has the highest rate of births to unmarried women at 64 percent. (See Figure 2.6.)

Among never-married women who gave birth, the number who elected to give the child up for adoption declined dramatically starting in the 1970s. Before 1973, 8.7 percent of all never-married pregnant women gave their child up for adoption. By the late 1970s, that rate had dropped by more than half. In the 1990s, only 0.9 percent of women chose adoption. (See Figure 2.7.)

Abortion Decreasing

The rate of abortion has also declined because of the shifting age distribution of pregnant women toward older women, a decrease in unplanned pregnancies, reduced access to abortion, and the increased use of contraceptives. In 1980, 10 percent of married women and 59 percent of unmarried women chose to end pregnancies with abortion. By 1995, 41 percent of unmarried women chose abortion. Among married women, since 1990, 8 percent have continued to elect abortion. (See Figure 2.8.) The steadily

FIGURE 2.2

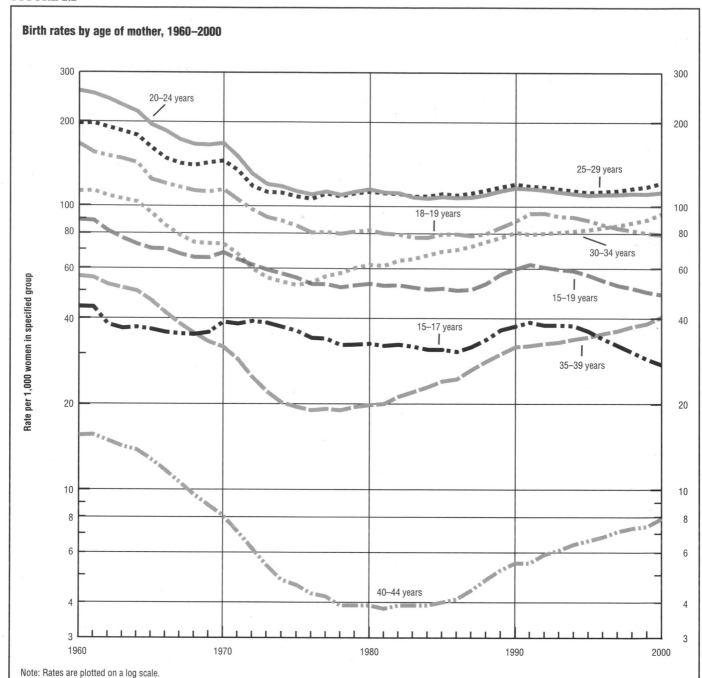

Birth rates by age of mother, 1960–2000

Note: Rates are plotted on a log scale.

SOURCE: J.A. Martin, B.E. Hamilton, S.J. Ventura, F. Menacker, and M.M. Park, "Figure 2. Birth rates by age of mother: United States, 1960–2000," in *Births: Final Data for 2000,* National Vital Statistics Reports, Vol. 50, No. 5, Centers for Disease Control and Prevention, National Center for Health Statistics, Hyattsville, MD, February 2002

declining birth rate among teenagers may be attributed to more effective contraceptives and reduced frequency of sex.

The availability of contraceptives has significantly impacted birth rates in the United States. In 1988, 18 percent of unmarried women reported they used no method of birth control, compared to 12 percent in 1995. In the 1980s, 48 percent of unmarried women used the pill. By the 1990s, that number had dropped to 36 percent. Implants and injectable birth control replaced the pill for

7 percent of women in the 1990s. Condom use increased from 15 percent in 1988 to 25 percent by the 1990s. Fear of sexually transmitted diseases, particularly AIDS, and the use of safe-sex advertisement and awareness programs increased the use of condoms. (See Figure 2.9.)

ARTIFICIAL REPRODUCTION

In the late 1980s and early 1990s, when an estimated 4,000 women became surrogate mothers by being artifi-

TABLE 2.2

Live births by plurality of birth and ratios, by age, race, and Hispanic origin of mother, 2000

Plurality and race and Hispanic origin of mother	All ages	Under 15 years	Age of mother 15-19 years Total	15-17 years	18-19 years	20-24 years	25-29 years	30-34 years	35-39 years	40-44 years	45-54 years
						Number					
All live births											
All races[1]	4,058,814	8,519	468,990	157,209	311,781	1,017,806	1,087,547	929,278	452,057	90,013	4,604
White, total	3,194,005	4,439	333,013	106,786	226,227	772,811	874,180	764,708	368,711	72,414	3,729
White, non-Hispanic	2,362,968	1,840	204,056	58,759	145,297	523,971	651,445	617,371	302,576	58,631	3,078
Black, total	622,598	3,808	118,954	44,618	74,336	202,596	141,968	94,808	49,295	10,699	470
Black, non-Hispanic	604,346	3,736	116,019	43,520	72,499	197,190	137,545	91,477	47,577	10,347	455
Hispanic[2]	815,868	2,638	129,469	48,423	81,046	247,552	218,167	141,493	62,993	12,987	569
Live births in single deliveries											
All races[1]	3,932,573	8,401	461,430	155,013	306,417	994,973	1,055,143	892,549	430,743	85,568	3,766
White, total	3,094,219	4,383	328,163	105,407	222,756	757,193	848,539	733,674	350,728	68,552	2,987
White, non-Hispanic	2,281,129	1,824	200,935	57,960	142,975	512,693	630,695	590,506	286,845	55,230	2,401
Black, total	601,451	3,750	116,434	43,851	72,583	196,054	136,595	90,808	47,035	10,345	430
Black, non-Hispanic	583,667	3,680	113,530	42,766	70,764	190,773	132,299	87,577	45,391	10,001	416
Hispanic[2]	798,739	2,596	127,765	47,848	79,917	243,274	213,457	137,593	60,922	12,607	525
Live births in twin deliveries											
All races[1]	118,916	115	7,452	2,178	5,274	22,383	30,628	33,873	19,648	4,071	746
White, total	93,235	56	4,765	1,364	3,401	15,289	24,046	28,407	16,486	3,522	664
White, non-Hispanic	76,018	16	3,071	790	2,281	11,023	19,339	24,486	14,365	3,103	615
Black, total	20,626	55	2,500	764	1,736	6,444	5,250	3,841	2,165	340	31
Black, non-Hispanic	20,173	53	2,469	751	1,718	6,319	5,123	3,744	2,103	332	30
Hispanic[2]	16,470	42	1,669	569	1,100	4,204	4,545	3,682	1,953	341	34
Live births in higher order multiple deliveries[3]											
All races[1]	7,325	3	108	18	90	450	1,776	2,856	1,666	374	92
White, total	6,551	-	85	15	70	329	1,595	2,627	1,497	340	78
White, non-Hispanic	5,821	-	50	9	41	255	1,411	2,379	1,366	298	62
Black, total	521	3	20	3	17	98	123	159	95	14	9
Black, non-Hispanic	506	3	20	3	17	98	123	156	83	14	9
Hispanic[2]	659	-	35	6	29	74	165	218	118	39	10
						Ratio per 1,000 live births					
All multiple births											
All races[1]	31.1	13.9	16.1	14.0	17.2	22.4	29.8	39.5	47.1	49.4	182.0
White, total	31.2	12.6	14.6	12.9	15.3	20.2	29.3	40.6	48.8	53.3	.199.0
White, non-Hispanic	34.6	*	15.3	13.6	16.0	21.5	31.9	43.5	52.0	58.0	219.9
Black, total	34.0	15.2	21.2	17.2	23.6	32.3	37.8	42.2	45.8	33.1	85.1
Black, non-Hispanic	34.2	15.0	21.5	17.3	23.9	32.5	38.1	42.6	45.9	33.4	85.7
Hispanic[2]	21.0	15.9	13.2	11.9	13.9	17.3	21.6	27.6	32.9	29.3	77.3
Twin births											
All races[1]	29.3	13.5	15.9	13.9	16.9	22.0	28.2	36.5	43.5	45.2	162.0
White, total	29.2	12.6	14.3	12.8	15.0	19.8	27.5	37.1	44.7	48.6	178.1
White, non-Hispanic	32.2	*	15.0	13.4	15.7	21.0	29.7	39.7	47.5	52.9	199.8
Black, total	33.1	14.4	21.0	17.1	23.4	31.8	37.0	40.5	43.9	31.8	66.0
Black, non-Hispanic	33.4	14.2	21.3	17.3	23.7	32.0	37.2	40.9	44.2	32.1	65.9
Hispanic[2]	20.2	15.9	12.9	11.8	13.6	17.0	20.8	26.0	31.0	26.3	59.8
						Ratio per 100,000 live births					
Higher order multiple births[3]											
All races[1]	180.5	*	23.0	*	28.9	44.2	163.3	307.3	368.5	415.5	1998.3
White, total	205.1	*	25.5	*	30.9	42.6	182.5	343.5	406.0	469.5	2091.7
White, non-Hispanic	246.3	*	24.5	*	28.2	48.7	216.6	385.3	451.5	508.3	2014.3
Black, total	83.7	*	16.8	*	*	48.4	86.6	167.7	192.7	*	*
Black, non-Hispanic	83.7	*	17.2	*	*	49.7	89.4	170.5	174.5	*	*
Hispanic[2]	80.8	*	27.0	*	35.8	29.9	75.6	154.1	187.3	300.3	*

- Quantity zero.
* Figure does not meet standards of reliability or precision; based on fewer than 20 births in the numerator.
[1] Includes races other than white and black and origin not stated.
[2] Includes all persons of Hispanic origin of any race.
[3] Births in greater than twin deliveries.

SOURCE: J.A. Martin, B.E. Hamilton, S.J. Ventura, F. Menacker, and M.M. Park, "Table 50. Live births by plurality of birth and ratios, by age and race and Hispanic origin of mother: United States, 2000," in *Births: Final Data for 2000*, National Vital Statistics Reports, Vol. 50, No. 5, Centers for Disease Control and Prevention, National Center for Health Statistics, Hyattsville, MD, February 2002

cially inseminated with sperm from men whose wives were infertile, many people were concerned that surrogate motherhood might threaten family stability. Who would be considered the child's mother? Also, some surrogate mothers refused to relinquish the child after delivery, resulting in long, bitter fights for custody of the child.

Rapid advances in fertility technology have made such family matters even more complicated. The use of

FIGURE 2.3

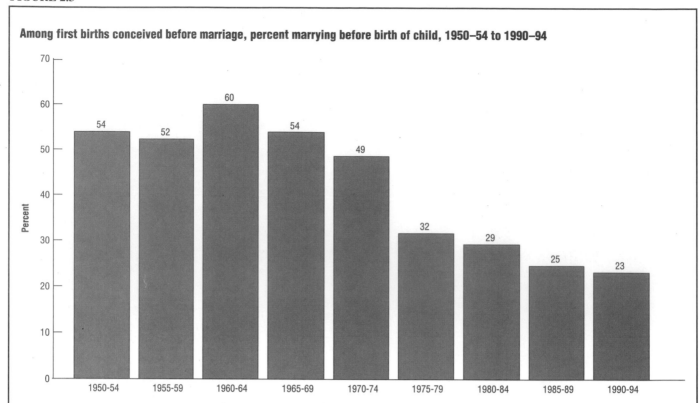

Among first births conceived before marriage, percent marrying before birth of child, 1950–54 to 1990–94

Note: Based on women aged 15–29 years at first birth.

SOURCE: S.J. Ventura and C.A. Bachrach, "Figure 16. Among first births conceived before marriage, percent marrying before birth of child: United States, 1950–54 to 1990–94," in *Nonmarital Childbearing in the United States, 1940–99,* National Vital Statistics Reports, Vol. 48, No. 16, Centers for Disease Control and Prevention, National Center for Health Statistics, Hyattsville, MD, October 2000

donor sperm and/or eggs could mean a child may have three or four parents—the donor or donors, the mother who carries the transplanted embryo in her uterus, and her spouse. While federal funding of human embryo research has been banned since the Reagan administration, private fertility enterprises continue to be unregulated in this country, and each fertility clinic has its own guidelines. Critics fear that fertility patients as well as donors may fall victim to unscrupulous clinics and doctors who may not have to answer to scientific and ethical review boards. To further complicate the issues, initial successes with cloning of sheep have led to reports about the cloning of humans.

Protecting the Family

In 1998, the New York State Task Force on Life and the Law, a 24-member panel of doctors, lawyers, ethicists, and clergy members, urged the formulation of more rigid standards to monitor reproductive technology. Past recommendations by this same panel have been included in U.S. Supreme Court rulings and state laws on issues in medical ethics, such as organ transplantation and the definition of death. Some of the task force's recommendations in regulating reproductive medicine include:

• Doctors cannot make embryos from donor sperm and eggs without permission from the donors who had intended those embryos for their own use.

• The birth mother should be considered the child's legal mother, even if a donor egg was used.

• There should be no discrimination in fertility technology when it comes to unmarried couples, including lesbians.

• The odds of consanguinity (blood relationship) should be studied. The task force believes children have the right to know of their genetic origin to avoid future mating with a blood relative from the same donors.

• Retrieval of gametes (sperm and eggs) from the dead should be banned.

Monitoring Fertility Technology

Because of the expense of fertility treatments (about $8,000 for each attempt), couples want to ensure a successful pregnancy. In most cases, the procedure must be repeated several times. Through ultrasound imaging, doctors can keep track of the number of maturing eggs. If too many eggs have matured, the doctor typically advises dis-

FIGURE 2.4

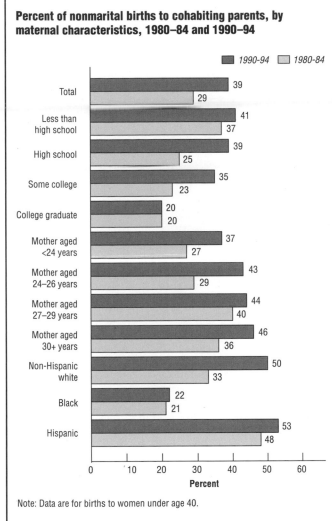

Percent of nonmarital births to cohabiting parents, by maternal characteristics, 1980–84 and 1990–94

Note: Data are for births to women under age 40.

SOURCE: S.J. Ventura and C.A. Bachrach, "Figure 15. Percent of nonmarital births to cohabiting parents, by maternal characteristics: United States, 1980–84 and 1990–94," in *Nonmarital Childbearing in the United States, 1940–99,* National Vital Statistics Reports, Vol. 48, No. 16, Centers for Disease Control and Prevention, National Center for Health Statistics, Hyattsville, MD, October 2000

FIGURE 2.5

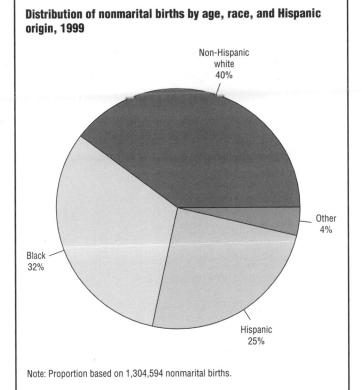

Distribution of nonmarital births by age, race, and Hispanic origin, 1999

Note: Proportion based on 1,304,594 nonmarital births.

SOURCE: S.J. Ventura and C.A. Bachrach, "Figure 11. Distribution of nonmarital births by age, race, and Hispanic origin: United States, 1999," in *Nonmarital Childbearing in the United States, 1940–99,* National Vital Statistics Reports, Vol. 48, No. 16, Centers for Disease Control and Prevention, National Center for Health Statistics, Hyattsville, MD, October 2000

continuing the treatment. Once sperm have been introduced, in cases in which it can be determined that a higher-order multiple birth will likely occur, many doctors consider destroying some of the embryos in order to improve viability of the remaining embryos. Generally, this may not be done without the permission of the parents. Some parents consider this act an abortion and refuse to permit it, a stance that often leads to a much higher level of multiple births.

WOMEN REDEFINE THEIR ROLE

Despite the nostalgia associated with the 1950s, many sociologists agree that the stereotypical family of the era, taken in the context of the historical American family, was more an exception than the rule. This "nuclear" family became insulated—and often, isolated—with women molding the children and doing more housework than women of past generations did.

While the husband's main role was that of breadwinner, by the 1960s many women were looking to redefine their own roles as homemakers. Many women who had experienced the economic independence of a paying job during World War II and who had attained personal satisfaction from working reentered the labor force. The availability of contraceptives enabled many young married women to postpone childbearing. The mothers of baby boomers, most of whom had given birth at a young age, saw the last of their children leave the nest. These mothers were ready to start a new chapter in life, which for many women meant finding a career.

More Education

Many older women performed service-oriented jobs traditionally held by females, such as secretaries and sales clerks, but many young women aspired to different careers. Realizing that higher education meant better wages, these young women pursued postsecondary education. In 1960, women earned about one-third of both

FIGURE 2.6

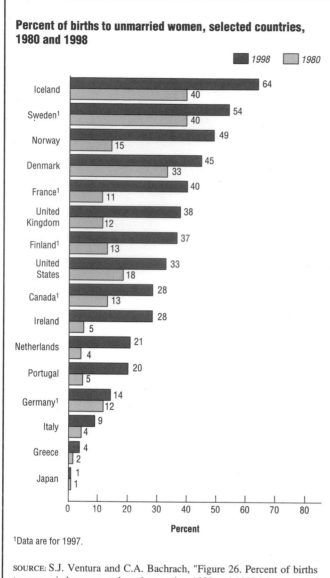

Percent of births to unmarried women, selected countries, 1980 and 1998

■ *1998* ▨ *1980*

Country	1998	1980
Iceland	64	40
Sweden[1]	54	40
Norway	49	15
Denmark	45	33
France[1]	40	11
United Kingdom	38	12
Finland[1]	37	13
United States	33	18
Canada[1]	28	13
Ireland	28	5
Netherlands	21	4
Portugal	20	5
Germany[1]	14	12
Italy	9	4
Greece	4	2
Japan	1	1

Percent

[1]Data are for 1997.

SOURCE: S.J. Ventura and C.A. Bachrach, "Figure 26. Percent of births to unmarried women, selected countries, 1980 and 1998," in *Nonmarital Childbearing in the United States, 1940–99,"* National Vital Statistics Reports, Vol. 48, No. 16, Centers for Disease Control and Prevention, National Center for Health Statistics, Hyattsville, MD, October 2000

FIGURE 2.7

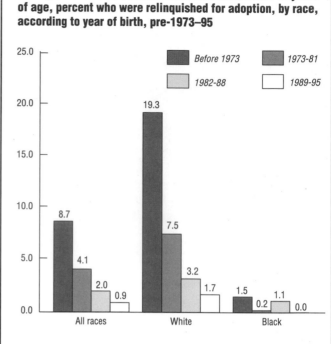

Among children born to never-married women under 45 years of age, percent who were relinquished for adoption, by race, according to year of birth, pre-1973–95

■ *Before 1973*   ▨ *1973-81*
▨ *1982-88*   □ *1989-95*

	Before 1973	1973-81	1982-88	1989-95
All races	8.7	4.1	2.0	0.9
White	19.3	7.5	3.2	1.7
Black	1.5	0.2	1.1	0.0

SOURCE: S.J. Ventura and C.A. Bachrach, "Figure 22. Among children born to never-married women under 45 years of age, percent who were relinquished for adoption, by race, according to year of birth," in *Nonmarital Childbearing in the United States, 1940–99,* National Vital Statistics Reports, Vol. 48, No. 16, Centers for Disease Control and Prevention, National Center for Health Statistics, Hyattsville, MD, October 2000

bachelor's (35.3 percent) and master's degrees (31.6 percent). By 1985, they were earning fully half of these degrees. The increase in the attainment of first professional degrees, such as medicine and law, was even more dramatic, doubling from 12.4 percent in 1975 to 24.8 percent in 1980 and soaring to 32.8 percent by 1985. By 1999, 23.1 percent of women and 27.4 percent of men had a college education. More than half of bachelor's and master's degrees, and 4 of 10 first professional degrees, went to women.

Into the Labor Force

In 1950, about one in three women participated in the labor force, that is, worked outside the home. By 1998, three of every five women of working age were in the workforce, an increase from a 33.9 percent participation rate in 1950 to 59.8 percent in 1998. The most significant increase was among those women in the 25 to 34 age range, who more than doubled their participation in the workforce after 1950. The only group to experience a decline in labor force participation was women age 65 and over. Between 1950 and 1998, the labor force participation rate for this group dropped from 9.7 percent to 8.6 percent. (See Figure 2.10.)

The number of women in the workforce continues to increase. In 1988, 57 percent of women age 16 and over were in the workforce, compared to 76 percent of men. The *Occupational Outlook Handbook* projects that by 2008, 62 percent of women and 74 percent of men will be working. Together, they will represent 68 percent of the population age 16 and over. (See Figure 2.11.) Between 1998 and 2008, the number of women in the labor force is projected to grow by 15 percent, compared to 12 percent for the growth of the total labor force. (See Figure 2.12.) By 2008, women may comprise 48 percent of the total workforce, coming close to the 52 percent share of men.

According to the U.S. Census Bureau study *We the American Women,* even though women have made progress in entering occupations predominately held by men (especially executive and professional specialty occupations), the majority of women are still in traditional "female" occupations. Women continue to be overrepresented in administrative support and service occupations and underrepresented in precision production, craft and repair occupations, and the transportation and material-moving occupations. For example, 79.3 percent of people involved in administrative support (including clerical) were female, and 95.5 percent of the 859,000 people employed as service workers in private homes were female.

Income Important to Family Well-being

Pay rates for all workers have increased as the workforce grew, but women's pay has not caught up with that of men. In 1967, the average full-time, year-round employed female earned about $18,000, compared to about $31,000 for men. By 2000, women's average earnings had increased 52 percent to $27,355, while the average men's salary rose 20.4 percent to $37,339. Women now received 73 percent of the wages paid to men. (See Figure 2.13.) For women with college degrees, the gap between their salaries and those of men with similar degrees was wider. The median salary for women with bachelor's degrees was 70.8 percent of that paid to men with bachelor's degrees ($35,408 for women, compared to $49,982 for men). And the $55,460 median salary for women with professional degrees was 61.2 percent of the $90,653 median salary for professional men.

Household incomes also increased over the past 30-plus years, but differences are seen by race and ethnicity. (See Figure 2.14.) Household income also varied by geographic region. In 2000, the median household income in the Northeast, Midwest, and West was about $45,000 (ranging from $44,646 to $45,106), compared to $38,410 in the South. (See Figure 2.15.)

CAREGIVERS

The U.S. Census Bureau defines a female-headed family as a family consisting of two or more persons living together who are related by birth, marriage, or adoption and in which the householder is a woman without a spouse present. Female-headed households may or may not have children present. Those that do not have children may consist of any combination of related persons, such as parents, grandparents, aunts, uncles, and in-laws.

In 2000, there were 14.7 million female-headed families (19.6 percent of family households). Female-headed families have grown continuously, from 5.5 million (11 percent) in 1970 and 10.9 million (16 percent) in 1990. This trend continues, reflecting the rising numbers of divorces, marital separations, and out-of-wedlock births. Of female heads of families, 14.4 percent in 2000 were young women in the 15–24 age range, while half (50.3

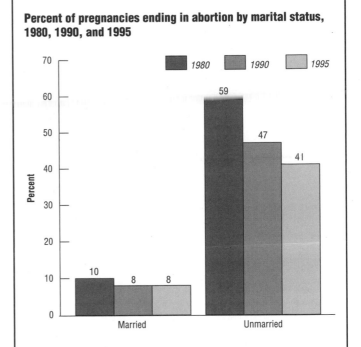

FIGURE 2.8

Percent of pregnancies ending in abortion by marital status, 1980, 1990, and 1995

SOURCE: S.J. Ventura and C.A. Bachrach, "Figure 20. Percent of pregnancies ending in abortion by marital status: United States, 1980, 1990, and 1995," in *Nonmarital Childbearing in the United States, 1940–99,* National Vital Statistics Reports, Vol. 48, No. 16, Centers for Disease Control and Prevention, National Center for Health Statistics, Hyattsville, MD, October 2000

percent) were in the traditional childbearing age range of 25 to 44. One-third (33.6 percent) of these women were divorced, and another 14.9 percent were separated, either legally or informally. Another third (35.2 percent) had never been married. Sixty percent of female heads of families had a high school education or less. (See Table 2.3.)

A somewhat unexpected result of better medical care and increased longevity is the phenomenon of the "sandwich generation"—adults who still have children living at home but who are also attending to the needs of their aging parents. While an increasing number of men have primary parental responsibility, women remain the traditional caregivers. In most cases, these women are employed and must meet the challenge of both family and work obligations.

Demands on Work

The demands of caregiving usually require some adjustments at work. Nearly two-thirds (64.1 percent) of caregivers surveyed by the National Alliance for Caregiving and the American Association of Retired Persons (*Family Caregiving in the U.S.: Findings from a National Survey,* Bethesda, Maryland, and Washington, D.C., 1997) were employed, most (51.8 percent) full-time. About one-half (54.2 percent) reported having to make

FIGURE 2.9

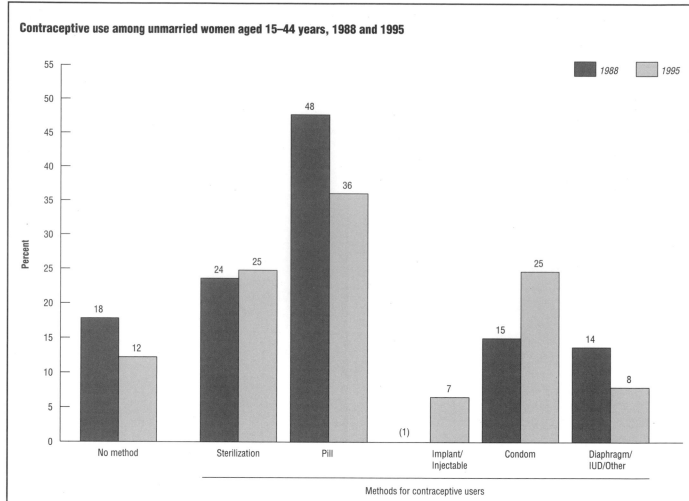

Contraceptive use among unmarried women aged 15–44 years, 1988 and 1995

¹Methods not available in 1988.

SOURCE: S.J. Ventura and C.A. Bachrach, "Figure 24. Contraceptive use among unmarried women aged 15–44 years: United States, 1988 and 1995," in *Nonmarital Childbearing in the United States, 1940–99,* National Vital Statistics Reports, Vol. 48, No. 16, Centers for Disease Control and Prevention, National Center for Health Statistics, Hyattsville, MD, October 2000

some type of adjustments at work as a result of caregiving responsibilities. Overall, nearly half (49.4 percent) of caregivers had to make changes to their daily work schedule, such as going in late, leaving early, or taking time off during the day. Some caregivers reported giving up their job either temporarily or permanently—10.9 percent took a leave of absence, 3.6 percent took early retirement, and 6.4 percent gave up their jobs altogether. About 7 percent worked fewer hours or took a less demanding job. A smaller percentage reported having lost some job benefits (4.2 percent) or having turned down a promotion (3.1 percent) because of caregiving.

Child Support

Inadequate, or lack of, financial support from noncustodial parents contributes to the high incidence of poverty among children living in single-parent families. When custodial parents are not paid the child support due them, they often turn to public welfare. According to *Child Support for Custodial Mothers and Fathers: 1997* (Timothy Grall, U.S. Bureau of the Census, Washington, D.C., 2000), a comprehensive report on child support, of the 13.7 million custodial parents, the majority (11.6 million, or 85.1 percent) were women, and 2.1 million (14.9 percent) were men.

MEN'S CHANGING ROLE

The number of single male heads of families is also increasing, growing from 3.9 million in 1998 to 4.3 million in 2000. Like female heads of families, one-third of single male heads of families were divorced (35 percent). Forty percent had never married, compared to 35.2 percent of female heads of families. Ten percent were widowed, compared to 16.3 percent of female heads of families. Quite similar to women, 58.5 percent of single male heads of families had high school educations or less. (See Table 2.3.)

FIGURE 2.10

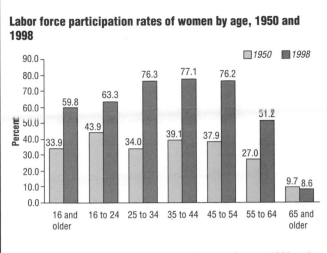

Labor force participation rates of women by age, 1950 and 1998

SOURCE: "Labor force participation rates of women by age, 1950 and 1998," in "Changes in women's labor force participation in the 20th century," *Monthly Labor Review: The Editor's Desk,* U.S. Department of Labor, Bureau of Labor Statistics, Washington, DC, February 16, 2000 [Online] http://www.bls.gov/opub/ted/2000/feb/wk3/art03.htm [accessed November 26, 2002]

FIGURE 2.11

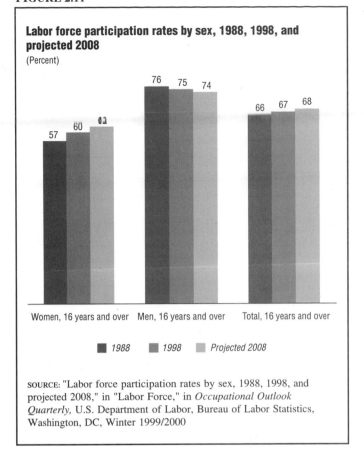

Labor force participation rates by sex, 1988, 1998, and projected 2008
(Percent)

SOURCE: "Labor force participation rates by sex, 1988, 1998, and projected 2008," in "Labor Force," in *Occupational Outlook Quarterly,* U.S. Department of Labor, Bureau of Labor Statistics, Washington, DC, Winter 1999/2000

FIGURE 2.12

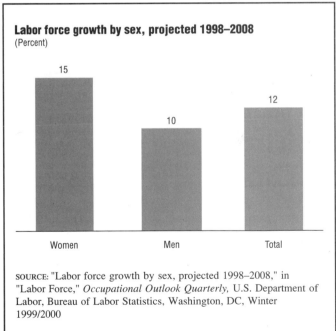

Labor force growth by sex, projected 1998–2008
(Percent)

SOURCE: "Labor force growth by sex, projected 1998–2008," in "Labor Force," *Occupational Outlook Quarterly,* U.S. Department of Labor, Bureau of Labor Statistics, Washington, DC, Winter 1999/2000

Contemporary Fathers

In a "Facts & Features" press release for Father's Day 2002, the U.S. Census Bureau provided a profile of contemporary fathers.

Of the 25.8 million fathers who were part of a married-couple family with children in 2000:

- 12 percent were under age 30.
- 61 percent had an annual family income of $50,000 or more.
- 22 percent were raising three or more of their own children under age 18.
- 9 percent were raising their own infants under age 1.

Of the 2 million single fathers with children in 2000:

- 22 percent were under age 30.
- 24 percent had an annual family income of $50,000 or more.
- 10 percent were raising three of more of their own children under age 18.
- 10 percent were raising their own infants under age 1.

The Future of Fatherhood

Researchers believe that more changes will occur in the roles of men and women in the twenty-first century. If mothers of young children continue to join the labor force, fathers may have to assume more child-care tasks. Researchers ask whether modern fathers will accept an increasing share of child-rearing responsibilities or flee from them. A bigger issue concerns the role and/or the commitment of noncustodial fathers in divorced families and fathers of children born out of wedlock.

According to the U.S. Department of Health and Human Services (HHS), the number of children growing up

FIGURE 2.13

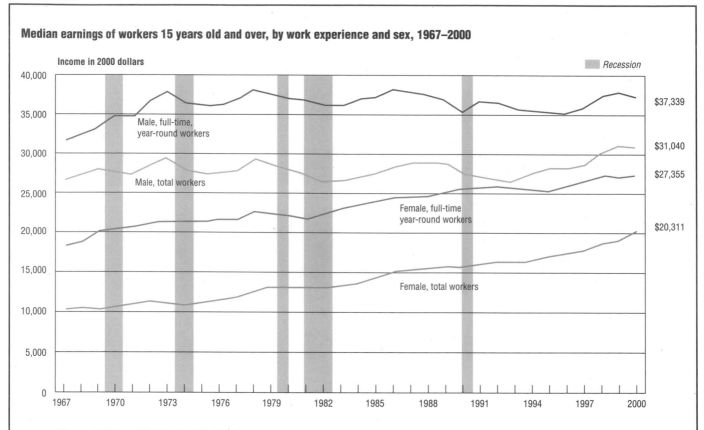

Median earnings of workers 15 years old and over, by work experience and sex, 1967–2000

Income in 2000 dollars

Recession

SOURCE: Carmen DeNavas-Walt, Robert W. Cleveland, and Marc I. Roemer, "Figure 3. Median earnings of workers 15 years old and over by work experience and sex: 1967–2000," in *Money Income in the United States 2000,* Current Population Reports, U.S. Census Bureau, Washington, DC, September 2001

in homes without fathers has increased dramatically since 1960. Nearly 25 million children today do not live with their fathers, compared to fewer than 10 million in 1960. More than one-third of these children will not see their fathers at all during the course of a year. Studies indicate that children who grow up without responsible fathers are significantly more likely to experience poverty, perform poorly in school, engage in criminal activity, and abuse drugs and alcohol. In addition to a number of programs to strengthen families and encourage the involvement of fathers for 2003, HHS has proposed a Fatherhood Initiative to:

- Promote responsible fatherhood through skill-based marriage and parenting education, job training, and other services to help fathers provide emotional and financial support to their children.

- Mentor children of prisoners who suffer disproportionate rates of substance abuse, gang involvement, early childbearing, and delinquency.

NEVER MARRIED

In 2000, 28.1 percent of the population age 15 or older had never been married, compared to 24.9 percent of the same population in 1970. The greatest difference in 2000 can be seen in the 20- to 29-year-old population, the group that is delaying marriage. In 1970, 44.5 percent of 20- to 24-year-olds had never been married; in 2000, 78.3 percent of this age group remained single. Only 14.7 percent of 25- to 29-year-olds had never been married in 1970; in 2000, 45.2 percent of this age group remained single. Of the 213.7 million people age 15 and over, 4.5 million were separated and 19.8 million were divorced. Another 13.6 million were widowed, and 11.0 million of these were female. (See Table 2.4.)

Since 1970, the percentage of the population age 15 and over that is married has steadily declined. The widowed population has declined more gradually, reflecting the aging of World War II couples as well as remarriage after the death of a spouse. Meanwhile, the percentage of the population who never married and of those who have separated or divorced has increased. In 1970, 28.1 percent of men and 22.1 percent of women had never been married. By 2000, 31.3 percent of men and 25.2 percent of women had never married. The growth of separation and divorce is significant. In 1970, 3.5 percent of men and 5.7 percent of women were separated or divorced. By 2000, those numbers had grown to 10.1 percent for men and

FIGURE 2.14

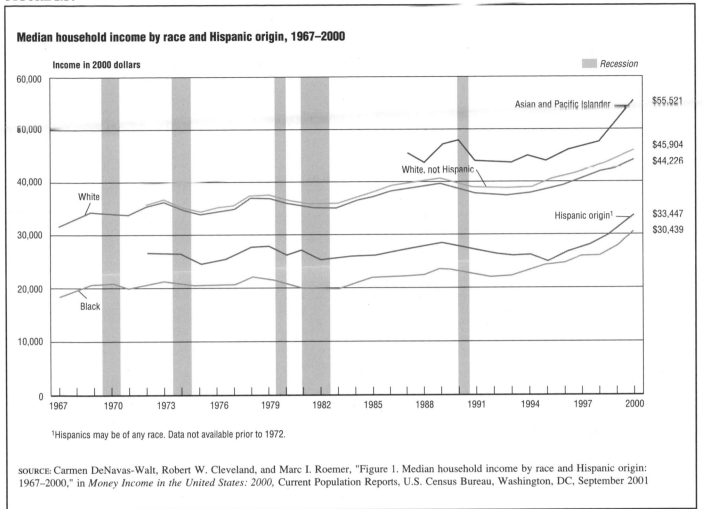

Median household income by race and Hispanic origin, 1967–2000

Income in 2000 dollars

Recession

Asian and Pacific Islander — $55,521

White, not Hispanic

$45,904

$44,226

White

Hispanic origin[1] — $33,447

$30,439

Black

[1]Hispanics may be of any race. Data not available prior to 1972.

SOURCE: Carmen DeNavas-Walt, Robert W. Cleveland, and Marc I. Roemer, "Figure 1. Median household income by race and Hispanic origin: 1967–2000," in *Money Income in the United States: 2000,* Current Population Reports, U.S. Census Bureau, Washington, DC, September 2001

12.6 percent for women. The percentage of widowed men has remained relatively stable at 2.4–2.5 percent of the population since 1980, while the number of widowed females has dropped from 12 percent in 1880 to 10 percent in 2000. (See Figure 2.16.)

Changes in marital and family patterns have contributed to more and more people, particularly women, living alone. (See Figure 2.17.)

DOMESTIC VIOLENCE

The U.S. Department of Justice reports that violence rates between intimate partners—current or former spous-es, boyfriends, or girlfriends—declined between 1993 and 1999. However, in 1999, the nonfatal intimate-partner violence rate among females age 16–24 was 15.6 victim-izations per 1,000, compared to 5.8 per 1,000 for all females over age 12. Younger victims were least likely to report the incidents to the police. Black and white women had similar rates of intimate-partner violence except in the 20–24 age group. Black women in this age range were victims at the rate of 29 per 1,000, compared to 20 per 1,000 for white women of the same age. Women separat-ed from their husbands were more likely to be victims of intimate-partner violence, while women age 35 to 49 were more susceptible to murder by an intimate partner.

FIGURE 2.15

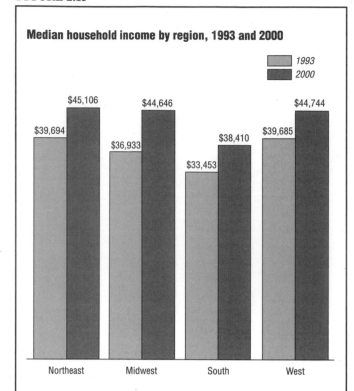

Median household income by region, 1993 and 2000

1993
2000

Northeast	Midwest	South	West
$39,694	$36,933	$33,453	$39,685
$45,106	$44,646	$38,410	$44,744

SOURCE: Carmen DeNavas-Walt, Robert W. Cleveland, and Marc I. Roemer, "Figure 2. Median household income by region: 1993 and 2000," in *Money Income in the United States 2000,* Current Population Reports, U.S. Census Bureau, Washington, DC, September 2001

TABLE 2.3

Family groups by type and selected characteristics of householder, March 2000

(In thousands)

Characteristic	Total	Married couple	Other family groups Total	Male	Female
All family groups	75,579	56,497	19,083	4,286	14,797
Age of reference person					
15 to 24 years old	4,396	1,663	2,733	609	2,124
25 to 34 years old	14,162	9,699	4,463	989	3,474
35 to 44 years old	19,509	14,361	5,148	1,177	3,971
45 to 54 years old	16,134	12,987	3,147	741	2,406
55 to 64 years old	9,675	8,234	1,441	354	1,087
65 years old and over	11,704	9,553	2,151	416	1,735
Race and ethnicity of reference person					
White	62,721	49,720	13,001	3,274	9,727
Non-Hispanic	54,711	44,431	10,280	2,597	7,683
Black	9,445	4,218	5,227	762	4,465
Asian and Pacific Islander	2,745	2,161	584	187	397
Hispanic (of any race)	8,420	5,505	2,915	725	2,190
Marital status of reference person					
Married (spouse present)	56,497	56,497	(X)	(X)	(X)
Married (spouse absent or separated)	2,821	(X)	2,821	604	2,217
Divorced	6,469	(X)	6,469	1,498	4,971
Widowed	2,845	(X)	2,845	440	2,405
Never Married	6,947	(X)	6,947	1,744	5,203
Education of reference person					
Less than high school	12,299	7,760	4,539	974	3,565
High school graduate	24,418	17,559	6,859	1,536	5,323
Some college	20,030	14,743	5,287	1,085	4,202
College graduate	18,832	16,434	2,398	691	1,707
Labor force status of reference person					
Employed	52,777	40,018	12,759	3,154	9,605
Unemployed	1,931	999	932	202	730
Not in labor force	20,872	15,479	5,393	931	4,462

X Not applicable.

Note: Data are not shown separately for the American Indian and Alaska Native population because of the small sample size in the Current Population Survey in March 2000.

SOURCE: Jason Fields and Lynne M. Casper, "Table 3. Family Groups by Type and Selected Characteristics of Householder: March 2000," in *America's Families and Living Arrangements: March 2000,* Current Population Reports, U.S. Census Bureau, Washington, DC, June 2001

TABLE 2.4

Marital status of people 15 years and over, March 1970 and March 2000

Characteristic	March 2000 Number							Percent never married	March 1970 percent never married[1]
	Total	Married spouse present	Married spouse absent	Sepa- rated	Divorced	Widowed	Never married		
Both sexes									
Total 15 years old and over	213,773	113,002	2,730	4,479	19,881	13,665	60,016	28.1	24.9
15 to 19 years old	20,102	345	36	103	64	13	19,541	97.2	93.9
20 to 24 years old	18,440	3,362	134	234	269	11	14,430	78.3	44.5
25 to 29 years old	18,269	8,334	280	459	917	27	8,252	45.2	14.7
30 to 34 years old	19,519	11,930	278	546	1,616	78	5,071	26.0	7.8
35 to 44 years old	44,804	29,353	717	1,436	5,967	399	6,932	15.5	5.9
45 to 54 years old	36,633	25,460	492	899	5,597	882	3,303	9.0	6.1
55 to 64 years old	23,388	16,393	308	441	3,258	1,770	1,218	5.2	7.2
65 years old and over	32,620	17,827	485	361	2,193	10,484	1,270	3.9	7.6
Males									
Total 15 years old and over	103,113	56,501	1,365	1,818	8,572	2,604	32,253	31.3	28.1
15 to 19 years old	10,295	69	3	51	29	3	10,140	98.5	97.4
20 to 24 years old	9,208	1,252	75	70	101	-	7,710	83.7	54.7
25 to 29 years old	8,943	3,658	139	170	342	9	4,625	51.7	19.1
30 to 34 years old	9,622	5,640	151	205	712	15	2,899	30.1	9.4
35 to 44 years old	22,134	14,310	387	585	2,775	96	3,981	18.0	6.7
45 to 54 years old	17,891	13,027	255	378	2,377	157	1,697	9.5	7.5
55 to 64 years old	11,137	8,463	158	188	1,387	329	612	5.5	7.8
65 years old and over	13,885	10,084	197	171	849	1,994	590	4.2	7.5
Females									
Total 15 years old and over	110,660	56,501	1,365	2,661	11,309	11,061	27,763	25.1	22.1
15 to 19 years old	9,807	276	33	52	35	10	9,401	95.9	90.3
20 to 24 years old	9,232	2,110	59	164	168	11	6,720	72.8	35.8
25 to 29 years old	9,326	4,676	141	289	575	18	3,627	38.9	10.5
30 to 34 years old	9,897	6,290	127	341	904	63	2,172	21.9	6.2
35 to 44 years old	22,670	15,043	330	851	3,192	303	2,951	13.0	5.2
45 to 54 years old	18,742	12,433	237	521	3,220	725	1,606	8.6	4.9
55 to 64 years old	12,251	7,930	150	253	1,871	1,441	606	4.9	6.8
65 years old and over	18,735	7,743	288	190	1,344	8,490	680	3.6	7.7

- Represents zero or rounds to zero.

[1]The 1970 percentages include 14-year-olds, and thus are for 14+ and 14-19.

SOURCE: Jason Fields and Lynne M. Casper, "Table 5. Marital Status of People 15 Years and Over: March 1970 and March 2000," in *America's Families and Living Arrangements: March 2000,* Current Population Reports, U.S. Census Bureau, Washington, DC, June 2001

FIGURE 2.16

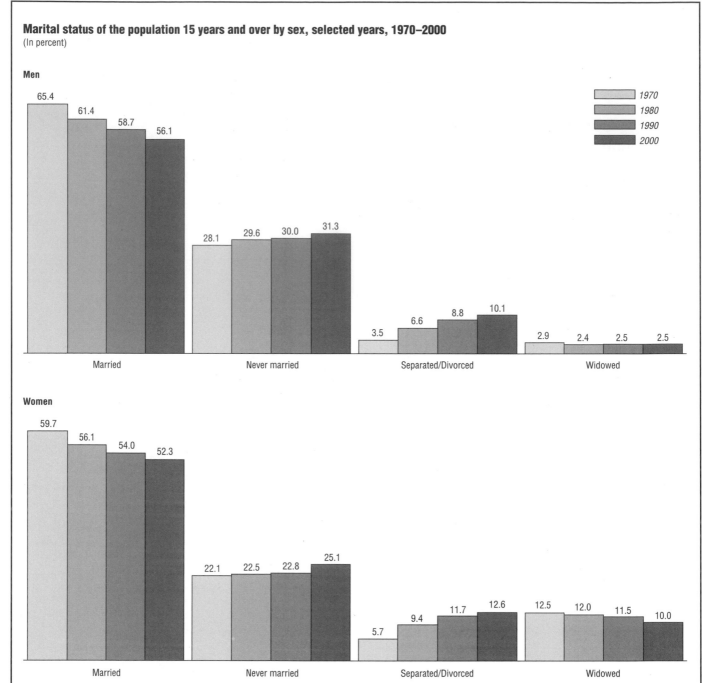

Marital status of the population 15 years and over by sex, selected years, 1970–2000
(In percent)

SOURCE: Jason Fields and Lynne M. Casper, "Figure 4. Marital Status of the Population 15 Years and Over by Sex: Selected Years, 1970 to 2000," in *America's Families and Living Arrangements: March 2000,* Current Population Reports, U.S. Census Bureau, Washington, DC, June 2001

FIGURE 2.17

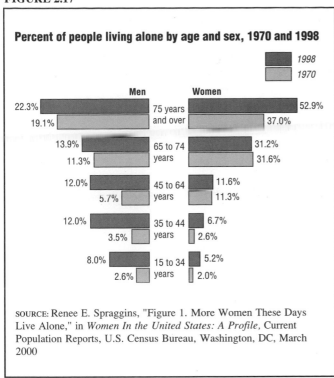

Percent of people living alone by age and sex, 1970 and 1998

| | 1998 |
| | 1970 |

Men — **Women**

75 years and over
Men 1998: 22.3%
Men 1970: 19.1%
Women 1998: 52.9%
Women 1970: 37.0%

65 to 74 years
Men 1998: 13.9%
Men 1970: 11.3%
Women 1998: 31.2%
Women 1970: 31.6%

45 to 64 years
Men 1998: 12.0%
Men 1970: 5.7%
Women 1998: 11.6%
Women 1970: 11.3%

35 to 44 years
Men 1998: 12.0%
Men 1970: 3.5%
Women 1998: 6.7%
Women 1970: 2.6%

15 to 34 years
Men 1998: 8.0%
Men 1970: 2.6%
Women 1998: 5.2%
Women 1970: 2.0%

SOURCE: Renee E. Spraggins, "Figure 1. More Women These Days Live Alone," in *Women In the United States: A Profile,* Current Population Reports, U.S. Census Bureau, Washington, DC, March 2000

CHAPTER 3
THE CHILDREN OF AMERICA

AMERICA'S CHILDREN: INDICATORS OF WELL-BEING

The sixth annual federal interagency report, *America's Children: Key National Indicators of Well-Being, 2002,* contains some good news. The mortality rate for infants and for children ages 5 to 14 has declined. Fewer births to teenage mothers occurred. Most children (82 percent) are in good to excellent health. The health of low-income children improved, with 70 percent in very good or excellent health, compared to 60 percent in 1984. More children have at least one parent working. The child poverty rate is at its lowest level since 1979, and the number of children suffering from hunger declined. Fewer children are smoking cigarettes. More young children are read to by a family member on a daily basis. Many other statistics remain unchanged from the previous year, indicating that, overall, the nation is making progress in improving the quality of life for its children.

The Children's Defense Fund presents more startling information about the challenges children face with its list of 25 Key Facts About American Children. While one-third of children are behind a year or more in school, 12.5 percent never graduate from high school and 40 percent will never complete a single year of college. One-third of children will be poor sometime during their childhoods, while 20 percent of children are born poor. (See Table 3.1.)

THE NUMBER OF CHILDREN

Since the mid-1960s, the number of children has been decreasing as a proportion of the total U.S. population. In 1950, 31 percent of the population was under age 18. In 1960, the population share of children peaked at 36 percent and began a decline to 26 percent by 1990. While the 72 million children under age 18 still represented 26 percent of the population in 2000, the U.S. Census Bureau projects that by 2010 only 24 percent of the population will be children under age 18.

TABLE 3.1

Twenty-five key facts about American children, 2001

1 in 2 will live in a single parent family at some point in childhood.
1 in 3 is born to unmarried parents.
1 in 3 will be poor at some point in their childhood.
1 in 3 is behind a year or more in school.
1 in 4 lives with only one parent.
2 in 5 never complete a single year of college.
1 in 5 was born poor.
1 in 5 is born to a mother who did not graduate from high school.
1 in 5 has a foreign-born mother.
3 in 5 preschoolers have their mother in the labor force.
1 in 6 is poor now.
1 in 6 is born to a mother who did not receive prenatal care in the first three months of pregnancy.
1 in 7 has no health insurance.
1 in 7 has a worker in their family but still is poor.
1 in 8 lives in a family receiving food stamps.
1 in 8 never graduates from high school.
1 in 8 is born to a teenage mother.
1 in 12 has a disability.
1 in 13 was born with low birthweight.
1 in 15 lives at less than half the poverty level.
1 in 24 lives with neither parent.
1 in 26 is born to a mother who received late or no prenatal care.
1 in 60 sees their parents divorce in any year.
1 in 139 will die before their first birthday.
1 in 1,056 will be killed by guns before age 20.

SOURCE: "25 Key Facts About American Children," in *The State of America's Children Yearbook 2001,* Children's Defense Fund, Washington, DC, 2001 [Online] http://www.childrensdefense.org/keyfacts.htm [accessed November 25, 2002]

Racial and Ethnic Diversity

Like the American population in general, America's children have become a more racially and ethnically diverse group over the past two decades. From 1980 to 2000, the proportion of Hispanic and Asian and Pacific Islander children increased significantly. In 1980, Hispanic children represented 9 percent of the population under age 18; by 2000, 16 percent of children were Hispanic. The Census Bureau predicts that by 2010, Hispanic children will make up 19 percent of America's children. The share of Asian and Pacific Islander children doubled from

TABLE 3.2

Native and foreign-born children under age 18 living in households and families by nativity of householder, 2000

(Numbers in thousands)

Item	All children		Native children		Foreign-born children		
	Total	Under age 6	Total	Under age 6	Total	Under age 6	Percent of all children
ALL HOUSEHOLDS							
Total	72,116	23,574	69,317	23,161	2,799	413	3.9
In family households	71,291	23,324	68,529	22,919	2,761	406	3.9
In families	70,469	23,099	67,764	22,698	2,705	401	3.8
Own child	64,965	20,784	62,560	20,435	2,405	348	3.7
Other related child	5,504	2,316	5,204	2,263	299	53	5.4
Not in families	822	225	765	220	56	5	6.8
Not in family households	825	250	788	243	38	8	4.6
Related child	70,469	23,099	67,764	22,698	2,705	401	3.8
Unrelated child	1,647	475	1,553	463	94	13	5.7
NATIVE HOUSEHOLDS							
Total	60,638	19,518	60,398	19,450	240	68	0.4
In family households	59,901	19,307	59,664	19,239	238	68	0.4
In families	59,226	19,139	59,008	19,071	218	68	0.4
Own child	54,785	17,320	54,590	17,252	195	68	0.4
Other related child	4,442	1,819	4,418	1,819	24	-	0.5
Not in families	675	168	656	168	19	-	2.8
Not in family households	737	211	734	211	3	-	0.4
Related child	59,226	19,139	59,008	19,071	218	68	0.4
Unrelated child	1,412	379	1,390	379	22	-	1.6
FOREIGN-BORN HOUSEHOLDS							
Total	11,478	4,056	8,919	3,711	2,558	345	22.3
In family households	11,389	4,018	8,866	3,680	2,523	338	22.2
In families	11,242	3,960	8,756	3,627	2,486	333	22.1
Own child	10,180	3,464	7,970	3,184	2,211	280	21.7
Other related child	1,062	496	787	444	275	53	25.9
Not in families	147	58	110	53	37	5	25.2
Not in family households	88	39	53	31	35	8	39.8
Related child	11,242	3,960	8,756	3,627	2,486	333	22.1
Unrelated child	235	97	163	84	72	13	30.6

- Represents zero.

SOURCE: "Figure 13-1. Native and Foreign-Born Children Under Age 18 Living in Households and Families by Nativity of Householder: 2000," in *Profile of Foreign-Born Population in the United States: 2000*, U.S. Census Bureau, Washington, DC, December 2001

2 percent in 1980 to 4 percent in 2000; the Census Bureau projects Asian and Pacific Islander children will represent 6 percent of the under-18 population by 2010.

Meanwhile, the proportion of white non-Hispanic children declined from 74 percent of all children in 1980 to 64 percent in 2000. By 2010, white non-Hispanic children are expected to represent only 59 percent of the population of children. Through all this change, black non-Hispanic children have remained a steady 15 percent and American Indian and Alaska Native children represent 1 percent of America's children.

AGE. Children under age 5 make up about one-third of the child population (33 percent), the 6–11 age group makes up another third (34 percent), and the remaining third are children age 12 to 17 (33 percent).

FAMILIES WITH CHILDREN

In 1970, despite the trend toward fewer children, married couples with children under the age of 18 made up 40

percent of all households. (By Census Bureau definition, "nonfamily" households do not contain "own children." However, the Census Bureau acknowledges that nonfamily households may contain persons under the age of 18 who are not relatives of the householder. These children are included in the total count of all children in the United States.) In 2000, 51.7 percent of households were married couples, but less than half (23.5 percent) had children under age 18 living in the home. Utah leads the nation with 63.2 percent married-couple households and 35.0 percent married couples with children under age 18. Utah was also the only state in 2000 with an average of more than three people per household.

Households headed by a female or a male without a spouse in 2000 were more likely to have children present. Female-headed family households represented 12.2 percent of households and 7.2 percent of households with children. The highest proportion of children living with a female householder (10.4 percent) was in Puerto Rico. Male-headed family households represented 4.2 percent of households, and half (2.1 percent) included children under age 18. In Alaska, where 5.5 percent of households are male family households, 3.6 percent include children.

Children of Foreign-Born Householders

Of the 72.1 million children under age 18 living in U.S. households in 2000, 11.5 million were living with a foreign-born householder. The majority of these children (98.7 percent) were the householder's own child, but a few were grandchildren, nieces, or nephews of the householder. (See Table 3.2.) The proportion of children living with at least one foreign-born parent increased from 15 percent in 1994 to 19 percent in 2001.

Foreign-born householders in 2000 had more children under age six who were born in the United States than were foreign born (41.6 percent native born, compared to 13.6 percent foreign born). Children of foreign-born householders were more likely to be in poverty (24 percent, compared to 14.9 percent for children of native-born householders). The "America's Children, 2000" report notes that children of foreign-born parents and their parents may need assistance to overcome language and cultural barriers both at school and at home in order for the children to succeed in school.

LIVING ARRANGEMENTS OF CHILDREN

Not surprisingly, the increasing number of divorces, marital separations, and out-of-wedlock births has significantly reshaped the living arrangements of American children. In the year 2000, children under 18 were considerably more likely to be living with only one parent than they had been 20 years earlier.

While the number of married-couple families with children declined from 87 percent in 1970 to 69 percent in 2000, single-mother families more than doubled during the same period, from 12 percent to 26 percent. The greatest increase was for male single-parent families with children, which quintupled from 1 percent of 1970 families to 5 percent of families in 2000.

Stepchildren

Many divorced parents eventually remarry and their children become part of stepfamilies, or blended families. The most common stepfamily consists of children living with a biological mother and a stepfather, with no other children present. The frequency of this arrangement is attributable to the large number of divorced women who gain custody of their children. Another type of stepfamily consists of at least one stepchild and one biological child of the couple. According to the U.S. Census Bureau, approximately 15 percent of all children live in stepfamilies and are included in the bureau's count of children in two-parent families.

Children and Grandparents

There were 3.9 million multigenerational households with children in 2000. These combination families included a variety of groupings of children, parents, and grandparents. Three-generation families with the householder, child, and grandchild accounted for 2.6 million multigenerational households. Another 1.3 million families included the householder with his or her parent and his or her child. In some cases, members of four generations lived in the same household. There were 78,000 such families in 2000. (See Table 3.3.)

In *Coresident Grandparents and Their Grandchildren: Grandparent-Maintained Families* (U.S. Bureau of the Census, Washington, D.C., 1998), Lynne M. Casper and Kenneth R. Bryson reported on the rising trend of grandparents raising grandchildren. They reported that in 1970, 3.2 percent (2.2 million) of all American children under the age of 18 lived in family households maintained by a grandparent. By 1997, this figure had grown to 3.9 million (5.5 percent of the population). The issue became significant enough that as early as 1992 the U.S. House of Representatives held hearings that focused on the causes of this growing phenomenon and issues of grandparents' rights and their access to public assistance.

DIVORCE, SUBSTANCE ABUSE, NEGLECT PUT GRANDPARENTS IN CHARGE. According to Casper and Bryson, some researchers attribute the growing trend in coresident grandparent/grandchildren families to the continuing incidence of divorce, the rise in single-parent households, parental substance abuse, teen pregnancy, AIDS, child abuse and neglect, and other similar factors.

GRANDPARENTS AND PARENTS. In 1997, 75 percent of coresident grandparent/grandchildren families were maintained by grandparents and 25 percent by parents. Casper and Bryson categorized these families into five basic types: both grandparents with some parents present (34 percent); both grandparents with no parents present (17 percent); grandmother-only with some parents present (29 percent); grandmother-only families with no parents present (14 percent); and grandfather-only families (6 percent). Overall, nearly two-thirds of grandparent-headed families had parents present. (See Figure 3.1.)

Sixty-three percent of coresident grandparents are grandmothers. The study suggests this may be because women live longer than men and women are less likely than men to remarry after the death of a spouse. Older women may also be financially less independent than men and may live with their children for economic reasons. Women are more likely than men to feel obliged to assume the caregiver role.

CHARACTERISTICS OF GRANDCHILDREN. Children living in grandparent-maintained homes are more likely to have family incomes below the poverty level (27 percent),

TABLE 3.3

Multigenerational households for the United States and Puerto Rico, 2000

	All households	Total[2]	Multigenerational households by type[1]		
			Householder with child and grandchild	Householder with parent and child	Householder with parent, child, and grandchild
United States	105,480,101	3,929,122	2,561,637	1,289,159	78,326
Alabama	1,737,080	64,841	50,679	12,925	1,237
Alaska	221,600	6,784	4,681	2,029	74
Arizona	1,901,327	75,296	50,817	22,957	1,522
Arkansas	1,042,696	33,158	25,614	6,911	633
California	11,502,870	642,474	353,682	273,017	15,775
Colorado	1,658,238	44,214	29,240	14,166	808
Connecticut	1,301,670	41,621	23,701	17,188	732
Delaware	298,736	10,992	7,741	3,063	188
District of Columbia	248,338	11,399	9,138	2,024	237
Florida	6,337,929	238,213	142,326	90,353	5,534
Georgia	3,006,369	129,162	90,413	36,053	2,696
Hawaii	403,240	33,106	20,462	11,391	1,253
Idaho	469,645	10,907	7,571	3,168	168
Illinois	4,591,779	184,505	120,437	60,202	3,866
Indiana	2,336,306	62,864	46,862	15,032	970
Iowa	1,149,276	17,906	13,512	4,174	220
Kansas	1,037,891	22,378	16,065	6,014	299
Kentucky	1,590,647	43,223	32,719	9,875	629
Louisiana	1,656,053	79,898	64,075	14,407	1,416
Maine	518,200	8,713	5,657	2,942	114
Maryland	1,980,859	88,923	56,832	30,211	1,880
Massachusetts	2,443,580	75,081	43,175	30,673	1,233
Michigan	3,785,661	116,662	84,832	29,987	1,843
Minnesota	1,895,127	31,076	21,087	9,648	341
Mississippi	1,046,434	54,262	44,319	8,826	1,117
Missouri	2,194,594	58,438	43,713	13,779	946
Montana	358,667	6,638	5,006	1,565	67
Nebraska	666,184	10,973	8,018	2,840	115
Nevada	751,165	30,005	16,978	12,371	656
New Hampshire	474,606	10,674	6,352	4,157	165
New Jersey	3,064,645	144,142	76,572	64,599	2,971
New Mexico	677,971	29,276	22,346	6,401	529
New York	7,056,860	312,270	178,039	127,841	6,390
North Carolina	3,132,013	101,544	74,032	25,699	1,813
North Dakota	257,152	2,799	2,190	594	15
Ohio	4,445,773	123,767	90,449	31,378	1,940
Oklahoma	1,342,293	38,306	29,286	8,492	528
Oregon	1,333,723	33,284	21,067	11,671	546
Pennsylvania	4,777,003	147,077	99,251	45,270	2,556
Rhode Island	408,424	12,972	7,264	5,485	223
South Carolina	1,533,854	63,722	49,252	13,212	1,258
South Dakota	290,245	5,169	4,143	973	53
Tennessee	2,232,905	75,753	56,307	18,106	1,340
Texas	7,393,354	353,682	244,216	101,898	7,568
Utah	701,281	25,673	18,198	7,038	437
Vermont	240,634	3,839	2,443	1,347	49
Virginia	2,699,173	92,471	60,693	30,097	1,681
Washington	2,271,398	57,193	35,324	20,983	886
West Virginia	736,481	19,011	14,661	4,099	251
Wisconsin	2,084,544	39,255	27,514	11,229	512
Wyoming	193,608	3,531	2,686	799	46
Puerto Rico	1,261,325	92,847	73,026	17,848	1,973

Note: Parent may be either parent or parent-in-law of the householder. Child may be the natural born, adopted or stepchild of the householder. Relationship refers to how each person is related to the householder.

[1]Individual types may include a small number of households with members from additional generations, for example, grandparents or great-grandparents of the householders for which tabulated data are not available.

[2]Total represents only those three types of households specified in the table.

SOURCE: "Multigenerational Households for the United States, States, and for Puerto Rico: 2000," U.S. Census Bureau, Washington, DC, September 2001 [Online] http://www.census.gov/population/cen2000/phc-t17.pdf [accessed December 4, 2002]

have no health insurance coverage (33 percent), and receive public assistance (56 percent). (See Figure 3.2.) Half of grandchildren living in grandparent-maintained homes are age six and under. Forty-three percent live in the South. Households led by a grandmother only with no parents of the grandchildren present appear to have the greatest financial challenges. The majority (60.4 percent) live in central cities, almost two-thirds (62.8 percent) have family incomes below the poverty level, and 84.4 percent receive some type of public assistance. (See Table 3.4.)

FIGURE 3.1

Families with coresident grandparents and grandchildren, 1997

Percent distribution of family type

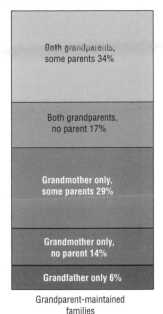

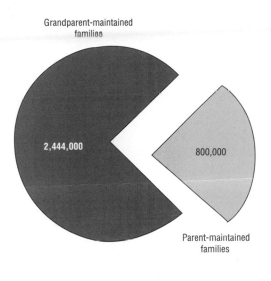

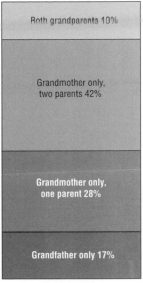

SOURCE: Ken Bryson and Lynne M. Casper, "Figure 3. Families With Coresident Grandparents and Grandchildren: 1997," in *Coresident Grandparents and Grandchildren*, Current Population Reports, U.S. Census Bureau, Washington, DC, May 1999

Families maintained by both grandparents with no parents present are more likely to have no health insurance. (See Figure 3.3.)

ADOPTED AND FOSTER CHILDREN

Many American families who want to adopt a child consider two groups of available children:

• Children, primarily infants, whose parents voluntarily give them up for adoption. The parents generally deal with private adoption agencies or make private placements with adoptive families. The number of these adoptees is unknown.

• Children who have been placed in foster care based on court determination that they were abused or neglected, and for whom placement with adoptive families would serve the children's best interests.

Adopted Children

In an attempt to make it easier for families to adopt, several laws have been enacted. The 1993 Family and Medical Leave Act (PL 103-3) enables parents to take time off work to adopt a child without losing their jobs or health insurance. The 1996 Adoption Tax Credit and Gross Income Exclusion, part of the Small Business Job Protection Act of 1996 (PL 104-188), provides a $5,000 tax credit to families adopting children and a $6,000 tax credit for families adopting children with special needs. The tax credit is designed to help middle-class families for whom adoption may be prohibitively expensive. The Inter-ethnic Adoption Provisions of the Small Business Job Protection Act of 1996 further amended the Multi-ethnic Placement Act of 1994 (PL 103-382) to ensure that the adoption process is free from discrimination and delays based on the race, culture, and ethnicity of the child or the prospective parents. The Child Citizenship Act of 2000 provides automatic citizenship to children adopted by U.S. citizens.

The National Adoption Information Clearinghouse (NAIC) reports that an adoption can be far more expensive (up to $30,000) than a birth (average cost of $6,430). The domestic adoption of a healthy infant through a private or independent agency can cost anywhere from $4,000 to $30,000. The costs of foreign adoptions can run between $12,000 and $25,000, not including travel and living expenses to visit the child's home country.

INTERCOUNTRY ADOPTION. Many American families choose to adopt children from other countries. In the 1970s, most children adopted from outside the United States were Korean. By the late 1990s, most were adopted from China

FIGURE 3.2

Percent of children in different living arrangements who are in poverty, without health insurance, and receiving public assistance, 1997

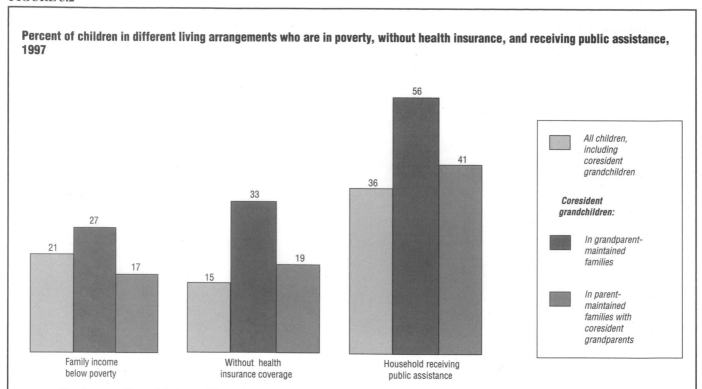

SOURCE: Ken Bryson and Lynne M. Casper, "Figure 4A. Percent of Children in Different Living Arrangements Who Are in Poverty, Without Health Insurance, and Receiving Public Assistance: 1997," in *Coresident Grandparents and Grandchildren,* Current Population Reports, U.S. Census Bureau, Washington, DC, May 1999

FIGURE 3.3

Percent of grandchildren in different family types who are in poverty, without health insurance, and receiving public assistance, 1997

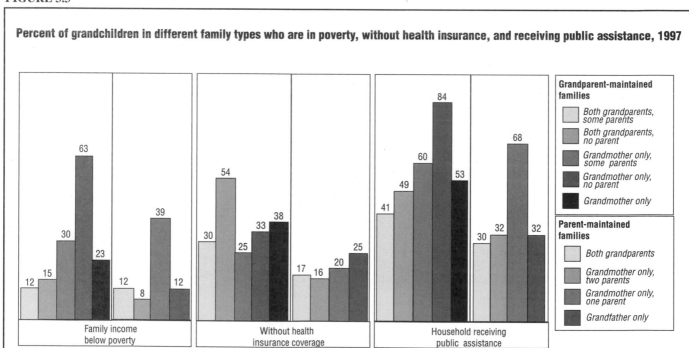

SOURCE: Ken Bryson and Lynne M. Casper, "Figure 4B. Percent of Grandchildren in Different Family Types Who Are In Poverty, Without Health Insurance, and Receiving Public Assistance, 1997," in *Coresident Grandparents and Grandchildren,* Current Population Reports, U.S. Census Bureau, Washington, DC, May 1999

TABLE 3.4

Characteristics of grandchildren who are coresident with grandparents, 1997

(Numbers in thousands. Percent distribution of characteristics)

Characteristics	All coresident grand-parent families	Grandparent-maintained families						Parent-maintained families				
		Total	Both grand-parents, some parents	Both grand-parents, no parent	Grand-mother only, some parents	Grand-mother only, no parent	Grand-father only	Total	Both grand-parents	Grand-mother only, two parents	Grand-mother only, one parent	Grand-father only
Grandchildren, total (number)	5,435	3,894	1,241	598	1,144	669	242	1,541	246	630	396	269
Percent distribution of grand-children	100.0	100.0	100.0	100.0	100.0	100.0	100.0	100.0	100.0	100.0	100.0	100.0
Race and ethnicity												
White, non-Hispanic	42.5	42.4	51.7	58.0	35.6	19.3	52.3	42.6	38.7	49.0	26.6	54.9
Black, non-Hispanic	30.1	35.9	18.8	22.3	48.6	62.7	23.8	15.2	3.2	7.9	40.7	5.9
Hispanic	18.2	16.5	21.0	15.2	12.5	14.7	20.6	22.6	20.0	21.4	23.7	26.5
Other, non-Hispanic	9.2	5.1	8.5	4.6	3.2	3.3	3.2	19.5	38.2	21.7	9.0	12.7
Age												
Under 6	46.0	50.8	66.3	36.1	56.7	27.1	45.6	33.7	49.0	25.8	39.4	29.7
6 to 11	30.9	28.8	24.5	28.9	26.6	40.0	29.8	36.4	33.8	38.5	33.7	38.2
12 to 17	23.1	20.4	9.2	35.0	16.7	32.8	24.7	29.9	17.2	35.7	26.9	32.1
Gender												
Male	48.8	48.3	51.1	43.3	48.6	45.8	50.8	50.1	39.9	55.5	43.1	57.2
Female	51.2	51.7	48.9	56.7	51.4	54.2	49.2	49.9	60.1	45.5	56.9	42.8
Nativity												
U.S. born, U.S. parents	77.7	86.7	80.1	87.8	90.2	92.7	84.2	55.0	43.7	48.1	68.1	62.1
U.S. born, 1 foreign parent	6.7	6.0	9.1	4.3	4.7	4.2	5.5	8.3	7.7	10.0	6.2	8.1
U.S. born, 2 foreign parents	12.8	5.8	9.6	6.1	3.5	2.1	6.1	30.5	45.7	32.4	22.4	23.9
Foreign born	2.9	1.5	1.1	1.7	1.6	0.9	4.2	6.2	3.0	9.5	3.3	5.8
General state of health												
Excellent	40.7	39.6	42.2	40.4	42.3	34.6	24.9	43.4	53.4	42.1	35.7	48.8
Very good	29.0	27.8	28.1	30.3	25.7	26.5	33.0	32.2	26.9	35.1	27.0	38.2
Good	25.7	27.5	26.5	24.4	27.2	29.5	36.6	21.2	16.3	19.4	34.0	11.0
Fair or poor	4.6	5.2	3.3	4.9	4.8	9.4	5.5	3.1	3.5	3.4	3.2	2.1
Insurance coverage												
Private insurance	39.5	30.3	38.2	18.6	38.1	14.0	27.5	62.5	66.4	75.3	42.6	58.2
Public insurance only	31.3	36.3	31.7	27.2	36.8	52.8	34.3	18.8	16.3	9.2	37.0	17.0
No health insurance	29.2	33.4	30.1	54.2	25.2	33.2	38.2	18.7	17.3	15.5	20.4	24.7
Region of U.S.												
Northeast	20.1	18.7	19.1	17.6	15.5	24.2	18.9	23.7	20.8	25.6	25.5	19.1
Midwest	16.1	16.9	15.0	19.1	18.7	17.7	9.4	14.3	7.2	12.6	21.2	14.3
South	39.3	43.3	38.2	44.8	49.6	44.0	34.8	29.0	23.8	22.8	41.2	30.4
West	24.5	21.1	27.7	18.4	16.2	14.0	37.0	33.0	48.2	38.9	12.1	36.2
Metropolitan area status												
Central city	37.8	38.9	31.1	23.9	44.2	60.4	31.2	35.1	33.3	29.7	50.4	26.6
Suburbs	44.5	41.3	51.4	43.4	35.6	26.6	51.8	52.5	50.7	62.6	35.1	56.1
Nonmetropolitan area	17.7	19.8	17.5	32.6	20.2	13.0	16.9	12.5	16.0	7.7	14.6	17.3
Household members under 18												
One	29.2	31.9	32.4	48.2	27.6	24.6	30.0	22.3	32.1	21.1	24.4	12.9
Two	31.8	29.2	34.8	15.2	31.4	24.7	37.9	38.2	26.9	37.8	39.1	48.3
Three or more	39.0	38.9	32.9	36.6	41.0	50.7	32.1	39.5	41.0	41.1	36.5	38.8
Earners in household												
None	11.7	14.4	4.1	11.3	10.7	43.9	10.6	4.8	0.9	0.8	15.1	2.5
One	26.2	27.3	14.6	31.9	31.6	37.9	31.8	23.5	11.7	12.5	47.2	25.2
Two	32.4	28.0	22.7	35.1	37.7	11.3	37.1	43.5	38.9	57.3	27.3	39.4
Three or more	29.7	30.3	58.6	21.7	19.9	6.9	20.5	28.2	48.4	29.4	10.3	33.0
Family income/poverty level												
Under 50 percent of poverty level	9.2	10.7	1.5	6.8	11.5	29.4	12.0	5.4	2.1	0.0	17.4	3.6
50 to 99 percent of poverty level	14.9	16.2	10.1	8.2	18.0	33.4	11.1	11.8	9.6	8.0	21.4	8.4
100 to 149 percent of poverty level	13.7	14.6	11.2	15.8	17.5	16.8	9.6	11.5	10.7	7.6	19.1	10.4
150 to 199 percent of poverty level	12.9	13.5	14.8	14.5	15.0	7.6	13.7	11.4	3.9	11.7	15.7	11.2
200 percent or more of poverty level	49.2	45.0	62.4	54.7	38.0	12.8	53.7	59.9	73.7	72.7	26.4	66.4

TABLE 3.4

Characteristics of grandchildren who are coresident with grandparents, 1997 [CONTINUED]

(Numbers in thousands. Percent distribution of characteristics)

Characteristics	All coresident grandparent families	Grandparent-maintained families						Parent-maintained families				
		Total	Both grand-parents, some parents	Both grand-parents, no parent	Grand-mother only, some parents	Grand-mother only, no parent	Grand-father only	Total	Both grand-parents	Grand-mother only, two parents	Grand-mother only, one parent	Grand-father only
Household public assistance												
No public assistance	48.1	43.8	58.7	50.7	39.8	15.6	47.2	59.1	69.7	68.1	32.3	67.9
Any public assistance program	51.9	56.2	41.3	49.3	60.2	84.4	52.8	40.9	30.3	31.9	67.7	32.1
School lunch program	37.5	40.0	26.0	34.1	40.3	73.5	32.5	31.1	20.4	24.4	52.4	25.2
Food stamps	26.6	30.3	20.3	20.0	37.6	48.3	22.5	17.3	10.1	10.8	37.9	8.7
AFDC, ADC, TANF, GA	20.6	24.5	18.1	20.8	26.4	40.3	14.1	10.5	2.5	4.1	30.4	3.5
SSI	14.9	15.5	9.9	13.2	16.9	28.1	8.7	13.4	5.3	12.7	22.2	9.7
Housing assistance	7.4	8.5	2.0	3.6	7.5	26.3	9.4	4.5	0.0	3.6	11.2	0.9
Energy assistance	5.2	6.7	3.8	2.9	7.0	17.4	0.0	1.3	0.0	1.3	2.9	0.1

SOURCE: Ken Bryson and Lynne M. Casper, "Table 2. Characteristics of Grandchildren Who Are Coresident With Grandparents: 1997," in *Coresident Grandparents and Grandchildren,* Current Population Reports, U.S. Census Bureau, Washington, DC, May 1999

and Russia. Because these foreign-born children require visas to enter the United States, the U.S. Department of State has current records of the number of foreign adoptees. During fiscal year 2001, American households adopted 19,237 orphaned children from other countries. Twenty-four percent were from China, 22 percent from Russia, 10 percent from South Korea, 8 percent from Guatemala, and 6 percent from the Ukraine. (See Table 3.5.)

Children in Foster Care

Foster care is an integral part of the child welfare system, designed to provide temporary respite and some stability for children whose families are having difficulties parenting or are no longer able to care for them. Some children remain in foster care until their parents resolve the problems that led to the children's placement in foster care. Other children cannot safely return home and, therefore, wait with their foster family until they are permanently placed with an adoptive family.

The median age of children in foster care on September 30, 2000, was 10.4 years. (See Table 3.6.) Forty percent of children in foster care were black non-Hispanic, 38 percent white non-Hispanic, and 15 percent Hispanic. (See Table 3.7.) Based on a variety of family situations, 10 percent of children who left foster care in fiscal year 2000 had been in the system for five years or more. (See Figure 3.4.) Forty-seven percent of children were living in nonrelative foster-family homes, and 25 percent were in foster care with relatives. (See Table 3.8.)

The primary goal of foster care is to reunite the child with parents or principal caretakers. However, this is not always possible. Some children may live with a guardian, and older children may seek emancipation at the eligible age. Another goal is adoption, which occurred for 17 percent of children exiting foster care in fiscal year 2000. (See Figure 3.5.)

Children Adopted from Foster Care

In 1997, the Clinton administration launched the "Adoption 2002" initiative with the goal of doubling the number of foster children adopted each year—from approximately 27,000 in 1996 to a projected 54,000 in 2002. To this end, on November 19, 1997, President William Clinton signed the Adoption and Safe Families Act of 1997 (PL 105-89), which requires, among other provisions, permanency hearings to be held no later than 12 months after a child enters foster care. The federal government offers financial incentives to states to increase adoption rates and provides technical assistance to states, courts, and communities in an effort to place children in adoptive homes within a shorter time frame.

Current or former foster youths 16 and older can obtain government assistance during their transition to independent living through the Independent Living Program. This program provides grants to states for education and employment aid, training in daily living skills, and individual and group counseling.

CHILDREN WAITING TO BE ADOPTED. In fiscal year 1998, 36,000 children were adopted from the public foster care system and 117,000 foster children who could not return safely to their birth families awaited adoption. In 2000, 51,000 children were adopted from the public foster care system and 131,000 were waiting to be adopted.

Of the children waiting to be adopted on September 30, 2000, 43 percent were black non-Hispanic, 34 percent white non-Hispanic, and 13 percent Hispanic. (See Table 3.9.) Of children adopted in 2000, 39 percent were black

TABLE 3.5

Immigrant Visas issued to orphans coming to the United States, by top countries of origin 1989–2001

	Fiscal Year 1989		Fiscal Year 1990		Fiscal Year 1991	
1	3,544	Korea	2,620	Korea	2,594	Romania
2	736	Colombia	631	Colombia	1,818	Korea
3	648	India	440	Peru	705	Peru
4	465	Philippines	421	Philippines	521	Colombia
5	253	Chile	348	India	445	India
6	252	Paraguay	302	Chile	393	Philippines
7	222	Peru	282	Paraguay	329	Guatemala
8	202	Guatemala	257	Guatemala	266	Chile
9	201	China	228	Brazil	234	Honduras
10	131	Honduras	197	Honduras	190	Paraguay
11	175	Brazil	121	Romania	175	Brazil
12	138	Romania	112	Mexico	131	Thailand
13	109	Thailand	105	Costa Rica	123	El Salvador
14	95	Cuba	103	El Salvador	97	Mexico
15	94	El Salvador	100	Thailand	92	Poland
16	91	Mexico	66	Poland	87	Japan
17	80	Haiti	66	Taiwan	61	China
18	78	Costa Rica	64	Haiti	60	Cambodia
19	75	Taiwan	59	Ecuador	56	Costa Rica
20	74	Japan	58	Dominican Rep	54	Taiwan
21	74	Poland	57	Japan	50	Dominican Rep

	Fiscal Year 1992		Fiscal Year 1993		Fiscal Year 1994	
1	1,840	Korea	1,775	Korea	1,795	Korea
2	418	Guatemala	746	Russia	1,530	Russia
3	404	Colombia	512	Guatemala	787	China
4	357	Philippines	426	Colombia	483	Paraguay
5	352	India	412	Paraguay	436	Guatemala
6	324	Russia	360	Philippines	412	India
7	309	Peru	331	India	351	Colombia
8	249	Honduras	330	China	314	Philippines
9	212	Paraguay	273	Ukraine	220	Vietnam
10	206	China	224	Peru	199	Romania
11	179	Chile	179	Honduras	164	Ukraine
12	138	Brazil	161	Brazil	149	Brazil
13	121	Romania	133	Bulgaria	97	Bulgaria
14	117	El Salvador	124	Bolivia	95	Lithuania
15	109	Poland	110	Vietnam	94	Poland
16	91	Bulgaria	100	El Salvador	85	Mexico
17	91	Mexico	97	Romania	79	Chile
18	86	Thailand	91	Mexico	77	Honduras
19	73	Bolivia	70	Poland	61	Haiti
20	68	Japan	69	Thailand	54	Ethiopia
21	64	Costa Rica	64	Japan	49	Japan

	Fiscal Year 1995		Fiscal Year 1996		Fiscal Year 1997	
1	2,130	China	3,333	China	3,816	Russia
2	1,896	Russia	2,454	Russia	3,597	China
3	1,666	Korea	1,516	Korea	1,654	South Korea
4	449	Guatemala	427	Guatemala	788	Guatemala
5	371	India	555	Romania	621	Romania
6	351	Paraguay	380	India	425	Vietnam
7	350	Colombia	354	Vietnam	352	India
8	318	Vietnam	258	Paraguay	233	Colombia
9	298	Philippines	255	Colombia	163	Philippines
10	275	Romania	229	Philippines	152	Mexico
11	146	Brazil	163	Bulgaria	148	Bulgaria
12	110	Bulgaria	103	Brazil	142	Haiti
13	98	Lithuania	82	Latvia	108	Latvia
14	90	Chile	78	Lithuania	91	Brazil
15	83	Mexico	77	Georgia	82	Ethiopia
16	67	Ecuador	76	Mexico	78	Lithuania
17	63	Ethiopia	68	Haiti	78	Poland
18	63	Japan	64	Poland	77	Bolivia
19	59	Latvia	63	Chile	72	Hungary
20	53	Thailand	55	Thailand	66	Cambodia
21	51	Georgia	51	Ecuador, Hungary		

TABLE 3.5

Immigrant Visas issued to orphans coming to the United States, by top countries of origin 1989–2001 [CONTINUED]

	Fiscal Year 1998		Fiscal Year 1999		Fiscal Year 2000	
1	4,491	Russia	4,348	Russia	5,053	China
2	4,206	China	4,101	China	4,269	Russia
3	1,829	South Korea	2,008	South Korea	1,794	South Korea
4	911	Guatemala	1,002	Guatemala	1,518	Guatemala
5	603	Vietnam	895	Romania	1,122	Romania
6	478	India	709	Vietnam	724	Vietnam
7	406	Romania	500	India	659	Ukraine
8	351	Colombia	323	Ukraine	503	India
9	249	Cambodia	248	Cambodia	402	Cambodia
10	200	Philippines	231	Colombia	399	Kazakhstan
11	180	Ukraine	221	Bulgaria	246	Colombia
12	168	Mexico	195	Philippines	214	Bulgaria
13	151	Bulgaria			173	Philippines
14	140	Dominican Rep			131	Haiti
15	121	Haiti			106	Mexico
16	103	Brazil			95	Ethiopia
17	96	Ethiopia			88	Thailand
18	84	Thailand			83	Poland
19	77	Poland			79	Moldova
20	76	Latvia			60	Bolivia

	Fiscal Year 2001		Fiscal Year 2002	
1	4,681	China (mainland born)	5,053	China (mainland)
2	4,279	Russia	4,939	Russia
3	1,870	South Korea	2,219	Guatemala
4	1,609	Guatemala	1,779	South Korea
5	1,246	Ukraine	1,106	Ukraine
6	782	Romania	819	Kazakhstan
7	737	Vietnam	766	Vietnam
8	672	Kazakhstan	466	India
9	543	India	334	Colombia
10	407	Cambodia	260	Bulgaria
11	297	Bulgaria	254	Cambodia
12	266	Colombia	221	Philippines
13	219	Philippines	187	Haiti
14	192	Haiti	169	Belarus
15	158	Ethiopia	168	Romania
16	129	Belarus	105	Ethiopia
17	86	Poland	101	Poland
18	74	Thailand	67	Thailand
19	73	Mexico	65	Peru
20	51	Jamaica and Liberia (both 51)	61	Mexico

World Total for Calendar Years

1989 - 8,102
1990 - 7,093
1991 - 8,481
1992 - 6,472
1993 - 7,377
1994 - 8,333
1995 - 8,987
1996 - 10,641
1997 - 12,743
1998 - 15,774
1999 - 16,363
2000 - 17,718
2001 - 19,237
2002 - 20,099

SOURCE: "Immigrant Visas Issued to Orphans Coming to the United States, Top Countries of Origin 1989-2001," U.S. Department of State, Washington, DC [Online] http://travel.state.gov/orphan_numbers.html [accessed December 11, 2002]

TABLE 3.6

Ages of children in foster care, fiscal year 2000

Mean Years	10.1	
Median Years	10.4	
Under 1 Year	4%	22,766
1 – 5 Years	24%	134,919
6 – 10 Years	25%	137,047
11 – 15 Years	29%	161,397
16 – 18 Years	16%	89,751
19 + Years	2%	10,120

SOURCE: "What were the ages of the children in foster care?," in *The AFCARS Report: Interim FY 2000 Estimates as of August 2002*, U.S. Department of Health and Human Services, Administration for Children and Families, Administration on Children, Youth and Families, Children's Bureau, Washington, DC, August 2002

FIGURE 3.4

Length of stay in foster care for children who exited foster care in fiscal year 2000

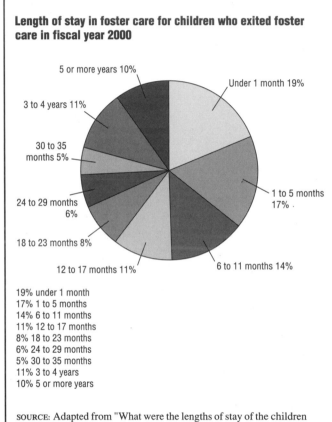

19% under 1 month
17% 1 to 5 months
14% 6 to 11 months
11% 12 to 17 months
8% 18 to 23 months
6% 24 to 29 months
5% 30 to 35 months
11% 3 to 4 years
10% 5 or more years

SOURCE: Adapted from "What were the lengths of stay of the children who exited foster care in FY 2000," in *The AFCARS Report: Interim FY 2000 Estimates as of August 2002*, U.S. Department of Health and Human Services, Administration for Children and Families, Administration on Children, Youth, and Families, Children's Bureau, Washington, DC, August 2002

TABLE 3.7

Race/ethnicity of children in foster care, fiscal year 2000

American Indian/Alaskan Native non-Hispanic	2%	10,994
Asian/Pacific Islander non-Hispanic	1%	5,978
Black non-Hispanic	40%	220,660
Hispanic	15%	81,890
White non-Hispanic	38%	208,632
Unknown/Unable to determine	4%	20,280
Two or more races non-Hispanic	1%	7,566

Note: Using U.S. Bureau of the Census standards, children of Hispanic origin may be of any race. Beginning in FY 2000, children could receive more than one race designation.

SOURCE: "What was the race/ethnicity of the children in foster care?," in *The AFCARS Report: Interim FY 2000 Estimates as of August 2002*, U.S. Department of Health and Human Services, Administration for Children and Families, Administration on Children, Youth and Families, Children's Bureau, Washington, DC, August 2002

TABLE 3.8

Placement settings of children in foster care, fiscal year 2000

What were the placement settings of children in foster care?		
Pre-Adoptive Home	4%	23,159
Foster Family Home (Relative)	25%	137,385
Foster Family Home (Non-Relative)	47%	260,636
Group Home	8%	43,893
Institution	10%	56,512
Supervised Independent Living	1%	5,108
Runaway	2%	9,964
Trial Home Visit	3%	19,343

SOURCE: "What were the placement settings of children in foster care?," in *The AFCARS Report: Interim FY 2000 Estimates as of August 2002*, U.S. Department of Health and Human Services, Administration for Children and Families, Administration on Children, Youth and Families, Children's Bureau, Washington, DC, August 2002

relatives of the child. Fewer than 20 percent of children adopted from the foster care system are placed with families not already familiar to the child. (See Table 3.12.)

CHILD VICTIMS OF ABUSE AND NEGLECT

According to *Child Maltreatment 1998: Reports from the States to the National Child Abuse and Neglect Data System* (Department of Health and Human Services, Administration for Children and Families), many children entering the foster care system are victims of abuse and/or neglect—a majority coming from families with substance-abuse problems. The child victimization rate has been on a slow decline since 1993 and reached a low of 11.8 victims per 1,000 children in 1999. In 2000, the victimization rate rose slightly to 12.2 per 1,000 children. (See Table 3.13 and Figure 3.6.) Maltreatment rates vary from state to state, from a low of 6 or fewer victims per 1,000 to more than 20 victims per 1,000. In 2000, Alaska, Florida, West Virginia, the District of Columbia, and Connecticut had child maltreatment rates greater than 20 per 1,000 children. (See Figure 3.7.)

non-Hispanic, 38 percent white non-Hispanic, and 14 percent Hispanic. (See Table 3.10.) The majority (66 percent) of adoptive families were married couples, but 1 percent were unmarried couples. (See Table 3.11.) In a majority of cases, the foster parents become adoptive parents, having formed a bond with the child after living together for a period of time. Of adoptive parents, 61 percent had previously been the child's foster parents and 21 percent were

FIGURE 3.5

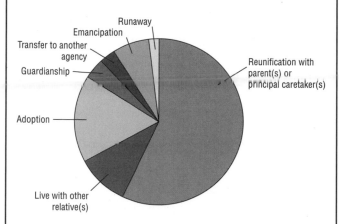

Outcomes for children who left foster care in fiscal year 2000

Reunification with parent(s) or prinicipal caretaker(s)	57%
Live with other relative(s)	10%
Adoption	17%
Guardianship	4%
Transfer to another agency	3%
Emancipation	7%
Death of a child	0%
Runaway	2%

SOURCE: Adapted from "What were the outcomes for the children exiting foster care during FY 2000?," in *The AFCARS Report: Interim FY 2000 Estimates as of August 2002*, U.S. Department of Health and Human Services, Administration for Children and Families, Administration on Children, Youth, and Families, Children's Bureau, Washington, DC, August 2002

TABLE 3.11

Adoptive family structures, fiscal year 2000

Married Couple	66%	33,440
Unmarried Couple	1%	451
Single Female	32%	16,083
Single Male	2%	1,026

SOURCE: "Adoptive Family Structure," in *The AFCARS Report: Interim FY 2000 Estimates as of August 2002*, U.S. Department of Health and Human Services, Administration for Children and Families, Administration on Children, Youth and Families, Children's Bureau, Washington, DC, August 2002

Child maltreatment is grouped into six types—physical abuse, neglect, medical neglect, sexual abuse, psychological maltreatment, and other abuse. There is variance in reporting among states and in categorizing types of abuse. Some states categorize "abandonment," "threats of harm," and "congenital drug addiction" as "other abuse." The most frequent type of child maltreatment, neglect, increased from 6.5 victims per 1,000 in 1999 to 7.3 in 2000. Abuse cases were at a five-year low in 2000. (See Figure 3.8.)

Parents Are Main Perpetrators of Maltreatment

Parents continue to be the main perpetrators of child maltreatment. A female parent acting alone is the most

TABLE 3.9

Racial/ethnic distribution of children waiting for adoption, fiscal year 2000

American Indian/Alaskan Native non-Hispanic	2%	2,306
Asian/Pacific Islander non-Hispanic	1%	1,119
Black non-Hispanic	43%	56,195
Hispanic	13%	17,441
White non-Hispanic	34%	45,130
Unknown/Unable to determine	5%	6,612
Two or more races non-Hispanic	2%	2,197

Note: Using U.S. Bureau of the Census standards, children of Hispanic origin may be of any race. Beginning in FY 2000, children could receive more than one race designation.

SOURCE: "What is the racial/ethnic distribution of the waiting children?," in *The AFCARS Report: Interim FY 2000 Estimates as of August 2002*, U.S. Department of Health and Human Services, Administration for Children and Families, Administration on Children, Youth and Families, Children's Bureau, Washington, DC, August 2002

TABLE 3.10

Racial/ethnic distribution of children adopted from the public foster care system, fiscal year 2000

American Indian/Alaskan Native non-Hispanic	1%	643
Asian/Pacific Islander non-Hispanic	1%	489
Black non-Hispanic	39%	19,659
Hispanic	14%	7,234
White non-Hispanic	38%	19,562
Unknown/Unable to determine	5%	2,463
Two or more races non-Hispanic	2%	951

Note: Using U.S. Bureau of the Census standards, children of Hispanic origin may be of any race. Beginning in FY 2000, children could receive more than one race designation

SOURCE: "What is the racial distribution of the children adopted from the public foster care system?," in *The AFCARS Report: Interim FY 2000 Estimates as of August 2002*, U.S. Department of Health and Human Services, Administration for Children and Families, Administration on Children, Youth and Families, Children's Bureau, Washington, DC, August 2002

TABLE 3.12

Relationship of adoptive parents to the adopted child prior to adoption, fiscal year 2000

Non-relative	18%	9,326
Foster parent	61%	30,969
Step-parent	0%	94
Other relative	21%	10,612

Note: Relatives who were also foster parents were counted as relatives.

SOURCE: "What was the relationship of the adoptive parents to the child prior to the adoption?," in *The AFCARS Report: Interim FY 2000 Estimates as of August 2002*, U.S. Department of Health and Human Services, Administration for Children and Families, Administration on Children, Youth and Families, Children's Bureau, Washington, DC, August 2002

common perpetrator of neglect and physical abuse. A male parent acting alone is the most frequent perpetrator of sexual abuse. Both parents acting together account for 21.9 percent of neglect cases, 13.5 percent of physical

TABLE 3.13

Victimization rates by selected characteristics, 1990–2000

Reporting year	Child population	Victim rate	Estimated number of victims[1]
1990	64,163,192	13.4	861,000
1991	65,069,507	14.0	912,000
1992	66,073,841	15.1	995,000
1993	66,961,573	15.3	1,026,000
1994	67,803,294	15.2	1,032,000
1995	68,437,378	14.7	1,006,000
1996	69,022,127	14.7	1,012,000
1997	69,527,944	13.8	957,000
1998	69,872,059	12.9	904,000
1999	70,199,435	11.8	829,000
2000	72,293,812	12.2	879,000

[1]Rounded to thousands

SOURCE: "Table 3-3. Victimization Rates, 1990-2000," in *Child Maltreatment 2000,* U.S. Department of Health and Human Services, Administration for Children and Families, Administration on Children, Youth and Families, Children's Bureau, Washington, DC, 2002

FIGURE 3.6

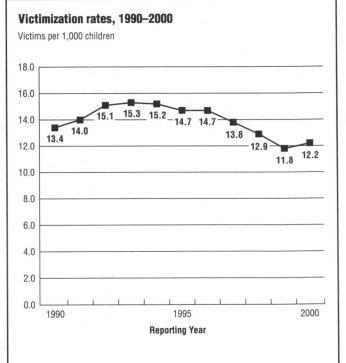

Victimization rates, 1990–2000

Victims per 1,000 children

SOURCE: "Figure 3-2. Victimization Rates, 1990-2000," in *Child Maltreatment 2000,* U.S. Department of Health and Human Services, Administration for Children and Families, Administration on Children, Youth and Families, Children's Bureau, Washington, DC, 2002

abuse cases, and 8.1 percent of sexual abuse cases. (See Figure 3.9.)

An estimated 1,200 children in the United States died from abuse and neglect during 2000, a rate of 1.71 deaths per 100,000 children. Child protective services in 45 states reported 32 deaths occurring in foster care. Very young children are at greatest risk of death from maltreatment. Children under one year of age accounted for 43.7 percent of fatalities, and 85 percent of all fatalities were under age six. Male children account for more deaths (56.7 percent) than female children (43.2 percent). (See Figure 3.10.)

While female parents are responsible for 40 percent of maltreatment, they cause less than a third of child fatalities. Male parents acting alone, both parents acting together, either parent with another person, day-care providers, foster parents, and unknown others all have higher fatality rates than maltreatment rates. (See Figure 3.11.)

CHILDREN WITH WORKING PARENTS

Since the 1970s, one of the most dramatic changes in the structure of the American family has been the increased employment of mothers outside the home. According to the sixth annual interagency report *America's Children: Key National Indicators of Well-Being, 2002,* the share of children with at least one parent working full-time increased from 70 percent in 1980 to 80 percent in 2000. For children living in two-parent households, 33 percent had both parents working, compared to 17 percent in 1980. (See Table 3.14.) Fifty percent of single mothers and 67 percent of single fathers were working in 2000.

CHILD CARE

As more and more mothers hold paying jobs, the issue of child care becomes a great concern, not only for parents but also for policymakers. The implementation of welfare-reform legislation, which requires welfare recipients to work, has further pushed the continuing problem of available child care to the forefront. In 1980, 33 percent of children had single mothers who were employed full-time all year. By 2000, half of single mothers were employed full-time all year. (See Figure 3.12.)

Child Care for the Working Poor

Since the 1930s, the federal government has subsidized child care for low-income families. The Child Care and Development Fund (CCDF), authorized by the Personal Responsibility and Work Opportunity Reconciliation Act of 1996 (PL 104-193), helps low-income families and those getting off welfare to obtain child care so they can pursue employment, job training, or education. Government-funded programs such as Head Start, which began as a nutritional and health program for poor children, offer educational readiness to prepare children for school as part of the child-care program.

Some Employers Address Child-Care Problems

In the United States, employer-sponsored child-care benefits continue to be rare, although the trend toward on-

FIGURE 3.7

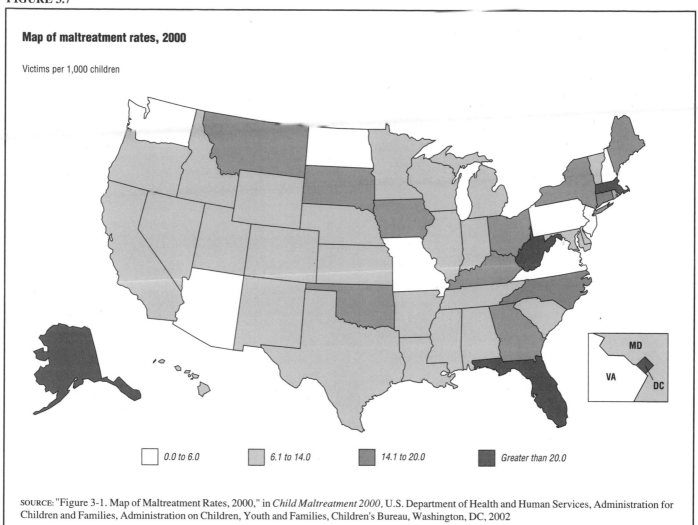

Map of maltreatment rates, 2000

Victims per 1,000 children

☐ 0.0 to 6.0	☐ 6.1 to 14.0	☐ 14.1 to 20.0	☐ Greater than 20.0

SOURCE: "Figure 3-1. Map of Maltreatment Rates, 2000," in *Child Maltreatment 2000,* U.S. Department of Health and Human Services, Administration for Children and Families, Administration on Children, Youth and Families, Children's Bureau, Washington, DC, 2002

site child care is increasing. Some employers offer child-care reimbursement accounts that are funded with employee pretax contributions. Employees in medium and large establishments are more likely than those in smaller establishments to receive child-care benefits.

According to the Bureau of Labor Statistics, in 2000, 13.8 percent of civilian workers in state and local governments and private industry had access to child-care resource and referral services through their employer. These services were provided by 3 percent of employers. Such services include information on child-care options, costs, schedules of availability, and qualifications of caregivers in the local community. Among employees of state and local governments, 13.5 percent had these services available, compared to 2.7 percent of employees in private industries. The larger the business establishment, the more likely it is to offer these services to employees. Only 2.5 percent of establishments with fewer than 100 workers offered child-care resources, compared to 25.5 percent of establishments with more than 500 workers and 44.4 percent of those with more

than 5,000 workers. Child-care resources were nearly twice as prevalent in establishments located in the West than any other region. (See Table 3.15.)

FINDING CHILD CARE RESOURCES CAN BE CHALLENGING. According to a June 2000 survey conducted by the Bureau of Labor Statistics, only 13.8 percent of workers in private industry and state and local governments had access to child-care resource and referral services. Most often, these services were provided to employees by outside resources rather than by their employers. People working for large establishments (those employing 5,000 or more workers) fare best when seeking child care. Data show that 45.8 percent of these employees had access to child-care resources and referral services, compared with only 4.5 percent of employees working in small businesses (those employing 99 or fewer workers). In 2002, a new Child Care Assistance Tax Credit became available to employers. Employers who provide child-care resources or facilities for employees can take a tax credit of up to $150,000 for actual expenses of the benefits provided.

FIGURE 3.8

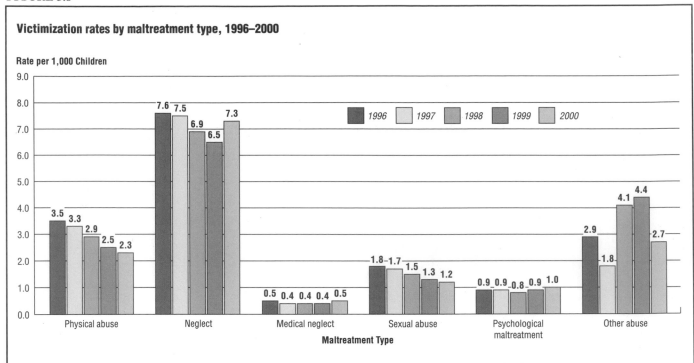

Victimization rates by maltreatment type, 1996–2000

SOURCE: "Figure 3-3. Victimization Rates by Maltreatment Type, 1996-2000," in *Child Maltreatment 2000,* U.S. Department of Health and Human Services, Administration for Children and Families, Administration on Children, Youth and Families, Children's Bureau, Washington, DC, 2002

FIGURE 3.9

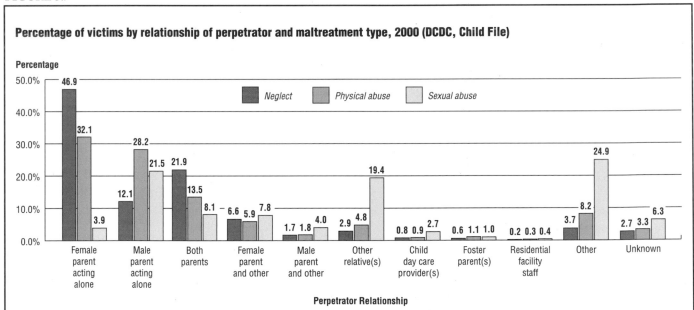

Percentage of victims by relationship of perpetrator and maltreatment type, 2000 (DCDC, Child File)

SOURCE: "Figure 4-3. Percentage of Victims by Relationship of Perpetrator and Maltreatment Type, 2000 (DCDC, Child File)," in *Child Maltreatment 2000,* U.S. Department of Health and Human Services, Administration for Children and Families, Administration on Children, Youth and Families, Children's Bureau, Washington, DC, 2002

FIGURE 3.10

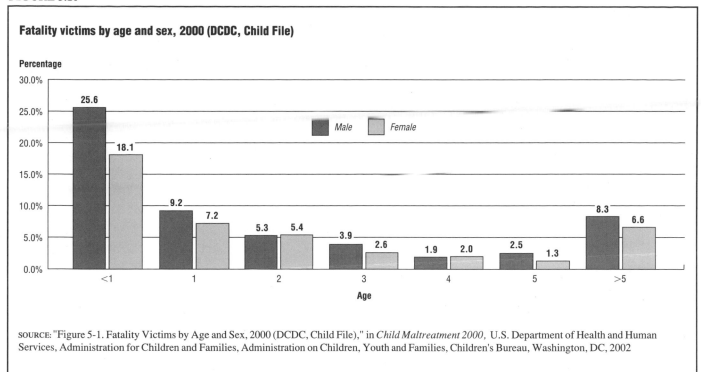

Fatality victims by age and sex, 2000 (DCDC, Child File)

Percentage

SOURCE: "Figure 5-1. Fatality Victims by Age and Sex, 2000 (DCDC, Child File)," in *Child Maltreatment 2000*, U.S. Department of Health and Human Services, Administration for Children and Families, Administration on Children, Youth and Families, Children's Bureau, Washington, DC, 2002

INCOME TAX CREDIT. Employees whose companies do not offer child-care benefits can offset child-care expenses through the Dependent Care Tax Credit (DCTC) when filing their federal income taxes. (This credit applies not only to child care but to costs of care for other dependents, such as a spouse or parent.) The amount of the DCTC increased for the 2003 tax year from a maximum credit of $2,400 to $3,000 for one child and from a maximum credit of $4,800 to $6,000 for two children. Some states offer tax credits as well. However, those who make too little money to pay income tax are not eligible to file for income tax credit.

CHILDREN IN POVERTY

The current poverty rate is at its lowest level since 1979, according to the "America's Children, 2002" report. The report notes a significant decline in child poverty for children in single-female families, which dropped from 51 percent in 1980 to 40 percent in 2000. However, children of single mothers are still more likely to be in poverty than children of married couples. Only 8 percent of children of married couples were identified as in poverty, compared to 39 percent of children of single mothers. Children of Hispanic parents are most likely to be in poverty. Of children of single Hispanic mothers, 49 percent were in poverty and twice as many children of Hispanic married couples were in poverty as any other racial/ethnic group. (See Figure 3.13.) The poverty rate for children living with single fathers was only slightly lower than that for children living with single mothers— 19 percent compared to 21 percent. (See Table 3.14.)

While child hunger dropped from 1.0 percent in 1998 to 0.8 percent in 2000, more than half a million children still live in households where they experience hunger, and many more live in households without continuous access to enough food to ensure an active and healthy life.

COST OF RAISING A CHILD

The U.S. Department of Agriculture (USDA) estimates the annual expenditures on children from birth through age 17 for husband-wife and single-parent families. These estimated expenses vary significantly according to family household income level. Expenditures include seven major budgetary components: housing, food, transportation, clothing, health care, child care and education, and miscellaneous expenses (personal-care items, entertainment, and reading materials). The study demonstrates a fact of life for these families—no matter what the income bracket, it is expensive to raise a family.

For a child who reached age one in 2001, a low-income family may spend $6,490 on the child in the first year, compared to $13,430 spent by a high-income family. While the overall cost increases as the child grows up, the ratio of expenditures on the child between low- and high-income families remains steady, with high-income family expenditures about double those of the low-income family. (See Table 3.16.) Housing accounts for the largest share of child-rearing expenses across income groups, accounting for 33 to 37 percent of expenses. Food is the second-largest child-rearing expense, accounting for 20 to 37 percent of expenses. Expenditures on children are

FIGURE 3.11

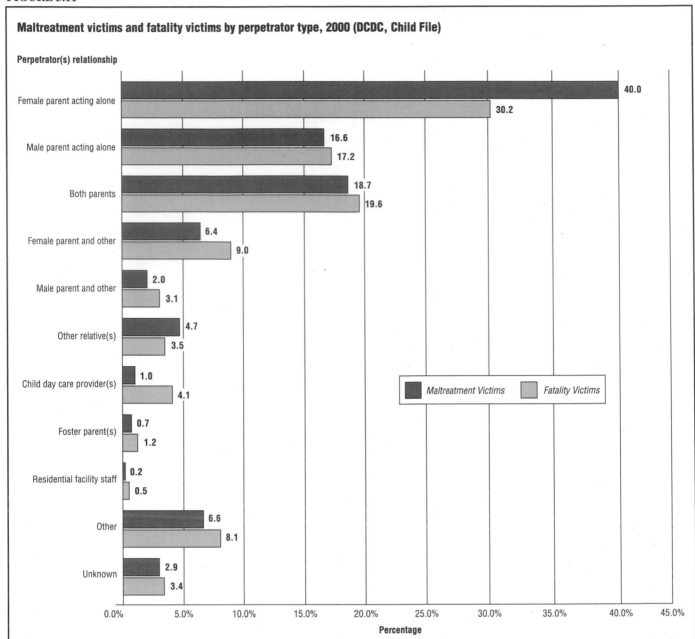

Maltreatment victims and fatality victims by perpetrator type, 2000 (DCDC, Child File)

Perpetrator(s) relationship

SOURCE: Figure 5-2. Maltreatment Victims and Fatality Victims by Perpetrator Type, 2000 (DCDC, Child File)," in *Child Maltreatment 2000*, U.S. Department of Health and Human Services, Administration for Children and Families, Administration on Children, Youth and Families, Children's Bureau, Washington, DC, 2002

lower in the younger age categories and higher in the older age categories. This held across all income groups.

In Married-Couple Families

A married couple with before-tax income of less than $39,100 is estimated to spend $124,800 on a child from birth to age 18. The greatest projected expense is housing at $41,520 over 17 years. Food cost is projected at a little more than half of housing cost ($24,600). (See Table 3.17.) The projected expenditures by a single parent in the same income range is less than 10 percent lower. (See Table 3.18.)

TABLE 3.14

Secure parental employment: percentage of children under 18 living with at least one parent employed full time all year by selected characteristics, selected years, 1980–2000

Characteristic	1980	1985	1990	1995	1996	1997	1998	1999	2000
All children living with parent(s)									
Total	70	70	72	74	76	76	77	79	80
Race and Hispanic origin									
White, non-Hispanic	75	77	79	81	82	82	84	84	85
Black, non-Hispanic	50	48	50	54	56	58	58	64	69
Hispanic[1]	59	55	60	61	64	67	68	71	72
Poverty status									
Below poverty	21	20	22	25	25	26	31	31	35
At or above poverty	81	82	85	86	87	88	87	88	89
Age									
Children under 6	67	67	68	69	71	72	74	76	77
Children ages 6-17	72	72	74	76	77	78	79	80	82
Children living in families maintained by two parents									
Total	80	81	85	87	88	88	89	90	91
Race and Hispanic origin									
White, non-Hispanic	81	83	86	89	90	91	91	91	92
Black, non-Hispanic	73	76	84	85	87	85	86	88	90
Hispanic[1]	71	70	74	77	79	80	82	83	85
Poverty status									
Below poverty	38	37	44	46	48	48	56	52	59
At or above poverty	84	87	89	91	92	92	92	93	94
Age									
Children under 6	76	79	83	86	87	87	88	89	90
Children ages 6-17	81	82	85	87	88	89	89	90	91
With both parents working full time all year	17	20	25	28	30	31	31	32	33
Children living in families maintained by single mothers[2]									
Total	33	32	33	38	39	41	44	47	50
Race and Hispanic origin									
White, non-Hispanic	39	39	40	46	47	46	52	52	53
Black, non-Hispanic	28	25	27	33	35	39	39	46	53
Hispanic[1]	22	22	24	27	27	34	36	39	37
Poverty status									
Below poverty	7	7	9	14	10	13	17	18	21
At or above poverty	59	59	60	61	64	66	66	66	67
Age									
Children under 6	20	20	21	24	27	28	31	35	37
Children ages 6-17	38	37	40	45	45	47	50	52	56
Children living in families maintained by single fathers[2]									
Total	57	60	64	67	67	70	70	70	67
Race and Hispanic origin									
White, non-Hispanic	61	62	68	72	69	72	72	76	72
Black, non-Hispanic	41	59	53	64	60	67	66	51	50
Hispanic[1]	53	53	59	58	66	68	69	65	67
Poverty status									
Below poverty	15	23	21	24	30	29	34	28	19
At or above poverty	68	69	74	79	77	80	79	79	79
Age									
Children under 6	48	57	58	54	61	62	65	66	66
Children ages 6-17	59	62	67	74	70	74	72	71	67

Note: Full-time, all-year employment is defined as usually working full time (35 hours or more per week) for 50 to 52 weeks.
[1] Persons of Hispanic origin may be of any race.
[2] Includes some families where both parents are present in the household, but living as unmarried partners.

SOURCE: Adapted from "Table ECON2. Secure parental employment: Percentage of children under age 18 living with at least one parent employed full time all year by family structure, race, Hispanic origin, poverty status, and age, selected years, 1980-2000," in *America's Children: Key National Indicators of Well-Being, 2002*, Federal Interagency Forum on Child and Family Statistics, Washington, DC, July 2002

FIGURE 3.12

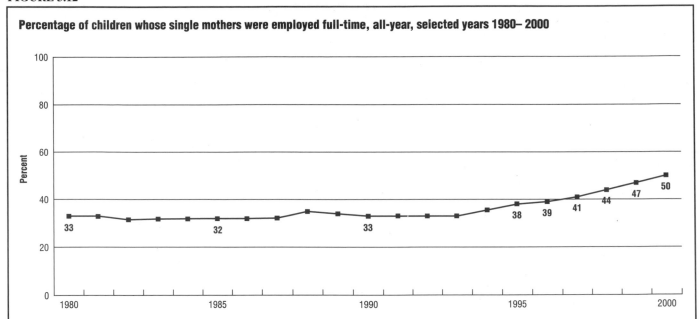

Percentage of children whose single mothers were employed full-time, all-year, selected years 1980– 2000

Note: Single Parent families includes where both parents are present in the household, but living as unmarried partners.

SOURCE: "Figure 1. Percentage of Children Whose Single Mothers Were Employed Full-Time, All-Year, Selected Years 1980-2000," Child Trends Databank [Online] http://www.childtrendsdatabank.org/figures/68-Figure-1.gif [accessed December 3, 2002]

TABLE 3.15

Incidence[1] of childcare resource and referral services by industry, establishment, size and region, June 2000

Category	Total	With childcare resource and referral services				Without childcare resource and referral services
		Total	Service contracted out	Provided internally	Other[2]	
Percent of workers						
Civilian workers	100.0	13.8	8.0	4.5	1.3	86.2
State and local governments	100.0	17.0	5.3	10.1	1.6	83.0
Private Industry	100.0	13.3	8.5	3.6	1.2	86.7
Goods producing	100.0	14.7	10.4	1.5	2.8	85.3
Service producing	100.0	12.8	7.9	4.3	0.7	87.2
Establishment size:						
1-99 workers	100.0	4.5	2.6	1.5	0.4	95.5
100-499 workers	100.0	14.6	8.5	5.2	1.0	85.4
500-999 workers	100.0	23.9	15.8	6.0	2.1	76.1
1,000-4,999 workers	100.0	32.3	20.2	8.9	3.3	67.7
5,000 workers or more	100.0	45.8	20.1	19.5	6.2	54.2
Region[3]:						
Northeast	100.0	16.0	9.3	5.9	0.8	84.0
South	100.0	10.3	6.4	3.5	0.5	89.7
Midwest	100.0	13.5	7.2	4.0	2.2	86.5
West	100.0	17.7	10.5	5.2	2.0	82.3
Percent of establishments						
All industries	100.0	3.0	1.7	1.1	0.1	97.0
State and local governments	100.0	13.5	6.7	5.8	1.0	86.5
Private Industry	100.0	2.7	1.6	1.0	0.1	97.3
Goods producing	100.0	1.9	1.4	0.4	0.1	98.1
Service producing	100.0	2.9	1.6	1.1	0.1	97.1
Establishment size:						
1-99 workers	100.0	2.5	1.4	1.0	0.1	97.5
100-499 workers	100.0	14.0	7.6	5.7	0.7	86.0
500-999 workers	100.0	25.5	18.5	4.9	2.1	74.5
1,000-4,999 workers	100.0	33.9	24.4	6.6	2.9	66.1
5,000 workers or more	100.0	44.4	20.0	14.3	10.1	55.6
Region[3]:						
Northeast	100.0	2.5	1.7	0.7	0.2	97.5
South	100.0	2.8	1.7	1.2	([4])	97.2
Midwest	100.0	2.2	0.9	1.2	0.1	97.8
West	100.0	4.6	2.8	1.4	0.4	95.4

[1]Incidence refers to the percent of workers eligible for childcare resource and referral services and the percent of establishments that provide this service.
[2]"Other" refers to establishments that provide childcare resource and referral services both internally and by contractors. For example, an establishment provides these services internally to nonmanagement workers and contracts the services for management workers.
[3]The regional breakout is as follows: Northeast: Connecticut, Maine, Massachusetts, New Hampshire, New Jersey, New York, Pennsylvania, Rhode Island, and Vermont. South: Alabama, Arkansas, Delaware, District of Columbia, Florida, Georgia, Kentucky, Louisiana, Maryland, Mississippi, North Carolina, Oklahoma, South Carolina, Tennessee, Texas, Virginia, and West Virginia. Midwest: Illinois, Indiana, Iowa, Kansas, Michigan, Minnesota, Missouri, Nebraska, North Dakota, Ohio, South Dakota, and Wisconsin. The West: Alaska, Arizona, California, Colorado, Hawaii, Idaho, Montana, Nevada, New Mexico, Oregon, Utah, Washington, and Wyoming.
[4]Less than 0.05 percent.

Note: Because of rounding, sums of individual items may not equal totals.

SOURCE: Jerome E. King and Cathy A. Baker, "Table 1. Incidence[1] of childcare resource and referral services by industry, establishment, size and region, June 2000," in *Childcare Benefits Continue to Evolve,* Compensation and Working Conditions Online, Bureau of Labor Statistics, Summer 2001 [Online] http://www.bls.gov/opub/cwc/2001/summer/art1full.pdf [accessed December 5, 2002]

FIGURE 3.13

Percentage of children in poverty, by family structure, race, and Hispanic origin, 2001

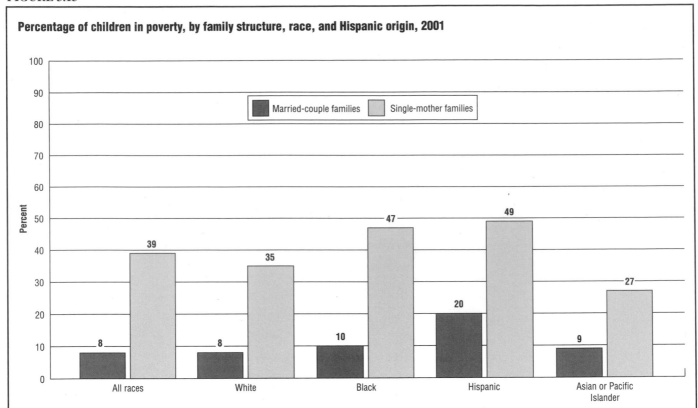

¹ Estimates are for children related to the householder who are under the age of 18.

SOURCE: "Figure 3. Percentage of Children in Poverty By Family Structure, Race, and Hispanic Origin 2001," Child Trends DataBank [Online] http://www.childtrendsdatabank.org/figures/4-Figure-3.gif [accessed December 3, 2002]

TABLE 3.16

Estimated annual expenditures* on children born in 2001, by income group

Year	Age	Income group		
		Lowest	Middle	Highest
2001	<1	$6,490	$9,030	$13,430
2002	1	6,710	9,340	13,890
2003	2	6,940	9,650	14,360
2004	3	7,330	10,240	15,170
2005	4	7,580	10,590	15,680
2006	5	7,840	10,940	16,220
2007	6	8,200	11,320	16,580
2008	7	8,480	11,700	17,150
2009	8	8,770	12,100	17,730
2010	9	9,090	12,420	18,120
2011	10	9,400	12,840	18,730
2012	11	9,720	13,280	19,370
2013	12	11,290	14,850	21,300
2014	13	11,680	15,350	22,020
2015	14	12,070	15,870	22,770
2016	15	12,350	16,740	24,220
2017	16	12,770	17,310	25,050
2018	17	13,210	17,900	25,900
Total		$169,920	$231,470	$337,690

*Estimates are for the younger child in husband-wife families with two children.

SOURCE: "Table 12. Estimated annual expenditures* on children born in 2001, by income group, overall United States," in *Expenditures on Children by Families, 2001 Annual Report,* U.S. Department of Agriculture, Center for Nutrition Policy and Promotion, Washington, DC, May 2002

TABLE 3.17

Estimated annual expenditures* on a child by husband-wife families, 2001

Age of child	Total	Housing	Food	Trans-portation	Clothing	Health care	Child care and education	Miscel-laneous†
Before-tax income: Less than $39,100 (Average = $24,400)								
0 - 2	$6,490	$2,500	$910	$780	$370	$460	$840	$630
3 - 5	6,630	2,470	1,010	750	360	440	950	650
6 - 8	6,710	2,380	1,300	880	400	510	560	680
9 - 11	6,730	2,150	1,560	950	450	560	340	720
12 - 14	7,560	2,400	1,640	1,070	750	560	240	900
15 - 17	7,480	1,940	1,780	1,440	660	600	400	660
Total	$124,800	$41,520	$24,600	$17,610	$8,970	$9,390	$9,990	$12,720
Before-tax income: $39,100 to $65,800 (Average = $52,100)								
0 - 2	$9,030	$3,380	$1,090	$1,160	$430	$610	$1,380	$980
3 - 5	9,260	3,350	1,260	1,130	420	580	1,530	990
6 - 8	9,260	3,260	1,600	1,260	470	660	980	1,030
9 - 11	9,190	3,030	1,890	1,330	520	720	640	1,060
12 - 14	9,940	3,280	1,900	1,450	870	720	470	1,250
15 - 17	10,140	2,820	2,110	1,840	780	770	810	1,010
Total	$170,460	$57,360	$29,550	$24,510	$10,470	$12,180	$17,430	$18,960
Before-tax income: More than $65,800 (Average = $98,600)								
0 - 2	$13,430	$5,370	$1,440	$1,630	$570	$700	$2,090	$1,630
3 - 5	13,720	5,340	1,630	1,600	560	670	2,270	1,650
6 - 8	13,570	5,250	1,970	1,720	610	770	1,560	1,690
9 - 11	13,410	5,020	2,290	1,800	670	820	1,090	1,720
12 - 14	14,260	5,270	2,400	1,920	1,100	830	840	1,900
15 - 17	14,670	4,810	2,530	2,330	1,000	870	1,470	1,660
Total	$249,180	$93,180	$36,780	$33,000	$13,530	$13,980	$27,960	$30,750

*Estimates are based on 1990-92 Consumer Expenditure Survey data updated to 2001 dollars using the Consumer Price Index. For each age category, the expense estimates represent average child-rearing expenditures for each age (e.g., the expense for the 3-5 age category, on average, applies to the 3-year-old, the 4-year-old, or the 5-year-old). The figures represent estimated expenses on the younger child in a two-child family. Estimates are about the same for the older child, so to calculate expenses for two children, figures should be summed for the appropriate age categories. To estimate expenses for an only child, multiply the total expense for the appropriate age category by 1.24. To estimate expenses for each child in a family with three or more children, multiply the total expense for each appropriate age category by 0.77. For expenses on all children in a family, these totals should be summed.
†Miscellaneous expenses include personal care items, entertainment, and reading materials.

SOURCE: "Table ES-1. Estimated annual expenditures* on a child by husband-wife families, overall United States, 2001," in *Expenditures on Children by Families, 2001 Annual Report,* U.S. Department of Agriculture, Center for Nutrition Policy and Promotion, Washington, DC, May 2002

TABLE 3.18

Estimated annual expenditures* on a child by single-parent families, 2001

Age of child	Total	Housing	Food	Trans-portation	Clothing	Health care	Child care and education	Miscel-laneous†
Before-tax income: Less than $39,100 (Average = $16,400)								
0 - 2	$5,440	$2,240	$1,010	$730	$330	$220	$530	$380
3 - 5	6,150	2,550	1,060	640	350	330	720	500
6 - 8	6,910	2,710	1,340	740	410	390	650	670
9 - 11	6,440	2,600	1,550	530	420	490	310	540
12 - 14	6,920	2,600	1,550	620	710	520	400	520
15 - 17	7,670	2,760	1,690	970	830	520	300	600
Total	$118,590	$46,380	$24,600	$12,690	$9,150	$7,410	$8,730	$9,630
Before-tax income: $39,100 or more (Average = $59,400)								
0 - 2	$12,450	$4,820	$1,560	$2,220	$470	$510	$1,290	$1,580
3 - 5	13,410	5,130	1,650	2,130	500	690	1,620	1,690
6 - 8	14,250	5,290	1,980	2,240	570	790	1,510	1,870
9 - 11	13,740	5,180	2,380	2,030	580	950	880	1,740
12 - 14	14,560	5,190	2,330	2,110	950	1,000	1,260	1,720
15 - 17	15,010	5,340	2,470	2,290	1,090	990	1,030	1,800
Total	$250,260	$92,850	$37,110	$39,060	$12,480	$14,790	$22,770	$31,200

*Estimates are based on 1990-92 Consumer Expenditure Survey data updated to 2001 dollars using the Consumer Price Index. For each age category, the expense estimates represent average child-rearing expenditures for each age (e.g., the expense for the 3-5 age category, on average, applies to the 3-year-old, the 4-year-old, or the 5-year-old). The figures represent estimated expenses on the younger child in a single-parent, two-child family. For estimated expenses on the older child, multiply the total expense for the appropriate age category by 0.93. To estimate expenses for two children, the expenses on the younger child and older child after adjusting the expense on the older child downward should be summed for the appropriate age categories. To estimate expenses for an only child, multiply the total expense for the appropriate age category by 1.35. To estimate expenses for each child in a family with three or more children, multiply the total expense for each appropriate age category by 0.72 after adjusting the expenses on the older children downward. For expenses on all children in a family, these totals should be summed.
†Miscellaneous expenses include personal care items, entertainment, and reading materials.

SOURCE: "Table 7. Estimated annual expenditures* on a child by single-parent families, overall United States, 2001," in *Expenditures on Children by Families, 2001 Annual Report,* U.S. Department of Agriculture, Center for Nutrition Policy and Promotion, Washington, DC, May 2002

CHAPTER 4
SOCIAL ISSUES AFFECTING AMERICA'S CHILDREN

In 1998, George Gallup Jr., the founder and chairman of the George H. Gallup International Institute, made several observations about American youth on the 20th anniversary of *The Gallup Youth Survey*. These observations included an enthusiasm among young people to help others, a desire to work toward world peace and health, and a positive perspective about the performance of their schools and, in particular, their teachers. Most had a happy and excited perspective about the future, a feeling of closeness with their families, a general satisfaction with their personal lives, a goal to attain the top of their chosen careers, and a belief that they would marry and have children.

Gallup also observed that, in contrast, these same youths understood they had many challenges to face. For example, the survey showed that 1 in 5 children lived below the poverty level, 10 million had no medical insurance, homicide and suicide killed approximately 7,000 of them each year, 1 in 4 had an unwed mother—some of these mothers being mere children themselves—and, at the time of the survey, 135 brought guns to school each day.

CHILD POVERTY

Poverty rates for all age groups declined significantly between 1959 and the early 1970s. Since the early 1980s, the poverty rates for adults aged 65 and over have nearly matched those for adults aged 18 to 64, demonstrating great improvement in the well-being of the elderly population. In 1974, for the first time children replaced the elderly as the poorest age group. As poverty rates for people aged 65 and over continued to decline, the poverty rate for children continued to climb to a 1992 peak of about 23 percent. The poverty rate for children then began a steady decline but leveled off around 1999 and remained unchanged from 2000 to 2001. (See Figure 4.1.)

The Census Bureau uses set income thresholds that vary by family size and composition to determine num-

bers of people at or below the poverty level. Income for this purpose is based on money income before taxes and does not include capital gains and noncash benefits such as public housing, Medicaid, and food stamps. This is a statistical measure of poverty; many government programs use different dollar amounts to determine eligibility for aid. In 2001, for a household with one adult under age 65, the income threshold is $11,859; for that adult with one child, it is $12,207. Two adults and one child have a poverty threshold of $14,255.

In 2001, 11.7 million children were poor. The poverty rate for all children under 18 years of age was 16.3 percent, higher than the rates for all people over age 18. (See Figure 4.1.) While children make up only one-fourth of the total population (25.6 percent), they represent 35.7 percent of the poor population.

Children under age six have been particularly vulnerable to poverty. In 2001, their poverty rate was 18.2 percent, unchanged from 2000. Of children under age six living with a female householder with no spouse present, 48.9 percent were poor, over five times the rate of children of the same age who lived in homes headed by married couples (9.2 percent).

Minority children continued to experience a higher poverty rate than their white peers. While the poverty rate for white children under 18 years of age was 13.5 percent of all poor children under 18, the rate for black children in the same age group was 33.1 percent. Hispanic children had a poverty rate of 30.3 percent. (Hispanics represent an ethnic group and may be of any race.)

Poverty is associated with a number of serious problems for children. In "The High Price of Poverty for Children of the South" (*CDF Reports,* Washington, D.C., May 1998), the Children's Defense Fund, a children's advocacy group, noted some of the consequences of child poverty.

FIGURE 4.1

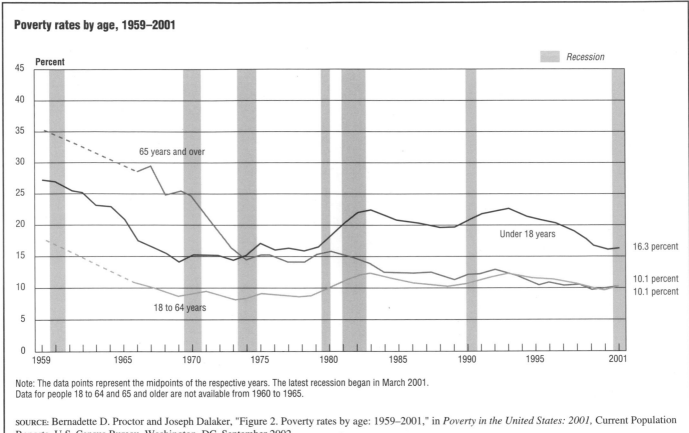

Poverty rates by age, 1959–2001

Note: The data points represent the midpoints of the respective years. The latest recession began in March 2001.
Data for people 18 to 64 and 65 and older are not available from 1960 to 1965.

SOURCE: Bernadette D. Proctor and Joseph Dalaker, "Figure 2. Poverty rates by age: 1959–2001," in *Poverty in the United States: 2001,* Current Population Reports, U.S. Census Bureau, Washington, DC, September 2002

- Poverty is a greater risk to children's overall health status than is living in a single-parent family.

- Poor children are twice as likely as nonpoor children to be born weighing too little or to suffer stunted growth.

- Poor children suffer more mental and physical disabilities.

- Poverty makes children hungry. Hungry children are more likely to be hyperactive and to have serious behavioral problems. They are also four times more likely to have difficulty concentrating in school.

- Poor children score lower on reading and math tests and are twice as likely to repeat a year of school as nonpoor children.

- Poor children earn 25 percent lower wages when they become young adults.

LACK OF HEALTH INSURANCE

Today, for too many parents, the emergency room is the family physician for children.

—Senator Edward Kennedy (D-MA), Children's Defense Fund's 17th annual conference, March 13, 1997

As the debate over health-care delivery, managed care, and the like rages on, children are all too often the innocent victims. Health insurance helps children obtain adequate health care, which helps ensure their physical well-being and optimum development. The social and economic changes that have affected children over the last several decades of the 20th century make access to health care even more essential. Changes in family composition and economic conditions have put children in situations that often require health services—hunger, poor housing conditions, violence, neglect, and others.

Uninsured Children

From 1987 to 1996, the number of American children without health insurance climbed from 8.2 million to 10.6 million, the highest levels ever recorded by the U.S. Bureau of the Census. That trend began to reverse in 1999, when the number of uninsured children declined to 10 million, the lowest rate since 1995. In 2000, 11.6 percent of children under age 18 were uninsured, down from 12.6 percent in 1999. (See Table 4.1.)

Children in poverty are far more likely to be uninsured than children who are not poor. While 11.6 percent of all children in America lack health insurance, 21.5 percent of poor children are uninsured. Children aged 12 to 17 are more often without insurance (12.3 percent) than are younger children. Children of Hispanic origin are far more likely to be uninsured than children of other racial or ethnic origins. Nearly one-fourth (24.9 percent) of His-

TABLE 4.1

People without health insurance for the entire year by selected characteristics: 1999 and 2000

Characteristic	2000 Total	2000 Uninsured Number	2000 Uninsured Percent[a]	2000 Uninsured Percent 90-pct. C.I. (±)	1999 Total	1999 Uninsured Number	1999 Uninsured Percent[2]	1999 Uninsured Percent 90-pct. C.I. (±)	Change[2] 1999 to 2000 Uninsured Number	Change Uninsured Percent	Change Uninsured Percent 90-pct. C.I. (±)
People											
Total	276,540	38,729	14.0	0.2	274,087	39,280	14.3	0.2	*−551	*−0.3	0.2
Sex											
Male	135,244	20,177	14.9	0.2	133,933	20,402	15.2	0.2	−226	*−0.3	0.3
Female	141,296	18,552	13.1	0.2	140,154	18,877	13.5	0.2	−325	*−0.3	0.3
Race and Ethnicity											
White	226,401	29,285	12.9	0.2	224,806	29,385	13.1	0.2	−99	−0.1	0.2
Non-Hispanic	194,161	18,898	9.7	0.2	193,633	19,237	9.9	0.2	−340	*−0.2	0.2
Black	35,919	6,629	18.5	0.5	35,509	6,963	19.6	0.5	*−333	*−1.2	0.7
Asian and Pacific Islander	11,384	2,051	18.0	1.0	10,925	2,080	19.0	1.0	−29	−1.0	1.2
Hispanic[1]	33,863	10,835	32.0	0.7	32,804	10,566	32.2	0.7	*269	−0.2	0.6
Age											
Under 18 years	72,556	8,451	11.6	0.3	72,325	9,145	12.6	0.3	*−693	*−1.0	0.3
18 to 24 years	26,962	7,349	27.3	0.7	26,532	7,199	27.1	0.7	150	0.1	0.8
25 to 34 years	37,440	7,926	21.2	0.5	37,786	8,188	21.7	0.5	*−262	−0.5	0.6
35 to 44 years	44,780	6,939	15.5	0.5	44,805	6,804	15.2	0.5	134	0.3	0.5
45 to 64 years	61,823	7,819	12.6	0.3	60,018	7,669	12.8	0.3	151	−0.1	0.4
65 years and over	32,979	245	0.7	0.2	32,621	276	0.8	0.2	−31	−0.1	0.1
Nativity											
Native	246,613	29,270	11.9	0.2	245,708	30,155	12.3	0.2	*−885	*−0.4	0.2
Foreign born	29,927	9,459	31.6	0.8	28,379	9,125	32.2	0.8	*334	−0.5	0.9
Naturalized citizen	11,390	1,807	15.9	1.0	10,622	1,764	16.6	1.0	43	−0.7	1.2
Not a citizen	18,538	7,652	41.3	1.0	17,758	7,361	41.5	1.0	*291	−0.2	1.2
Region											
Northeast	52,809	6,019	11.4	0.3	52,038	5,988	11.5	0.3	31	−0.1	0.4
Midwest	62,953	6,787	10.8	0.3	63,595	6,412	10.1	0.3	*375	*0.7	0.4
South	97,444	15,357	15.8	0.3	95,928	15,767	16.4	0.3	*−410	*−0.7	0.4
West	63,334	10,566	16.7	0.3	62,526	11,112	17.8	0.3	*−547	*−1.1	0.5
Household Income											
Less than $25,000	61,130	13,898	22.7	0.5	64,628	15,003	23.2	0.3	*−1,105	−0.5	0.5
$25,000 to $49,999	75,351	12,783	17.0	0.3	77,119	13,176	17.1	0.3	*−393	−0.1	0.4
$50,000 to $74,999	59,237	6,496	11.0	0.3	56,873	5,827	10.2	0.3	*668	*0.7	0.4
$75,000 or more	80,822	5,552	6.9	0.2	75,467	5,273	7.0	0.2	*279	−0.1	0.3
Education (18 years and older)											
Total	203,985	30,278	14.8	0.2	201,762	30,135	14.9	0.2	143	−0.1	0.2
No high school diploma	33,950	9,026	26.6	0.7	34,087	8,780	25.8	0.7	246	*0.8	0.7
High school graduate only	65,833	10,816	16.4	0.3	66,141	10,812	16.3	0.3	3	0.1	0.4
Some college, no degree	40,068	5,369	13.4	0.5	39,940	5,571	13.9	0.5	−202	*−0.5	0.5
Associate degree	15,702	1,619	10.3	0.7	14,715	1,680	11.4	0.7	−61	*−1.1	0.8
Bachelor's degree or higher	48,432	3,448	7.1	0.3	46,880	3,292	7.0	0.3	156	0.1	0.4
Work Experience (18 to 64 years old)											
Total	171,006	30,033	17.6	0.2	169,141	29,860	17.7	0.2	173	−0.1	0.3
Worked during year	140,403	22,806	16.2	0.2	139,218	22,568	16.2	0.3	238	−	0.3
Worked full-time	117,478	18,057	15.4	0.3	115,973	17,660	15.2	0.3	397	0.1	0.3
Worked part-time	22,925	4,749	20.7	0.7	23,245	4,908	21.1	0.8	−159	−0.4	0.8
Did not work	30,603	7,227	23.6	0.7	29,923	7,292	24.4	0.7	−65	−0.8	0.8

- Represents zero or rounds to zero.
*Statistically significant at the 90-percent confidence level.
[1]Hispanics may be of any race.
[2]All numbers are derived from unrounded numbers. Some numbers and percentages may therefore appear to be slightly higher or lower than those computed with rounded figures from other columns.

SOURCE: Robert J. Mills, "Table A. People Without Health Insurance for the Entire Year by Selected Characteristics: 1999 and 2000," *Health Insurance Coverage: 2000,* Current Population Reports, U.S. Census Bureau, Washington, DC, September 2001

panic children were uninsured in 2000, compared to 7.3 percent of white non-Hispanic children. (See Figure 4.2.)

Medicaid covers 20.4 percent of all children. Black children are most likely to participate in Medicaid insurance (35.8 percent), compared to 13.2 percent of white non-Hispanic children. Medicaid is the insurance resource

for 32.8 percent of Hispanic children (who may also be of any race). (See Figure 4.3.)

Children in Low-Income Working Families

Most uninsured children are from low-income working families, where the children are not eligible for public

FIGURE 4.2

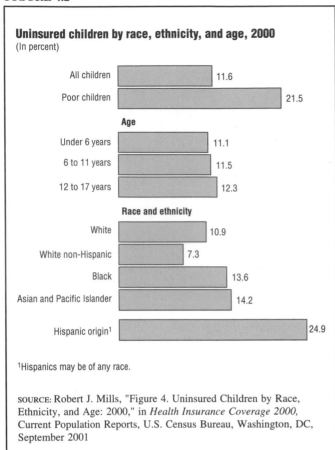

Uninsured children by race, ethnicity, and age, 2000
(In percent)

All children	11.6
Poor children	21.5

Age

Under 6 years	11.1
6 to 11 years	11.5
12 to 17 years	12.3

Race and ethnicity

White	10.9
White non-Hispanic	7.3
Black	13.6
Asian and Pacific Islander	14.2
Hispanic origin[1]	24.9

[1]Hispanics may be of any race.

SOURCE: Robert J. Mills, "Figure 4. Uninsured Children by Race, Ethnicity, and Age: 2000," in *Health Insurance Coverage 2000,* Current Population Reports, U.S. Census Bureau, Washington, DC, September 2001

FIGURE 4.3

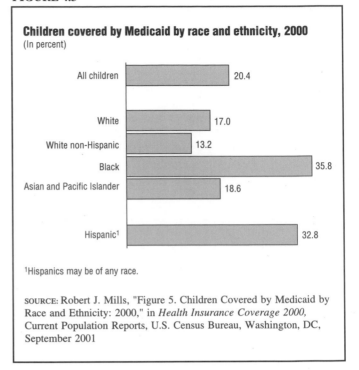

Children covered by Medicaid by race and ethnicity, 2000
(In percent)

All children	20.4
White	17.0
White non-Hispanic	13.2
Black	35.8
Asian and Pacific Islander	18.6
Hispanic[1]	32.8

[1]Hispanics may be of any race.

SOURCE: Robert J. Mills, "Figure 5. Children Covered by Medicaid by Race and Ethnicity: 2000," in *Health Insurance Coverage 2000,* Current Population Reports, U.S. Census Bureau, Washington, DC, September 2001

assistance because their families earn too much to qualify for Medicaid, despite not earning enough to pay for their own insurance. In most cases, the parents work for small companies, which are the least likely to provide health insurance. When these companies do offer insurance plans, the cost to employees may be too much for low-income workers.

STATE CHILDREN'S HEALTH INSURANCE PROGRAM (CHIP). The State Children's Health Insurance Program (CHIP), part of the Balanced Budget Act of 1997 (PL 105-33) under Title XXI of the Social Security Act (PL 89-97), is intended to improve access to health-care coverage for uninsured children from low-income families who are not Medicaid eligible. States may use CHIP funding to expand their Medicaid programs or develop other initiatives.

Expanding access to health coverage, however, does not necessarily mean that children from low-income families will get appropriate health-care services. According to the Institute of Medicine, these families have a number of additional barriers to overcome—difficulty in scheduling appointments, cultural differences with medical providers, or a lack of easily accessible services. States may need to go one step further by providing culturally appropriate services and assisting with child care and transportation.

Weight a Health Issue for Children

In July 2002, a New York man filed a class-action suit on behalf of himself and an unknown number of other people in New York who are obese or ill, allegedly due to the failure of a number of fast-food restaurants to properly disclose ingredients in their food items and the risks of eating too much. He claimed that the fast-food companies contributed to his obesity.

This legal action brought news media attention to the problem of obesity in America. According to the Centers for Disease Control, obesity has risen at an epidemic rate during the past 20 years. Half of the nation's adults are considered overweight. Related problems include a dramatic rise in the incidence of diabetes. Research indicates that the situation is worsening rather than improving.

Children are similarly affected by obesity. A 2002 report by the National Center for Health Statistics indicates that in the 1960s, 4.2 percent of children aged 6 to 11 and 4.6 percent of children aged 12 to 19 were overweight. By the late 1970s, the percent of overweight children aged 6 to 11 had jumped to 6.5 percent. By 2000, more than 15 percent of children aged 6 to 19 were overweight. (See Figure 4.4.)

For Americans, prepackaged foods and fast-food restaurants offer convenience but often do not provide good nutrition. The CDC reports that food portions in restaurants and at home have become larger. Adding to the potential for overeating and choosing a poor diet, technology has created many time- and labor-saving products that have helped Americans of all ages to become sedentary.

FIGURE 4.4

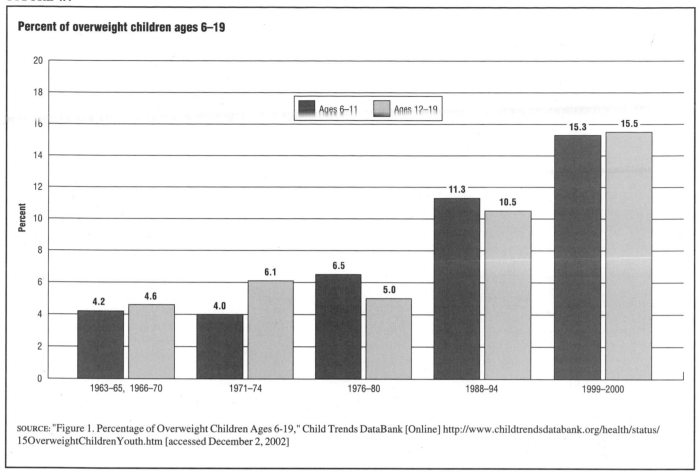

Percent of overweight children ages 6–19

SOURCE: "Figure 1. Percentage of Overweight Children Ages 6-19," Child Trends DataBank [Online] http://www.childtrendsdatabank.org/health/status/15OverweightChildrenYouth.htm [accessed December 2, 2002]

"The Surgeon General's Call to Action to Prevent and Decrease Overweight and Obesity" (Office of the Surgeon General, U.S. Department of Health and Human Services, Washington, D.C., 2002) noted the risk factors for overweight children:

- Risk factors for heart disease, such as high cholesterol and high blood pressure, occur with increased frequency in overweight children and adolescents compared to children with a healthy weight.

- Type 2 diabetes, previously considered an adult disease, has increased dramatically in children and adolescents. Being overweight and obese is closely linked to type 2 diabetes.

- Overweight adolescents have a 70 percent chance of becoming overweight or obese adults. This increases to 80 percent if one or more parents is overweight or obese. Overweight or obese adults are at risk for a number of health problems, including heart disease, type 2 diabetes, high blood pressure, and some forms of cancer.

- The most immediate consequence of being overweight as perceived by the children themselves is social discrimination. This is associated with poor self-esteem and depression.

The surgeon general asked schools to take three specific actions to assist in the effort to combat the problem of overweight children:

- Ensure that school breakfast and lunch programs meet nutrition standards.

- Provide food options that are low in fat, calories, and added sugars.

- Provide all children, from prekindergarten through grade 12, with quality daily physical education.

TEEN SEXUALITY

By the late 20th century, American teens were more sexually active than previous generations. While sexual activity was rare in young teens, it increased as teens grew older; by the age of 17, most teens reported at least one sexual experience. Concurrent with sexual activity are risks of sexually transmitted diseases (STDs), pregnancy, and dropping out of school.

Sexual Risk Behaviors

Unprotected sexual intercourse and multiple sex partners place young people at high risk for the human immunodeficiency virus (HIV) infection, other STDs, and pregnancy. Each year about 3 million teens contract STDs and approximately 1 million—1 of every 10—females aged 15 to 19 gets pregnant.

In "Trends in Sexual Risk Behaviors Among High School Students—United States, 1991–2001" (*Morbidity and Mortality Weekly Report,* vol. 51, no. 38, September 2002), the Centers for Disease Control and Prevention (CDC) reported that, in 2001, the percentage of U.S. high school students who ever had sexual intercourse and the percentage who had multiple sex partners decreased. Among students who are currently sexually active, the use of condoms increased. However, the percentage of these students who used alcohol or drugs before their last sexual intercourse increased. Between 1991 and 2001, sexual activity dropped 16 percent and the prevalence of multiple partners among sexually active teens decreased 24 percent. (See Table 4.2.) Drug or alcohol use prior to sexual intercourse increased 18 percent among students who are currently sexually active. This trend appeared to be most prevalent among male black and Hispanic students in 11th and 12th grades.

Increased Risk Education

Overall, the CDC report concludes that fewer high school students are engaging in sexual risk behaviors, and the decrease corresponds to a decline in gonorrhea, pregnancy, and birth rates among adolescents. The CDC report attributes these improvements in health outcomes to combined efforts of parents and families, schools, community organizations that serve young persons, health-care providers, religious organizations, the media, and government agencies. HIV-prevention education in schools increased from 83 percent in 1991 to 92 percent in 1997 and leveled off at 89 percent in 2001. The data is limited to adolescents who attend high school.

The decline in risk behaviors among high school students between 1991 and 2001 corresponded with the increase in the proportion of students who participated in HIV/AIDS education in school. Dr. Lloyd Kolbe, director of the CDC's Division of Adolescent and School Health, claims that the survey findings showed that teaching teenagers about safe sex does not result in more promiscuity.

One of the national health objectives for 2010 is to increase from 85 percent to 95 percent the proportion of adolescents in grades 9 to 12 who have never had sexual intercourse, have had sexual intercourse but not during the past three months, or used a condom during sexual intercourse. At least in 2001, this goal has been met, according to the CDC, which reports that 96 percent of high school students met this objective, compared to 80 percent in 1991.

Noncoital Behaviors

The growing perception among young people that noncoital behaviors are not "sex" is placing more teens at

risk. A new study by the Urban Institute, a nonprofit policy research organization based in Washington, D.C., that investigates social and economic problems, provided the first data on the sexual practices of 15- to 19-year-old boys. The study said that health educators have focused on sexual intercourse by young teens but not on other sexual behaviors (oral sex, anal sex, and masturbation) that can also pose a danger of STDs. Most STDs—such as herpes, hepatitis B, gonorrhea, syphilis, and chlamydia—can be transmitted orally or genitally. And, although HIV is not easily transmitted through oral sex, researchers say such transmission is possible.

The study also showed that while 55 percent of teenage males stated they had had vaginal sex, two-thirds had experienced oral or anal sex or had been masturbated by a female. More than 1 in 10 boys had engaged in oral intercourse, one-half had received oral sex from a girl, and slightly more than one-third had performed oral sex on a girl.

Researchers and public health experts found that many young people perceived these noncoital behaviors as something other than sex—and sometimes even believed they were being sexually abstinent while participating in noncoital sexual behavior.

Racial and Ethnic Differences

The survey also found significant differences among racial and ethnic groups. Black and Hispanic boys were almost twice as likely as white boys to have had anal intercourse, and white and Hispanic boys were about twice as likely as black boys to have performed oral sex on a girl. The percentage of black boys receiving oral sex more than doubled from 1988 to 1995, while that percentage stayed stable among white and Hispanic boys.

Teens' First Sexual Experiences

Contrary to popular belief that the after-school hours (3:00 P.M. to 6:00 P.M.), when parents may be at work and teens unsupervised, were the high-risk period for teen sexual encounters, only 15 percent of teens in a recent survey reported having their first sexual experience during this time. Forty-two percent of teens reported their first sexual experience took place between 10:00 P.M. and 7:00 A.M. (See Figure 4.5.) Half of teens reported having their first sexual experience in their own home (22 percent) or the home of their sexual partner (34 percent). Only 4 percent reported having their first sexual experience in a car or truck, as seemed to be so common in the 1940s and 1950s. (See Figure 4.6.)

TEENAGE PREGNANCY

The pregnancy rate among teenagers 15 to 19 years old generally rose during the 1970s and 1980s and peaked at 116.5 pregnancies per 1,000 females in 1991. Between

TABLE 4.2

Percentage of high school students who reported sexual risk behaviors by selected characteristics, and survey year–United States Youth Risk Behavior Survey, 1991, 1993, 1995, 1997, 1999, and 2001

Characteristic	Ever had sexual intercourse		≥4 sex partners during lifetime		Currently sexually active[2]		Condom use during last sexual intercourse[3]		Alcohol or drug use before last sexual intercourse[3]	
	%	(95% CI[1])	%	(95% CI)	%	(95% CI)	%	(95% CI)	%	(95% CI)
Sex										
Female										
1991	50.8	(±4.0)	13.8	(±1.8)	38.2	(±3.4)	38.0	(±4.3)	16.8	(±3.2)
1993	50.2	(±2.5)	15.0	(+1.9)	37.5	(±1.8)	46.0	(±2.8)	16.6	(±2.2)
1995	52.1	(±5.0)	14.4	(±3.5)	40.4	(±4.2)	48.6	(±5.2)	16.8	(±3.0)
1997	47.7	(±3.7)	14.1	(±2.0)	36.5	(±2.7)	50.8	(±3.0)	18.5	(±3.0)
1999	47.7	(±4.1)	13.1	(±2.2)	36.3	(±4.1)	50.7	(±5.8)	18.6	(±3.4)
2001	42.9	(±2.8)[4]	11.4	(±1.5)	33.4	(±2.5)	51.3	(±3.4)[4,5]	20.7	(±2.7)
Male										
1991	57.4	(±4.1)	23.4	(±3.0)	36.8	(±3.4)	54.5	(±3.8)	26.3	(±3.3)
1993	55.6	(±3.5)	22.3	(±2.7)	37.5	(±3.0)	59.2	(±3.8)	25.7	(±3.0)
1995	54.0	(±4.7)	20.9	(±2.6)	35.5	(±3.5)	60.5	(±4.3)	32.8	(±4.1)
1997	48.8	(±3.4)	17.6	(±1.5)	33.4	(±2.6)	62.5	(±2.8)	30.5	(±2.8)
1999	52.2	(±4.0)	19.3	(±3.6)	36.2	(±3.9)	65.5	(±4.3)	31.2	(±4.0)
2001	48.5	(±2.7)[4]	17.2	(±1.6)[4]	33.4	(±2.3)	65.1	(±2.7)[4]	30.9	(±2.9)[4]
Grade										
9										
1991	39.0	(±5.0)	12.5	(±2.9)	22.4	(±3.9)	53.3	(±6.2)	20.9	(±6.9)
1993	37.7	(±4.2)	10.9	(±2.0)	24.8	(±3.2)	61.6	(±5.7)	22.4	(±3.9)
1995	36.9	(±5.9)	12.9	(±3.0)	23.6	(±4.0)	62.9	(±5.5)	29.7	(±5.7)
1997	38.0	(±3.8)	12.2	(±2.5)	24.2	(±3.3)	58.8	(±5.6)	33.2	(±8.3)
1999	38.6	(±6.1)	11.8	(±2.3)	26.6	(±5.7)	66.6	(±7.8)	25.6	(±5.2)
2001	34.4	(±3.6)	9.6	(±1.6)	22.7	(±3.1)	67.5	(±3.3)[4]	24.0	(±4.4)[5]
10										
1991	48.2	(±5.7)	15.1	(±2.8)	33.2	(±4.6)	46.3	(±4.7)	22.3	(±4.9)
1993	46.1	(±3.6)	15.9	(±2.0)	30.1	(±3.0)	54.7	(±4.5)	24.2	(±4.2)
1995	48.0	(±5.1)	15.6	(±2.0)	33.7	(±3.1)	59.7	(±4.6)	28.6	(±5.9)
1997	42.5	(±4.3)	13.8	(±2.7)	29.2	(±2.9)	58.9	(±3.6)	22.9	(±3.3)
1999	46.8	(±5.6)	15.6	(±5.0)	33.0	(±5.2)	62.6	(±6.1)	23.1	(±4.2)
2001	40.8	(±3.0)[4]	12.6	(±1.8)	29.7	(±2.9)	60.1	(±4.5)[4,5]	27.7	(±3.1)
11										
1991	62.4	(±3.2)	22.1	(±3.6)	43.3	(±3.6)	48.7	(±5.8)	22.2	(±3.5)
1993	57.5	(±3.5)	19.9	(±3.1)	40.0	(±3.6)	55.3	(±3.0)	22.0	(±2.6)
1995	58.6	(±5.0)	19.0	(±3.7)	42.4	(±4.4)	52.3	(±6.2)	24.3	(±3.1)
1997	49.7	(±5.2)	16.7	(±2.9)	37.8	(±4.8)	60.1	(±5.2)	23.1	(±4.1)
1999	52.5	(±3.8)	17.3	(±4.1)	37.5	(±3.4)	59.2	(±4.8)	28.6	(±5.8)
2001	51.9	(±2.9)[4,5]	15.2	(±1.5)[4]	38.1	(±2.6)[4]	58.9	(±4.0)[4]	24.7	(±2.9)[4]
12										
1991	66.7	(±4.4)	25.0	(±4.0)	50.6	(±4.5)	41.4	(±3.6)	20.8	(±3.7)
1993	68.3	(±4.6)	27.0	(±3.6)	53.0	(±3.9)	46.5	(±4.0)	19.1	(±3.3)
1995	66.4	(±4.0)	22.9	(±3.5)	49.7	(±3.9)	49.5	(±4.4)	20.3	(±3.6)
1997	60.9	(±6.5)	20.6	(±3.5)	46.0	(±5.0)	52.4	(±3.5)	23.2	(±1.8)
1999	64.9	(±4.9)	20.6	(±2.8)	50.6	(±5.1)	47.9	(±5.7)	22.0	(±3.8)
2001	60.5	(±4.0)[4]	21.6	(±2.4)[4]	47.9	(±4.0)	49.3	(±3.1)[4,5]	25.4	(±2.6)[4]
Race/Ethnicity[6]										
Black										
1991	81.4	(±3.2)	43.1	(±3.5)	59.3	(±3.8)	48.0	(±3.8)	13.7	(±2.9)
1993	79.7	(±3.2)	42.7	(±3.8)	59.1	(±4.4)	56.5	(±3.8)	12.2	(±3.5)
1995	73.4	(±4.5)	35.6	(±4.4)	54.2	(±4.7)	66.1	(±4.8)	19.2	(±4.6)
1997	72.6	(±2.8)	38.5	(±3.6)	53.6	(±3.2)	64.0	(±2.8)	18.1	(±3.1)
1999	71.2	(±8.2)	34.4	(±10.3)	53.0	(±8.9)	70.0	(±5.4)	18.1	(±7.9)
2001	60.8	(±6.6)[4]	26.6	(±3.7)[4]	45.6	(±5.4)[4]	67.1	(±3.5)[4,5]	17.8	(±2.6)[4]
Hispanic										
1991	53.1	(±3.5)	16.8	(±2.6)	37.0	(±3.6)	37.4	(±6.2)	17.8	(±4.2)
1993	56.0	(±4.1)	18.6	(±3.1)	39.4	(±3.7)	46.1	(±4.4)	18.2	(±4.8)
1995	57.6	(±8.6)	17.6	(±3.7)	39.3	(±7.1)	44.4	(±11.1)	24.9	(±5.2)
1997	52.2	(±3.6)	15.5	(±2.4)	35.4	(±3.9)	48.3	(±5.6)	25.3	(±5.3)
1999	54.1	(±4.8)	16.6	(±3.6)	36.3	(±4.0)	55.2	(±6.8)	22.5	(±4.0)
2001	48.4	(±4.5)	14.9	(±1.7)	35.9	(±3.2)	53.5	(±5.1)[4]	24.1	(±2.8)[4]
White										
1991	50.0	(±3.2)	14.7	(±1.8)	33.9	(±2.8)	46.5	(±4.6)	25.3	(±3.7)
1993	48.4	(±2.8)	14.3	(±2.1)	34.0	(±2.1)	52.3	(±3.9)	24.4	(±2.7)
1995	48.9	(±5.0)	14.2	(±2.4)	34.8	(±3.9)	52.5	(±4.0)	26.6	(±3.1)
1997	43.6	(±4.2)	11.6	(±1.5)	32.0	(±3.1)	55.8	(±2.0)	26.0	(±2.5)
1999	45.1	(±3.9)	12.4	(±2.1)	33.0	(±3.3)	55.0	(±5.1)	27.4	(±4.8)
2001	43.2	(±2.5)[4]	12.0	(±1.4)[4]	31.3	(±2.2)	56.8	(±3.0)[4]	27.8	(±2.2)

TABLE 4.2

Percentage of high school students who reported sexual risk behaviors by selected characteristics, and survey year–United States Youth Risk Behavior Survey, 1991, 1993, 1995, 1997, 1999, and 2001 [CONTINUED]

Characteristic	Ever had sexual intercourse		≥4 sex partners during lifetime		Currently sexually active[2]		Condom use during last sexual intercourse[3]		Alcohol or drug use before last sexual intercourse[3]	
	%	(95% CI[1])	%	(95% CI)	%	(95% CI)	%	(95% CI)	%	(95% CI)
Total										
1991	54.1	(±3.5)	18.7	(±2.1)	37.4	(±3.1)	46.2	(±3.3)	21.6	(±2.9)
1993	53.0	(±2.7)	18.7	(±2.0)	37.5	(±2.1)	52.8	(±2.7)	21.3	(±2.0)
1995	53.1	(±4.5)	17.8	(±2.6)	37.9	(±3.4)	54.4	(±3.5)	24.8	(±2.8)
1997	48.4	(±3.1)	16.0	(±1.4)	34.8	(±2.2)	56.8	(±1.6)	24.7	(±1.8)
1999	49.9	(±3.7)	16.2	(±2.6)	36.3	(±3.5)	58.0	(±4.2)	24.8	(±3.0)
2001	45.6	(±2.3)[4]	14.2	(±1.2)[4]	33.4	(±2.0)	57.9	(±2.2)[4,5]	25.6	(±1.7)[4]

[1]Confidence interval.
[2]Sexual intercourse during the 3 months preceding the survey.
[3]Among students who are currently sexually active.
[4]Significant linear effect (p<0.05).
[5]Significant quadratic effect (p<0.05).
[6]Numbers of students in racial/ethnic groups other than white, black, or Hispanic were too small for meaningful analysis.

SOURCE: "Table. Percentage of high school students who reported sexual risk behaviors, by sex, grade, race/ethnicity, and survey year–United States, Youth Risk Behavior Survey, 1991, 1993, 1995, 1997, 1999, and 2001," in *Trends in Sexual Risk Behaviors among High School Students—United States, 1991—2001*, Morbidity and Mortality Weekly Report, Vol. 51, No. 38, Centers for Disease Control and Prevention, Atlanta, GA, September 2002

1991 and 2000, the birth rate for teens aged 15 to 19 dropped 21.9 percent overall. The decline in teen birth rates varies significantly by state and region. Vermont recorded the greatest decline (38.5 percent) in teen birth rates between 1991 and 2000, while Texas and Nebraska recorded the smallest decline, 12.3 percent. (See Table 4.3.) Teen birth rates vary by state and by region, with the highest rates in southern states (plus Puerto Rico, Guam, and the Northern Mariana Islands). The 10 states with the lowest rates of teen births are Maine, Vermont, New Hampshire, Massachusetts, Connecticut, New Jersey, Wisconsin, Iowa, Minnesota, and North Dakota. (See Figure 4.7.) Between 1991 and 2000, Maine, Vermont, New Hampshire, Massachusetts, the District of Columbia, Michigan, Washington, and California all saw reductions in teen birth rates of 25 percent or more.

Some analysts ascribe the declining pregnancy trend to the increasing use of birth control methods, especially longer-lasting contraceptives such as Norplant and Depo-Provera. The increasing use of condoms due to fear of contracting AIDS is also thought to contribute to the lower pregnancy rate. Conservative analysts, however, discount the increasing use of contraception as responsible for the lower pregnancy rates, ascribing the drop in teen pregnancy to the increasing practice of abstinence.

Many experts believe that the factors that predispose adolescents to drug use are the same ones that predispose them to teen pregnancy—poverty, family dysfunction, child abuse, and early education difficulties.

Births and Induced Abortions

In 1940, 54.1 out of every 1,000 women aged 15 to 19 years gave birth. The teen birth rate peaked in 1960 at 89.1 births per 1,000 teens and reached an all-time low of 45.9 in 2001. (See Table 4.4.) Along with the decline in birth rates for teens in this age group came a decline in the rate of induced abortions, which fell 33 percent between 1988 and 1996, from 43.5 abortions per 1,000 teenage women in 1988 to 29.2 in 1996.

FAMILY STRUCTURE AND TEEN SEXUALITY

In *Not Just for Girls: The Roles of Boys and Men in Teen Pregnancy Prevention* (Kristin A. Moore, Anne K. Driscoll, and Theodora Ooms, National Campaign to Prevent Teen Pregnancy, Washington, D.C., 1997), researchers analyzed the 1995 National Survey of Family Growth (NSFG) to study the impact of family structure on teen sexuality. The NSFG is a periodic survey conducted by the National Center for Health Statistics of the U.S. Department of Health and Human Services to collect information on the reproductive health of women in the United States.

The researchers found that girls who were raised during their entire childhood by both biological parents were less likely to have sex in their teens than were those raised in a different family structure. Slightly more than two of five female teens (42.8 percent) who grew up with both parents had had sex by the age of 20, compared with three of five female teens (60 percent) who grew up in a different living arrangement.

TEEN MOTHERS

The U.S. General Accounting Office (GAO), in *Teen Mothers—Selected Socio-Demographic Characteristics and Risk Factors* (Washington, D.C., 1998), reported on

FIGURE 4.5

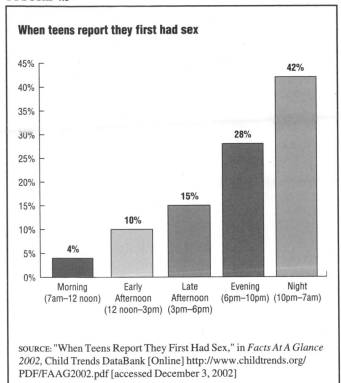

When teens report they first had sex

SOURCE: "When Teens Report They First Had Sex," in *Facts At A Glance 2002*, Child Trends DataBank [Online] http://www.childtrends.org/PDF/FAAG2002.pdf [accessed December 3, 2002]

FIGURE 4.6

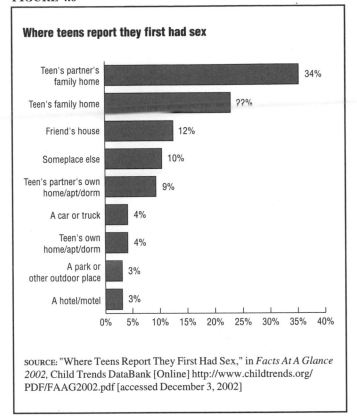

Where teens report they first had sex

SOURCE: "Where Teens Report They First Had Sex," in *Facts At A Glance 2002*, Child Trends DataBank [Online] http://www.childtrends.org/PDF/FAAG2002.pdf [accessed December 3, 2002]

the profile of teenage mothers who gave birth in the 1990s. Nearly one-half (47 percent) were white, three of five were 18 to 19 years old, and three-quarters were unmarried. About two-thirds were not planning to have a child, and about one-fifth already had a child. Teen mothers graduated from high school at lower rates than all female teens: 64 percent, compared with 90 percent of all female adolescents. Nearly half (49 percent) received welfare within five years of giving birth, and more than two-thirds of births (69 percent) were paid for by Medicaid.

Unmarried Teen Mothers

For most observers, the issue is not specifically teen births but rather the impact of early motherhood on unmarried young girls. Until the 1960s, it was normal for young people who were not going on to college to graduate from high school, acquire a job, and get married. Quite often, these young people were teenagers when their first, or even second, child was born.

Douglas Kirby, in *No Easy Answers: Research Findings on Programs to Reduce Teen Pregnancy* (National Campaign to Prevent Teen Pregnancy, Washington, D.C., 1997), pointed out the serious consequences that high teen pregnancy rates have on adolescents, their children, and society at large. According to Kirby, the future prospects for teen women who give birth decline considerably. He says they achieve a lower standard of education, usually have larger families, and are more likely to be single parents. He also believes that children born to teens live in a less supportive and stimulating home environment, are less healthy, do not develop as well cognitively, and do worse in school. These children seem to display higher rates of behavioral problems and of teen pregnancies themselves.

Kirby also believes that adolescent births result in a high cost to society, with an annual estimated cost to taxpayers of at least $6.9 billion. This figure includes lost tax revenues because teen parents are usually lower income earners, as well as expenditure of tax dollars on public assistance, health care, foster care, and the criminal justice system.

SUBSTANCE ABUSE AND THE CHANGING FAMILY STRUCTURE

Substance use and abuse by adolescents are risk-taking behaviors that can have serious consequences not only for the adolescents but also for their families, communities, and society. Young people who abuse substances appear to experience varied problems ranging from difficulties in school to increased risk of injuries and diseases. They may also experience significant mental health problems, including depression, withdrawal, and suicidal tendencies.

Teen abuse of alcohol and other drugs also disrupts many aspects of family life, resulting in family dysfunction and taxing financial and emotional resources. In addition, society bears the consequences of adolescent substance abuse, such as gang activities, prostitution, drug trafficking, more crime, and even youth homicides.

TABLE 4.3

Birth rates for teenagers aged 15–19 years by age group, state and territory and percent change by age, 1991 and 2000

	1991			2000			Percent change between 1991 and 2000		
State	**15–19 years**	**15–17 years**	**18–19 years**	**15–19 years**	**15–17 years**	**18–19 years**	**15–19 years**	**15–17 years**	**18–19 years**
United States[3]	62.1	38.7	94.4	48.5	27.4	79.2	−21.9	−29.2	−16.1
Alabama	73.9	47.7	109.5	62.9	37.9	97.3	−14.9	−20.5	−11.1
Alaska	65.4	35.3	111.7	42.4	23.6	69.4	−35.2	−33.1	−37.9
Arizona	80.7	51.4	122.6	69.1	41.1	111.3	−14.4	−20.0	−9.2
Arkansas	79.8	49.4	122.8	68.5	36.7	114.1	−14.2	−25.7	−7.1
California	74.7	46.9	113.6	48.5	28.6	75.6	−35.1	−39.0	−33.5
Colorado	58.2	35.3	91.4	49.2	28.6	79.8	−15.5	−19.0	−12.7
Connecticut	40.4	26.3	59.4	31.9	16.9	56.3	−21.0	−35.7	[2]−5.2
Delaware	61.1	40.3	87.1	51.6	30.5	80.2	−15.5	−24.3	[2]−7.9
District of Columbia	114.4	102.8	125.5	80.7	60.7	101.8	−29.5	−41.0	−18.9
Florida	68.8	44.0	102.9	52.6	29.7	88.0	−23.5	−32.5	−14.5
Georgia	76.3	50.6	110.9	64.2	36.8	104.3	−15.9	−27.3	−6.0
Hawaii	58.7	34.7	91.5	45.1	24.7	70.5	−23.2	−28.8	−23.0
Idaho	53.9	29.3	90.8	43.1	21.3	72.8	−20.0	−27.3	−19.8
Illinois	64.8	40.6	99.1	49.5	28.5	81.1	−23.6	−29.8	−18.2
Indiana	60.5	35.2	95.2	50.3	26.2	85.9	−16.9	−25.6	−9.8
Iowa	42.6	22.8	71.5	34.7	17.4	60.3	−18.5	−23.7	−15.7
Kansas	55.4	29.4	94.1	45.3	22.4	78.5	−18.2	−23.8	−16.6
Kentucky	68.9	42.6	105.5	55.3	29.2	92.2	−19.7	−31.5	−12.6
Louisiana	76.1	51.1	111.4	62.1	36.3	97.1	−18.4	−29.0	−12.8
Maine	43.5	23.8	70.1	28.7	13.4	52.8	−34.0	−43.7	−24.7
Maryland	54.3	35.2	79.8	41.6	23.8	68.8	−23.4	−32.4	−13.8
Massachusetts	37.8	25.2	52.9	27.1	15.0	44.9	−28.3	−40.5	−15.1
Michigan	59.0	35.5	91.1	39.2	21.3	66.3	−33.6	−40.0	−27.2
Minnesota	37.3	20.7	61.4	29.6	15.6	51.0	−20.6	−24.6	−16.9
Mississippi	85.6	60.1	120.4	72.0	45.0	109.9	−15.9	−25.1	−8.7
Missouri	64.5	38.7	100.7	48.8	26.5	82.2	−24.3	−31.5	−18.4
Montana	46.7	23.6	83.0	35.8	19.1	60.8	−23.3	−19.1	−26.7
Nebraska	42.4	23.6	69.2	37.2	19.3	62.7	−12.3	−18.2	−9.4
Nevada	75.3	43.9	119.1	62.2	34.2	106.7	−17.4	−22.1	−10.4
New Hampshire	33.3	17.1	53.8	23.4	9.8	45.4	−29.7	−42.7	−15.6
New Jersey	41.6	26.3	62.9	31.7	17.0	54.9	−23.8	−35.4	−12.7
New Mexico	79.8	50.0	124.4	66.2	40.2	105.1	−17.0	−19.6	−15.5
New York	46.0	29.1	69.0	35.6	20.1	58.1	−22.6	−30.9	−15.8
North Carolina	70.5	46.2	101.7	59.9	32.8	101.4	−15.0	−29.0	[2]−0.3
North Dakota	35.6	18.1	62.4	28.2	12.5	51.4	−20.8	−30.9	−17.6
Ohio	60.5	36.2	93.8	45.6	24.1	77.2	−24.6	−33.4	−17.7
Oklahoma	72.1	41.7	115.6	60.1	32.9	99.8	−16.6	−21.1	−13.7
Oregon	54.9	31.3	90.7	43.2	23.5	72.8	−21.3	−24.9	−19.7
Pennsylvania	46.9	29.2	70.5	35.2	19.6	58.8	−24.9	−32.9	−16.6
Rhode Island	45.4	30.1	63.6	38.4	21.3	64.0	−15.4	−29.2	[2]0.6
South Carolina	72.9	48.0	105.4	60.6	36.7	92.9	−16.9	−23.5	−11.9
South Dakota	47.5	26.3	79.2	37.2	19.4	62.2	−21.7	−26.2	−21.5
Tennessee	75.2	47.8	112.1	61.5	34.2	101.6	−18.2	−28.5	−9.4
Texas	78.9	50.4	119.3	69.2	42.7	107.1	−12.3	−15.3	−10.2
Utah	48.2	27.0	79.8	40.0	22.0	62.7	−17.0	−18.5	−21.4
Vermont	39.2	21.3	62.0	24.1	10.6	44.5	−38.5	−50.2	−28.2
Virginia	53.5	31.8	81.2	40.8	21.7	66.9	−23.7	−31.8	−17.6
Washington	53.7	31.0	86.5	38.2	20.3	64.5	−28.9	−34.5	−25.4
West Virginia	57.8	32.4	93.2	46.4	22.8	79.8	−19.7	−29.6	−14.4
Wisconsin	43.7	24.8	71.2	34.5	18.3	58.8	−21.1	−26.2	−17.4
Wyoming	54.2	26.4	98.6	40.8	19.0	73.4	−24.7	−28.0	−25.6
Puerto Rico	72.4	50.8	105.9	71.5	49.1	103.8	[2]−1.2	[2]−3.3	[2]−2.0
Virgin Islands	77.9	48.6	124.0	51.9	29.2	86.6	−33.4	−39.9	−30.2
Guam	95.7	55.0	156.1	80.3	55.0	120.5	−16.0	[2]0.0	−22.8
American Samoa	[1]	[1]	[1]	44.8	20.4	83.8	[1]	[1]	[1]
Northern Marianas	[1]	[1]	[1]	54.0	40.8	70.9	[1]	[1]	[1]

[1]Data not available.
[2]Not significant at $p < 0.05$.
[3]Excludes data for the territories.

Note: Birth rates by state shown in this table are based on population estimates provided by the U.S. Bureau of the Census, projected from the 1990 census; see reference 2. Therefore, the rates shown here may differ from rates computed on the basis of other population estimates.

SOURCE: S.J. Ventura, T.J. Mathews, and B.E. Hamilton, "Table 1. Birth rates for teenagers aged 15–19 years, by age group and state territory, and percent change by age: United States, 1991 and 2000," *Teenage Births in the United States: State Trends 1991–2000, an Update,* National Vital Statistics Reports, Vol. 50, No. 9, Centers for Disease Control and Prevention, National Center for Health Statistics, Hyattsville, MD, May 2002

FIGURE 4.7

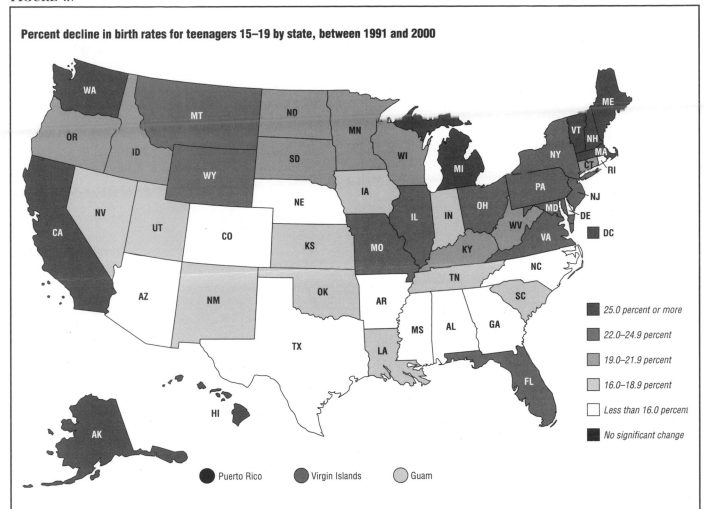

Percent decline in birth rates for teenagers 15–19 by state, between 1991 and 2000

Legend:
- 25.0 percent or more
- 22.0–24.9 percent
- 19.0–21.9 percent
- 16.0–18.9 percent
- Less than 16.0 percent
- No significant change

Puerto Rico Virgin Islands Guam

SOURCE: S.J. Ventura, T.J. Mathews, and B.E. Hamilton, "Figure 2. Percent Decline in Birth Rates for Teenagers 15–19 by State, Between 1991 and 2000," *Teenage Births in the United States: State Trends 1991–2000, an Update,* National Vital Statistics Reports, Vol. 50, No. 9, Centers for Disease Control and Prevention, National Center for Health Statistics, Hyattsville, MD, May 2002

TABLE 4.4

Teen birth rate, 1940–2001

Ages:	1940	1950	1960	1970	1980	1986	1990	1991	1995	1996	1997	1998	1999	2000	2001
15-19	54.1	81.6	89.1	68.3	53.0	50.2	59.9	62.1	56.8	54.4	52.3	51.1	49.6	48.5	45.9
15-17	—	—	43.9	38.8	32.5	30.5	37.5	38.7	36.0	33.8	32.1	30.4	28.7	27.4	25.3
18-19	—	—	166.7	114.7	82.1	79.6	88.6	94.4	89.1	86.0	83.6	82.0	80.3	79.2	75.8

SOURCE: "Teen Birth Rate (Births per 1,000 Females Aged 15-19, 15-17, and 18-19)," in *Facts At A Glance 2002,* Child Trends DataBank [Online] http://www.childtrends.org/PDF/FAAG2002.pdf [accessed December 3, 2002]

On September 5, 2002, the U.S. Department of Health and Human Services released its 2001 National Household Survey on Drug Abuse (NHSDA), conducted by the Substance Abuse and Mental Health Services Administration. This report provides data on the prevalence, consequences, trends, and demographic patterns of substance use and abuse among the civilian, noninstitutionalized American population aged 12 years and older. The survey found that among youth aged 12 to 17, 28.4 percent had used "any illicit drug"—marijuana/hashish, cocaine (including crack), heroin, hallucinogens, inhalants, or prescription-type medicines for nonmedical purposes—during his or her lifetime.

An earlier version of this survey (1996) examined some implications of the changing family living arrangements for

FIGURE 4.8

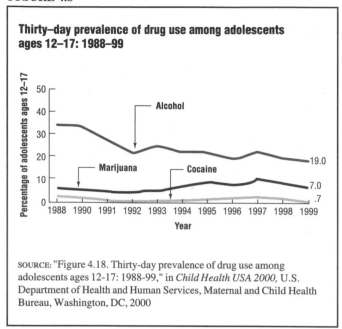

Thirty–day prevalence of drug use among adolescents ages 12–17: 1988–99

SOURCE: "Figure 4.18. Thirty-day prevalence of drug use among adolescents ages 12-17: 1988-99," in *Child Health USA 2000,* U.S. Department of Health and Human Services, Maternal and Child Health Bureau, Washington, DC, 2000

FIGURE 4.9

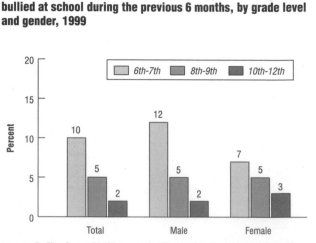

Percentage of students ages 12–18 who reported being bullied at school during the previous 6 months, by grade level and gender, 1999

SOURCE: P. Kaufman, X. Chen, et al, "Figure 6.1. Percentage of students ages 12 through 18 who reported being bullied at school during the previous 6 months, by grade level and gender: 1999," in *Indicators of School Crime and Safety: 2001,* U.S. Department of Education, National Center for Education Statistics, and U.S. Department of Justice, Bureau of Justice Statistics, Washington, DC, 2001

substance use (including alcohol and cigarettes) among American adolescents. This included the effects of family structure on adolescent substance use, dependence, and need for illicit drug-abuse treatment. The NHSDA found that, regardless of the specific substance, adolescents who lived with two biological parents reported lower risks of substance use during the previous year than those in other family structures. Approximately one-third (32.1 percent) of adolescents living with both their mother and father indicated using alcohol during the previous year, compared with more than one-half (50.8 percent) of those living with their father and stepmother. Similarly, children living with their biological parents were less likely to abuse substances than those living in stepfamilies or with either their father or mother.

Between 1988 and 1999, teen use of alcohol dropped from more than 30 percent to 19 percent, and use of cocaine by teens remained relatively flat at 0.7 percent. However, the use of marijuana rose from about 7 percent in 1988 to a peak of more than 10 percent in 1997. Since that time, the percent of marijuana use among teens has dropped back to the 1988 level of 7.0 percent. (See Figure 4.8.) The NHSDA study found that a higher percentage of younger youth indicated they had tried hallucinogens. While the number of 12th graders who had ever tried hallucinogens dropped from 13.6 percent in 1999 to 12.7 percent in 2001, the number of 8th graders who had ever tried hallucinogens rose from 2.7 percent in 1999 to 3.8 percent in 2001.

Alcohol Dependence

Although in most states the sale of alcohol to persons under the age of 21 years is illegal, alcohol is the most widely used drug among, and the greatest threat to, Amer-

ican youth. The 2001 NHSDA reports that of the 10.1 million youth aged 12 to 20 who said they had drunk alcohol in the previous month, 19 percent said they were binge drinkers and 6 percent identified themselves as heavy drinkers. Of those who said they had drunk in the previous month, 31.6 percent were white, compared to 19.8 percent black and 19.7 percent Asian American.

Cigarette Use

According to the NHSDA study, 15.1 percent of youth aged 12 to 17 reported they used some form of tobacco. This represents a continuing decline from 17.3 percent in 1999 and 15.6 percent in 2000 and marks a change from the increasing patterns of tobacco use by teens seen during the 1990s.

SCHOOL VIOLENCE

According to Gallup Youth Surveys, as many as 4 in 10 teenagers think that at some point in their lifetime, someone is likely to fire a gun at them. Four in 10 teens are fearful of walking alone at night in certain areas within a mile of their homes. Half believe they will at some point be mugged.

At the same time that young people held these more negative perceptions, a Gallup Youth Survey completed just before the April 1999 tragedy at Columbine High School in Littleton, Colorado, revealed that the percentage of teens who consider school a safe place was significantly higher than in earlier years. In early 1999, only 15 percent of teens said they sometimes feared for their phys-

FIGURE 4.10

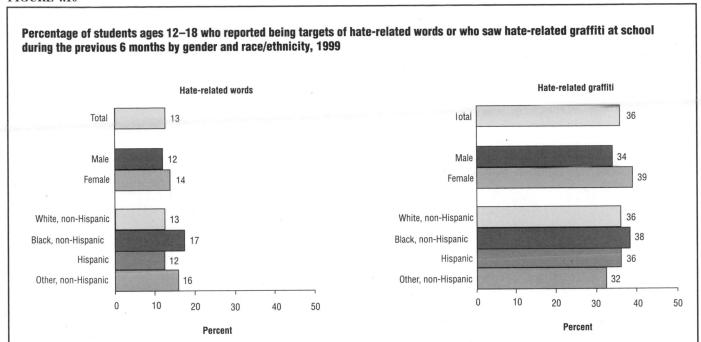

Percentage of students ages 12–18 who reported being targets of hate-related words or who saw hate-related graffiti at school during the previous 6 months by gender and race/ethnicity, 1999

Hate-related words

	Percent
Total	13
Male	12
Female	14
White, non-Hispanic	13
Black, non-Hispanic	17
Hispanic	12
Other, non-Hispanic	16

Hate-related graffiti

	Percent
Total	36
Male	34
Female	39
White, non-Hispanic	36
Black, non-Hispanic	38
Hispanic	36
Other, non-Hispanic	32

SOURCE: P. Kaufman, X. Chen, et al, "Figure 14.1. Percentage of students ages 12 through 18 who reported being targets of hate-related words or who saw hate-related graffiti at school during the previous 6 months, by gender and race/ethnicity: 1999," in *Indicators of School Crime and Safety: 2001,* U.S. Department of Education, National Center for Education Statistics, and U.S. Department of Justice, Bureau of Justice Statistics, Washington, DC, 2001

ical safety at school, compared to 28 percent of teens in 1996. However, teens said they were aware of the potential for violence at school. Seventeen percent said that "students carrying weapons to school" was a "very big" or "big" problem in their school, and 3 in 10 said they were aware of peers who had carried or regularly carried guns and knives at school.

Report on School Crime and Violence

The recently released report *Indicators of School Crime and Safety, 2002* (U.S. Departments of Education and Justice, NCES 2003-009/NCJ 196753, Washington, D.C., 2002.) reveals a 46 percent drop in violent crime victimization rates in schools from 1991 to 2000. According to the report, students were twice as likely to become victims of serious violent crime away from school than at school. However, violence, theft, bullying, drugs, and firearms continue to be problems in many schools. Students in the 12 to 18 age group were victims of 700,000 violent crimes and 1.2 million thefts that occurred at school during 2000. Students continue to report they are more afraid of being attacked at school than away from school.

The report offers key findings on violence in schools and children's perceptions of their safety at school:

• In 1999, 10 percent of students in 6th to 7th grade reported being bullied at school, compared to 5 percent of 8th to 9th graders and 2 percent of 10th to 12th graders. (See Figure 4.9.)

• In 1999, 13 percent of students aged 12 to 18 reported someone at school used hate-related words against them and 36 percent of students saw hate-related graffiti at school. (See Figure 4.10.)

• Five percent of all students aged 12 to 18 in 1999 reported fear of being attacked at school. The concern was greater among black (9 percent) and Hispanic (8 percent) students than white or other non-Hispanic students. (See Figure 4.11.)

• In 1999, 5 percent of students reported that they avoided one or more places in their school, down from 9 percent in 1995. (See Figure 4.12.)

• The percentage of students who reported being involved in a fight on school property declined from 16 to 14 percent from 1993 to 1999. Away from school, 36 percent of students reported being in a fight. (See Figure 4.13.)

• Between 7 and 12 percent of students in grades 9 to 12 reported being threatened or injured with a weapon such as a gun, knife, or club on school property in the previous 12 months.

• Between 1993 and 1999, the percentage of students in grades 9 to 12 who reported carrying a weapon such as a gun, knife, or club on school property within the previous 30 days dropped from 12 percent to 7 percent. (See Figure 4.14.) Student possession of weapons was reported as a serious or moderate problem by 1 percent of public school principals.

FIGURE 4.11

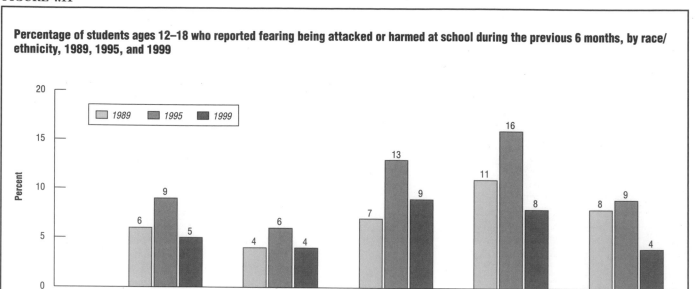

Percentage of students ages 12–18 who reported fearing being attacked or harmed at school during the previous 6 months, by race/ethnicity, 1989, 1995, and 1999

*The response rate for this survey was less than 70 percent and a full nonresponse bias analysis has been done to date.
Note: "On school property" was not defined for survey respondents. The term "anywhere" is not used in the questionnaire. Rather, students are simply asked during the past 30 days, on how many days they carried a weapon.

SOURCE: P. Kaufman, X. Chen, et al, "Figure 12.1. Percentage of students ages 12 through 18 who reported fearing being attacked or harmed at school during the previous 6 months, by race/ethnicity: 1989, 1995, and 1999," in *Indicators of School Crime and Safety: 2001,* U.S. Department of Education, National Center for Education Statistics, and U.S. Department of Justice, Bureau of Justice Statistics, Washington, DC, 2001

FIGURE 4.12

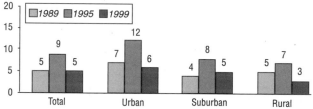

Percentage of students ages 12–18 who reported that they avoided one or more places in school during the previous 6 months, by urbanicity: 1989, 1995, and 1999

SOURCE: P. Kaufman, X. Chen, et al, "Figure 13.2. Percentage of students ages 12 through 18 who reported that they avoided one or more places in school during the previous 6 months, by urbanicity: 1989, 1995, and 1999," in *Indicators of School Crime and Safety: 2001,* U.S. Department of Education, National Center for Education Statistics, and U.S. Department of Justice, Bureau of Justice Statistics, Washington, DC, 2001

• Schools in urban, suburban, and rural communities all report the presence of street gangs. The peak year for gang presence was 1995 for all types of communities, with the high in urban schools, where 41 percent of students reported the presence of gangs. By 1999, gang presence declined almost to the level of a decade earlier. (See Figure 4.15.) However, in 2001, reports of gang presence rose slightly to 29 percent in urban

schools, 18 percent in suburban schools, and 13 percent in rural schools.

Indicators of School Crime and Safety, 2002 also considered the safety of teachers. In the 1999 to 2000 school year, 305,000 (9 percent) of all elementary and secondary school teachers were threatened with injury by a student, and 135,000 (4 percent) were physically attacked by a student. From 1996 through 2000, teachers were victims of more than 1 million thefts and 599,000 violent crimes (rape or sexual assault, robbery, aggravated assault, and simple assault) at school. In 2001, 49 senior high teachers per 1,000 were victims of violent crimes at school—mostly simple assaults—compared to 49 middle/junior high teachers per 1,000 and 15 elementary teachers per 1,000. Urban teachers were twice as likely as rural teachers to be victims of violence at school—36 per thousand compared to 17 per thousand.

Other Factors Contributing to Violence

In a report entitled *Youth Gangs in Schools* (Office of Juvenile Justice and Delinquency Prevention, 2000), one-half of teens surveyed said there were guns in their homes and about half said it is at least somewhat important to know how to shoot a gun. Growing alienation from family or attraction to the family-type environment or acceptance of a gang is also an issue. Six percent of teens surveyed said it was very or somewhat important to belong to a

FIGURE 4.13

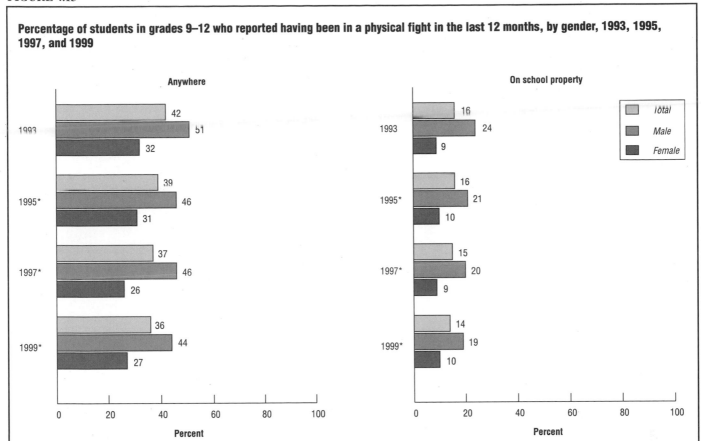

Percentage of students in grades 9–12 who reported having been in a physical fight in the last 12 months, by gender, 1993, 1995, 1997, and 1999

*The response rate for this survey was less than 70 percent and a full nonresponse bias analysis has not been done to date.
Note: "On school property" was not defined for survey respondents. The term "anywhere" is not used in the questionnaire. Rather, students are simply asked how many times in the last 12 months they had been in a physical fight.

SOURCE: P. Kaufman, X. Chen, et al, "Figure 5.1. Percentage of students in grades 9 through 12 who reported having been in a physical fight in the last 12 months, by gender: 1993, 1995, 1997 and 1999," in *Indicators of School Crime and Safety: 2001,* U.S. Department of Education, National Center for Education Statistics, and U.S. Department of Justice, Bureau of Justice Statistics, Washington, DC, 2001

gang or "posse." Thirty-seven percent of students reported there was a gang presence at their school.

Gallup's Youth Surveys shed light not only on the extent of teen violence but also on the factors that may contribute to violence and possible strategies to deal with this situation. More than half of U.S. teens believed that television shows, movies, or news programs containing violence may play a role in violent behavior by teens, such as gang warfare or shootings at schools. Seven in 10 teens admitted they watched too much television, 6 in 10 believed "gangsta rap" encouraged violence, and 4 in 10 said they "liked to live dangerously."

Teens were also likely to perceive an influence by the media and Internet in terms of lifestyles. More than 6 in 10 said they had noticed changes in their friends, such as the way they talk, dress, or act, because of something they saw or heard in the media or on the Internet. One-third of teens (35 percent) said they were under a "great deal" or "some" pressure from their peers to "break rules," and many reported being teased about their appearance.

One-half said they received "too little" respect from adults, and many felt misunderstood. One teen in eight reported that he or she had been physically abused; one-third could not talk about "life with father." When asked what relatives lived at home with them, although 91 percent said their mother, only 67 percent said their father.

How America Sees Teen Violence

Poor upbringing is identified by 42 percent of the public as the main reason for teen violence. While only 25 percent of mothers identified upbringing as a cause, 46 percent of fathers thought poor upbringing contributed to violence. In contrast, 41 percent of mothers associated violence in the media with teen violence, while only 24 percent of fathers and 26 percent of the public agreed. All agreed that peer pressure was a contributing factor. (See Table 4.5.) When asked for ways to reduce violent crime among teens, jobs and community programs to occupy free time led the list for 63 percent of respondents. Longer jail terms and less violence on TV appeared on the list for nearly half of respondents. (See Table 4.6.)

FIGURE 4.14

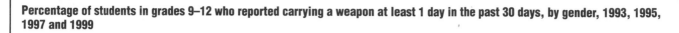

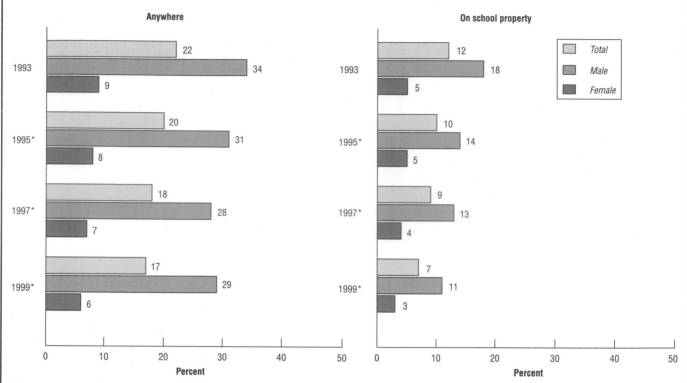

Percentage of students in grades 9–12 who reported carrying a weapon at least 1 day in the past 30 days, by gender, 1993, 1995, 1997 and 1999

*The response rate for this survey was less than 70 percent and a full nonresponse bias analysis has not been done to date.
Note: "On school property" was not defined for survey respondents. The term "anywhere" is not used in the questionnaire. Rather, students are simply asked during the past 30 days, on how many days they carried a weapon.

SOURCE: P. Kaufman, X. Chen, et al, "Figure 11.1. Percentage of students in grades 9 through 12 who reported carrying a weapon at least 1 day in the past 30 days, by gender, 1993, 1995, 1997 and 1999," in *Indicators of School Crime and Safety: 2001,* U.S. Department of Education, National Center for Education Statistics, and U.S. Department of Justice, Bureau of Justice Statistics, Washington, DC, 2001

FIGURE 4.15

Percentage of students ages 12–18 who reported that street gangs were present at school during the previous 6 months, by urbanicity, 1989, 1995, and 1999

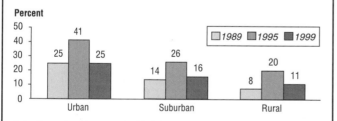

Note: Comparisons between the 1989 data and the 1995 and 1999 data should be made with caution due to changes in the questionnaire. Also the 1989 data include students ages 12 through 19. This indicator is based on an item from earlier in the SCS questionnaire, before "at school" was defined for the respondent.

SOURCE: P. Kaufman, X. Chen, et al, "Figure 15.2. Percentage of students ages 12 through 18 who reported that street gangs were present at school during the previous 6 months, by urbanicity: 1989, 1995, and 1999," in *Indicators of School Crime and Safety: 2001,* U.S. Department of Education, National Center for Education Statistics, and U.S. Department of Justice, Bureau of Justice Statistics, Washington, DC, 2001

JUVENILE VIOLENCE DECLINES

The level of juvenile violence in America during the 1980s and early 1990s caused predictions of a national crisis of violent youth. The number of juvenile arrests for violent crimes—murder, rape, robbery, and aggravated assault—rose 64 percent between 1980 and 1994. The tide turned in 1994, and by 2000 arrests for violent crimes by all age groups had declined significantly. (See Figure 4.16.) Arrests for murder declined most significantly for the under-18 age group (71 percent) and the 18 to 24 age group (41 percent). (See Figure 4.17.)

Juvenile violent crimes declined more than crimes by young adults and older adults. (See Figure 4.18.) Between 1994 and 2000, juvenile arrests for all types of offenses dropped 13 percent. Juvenile arrests for violent crimes dropped 34 percent, and arrests for property violations dropped 31 percent. However, during that same period juvenile arrests for driving under the influence rose 54 percent; for violation of liquor laws, 33 percent; and drug abuse violations, 29 percent. (See Table 4.7.)

TABLE 4.5

Public opinion on why kids commit violence, April 2000

Main reasons:	Total %	Moms %	Dads %
Poor upbringing	42	25	46
Violence in media	26	41	24
Peer pressure	14	16	15
Genetic/biological tendencies	4	4	2
Other	7	7	7
Don't know	7	7	6
	100	100	100

SOURCE: "Why Kids Commit Violence," in *A Year After Columbine Public Looks To Parents More Than Schools To Prevent Violence,* The Pew Research Center for the People and the Press, Washington, DC, April 19, 2000 [Online] http://people-press.org/reports/display.php3?ReportID=40 [accessed December 12, 2002]. Materials may be obtained free of charge at www.people-press.org.

According to the FBI publication series *Crime in the United States,* juveniles and young adults (all youth under age 24) were responsible for 32 percent of the rise in violent crime between 1980 and 1994, but they accounted for 58 percent of the subsequent decrease from 1994 to 2000. (See Figure 4.19 and Figure 4.20.)

Arrests of Juvenile Girls Increase

A 2001 report, *Justice By Gender* by the American Bar Association and the National Bar Association, noted that between 1990 and 1999, arrest rates for juvenile girls increased and exceeded the arrest rates of juvenile males in most offense categories. While arrests of juvenile males for aggravated assault declined about 8 percent, arrests of juvenile females for the same crimes rose more than 50 percent. And while drug abuse arrests rose 125 percent for juvenile males, the increase for juvenile females approached 200 percent. (See Figure 4.21.)

TABLE 4.6

Public opinion on the future of the nation, April–May 1999

	Optimistic %	Pessimistic %	Don't know %
All	70	27	3 =100
Men	70	27	3 =100
Women	69	28	3 =100
18–29	68	28	4 =100
30–49	70	28	2 =100
50–64	73	24	3 =100
65+	68	26	6 =100
Men 18–29	67	30	3 =100
Women 18–29	70	26	4 =100
College grad	75	24	1 =100
Some college	74	25	1 =100
HS graduate	68	28	4 =100
Less than HS	60	32	8 =100
$75,000+	77	22	1 =100
$50,000–74,999	72	27	1 =100
$30,000–49,999	70	28	2 =100
$20,000–29,999	67	30	3 =100
<$20,000	64	31	5 =100
East	78	18	4 =100
Midwest	69	27	4 =100
South	67	30	3 =100
West	67	31	2 =100

SOURCE: "Looking at the Nation's Future: The Optimists and Pessimists," in *Optimism Reigns, Technology Plays Key Role*, The Pew Research Center for the People and the Press, Washington, DC, October 24, 1999 [Online] http://people-press.org/reports/display.php3?PageID=258 [accessed December 12, 2002]. Materials may be obtained free of charge at www.people-press.org.

TABLE 4.7

Juvenile arrests and percent change, 1994–2000

	National estimate of juvenile arrests, 2000	Change: 1994–2000
All offenses	**2,369,400**	**−13%**
Violent Crime Index offenses	**98,900**	**−34**
Murder/non-negligent manslaughter	1,200	−68
Forcible rape	4,500	−25
Robbery	26,800	−51
Aggravated assault	66,300	−22
Index property	**518,800**	**−31**
Burglary	95,800	−33
Larceny-theft	363,500	−28
Motor vehicle theft	50,800	−42
Arson	8,700	−25
Selected other offenses		
Other assaults	236,800	+12
Weapons	37,600	−41
Drug abuse violations	203,900	+29
Driving under the influence	21,000	+54
Liquor laws	159,400	+33
Disorderly conduct	165,700	−3
Curfew/loitering	154,700	+20
Runaways	142,000	−43

Note: Juvenile arrests declined 13% between 1994 and 2000, with larger decreases in violent offenses.

SOURCE: Jeffrey Butts and Jeremy Travis, "Juvenile arrests declined 13% between 1994 and 2000, with larger decreases in violent offenses," in *The Rise and Fall of American Youth Violence 1980–2000*, Urban Institute, Justice Policy Center, Washington, DC, March 2002

FIGURE 4.16

Violent crime arrest rates, 1980, 1994, and 2000
Violent Crime Index arrests per 100,000 population

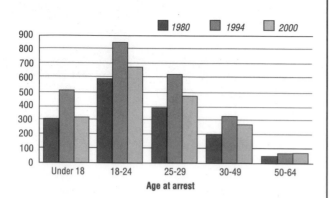

Percent change in arrest rates, 1994–2000

Age at arrest	All Violent Crime Index
Under 18 (juvenile)	−41%
18–24 (young adult)	−20
25–29	−24
30–49	−16
50–64	−7

Note: In 2000, the violent crime arrest rate for juveniles was nearly as low as it had been in 1980.

SOURCE: Jeffrey Butts and Jeremy Travis, "In 2000, the violent crime arrest rate for juveniles was nearly as low as it had been in 1980," in *The Rise and Fall of American Youth Violence 1980–2000,* Urban Institute, Justice Policy Center, Washington, DC, March 2002

FIGURE 4.17

Murder arrest rates for juveniles and adults, 1980, 1994, and 2000
Murder arrests per 100,000 population

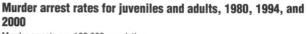
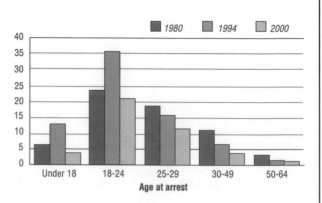

Percent change in arrest rates, 1994–2000

Age at arrest	Murder
Under 18 (juvenile)	−71%
18–24 (young adult)	−41
25–29	−28
30–49	−36
50–64	−26

Note: The rise in murder arrest rates for juveniles and young adults had completely vanished by 2000.

SOURCE: Jeffrey Butts and Jeremy Travis, "The rise in murder arrest rates for juveniles and young adults had completely vanished by 2000," in *The Rise and Fall of American Youth Violence 1980–2000,* Urban Institute, Justice Policy Center, Washington, DC, March 2002

FIGURE 4.18

Change in violent crime among juveniles and adults, 1994–2000
Percent change in arrests for selected offenses, 1994–2000

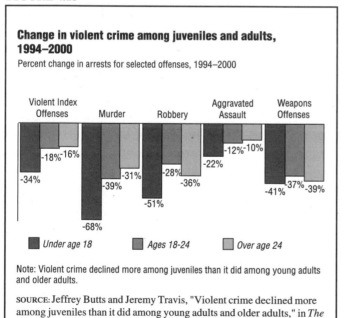

Note: Violent crime declined more among juveniles than it did among young adults and older adults.

SOURCE: Jeffrey Butts and Jeremy Travis, "Violent crime declined more among juveniles than it did among young adults and older adults," in *The Rise and Fall of American Youth Violence 1980–2000,* Urban Institute, Justice Policy Center, Washington, DC, March 2002

FIGURE 4.19

Estimated arrests for Violent Crime Index offenses, 1980, 1994, and 2000

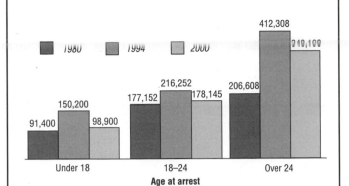

Increase: 1980 to 1994

	Arrests		Size of	Share of
Age	1980	1994	change	change
Under 18	91,400	150,200	58,800	19%
18 to 24	177,152	216,252	39,100	13%
Over 24	206,608	412,308	205,700	68%
Total	475,160	778,760	303,600	

SOURCE: Jeffrey Butts and Jeremy Travis, "Estimated arrests for Violent Crime Index offenses," in *The Rise and Fall of American Youth Violence 1980–2000,* Urban Institute, Justice Policy Center, Washington, DC, March 2002

FIGURE 4.20

Contribution to change in Violent Crime Index arrests, 1980–1994

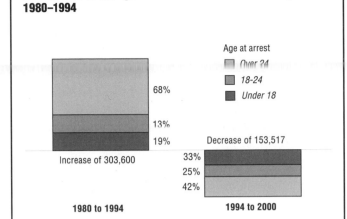

Decrease: 1994 to 2000

	Arrests		Size of	Share of
Age	1994	2000	change	change
Under 18	150,200	98,900	−51,300	33%
18 to 24	216,252	178,145	−38,108	25%
Over 24	412,308	348,198	−64,109	42%
Total	778,760	625,243	−153,517	

SOURCE: Jeffrey Butts and Jeremy Travis, "Contribution to change in Violent Crime Index arrests," in *The Rise and Fall of American Youth Violence 1980–2000,* Urban Institute, Justice Policy Center, Washington, DC, March 2002

FIGURE 4.21

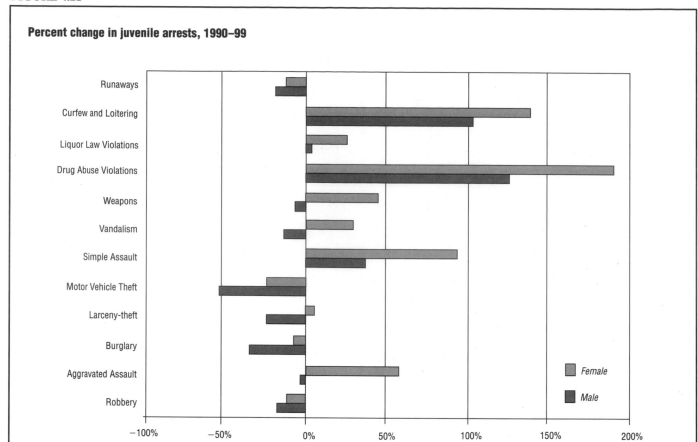

Percent change in juvenile arrests, 1990–99

SOURCE: "Percent Change in Juvenile Arrests 1990-99," in *Justice By Gender,* American Bar Association, Washington, DC, and National Bar Association, Washington, DC, May 1, 2001. ©The American Bar Association. All rights reserved. Reprinted by permission.

CHAPTER 5
FAMILY EMPLOYMENT, INCOME, COMPUTER USE, POVERTY, AND HOUSING

EMPLOYMENT

Secretary of Labor Elaine Chao titled her August 30, 2001, address to the Council for Excellence in Government "State of the Workforce." She reported that the American workforce is strong. However, workplaces have

> transformed overnight from physical plants and offices to mobile packages of 21st century technology and work trends that tell us old notions of the workforce cannot meet the needs and expectations of a new generation of workers.... Years ago, unemployment meant no jobs. Today, in many cases, unemployment means a disconnect between the new jobs our economy is producing—and the current skill levels of Americans in the workforce. The 'skills gap' is too wide for too many Americans.

Chao went on to discuss future anticipated labor shortages. As the baby boomers move into retirement, the number of people aged 25 to 34 in the labor force is projected to decline by 2.7 million.

Over the last four decades of the 20th century, the massive numbers of baby boomers and women entering the workplace have accounted for substantial growth in the American labor force. ("Labor force" includes persons who hold part- or full-time jobs and those who are unemployed but looking for work.) In 1999, 83.1 percent of the 71.3 million American families had at least one employed member; 93 percent of those families had at least one member who worked full-time (35 hours or more). The Bureau of Labor Statistics reports that in October 2002 143.1 million people were in the civilian labor force, with 134.9 million employed and 8.2 million unemployed.

Technology is changing the way American industry does business and the way jobs are performed. The economic boom of the 1990s took unemployment to record low levels and opened the door for many Americans to gain new training and move up into higher paying jobs. As workers abandoned labor-intensive jobs for new opportu-

nities, many low-paying service-industry jobs were filled by immigrants, who often lacked English-language skills.

On the other end of the spectrum, many highly educated and highly skilled foreign-born residents were recruited for professional and technical positions. According to the Bureau of Labor Statistics, the overall share of jobs held by foreign-born residents increased from 10.6 percent in 1996 to 13.0 percent in 2001. By 2001, 27 percent of physicians were foreign born, as were 54.5 percent of medical scientists. Foreign-born residents held over 20 percent of mathematics, computer science, and computer programmer positions. In the service sector, foreign-born residents held 37.1 percent of private household service positions and 22.1 percent of food-service jobs. Thirty-two percent of construction laborers and 16.3 percent of construction trades workers were foreign born.

INCOME

In 1999 the Census Bureau reported that the median income (the level at which half earned more and half earned less) for all U.S. households (family and nonfamily) had increased for all groups since 1989, with 1999 levels reaching or tying record highs. The 1999 average median income for all households (family and nonfamily) was $40,816, higher than the 1989 median income of $38,721 (in 1999 dollars).

Families

In 1999 married-couple families earned a median income of $56,827. Working wives contributed substantially to this income. For example, in 1997 working wives contributed an average of 36.5 percent of total family earnings. White wives contributed 35.8 percent, black wives 43.7 percent, and Hispanic wives 37.5 percent. (See Table 5.1.)

Families maintained by women with no husband present traditionally earn the lowest median income of all

TABLE 5.1

Percent of family earnings contributed by wives, 1997

SOURCE: Ida L. Castro, "Figure 6. Percent of Family Earnings Contributed by Wives, 1997," in *Equal Pay: A Thirty-Five Year Perspective,* U.S. Department of Labor, Women's Bureau, Washington, DC, 1998

families. In 1989 female householders with no husband present earned 45 percent of the income of married-couple households and 57 percent of that of male-headed households with no wife present. In 1999 the comparable proportions were 46 percent and 62.5 percent, respectively. Also in 1999, female-headed families with no husband present earned a median income of $26,164, while male householders with no wife present earned $41,838.

Racial and Ethnic Differences

In 1999 the typical white family earned considerably more ($42,504) than the typical black ($27,910) or Hispanic ($30,735) family. Asian/Pacific Islander families were the highest income earners ($51,205). According to *Income 1999, Comparison of Summary Measures of Income by Selected Characteristics 1989, 1998 and 1999* (U.S. Census Bureau, December 2000), the large proportion of minority families maintained by females without a husband present accounted for this great disparity. Female-headed families of all racial and ethnic groups with no husband present earned well below their male counterparts. However, black ($18,244) and Hispanic ($18,701) female householders earned much less than white female householders ($26,529).

In married-couple families, incomes were much higher ($57,089 for whites, $50,656 for blacks, and $37,132 for Hispanics).

NEW TREND IN HOME WORKERS

A growing new trend is working from home. In 1960, 4.6 million workers worked from home. Those numbers declined more than 50 percent to a low of 2.1 million in 1980, primarily reflecting a decrease in the number of family farmers. By 1990, however, 3.4 million people worked from home. Advances in personal computers and the Internet fueled this change.

A survey conducted for Telecommute America indicated that by 1997, 11 million people were working from home. A November 1997 Census Bureau report, *Characteristics of Business Owners,* reported that by 1992 nearly half of the 17 million small businesses in the United States were home based. Census Bureau demographer Phillip A. Salopek said in *Increase in At-Home Workers Reverses Earlier Trend* (March 1998) that "...the decade of the 1980s marked a rebirth of work at home in the United States. It is noteworthy that this impressive growth occurred before the expansion of the Internet." (See Figure 5.1.) Women in particular took advantage of opportunities to work from home either through their own businesses or telecommuting options offered by employers. Women represented 52 percent of the work-from-home group, compared to 45 percent of those who worked away from home. More than half (54 percent) of persons who worked at home in 1990 were self-employed, compared to 36 percent employed by private-sector companies and 6 percent who worked for government agencies. (See Figure 5.2.)

In 1997, 93 percent of workers never worked at home, 2 percent worked at home for part of their work week (mixed workers), and 5 percent worked at home exclusively (home workers). Figure 5.3 displays the distribution of days worked at home for mixed workers and home workers. Most (60 percent) mixed workers worked only one day at home; 28 percent worked two or three days at home. Some of these workers may be working parents who gain relief from child-care expense by such flexible work arrangements. Fifty-six percent of home workers spent five days a week working at home, and 25 percent worked six or seven days at home.

The greatest number of home workers hold executive, administrative, managerial, and professional positions. (See Figure 5.4.) The typical home worker is white (89.9 percent), lives in a metropolitan area (78.1 percent), is married (68.6 percent), has at least one child at home (57.4 percent), is female (53.9 percent), and has a bachelor's degree or more education (38.1 percent). (See Table 5.2.) Home workers in 1997 had an average personal income of $27,641, slightly higher than the $27,536 average for all types of workers. Mixed workers (who worked part of the time from home and part at the office) had average personal earnings of $42,821. Average family income was highest ($72,343) for mixed workers, followed by $64,165 for families that included a full-time at-home worker. The average family income for all workers in the study was $55,286. (See Figure 5.5.)

Number of Home Workers Expected to Grow

In a July 1999 article for *American Demographics* magazine, Norman Nie of the Stanford Institute predicted that "by 2005, at least 25 percent of the American workforce will be telecommuters or home office workers." Nie said "telecommuting may be the first social transformation in centuries that pulls working fathers and mothers back into the home rather than pushing them out."

Data varies on how many people actually telecommute. Flexible work schedules offered by employers have become more common. Besides options to work from home all or part of the time, some employers offer flexible starting times with requirements that employees be present during certain core hours. In 1997 the Bureau of Labor Statistics estimated that 28 percent of full-time wage and salary workers had flexible work schedules.

FIGURE 5.1

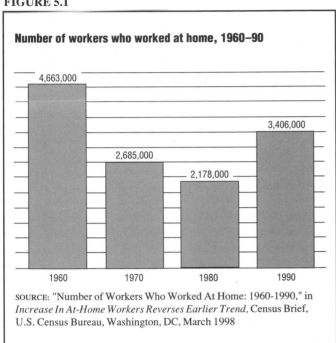

Number of workers who worked at home, 1960–90

SOURCE: "Number of Workers Who Worked At Home: 1960-1990," in *Increase In At-Home Workers Reverses Earlier Trend,* Census Brief, U.S. Census Bureau, Washington, DC, March 1998

FIGURE 5.2

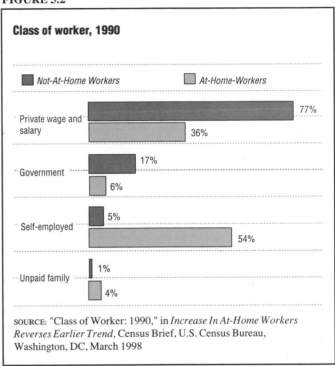

Class of worker, 1990

SOURCE: "Class of Worker: 1990," in *Increase In At-Home Workers Reverses Earlier Trend,* Census Brief, U.S. Census Bureau, Washington, DC, March 1998

FIGURE 5.3

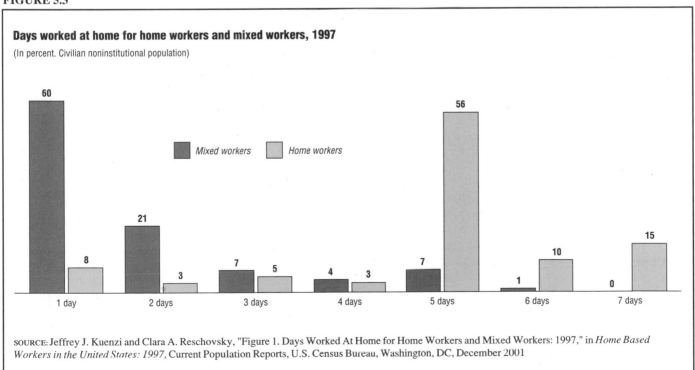

Days worked at home for home workers and mixed workers, 1997

(In percent. Civilian noninstitutional population)

SOURCE: Jeffrey J. Kuenzi and Clara A. Reschovsky, "Figure 1. Days Worked At Home for Home Workers and Mixed Workers: 1997," in *Home Based Workers in the United States: 1997,* Current Population Reports, U.S. Census Bureau, Washington, DC, December 2001

FIGURE 5.4

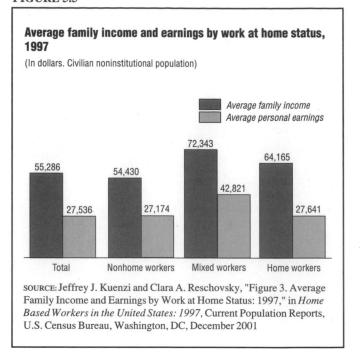

Work at home status by occupation, 1997
(Percent of workers. Civilian noninstitutional population)

Legend:
- Total
- Nonhome workers
- Mixed workers
- Home workers

Operators, transportation, and laborers
- Total: 15
- Nonhome workers: 15
- Mixed workers: 4
- Home workers: 5

Precision production, craft, and repair
- Total: 10
- Nonhome workers: 11
- Mixed workers: 6
- Home workers: 5

Farming, forestry, and fishing
- Total: 3
- Nonhome workers: 3
- Mixed workers: 3
- Home workers: 9

All services
- Total: 14
- Nonhome workers: 14
- Mixed workers: 5
- Home workers: 14

Administrative support
- Total: 15
- Nonhome workers: 15
- Mixed workers: 7
- Home workers: 11

Technician and sales
- Total: 15
- Nonhome workers: 15
- Mixed workers: 23
- Home workers: 16

Executive, administrative, managerial and professional
- Total: 28
- Nonhome workers: 27
- Mixed workers: 52
- Home workers: 40

SOURCE: Jeffrey J. Kuenzi and Clara A. Reschovsky, "Figure 2. Work at Home Status by Occupation: 1997," in *Home Based Workers in the United States: 1997,* Current Population Reports, U.S. Census Bureau, Washington, DC, December 2001

FIGURE 5.5

Average family income and earnings by work at home status, 1997

(In dollars. Civilian noninstitutional population)

Legend:
- Average family income
- Average personal earnings

	Average family income	Average personal earnings
Total	55,286	27,536
Nonhome workers	54,430	27,174
Mixed workers	72,343	42,821
Home workers	64,165	27,641

SOURCE: Jeffrey J. Kuenzi and Clara A. Reschovsky, "Figure 3. Average Family Income and Earnings by Work at Home Status: 1997," in *Home Based Workers in the United States: 1997,* Current Population Reports, U.S. Census Bureau, Washington, DC, December 2001

The high-tech research firm Cahners In-Stat Group suggests that in 2000 more than 10 percent of the U.S. workforce telecommuted. The company predicts that by 2004, 28 percent of workers, or 40 million people, will be telecommuters. While most telecommuting is thought of as Internet-based, some workers use CDs, computer disks, fax, and even the mail service to exchange information and completed work with the workplace.

AMERICAN FAMILIES USE COMPUTERS

Home computers and the Internet have changed a variety of things for the American family. The proportion of households with computers has grown from 8.2 percent in 1984 to 51 percent in 2000. While only 18 percent of homes had Internet access in 1997, 41.5 percent of homes were Internet linked in 2000. (See Figure 5.6.) In 2000, 53.7 million homes had a computer and 43.6 had Internet access.

People in the 25 to 44 age group are most likely to have a computer (61 percent). Of people with college degrees, 75.7 percent have computers, compared to 39.6 percent of those with high school diplomas and 18.2 percent with less than a high school diploma. Family households are more likely to have computers (58.6 percent) compared to nonfamily households (34.6 percent). Not surprisingly, the likelihood of a computer in the home increases with family income; 23.4 percent of families with incomes under $15,000 had computers, compared to 87.8 percent of households with family incomes of $75,000 or more. (See Table 5.3.)

Among school-age children in 2000, 56.9 percent had access to a computer both at home and at school. While 22.8

FIGURE 5.6

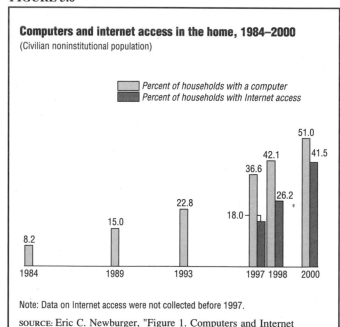

Computers and internet access in the home, 1984–2000
(Civilian noninstitutional population)

Legend:
- Percent of households with a computer
- Percent of households with Internet access

Year	Computer	Internet access
1984	8.2	
1989	15.0	
1993	22.8	
1997	36.6	18.0
1998	42.1	26.2
2000	51.0	41.5

Note: Data on Internet access were not collected before 1997.

SOURCE: Eric C. Newburger, "Figure 1. Computers and Internet Access in the Home: 1984–2000," in *Home Computers and Internet Use In the United States: August 2000,* Current Population Reports, U.S. Census Bureau, Washington, DC, September 2001

TABLE 5.2

Employed people by selected characteristics, 1997

(Numbers in thousands, civilian noninstitutional population)

Characteristic	Total		Nonhome workers		Mixed workers		Home workers	
	Number	Percent	Number	Percent	Number	Percent	Number	Percent
Total	132,692	100.0	123,432	100.0	2,875	100.0	6,385	100.0
Age								
15 to 24 years	19,495	14.7	18,899	15.3	147	5.1	450	7.1
25 to 34 years	32,783	24.7	30,819	25.0	731	25.4	1,233	19.3
35 to 44 years	36,386	27.4	33,719	27.3	889	30.9	1,777	27.8
45 to 54 years	26,846	20.2	24,696	20.0	658	22.9	1,491	23.4
55 to 64 years	12,734	9.6	11,529	9.3	327	11.4	878	13.7
65 years and over.	4,449	3.4	3,770	3.1	123	4.3	556	8.7
Sex								
Male	71,036	53.5	66,457	53.8	1,637	57.0	2,942	46.1
Female	61,656	46.5	56,975	46.2	1,237	43.0	3,444	53.9
Race and Hispanic origin								
White	112,915	85.1	104,575	84.7	2,597	90.3	5,742	89.9
White non-Hispanic	101,241	76.3	93,320	75.6	2,481	86.3	5,440	85.2
Black	14,005	10.6	13,430	10.9	178	6.2	397	6.2
American Indian and Alaska Native	1,272	1.0	1,161	0.9	10	0.4	101	1.6
Asian and Pacific Islander	4,500	3.4	4,265	3.5	89	3.1	146	2.3
Hispanic (of any race)	12,689	9.6	12,238	9.9	129	4.5	322	5.0
Marital status								
Married	77,565	58.5	71,227	57.7	1,958	68.1	4,380	68.6
Widowed	2,691	2.0	2,476	2.0	18	0.6	196	3.1
Divorced	14,182	10.7	13,250	10.7	303	10.5	629	9.9
Separated	3,284	2.5	3,103	2.5	54	1.9	127	2.0
Never married	34,970	26.4	33,376	27.0	541	18.8	1,053	16.5
Own children under 18								
At least one	75,685	57.0	70,364	57.0	1,659	57.7	3,662	57.4
None	57,007	43.0	53,067	43.0	1,216	42.3	2,723	42.6
Family income								
Under $25,000	32,049	24.2	29,781	24.1	468	16.3	1,801	28.2
$25,000 to $49,999	44,023	33.2	41,441	33.6	813	28.3	1,769	27.7
$50,000 to $74,999	28,637	21.6	26,828	21.7	634	22.0	1,175	18.4
$75,000 and over	27,983	21.1	25,382	20.6	961	33.4	1,641	25.7
Metropolitan status								
Metropolitan	109,654	82.6	102,260	82.8	2,406	83.7	4,988	78.1
Nonmetropolitan	22,410	16.9	20,552	16.7	468	16.3	1,390	21.8
Educational attainment								
Less than high school diploma	17,127	12.9	16,374	13.3	105	3.7	648	10.2
High school graduate	40,979	30.9	39,044	31.6	430	14.9	1,505	23.6
Some college/Associate degree	41,121	31.0	38,474	31.2	848	29.5	1,800	28.2
Bachelor's degree or more	33,465	25.2	29,539	23.9	1,493	51.9	2,433	38.1

SOURCE: Jeffrey J. Kuenzi and Clara A. Reschovsky, "Table 4. Employed People by Selected Characteristics: 1997," in *Home Based Workers in the United States: 1997*, Current Population Reports, U.S. Census Bureau, Washington, DC, December 2001

percent had access only at school and 9.9 percent had access only at home, just 10.4 percent of children had no computer access. (See Figure 5.7.) Children of white non-Hispanic families were more likely to have computer access at home (78.9 percent), with Asian and Pacific Islanders following closely at 73.7 percent. Only 44.6 percent of black children and 38.4 percent of Hispanic children had home computers. Schools help to level the playing field, with 70 percent of Hispanic children and 72.4 percent of black children having access to a computer at school. (See Figure 5.8.)

Sending and receiving e-mail is the most frequent use of at-home computers with Internet access (72.9 percent for children aged 3 to 17 and 87.7 percent for adults). However, 68.1 percent of children use the Internet to do school-related research. (See Table 5.4.)

TECHNOLOGY ENABLES DISTANCE LEARNING

Technology has provided opportunities to deliver education to people in their homes. Many community colleges and universities offer distance learning courses through the Internet or through classes broadcast on television. This makes education more accessible to working people, who can take courses at times that fit their own schedules. It also brings educational access to people who do not have a college nearby or who live in very rural areas. The United States Distance Learning Association estimates that 2.3 million students will take distance learning courses over the next few years.

Distance learning encompasses all technologies and supports the pursuit of lifelong learning for all. It is used

TABLE 5.3

Households with computers and internet access by selected characteristics, August 2000

(Numbers in thousands. Civilian noninstitutional population)

Characteristic	Total households Number	Computer in household Number	Computer in household Percent	Computer in household 90 percent C.I. (+ −)[1]	Home Internet access Number	Home Internet access Percent	Home Internet access 90 percent C.I. (+ −)[1]
TOTAL HOUSEHOLDS	105,247	53,716	51.0	0.4	43,639	41.5	0.4
AGE OF HOUSEHOLDER							
Under 25 years	6,104	2,675	43.8	1.5	2,179	35.7	1.5
25 to 44 years	42,545	25,944	61.0	0.6	21,353	50.2	0.6
45 to 64 years	34,800	19,800	56.9	0.6	16,251	46.7	0.6
65 years and over	21,798	5,297	24.3	0.7	3,856	17.7	0.6
RACE AND HISPANIC ORIGIN OF HOUSEHOLDER							
White	87,746	46,846	53.4	0.4	38,380	43.7	0.4
White non-Hispanic	78,719	43,829	55.7	0.4	36,260	46.1	0.4
Black	13,171	4,317	32.8	0.9	3,111	23.6	0.8
Asian and Pacific Islander	3,457	2,250	65.1	1.8	1,944	56.2	1.9
Hispanic (of any race)	9,565	3,224	33.7	1.4	2,255	23.6	1.3
HOUSEHOLDER'S EDUCATIONAL ATTAINMENT							
Less than high school diploma	17,402	3,162	18.2	0.7	2,032	11.7	0.6
High school diploma/GED	32,278	12,783	39.6	0.6	9,666	29.9	0.6
Some college	27,883	16,807	60.3	0.7	13,661	49.0	0.7
Bachelors degree or more	27,684	20,963	75.7	0.6	18,279	66.0	0.7
SIZE OF HOUSEHOLD							
One person	27,167	8,165	30.1	0.7	6,533	24.0	0.6
Two to four people	67,461	38,853	57.6	0.5	31,829	47.2	0.5
Five or more people	10,619	6,697	63.1	1.1	5,277	49.7	1.1
HOUSEHOLD TYPE							
Family households	72,044	42,238	58.6	0.4	34,315	47.6	0.4
Married-couple household	54,830	34,875	63.6	0.5	28,872	52.7	0.5
Male householder	4,179	1,879	45.0	1.8	1,455	34.8	1.7
Female householder	13,035	5,484	42.1	1.0	3,988	30.6	1.0
Nonfamily household	33,203	11,478	34.6	0.6	9,323	28.1	0.6
PRESENCE OF SCHOOL-AGE CHILDREN IN HOUSEHOLD							
Without children 6 to 17 years	76,558	34,537	45.1	0.4	28,360	37.0	0.4
With children 6 to 17 years	28,689	19,179	66.8	0.7	15,279	53.3	0.7
REGION							
Northeast	20,051	10,283	51.3	0.8	8,620	43.0	0.8
Midwest	24,276	12,442	51.3	0.8	9,929	40.9	0.8
South	38,009	17,891	47.1	0.6	14,404	37.9	0.6
West	22,912	13,099	57.2	0.8	10,685	46.6	0.8
METROPOLITAN STATUS							
Metropolitan	84,646	45,110	53.3	0.4	37,124	43.9	0.4
Inside central city	31,806	14,727	46.3	0.7	11,987	37.7	0.6
Outside central city	52,840	30,382	57.5	0.5	25,137	47.6	0.5
Nonmetropolitan	20,601	8,606	41.8	1.0	6,515	31.6	0.9
FAMILY INCOME							
TOTAL FAMILIES	72,044	42,238	58.6	0.5	34,315	47.6	0.5
Under $15,000	7,458	1,747	23.4	1.2	1,068	14.3	1.0
15,000-19,999	3,298	1,021	30.9	2.0	674	20.4	1.7
20,000-24,999	4,173	1,437	34.4	1.8	1,040	24.9	1.6
25,000-34,999	8,553	4,031	47.1	1.3	2,982	34.9	1.3
35,000-49,999	9,918	6,131	61.8	1.2	4,766	48.1	1.2
50,000-74,999	12,555	9,424	75.1	1.0	7,825	62.3	1.1
75,000+	15,040	13,198	87.8	0.7	11,886	79.0	0.8
Not reported	11,050	5,249	47.5	1.2	4,074	36.9	1.1

[1]This figure added to or subtracted from the estimate provides the 90-percent confidence interval.

SOURCE: Eric C. Newburger, "Table A. Households With Computers and Internet Access by Selected Characteristics: August 2000," in *Home Computers and Internet Use In the United States: August 2000*, Current Population Reports, U.S. Census Bureau, Washington, DC, September 2001

in all areas of education, including pre-K through grade 12, higher education, home-school education, continuing education, corporate training, military and government training, and telemedicine. Providing course content and electronic field trips are some of the principal applications for distance learning in pre-K through grade 12 education. Distance learning is also used to support rural and inner-city classes with student enrichment programs and to provide staff development and in-service training for teachers and administrators. People can receive college credit and earn degrees by satellite, audio, and Internet courses.

Faced with retraining 50 million American workers, corporate America is using distance learning, both internal-

FIGURE 5.7

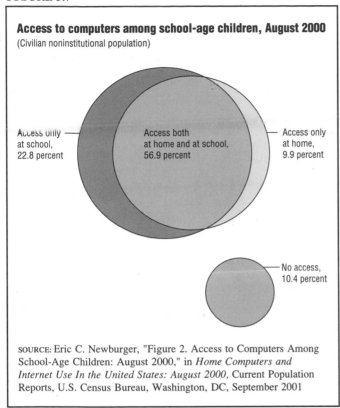

Access to computers among school-age children, August 2000

(Civilian noninstitutional population)

Access only at school, 22.8 percent

Access both at home and at school, 56.9 percent

Access only at home, 9.9 percent

No access, 10.4 percent

SOURCE: Eric C. Newburger, "Figure 2. Access to Computers Among School-Age Children: August 2000," in *Home Computers and Internet Use In the United States: August 2000*, Current Population Reports, U.S. Census Bureau, Washington, DC, September 2001

TABLE 5.4

Specific uses of the internet at home by adults and children, August 2000

(Numbers in thousands. Civilian noninstitutional population)

| | People using the Internet at home | | | |
| | Children 3 to 17 years | | Adults 18 years and over | |
Specific use	Number	Percent	Number	Percent
Any Internet use	**18,437**	**100.0**	**75,322**	**100.0**
E-mail	13,438	72.9	66,046	87.7
School research or courses	12,560	68.1	18,080 ·	24.0
Check news, weather, sports	3,658	19.8	39,528	52.5
Make phone calls	630	3.4	4,831	6.4
Information search	6,079	33.0	48,358	64.2
Job search	418	2.3	14,930	19.8
Job-related tasks	272	1.5	25,347	33.7
Shop or pay bills	1,467	8.0	30,014	39.8
Play games, entertainment, fun	1,981	10.7	3,655	4.9
Other	1,099	6.0	7,051	9.4

SOURCE: Eric C. Newburger, "Table D. Specific Uses of the Internet at Home by Adults and Children: August 2000," in *Home Computers and Internet Use In the United States: August 2000*, Current Population Reports, U.S. Census Bureau, Washington, DC, September 2001

FIGURE 5.8

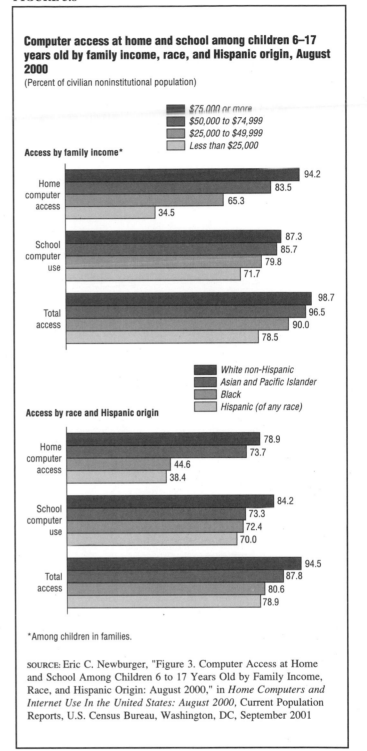

Computer access at home and school among children 6–17 years old by family income, race, and Hispanic origin, August 2000

(Percent of civilian noninstitutional population)

- $75,000 or more
- $50,000 to $74,999
- $25,000 to $49,999
- Less than $25,000

Access by family income*

Home computer access — 94.2 / 83.5 / 65.3 / 34.5

School computer use — 87.3 / 85.7 / 79.8 / 71.7

Total access — 98.7 / 96.5 / 90.0 / 78.5

- White non-Hispanic
- Asian and Pacific Islander
- Black
- Hispanic (of any race)

Access by race and Hispanic origin

Home computer access — 78.9 / 73.7 / 44.6 / 38.4

School computer use — 84.2 / 73.3 / 72.4 / 70.0

Total access — 94.5 / 87.8 / 80.6 / 78.9

*Among children in families.

SOURCE: Eric C. Newburger, "Figure 3. Computer Access at Home and School Among Children 6 to 17 Years Old by Family Income, Race, and Hispanic Origin: August 2000," in *Home Computers and Internet Use In the United States: August 2000*, Current Population Reports, U.S. Census Bureau, Washington, DC, September 2001

ly and externally, for all aspects of training. Many major corporations save millions of dollars in travel and facilities expenses each year by delivering training to employees more efficiently through telecommunications technology.

POVERTY

The economic growth following World War II (1939–45) spilled into the next two decades, but not every American reaped the economic benefits. In 1965 newly elected President Lyndon B. Johnson declared a "War on Poverty," calling for sweeping legislative changes to help the disadvantaged. From a high of about 23 percent in 1959, when data on poverty were first tabulated, the overall poverty rate declined to a low of about 11 percent in the mid-1970s. After that the rate fluctuated, hitting 15 percent peaks in 1982–83 and 1993. In 2001 the poverty rate rose slightly to 11.7 percent. (See Figure 5.9.)

FIGURE 5.9

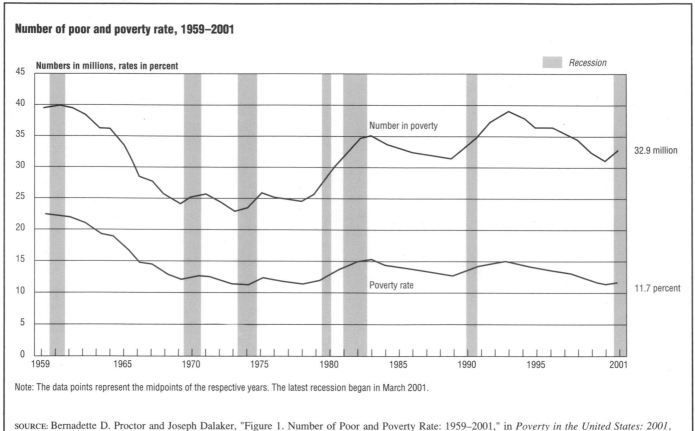

Number of poor and poverty rate, 1959–2001

Note: The data points represent the midpoints of the respective years. The latest recession began in March 2001.

SOURCE: Bernadette D. Proctor and Joseph Dalaker, "Figure 1. Number of Poor and Poverty Rate: 1959–2001," in *Poverty in the United States: 2001*, Current Population Reports, U.S. Census Bureau, Washington, DC, September 2002

Minorities experience a higher poverty rate than the white population. In 1959 the poverty rate for blacks was 55 percent, compared to 18 percent for whites. The black poverty rate tumbled in the 1960s and made another significant decline during the 1990s. In 2001, however, the poverty rate for blacks was 22.7 percent and that for Hispanics 21.4 percent, while the rates for Asian and Pacific Islanders, white, and non-Hispanic white populations were at or below 10 percent. (See Figure 5.10.)

Poor Families

Poverty rates for families have followed the same trends as for the general population. However, while 23,215 families (9.9 percent of all families) were below the poverty level in 2001, 28.6 percent of families with a female householder and no husband present were below the poverty level. (See Table 5.5.)

Married-Couple Families

In 1999 married-couple families had a poverty rate of 4.8 percent, down from 5.3 percent in 1998. The Census Bureau points out that although married-couple families had the lowest poverty rate, they still accounted for a large proportion of poor families (40 percent) because they were the most common family type. Hispanic married-couple families have a much higher poverty rate (14.2 percent) than black (7.1 percent) or white (4.4 percent) married-couple families.

Families Maintained by Women

Historically, the incidence of poverty among families headed by women has been very high. The 28.6 percent poverty rate for all families headed by females in 2001 is worse for most families headed by a minority female. Households headed by a black female had a 37.4 percent poverty rate, and the rate was 37.8 for Hispanic female-headed households. White female family households had a 19.9 percent poverty rate, and the lowest rate (14.8 percent) was found in households headed by female Asian and Pacific Islanders. (See Table 5.5.)

Poor Families with Children

Families with children are more likely to be at risk of poverty than families without children. Children add to expenses, stretching the family income to accommodate their needs.

Working and Non-Working Poor Families

Having a job does not necessarily solve the problem of poverty. In 2001, 5.6 percent of all workers were below the poverty level, compared to 20.6 percent of people who did

FIGURE 5.10

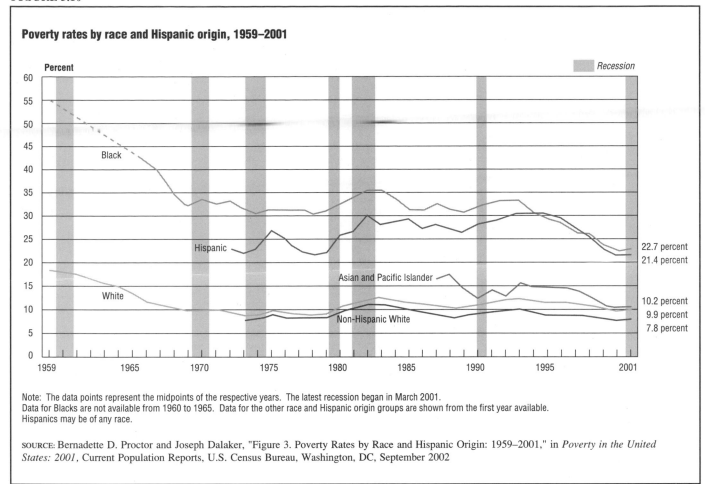

Poverty rates by race and Hispanic origin, 1959–2001

Note: The data points represent the midpoints of the respective years. The latest recession began in March 2001.
Data for Blacks are not available from 1960 to 1965. Data for the other race and Hispanic origin groups are shown from the first year available.
Hispanics may be of any race.

SOURCE: Bernadette D. Proctor and Joseph Dalaker, "Figure 3. Poverty Rates by Race and Hispanic Origin: 1959–2001," in *Poverty in the United States: 2001*, Current Population Reports, U.S. Census Bureau, Washington, DC, September 2002

not work during the year. Only 2.6 percent of those who worked full-time year-round were below the poverty level, but 11.8 percent of those who either worked part-time, seasonally, or intermittently fell below the poverty mark.

Seventy percent of female householder families with no workers in the family were in poverty, compared to 15.1 percent of married-couple families with no workers. Family households headed by a single male with no workers had the second highest poverty rate, 48 percent. The lowest poverty rate (4.7 percent) was among married-couple households with one or more workers. (See Figure 5.11.)

Health Insurance Challenges

The availability of affordable health insurance is a national concern. For people in poverty who can least afford medical expenses, obtaining adequate health coverage is a significant challenge. Among people who were employed in 2000, only 57.1 percent had health insurance provided by their employer. Those who worked for large employers with more than 1,000 employees were more likely to have company insurance (70.0 percent) compared to those who worked for small employers with fewer than 25 employees (31.6 percent). (See Figure 5.12.)

The higher a person's income, the more likely he or she is to have health insurance. Seventy-one percent of people with household incomes less than $25,000 were insured, compared to 93.1 percent of people with household incomes of $75,000 or more. However, even in households with high incomes, 6.9 percent had no medical insurance coverage in 2000. Of those people who did not work, 52.4 percent had private health insurance and 43.6 percent had employment-based insurance from retirement plans, severance benefits, or COBRA (temporary insurance provided under the Consolidated Omnibus Budget Reconciliation Act of 1986). Another 19.5 percent had Medicaid, 13.0 percent had Medicare, and 4.0 percent had military health care. (See Table 5.6.)

Of people without insurance, based on a three-year average from 1998 to 2000, 32.8 percent were Hispanic and 26.8 percent were American Indian or Alaska Native, compared to 10.1 percent who were white non-Hispanic. (See Table 5.7.) Almost 30 percent of people without health insurance in 2000 were poor. The foreign born and noncitizens had the highest rates of noninsurance—31.6 percent and 41.3 percent, respectively. Of noncitizens who were poor, 60.9 percent lacked health insurance. Educational attainment appeared to have the least correlation with lack

TABLE 5.5

Poverty status of people by family relationship, race, and Hispanic origin, 1959–2001

[Numbers in thousands. People as of March of the following year]

	All people			People in families						Unrelated individuals		
				All families			Families with female householder, no husband present					
		Below poverty level			Below poverty level			Below poverty level			Below poverty level	
Year and characteristic	Total	Number	Percent	Total	Number	Percent	Total	Number	Percent	Total	Number	Percent
All Races												
2001	281,475	32,907	11.7	233,911	23,215	9.9	39,261	11,223	28.6	46,392	9,226	19.9
2000¹	278,944	31,581	11.3	231,909	22,347	9.6	38,375	10,926	28.5	45,624	8,653	19.0
2000ʳ	275,924	31,054	11.3	229,482	22,015	9.6	37,422	10,425	27.9	45,117	8,529	18.9
1999	273,493	32,258	11.8	228,633	23,396	10.2	38,223	11,607	30.4	43,432	8,305	19.1
1998	271,059	34,476	12.7	227,229	25,370	11.2	39,000	12,907	33.1	42,539	8,478	19.9
1997	268,480	35,574	13.3	225,369	26,217	11.6	38,412	13,494	35.1	41,672	8,687	20.8
1996	266,218	36,529	13.7	223,955	27,376	12.2	38,584	13,796	35.8	40,727	8,452	20.8
1995	263,733	36,425	13.8	222,792	27,501	12.3	38,908	14,205	36.5	39,484	8,247	20.9
1994	261,616	38,059	14.5	221,430	28,985	13.1	37,253	14,380	38.6	38,538	8,287	21.5
1993	259,278	39,265	15.1	219,489	29,927	13.6	37,861	14,636	38.7	38,038	8,388	22.1
1992ʳ	256,549	38,014	14.8	217,936	28,961	13.3	36,446	14,205	39.0	36,842	8,075	21.9
1991ʳ	251,192	35,708	14.2	212,723	27,143	12.8	34,795	13,824	39.7	36,845	7,773	21.1
1990	248,644	33,585	13.5	210,967	25,232	12.0	33,795	12,578	37.2	36,056	7,446	20.7
1989	245,992	31,528	12.8	209,515	24,066	11.5	32,525	11,668	35.9	35,185	6,760	19.2
1988ʳ	243,530	31,745	13.0	208,056	24,048	11.6	32,164	11,972	37.2	34,340	7,070	20.6
1987ʳ	240,982	32,221	13.4	206,877	24,725	12.0	31,893	12,148	38.1	32,992	6,857	20.8
1986	238,554	32,370	13.6	205,459	24,754	12.0	31,152	11,944	38.3	31,679	6,846	21.6
1985	236,594	33,064	14.0	203,963	25,729	12.6	30,878	11,600	37.6	31,351	6,725	21.5
1984	233,816	33,700	14.4	202,288	26,458	13.1	30,844	11,831	38.4	30,268	6,609	21.8
1983	231,700	35,303	15.2	201,338	27,933	13.9	30,049	12,072	40.2	29,158	6,740	23.1
1982	229,412	34,398	15.0	200,385	27,349	13.6	28,834	11,701	40.6	27,908	6,458	23.1
1981	227,157	31,822	14.0	198,541	24,850	12.5	28,587	11,051	38.7	27,714	6,490	23.4
1980	225,027	29,272	13.0	196,963	22,601	11.5	27,565	10,120	36.7	27,133	6,227	22.9
1979	222,903	26,072	11.7	195,860	19,964	10.2	26,927	9,400	34.9	26,170	5,743	21.9
1978	215,656	24,497	11.4	191,071	19,062	10.0	26,032	9,269	35.6	24,585	5,435	22.1
1977	213,867	24,720	11.6	190,757	19,505	10.2	25,404	9,205	36.2	23,110	5,216	22.6
1976	212,303	24,975	11.8	190,844	19,632	10.3	24,204	9,029	37.3	21,459	5,344	24.9
1975	210,864	25,877	12.3	190,630	20,789	10.9	23,580	8,846	37.5	20,234	5,088	25.1
1974	209,362	23,370	11.2	190,436	18,817	9.9	23,165	8,462	36.5	18,926	4,553	24.1
1973	207,621	22,973	11.1	189,361	18,299	9.7	21,823	8,178	37.5	18,260	4,674	25.6
1972	206,004	24,460	11.9	189,193	19,577	10.3	21,264	8,114	38.2	16,811	4,883	29.0
1971	204,554	25,559	12.5	188,242	20,405	10.8	20,153	7,797	38.7	16,311	5,154	31.6
1970	202,183	25,420	12.6	186,692	20,330	10.9	19,673	7,503	38.1	15,491	5,090	32.9
1969	199,517	24,147	12.1	184,891	19,175	10.4	17,995	6,879	38.2	14,626	4,972	34.0
1968	197,628	25,389	12.8	183,825	20,695	11.3	18,048	6,990	38.7	13,803	4,694	34.0
1967	195,672	27,769	14.2	182,558	22,771	12.5	17,788	6,898	38.8	13,114	4,998	38.1
1966	193,388	28,510	14.7	181,117	23,809	13.1	17,240	6,861	39.8	12,271	4,701	38.3
1965	191,413	33,185	17.3	179,281	28,358	15.8	16,371	7,524	46.0	12,132	4,827	39.8
1964	189,710	36,055	19.0	177,653	30,912	17.4	(NA)	7,297	44.4	12,057	5,143	42.7
1963	187,258	36,436	19.5	176,076	31,498	17.9	(NA)	7,646	47.7	11,182	4,938	44.2
1962	184,276	38,625	21.0	173,263	33,623	19.4	(NA)	7,781	50.3	11,013	5,002	45.4
1961	181,277	39,628	21.9	170,131	34,509	20.3	(NA)	7,252	48.1	11,146	5,119	45.9
1960	179,503	39,851	22.2	168,615	34,925	20.7	(NA)	7,247	48.9	10,888	4,926	45.2
1959	176,557	39,490	22.4	165,858	34,562	20.8	(NA)	7,014	49.4	10,699	4,928	46.1
White												
2001	229,675	22,739	9.9	190,413	15,369	8.1	24,619	5,972	24.3	38,294	6,996	18.3
2000¹	227,846	21,645	9.5	188,966	14,692	7.8	24,166	5,609	23.2	37,699	6,454	17.1
2000ʳ	225,997	21,242	9.4	187,677	14,392	7.7	23,591	5,211	22.1	37,211	6,402	17.2
1999	224,373	21,922	9.8	187,139	15,141	8.1	23,895	5,891	24.7	36,151	6,375	17.6
1998	222,837	23,454	10.5	186,184	16,549	8.9	24,211	6,674	27.6	35,563	6,386	18.0
1997	221,200	24,396	11.0	185,147	17,258	9.3	23,773	7,296	30.7	34,858	6,593	18.9
1996	219,656	24,650	11.2	184,119	17,621	9.6	23,744	7,073	29.8	34,247	6,463	18.9
1995	218,028	24,423	11.2	183,450	17,593	9.6	23,732	7,047	29.7	33,399	6,336	19.0
1994	216,460	25,379	11.7	182,546	18,474	10.1	22,713	7,228	31.8	32,569	6,292	19.3
1993	214,899	26,226	12.2	181,330	18,968	10.5	23,224	7,199	31.0	32,112	6,443	20.1
1992ʳ	213,060	25,259	11.9	180,409	18,294	10.1	22,453	6,907	30.8	31,170	6,147	19.7
1991ʳ	210,133	23,747	11.3	177,619	17,268	9.7	21,608	6,806	31.5	31,207	5,872	18.8
1990	208,611	22,326	10.7	176,504	15,916	9.0	20,845	6,210	29.8	30,833	5,739	18.6
1989	206,853	20,785	10.0	175,857	15,179	8.6	20,362	5,723	28.1	29,993	5,063	16.9
1988ʳ	205,235	20,715	10.1	175,111	15,001	8.6	20,396	5,950	29.2	29,315	5,314	18.1
1987ʳ	203,605	21,195	10.4	174,488	15,593	8.9	20,244	5,989	29.6	28,290	5,174	18.3

TABLE 5.5

Poverty status of people by family relationship, race, and Hispanic origin, 1959–2001 [CONTINUED]

[Numbers in thousands. People as of March of the following year]

Year and characteristic	All people Total	Below poverty level Number	Percent	People in families All families Total	Below poverty level Number	Percent	Families with female householder, no husband present Total	Below poverty level Number	Percent	Unrelated individuals Total	Below poverty level Number	Percent
1986	202,282	22,183	11.0	174,024	16,393	9.4	20,163	6,171	30.6	27,143	5,198	10.2
1985	200,918	22,860	11.4	172,863	17,125	9.9	20,105	5,990	29.8	27,067	5,299	19.6
1984	198,941	22,955	11.5	171,839	17,299	10.1	19,727	5,866	29.7	26,094	5,181	19.9
1983	197,496	23,984	12.1	171,407	18,377	10.7	19,256	6,017	31.2	25,206	5,189	20.6
1982	195,919	23,517	12.0	170,748	18,015	10.6	18,374	5,686	30.9	24,300	5,041	20.7
1981	194,504	21,553	11.1	169,868	16,127	9.5	18,795	5,600	29.8	23,913	5,061	21.2
1980	192,912	19,699	10.2	168,756	14,587	8.6	17,642	4,940	28.0	23,370	4,760	20.4
1979	191,742	17,214	9.0	168,461	12,495	7.4	17,349	4,375	25.2	22,587	4,452	19.7
1978	186,450	16,259	8.7	165,193	12,050	7.3	16,877	4,371	25.9	21,257	4,209	19.8
1977	185,254	16,416	8.9	165,385	12,364	7.5	16,721	4,474	26.8	19,869	4,051	20.4
1976	184,165	16,713	9.1	165,571	12,500	7.5	15,941	4,463	28.0	18,594	4,213	22.7
1975	183,164	17,770	9.7	165,661	13,799	8.3	15,577	4,577	29.4	17,503	3,972	22.7
1974	182,376	15,736	8.6	166,081	12,181	7.3	15,433	4,278	27.7	16,295	3,555	21.8
1973	181,185	15,142	8.4	165,424	11,412	6.9	14,303	4,003	28.0	15,761	3,730	23.7
1972	180,125	16,203	9.0	165,630	12,268	7.4	13,739	3,770	27.4	14,495	3,935	27.1
1971	179,398	17,780	9.9	165,184	13,566	8.2	13,502	4,099	30.4	14,214	4,214	29.6
1970	177,376	17,484	9.9	163,875	13,323	8.1	13,226	3,761	28.4	13,500	4,161	30.8
1969	175,349	16,659	9.5	162,779	12,623	7.8	12,285	3,577	29.1	12,570	4,036	32.1
1968	173,732	17,395	10.0	161,777	13,546	8.4	12,190	3,551	29.1	11,955	3,849	32.2
1967	172,038	18,983	11.0	160,720	14,851	9.2	12,131	3,453	28.5	11,318	4,132	36.5
1966	170,247	19,290	11.3	159,561	15,430	9.7	12,261	3,646	29.7	10,686	3,860	36.1
1965	168,732	22,496	13.3	158,255	18,508	11.7	11,573	4,092	35.4	10,477	3,988	38.1
1964	167,313	24,957	14.9	156,898	20,716	13.2	(NA)	3,911	33.4	10,415	4,241	40.7
1963	165,309	25,238	15.3	155,584	21,149	13.6	(NA)	4,051	35.6	9,725	4,089	42.0
1962	162,842	26,672	16.4	153,348	22,613	14.7	(NA)	4,089	37.9	9,494	4,059	42.7
1961	160,306	27,890	17.4	150,717	23,747	15.8	(NA)	4,062	37.6	9,589	4,143	43.2
1960	158,863	28,309	17.8	149,458	24,262	16.2	(NA)	4,296	39.0	9,405	4,047	43.0
1959	156,956	28,484	18.1	147,802	24,443	16.5	(NA)	4,232	40.2	9,154	4,041	44.1
White Non-Hispanic												
2001	194,538	15,271	7.8	159,178	9,122	5.7	18,365	3,661	19.9	34,603	5,882	17.0
2000[1]	193,691	14,366	7.4	158,838	8,664	5.5	18,196	3,412	18.8	33,943	5,356	15.8
2000[r]	193,917	14,532	7.5	159,143	8,753	5.5	18,011	3,252	18.1	33,881	5,445	16.1
1999	193,334	14,875	7.7	159,362	9,118	5.7	18,233	3,618	19.8	33,136	5,440	16.4
1998	192,754	15,799	8.2	159,301	10,061	6.3	18,547	4,074	22.0	32,573	5,352	16.4
1997	191,859	16,491	8.6	158,796	10,401	6.5	18,474	4,604	24.9	32,049	5,632	17.6
1996	191,459	16,462	8.6	159,044	10,553	6.6	18,597	4,339	23.3	31,410	5,455	17.4
1995	190,951	16,267	8.5	159,402	10,599	6.6	18,340	4,183	22.8	30,586	5,303	17.3
1994	192,543	18,110	9.4	161,254	12,118	7.5	18,186	4,743	26.1	30,157	5,500	18.2
1993	190,843	18,882	9.9	160,062	12,756	8.0	18,508	4,724	25.5	29,681	5,570	18.8
1992[r]	189,001	18,202	9.6	159,102	12,277	7.7	18,016	4,640	25.8	28,775	5,350	18.6
1991[r]	189,116	17,741	9.4	158,850	11,998	7.6	17,609	4,710	26.7	29,215	5,261	18.0
1990	188,129	16,622	8.8	158,394	11,086	7.0	17,160	4,284	25.0	28,688	5,002	17.4
1989	186,979	15,599	8.3	158,127	10,723	6.8	16,827	3,922	23.3	28,055	4,466	15.9
1988[r]	185,961	15,565	8.4	157,687	10,467	6.6	16,828	3,988	23.7	27,552	4,746	17.2
1987[r]	184,936	16,029	8.7	157,785	11,051	7.0	16,787	4,075	24.3	26,439	4,613	17.4
1986	184,119	17,244	9.4	157,665	12,078	7.7	16,739	4,350	26.0	25,525	4,668	18.3
1985	183,455	17,839	9.7	157,106	12,706	8.1	16,749	4,136	24.7	25,544	4,789	18.7
1984	182,469	18,300	10.0	156,930	13,234	8.4	16,742	4,193	25.0	24,671	4,659	18.9
1983	181,393	19,538	10.8	156,719	14,437	9.2	16,369	4,448	27.2	23,894	4,746	19.9
1982	181,903	19,362	10.6	157,818	14,271	9.0	15,830	4,161	26.3	23,329	4,701	20.2
1981	180,909	17,987	9.9	157,330	12,903	8.2	16,323	4,222	25.9	22,950	4,769	20.8
1980	179,798	16,365	9.1	156,633	11,568	7.4	15,358	3,699	24.1	22,455	4,474	19.9
1979	178,814	14,419	8.1	156,567	10,009	6.4	15,410	3,371	21.9	21,638	4,179	19.3
1978	174,731	13,755	7.9	154,321	9,798	6.3	15,132	3,390	22.4	20,410	3,957	19.4
1977	173,563	13,802	8.0	154,449	9,977	6.5	14,888	3,429	23.0	19,114	3,825	20.0
1976	173,235	14,025	8.1	155,324	10,066	6.5	14,261	3,516	24.7	17,912	3,959	22.1
1975	172,417	14,883	8.6	155,539	11,137	7.2	13,809	3,570	25.9	16,879	3,746	22.2
1974	171,463	13,217	7.7	155,764	9,854	6.3	13,763	3,379	24.6	15,699	3,364	21.4
1973	170,488	12,864	7.5	155,330	9,262	6.0	12,731	3,185	25.0	15,158	3,602	23.8

TABLE 5.5

Poverty status of people by family relationship, race, and Hispanic origin, 1959–2001 [CONTINUED]

[Numbers in thousands. People as of March of the following year]

Year and characteristic	All people Total	All people Below poverty level Number	All people Below poverty level Percent	People in families All families Total	People in families All families Below poverty level Number	People in families All families Below poverty level Percent	Families with female householder, no husband present Total	Families with female householder, no husband present Below poverty level Number	Families with female householder, no husband present Below poverty level Percent	Unrelated individuals Total	Unrelated individuals Below poverty level Number	Unrelated individuals Below poverty level Percent
Black												
2001	35,871	8,136	22.7	29,869	6,389	21.4	12,550	4,694	37.4	5,873	1,692	28.8
2000[1]	35,425	7,982	22.5	29,378	6,221	21.2	12,383	4,774	38.6	5,885	1,702	28.9
2000[r]	35,752	7,862	22.0	29,497	6,108	20.7	12,172	4,697	38.6	6,099	1,708	28.0
1999	35,373	8,360	23.6	29,488	6,688	22.7	12,644	5,179	41.0	5,619	1,552	27.6
1998	34,877	9,091	26.1	29,333	7,259	24.7	13,156	5,629	42.8	5,390	1,752	32.5
1997	34,458	9,116	26.5	28,962	7,386	25.5	13,218	5,654	42.8	5,316	1,645	31.0
1996	34,110	9,694	28.4	28,933	7,993	27.6	13,193	6,123	46.4	4,989	1,606	32.2
1995	33,740	9,872	29.3	28,777	8,189	28.5	13,604	6,553	48.2	4,756	1,551	32.6
1994	33,353	10,196	30.6	28,499	8,447	29.6	12,926	6,489	50.2	4,649	1,617	34.8
1993	32,910	10,877	33.1	28,106	9,242	32.9	13,132	6,955	53.0	4,608	1,541	33.4
1992[r]	32,411	10,827	33.4	27,790	9,134	32.9	12,591	6,799	54.0	4,410	1,569	35.6
1991[r]	31,313	10,242	32.7	26,565	8,504	32.0	11,960	6,557	54.8	4,505	1,590	35.3
1990	30,806	9,837	31.9	26,296	8,160	31.0	11,866	6,005	50.6	4,244	1,491	35.1
1989	30,332	9,302	30.7	25,931	7,704	29.7	11,190	5,530	49.4	4,180	1,471	35.2
1988[r]	29,849	9,356	31.3	25,484	7,650	30.0	10,794	5,601	51.9	4,095	1,509	36.8
1987[r]	29,362	9,520	32.4	25,128	7,848	31.2	10,701	5,789	54.1	3,977	1,471	37.0
1986	28,871	8,983	31.1	24,910	7,410	29.7	10,175	5,473	53.8	3,714	1,431	38.5
1985	28,485	8,926	31.3	24,620	7,504	30.5	10,041	5,342	53.2	3,641	1,264	34.7
1984	28,087	9,490	33.8	24,387	8,104	33.2	10,384	5,666	54.6	3,501	1,255	35.8
1983	27,678	9,882	35.7	24,138	8,376	34.7	10,059	5,736	57.0	3,287	1,338	40.7
1982	27,216	9,697	35.6	23,948	8,355	34.9	9,699	5,698	58.8	3,051	1,229	40.3
1981	26,834	9,173	34.2	23,423	7,780	33.2	9,214	5,222	56.7	3,277	1,296	39.6
1980	26,408	8,579	32.5	23,084	7,190	31.1	9,338	4,984	53.4	3,208	1,314	41.0
1979	25,944	8,050	31.0	22,666	6,800	30.0	9,065	4,816	53.1	3,127	1,168	37.3
1978	24,956	7,625	30.6	22,027	6,493	29.5	8,689	4,712	54.2	2,929	1,132	38.6
1977	24,710	7,726	31.3	21,850	6,667	30.5	8,315	4,595	55.3	2,860	1,059	37.0
1976	24,399	7,595	31.1	21,840	6,576	30.1	7,926	4,415	55.7	2,559	1,019	39.8
1975	24,089	7,545	31.3	21,687	6,533	30.1	7,679	4,168	54.3	2,402	1,011	42.1
1974	23,699	7,182	30.3	21,341	6,255	29.3	7,483	4,116	55.0	2,359	927	39.3
1973	23,512	7,388	31.4	21,328	6,560	30.8	7,188	4,064	56.5	2,183	828	37.9
1972	23,144	7,710	33.3	21,116	6,841	32.4	7,125	4,139	58.1	2,028	870	42.9
1971	22,784	7,396	32.5	20,900	6,530	31.2	6,398	3,587	56.1	1,884	866	46.0
1970	22,515	7,548	33.5	20,724	6,683	32.2	6,225	3,656	58.7	1,791	865	48.3
1969	22,011	7,095	32.2	20,192	6,245	30.9	5,537	3,225	58.2	1,819	850	46.7
1968	21,944	7,616	34.7	(NA)	6,839	33.7	(NA)	3,312	58.9	(NA)	777	46.3
1967	21,590	8,486	39.3	(NA)	7,677	38.4	(NA)	3,362	61.6	(NA)	809	49.3
1966	21,206	8,867	41.8	(NA)	8,090	40.9	(NA)	3,160	65.3	(NA)	777	54.4
1959	18,013	9,927	55.1	(NA)	9,112	54.9	(NA)	2,416	70.6	1,430	815	57.0
Hispanic[2]												
2001	37,312	7,997	21.4	33,110	6,674	20.2	6,830	2,585	37.8	3,981	1,211	30.4
2000[1]	35,955	7,747	21.5	31,700	6,430	20.3	6,469	2,444	37.8	3,978	1,163	29.2
2000[r]	33,716	7,153	21.2	29,976	6,025	20.1	6,048	2,210	36.5	3,521	1,013	28.8
1999	32,669	7,439	22.8	29,198	6,349	21.7	6,113	2,488	40.7	3,207	991	30.9
1998	31,515	8,070	25.6	28,055	6,814	24.3	6,074	2,837	46.7	3,218	1,097	34.1
1997	30,637	8,308	27.1	27,467	7,198	26.2	5,718	2,911	50.9	2,976	1,017	34.2
1996	29,614	8,697	29.4	26,340	7,515	28.5	5,641	3,020	53.5	2,985	1,066	35.7
1995	28,344	8,574	30.3	25,165	7,341	29.2	5,785	3,053	52.8	2,947	1,092	37.0
1994	27,442	8,416	30.7	24,390	7,357	30.2	5,328	2,920	54.8	2,798	926	33.1
1993	26,559	8,126	30.6	23,439	6,876	29.3	5,333	2,837	53.2	2,717	972	35.8
1992[r]	25,646	7,592	29.6	22,695	6,455	28.4	4,806	2,474	51.5	2,577	881	34.2
1991[r]	22,070	6,339	28.7	19,658	5,541	28.2	4,326	2,282	52.7	2,146	667	31.1
1990	21,405	6,006	28.1	18,912	5,091	26.9	3,993	2,115	53.0	2,254	774	34.3
1989	20,746	5,430	26.2	18,488	4,659	25.2	3,763	1,902	50.6	2,045	634	31.0
1988[r]	20,064	5,357	26.7	18,102	4,700	26.0	3,734	2,052	55.0	1,864	597	32.0
1987[r]	19,395	5,422	28.0	17,342	4,761	27.5	3,678	2,045	55.6	1,933	598	31.0
1986	18,758	5,117	27.3	16,880	4,469	26.5	3,631	1,921	52.9	1,685	553	32.8
1985	18,075	5,236	29.0	16,276	4,605	28.3	3,561	1,983	55.7	1,602	532	33.2
1984	16,916	4,806	28.4	15,293	4,192	27.4	3,139	1,764	56.2	1,481	545	36.8
1983	16,544	4,633	28.0	15,075	4,113	27.3	3,032	1,670	55.1	1,364	457	33.5
1982	14,385	4,301	29.9	13,242	3,865	29.2	2,664	1,601	60.1	1,018	358	35.1
1981	14,021	3,713	26.5	12,922	3,349	25.9	2,622	1,465	55.9	1,005	313	31.1

TABLE 5.5

Poverty status of people by family relationship, race, and Hispanic origin, 1959–2001 [CONTINUED]

[Numbers in thousands. People as of March of the following year]

Year and characteristic	All people Total	All people Below poverty level Number	All people Below poverty level Percent	People in families All families Total	People in families All families Below poverty level Number	People in families All families Below poverty level Percent	Families with female householder, no husband present Total	Families with female householder, no husband present Below poverty level Number	Families with female householder, no husband present Below poverty level Percent	Unrelated individuals Total	Unrelated individuals Below poverty level Number	Unrelated individuals Below poverty level Percent
1980	13,600	3,491	25.7	12,547	3,143	25.1	2,421	1,319	54.5	970	312	32.2
1979	13,371	2,921	21.8	12,291	2,599	21.1	2,058	1,053	51.2	991	286	28.8
1978	12,079	2,607	21.6	11,193	2,343	20.9	1,817	1,024	56.4	886	264	29.8
1977	12,046	2,700	22.4	11,249	2,463	21.9	1,901	1,077	56.7	797	237	29.8
1976	11,269	2,783	24.7	10,552	2,516	23.8	1,766	1,000	56.6	716	266	37.2
1975	11,117	2,991	26.9	10,472	2,755	26.3	1,842	1,053	57.2	645	236	36.6
1974	11,201	2,575	23.0	10,584	2,374	22.4	1,723	915	53.1	617	201	32.6
1973	10,795	2,366	21.9	10,269	2,209	21.5	1,534	881	57.4	526	157	29.9
1972	10,588	2,414	22.8	10,099	2,252	22.3	1,370	733	53.5	488	162	33.2
Asian and Pacific Islander												
2001	12,465	1,275	10.2	10,745	873	8.1	1,333	198	14.8	1,682	393	23.4
2000[1]	12,672	1,258	9.9	11,044	895	8.1	1,231	289	23.4	1,588	350	22.0
2000[r]	11,305	1,214	10.7	9,894	932	9.4	1,052	206	19.6	1,375	271	19.7
1999	10,916	1,163	10.7	9,618	919	9.6	1,097	253	23.0	1,267	238	18.8
1998	10,873	1,360	12.5	9,576	1,087	11.4	1,123	373	33.2	1,266	257	20.3
1997	10,482	1,468	14.0	9,312	1,116	12.0	932	313	33.6	1,134	327	28.9
1996	10,054	1,454	14.5	8,900	1,172	13.2	1,018	300	29.5	1,120	255	22.8
1995	9,644	1,411	14.6	8,582	1,112	13.0	919	266	28.9	1,013	260	25.6
1994	6,654	974	14.6	5,915	776	13.1	582	137	23.6	696	179	25.7
1993	7,434	1,134	15.3	6,609	898	13.6	725	126	17.4	791	228	28.8
1992[r]	7,779	985	12.7	6,922	787	11.4	729	183	25.0	828	193	23.3
1991[r]	7,192	996	13.8	6,367	773	12.1	721	177	24.6	785	209	26.6
1990	7,014	858	12.2	6,300	712	11.3	638	132	20.7	668	124	18.5
1989	6,673	939	14.1	5,917	779	13.2	614	212	34.6	712	144	20.2
1988[r]	6,447	1,117	17.3	5,767	942	16.3	650	263	40.5	651	160	24.5
1987[r]	6,322	1,02	116.1	5,785	875	15.1	584	187	32.0	516	138	26.8

[r]For 2000, figures are based on a November 2001 weighting correction. For 1992, figures are based on 1990 census population controls. For 1991, figures are revised to correct for nine omitted weights from the original March 1992 CPS file. For 1988 and 1987, figures are based on new processing procedures and are also revised to reflect corrections to the files after publication of the 1988 advance report, *Money Income and Poverty Status in the United States: 1988*, P-60, No. 166.

NA = Not available.

[1]Consistent with 2001 data through implementation of Census 2000-based population controls and a 28,000 household sample expansion.

[2]Hispanics may be of any race.

Note: Prior to 1979, people in unrelated subfamilies were included in people in families. Beginning in 1979, people in unrelated subfamilies are included in all people but are excluded from people in families.

SOURCE: Bernadette D. Proctor and Joseph Dalaker, "Table A-1. Poverty Status of People by Family Relationship, Race, and Hispanic Origin, 1959–2001," in *Poverty in the United States: 2001*, Current Population Reports, U.S. Census Bureau, Washington, DC, September 2002

of health insurance, as 31.2 percent of those who were poor and held bachelor's degrees or higher were uninsured, compared to 36.5 percent of those who were poor and had not earned a high school diploma. (See Figure 5.13.)

FOREIGN-BORN POPULATION

In 1960 the foreign-born population in the United States totaled 9.7 million; by 2000 it had grown to 28.4 million. Since 1970 the number of foreign-born residents more than tripled. The composition of the foreign-born population has changed over time as immigration patterns shifted. From 1850 to 1960 the majority of immigrants came from European countries. In 1980 just under 40 percent of the foreign-born population came from Europe, while 33 percent came from Latin America and 19.3 percent from Asia. By 2000, 51.0 percent of foreign-born residents were from Latin America, 25.5 percent from Asia, and only 15.3 percent from Europe. (See Figure 5.14.)

From 1900 through 1930 more than 80 percent of foreign-born residents lived in the Northeast and Midwest. In 1930 New York had more than twice the foreign-born population of any other state. Between 1960 and 2000 growth of the foreign-born population shifted to the West and the South. While New York still has a significant foreign-born population, California led the nation in 2000 with 25.9 percent of its population coming from outside the United States. (See Figure 5.15.)

The median length of U.S. residence of foreign-born populations was 14.4 years in 2000, a significant decrease from 20.3 years in 1970. The Census Bureau attributes this change to the high level of international migration during this time and the death of the majority of migrants who came to the United States before 1930. (See Figure 5.16.) While Figure 5.17 shows that the number of foreign-born residents has more than tripled since 1970, the proportion of naturalized citizens dropped from 63.6 percent in 1970

FIGURE 5.11

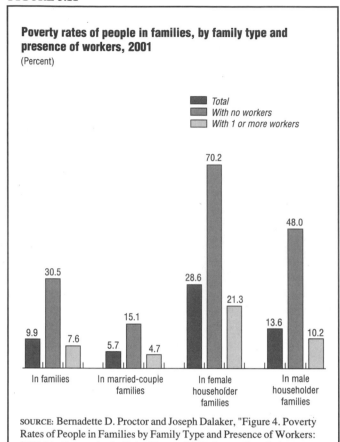

Poverty rates of people in families, by family type and presence of workers, 2001

(Percent)

Legend:
- Total
- With no workers
- With 1 or more workers

In families: 9.9 / 30.5 / 7.6

In married-couple families: 5.7 / 15.1 / 4.7

In female householder families: 28.6 / 70.2 / 21.3

In male householder families: 13.6 / 48.0 / 10.2

SOURCE: Bernadette D. Proctor and Joseph Dalaker, "Figure 4. Poverty Rates of People in Families by Family Type and Presence of Workers: 2001," in *Poverty in the United States: 2001*, Current Population Reports, U.S. Census Bureau, Washington, DC, September 2002

FIGURE 5.12

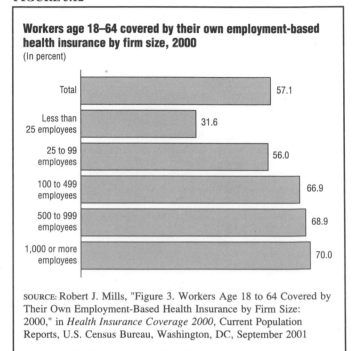

Workers age 18–64 covered by their own employment-based health insurance by firm size, 2000

(In percent)

Total: 57.1

Less than 25 employees: 31.6

25 to 99 employees: 56.0

100 to 499 employees: 66.9

500 to 999 employees: 68.9

1,000 or more employees: 70.0

SOURCE: Robert J. Mills, "Figure 3. Workers Age 18 to 64 Covered by Their Own Employment-Based Health Insurance by Firm Size: 2000," in *Health Insurance Coverage 2000*, Current Population Reports, U.S. Census Bureau, Washington, DC, September 2001

to 37.4 percent in 2002. In 2000, 52.0 percent of the population born in Europe were naturalized citizens, compared to 47.1 percent of the population from Asia and 28.3 percent of the population from Latin America.

On average, foreign-born households are larger than native-born households. In 2000, 11.1 percent of U.S. households had a foreign-born householder. The average foreign-born household had 3.26 people, compared to 2.54 people in native-born households. (See Figure 5.18.) One-third of the members of households headed by foreign-born householders are native born, indicating children born in the United States.

HOMELESS FAMILIES

Since the 1980s, the incidence of homelessness has increased, and by the beginning of the 21st century, homeless people could be found on the streets of virtually every American city. While the number of homeless people is based largely on estimates, families with children have reportedly become the fastest growing segment of the homeless population, making up 37 percent of all homeless people. Children (27 percent), including unaccompanied youth (7 percent), made up more than one-quarter of homeless persons in 1999.

Between 1990 and 2000 the number of people living in emergency and transitional shelters decreased 4.4 percent, from 178,638 to 170,706. (See Table 5.8.) One-fourth of the population living in emergency and transitional shelters were children under 18 years of age. While the total population residing in shelters is fairly evenly spread among regions of the United States, the Northeast has the largest proportion of children living in shelters (30.1 percent). (See Figure 5.19.) The white and black populations living in shelters are fairly evenly matched at a little over 40 percent each. Another 19.9 percent of shelter populations are identified as Hispanic, but they may be of any race. (See Figure 5.20.) Among children, 44.4 percent of shelter residents under age 18 are black, compared to 31.8 percent who are white and 26.1 percent who are Hispanic. (See Table 5.9.)

Although studies show that battered women who leave their homes may end up in the streets, there are 59 percent more males (104,879) than females (65,827) among the shelter population. In its latest survey of hunger and homelessness in 26 American cities, the U.S. Conference of Mayors reported that domestic violence was cited as the main cause of homelessness by 58 percent of responding cities. Many of the mayors who participated in the survey also reported that the strong economy of the late 1990s had not benefited the homeless in their city. They cited increasing housing costs, for example, which made it more difficult for the poor to afford housing. In 1999 every participating city reported a lack of affordable housing. Low-skill jobs, generally the only type of work for which many homeless people would qualify, were also difficult to find. Welfare reform had

TABLE 5.6

Health insurance coverage status and type of coverage by selected characteristics, 2000

(Numbers in thousands)

| Characteristic | Total people | Covered by private or government health insurance | | | | | | | Not covered |
| | | Total | Private health insurance | | Government health insurance | | | | |
			Total	Employment based	Total	Medicaid	Medicare	Military health care[1]	
NUMBERS									
People									
Total	276,540	237,812	200,171	177,226	66,936	28,648	37,015	8,301	38,729
Sex									
Male	135,244	115,067	98,404	88,290	30,088	12,670	16,209	4,401	20,177
Female	141,296	122,744	101,767	88,935	36,849	15,978	20,806	3,900	18,552
Race and Ethnicity									
White	226,401	197,116	169,691	149,273	52,791	19,462	32,043	6,526	29,285
Non-Hispanic	194,161	175,263	154,238	134,891	45,081	13,560	29,938	6,068	18,898
Black	35,919	29,289	21,146	19,522	11,144	7,293	3,811	1,359	6,629
Asian and Pacific Islander	11,384	9,333	7,952	7,157	2,085	1,292	852	294	2,051
Hispanic[2]	33,863	23,027	16,217	15,088	8,236	6,306	2,187	534	10,835
Age									
Under 18 years	72,556	64,105	51,122	48,027	16,909	14,767	504	2,098	8,451
18 to 24 years	26,962	19,614	17,466	14,399	3,202	2,349	161	777	7,349
25 to 34 years	37,440	29,514	27,008	25,496	3,368	2,355	425	822	7,926
35 to 44 years	44,780	37,841	35,210	33,252	3,887	2,400	816	1,168	6,939
45 to 64 years	61,823	54,004	49,070	44,889	7,723	3,485	3,377	2,041	7,819
65 years and over	32,979	32,734	20,295	11,163	31,847	3,291	31,734	1,395	245
Nativity									
Native	246,613	217,343	183,733	162,637	61,163	25,682	33,693	7,858	29,270
Foreign born	29,927	20,468	16,438	14,589	5,774	2,965	3,322	443	9,459
Naturalized citizen	11,390	9,583	7,610	6,615	3,160	1,076	2,433	276	1,807
Not a citizen	18,538	10,886	8,828	7,974	2,613	1,889	889	167	7,652
Region									
Northeast	52,809	46,791	39,646	35,493	13,087	6,108	7,488	869	6,019
Midwest	62,953	56,166	49,568	43,741	13,617	5,277	8,337	1,188	6,787
South	97,444	82,087	67,777	60,079	24,715	9,731	13,894	4,010	15,357
West	63,334	52,769	43,180	37,912	15,517	7,531	7,296	2,234	10,566
PERCENTS									
People									
Total	100.0	86.0	72.4	64.1	24.2	10.4	13.4	3.0	14.0
Sex									
Male	100.0	85.1	72.8	65.3	22.2	9.4	12.0	3.3	14.9
Female	100.0	86.9	72.0	62.9	26.1	11.3	14.7	2.8	13.1
Race and Ethnicity									
White	100.0	87.1	75.0	65.9	23.3	8.6	14.2	2.9	12.9
Non-Hispanic	100.0	90.3	79.4	69.5	23.2	7.0	15.4	3.1	9.7
Black	100.0	81.5	58.9	54.4	31.0	20.3	10.6	3.8	18.5
Asian and Pacific Islander	100.0	82.0	69.9	62.9	18.3	11.3	7.5	2.6	18.0
Hispanic[2]	100.0	68.0	47.9	44.6	24.3	18.6	6.5	1.6	32.0
Age									
Under 18 years	100.0	88.4	70.5	66.2	23.3	20.4	0.7	2.9	11.6
18 to 24 years	100.0	72.7	64.8	53.4	11.9	8.7	0.6	2.9	27.3
25 to 34 years	100.0	78.8	72.1	68.1	9.0	6.3	1.1	2.2	21.2
35 to 44 years	100.0	84.5	78.6	74.3	8.7	5.4	1.8	2.6	15.5
45 to 64 years	100.0	87.4	79.4	72.6	12.5	5.6	5.5	3.3	12.6
65 years and over	100.0	99.3	61.5	33.8	96.6	10.0	96.2	4.2	0.7
Nativity									
Native	100.0	88.1	74.5	65.9	24.8	10.4	13.7	3.2	11.9
Foreign born	100.0	68.4	54.9	48.7	19.3	9.9	11.1	1.5	31.6
Naturalized citizen	100.0	84.1	66.8	58.1	27.7	9.4	21.4	2.4	15.9
Not a citizen	100.0	58.7	47.6	43.0	14.1	10.2	4.8	0.9	41.3
Region									
Northeast	100.0	88.6	75.1	67.2	24.8	11.6	14.2	1.6	11.4
Midwest	100.0	89.2	78.7	69.5	21.6	8.4	13.2	1.9	10.8
South	100.0	84.2	69.6	61.7	25.4	10.0	14.3	4.1	15.8
West	100.0	83.3	68.2	59.9	24.5	11.9	11.5	3.5	16.7

TABLE 5.6

Health insurance coverage status and type of coverage by selected characteristics, 2000 [CONTINUED]

(Numbers in thousands)

Characteristic	Total people	Covered by private or government health insurance								Not covered
		Total	Private health insurance		Government health insurance					
			Total	Employment based	Total	Medicaid	Medicare	Military health care[1]		

Characteristic	Total people	Total	Total	Employment based	Total	Medicaid	Medicare	Military health care[1]	Not covered
NUMBERS									
Household Income									
Less than $25,000	61,130	47,232	25,165	16,889	32,007	16,958	17,554	1,564	13,898
$25,000 to $49,999	75,351	62,568	52,862	45,907	19,390	7,401	11,052	2,671	12,783
$50,000 to $74,999	59,237	52,741	49,315	45,847	8,024	2,544	4,222	1,894	6,496
$75,000 or more	80,822	75,270	72,828	68,583	7,515	1,744	4,186	2,172	5,552
Education (18 years and older)									
Total	203,985	173,707	149,049	129,199	50,027	13,880	36,511	6,203	30,278
No high school diploma	33,950	24,924	15,561	12,106	14,624	5,593	11,074	667	9,026
High school graduate only	65,833	55,018	46,739	40,121	17,779	4,771	13,060	2,016	10,816
Some college, no degree	40,068	34,699	31,104	26,610	7,912	1,939	5,219	1,613	5,369
Associate degree	15,702	14,083	12,954	11,691	2,698	586	1,733	667	1,619
Bachelor's degree or higher	48,432	44,984	42,691	38,671	7,014	991	5,426	1,240	3,448
Work Experience (18 to 64 years old)									
Total	171,006	140,973	128,754	118,036	18,181	10,589	4,777	4,808	30,033
Worked during year	140,403	117,597	112,713	104,705	8,696	4,622	798	3,589	22,806
Worked full-time	117,478	99,421	96,298	90,960	6,135	2,944	426	2,911	18,057
Worked part-time	22,925	18,176	16,415	13,744	2,562	1,678	372	677	4,749
Did not work	30,603	23,376	16,040	13,331	9,484	5,967	3,979	1,219	7,227
PERCENTS									
Household Income									
Less than $25,000	100.0	77.3	41.2	27.6	52.4	27.7	28.7	2.6	22.7
$25,000 to $49,999	100.0	83.0	70.2	60.9	25.7	9.8	14.7	3.5	17.0
$50,000 to $74,999	100.0	89.0	83.3	77.4	13.5	4.3	7.1	3.2	11.0
$75,000 or more	100.0	93.1	90.1	84.9	9.3	2.2	5.2	2.7	6.9
Education (18 years and older)									
Total	100.0	85.2	73.1	63.3	24.5	6.8	17.9	3.0	14.8
No high school diploma	100.0	73.4	45.8	35.7	43.1	16.5	32.6	2.0	26.6
High school graduate only	100.0	83.6	71.0	60.9	27.0	7.2	19.8	3.1	16.4
Some college, no degree	100.0	86.6	77.6	66.4	19.7	4.8	13.0	4.0	13.4
Associate degree	100.0	89.7	82.5	74.5	17.2	3.7	11.0	4.2	10.3
Bachelor's degree or higher	100.0	92.9	88.1	79.8	14.5	2.0	11.2	2.6	7.1
Work Experience (18 to 64 years old)									
Total	100.0	82.4	75.3	69.0	10.6	6.2	2.8	2.8	17.6
Worked during year	100.0	83.8	80.3	74.6	6.2	3.3	0.6	2.6	16.2
Worked full-time	100.0	84.6	82.0	77.4	5.2	2.5	0.4	2.5	15.4
Worked part-time	100.0	79.3	71.6	60.0	11.2	7.3	1.6	3.0	20.7
Did not work	100.0	76.4	52.4	43.6	31.0	19.5	13.0	4.0	23.6

[1]Includes CHAMPUS (Comprehensive Health and Medical Plan for Uniformed Services)/Tricare, Veterans', and military health care.

[2]Hispanics may be of any race.

SOURCE: Robert J. Mills, "Table A-2. Health Insurance Coverage Status and Type of Coverage by Selected Characteristics: 2000," in *Health Insurance Coverage 2000*, Current Population Reports, U.S. Census Bureau, Washington, DC, September 2001

also sparked an increase in the number of requests for emergency food assistance.

HOUSING

Owning one's own home is a cornerstone of the "American Dream." In 1890 less than half of householders owned their homes. Home ownership dwindled slowly until 1920, when a robust economy spurred greater home buying. The Great Depression dashed many dreams and drove the rate of home ownership to the century's low of 43.6 percent in 1940. The post–World War II economic boom, favorable tax laws, easier financing, and a revived home-building industry started a home ownership explo-

sion that exceeded 60 percent within two decades. By 2000 at least two out of three householders had attained the goal of home ownership. (See Figure 5.21.)

According to Census 2000, there were 115.9 million housing units—defined as a house, an apartment, a mobile home, a group of rooms, or a single room intended as separate living quarters—in the United States. Owner occupancy accounted for 66.2 percent of all units. (See Figure 5.21.) The District of Columbia had the lowest owner occupancy at 40.8 percent; West Virginia had the most owner occupants at 75.2 percent. Between 1990 and 2000, the U.S. housing inventory increased by 13.3 percent. Nine percent of available housing units in 2000 (10.4 mil-

TABLE 5.7

People without health insurance for the entire year by race and ethnicity (3-year average), 1998–2000
(Numbers in thousands)

Characteristic	Total	Uninsured	
		Number	Percent
Total	274,123	39,573	14.4
White	224,834	29,843	13.3
Non-Hispanic	193,623	19,536	10.1
Black	35,499	6,919	19.5
American Indian or Alaska Native	2,722	730	26.8
Asian or Pacific Islander	11,069	2,079	18.8
Hispanic[1]	32,785	10,739	32.8

[1]Hispanics may be of any race.

SOURCE: Robert J. Mills, "Table C. People Without Health Insurance for the Entire Year by Race and Ethnicity (3-Year Average): 1998 to 2000," in *Health Insurance Coverage 2000,* Current Population Reports, U.S. Census Bureau, Washington, DC, September 2001

lion units) were vacant. (See Table 5.10.) Of these, 3.8 million were available for sale or rent. Another 0.7 million were rented or sold and awaiting occupancy. There were 3.6 million vacation or recreational-use housing units and 25,000 units intended for seasonal use by migrant farmworkers. The remaining 2.3 million vacant units were held for other reasons by the owners.

Home ownership varies by region. The Midwest has the largest number of home owners, 70.2 percent; in the West, 61.5 percent of householders are home owners. (See Figure 5.22.) Married couples without children are more likely to own their homes (84.8 percent), while female householders with children were least likely to own their homes (37.7 percent). Nearly twice as many females with children rent as own homes. (See Table 5.11.) Home ownership is also closely related to age. Young adults just beginning their working careers have the lowest home ownership rate, 45.6 percent. Ownership increases with age and peaks between ages 65 and 74. (See Figure 5.23.)

Aided by low interest rates, the single family housing market remained strong in most areas of the country into 2001 despite rising prices. Home sales in the South accounted for more than one–third (38.9 percent) of all nationwide single family home sales in 2000. The median sale price of single family homes rose 4.3 percent from 1999 to 2000. Single family home prices increased most dramatically in the active Southern market, from a median of $120,300 in 1999 to $128,300 in 2000, an increase of 6.7 percent. The highest home prices were found in the West where the median sale price of existing single family homes was $183,000 in 2000. (See Table 5.12.)

The cost of housing, whether owned or rented, presents a challenge to many families. Housing costs include utilities, fuel, water, garbage collection, and rent or mortgage

TABLE 5.8

Population in emergency and transitional shelters by region, state, and Puerto Rico, 1990 and 2000

Area	1990		2000	
	Number	Percent	Number	Percent
United States	**178,638**	**100.0**	**170,706**	**100.0**
Region				
Northeast	60,077	33.6	52,369	30.7
Midwest	27,245	15.3	28,438	16.7
South	42,407	23.7	42,471	24.9
West	48,909	27.4	47,428	27.8
State				
Alabama	1,530	0.9	1,177	0.7
Alaska	447	0.3	558	0.3
Arizona	2,735	1.5	2,312	1.4
Arkansas	489	0.3	754	0.4
California	30,806	17.2	27,701	16.2
Colorado	2,554	1.4	2,281	1.3
Connecticut	4,194	2.3	2,291	1.3
Delaware	313	0.2	847	0.5
District of Columbia	4,682	2.6	1,762	1.0
Florida	7,110	4.0	6,766	4.0
Georgia	3,930	2.2	4,774	2.8
Hawaii	854	0.5	747	0.4
Idaho	461	0.3	703	0.4
Illinois	7,481	4.2	6,378	3.7
Indiana	2,251	1.3	2,384	1.4
Iowa	989	0.6	1,013	0.6
Kansas	940	0.5	587	0.3
Kentucky	1,284	0.7	1,626	1.0
Louisiana	1,559	0.9	1,986	1.2
Maine	419	0.2	458	0.3
Maryland	2,507	1.4	2,545	1.5
Massachusetts	6,207	3.5	5,405	3.2
Michigan	3,784	2.1	4,745	2.8
Minnesota	2,253	1.3	2,738	1.6
Mississippi	383	0.2	572	0.3
Missouri	2,276	1.3	2,164	1.3
Montana	445	0.2	477	0.3
Nebraska	764	0.4	913	0.5
Nevada	1,013	0.6	1,553	0.9
New Hampshire	377	0.2	523	0.3
New Jersey	7,470	4.2	5,500	3.2
New Mexico	667	0.4	934	0.5
New York	32,472	18.2	31,856	18.7
North Carolina	2,637	1.5	3,579	2.1
North Dakota	279	0.2	178	0.1
Ohio	4,277	2.4	5,224	3.1
Oklahoma	2,222	1.2	1,478	0.9
Oregon	3,254	1.8	3,011	1.8
Pennsylvania	8,237	4.6	5,463	3.2
Rhode Island	469	0.3	634	0.4
South Carolina	973	0.5	1,528	0.9
South Dakota	396	0.2	414	0.2
Tennessee	1,864	1.0	2,252	1.3
Texas	7,816	4.4	7,608	4.5
Utah	925	0.5	1,494	0.9
Vermont	232	0.1	239	0.1
Virginia	2,657	1.5	2,692	1.6
Washington	4,565	2.6	5,387	3.2
West Virginia	451	0.3	525	0.3
Wisconsin	1,555	0.9	1,700	1.0
Wyoming	183	0.1	270	0.2
Puerto Rico	**445**	**(X)**	**586**	**(X)**

X Not applicable.

SOURCE: Annette C. Smith and Denise I. Smith, "Table 1. Population in Emergency and Transitional Shelters for the United States, Regions, States, and Puerto Rico: 1990 and 2000," in *Emergency and Transitional Shelter Population: 2000,* Census 2000 Special Reports, U.S. Census Bureau, Washington, DC, October 2001

FIGURE 5.13

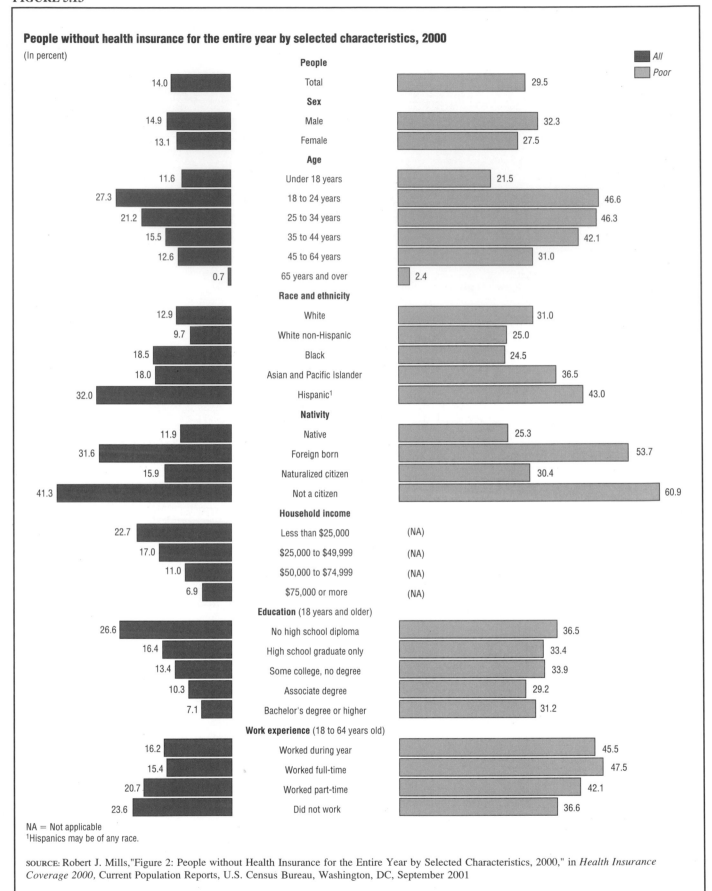

People without health insurance for the entire year by selected characteristics, 2000

(In percent)

■ All
▨ Poor

	People	
14.0	Total	29.5
	Sex	
14.9	Male	32.3
13.1	Female	27.5
	Age	
11.6	Under 18 years	21.5
27.3	18 to 24 years	46.6
21.2	25 to 34 years	46.3
15.5	35 to 44 years	42.1
12.6	45 to 64 years	31.0
0.7	65 years and over	2.4
	Race and ethnicity	
12.9	White	31.0
9.7	White non-Hispanic	25.0
18.5	Black	24.5
18.0	Asian and Pacific Islander	36.5
32.0	Hispanic[1]	43.0
	Nativity	
11.9	Native	25.3
31.6	Foreign born	53.7
15.9	Naturalized citizen	30.4
41.3	Not a citizen	60.9
	Household income	
22.7	Less than $25,000	(NA)
17.0	$25,000 to $49,999	(NA)
11.0	$50,000 to $74,999	(NA)
6.9	$75,000 or more	(NA)
	Education (18 years and older)	
26.6	No high school diploma	36.5
16.4	High school graduate only	33.4
13.4	Some college, no degree	33.9
10.3	Associate degree	29.2
7.1	Bachelor's degree or higher	31.2
	Work experience (18 to 64 years old)	
16.2	Worked during year	45.5
15.4	Worked full-time	47.5
20.7	Worked part-time	42.1
23.6	Did not work	36.6

NA = Not applicable
[1]Hispanics may be of any race.

SOURCE: Robert J. Mills,"Figure 2: People without Health Insurance for the Entire Year by Selected Characteristics, 2000," in *Health Insurance Coverage 2000,* Current Population Reports, U.S. Census Bureau, Washington, DC, September 2001

payments plus real estate taxes and property insurance for those who own their homes. In 1999 home owners spent a median per month of 17 percent of before tax income on housing costs, as compared to renters, who spent a median of 28 percent. Minority home owners and renters spent a slightly higher percentage of their income on housing costs. While housing costs for elderly home owners accounted for the same percentage of income as the general population, elderly renters spent 38 percent of their before tax income on housing. Housing costs for households below the poverty level exceeded half of their income whether they owned or rented. (See Table 5.13.)

According to the U.S. Census Bureau, there were 37.5 million households with children in 1999. Of these, 35 percent experienced housing problems and 11 percent suffered severe problems. The most common problems were related to inadequate plumbing, unvented heaters, water leaks, cracks, holes, broken plaster, and evidence of rats. The greatest problem was the cost of housing, whether owned or rented. Of households with children, 28 percent spent more than 30 percent of their resources on housing, while 11 percent spent more than half of their resources. The challenges were far greater for the 6.2 million very-low-income renter households with children. Of these households, 80 percent expressed problems with their living situation. Government assistance programs do not solve all of the problems for these families. While 31 percent received some type of rental assistance, 37 percent still spent more than half of their resources on housing costs. (See Table 5.14.)

FIGURE 5.14

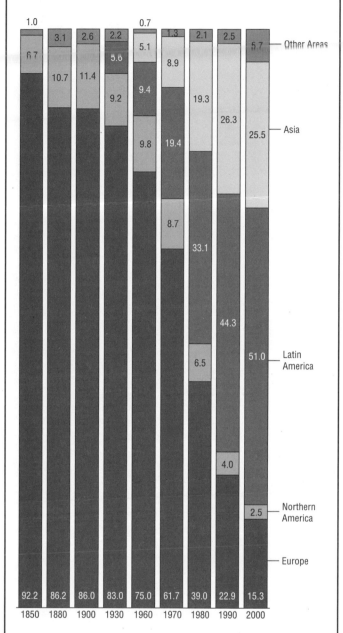

Foreign-born population by region of birth, selected years 1850–2000

Note: Percent distribution. For 1960–90, resident population. For 2000, civilian noninstitutional population plus Armed Forces living off post or with their families on post.

SOURCE: "Figure 2-2. Foreign-Born Population by Region of Birth: Selected Years, 1850–2000," in *Profile of Foreign-Born Population in the United States: 2000,* U.S. Census Bureau, Washington, DC, December 2001

FIGURE 5.15

Foreign-born population for states, 2000

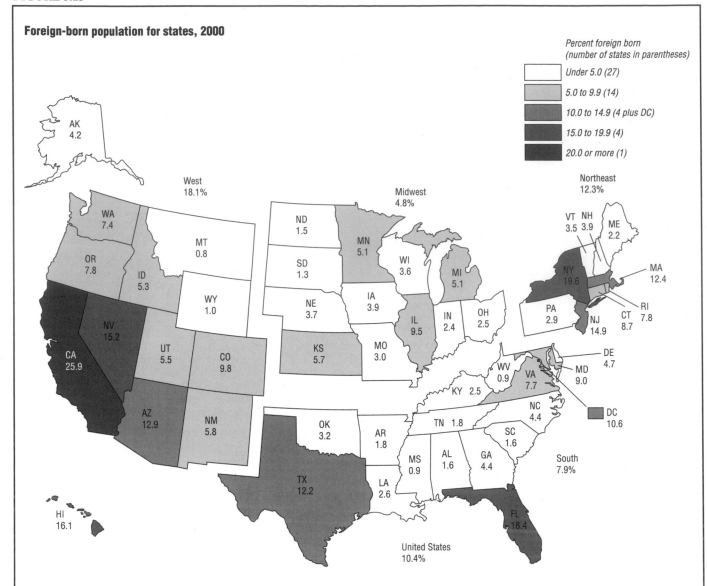

*Percent foreign born
(number of states in parentheses)*

- Under 5.0 (27)
- 5.0 to 9.9 (14)
- 10.0 to 14.9 (4 plus DC)
- 15.0 to 19.9 (4)
- 20.0 or more (1)

AK 4.2

West 18.1%

WA 7.4
OR 7.8
ID 5.3
MT 0.8
WY 1.0
NV 15.2
CA 25.9
UT 5.5
CO 9.8
AZ 12.9
NM 5.8

Midwest 4.8%

ND 1.5
SD 1.3
NE 3.7
KS 5.7
MN 5.1
WI 3.6
IA 3.9
MO 3.0
IL 9.5
IN 2.4
MI 5.1
OH 2.5

Northeast 12.3%

VT 3.5
NH 3.9
ME 2.2
NY 19.6
MA 12.4
PA 2.9
NJ 14.9
RI 7.8
CT 8.7

WV 0.9
VA 7.7
DE 4.7
MD 9.0
DC 10.6

KY 2.5
NC 4.4

OK 3.2
AR 1.8
TN 1.8
SC 1.6
South 7.9%

TX 12.2
LA 2.6
MS 0.9
AL 1.6
GA 4.4

HI 16.1

FL 18.4

United States 10.4%

Note: Civilian noninstitutional population plus Armed Forces living off post or with their families on post.

SOURCE: "Figure 4-2. Foreign-Born Population for States: 2000," in *Profile of Foreign-Born Population in the United States: 2000,* U.S. Census Bureau, Washington, DC, December 2001

FIGURE 5.16

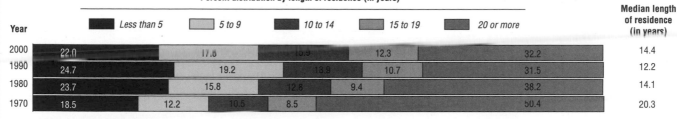

Length of residence for the foreign-born population, 1970–2000

Percent distribution by length of residence (in years)

Year	Less than 5	5 to 9	10 to 14	15 to 19	20 or more	Median length of residence (in years)
2000	22.0	17.6	15.9	12.3	32.2	14.4
1990	24.7	19.2	13.9	10.7	31.5	12.2
1980	23.7	15.8	12.8	9.4	38.2	14.1
1970	18.5	12.2	10.5	8.5	50.4	20.3

[1]Census data for 1970–90 do not include persons who did not report length of residence information.

Note: For 1970–90, resident population. For 2000, civilian noninstitutional population plus Armed Forces living off post or with their families on post.

SOURCE: "Figure 6-1. Length of Residence in the United States for the Foreign-Born Population: 1970–2000," in *Profile of Foreign-Born Population in the United States: 2000,* U.S. Census Bureau, Washington, DC, December 2001

FIGURE 5.17

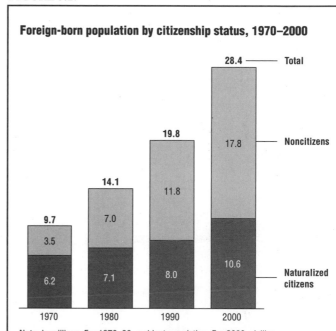

Foreign-born population by citizenship status, 1970–2000

Note: In millions. For 1970–90, resident population. For 2000, civilian noninstitutional population plus Armed Forces living off post or with their families on post.

SOURCE: "Figure 7-1. Foreign-Born Population by Citizenship Status: 1970–2000," in *Profile of Foreign-Born Population in the United States: 2000,* U.S. Census Bureau, Washington, DC, December 2001

FIGURE 5.18

Households by nativity, length of residence, and citizenship status of the householder, 2000

Percent distribution of households by type

	Households (in millions)	Family households			Nonfamily households		Average household size
		Married couple	Male householder[1]	Female householder[2]	Male householder	Female householder	
Total	104.7	52.8	3.8	12.1	14.0	17.2	2.62
Native	93.1	52.1	3.5	12.0	14.2	18.1	2.54
Foreign born	11.6	58.7	6.2	12.7	11.9	10.6	3.26
Length of residence in U.S.							
Less than 10 years	3.4	54.0	8.6	11.3	17.2	8.9	3.25
10 to 19 years	3.3	62.9	7.5	13.9	9.5	6.2	3.70
20 years and over	4.9	59.0	3.8	12.8	9.8	14.7	2.97
Citizenship status							
Naturalized citizen	5.4	60.3	4.6	12.1	9.5	13.5	3.05
Not a citizen	6.3	57.3	7.6	13.1	13.9	8.0	3.44

[1]Male householder, no spouse present.
[2]Female householder, no spouse present.

Note: Civilian noninstitutional population plus Armed Forces living off post or with their families on post.

SOURCE: "Figure 11-1. Households by Nativity, Length of Residence in the United States, and Citizenship Status of the Householder: 2000," in *Profile of Foreign-Born Population in the United States: 2000,* U.S. Census Bureau, Washington, DC, December 2001

FIGURE 5.19

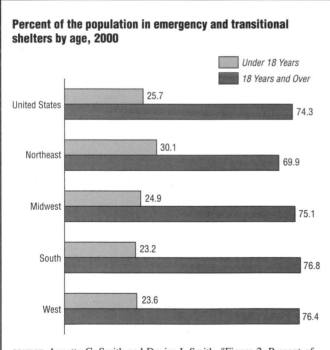

Percent of the population in emergency and transitional shelters by age, 2000

SOURCE: Annette C. Smith and Denise I. Smith, "Figure 2. Percent of the Population in Emergency and Transitional Shelters by Age, for the United States and Regions: 2000," in *Emergency and Transitional Shelter Population: 2000,* Census 2000 Special Reports, U.S. Census Bureau, Washington, DC, October 2001

FIGURE 5.20

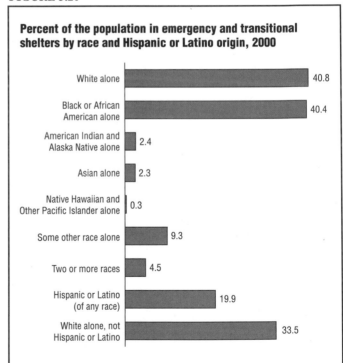

Percent of the population in emergency and transitional shelters by race and Hispanic or Latino origin, 2000

SOURCE: Annette C. Smith and Denise I. Smith, "Figure 3. Percent of the Population in Emergency and Transitional Shelters by Race and Hispanic or Latino Origin, for the United States: 2000," in *Emergency and Transitional Shelter Population: 2000,* Census 2000 Special Reports, U.S. Census Bureau, Washington, DC, October 2001

TABLE 5.9

Population in emergency or transitional shelters by sex, age, race, and Hispanic or Latino origin, 2000

Sex and age	Total population	Race One race Total	White	Black or African American	American Indian and Alaska Native	Asian	Native Hawaiian and Other Pacific Islander	Some other race	Two or more races	Hispanic or Latino (of any race)	White alone, not Hispanic or Latino
NUMBER											
Both sexes	170,706	163,028	69,637	69,046	4,092	3,922	489	15,842	7,678	34,013	57,173
Under 18 years	43,887	41,049	13,935	19,475	1,030	897	188	5,524	2,838	11,475	10,005
18 years and over	126,819	121,979	55,702	49,571	3,062	3,025	301	10,318	4,840	22,538	47,168
Male	104,879	100,595	45,028	41,544	2,506	2,088	259	9,170	4,284	20,153	37,356
Under 18 years	22,465	21,057	7,262	9,886	538	446	104	2,821	1,408	5,847	5,245
18 years and over	82,414	79,538	37,766	31,658	1,968	1,642	155	6,349	2,876	14,306	32,111
Female	65,827	62,433	24,609	27,502	1,586	1,834	230	6,672	3,394	13,860	19,817
Under 18 years	21,422	19,992	6,673	9,589	492	451	84	2,703	1,430	5,628	4,760
18 years and over	44,405	42,441	17,936	17,913	1,094	1,383	146	3,969	1,964	8,232	15,057
PERCENT BY AGE											
Both sexes	100.0	100.0	100.0	100.0	100.0	100.0	100.0	100.0	100.0	100.0	100.0
Under 18 years	25.7	25.2	20.0	28.2	25.2	22.9	38.4	34.9	37.0	33.7	17.5
18 years and over	74.3	74.8	80.0	71.8	74.8	77.1	61.6	65.1	63.0	66.3	82.5
Male	100.0	100.0	100.0	100.0	100.0	100.0	100.0	100.0	100.0	100.0	100.0
Under 18 years	21.4	20.9	16.1	23.8	21.5	21.4	40.2	30.8	32.9	29.0	14.0
18 years and over	78.6	79.1	83.9	76.2	78.5	78.6	59.8	69.2	67.1	71.0	86.0
Female	100.0	100.0	100.0	100.0	100.0	100.0	100.0	100.0	100.0	100.0	100.0
Under 18 years	32.5	32.0	27.1	34.9	31.0	24.6	36.5	40.5	42.1	40.6	24.0
18 years and over	67.5	68.0	72.9	65.1	69.0	75.4	63.5	59.5	57.9	59.4	76.0
PERCENT BY RACE AND HISPANIC OR LATINO ORIGIN											
Both sexes	100.0	95.5	40.8	40.4	2.4	2.3	0.3	9.3	4.5	19.9	33.5
Under 18 years	100.0	93.5	31.8	44.4	2.3	2.0	0.4	12.6	6.5	26.1	22.8
18 years and over	100.0	96.2	43.9	39.1	2.4	2.4	0.2	8.1	3.8	17.8	37.2
Male	100.0	95.9	42.9	39.6	2.4	2.0	0.2	8.7	4.1	19.2	35.6
Under 18 years	100.0	93.7	32.3	44.0	2.4	2.0	0.5	12.6	6.3	26.0	23.3
18 years and over	100.0	96.5	45.8	38.4	2.4	2.0	0.2	7.7	3.5	17.4	39.0
Female	100.0	94.8	37.4	41.8	2.4	2.8	0.3	10.1	5.2	21.1	30.1
Under 18 years	100.0	93.3	31.2	44.8	2.3	2.1	0.4	12.6	6.7	26.3	22.2
18 years and over	100.0	95.6	40.4	40.3	2.5	3.1	0.3	8.9	4.4	18.5	33.9

SOURCE: Annette C. Smith and Denise I. Smith, "Table 3. Population in Emergency or Transitional Shelters by Sex, Age, Race, and Hispanic or Latino Origin for the United States: 2000," in *Emergency and Transitional Shelter Population: 2000,* Census 2000 Special Reports, U.S. Census Bureau, Washington, DC, October 2001

FIGURE 5.21

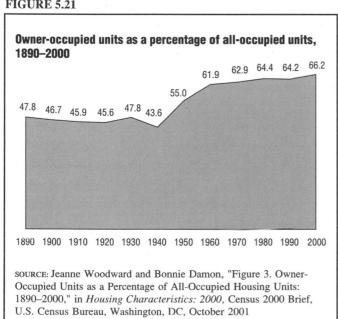

Owner-occupied units as a percentage of all-occupied units, 1890–2000

SOURCE: Jeanne Woodward and Bonnie Damon, "Figure 3. Owner-Occupied Units as a Percentage of All-Occupied Housing Units: 1890–2000," in *Housing Characteristics: 2000,* Census 2000 Brief, U.S. Census Bureau, Washington, DC, October 2001

FIGURE 5.22

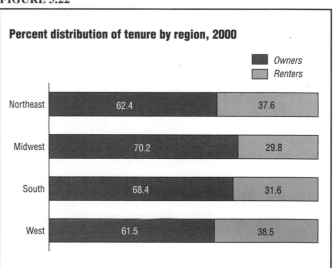

Percent distribution of tenure by region, 2000

SOURCE: Jeanne Woodward and Bonnie Damon, "Figure 4. Percent Distribution of Tenure by Region: 2000," in *Housing Characteristics: 2000,* Census 2000 Brief, U.S. Census Bureau, Washington, DC, October 2001

TABLE 5.10

General housing characteristics by region, state, and Puerto Rico, 1990 and 2000

Area	Total housing units in 1990	Housing units in 2000				Percent change, 1990 to 2000				
		Total	Percent vacant	Occupied	Percent owner-occupied	All housing units	Vacant units	Occupied units		
								Total	Owner	Renter
United States	102,263,678	115,904,641	9.0	105,480,101	66.2	13.3	1.0	14.7	18.3	8.3
Region										
Northeast	20,810,637	22,180,440	8.5	20,285,622	62.4	6.6	−2.2	7.5	9.3	4.6
Midwest	24,492,718	26,963,635	8.3	24,734,532	70.2	10.1	2.5	10.8	14.3	3.4
South	36,065,102	42,382,546	10.3	38,015,214	68.4	17.5	2.9	19.5	23.3	11.9
West	20,895,221	24,378,020	7.9	22,444,733	61.5	16.7	−1.4	18.5	23.5	11.4
State										
Alabama	1,670,379	1,963,711	11.5	1,737,080	72.5	17.6	38.5	15.3	18.5	7.5
Alaska	232,608	260,978	15.1	221,600	62.5	12.2	−9.9	17.3	30.7	0.2
Arizona	1,659,430	2,189,189	13.1	1,901,327	68.0	31.9	−0.9	38.9	47.2	24.0
Arkansas	1,000,667	1,173,043	11.1	1,042,696	69.4	17.2	19.1	17.0	16.7	17.7
California	11,182,882	12,214,549	5.8	11,502,870	56.9	9.2	−11.2	10.8	13.4	7.6
Colorado	1,477,349	1,808,037	8.3	1,658,238	67.3	22.4	−23.1	29.3	39.8	12.0
Connecticut	1,320,850	1,385,975	6.1	1,301,670	66.8	4.9	−6.7	5.8	7.7	2.1
Delaware	289,919	343,072	12.9	298,736	72.3	18.3	4.5	20.7	24.3	12.2
District of Columbia	278,489	274,845	9.6	248,338	40.8	−1.3	−8.1	−0.5	4.2	−3.5
Florida	6,100,262	7,302,947	13.2	6,337,929	70.1	19.7	–	23.4	28.7	12.7
Georgia	2,638,418	3,281,737	8.4	3,006,369	67.5	24.4	1.3	27.0	32.0	17.8
Hawaii	389,810	460,542	12.4	403,240	56.5	18.1	70.8	13.2	18.7	6.7
Idaho	413,327	527,824	11.0	469,645	72.4	27.7	10.6	30.2	34.5	20.1
Illinois	4,506,275	4,885,615	6.0	4,591,779	67.3	8.4	−3.4	9.3	14.4	–
Indiana	2,246,046	2,532,319	7.7	2,336,306	71.4	12.7	8.5	13.1	15.0	8.6
Iowa	1,143,669	1,232,511	6.8	1,149,276	72.3	7.8	4.9	8.0	11.5	−0.3
Kansas	1,044,112	1,131,200	8.2	1,037,891	69.2	8.3	−6.1	9.9	12.0	5.4
Kentucky	1,506,845	1,750,927	9.2	1,590,647	70.8	16.2	26.1	15.3	17.2	11.0
Louisiana	1,716,241	1,847,181	10.3	1,656,053	67.9	7.6	−11.9	10.5	13.9	3.8
Maine	587,045	651,901	20.5	518,200	71.6	11.0	9.8	11.4	13.1	7.2
Maryland	1,891,917	2,145,283	7.7	1,980,859	67.7	13.4	15.0	13.3	18.0	4.5
Massachusetts	2,472,711	2,621,989	6.8	2,443,580	61.7	6.0	−20.9	8.7	13.3	2.2
Michigan	3,847,926	4,234,279	10.6	3,785,661	73.8	10.0	4.7	10.7	15.1	0.1
Minnesota	1,848,445	2,065,946	8.3	1,895,127	74.6	11.8	−14.8	15.0	19.4	3.9
Mississippi	1,010,423	1,161,953	9.9	1,046,434	72.3	15.0	16.6	14.8	16.2	11.4
Missouri	2,199,129	2,442,017	10.1	2,194,594	70.3	11.0	4.0	11.9	14.3	6.5
Montana	361,155	412,633	13.1	358,667	69.1	14.3	−1.9	17.1	20.3	10.7
Nebraska	660,621	722,668	7.8	666,184	67.4	9.4	−3.0	10.6	12.2	7.4
Nevada	518,858	827,457	9.2	751,165	60.9	59.5	45.1	61.1	79.0	39.4
New Hampshire	503,904	547,024	13.2	474,606	69.7	8.6	−21.9	15.4	18.0	10.0
New Jersey	3,075,310	3,310,275	7.4	3,064,645	65.6	7.6	−12.5	9.7	10.9	7.3
New Mexico	632,058	780,579	13.1	677,971	70.0	23.5	14.8	24.9	29.6	15.2
New York	7,226,891	7,679,307	8.1	7,056,860	53.0	6.3	5.9	6.3	7.9	4.5
North Carolina	2,818,193	3,523,944	11.1	3,132,013	69.4	25.0	30.1	24.4	26.9	19.2
North Dakota	276,340	289,677	11.2	257,152	66.6	4.8	−8.3	6.8	8.5	3.5
Ohio	4,371,945	4,783,051	7.1	4,445,773	69.1	9.4	18.6	8.8	11.4	3.3
Oklahoma	1,406,499	1,514,400	11.4	1,342,293	68.4	7.7	−14.1	11.3	11.8	10.2
Oregon	1,193,567	1,452,709	8.2	1,333,723	64.3	21.7	31.8	20.9	23.1	17.0
Pennsylvania	4,938,140	5,249,750	9.0	4,777,003	71.3	6.3	6.9	6.3	7.2	3.9
Rhode Island	414,572	439,837	7.1	408,424	60.0	6.1	−14.2	8.1	9.1	6.6
South Carolina	1,424,155	1,753,670	12.5	1,533,854	72.2	23.1	32.3	21.9	26.1	12.4
South Dakota	292,436	323,208	10.2	290,245	68.2	10.5	−1.3	12.0	15.6	5.0
Tennessee	2,026,067	2,439,443	8.5	2,232,905	69.9	20.4	19.8	20.5	23.8	13.3
Texas	7,008,999	8,157,575	9.4	7,393,354	63.8	16.4	−18.5	21.8	27.7	12.7
Utah	598,388	768,594	8.8	701,281	71.5	28.4	10.1	30.5	37.0	16.6
Vermont	271,214	294,382	18.3	240,634	70.6	8.5	−11.3	14.2	16.8	8.5
Virginia	2,496,334	2,904,192	7.1	2,699,173	68.1	16.3	0.3	17.8	21.0	11.5
Washington	2,032,378	2,451,075	7.3	2,271,398	64.6	20.6	12.3	21.3	25.2	14.8
West Virginia	781,295	844,623	12.8	736,481	75.2	8.1	16.6	7.0	8.6	2.4
Wisconsin	2,055,774	2,321,144	10.2	2,084,544	68.4	12.9	1.3	14.4	17.4	8.5
Wyoming	203,411	223,854	13.5	193,608	70.0	10.1	−12.5	14.7	18.3	7.0
Puerto Rico	1,188,985	1,418,476	11.1	1,261,325	72.9	19.3	17.2	19.6	21.0	15.9

– Percentage rounds 0.0.

SOURCE: Jeanne Woodward and Bonnie Damon, "Table 1. General Housing Characteristics for the United States, Regions, and States, and for Puerto Rico: 1990 and 2000," in *Housing Characteristics: 2000,* Census 2000 Brief, U.S. Census Bureau, Washington, DC, October 2001

FIGURE 5.23

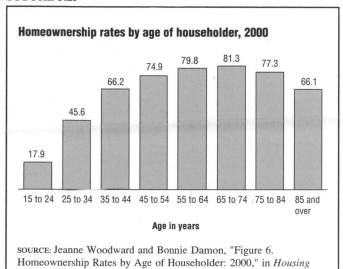

Homeownership rates by age of householder, 2000

Age in years	Rate
15 to 24	17.9
25 to 34	45.6
35 to 44	66.2
45 to 54	74.9
55 to 64	79.8
65 to 74	81.3
75 to 84	77.3
85 and over	66.1

SOURCE: Jeanne Woodward and Bonnie Damon, "Figure 6. Homeownership Rates by Age of Householder: 2000," in *Housing Characteristics: 2000,* Census 2000 Brief, U.S. Census Bureau, Washington, DC, October 2001

TABLE 5.11

Family type by tenure, 2000

Family characteristic	Occupied units			
	Total	Owner	Percent owner	Renter
Total housing units	105,480,101	69,815,733	66.2	35,664,348
Total families	71,787,347	53,071,538	73.9	18,715,809
Married-couple families	54,493,232	44,240,872	81.2	10,252,360
With children[1]	24,835,505	19,103,921	76.9	5,731,584
Without children[1]	29,657,727	25,136,951	84.8	4,520,776
Male householder, no spouse present	4,394,012	2,433,530	55.4	1,960,482
With children[1]	2,190,989	1,113,804	50.8	1,077,185
Without children[1]	2,203,023	1,319,726	59.9	883,297
Female householder, no spouse present	12,900,103	6,397,136	49.6	6,502,967
With children[1]	7,561,874	2,851,607	37.7	4,710,267
Without children[1]	5,338,229	3,545,529	66.4	1,792,700
Total nonfamily households	33,692,754	16,744,215	49.7	16,948,539
Male householder	15,556,103	7,004,848	45.0	8,551,255
Living alone	11,779,106	5,530,759	47.0	6,248,347
Living with nonrelative	3,776,997	1,474,089	39.0	2,302,908
Female householder	18,136,651	9,739,367	53.7	8,397,284
Living alone	15,450,969	8,659,549	56.0	6,791,420
Living with nonrelative	2,685,682	1,079,818	40.2	1,605,864

[1]Children represent own children under 18 years.

SOURCE: Jeanne Woodward and Bonnie Damon, "Table 5. Family Type by Tenure: 2000," in *Housing Characteristics: 2000,* Census 2000 Brief, U.S. Census Bureau, Washington, DC, October 2001

TABLE 5.12

Existing one-family houses sold and price, by region, 1970–2000

[1,612 represents 1,612,000. Based on data (adjusted and aggregated to regional and national totals) reported by participating real estate multiple listing services.]

Year	Houses sold (1,000)					Median sales price (dollars)				
	Total	North-east	Mid-west	South	West	Total	North-east	Mid-west	South	West
1970	1,612	251	501	568	292	23,000	25,700	20,100	22,200	24,300
1975	2,476	370	701	862	543	35,300	39,300	30,100	34,800	39,600
1980	2,973	403	806	1,092	672	62,200	60,800	51,900	58,300	89,300
1981	2,419	353	632	917	516	66,400	63,700	54,300	64,400	96,200
1982	1,990	354	490	780	366	67,800	63,500	55,100	67,100	98,900
1983	2,697	477	692	1,004	524	70,300	72,200	56,600	69,200	94,900
1984	2,829	478	720	1,006	624	72,400	78,700	57,100	71,300	95,800
1985	3,134	561	806	1,063	704	75,500	88,900	58,900	75,200	95,400
1986	3,474	635	922	1,145	773	80,300	104,800	63,500	78,200	100,900
1987	3,436	618	892	1,163	763	85,600	133,300	66,000	80,400	113,200
1988	3,513	606	865	1,224	817	89,300	143,000	68,400	82,200	124,900
1989[1]	3,325	490	832	1,185	818	89,500	127,700	71,800	84,400	127,100
1990	3,219	458	809	1,193	759	92,000	126,400	75,300	85,100	129,600
1991	3,186	463	812	1,173	737	97,100	129,100	79,500	88,500	135,300
1992	3,479	521	913	1,242	802	99,700	128,900	83,000	91,500	131,500
1993	3,786	550	967	1,386	882	103,100	129,100	86,000	94,300	132,500
1994	3,916	552	965	1,436	962	107,200	129,100	89,300	95,700	139,400
1995	3,888	547	945	1,433	964	110,500	126,700	94,800	97,700	141,000
1996	4,196	584	986	1,511	1,116	115,800	127,800	101,000	103,400	147,100
1997	4,382	607	1,005	1,595	1,174	121,800	131,800	107,000	109,600	155,200
1998	4,970	662	1,130	1,868	1,309	128,400	135,900	114,300	116,200	164,800
1999	5,205	656	1,148	2,015	1,386	133,300	139,000	119,600	120,300	173,900
2000	5,113	645	1,115	1,992	1,362	139,000	139,400	123,600	128,300	183,000

[1]Beginning 1989 data not comparable to earlier years due to rebenchmarking.

SOURCE: "No. 942. Existing One-Family Houses Sold at Price by Region: 1970–2000," in *Statistical Abstract of the United States 2001,* U.S. Census Bureau, Washington, DC, 2001

TABLE 5.13

Occupied housing units—Financial summary by selected characteristics of the householder, fall 1999

[In thousands of units (102,803 represents 102,803,000), except as indicated. Housing costs include real estate taxes, property insurance, utilities, fuel, water, garbage collection, and mortgage. Based on the American Housing Survey.]

Characteristic	Total occupied units	Tenure		Black		Hispanic origin[1]		Elderly[2]		Households below poverty level	
		Owner	Renter	Owner	Renter	Owner	Renter	Owner	Renter	Owner	Renter
Total units[3]	102,803	68,796	34,007	6,013	6,923	4,087	4,955	17,196	4,227	6,276	7,988
Monthly housing costs:											
Less than $300	22,541	18,810	3,730	1,890	1,161	1,053	481	8,931	980	3,272	2,005
$300-$399	10,098	6,758	3,340	615	751	293	448	2,647	494	725	975
$400-$499	9,749	5,096	4,654	498	1,122	241	709	1,603	526	557	1,197
$500-$599	9,882	4,593	5,289	425	1,064	265	892	1,019	528	361	1,025
$600-$699	8,770	4,215	4,554	393	893	308	776	654	375	298	768
$700-$799	7,485	4,071	3,414	400	594	300	573	468	312	223	487
$800-$999	10,886	7,205	3,681	611	585	418	540	610	279	257	416
$1,000 or more	21,292	18,048	3,244	1,181	350	1,208	333	1,266	309	583	413
Median amount (dol.)	581	581	580	501	521	662	583	292	481	290	459
Monthly housing costs as percent of income:[4]											
Less than 5 percent	5,457	5,163	293	365	68	249	27	1,040	44	33	7
5 to 9 percent	13,195	11,992	1,203	931	212	614	120	3,213	85	103	59
10 to 14 percent	15,070	11,948	3,122	922	518	574	395	3,062	173	233	144
15 to 19 percent	15,333	11,108	4,226	833	708	595	575	2,353	271	280	179
20 to 24 percent	11,996	7,761	4,235	654	811	422	548	1,578	268	266	214
25 to 29 percent	9,066	5,503	3,562	516	718	394	530	1,170	455	380	432
30 to 34 percent	6,281	3,450	2,832	344	589	247	426	769	408	284	438
35 to 39 percent	4,495	2,428	2,067	285	435	198	367	697	281	303	383
40 percent or more	17,539	8,251	9,287	1,016	2,197	724	1,580	2,877	1,720	3,227	4,430
Median amount (percent)	20	17	28	19	31	20	31	17	38	56	64
Median monthly costs (dol.):											
Electricity	60	67	45	72	49	63	42	60	38	59	44
Piped gas	40	43	28	47	33	33	25	43	28	42	29
Fuel oil	56	58	44	58	45	56	32	58	42	49	53

[1]Persons of Hispanic origin may be of any race.
[2]Householders 65 years old and over.
[3]Includes units with mortgage payment not reported and no cash rent not shown separately.
[4]Money income before taxes.

SOURCE: "No. 959. Occupied Housing Units—Financial Summary by Selected Characteristics of the Householder: 1999," in *Statistical Abstract of the United States 2001*, U.S. Census Bureau, Washington, DC, 2001

TABLE 5.14

Percentage of households with children under age 18 that report housing problems by type of problem, selected years 1978–99

Household type	1978	1983	1989	1993	1995	1997	1999
All households with children							
Number of households (in millions)	32.3	33.6	35.4	35.4	37.2	37.0	37.5
Percent with							
Any problems	00	33	33	34	36	36	35
Inadequate housing[a]	9	8	9	7	7	7	7
Crowded housing	9	8	7	6	7	7	7
Cost burden greater than 30 percent	15	21	24	26	28	28	28
Cost burden greater than 50 percent	6	11	9	11	12	12	11
Severe problems	8	12	10	11	12	11	11
Very-low-income renter households with children[b]							
Number of households (in millions)	4.2	5.1	5.9	6.6	6.5	6.4	6.2
Percent with							
Any problems	79	83	77	75	77	82	80
Inadequate housing[a]	18	18	18	14	13	16	15
Crowded housing	22	18	17	14	17	17	17
Cost burden greater than 30 percent	59	68	67	67	69	73	70
Cost burden greater than 50 percent	31	38	36	38	38	41	37
Severe problems	33	42	31	33	31	32	29
Rental assistance	23	23	33	33	33	31	31

[a]Inadequate housing refers to housing with "moderate or severe physical problems." The most common problems meeting the definition are lacking complete plumbing for exclusive use, having unvented room heaters as the primary heating equipment, and multiple upkeep problems such as water leakage, open cracks or holes, broken plaster, or signs of rats.
[b]Very-low-income households are those with incomes at or below one-half the median in a geographic area.

Note: Data are available for 1978, 1983, 1989, 1993, 1995, 1997, and 1999 (1978 data based on 1970 Census weights; 1983 and 1989 data on 1980 weights; 1993, 1995, and 1997 data on 1990 weights). Cost burden: Expenditures on housing and utilities are greater than 30 percent of reported income. Rental assistance: Renters are either in a public housing project or have a subsidy (i.e., pay a lower rent because a federal, state, or local government program pays part of the cost of construction, mortgage, or operating expenses). Severe problems: Cost burden is greater than 50 percent of income or severe physical problems among those not reporting housing assistance. Because of questionnaire changes, 1997 and 1999 data on assisted families, priority problems, and severe physical problems are not comparable to earlier data.

SOURCE: "Table ECON3. Housing Problems: Percentage of households with children under age 18 that report housing problems by type of problem, selected years 1978–99," in *Childstats*, U.S. Census Bureau, Washington, DC, 2001 [Online] http://www.childstats.gov/ac2001/econ3.asp [accessed January 17, 2003]

CHAPTER 6
CHANGING FAMILY PATTERNS

THE COMPOSITION OF THE FAMILY

The American family has evolved into an incredibly diverse one. The traditional married couple with children, while still the majority of families, has declined from 87 percent of families in 1970 to 51.7 percent in 2000. Only in Utah and Idaho did married couples account for more than 57 percent of families statewide. (See Figure 6.1.) Twenty-six percent of families are headed by single females, while single males head 5 percent of families. Single parents may be separated, divorced, widowed, or never married. Single women and men and same-sex partners now adopt children, a privilege once reserved only for married couples. More than two-thirds of single heads of families are divorced (33.9 percent) or never married (36.4 percent). Males are more often never married (40.7 percent) than women (35.2 percent). (See Table 2.3 in Chapter 2.)

More than 63 percent of single fathers have one child under age 18, compared to 54 percent of single mothers. Only 2.7 percent of single fathers have four or more children under 18, compared to 4.9 percent of single mothers. More than two-thirds of single fathers are white non-Hispanic, compared to less than half of single mothers. Black women account for 31.6 percent of single mothers, while only 16.4 percent of single fathers are black. A fairly equal proportion of single parents are Hispanic—15.3 percent of fathers and 16.1 percent of mothers. Single-mother households are twice as likely as single-father households to live in poverty (34 percent, compared to 15.9 percent). (See Table 6.1.)

While most Americans are delaying marriage, more teenagers were married between 1990 and 2000. The median age of first marriage rose from 26.8 for men and 25.1 for women during this period. Yet in 2000, 4.5 percent of teens aged 15 to 19 were married, compared to 3.4 percent in 1990. Some researchers suggest that this is a result of less premarital sex and more fear of sexually transmitted diseases. Others suggest that the change is the result of

children of immigrant families from countries where the teenage years are the expected time of marriage.

Multigenerational Families

While they represent a small segment of families, 3.9 million families, or 3.7 percent of all households in 2000, contained three or four generations. The most common grouping (65 percent) of multigenerational households included the householder and his or her children and grandchildren. Immigrant families were more likely to have more than three generations in the household. In some cases, this may be cultural, while in others it is because many immigrant families cannot afford separate housing accommodations.

Grandparents Raising Grandchildren

A growing trend in families is grandparents who have taken responsibility for raising grandchildren and sometimes great-grandchildren. In 17 states in 2000, more than 50 percent of grandparents who lived in the same household with their grandchildren were responsible for the grandchildren. In Wyoming, 58.6 percent of such coresident grandparents were raising their grandchildren. Massachusetts had the lowest rate (28.4 percent) of grandparents responsible for grandchildren. (See Table 6.2.)

GRANDPARENTS RAISING CHILDREN ARE YOUNGER AND HEALTHIER. Grandparents maintaining homes for their grandchildren tend to be younger, healthier, and more likely to work full- or part-time than those grandparents who share the home with grandchildren and one or both of their parents. Of coresident grandparents, only 22.7 percent of grandmothers and 27.5 percent of grandfathers were 65 or over; 16.6 percent of grandmothers and 13.3 percent of grandfathers were under age 45. Roughly two-thirds of both grandmothers and grandfathers were identified as in excellent to good health and one-third were in fair to poor health. Thirty-two percent of all

FIGURE 6.1

Percent married-couple households, 2000

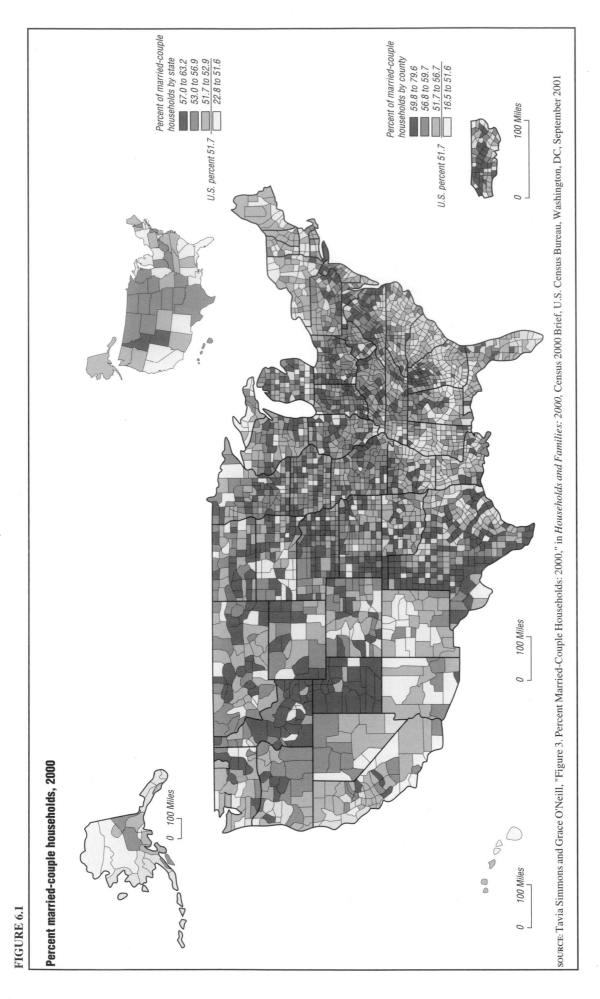

Percent of married-couple
households by state

- 57.0 to 63.2
- 53.0 to 56.9
- 51.7 to 52.9
- 22.8 to 51.6

U.S. percent 51.7

Percent of married-couple
households by county

- 59.8 to 79.6
- 56.8 to 59.7
- 51.7 to 56.7
- 16.5 to 51.6

U.S. percent 51.7

0   100 Miles

0   100 Miles

0   100 Miles

0   100 Miles

SOURCE: Tavia Simmons and Grace O'Neill, "Figure 3. Percent Married-Couple Households: 2000," in *Households and Families: 2000*, Census 2000 Brief, U.S. Census Bureau, Washington, DC, September 2001

TABLE 6.1

Single parents by sex and selected characteristics, March 2000

(In thousands)

Characteristic	Single fathers Total	White	Race and ethnicity White non-Hispanic	Black	Hispanic (of any race)	Single mothers Total	White	Race and ethnicity White non-Hispanic	Black	Hispanic (of any race)
All single parents	2,044	1,622	1,331	335	313	9,681	6,216	4,766	3,060	1,565
Type of family group										
Family household	1,786	1,429	1,202	280	246	7,571	4,869	3,815	2,409	1,145
Related subfamily	201	140	87	50	55	1,633	995	665	550	347
Unrelated subfamily	57	53	42	5	11	477	352	286	101	73
Presence of children										
With own children under 18	2,044	1,622	1,331	335	313	9,681	6,216	4,766	3,060	1,565
With own children under 12	1,441	1,145	900	225	260	7,337	4,558	3,459	2,484	1,190
With own children under 6	819	647	466	138	189	4,115	2,519	1,855	1,459	720
With own children under 3	511	393	269	95	129	2,319	1,396	1,027	846	409
With own children under 1	196	152	103	38	51	824	499	372	307	141
Number of own children under 18										
1 child	1,300	1,016	849	233	182	5,239	3,544	2,819	1,493	774
2 children	543	441	364	74	80	2,954	1,848	1,423	983	463
3 children	146	126	91	12	37	1,013	592	390	377	223
4 or more children	55	39	27	16	13	475	232	134	207	105
Marital status										
Never married	693	497	333	164	168	4,181	2,039	1,422	1,984	686
Married spouse absent[1]	350	236	184	84	61	1,716	1,146	782	474	386
Divorced	913	824	757	71	74	3,392	2,748	2,369	524	394
Widowed	88	65	56	17	10	391	283	193	79	99
Poverty status										
Below poverty level	326	225	135	84	99	3,305	1,817	1,190	1,344	678
At or above poverty level	1,718	1,397	1,196	251	214	6,376	4,399	3,576	1,716	887
Metropolitan residence										
Metropolitan	1,635	1,278	1,014	289	282	8,047	5,005	3,647	2,727	1,464
In central cities	631	421	282	169	146	3,790	1,906	1,115	1,727	865
Outside central cities	1,004	857	732	120	136	4,257	3,099	2,532	1,000	599
Nonmetropolitan	409	344	317	47	31	1,634	1,211	1,119	333	101

[1]Married spouse absent, includes separated.

Note: Data are not shown separately for the American Indian and Alaska Native population or the Asian and Pacific Islander population because of the small sample size in the Current Population Survey in March 2000.

SOURCE: Jason Fields and Lynne M. Casper, "Table 4. Single Parents by Sex and Selected Characteristics: March 2000," in *America's Families and Living Arrangements: March 2000*, Current Population Reports, U.S. Census Bureau, Washington, DC, June 2001

coresident grandmothers and 48.1 percent of grandfathers worked full-time all year. (See Table 6.3.)

Nearly half (46.9 percent) of coresident grandmothers are white non-Hispanic, and a little over one-fourth (27.8 percent) are black. Almost half (48.6 percent) are married. A small segment of coresident grandmothers (5.9 percent) have never been married. Twelve percent of coresident grandmother families live in poverty. (See Table 6.3.)

Denver's *Rocky Mountain News* focused on the challenges faced by grandparents raising their grandchildren in a November 9, 2002, feature, "Grandparents As Parents: The Second Time Around." In Colorado, 43 percent of grandparents living with grandchildren were actually raising the children. In census tract 9.02 on the south side of Pueblo, Colorado, reporter Burt Hubbard discovered a total of 140 grandparents living with grandchildren. One hundred percent of these grandparents are raising one or more grandchildren, some since birth. The reasons range from deceased parents, to parents in prison or addicted to drugs, to parents

who could not handle the responsibility of a child. The oldest grandparent interviewed was past 90 years of age and had raised her 10-year-old grandchild since birth.

These grandparents face financial challenges. Many are living on retirement income or Social Security; some have had to return to the workforce. Expecting to coddle and spoil their grandchildren, they find themselves instead in the role of disciplinarians. They also face the challenges of a changed school system and new cultural attitudes among the younger generation.

THE FAMILY'S FLIGHT TO THE SUBURBS

The economic prosperity following World War II enabled many American families to pursue what was perceived to be a better life in the wide-open spaces of the outlying, newly developing suburbs. The ties that bound the nuclear family, the extended family, and the ethnic neighborhood—all of which existed before the war— were loosened. With government aid, most notably

TABLE 6.2

Percent of grandparents living with own grandchildren who are responsible for their own grandchildren, 2000

National rank	Geographic area	Percent
1	Wyoming	58.6
2	Oklahoma	58.5
3	Arkansas	58.1
4	South Dakota	57.8
5	Mississippi	57.1
6	Alabama	55.9
7	Louisiana	54.9
8	North Dakota	54.8
9	Montana	54.5
10	West Virginia	52.4
11	New Mexico	52.2
12	Alaska	52.0
12	South Carolina	52.0
14	Kentucky	51.5
15	Tennessee	51.1
16	Kansas	50.7
17	Indiana	50.1
18	North Carolina	49.7
19	Missouri	48.7
20	District of Columbia	48.6
20	Nebraska	48.6
22	Georgia	47.6
23	Texas	46.7
24	Idaho	46.5
25	Ohio	46.4
25	Iowa	46.4
27	Arizona	45.4
28	Oregon	43.2
28	Delaware	43.2
30	Florida	42.7
31	Colorado	42.6
32	Virginia	42.5
33	Wisconsin	42.3
34	Michigan	42.0
35	Washington	41.8
36	Nevada	41.3
37	Maryland	40.6
38	Utah	40.4
39	Illinois	40.2
40	Pennsylvania	39.2
41	Minnesota	39.1
42	Maine	38.9
43	Vermont	36.3
44	New York	34.7
45	Connecticut	34.1
46	California	31.8
47	New Jersey	31.6
48	New Hampshire	30.9
49	Rhode Island	29.8
50	Hawaii	28.5
51	Massachusetts	28.4

N/A = Not Applicable or Not Yet Available

SOURCE: "Percent of Grandparents Living With Own Grandchildren Who Are Responsible for Their Own Grandchildren, 2000," Kids Count Census Data Online, The Annie E. Casey Foundation, Baltimore, MD, November 2002 [Online] http://www.aecf.org/cgi-bin/aeccensus.cgi?action=submit_rankvariable&ranktype=ALL_state&rankarea=&rankvariable=977 [accessed December 4, 2002]. The Annie E. Casey Foundation, www.aecf.org, 2002. Reproduced by permission.

Veterans' Administration (VA) mortgages, newlyweds and young couples with children bought homes in the suburbs. Leaving their parents and relatives, these young families soon became self-sufficient entities tending to their own needs. By 1960, suburban residents for the first time outnumbered those living in cities.

Additionally, in 1956, the federal government enacted the National Defense Highway Act, which provided for the construction of more than 40,000 miles of interstate highway. The expansion of the nation's highway system, coupled with low gas prices, also facilitated the suburbanization of America. By 1960, 75 percent of families in the United States owned a car, compared with about 50 percent in the late 1940s. Many businesses also left cities to move to the suburbs. It did not take long for shopping and entertainment centers to follow.

Decades of Decline

During the 1970s and 1980s, more middle-class and affluent families migrated to the suburbs. With the loss of many businesses and jobs to the suburbs, city dwellers began to see their quality of life diminish. Cities struggled with fewer jobs, poverty, high crime rates, and drug-related problems.

Migration to Suburbs Continues

According to the U.S. Department of Housing and Urban Development (HUD), in 1996 alone, 2.7 million people moved from cities to the suburbs, while only 800,000 people moved from the suburbs to cities. HUD Secretary Andrew Cuomo, in *The State of the Cities 1998* (Washington, D.C., 1998), noted that "the long-run trend is more stark—a 60 percent jump in the number of suburban families between 1970 and 1997 versus the modest 12 percent increase for cities over that period." In *The State of the Cities 2000* (Washington, D.C., 2000), Cuomo noted that "compared with the suburbs, city population growth was quite modest."

According to HUD, growth in metropolitan areas is continuing at a faster pace in suburbs than in central cities. The 2000 U.S. population of 281 million is projected to rise to 350 million by 2030, with 75 million being new immigrants, and many immigrants are already moving to the suburbs.

HOME OWNERSHIP

The national home ownership rate reached 66.8 percent in 1999 and rose even higher in the first quarter of 2000 to an all-time high of 67.1 percent. According to the U.S. Census Bureau and HUD, all racial and ethnic groups have shared in this trend. Minorities comprise 30 percent of first-time home buyers and 40 percent of the increase in home ownership.

AMERICANS HAVE BECOME MOBILE

America has a very mobile society. Between March 1999 and March 2000, 43.4 million Americans (16.1 percent) moved. Over half of these moves (56.2 percent) were within the same county, and another 20.3 percent were to another county within in the same state. Less than one-fifth (19.4

TABLE 6.3

Characteristics of grandparents who are coresident with grandchildren, 1997

(Numbers in thousands. Percent distribution of characteristics)

Characteristics	All coresident grandparent families	Grandparent-maintained families						Parent-maintained families				
		Total	Both grandparents, some parents	Both grandparents, no parent	Grandmother only, some parents	Grandmother only, no parent	Grandfather only	Total	Both grandparents	Grandmother only, two parents	Grandmother only, one parent	Grandfather only
Grandparents, total (number)	4,674	3,694	1,676	824	702	340	152	980	204	324	211	242
Grandmothers, total (number)	2,928	2,292	838	412	702	340	(X)	636	101	324	211	(X)
Percent distribution of grandmothers	100.0	100.0	100.0	100.0	100.0	100.0	(X)	100.0	100.0	100.0	100.0	(X)
Race and ethnicity												
White, non-Hispanic	46.9	48.0	56.7	62.8	38.6	27.9	(X)	42.8	40.7	51.0	31.2	(X)
Black, non-Hispanic	27.8	31.0	16.0	18.8	45.4	53.5	(X)	16.2	3.4	6.3	37.6	(X)
Hispanic	17.7	16.4	20.5	15.3	12.5	15.8	(X)	22.3	25.6	20.5	23.4	(X)
Other, non-Hispanic	7.6	4.5	6.8	3.2	3.5	2.8	(X)	18.7	30.2	22.2	7.8	(X)
Age												
Under 45	16.6	19.4	22.9	14.8	24.2	6.9	(X)	6.3	6.8	0.7	14.5	(X)
45 to 54	31.9	36.0	42.0	35.2	30.1	34.1	(X)	17.2	22.9	13.0	20.9	(X)
55 to 64	28.9	29.5	26.5	36.4	25.4	36.9	(X)	26.7	46.4	22.6	23.7	(X)
65 and older	22.7	15.1	8.6	13.6	20.3	22.2	(X)	49.8	23.9	63.7	40.9	(X)
Marital status												
Married, spouse present	48.6	56.1	100.0	100.0	4.8	0.9	(X)	21.4	97.8	5.6	9.1	(X)
Divorced, separated	23.5	22.9	(X)	(X)	50.4	50.3	(X)	25.8	0.0	24.1	40.8	(X)
Widowed	22.0	15.4	(X)	(X)	32.9	36.1	(X)	45.5	0.0	66.1	35.8	(X)
Never married	5.9	5.5	(X)	(X)	11.9	12.7	(X)	7.3	2.2	4.3	14.3	(X)
Education												
Not high school graduate	38.0	35.5	27.7	41.0	36.6	45.9	(X)	46.8	41.9	49.6	44.8	(X)
High school graduate	39.8	40.2	45.9	39.3	38.5	30.4	(X)	38.6	46.1	35.0	40.4	(X)
At least some college	22.2	24.3	26.4	19.7	25.0	23.7	(X)	14.6	12.0	15.3	14.8	(X)
Work experience in 1996												
Worked full-time, full-year	32.2	36.9	38.3	32.2	45.6	21.4	(X)	15.3	16.1	11.6	20.5	(X)
Less than full-time, full-year	17.2	19.6	22.5	21.5	16.3	16.8	(X)	8.6	18.6	3.9	11.1	(X)
Did not work	50.6	43.6	39.3	46.3	38.2	61.8	(X)	76.1	65.3	84.5	68.4	(X)
General state of health												
Excellent	12.4	13.3	14.9	11.6	14.3	9.1	(X)	9.2	11.0	6.5	12.4	(X)
Very Good	21.2	21.9	22.6	27.2	22.9	12.0	(X)	18.5	15.6	22.4	14.0	(X)
Good	31.4	31.2	36.0	32.4	26.4	27.9	(X)	32.1	41.1	33.8	25.1	(X)
Fair or Poor	35.1	33.6	26.5	28.9	36.4	51.0	(X)	40.3	32.3	37.4	48.5	(X)
Poverty status												
Poor	20.9	23.0	10.0	14.4	26.9	57.2	(X)	13.6	9.5	5.3	28.2	(X)
Not poor	79.1	77.0	90.0	85.6	73.1	42.8	(X)	86.4	90.5	94.7	71.8	(X)
Grandfathers, total (number)	1,746	1,402	838	412	(X)	(X)	152	344	103	(X)	(X)	242
Percent distribution of grandfathers	100.0	100.0	100.0	100.0	(X)	(X)	100.0	100.0	100.0	(X)	(X)	100.0
Race and ethnicity												
White, non-Hispanic	57.8	60.3	59.0	63.6	(X)	(X)	58.1	47.9	42.4	(X)	(X)	50.3
Black, non-Hispanic	15.6	18.3	16.2	19.5	(X)	(X)	26.0	4.8	3.4	(X)	(X)	5.4
Hispanic	19.7	17.3	19.2	14.6	(X)	(X)	14.1	29.7	24.2	(X)	(X)	32.1
Other, non-Hispanic	6.8	4.2	5.6	2.2	(X)	(X)	1.7	17.5	29.9	(X)	(X)	12.3
Age												
Under 45	13.3	14.9	16.9	11.0	(X)	(X)	13.8	7.2	11.7	(X)	(X)	5.2
45 to 54	28.3	32.0	38.4	23.7	(X)	(X)	19.3	13.2	12.4	(X)	(X)	13.6
55 to 64	30.8	32.6	29.9	38.8	(X)	(X)	31.0	23.6	34.3	(X)	(X)	19.0
65 and older	27.5	20.5	14.8	26.5	(X)	(X)	35.9	56.1	41.6	(X)	(X)	62.2
Marital status												
Married, spouse present	79.8	90.1	100.0	100.0	(X)	(X)	8.6	38.1	96.7	(X)	(X)	13.2
Divorced, separated	9.9	6.1	(X)	(X)	(X)	(X)	56.0	25.5	0.0	(X)	(X)	36.3
Widowed	9.1	3.2	(X)	(X)	(X)	(X)	29.0	33.4	0.0	(X)	(X)	47.5
Never married	1.2	0.7	(X)	(X)	(X)	(X)	6.4	3.0	3.3	(X)	(X)	2.9
Education												
Not high school graduate	39.9	37.1	35.3	40.6	(X)	(X)	37.7	51.2	36.4	(X)	(X)	57.5
High school graduate	36.8	37.1	37.6	36.1	(X)	(X)	36.6	35.6	41.7	(X)	(X)	33.1
At least some college	23.3	25.8	27.1	23.3	(X)	(X)	25.6	13.1	21.9	(X)	(X)	9.4

TABLE 6.3

Characteristics of grandchildren who are coresident with grandparents, 1997 [CONTINUED]

(Numbers in thousands. Percent distribution of characteristics)

Characteristics	All coresident grandparent families	Grandparent-maintained families						Parent-maintained families				
		Total	Both grandparents, some parents	Both grandparents, no parent	Grandmother only, some parents	Grandmother only, no parent	Grandfather only	Total	Both grandparents	Grandmother only, two parents	Grandmother only, one parent	Grandfather only
Household public assistance												
No public assistance	48.1	43.8	58.7	50.7	39.8	15.6	47.2	59.1	69.7	68.1	32.3	67.9
Any public assistance program	51.9	56.2	41.3	49.3	60.2	84.4	52.8	40.9	30.3	31.9	67.7	32.1
School lunch program	37.5	40.0	26.0	34.1	40.3	73.5	32.5	31.1	20.4	24.4	52.4	25.2
Food stamps	26.6	30.3	20.3	20.0	37.6	48.3	22.5	17.3	10.1	10.8	37.9	8.7
AFDC, ADC, TANF, GA	20.6	24.5	18.1	20.8	26.4	40.3	14.1	10.5	2.5	4.1	30.4	3.5
SSI	14.9	15.5	9.9	13.2	16.9	28.1	8.7	13.4	5.3	12.7	22.2	9.7
Housing assistance	7.4	8.5	2.0	3.6	7.5	26.3	9.4	4.5	0.0	3.6	11.2	0.9
Energy assistance	5.2	6.7	3.8	2.9	7.0	17.4	0.0	1.3	0.0	1.3	2.9	0.1

SOURCE: Ken Bryson and Lynne M. Casper, "Table 2. Characteristics of Grandchildren Who Are Coresident With Grandparents: 1997," in *Coresident Grandparents and Grandchildren,* Current Population Reports, U.S. Census Bureau, Washington, DC, May 1999

---

percent) of Americans moved to a different state, and 4.0 percent moved from outside the country. (See Figure 6.2.)

While the portion of the population that moves each year has remained relatively constant for the past decade, moves within the same county have declined and long-distance moves have increased. In 1998, 64 percent of moves were within the same county, compared to 56 percent in 2000. Fifteen percent of all movers went to another state in 1998, compared to 19 percent in 2000.

Who Moves?

People in the 20 to 29 age range are most likely to move. About one-third of this age group moved between March 1999 and March 2000, twice the moving rate of the total population, and they moved to other states at twice the rate of the overall population. Least likely to move are the 65 to 84 age group, with only a 4.3 percent moving rate.(See Figure 6.3.)

White non-Hispanic residents are the least mobile; 14.4 percent moved between 1999 and 2000, compared to 21 percent of Hispanics (of any race), 20.4 percent of Asians and Pacific Islanders, and 19.2 percent of blacks. People who rent move more than three times as often as people who own their homes. While one-fifth of people who never married (22.9 percent) and people who are separated or divorced (20.5 percent) move, only 12 percent of married people and 6.9 percent of widowed people moved. Moving rates decrease as household income increases; 21.1 percent of households with incomes under $25,000 moved, compared to 12.1 percent of households with incomes in excess of $100,000. (See Table 6.4.)

Interstate moves (along with births, deaths, and immigration) have contributed to the shifting distribution of the population. From 1999 to 2000, the primary population movement was out of the Northeast. However, a large number of people moved from the South to the Midwest and the West. (See Figure 6.4.)

Why People Move

Housing is the most common reason for moving (65.4 percent of local and 31.9 percent of long-distance moves). Family reasons account for about 25 percent of both local and long-distance moves. Only 5.6 percent of moves within a county were related to work, but 31.1 of long-distance moves were job related. (See Figure 6.5.) Of housing-related moves, 17.8 percent were for newer or better housing, while 11.5 percent were to purchase a home rather than renting.

Educational attainment has little bearing on intra-county moves but is a definite factor in longer distance moves. Work-related reasons are more likely to prompt intercounty moves by people with higher educational levels. More than 70 percent of moves to another county or state by people with less than a high school education were related to family or housing, compared to 42.0 percent of moves by graduates and people with professional degrees. (See Figure 6.6.)

Poor people are more likely to move for family-related reasons (30.8 percent), compared to those who are above the poverty level (25.2 percent); they are also less likely to move for work-related reasons (11.6 percent, compared to 17.3 percent). (See Figure 6.7.) One of the marked contrasts between the poor and the non-poor is that 13.2 percent of the nonpoor move in order to become home owners, compared to only 4.5 percent of poor people.

FIGURE 6.2

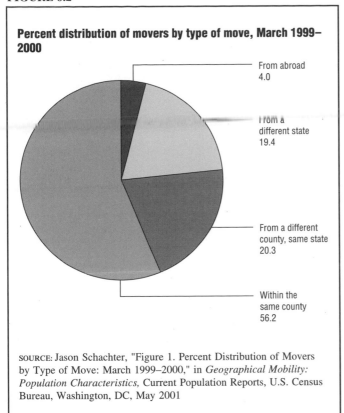

Percent distribution of movers by type of move, March 1999–2000

- From abroad 4.0
- From a different state 19.4
- From a different county, same state 20.3
- Within the same county 56.2

SOURCE: Jason Schachter, "Figure 1. Percent Distribution of Movers by Type of Move: March 1999–2000," in *Geographical Mobility: Population Characteristics,* Current Population Reports, U.S. Census Bureau, Washington, DC, May 2001

FIGURE 6.3

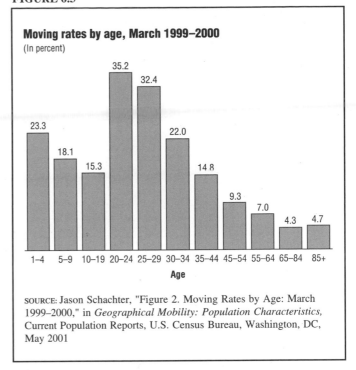

Moving rates by age, March 1999–2000
(In percent)

Age	Percent
1–4	23.3
5–9	18.1
10–19	15.3
20–24	35.2
25–29	32.4
30–34	22.0
35–44	14.8
45–54	9.3
55–64	7.0
65–84	4.3
85+	4.7

SOURCE: Jason Schachter, "Figure 2. Moving Rates by Age: March 1999–2000," in *Geographical Mobility: Population Characteristics,* Current Population Reports, U.S. Census Bureau, Washington, DC, May 2001

POVERTY

Poverty is a particular concern for the elderly and children. While an increasing share of residents in both cities and suburbs are getting older, a disproportionate number of the elderly poor live in cities. People over age 65 accounted for 10.1 percent of people in poverty in 2001, representing a slight increase from 2000. In 2030, the elderly population will reach 70 million, doubling the current number of elderly Americans and accounting for 20 percent of the overall U.S. population. Cities will continue to house disproportionate numbers of the nation's seniors who live below or near the poverty line.

Of persons in poverty in 2001, 9.9 percent were part of a family, and 19.9 percent lived with an unrelated individual. Children represented 16.3 percent of people in poverty in 2001. A little over 18 percent of families in poverty included children under age six. People in poverty are more likely to live inside central cities (16.5 percent) and in the South (13.5 percent). (See Table 6.5.)

Homelessness

In 2000, more than 170,000 homeless people were housed in emergency and transitional shelters. One-fourth of the population living in shelters were children under age 18. Just over three out of five shelter residents were male (61.4 percent, compared to 38.6 percent for females). Thirty percent of shelter residents were located

in the Northeast, and almost 28 percent were found in the West. Two states accounted for 35 percent of all shelter populations—California (31,856) and New York (27,701), with a majority of the homeless populations found in large cities. The next largest shelter population was in Texas, with only 7,608 shelter residents. (See Table 6.6.)

THE MULTIRACIAL SOCIETY

The Census Bureau in 2000 changed the way information on race was gathered. For the first time, individuals were allowed to identify themselves as of more than one race or of a race other than the standard choices—white, black or African American, American Indian and Alaska Native, Asian, Native Hawaiian, and Other Pacific Islander. While 97.6 percent of the population identified themselves with one race, 2.4 percent identified themselves with two or more races. (See Table 6.7.) Of people identifying with two or more races, 40 percent lived in the West; only 15 percent lived in the Midwest. (See Figure 6.8.) Nearly two-thirds of people reporting more than one race lived in just 10 states—California, New York, Texas, Florida, Hawaii, Illinois, New Jersey, Washington, Michigan, and Ohio. The trend in multiracial identification is most apparent among youth. Of persons reporting two or more races, 42 percent were under age 18. (See Figure 6.9.)

Interracial marriages have increased. In 1980, 651,000 couples, 1.3 percent of all married couples, were identified as interracial. In 1990, 1.8 percent of couples were interracial, and by 2000 interracial couples accounted for 2.6 percent of married couples. The most common interracial

TABLE 6.4

Geographical mobility by selected characteristics, March 1999–2000

(Numbers in thousands)

Selected characteristics	Total	Same residence (non-movers)	Total movers	Percent moved				
				Total	Within same county	From different county		From abroad
						Same state	Different state	
Total, age 1 and older	270,219	226,831	43,388	16.1	9.0	3.3	3.1	0.6
Age								
1 to 4 years	15,740	12,075	3,665	23.3	14.1	4.4	4.0	0.8
5 to 9 years	20,379	16,685	3,694	18.1	11.0	3.2	3.3	0.7
10 to 19 years	40,430	34,226	6,204	15.3	8.6	3.0	3.1	0.7
20 to 24 years	18,441	11,942	6,499	35.2	20.4	7.1	6.2	1.6
25 to 29 years	18,268	12,358	5,910	32.4	18.0	7.1	6.0	1.3
30 to 34 years	19,518	15,216	4,302	22.0	12.4	4.6	4.0	1.1
35 to 44 years	44,805	38,178	6,627	14.8	8.3	3.0	3.0	0.6
45 to 54 years	36,631	33,211	3,420	9.3	4.9	2.1	1.9	0.4
55 to 64 years	23,387	21,744	1,643	7.0	3.4	1.5	1.9	0.2
65 to 84 years	29,482	28,205	1,277	4.3	2.2	0.9	1.1	0.1
85 years and older	3,140	2,992	148	4.7	2.3	1.3	1.0	0.1
Sex								
Male	131,969	110,396	21,573	16.3	9.1	3.4	3.2	0.7
Female	138,250	116,435	21,815	15.8	8.9	3.2	3.1	0.6
Race and Hispanic origin								
White	221,703	187,810	33,893	15.3	8.5	3.2	3.0	0.6
Non-Hispanic	191,197	163,595	27,602	14.4	7.8	3.3	3.1	0.4
Black	34,948	28,226	6,722	19.2	11.7	3.5	3.6	0.5
Asian and Pacific Islander	10,779	8,577	2,202	20.4	10.5	3.4	3.6	3.0
Hispanic (of any race)	32,103	25,347	6,756	21.0	13.3	3.1	2.7	2.0
Nativity								
Native	241,867	204,777	37,090	15.3	8.8	3.2	3.1	0.2
Foreign born (naturalized and non U.S. citizen)	28,352	22,054	6,298	22.2	11.1	3.4	3.2	4.4
Poverty status (in 1999)								
Below poverty level	32,100	23,229	8,871	27.6	16.8	4.6	4.4	1.9
100 percent to 149 percent above poverty level	24,637	19,410	5,227	21.2	13.1	3.5	3.9	0.7
Above 149 percent of poverty level	213,482	184,192	29,290	13.7	7.4	3.0	2.8	0.5
Housing tenure								
Owner-occupied	189,408	172,258	17,150	9.1	5.0	2.1	1.7	0.3
Renter-occupied	80,811	54,573	26,238	32.5	18.6	5.9	6.4	1.6
Household type								
In married-couple family households	176,427	155,022	21,405	12.1	6.4	2.5	2.6	0.7
In other households	93,792	71,809	21,983	23.4	14.0	4.7	4.1	0.6
Household income (in 1999)								
Less than $25,000	63,680	50,228	13,452	21.1	12.9	3.6	3.6	1.1
$25,000 to $49,999	75,986	62,624	13,362	17.6	10.4	3.3	3.3	0.6
$50,000 to $99,999	89,674	78,031	11,643	13.0	6.7	3.1	2.8	0.4
$100,000 and over	40,879	35,948	4,931	12.1	5.6	3.0	2.8	0.7
Marital status (age 16 and older)								
Never married	56,182	43,316	12,866	22.9	12.9	4.9	4.2	1.0
Married	115,719	101,871	13,848	12.0	6.3	2.6	2.6	0.6
Divorced or separated	24,282	19,293	4,989	20.5	12.5	4.0	3.8	0.3
Widowed	13,662	12,718	944	6.9	3.8	1.5	1.5	0.2
Education (age 25 and older)								
Not a high school graduate	27,853	24,221	3,632	13.0	7.9	2.5	2.0	0.7
High school graduate	58,086	50,934	7,152	12.3	7.0	2.4	2.5	0.4
Some college or Associate degree	44,445	38,394	6,051	13.6	7.6	3.1	2.6	0.3
Bachelor's degree	29,840	25,259	4,581	15.4	7.4	3.6	3.5	0.8
Graduate degree	15,006	13,094	1,912	12.7	5.6	2.7	3.5	1.0

SOURCE: Jason Schachter, "Table B. Geographical Mobility by Selected Characteristics: March 1999–2000," in *Geographical Mobility: Population Characteristics*, Current Population Reports, U.S. Census Bureau, Washington, DC, May 2001

marriages (71.7 percent) were between a white person and a spouse who was neither white nor black. (See Table 6.8.)

ADOPTION IN AMERICA

Historically, adoption in the United States involved homeless, orphaned, abandoned, and older children. Dur-

ing the mid-1800s, adoption laws were enacted to regulate the adoption of children born out of wedlock. State laws further protected the privacy of unmarried mothers and their children, who were often stigmatized by society. The adoption of newborns did not occur until the early 1900s, when the introduction of infant formula gave pregnant

FIGURE 6.4

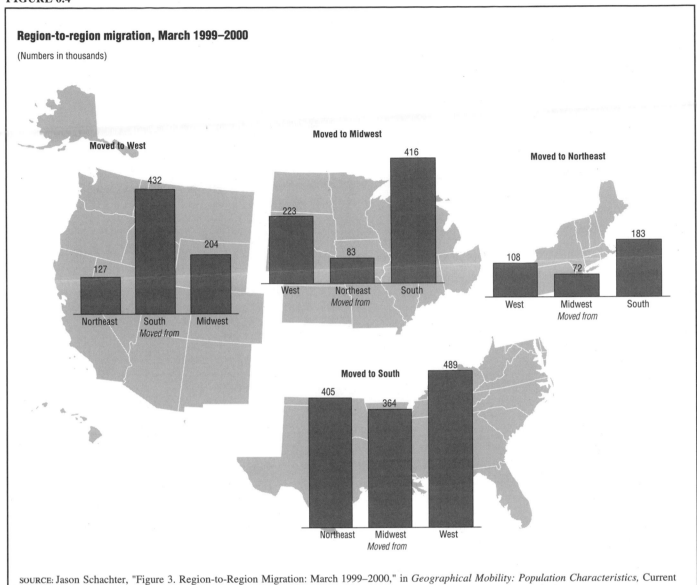

Region-to-region migration, March 1999–2000

(Numbers in thousands)

Moved to West
- Northeast: 127
- South: 432
- Midwest: 204
- *Moved from*

Moved to Midwest
- West: 223
- Northeast: 83
- South: 416
- *Moved from*

Moved to Northeast
- West: 108
- Midwest: 72
- South: 183
- *Moved from*

Moved to South
- Northeast: 405
- Midwest: 364
- West: 489
- *Moved from*

SOURCE: Jason Schachter, "Figure 3. Region-to-Region Migration: March 1999–2000," in *Geographical Mobility: Population Characteristics,* Current Population Reports, U.S. Census Bureau, Washington, DC, May 2001

women the option of giving up their babies for adoption immediately after birth.

After World War II (1939–45) and the Korean War (1950–53), the international adoption of "war orphans" provided an option for the parentless children who had survived. During the 1950s, America's child welfare system considered adoption as an alternative for "hard-to-place" children who had spent many years in foster care. These toddlers and older children are now known as children with "special needs." They are generally children with physical, mental, or emotional disabilities; minority children; and sibling groups.

Legal and Societal Changes Affect Adoption

In 1973, the historic U.S. Supreme Court decision *Roe v. Wade* (410 U.S. 113), which legalized abortion, gave women with unwanted pregnancies another legal option besides adoption. During the 1970s, unmarried fathers' legal rights were upheld by the High Court. *Stanley v. Illinois* (405 U.S. 645, 1972) required paternal notification, and *Caban v. Mohammed* (441 U.S. 380, 1979) required paternal consent in adoption cases, regardless of the fathers' responsibility before the adoption.

During the last few decades of the 20th century, the rise in nonmarital childbearing and divorce led to a reduction in the stigma attached to single motherhood. Consequently, many unwed mothers chose to raise their children instead of giving them up for adoption. Moreover, welfare benefits provided economic support for many single-parent families. These factors have contributed to a decline in the number of infants available for adoption.

FIGURE 6.5

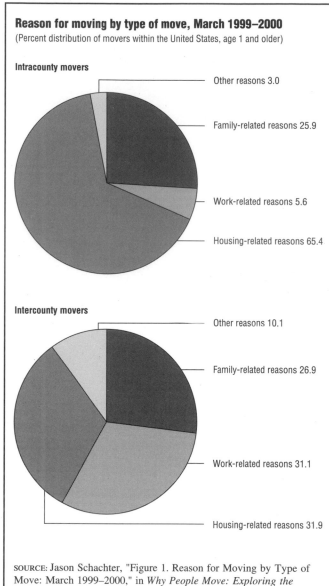

Reason for moving by type of move, March 1999–2000
(Percent distribution of movers within the United States, age 1 and older)

Intracounty movers

Other reasons 3.0

Family-related reasons 25.9

Work-related reasons 5.6

Housing-related reasons 65.4

Intercounty movers

Other reasons 10.1

Family-related reasons 26.9

Work-related reasons 31.1

Housing-related reasons 31.9

SOURCE: Jason Schachter, "Figure 1. Reason for Moving by Type of Move: March 1999–2000," in *Why People Move: Exploring the March 2000 Current Populations Survey,* Current Population Reports, U.S. Census Bureau, Washington, DC, May 2001

FIGURE 6.6

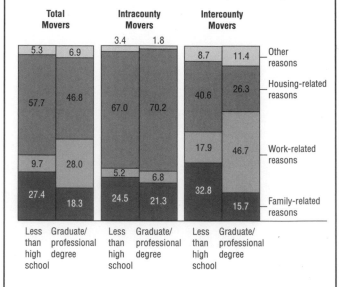

Reason for moving by educational status and type of move, March 1999–2000
(Percent distribution of movers within the United States, age 18 and older)

	Total Movers		Intracounty Movers		Intercounty Movers	
Other reasons	5.3	6.9	3.4	1.8	8.7	11.4
Housing-related reasons	57.7	46.8	67.0	70.2	40.6	26.3
Work-related reasons	9.7	28.0	5.2	6.8	17.9	46.7
Family-related reasons	27.4	18.3	24.5	21.3	32.8	15.7
	Less than high school	Graduate/ professional degree	Less than high school	Graduate/ professional degree	Less than high school	Graduate/ professional degree

SOURCE: Jason Schachter, "Figure 2. Reason for Moving by Educational Status and Type of Move: March 1999–2000," in *Why People Move: Exploring the March 2000 Current Populations Survey,* Current Population Reports, U.S. Census Bureau, Washington, DC, May 2001

FIGURE 6.7

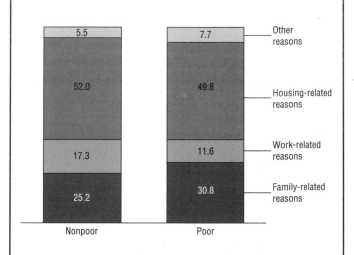

Reason for moving by poverty status, March 1999–2000
(Percent distribution of movers within the United States, age 1 and older)

	Nonpoor	Poor
Other reasons	5.5	7.7
Housing-related reasons	52.0	49.8
Work-related reasons	17.3	11.6
Family-related reasons	25.2	30.8

SOURCE: Jason Schachter, "Figure 3. Reason for Moving by Poverty Status: March 1999–2000," in *Why People Move: Exploring the March 2000 Current Populations Survey,* Current Population Reports, U.S. Census Bureau, Washington, DC, May 2001

Single-Parent Adoption

During the 1980s and 1990s, the fastest-growing trend in adoption was single-parent adoption. According to the National Adoption Center, about 25 percent of all "special needs" adoptions were by single people. An estimated 5 percent of all other adoptions were also by single men and women. Such adoptions have become more widely accepted. There is now less stigma attached to single-parent families, and the child welfare system and adoption agencies are more open to considering single people as potential adoptive parents. They now believe it better for a child to have a single parent than no family at all.

ISSUES AFFECTING GAYS AND LESBIANS

Gay and lesbian couples have gained recognition as couples in some states and family benefits from many major employers. In a November 7, 2002, edition of "All Things Considered" on National Public Radio, reporter Tovia Smith announced that Nevada had become the

TABLE 6.5

People and families in poverty by selected characteristics, 2000 and 2001

(Numbers in thousands)

Characteristic	2001 below poverty				2000 below poverty[1]				Difference (2001 minus 2000)[2]			
	Number	90-percent C.I. (±)	Percent	90-percent C.I. (±)	Number	90-percent C.I. (±)	Percent	90-percent C.I. (±)	Number	90-percent C.I. (±)	Percent	90-percent C.I. (±)
People												
Total	32,907	644	11.7	0.2	31,581	633	11.3	0.2	*1,325	669	*0.4	0.2
Family Status												
In families	23,215	551	9.9	0.2	22,347	542	9.6	0.2	*868	623	*0.3	0.3
Householder	6,813	172	9.2	0.2	6,400	165	8.7	0.2	*413	192	*0.5	0.3
Related children under 18	11,175	323	15.8	0.5	11,005	321	15.6	0.5	170	367	0.1	0.5
Related children under 6	4,188	207	18.2	1.0	4,066	204	17.8	0.9	121	235	0.4	1.1
In unrelated subfamilies	466	82	39.8	7.6	581	45	41.2	3.7	*-116	78	−1.4	7.2
Reference person	172	50	36.4	11.4	223	27	39.0	5.6	*-50	48	−2.7	10.8
Children under 18	292	57	44.6	9.8	348	62	43.7	8.8	−57	68	0.9	10.6
Unrelated individual	9,226	207	19.9	0.5	8,653	199	19.0	0.5	*573	213	*0.9	0.5
Male	3,833	122	17.3	0.6	3,426	115	15.7	0.6	*407	124	*1.6	0.6
Female	5,393	149	22.3	0.7	5,227	146	22.0	0.7	*165	155	0.3	0.7
Race[3] and Hispanic Origin												
White	22,739	546	9.9	0.2	21,645	534	9.5	0.2	*1,094	616	*0.4	0.3
Non-Hispanic	15,271	454	7.8	0.2	14,366	441	7.4	0.2	*905	511	*0.4	0.3
Black	8,136	300	22.7	0.8	7,982	297	22.5	0.8	154	313	0.1	0.9
Asian and Pacific Islander	1,275	129	10.2	1.0	1,258	129	9.9	1.0	17	135	0.3	1.1
Hispanic[4]	7,997	300	21.4	0.8	7,747	295	21.5	0.8	*250	249	−0.1	0.7
Age												
Under 18 years	11,733	329	16.3	0.5	11,587	328	16.2	0.5	146	344	0.1	0.5
18 to 64 years	17,760	483	10.1	0.3	16,671	469	9.6	0.3	*1,089	500	*0.5	0.3
65 years and over	3,414	129	10.1	0.4	3,323	127	9.9	0.4	91	134	0.2	0.4
Nativity												
Native	27,698	597	11.1	0.2	26,680	587	10.8	0.2	*1,018	621	*0.3	0.3
Foreign born	5,209	308	16.1	1.0	4,901	299	15.4	0.9	307	319	0.6	1.0
Naturalized citizen	1,186	148	9.9	1.2	1,060	140	9.0	1.2	126	151	0.9	1.3
Not a citizen	4,023	271	19.7	1.3	3,841	265	19.2	1.3	181	281	0.5	1.4
Region												
Northeast	5,687	266	10.7	0.5	5,474	261	10.3	0.5	212	277	0.4	0.5
Midwest	5,966	278	9.4	0.4	5,916	274	9.3	0.4	50	290	-	0.5
South	13,515	458	13.5	0.5	12,705	444	12.8	0.5	*810	473	*0.7	0.5
West	7,739	364	12.1	0.6	7,485	358	11.8	0.6	254	379	0.2	0.6
Residence												
Inside metropolitan areas	25,446	575	11.1	0.3	24,603	566	10.8	0.3	*843	598	*0.3	0.3
Inside central cities	13,394	427	16.5	0.5	13,257	425	16.3	0.5	137	447	0.2	0.6
Outside central cities	12,052	406	8.2	0.3	11,346	394	7.8	0.3	*706	420	*0.4	0.3
Outside metropolitan areas	7,460	394	14.2	0.8	6,978	382	13.4	0.7	*482	407	0.8	0.8
Families												
Total	6,813	172	9.2	0.2	6,400	165	8.7	0.2	*413	192	*0.5	0.3
White	4,579	135	7.4	0.2	4,333	131	7.1	0.2	*246	158	*0.4	0.3
Non-Hispanic	3,051	108	5.7	0.2	2,896	105	5.4	0.2	*155	125	*0.3	0.2
Black	1,829	81	20.7	1.0	1,686	78	19.3	0.9	*144	91	*1.4	1.1
Asian and Pacific Islander	234	28	7.8	1.0	233	28	7.8	1.0	-	32	-	1.1
Hispanic[4]	1,649	77	19.4	0.9	1,540	74	19.2	1.0	*109	72	0.2	0.9
Type of Family												
Married-couple	2,760	102	4.9	0.2	2,637	99	4.7	0.2	*124	115	*0.2	0.2
White	2,242	91	4.5	0.2	2,181	89	4.4	0.2	61	107	0.1	0.2
Non-Hispanic	1,477	73	3.3	0.2	1,435	72	3.2	0.2	42	85	0.1	0.2
Black	328	33	7.8	0.8	266	30	6.3	0.7	*62	36	*1.4	0.9
Asian and Pacific Islander	156	23	6.6	1.0	142	22	5.9	0.9	13	26	0.7	1.1
Hispanic[4]	799	53	13.8	0.9	772	52	14.2	1.0	26	50	−0.4	0.9
Female householder, no husband present	3,470	116	26.4	1.0	3,278	112	25.4	0.9	*191	130	1.0	1.1
White	1,939	84	22.4	1.1	1,820	81	21.2	1.0	*118	98	1.2	1.2
Non-Hispanic	1,305	68	19.0	1.1	1,226	66	17.8	1.0	*80	79	1.2	1.2
Black	1,351	69	35.2	2.0	1,300	68	34.3	2.0	51	78	0.9	2.3
Asian and Pacific Islander	61	14	14.6	3.6	81	16	22.2	5.0	*-20	18	*-7.6	5.1
Hispanic[4]	711	50	37.0	2.9	664	48	36.4	3.0	*47	46	0.6	2.8
Male householder, no wife present	583	45	13.1	1.1	485	41	11.3	1.0	*98	49	*1.8	1.2
White	398	37	11.7	1.1	332	34	10.1	1.1	*66	42	*1.6	1.3
Non-Hispanic	270	30	10.3	1.2	236	28	9.2	1.2	34	35	1.1	1.4
Black	150	23	19.4	3.1	120	20	16.3	3.0	*31	24	3.1	3.5
Asian and Pacific Islander	17	8	9.1	4.2	10	6	5.4	3.1	7	8	3.7	4.2
Hispanic[4]	139	22	17.0	2.9	104	19	13.6	2.6	*35	19	*3.5	2.6

-Represents zero. *Statistically significant at the 90-percent confidence level.
[1]Consistent with 2001 data through implementation of Census 2000-based population controls and a 28,000 household sample expansion.
[2]As a result of rounding, some differences may appear to be slightly higher or lower than the differences of the reported rates.
[3]Data for American Indians and Alaska Natives are not shown separately in this table because of the small sample of that population.
[4]Hispanics may be of any race.

SOURCE: Bernadette D. Proctor and Joseph Dalaker, "Table 1. People and Families in Poverty by Selected Characteristics: 2000 and 2001," in *Poverty in the United States: 2001,* Current Population Reports, U.S. Census Bureau, Washington, DC, September 2002

TABLE 6.6

Population in emergency and transitional shelters by sex and age, for region, states, and Puerto Rico, 2000

Area	Both sexes			Male			Female		
	All ages	Under 18 years	18 years and over	All ages	Under 18 years	18 years and over	All ages	Under 18 years	18 years and over
United States	170,706	43,887	126,819	104,879	22,465	82,414	65,827	21,422	44,405
Region									
Northeast	52,369	15,776	36,593	29,929	8,052	21,877	22,440	7,724	14,716
Midwest	28,438	7,086	21,352	17,836	3,673	14,163	10,602	3,413	7,189
South	42,471	9,848	32,623	27,437	5,034	22,403	15,034	4,814	10,220
West	47,428	11,177	36,251	29,677	5,706	23,971	17,751	5,471	12,280
State									
Alabama	1,177	258	919	811	121	690	366	137	229
Alaska	558	144	414	381	81	300	177	63	114
Arizona	2,312	641	1,671	1,659	402	1,257	653	239	414
Arkansas	754	233	521	521	128	393	233	105	128
California	27,701	6,841	20,860	16,573	3,431	13,142	11,128	3,410	7,718
Colorado	2,281	385	1,896	1,589	213	1,376	692	172	520
Connecticut	2,291	543	1,748	1,447	290	1,157	844	253	591
Delaware	847	219	628	497	114	383	350	105	245
District of Columbia	1,762	287	1,475	991	127	864	771	160	611
Florida	6,766	1,751	5,015	4,336	903	3,433	2,430	848	1,582
Georgia	4,774	886	3,888	3,145	415	2,730	1,629	471	1,158
Hawaii	747	246	501	431	138	293	316	108	208
Idaho	703	203	500	430	106	324	273	97	176
Illinois	6,378	1,464	4,914	4,023	775	3,248	2,355	689	1,666
Indiana	2,384	615	1,769	1,497	314	1,183	887	301	586
Iowa	1,013	314	699	646	155	491	367	159	208
Kansas	587	185	402	377	100	277	210	85	125
Kentucky	1,626	326	1,300	1,098	167	931	528	159	369
Louisiana	1,986	437	1,549	1,251	209	1,042	735	228	507
Maine	458	91	367	295	47	248	163	44	119
Maryland	2,545	608	1,937	1,552	297	1,255	993	311	682
Massachusetts	5,405	1,169	4,236	3,581	632	2,949	1,824	537	1,287
Michigan	4,745	1,140	3,605	2,920	578	2,342	1,825	562	1,263
Minnesota	2,738	790	1,948	1,678	414	1,264	1,060	376	684
Mississippi	572	202	370	328	89	239	244	113	131
Missouri	2,164	569	1,595	1,319	293	1,026	845	276	569
Montana	477	109	368	313	53	260	164	56	108
Nebraska	913	281	632	518	142	376	395	139	256
Nevada	1,553	188	1,365	1,158	99	1,059	395	89	306
New Hampshire	523	120	403	308	56	252	215	64	151
New Jersey	5,500	1,494	4,006	3,198	776	2,422	2,302	718	1,584
New Mexico	934	181	753	633	98	535	301	83	218
New York	31,856	10,465	21,391	17,268	5,267	12,001	14,588	5,198	9,390
North Carolina	3,579	643	2,936	2,466	337	2,129	1,113	306	807
North Dakota	178	15	163	143	8	135	35	7	28
Ohio	5,224	1,096	4,128	3,406	575	2,831	1,818	521	1,297
Oklahoma	1,478	396	1,082	974	211	763	504	185	319
Oregon	3,011	467	2,544	2,128	243	1,885	883	224	659
Pennsylvania	5,463	1,732	3,731	3,250	899	2,351	2,213	833	1,380
Rhode Island	634	122	512	417	65	352	217	57	160
South Carolina	1,528	329	1,199	1,082	177	905	446	152	294
South Dakota	414	203	211	240	111	129	174	92	82
Tennessee	2,252	592	1,660	1 536	354	1,182	716	238	478
Texas	7,608	1,778	5,830	4,927	918	4,009	2,681	860	1,821
Utah	1,494	298	1,196	1,034	126	908	460	172	288
Vermont	239	40	199	165	20	145	74	20	54
Virginia	2,692	757	1,935	1,582	376	1,206	1,110	381	729
Washington	5,387	1,401	3,986	3,203	680	2,523	2,184	721	1,463
West Virginia	525	146	379	340	91	249	185	55	130
Wisconsin	1,700	414	1,286	1,069	208	861	631	206	425
Wyoming	270	73	197	145	36	109	125	37	88
Puerto Rico	586	209	377	319	116	203	267	93	174

SOURCE: Annette C. Smith and Denise I. Smith, "Table 2. Population in Emergency and Transitional Shelters by Sex and Age for the United States, Regions, States, and Puerto Rico: 2000," in *Emergency and Transitional Shelter Population: 2000,* Census 2000 Special Reports, U.S. Census Bureau, Washington, DC, October 2001

TABLE 6.7

Total population by number of races reported, 2000

Number of races	Number	Percent of total population	Percent of total Two or more races population
Total population	281,421,906	100.0	(X)
One race	274,595,678	97.6	(X)
Two or more races	6,826,228	2.4	100.0
Two races	6,368,075	2.3	93.3
Three races	410,285	0.1	6.0
Four races	38,408	–	0.6
Five races	8,637	–	0.1
Six races	823	–	–

– Percentage rounds to 0.0.
X Not applicable.
SOURCE: Nicholas A. Jones and Amy Symens Smith, "Table 1. Total Population by Number of Races Reported: 2000," in *The Two Or More Races Population: 2000,* Census 2000 Brief, U.S. Census Bureau, Washington, DC, November 2001

FIGURE 6.8

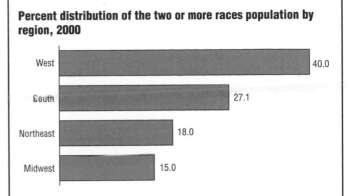

Percent distribution of the two or more races population by region, 2000

West	40.0
South	27.1
Northeast	18.0
Midwest	15.0

SOURCE: Nicholas A. Jones and Amy Symens Smith, "Figure 2. Percent Distribution of the Two or More Races Population by Region: 2000," in *The Two Or More Races Population: 2000,* Census 2000 Brief, U.S. Census Bureau, Washington, DC, November 2001

FIGURE 6.9

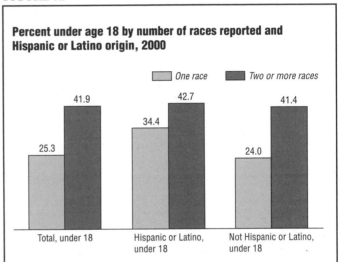

Percent under age 18 by number of races reported and Hispanic or Latino origin, 2000

☐ One race ■ Two or more races

	One race	Two or more races
Total, under 18	25.3	41.9
Hispanic or Latino, under 18	34.4	42.7
Not Hispanic or Latino, under 18	24.0	41.4

SOURCE: Nicholas A. Jones and Amy Symens Smith, "Figure 6. Percent Under Age 18 by Number of Races Reported and Hispanic or Latino Origin: 2000," in *The Two Or More Races Population: 2000,* Census 2000 Brief, U.S. Census Bureau, Washington, DC, November 2001

36th state to ban gay marriages. Vermont is the only state to sanction "civil unions" between homosexual partners. Like heterosexual couples, gay and lesbian couples sometimes go their separate ways. But, they have no divorce. Vermont grants divorces to same-sex couples but only those who reside in the state. One problem for same-sex partners is that unless they have made private contractual arrangements specifying how property will be divided in the event of separation or death, one partner can be left out in the cold after years of contributing to family finances or staying at home to raise children.

Marriage

The issue of same-sex marriage continues to be hotly debated as more gay couples demand legal recognition of their unions. In 2000, Vermont became the first state to officially sanction same-sex marriages. In other states, gay and lesbian couples continue to go to court for the right to get married.

Dependent Benefits for Domestic Partners

Many local governments have begun to provide benefits to domestic partners of gay and lesbian employees. In 1997, in the first state law of its kind, the Hawaii legislature gave gays and lesbians the right to participate in their partners' medical insurance and state pensions. Lesbian and gay couples were also granted inheritance rights, joint property ownership rights, and the right to sue for wrongful death.

Many private companies have extended to their employees' same-sex partners and live-in heterosexual partners the same dependent benefits provided to legal spouses. In the "2001 Benefits Survey" conducted by the Society for Human Resource Management, 25 percent of respondents offered domestic-partner benefits to opposite-sex partners and 16 percent offered these benefits to same-sex partners. This represented a significant increase from 10 percent of respondents who offered these benefits in 2000.

In August 2000, the big three Detroit automakers—Ford, General Motors, and DaimlerChrysler—added full health-care benefits for the domestic partners of their 500,000 U.S. employees. Gannett, the largest newspaper publisher in the country (98 U.S. papers plus 22 television stations), introduced domestic-partner benefits beginning January 1, 2002. In September 2002, Purdue University announced that it would become the seventh Big Ten school to offer benefits to same-sex domestic partners of university employees. Several employers noted that this benefit change would enhance efforts to recruit new employees in a tight labor market.

Most options for domestic-partner benefits require that the relationship has been established for some period

TABLE 6.8

Interracial married couples, 1980–2000

(Numbers in thousands. Includes all interracial married couples with at least one spouse of White or Black race.)

| | | Interracial married couples | | | | | |
| | | | Black/White | | | | |
Year	Total married couples	Total	Total	Black husband White wife	White husband Black wife	White/ Other race*	Black/ Other race*
2000	56,497	1,464	363	268	95	1,051	50
1999	55,849	1,481	364	240	124	1,086	31
1998	55,305	1,348	330	210	120	975	43
1997	54,666	1,264	311	201	110	896	57
1996	54,664	1,260	337	220	117	884	39
1995	54,937	1,392	328	206	122	988	76
1994	54,251	1,283	296	196	100	909	78
1993	54,199	1,195	242	182	60	920	33
1992	53,512	1,161	246	163	83	883	32
1991	53,227	994	231	156	75	720	43
1990	53,256	964	211	150	61	720	33
1989	52,924	953	219	155	64	703	31
1988	52,613	956	218	149	69	703	35
1987	52,286	799	177	121	56	581	41
1986	51,704	827	181	136	45	613	33
1985	51,114	792	164	117	47	599	29
1984	50,864	762	175	111	64	564	23
1983	50,665	719	164	118	46	522	33
1982	50,294	697	155	108	47	515	27
1981	49,896	639	132	104	28	484	23
1980	49,714	651	167	122	45	450	34

* "Other race" is any race other than White or Black, such as American Indian, Japanese, Chinese, etc.

SOURCE: "Interracial Married Couples: 1980 to Present," *Current Population Reports,* U.S. Census Bureau, Washington, DC, February 2002 [Online] http://www.census.gov/population/socdemo/hh-fam/tabMS-3.txt [accessed December 4, 2002]

of time, usually 6 or 12 months. The employee may be required to file a domestic-partner affidavit certifying that the relationship meets the rules established by the employer. The same type of certification is required of opposite-sex partners as a substitute for the legal marriage certificate required for married employees to establish their spouses' eligibility for benefits.

The plight of domestic partners made headlines after September 11, 2001, as domestic partners of individuals who died in the terrorist attacks found themselves ineligible for survivor benefits from Social Security, workers' compensation, and potentially from victims compensation funds. If the deceased left no will, the partner had no legal claim to the estate. Since September 11, 2001, the Red Cross, the United Way, and several other relief agencies have taken steps to assure that gay and lesbian partners are treated equally. New York governor George Pataki issued an Executive Order on October 11, 2001, granting same-sex partners the same benefits as spouses from the New York State Crime Victims Board.

In June 2002, President George W. Bush signed a bill making domestic partners eligible for death benefits paid to survivors of firefighters and police officers who die in the line of duty. Retroactive to September 11, 2001, the new law allows a $250,000 federal benefit paid to any beneficiary listed on the victim's life insurance policy, previously restricted to spouses, children, and parents.

The new law is named for the Reverend Mychal Judge, the New York Fire Department's chaplain who died in the collapse of the World Trade Center. The law marks the first extension of federal benefits to domestic partners.

With this crack in the door to federal benefits, Senator Mark Dayton (Democrat, Minnesota) introduced legislation to extend health, retirement, and life insurance benefits to same-sex partners of federal employees.

Adoption

The National Adoption Information Clearinghouse (NAIC) reports that gays and lesbians have always adopted children but that the number of adoptive parents is unknown. The last several years of the 1990s saw more gay and lesbian individuals and/or couples raising children, and many more interested in adoption.

THE LAW AND ADOPTION BY GAYS AND LESBIANS. Ten states (California, Massachusetts, New Jersey, New Hampshire, New Mexico, New York, Ohio, Vermont, Washington, and Wisconsin) and the District of Columbia have allowed openly gay and lesbian individuals or couples to adopt. Although some joint adoptions have been successful, the most common practice is for a single person to apply as the legal adoptive parent of the child.

Some jurisdictions now allow second-parent adoption. In second-parent adoption, a child's nonbiological parent is permitted to adopt the child without severing the rights of the biological parent. According to the National Adoption Information Clearinghouse, as of 2000, Alaska, California, Colorado, Connecticut, the District of Columbia, Illinois, Indiana, Iowa, Maryland, Massachusetts, Minnesota, Michigan, Nevada, New Jersey, New York, Ohio, Oregon, Pennsylvania, Rhode Island, Texas, Vermont, and Washington allowed second-parent adoptions for same-sex couples.

In 2000, Florida and Utah were joined by Mississippi as the only states banning lesbians and gays from adopting children. Other states maintain strict regulations for adoptive parents. For instance, North Dakota considers only married couples as prospective adopters of foster children, while Massachusetts requires adoption applicants to reveal their sexual orientation. Each state decides its own adoption rules, with the courts ruling on the legality of those rules.

CHAPTER 7

PUBLIC OPINION ON THE FAMILY

Families provide a loving environment where children can flourish; and they help ensure that cultural traditions and timeless values are passed on to future generations.... Strong families play a critical role in developing the character of our Nation. They teach children important standards of conduct such as accepting responsibility, respecting others, and distinguishing the difference between right and wrong. By helping America's youth to grow into mature, thoughtful, and caring citizens, families help make our communities and our Nation safer and more civilized.

— President George W. Bush, Proclamation of National Family Week 2002

STATUS OF THE FAMILY

"The vast majority of Americans believe that preservation of the family is critical to the future survival of the United States," according to a 2000 survey by Wirthlin Worldwide. (See Figure 7.1.) However, when asked to characterize the state of the American family, just 7 percent said it is "very strong and growing." Nearly one-third (32 percent) said the family is "weak and losing ground." While sounding pessimistic, the survey shows an improved perception of the strength of the family compared to a 1995 survey in which 44 percent categorized the family as "weak." (See Figure 7.2.)

When asked to identify the causes of the decline of the family, two of the most frequent responses focused on parents' failure to teach their children discipline and respect (12 percent) and moral values (11 percent). The greater work demands on parents also ranked as one of the most frequent responses (11 percent). Other factors cited include divorce (9 percent), economic and financial pressures (8 percent), decline in religious faith and church attendance (7 percent), mothers working outside the home (6 percent), and the availability of drugs (6 percent). (See Figure 7.3.) According to Wirthlin Worldwide, survey respondents in recent years have named "a decline in moral values" as the most important problem facing the nation.

FIGURE 7.1

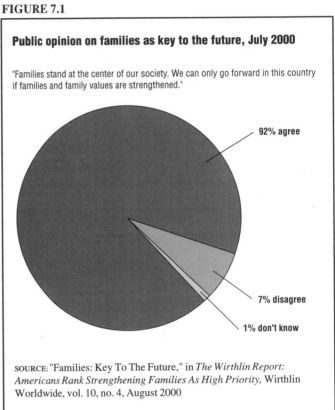

Public opinion on families as key to the future, July 2000

"Families stand at the center of our society. We can only go forward in this country if families and family values are strengthened."

92% agree

7% disagree

1% don't know

SOURCE: "Families: Key To The Future," in *The Wirthlin Report: Americans Rank Strengthening Families As High Priority*, Wirthlin Worldwide, vol. 10, no. 4, August 2000

Strengthening the Family a Priority

Americans surveyed about priorities for political leaders named "strengthening the family" as twice as important as job opportunities and three times as important as the environment. (See Figure 7.4.) Hispanic and African American respondents, who traditionally have strong extended families, placed more importance on political leaders working to increase job opportunities than strengthening the family. (See Table 7.1.) Concern about jobs was also a stronger focus for respondents living in the northeastern United States (45 percent) than in other areas of the country.

FIGURE 7.2

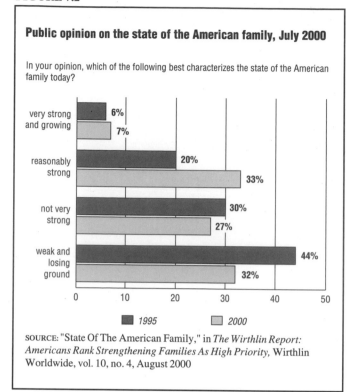

Public opinion on the state of the American family, July 2000

In your opinion, which of the following best characterizes the state of the American family today?

SOURCE: "State Of The American Family," in *The Wirthlin Report: Americans Rank Strengthening Families As High Priority,* Wirthlin Worldwide, vol. 10, no. 4, August 2000

TABLE 7.1

Public opinion on issue priority, July 2000

Which is more important...?	TOT	White	Black	Hispanic	Other
Strengthening families	64%	70%	46%	30%	68%
Increasing job opportunities	35%	29%	53%	70%	31%
Strengthening families	77%	76%	90%	64%	79%
Creating a cleaner environment	22%	23%	10%	36%	18%

SOURCE: "Issue Priority Varies Among Ethnic Groups," in *The Wirthlin Report: Americans Rank Strengthening Families As High Priority,* Wirthlin Worldwide, vol. 10, no. 4, August 2000

Among possible initiatives to strengthen the family, support for voluntary action by businesses led the way. A strong majority (87 percent) of persons surveyed believe business can strengthen marriages and parental attention to families by providing flexible work schedules. Recognizing the power of the media on young people's attitudes, respondents gave strong support (80 percent) to commending the media when efforts are made to portray positive influences of marriage. More than three-fourths (78 percent) of respondents supported legislation requiring counseling for couples with children before a divorce could be granted. (See Figure 7.5.)

TEACHING CHILDREN MORAL VALUES

Questions about family values generally include issues concerning the current diversity of family structures. In 1998, Lou Harris and Associates prepared a survey on family values for the Families and Work Institute and the Whirlpool Foundation. They asked women, "Do you think that society should value only certain types of families, like those with two parents, or should society value all types of families?" More than 9 of 10 respondents (93 percent) thought that society should value all types of families. Only 5 percent indicated that society should value certain types of families, such as those with two parents.

In the same survey 52 percent of women and 42 percent of men thought family values meant "loving, taking care of, and supporting each other." The term *family values* was

described as "knowing right from wrong and having good values" by 38 percent of women and 35 percent of men. Only 2 percent of women and 1 percent of men defined family values in terms of the traditional nuclear family.

By the year 2003, families had indeed become diverse. In addition to the shrinking number of nuclear families, there are blended families that combine children from past marriages with offspring of the current marriage, cohabiting couples with children, multigenerational families, families headed by gay or lesbian couples, single-parent families, and various combinations of related and unrelated individuals who consider themselves a family.

The Influence of Television

The Statistical Abstract of the United States: 2001 (U.S. Census Bureau, 121st Edition, Washington, D.C., 2001) reports that more American households have at least one television set (98 percent) than have telephones (94 percent). Many homes have multiple sets, and cable access brings a vast array of program options into American homes. Parents have become increasingly concerned about the influence of television on children's attitudes and behavior.

According to a survey by the National Parent Teacher Association, parents of small children (3- to 7-year-olds) are most worried about their children's exposure to sexual content and profanity on television. Parents of boys have almost equal fears about the effects of violence, while parents of girls are even more concerned about programs with frightening content. (See Figure 7.6.) Parental concerns diminish with the 8 to 12 age group, although worries about sexual content remain. (See Figure 7.7.) For 13- to 18-year-olds, however, parents express greater distress about TV's influence on girls. Sexual content remains the top concern with both boys and girls, but parental anxiety about programs that promote risk-taking behaviors rises dramatically. (See Figure 7.8.)

Concerned parents want to be warned in advance about program content. And they want enough information so they can decide which shows are appropriate for

FIGURE 7.3

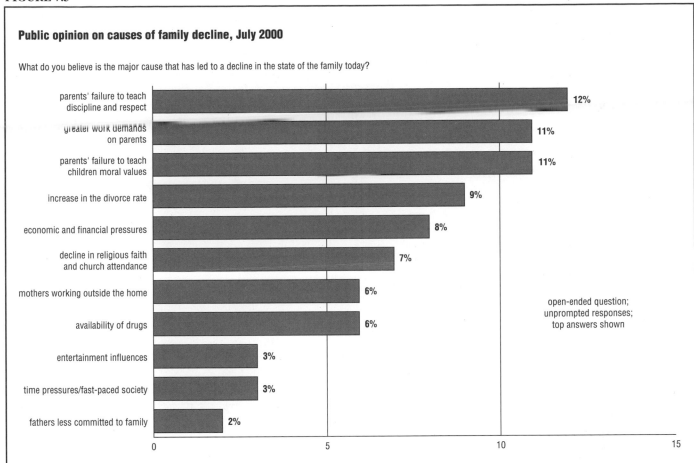

Public opinion on causes of family decline, July 2000

What do you believe is the major cause that has led to a decline in the state of the family today?

parents' failure to teach discipline and respect	12%
greater work demands on parents	11%
parents' failure to teach children moral values	11%
increase in the divorce rate	9%
economic and financial pressures	8%
decline in religious faith and church attendance	7%
mothers working outside the home	6%
availability of drugs	6%
entertainment influences	3%
time pressures/fast-paced society	3%
fathers less committed to family	2%

open-ended question; unprompted responses; top answers shown

SOURCE: "Causes of Family Decline," in *The Wirthlin Report: Americans Rank Strengthening Families As High Priority,* Wirthlin Worldwide, vol. 10, no. 4, August 2000

their children. Both the television and movie industries, as well as publications offering programming schedules, have developed ratings guides. In the PTA survey, more than 65 percent of parents preferred guidelines like those developed in 1996 by the cable networks over those developed by the Movie Producers Association of America (MPAA) and guidelines based only on age. (See Figure 7.9.) The MPAA ratings use four broad categories: G—General Audiences; PG—Parental Guidance Suggested; PG-13—Parents Strongly Cautioned; and R—Restricted. Descriptions of these categories are broad, and even the General Audience rating carries a disclaimer that "some material may be unsuitable for children."

The cable networks' TV Parental Guidelines include seven categories, with three specific to programs designed for children.

• TV–Y All Children. Whether animated or live action, the themes and elements in this program are specifically designed for a very young audience, including children from ages two to six. This program is not expected to frighten younger children.

FIGURE 7.4

Public opinion on importance of strengthening family, July 2000

Which is more important...?

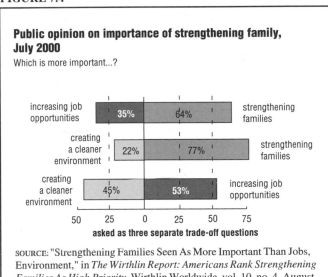

increasing job opportunities	35% / 64%	strengthening families
creating a cleaner environment	22% / 77%	strengthening families
creating a cleaner environment	45% / 53%	increasing job opportunities

asked as three separate trade-off questions

SOURCE: "Strengthening Families Seen As More Important Than Jobs, Environment," in *The Wirthlin Report: Americans Rank Strengthening Families As High Priority,* Wirthlin Worldwide, vol. 10, no. 4, August 2000

FIGURE 7.5

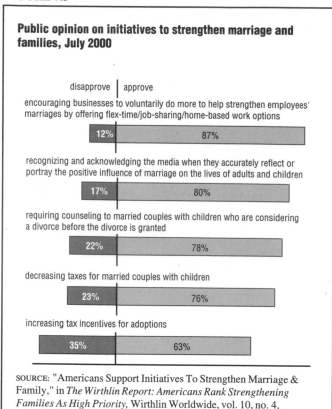

Public opinion on initiatives to strengthen marriage and families, July 2000

SOURCE: "Americans Support Initiatives To Strengthen Marriage & Family," in *The Wirthlin Report: Americans Rank Strengthening Families As High Priority,* Wirthlin Worldwide, vol. 10, no. 4, August 2000

FIGURE 7.6

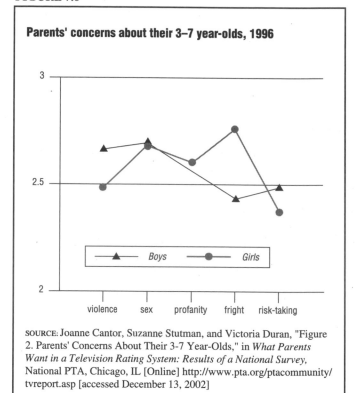

Parents' concerns about their 3–7 year-olds, 1996

SOURCE: Joanne Cantor, Suzanne Stutman, and Victoria Duran, "Figure 2. Parents' Concerns About Their 3-7 Year-Olds," in *What Parents Want in a Television Rating System: Results of a National Survey,* National PTA, Chicago, IL [Online] http://www.pta.org/ptacommunity/tvreport.asp [accessed December 13, 2002]

FIGURE 7.7

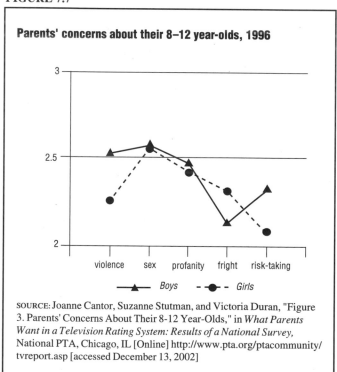

Parents' concerns about their 8–12 year-olds, 1996

SOURCE: Joanne Cantor, Suzanne Stutman, and Victoria Duran, "Figure 3. Parents' Concerns About Their 8-12 Year-Olds," in *What Parents Want in a Television Rating System: Results of a National Survey,* National PTA, Chicago, IL [Online] http://www.pta.org/ptacommunity/tvreport.asp [accessed December 13, 2002]

FIGURE 7.8

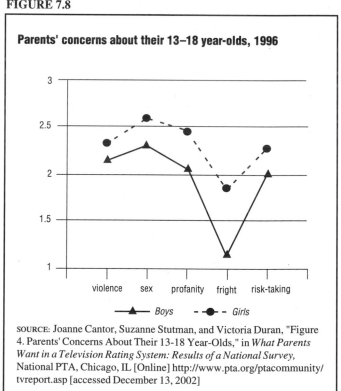

Parents' concerns about their 13–18 year-olds, 1996

SOURCE: Joanne Cantor, Suzanne Stutman, and Victoria Duran, "Figure 4. Parents' Concerns About Their 13-18 Year-Olds," in *What Parents Want in a Television Rating System: Results of a National Survey,* National PTA, Chicago, IL [Online] http://www.pta.org/ptacommunity/tvreport.asp [accessed December 13, 2002]

• TV–Y7 Directed to Older Children. This program is designed for children aged seven and above. It may be more appropriate for children who have acquired the developmental skills needed to distinguish between make-believe and reality. Themes and elements in this program may include mild fantasy or comedic violence, or may frighten children under the age of seven. Therefore, parents may wish to consider the suitability of this program for their very young children.

- TV–Y7–FV Programs where fantasy violence may be more intense or more combative than other programs in the TV–Y7 category.

- TV–G General Audiences. Although this rating does not signify a program designed specifically for children, most parents may let younger children watch this program unattended. It contains little or no violence, no strong language, and little or no sexual dialogue or situations.

- TV–PG Parental Guidance Suggested. This program contains material that parents may find unsuitable for younger children, including one or more of the following: moderate violence (V), some sexual situations (S), infrequent coarse language (L), or some suggestive dialogue (D).

- TV–14 Parents Strongly Cautioned. This program contains some material that parents would find unsuitable for children under 14 years of age, including one or more of the following: intense violence (V), intense sexual situations (S), strong coarse language (L), or intensely suggestive dialogue (D).

- TV–MA Mature Audience Only. This program is specifically designed to be viewed by adults and therefore may be unsuitable for children under 17. It contains one or more of the following: graphic violence (V), explicit sexual activity (S), or crude indecent language (L).

A further aid to parents is the V-chip, which allows parents to block programs they do not want their children to watch. Broadcast and cable networks encode the ratings information into their television signals to be "read" by V-chip-equipped television sets that parents have programmed. As of January 1, 2000, all television sets manufactured with screens larger than 13 inches contain V-chip technology.

Parents of Teenagers

Parents of teenagers have many worries. Prominent among them is concern about teenagers driving cars and riding in cars with teenage friends. According to the National Transportation Safety Board (NTSB), traffic accidents are the leading cause of death for 15- to 20-year-olds. In 1994, youth highway safety was placed on the NTSB's "Most Wanted List" of safety improvements, and it has remained on the list ever since. The NTSB recently requested that all states adopt new restrictions limiting to one the number of passengers under age 20 who may ride with a novice driver unless accompanied by a supervising adult driver. In the November 2002 press

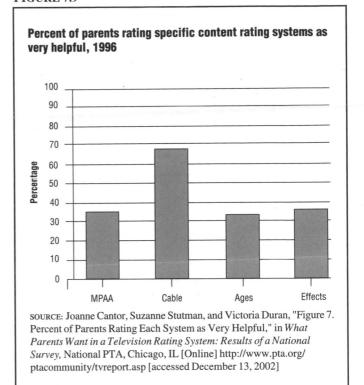

FIGURE 7.9

Percent of parents rating specific content rating systems as very helpful, 1996

SOURCE: Joanne Cantor, Suzanne Stutman, and Victoria Duran, "Figure 7. Percent of Parents Rating Each System as Very Helpful," in *What Parents Want in a Television Rating System: Results of a National Survey,* National PTA, Chicago, IL [Online] http://www.pta.org/ptacommunity/tvreport.asp [accessed December 13, 2002]

release announcing this request, the NTSB reports that in 2000, 6.8 percent of the driving population was 20 years old or less, yet they were involved in 14 percent of fatal crashes. Single-vehicle crashes involving teenagers accounted for 67 percent of fatally injured passengers between the ages of 15 and 19.

WORK DEMANDS ON PARENTS

Parents Find Little Time to Relax

Stress has become a common part of everyday life in America. According to an October 2002 CNN/*USA Today*/Gallup poll, 40 percent of Americans report they have limited time to relax. One out of 10 say they "never have time to relax." Those with the least time to relax are all parents. The most stressed group are working mothers, 65 percent of whom report having little time for relaxation. On the other end of the scale, the people with the most time available for relaxation are aged 65 and above.

Employers Can Assist Working Parents

Parents, and particularly working mothers, look to employers to offer family-friendly benefits such as flexible work schedules and time off for certain family needs. Many employers today have implemented creative options to assist working parents. Consolidated annual leave plans no longer categorize available paid time off into vacation, personal, and sick time. This gives employees discretion about how best to use paid time off to meet their individual circumstances. Some companies have

TABLE 7.2

Public opinion on the nation's number one problem, February and May 2001

Volunteered problems:	Feb 2001 %	May 2001 %
Energy crisis	4	22
Education	11	8
Economy	7	7
Morality	12	6
Unemployment	6	5
Teen violence	1	5
Health care	6	4
Crime	8	4
Drugs	6	4
Poverty	3	3

SOURCE: "It's Energy, Stupid," in *From News Interest To Lifestyles, Energy Takes Hold: America's New Number One Problem,* The Pew Research Center for the People and the Press, Washington, DC, May 24, 2001 [Online] http://people-press.org/reports/display.php3?PageID=67 [accesssed December 12, 2002]. Materials may be obtained free of charge at www.people-press.org.

TABLE 7.3

Public opinion on the impact of rising gasoline prices, increasing utility costs, and energy shortages, by income group, May 2001

	Serious problem...		
	Rising gasoline prices %	Increasing utility costs %	Energy shortages %
Total public	49	41	16
Family income:			
$75,000 +	33	29	11
$50,000–$74,999	46	37	13
$30,000–$49,999	52	45	15
$20,000–$29,999	53	46	17
<$20,000	63	52	26

SOURCE: "Poor Hit Hardest," in *From News Interest To Lifestyles, Energy Takes Hold: America's New Number One Problem,* The Pew Research Center for the People and the Press, Washington, DC, May 24, 2001 [Online] http://people-press.org/reports/display.php3?PageID=67 [accesssed December 12, 2002]. Materials may be obtained free of charge at www.people-press.org.

on-site day-care centers for children of employees. Part-time work, job sharing, and flexible work schedules help parents accommodate the needs of the job and the family. Telecommuting options allow parents to perform part or all of their work from home.

The government has also offered some relief for working parents. Employer-sponsored Flexible Spending Accounts allow working parents to set aside part of their pretax earnings to pay for specified medical and dependent-care expenses.

The Family and Medical Leave Act of 1993 requires employers with 50 or more employees to grant up to 12 weeks of unpaid leave during any 12-month period (to an employee who has been employed by the employer for at least 12 months and has worked at least 1,250 hours during the 12 months preceding the leave) for one or more of the following reasons:

- For birth and care of the newborn child of the employee;

- For placement with the employee of a son or daughter for adoption or foster care;

- To care for an immediate family member (spouse, child, or parent) with a serious health condition, or;

- To take medical leave when the employee is unable to work due to a serious health condition.

ECONOMIC AND FINANCIAL PRESSURES

Changes in the cost of goods and services can quickly upset tight family budgets. Rising energy costs topped a list of national concerns in a 2001 survey by the Pew Research Center. About half of Americans listed the rising cost of gasoline as serious, and 4 in 10 were concerned about the cost of electricity and other home utilities. (See Table 7.2.) Almost 40 percent of parents in the survey reported they had changed summer vacation plans and cut back on long-distance driving because of the increased cost of gasoline, compared to 26 percent of nonparents. Hardest hit are low-income families; 52 percent of families with incomes below $20,000 rated increased utility costs as a serious problem. (See Table 7.3.)

In proclaiming November 24 through November 30, 2002, as National Family Week, President Bush noted that earlier in the year he signed bipartisan legislation:

to expand the Promoting Safe and Stable Families Program, which provides States with vital resources to help families stay together and to promote adoption. The Program seeks to prevent child abuse and neglect, avoid removing children from their homes, support family reunification services, and help those children who are unable to return home by providing crucial adoption and post-adoptive services.

Despite government-aid programs, many families, especially those with children, struggle to meet basic expenses of living and continue to fall behind in living the American dream.

RELIGIOUS FAITH AND CHURCH ATTENDANCE

Religion Among Adults

Periodically, the Gallup organization interviews Americans on the role of religion in their lives. In 2000, the poll found that 68 percent of Americans claimed to be members of a church or synagogue, a percentage that has changed little over the past 60 years. About one-third of Americans claimed they went to church or synagogue at least once a week, and 11 percent said they went almost every week. On the other hand, a slightly smaller proportion, 27 percent, attended seldom and 11 percent never attended religious services. A majority of Americans believed that "religion can answer all or most of today's problems," while only 17 percent thought it is "old-fashioned."

In August 2000, the overwhelming majority of Americans said religion was either very important (57 percent) or fairly important (31 percent) in their own lives. Only 12 percent considered religion not very important in their lives. On the other hand, more than half of Americans believe that religion is losing influence in society. Fifty-eight percent of respondents thought the influence of religion was declining.

Religion Among Young People

Public Agenda, in *Kids These Days: What Americans Really Think About the Next Generation,* found that in 1997, two-thirds of teens said, "faith in God is an important part of my life." A 1998 Gallup International poll found that 49 percent of teens believe their life belongs to God or another high power. Nearly two-thirds (64 percent) of teens aged 13 to 17 belonged to a church, synagogue, mosque, or other organized religious group, and 42 percent of teens reported that they had attended religious worship services in the week prior to the survey.

More recent data from the 2000 Barna Research Organization shows that 56 percent of teens believe their religious faith is very important in their lives and about 34 percent believe they have been born again. American teens also perceive themselves as deeply spiritual. Over one-quarter of respondents feel a personal responsibility to tell others about their religious beliefs, 64 percent consider themselves religious, and 60 percent say they are spiritual. Nearly 9 of 10 teens (89 percent) say that they pray at least weekly, and 56 percent say they have attended church or synagogue in the last week.

WORKING MOTHERS

Working Mothers Think Their Working Benefits Children

In *Report Card on the New Providers: Kids and Moms Speak* (Irene Natividad, National Commission on Working Women, Benton Harbor, Michigan, 1998), Roper Starch Worldwide surveyed school-age children and their mothers for the Whirlpool Foundation. The study found that "Children [continue to be] the key to women's choices." Women's lives have dramatically changed, but their children are as important to them as they were to women 50 years ago. More than 9 of 10 working mothers believed that their job allowed them to provide better opportunities for their children. At the same time, 83 percent of these women reported that they got personal fulfillment from working.

When asked, "All things being equal, do you think it is better if the mother or the father stays home and takes

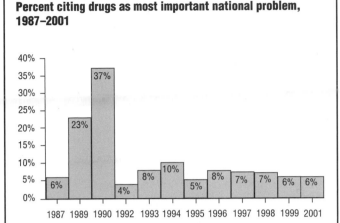

FIGURE 7.10

Percent citing drugs as most important national problem, 1987–2001

SOURCE: "Percent Citing Drugs As Most Important National Problem," in *Interdiction and Incarceration Still Top Remedies,* The Pew Research Center for the People and the Press, Washington, DC, March 21, 2001 [Online] http://people-press.org/reports/display.php3?ReportID=16 [accessed December 11, 2002]. Materials may be obtained free of charge at www.people-press.org.

care of the house and children?" 69 percent thought it better that the mother stays home and only 2 percent thought the father staying home was the best option.

Nonetheless, when the September 1997 survey prepared by the *Washington Post* for the Kaiser Family Foundation asked whether "A woman can have a successful career and be a good mother or a woman must decide between having a successful career and being a good mother?" a large majority thought that women could have both. Among working women, 82 percent thought they could have both career and motherhood. Among all women, 74 percent thought they could have both, while 68 percent of the men thought this was possible.

AVAILABILITY OF DRUGS

After the intense media attention given to crack cocaine and drug-related violence in the early 1990s, the problem of illegal drug use has slipped from the national consciousness. (See Figure 7.10.) Yet three-fourths of Americans say the nation is losing the drug war, according to a study by the Pew Research Center. The importance of the drug problem varies by type of community. Both rural residents and people living in large cities consider drugs an important community problem, while drugs have slipped to fourth and fifth place on the concern list for small-town and suburban residents. (See Table 7.4.)

Age is also a factor in perspective on the drug problem. Almost one-fourth of people under age 30 consider drug and alcohol abuse the most important problem in their community, compared to just 10 percent of those age 30 to 64 and 5 percent of those 64 and older. There is consensus, however, that peer pressure and bad parents are to blame for drug use

TABLE 7.4

Most important community problem by size

Large city	Suburb	Small city/town	Rural area
1. Crime	1. Education	1. Education	**1. Drugs**
2. Drugs	2. Crime	2. Unemployment	2. Unemployment
3. Education	3. Sprawl	3. Crime	3. Education
4. Problems with kids	4. Taxes	**4. Drugs**	4. Taxes
5. Infrastructure	**5. Drugs**	5. Sprawl	5. Infrastructure

SOURCE: "Most Important Community Problem," in *Interdiction and Incarceration Still Top Remedies,* The Pew Research Center for the People and the Press, Washington, DC, March 21, 2001 [Online] http://people-press .org/reports/display.php3?ReportID=16 [accessed December 11, 2002]. Materials may be obtained free of charge at www.people-press.org.

FIGURE 7.11

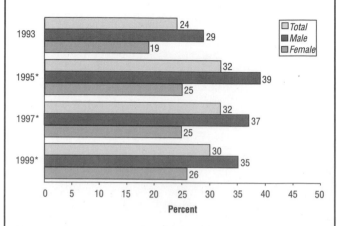

Percentage of students in grades 9–12 who reported that drugs were made available to them on school property during the last 12 months, by gender, 1993, 1995, 1997, and 1999

*The response rate for this survey was less than 70 percent and a full nonresponse bias analysis has not been done to date.
Note: "On school property" was not defined for survey respondents.

SOURCE: P. Kaufman, X. Chen, et al, "Figure 19.1. Percentage of students in grades 9 through 12 who reported that drugs were made available to them on school property during the last 12 months, by gender: 1993, 1995, 1997 and 1999," in *Indicators of School Crime and Safety: 2001,* U.S. Department of Education, National Center for Education Statistics, and U.S. Department of Justice, Bureau of Justice Statistics, Washington, DC, 2001

among teenagers, according to 8 of 10 Americans surveyed. The easy availability of drugs is also included as a factor by three-fourths of those surveyed. The study *Indicators of School Crime and Safety: 2001* (U.S. Departments of Education and Justice, NCES 2003-009/NCJ 196753, Washington, D.C., 2002) reports that in 1999, 30 percent of students surveyed in grades 9 to 12 said that during the previous 12 months drugs had been made available to them on school property. This level of drug availability has been fairly consistently reported since 1995. (See Figure 7.11.)

The 2001 data for the national survey series "Monitoring the Future" was jointly released in December 2001 by the Department of Health and Human Services and the University of Michigan Institute for Social Research (ISR). The survey revealed that use of the drug "ecstasy" continues to increase among teenagers, although the rate of increase is beginning to slow. Ecstasy first became popular in "rave" parties by the 16 to 26 age group, and by 2000 its use increased among eighth-graders. In 2001, 5 percent of 8th-graders, 8 percent of 10th-graders, and 12 percent of 12th-graders reported having used ecstasy during the year. The increasing availability of ecstasy has fueled expanded use. In 2001, 62 percent of 12th-graders said the drug was "fairly" or "very" easy to get, compared to 40 percent in 1999. The use of other drugs such as heroin, cocaine and crack, and inhalants (solvents and aerosols) has declined. (See Table 7.5.)

Teenagers' attitudes toward various drugs change over time. Among high school seniors in 1975, 47 percent disapproved of trying marijuana once or twice. Disapproval rose gradually to 69.9 percent in 1992, then dropped back to 49.1 percent by 2001. The class of 1997 was the first surveyed about ecstasy. In 1997, 82.2 percent of seniors disapproved of trying the drug, but 79.5 percent of the class of 2001 disapproved. Teen disapproval of drugs like heroin, cocaine, and barbiturates remains high in comparison to disapproval of alcohol use. In 1975, 60.3 percent of seniors disapproved of having five or more drinks once or twice on a weekend, and in 2001 62.9 percent disapproved. (See Table 7.6.)

EDUCATION

A 2001 Roper Center report, "To The Test," includes a Gallup survey that asked what national issues were most important for the president and Congress to address. Education topped the list, with 93 percent of respondents listing it as very important or extremely important. As recently as 1993, education ranked fifth on the survey list after health care, the economy, employment, and the federal budget deficit.

More than two-thirds of respondents stated that change was needed in public schools; 34 percent said major change was needed, and 36 percent said some change was needed. When respondents were asked to identify the problems in schools, lack of parental involvement topped the list (78 percent). Undisciplined and disruptive students (73 percent), drugs and alcohol (69 percent), violence (64 percent), and overcrowded classrooms (61 percent) were identified as concerns by more than half of respondents. While 25 percent of respondents in another survey cited in the Roper study thought students should gain an academic background in high school, nearly half (48 percent) expected high school to instill discipline, morals, character, and responsibility.

FAMILY LIFE IN THE TECHNOLOGY AGE

Technology has dramatically altered the lives of most Americans, and the pace of new innovations is often

TABLE 7.5

Trends in lifetime prevalence of use of various drugs for eighth, tenth, and twelfth graders, 1991–2001

(Entries are percentages)

						Lifetime						
	1991	1992	1993	1994	1995	1996	1997	1998	1999	2000	2001	'00–'01 change
Any Illicit Drug												
8th Grade	18.7	20.6	22.5	25.7	28.5	31.2	29.4	29.0	28.3	26.8	26.8	0.0
10th Grade	30.6	29.8	32.8	37.4	40.9	45.4	47.3	44.9	46.2	45.6	45.6	+0.1
12th Grade	44.1	40.7	42.9	45.6	48.4	50.8	54.3	54.1	54.7	54.0	53.9	-0.1
Any Illicit Drug Other Than Marijuana												
8th Grade	14.3	15.6	16.8	17.5	18.8	19.2	17.7	16.9	16.3	15.8	14.8	-1.0
10th Grade	19.1	19.2	20.9	21.7	24.3	25.5	25.0	23.6	24.0	23.1	23.4	+0.3
12th Grade	26.9	25.1	26.7	27.6	28.1	28.5	30.0	29.4	29.4	29.0	28.5	-0.5
Any Illicit Drug Including Inhalants												
8th Grade	28.5	29.6	32.3	35.1	38.1	39.4	38.1	37.8	37.2	35.1	34.5	-0.6
10th Grade	36.1	36.2	38.7	42.7	45.9	49.8	50.9	49.3	49.9	49.3	48.8	-0.5
12th Grade	47.6	44.4	46.6	49.1	51.5	53.5	56.3	56.1	56.3	57.0	56.0	-1.1
Marijuana/Hashish												
8th Grade	10.2	11.2	12.6	16.7	19.9	23.1	22.6	22.2	22.0	20.3	20.4	+0.1
10th Grade	23.4	21.4	24.4	30.4	34.1	39.8	42.3	39.6	40.9	40.3	40.1	-0.2
12th Grade	36.7	32.6	35.3	38.2	41.7	44.9	49.6	49.1	49.7	48.8	49.0	+0.2
Inhalants												
8th Grade	17.6	17.4	19.4	19.9	21.6	21.2	21.0	20.5	19.7	17.9	17.1	-0.8
10th Grade	15.7	16.6	17.5	18.0	19.0	19.3	18.3	18.3	17.0	16.6	15.2	-1.4
12th Grade	17.6	16.6	17.4	17.7	17.4	16.6	16.1	15.2	15.4	14.2	13.0	-1.2
Nitrites												
8th Grade	—	—	—	—	—	—	—	—	—	—	—	—
10th Grade	—	—	—	—	—	—	—	—	—	—	—	—
12th Grade	1.6	1.5	1.4	1.7	1.5	1.8	2.0	2.7	1.7	0.8	1.9	+1.1s
Hallucinogens												
8th Grade	3.2	3.8	3.9	4.3	5.2	5.9	5.4	4.9	4.8	4.6	4.0	-0.7
10th Grade	6.1	6.4	6.8	8.1	9.3	10.5	10.5	9.8	9.7	8.9	7.8	-1.1
12th Grade	9.6	9.2	10.9	11.4	12.7	14.0	15.1	14.1	13.7	13.0	12.8	-0.2
LSD												
8th Grade	2.7	3.2	3.5	3.7	4.4	5.1	4.7	4.1	4.1	3.9	3.4	-0.4
10th Grade	5.6	5.8	6.2	7.2	8.4	9.4	9.5	8.5	8.5	7.6	6.3	-1.2
12th Grade	8.8	8.6	10.3	10.5	11.7	12.6	13.6	12.6	12.2	11.1	10.9	-0.2
Hallucinogens Other Than LSD												
8th Grade	1.4	1.7	1.7	2.2	2.5	3.0	2.6	2.5	2.4	2.3	1.8	-0.5
10th Grade	2.2	2.5	2.8	3.8	3.9	4.7	4.8	5.0	4.7	4.8	4.0	-0.8
12th Grade	3.7	3.3	3.9	4.9	5.4	6.8	7.5	7.1	6.7	6.9	7.0	+0.1
PCP												
8th Grade	—	—	—	—	—	—	—	—	—	—	—	—
10th Grade	—	—	—	—	—	—	—	—	—	—	—	—
12th Grade	2.9	2.4	2.9	2.8	2.7	4.0	3.9	3.9	3.4	3.4	3.5	+0.2
MDMA (Ecstasy)												
8th Grade	—	—	—	—	—	3.4	3.2	2.7	2.7	4.3	5.2	+1.0
10th Grade	—	—	—	—	—	5.6	5.7	5.1	6.0	7.3	8.0	+0.7
12th Grade	—	—	—	—	—	6.1	6.9	5.8	8.0	11.0	11.7	+0.7
Cocaine												
8th Grade	2.3	2.9	2.9	3.6	4.2	4.5	4.4	4.6	4.7	4.5	4.3	-0.2
10th Grade	4.1	3.3	3.6	4.3	5.0	6.5	7.1	7.2	7.7	6.9	5.7	-1.2s
12th Grade	7.8	6.1	6.1	5.9	6.0	7.1	8.7	9.3	9.8	8.6	8.2	-0.4
Crack												
8th Grade	1.3	1.6	1.7	2.4	2.7	2.9	2.7	3.2	3.1	3.1	3.0	-0.2
10th Grade	1.7	1.5	1.8	2.1	2.8	3.3	3.6	3.9	4.0	3.7	3.1	-0.6s
12th Grade	3.1	2.6	2.6	3.0	3.0	3.3	3.9	4.4	4.6	3.9	3.7	-0.2
Other Cocaine												
8th Grade	2.0	2.4	2.4	3.0	3.4	3.8	3.5	3.7	3.8	3.5	3.3	-0.2
10th Grade	3.8	3.0	3.3	3.8	4.4	5.5	6.1	6.4	6.8	6.0	5.0	-1.1
12th Grade	7.0	5.3	5.4	5.2	5.1	6.4	8.2	8.4	8.8	7.7	7.4	-0.3

TABLE 7.5

Trends in lifetime prevalence of use of various drugs for eighth, tenth, and twelfth graders, 1991–2001 [CONTINUED]

(Entries are percentages)

	1991	1992	1993	1994	1995	1996	1997	1998	1999	2000	2001	'00–'01 change
					Lifetime							
Heroin												
8th Grade	1.2	1.4	1.4	2.0	2.3	2.4	2.1	2.3	2.3	1.9	1.7	-0.2
10th Grade	1.2	1.2	1.3	1.5	1.7	2.1	2.1	2.3	2.3	2.2	1.7	-0.6s
12th Grade	0.9	1.2	1.1	1.2	1.6	1.8	2.1	2.0	2.0	2.4	1.8	-0.6s
With a needle												
8th Grade	—	—	—	—	1.5	1.6	1.3	1.4	1.6	1.1	1.2	0.0
10th Grade	—	—	—	—	1.0	1.1	1.1	1.2	1.3	1.0	0.8	-0.2
12th Grade	—	—	—	—	0.7	0.8	0.9	0.8	0.9	0.8	0.7	-0.1
Without a needle												
8th Grade	—	—	—	—	1.5	1.6	1.4	1.5	1.4	1.3	1.1	-0.2
10th Grade	—	—	—	—	1.1	1.7	1.7	1.7	1.6	1.7	1.3	-0.4s
12th Grade	—	—	—	—	1.4	1.7	2.1	1.6	1.8	2.4	1.5	-0.9ss
Other Narcotics												
8th Grade	—	—	—	—	—	—	—	—	—	—	—	—
10th Grade	—	—	—	—	—	—	—	—	—	—	—	—
12th Grade	6.6	6.1	6.4	6.6	7.2	8.2	9.7	9.8	10.2	10.6	9.9	-0.8
Amphetamines												
8th Grade	10.5	10.8	11.8	12.3	13.1	13.5	12.3	11.3	10.7	9.9	10.2	+0.3
10th Grade	13.2	13.1	14.9	15.1	17.4	17.7	17.0	16.0	15.7	15.7	16.0	+0.3
12th Grade	15.4	13.9	15.1	15.7	15.3	15.3	16.5	16.4	16.3	15.6	16.2	+0.6
Methamphetamine												
8th Grade	—	—	—	—	—	—	—	—	4.5	4.2	4.4	+0.2
10th Grade	—	—	—	—	—	—	—	—	7.3	6.9	6.4	-0.5
12th Grade	—	—	—	—	—	—	—	—	8.2	7.9	6.9	-0.9
Ice												
8th Grade	—	—	—	—	—	—	—	—	—	—	—	—
10th Grade	—	—	—	—	—	—	—	—	—	—	—	—
12th Grade	3.3	2.9	3.1	3.4	3.9	4.4	4.4	5.3	4.8	4.0	4.1	+0.1
Barbiturates												
8th Grade	—	—	—	—	—	—	—	—	—	—	—	—
10th Grade	—	—	—	—	—	—	—	—	—	—	—	—
12th Grade	6.2	5.5	6.3	7.0	7.4	7.6	8.1	8.7	8.9	9.2	8.7	-0.5
Tranquilizers												
8th Grade	3.8	4.1	4.4	4.6	4.5	5.3	4.8	4.6	4.4	4.4	4.7	+0.3
10th Grade	5.8	5.9	5.7	5.4	6.0	7.1	7.3	7.8	7.9	8.0	8.1	+0.1
12th Grade	7.2	6.0	6.4	6.6	7.1	7.2	7.8	8.5	9.3	8.9	9.2	+0.4
Rohypnol												
8th Grade	—	—	—	—	—	1.5	1.1	1.4	1.3	1.0	1.1	+0.1
10th Grade	—	—	—	—	—	1.5	1.7	2.0	1.8	1.3	1.5	+0.2
12th Grade	—	—	—	—	—	1.2	1.8	3.0	2.0	1.5	1.7	+0.3
Alcohol **Any use**												
8th Grade	70.1	69.3	67.1	—	—	—	—	—	—	—	—	—
			55.7	55.8	54.5	55.3	53.8	52.5	52.1	51.7	50.5	-1.2
10th Grade	83.8	82.3	80.8	—	—	—	—	—	—	—	—	—
			71.6	71.1	70.5	71.8	72.0	69.8	70.6	71.4	70.1	-1.3
12th Grade	88.0	87.5	87.0	—	—	—	—	—	—	—	—	—
			80.0	80.4	80.7	79.2	81.7	81.4	80.0	80.3	79.7	-0.6
Been Drunk												
8th Grade	26.7	26.8	26.4	25.9	25.3	26.8	25.2	24.8	24.8	25.1	23.4	-1.7
10th Grade	50.0	47.7	47.9	47.2	46.9	48.5	49.4	46.7	48.9	49.3	48.2	-1.1
12th Grade	65.4	63.4	62.5	62.9	63.2	61.8	64.2	62.4	62.3	62.3	63.9	+1.6
Cigarettes **Any use**												
8th Grade	44.0	45.2	45.3	46.1	46.4	49.2	47.3	45.7	44.1	40.5	36.6	-3.9ss
10th Grade	55.1	53.5	56.3	56.9	57.6	61.2	60.2	57.7	57.6	55.1	52.8	-2.3s
12th Grade	63.1	61.8	61.9	62.0	64.2	63.5	65.4	65.3	64.6	62.5	61.0	-1.5

overwhelming. Eight of the 10 fastest growing occupations identified by the U.S. Bureau of Labor Statistics (BLS) in its "2000–2010 Employment Projections" report are in the technology field. The BLS anticipates that the number of jobs in the largest growth category—computer software applications engineers—will double by 2010.

Communications technology in particular has impacted family life. Cell phones allow people to carry on con-

TABLE 7.5

Trends in lifetime prevalence of use of various drugs for eighth, tenth, and twelfth graders, 1991–2001 [CONTINUED]

(Entries are percentages)

						Lifetime						
	1991	1992	1993	1994	1995	1996	1997	1998	1999	2000	2001	'00–'01 change
Smokeless Tobacco												
8th Grade	22.2	20.7	18.7	19.9	20.0	20.4	16.0	15.0	14.4	12.8	11.7	-1.1
10th Grade	28.2	26.6	28.1	29.2	27.6	27.4	26.3	22.7	20.4	19.1	19.5	+0.4
12th Grade	—	32.4	31.0	30.7	30.9	29.8	25.3	26.2	23.4	23.1	19.7	-3.4
Steroids												
8th Grade	1.9	1.7	1.6	2.0	2.0	1.8	1.8	2.3	2.7	3.0	2.8	-0.2
10th Grade	1.8	1.7	1.7	1.8	2.0	1.8	2.0	2.0	2.7	3.5	3.5	0.0
12th Grade	2.1	2.1	2.0	2.4	2.3	1.9	2.4	2.7	2.9	2.5	3.7	+1.2s

Notes: Level of significance of difference between the two most recent classes: s = .05, ss = .01, sss = .001. '—' indicates data not available.
Any apparent inconsistency between the change estimate and the prevalence of use estimates for the two most recent classes is due to rounding error.

SOURCE: L.D. Johnston, P.M. O'Malley, and J.G. Bachman, "Table 1. Trends in Lifetime Prevalence of Use of Various Drugs for Eighth, Tenth, and Twelfth Graders," in *Rise in ecstasy use among American teens begins to slow,* U.S. Department of Health and Human Services, Washington, DC, and The University of Michigan, Ann Arbor, MI, December 19, 2001 [Online] http://monitoringthefuture.org/data/01data.html#2001data-drugs [accessed December 13, 2002]

versations while driving, shopping, dining out, working, or playing. Many public forums are disrupted by the ringing of cell phones. Some houses of worship have even found it necessary to remind participants to "please turn off your cell phone during the service."

Cell Phones Put Families in Touch

Cell phones provide go-everywhere portable access that allows working parents and their children to keep in touch anywhere and anytime. The *New York Times* on November 18, 2002, reported that 56 percent of American households have wireless telephone service. Many teachers report that "every kid seems to have a cell phone in his/her pocket or backpack." Tragedies like the 1999 Columbine High School shootings gave evidence of the proliferation of cell phones, as frightened students called their parents from inside the school and parents called their children as soon as they heard the news reports. Media coverage of the role of cell phones in this incident perhaps spurred more parents to equip their children with cell phones. Following the September 11, 2001, terrorist attacks, news media reported victims' last calls on cell phones and increased calls between family members and friends as Americans were touched by the need to make contact with everyone who was important to them.

Internet Access Is More Controversial

The Internet is perhaps a more controversial source of communication. In 1996, only 18 percent of all women and 27 percent of all men in the United States used the Internet. By 2000, 46 percent of all women and 51 percent of all men were online. (See Table 7.7.) On an average day, 55 million Americans log on to the Internet. Most daily Internet users are in the 30 to 49 age range. (See Table 7.8.)

There are some concerns about just how much time Americans spend online. In a 2000 survey by the Pew Internet and American Life Project, just over one-third of all users reported spending half an hour to one hour per day online. People who used online resources both from home and from work were most likely to spend three or more hours online. (See Table 7.9.)

E-mail, the most common Internet activity, is used by 91 percent of all homes with Internet access. (See Table 7.10.) Research by the Pew Internet and American Life Project indicates that Internet users tend to have increased contact with family members by e-mail. (See Table 7.11.) Almost one-third (31 percent) of e-mail users report that they have renewed contact with a family member they did not keep up with very often before Internet access. (See Table 7.12.)

Uses of the Internet vary by age groups, although 90 percent or more of users in each age group send and receive e-mail. Not surprisingly, Internet use is more common among younger people. However, about 4 percent of people aged 81–90 are Internet savvy. (See Figure 7.12.) Individuals in the 18 to 29 age range are more likely than those in other age groups to browse the Internet just for fun, such as using it to look for information about books, music, or leisure activities. People in the 30 to 49 age group are the most likely to research product and religious information or do work-related research. Those in the 50 to 64 age range are most likely to search for health and financial information. Those over 65 are the least likely to engage in online transactions such as banking or use the Internet for job-related purposes. The most popular use of the Internet by all age groups, after e-mail, is to get hobby-related information. (See Table 7.13.)

The Internet plays a pivotal role in the lives of American teenagers, according to the Pew Internet and American Life Project. About 73 percent of youth ages 12 through 17

TABLE 7.6

Long-term trends in disapproval of drug use by twelfth graders, 1975–2001

Percentage "disapproving"[2]

12th grade

Do you disapprove of people (who are 18 or older) doing each of the following?[1]	Class of 1975	Class of 1976	Class of 1977	Class of 1978	Class of 1979	Class of 1980	Class of 1981	Class of 1982	Class of 1983	Class of 1984	Class of 1985	Class of 1986	Class of 1987	Class of 1988
Try marijuana once or twice	47.0	38.4	33.4	33.4	34.2	39.0	40.0	45.5	46.3	49.3	51.4	54.6	56.6	60.8
Smoke marijuana occasionally	54.8	47.8	44.3	43.5	45.3	49.7	52.6	59.1	60.7	63.5	65.8	69.0	71.6	74.0
Smoke marijuana regularly	71.9	69.5	65.5	67.5	69.2	74.6	77.4	80.6	82.5	84.7	85.5	86.6	89.2	89.3
Try LSD once or twice	82.8	84.6	83.9	85.4	86.6	87.3	86.4	88.8	89.1	88.9	89.5	89.2	91.6	89.8
Take LSD regularly	94.1	95.3	95.8	96.4	96.9	96.7	96.8	96.7	97.0	96.8	97.0	96.6	97.8	96.4
Try MDMA (Ecstasy) once or twice	—	—	—	—	—	—	—	—	—	—	—	—	—	—
Try cocaine once or twice	81.3	82.4	79.1	77.0	74.7	76.3	74.6	76.6	77.0	79.7	79.3	80.2	87.3	89.1
Take cocaine regularly	93.3	93.9	92.1	91.9	90.8	91.1	90.7	91.5	93.2	94.5	93.8	94.3	96.7	96.2
Try crack once or twice	—	—	—	—	—	—	—	—	—	—	—	—	—	—
Take crack occasionally	—	—	—	—	—	—	—	—	—	—	—	—	—	—
Take crack regularly	—	—	—	—	—	—	—	—	—	—	—	—	—	—
Try cocaine powder once or twice	—	—	—	—	—	—	—	—	—	—	—	—	—	—
Take cocaine powder occasionally	—	—	—	—	—	—	—	—	—	—	—	—	—	—
Take cocaine powder regularly	—	—	—	—	—	—	—	—	—	—	—	—	—	—
Try heroin once or twice	91.5	92.6	92.5	92.0	93.4	93.5	93.5	94.6	94.3	94.0	94.0	93.3	96.2	95.0
Take heroin occasionally	94.8	96.0	96.0	96.4	96.8	96.7	97.2	96.9	96.9	97.1	96.8	96.6	97.9	96.9
Take heroin regularly	96.7	97.5	97.2	97.8	97.9	97.6	97.8	97.5	97.7	98.0	97.6	97.6	98.1	97.2
Try heroin once or twice without using a needle	—	—	—	—	—	—	—	—	—	—	—	—	—	—
Take heroin occasionally without using a needle	—	—	—	—	—	—	—	—	—	—	—	—	—	—
Try amphetamines once or twice	74.8	75.1	74.2	74.8	75.1	75.4	71.1	72.6	72.3	72.8	74.9	76.5	80.7	82.5
Take amphetamines regularly	92.1	92.8	92.5	93.5	94.4	93.0	91.7	92.0	92.6	93.6	93.3	93.5	95.4	94.2
Try barbiturates once or twice	77.7	81.3	81.1	82.4	84.0	83.9	82.4	84.4	83.1	84.1	84.9	86.8	89.6	89.4
Take barbiturates regularly	93.3	93.6	93.0	94.3	95.2	95.4	94.2	94.4	95.1	95.1	95.5	94.9	96.4	95.3
Try one or two drinks of an alcoholic beverage (beer, wine, liquor)	21.6	18.2	15.6	15.6	15.8	16.0	17.2	18.2	18.4	17.4	20.3	20.9	21.4	22.6
Take one or two drinks nearly every day	67.6	68.9	66.8	67.7	68.3	69.0	69.1	69.9	68.9	72.9	70.9	72.8	74.2	75.0
Take four or five drinks nearly every day	88.7	90.7	88.4	90.2	91.7	90.8	91.8	90.9	90.0	91.0	92.0	91.4	92.2	92.8
Have five or more drinks once or twice each weekend	60.3	58.6	57.4	56.2	56.7	55.6	55.5	58.8	56.6	59.6	60.4	62.4	62.0	65.3
Smoke one or more packs of cigarettes per day	67.5	65.9	66.4	67.0	70.3	70.8	69.9	69.4	70.8	73.0	72.3	75.4	74.3	73.1
Take steroids	—	—	—	—	—	—	—	—	—	—	—	—	—	—
Approx. N =	2677	2957	3085	3686	3221	3261	3610	3651	3341	3254	3265	3113	3302	3311

TABLE 7.6

Long-term trends in disapproval of drug use by twelfth graders, 1975–2001 [CONTINUED]

Percentage "disapproving"

12th grade

Do you disapprove of people (who are 18 or older) doing each of the following?	Class of 1989	Class of 1990	Class of 1991	Class of 1992	Class of 1993	Class of 1994	Class of 1995	Class of 1996	Class of 1997	Class of 1998	Class of 1999	Class of 2000	Class of 2001	Change '00–'01
Try marijuana once or twice	64.6	67.8	68.7	69.9	63.3	57.6	56.7	52.5	51.0	51.6	48.8	52.5	49.1	−3.4
Smoke marijuana occasionally	77.2	80.5	79.4	79.7	75.5	68.9	66.7	62.9	63.2	64.4	62.5	65.8	63.2	−2.7
Smoke marijuana regularly	89.8	91.0	89.3	90.1	87.6	82.3	81.9	80.0	78.8	81.2	78.6	79.7	79.3	−0.4
Try LSD once or twice	89.7	89.8	90.1	88.1	85.9	82.5	81.1	79.6	80.5	82.1	83.0	82.4	81.8	−0.6
Take LSD regularly	96.4	96.3	96.4	95.5	95.8	94.3	92.5	93.2	92.9	93.5	94.3	94.2	94.0	−0.2
Try MDMA (Ecstasy) once or twice	—	—	—	—	—	—	—	—	82.2	82.5	82.1	81.0	79.5	−1.5
Try cocaine once or twice	90.5	91.5	93.6	93.0	92.7	91.6	90.3	90.0	88.0	89.5	89.1	88.2	88.1	−0.1
Take cocaine regularly	96.4	96.7	97.3	96.9	97.5	96.6	96.1	95.6	96.0	95.6	94.9	95.5	94.9	−0.6
Try crack once or twice	—	92.3	92.1	93.1	89.9	89.5	91.4	87.4	87.0	86.7	87.6	87.5	87.0	−0.5
Take crack occasionally	—	94.3	94.2	95.0	92.8	92.8	94.0	91.2	91.3	90.9	92.3	91.9	91.6	−0.3
Take crack regularly	—	94.9	95.0	95.5	93.4	93.1	94.1	93.0	92.3	91.9	93.2	92.8	92.2	−0.6
Try cocaine powder once or twice	—	87.9	88.0	89.4	86.6	87.1	88.3	83.1	83.0	83.1	84.3	84.1	83.3	−0.8
Take cocaine powder occasionally	—	92.1	93.0	93.4	91.2	91.0	92.7	89.7	89.3	88.7	90.0	90.3	89.8	−0.5
Take cocaine powder regularly	—	93.7	94.4	94.3	93.0	92.5	93.8	92.9	91.5	91.1	92.3	92.6	92.5	−0.1
Try heroin once or twice	95.4	95.1	96.0	94.9	94.4	93.2	92.8	92.1	92.3	93.7	93.5	93.0	93.1	+0.1
Take heroin occasionally	97.2	96.7	97.3	96.8	97.0	96.2	95.7	95.0	95.4	96.1	95.7	96.0	95.4	−0.6
Take heroin regularly	97.4	97.5	97.8	97.2	97.5	97.1	96.4	96.3	96.4	96.6	96.4	96.6	96.2	−0.4
Try heroin once or twice without using a needle	—	—	—	—	—	—	92.9	90.8	92.3	93.0	92.6	94.0	91.7	−2.3s
Take heroin occasionally without using a needle	—	—	—	—	—	—	94.7	93.2	94.4	94.3	93.8	95.2	93.5	−1.7s
Try amphetamines once or twice	83.3	85.3	86.5	86.9	84.2	81.3	82.2	79.9	81.3	82.5	81.9	82.1	82.3	+0.2
Take amphetamines regularly	94.2	95.5	96.0	95.6	96.0	94.1	94.3	93.5	94.3	94.0	93.7	94.1	93.4	−0.7
Try barbiturates once or twice	89.3	90.5	90.6	90.3	89.7	87.5	87.3	84.9	86.4	86.0	86.6	85.9	85.9	0.0
Take barbiturates regularly	95.3	96.4	97.1	96.5	97.0	96.1	95.2	94.8	95.3	94.6	94.7	95.2	94.5	−0.7
Try one or two drinks of an alcoholic beverage (beer, wine, liquor)	27.3	29.4	29.8	33.0	30.1	28.4	27.3	26.5	26.1	24.5	24.6	25.2	26.6	+1.4
Take one or two drinks nearly every day	76.5	77.9	76.5	75.9	77.8	73.1	73.3	70.8	70.0	69.4	67.2	70.0	69.2	−0.9
Take four or five drinks nearly every day	91.6	91.9	90.6	90.8	90.6	89.8	88.8	89.4	88.6	86.7	86.9	88.4	86.4	−2.0
Have five or more drinks once or twice each weekend	66.5	68.9	67.4	70.7	70.1	65.1	66.7	64.7	65.0	63.8	62.7	65.2	62.9	−2.3
Smoke one or more packs of cigarettes per day	72.4	72.8	71.4	73.5	70.6	69.8	68.2	67.2	67.1	68.8	69.5	70.1	71.6	+1.5
Take steroids	—	90.8	90.5	92.1	92.1	91.9	91.0	91.7	91.4	90.8	88.9	88.8	86.4	−2.4s
Approx. N =	2799	2566	2547	2645	2723	2588	2603	2399	2601	2545	2310	2150	2144	

[1] The 1975 question asked about people who are "20 or older."

[2] Answer alternatives were: (1) Don't disapprove, (2) Disapprove, and (3) Strongly disapprove. Percentages are shown for categories (2) and (3) combined.

Notes: Level of significance of difference between the two most recent classes: s = .05, ss = .01, sss = .001. '—' indicates data not available. Any apparent inconsistency between the change estimate and the prevalence of use estimates for the two most recent classes is due to rounding error.

SOURCE: L.D. Johnston, P.M. O'Malley, and J.G. Bachman, "Table 11. Long-Term Trends in Disapproval of Drug Use by Twelfth Graders," in Rise in ecstasy use among American teens begins to slow, U.S. Department of Health and Human Services, Washington, DC, and The University of Michigan, Ann Arbor, MI, December 19, 2001 [Online] http://monitoringthefuture.org/data/01data.html#2001data-drugs [accessed December 13, 2002]

TABLE 7.7

Percent of women and men who use the internet, 1996, 1998, and 2000

	Percentage who use the Internet	
	All Women	All Men
1996	18%	27%
1998	34%	41%
2000	46%	51%

SOURCE: "Growth Rate: Percentage Who Use the Internet," in *Tracking Online Life: How Women Use the Internet to Cultivate Relationships with Family and Friends,* The Pew Internet & American Life Project, Washington, DC, May 10, 2000 [Online] http://www.pewinternet.org/reports/toc.asp?Report=11 [accessed January 29, 2003]

TABLE 7.9

Time spent online in a typical day, 2000
HOW MUCH TIME DID YOU SPEND ONLINE YESTERDAY?

Time spent online on a typical day...	All users who went online	Users who went online from work	Users who went online from home	Users who went online at both home and work
Half hour or less	25%	38%	26%	12%
Half hour to one hour	36%	37%	38%	28%
One to three hours	22%	13%	24%	27%
More than three hours	16%	11%	12%	34%

SOURCE: "How much time did you spend online yesterday?," in *Tracking Online Life: How Women Use the Internet to Cultivate Relationships with Family and Friends,* The Pew Internet & American Life Project, Washington, DC, May 10, 2000 [Online] http://www.pewinternet.org/reports/toc.asp?Report=11 [accessed January 29, 2003]

FIGURE 7.12

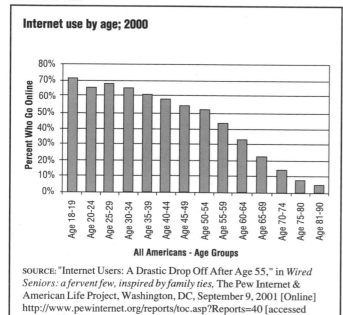

Internet use by age; 2000

SOURCE: "Internet Users: A Drastic Drop Off After Age 55," in *Wired Seniors: a fervent few, inspired by family ties,* The Pew Internet & American Life Project, Washington, DC, September 9, 2001 [Online] http://www.pewinternet.org/reports/toc.asp?Reports=40 [accessed January 29, 2003]

TABLE 7.8

Daily internet use and specific population groups, 2000

On an average day, 55 million Americans are online. Here is a portrait of wired America on a typical day:	Percentage of Internet users in this group who are online each day	Number of Americans who are daily users (in millions)
Sex		
Men	63%	29
Women	57	26
Race		
Whites	62	50
Blacks	37	3
Hispanic Origin*		
Non-Hispanics	60	52
Hispanics	51	4
Age		
18-29	54	15
30-49	62	28
50-64	63	10
65+	67	3
Education		
Less than high school	49	3
High school graduate	53	13
Some college	59	17
College degree +	66	22

*The survey and the table follow the practice of the Census Bureau in presenting data on the Hispanic population, which distinguishes between racial and ethnic classifications.

SOURCE: "Daily Internet & Specific Population Groups," in *Tracking Online Life: How Women Use the Internet to Cultivate Relationships with Family and Friends,* The Pew Internet & American Life Project, Washington, DC, May 10, 2000 [Online] http://www.pewinternet.org/reports/toc.asp?Report=11 [accessed January 29, 2003]

use the Internet. Many (48 percent) say the Internet improves their relationships with friends, and 32 percent believe it helps them make new friends. However, 64 percent say that the Internet takes away time they might otherwise spend with their families. More than half (55 percent) of parents of these online teens say the Internet is a good thing for their children, while 6 percent believe the Internet is a bad thing. A full 95 percent of parents of online teens believe it is important for today's children to learn to use the Internet in order to be successful.

The Internet appears to foster extended family communication. Some 16 percent of Americans say they or another family member has a family Web page with pictures or information about the clan. Almost one-third (29 percent) say they have used the Internet to do family history research. A fourth of those who e-mail relatives say they have learned more about their family since they began e-mailing family members.

WHAT YOUNG AMERICANS THINK ABOUT MARRIAGE AND FAMILY ISSUES

Just before the dawn of the 21st century, the interviewers for the Roper Institute asked Americans whether life for their family had improved since 1950. Regardless of

TABLE 7.10

Survey of internet activities, 2000

More than 90 million Americans have gone online. Here are the kinds of things they do:	Based on those with Internet access Percent	Number in millions
Send email	91%	84
Look for info on a hobby	76	70
Research a product or service before buying it	74	68
Get travel information	64	59
Surf the Web for fun	63	58
Check the weather	62	57
Look for info about movies, books, or other leisure activities	62	57
Get news	60	55
Research for school or training	55	51
Look for health/medical information	54	50
Do any type of research	49	45
Buy a product	48	44
Visit a government Web site	47	43
Send an instant message	45	41
Get financial information	44	41
Look for information about a job	38	35
Buy or make a reservation for travel	36	33
Check sports scores	35	32
Look for political news/information	35	32
Listen to or download music	35	32
Play a game	34	31
Chat in a chat room or in an online discussion	28	26
Look for information about a place to live	27	25
Look for religious/spiritual information	21	19
Bank online	17	16
Participate in an online auction	15	14
Buy or sell stocks, bonds, or mutual funds	12	11
Gamble	5	5

SOURCE: "Internet Activities," in *Tracking Online Life: How Women Use the Internet to Cultivate Relationships with Family and Friends,* The Pew Internet & American Life Project, Washington, DC, May 10, 2000 [Online] http://www.pewinternet.org/reports/toc.asp?Report=11 [accessed January 29, 2003]

TABLE 7.12

The internet and family connections, 2000

Percent of email users who	
...have an email group list for family or friends	54%
...have started emailing a family member with whom they did not keep up with very much before	31%

SOURCE: "The Internet and Family Connections," in *Tracking Online Life: How Women Use the Internet to Cultivate Relationships with Family and Friends,* The Pew Internet & American Life Project, Washington, DC, May 10, 2000 [Online] http://www.pewinternet.org/reports/toc.asp?Report=11 [accessed January 29, 2003]

age, gender, race, religion, or educational level, two-thirds (63 percent) said that life was better at the close of the century than it had been back in the middle. The researchers went on to ask whether life was better for 15 demographic groups (such as children or the disabled). Respondents believed 13 of the 15 groups had better lives in 1999 than they did in 1950. In the public perception, women, persons with disabilities, and African Americans had seen the

TABLE 7.11

Internet users' contact with family members, 2000

	Every day	Once a week	Less often
Get together	8%	17%	74%
Speak on the phone	16%	38%	46%
Exchange email	22%	49%	29%

SOURCE: "Internet users' contact with family members," in *Tracking Online Life: How Women Use the Internet to Cultivate Relationships with Family and Friends,* The Pew Internet & American Life Project, Washington, DC, May 10, 2000 [Online] http://www.pewinternet.org/reports/toc.asp?Report=11 [accessed January 29, 2003]

TABLE 7.13

Internet activities by age groups, 2000

SENIORS ENJOY GATHERING INFORMATION AND PLAYING GAMES, BUT ARE LESS LIKELY THAN YOUNGER USERS TO CHAT, LISTEN TO MUSIC, OR SHOP ONLINE. THIS IS THE PERCENT OF INTERNET USERS WHO HAVE EVER DONE THE FOLLOWING ACTIVITIES:

Activity	All Internet users	Age Groups 18–29	30–49	50–64	65+
Send and read email	92%	90%	92%	94%	93%
Fun					
Get hobby information	76	81	77	72	58
Browse just for fun	64	75	62	53	53
Look for info about music, books, or other leisure activities	63	72	64	55	36
Play a game	34	44	31	25	32
Check sports scores	37	42	37	31	31
Send an instant message	45	57	43	35	30
Use a video or audio clip	48	61	47	35	23
Listen to music	37	51	34	24	18
Chat online	28	46	22	16	12
Play lottery or gamble	5	5	5	5	4
Information Seeking					
Get news	61	59	62	60	55
Get weather reports	62	57	65	62	53
Look for travel info	65	66	66	66	51
Research product info	73	72	77	66	48
Get financial info	44	35	48	50	44
Visit a government Web site	49	40	54	53	40
Get political news or info	39	37	40	39	36
Seek religious info	22	19	25	18	11
Major Life Activities					
Seek health info	56	48	60	60	53
Do work research	50	46	57	50	20
Do school research or job training	54	69	53	39	18
Look for a place to live	27	34	27	18	11
Look for job info	38	51	39	20	5
Transactions					
Buy a product	48	47	51	45	36
Make a travel reservation	36	35	38	37	25
Buy or sell stocks	13	10	14	15	12
Participate in online auction	15	17	16	13	8
Bank online	18	18	19	16	8

SOURCE: "Internet Activities," in *Wired Seniors: a fervent few, inspired by family ties,* The Pew Internet & American Life Project, Washington, DC, September 9, 2001 [Online] http://www.pewinternet.org/reports/toc.asp?Report=40 [accessed January 29, 2003]

TABLE 7.14

Opinions of college freshmen on legal and social issues as of January 26, 2001

Agree strongly or somewhat that:	Total	Men	Women
There is too much concern in the courts for the rights of criminals	66.5%	67.8%	65.5%
Abortion should be legal	53.9%	54.5%	53.5%
The death penalty should be abolished	31.2%	27.4%	34.3%
If two people really like each other, it's all right for them to have sex even if they've known each other for only a very short time	41.8%	54.6%	31.3%
Marijuana should be legalized	34.2%	40.4%	29.1%
It is important to have laws prohibiting homosexual relationships	27.2%	36.0%	20.1%
Employers should be allowed to require drug testing of employees or job applicants	76.5%	73.3%	79.2%
The federal government should do more to control the sale of handguns	82.0%	72.6%	89.6%
Racial discrimination is no longer a major problem in America	20.5%	24.4%	17.3%
Realistically, an individual can do little to bring about changes in our society	27.2%	31.6%	23.6%
Wealthy people should pay a larger share of taxes than they do now	52.2%	53.0%	51.5%
Colleges should prohibit racist/sexist speech on campus	61.8%	56.4%	66.1%
Same-sex couples should have the right to legal marital status	56.0%	47.2%	63.1%
Affirmative action in college admissions should be abolished	49.9%	56.2%	44.7%
The activities of married women are best confined to the home and family	22.2%	28.7%	16.8%
People have a right to know about the personal lives of public figures	26.4%	28.7%	24.5%

Note: The statistics are based on survey responses of 269,413 freshmen entering 434 four-year colleges and universities in the fall of 2000. In a change from previous years, the statistics do not include two-year colleges because too few such institutions participated in the survey to allow for meaningful analysis. (Because of that change, the figures are not directly comparable to freshman-survey statistics previously published by *The Chronicle*.) The figures were statistically adjusted to represent the total population of approximately 1.1 million first-time, full-time freshmen at four-year institutions. Because of rounding or multiple responses, figures may add to more than 100 percent.

SOURCE: Sax, L. J., Astin, A. W., Korn, W. S., Mahoney, K. M. (2000) *The American Freshman: National Norms for Fall 2000*. Los Angeles: Higher Education Research Institute, UCLA

TABLE 7.15

Predictions for the future, April–May 1999

Will probably happen over next 50 years...	Yes %	No %	Don't know %
Cure for cancer	81	18	1 =100
Cure for AIDS	79	20	1 =100
Manned spacecraft on Mars	76	22	2 =100
Ordinary people in space	57	41	2 =100
Epidemic worse than AIDS	56	41	3 =100
Clone humans	51	45	4 =100
Major earthquake in California	91	6	3 =100
Environment will improve	78	20	2 =100
Earth will get warmer	76	19	5 =100
Major energy crisis	63	34	3 =100
Asteroid hitting Earth	31	62	7 =100
Terrorist attack on U.S.	64	32	4 =100
A nuclear war	41	57	2 =100
A nuclear war involving the U.S.	37	58	5 =100
Democracy continues to spread	79	16	5 =100
China a rival superpower	67	29	4 =100
U.S. the only superpower	44	53	3 =100
More countries ruled by dictators	41	55	4 =100
Woman President	80	19	1 =100
African American President	76	22	2 =100
Only two major parties	52	45	3 =100
Women ordained as priests	43	50	7 =100
Priests allowed to marry	43	50	7 =100
The return of Jesus Christ	44	44	12 =100
Contact with alien life	27	69	4 =100

SOURCE: "Predictions for the Future," in *Optimism Reigns, Technology Plays Key Role*, The Pew Research Center for the People and the Press, Washington, DC, October 24, 1999 [Online] http://people-press.org/reports/display.php3?PageID=258 [accessed December 12, 2002]. Materials may be obtained free of charge at www.people-press.org.

60 percent thought that living together as a couple before marriage was a good idea, and nearly 70 percent felt that premarital sex is all right when two people love each other. On the other hand, only 2 of 10 respondents believed that divorce was an acceptable solution if two people were unhappy in their marriage.

Of freshmen entering the class of 2004, 54.6 percent of men and 31.3 percent of women thought that if two people really like each other, it is all right for them to have sex, even if they have known each other only for a very short time. On the issue of legalizing abortion, however, men and women had more similar opinions, with 54.5 percent of men and 53.5 percent of women supporting legal abortions. Women were more supportive than men of same-sex couples having the right to legal marital status, with 63.1 percent of women but 47.2 percent of men favoring the idea. (See Table 7.14.)

Surveys of entering freshmen have been conducted regularly since 1968 by the Higher Education Research Institute of the University of California. A look at the data for the past 30 or more years shows significant shifts in the views of these emerging adults. The desire to help others has hovered consistently in the mid-60 percent range since 1968. The greatest decline has been in the importance of

greatest improvement over the past 50 years. On the other end of the scale, 65 percent of respondents said farmers were in worse condition than they were in 1950, given that three out of five family farms have disappeared since 1950. The demographic group of greatest concern for the family, however, are the children. More than half (56 percent) of respondents felt life had become worse for teenagers, and 44 percent thought it worse for children.

College freshmen provide a glimpse of the ideas of the next generation. In 1997, Northwestern Mutual Life sponsored a survey conducted by Louis Harris and Associates that questioned incoming college freshmen on a variety of subjects, including family values. Most (94 percent) of the students entering the class of 2001 planned to be married by the time they were 26 years old, and 89 percent intended to have children. Most of these future parents favored three children. Some 90 percent felt that "marriage is a cornerstone of societal values." More than

developing a philosophy of life, which dropped from 80 percent in 1968 to 42 percent in 2000. As noted in a Roper Institute study, in an opposite trend, the importance of being well off financially climbed from 41 percent in 1968 to 73 percent in 1986, where it has remained ever since. Interest in raising a family dipped in the mid-1970s but by 2000 was equal in importance with financial well-being.

OPTIMISM FOR THE FUTURE

Despite predictions of natural disasters, terrorism, and environmental calamities, Americans at the turn of the new century expressed confidence that life will con-tinue to get better. More than four-fifths of Americans (81 percent) are optimistic about the welfare of themselves and their families, and 70 percent believe the country as a whole will do well. (See Table 4.6 in Chapter 4.) Their predictions for the future include good and bad. Eight in 10 people believe there will be a cure for cancer and for AIDS in the next 50 years. Nine in ten (91 percent) also believe there will be a major earthquake in California, and 41 percent believe there will be a nuclear war. More than three-fourths believe a woman (80 percent) and an African American (76 percent) will be elected president in the next 50 years. (See Table 7.15.)

IMPORTANT NAMES AND ADDRESSES

Administration for Children and Families
U.S. Department of Health and
Human Services
370 L'Enfant Promenade SW
Washington, DC 20447
(202) 619-0257
(877) 696-6775
E-mail: hhsmail@os.dhhs.gov
URL: http://www.hhs.gov

Annie E. Casey Foundation
701 Saint Paul St.
Baltimore, MD 21202
(410) 547-6600
FAX: (410) 547-6624
E-mail: webmail@aecf.org
URL: http://www.aecf.org

Barna Research
5528 Everglades St.
Ventura, CA 93003
(805) 658-8885
FAX: (805) 658-7298
E-mail: pjacobs@barna.org
URL: http://www.barna.org

**Center for Nutrition Policy and
Promotion**
U.S. Department of Agriculture
3101 Park Center Dr., Rm. 1034
Alexandria, VA 22302-1594
(703) 305-7600
E-mail: infocnpp@cnpp.usda.gov
URL: http://www.usda.gov/cnpp

**Center for Research for Mothers
and Children**
National Institute of Child Health and
Human Development
Bldg. 31, Rm. 2A32, MSC 2425
31 Center Dr.
Bethesda, MD 20892-2425
(301) 496-5097
FAX: (301) 402-2085
E-mail: NICHDClearinghouse@mail.nih.gov
URL: http://www.nichd.nih.gov/

Center on Budget and Policy Priorities
820 1st St. NE, #510
Washington, DC 20002
(202) 408-1080
FAX: (202) 408-1056
E-mail: bazie@cbpp.org
URL: http://www.cbpp.org

**Center on Fathers, Families, and
Public Policy**
23 N. Pinckney St., Suite 210
Madison, WI 53703
(608) 257-3148
FAX: (608) 257-4686
URL: http://www.cffpp.org

**Centers for Disease Control
and Prevention**
1600 Clifton Rd.
Atlanta, GA 30333
(404) 639-3311
Toll-free: (800) 311-3435
URL: http://www.cdc.gov

Child Care Bureau
Administration on Children, Youth,
and Families
U.S. Department of Health and
Human Services
200 Independence Ave. SW
Washington, DC 20201
(202) 619-0257
(877) 696-6775
E-mail: hhsmail@os.dhhs.gov
URL: http://www.hhs.gov

Child Trends, Inc.
4301 Connecticut Ave. NW, Suite 100
Washington, DC 20008
(202) 362-5580
FAX: (202) 362-5533
E-mail: webmaster@childtrends.org
URL: http://www.childtrends.org

Children's Defense Fund
25 E St. NW
Washington, DC 20001
(202) 628-8787
FAX: (202) 662-3520
E-mail: cdfinfo@childrensdefense.org
URL: http://www.childrensdefense.org

Families and Work Institute
267 Fifth Ave., Fl. 2
New York, NY 10016
(212) 465-2044
FAX: (212) 465-8637
E-mail: mlambert@familiesandwork.org
URL: http://www.familiesandwork.org

Gallup Organization
901 F St. NW
Washington, DC 20004
(202) 715-3030
FAX: (202) 715-3041
URL: http://www.gallup.com

Hartford Institute for Religion Research
Hartford Seminary
77 Sherman St.
Hartford, CT 06105-2260
(860) 509-9543
FAX: (860) 509-9551
E-mail: hirr@hartsem.edu
URL: http://www.hirr.hartsem.edu

Head Start
Administration for Children and Families
U.S. Department of Health and
Human Services
1133 15th St. NW, Suite 450
Washington, DC 20005
(703) 739-0875
FAX: (202) 737-1151
Toll-free: (866) 763-6481
E-mail: askus@headstartinfo.org
URL: http://www.acf.hhs.gov/programs/hsb/

Joint Center for Housing Studies
Harvard University
1033 Massachusetts Ave.
Cambridge, MA 02138
(617) 495-7908
FAX: (617) 496-9957
URL: http://www.jchs.harvard.edu

Joint Center for Poverty Research
Institute for Policy Research
Northwestern University
2046 Sheridan Rd.
Evanston, IL 60208
(847) 491-4145
FAX: (847) 467-2459
E-mail: povcen@northwestern.edu
URL: http://www.jcpr.org

**Lambda Legal Defense and
Education Fund**
120 Wall St., Suite 1500
New York, NY 10005-3904
(212) 809-8585
FAX: (212) 809-0055
E-mail: lambdalegal@lambdalegal.org
URL: http://www.lambdalegal.org

**National Adoption
Information Clearinghouse**
330 C St. SW
Washington, DC 20447
(703) 352-3488
FAX: (703) 385-3206
Toll-free: (888) 251-0075
E-mail: naic@calib.com.
URL: http://www.calib.com/naic

National Alliance for Caregiving
4720 Montgomery Ln., 5th Fl.
Bethesda, MD 20814
(301) 718-8444
FAX: (301) 652-7711
E-mail: info@caregiving.org
URL: http://www.caregiving.org

**National Campaign to Prevent
Teen Pregnancy**
1776 Massachusetts Ave. NW, Suite 200
Washington, DC 20036
(202) 478-8500
FAX: (202) 478-8588
E-mail: campaign@teenpregnancy.org
URL: http://www.teenpregnancy.org

National Center for Children in Poverty
Mailman School of Public Health, Columbia
University
154 Haven Ave.
New York, NY 10032
(212) 304-7100
FAX: (212) 544-4200
E-mail: nccp@columbia.edu
URL: http://www.nccp.org

National Center for Education Statistics
1990 K St. NW
Washington, DC 20006
(202) 502-7300
E-mail: NCESWebMaster@ed.gov
URL: http://www.nces.ed.gov

**National Clearinghouse on Child Abuse
and Neglect Information**
330 C St. SW
Washington, DC 20447
(703) 385-7565
FAX: (703) 385-3206
Toll-free: (800) 394-3366
E-mail: nccanch@calib.com
URL: http://www.calib.com/nccanch/

National Fatherhood Initiative
101 Lake Forest Blvd., Suite 360
Gaithersburg, MD 20877
(301) 948-0599
FAX: (301) 948-4325
E-mail: nfi1995@aol.com
URL: http://www.fatherhood.org

National Low Income Housing Coalition
1012 14th St. NW, Suite 610
Washington, DC 20005
(202) 662-1530
FAX: (202) 393-1973
E-mail: info@nlihc.org
URL: http://www.nlihc.org

Public Agenda
6 E. 39th St.
New York, NY 10016
(212) 686-6610
FAX: (212) 889-3461
URL: http://www.publicagenda.org

Urban Institute
2100 M St. NW
Washington, DC 20037
(202) 833-7200
FAX: (202) 223-3043
E-mail: webmaster@ui.urban.org
URL: http://www.urban.org

U.S. Census Bureau
Washington, DC 20233
(301) 457-4608
FAX: (301) 457-4714
E-mail: webmaster@census.gov
URL: http://www.census.gov

U.S. Conference of Mayors
1620 I St. NW
Washington, DC 20006
(202) 293-7330
FAX: (202) 293-2352
E-mail: info@usmayors.org
URL: http://www.usmayors.org/uscm/

U.S. General Accounting Office
441 G St. NW
Washington, DC 20548
(202) 512-4800
E-mail: webmaster@gao.gov
URL: http://www.gao.gov

Women's Bureau
U.S. Department of Labor
200 Constitution Ave. NW
Room S-3002
Washington, DC 20210
(202) 693-6710
FAX: (202) 693-6725
Toll-free: (800) 827-5335
URL: http://www.dol.gov/wb

RESOURCES

The Bureau of the Census of the U.S. Department of Commerce is probably the single most important collection point for demographic information about American life. Many of its publications were essential for the preparation of this book, including *Multigenerational Households for the United States, and for Puerto Rico: 2000* (2001), *America's Families and Living Arrangements: March 2000* (2001), *Household and Family Characteristics: 1998* (1999), *Households by Type 1940—Present* (2001), *Households and Families: 2000* (2001), *Households by Size 1960 to Present* (2001), *Fertility of American Women* (2000), *Coresident Grandparents and Their Grandchildren: Grandparent Maintained Families* (1999), *Money Income in the United States: 2000* (2001), *Poverty in the United States: 2001* (2002), *Health Insurance Coverage: 2000* (2001), *Geographic Mobility* (2001), *Why People Move: Exploring the March 2000 Current Population Survey* (2001), *Profile of Foreign-Born Population in the United States 2000* (2001), *Home Computers and Internet Use in the United States: August 2000* (2001), *Emergency and Transitional Shelter Population: 2000* (2001), *The Two or More Races Population: 2000* (2001), *Housing Characteristics: 2000* (2001), *Women in the United States: A Profile* (2000), *Population Change and Distribution* (2001), *Increase in At-Home Workers Reverses Earlier Trend* (1998), *Home Based Workers in the United States 1997* (1997), *Unmarried Partner Households By Sex 2000* (2000), *Estimated Age at First Marriage, by Sex, 1890 to the Present* (2001), and *Interracial Married Couples: 1980 to Present* (2002).

The different agencies of the U.S. Department of Health and Human Services (HHS) produce important publications on a wide variety of statistical data. Its Substance Abuse and Mental Health Service Administration (SAMHSA) published *The Relationship Between Family Structure and Adolescent Substance Abuse* (1996). The department's Maternal and Child Health Bureau published *Child Health USA 2000* (2000), part of an annual series that reports on the health status and service needs of America's children; and it disseminated data collected through the Adoption and Foster Care Analysis and Reporting System (AFCARS). The Federal Interagency Forum on Child and Family Statistics presented an overview of the well-being of the nation's children in *America's Children: Key National Indicators of Well-Being* (2002). The National Child Abuse and Neglect Data System (NCANDS) of the HHS reported on child abuse and neglect statistics submitted by state child protective services agencies in *Child Maltreatment 2000: Reports from the States to the National Child Abuse and Neglect Data System* (2000).

Another agency of the HHS, the Centers for Disease Control and Prevention (CDC), provided sobering data on young adults who have died of AIDS in its publication *HIV/AIDS Surveillance Report* (2000). The CDC's *Morbidity and Mortality Weekly Report* discussed "Trends in Sexual Risk Behaviors Among High School Students; United States, 1991–1997" (1998); and youth risk behaviors were further studied in *Youth Risk Behavior Surveillance; United States, 1999* (2000). The CDC's National Center for Health Statistics (NCHS) is another valuable resource. In *Health, United States, 2000* (2000) it provided a statistical overview of the nation's fertility. The NCHS periodical *National Vital Statistics Report*, formerly called the *Monthly Vital Statistics Report*, supplied data on marriage, divorce, and births. Additionally, some data was gleaned from *Provisional Vital Statistics for the United States; Births, Marriages, Divorces, and Deaths: Provisional Data for 2001* (2002), *Births: Preliminary Data for 1999* (2000), *Teenage Births in the United States: State Trends, 1991–2000, an Update* (2002), and *Nonmarital Childbearing in the United States 1940–1999* (2000).

Trends in multiple births were researched using data from the CDC's report *Trends in Twin and Triplet Births:*

1980–97 (1999), as well as *1997 Assisted Reproductive Technology Success Rates, National Summary and Fertility Clinic Reports* (1999), released by the U.S. Department of Health and Human Services. The U.S. Department of Education, in conjunction with the Bureau of Justice Statistics report *Indicators of School Crime and Safety: 2001*, provided important information on student attitudes toward safety in the school setting.

The U.S. Department of Labor (DOL) was also a vital source for this work. The DOL's *Pilot Survey on the Incidence of Child Care Resource and Referral Services in June 2000* (2000), released through the Bureau of Labor Statistics, was very helpful. The bureau also provides a historical analysis of the economic trends affecting female workers from the years leading to the Equal Pay Act to the present in *Equal Pay: A Thirty-five Year Perspective* (1998) and *Women's Jobs 1964–1999: More Than 30 Years of Progress* (2000). The Bureau of Labor Statistics of the DOL published "Employer-sponsored Childcare Benefits" in *Issues in Labor Statistics* (1998); "Childcare Benefits Continue to Evolve" in *Compensation and Working Conditions* (Summer 2001); *Employment Characteristics of Families: 1999* (2000); *Changes in Women's Labor Force Participation in the 20th Century* (2000); and "Labor Force" data from the *Occupational Outlook Quarterly* (Winter 1999/2000).

We are also grateful for the in-depth research of the U.S. Department of Agriculture's (USDA) Center for Nutrition Policy and Promotion, which released the report *Expenditures on Children by Families, 2001*, part of an annual series that helps quantify how much it costs to raise a child in today's economy. The Alabama Center for Health Statistics compiled national divorce statistics presented in *Divorces and Divorce Rates: Alabama and the United States: 1945–2000*.

The Gale Group thanks the Department for Professional Employees of the AFL-CIO for permission to reprint graphics from *Salaried and Professional Women, Relevant Statistics: 1997 Edition* (1997). The Gale Group is also grateful to the National Adoption Information Clearinghouse for its in-depth information and statistics on adoption and foster care in America.

The Gale Group appreciates the permission of Child Trends DataBank to reproduce information from *Facts at a Glance 2002* and the graphics "Percentage of Overweight Children Ages 6–19," "Percentage of Children in Poverty by Family Structure, Race and Hispanic Origin 2001," "Secure Parental Employment: Percentage of Children Under Age 18 Living with at Least One Parent Employed Full-Time All-Year by Family Structure, Race, Hispanic Origin, Poverty State, and Age, 1980–2000," and "Percentage of Children Whose Single Mothers Were Employed Full-Time, All-Year, Selected Years 1980–2000."

The Gale Group thanks the Pew Charitable Trust for permission to reproduce graphics from the *Pew Internet & American Life Project* (2002), and the Pew Research Center for permission to reproduce graphics from *Interdiction and Incarceration Still Top Remedies* (2001), *From New Interest to Lifestyles, Energy Takes Hold* (2001), *A Year After Columbine Public Looks to Parents More Than Schools to Prevent Violence* (2000), and *Optimism Reigns, Technology Plays Key Role* (2002). We also thank the University of California at Los Angeles Higher Education Research Institute for permission to reprint data from "This Year's Freshmen at 4-Year Colleges: Their Opinions, Activities and Goals" (2000).

The Gale Group appreciates the permission of the Urban Institute to reproduce graphics from *The Rise and Fall of American Youth Violence, 1890–2000* (2002). The American Bar Association and National Bar Association graciously allowed us to reproduce graphics from *Justice by Gender* (2001). We also thank the Joint Center for Housing Studies of Harvard University for permission to reproduce graphics from *The State of the Nation's Housing 2002*. The Annie E. Casey Foundation kindly granted permission to reproduce "Percent of Grandparents Living with Own Grandchildren Who Are Responsible for Their Own Grandchildren" from *Kids Count Census Data Online*.

The Gale Group extends a special thanks to the Gallup Organization for permission to use data from their opinion polls, including permission to publish information from the survey "Parents of Young Children Are Most Stressed Americans" (2002) and from the *Gallup Monthly Poll* (December 2000) survey of attitudes toward religion in America. Additionally, we are grateful to Barna Research for use of their extensive surveys on teens' views of religion and spirituality. Also of help were the Roper Center for Public Opinion Research's studies *Faces of Youth* (2001) and "To the Test" in *Public Perspective* (September/October 2001).

The Gale Group appreciates the permission of the National Parent Teachers Association to reproduce graphics from *What Parents Want in a Television Rating System: Results of a National Survey*. We also thank Worthlin Worldwide for permission to reproduce graphics from "Americans Rank Strengthening Families as High Priority" (2000). The University of Michigan Institute for Social Research ongoing survey "Monitoring the Future" provided valuable 2001 data and graphics.

INDEX

Children's Defense Fund, 31, 55
China, 35
Clinton, Bill, 38
Columbine High School, Colorado, 66, 129
Computers, 75, 78-81
    See also Technology
Consolidated Omnibus Budget
    Reconciliation Act (1986) (COBRA), 83
Contraceptives, 16, 22*f*, 60, 62
Court cases, 111
    Caban v. Mohammed, 111
    Roe v. Wade, 111
    Stanley v. Illinois, 111
Crime, 63, 66-74
    See also Violence among children
Cuomo, Andrew, 106

D
DaimlerChrysler (company), 115
Dayton, Mark, 116
Death rates, 6(*t*1.4), 45*f*, 46*f*
Distance learning, 79-81
Divorce rates, 8, 10*t*, 24-25
Domestic violence, 25
Driscoll, Anne K., 62
Drug use, 62*t*, 66(*t*4.8)
    See also Substance abuse

E
E-mail, 129
Education
    computer and Internet access influenced
        by, 80*t*
    expenditures on children, 52*t*
    influence on computer access, 78
    influence on telecommuting, 79*t*
    insurance coverage, 83, 87, 90*t*, 92*f*
    Internet usage by, 132*t*
    lack of insurance coverage for children,
        57*t*
    married and unmarried people, 11(*t*1.9)
    mobility of families, 108, 110*t*, 112*f*
    nonmarital births by, 19(*f*2.4)
    public opinion on, 126
    on sexual risks, 60
    types of family groups by, 26*t*
    of women, 19-20
Employment, 75
    poverty, 82-83
    work demands on parents, 123-124
    See also Labor force
Energy costs, 124
Expenditures on children, 45-46, 51*t*, 52*t*,
    53*t*

F
Family and Medical Leave Act (1993), 35,
    124
Family households, 1, 26*t*
    See also Households
Family values, 120
    See also Values
Fatalities among abused children, 45*f*, 46*f*
Fertility rates, 6, 14-15
Flexible work schedules, 77
Ford (company), 115

Foreign-born populations, 87-88, 96(*f*5.18)
    children in foreign-born households, 32*t*,
        33
    citizenship status, 95(*f*5.17)
    foreign-born workers, 75
    immigrants, 10, 12(*t*1.10), 12(*t*1.11)
    insurance coverage, 89*t*–90*t*, 92*f*
    lack of insurance coverage for children, 57*t*
    length of residence, 95(*f*5.16)
    mobility of families, 110*t*
    orphans adopted by U.S. natives, 39
    poverty, 113*t*
    by region of origin, 93*f*
    by state, 94*f*
Foster care children, 38, 40, 41(*f*3.10)
Future optimism, 135

G
Gallup, George Jr., 55
Gallup International Poll, 124-125
Gallup Youth Surveys, 55, 66, 69
Gangs, 68-69, 70(*f*4.15)
Gangsta rap, 69
Gannett (company), 115
Gasoline prices, 124(*t*7.3)
Gay partners, 9-10, 112, 115-117
Gender and family, 13-29
    childbearing, 13-19
    domestic violence, 25
    marital status, 26-29
    men, 22-24
    women, 19-22
    See also Marriage/Marital status; Men;
        Women
General Motors (company), 115
Government health insurance, 89*t*–90*t*
Grandparents, 33-35, 34*t*, 35*f*
    characteristics of grandchildren residing
        with, 37*t*–38*t*
    in poverty, 36*f*
    raising children, 103, 105, 106*t*
    residing with grandchildren, 107*t*–108*t*

H
Hate-related behavior at school, 67*f*
Hawaii, 115
Head Start, 42
Health
    expenditures on children, 52*t*
    grandparents residing with
        grandchildren, 107*t*–108*t*
    lack of insurance, 56-59
    of members of multigenerational
        households, 37*t*–38*t*
    obesity in children, 58-59
    See also Insurance coverage
Hispanics
    birth rate among teenagers, 14*t*
    Census Bureau report, 115(*f*6.9)
    children, 31-32
    children in poverty, 50*f*
    income earned by, 76
    lack of insurance for children, 56-57
    sexual risk behaviors, 61*t*–62*t*
Home computers, 78-81
Home ownership, 99, 106, 110*t*
    See also Housing

Home working, 76-78, 77*t*, 78*t*, 79*t*
Homelessness, 88, 90
    by age, 96(*f*5.19)
    by race/ethnicity, 96(*f*5.20)
    by state, 91(*t*5.7), 109, 114*t*
Homosexual partners, 9-10, 112, 115-117
Households, 1-4
    by characteristics of, 2*t*, 3*t*, 9*t*, 26*t*
    children in, 32-33
    foreign and native-born, 32*t*
    multigenerational, 33-35, 34*t*, 36*f*
    people living alone, 29*f*
    by size, 4-8, 4(*f*1.3), 5*t*
    by type and year, 4(*f*1.2)
    unmarried partners 11(*t*1.10)
Housing, 90-91, 93
    characteristics by state, 98*t*
    costs of, 100-101
    home ownership, 99, 106
    mobility of families, 108
    tenure of stay at residence, 97(*f*5.22)
Hubbard, Burt, 105
Human immunodeficiency virus (HIV), 59

I
Illinois, Stanley v., 111
Immigration, 10, 12*t*
    See also Foreign-born populations
Income
    computer and Internet access, 78, 80*t*,
        81(*f*5.8)
    of families, 9*t*
    by family structure, 75-76
    by gender and experience, 24*f*
    influencing expenditures on children, 51*t*,
        52*t*, 53*t*
    insurance coverage, 57*t*, 83, 90*t*, 92*f*
    married and unmarried people, 11(*t*1.9)
    mobility of families, 110*t*
    in multigenerational households, 37*t*–38*t*
    public opinion on the future of the nation,
        71(*t*4.6)
    by race/ethnicity, 76
    by region, 26*f*
    of telecommuters, 76, 78(*f*5.5), 79*t*
    of women, 21
    See also Poverty
Indicators of School Crime and Safety, 67, 68
Insurance coverage, 89*t*–90*t*, 92*f*
    for the impoverished, 83, 87
    lack of for children, 56-59, 57*t*
    for multigenerational households,
        37*t*–38*t*
    by race/ethnicity, 91(*t*5.7)
    in same-sex marriages, 115-116
    workers covered by firm size, 88(*f*5.12)
International statistics
    adoption from other countries, 35, 38
    birth rates among unmarried women, 20*f*
Internet, 69, 78(*f*5.6), 80(*t*5.4), 81*f*, 129,
    132-133, 132*t*, 133*t*
Interracial marriages, 109-110, 116*t*

J
Johnson, Lyndon B., 81
Judge, Mychal, 116
Justice By Gender, 71

of children, 31-32
of children in foster care, 40(*t*3.7)
children in poverty, 50*f*, 55
children waiting to be adopted, 38, 40
computer and Internet access by, 80*t*,
    81(*f*5.8)
employment of parents by, 47*t*
fears of being attacked at school,
    68(*f*4.11)
grandparents residing with
    grandchildren, 107*t*–108*t*
hate-related behavior at school, 67*f*
homelessness by, 96(*f*5.20), 97*t*
householders by, 2*t*
housing costs, 100*t*
importance of family, 119
income, 76
insurance coverage, 89*t*–90*t*, 91(*t*5.7), 92*f*
Internet usage, 132*t*
interracial marriages, 109-110, 116*t*
lack of insurance coverage for children,
    57*t*, 58(*f*4.2)
married and unmarried people, 11(*t*1.9)
Medicaid coverage, 58(*f*4.3)
of members of multigenerational
    households, 37*t*–38*t*
mobility of families, 108, 110*t*
nonmarital births by, 19(*f*2.5)
poverty, 82, 83*f*, 84*t*–87*t*, 113*t*
sexual risk behaviors, 61*t*–62*t*
single parents, 105*t*
teen sexuality, 60
teenage birth rate, 14*t*, 15*f*
telecommuting, 79*t*
types of family groups by, 26*t*
Rating systems for media, 123*f*
Regional distributions
    child care provided by place of
        employment by industry, 49*t*
    computer and Internet access, 80*t*
    foreign-born populations in, 87
    home ownership, 91
    homelessness, 91(*t*5.8), 96(*f*5.20)
    housing characteristics, 98*t*
    housing prices, 99(*t*5.12)
    insurance coverage, 89*t*–90*t*
    lack of insurance coverage for children,
        57*t*
    median income, 26*f*
    mobility of families, 111*f*
    multigenerational households, 37*t*
    poverty, 113*t*
    public opinion on the future of the nation,
        71(*t*4.6)
Religion, 124-125
Renters, 97(*f*5.22), 100*t*, 108
Risk behaviors for sexuality, 59-60, 61*t*–62*t*
    See also Sexuality
Roe v. Wade, 111
Roper Center, 126

S

School violence, 66-70
September 11, 2001, 116
Sexual abuse, 44*f*
Sexuality
    among teens, 59-62, 63*f*, 134

contraceptives, 16, 22*f*
gay and lesbian partners, 9-10, 112, 115-
    117
Single people, 24-25
    adoptions by, 112
    with children, 47*t*, 53*t*
    living alone, 29*f*
Small Business Job Protection Act (1996),
    35
Smith, Tovia, 112
Social issues affecting children, 55-74
    See also under Children
Stanley v. Illinois, 111
State Children's Health Insurance Program
    (CHIP), 58
The State of the Cities 1998, 106
State statistics
    abuse of children, 43*f*
    birth rate among teenagers, 64*t*, 65*f*
    foreign-born populations, 94*f*
    gays and lesbian adoption laws, 117
    grandparents raising children, 106*t*
    homelessness, 91(*t*5.8), 114*t*
    housing characteristics, 98*t*
    married couple households, 104*f*
    multigenerational households, 34
Statistical information
    age of children in foster care, 40(*t*3.6)
    arrests of juveniles, 71(*t*4.7)
    birth rate among teenagers, 14*t*, 64*t*, 65*f*,
        65*t*
    birth rates by age and race/ethnicity, 17*t*
    characteristics of children in
        multigenerational households, 37*t*–38*t*
    characteristics of married and unmarried,
        11(*t*1.9)
    child care provided by place of
        employment by industry, 49*t*
    children in foreign and native-born
        households, 32
    children in poverty, 50*f*
    community problems, public opinion on,
        126*t*
    computer and Internet access, 80*t*
    divorce rates, 10*t*
    drug use amongst teenagers, 127*t*–129*t*
    employment of parents, 47*t*
    expenditures on children, 51*t*, 52*t*, 53*t*
    family households by characteristics, 26*t*
    family structure and owning/renting
        housing, 99(*t*5.11)
    fertility rates, 6(*t*1.5)
    gasoline prices, public opinion on,
        124(*t*7.3)
    grandparents raising children, 106*t*
    grandparents residing with
        grandchildren, 107*t*–108*t*
    homelessness, 91(*t*5.8), 97*t*, 114*t*
    households by characteristics of, 2*t*, 3*t*, 9*t*
    households by size, 5*t*
    housing characteristics by state, 98*t*
    housing costs, 100*t*
    housing difficulties, 101*t*
    housing prices by region, 99(*t*5.12)
    insurance coverage, 89*t*–90*t*, 91(*t*5.7)
    Internet usage, 81*t*, 133*t*
    Internet usage by gender, 132(*t*7.7)

Internet usage by race/ethnicity, 132(*t*7.8)
Internet usage by time spent online,
    132(*t*7.9)
interracial marriages, 116*t*
lack of insurance coverage for children,
    57*t*
living arrangements, 7*t*
marriage status comparison by year, 27*t*
mobility of families, 110*t*
multigenerational households, 34*t*
opinions of college freshman on legal and
    social issues, 134(*t*7.14)
placement of foster care children,
    40(*t*3.8)
poverty, 113*t*
predictions for the future, 134(*t*7.15)
public opinion on juvenile violence,
    71(*t*4.5)
public opinion on priorities of issues,
    120*t*
public opinion on the future of the nation,
    71(*t*4.6)
race/ethnicity of children in foster care,
    40(*t*3.7)
race/ethnicity reported to Census Bureau,
    115*t*
racial/ethnic distribution of adoption
    rates, 41(*t*3.10)
relationship between children and
    adoptive parents, 41(*t*3.12)
sexual risk behaviors among teenagers,
    61*t*–62*t*
single parents, 105*t*
teenagers' disapproval of drug use,
    130*t*–131*t*
telecommuting, 79*t*
twenty-five key facts about children, 31*t*
victimization of children, 42*t*
visas issued to orphans, 39*t*
vital statistics, 6(*t*1.4)
women contributing to family earnings, 76*t*
Stepchildren, 33
Structure of families, 2, 4, 103-117
    adoption, 110-112
    computer and Internet access, 80*t*
    gays and lesbians, 112, 115-117
    income, 75-76
    influence on substance abuse, 65-66
    mobility, 105-106, 108
    multigenerational families, 10-11, 103,
        105, 106*t*
    owning/renting housing, 99(*t*5.11)
    poverty, 84*t*–87*t*, 88(*f*5.11), 109, 113*t*
    single parents, 103
Substance abuse, 63, 65-66
    drug use amongst teenagers, 127*t*–129*t*
    public opinion on, 125-126
    sexual risk behaviors, 62*t*
    teenagers' disapproval of, 130*t*–131*t*
Suburban migration, 105-106

T

Taxes, credits for child care, 45
Technology, 126, 128-129, 132-133
    computers, 75, 78-81, 81*f*
    distance learning, 79-81
    Internet, 69, 80, 81*t*

GARBAGE AND OTHER POLLUTION

ISSN 1538-6651

GARBAGE AND OTHER POLLUTION

Kim Masters Evans

INFORMATION PLUS® REFERENCE SERIES
Formerly published by Information Plus, Wylie, Texas

THOMSON

GALE

Detroit • New York • San Francisco • San Diego • New Haven, Conn. • Waterville, Maine • London • Munich

Garbage and Other Pollution
Kim Masters Evans

Project Editor
Ellice Engdahl

Editorial
Beverly Baer, Paula Cutcher-Jackson, Pamela A. Dear, Kathleen Edgar, Debra Kirby, Prindle LaBarge, Elizabeth Manar, Kathleen Meek, Charles B. Montney, Heather Price

Permissions
Margaret Abendroth, William Sampson, Sheila Spencer

Composition and Electronic Prepress
Evi Seoud

Manufacturing
Keith Helmling

Since this page cannot legibly accommodate all copyright notices, the acknowledgments constitute an extension of the copyright notice.

While every effort has been made to ensure the reliability of the information presented in this publication, The Gale Group, Inc. does not guarantee the accuracy of the data contained herein. The Gale Group, Inc. accepts no payment for listing; and inclusion in the publication of any organization, agency, institution, publication, service, or individual does not imply endorsement of the editors or publisher. Errors brought to the attention of the publisher and verified to the satisfaction of the publisher will be corrected in future editions.

LIBRARY OF CONGRESS CATALOGING-IN-PUBLICATION DATA

ISBN 0-7876-5103-6 (set)
ISBN 0-7876-7520-2
ISSN 1538-6651

Printed in the United States of America
10 9 8 7 6 5 4 3 2 1

TABLE OF CONTENTS

This chapter describes the history of waste management from ancient to modern times. Early efforts at recycling, the modern-day American "throwaway society," total amounts of waste generated, and federal laws concerning waste are also explained.

Chapter 2 defines municipal solid waste (MSW) and examines how it is generated and dealt with. A substantial section details landfills, into which a majority of MSW goes. Also covered are alternative treatments for MSW, including combustion and recycling; packaging as MSW; and recent trends and future projections about waste management.

Recycling and composting are two ways to reduce the amount of waste that has to be disposed. Types of recycling programs and facilities are looked at, and recycling rates of specific wastes are analyzed. Also included are brief accounts of recycling around the world and projections for future waste recovery.

Conveyed in this chapter are facts about pollution that exists in the air. Smog and the health effects of air pollution are covered, and there is detailed treatment of the major air pollutants. Also described are the effects of automobiles on air pollution, national and international laws and treaties on the topic, and the quality of air indoors.

This chapter explains why water pollution is such a serious issue, detailing health risks for humans and whole ecosystems. The Clean Water Act is covered, and the current state of pollution in oceans, estuaries, lakes, reservoirs, ponds, rivers, streams, and wetlands in the United States is explored in depth.

Groundwater is distinct from surface water in that it is found only below Earth's surface; however, it may still become polluted. In this chapter are found the factors that affect ground pollution, sources and types of such pollution, and strategies for protecting or cleaning up groundwater.

Solid waste that can be considered dangerous is classified as hazardous waste. Information on the management and government regulation of hazardous waste is included in this chapter, and the topics of Brownfields, environmental justice, and groundwater contamination are also tackled. The latter two-thirds of the chapter describes various aspects of radioactive waste, including what it is, how it is disposed of, how it is transported, and how other countries deal with its disposal.

Various polls discussed in this chapter display how Americans feel about waste management issues. Poll results presented include how sympathetic people feel to the environmental movement, what Americans' major environmental concerns are, how well the public feels the government is addressing these concerns, how much environmental knowledge people have, and how the importance of environmental protection compares to that of economic growth.

PREFACE

Garbage and Other Pollution is one of the latest volumes in the Information Plus Reference Series. The purpose of each volume of the series is to present the latest facts on a topic of pressing concern in modern American life. These topics include today's most controversial and most studied social issues: abortion, capital punishment, care for the elderly, crime, health care, the environment, immigration, minorities, social welfare, women, youth, and many more. Although written especially for the high school and undergraduate student, this series is an excellent resource for anyone in need of factual information on current affairs.

By presenting the facts, it is Thomson Gale's intention to provide its readers with everything they need to reach an informed opinion on current issues. To that end, there is a particular emphasis in this series on the presentation of scientific studies, surveys, and statistics. These data are generally presented in the form of tables, charts, and other graphics placed within the text of each book. Every graphic is directly referred to and carefully explained in the text. The source of each graphic is presented within the graphic itself. The data used in these graphics are drawn from the most reputable and reliable sources, in particular from the various branches of the U.S. government and from major independent polling organizations. Every effort has been made to secure the most recent information available. The reader should bear in mind that many major studies take years to conduct, and that additional years often pass before the data from these studies are made available to the public. Therefore, in many cases the most recent information available in 2004 dated from 2001 or 2002. Older statistics are sometimes presented as well if they are of particular interest and no more recent information exists.

Although statistics are a major focus of the Information Plus Reference Series, they are by no means its only content. Each book also presents the widely held positions and important ideas that shape how the book's subject is discussed in the United States. These positions are explained in detail and, where possible, in the words of their proponents. Some of the other material to be found in these books includes: historical background; descriptions of major events related to the subject; relevant laws and court cases; and examples of how these issues play out in American life. Some books also feature primary documents or have pro and con debate sections giving the words and opinions of prominent Americans on both sides of a controversial topic. All material is presented in an even-handed and unbiased manner; the reader will never be encouraged to accept one view of an issue over another.

HOW TO USE THIS BOOK

Modern American society is consumption-driven, which means that goods and materials are produced and discarded. The production and consumption of goods results in pollution and waste. This book provides a snapshot of the current condition of garbage and other pollution in the United States. Included is information on the makeup of solid waste, including ways in which it is disposed and/or recycled; the pollution found in air and water; hazardous waste; and the opinions of Americans on various environmental concerns.

Garbage and Other Pollution consists of eight chapters and three appendices. Each of the chapters is devoted to a particular aspect of garbage and pollution. For a summary of the information covered in each chapter, please see the synopses provided in the Table of Contents at the front of the book. Chapters generally begin with an overview of the basic facts and background information on the chapter's topic, then proceed to examine sub-topics of particular interest. For example, Chapter 6: Pollution of Groundwater begins with a definition of groundwater, an explanation of the water cycle, and a list of factors that can affect the pollution of groundwater. It then goes on to provide in-depth coverage of the major sources of ground-water contamination, including underground storage tanks; septic systems and sewage disposal; landfills and hazardous waste sites; pesticides, herbicides, and fertilizers; and surface impoundments. Also included is a section on state and federal legislation. Readers can find their way through a chapter by looking for the section and subsection headings, which are clearly set off from the text. They can also refer to the book's extensive index if they already know what they are looking for.

Statistical Information

The tables and figures featured throughout *Garbage and Other Pollution* will be of particular use to the reader in learning about this issue. These tables and figures represent an extensive collection of the most recent and important statistics on garbage and pollution, as well as related issues—for example, graphics in the book cover materials generated in the municipal waste stream, glass generation and recovery, nitrogen dioxide emissions by source category, characteristics of alternative transportation fuels, fish consumption advisories by state, the nuclear fuel cycle, and public attitudes concerning the priority of various environmental problems. Thomson Gale believes that making this information available to the reader is the most important way in which we fulfill the goal of this book: to help readers understand the issues and controversies surrounding garbage and other pollution in the United States and to reach their own conclusions.

Each table or figure has a unique identifier appearing above it for ease of identification and reference. Titles for the tables and figures explain their purpose. At the end of each table or figure, the original source of the data is provided.

In order to help readers understand these often complicated statistics, all tables and figures are explained in the text. References in the text direct the reader to the relevant statistics. Furthermore, the contents of all tables and figures are fully indexed. Please see the opening section of the index at the back of this volume for a description of how to find tables and figures within it.

Appendices

In addition to the main body text and images, *Garbage and Other Pollution* has three appendices. The first is the Important Names and Addresses directory.

Here the reader will find contact information for a number of government and private organizations that can provide information on garbage and/or pollution in America. The second appendix is the Resources section, which can also assist the reader in conducting his or her own research. In this section, the author and editors of *Garbage and Other Pollution* describe some of the sources that were most useful during the compilation of this book. The final appendix is the detailed index, which facilitates reader access to specific topics in this book.

ADVISORY BOARD CONTRIBUTIONS

The staff of Information Plus would like to extend their heartfelt appreciation to the Information Plus Advisory Board. This dedicated group of media professionals provides feedback on the series on an ongoing basis. Their comments allow the editorial staff who work on the project to make the series better and more user-friendly. Our top priority is to produce the highest-quality and most useful books possible, and the Advisory Board's contributions to this process are invaluable.

The members of the Information Plus Advisory Board are:

- Kathleen R. Bonn, Librarian, Newbury Park High School, Newbury Park, California

- Madelyn Garner, Librarian, San Jacinto College—North Campus, Houston, Texas

- Anne Oxenrider, Media Specialist, Dundee High School, Dundee, Michigan

- Charles R. Rodgers, Director of Libraries, Pasco-Hernando Community College, Dade City, Florida

- James N. Zitzelsberger, Library Media Department Chairman, Oshkosh West High School, Oshkosh, Wisconsin

COMMENTS AND SUGGESTIONS

The editors of the Information Plus Reference Series welcome your feedback on *Garbage and Other Pollution*. Please direct all correspondence to:

Editors
Information Plus Reference Series
27500 Drake Rd.
Farmington Hills, MI 48331-3535

ACKNOWLEDGMENTS

The editors wish to thank the copyright holders of material included in this volume and the permissions managers of many book and magazine publishing companies for assisting us in securing reproduction rights. We are also grateful to the staffs of the Detroit Public Library, the Library of Congress, the University of Detroit Mercy Library, Wayne State University Purdy/Kresge Library Complex, and the University of Michigan Libraries for making their resources available to us.

Following is a list of the copyright holders who have granted us permission to reproduce material in Garbage and Other Pollution. *Every effort has been made to trace copyright, but if omissions have been made, please let us know.*

For more detailed source citations, please see the sources listed under each individual table and figure.

Bay County Solid Waste Management Department: Figure 3.8

BFI Waste Services: Table 1.1

The Gallup Organization: Figure 8.1, Figure 8.2, Figure 8.3, Figure 8.4, Figure 8.5, Figure 8.6, Figure 8.9, Figure 8.10, Table 8.1, Table 8.2

The JG Press, Inc.: Table 2.4, Table 2.5, Table 2.6, Table 3.3

The Library of Congress, Congressional Research Service: Table 2.9

Mid-America Glass Recycling Program: Figure 3.3

The National Environmental Education & Training Foundation: Figure 8.7, Figure 8.8

Natural Resources Defense Council: Table 5.3

Northwest Environment Watch: Table 1.4

The Ocean Conservancy: Table 5.5

Rubber Manufacturers Association: Figure 2.9

U.S. Congress, Office of Technology Assessment: Table 5.4

U.S. Department of Agriculture: Table 4.1

U.S. Department of Agriculture, Economic Research Service: Figure 5.3

U.S. Department of Energy, Energy Information Administration: Figure 2.12, Table 2.7, Figure 6.9

U.S. Department of Energy, Office of Energy Efficiency and Renewable Energy, Office of Industrial Technologies: Figure 1.4

U.S. Department of Energy, Office of Energy Efficiency and Renewable Energy, Office of Transportation Technologies: Table 4.4

U.S. Department of Energy, Office of Energy Efficiency and Renewable Energy, Office of Transportation Technologies, Alternative Fuels Data Center: Table 4.3

U.S. Department of Energy, Office of Public Affairs: Figure 7.11

U.S. Environmental Protection Agency: Figure 2.11, Figure 2.14, Table 2.8, Table 2.10, Figure 3.7, Figure 3.9, Figure 4.13, Figure 4.20, Figure 5.1, Figure 5.2, Figure 5.4, Figure 5.5, Figure 5.9, Table 5.1, Table 5.2, Figure 6.1, Figure 6.3, Figure 6.4, Figure 6.6, Figure 6.7, Figure 6.8, Figure 6.10, Table 6.1, Figure 7.1, Table 7.6

U.S. Environmental Protection Agency, Landfill Methane Outreach Program: Figure 2.10

U.S. Environmental Protection Agency, Office of Air and Radiation: Figure 4.1, Figure 4.12, Figure 4.17

U.S. Environmental Protection Agency, Office of Air Quality and Standards: Figure 4.2, Figure 4.3, Figure 4.4, Figure 4.5, Figure 4.6, Figure 4.7, Figure 4.8, Figure 4.9, Figure 4.10, Figure 4.11, Figure 4.14, Figure 4.15, Figure 4.16, Figure 4.18, Figure 4.19, Figure 4.21, Table 4.2

U.S. Environmental Protection Agency, Office of Environmental Information: Figure 7.5, Figure 7.6, Table 7.4, Table 7.5

U.S. Environmental Protection Agency, Office of Solid Waste and Emergency Response: Figure 1.1, Figure 1.2, Figure 1.5, Table 1.2, Table 1.3, Table 1.5, Figure 2.1, Figure 2.2, Figure 2.3, Figure 2.4, Figure 2.5, Figure 2.6, Figure 2.7, Figure 2.8, Figure 2.13, Table 2.1, Table 2.2, Table 2.3, Figure 3.1, Figure 3.2, Figure 3.4, Figure 3.5, Figure 3.6, Table 3.1, Table 3.2, Table 3.4, Figure 6.2, Figure 6.11, Figure 6.12, Figure 7.2, Figure 7.4, Table 7.1, Table 7.2, Table 7.3

U.S. Environmental Protection Agency, Office of Water: Figure 5.6, Figure 5.7, Figure 5.8, Figure 5.10, Figure 5.11, Figure 5.12, Figure 5.13, Figure 5.14, Figure 5.15, Figure 5.16, Figure 5.17, Figure 5.18, Figure 5.19, Figure 5.20, Figure 5.21, Figure 5.22, Figure 5.23, Figure 5.24, Figure 6.5, Table 6.2, Figure 7.3

U.S. General Accounting Office: Figure 1.3, Figure 4.22, Figure 7.7, Figure 7.8, Figure 7.9, Figure 7.10, Figure 7.12, Table 7.7, Table 7.8

U.S. Geological Survey, prepared in cooperation with the U.S. Environmental Protection Agency: Figure 6.13, Figure 6.14

CHAPTER 1
HISTORICAL PERSPECTIVE—GARBAGE THEN AND NOW

Garbage, trash, refuse, rubbish, and waste—these terms are often used interchangeably. What do they mean? Are they all the same thing?

Garbage is "wet" discarded matter that is generally edible by animals. Food remains and yard clippings are examples of garbage. Trash is "dry" discarded matter that is generally inedible. Newspapers, bottles, and cans are examples of trash. Refuse refers to both garbage and trash, while rubbish is refuse plus construction and demolition debris. Waste (which is more properly termed solid waste) includes rubbish along with semisolids, liquids, and gases from mining, agricultural, commercial, and industrial activities. All animals produce garbage when they eat food and then cast aside the remains. However, only humans produce trash, refuse, rubbish, and solid waste.

THE FIRST GARBAGE DUMPS

The earliest humans did not have garbage disposal problems. They lived in nomadic tribes, wandering the countryside and following herds of wild animals that they hunted and killed for food and clothing. Scavengers and insects ate their discarded food remains, and what was left decomposed. About 12,000 years ago, people began to form villages and become farmers. For the first time, they had to live with their garbage, which smelled bad and attracted wild animals. Therefore, some villagers dug pits into which they tossed garbage. One of the best ways scientists learn about such prehistoric communities is by studying their garbage pits. See Table 1.1 for a historical timeline of waste management practices through the centuries.

CLEANING UP ANCIENT CITIES

About 4,500 years ago, one of the world's first great civilizations began to develop in what is now Pakistan and northwestern India. Ruins show that the two major cities in this area were large and well planned. One of the cities, Mahenjo-Daro, was built using a design that called for

homes to contain built-in rubbish chutes and trash bins. A few hundred years after that, in the ancient Egyptian city of Heracleopolis, religious leaders and the wealthy had their refuse collected and then dumped into the Nile River. At about the same time in Crete, the bathrooms of the kings were connected to sewers.

About 1,300 years later, Jerusalem developed a sewer system that served the entire city—not just the rich or powerful. A few hundred years later (approximately 400 B.C.), the city of Athens, Greece, passed the first garbage dump law in the Western world, requiring that garbage be dumped at least one mile outside the city walls. The Roman Empire is famous for its innovative water and sewage systems in major cities. The Romans also created a garbage collection service.

The fall of the Roman Empire around 400 A.D. ushered in a period of time called the Middle Ages, which lasted until around the year 1500. In Europe during the Middle Ages, refuse collection and disposal took a step backward. These systems were not considered important and people threw their garbage and trash into the streets and rivers. Disease spread quickly, as poor sanitation practices and rotting garbage piles throughout Europe attracted disease-spreading vermin and insects. A horrible epidemic called the Black Death was spread by rats and killed millions of people during the Middle Ages. In 1388 the English Parliament made it illegal to throw garbage into the rivers. However, by 1400 the piles of garbage outside the city gates of Paris were so high that it was hard to defend the city because the mounds of garbage were as tall as the city walls.

THE COMING OF THE INDUSTRIAL REVOLUTION

From the 1700s through the early 1800s, the Western world experienced an Industrial Revolution. The development of factories and the congestion of cities with factory workers characterized this period. People lived in

TABLE 1.1

Trash timeline, 10,000 BC–2000 AD

10000 BC	Garbage becomes an issue as people first begin to establish permanent settlements
400 BC	The first municipal dump is established in ancient Athens
200	The first sanitation force is created by the Romans. Teams of two men walk along the streets, pick up garbage and throw it in a wagon.
1388	The English Parliament bans dumping of waste in ditches and public waterways.
1551	The first recorded use of packaging: German papermaker Andreas Bernhart begins placing his paper in wrappers labeled with his name and address.
1657	New Amsterdam (now Manhattan) passes a law against casting waste in the streets.
1690	The Rittenhouse Mill, America's first paper mill, opens in Philadelphia making paper from recycled cotton and linen as well as used paper.
1710	Colonists in Virginia commonly bury their trash. Holes are filled with building debris, broken glass or ceramic objects, oyster shells and animal bones. They also throw away hundreds of suits of armor that were sent to protect colonists from arrows of native inhabitants.
1776	The first metal recycling in America occurs when patriots in New York City melt down a statue of King George III and make it into bullets.
1792	Benjamin Franklin uses slaves to carry Philadelphia's waste downstream.
1800	Pigs loose in city streets throughout the country eat garbage and leave their own wastes behind.
1800	Visitors describe New York City as a "nasal disaster, where some streets smell like bad eggs dissolved in ammonia."
1810	The tin can is patented in London by Peter Durand.
1834	Charleston, West Virginia, enacts a law protecting vultures from hunters. The birds help eat the city's garbage.
1850	Junk dealers in Reno, Nevada scavenge personal belongings from the Oregon, Santa Fe and California trails. Pioneers abandoned the items on the long trek west.
1860	American newspapers are now printed on paper made from wood pulp fibers rather than rags.
1860	Residents of Washington, D.C. dump garbage and slop into alleys and streets, pigs roam freely, slaughterhouses spew nauseating fumes and rats and cockroaches infest most dwellings including the White House.
1866	New York City's Metropolitan Board of Health declares war on garbage, forbidding the "throwing of dead animals, garbage or ashes into the streets."
1872	New York City stops dumping its garbage from a platform built over the East River.
1873	John Wesley Hyatt successfully manufactures "celluloid," the first commercial synthetic plastic. It replaces wood, ivory, metal and linen in such items as combs, billiard balls, eyeglasses and shirt collars.
1879	Frank Woolworth opens the first five and dime store in Utica, New York. He pioneers the idea of displaying goods on open counters so customers can see and feel merchandise (a practice that later makes larger, theft proof packaging necessary).
1879	"Thither were brought the dead dogs and cats, the kitchen garbage and the like, and duly dumped. This festering, rotten mess were picked over by rag pickers and wallowed over by pigs, pigs and humans contesting for a living from it, and as the heaps increased, the odors increased also, and the mass lay corrupting under a tropical sun, dispersing the pestilential fumes where the winds carried them." - Minister describing the New Orleans dump to the American Public Health Association.
1880	Many Americans still believe that diseases such as typhoid fever are caused by "miasma" or gases coming from garbage and sewers.
1880	New York City scavengers remove 15,000 horse carcasses from the streets.
1885	The first garbage incinerator in the U.S. is built on Governors Island in New York Harbor.
1885-1908	180 garbage incinerators are built in the United States.
1889	"Appropriate places for (refuse) are becoming scarcer year by year, and the question as to some other method of disposal…must soon confront us. Already the inhabitants in proximity to the public dumps are beginning to complain." - Health Officer's report, Washington, D.C.
1892	Beer bottles now sport a metal cap to prevent spoilage.
1893	"The means resorted to by a large number of citizens to get rid of their garbage and avoid paying for its collection would be very amusing were it not such a menace to public health. Some burn it, while others wrap it up in paper and carry it on their way to work and drop it when unobserved, or throw it into vacant lots or into the river." - Boston Sanitary Committee
1894	The citizens of Alexandria, Virginia are disgusted by the sight of barge loads of garbage floating down the Potomac River from Washington, D.C. They take to sinking the barges upriver from their community.
1895	King C. Gillette, a traveling salesman, invents a razor with disposable blades.
1896	Chicago's City Council records its concern for the death rate in the 19th Ward, which has eight miles of unpaved roads that can't be swept, roads "polluted to the last degree with trampled garbage, excreta and other vegetables and animal refuse of the vilest description."
1897	The first recycling center is established in New York City.
1898	Colonel George Waring, New York's Street Cleaning Commissioner, organizes the country's first rubbish sorting plant for recycling.
1899	The federal Rivers and Harbors Act restricts dumping in navigable rivers, to keep them open for shipping.
1900	American cities begin to estimate and record collected wastes. According to one estimate, each American produces annually: 80 - 100 pounds of food waste; 50 - 100 pounds of rubbish; 300 - 1,200 pounds of wood or coal ash - up to 1,400 pounds per person.
1900	Greater acceptance of the germ theory of disease begins to shift the job of garbage removal from health departments to public works departments. Health officers, it is felt, should spend their time battling infectious diseases, not cleaning up "public nuisances" such as garbage.
1900	Hills Brothers Coffee in San Francisco puts the first vacuum-packed coffee on the market.
1900	Small and medium sized towns build piggeries, where swine are fed fresh or cooked garbage. One expert estimates that 75 pigs can eat one ton of refuse per day.
1900	There are over 3 million horses working in American cities, each producing over 20 pounds of manure and gallons of urine per day, most of which is left on the streets.
1902	A survey of 161 cities by the Massachusetts Institute of Technology finds that 79% of them provide regular collection of refuse.
1903	Corrugated paperboard containers are now used commercially.
1904	Large-scale aluminum recycling begins in Chicago and Cleveland.
1904	Montgomery Ward mails out 3 million catalogues weighing four pounds each.
1904	Postmaster General Henry Clay Payne authorizes permit mail. This means that with a single fee, 2,000 or more pieces of third or fourth class mail can be posted without stamps. This opens the door for direct mail advertising and mass solicitations.
1905	New York City begins using a garbage incinerator to generate electricity to light the Williamsburg Bridge.
1907	An unexpectedly thick run of toilet paper is converted to become the first paper towels.
1908	Paper cups replace tin cups at water vending machines on trains and in public buildings.

TABLE 1.1

Trash timeline, 10,000 BC–2000 AD [CONTINUED]

1909	102 of 180 incinerators built since 1885 are abandoned or dismantled. Many had been inadequately built or run. Also, American's abundant land and widely spaced population made dumping garage cheaper and more practical.
1909	Kraft paper pulp first made in the United States, a process developed in Germany in 1883.
1910	City beautification programs become more and more popular. Many cities have juvenile sanitation leagues whose members promise to help keep streets and neighborhoods clean. Sanitation workers wear white uniforms, reminiscent of other public workers such as doctors and nurses.
1912	Cellophane (clear plastic) is invented by Swiss chemist Dr. Jacques Brandenberger, which encourages the use of plastic packaging.
1914	W.K. Kellogg invents a wax paper wrapper for Corn Flakes boxes.
1915	The National Clean-Up and Paint-Up bureau sponsors 5,000 local clean-up campaigns.
1916	Dr. Thomas Jasperson obtains a patent for making paper from de-inked wastepaper.
1916	Major cities estimate that of the 1,000 to 1,750 pounds of waste generated by each person per year, 80% is coal and wood ash.
1916	Waxed paper is commonly used to wrap bread.
1917	Shortages of raw materials during World War I prompt the federal government to start the Waste Reclamation Service, part of the War Industries Board. Its motto is "Don't Waste Waste - Save it." Every article of waste is considered valuable for industry.
1920	During this decade, "reclaiming" or filling wetlands near cities with garbage, ash and dirt becomes a popular disposal method.
1920	The first commercial radio broadcast. The technology held far reaching implications for advertising and purchasing. Americans buy 1.5 million radios within the year.
1924	The Kleenex facial tissue is introduced.
1926	Clarence Saunders opens the first supermarket. Pre-packaged food and self service packaging increases selection for consumers and lowers the cost of food.
1928	Moisture-proof cellophane is invented by the DuPont Cellophane Company. The transparent material is used as a protective wrapping for food and other products.
1928	Teleprinters and teletypewriters come into use.
1929	Aluminum foil is invented.
1930	A new plastic, polyvinyl chloride, is patented by B.F. Goodrich. It is used as a replacement for rubber, as protection against corrosion and for adhesives.
1930	Another plastic, polystyrene, is put on the market by a German firm, I.G. Farben, and also produced by Dow Chemical Company. The hard, shiny material is molded into tackle boxes, refrigerator linings and other items.
1930	Kimberly Clark develops disposable sanitary pads.
1932	The development of compactor garbage trucks increases vehicle capacity.
1933	Communities on the New Jersey shore obtain a court order forcing New York City to stop dumping garbage in the Atlantic Ocean. On July 1, 1934, the Supreme Court upholds the lower court action, but applies it only to municipal waste, not commercial or industrial wastes.
1935	Rohm and Haas invents Plexiglass, a clear plastic used in headlights, lenses, windows, clocks and jewelry.
1935	General Electric begins producing and marketing a garbage "Disposal."
1935	The first beer can is produced by Kreuger's Cream Ale in Richmond, VA. Over the next six months, company sales increased 550% because customers loved the convenience.
1936	Milk products are now commonly sold in paper packaging.
1937	The DuPont Company patents nylon, the world's first synthetic fiber. Its strength, resistance to moisture and mildew, and good recovery after stretching lead to its use in stockings, electrical parts, power tools and car accessories.
1939	Coal and wood ash make up 43% of New York City's refuse, down from 80% in 1916.
1939	Paperback books are introduced, selling for 25 cents.
1939	Wisconsin Select beer is sold in no deposit, no return bottles to compete with the recent introduction of beer in no return cans.
1939	Birds Eye introduces the first pre-cooked frozen foods - chicken fricassee and criss cross steak.
1940	Japanese conquests in Southeast Asia cut off America's supply of tin, hampering canned food production.
1941	America enters World War II. Rationing of such materials as wood and metal forces an increased reliance on synthetic materials such as plastics. Low-density polyethylene film, developed during wartime, replaces cellophane as the favorite food wrap by 1960.
1942	Americans collect rubber, paper, glass, metals and fats to help the war effort. Paper collections are so successful they overwhelm the markets by the spring of 1942.
1942	Methods and materials for wartime shipment of food make World War II "the great divide" in the packaging and storage industry.
1943	The aerosol can is invented by two researchers at the U.S. Department of Agriculture.
1944	Styrofoam is invented by Dow Chemical Co.
1945	The first American ballpoint pens go on sale for $12.50 each at Gimbel's in New York.
1946	Fortune Magazine heralds the arrival of the "dream era...The Great American Boom is on."
1947	"Our willingness to part with something before it is completely worn out is a phenomenon noticeable in no other society in history...It is soundly based on our economy of abundance. It must be further nurtured even though it runs contrary to one of the oldest inbred laws of humanity, the law of thrift." - J. Gordon Lippincott, industrial designer
1948	American Public Health Association predicts that the garbage disposal will cause the garbage can to "ultimately follow the privy" and become an "anachronism."
1948	Fresh Kills landfill is opened in Staten Island, New York. It later becomes the world's largest city dump. Fresh Kills and the Great Wall of China are the only man-made objects visible from space.
1950	A second hydraulic system to eject garbage is added to garbage trucks.
1950	An improved paper cup for hot beverages is introduced. It is lined with polyethylene instead of wax.
1950	The growth of convenience foods (frozen, canned, dried, boxed, etc) increases the amounts and changes the types of packaging thrown away.
1953	The American economy's "ultimate purpose is to produce more consumer goods." - Chairman of President Eisenhower's Council of Economic Advisors.
1953	Swanson introduces the first successful TV dinner: turkey, mashed potatoes and peas.
1954	"Never underestimate the buying power of a child under seven. He has brand loyalty and the determination to see that his parents purchase the products of his choice." - Dr. Frances Horwitch ("Miss Frances" of TV's Ding Dong School) at Chicago advertising conference.

TABLE 1.1

Trash timeline, 10,000 BC–2000 AD [CONTINUED]

1957	High-density polyethylene (HDPE) is developed by Standard Oil of Indiana and Phillips Petroleum (now used for milk containers).
1958	The Bic Crystal Company introduces the throwaway pen.
1959	Philadelphia closes its reduction plant (a facility for turning organic wastes into fats, grease and oils) the last one in the country.
1959	The American Society of Civil Engineers publishes a standard guide to sanitary landfilling. To guard against rodents and odors, it suggests compacting the refuse and covering it with a layer of soil each day.
1959	The first photocopier, the Xerox 914, is introduced - 22 years after it was patented.
1960	Bead molded polystyrene cups are introduced. They provide better insulation for hot drinks.
1960	Bread is sold bagged in polyethylene rather than wrapped in waxed paper.
1960	Easy open tops (pop tops) for beverage cans are invented. Iron City Beer in Pittsburgh is the first to try the invention and sales increase immediately.
1960	The first disposable razors are sold.
1961	Sam Yorty runs successfully for mayor of Los Angeles on a platform to end the inconvenience of separating refuse. A city ordinance eliminates the sorting of recyclables.
1963	The aluminum can for beverages is developed.
1965	The federal government realizes that garbage has become a major problem and enacts the Solid Waste Disposal Act. This calls for the nation to find better ways of dealing with trash.
1968	President Lyndon Johnson commissions the National Survey of Community Solid Waste Practices, which provides the first comprehensive data on solid waste since cities began to record amounts and types of waste in the early 1900s.
1968	The U.S. aluminum industry begins recycling discarded aluminum products, from beverage cans to window blinds.
1969	Seattle, Washington institutes a new fee structure for garbage pick up. Residents pay a base rate for one to four cans and an additional fee for each additional bundle or can.
1970	The Federal Clean Air Act enacted. New regulations lead to incineration shut downs.
1970	The first Earth Day. Millions of people rally nationwide on April 22.
1970	United States Environmental Protection Agency is created.
1971	Oregon passes the nation's first bottle bill. By offering cash for aluminum, glass and plastic containers, it removes about 7% of its garbage from the waste stream.
1972	According to William Ruckelshaus, head of EPA, solid waste management is a "fundamental ecological issue. It illustrates, perhaps more clearly than any other environmental problem, that we must change many of our traditional attitudes and habits."
1972	The Federal Clean Water Act is enacted to restore and maintain the chemical, physical and biological integrity of the nation's waters.
1972	The first buy-back centers for recyclables are opened in Washington State. They accept beer bottles, aluminum cans and newspapers.
1974	The first city-wide use of curbside recycling bins occurs in University City, Missouri for collecting newspapers.
1975	"That happiness is to be attained through limitless material acquisition is denied by every religion and philosophy known to humankind, but is preached incessantly by every American television set." - Robert Bellah, The Broken Covenant.
1976	The Resource Conservation and Recovery Act creates the first significant role for federal government in waste management. It emphasizes recycling and conservation of energy. It also requires all dumps to be replaced with "sanitary landfills." The enforcement of this act will increase the cost of landfill disposal, and that will make resource-conserving options like recycling more appealing.
1976	The Toxic Substances Control Act is passed. Before this and the Resource Conservation and Recovery Act went into effect, any individual or business could legally dump any kind and amount of hazardous chemicals in landfills.
1976	Three people from Bartlesville, Oklahoma get a patent on a method for purifying and reusing lubricating oils.
1977	Polyethylene terephthalate (PET) soda bottles are introduced to replace glass bottles. The plastic was first developed in England in 1941.
1978	The Supreme Court rules that garbage is protected by the Interstate Commerce Clause; therefore, one state cannot ban shipments of waste from another.
1979	EPA issues landfill criteria that prohibit open dumping.
1980	Polypropylene is introduced and used for butter and margarine tubs and for drinking straws.
1983	The space shuttle is pulled out of service to replace a window that had been severely pitted by a chip of paint from space junk.
1984	During the Olympic Games in Los Angeles, athletes, trainers, coaches and spectators produce 6.5 million pounds of trash in 22 days, more than six pounds per person per day.
1984	Hazardous and Solid Waste Act amendments and reauthorization to the Resource Conservation and Recovery Act require tougher federal regulation of landfills.
1986	Fresh Kills, in Staten Island, New York, becomes the largest landfill in the world.
1986	Rhode Island becomes the first state to pass mandatory recycling laws for aluminum and steel cans, glass, newspapers and some plastics.
1986	The city of San Francisco meets its goal of recycling 25% of its commercial and residential waste.
1987	The Garbage Project at the University of Arizona, Tucson begins to excavate modern landfills as if they were ancient archaeological sites. The goal is to determine exactly what is inside landfills and how much of it biodegrades.
1987	The Mobro, a Long Island garbage barge, is turned away by six states and three countries. The garbage (mostly paper) is finally incinerated in Brooklyn and the ash buried in a landfill near Islip.
1988	"Nobody ever has enough." - Lewis Lapham, Money and Class in America.
1988	The EPA estimates that more than 14,000 landfills have closed since 1978, more than 70% of those operating at that time. The landfills were full, unsafe or the owners declined to adhere to new standards.
1988	The Plastic Bottle Institute develops a material-identification code system for plastic bottle manufacturers (this is our current #1-#7 system).
1989	EPA issues "An Agenda for Action," calling for an integrated solid waste management approach to solving solid waste problems with waste problems, with waste prevention and recycling as its first two priorities.
1990	140 recycling laws enacted in 38 states and the District of Columbia.
1990	McDonald's announces plans to stop the use of Styrofoam packaging of its food due to consumer protests.
1990	"Neither shortening nor lengthening product life can be a general principle. The strategy, rather, is to fine tune the durations of things, now avoiding cheap things that break too soon and clog our trash cans, now expensive objects that last too long and clog our lives." - Kevin Lynch, Wasting Away.

TABLE 1.1

Trash timeline, 10,000 BC–2000 AD [CONTINUED]

1990	On December 4, both Coca-Cola and Pepsi announced that they will begin using a recycled PET (#1 plastic) bottle made of about 25% recycled plastic resin.
1991	EPA issues comprehensive municipal solid waste landfill criteria required by the Hazardous and Solid Waste Amendment.
1991	"Our economy is such that we cannot 'afford' to take care of things: labor is expensive, time is expensive, money is expensive, but materials —the stuff of creation— are so cheap that we cannot afford to take care of them." - Wendell Berry
1993	Municipal Solid Waste landfill criteria become effective for most landfills in the U.S.
1993	"We're reminded a hundred times a day to buy things, but we're not reminded to take care of them, repair them, reuse them or give them away." - Michael Jacobson, Center for the Study of Commercialism
2000	Cities in California are required to recycle 50% of their waste.

SOURCE: "Trash Timeline," in *BFI Kids,* BFI Waste Services, Salinas, CA, 2003 [Online] http://www.bfi-salinas.com/kids_trash_timeline-printer.cfm [accessed October 20, 2003]. Data from the Association of Science-Technology Centers Incorporated and the Smithsonian Institution Traveling Exhibition Service.

crowded housing and the sanitation was poor, allowing raw sewage to get into water supplies in some cities. The polluted water caused typhoid fever and other illnesses. Additionally, the burning of coal, which powered most factories and heated most city homes, filled the air of industrial cities with smoke and soot.

It was finally during the 1800s that scientists figured out the link between germs and poor sanitation. By 1869 England had created a Sanitary Commission to improve sanitation and garbage disposal in English cities.

IN THE UNITED STATES

During the 1600s and 1700s in colonial America, people dumped their refuse into the streets as they did in European cities. Pigs roamed the streets and ate the garbage. In 1657 New Amsterdam (now New York City) became the first city to pass laws against street disposal. Nonetheless, as late as the 1860s residents of New York City and Washington, D.C. still threw their garbage into the streets.

When the United States became industrialized in the 1800s, most Americans did not think that what they were doing would hurt the environment. Factories often dumped their chemicals directly into rivers and lakes. Cities poured their sewage into the same rivers and lakes. Garbage was deposited into nearby garbage dumps without any concern that it might harm groundwater. Ships dumped garbage overboard into rivers, lakes, and oceans.

The air became polluted, as did the land and the water. Postcards proudly showed factories pouring smoke into the air. By the early 1900s, air pollution problems became particularly serious; smoke and soot filled the air over many Eastern and Midwestern cities. In some industrial cities, the air frequently became so hazy that drivers needed streetlights and headlights to see during the day.

This lack of concern for the environment led to serious problems. New Orleans had typhoid epidemics because sewage was poured into streets and canals. Memphis lost nearly 10 percent of its population to yellow fever. Infant mortality was very high in large cities.

It was not only people that produced waste. In New York City more than 100,000 horses drew carriages, hauled wagons, and pulled streetcars. Thousands more horses did such work in other major cities, generating massive amounts of manure that dirtied the streets. This waste had to be cleaned up and dumped elsewhere.

EARLY EFFORTS TO REUSE GARBAGE AND TRASH

Although pre-1900s refuse disposal practices were poor, most Americans produced much less garbage and trash than they do today. Food scraps were boiled to make soups or were fed to farm animals. Durable items were passed on to the next generation or to people in need. Objects that were of no further use to adults became toys for children. Broken items were repaired or dismantled for reuse. Things that could no longer be used were burned for fuel, especially in the homes of the poor. Even middle-class Americans traded rags to peddlers in exchange for buttons or teakettles. The ragmen worked the streets, begging for or buying at low prices items such as bones, paper, old iron, rags, and bottles. They then sold the junk to dealers who marketed it to manufacturers.

Using scraps and prolonging the useful lives of items saved money. In 1919 in the publication *Save and Have, A Book of 'Saving Graces' for American Homes* (New York), the University Society discussed habits of thrift. The Society recommended keeping cake fresh by storing it with an apple and "turning" worn sheets by tearing them down the middle and sewing up the good sides. Other suggestions included collecting grease to make soap, reusing flour sacks for dishtowels or clothing, using jars for drinking glasses, and keeping a can on the stove for grease that was used over and over.

Besides giving away clothes, mending and remaking them, and using them as rags for work, women reworked textiles into useful household furnishings, such as quilts, rugs, and upholstery. In the American culture of the time, such activities demonstrated a woman's frugality and creative skill and came to represent an aspect of a woman's virtue. A growing paper

TABLE 1.2

Outline of the Resource Conservation and Recovery Act

Subtitle	Provisions
A	General provisions
B	Office of Solid Waste; authorities of the administrator and Interagency Coordinating Committee
C	Hazardous waste management
D	State or regional solid waste plans
E	Duties of the Secretary of Commerce in resource and recovery
F	Federal responsibilities
G	Miscellaneous provisions
H	Research, development, demonstration, and information
I	Regulation of underground storage tanks
J	Standards for the tracking and management of medical waste

SOURCE: "Figure I-3: Outline of the Act," in *RCRA Orientation Manual,* EPA530-R-02-016, U.S. Environmental Protection Agency, Office of Solid Waste and Emergency Response, Washington, DC, January 2003

TABLE 1.3

Resource Conservation and Recovery Act's interrelated programs

Subtitle D	Subtitle C	Subtitle I
Solid waste program	Hazardous waste program	Underground storage tank program

SOURCE: "Figure I-1: RCRA's Three Interrelated Programs," in *RCRA Orientation Manual,* EPA530-R-02-016, U.S. Environmental Protection Agency, Office of Solid Waste and Emergency Response, Washington, DC, January 2003

industry also made it profitable for thrifty housewives to save rags, which were used by paper mills to make paper.

A trade in used goods such as rags provided crucial resources for early industrialization. However, these early systems of recycling diminished in the early 1900s. Sanitary reformers and municipal trash collection did away with scavenging. Technology made cheap and new alternatives available. People made fewer things and bought more than previous generations. They also saved and repaired less and threw out more. In *A Social History of Trash* (Henry Holt and Co., New York, 1999), Susan Strasser describes this change in the nation's mindset:

> The rhetoric of convenience, luxury, and cleanliness was potent. It sold a wide variety of products that transformed Americans' relationship to waste and, in general, to the material world. In a few decades, the ideal of the durable and reusable was displaced by aspirations of leisure and luxury, ease and cleanliness. The new ways were entrenched by 1929, in principle if not always in practice, and neither a depression nor the material shortages of a world war were enough to reverse what most people saw as progress.

Old-fashioned reuse and recycling did not cease overnight. During the first decades of the twentieth century, most people still threw away relatively little. Publications such as the aforementioned *Save and Have* were popular. Nonetheless, as the century progressed, middle-class people learned to discard things, attracted by convenience and a desire to avoid any association with scavenging and poverty. Success often meant that one did not have to use secondhand goods. As municipalities became responsible for collecting and disposing of refuse, Americans found it easier to throw things away.

WASTE MANAGEMENT

Throughout the 1800s, many cities passed anti-dumping ordinances, but they were often ignored. Some landowners and merchants resented ordinances, which they considered an infringement on their rights. Therefore, as cities grew, refuse piles grew, becoming not only public eyesores but also threats to public health.

By the end of the 1800s, city leaders began to recognize that they had to do something about proper refuse disposal. As a result, most major cities had set up refuse collection systems by the turn of the century. Many cities introduced incinerators to burn some of the refuse. When World War I began in 1914, about 300 incinerators were operating in the United States and Canada. By the 1920s, landfilling had become a popular refuse disposal method. As shown in Table 1.1 cities often dumped their trash in nearby marshes and swamps, areas that were considered useless for development purposes.

In 1959 the American Society of Civil Engineers published *Landfill Practice,* a comprehensive manual about sanitary landfilling. The manual suggests that landfill waste be compacted and covered daily to prevent problems with rodents and odors.

LAWS GOVERNING WASTE AND OTHER POLLUTION

In 1965 the United States government passed the Solid Waste Disposal Act, the first of many solid waste management laws. It was amended several times, most notably in 1976, with the Resource Conservation and Recovery Act (RCRA). The RCRA consists of 10 subtitles. (See Table 1.2.) As shown in Table 1.3, there are three subtitles covering the major programs regulated under RCRA: the solid waste program (Subtitle D), the hazardous waste program (Subtitle C), and the underground storage tank program (Subtitle I).

Subtitle D of RCRA assigns to the states responsibility for permitting and monitoring landfills for municipal solid waste and other nonhazardous wastes. Regulations established under Subtitle D describe minimum federal standards for the design, location, and operation of solid waste landfills to protect the environment. The states can develop their own permitting programs, so long as they

FIGURE 1.1

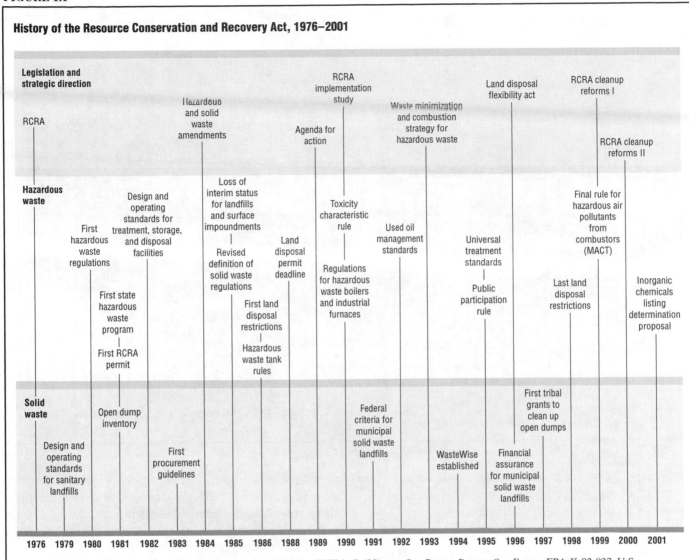

History of the Resource Conservation and Recovery Act, 1976–2001

Legislation and strategic direction

RCRA

Hazardous and solid waste amendments

RCRA implementation study

Agenda for action

Waste minimization and combustion strategy for hazardous waste

Land disposal flexibility act

RCRA cleanup reforms I

RCRA cleanup reforms II

Hazardous waste

First hazardous waste regulations

Design and operating standards for treatment, storage, and disposal facilities

First state hazardous waste program

First RCRA permit

Loss of interim status for landfills and surface impoundments

Revised definition of solid waste regulations

Land disposal permit deadline

First land disposal restrictions

Hazardous waste tank rules

Toxicity characteristic rule

Regulations for hazardous waste boilers and industrial furnaces

Used oil management standards

Universal treatment standards

Public participation rule

Final rule for hazardous air pollutants from combustors (MACT)

Last land disposal restrictions

Inorganic chemicals listing determination proposal

Solid waste

Open dump inventory

Design and operating standards for sanitary landfills

First procurement guidelines

Federal criteria for municipal solid waste landfills

WasteWise established

First tribal grants to clean up open dumps

Financial assurance for municipal solid waste landfills

1976 1979 1980 1981 1982 1983 1984 1985 1986 1988 1989 1990 1991 1992 1993 1994 1995 1996 1997 1998 1999 2000 2001

SOURCE: "25 Years: Preserving, Preventing, Protecting," in *25 Years of RCRA: Building on Our Past to Protect Our Future*, EPA-K-02-027, U.S. Environmental Protection Agency, Office of Solid Waste and Emergency Response, Washington, DC, April 2002

include the federal landfill criteria. The U.S. Environmental Protection Agency (EPA) has the authority to review and approve the state programs.

Subtitle C of RCRA give the EPA primary responsibility for permitting facilities that treat, store, and/or dispose of hazardous waste. However, the EPA can allow states to operate their own permitting programs. Subtitle C regulations cover hazardous waste from the time it is created to the time of its final disposal. This is commonly called "cradle to grave" coverage.

The Subtitle C regulations exempt certain kinds of hazardous waste (for example, hazardous wastes generated by households). Exempted hazardous wastes are covered by Subtitle D.

Subtitle I is concerned with preventing, detecting, and cleaning up any releases from underground storage tanks holding petroleum products and hazardous substances.

Subtitle I regulations include design standards for new tanks and upgrade requirements for existing tanks. The states can establish their own permitting programs with the approval of the EPA.

The RCRA's primary goals are to:

1) protect human health and the environment from the potential hazards of waste disposal,

2) conserve energy and natural resources,

3) reduce the amount of waste generated, and

4) ensure that wastes are managed in an environmentally sound manner.

Figure 1.1 shows the legislative milestones associated with RCRA between 1976 and 2001.

Besides RCRA, other federal laws indirectly regulate waste disposal by protecting against pollution that can result

Example of multi-exposure contamination pathways

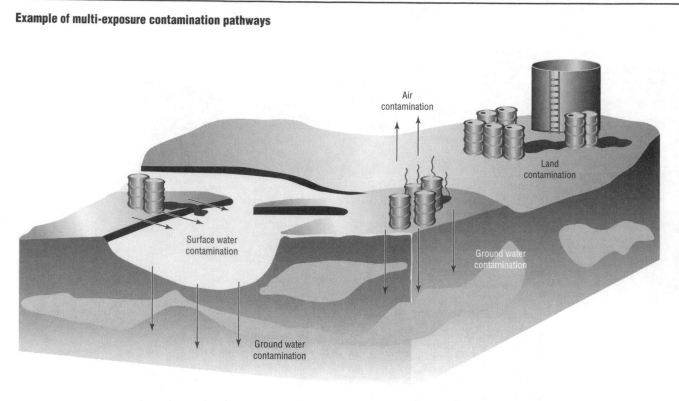

Air contamination

Land contamination

Surface water contamination

Ground water contamination

Ground water contamination

SOURCE: "Figure VI-1: Multi-Exposure Pathways," in *RCRA Orientation Manual*, EPA530-R-02-016, U.S. Environmental Protection Agency, Office of Solid Waste and Emergency Response, Washington, DC, January 2003

from improper waste disposal practices. As shown in Figure 1.2, improper waste disposal can endanger the nation's land, air, surface water, and groundwater resources.

The Federal Water Pollution Control Act was originally enacted in 1948 and totally revised by amendments in 1972, giving the Clean Water Act its current form. Another set of amendments to this law is the Water Quality Act of 1987. These acts provide legislation to protect against the pollution of America's lakes, rivers, coastal areas, and aquifers (underground areas of water). The Safe Drinking Water Act, enacted in 1974, protects the quality of drinking water in the United States.

The Clean Air Act of 1990 establishes federal standards for autos and other mobile sources of air pollution; for sources of hazardous air pollutants; and for the emissions that cause acid rain. This legislation began as the Air Pollution Control Act of 1955 and the Clean Air Act of 1963, with a major revision of the legislation in 1970.

HOW MUCH WASTE?

It is difficult to calculate exactly how much waste is generated in the United States and what becomes of it. Under RCRA the federal government collects data on the production and management of hazardous waste. These data are supplied by the industries and businesses generating the waste. The EPA estimates the production of

municipal solid waste (common garbage) each year using surveys, studies, population data, and other information. However, both of these wastestreams are thought to be very small in comparison to the amount of industrial nonhazardous waste that is generated.

The EPA reported that the country generated a total of 13 billion tons of solid waste in 1992 (*Solid Waste: State and Federal Efforts to Manage Nonhazardous Waste*, U.S. General Accounting Office, Washington, DC, 1995). Municipal solid waste and industrial hazardous waste made up only small fractions of this total, as shown in Figure 1.3. The vast majority of the waste was estimated to be industrial nonhazardous waste and special waste. Special waste comes from mining, oil and gas production, electric utilities, and cement kilns.

Industrial Nonhazardous Waste

RCRA does not apply to industrial nonhazardous waste, which includes nonhazardous chemicals, paper and metal scraps, and other wastes generated during manufacturing. These wastes are regulated by various state, tribal, and local regulatory agencies. This makes it difficult to know exactly how much industrial nonhazardous waste is generated. In 1988 the EPA estimated that 7.6 billion tons of industrial nonhazardous wastes are generated each year. In 1997 the federal government's Office of Industrial

FIGURE 1.3

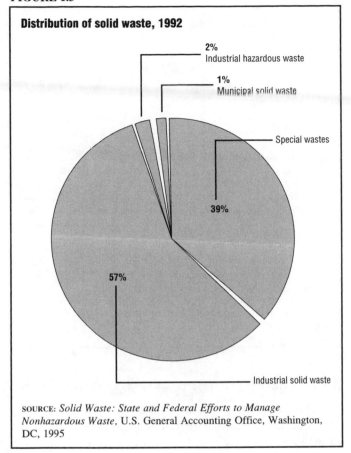

Distribution of solid waste, 1992

- 2% Industrial hazardous waste
- 1% Municipal solid waste
- Special wastes 39%
- Industrial solid waste 57%

SOURCE: *Solid Waste: State and Federal Efforts to Manage Nonhazardous Waste,* U.S. General Accounting Office, Washington, DC, 1995

FIGURE 1.4

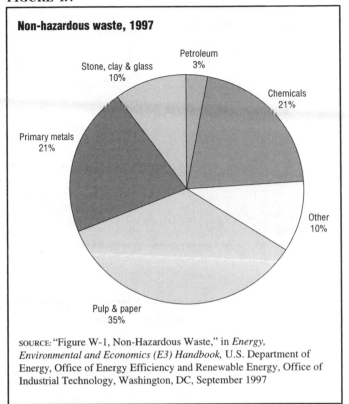

Non-hazardous waste, 1997

- Petroleum 3%
- Stone, clay & glass 10%
- Chemicals 21%
- Primary metals 21%
- Other 10%
- Pulp & paper 35%

SOURCE: "Figure W-1, Non-Hazardous Waste," in *Energy, Environmental and Economics (E3) Handbook,* U.S. Department of Energy, Office of Energy Efficiency and Renewable Energy, Office of Industrial Technology, Washington, DC, September 1997

Technology published an estimated breakdown of this wastestream, as shown in Figure 1.4.

Manufacturing produces huge amounts of waste. The paper industry, which uses many chemicals to produce paper, accounts for the largest proportion of manufacturing wastes—35 percent of the total. The iron and steel (20 percent) and chemical industries (14 percent) produce most of the rest. Many of the big manufacturing plants have sites on their own property where they can discard waste or treat it so it will not pollute the groundwater, rivers, or streams. Still others ship it to private disposal sites for dumping or for treatment. Smaller manufacturers often use private waste disposal companies or the city waste collection and disposal facilities.

Mining also produces much waste, most of it waste rock and tailings. In the mining process, waste rock is separated from ore. Ore is rock that contains enough metal to make it worth processing. Tailings are the leftovers after ore is processed to remove the metal. Chemicals are often used to remove metals from ore. After these chemicals have done their job, they become waste. Sometimes the chemical wastes are liquid, and sometimes they are solid.

Almost all (96 to 98 percent) of the waste from gas and oil drilling is wastewater that is pumped out of the ground before oil is found, or water that is mixed with oil.

Wastewater must be separated from oil and gas before these crude products can be processed into refined oil or gas for automobiles or home heating. The rest of the oil and gas waste comes from mud and rock that surfaces during drilling. Most oil and gas companies dispose of their own wastes. One of the most common disposal methods is the use of surface impoundments. These are large ponds in which liquid wastes are stored and treated before being discharged to surface water or groundwater.

Hazardous Waste

Hazardous waste is that which burns readily, is explosive, is corrosive, or contains certain amounts of toxic chemicals. It is produced by large industrial facilities (such as chemical manufacturers and petroleum refineries), and by more common businesses, such as dry cleaners, auto repair shops, and photo processing centers. The EPA reports that U.S. industry produced 40.8 million tons of hazardous waste in 2001 (*National Biennial RCRA Hazardous Waste Report: Based on 2001 Data,* Environmental Protection Agency, Washington, DC, 2003).

Municipal Solid Waste

Municipal solid waste is common garbage and trash that people throw away in everyday life. This includes paper and plastic products, food scraps, household goods, and other consumer items. In 2000 the EPA estimates that Americans generated nearly 232 million tons of municipal solid waste.

TABLE 1.4

Per capita resource consumption, mid-1990s

Material	Pounds per day
Stone and cement	27
Coal	19
Miscellaneous minerals	17
Oil	16
Farm products	12
Wood	11
Range grass	10
Metals	8
Natural gas	1
Total	**121**

SOURCE: John C. Ryan and Alan Thein Durning, *Stuff: The Secret Lives of Everyday Things,* Northwest Environment Watch, Seattle, WA, 1997

TABLE 1.5

Estimated life of selected consumer electronics

(In years)

	Range of primary and secondary use (reuse) life expectancy
Video products	
Direct view color TV	13 to 15
Projection TV	13 to 15
LCD color TV	13 to 15
Videocassette players	7 to 10
VCR decks	7 to 10
Camcorders	7 to 10
Laserdisc players	7 to 10
Audio products	
Rack audio system	3 to 15
Compact audio system	3 to 15
Portable CD	3 to 15
Portable headset audio	3 to 15
Total CD players	3 to 15
Home radios	3 to 15
Information products	
Cordless/corded telephones	3 to 6
Wireless telephones	2 to 4
Telephone answering machines	3 to 6
Fax machines	3 to 6
Personal word processors	3 to 6
Personal computers	3 to 6
Computer printers	3 to 5
Computer monitors	6 to 7
Modem/fax modems	3 to 6

SOURCE: "Table C-3: Estimated Life of Selected Consumer Electronics," in *Municipal Solid Waste in the United States: 2000 Facts and Figures,* EPA530-R-02-001, U.S. Environmental Protection Agency, Office of Solid Waste and Emergency Response, Washington, DC, June 2002. Data from Franklin Associates, Ltd.

Between 1960 and 2000 the U.S. population increased from 178.5 million to 281.4 million, an increase of almost 58 percent. However, the amount of municipal solid waste generated increased by 163 percent. In 1960 Americans generated 88.1 million tons of garbage or 2.68 pounds per person per day. By 2000 this figure had climbed to 4.5 pounds per person per day.

FIGURE 1.5

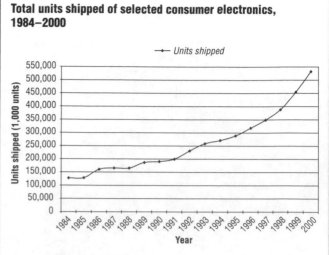

Total units shipped of selected consumer electronics, 1984–2000

SOURCE: "Figure C-1: Selected Consumer Electronics: Total Units Shipped 1984–2000," in *Municipal Solid Waste in the United States: 2000 Facts and Figures,* EPA530-R-02-001, U.S. Environmental Protection Agency, Office of Solid Waste and Emergency Response, Washington, DC, June 2002

A CONSUMER SOCIETY—A GLUT OF WASTE

The United States produces billions of tons of waste each year including a wide variety of materials. In fact, the variety of materials used by people in the United States, Europe, Japan, and other industrialized countries dwarfs that of a century ago. Today's materials draw from all 92 naturally occurring elements in the periodic table, compared with approximately 20 at the turn of the century. The United States Geological Survey (USGS) estimates that U.S. consumption of metal, glass, wood, cement, and chemicals has grown eighteen-fold since 1900. The United States alone uses one-third of the world's materials. Table 1.4 shows the per capita resource consumption of Americans in the mid-1990s.

One reason that Americans produce so much waste is that consumer goods are designed for short-term use. In fact, this concept has fostered one of America's nicknames—"the throwaway society." This situation contrasts sharply with the practices of earlier eras, when materials were reused or transformed for other uses. In her aforementioned book *A Social History of Trash,* Strasser notes that American society developed a "throwaway" mentality during the 20th century as "more and more things were made and sold with the understanding that they would soon be worthless or obsolete."

Consumer electronics provide an excellent example of this. Table 1.5 shows the estimated life expectancy of some popular electronic products. None are expected to last for more than 15 years. Sales of these products skyrocketed during the 1990s as shown in Figure 1.5. More than half a million units were shipped during 2000 alone. This means that millions of these products will enter the country's wastestream over the next two decades.

Municipal solid waste comprises only a small fraction of the total waste generated in this country. However, the "throwaway society" mindset spurs industry to produce more. This results in greater amounts of industrial waste and greater usage of fossil fuels to generate power. All of these actions have profound effects on the nation's environment.

CHAPTER 2

MUNICIPAL SOLID WASTE

The U.S. Environmental Protection Agency (EPA) defines municipal solid waste (MSW) as "common garbage or trash." MSW includes items like food scraps, paper, containers and packaging, appliances, batteries, and yard trimmings. These types of wastes are generally collected and managed by local municipal agencies. MSW does not include construction and demolition wastes, automobile bodies, sludge, combustion ash, and industrial process wastes.

THE ROLE OF OBSOLESCENCE IN MSW GENERATION

At one time, goods were scarce and were made to last a long time. That was considered part of their inherent workmanship. Henry Ford believed that "a Ford was forever." He insisted that his Model T and Model A cars were "so strong and so well-made that no one ought ever to have to buy a second one." Soon, however, it became evident that there was a substantial resale market for secondhand cars. Furthermore, it was quickly recognized that the industry could be more profitable if a person bought nine or ten cars over his or her lifetime rather than one or two.

By the 1920s technological and stylistic obsolescence began to characterize a growing number of consumer products. American markets were flooded with goods manufactured with the knowledge that they would become obsolete in a relatively short time.

MSW GENERATION RATES

Determining the amount and types of MSW generated in the United States is a very difficult task. People are not required to track or report how much MSW they produce or what it contains. There are two reliable sources of national information: the EPA and the journal *BioCycle,* a waste industry publication.

EPA Data

The EPA publication *Municipal Solid Waste in the United States: 2000 Facts and Figures* (June 2002) reports that Americans produced nearly 232 million tons of MSW in 2000, up from 231 million tons in 1999. (See Table 2.1.) The tons of MSW generated increased dramatically between 1960 and 2000. Most of this increase occurred during the 1960s, 1970s, and 1980s. In 1960 just over 88 million tons of MSW were generated. Over the next three decades, MSW generation increased on average by 32 percent per decade. However, the 1990s witnessed a slowdown in this rate of increase. MSW generation increased by only 13 percent between 1990 and 2000.

This trend is also reflected in the per capita (per person) values for MSW generation. In 1960 each American generated on average 2.68 pounds of MSW per day. That value steadily increased until 1990, when it reached 4.50 pounds per day. The rate leveled off during the 1990s as shown in Figure 2.1, fluctuating between 4.40 and 4.64 pounds. In 2000 per capita generation was 4.51 pounds per day, down from 4.64 pounds per day in 1999.

BioCycle Data

In December 2001 the journal *BioCycle* published part I of its 13th nationwide survey on MSW in "The State of Garbage in America" by Nora Goldstein and Celeste Madtes.

The authors report that in 2000 there were 409 million tons of MSW generated in the United States. This number is quite different from the 232 million tons reported by the EPA. The differences lie in the methods used to estimate generation rates.

The *BioCycle* authors relied on data provided to them by state solid waste management and recycling officials in response to questionnaires sent out by the journal's editors. Responses were received from all states, except Montana. In addition, officials in some states were unable

TABLE 2.1

Municipal solid waste generation and outcomes, 1960–2000

IN THOUSANDS OF TONS AND PERCENT OF TOTAL GENERATION

	Thousands of tons								
	1960	1970	1980	1990	1994	1995	1998	1999	2000
Generation	88,120	121,060	151,640	205,210	214,360	211,360	223,360	230,940	231,850
Recovery for recycling	5,610	8,020	14,520	29,040	42,150	45,340	47,950	50,060	53,420
Recovery for composting[1]	Neg.	Neg.	Neg.	4,200	8,480	9,570	13,140	14,720	16,450
Total materials recovery	5,610	8,020	14,520	33,240	50,630	54,910	61,090	64,780	69,870
Discards after recovery	82,510	113,040	137,120	171,970	163,730	156,450	162,270	166,160	161,980
Combustion[2]	27,000	25,100	13,700	31,900	32,490	35,540	34,410	34,040	33,730
Discards to landfill, other disposal[3]	55,510	87,940	123,420	140,070	131,240	120,910	127,860	132,120	128,250

	Pounds per person per day								
	1960	1970	1980	1990	1994	1995	1998	1999	2000
Generation	2.68	3.25	3.66	4.50	4.51	4.40	4.52	4.64	4.51
Recovery for recycling	0.17	0.22	0.35	0.64	0.89	0.94	0.97	1.01	1.04
Recovery for composting[1]	Neg.	Neg.	Neg.	0.09	0.18	0.20	0.27	0.30	0.32
Total materials recovery	0.17	0.22	0.35	0.73	1.06	1.14	1.24	1.31	1.36
Discards after recovery	2.51	3.04	3.31	3.77	3.44	3.26	3.29	3.33	3.15
Combustion[2]	0.82	0.67	0.33	0.70	0.68	0.74	0.70	0.68	0.66
Discards to landfill, other disposal[3]	1.69	2.36	2.98	3.07	2.76	2.52	2.59	2.65	2.50
Population (thousands)	179,979	203,984	227,255	249,907	260,682	263,168	270,561	272,691	281,422

	Percent of total generation								
	1960	1970	1980	1990	1994	1995	1998	1999	2000
Generation	100.0%	100.0%	100.0%	100.0%	100.0%	100.0%	100.0%	100.0%	100.0%
Recovery for recycling	6.4%	6.6%	9.6%	14.2%	19.7%	21.5%	21.5%	21.7%	23.0%
Recovery for composting[1]	Neg.	Neg.	Neg.	2.0%	4.0%	4.5%	5.9%	6.4%	7.1%
Total materials recovery	6.4%	6.6%	9.6%	16.2%	23.6%	26.0%	27.4%	28.1%	30.1%
Discards after recovery	93.6%	93.4%	90.4%	83.8%	76.4%	74.0%	72.6%	71.9%	69.9%
Combustion[2]	30.6%	20.7%	9.0%	15.5%	15.2%	16.8%	15.4%	14.7%	14.5%
Discards to landfill, other disposal[3]	63.0%	72.6%	81.4%	68.3%	61.2%	57.2%	57.2%	57.2%	55.3%

[1]Composting of yard trimmings and food scraps. Does not include mixed MSW composting or backyard composting.
[2]Includes combustion of MSW in mass burn or refuse-derived fuel form, and combustion with energy recovery of source separated materials in MSW (e.g., wood pallets and tire-derived fuel).
[3]Discards after recovery minus combustion.
Details may not add to totals due to rounding.
Neg. = Negligible; less than 50,000 tons or 0.05 percent.
MSW = Municipal solid waste

SOURCE: "Table 29. Generation, Materials Recovery, Composting, Combustion, and Discards of Municipal Solid Waste, 1960 to 2000," in *Municipal Solid Waste in the United States: 2000 Facts and Figures,* EPA530-R-02-001, U.S. Environmental Protection Agency, Office of Solid Waste and Emergency Response, Washington, DC, June 2002. Data from Franklin Associates, Ltd.

to provide complete data, thus in those cases data were estimated by the editors. Some states included certain wastes (for example, construction debris) in their data totals that the EPA does not include in its data totals.

The EPA uses information supplied by trade groups and industrial sources, combined with estimated product life spans and population and sales data, to estimate how much and what types of MSW are generated.

MSW COMPOSITION

Figure 2.2 shows EPA estimates of the breakdown of MSW produced in 2000 by waste type. Paper was the largest single component by weight, comprising 37 percent of the wastestream. It was followed by yard trimmings (12 percent), food scraps (11 percent), plastics (11 percent), metals (8 percent), rubber, leather, and textiles (7 percent), glass (6 percent), wood (6 percent), and other MSW (3 percent).

The top five categories—paper, yard trimmings, food scraps, plastics, and metals—together comprise more than three-fourths of the MSW generated in 2000.

Paper

The EPA estimates that in 2000 there were 86.7 million tons of paper generated as MSW.

FIGURE 2.1

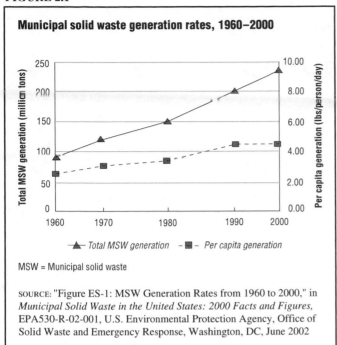

Municipal solid waste generation rates, 1960–2000

SOURCE: "Figure ES-1: MSW Generation Rates from 1960 to 2000," in *Municipal Solid Waste in the United States: 2000 Facts and Figures*, EPA530-R-02-001, U.S. Environmental Protection Agency, Office of Solid Waste and Emergency Response, Washington, DC, June 2002

FIGURE 2.2

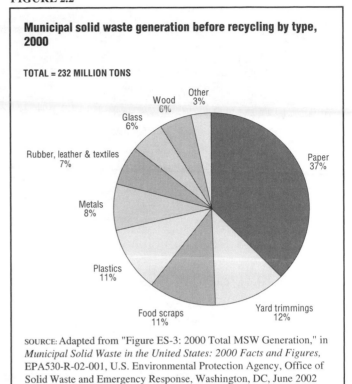

Municipal solid waste generation before recycling by type, 2000

SOURCE: Adapted from "Figure ES-3: 2000 Total MSW Generation," in *Municipal Solid Waste in the United States: 2000 Facts and Figures*, EPA530-R-02-001, U.S. Environmental Protection Agency, Office of Solid Waste and Emergency Response, Washington, DC, June 2002

The paper category includes numerous paper and paperboard (boxboard and containerboard) products as shown in Figure 2.3. Corrugated boxes make up the bulk of this category in terms of the tons generated. In 2000 MSW included just over 30 million tons of corrugated boxes, representing 35 percent of the entire paper category. Newspapers, office papers, commercial printing papers, milk cartons, and junk mail are other major contributors to the paper category. This category does not include gypsum wallboard facings (which are classified as construction and demolition debris) or toilet tissue (which goes to sewage treatment plants).

The EPA based its estimates of paper and paperboard generation on statistics published by the American Forest and Paper Association.

Yard Trimmings

EPA estimates show that in 2000 there were 27.7 million tons of yard trimmings generated as MSW.

Yard trimmings include grass, leaves, and tree and brush trimmings from residential, commercial, and institutional sources. According to the EPA, yard trimmings are assumed to contain an average by weight of 50 percent grass, 25 percent leaves, and 25 percent brush.

The EPA reports that in the past it based its estimates of yard trimming generation on only sampling studies and population and housing data. During the 1990s it began to take into account the expected effects of local and state legislation on yard trimmings disposal in landfills. For example, in 1992 only 11 states and the District of Columbia had laws prohibiting or discouraging residents from

disposing yard trimmings at landfills. By 1997 another 12 states had such legislation in place. The EPA believes that this increased the use of mulching lawnmowers and the practice of backyard composting of yard trimmings, thus reducing the amount of yard trimmings in MSW.

Food Scraps

The EPA estimates that in 2000 there were 25.9 million tons of food wastes generated in MSW.

Included in EPA's definition of food scraps are uneaten food and food preparation scraps from residences, commercial establishments (such as restaurants and grocery stores), institutional sources (such as school cafeterias and prisons), and industrial sources (such as factory cafeterias). Food scraps generated by industrial sources that produce and package food products are not included in MSW.

The EPA made its estimates on food scrap generation using data from sampling studies combined with demographic data on population, grocery store sales, restaurant sales, and the number of students, prisoners, and employees serviced by institutional and industrial cafeterias.

Plastics

The EPA estimates that in 2000 there were 24.7 million tons of plastic materials in the MSW wastestream.

The term plastics refers to materials made from particular chemical resins that can be molded or shaped into various products. Plastic materials are found in a wide

FIGURE 2.3

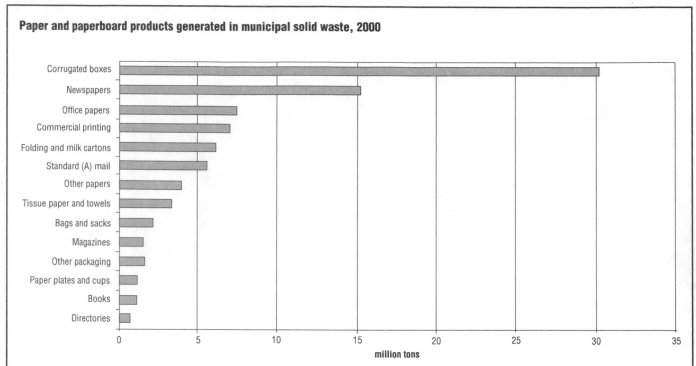

Paper and paperboard products generated in municipal solid waste, 2000

SOURCE: "Figure 2. Paper and Paperboard Products Generated in MSW, 2000," in *Municipal Solid Waste in the United States: 2000 Facts and Figures*, EPA530-R-02-001, U.S. Environmental Protection Agency, Office of Solid Waste and Emergency Response, Washington, DC, June 2002

variety of products, including containers, packaging, trash bags, milk jugs, cups, eating utensils, disposable diapers, sporting and recreational equipment, and many common household items (such as shower curtains). In addition there are plastic components in appliances, computers, furniture, luggage, and many other consumer products.

The EPA classifies plastic materials generated in the MSW in two ways—by product type and by resin. The product types are listed below along with the corresponding percentage that each comprised of the plastics wastestream:

• Durable goods—30 percent

• Nondurable goods—24 percent

• Bags, sacks, and wraps—17 percent

• Other packaging—12 percent

• Other containers—11 percent

• Soft drink, water, and milk containers—6 percent

Durable goods are those with a life expectancy in excess of three years (such as appliances and luggage). Nondurable goods are items with a life expectancy of less than three years (such as disposable diapers). Note that plastics used in automobiles and other vehicles are not included in these totals.

In addition the EPA classifies plastics by their resin type. Although there are dozens of resin types, the most common are listed below along with the corresponding percentage of each found in the plastics wastestream:

• Low-density polyethylene (LDPE)/Linear low-density polyethylene (LLDPE)—23 percent

• High-density polyethylene (HDPE)—19 percent

• Other resins—19 percent

• Polypropylene (PP)—14 percent

• Polyethylene terephthalate (PET)—10 percent

• Polystyrene (PS)—9 percent

• Polyvinyl chloride (PVC)—6 percent

PET is widely used to make soft drink bottles, while HDPE is commonly used in milk jugs. Many people are familiar with the plastic PVC, because household piping is made from it.

The EPA bases its estimates of plastics generated in MSW on data from industrial sources.

Metals

EPA estimates show that in 2000 there were 18 million tons of metals generated in MSW.

Ferrous metals (iron and steel) comprised 75 percent of this category by weight, followed by aluminum at 17 percent and other nonferrous (non-iron) metals at 8 percent. Ferrous metals are widely used in durable goods

TABLE 2.2

Total generation of consumer electronics by material in the municipal waste stream, 2000

(In percent of total generation)

Type of consumer electronics	Steel	Copper & brass	Alumi-num	Lead	Other metals	Glass	Wood	Plastic	Other
Video products	22%	3%	0%	7%	10%	27%	20%	11%	0%
Audio products	21%	0%	0%	0%	30%	0%	3%	47%	0%
Information products	27%	5%	4%	3%	4%	8%	0%	46%	2%
Total	24%	3%	2%	4%	11%	15%	9%	32%	1%

SOURCE: "Table C-4: Total Generation of Consumer Electronics by Material in the Municipal Waste Stream," in *Municipal Solid Waste in the United States: 2000 Facts and Figures,* EPA530-R-02-001, U.S. Environmental Protection Agency, Office of Solid Waste and Emergency Response, Washington, DC, June 2002. Data from Franklin Associates, Ltd.

such as appliances and furniture. Ferrous metals used in transportation vehicles (such as automobiles) are not included in this category. Steel is also used to manufacture food cans, barrels, and drums. Aluminum found in MSW is most commonly in beer and soft drink cans, food cans, and as foil wrap.

CONSUMER ELECTRONICS. The EPA included a discussion about consumer electronic products in an appendix to *Municipal Solid Waste in the United States: 2000 Facts and Figures.* Consumer electronics include televisions, computers, VCRs, CD and DVD players, digital and video cameras, radios, answering machines, telephones and cellular phones, fax machines, printers, scanners, and miscellaneous other equipment. Historically, such products have been lumped with other products under the category "other miscellaneous durable goods."

In 1999 for the first time consumer electronics were categorized separately and it was estimated that 1.7 million tons entered the MSW stream. In 2000 this value climbed to 2.1 million tons, representing 0.9 percent of the total MSW generated. Although this percentage is small, it is expected to increase quickly during the 2000s as more products reach the end of their useful lives.

EPA estimates of the breakdown by material in consumer electronic products in MSW are shown in Table 2.2. The average electronic product is assumed to be 44 percent metal, 32 percent plastic, 15 percent glass, 9 percent wood, and 1 percent other components. (Note that the total exceeds 100 percent due to rounding).

Historical Trends in MSW Composition

Table 2.3 and Figure 2.4 show EPA estimates of MSW composition for various years between 1960 and 2000. Paper has consistently been the largest single component of MSW generated. Its share of the total increased slightly from 34 percent in 1960 to 37.4 percent in 2000. Most of the other categories have also experienced small changes

FIGURE 2.4

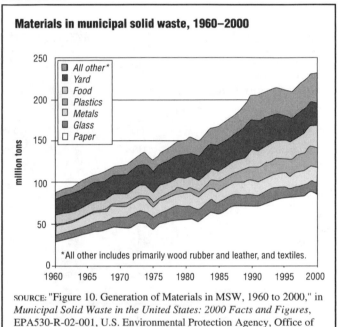

Materials in municipal solid waste, 1960–2000

Legend:
■ All other*
■ Yard
□ Food
□ Plastics
□ Metals
■ Glass
□ Paper

*All other includes primarily wood rubber and leather, and textiles.

SOURCE: "Figure 10. Generation of Materials in MSW, 1960 to 2000," in *Municipal Solid Waste in the United States: 2000 Facts and Figures,* EPA530-R-02-001, U.S. Environmental Protection Agency, Office of Solid Waste and Emergency Response, Washington, DC, June 2002

(either up or down) in percentage of total generation. The notable exceptions are plastics and yard trimmings.

In 1960 plastics comprised only 0.4 percent of the total MSW generated. By 2000 they comprised 10.7 percent of the MSW total. This is an enormous increase. Manufacturers are increasingly using plastic to package their products because plastic is so easy to use and to shape. As a result, plastics are the fastest-growing proportion of MSW in the United States.

The total number of pounds of plastic in MSW increased from only 390,000 tons in 1960 to 24.7 million tons in 2000. This is significant because plastics are not biodegradable. They do not break down through organic processes. The percentage of yard trimmings in the MSW total decreased from 22.7 percent in 1960 to 12 percent in 2000. However, the tons of yard trimmings in MSW actually increased over this time period.

TABLE 2.3

Materials generated in the municipal waste stream, 1960–2000

IN THOUSANDS OF TONS AND PERCENT OF TOTAL GENERATION

Materials	Thousands of tons							
	1960	1970	1980	1990	1995	1998	1999	2000
Paper and paperboard	29,990	44,310	55,160	72,730	81,670	84,160	88,260	86,740
Glass	6,720	12,740	15,130	13,100	12,830	12,640	12,910	12,770
Metals								
Ferrous	10,300	12,360	12,620	12,640	11,640	12,380	13,290	13,460
Aluminum	340	800	1,730	2,810	2,960	3,070	3,120	3,170
Other nonferrous	180	670	1,160	1,100	1,260	1,360	1,380	1,390
Total metals	10,820	13,830	15,510	16,550	15,860	16,810	17,790	18,020
Plastics	390	2,900	6,830	17,130	18,900	22,370	24,080	24,710
Rubber and leather	1,840	2,970	4,200	5,790	6,030	6,860	6,210	6,370
Textiles	1,760	2,040	2,530	5,810	7,400	8,600	9,060	9,380
Wood	3,030	3,720	7,010	12,210	10,440	12,090	12,360	12,700
Other*	70	770	2,520	3,190	3,650	3,900	4,000	4,030
Total materials in products	54,620	83,280	108,890	146,510	156,780	167,430	174,670	174,720
Other wastes								
Food scraps	12,200	12,800	13,000	20,800	21,740	24,910	25,160	25,900
Yard trimmings	20,000	23,200	27,500	35,000	29,690	27,730	27,730	27,730
Miscellaneous inorganic wastes	1,300	1,780	2,250	2,900	3,150	3,290	3,380	3,500
Total other wastes	33,500	37,780	42,750	58,700	54,580	55,930	56,270	57,130
Total MSW generated - weight	88,120	121,060	151,640	205,210	211,360	223,360	230,940	231,850

Materials	Percent of total generation							
	1960	1970	1980	1990	1995	1998	1999	2000
Paper and paperboard	34.0%	36.6%	36.4%	35.4%	38.6%	37.7%	38.2%	37.4%
Glass	7.6%	10.5%	10.0%	6.4%	6.1%	5.7%	5.6%	5.5%
Metals								
Ferrous	11.7%	10.2%	8.3%	6.2%	5.5%	5.5%	5.8%	5.8%
Aluminum	0.4%	0.7%	1.1%	1.4%	1.4%	1.4%	1.4%	1.4%
Other nonferrous	0.2%	0.6%	0.8%	0.5%	0.6%	0.6%	0.6%	0.6%
Total metals	12.3%	11.4%	10.2%	8.1%	7.5%	7.5%	7.7%	7.8%
Plastics	0.4%	2.4%	4.5%	8.3%	8.9%	10.0%	10.4%	10.7%
Rubber and leather	2.1%	2.5%	2.8%	2.8%	2.9%	3.1%	2.7%	2.7%
Textiles	2.0%	1.7%	1.7%	2.8%	3.5%	3.9%	3.9%	4.0%
Wood	3.4%	3.1%	4.6%	6.0%	4.9%	5.4%	5.4%	5.5%
Other *	0.1%	0.6%	1.7%	1.6%	1.7%	1.7%	1.7%	1.7%
Total materials in products	62.0%	68.8%	71.8%	71.4%	74.2%	75.0%	75.6%	75.4%
Other wastes								
Food scraps	13.8%	10.6%	8.6%	10.1%	10.3%	11.2%	10.9%	11.2%
Yard trimmings	22.7%	19.2%	18.1%	17.1%	14.0%	12.4%	12.0%	12.0%
Miscellaneous inorganic wastes	1.5%	1.5%	1.5%	1.4%	1.5%	1.5%	1.5%	1.5%
Total other wastes	38.0%	31.2%	28.2%	28.6%	25.8%	25.0%	24.4%	24.6%
Total MSW generated - %	100.0%	100.0%	100.0%	100.0%	100.0%	100.0%	100.0%	100.0%

Note: Generation calculated in table is before materials recovery or combustion. Does not include construction & demolition debris, industrial process wastes, or certain other wastes.
*Includes electrolytes in batteries and fluff pulp, feces, and urine in disposable diapers.
Details may not add to totals due to rounding.
MSW = Municipal solid waste

SOURCE: "Table 1. Materials Generated in the Municipal Waste Stream, 1960 to 2000," in *Municipal Solid Waste in the United States: 2000 Facts and Figures,* EPA530-R-02-001, U.S. Environmental Protection Agency, Office of Solid Waste and Emergency Response, Washington, DC, June 2002. Data from Franklin Associates, Ltd.

Focus on Containers and Packaging

The EPA reports that containers and packaging accounted for 32.2 percent of all municipal waste in 2000. A total of 74.7 million tons were generated. Containers and packaging are made of a number of materials: paper and paperboard, glass, steel, aluminum, plastics, wood, and small amounts of other materials.

Three-quarters of all products require a package, and 90 percent of those products requiring packaging are in the food and drink industry. Additional items requiring packaging are automotive products, hardware, housewares, and tobacco products.

For any product, from one to three types of packaging may be required depending on its purpose and the way in which it is shipped. The container that directly holds the product, such as a can, bottle, tube, or carton, is the primary packaging. Outer wrappings, such as a decorated carton or gift box, are secondary packaging. Tertiary packaging, such as divided cartons or shrink-wrapping of multiple products on a pallet, is used with products that are grouped for shipping and storage.

The cost of packaging as a percentage of total selling price varies greatly among products, from 1.4 to 40 percent. The average cost of packaging for a consumer item is about 9 percent. In other words roughly 9 cents out of every dollar spent on an item is for the cost of the packaging.

Aluminum

According to the U.S. Department of Agriculture's Economic Research Service, soft-drink consumption has risen in the past few decades, from 24.3 gallons per person in 1970 to twice that, 50.8 gallons per person, in 1999. Additionally, the population has grown from about 205.1 million persons in 1970 to about 272.7 million persons in 1999. Therefore, can and plastic container usage has increased even beyond what soft drink per capita consumption figures predicted.

Beverage cans are made out of aluminum. In fact, beverage cans are currently the largest single use of aluminum.

Plastics

The word "plastics" comes from the Greek word "plastikos," which means "to form." Today, the term refers to a wide range of flexible materials that can be molded or shaped into products such as fast-food packages, compact discs, contact lenses, and surgical sutures.

The advent of low-priced petrochemicals ushered in the age of plastics. Petrochemicals are substances derived from petroleum or natural gas. Plastics are made primarily from petroleum.

The plastics industry in the United States dates from the work of researcher John Wesley Hyatt in the 1860s. In 1939 nylon stockings were introduced at the World's Fair, and in 1940 plastic ornaments decorated the Christmas tree in Rockefeller Center. World War II spurred the development of new kinds of plastics and major growth in the industry. The 1955 Corvette was the first car to use plastic parts, and in 1982 Dr. Robert Jarvik designed the first artificial heart made largely of plastic.

Today, more plastics are produced in the United States than aluminum and all other nonferrous metals combined. Most of these plastics (a family of more than 45 types) are nonbiodegradable and, once discarded, remain relatively intact for many years. The EPA predicts that the amount of plastic thrown away will continue to increase.

The Positive Side of Packaging

No one ever buys just a package. The package is a conveyor, a piece of the distribution system that protects, preserves, and holds the product on its journey from the manufacturer to the store and, ultimately, the consumer. In developing countries where product packaging is poor or nonexistent, 30 to 50 percent of food is lost between producer and consumer. For example, approximately 20 percent of China's food supplies spoil before reaching the consumer. The United Nations estimates that improved packaging would reduce crop losses by 5 percent.

Packaging also helps reduce disease. Packaging helps prevent contamination of food by bacteria and ensures that medical supplies reach hospitals undamaged. While packaging represents 9 percent of the price of food and beverages, without the protection of packaging, food and beverages would cost even more due to spoilage and damage, perhaps as much as 20 percent more. Packaging reduces the amount of inedible food waste in the municipal wastestream and makes "seasonal" produce available nearly year-round.

Packaging protects against tampering of medications and foods, provides convenience in preparing meals, and enables the fast-food industry to give Americans the precious commodity of time. Latchkey children, single adults, and the elderly all benefit from single-serve, small-quantity packages. In addition, the packaging industry employs 2 million people in the United States, a $75 to $80 billion a year business.

Distribution Packaging

Part of the packaging and distribution system is largely unseen. About one-half of all packaging is primary and secondary consumer packaging—the familiar bottles, jars, cartons, wraps, and other containers found on a typical store shelf. The other half of packaging is distribution or tertiary packaging, which is used to transport products from manufacturers to retailers and consumers.

Distribution packaging can take many forms, such as corrugated boxes and trays, wood or plastic pallets, stretch film ("shrink-wrap"), molded plastic foam, or plastic and paper bags. The primary purpose of distribution packaging is to ensure that products arrive at their destination safely and securely, unharmed by hazards in transport and warehousing—such as temperature changes, vibration, compression, puncturing, biological contamination, and pilferage.

The fresh meat industry reflects changes in the packaging and distribution system in the United States. Beef is no longer shipped from processors to stores as sides of beef on hooks swinging in refrigerated trucks or railcars, as it was until the 1960s. Since fresh meat is sensitive to dehydration, oxygen, and bacterial contamination, its shelf life was about one week, and maintaining a large inventory was impossible. Today, beef is vacuum-packed in thin multi-layer plastic bags with an oxygen barrier. Packaging beef at the processor, instead of at the store, lowers transportation and processing costs since less waste—bones,

FIGURE 2.5

Municipal solid waste handling methods, 2000

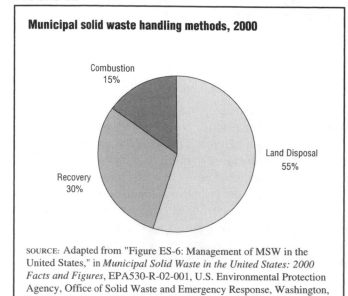

SOURCE: Adapted from "Figure ES-6: Management of MSW in the United States," in *Municipal Solid Waste in the United States: 2000 Facts and Figures*, EPA530-R-02-001, U.S. Environmental Protection Agency, Office of Solid Waste and Emergency Response, Washington, DC, June 2002

fat, etc.—is shipped and rail cars can be packed more efficiently. The shelf life for vacuum-packaged beef is four to six weeks. About 95 percent of beef is now shipped in vacuum barrier bags. Although the use of tertiary packaging in the beef industry has increased, the quality of the product and its shelf life has increased as well.

About 48 percent of products sold in grocery stores in the United States are nonperishables packed in cans, bottles, boxes, and jars. To ensure that packages arrive undamaged at the stores, manufacturers use corrugated boxing and wood pallets. While packaging is absolutely essential in getting food to the table, manufacturers of nonperishables are reassessing their delivery systems to see if some packaging can be modified, or even eliminated, to cut down on waste.

One way to reduce the quantity of plastics waste is to trim the amount of packaging. Manufacturers have already taken steps to reduce the weight of plastic containers. Other packaging design changes may help reduce plastics waste as well.

MSW MANAGEMENT

The three primary methods for the management of MSW are:

- Land Disposal

- Combustion (or Incineration), and

- Recovery through Recycling or Composting

Land disposal involves piling or burying waste materials on or below the ground surface. This is primarily done at facilities called landfills. Combustion is the burning of waste to produce energy. Incineration is a disposal method in which MSW is burned at high temperatures. Recycling

TABLE 2.4

Municipal solid waste (MSW) tonnages, recycling, incineration, and landfilling rates by state, 2000 unless noted

State	MSW (tons/yr)	Recycled[1] (%)	Incinerated (%)	Landfilled (%)
Alabama	4,500,000	23	6	71
Alaska	686,000	8	10	82
Arizona[2]	5,750,000	17	0	83
Arkansas	2,056,000[3]	45	1	54
California	66,100,000	42	1	57[4]
Colorado[5]	6,535,000	<10	0	>90
Connecticut	3,234,000	23[6]	65	12
Delaware	2,065,000	59	0	41
District of Columbia	500,000	16	79	5
Florida[7]	24,800,000	28	16	56
Georgia	10,236,000	n/a	n/a	n/a
Hawaii[3]	1,884,000	24	32	44
Idaho	1,086,000	n/a	n/a	n/a
Illinois	15,102,000	28	1	71
Indiana	13,571,000	35[8]	4	61
Iowa	2,866,000	35[8]	<1	65
Kansas	3,000,000	9	<1	91
Kentucky	4,376,000	30	0	70
Louisiana	3,361,000	17	0	83
Maine[3]	1,696,000	40	39	21
Maryland	6,268,000	37	21	42
Massachusetts[3]	8,141,000	38	36	26[9]
Michigan	18,717,000	18[10]	9	73
Minnesota[11]	5,634,000	42	23	35
Mississippi	4,400,000	16	0	84
Missouri	10,288,000	38[8]	0	62
Montana	757,000	n/a	n/a	n/a
Nebraska	1,848,000	23	0	77
Nevada	3,356,000	14	0	86
New Hampshire	1,068,000	21	17	62
New Jersey	9,200,000	38	17	45
New Mexico	3,418,000	9	0	91
New York[12]	31,100,000	42	12	46
North Carolina	13,500,000	26	1	73
North Dakota	573,000	11[3,13]	0	89
Ohio[14]	14,335,000	21	0	79
Oklahoma	3,787,000	1[15]	10	89
Oregon	4,544,000	39	5	56
Pennsylvania	11,620,000[3]	33	17	50
Rhode Island	1,561,000	24	0	76
South Carolina	4,483,000	31	6	63
South Dakota	514,000[3]	n/a	n/a	n/a
Tennessee	5,200,000	34[16]	11	55
Texas	44,791,000	35[17]	<1	65
Utah[18]	2,433,000	5	5	90
Vermont	578,000	33	10[19]	57
Virginia	10,661,000	29	9	62

is the reuse of a material in another product or application. Composting is a method of decomposing yard trimmings and other biodegradable wastes for reuse as fertilizer.

According to the EPA, in 2000 land disposal was the most common method used to manage MSW in the United States. (See Figure 2.5.) More than half (55 percent) of the MSW generated went to land disposal, while 30 percent was recovered, and 15 percent was combusted.

By contrast, *BioCycle* data for 2000 indicate that 61 percent of MSW was landfilled, 32 percent was recycled, and 7 percent was incinerated on a national basis.

BioCycle's state-by-state breakdown is presented in Table 2.4. States with very high landfill percentages include Kansas (91 percent), New Mexico (91 percent), and

TABLE 2.4

Municipal solid waste (MSW) tonnages, recycling, incineration, and landfilling rates by state, 2000 unless noted [CONTINUED]

State	MSW (tons/yr)	Recycled[1] (%)	Incinerated (%)	Landfilled (%)
Washington	7,072,000	35	5	60
West Virginia	1,500,000	25	0	75
Wisconsin[20]	3,710,000	36	4	60
Wyoming[21]	568,000	10	1	89
Total	**409,029,000**	**32**	**7**	**61**

n/a: Information not available
[1]Rate includes yard trimmings composting.
[2]Landfilled data is from 4/00-3/01. Public recycling activity is from 7/00-6/01. Private recycling activity is from 7/98-6/99, therefore diversion, recycling and generation rates are expected to rise when private data from 2000 and 2001 are compiled.
[3]1999 data.
[4]State included MSW incinerated in its landfill rate, but also provided incinerated tonnage used by BioCycle to calculate incinerated rate.
[5]Recycled rate estimated using local program information. Landfilled rate calculated using data provided by state.
[6]Does not include bottle bill material recycled nor complete data on commercial MSW recycled.
[7]1998 data.
[8]Diversion rate includes MSW recycled, composted, reused (i.e.. not disposed or incinerated).
[9]12% is landfilled in state. 14% is exported out of state primarily to landfill disposal.
[10]Recycled rate provided by Michigan Recycling Coalition based on MRC survey data.
[11] State reports 3.7% of MSW disposed on-site (mostly illegally) through burning or burying. Recycled, incinerated, landfilled rates adjusted to account for on-site disposal.
[12]1998 data for recycled. 2000 data for incinerated and landfilled.
[13]Recycled data does not include any composting. State reports about 85 yard trimmings composting facilities.
[14]Preliminary data for 2000.
[15]Recycled rate estimated using local program information.
[16]Waste reduction rate.
[17]Rate based on 1997 study (landfill data is 2000). State provided data to estimate incinerated and landfilled rates.
[18]Recycled rate estimated using local program information. State provided data for composted, incinerated and landfilled rates.
[19]MSW incinerated out-of-state.
[20]1995 data.
[21]Rates estimated using combination of state data and local recycling program data.

SOURCE: Nora Goldstein and Celeste Madtes, "Table 3. Municipal Solid Waste (MSW) Tonnages, Recycling, Incineration and Landfilling Rates by State," in "The State of Garbage in America," *BioCycle*, vol. 42, no. 12, December 2001. The JG Press, Inc. (www.BioCycle.net). Reproduced with permission.

Colorado (in excess of 90 percent). In general, these states are less densely populated, thus they generate less MSW and have more space for landfills than many other states.

The states reporting the greatest recycling rates were Delaware (59 percent), Arkansas (45 percent), and California, Minnesota, and New York (all 42 percent). Incineration rates were highest in the District of Columbia (79 percent), Connecticut (65 percent), and Maine (39 percent).

Figure 2.6 shows EPA's estimates of landfill, combustion, and recovery data in millions of tons from 1960 to 2000. The proportion of MSW that is recovered through recycling and composting has grown over the decades, especially during the 1990s. Landfill use leveled off during the mid-1980s.

MUNICIPAL (OR SANITARY) LANDFILLS

Municipal (or sanitary) landfills are areas where MSW waste is placed into and onto the land. While some landfilled organic wastes will decompose, many of the

FIGURE 2.6

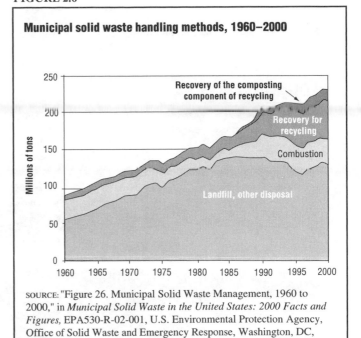

Municipal solid waste handling methods, 1960–2000

SOURCE: "Figure 26. Municipal Solid Waste Management, 1960 to 2000," in *Municipal Solid Waste in the United States: 2000 Facts and Figures*, EPA530-R-02-001, U.S. Environmental Protection Agency, Office of Solid Waste and Emergency Response, Washington, DC, June 2002

wastes in MSW are not biodegradable. Landfills provide a centralized location in which these wastes can be contained. Landfills are not open dumps, but rather managed facilities in which wastes are controlled. MSW is often compacted before it is placed in a landfill, and it is covered with soil. Modern landfills have liner systems and other safeguards to prevent groundwater contamination. When they are full, landfills are usually capped with a clay liner to prevent contamination. (See Figure 2.7.)

How Organic Matter Decomposes in Landfills

Organic material (material that was once alive, such as paper and wood products, food scraps, and clothing made of natural fibers) decomposes in the following way: First, aerobic (oxygen-using) bacteria use the material as food and begin the decomposition process. Principal byproducts of this aerobic stage are water, carbon dioxide, nitrates, and heat. This stage lasts about two weeks. However, in compacted, layered, and covered landfills, the availability of oxygen may be low.

After the available oxygen is used, anaerobic bacteria (those that do not use oxygen) continue the decomposition. They generally produce carbon dioxide and organic acids. This stage can last up to one to two years. During a final anaerobic stage of decomposition lasting several years or decades, methane gas is formed along with carbon dioxide. The duration of this stage and the amount of decomposition depend on landfill conditions, including temperature, soil permeability, and water levels.

In July 1992 *The Smithsonian* reported on a 20-year study called the Garbage Project. Conceived in 1971 and

FIGURE 2.7

Example of a properly closed landfill

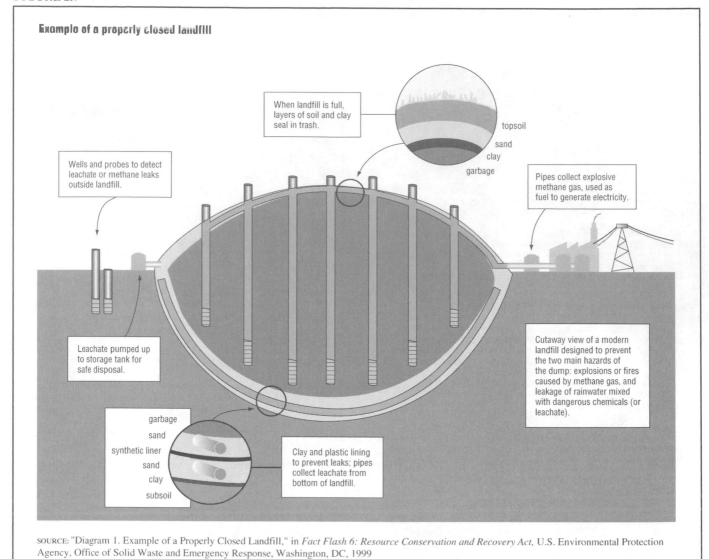

When landfill is full, layers of soil and clay seal in trash.

topsoil
sand
clay
garbage

Wells and probes to detect leachate or methane leaks outside landfill.

Pipes collect explosive methane gas, used as fuel to generate electricity.

Leachate pumped up to storage tank for safe disposal.

Cutaway view of a modern landfill designed to prevent the two main hazards of the dump: explosions or fires caused by methane gas, and leakage of rainwater mixed with dangerous chemicals (or leachate).

garbage
sand
synthetic liner
sand
clay
subsoil

Clay and plastic lining to prevent leaks; pipes collect leachate from bottom of landfill.

SOURCE: "Diagram 1. Example of a Properly Closed Landfill," in *Fact Flash 6: Resource Conservation and Recovery Act,* U.S. Environmental Protection Agency, Office of Solid Waste and Emergency Response, Washington, DC, 1999

officially established at the University of Arizona in 1973, the Garbage Project was an attempt to apply archaeological principles to the study of solid waste. About 750 people processed more than 250,000 pounds of waste, excavating 14 tons of it from landfills.

Among the Garbage Project's findings was the discovery that although some degradation takes place initially (sufficient to produce large amounts of methane and other gases), it then slows to a virtual standstill. Study results revealed that an astonishingly high volume of old organic matter remained largely intact. Even after two decades, one-third to one-half of supposedly degradable organics remained in recognizable condition. The Smithsonian Institution concluded that well-designed and well-managed landfills, in particular, seemed more likely to preserve their contents than to transform them into humus or mulch.

Decreasing Numbers of Landfills

Prior to using landfills, cities used open dumps, areas in which garbage and trash were simply discarded in huge piles. However, open dumps produced unpleasant odors and attracted animals. In the early 1970s the number of operating landfills in the United States was estimated at about 20,000. In 1979, as part of the Resource Conservation and Recovery Act (RCRA), the EPA designated conditions under which solid waste disposal facilities and practices would not pose adverse effects to human health and the environment. As a result of the implementation of these criteria, open dumps had to be closed or upgraded to meet the criteria for landfills.

Additionally, many more landfills closed in the early 1990s because they could not conform to the new standards that took effect in 1993 under the 1992 RCRA amendment. Other landfills closed as they became full.

According to the EPA, the number of landfills available for MSW disposal decreased dramatically between 1988 and 2000 from 7,924 to 1,967. (See Figure 2.8.)

BioCycle estimates that in 2000 there were 2,142 MSW landfills in operation. A state-by-state breakdown is

FIGURE 2.8

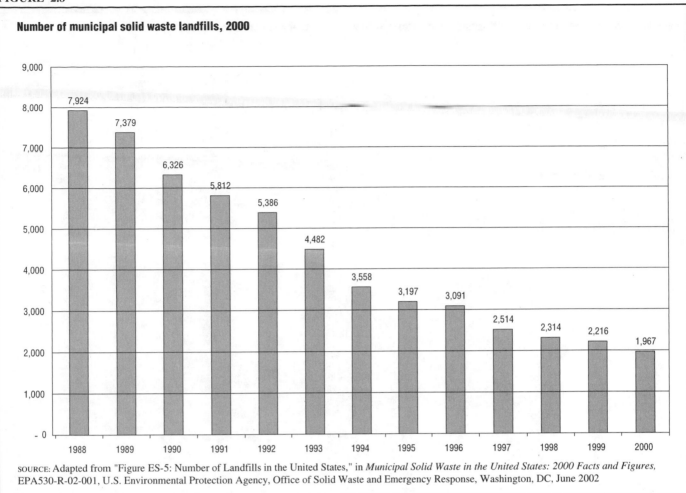

Number of municipal solid waste landfills, 2000

SOURCE: Adapted from "Figure ES-5: Number of Landfills in the United States," in *Municipal Solid Waste in the United States: 2000 Facts and Figures*, EPA530-R-02-001, U.S. Environmental Protection Agency, Office of Solid Waste and Emergency Response, Washington, DC, June 2002

provided in Table 2.5. The table also provides information on landfill capacity and tip fees. Landfills charge disposers "tip fees" to use their facilities. Tip fees range from a low of $11 per ton in Colorado to a high of $75 per ton in Vermont. In general, the highest tip fees are in the Northeast, and the lowest are in the Midwest and Southwest.

Although the United States is one of the least crowded industrialized nations in the world, in terms of population density per acre, population density and available landfill space vary widely across the country. New areas for landfills are becoming increasingly hard to find in some areas of the country (such as the Northeast), while other states have plenty of landfill space available. A few states (Connecticut, Massachusetts, New Jersey, and Rhode Island) have insufficient land with suitable soil and water conditions for landfills. Since landfills are not welcome in most neighborhoods, useable land must be found away from residential areas. Several states in the Northeast and Midwest have very little landfill capacity remaining. Missouri, New Hampshire, Minnesota, New York, Vermont, Wisconsin, Connecticut, and Massachusetts all have less than 10 years of in-state landfill capacity. Connecticut (2–3 years) and Massachusetts (less than 2 years) are particularly short of time.

Landfill Design Standards

The RCRA standards require landfill operators to do several things to lessen the chance of polluting the underlying groundwater. Groundwater can become contaminated when liquid chemicals or contaminated rainfall runoff seep down through the ground underneath the landfill. This liquid is called leachate.

The RCRA requirements are as follows:

- Landfill operators must monitor the groundwater for pollutants. This is usually accomplished with a groundwater monitoring well system.

- Landfills must have plastic liners underneath their waste, as well as a leachate collection system. (See Figure 2.7.)

- Debris must be covered daily with soil to prevent odors and stop refuse from being blown away.

- Methane gas (a byproduct of decomposition) must be monitored, which is usually accomplished with an explosive-gas monitoring well.

- Landfill owners are responsible for cleanup of any contamination.

TABLE 2.5

Number of municipal solid waste landfills and incinerators, average tip fees, and capacity by state, 2000

State	Landfills			Incinerators		
	Number	Average tip fee ($/ton)	Remaining capacity (years)	Number	Average tip fee ($/ton)	Daily capacity (tons/day)
Alabama	29	30	10	1	n/a	700
Alaska	275	n/a	0-100	1	140	70
Arizona	49	26.11	n/a	0	—	—
Arkansas	23	n/a	30	2	n/a	72
California	175	35.14	18[1]	3	34.66	6,440
Colorado	70	11	n/a	1	n/a	n/a
Connecticut	2	n/a	2-3	6	57	7358
Delaware	3	58.50	30	0	—	—
District of Columbia	0	—	—	0	—	—
Florida	61	42.85	n/a	13	55.22	19,000
Georgia	69	29.18	23.5	1	n/a	500
Hawaii	9	50	1-15	1	n/a	2,000
Idaho	29	n/a	n/a	0	—	—
Illinois	52	30.68	15	1	n/a	1,200
Indiana	36	29.92	13.5	3	27	n/a
Iowa	61	33	60	1	n/a	n/a
Kansas	51	n/a	20+	1	50	15
Kentucky	26	27.24	15.2	1	27.24	30
Louisiana	23	22.85	n/a	0	—	—
Maine	8	65	12-15	4	60	2,850
Maryland	23	49	>10	4	49	3,650
Massachusetts	21	67	<2[2]	7	66	8,400[3]
Michigan	54	n/a	15	4	n/a	3,800
Minnesota	22	40	7[4]	9	40	3,300
Mississippi	20	25	20	2	30	150
Missouri	25	29.53	9	0	—	—
Montana	n/a	n/a	n/a	n/a	n/a	n/a
Nebraska	23	25	n/a	0	—	—
Nevada	24	18	>50	0	—	—
New Hampshire	15	66	8	8	74	746
New Jersey	12	55	12	5	55	6,490
New Mexico	44	32	20	0	—	—
New York	27	n/a	7[5]	10	n/a	11,000[6]
North Carolina	42	31	n/a	1	34	380
North Dakota	14	25	20	0	—	—
Ohio	44	29	22	0	—	—
Oklahoma	40	20	20	1	52.29	1,125
Oregon	29	25	40	2	n/a	570
Pennsylvania	49	n/a	12	5	n/a	9,450
Rhode Island	4	40	10	0	—	—
South Carolina	19	n/a	>13	4	n/a	700[7]
South Dakota	15	31	25-30	0	—	—
Tennessee	48	28.76	n/a	2	28.75	1,500
Texas	227[8]	25.46	32	16[9]	n/a	n/a
Utah	37	n/a	100	1	n/a	342[10]
Vermont	5	75	6.3	0	—	—
Virginia	67	n/a	20	5	n/a	n/a
Washington	21	49.72	51	3	n/a	1,520
West Virginia	18	42.37	30	0	—	—
Wisconsin	44	38	5	2	45	22.4
Wyoming	58	n/a	n/a	1	n/a	20
Total	**2,142**			**132**		

[1]Landfill capacity reported as 1.35 billion cubic yards or about 677 million tons. About 37 million tons were landfilled in 2000. At that rate, California has about 18 years of landfill capacity remaining.

[2]1,808,669 tons of landfill capacity was permitted in 2000. About 1,000,000 tons were landfilled in-state in 1999. Thus in-state capacity is <2 years

[3]Capacity reported as 3,068,975 tons/year (tpy).

[4]State did 120 mile radius capacity search that included some out-of-state landfills mostly made up of Minnesota waste. Total capacity (when combined with in-state facilities) is 40 years.

[5]Landfill capacity reported as 68 million tons. In 2000, 9.3 million tons were landfilled in-state. At that rate, New York has about 7 years of in-state landfill capacity remaining.

[6]Capacity reported as 3,886,200 tpy.

[7]Capacity reported as 255,000 tpy.

[8]227 MSW landfills provided data in 2000. Of those, 183 were active and 44 were inactive.

[9]16 permitted incinerators - 9 active, 5 inactive and 2 closed in 2000.

[10]Capacity reported as 125,000 tpy.

SOURCE: Nora Goldstein and Celeste Madtes, "Table 7. Number of Municipal Solid Waste Landfills and Incinerators, Average Tip Fees, and Capacity by State for 2000," in "The State of Garbage in America," *BioCycle,* vol. 42, no. 12, December 2001. The JG Press, Inc. (www.BioCycle.net). Reproduced with permission.

TABLE 2.6

Waste imports and exports by state, 2000 unless noted

State	Imported (tons/yr)	Exported (tons/yr)
Alabama	382,000	n/a
Alaska	0	24,500
Arizona	424,000	5,000
California	29,000	746,000
Connecticut	110,000	247,000
Delaware	0	0
Georgia	511,000	n/a
Hawaii	0	0
Idaho	n/a	65,530
Illinois	1,548,000	n/a
Indiana	1,531,000	290,000
Iowa	580,000	265,000
Kansas	500,000	40,000
Kentucky	515,000	196,000
Maryland	66,000	1,547,000
Massachusetts[1]	43,000	1,218,000
Michigan	3,124,000	n/a
Minnesota	n/a[2]	705,000
Mississippi	334,000	n/a
Missouri	183,000	1,793,000
Nevada	541,000	n/a
New Hampshire	255,000	60,000
New Jersey	900,000	1,800,000
New Mexico	572,000	0
New York	447,500	5,600,000
North Carolina	42,000	1,107,000
North Dakota	103,000	5,000
Ohio	1,092,000	598,000
Oregon	1,312,000	19,000
Pennsylvania	9,764,000[3]	300,000
Rhode Island	0	133,000
South Carolina	562,000	77,000
Texas	54,000	519,000
Utah	66,000	n/a
Vermont	<2,000	122,000
Virginia	3,891,000	100,000
Washington	116,000	1,243,000
West Virginia	215,000	250,000
Wisconsin[1]	1,068,000	180,000

[1]1999 data.
[2]Very small amount of waste is imported due to lower tip fees in all four states bordering Minnesota. The amount exported has increased every year.
[3]If sludge, industrial/commercial and ash included, the amount imported is 10,992,262.

SOURCE: Nora Goldstein and Celeste Madtes, "Table 9. Waste Imports and Exports by State for 2000," in "The State of Garbage in America," *BioCycle,* vol. 42, no. 12, December 2001. The JG Press, Inc. (www.BioCycle.net). Reproduced with permission.

Imports and Exports of Garbage

The combination of fewer landfills and high tipping fees in some states has encouraged some municipalities to send their garbage to other states. Although shipments do occur across the Mexican and Canadian borders, the vast majority of American MSW is managed within the United States.

According to *BioCycle,* importing and exporting MSW from state to state is very common. Table 2.6 shows the number of tons imported and exported in 2000 for each state. New York exported the most MSW (5.6 million tons), followed by New Jersey (1.8 million tons), and Missouri (1.79 million tons). The chief MSW importers were Pennsylvania (9.8 million tons), Virginia (3.9 million tons), and Michigan (3.1 million tons).

FIGURE 2.9

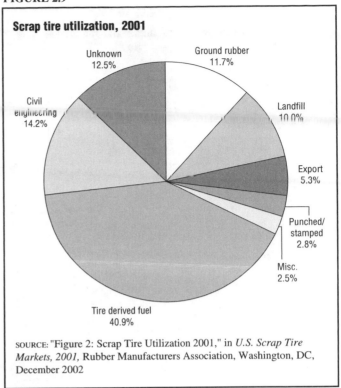

Scrap tire utilization, 2001

- Unknown 12.5%
- Ground rubber 11.7%
- Landfill 10.0%
- Export 5.3%
- Punched/stamped 2.8%
- Misc. 2.5%
- Tire derived fuel 40.9%
- Civil engineering 14.2%

SOURCE: "Figure 2: Scrap Tire Utilization 2001," in *U.S. Scrap Tire Markets, 2001,* Rubber Manufacturers Association, Washington, DC, December 2002

New York's large amount of exported waste is dominated by New York City's commercial waste. Furthermore, waste exports from New York grew rapidly after the New York City's Fresh Kills landfill closed on March 22, 2001. It reopened on September 13, 2001, after the September 11, 2001 terrorist attack on the World Trade Center, in order to receive the debris from the cleanup, but it is not accepting other MSW.

Several states have tried to ban the importing of garbage into their states. In 1992 the Supreme Court ruled in *Chemical Waste Management, Inc. v. Hunt* (504 U.S. 334, 1992) that the constitutional right to conduct commerce across state borders protects such shipments. Experts point out that newer, state-of-the-art landfills with multiple liners and sophisticated pollution control equipment have to accept waste from a wide region to be financially viable.

Special Wastes

Certain types of MSW are particularly challenging for waste management facilities to process, either because of their volume or because they pose specific contamination problems.

SCRAP TIRES. The Rubber Manufacturers Association (RMA) is a trade organization based in Washington, D.C., that collects and reports data on scrap tires. In December 2002 the RMA published *U.S. Scrap Tire Markets—2001,* which estimated that 281 million scrap tires were generated in 2001. The vast majority of these tires (77.6 percent) were recycled in some way. This value has increased dramatically

FIGURE 2.10

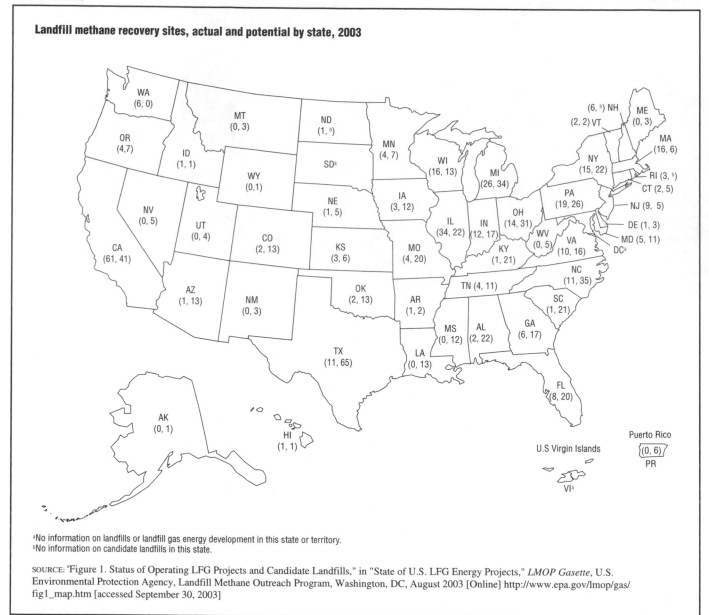

Landfill methane recovery sites, actual and potential by state, 2003

[a]No information on landfills or landfill gas energy development in this state or territory.
[b]No information on candidate landfills in this state.

SOURCE: "Figure 1. Status of Operating LFG Projects and Candidate Landfills," in "State of U.S. LFG Energy Projects," *LMOP Gasette*, U.S. Environmental Protection Agency, Landfill Methane Outreach Program, Washington, DC, August 2003 [Online] http://www.epa.gov/lmop/gas/fig1_map.htm [accessed September 30, 2003]

since 1990 when only 24 percent of scrap tires were recycled. The RMA estimates that 10 percent of the scrap tires generated in 2001 went to landfills. The fate of the remaining 12.5 percent is unknown. (See Figure 2.9.) (Note that the figures do not add to 100 percent due to rounding.)

Prior to the 1980s, scrap tires were either landfilled, illegally dumped, or stockpiled. In 1985 Minnesota passed the first state legislation dealing with scrap tires. Other states followed suit. Several waste management companies invested in tire-to-fuel projects, and by 1990 up to 25 million scrap tires per year were burned for fuel. During the 1990s new markets emerged for shredded rubber from scrap tires in civil engineering applications (for example, road building and landfill cover).

The RMA estimates that in 2001 approximately 41 percent of the scrap tires generated were burned for fuel.

Another 14 percent were used in civil engineering applications. Both markets are expected to expand in the future. Up to 300 million scrap tires are believed to be in stockpiles around the country. According to the RMA, 85 percent of stockpiled scrap tires are in only nine states: Alabama, Colorado, Connecticut, Michigan, New York, Ohio, Pennsylvania, Texas, and West Virginia.

Scrap tires accumulated in landfills or uncontrolled tire dumps can pose health and fire hazards. Scrap tires are highly combustible, do not compost, and do not degrade easily. The material, primarily hydrocarbons, burns easily, producing toxic, bad-smelling air pollutants and toxic runoff when burned in the open. Health effects that can result from exposure to an open tire fire include irritation of the skin, eyes, and mucous membranes; respiratory effects; central nervous system depression; and cancer. (The controlled combustion of scrap tires in special incinerators does not produce these toxic emissions.) Scrap tires do not compress in landfills and provide breeding grounds for a variety of pests. In fact, some states ban the disposal of tires in landfills.

USED MOTOR OIL. Used oil is generated by large manufacturing facilities, industrial operations, service stations, quick-lube shops, and do-it-yourselfers who change the oil in their cars at home. Approximately 1.4 billion gallons of used oil is discarded by these sources per year (*RCRA Orientation Manual*, Environmental Protection Agency, Washington, DC, 1998).

In 1980 Congress passed the Used Oil Recycling Act, and in 1992 developed a more comprehensive used oil recycling program. The Act and associated program include used oil management standards for all facilities that handle used oil.

The problem with used oil disposal is primarily with do-it-yourselfers. In 1994 the EPA estimated that about 200 million gallons of used oil was discarded each year by do-it-yourselfers, rather than recycled via a community program. That amount of discarded oil is equivalent to 18 *Exxon Valdez* spills dumped on the ground, poured down the sewers, or thrown in the trash where it will likely end up in landfills. All these disposal methods are likely to result in the used oil tainting water supplies. A small volume of motor oil can contaminate a large volume of water. One gallon of motor oil from a single oil change can pollute 1 million gallons of fresh water. Contaminants often found in used motor oil add to its toxicity.

Landfills and the Environment

METHANE. Methane, a flammable gas, is produced when organic matter decomposes in the absence of oxygen. If not properly vented or controlled, it can cause explosions and underground fires that smolder for years. Methane is also deadly to breathe. The RCRA requires landfill operators to monitor methane gas.

The Smithsonian Garbage Project found that for 15 or 20 years after a landfill stops accepting garbage, the wells still vent methane in fairly substantial amounts. Thereafter, methane production drops off rapidly, indicating that the landfill has stabilized.

Methane gas can be recovered through pipes inserted into landfills, and the gas can be used to generate energy. As of May 2003, there are 339 operational landfill gas-to-energy projects in the United States. The EPA's Landfill Methane Outreach Program estimates that more than 600 other landfill sites present attractive opportunities for project development. Figure 2.10 shows the number of operational landfills in each state (first number inside parentheses) and the number of candidate landfills (second number inside parentheses).

CADMIUM. Cadmium is a natural element in the earth's crust that is frequently found in municipal waste. It has uses in many products, including batteries, pigments, plastics, and metal coatings. The EPA estimates that 2,680 tons of cadmium had been deposited in MSW by 2000. Most cadmium in MSW comes from the disposal of batteries. The remainder comes from plastics, consumer electronics, pigments, appliances, glass, and ceramics.

When ingested by humans in polluted air or water, cadmium can build up in the human body over years, damaging the lungs, kidneys, nervous system, and stomach. It is also associated with the development of lung cancer.

LEAD. Lead is an environmental contaminant found in municipal waste that can damage virtually every human organ system. A naturally occurring metal found in small amounts in the earth's surface, lead is used in many products including lead-acid batteries, consumer electronics, glass and ceramics, plastics, cans, and pigments. The EPA estimates in 2000 there were 1.9 million tons of lead-acid batteries in MSW.

MERCURY. Another component of MSW is mercury. Mercury is a naturally occurring metal that is found both in liquid and gas form. It is used to produce chlorine gas and is used in the manufacturing of many products. Once in ground and surface water, it accumulates in fish that humans may eat. It harms the human nervous system and other body organs. The EPA estimates that 172.7 tons of mercury was discarded in waste in 2000. Most of that came from household batteries, thermometers, electronics, paint residues, and pigments.

In 1996 Congress passed the Mercury-Containing and Rechargeable Battery Management Act (known as the "battery recycling bill"). This law phased out the use of mercury in batteries.

Trends in Landfill Development

Landfilling is expected to continue to be the single most predominant MSW management method. In the coming decades, it will be economically prohibitive to develop and maintain small-scale, local landfills. There will likely be fewer, larger, and more regional operations. More MSW is expected to move away from its point of generation, resulting in increased import and export rates.

Landfill protection methods will likely become stronger in the future with more options for leachate and gas recovery. To make landfills more acceptable to neighborhoods, operators will likely establish larger buffer zones, use more green space, and show more sensitivity to land-use compatibility and landscaping.

INCINERATION AND COMBUSTION

Incineration and combustion both include heating MSW to very high temperatures. In the past, MSW was

FIGURE 2.11

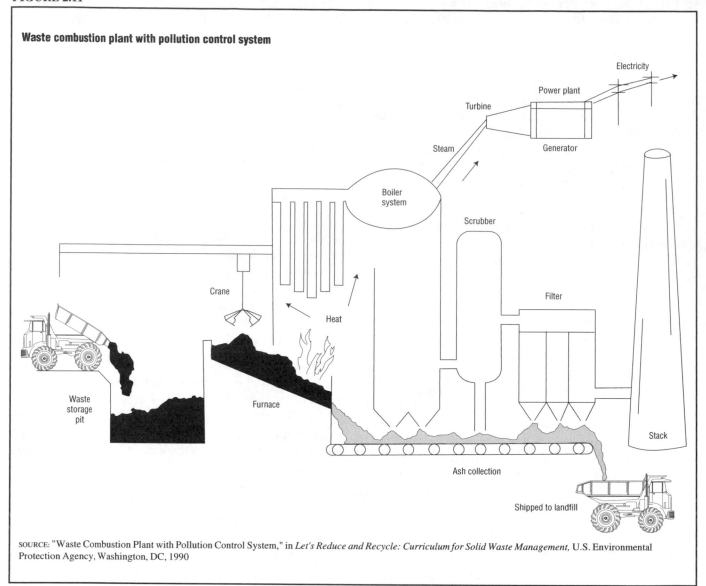

Waste combustion plant with pollution control system

SOURCE: "Waste Combustion Plant with Pollution Control System," in *Let's Reduce and Recycle: Curriculum for Solid Waste Management*, U.S. Environmental Protection Agency, Washington, DC, 1990

burned in incinerators primarily to reduce its volume. During the 1980s, technology was developed that allowed MSW to be burned for energy recovery. Use of MSW as a fuel is more commonly termed combustion, however both terms are used interchangeably. The EPA refers to MSW combustion as a waste-to-energy (WTE) process.

Figure 2.11 shows a typical waste-to-energy system. At this incinerator, the trucks dump waste into a pit. The waste is moved to the furnace by a crane. The furnace burns the waste at a very high temperature, heating a boiler that produces steam for generating electricity and heat. Ash collects at the bottom of the furnace, where it is later removed and taken to a landfill for disposal.

According to the EPA, in 2000 approximately 15 percent of MSW was incinerated. (See Figure 2.5.) The journal *BioCycle* estimates the value at only 7 percent.

Data from the EPA document 102 WTE facilities operating in the United States, with the ability to burn up

to 97,500 tons of MSW per day. The total MSW burned during 2000 is estimated at 33.7 million tons. Another 2.3 million tons of source-specific MSW (primarily tires) were burned as fuel in specialized facilities. As shown in Table 2.7, tires have a very high average heat content compared to typical MSW.

BioCycle's data in the year 2000 document 132 incinerators in the United States as shown on the right-hand side of Table 2.5. Texas had the greatest number of incinerators (16), followed by Florida (13) and New York (10). However, note that only nine of the Texas facilities are actually active. Florida has the greatest daily incineration capacity at 19,000 tons/day, followed by New York with 11,000 tons/day. Although data for incinerator tip fees are sketchy, the tip fees shown range from a low of around $27 per ton in Indiana and Kentucky to a high of $140 per ton in Alaska.

Some experts think that incinerators are the best alternative to landfills, while others believe that they are good

TABLE 2.7

Average heat content of selected biomass fuels

Fuel type	Heat content	Units
Agricultural byproducts	8.248	Million Btu/short ton
Black liquor	11.758	Million Btu/short ton
Digester gas	0.619	Million Btu/thousand cubic foot
Landfill gas	0.490	Million Btu/thousand cubic feet
Methane	0.841	Million Btu/thousand cubic feet
Municipal solid waste	9.945	Million Btu/short ton
Paper pellets	13.029	Million Btu/short ton
Peat	8.000	Million Btu/short ton
Railroad ties	12.618	Million Btu/short ton
Sludge waste	7.512	Million Btu/short ton
Sludge wood	10.071	Million Btu/short ton
Solid byproducts	25.830	Million Btu/short ton
Spent sulfite liquor	12.720	Million Btu/short ton
Tires	26.865	Million Btu/short ton
Utility poles	12.500	Million Btu/short ton
Waste alcohol	3.800	Million Btu/barrel
Wood/wood waste	9.961	Million Btu/short ton

SOURCE: "Table B6. Average Heat Content of Selected Biomass Fuels," in *Renewable Energy Trends 2002*, U.S. Department of Energy, Energy Information Administration, Washington, DC, August 2003

FIGURE 2.12

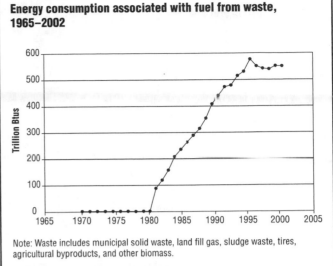

Energy consumption associated with fuel from waste, 1965–2002

Note: Waste includes municipal solid waste, land fill gas, sludge waste, tires, agricultural byproducts, and other biomass.

SOURCE: Adapted from "Table 10.1 Renewable Energy Consumption by Source, 1949–2001," in *Annual Energy Review, 2001*, U.S. Department of Energy, Energy Information Administration, Washington, DC, November 2002

additions to landfills. WTE facilities do provide an alternative energy source to traditional fossil fuels, and the sale of the energy they produce helps offset the cost of operating the facilities. Incinerators are very expensive to build. The country's largest incinerator, located in Detroit, cost $438 million. This huge incinerator produces enough steam to heat half of the city's central business district and enough electricity to supply 40,000 homes.

According to the Department of Energy (DOE), in 2002 waste-derived energy comprised just over one-half of 1 percent of the nation's total energy supply, producing 550 trillion British thermal units (BTUs) of power. (See Figure 2.12.) The DOE hopes to increase this value to 2 percent by the year 2010.

Incinerator Emissions

During MSW combustion, certain metals and other toxic materials can be released in gaseous emissions. (See Figure 2.13.) The contaminants of greatest concern are mercury and dioxins.

Mercury is released as a gaseous vapor when paints, fluorescent lights, batteries, electronics, and medical wastes are incinerated. The metal is a hazard to the environment and to human health. The EPA estimates that WTE mercury emissions account for less than 3 percent of the country's total human-made mercury emissions.

Dioxin is the common name for a family of several hundred toxic compounds with similar chemical structures and biological characteristics. Dioxins are not deliberately manufactured—they are the unintended by-products of industrial processes that involve chlorine (such as chlorine bleaching of pulp and paper) or processes that burn chlorine with organic matter. Dioxins are also released in small amounts when sewage sludge, medical waste, hazardous waste, MSW, or fuels, such as wood, oil, and coal, are burned. Even car exhaust and cigarette smoke contain dioxins.

Dioxins are stable compounds that accumulate in the human body over a lifetime. In 1997 the International Agency for Research on Cancer listed dioxin as a known carcinogen (cancer-causing substance). The EPA estimates that WTE dioxin emissions account for less than 1 percent of the country's total dioxin emissions.

WTE facilities are required to use air pollution control equipment to reduce emissions of toxic chemicals. In 2002 the EPA reported that emissions of organic, metal, and acid gases from 66 large MSW incinerators were reduced by more than 90 percent between 1990 and 2000. Mercury emissions were reduced by 95.1 percent, while emissions of dioxins were reduced by more than 99 percent.

RECOVERY AND RECYCLING

The terms "recovery" and "recycling" are often used interchangeably. Both mean that a waste material is being reused rather than landfilled. In general, reuse as a fuel does not fall under the definition of recovery, while composting does.

According to the EPA, in 2000 approximately 30 percent of MSW was recovered. (See Figure 2.5.) *BioCycle* estimates the value at 32 percent.

The recovery and recycling of MSW will be discussed in detail in Chapter 3.

FIGURE 2.13

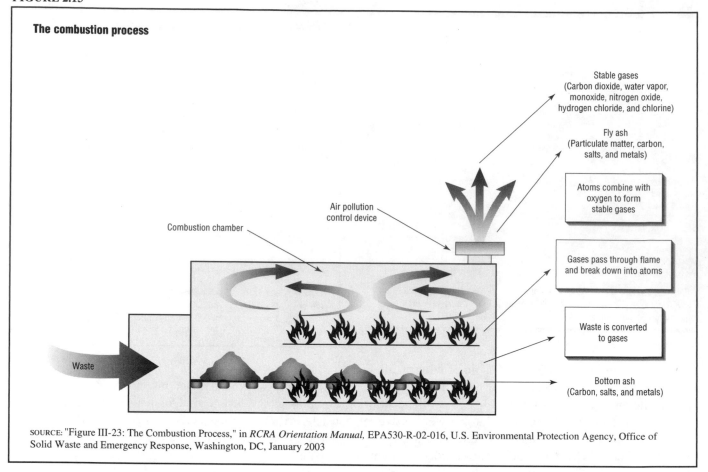

The combustion process

SOURCE: "Figure III-23: The Combustion Process," in *RCRA Orientation Manual*, EPA530-R-02-016, U.S. Environmental Protection Agency, Office of Solid Waste and Emergency Response, Washington, DC, January 2003

SOURCE REDUCTION

Source reduction means reducing the amount of waste that requires disposal in the first place. (See Figure 2.14.) This process is also called waste prevention or waste minimization.

Source reduction measures include:

• redesigning products or packages to reduce the quantity of materials or the toxicity of materials used, substituting lighter materials for heavier ones, and lengthening the life of products to postpone disposal,

• using packaging that reduces damage or spoilage to a product,

• reusing packages or products already manufactured, and

• managing non-product organic wastes (food wastes, yard trimmings) through composting or other on-site alternatives to disposal.

Table 2.8 shows specific examples of source reduction practices.

Pay-As-You-Throw

Rather than pay for waste collection services through a flat tax or monthly fee, some communities have institut-

FIGURE 2.14

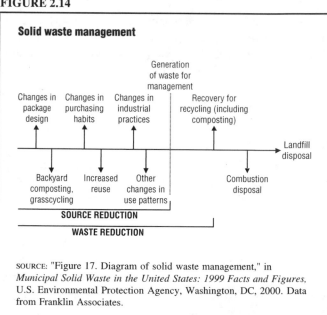

Solid waste management

SOURCE: "Figure 17. Diagram of solid waste management," in *Municipal Solid Waste in the United States: 1999 Facts and Figures*, U.S. Environmental Protection Agency, Washington, DC, 2000. Data from Franklin Associates.

ed "unit pricing," a fee for the amount of waste set on the curb. These programs are called Pay-As-You-Throw (PAYT) and encourage recycling. According to the EPA, the agency that instituted PAYT programs, there are more than 6,000 PAYT programs operating around the country in 2003. The EPA estimates that PAYT communities

TABLE 2.8

Selected examples of municipal solid waste source reduction practices

| | MSW product categories | | | |
Source reduction practice	Durable goods	Nondurable goods	Containers & packaging	Organics
Redesign				
Materials reduction	• Downgauge metals in appliances	• Paperless purchase orders	• Concentrates	• Xeriscaping
Materials substitution	• Use of composites in appliances and electronic circuitry		• Cereal in bags • Coffee brick • Multi-use products	
Lengthen life	• High mileage tires • Electronic components reduce moving parts	• Regular servicing • Look at warranties • Extend warranties	• Design for secondary uses	
Consumer practices				
	• Purchase long lived products	• Repair • Duplexing • Sharing • Reduce unwanted mail	• Purchasing: products in bulk, concentrates	
Reuse				
By design	• Modular design	• Envelopes	• Pallets • Returnable secondary packaging	
Secondary	• Borrow or rent for temporary use • Give to charity • Buy or sell at garage sales	• Clothing • Waste paper scratch pads	• Loosefill • Grocery sacks • Dairy containers • Glass and plastic jars	
Reduce/eliminate toxins				
	• Eliminate PCBs	• Soy ink, waterbased • Waterbased solvents • Reduce mercury	• Replace lead foil on wine bottles	
Reduce organics				
Food wastes				• Backyard composting • Vermi-composting
Yard trimmings				• Backyard composting • Grasscycling

SOURCE: "Table 24: Selected Examples of Source Reduction Practices," in *Municipal Solid Waste in the United States: 1999 Facts and Figures,* U.S. Environmental Protection Agency, Washington, DC, 2000. Data from Franklin Associates.

reduce their waste by 14 to 17 percent and increase recycling by 32 to 59 percent.

Illegal Dumping

Illegal dumping is a continuing problem. One major reason for illegal dumping is the cost of legally disposing of waste in landfills. In addition, the declining number of landfills, with those remaining often sited at a distance, has led to increased illegal dumping. Illegal dumping endangers human health and the environment because the dump sites become breeding grounds for animal and insect pests, present safety hazards for children, are sources of pollutants, and disrupt wildlife habitats.

The Federal Role in MSW Management

The federal government plays a key role in waste management. Its legislation has set landfill standards under the RCRA and incinerator and landfill emission standards under The Clean Air Act. Table 2.9 lists and describes federal regulations involving waste management.

Some waste management laws have been controversial, resulting in legal challenges. Consequently, the federal government has also had an effect on waste management programs through federal court rulings. In a series of rulings, including Supreme Court decisions such as *Chemical Waste Management, Inc. v. Hunt* (504 U.S. 334, 1992), federal courts have held that shipments of waste are protected under the interstate commerce clause of the U.S. Constitution. As a result, state and local governments may not prohibit landfills from accepting waste from other states, nor may they impose fees on waste disposal that discriminate on the basis of origin.

FLOW CONTROL LAWS. Municipalities nationwide have upgraded waste management programs and attempted to deal with public concern over waste issues. In most areas of the country, state and local governments have played the lead role in transforming solid waste management. Private waste management firms have also been involved, often under contract or franchise agreements with local governments. Private firms manage most of the commercial waste, which comprises about 40 percent of

TABLE 2.9

Federal regulations on solid waste management

Authority	Regulation	Status	EPA annual cost estimate
RCRA Subtitle D	Municipal Solid Waste Landfill Criteria: location, design, and operating groundwater monitoring, and corrective action closure and post-closure care financial assurance criteria	Promulgated 10/9/91, with some subsequent modifications effective 10/9/93 for large landfills, 4/9/94 for others requirements phased in; final compliance deadline 10/9/97 effective 10/9/93 for large landfills, 4/9/94 for others effective 4/97	$330,000,000
RCRA Subtitle D	Non-Municipal Solid Waste Landfill Criteria	Promulgated 7/1/96; requirements took effect 18 months to 2 years after promulgation	$12,650,000 - 51,000,000
Clean Air Act, Section 111	Air Emissions from Municipal Solid Waste Landfills	Promulgated 3/12/96; effective immediately for new landfills	$94,000,000
Clean Air Act, Sections 111 and 129	Emissions from Municipal Solid Waste Combustors (Incinerators): combustion practices, carbon monoxide, dioxins/furans, particulates, acid gases, nitrogen oxides; applied only to combustors with capacity of 250 tons per day or more	Promulgated 2/11/91; effective 8/12/91	$472,000,000
	maximum achievable control technology for carbon monoxide, dioxins, particulate matter, cadmium, lead, mercury, sulfur dioxide, hydrogen chloride, nitrogen oxides; applies to incinerators with capacity of 35 tons per day or more	Originally promulgated 12/19/95; as the result of a court decision, EPA repromulgated the standards for combustors with capacity >250 tons per day 8/25/97; regulations for smaller combustors were reproposed 8/30/99. Effective date of requirements varies.	$405,000,000
RCRA Sections 3001 - 3005	Management of Ash from Municipal Waste Combustors (Incinerators)	Supreme Court ruled May 2, 1994, that ash was not exempt from hazardous waste management regulations, despite EPA guidance to the contrary. Hazardous waste testing and management regulations were promulgated 5/19/80, with many subsequent amendments.	not available
Executive Orders 12873 and 13101; RCRA Section 6002	Federal Procurement of Recycled Products	Procurement guidelines for paper, retread tires, used oil and insulation materials took effect in 1988. Executive Orders 12873 (10/20/93) and 13101 (9/14/98) strengthened paper requirements. EPA designated an additional 19 recycled content product categories for procurement preferences 5/1/95; 12 product categories were added 11/13/97; and 19 more were proposed for addition 8/26/98.	not available

SOURCE: James E. McCarthy, "Table 1. Regulations on Solid Waste Management," in *Solid Waste Issues in the 106th Congress,* Congressional Research Service, The Library of Congress, Washington, DC, April 27, 2000

MSW. Increasingly, they also collect residential waste, the remaining 60 percent of MSW.

Flow control laws require private waste collectors to dispose of their waste in specific landfills. State and/or local governments institute these laws to guarantee that any new landfill they build will be used. That way, when they sell bonds to get the money to build a new landfill, the bond purchasers will not worry that they will not be repaid. Since 1980 about $10 billion in municipal bonds have been issued to pay for the construction of solid waste facilities. In many of those cases, flow control authority was used to guarantee the investment. Flow control also benefits recycling plants where recycling is financed by fees collected at incinerators or landfills. In the process, however, a monopoly is created, prohibiting facilities outside a jurisdiction from offering competitive services. As a result, there have been a number of court challenges to flow control laws.

In 1994 the Supreme Court, in *C & A Carbone v. Clarkstown* (511 US 383), held that flow control violates the interstate commerce clause. In response, however, many local governments have strongly pushed for the restoration of flow control authority. They have appealed

TABLE 2.10

Projections of materials generated* in the municipal waste stream, 2000 and 2005

Materials	Million tons		% of total	
	2000	2005	2000	2005
Paper and paperboard	87.7	94.8	39.3%	39.6%
Glass	11.9	11.2	5.3%	4.7%
Metals	17.6	18.7	7.9%	7.8%
Plastics	23.4	26.7	10.5%	11.2%
Wood	14.0	15.8	6.3%	6.6%
Others	19.7	22.2	8.8%	9.3%
Total materials in products	174.3	189.4	78.1%	79.1%
Other Wastes				
Food wastes	22.5	23.5	10.1%	9.8%
Yard trimmings	23.0	23.0	10.3%	9.6%
Miscellaneous inorganic wastes	3.4	3.6	1.5%	1.5%
Total other wastes	48.9	50.1	21.9%	20.9%
Total MSW generated	223.2	239.5	100.0%	100.0%

* Generation before materials recovery or combustion.
Details may not add to totals due to rounding.

SOURCE: "Projections of materials generated* in the municipal waste stream: 2000 and 2005," in *Characterization of Municipal Solid Waste in the United States: 1998 Update,* U.S. Environmental Protection Agency, Washington, DC, 1999

to Congress, with its authority to regulate interstate commerce, to restore the use of flow control. Thus far, bills proposed to address flow control have failed.

In 1997 a federal district court, in *Atlantic Coast Demolition and Recycling Inc. v. Atlantic County* (112 F 3d 652), overturned New Jersey's flow control requirements. As a result, much of New Jersey's waste leaves the state for cheaper disposal elsewhere.

In Minnesota, a federal district court, in *Ben Oehrleins, Inc. v. Hennepin County* (GA8 N.96-2120, 1997), ruled in favor of waste haulers who claimed that the county was liable for damages resulting from enforcement of flow control ordinances. The jury awarded the plaintiffs $7.1 million as compensation for the higher costs they were forced to pay as a result of flow control programs. In March 1998 Hennepin County agreed to pay $3.45 million to settle the suit and agreed to lift its garbage delivery restrictions for the next five years.

PROJECTIONS OF MUNICIPAL SOLID WASTE GENERATION

In 1999 the EPA issued its projections for expected MSW generation rates through 2005 based on the trend in historical levels. (See Table 2.10.) This estimate places total MSW generation near 250 million tons per year by 2005.

CHAPTER 3

MATERIALS RECOVERY—RECYCLING AND COMPOSTING

Materials recovery is the removal of municipal solid waste (MSW) from the wastestream for recycling and composting. Recycling involves the sorting, collecting, and processing of wastes such as paper, glass, plastic, and metals, which are then refashioned or incorporated into new marketable products. Composting is the decomposition of organic wastes, such as food scraps and yard trimmings, in a manner that produces a humus-like substance for fertilizer or mulch.

As shown in Figure 3.1, the percentage of MSW recovered for recycling or composting increased from 6 percent in 1960 to 30 percent in 2000. However, the largest gains were obtained during the 1980s and early 1990s. The recovery rate leveled off during the late 1990s, changing very little between 1995 and 2000.

MSW recovery offers many advantages. It conserves energy otherwise used to incinerate the waste; reduces the amount of landfill space needed for disposal of waste; reduces possible environmental pollution due to waste disposal; generates jobs and small-scale enterprises; reduces dependence on foreign imports of raw materials; and replaces some chemical fertilizers with composting material, which further lessens possible environmental pollution.

Many Americans view waste recovery primarily as a way to help the environment. For example, if paper is recycled, fewer trees have to be cut down to make paper. State and local governments see recycling as a way to save money on waste disposal costs and prolong the life of landfill space. Thus, MSW recovery has both environmental and economic components.

MATERIAL RECOVERY RATES

Table 3.1 shows the U.S. Environmental Protection Agency (EPA) estimates for the year 2000 of the materials recovered from all MSW generated. On a weight basis, the

TABLE 3.1

Generation and recovery of materials in municipal solid waste, 2000

IN MILLONS OF TONS AND PERCENT OF GENERATION OF EACH MATERIAL

	Weight generated	Weight recovered	Recovery as a percent of generation
Paper and paperboard	86.7	39.4	45.4%
Glass	12.8	2.9	23.0%
Metals			
Steel	13.5	4.6	34.0%
Aluminum	3.2	0.9	27.4%
Other nonferrous metals[1]	1.4	0.9	66.9%
Total metals	18.0	6.4	35.4%
Plastics	24.7	1.3	5.4%
Rubber and leather	6.4	0.8	12.2%
Textiles	9.4	1.3	13.5%
Wood	12.7	0.5	3.8%
Other materials	4.0	0.9	21.3%
Total materials in products	174.7	53.4	30.6%
Other wastes			
Food, other[2]	25.9	0.7	2.6%
Yard trimmings	27.7	15.8	56.9%
Miscellaneous inorganic wastes	3.5	Neg.	Neg.
Total other wastes	57.1	16.5	28.8%
Total municipal solid waste	**231.9**	**69.9**	**30.1%**

Note: Table includes waste from residential, commercial, and institutional sources.
[1] Includes lead from lead-acid batteries.
[2] Includes recovery of paper for composting.
Neg. = Less than 50,000 tons or 0.05 percent.

SOURCE: "Table ES-4: Generation and Recovery of Materials in MSW, 2000," in *Municipal Solid Waste in the United States: 2000 Facts and Figures*, EPA530-R-02-001, U.S. Environmental Protection Agency, Office of Solid Waste and Emergency Response, June 2002. Data from Franklin Associates, Ltd.

recovery of nonferrous metals (excluding aluminum) had the highest rate (66.9 percent), followed by yard trimmings (56.9 percent), paper and paperboard (45.4 percent), steel (34 percent), and aluminum (27.4 percent). At least a quarter of each of these materials was recovered from the national MSW stream. By contrast, recovery rates for plastic (5.4 percent) and wood (3.8 percent) were very low.

FIGURE 3.1

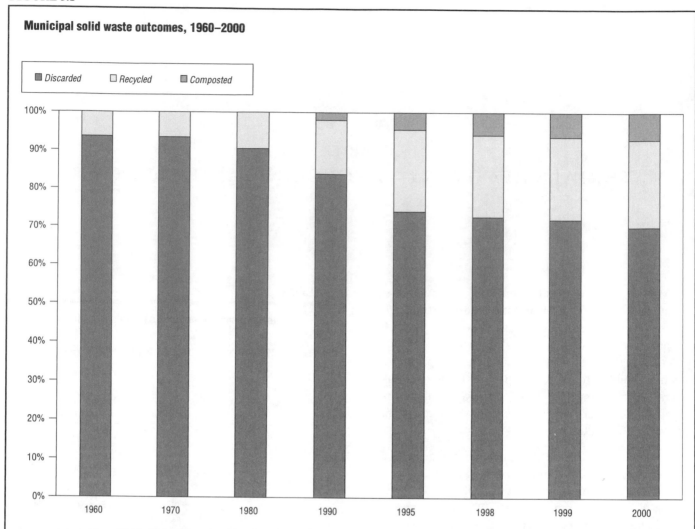

Municipal solid waste outcomes, 1960–2000

□ Discarded   □ Recycled   ■ Composted

SOURCE: Adapted from "Table ES-3: Generation, Materials Recovery, Composting, and Discards of Municipal Solid Waste, 1960–2000," in *Municipal Solid Waste in the United States: 2000 Facts and Figures,* EPA530-R-02-001, U.S. Environmental Protection Agency, Office of Solid Waste and Emergency Response, Washington, DC, June 2002

Table 3.2 provides historical rates of recovery for various materials. Recovery rates for most materials grew quickly between 1960 and 1995 and then leveled off or decreased slightly through the remainder of the decade. Two exceptions are yard trimmings and paper and paperboard. The recovery rate for yard trimmings increased from 30.3 percent in 1995 to 56.9 percent in 2000. This was the largest increase by far for any material over that time period. Paper and paperboard recovery increased from 40 percent in 1995 to 45.4 percent in 2000.

Paper

The paper industry has been at the leading edge of the recycling revolution. Used paper-based products can be de-inked in chemical baths and reduced to a fibrous slurry that can be reformulated into new paper products. Paper can undergo this process several times before the fibers become too damaged for reuse. Paper products vary greatly in the type (hardwood versus softwood) and length of fibers that are used to make them. Recycled papers must typically be sorted into particular usage categories (for example, newsprint or fine writing papers) before being reprocessed.

Figure 3.2 shows EPA estimates of the tons of paper (and paperboard) products generated as MSW and the tons recovered between 1960 and 2000. Overall the recovery rate for the year 2000 was 45.4 percent. However, examination of detailed data shows that there were wide variations in rates for specific paper products. For example, corrugated boxes had a recovery rate of 71 percent. This was the highest rate for any product within the category. Recovery rates were also high for newspapers (58 percent) and office papers (54 percent). Most other paper products had moderate recovery rates falling within the 20–40 percent range. By contrast, paper products such as tissue papers and towels and paper plates and cups had negligible recovery rates (less than 0.05 percent).

Even though paper and paperboard recovery is high, only about 10 percent of the paper used in printing and

TABLE 3.2

Recovery of municipal solid waste, 1960–2000

IN THOUSANDS OF TONS AND PERCENT OF GENERATION OF EACH MATERIAL

Materials	Thousands of tons							
	1960	1970	1980	1990	1995	1998	1999	2000
Paper and paperboard	5,080	6,770	11,740	20,230	32,700	34,360	36,080	39,370
Glass	100	160	750	2,630	3,140	2,940	3,000	2,940
Metals								
Ferrous	50	150	370	2,230	4,130	4,310	4,530	4,580
Aluminum	Neg.	10	310	1,010	930	880	880	870
Other nonferrous	Neg.	320	540	730	810	930	930	930
Total metals	50	480	1,220	3,970	5,870	6,120	6,340	6,380
Plastics	Neg.	Neg.	20	370	990	1,200	1,280	1,340
Rubber and leather	330	250	130	370	540	860	780	780
Textiles	50	60	160	660	900	1,120	1,230	1,270
Wood	Neg.	Neg.	Neg.	130	450	490	490	480
Other[1]	Neg.	300	500	680	750	860	860	860
Total materials in products	5,610	8,020	14,520	29,040	45,340	47,950	50,060	53,420
Other wastes								
Food, other[2]	Neg.	Neg.	Neg.	Neg.	570	580	550	680
Yard trimmings	Neg.	Neg.	Neg.	4,200	9,000	12,560	14,170	15,770
Miscellaneous inorganic wastes	Neg.	Neg.	Neg.	Neg.	Neg.	Neg.	Neg.	Neg.
Total other wastes	**Neg.**	**Neg.**	**Neg.**	**4,200**	**9,570**	**13,140**	**14,720**	**16,450**
Total MSW recovered - weight	**5,610**	**8,020**	**14,520**	**33,240**	**54,910**	**61,090**	**64,780**	**69,870**

Materials	Percent of generation of each material							
	1960	1970	1980	1990	1995	1998	1999	2000
Paper and paperboard	16.9%	15.3%	21.3%	27.8%	40.0%	40.8%	40.9%	45.4%
Glass	1.5%	1.3%	5.0%	20.1%	24.5%	23.3%	23.2%	23.0%
Metals								
Ferrous	0.5%	1.2%	2.9%	17.6%	35.5%	34.8%	34.1%	34.0%
Aluminum	Neg.	1.3%	17.9%	35.9%	31.4%	28.7%	28.2%	27.4%
Other nonferrous	Neg.	47.8%	46.6%	66.4%	64.3%	68.4%	67.4%	66.9%
Total metals	0.5%	3.5%	7.9%	24.0%	37.0%	36.4%	35.6%	35.4%
Plastics	Neg.	Neg.	0.3%	2.2%	5.2%	5.4%	5.3%	5.4%
Rubber and leather	17.9%	8.4%	3.1%	6.4%	9.0%	12.5%	12.6%	12.2%
Textiles	2.8%	2.9%	6.3%	11.4%	12.2%	13.0%	13.6%	13.5%
Wood	Neg.	Neg.	Neg.	1.1%	4.3%	4.1%	4.0%	3.8%
Other[1]	Neg.	39.0%	19.8%	21.3%	20.5%	22.1%	21.5%	21.3%
Total materials in products	**10.3%**	**9.6%**	**13.3%**	**19.8%**	**28.9%**	**28.6%**	**28.7%**	**30.6%**
Other wastes								
Food, other[2]	Neg.	Neg.	Neg.	Neg.	2.6%	2.3%	2.2%	2.6%
Yard trimmings	Neg.	Neg.	Neg.	12.0%	30.3%	45.3%	51.1%	56.9%
Miscellaneous inorganic wastes	Neg.	Neg.	Neg.	Neg.	Neg.	Neg.	Neg.	Neg.
Total other wastes	**Neg.**	**Neg.**	**Neg.**	**7.2%**	**17.5%**	**23.5%**	**26.2%**	**28.8%**
Total MSW recovered - %	**6.4%**	**6.6%**	**9.6%**	**16.2%**	**26.0%**	**27.4%**	**28.1%**	**30.1%**

Note: Recovery in table refers to postconsumer wastes; does not include converting/fabrication scrap.
[1]Recovery of electrolytes in batteries; probably not recycled.
[2]Includes recovery of paper for composting.
Details may not add to totals due to rounding.
Neg. = Less than 5,000 tons or 0.05 percent.

SOURCE: "Table 2. Recovery of Municipal Solid Waste, 1960 to 2000," in *Municipal Solid Waste in the United States: 2000 Facts and Figures*, EPA530-R-02-001, U.S. Environmental Protection Agency, Office of Solid Waste and Emergency Response, Washington, DC, June 2002. Data from Franklin Associates, Ltd.

writing is recycled paper because it is slightly more costly to produce than "virgin" paper.

Glass

Waste glass can be melted down and formed into new glass products over and over without losing its structural integrity. (See Figure 3.3.) However, colored glass cannot be easily de-colored, as paper is de-inked. This means that glass products must be sorted by color prior to reprocessing.

Figure 3.4 shows EPA estimates of the tons of glass products generated as MSW and the tons recovered between 1960 and 2000. Most glass that becomes MSW is from bottles and jars manufactured for food and drink products. Glass generation rates generally declined

FIGURE 3.2

Paper generation and recovery, 1960–2000

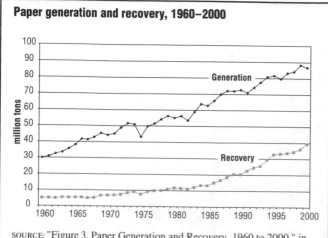

SOURCE: "Figure 3. Paper Generation and Recovery, 1960 to 2000," in *Municipal Solid Waste in the United States: 2000 Facts and Figures,* EPA530-R-02-001, U.S. Environmental Protection Agency, Office of Solid Waste and Emergency Response, Washington, DC, June 2002

FIGURE 3.4

Glass generation and recovery, 1960–2000

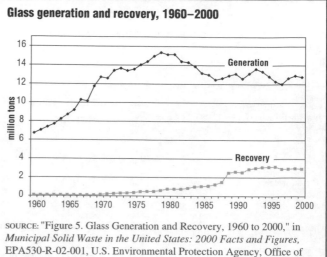

SOURCE: "Figure 5. Glass Generation and Recovery, 1960 to 2000," in *Municipal Solid Waste in the United States: 2000 Facts and Figures,* EPA530-R-02-001, U.S. Environmental Protection Agency, Office of Solid Waste and Emergency Response, Washington, DC, June 2002

FIGURE 3.3

Glass recycling process

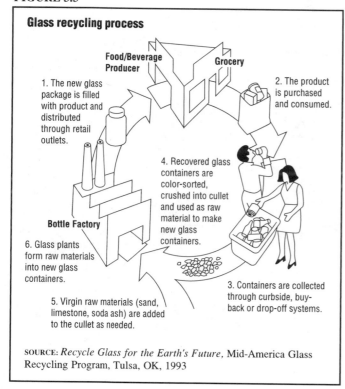

Food/Beverage Producer

Grocery

1. The new glass package is filled with product and distributed through retail outlets.

2. The product is purchased and consumed.

4. Recovered glass containers are color-sorted, crushed into cullet and used as raw material to make new glass containers.

Bottle Factory

6. Glass plants form raw materials into new glass containers.

3. Containers are collected through curbside, buy-back or drop-off systems.

5. Virgin raw materials (sand, limestone, soda ash) are added to the cullet as needed.

SOURCE: *Recycle Glass for the Earth's Future,* Mid-America Glass Recycling Program, Tulsa, OK, 1993

FIGURE 3.5

Metals generation and recovery, 1960–2000

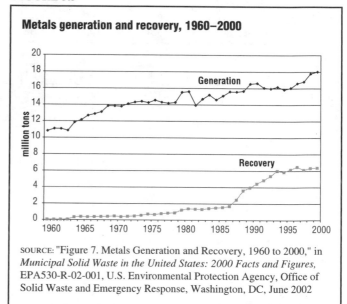

SOURCE: "Figure 7. Metals Generation and Recovery, 1960 to 2000," in *Municipal Solid Waste in the United States: 2000 Facts and Figures,* EPA530-R-02-001, U.S. Environmental Protection Agency, Office of Solid Waste and Emergency Response, Washington, DC, June 2002

between 1980 and 2000 due to competition from the plastics industry for these markets. However, glass recovery increased throughout the 1980s and early 1990s before leveling off during the mid-1990s.

Metals

Metal recycling is as old as metalworking. Coins and jewelry made of gold and silver were melted down in ancient times to make new coins with images of the latest ruler. Metal objects were generally considered valuable and were frequently sold or given away, rarely simply discarded. When metal objects could not be repaired, they could be melted down and fashioned into something else. This practice continues in modern society. In general, metals must be sorted by composition prior to reprocessing.

Figure 3.5 shows EPA estimates of the tons of metal products generated as MSW and the tons recovered between 1960 and 2000. Ferrous metals (iron and steel) comprise the largest category of metals in MSW. They are primarily used in durable goods such as appliances, furniture, and tires. Aluminum is used extensively in drink and food cans and packaging materials. Lead, zinc, and copper fall under the category "other nonferrous metals." They are found in batteries, appliances, and consumer electronics.

Metals recovery was relatively flat until the mid-1980s when it began increasing dramatically. Recovery leveled off during the late 1990s. Detailed EPA data show that recovery rates differ greatly from metal to metal. Nearly 67 percent of nonferrous metals (excluding aluminum) in the 2000 MSW stream were recovered, compared to only 34 percent of ferrous metals (iron and steel) and 27.4 percent of aluminum.

The Aluminum Association reports that the average aluminum can contains about 51 percent recycled content. Additionally, the manufacturers of aluminum cans have reduced can weight by 52 percent since 1972 and continue to find methods to reduce the weight further. Thus, each aluminum can produced in 2000 contained less aluminum than the average can from years past. Because the number of aluminum cans produced each year was fairly constant between 1995 and 2000, the number of pounds of aluminum entering MSW each year due to aluminum cans went down over this time period.

Plastics

Plastic products are manufactured from chemical resins molded into various shapes. There are dozens of different resins in common use, each with a different chemical formulation. Although waste plastic products can be melted down and reformulated into new products, sorting by resin type must first be performed.

Figure 3.6 shows EPA estimates of the tons of plastic products generated as MSW and the tons recovered between 1960 and 2000. In 1960 there were virtually no plastic products in MSW. In the year 2000, MSW contained nearly 25 million tons of plastic products. This massive increase in generation was accompanied by incredibly low rates of recovery. Only 5.4 percent of all plastic products generated in MSW during 2000 were recovered. This is less than 2 tons of plastic recovered.

Detailed EPA data show that recovery of some plastic products is much higher than others. In 2000 nearly 35 percent of PET soft drink bottles were recovered from MSW. PET stands for polyethylene terephthalate, a particular plastic resin. Likewise, just over 30 percent of HDPE milk and water bottles were recovered. HDPE is another plastic resin known as high-density polyethylene.

Recovery rates for other plastic products were very low. The EPA reported a zero recovery rate for plastic plates and cups, trash bags, and similar nondurable goods.

Packaging and Containers

The American way of life has changed greatly over the past few decades, as reflected in increases in the number of elderly and disabled living independently at home, women in the workforce, and latchkey children. Many products and packages have been developed to meet the changing needs of these American consumers—single-

FIGURE 3.6

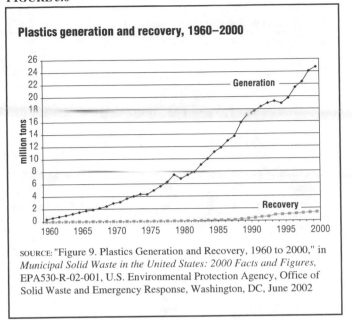

Plastics generation and recovery, 1960–2000

SOURCE: "Figure 9. Plastics Generation and Recovery, 1960 to 2000," in *Municipal Solid Waste in the United States: 2000 Facts and Figures*, EPA530-R-02-001, U.S. Environmental Protection Agency, Office of Solid Waste and Emergency Response, Washington, DC, June 2002

serve meals, easy-to-open bottles and cans, and reclosable containers.

Packaging and containers comprise a large proportion of MSW (32.2 percent in 2000). A total of 74.7 million tons of packaging and containers were generated that year. Therefore, one of the major ways to reduce the amount of MSW is to reduce the amount of packaging used for products or to use materials that recycle or biodegrade easily.

As an example of source reduction in packaging, until recently CDs and cassettes were sold in packages far larger than needed. Many customers and recording artists complained to the manufacturers, who now put CDs and cassettes in smaller packages. Many other industries are also using less plastic and paper to package their products.

The EPA reported that 38.9 percent of packaging and containers were recovered in 2000, up from 36.7 percent in 1999. The packaging and container recovery rate was only 10.5 percent in 1960. The 2000 recovery figures for packaging and containers included 26.3 percent of glass, 58 percent of steel, 44.6 percent of aluminum, 56.1 percent of paper and paperboard, 9.2 percent of plastics, and 6.1 percent of wood.

"GREEN" PRODUCT DESIGN

Designing and manufacturing products with conservation and consideration for the environment in mind is called "green" product design. Figure 3.7 contrasts conventional and green design methods. Although costs of green design systems are generally greater initially, experts think that the long-term expense will be no greater and may be offset by recycling savings.

FIGURE 3.7

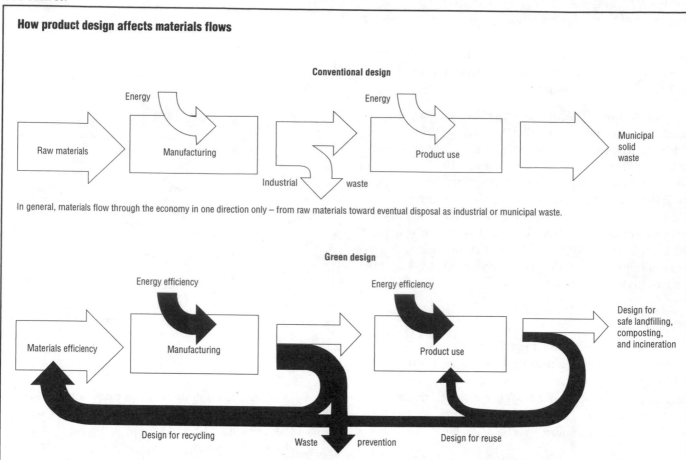

How product design affects materials flows

Conventional design

Raw materials → Manufacturing (Energy) → Industrial waste → Product use (Energy) → Municipal solid waste

In general, materials flow through the economy in one direction only – from raw materials toward eventual disposal as industrial or municipal waste.

Green design

Materials efficiency → Manufacturing (Energy efficiency) → Product use (Energy efficiency) → Design for safe landfilling, composting, and incineration

Design for recycling | Waste prevention | Design for reuse

By making changes in a product's design, overall environmental impact can be reduced. Green design emphasizes efficient use of materials and energy, reduction of waste toxicity, and reuse and recycling of materials.

SOURCE: "How Product Design Affects Materials Flows," in *Characterization of Municipal Solid Waste in the US: 1998 Update*, U.S. Environmental Protection Agency, Washington, DC, 1999

RECYCLING PROGRAMS

The successful recycling of any product within MSW is dependent on the success of three key components in the recycling process:

- Collection and sorting of the products to be recycled

- Processing and manufacturing technologies to convert waste materials into new products

- Consumer demand for recycled products and those containing recycled materials

Lack of any one of these components seriously jeopardizes recovery efforts for a particular material within the MSW stream. These three factors are represented by the three arrows in the international symbols used to show that a product is recyclable or contains recycled materials. (See Figure 3.8.)

Collection and Sorting

Before recyclable materials can be refashioned into new products, they must be collected. Most residential recycling involves curbside collection, drop-off programs,

FIGURE 3.8

The International Recycling Symbols

Made from recycled materials

May be recycled

As the three arrows of the international recycling symbol show, recycling involves three distinct steps:

1. The seperation and collection of recyclable materials,
2. The processing and manufacturing of these materials into new products and,
3. The purchase and use of recyled products.

SOURCE: "The International Recycling Symbols," in *Talkin' Trash!: A Guide to Solid Waste Disposal and Recycling in Bay County, Florida*, Bay County Solid Waste Management Department, Panama City, FL [Online] http://recycle.co.bay.fl.us/recycling_symbols.html [accessed November 6, 2003]

TABLE 3.3

Number of residential curbside recycling programs and yard trimmings composting sites by state, 2000 unless noted[1]

State	Curbside programs[2]	Curbside population served[3]	Population served (%)	Yard trimmings composting sites
Alabama	39	1,100,000	25	20
Alaska	0	0	0	0
Arizona	27	2,430,000	47	21
Arkansas	n/a	n/a	n/a	25
California	546[4]	31,146,000[5]	89	90
Colorado	n/a	n/a	n/a	n/a
Connecticut	169	3,406,000	100	88
Delaware	2	4,000	<1	4
District of Columbia	1	n/a	n/a	0
Florida	299	8,500,000	57	26
Georgia	459	n/a	n/a	15
Hawaii	5	400,000	33	9
Idaho	20	n/a	n/a	10
Illinois[6]	474	8,051,000	65	46
Indiana	168	4,170,000	73	81
Iowa	608	1,983,000	66	43
Kansas	109	1,223,000	46	91
Kentucky	45	590,000	15	37
Louisiana	25	n/a	n/a	3
Maine	34	487,000	37	30
Maryland	99	3,600,000	70	17
Massachusetts	159	4,832,000	78	219
Michigan[7]	347	2,951,000	30	164
Minnesota	765	3,700,000	75	454
Mississippi	14	325,000	12	7
Missouri	177	n/a	n/a	100[8]
Montana	n/a	n/a	n/a	n/a
Nebraska	11	500,000	29	2[9]
Nevada	3	1,622,000	81	0
New Hampshire	39	511,000	41	192
New Jersey	510	7,500,000	90	170
New Mexico	8	400,000	21	10
New York	1,500	17,230,000	95	105
North Carolina	279	3,500,000	46	120
North Dakota	50	100,000	16	85
Ohio	232[9]	n/a	n/a	519
Oklahoma	7	1,057,000	31	2
Oregon	139	2,633,000	77	30
Pennsylvania	892	8,800,000	72	313[10]
Rhode Island	25	890,000	85	15
South Carolina	135	1,676,000[11]	42	128
South Dakota	n/a	n/a	n/a	126
Tennessee	n/a	n/a	n/a	n/a
Texas	160	5,000,000	25	166
Utah	7	n/a	n/a	17
Vermont[12]	93[13]	325,000	55	12
Virginia	62	1,144,000[14]	16	14
Washington	283	4,787,000	82	32
West Virginia	51	n/a	n/a	23
Wisconsin	631[15]	3,173,000	60	140
Wyoming	1	20,000	4	>25
Total	**9,709**	**139,766,000**		**3,846**

n/a - Information not available.
[1]Many states also offer recycling services via drop-off sites. The numbers of that population are not reflected in this table.
[2]Municipal, county and other curbside programs available to residents.
[3]Conversion of 2.86 people/household used to determine population served by curbside when state provided number of households.
[4]Data collected continually by Department of Conservation, Division of Recycling, thus 546 is current number of curbside programs.
[5]Based on 11,163,287 households served.
[6]1998 data from Illinois Recycling Association.
[7]Data provided by Michigan Recycling Coalition.
[8]15 permitted facilities but state estimates total of 100 because a solid waste permit is not required, making tracking difficult.
[9]1999 data.
[10]Number of sites reported in BioCycle 2000 State of Garbage in America report (November 2000).
[11]Based on 585,916 households.
[12]1998 data.
[13]93 towns have publicly owned curbside or are under an ordinance that requires haulers to pick up some recyclables.
[14]Based on 400,000 households.
[15]Based on a January 2001 Wisconsin Legislative Audit Bureau report.

SOURCE: Nora Goldstein and Celeste Madtes, "Table 6. Number of Residential Curbside Recycling Programs and Yard Trimmings Composting Sites by State," in "The State of Garbage in America," *BioCycle*, vol. 42, no. 12, December 2001. The JG Press, Inc. (www.BioCycle.net). Reproduced with permission.

buy-back operations, and/or container deposit systems. In some cases, people are required to sort their recyclables prior to collection. Large-scale sorting of recyclable materials is performed at materials recovery facilities (MRFs).

CURBSIDE PROGRAMS. Curbside programs are those in which recyclable items are collected from bins placed outside residences.

According to the journal *BioCycle* only 1,042 curbside programs were operating in the United States in 1988. In 2000 this number climbed to 9,709 as shown in Table 3.3. New York had the highest number of curbside programs (1,500), followed by Pennsylvania (892), and Minnesota (765). Although California had only 546 curbside programs, they serviced more than 31 million residents, the highest number for any state. Together, all curbside programs serviced nearly 140 million people,

approximately half of the country's total population that year.

The state of Connecticut claims it serviced 100 percent of its population with curbside recycling programs. Other states with high percentages include New York (95 percent of population serviced) and New Jersey (90 percent of population serviced).

DROP-OFF CENTERS. Drop-off centers typically collect residential waste, although some accept commercial waste. They are found in grocery stores, charitable organizations, city-sponsored sites, and apartment complexes. The types of materials accepted vary, although drop-off centers generally accept a greater variety of materials than do curbside collection services. The EPA estimates that more than 10,000 drop-off centers are operated around the United States.

COMMERCIAL RECYCLABLES COLLECTION. The largest quantity of recovered materials comes from the commercial sector. Old corrugated containers and office papers are widely collected from businesses. Grocery stores and other retail outlets that use corrugated packaging return large amounts of recovered materials.

Buy-Back Centers and Deposit Systems

A buy-back center is usually a commercial operation that pays individuals for recovered materials. Examples include scrap metal dealers, paper dealers, waste haulers, and aluminum can centers.

Deposit systems are programs in which consumers pay a deposit on beverage containers at the time of purchase. This deposit can be redeemed if the container is returned empty for reuse. According to the EPA in 2000 there were nine states operating deposit programs: Connecticut, Delaware, Iowa, Maine, Massachusetts, Michigan, New York, Oregon, and Vermont. California operates a similar system in which consumers pay a redemption fee.

Materials Recovery Facilities

Materials recovery facilities (MRFs) sort collected recyclables, process them, and ship them to companies that can use them to produce new or reformulated products. For example, an MRF may sort and crush various types of glass recovered from curbside programs and then ship the processed glass to a bottle factory where it can be used to produce new bottles.

According to EPA estimates there were 480 MRFs operating in the United States during 2000, with an estimated total throughput of 62,000 tons per day.

MRFs vary widely in the types of materials they accept and the technology and labor they use to sort and process recyclables. Most MRFs are classified as low-technology, meaning that most of the sorting is done manually. High-technology MRFs sort recyclables using eddy currents (swirling air or water), magnetic pulleys, optical sensors, and air classifiers.

Newspaper is the major paper commodity processed at MRFs, along with corrugated boxes, used telephone books, magazines, and mixed waste paper. Non-paper commingled recyclables consist of aluminum beverage containers, food cans, glass food and beverage containers, and certain plastics. Most MRFs have separate processing lines for paper and commingled container streams. The type of processing equipment found in a particular plant depends upon the markets for which the processed recyclables are destined and the distances they must be transported.

The Role of Government

The oldest recycling law in the United States is the Oregon Recycling Opportunity Act, which was passed in 1983 and went into effect in 1986. The Act established curbside residential recycling opportunities in large cities and set up drop-off depots in small towns and rural areas.

A growing number of states require that many consumer goods sold must be made from recycled products. In addition, many states have set recycling/recovery goals for their MSW.

For recycling programs to work, there must be markets for recycled products. To help create demand, some states require that newspaper publishers use a minimum proportion of recycled paper. Many states require that recycled materials be used in making products such as telephone directories, trash bags, glass, and plastic containers. All states have some kind of "buy recycled" program that requires them to purchase recycled products when possible.

The states also use other incentives for recycling. Most states have introduced curbside collection or public drop-off sites for recyclables. Some states provide financial assistance, incentive money, or tax credits or exemptions for recycling businesses. And almost all states bar certain recyclable materials (such as car and boat batteries, grass cuttings, tires, used motor oil, glass, plastic containers, and newspapers) from entering their landfills.

The federal government also helps create a market for recycled goods. Under the Resource Conservation and Recovery Act (RCRA), federal government agencies are required to buy recycled-content products as directed by the EPA. In September 1998 President Clinton signed Executive Order 13101, which called for an increase in the federal government's use of recycled-content products. For example, it required the purchase of paper containing 30 percent post-consumer content. Post-consumer content comes from used paper that has been recycled.

Table 3.4 features the Recovered Materials Advisory Notice (RMAN) issued by the EPA, which shows the recommended recovered content and post-consumer content for various paper products. Recovered content refers to all recovered fibers used in making paper (for example, scraps recovered during manufacturing). Recovered content can also include post-consumer papers.

Additionally, almost all books and pamphlets released by the U.S. Government Printing Office (GPO) are printed on recycled paper.

In 1995 Congress passed the National Highway System Designation Act. This legislation repealed federal requirements that up to 20 percent of the asphalt pavement used in federal highway projects had to contain rubber-modified asphalt made from scrap tires or other recovered materials. The original mandate was part of the Intermodal Surface Transportation Efficiency Act of 1991. The purpose was to encourage reuse of scrap tires. According to the Rubber Pavement Association (RPA) the mandate was repealed due to cost and performance problems. Rubber-containing asphalt turned out to be more

TABLE 3.4

Recovered Materials Advisory Notice levels for paper products, April 2000

Item	Notes	Recovered content (%)	Post-consumer content (%)
Printing and writing papers			
Reprographic	Business papers such as bond, electrostatic, copy, mimeo, duplicator, and reproduction	30	30
Offset	Used for book publishing, commercial printing, direct mail, technical documents, and manuals	30	30
Tablet	Office paper such as note pads and notebooks continuous, cash register, sales book,	30	30
Forms bond	Bond type papers used for business forms such as unit sets, and computer printout, excluding carbonless	30	30
Envelope	Wove	30	30
	Kraft, white and colored (including manila)	10–20	10–20
	Kraft, unbleached	10	10
	Excludes custom envelopes		
Cotton fiber	High-quality papers used for stationery, invitations, currency, ledgers, maps, and other specialty items	30	30
Text and cover	Premium papers used for cover stock, books, and stationery and matching envelopes	30	30
Supercalendered	Groundwood paper used for advertising and mail order inserts, catalogs, and some magazines	10	10
Machine finished groundwood	Groundwood paper used in magazines and catalogs	10	10
Papeteries	Used for invitations and greeting cards	30	30
Check safety	Used in the manufacture of commercial and government checks	10	10
Coated	Used for annual reports, posters, brochures, and magazines. Have gloss, dull, or matte finishes	10	10
Carbonless	Used for multiple-impact copy forms	30	30
File folders	Manila or colored	30	30
Dyed filing products	Used for multicolored hanging folders and wallet files	20–50	20
Index and card stock	Used for index cards and postcards	50	20
Pressboard	High-strength paperboard used in binders and report covers	50	20
Tags and tickets	Used for toll and lottery tickets, licenses, and identification and tabulating cards	20–50	20
Newsprint			
Newsprint	Groundwood paper used in newspapers	20–100	20–85
Commercial sanitary tissue products			
Bathroom tissue	Used in rolls or sheets	20–100	20–60
Paper towels	Used in rolls or sheets	40–100	40–60
Paper napkins	Used in food service applications	30–100	30–60
Facial tissue	Used for personal care	10–100	10–15
General-purpose industrial wipers	Used in cleaning and wiping applications	40–100	40
Paperboard and packaging products			
Corrugated containers	Used for packaging and shipping a variety of goods		
(<300 psi)		25–50	25–50
(300 psi)		25–30	25–30
Solid fiber boxes	Used for specialized packaging needs such as dynamite packaging and army ration boxes	40	40
Folding cartons	Used to package a wide variety of foods, household products, cosmetics, pharmaceuticals, detergent, and hardware	100	40–80
Industrial paperboard	Used to create tubes, cores, cans, and drums	100	45–100
Miscellaneous	Includes "chipboard" pad backings, book covers, covered binders, mailing tubes, game boards, and puzzles	90–100	75–100
Padded mailers	Made from kraft paper that is usually brown but can be bleached white	5–15	5–15
Carrierboard	A type of folding carton designed for multipack beverage cartons	10–100	10–15
Brown papers	Used for bags and wrapping paper	5–40	5–20
Miscellaneous paper products			
Tray liners	Used to line food service trays. Often contain printed information	100	50–75

SOURCE: "RMAN Levels for Paper Products," in *2000 Buy-Recycled Series: Paper Products*, EPA530-F-00-013, U.S. Environmental Protection Agency, Office of Solid Waste and Emergency Response, Washington, DC, April 2000

expensive to produce than conventional asphalt. To make matters worse, some road applications failed to provide good results. The goal of repealing the requirements was to enable federal transportation officials to focus on the most useful and cost-effective ways of achieving important safety aims and to increase states' discretion to implement their highway programs in ways best suited to their own circumstances.

In 1996 Congress passed the Mercury-Containing and Rechargeable Battery Management Act (known as the "battery recycling bill"). This law phased out the use of mercury in batteries and provided for efficient and cost-effective collection and recycling or proper disposal of used nickel cadmium batteries, small sealed lead-acid batteries, and certain other batteries. It also exempted certain battery collection and recycling programs from some hazardous waste requirements.

COMPOSTING

In 2000 approximately 23 percent of the total MSW generated was food and yard waste. All plant-based materials in these categories can be recycled by means of composting. The substances most commonly composted are grass cuttings, garden clippings, leaves, and coffee grounds, but well-chopped plant-based food wastes are suitable as well. Using meat-based food scraps is usually discouraged because they are likely to attract animals.

To prepare a compost heap or pile, plant wastes are layered with manure or soil to speed decomposition (decay). Each six inches or so of plant material is layered with about an inch of soil. Watering the mixture and aerating it (turning it) also speeds decomposition. The compost should decay for five to seven months before it is used.

Gardeners mix compost with the soil to loosen the structure of the soil and provide it with nutrients, or spread it on top of the soil as a mulch to keep in moisture. Since compost adds nutrients to the soil, slows soil erosion, and improves water retention, it is an alternative to the use of chemical fertilizers. Compost created on a large scale is often used in landscaping, land reclamation, and landfill cover, and to provide high-nutrient soil for farms and nurseries.

Yard waste is especially suitable for composting due to its high moisture content. Over the past decade, composting yard trimmings has become an accepted waste management method in many U.S. locations. The practice got a huge boost beginning in the late 1980s when many states banned yard trimmings from disposal facilities. The 2000 *BioCycle* report revealed that in 2000 there were 3,846 public yard trimming composting sites in the United States. (See Table 3.3.)

THE HISTORY AND CURRENT STRENGTH OF RECYCLING

Recycling has become a major part of MSW management in the United States, and it will likely continue to grow, although at a slower pace than in the past. Recycling, however, did not enjoy immediate success. It started out as a "do-good" activity but eventually became a necessity for municipal governments.

For a quarter-century after the first Earth Day (April 22, 1970), recycling advocates pleaded their case to skeptical decision-makers in the interest of environmental benefit. In the early years of recycling, the economy was unable to use all the plastic, paper, and other materials that were recovered. Many private recycling companies were not able to make a profit. Instead of earning money from recycling, the programs cost them money. Some cities even started dumping their recycled materials into landfills because they could not sell them. Many city leaders felt that money spent on recycling should be used in other areas instead, such as education.

Critics of recycling pointed to the problems that recycling was experiencing as evidence that recycling programs could not work. But supporters of recycling suspected that recycling problems stemmed from the success of collection programs, which recouped more than manufacturers were initially able to handle. Advocates of recycling programs had underestimated the wellspring of support for recycling that existed among the American people.

In fact, by the mid-1990s, that support translated into marketing success. Recycling had become a revenue-producer, and prices for nearly all recyclables skyrocketed. Cities that were once paying to get rid of waste could earn millions from selling the same material. Recycling programs began to prosper. Theft of recyclables became commonplace. And private industry began to consider recycling as a way to cut expenses and even to add income, rather than as a nuisance that increased overhead costs. The new economics of recycling made it increasingly attractive to many city waste administrators.

As with any business, recycling is subject to the cyclical highs and lows of supply and demand. In the early 2000s, the recycling boom has leveled off, and prices have dropped. However, most Americans have come to understand that recovery is a viable industry as well as a necessary service.

There are several barriers, however, that continue to hinder the development of the recycling market:

- Consumers are often unaware of recycled products.

- Consumers often lack confidence in the quality of recycled products.

- The transportation costs of carrying recyclables to processing plants are high.

- Questions about supply and demand deter investors.

- It is difficult to recover or sort certain materials, such as oil, tires, and plastics.

- Recycled products are generally more expensive.

RECYCLING AROUND THE WORLD

The United States is not the only country facing waste disposal problems. Other industrial nations are con-

FIGURE 3.9

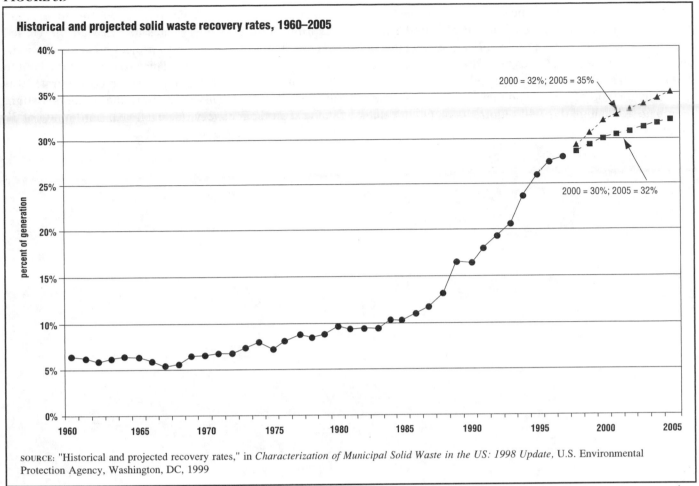

Historical and projected solid waste recovery rates, 1960–2005

SOURCE: "Historical and projected recovery rates," in *Characterization of Municipal Solid Waste in the US: 1998 Update*, U.S. Environmental Protection Agency, Washington, DC, 1999

fronting similar situations. Some landfills in Europe are reaching capacity, and most European countries are passing laws requiring more control over them. Unlike the United States, which still has much undeveloped territory, those nations do not. As a result, many European countries, like many American cities, are sending their waste to Africa and Latin America.

Several European countries, most notably Germany, require manufacturers to collect and recycle packaging they use for their products. A green dot is put on products sold in German supermarkets to show that the packaging is recyclable. Between one-half and two-thirds of products carry the green dot. France, Austria, and the United Kingdom have similar laws.

The Organisation for Economic Co-operation and Development (OECD) is comprised of 30 member countries, including the United States. In 2002 the OECD published MSW generation and disposal statistics for its members in the *OECD Environmental Data Compendium 2002*. The publication includes a comparison of recycling rates for paper and cardboard products within each country's MSW stream for the year 1999. The recycling rates range from a low of 2 percent in Poland to a high of 73 percent in Germany. The overall recycling rate for paper

and cardboard for the European Union was 51 percent. This was somewhat higher than the rate of 42 percent reported for the United States that year.

The European Union Parliament reached agreement on a new End of Life Vehicle (ELV) Directive in January 2001. Member states had 18 months from that time to introduce the final version of the Directive nationally. Under this law, manufacturers of cars face a 2007 deadline for recycling all scrap vehicles manufactured prior to January 1, 2001, and an immediate deadline for recycling all scrap vehicles manufactured after January 1, 2001. By 2015, 85 percent of the total weight of scrap vehicles will have to be recycled. The automobile manufacturers have the responsibility for arranging the take-back of cars. The ELV Directive also mandated that a number of metals, including lead, mercury, and cadmium, were banned in the manufacture of vehicles beginning July 2003.

Sometimes cultural traditions can make it more difficult to control the amount of MSW a country produces. According to a July 22, 2001, report in the *Japan Economic Newswire,* Japan uses 2 billion tons of materials annually and buries 80 million tons of refuse in landfills. One of the major reasons for Japan's huge materials use and waste disposal is the amount of wrapping and packaging that manufacturers use. Often, the amount of wrapping on a gift shows the amount of respect or love the gift-giver has for the person receiving the gift; the more wrapping, the more respect or love. For example, it is not unusual to have a gift of cookies individually wrapped, laid in corrugated paper, put inside a plastic wrap, covered with fancy wrapping paper, and then delivered in a shopping bag. To change this will require a change in values for many Japanese.

PROJECTIONS FOR SOLID WASTE RECOVERY

Figure 3.9 shows EPA projections made in 1999 regarding future recovery rates of MSW in the United States. The more conservative projection is the one indicated by a line with squares. This projection turned out to be accurate, in that a 30 percent recovery rate was achieved in 2000. This projection line predicts a slight increase in the recovery rate each year until a rate of 32 percent is achieved in the year 2005.

CHAPTER 4

AIR POLLUTION

Air pollution is unwanted chemicals or other materials (pollutants) in the air. Many air pollutants are gases or vapors, but some are solid particles, such as dust and soot. The U.S. Environmental Protection Agency (EPA) estimates that approximately 160 million tons of air pollutants were emitted into the atmosphere during 2002 in the United States.

Air pollution is a serious concern, because it poses many dangers to human health and the environment. The quality of the air plays a role in public health. Focusing on air quality is an obvious and often successful approach to improving public health; however, it can be complex. Among the factors that must be considered are the levels of pollutants in the air, levels of individual exposure to these pollutants, individual susceptibility to toxic substances, and exposure times to substances. In addition, attributing health problems to specific pollutants is complicated by the effects on health of non-environmental factors, such as smoking, heredity, and diet.

Air pollution is related to a number of respiratory diseases, including bronchitis, pulmonary emphysema, lung cancer, bronchial asthma, and premature lung tissue aging. In addition, air pollution may cause eye irritation and weaken the immune system. Lead contamination in the air can cause neurological and kidney disease and can be responsible for impaired fetal development and impaired cognitive development in children.

Air pollutants can make people sick and harm forests and food crops. Pollutants in the atmosphere make precipitation too acidic, damaging fragile ecosystems. Air pollution is also blamed for global warming and reducing the protective ozone layer around Earth. Air pollutants eat away the stone in buildings, monuments, and statues and cause hazy conditions that reduce visibility.

Air pollution comes from a variety of sources, both natural and human-made. Natural sources include wildfires and windblown dust. Human-made sources include factories, power plants, and transportation vehicles. The burning of fossil fuels and other releases of chemicals into the air are associated with economic growth and development of industrial societies. However, the consequences of these actions must be addressed. Air pollution can alter the earth's chemistry and threaten the food, water, and air supplies on which life depends.

CRITERIA AIR POLLUTANTS AND SOURCES

Under the Clean Air Act (CAA) of 1970 and the Clean Air Act Amendments of 1990, the EPA established standards to protect the ambient air (the air that naturally surrounds us). There are national ambient air quality standards (NAAQS) for six air pollutants:

- Nitrogen Dioxide (NO_2)

- Sulfur Dioxide (SO_2)

- Lead (Pb)

- Carbon Monoxide (CO)

- Particulate Matter (PM)

- Ozone (O_3)

These are called the criteria air pollutants. The NAAQS are designed to protect human health, ecosystems, plants, animals, property, and visibility from the damaging effects of these pollutants.

Pollutants directly emitted into the air are termed primary pollutants. Those formed by reactions with other air pollutants are termed secondary pollutants. NO_2, SO_2, Pb, CO, and PM are primary pollutants—meaning that they are directly emitted into the atmosphere. Ozone is considered a secondary pollutant, because it is not emitted directly, but forms due to complex chemical reactions in the atmosphere.

FIGURE 4.1

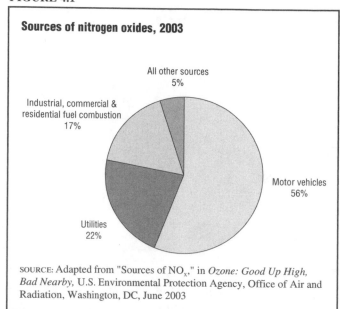

Sources of nitrogen oxides, 2003

All other sources 5%

Industrial, commercial & residential fuel combustion 17%

Motor vehicles 56%

Utilities 22%

SOURCE: Adapted from "Sources of NO$_x$," in *Ozone: Good Up High, Bad Nearby,* U.S. Environmental Protection Agency, Office of Air and Radiation, Washington, DC, June 2003

FIGURE 4.2

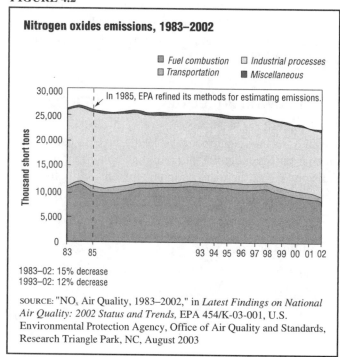

Nitrogen oxides emissions, 1983–2002

■ Fuel combustion   □ Industrial processes
□ Transportation   ■ Miscellaneous

In 1985, EPA refined its methods for estimating emissions.

1983–02: 15% decrease
1993–02: 12% decrease

SOURCE: "NO$_x$ Air Quality, 1983–2002," in *Latest Findings on National Air Quality: 2002 Status and Trends,* EPA 454/K-03-001, U.S. Environmental Protection Agency, Office of Air Quality and Standards, Research Triangle Park, NC, August 2003

The EPA tracks emissions of the primary air pollutants and ozone precursors (chemicals known to contribute to ozone formation). Ozone precursors include volatile organic compounds (VOCs) and nitrogen oxides (NO$_x$). NO$_x$ is a generic label designating any of the groups of gases that contain nitrogen and oxygen in varying amounts.

The EPA has documented air pollution trends in the United States annually since 1970. Two kinds of trends are reported for criteria pollutants. Emissions of the total tonnage of pollutants released into the air annually are

FIGURE 4.3

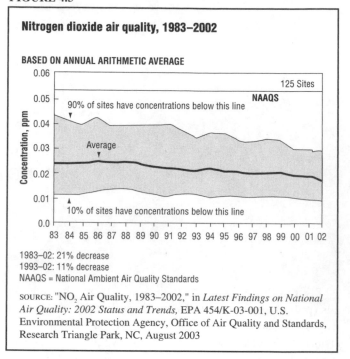

Nitrogen dioxide air quality, 1983–2002

BASED ON ANNUAL ARITHMETIC AVERAGE

125 Sites
NAAQS

90% of sites have concentrations below this line

Average

10% of sites have concentrations below this line

1983–02: 21% decrease
1993–02: 11% decrease
NAAQS = National Ambient Air Quality Standards

SOURCE: "NO$_2$ Air Quality, 1983–2002," in *Latest Findings on National Air Quality: 2002 Status and Trends,* EPA 454/K-03-001, U.S. Environmental Protection Agency, Office of Air Quality and Standards, Research Triangle Park, NC, August 2003

calculated based on monitoring data or are estimated. Air quality concentrations represent pollutant concentrations measured in the air at monitoring stations located around the country.

Nitrogen Dioxide

Nitrogen dioxide (NO$_2$) is a reddish brown gas that is highly reactive. It forms easily in the ambient air when nitric oxide (NO) is oxidized. The EPA tracks national emissions of NO$_x$ and measures ambient concentrations of NO$_2$ for comparison to the NAAQS.

As shown in Figure 4.1, operation of motor vehicles accounted for 56 percent of NO$_x$ emissions in the United States during 2003. Historically, the burning of fossil fuels in transportation vehicles has been the major cause of NO$_x$ emissions. (See Figure 4.2.) These fossil fuels include coal, oil, natural gas, and gasoline. Industrial processes account for only a tiny fraction of NO$_x$ emissions. EPA data show that national NO$_x$ emissions decreased by 15 percent between 1983 and 2002. NO$_2$ air quality concentrations decreased by 21 percent over the same time period. (See Figure 4.3.) The national average NO$_2$ concentration in 2002 was well below the NAAQS.

In its 2003 report *Latest Findings on National Air Quality: 2002 Status and Trends,* the EPA noted that NO$_x$ emissions from nonroad diesel engines increased between 1983 and 2002, even as all other emission sources declined. Nonroad diesel engines are used as backup fuel sources by industries and power plants.

NO$_x$ contributes to many other air pollution problems, including haze, acid rain, and the formation of particulate

FIGURE 4.4

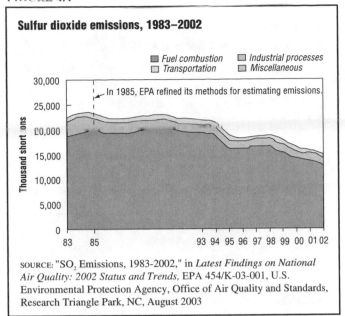

Sulfur dioxide emissions, 1983–2002

SOURCE: "SO₂ Emissions, 1983-2002," in *Latest Findings on National Air Quality: 2002 Status and Trends,* EPA 454/K-03-001, U.S. Environmental Protection Agency, Office of Air Quality and Standards, Research Triangle Park, NC, August 2003

FIGURE 4.5

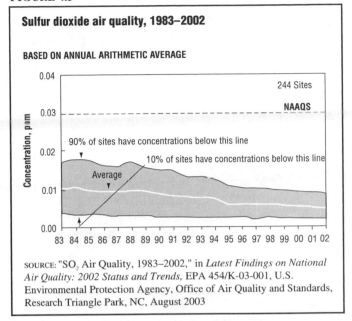

Sulfur dioxide air quality, 1983–2002

SOURCE: "SO₂ Air Quality, 1983–2002," in *Latest Findings on National Air Quality: 2002 Status and Trends,* EPA 454/K-03-001, U.S. Environmental Protection Agency, Office of Air Quality and Standards, Research Triangle Park, NC, August 2003

matter and ozone. Nitrogen compounds that reach the ground and surface waters can be particularly damaging to plant life and aquatic ecosystems. High nitrogen concentrations in surface waters can lead to eutrophication—a condition in which too much algae grows and levels of dissolved oxygen are severely lowered. Excessive nitrogen also acidifies soil causing damage to plants and trees.

The EPA warns that even short-term exposure (less than three hours) to low NO_2 levels can damage airway and lung functions in humans with existing respiratory illnesses. Long-term exposure to NO_2 can cause increased susceptibility to respiratory infections and may cause serious alterations in lung structure.

Sulfur Dioxide

Sulfur dioxide (SO_2) is a gas that is formed when sulfur-containing fuels (mainly coal and oil) are burned. As shown in Figure 4.4, power plants combusting fossil fuels to generate power have historically been the primary source of SO_2 emissions. Transportation and industrial processes (such as metal smelting) account for only a very small fraction of SO_2 emissions.

The EPA reports that SO_2 emissions decreased by 33 percent between 1983 and 2002. SO_2 air quality concentrations decreased by 54 percent over the same time period. (See Figure 4.5.) The national average in 2002 was well below the NAAQS. The historical decline in SO_2 levels is attributed to greater use of low-sulfur coal at power plants and implementation of pollution control devices, such as scrubbers, that clean factory emissions.

Inhaling sulfur dioxide in polluted air can impair breathing in those with asthma or even in healthy adults who are active outdoors. As with other air pollutants, chil-

dren, the elderly, and those with preexisting respiratory and cardiovascular diseases and conditions are most susceptible to adverse effects from breathing this gas.

SO_2 is also a major contributor to acid rain, haze, and particulate matter. Acid rain is of particular concern, because acid deposition harms aquatic life by lowering the pH of surface waters, impairs the growth of forests, causes depletion of natural soil nutrients, and corrodes buildings, cars, and monuments. Acid rain is largely associated with the eastern United States, because eastern coal tends to be higher in sulfur content than coal mined in the western United States.

In 1990 the United States Congress established the Acid Rain Program under Title IV of the 1990 Clean Air Act Amendments. The goal of the program is to reduce annual emission of SO_2 by 10 million tons and of NO_x by 2 million tons between 1980 and 2010. A permanent national cap of 8.95 million tons of SO_2 per year is to be in effect for electric utilities by 2010. The program expects to meet its goals by tightening annual emission limits on thousands of power plants around the country.

Lead

Lead is a metal that can enter the atmosphere via combustion or industrial processing of lead-containing materials. Prior to 1985, the major source of lead emissions in the United States was the use of leaded gasoline in automobiles. As shown in Figure 4.6, this source has virtually been eliminated. Industrial processes (chiefly metals smelting and battery manufacturing) were responsible for the bulk of lead emissions from the early 1990s through 2002.

The EPA reports that lead emissions declined by 93 percent between 1982 and 2002. Lead air concentrations

FIGURE 4.6

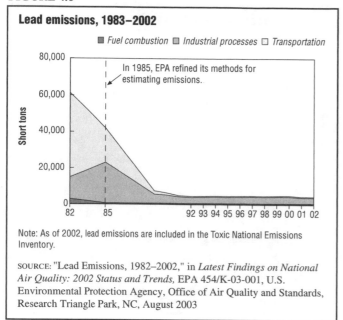

Lead emissions, 1983–2002

Note: As of 2002, lead emissions are included in the Toxic National Emissions Inventory.

SOURCE: "Lead Emissions, 1982–2002," in *Latest Findings on National Air Quality: 2002 Status and Trends,* EPA 454/K-03-001, U.S. Environmental Protection Agency, Office of Air Quality and Standards, Research Triangle Park, NC, August 2003

FIGURE 4.7

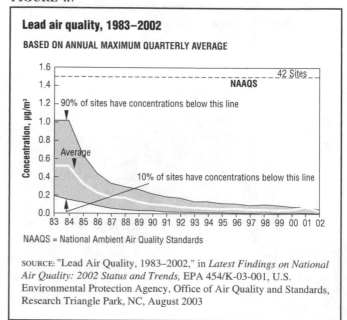

Lead air quality, 1983–2002

NAAQS = National Ambient Air Quality Standards

SOURCE: "Lead Air Quality, 1983–2002," in *Latest Findings on National Air Quality: 2002 Status and Trends,* EPA 454/K-03-001, U.S. Environmental Protection Agency, Office of Air Quality and Standards, Research Triangle Park, NC, August 2003

measured at monitoring sites around the country decreased by 94 percent between 1983 and 2002. (See Figure 4.7).

Lead is a particularly dangerous pollutant, because it accumulates in the blood, bones, and soft tissues of the body. It can be harmful to the nervous system, kidneys, liver, and other organs. Excessive concentrations are associated with neurological damage, leading to such impairments as seizures, mental retardation, and behavioral disorders. Even low doses of lead can cause damage to the brains and nervous systems of fetuses and young children. Atmospheric lead that falls onto vegetation poses potential harm to humans and animals if it is eaten.

Carbon Monoxide

Carbon monoxide (CO) is a colorless, odorless gas formed when the carbon in a fuel is not burned completely. Examples include coal, natural gas, oil, gasoline, and wood. Motor vehicle exhaust has historically been the primary source of CO emissions in the United States. (See Figure 4.8.)

In 1940 cars and trucks created only about 28 percent of carbon monoxide emissions, while homes burning coal and oil made up about 50 percent. From 1940 through 1970, emissions from cars and trucks nearly tripled. By 1970 cars and trucks accounted for 71 percent of all carbon monoxide, and a dozen years later, in 1982, they produced 80 percent of the total carbon monoxide emissions.

The EPA estimates that in 2002 as much as 95 percent of all CO emissions in urban areas came from automobile exhaust. Wildfires are the second largest source of CO emissions at the national level. Overall CO emissions decreased by 41 percent between 1983 and 2002. The

largest decrease has been obtained in the transportation sector due to increased focus on vehicle emission control programs. CO air concentrations decreased by 65 percent between 1983 and 2002, as shown in Figure 4.9.

Breathing carbon monoxide (CO) is harmful, because it reduces the ability of blood to carry oxygen to organs and tissues. The health threat is most serious for people who suffer from cardiovascular disease. At high levels of exposure, even healthy people are at risk and can experience impaired vision, disruptions in hand-eye coordination, and other motor skill problems. Very high levels of CO are deadly. Fortunately, such high levels are not associated with ambient air pollution. They can occur when people are enclosed in a room or other confined space with an improperly vented fuel source, such as a propane stove.

Particulate Matter

Particulate matter (PM) is the general term for the mixture of solid particles and/or liquid droplets found in the air. Primary particles are those emitted directly into the atmosphere, for example, dust, dirt, and soot (black carbon). Secondary particles form in the atmosphere due to complex chemical reactions among gaseous emissions, such as sulfates, nitrates, and organic carbon compounds. For example, sulfate particulates can form when sulfur dioxide emissions from industrial facilities and power plants undergo chemical reactions in the atmosphere.

Sources of particulate matter include unpaved roads, agriculture and forestry, residential wood stoves and fireplaces, and fuel combustion in vehicles, power plants, and industry.

The EPA tracks two sizes of particulate matter: PM_{10} and $PM_{2.5}$. PM_{10} are relatively coarse particles that

FIGURE 4.8

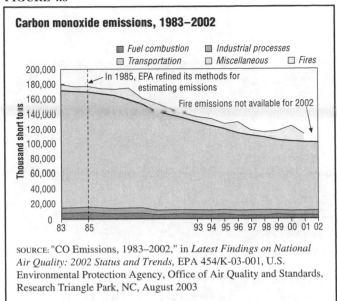

Carbon monoxide emissions, 1983–2002

SOURCE: "CO Emissions, 1983–2002," in *Latest Findings on National Air Quality: 2002 Status and Trends,* EPA 454/K-03-001, U.S. Environmental Protection Agency, Office of Air Quality and Standards, Research Triangle Park, NC, August 2003

FIGURE 4.9

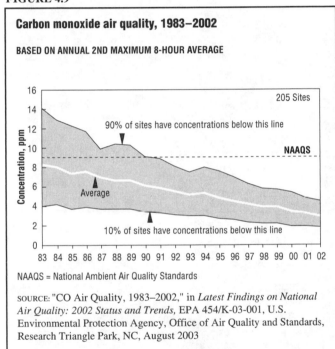

Carbon monoxide air quality, 1983–2002

NAAQS = National Ambient Air Quality Standards

SOURCE: "CO Air Quality, 1983–2002," in *Latest Findings on National Air Quality: 2002 Status and Trends,* EPA 454/K-03-001, U.S. Environmental Protection Agency, Office of Air Quality and Standards, Research Triangle Park, NC, August 2003

FIGURE 4.10

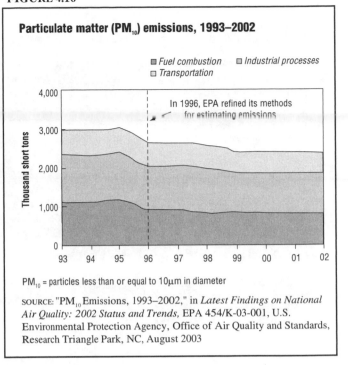

Particulate matter (PM$_{10}$) emissions, 1993–2002

PM$_{10}$ = particles less than or equal to 10μm in diameter

SOURCE: "PM$_{10}$ Emissions, 1993–2002," in *Latest Findings on National Air Quality: 2002 Status and Trends,* EPA 454/K-03-001, U.S. Environmental Protection Agency, Office of Air Quality and Standards, Research Triangle Park, NC, August 2003

FIGURE 4.11

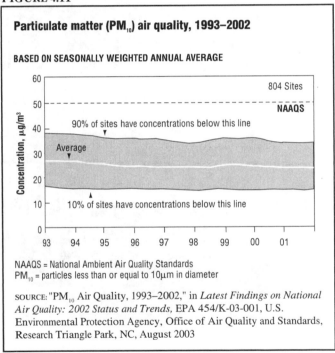

Particulate matter (PM$_{10}$) air quality, 1993–2002

NAAQS = National Ambient Air Quality Standards
PM$_{10}$ = particles less than or equal to 10μm in diameter

SOURCE: "PM$_{10}$ Air Quality, 1993–2002," in *Latest Findings on National Air Quality: 2002 Status and Trends,* EPA 454/K-03-001, U.S. Environmental Protection Agency, Office of Air Quality and Standards, Research Triangle Park, NC, August 2003

are less than or equal to 10 micrometers in diameter. That is roughly one-seventh the diameter of a human hair. Particles of this size are small enough that they can be breathed into the lungs. This can aggravate respiratory conditions, such as bronchitis and asthma, and endanger the circulatory system. PM$_{2.5}$ are even smaller particles (less than or equal to 2.5 micrometers in diameter). They have been linked with the most serious health effects in humans.

Particulates pose the greatest health risk to those with heart or lung problems, the elderly, and children. Children are particularly susceptible when they spend a great deal

of time outside and their lungs are still developing. Particulates are also a major contributor to haze and can damage painted surfaces, buildings, and monuments.

Figure 4.10 shows historical sources of PM$_{10}$ emissions in the United States. Industrial processes are the largest source, followed closely by fuel combustion and transportation. From 1940 to 1971, the amount of particulate matter in the air increased. During the 1970s, however, pollution control laws led to a drop in particulate

FIGURE 4.12

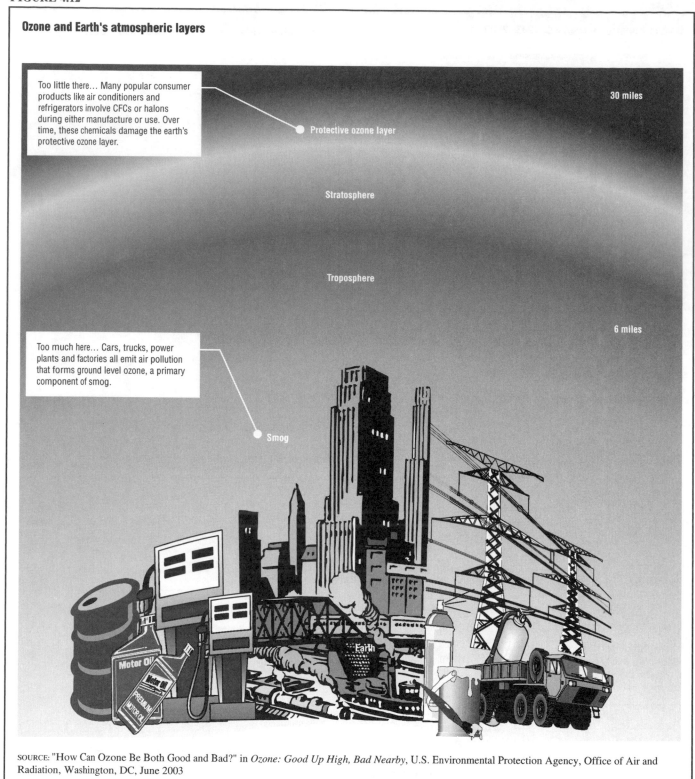

Ozone and Earth's atmospheric layers

Too little there… Many popular consumer products like air conditioners and refrigerators involve CFCs or halons during either manufacture or use. Over time, these chemicals damage the earth's protective ozone layer.

Protective ozone layer

30 miles

Stratosphere

Troposphere

6 miles

Too much here… Cars, trucks, power plants and factories all emit air pollution that forms ground level ozone, a primary component of smog.

Smog

SOURCE: "How Can Ozone Be Both Good and Bad?" in *Ozone: Good Up High, Bad Nearby*, U.S. Environmental Protection Agency, Office of Air and Radiation, Washington, DC, June 2003

matter concentrations in the air. Direct PM_{10} emissions decreased by 22 percent between 1993 and 2002. PM_{10} air quality concentrations decreased by 13 percent over the same time period, as shown in Figure 4.11.

The EPA also tracks direct $PM_{2.5}$ emissions and reports that they decreased by 17 percent nationally between 1993 and 2002. However, direct emissions account for only a small percentage of the $PM_{2.5}$ found in the atmosphere. The vast majority of small particulates form from other emissions.

The Interagency Monitoring of Protected Visual Environments (IMPROVE) network was established by the EPA in 1987 to track $PM_{2.5}$ trends. The network includes monitoring sites located in rural areas around the country.

IMPROVE data for the period September 2001 to August 2002 show that PM$_{2.5}$ levels were highest in southern California and the eastern United States. Particulates found in southern California were usually composed of carbon and nitrates, while eastern U.S. particulates were more likely to be of sulfates, ammonium, and carbon. The EPA reports that parts of California and many areas in the eastern United States have annual average PM$_{2.5}$ air quality concentrations that are above the national standard.

Ozone

Ozone (O$_3$) is a gas that is naturally present in Earth's upper atmosphere. Approximately 90 percent of the planet's ozone lies in the stratosphere at altitudes greater than about 20 miles. Stratospheric ozone plays a useful role by absorbing ultraviolet (UV) radiation from the sun and preventing it from reaching Earth's surface. Beneath the stratosphere lies the troposphere. (See Figure 4.12.) Ozone trapped within this layer of the atmosphere is a potent air pollutant with serious health consequences. Tropospheric ozone is also called terrestrial or ground-level ozone.

Ground-level ozone is not emitted into the air from sources on the ground, but forms due to complex chemical reactions initiated by sunlight. These reactions are known as photochemical reactions. Ozone formation is greatest on sunny hot days when the atmosphere contains other pollutants, primarily volatile organic compounds (VOCs) and nitrogen oxide. Emissions of these ozone precursors result from chemical use in factories and fossil fuel combustion.

Ground-level ozone is the principal component of smog—a word derived from "smoke" and "fog." Smog is probably the most well-known form of air pollution.

Weather and location determine where smog goes and how bad it will become. When thermal inversions occur (a layer of warm air over cool air), they trap air pollution near the ground. If winds are light as well, smog may stay in one place for days. As traffic and other pollution sources add more primary pollutants to the air, the smog gets worse. Some of the worst smog in the United States occurs in cities such as Los Angeles, Chicago, Houston, and New York. Mexico City, the capital city of neighboring Mexico, is generally considered to have the most polluted air in the world.

Many people are familiar with smoggy conditions around major cities, but smog is increasingly a problem in rural areas also. Wind often blows primary pollutants away from their sources of emission. The chemical reactions that create the photochemical pollutants of smog can occur while primary pollutants are being blown through the air by the wind. For this reason, smog can be more serious miles away from the location where primary pollutants are emitted than at their source.

TABLE 4.1

Air pollutants, in order of harm to plants

Pollutant	Primary or secondary pollutant	Form	Major source(s)
Ozone (O$_3$)	Secondary	Gas	Product of chemical reactions in the atmosphere
Acidic deposition (sulfates and nitrates)	Secondary	Particulate	Product of chemical reactions in the atmosphere
Sulfur dioxide (SO$_2$)	Primary	Gas	Power generation, smelter operation
Nitrogen dioxides (NO$_x$)	Primary and secondary	Gas	From direct release and atmospheric transformation
Hydrogen fluoride (HF)	Primary	Gas/ Particulate	Superphosphate production, and aluminum smelters
Ethylene	Primary	Gas	Combustion, natural causes

SOURCE: "Air pollutants, in order of harm to plants," in *Agriculture and the Environment*, U.S. Department of Agriculture, Washington, DC, 1992

During the 1990s EPA researchers monitored ozone levels at national parks around the country. They found that ozone levels increased by more than 4 percent in 29 of the parks. Ozone exposure in forests is a concern, because the chemical is harmful to vegetation. It stunts the growth of seedlings and stresses trees. Smog also impairs visibility in national parks and forests, a problem that reduces visitor enjoyment and harms tourism. Ozone is damaging to agricultural crops and other plants as well. It increases their susceptibility to diseases, pests, and other environmental stresses. Table 4.1 is a list compiled by the U.S. Department of Agriculture that ranks air pollutants in terms of their harmful effects on plant life. Ozone ranks at the top of the list.

Ozone exposure in humans causes and aggravates respiratory problems, such as lung inflammation and asthma. This is particularly true for children, elderly people, and people who spend a great deal of time outside. Children are of particular concern, because their developing lungs are particularly susceptible to harm. The prevalence of childhood asthma doubled between 1980 and 1995, as shown in Figure 4.13. Researchers are not sure why asthma cases have increased, even as overall air quality in this country has improved. However, it is known that reductions in ozone levels should help reduce the severity of asthma attacks in children that have the disease.

Long-term human exposure to even moderate levels of ozone is believed to cause irreversible lung damage due to premature aging of the tissues. Ozone has different health and environmental effects depending on the time of exposure. The EPA monitors average 8-hour and 1-hour ozone levels and sets different standards for each. As shown in Figure 4.14, the average national ozone concentration, based on an 8-hour average, increased by 4

FIGURE 4.13

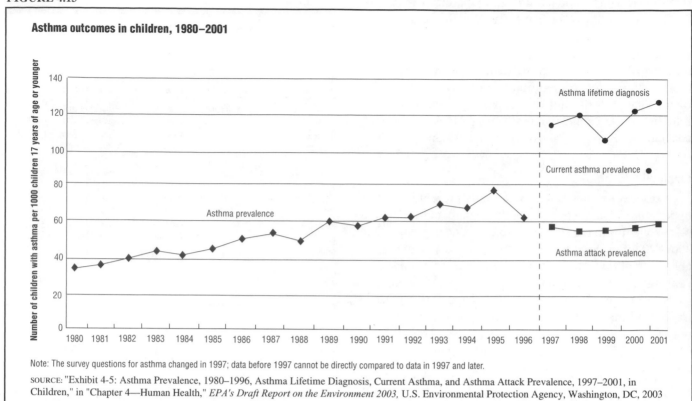

Asthma outcomes in children, 1980–2001

Note: The survey questions for asthma changed in 1997; data before 1997 cannot be directly compared to data in 1997 and later.

SOURCE: "Exhibit 4-5: Asthma Prevalence, 1980–1996, Asthma Lifetime Diagnosis, Current Asthma, and Asthma Attack Prevalence, 1997–2001, in Children," in "Chapter 4—Human Health," *EPA's Draft Report on the Environment 2003,* U.S. Environmental Protection Agency, Washington, DC, 2003

FIGURE 4.14

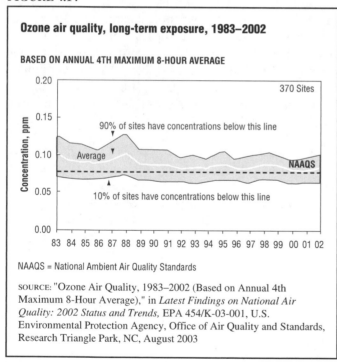

Ozone air quality, long-term exposure, 1983–2002

BASED ON ANNUAL 4TH MAXIMUM 8-HOUR AVERAGE

NAAQS = National Ambient Air Quality Standards

SOURCE: "Ozone Air Quality, 1983–2002 (Based on Annual 4th Maximum 8-Hour Average)," in *Latest Findings on National Air Quality: 2002 Status and Trends,* EPA 454/K-03-001, U.S. Environmental Protection Agency, Office of Air Quality and Standards, Research Triangle Park, NC, August 2003

percent between 1993 and 2002. The average 1-hour concentration decreased by 2 percent during the same time period. (See Figure 4.15.) However, both averages exceeded the NAAQS in 2002.

Ground-level ozone has historically been the most complex, pervasive, and difficult to control of the six criteria pollutants. Because ozone is not emitted directly from human-made sources, researchers track emissions of ozone precursors, such as VOCs.

Volatile Organic Compounds

Volatile organic compounds (VOCs) are carbon-containing chemicals that convert easily from a liquid to gaseous state. Examples include benzene, toluene, and formaldehyde. These gases are released during the combustion of fossil fuels and from many industrial processes. As shown in Figure 4.16, industrial processes and transportation have historically been the two leading sources of VOC emissions in the United States. The widespread use of solvents is blamed for most of the VOC emissions associated with industrial processes.

From 1940 through 1970, VOC emissions increased about 77 percent, mainly because of the increase in car and truck traffic, and in industrial production. Since 1970 national VOC emissions have decreased as a result of emission controls on cars and trucks, and less open burning of solid waste. From 1980 to 1999, VOC emissions decreased 31 percent. From 1990 to 1999, VOC emissions from highway vehicles dropped 18 percent. During that time, industrial VOC emissions decreased 21 percent, in part due to the implementation of controls that affect specific chemical and solvent industries.

Figure 4.17 shows the primary sources of VOC emissions in 2003. Industrial and commercial processes and motor vehicles accounted for 95 percent of all VOC

FIGURE 4.15

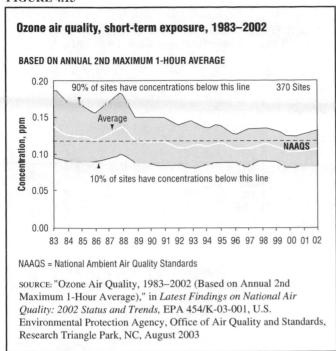

Ozone air quality, short-term exposure, 1983–2002

BASED ON ANNUAL 2ND MAXIMUM 1-HOUR AVERAGE

NAAQS = National Ambient Air Quality Standards

SOURCE: "Ozone Air Quality, 1983–2002 (Based on Annual 2nd Maximum 1-Hour Average)," in *Latest Findings on National Air Quality: 2002 Status and Trends,* EPA 454/K-03-001, U.S. Environmental Protection Agency, Office of Air Quality and Standards, Research Triangle Park, NC, August 2003

FIGURE 4.17

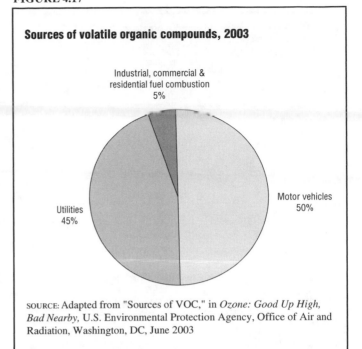

Sources of volatile organic compounds, 2003

SOURCE: Adapted from "Sources of VOC," in *Ozone: Good Up High, Bad Nearby,* U.S. Environmental Protection Agency, Office of Air and Radiation, Washington, DC, June 2003

FIGURE 4.16

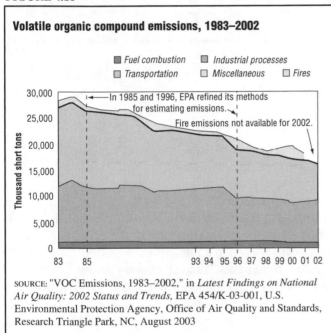

Volatile organic compound emissions, 1983–2002

SOURCE: "VOC Emissions, 1983–2002," in *Latest Findings on National Air Quality: 2002 Status and Trends,* EPA 454/K-03-001, U.S. Environmental Protection Agency, Office of Air Quality and Standards, Research Triangle Park, NC, August 2003

FIGURE 4.18

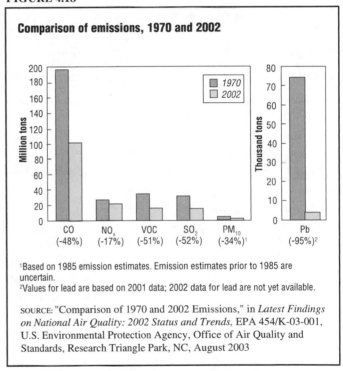

Comparison of emissions, 1970 and 2002

[1] Based on 1985 emission estimates. Emission estimates prior to 1985 are uncertain.
[2] Values for lead are based on 2001 data; 2002 data for lead are not yet available.

SOURCE: "Comparison of 1970 and 2002 Emissions," in *Latest Findings on National Air Quality: 2002 Status and Trends,* EPA 454/K-03-001, U.S. Environmental Protection Agency, Office of Air Quality and Standards, Research Triangle Park, NC, August 2003

emissions. The remaining 5 percent are attributed to consumer usage of solvents, for example, in cleaning chemicals.

The health and environmental effects of VOCs are similar to those of ozone.

Overall Trends for Criteria Pollutants

As shown in Figure 4.18, emissions of all criteria air pollutants decreased between 1970 and 2002. However, decreases in emissions do not necessarily result in lower air concentrations. Table 4.2 compares the percent decreases in emissions and air concentrations of the principal air pollutants between 1983 and 2002 and between 1993 and 2002. The table shows that 8-hour ozone concentrations increased by 4 percent between 1993 and 2002, despite the fact that emissions of ozone precursors (VOCs and NO$_x$) decreased during the same time period.

The EPA reports that emission and air quality data trends do not always match for a variety of reasons. Atmospheric chemistry and weather play a major role in air pollutant formation; however, these factors are not easily measured. Although emissions from factories and

TABLE 4.2

Percent change in air quality and emissions, 1983–2002

Air quality

	1983-2002	1993-2002
NO_2	-21	-11
O_3 1-h	-22	-2[1]
8-h	-14	+4[1]
SO_2	-54	-39
PM_{10}	—	-13
$PM_{2.5}$	—	-8[2]
CO	-65	-42
Pb	-94	-57

Emissions

	1983-2002	1993-2002
NO_x	-15	-12
VOC	-40	-25
SO_2	-33	-31
PM_{10}[3]	-34[5]	-22
$PM_{2.5}$[3]	—	-17
CO	-41	-21
Pb[5]	-93	-5

Note: Negative numbers indicate improvements in air quality or reductions in emissions. Positive numbers show where emissions have increased or air quality has gotten worse.
—Trend data not available.
[1] Not statistically significant.
[2] Based on percentage change from 1999.
[3] Includes only directly emitted particles.
[4] Based on percentage change from 1985. Emission estimates prior to 1985 are uncertain.
[5] Lead emissions are included in the toxic air pollutant emissions inventory and are presented for 1982-2001.

SOURCE: "Percent Change in Air Quality" and "Percent Change in Emissions," in *Latest Findings on National Air Quality: 2002 Status and Trends,* EPA 454/K-03-001, U.S. Environmental Protection Agency, Office of Air Quality and Standards, Research Triangle Park, NC, August 2003

FIGURE 4.19

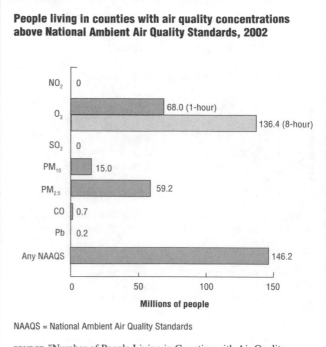

People living in counties with air quality concentrations above National Ambient Air Quality Standards, 2002

NAAQS = National Ambient Air Quality Standards

SOURCE: "Number of People Living in Counties with Air Quality Concentrations Above the Level of the NAAQS in 2002," in *Latest Findings on National Air Quality: 2002 Status and Trends,* EPA 454/K-03-001, U.S. Environmental Protection Agency, Office of Air Quality and Standards, Research Triangle Park, NC, August 2003

other stationary sources are monitored directly, emissions from mobile sources (such as cars, trains, and planes) have to be estimated. This introduces some uncertainty into data analysis and comparison.

In 2002 approximately 146 million Americans (about 47 percent of the population) lived in counties that failed to meet the NAAQS for at least one of the criteria pollutants. (See Figure 4.19.) The vast majority (93 percent) of these people were exposed to levels of ozone greater than the acceptable 8-hour standard. The 1-hour ozone standard was also exceeded in a number of counties, exposing 68 million people to high levels of this pollutant. Particulate matter was the second most problematic of the NAAQS. Only a small fraction of people lived in counties where carbon monoxide and lead NAAQS were exceeded. Areas where NAAQS are exceeded are called nonattainment areas. There were no nonattainment areas reported for NO_2 and SO_2 in 2002.

HAZARDOUS AIR POLLUTANTS AND SOURCES

Hazardous air pollutants (HAPs), or air toxics, are pollutants that cause or may cause cancer or other serious health effects, such as damage to the immune system, birth defects or reproductive disorders, or serious neurological, developmental, or respiratory problems. HAPs are also associated with adverse effects on the environment

and ecological systems. Examples of air toxics include benzene, perchloroethylene, methylene chloride, dioxin, asbestos, toluene, and metals such as mercury, chromium, cadmium, and lead compounds.

Overall, the CAA lists 188 substances as hazardous air pollutants and directs the EPA to regulate sources emitting major amounts of these pollutants. Air toxics are emitted from many sources. For example, benzene is found in gasoline. Perchloroethylene is emitted by some dry cleaning facilities. Methylene chloride is a common solvent and paint stripper used in a number of industries. Most HAPs originate from human-made sources. Factories, refineries, power plants, dry cleaners, cars, trucks, and construction vehicles are common examples. The use of certain building materials and solvents can also lead to HAP emissions. Natural sources of HAPs include volcanoes and wildfires.

HAPs can be a health hazard to humans and animals via inhalation or via ingestion of vegetation that becomes contaminated through deposition onto the soil or surface waters. Some HAPs are bioaccumulative, meaning that they can work their way up the food chain from vegetation through animals to humans. The EPA does not operate an extensive nationwide monitoring network for air toxics as is done for the priority pollutants. In 2003 the agency created the National Air Toxic Trend Site (NATTS) network to monitor trends in high-risk air toxics such as benzene, formaldehyde, chromium, acrolein, and 1,3-butadiene. The network is expected to begin collecting data in 2004.

Certain manufacturing facilities are required to report to the EPA their estimated releases of 650 listed chemicals each year. These reports are compiled into an annual database called the Toxics Release Inventory (TRI), which was established under the Emergency Planning and Community Right-to-Know Act of 1986. Data were first collected in 1987 and compiled in 1988.

TRI data do have limitations, because the data are self-reported and certain facilities are not required to participate. However, TRI estimates help show trends in toxic air emissions. The *2001 Toxics Release Inventory Executive Summary* was released by the EPA in July 2003. It reports that nearly 25,000 registered facilities released 1.7 billion pounds of materials from their sites directly into the air in 2001. These are called on-site air releases. The states with the highest TRI on-site air releases in 2001 were Ohio, North Carolina, and Texas. Each state released more than 100 million pounds of materials into the air. Hydrochloric acid was by far the predominant air toxic released. It accounted for 35 percent of all toxic air releases. Hydrochloric acid emissions are primarily a by-product of pulp and paper production, metal cleaning, and the production or combustion of chlorine-containing chemicals.

The Clinton Administration expanded "right to know" initiatives, which are environmental programs designed to inhibit pollution, not with legislation and regulation, but by exposing polluters to pressure from a well-informed public. One of these initiatives is the Sector Facility Indexing Project (SFIP), which was launched by the EPA in early 1995. SFIP expands on the Toxics Release Inventory by providing data on the Internet in one location (http://www.epa.gov/sfip/intro_and_overview.html) about 617 facilities in five industry sectors:

• Automobile assembly

• Pulp manufacturing for the paper industry

• Iron and steel production

• Petroleum refining

• Primary smelting and refining of aluminum, copper, lead, and zinc

In June 2001 data for hundreds of major federal facilities in the United States were added to the SFIP. As of December 2003 the database includes data for 273 of these facilities. These facilities are operated by a variety of federal agencies, including the Department of Defense, Department of Energy, and the National Aeronautics and Space Administration (NASA). The SFIP provides environmental data about each facility, such as the number of inspections, noncompliance issues, enforcement actions, chemical releases, and pollution spills. SFIP also includes information on the location of each facility and the population of the surrounding area.

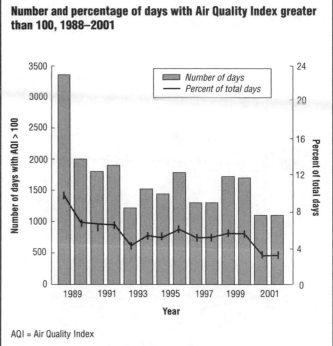

FIGURE 4.20

Number and percentage of days with Air Quality Index greater than 100, 1988–2001

AQI = Air Quality Index

SOURCE: "Exhibit 1-3: Number and Percentage of Days with Air Quality Index (AQI) Greater Than 100, 1988–2001," in "Chapter 1—Cleaner Air," *EPA's Draft Report on the Environment 2003,* U.S. Environmental Protection Agency, Washington, DC, 2003

THE AIR QUALITY INDEX

The air quality index is a means for describing the health effects of air quality due to ozone, particulate matter, carbon monoxide, SO_2, and NO_2. The AQI scale runs from 0 to 500, where higher values indicate greater health danger. An AQI value of 100 is considered equivalent to the NAAQS for a particular pollutant. Values higher than 100 indicate that air quality is unhealthy. Figure 4.20 shows the number and percentage of days each year between 1988 and 2001 when the AQI exceeded 100.

TRANSPORTATION AND AIR POLLUTION

Automobiles and Trucks

In the early 1950s, a California researcher studying the smog over Los Angeles made the first link between air pollution and automobiles. Since that initial discovery, the federal government has set standards to bring down levels of automobile emissions.

In 1970 Congress enacted the CAA, which gave the EPA broad responsibility for regulating motor vehicle pollution. The law called for a 90 percent reduction in auto emissions. In response to these standards, the auto industry developed new emission control technologies. For example, by 1971, auto manufacturers developed charcoal canisters to trap gasoline vapors. Exhaust gas recirculation valves, which reduced nitrogen dioxide emissions, appeared in cars by 1972. And by 1975, the

FIGURE 4.21

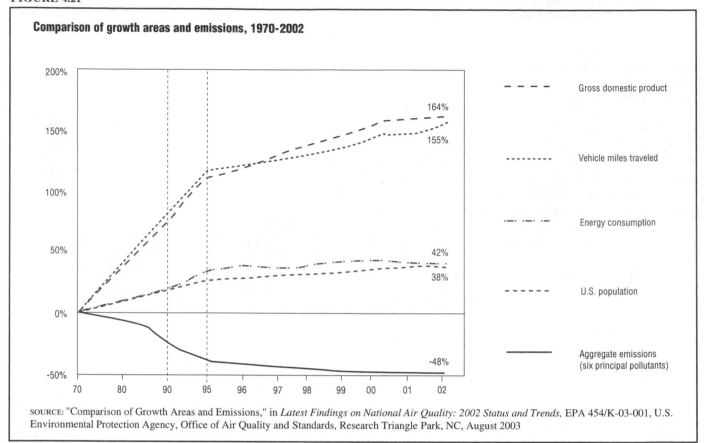

Comparison of growth areas and emissions, 1970-2002

SOURCE: "Comparison of Growth Areas and Emissions," in *Latest Findings on National Air Quality: 2002 Status and Trends,* EPA 454/K-03-001, U.S. Environmental Protection Agency, Office of Air Quality and Standards, Research Triangle Park, NC, August 2003

first generation of catalytic converters were in use. Catalytic converters cut down on emissions of VOCs (hydrocarbons) and carbon monoxide. Unleaded gasoline was introduced that same year, which reduced lead emissions.

In 1985 the EPA adopted stringent emission standards for diesel-powered trucks and buses. These standards took effect in 1991 and 1994. In 1990 the Clean Air Act Amendments required further reduction in VOC, carbon monoxide, nitrogen dioxide, and particulate emissions. The Clean Air Act Amendments also developed programs aimed at reducing pollution from cars by such approaches as more stringent emission testing procedures, new vehicle technologies, and clean fuels programs.

The CAA and the resultant response from the auto industry have had a tremendous effect on reducing automobile emissions. Figure 4.21 shows that between 1970 and 2002, total emissions of the six criteria air pollutants fell by 48 percent while vehicle miles traveled increased 155 percent. However, millions of vehicles still pollute the air. Some experts believe that additional efforts are needed to eliminate emissions further, by promoting alternative fuels for cars and alternative transportation, such as mass transit systems, carpools, and bicycles.

In addition to reducing emissions, a governmental goal is to conserve energy and reduce America's dependence on foreign oil. In 1973 the Organization of Petroleum Exporting Countries (OPEC) imposed an oil embargo that reminded America how dependent it had become on foreign sources of fuel. In 1972, the year before the embargo, the United States had consumed 31 percent of the world's oil, and depended on foreign sources—particularly the Middle East—for 28 percent of that oil. As a result of the embargo, and in an effort to make the United States less dependent on foreign oil, Congress passed the 1975 Automobile Fuel Efficiency Act, which set the initial Corporate Average Fuel Efficiency (CAFE) standards.

The CAFE standards required each domestic automaker to increase the average fuel economy of its new cars each year, until achieving 27.5 miles per gallon (mpg) by 1985. In the aftermath of the Persian Gulf War in the early 1990s, another strong reminder of U.S. dependence on foreign oil, some members of Congress wanted to raise the CAFE standards by as much as 40 percent, to 45 mpg for cars and 35 mpg for light trucks. Those in favor of raising the standards claimed that it would save about 2.8 million barrels of oil a day.

They also noted that if cars became even more fuel-efficient, emissions of carbon dioxide would be significantly reduced. Some scientists have blamed carbon dioxide for being the main "greenhouse" gas contributing to global warming. This gas (along with other greenhouse gases) traps some of the earth's outgoing energy, retaining heat in

TABLE 4.3

Characteristics of alternative transportation fuels

	Biodiesel	Compressed natural gas (CNG)	Ethanol (E85)	Liquefied natural gas (LNG)	Liquefied petroleum gas (LPG)	Methanol (M85)
Chemical structure	Methyl esters of C16-C18 fatty acids	CH_4	CH_3CH_2OH	CH_4	C_3H_8	CH_3UH
Primary components	Vegetable oil, animal fats, or recycled restaurant grease	Methane	Denatured ethanol and gasoline	Methane that is cooled cryogenically	Propane	Methanol and gasoline
Main fuel source	Soybean oil	Under-ground reserves	Corn, grains, or agricultural waste	Underground reserves	A by-product of petroleum refining or natural gas processing	Natural gas, coal, or woody biomass
Energy content per gallon	117,000 to 120,000 Btu	33,000 to 38,000 Btu @3000 psi	80,460 Btu	73,500 Btu	84,000 Btu	65,350 Btu
Energy ratio compared to gasoline	1.1 to 1 or 90%	3.94 to 1 or 25% @3000 psi	1.42 to 1 or 70%	1.55 to 1 or 66%	1.36 to 1 or 74%	1.75 to 1 or 57%
Liquid or gas	Liquid	Gas	Liquid	Liquid	Liquid	Liquid

SOURCE: "What are characteristics of alternative fuels?" in *Alternative Fuels Data Center: Frequently Asked Questions,* U.S. Department of Energy, Office of Transportation Technology, Alternative Fuels Data Center, Washington, DC [Online] http://www.afdc.nrel.gov/p_single_faq.cgi?2 [accessed November 10, 2003]

the atmosphere like the glass panels of a greenhouse. Global warming is a controversial subject, and not all scientists are convinced that recent warming trends are out of the ordinary or are due to emissions of greenhouse gases.

Opponents of raising CAFE standards believe that the congressional fuel economy campaign would saddle American motorists with car features they would not like and would not buy. They also point out that the only way to additionally raise fuel efficiency levels is to manufacture much smaller cars and trucks and to limit the number of larger vehicles. They claim smaller cars would limit consumer choice of larger and family-sized vehicles and place thousands of auto-related jobs at risk.

Thus far, legislators have not passed further legislation to increase CAFE standards. The required efficiency standards are still being met, but average fuel efficiency has not increased much beyond the original standards. In contrast, the European Commission (the executive board of the European Union, a league of European countries) has proposed an ambitious target of 47 mpg for gasoline-driven European cars (compared to the current average of 29 mpg) and 52 mpg for diesel-powered European cars by 2005.

In recent years, passenger cars have been losing market share to sport utility vehicles (SUVs). Because SUVs are classified as light trucks, they are subject to a less stringent fuel economy standard of 20.7 mpg. Additionally, SUVs and light trucks fall under less stringent emissions standards and are allowed to emit three times more

nitrogen dioxide than cars. However, in December 1999, the EPA announced tougher pollution regulations on new cars, including SUVs, minivans, and light trucks, which together currently account for half of the new vehicles sold. The regulations are aimed at slashing tailpipe releases by 90 percent by 2009 and reducing sulfur in gasoline by 90 percent. The regulations will be phased in beginning in 2004.

Alternative Fuels

The use of alternative (nonpetroleum-based) fuels is becoming an increasingly popular way to reduce vehicle emissions and overall energy use. The U.S. Department of Energy (DOE) defines alternative fuels as those that are substantially nonpetroleum, yield energy security (lower our dependence on foreign oil), and offer environmental benefits.

The DOE currently recognizes the following as alternative fuels: methanol and denatured ethanol (which are both mixed with gasoline to yield a fuel containing no less than 70 percent alcohol), compressed natural gas (CNG), liquefied natural gas (LNG), liquefied petroleum gas (LPG), hydrogen, coal-derived liquid fuels, fuels derived from biological materials (such as biodiesel), and electricity (including solar energy). The characteristics of the most common alternative fuels are shown in Table 4.3. Note that E85 is a mixture of 85 percent ethanol and 15 percent gasoline. Likewise, M85 is a similar mixture of methanol and gasoline. Table 4.4 compares the fuels in

TABLE 4.4

Alternative fuels comparison

Fuel	Ultimate availability	Source	State of technology	Infrastructure needs/cost	Other barriers
1 Conventional liquid fuels from:					Continued high carbon emissions
Petroleum	Finite	Largely foreign	Mature	None	
Natural gas	Finite	Largely foreign	Near term (2-7 years)	Moderate	Rising U.S. NG cost
Unconventional oil	Finite but large	Foreign and domestic	Near to medium term (5-10 years)	Minimal	High extraction cost
Methane hydrates	Finite but vast	Foreign and domestic	Far term (7-12 years)	Moderate technology	Unknown
2 Bio-ethanol	Renewable, land limited	Domestic	Near term (2-7 years)	Minimal	High cost
3 Bio-diesel	Renewable, land limited	Domestic	Near term (2-7 years)	Minimal	High cost
4 Methanol	Finite but large	Foreign and Domestic	Mature	Moderate	Toxicity
5 Natural gas	Finite	Largely foreign	Mature	Substantial	Storage, range, rising U.S. price
6 Grid electricity	Depends on primary fuel	Diversified	Mature	Substantial	Storage, range
7 Hydrogen	Potentially vast, depending on source	Depends on feedstock and production process	Near to long term (5-12 years)	Very high	Storage, range, safety

SOURCE: Alicia Birky et al., "Table 3, Alternative Fuels Comparison," in *Future U.S. Highway Energy Use: A Fifty Year Perspective, Draft,* U.S. Department of Energy, Office of Energy Efficiency and Renewable Energy, Office of Transportation Technologies, Washington, DC, May 3, 2001

terms of their availability, infrastructure needs, and other technological factors.

All the alternative fuels recognized by the DOE reduce ozone-forming tailpipe emissions. Additionally, some of them have been shown to produce less combined carbon monoxide and nitrogen dioxide emissions than reformulated gasoline. Reformulated gasoline is gas that is specially blended to reduce emissions and smog formation.

According to the DOE, in 2002 there were 519,000 alternative-fuel vehicles on American roads. More than half (54 percent) were fueled with LPG, 24 percent with CNG, 16 percent with E85, 4 percent with electricity, and 2 percent with other alternative fuels.

LIQUEFIED PETROLEUM GAS. LPG (or propane) has been the most successful alternative fuel to date. It is a by-product of petroleum refining or natural gas processing. In 2002 the DOE reported 4,004 LPG fuel stations around the country.

COMPRESSED NATURAL GAS. Natural gas requires less refinery work than gasoline and is already distributed around the continental United States; it also burns cleaner than gasoline. However, the public has been slow to embrace it.

CNG fueling stations have been built across the country, but they are not yet commonplace. In 2002 there were 1,055 natural gas refueling stations in the country. In some cases, local natural gas companies build the CNG stations; large companies that have their own fleets of natural gas vehicles build others. Still, it is difficult to sell CNG technology with few fueling stations, and even more difficult to establish a network of fueling stations without a mass market for the fuel.

GASOHOL. To help reduce the nation's dependence on imported oil, Congress enacted the National Defense Authorization Act in 1991. The law includes a provision directing federal agencies to purchase gasohol when it is available at prices equal to or lower than those of gasoline.

Gasohol is made from a mixture of gasoline with ethanol or methanol. Gasohol burns slower, cooler, and more completely than gasoline, resulting in reduced emissions of some pollutants. However, gasohol has negative aspects. It vaporizes more readily than gasoline, potentially aggravating ozone pollution in warm weather. Ethanol-based gasohol can damage rubber seals, diaphragms, and certain finishes. Methanol-based gasohol is toxic and corrosive, and its emissions produce cancer-causing formaldehyde.

Nevertheless, federal agencies have taken a number of steps to encourage the use of gasohol. In 1991 Executive Order 12759 required federal agencies that operate more than 300 vehicles to reduce their gas consumption by 10 percent—an incentive to use gasohol. Despite these measures, however, use of gasohol has increased only slightly, mainly because gasohol costs more than gasoline and is sometimes unavailable due to the high cost of transporting and storing it. Most support for gasohol seems to come from farm states, where the main ingredients for ethanol are grown. In 2002 there were 179 fueling stations around the country for E85 fuel.

The major American automobile manufacturers all produce flexible-fuel vehicles that can run on ethanol, gasoline, or a mixture of the two. These flex-fuel systems are available on several regular-production models.

ELECTRICITY. In the early days of the automobile, electric cars outnumbered internal-combustion vehicles. With the introduction of technology for producing low-cost gasoline, however, electric vehicles fell out of favor. But as cities became choked with air pollution, the idea of an efficient electric car once again emerged. In order to make it acceptable to the public, however, several considerations had to be addressed: How many miles could an electric car be driven before needing to be recharged? How light would the vehicle need to be? And could the car keep up with the speed and driving conditions of busy freeways and highways?

In 1993 tax breaks became available for people who buy cars that run on alternative energy sources; these breaks are especially generous for purchasers of electric cars. The breaks are intended to compensate for the price difference between electric cars and the average gas-powered car, and to jump-start production of these vehicles. As of 2003, 10 percent of all new cars offered for sale in California must be zero-emission vehicles. New York, Massachusetts, Maine, and Vermont each have similar laws.

Electric vehicles (EVs) come in three types: battery-powered; fuel cell; and hybrids, which are powered by both an electric motor and a small conventional engine. In 2002 there were 875 stations around the country servicing electric vehicles.

The EV1, a two-seater by General Motors (GM), was the first commercially available electric car. In 1999 GM introduced its second-generation EV1, the Gen II. It uses a lead-acid battery pack and has a driving range of approximately 95 miles. The Gen II is also offered with an optional nickel-metal hydride battery pack, which increases its range to 130 miles. Ford is currently producing a Ranger in an EV model. EV drivers have a charger installed at their home, allowing them to recharge the car overnight. There are also some public places where chargers are available.

Fuel-cell electric vehicles use an electrochemical process that converts a fuel's energy into usable electricity. Some experts think that, in the future, vehicles driven by fuel cells could replace vehicles with combustion engines.

Fuel cells produce very little sulfur and nitrogen dioxide, and generate less than half the carbon dioxide of internal-combustion engines. Rather than needing to be recharged, they are simply refueled. Hydrogen, natural gas, methanol, and gasoline can all be used with a fuel cell.

DaimlerChrysler's Mercedes-Benz division has produced the first prototype fuel-cell car. The NECAR4 produces zero emissions and runs on liquid hydrogen. The hydrogen must be kept cold at all times, which makes the design impractical for widespread use. However, the company plans to introduce another model, which runs on methanol and should be more practical. The NECAR4 travels 280 miles on a full 11-gallon tank. The prototype was introduced in 1999, and consumers may be able to purchase a production version in 2004.

Ecostar, an alliance between Ford, DaimlerChrysler, and Ballard Power Systems, is working on developing new fuel cells to power vehicles. Other automakers have experimented with fuel-cell prototype cars as well, but these vehicles are not yet commercially available.

Hybrid Vehicles

Hybrid vehicles have both an electric motor and a small internal-combustion engine. A sophisticated computer system automatically shifts from using the electric motor to the gas engine, as needed, for optimum driving. The electric motor is recharged while the car is driving and braking. Because the gasoline engine does only part of the work, the car gets very good fuel economy, generally two to three times that of a vehicle powered by gasoline only. The engine is also designed for ultra-low emissions. However, hybrid vehicles are not considered alternative fuel vehicles by the DOE.

In 2003 there were three hybrid vehicles on the market in the United States: the Toyota Prius, Honda Insight, and Honda Civic Hybrid. Ford has created a hybrid SUV, the Ford Escape, which will be available in 2004.

Mandating the Use of Alternative Fuel Vehicles

The Energy Policy Act of 1992, which passed in the wake of the 1991 Persian Gulf War, required that federal and state governments and fleet owners increase the percentages of vehicles powered by alternative fuels. The fleet requirements affect those who own or control at least 50 vehicles in the United States and fleets of at least 20 vehicles that are centrally fueled or capable of being centrally fueled within a metropolitan area of 250,000 or more. Many municipal governments and the U.S. Postal Service have put into operation fleets of natural gas and electric vehicles, such as garbage trucks, transit buses, and postal vans.

Airplanes

Flying carries an environmental price; it is the most energy-intensive form of transport. In much of the industrialized world, air travel is replacing more energy-efficient rail or bus travel. Despite a rise in fuel efficiency of jet engines, jet fuel consumption has risen 65 percent since 1970.

Another problem with air travel cited by some scientists is its possible impact on global warming due to aircraft emissions of nitrogen oxide. Results from a study of 10 regional areas by the EPA's Office of Mobile Sources show that in 1990, for nitrogen oxide, the aircraft component of the regional mobile source emissions ranged from 0.6 percent to 3.6 percent. Projected nitrogen oxide emissions from aircraft for 2010 range from 1.9 percent to 10.4 percent of the regional mobile source emissions (*Evaluation of Air Pollutant Emissions from Subsonic Commercial Jet Aircraft,* 1999). The Intergovernmental Panel on Climate Change (IPCC) notes that greenhouse gas emissions deposited in the upper atmosphere do greater harm than those released at the earth's surface.

There is also a movement toward action on other engines in the airline industry—those in trucks, cars, and carts that service airplane fleets. The Electric Power Research Institute launched a research study in 1993 to show that the use of electric vehicles can significantly reduce total airport emissions. In mid-1998, at the completion of the study, researchers concluded that the use of electric vehicles and equipment at airports was an economically and environmentally viable method for reducing current airport emissions or for offsetting future emissions. Many large airports, such as Los Angeles International, San Francisco International, and Dallas/Fort Worth, have already replaced or currently are replacing high-pollution ground vehicles with zero-emission (electric) vehicles.

Boats and Air Pollution

Boat engines have not changed much since the 1930s. Running an outboard motor for an hour is estimated to pollute as much as driving 800 miles. In 1996 the EPA adopted standards to slash emissions from boats and other water vehicles, such as jet skis, which, according to the EPA, can sometimes account for up to 15 percent of total smog. The new standards set a goal of a 75 percent emissions reduction by 2006. Under the new regulations, engine prices have risen approximately 14 percent, but these new engines will make up some of this extra expense by using less gas.

In 1998 air-quality regulators in California proposed state rules tougher than federal standards to limit emissions from personal watercraft and motorboats. The rules went into effect in 2001 and will be completely phased in by 2008. California is the nation's second largest boating state after Michigan.

THE CLEAN AIR ACT—A HUGE SUCCESS

In 1970 the United States Congress passed the landmark Clean Air Act (CAA), proclaiming that it would restore urban air quality. It was no coincidence that the law was passed during a 14-day Washington, D.C., smog alert. Although the CAA has had mixed results and many goals still have not been met, most experts credit it with making great strides toward cleaning up the air (*Air Pollution: Status of Implementation and Issues of the Clean Air Act Amendments of 1990,* United States General Accounting Office, 2000).

Since its adoption, concentrations of all six priority pollutants have dropped by 48 percent. (See Figure 4.21.) Air quality around the country is improving. Los Angeles, for example, while still far from attaining air quality standards, has cleaner air than at any time since measurements were first taken in the 1940s.

The Clean Air Act Amendments of 1990

The overall goal of the Clean Air Act Amendments of 1990 is to reduce the pollutants in the air by 56 billion pounds a year when the law is fully in effect by the year 2005. Other aims are to cut acid precipitation in half by the year 2000, reduce smog and other pollutants, and protect the ozone layer by phasing out chlorofluorocarbons (CFCs) and related chemicals.

The Economic Value of the Clean Air Act and Its Amendments

In *The Benefits and Costs of the Clean Air Act, 1970 to 1990* (1997), the first report mandated by the CAA on the monetary costs and benefits of controlling pollution, the EPA concludes that the economic value of clean air programs was 42 times greater than the total costs of air pollution control over the 1970 to 1990 period. The study found numerous positive consequences in the U.S. economy because of CAA programs and regulations. The CAA affected industrial production, investment, productivity, consumption, employment, and economic growth. In fact, the study estimated total agricultural benefits from the CAA at almost 10 billion dollars. The EPA compared benefits to direct costs or expenditures. The total costs of the CAA were $523 billion for the 20-year period; total benefits equaled $22.2 trillion—a net benefit of approximately $21.7 trillion.

The National Conference of State Legislatures, in its *Two Decades of Clean Air: EPA Assesses Costs and Benefits* (1998), used data from the EPA analysis and found that the Act produced major reductions in pollution that caused illness and disease, smog, acid rain, haze, and damage to the environment.

The second mandated review of the CAA, *The Benefits and Costs of the Clean Air Act Amendments of 1990* (2000), the most comprehensive and thorough review of the CAA's amendments ever conducted, found similar results. Using a sophisticated array of computer models and the latest cost data, the EPA found that by 2010 the

Act will have prevented 23,000 Americans from dying prematurely and averted more than 1.7 million asthma attacks. The CAA will prevent 67,000 episodes of acute bronchitis, 91,000 occurrences of shortness of breath, 4.1 million lost work days, and 31 million days in which Americans would have had to restrict activity because of illness. Another 22,000 respiratory-related hospital admissions will be averted, as well as 42,000 admissions for heart disease and 4,800 emergency room visits.

The EPA estimated that the benefits of CAA amendment programs totaled about $110 billion in reduction of illness and premature death. The study found that the costs of achieving these benefits were only about $27 billion, a fraction of the value of the benefits. In addition, the study reported that there were other benefits that scientists and economists cannot quantify and express in dollar terms, such as controlling cancer-causing air toxics and benefiting crops and ecosystems by reducing pollutants.

The Continuing Problem of Ozone and Particulates

The CAA requires the EPA to review public health standards at least every five years to ensure that they reflect the best current science. In 1997, in response to what many consider compelling scientific evidence of the harm caused by ozone and fine particles to human health, the EPA issued new, stricter air quality standards for ozone and particulate matter.

This was the first revision in ozone standards in 20 years and the first-ever standard for fine particulates. The provisions tightened the standard for ground-level ozone from the level of 0.12 parts per million (ppm) at the highest daily measurement to 0.08 ppm average over an 8-hour period. The new particulate matter standard included particles larger than 2.5 microns in diameter instead of the original standard of those larger than 10 microns.

In May 1999 a three-judge federal appeals panel overturned the new standards. The EPA appealed, but in October 1999 the full U.S. Court of Appeals for the District of Columbia refused to overturn the decision. Finally, in February 2001, the Supreme Court returned a unanimous decision reaffirming the federal government's authority to set clean air standards. The court ordered the EPA to adopt a more reasonable interpretation for enforcing ozone standards in some areas, but they agreed that the agency has the right to enforce the stringent regulations set in 1997.

Despite improvements in ozone levels, few large urban areas in the United States comply with ozone standards. These are known as nonattainment areas for ozone. Likewise, areas that cannot meet the $PM_{2.5}$ standard will be considered nonattainment areas for $PM_{2.5}$.

Under the new standards, many smaller population centers may also become nonattainment areas for either ozone or $PM_{2.5}$. The EPA expects to publish the lists of nonattainment areas for ozone by April 30, 2004, and for $PM_{2.5}$ by December 15, 2004. These designations will be based on data collected between 2001 and 2003. Experts within the environmental industry are predicting that many states, particularly those in the eastern part of the country, will have a significant increase in their number of nonattainment areas.

The CAA requires state and local governments to take particular actions regarding nonattainment areas within their boundaries. The states with new nonattainment areas under the new ozone and $PM_{2.5}$ standards will have three years to submit plans known as state implementation plans (SIPs) that detail the steps that will be taken to meet the standards. These steps will likely include a variety of control measures on new and existing sources of air pollution.

THE COST OF CUTTING EMISSIONS FURTHER

In the United States, an increasing problem in the effort to reduce air pollution further is that most of the cheap fixes have already been made. Many economists argue that the expensive ones may not be worth the price. The very premise that air pollution can be reduced to levels at which it no longer poses any health risk is now being questioned by some academics as well as by industry analysts.

Virtually all gains in the war on ozone have been achieved by reducing auto emissions. The costs for future air quality improvements may exceed, from some points of view, the value of any improvement, and the disparity may only get worse over time. For example, by 1994 the tailpipe pollution standard had reduced the exhaust of volatile organic compounds (VOCs) by 98 percent. Reducing the figure by a total of 99.5 percent will at least double the cost.

Some cheap fixes are still available, however. The steps by the EPA in 1999 to toughen pollution regulations on new cars, including SUVs, minivans, and light trucks, will help improve air quality when the regulations take effect in 2004. Other possible improvements could come from changes in grandfather clauses—loopholes that exempt companies from compliance with laws because the companies existed prior to the law. Power plants rank first in grandfathered emissions. Other top industries affected by grandfather clauses include aluminum smelters and oil refineries.

REDUCING MANY POLLUTANTS BUT MISSING SOME

The equilibrium of CO_2 in the atmosphere has been altered since the Industrial Revolution, which began in the United States in the early 1800s. Since that time, atmospheric concentrations of carbon dioxide have risen about 28 percent, principally because of fossil fuel combustion (the burning of fuels such as gasoline and coal). Carbon dioxide emissions are long-lasting, with an atmospheric lifetime ranging from 50 to 200 years. (See Figure 4.22.)

FIGURE 4.22

Sources and lifetime of selected substances affecting climate

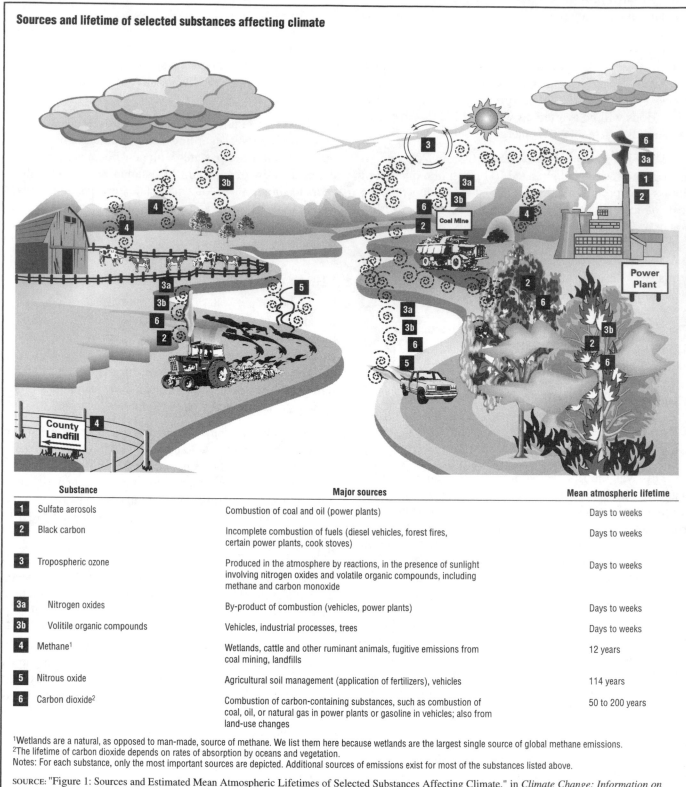

	Substance	Major sources	Mean atmospheric lifetime
1	Sulfate aerosols	Combustion of coal and oil (power plants)	Days to weeks
2	Black carbon	Incomplete combustion of fuels (diesel vehicles, forest fires, certain power plants, cook stoves)	Days to weeks
3	Tropospheric ozone	Produced in the atmosphere by reactions, in the presence of sunlight involving nitrogen oxides and volatile organic compounds, including methane and carbon monoxide	Days to weeks
3a	Nitrogen oxides	By-product of combustion (vehicles, power plants)	Days to weeks
3b	Volitile organic compounds	Vehicles, industrial processes, trees	Days to weeks
4	Methane[1]	Wetlands, cattle and other ruminant animals, fugitive emissions from coal mining, landfills	12 years
5	Nitrous oxide	Agricultural soil management (application of fertilizers), vehicles	114 years
6	Carbon dioxide[2]	Combustion of carbon-containing substances, such as combustion of coal, oil, or natural gas in power plants or gasoline in vehicles; also from land-use changes	50 to 200 years

[1]Wetlands are a natural, as opposed to man-made, source of methane. We list them here because wetlands are the largest single source of global methane emissions.
[2]The lifetime of carbon dioxide depends on rates of absorption by oceans and vegetation.
Notes: For each substance, only the most important sources are depicted. Additional sources of emissions exist for most of the substances listed above.

SOURCE: "Figure 1: Sources and Estimated Mean Atmospheric Lifetimes of Selected Substances Affecting Climate," in *Climate Change: Information on Three Air Pollutants' Climate Effects and Emissions Trends*, GAO-03-25, U.S. General Accounting Office, Washington, DC, April 28, 2003

Carbon dioxide emissions from fossil fuel combustion have gone up even within the last decade. From 1990 to 1999, emissions of CO_2 from fossil fuel combustion increased at an average annual rate of 1.4 percent. Of the total carbon dioxide emissions in 1999, fossil fuel combustion accounted for 98 percent (*Inventory of U.S.*

Greenhouse Gas Emissions and Sinks: 1990–1999, Office of Atmospheric Programs, EPA, 2001).

Although a car built today produces only one-tenth the pollution per mile traveled as one built two decades ago, fuel efficiency standards have not been tightened in years, Americans are buying less-efficient vehicles, and total miles traveled increase each year. This is just the opposite of what was promised at the 1992 United Nations Conference on the Environment in Rio de Janeiro (also known as the Rio Earth Summit). The U.S. goal of reducing carbon dioxide emissions to 1990 levels by 2000, as agreed at the Conference, was not reached. Other industrialized nations also fell short of this voluntary treaty goal.

The 1997 Kyoto Global Warming Treaty

In December 1997 the United Nations convened a 160-nation conference on global warming in Kyoto, Japan, in the hopes of producing a new treaty on climate change that would place binding caps on industrial emissions. Participants hoped to ratify the treaty and have it enacted in 2002, the 10th anniversary of the Rio Earth Summit. In 2003, ratification of the treaty was tenuous.

The treaty, called the Kyoto Protocol to the United Nations Framework Convention on Climate Change (or simply the Kyoto Protocol), binds industrialized nations to reducing their emissions of six greenhouse gases below 1990 levels by 2012, with each country having a different target. The six greenhouse gases are: carbon dioxide, methane, nitrogen oxide, hydrofluorocarbons, sulfur dioxides, and perfluorocarbons. Under the terms of initial drafts of the treaty, the United States must cut emissions by 7 percent, most European nations by 8 percent, and Japan by 6 percent. Reductions must begin by 2008 and be achieved by 2012. Developing nations are not required to make such pledges.

The United States had proposed a program of voluntary pledges by developing nations, but that proposal was rejected, as was a tough system of enforcement. Instead, each country decides for itself how to achieve its goal. The treaty provides market-driven tools, such as buying and selling credits, for reducing emissions. It also sets up a Clean Development Fund to help provide poorer nations with technology to reduce their emissions.

Although it is the first time nations have made such sweeping pledges, many sources expect difficulty in getting ratification. In the United States, President Bill Clinton signed the Protocol, but the Senate did not ratify it. Business leaders believe the treaty goes too far, while environmentalists believe standards do not go far enough. Some experts doubt that any action emerging from Kyoto will be sufficient to prevent the doubling of greenhouse gases. Representatives of the oil industry and business community contend the treaty will spell economic hardship for the United States. The fossil-fuel industry and conservative politicians portray the Protocol as unworkable and too costly to the American economy.

By 2001 the Kyoto Protocol was near collapse. However, diplomats from 178 nations met in Bonn, Germany, in July 2001 and drafted a compromise to preserve the global-warming treaty. U.S. President George W. Bush stood firm on rejecting the Kyoto Protocol and characterized it as "fatally flawed," stating that implementing it would harm the economy and unfairly require only the industrial nations to cut emissions. Australia also refused to support the Protocol.

To take effect, the treaty must be ratified by 55 of the countries that were responsible for 55 percent of industrialized nations' carbon dioxide emissions in 1990. The European Union, Japan, and Canada all ratified the Protocol during 2002. Russia was expected to ratify it during 2003, which would have put the Protocol into effect. However, in September 2003, Russian President Vladimir Putin announced that his government needed additional time to study the ramifications of the Protocol and would not be ratifying it within the near future.

Although President Bush has rejected the Kyoto Protocol, he has promised to address the issues of greenhouse gas emissions and global warming. Thus far, he has proposed studying the problem and funding new technologies to reduce carbon dioxide emissions.

Fossil Fuel Use in the Developing World

Environmental pollution is worldwide and environmental problems are expected to become increasingly regional and global in the future. Evidence mounts that human activities—especially the production of gases from the combustion of coal, oil, and natural gas—may be causing atmospheric warming worldwide. Developing countries stand on the brink of economic growth, but that explosion of growth will undoubtedly be fueled by fossil fuels, as was the case in America and Europe earlier. The filthiest smoke and water generally arise in the early stages of industrialization.

China, especially, faces a dilemma—coal harms the environment but it just as surely fuels economic growth. China's heavy reliance on coal, along with its inefficient and wasteful patterns of energy use, will make it the largest single producer of carbon dioxide by 2020, surpassing even the United States. Between 1970 and 1990, energy consumption in China rose 208 percent, compared with an average rise of 28 percent in developed countries during the same period. More than 5 million Chinese participate in coal extraction, feeding China's enormous and growing appetite for energy.

Five of China's largest cities are among the world's ten most polluted cities. Polluted air reportedly kills 178,000 Chinese people prematurely each year, primarily from emphysema and bronchitis.

China's situation is repeated, on a lesser scale, in India, Brazil, and the rest of the developing world, where meeting environmental goals is considered a rich country's luxury. Chinese officials believe, as do officials in many other developing nations, that developed countries cause 80 percent of the world's pollution. Chinese leadership believes the developed nations should be held responsible for the problems and, as a result, should help pay for cleaner coal-burning technologies in the third world, as well as financing hydroelectric plants, nuclear power stations, and alternative energy sources.

In India, the population has adjusted to living in a haze of dust and fumes. In December 2000 the World Health Organization reported that the level of microscopic particles in the air was nearly seven times the amount the organization deems healthy. On the streets, pedestrians cover their faces as protection against airborne pollutants. In 1994 the Indian Supreme Court ruled that cars sold in the largest cities must run on unleaded fuel and have catalytic converters. But unleaded fuel is expensive and hard to find—less than 1 percent of the fuel sold in New Delhi, India's capital, is unleaded. Inefficient two-wheeled scooters spew out pollution and, with 400 new scooters added every day in New Delhi alone, the air quality continues to deteriorate.

INDOOR AIR QUALITY

Although most people think of the outdoor air when they think of air pollution, studies have shown that indoor environments are not necessarily safe havens from air pollution. In fact, certain pollutants are often found in greater concentrations indoors than out. This fact is especially important since 90 percent of people's time is spent in indoor environments, including residences, workplaces, public transportation, and public and commercial establishments. Particularly vulnerable groups, such as infants, the elderly, and the ill, may be inside virtually all the time.

Modern indoor environments contain a variety of sources for pollution, including synthetic building materials, consumer products, and dust mites (microscopic insects that live on house dust and human skin residue). People, pets, and indoor plants also contribute to airborne pollution. Efforts to lower energy costs by tightly sealing and insulating buildings have increased the likelihood that pollutants will accumulate.

Reports of illness and allergy among building occupants have become commonplace. Scientific evidence suggests that respiratory diseases, allergies, mucous membrane irritation, nervous system defects, cardiovascular symptoms, reproductive problems, and lung cancer may be linked to exposure to indoor air pollution. Scientists consistently rank indoor air pollution among the top environmental health risks, although public opinion polls report that most Americans do not perceive the risks of indoor pollution to be great.

Providing healthful air quality is not only a complex scientific and technical issue, but also a complicated issue of public policy, in determining the proper role of the government in safeguarding people's health. For example, the EPA estimates that exposure of nonsmokers to cigarette smoke may cause as many as 3,000 lung-cancer deaths annually in the United States. It also contributes to a wide range of diseases, including asthma, pneumonia, and bronchitis, and incurs enormous expense in work-time loss and medical and insurance expenses.

The first legislation to deal specifically with indoor air quality was Title IV of the Superfund Amendments and Reauthorization Act of 1986, which called for the EPA to establish an advisory committee to conduct research and disseminate information. In October 1991 the General Accounting Office (GAO) reported on the progress of the legislation in *Indoor Air Pollution: Federal Efforts Are Not Effectively Addressing a Growing Problem.* The GAO concluded that not only was the EPA's emphasis on indoor pollution not commensurate with the health risks posed by the problem, but also that research had been, and would likely continue to be, constrained by lack of funding. Accordingly, the proposed Indoor Air Quality Act of 1991 was not enacted by Congress.

In 1999 the GAO once again reviewed the status of indoor air quality in its *Indoor Pollution: Status of Federal Research Activities,* its latest publication on this topic. It found that significant strides have been made in understanding the risks posed by chemicals and other contaminants commonly found in homes, offices, and schools. Nonetheless, it concluded that "many gaps and uncertainties remain in the assessment of exposures to known indoor pollutants." These gaps include specific sources of exposures; the magnitude of exposures; the relative role of specific exposures such as inhalation, ingestion, and skin contact; the nature, duration, and frequency of human activities that contribute to exposures; and the geographic distribution of exposures to certain pollutants for the U.S. population as a whole.

CHAPTER 5
POLLUTION OF SURFACE WATERS

Surface water pollution is the presence of unwanted chemicals, biological agents, or other contaminants in oceans, rivers, lakes, streams, ponds, estuaries, and wetlands. Estuaries are located at the intersection of fresh and saline waters, for example, at the mouths of rivers feeding into the ocean. Wetlands are low-lying areas, such as swamps, that retain some water at least part of the year.

The amount of water on Earth remains constant. It moves around and changes forms as part of the hydrologic cycle. (See Figure 5.1.) Rain, snow, and dew droplets fall on the earth. Some of this precipitation seeps into the soil where it is taken up by the roots of vegetation. Some precipitation runs off saturated land into rivers, streams, lakes, and oceans. Some precipitation seeps deep underground into spaces and voids in subsurface rock formations.

On the surface, plants return moisture to the atmosphere from their leaves in a process called transpiration. Some water also returns to the atmosphere via evaporation from the land and surface water. This natural process repeats itself over and over. Precipitation can wash contaminants out of the atmosphere and across land surfaces into surface water bodies. Human activities also result in direct discharges or leaks of contaminants into surface waters.

Surface waters are considered polluted when they become unsuitable for their intended purposes. Different purposes have different requirements for water purity. For example, water intended for drinking water has much more stringent requirements for purity than does water intended for industrial use. The primary surface water uses include drinking water supply, supporting aquatic life and vegetation, agricultural and industrial uses, and recreation and tourism. These intended uses can be spoiled by a variety of water pollutants.

Water pollutants fall into eight general categories:

1) Wastes that deplete dissolved oxygen in the water,

2) Infectious agents, such as bacteria and viruses,

3) Nutrients, such as fertilizers,

4) Organic chemicals, such as pesticides,

5) Inorganic chemicals, such as metals and acids,

6) Sediment, soil, and dust,

7) Radioactive substances, and

8) Heat from industrial sources, such as heated water discharged from power plants during electricity generation.

Table 5.1 lists many of the various sources of these water pollutants.

Surface waters cover nearly three-fourths of the planet. They are an enormous and vital resource. Good water quality is essential for the health of humans, animals, and plant life. It is also crucial to activities in industry, farming, fishing, and transportation, and provides opportunities for recreation. Since water plays critical roles in the lives of all Americans, it is an extremely serious situation when the nation's waterways become polluted.

GROWTH AND WATER POLLUTION

Throughout much of history, wastes were discharged directly into rivers, streams, and oceans without any treatment at all. As America grew and cities increased in size, water pollution became increasingly worse. In the 1800s and early 1900s, factories poured chemicals directly into rivers. People threw garbage onto the streets or piled it in open dumps. Pollution from that waste contaminated surface waters and seeped into the groundwater. Many cities poured raw sewage directly into rivers. Cities along the coast dumped their garbage and raw sewage into the ocean. People believed that water bodies would dilute the waste materials and render them harmless.

FIGURE 5.1

The water cycle

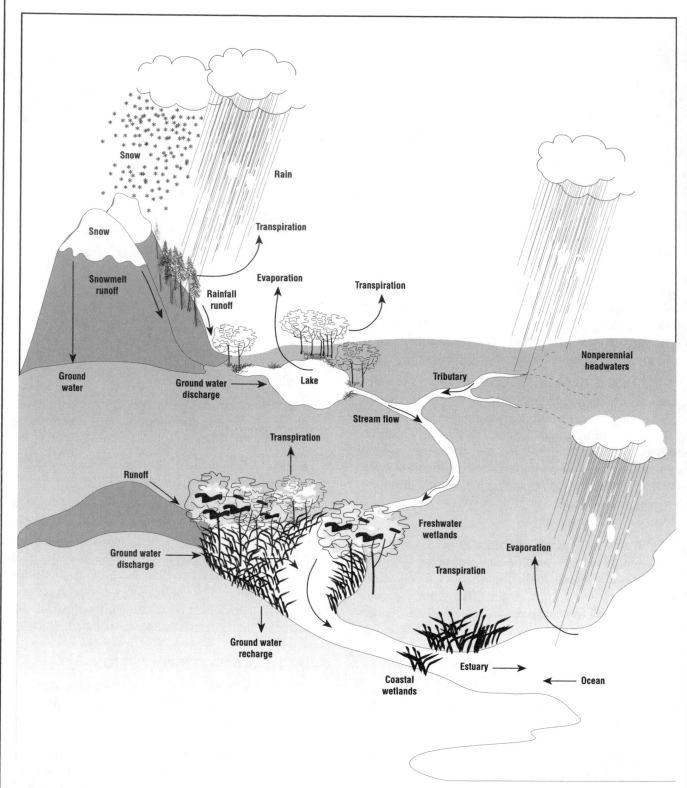

SOURCE: "The Water Cycle," in *National Water Quality Inventory: 1998 Report to Congress,* U.S. Environmental Protection Agency, Washington, DC, 2000

TABLE 5.1

Pollution sources

Category	Examples
Industrial	Pulp and paper mills, chemical manufacturers, steel plants, metal process and product manufacturers, textile manufacturers, food processing plants
Municipal	Publicly owned sewage treatment plants that may receive indirect discharges from industrial facilities or businesses
Combined sewer overflows	Single facilities that treat both storm water and sanitary sewage, which may become overloaded during storm events and discharge untreated wastes into surface waters
Storm sewers/urban runoff	Runoff from impervious surfaces including streets, parking lots, buildings, and other paved areas
Agricultural	Crop production, pastures, rangeland, feedlots, animal operations
Silvicultural	Forest management, tree harvesting, logging road construction
Construction	Land development, road construction
Resource extraction	Mining, petroleum drilling, runoff from mine tailing sites
Land disposal	Leachate or discharge from septic tanks, landfills, and hazardous waste sites
Hydrologic modification	Channelization, dredging, dam construction, flow regulation
Habitat modification	Removal of riparian vegetation, streambank modification, drainage/filling of wetlands

SOURCE: "Table 1-1. Pollution Source Categories Used in This Report," in *National Water Quality Inventory: 1998 Report to Congress*, U.S. Environmental Protection Agency, Washington, DC, 2000

TABLE 5.2

Effects of pH on aquatic life

pH range	General biological effects
6.5 to 6.0	Some adverse effects for highly acid-sensitive species
6.0 to 5.5	Loss of sensitive minnows and forage fish; decreased reproductive success for trout and walleye
5.5 to 5.0	Loss of many common sports fish and additional nongame species
5.0 to 4.5	Loss of most sports fish; very few fishes able to survive and reproduce where pH levels commonly below 4.5

SOURCE: "Effects of pH on aquatic life," in *National Water Quality Inventory: 1996 Report to Congress*, U.S. Environmental Protection Agency, Washington, DC, 1998

Gradually people began to figure out that there was a link between raw sewage and disease. That's when domestic wastewaters (sewage) came under government control. It took a little longer for industrial wastewaters to receive the same regulatory attention. Prior to the 1940s the U.S. government didn't pay much attention to water quality. It was more concerned with developing dams, reservoirs, and canals. In 1948 Congress passed the Federal Water Pollution Control Act. This Act was concerned with protecting public health from bacteria in water bodies.

The Act designated funds to state and local governments for water pollution control and emphasized the role of state governments in controlling and protecting water resources. There were few federal goals, limits, or guidelines. It authorized the surgeon general to work with federal, state, and local agencies to develop programs to eliminate or reduce pollution of interstate waters and to improve the sanitary condition of surface waters and groundwater. The Act also authorized the Federal Works Administrator to help state and local agencies construct treatment plants for sewage and other wastewaters.

Congress passed four more laws between 1956 and 1966 to strengthen the federal government's role in water pollution control, including the Water Pollution Control Act Amendments of 1956 and the Federal Water Pollution Control Act Amendments of 1961. These measures provided additional funding to local governments for the con-

struction of wastewater treatment plants. In 1965 the Water Quality Act was passed. It required the states to develop water quality standards for interstate waters by 1967. The Act also called upon the states to develop waste load allocations. A waste load allocation, or WLA, is the amount of a pollutant that a facility could discharge without exceeding the water quality standard.

The Clean Water Act

Despite all of these measures, only about half of the states had developed water quality standards by the end of the 1960s. At the federal level there were no criminal or civil penalties in place to enforce the regulations. Two major events happened in 1969 to change all this. In January 1969 an offshore oil-drilling rig located six miles off the California coast tapped an oil reserve thousands of feet beneath the ocean floor. A blowout occurred, and over the next several weeks more than 200,000 gallons of crude oil bubbled up to the surface and washed up on California beaches. Thousands of birds and sea creatures were killed.

On June 22, 1969, an oil slick on the Cuyahoga River near downtown Cleveland, Ohio, burst into flames. Witnesses claim that the flames were 5 stories high. Actually the river had caught fire several times before, because there was so much oil and debris floating in it. Luckily no one was hurt in the 1969 blaze, and it was extinguished quickly. It did result in $50,000 worth of damage to some overhanging railroad trestles. Officials concluded that sparks from a passing train had ignited the oil slick.

Both events made national headlines, and the public demanded action on water quality protection. In 1970 the U.S. Environmental Protection Agency (EPA) was formed to oversee pollution control efforts at the federal level and to enforce compliance with them. In 1972 Congress amended the Federal Water Pollution Control Act once again to create what is commonly known as the Clean Water Act (CWA).

The CWA set some very lofty goals, as follows:

1) "It is the national goal that the discharge of pollutants into navigable waters be eliminated by 1985;"

FIGURE 5.2

The Potential Hydrogen (pH) scale

Mean pH of Adirondack Lakes–1975

"Pure" rain (5.6)

Mean pH of Adirondack Lakes–1930s

Lemon juice

Vinegar

Distilled water

Baking soda

| 0 | 1 | 2 | 3 | 4 | 5 | 6 | 7 | 8 | 9 | 10 | 11 | 12 | 13 | 14 |

Acidic   Neutral   Basic

The pH Scale

The pH ("potential hydrogen") scale is a measure of hydrogen ion concentration. Hydrogen ions have a positive electrical charge and are called cations; ions with a negative electrical charge are known as anions. A substance containing equal concentrations of cations and anions so that the electrical charges balance is neutral and has a pH of 7. However, a substance with more hydrogen ions than anions is acidic and has a pH less than 7; substances with more anions than cations are alkaline and have pH measures above 7. Thus, as the concentration of hydrogen ions increases, the pH decreases. But the pH scale says nothing about whether the cations or anions are from natural or manmade sources; a hydrogen ion from an industrial smokestack measures the same on the scale as a hydrogen ion from natural minerals.

| PH 4 | PH 5 | PH 6 | PH 7 |

= Acid Content

Remember

The lower the pH value, the higher the acid content. Each full pH unit drop represents a tenfold increase in acidity.

SOURCE: "The Potential Hydrogen (pH) Scale," in *Acid Rain*, U.S. Environmental Protection Agency, 1980

FIGURE 5.3

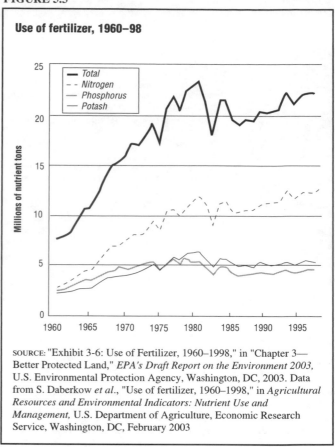

Use of fertilizer, 1960–98

SOURCE: "Exhibit 3-6: Use of Fertilizer, 1960–1998," in "Chapter 3—Better Protected Land," *EPA's Draft Report on the Environment 2003*, U.S. Environmental Protection Agency, Washington, DC, 2003. Data from S. Daberkow *et al.*, "Use of fertilizer, 1960–1998," in *Agricultural Resources and Environmental Indicators: Nutrient Use and Management*, U.S. Department of Agriculture, Economic Research Service, Washington, DC, February 2003

2) "It is the national goal that wherever attainable an interim goal of water quality which provides for the protection and propagation of fish, shellfish, and wildlife and provides for recreation in and on the water be achieved by July 1, 1983"; and

3) "It is the national policy that the discharge of toxic pollutants in toxic amounts be prohibited."

The stated overall goal of the CWA was to "restore and maintain the chemical, physical, and biological integrity of the nation's waters" and to make all waters at least safe enough for swimming and fishing.

The 1972 Act called for eliminating all pollutant discharges into navigable waters. Virtually every city in the country was required to build a wastewater treatment plant with the help of the EPA. Every state had to adopt water quality standards and come up with plans for limiting discharges of municipal and industrial wastewaters. Section 307(a)(1) of the Act required the development of a list of toxic pollutants called the Priority Pollutants. These are pollutants commonly found in wastewaters. As of late 2003 there were 126 Priority Pollutants, including asbestos, arsenic, heavy metals, organics, pesticides, and polychlorinated biphenyls (PCBs).

Toxic pollutants are defined by the CWA as those that "cause death, disease, behavioral abnormalities, cancer, genetic mutations, physiological malfunctions (including malfunctions in reproduction) or physical deformities."

The toxic pollutants are divided into two broad categories: metals and organics. The metals, including lead, mercury, chromium, and cadmium, cannot be destroyed or broken down through treatment or environmental degradation and can cause various human health problems as well as contamination of seafood and land-grown crops. The organics, including solvents, pesticides, dioxins, and PCBs can cause cancer and other serious health problems, including damage to major organs.

THE CONSEQUENCES OF WATER POLLUTION

Water pollution can have dire consequences for vegetation, animal life, and human health. Some waterways become contaminated to the point of ecological death. In other words, they are unable to sustain vegetative or aquatic life. Water pollution also poses a serious threat to the health and well-being of humans.

Acidic Surface Waters

Acid pollutes waterways, because excessive amounts lower the pH of the water. Acidity is measured using the pH

FIGURE 5.4

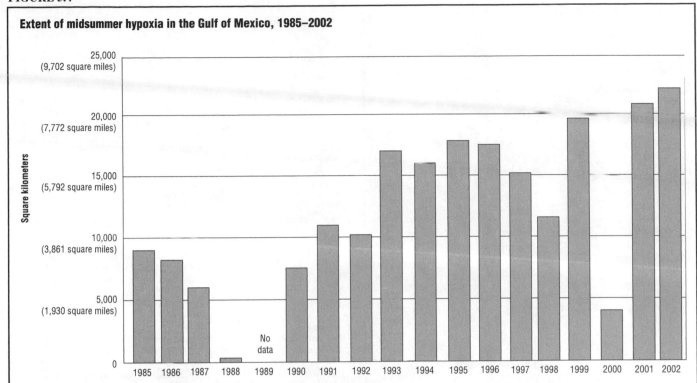

Extent of midsummer hypoxia in the Gulf of Mexico, 1985–2002

Note: Hypoxia in the Gulf is defined as less than 2.0 parts per million (ppm). Hypoxia is oxygen deficiency.
Annual midsummer cruises have been conducted systematically over the past 15 years (with the exception of 1989). Hypoxia in bottom waters covered an average of 8,000–9,000 km² in 1985–92 but increased to 16,000–20,000 km² in 1993–99.

SOURCE: "Exhibit 2-3: Areal Extent of Midsummer Hypoxia in the Gulf of Mexico, 1985–2002," in "Chapter 2—Purer Water," *EPA's Draft Report on the Environment 2003,* U.S. Environmental Protection Agency, Washington, DC, 2003.

scale. (See Figure 5.2.) Pure water has a neutral pH value of 7. Acidic waters can have pH values that are much lower. This can have some very negative consequences on aquatic organisms, particularly fish. Table 5.2 lists the general biological effects of pH values less than 6.5. Even small pH decreases in a body of water can affect physiological processes, making it more difficult for fish to reproduce. Large decreases can kill aquatic life. Most aquatic organisms cannot live outside the pH range of 5 to 9.

Surface waters with low pH are usually caused by two major sources introducing acids to the environment: acid precipitation and acid mine drainage.

ACID PRECIPITATION. Acid precipitation (rain, snow, or fog) is produced when industrial emissions containing sulfur dioxide, nitrogen oxides, and hydrocarbons mix with the water in the air to form a mild acid. These emissions are produced by many factories and by power plants burning coal. Acid precipitation may fall close to the factories or power plants, or it may be carried many hundreds of miles away by winds high in the atmosphere. If there is no water in the air, the acid may fall to the earth as particles. This is called dry deposition.

Acid precipitation falls everywhere—on cities, on forests, and into bodies of water. When it falls in cities, it can damage stone statues and buildings as well as vegeta-

tion. When it is in smog, it can harm people's lungs. When it falls in forests, it can kill trees and other vegetation. When it falls into bodies of water, it acidifies the water. That, in turn, harms aquatic plants and animals.

In 1980 the National Acid Precipitation Assessment Program (NAPAP) was created by the United States Congress to assess the damage caused by acid precipitation. The NAPAP released its findings in April 1999 in the study, *National Acid Precipitation Assessment Program Biennial Report to Congress: An Integrated Assessment.* The report noted that the country had made important strides in reducing air pollution. However, it warned that acid precipitation remains a serious problem, particularly in sensitive areas. Among the findings were:

- New York's Adirondack Mountain waterways suffer from serious levels of acid. Even though sulfur levels are declining, nitrogen levels are still climbing. The agency predicted that by 2040, about half the region's 2,800 lakes and ponds would be too acidic to sustain life.

- The Chesapeake Bay is suffering from excess nitrogen, which is causing algal blooms (sharp increases in the growth of algae) that can suffocate other life forms.

- High elevation forests in Colorado, West Virginia, Tennessee, and Southern California are nearly saturated

FIGURE 5.5

Bioaccumulation of pollutants in the food chain

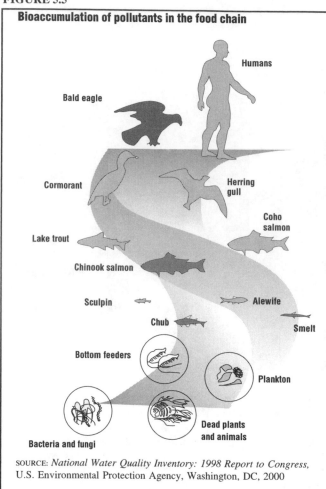

SOURCE: *National Water Quality Inventory: 1998 Report to Congress,* U.S. Environmental Protection Agency, Washington, DC, 2000

TABLE 5.3

Pathogens and swimming-related illnesses

Pathogenic Agent	Disease
Bacteria	
E. coli	Gastroenteritis
Salmonella typhi	Typhoid fever
Other salmonella species	Various enteric fevers (often called paratyphoid), gastroenteritis, septicemia (generalized infections in which organisms multiply in the bloodstream)
Shigella dysenteriae	Bacterial dysentery and other species
Vibrio cholera	Cholera
Viruses	
Rotavirus	Gastroenteritis
Norwalkvirus	Gastroenteritis
Poliovirus	Poliomyelitis
Coxsackievirus (some strains)	Various, including severe respiratory diseases, fevers, rashes, paralysis, aseptic meningitis, myocarditis
Echovirus	Various, similar to coxsackievirus (evidence is not definitive except in experimental animals)
Adenovirus	Respiratory and gastrointestinal infections
Hepatitis	Infectious hepatitis (liver malfunction), also may affect kidneys and spleen
Protozoa	
Cryptosporidium	Gastroenteritis
Giardia lamblia	Diarrhea (intestinal parasite)
Entamoeba histolytica	Amoebic dysentery, infections of other organs
Isospora belli and *Isospora hominus*	Intestinal parasites, gastrointestinal infection
Balantidium coli	Dysentery, intestinal ulcers

SOURCE: Mark Dorfman, "Table 4: Pathogens and Swimming-Related Illnesses," in *Testing the Waters XI: A Guide to Beach Water Quality at Vacation Beaches,* Natural Resources Defense Council, New York, NY, August 2001

with nitrogen, a key ingredient in acid precipitation. (Nitrogen saturation is a condition in which the nitrogen levels in the soil exceed the plant needs with the result that excess nitrogen is flushed into streams where it can cause undesirable plant growth. As the nitrogen moves through the soil, it strips away chemicals essential for forest fertility, increasing lake and stream acidity.)

• High elevation lakes and streams in the Sierra Nevada, the Cascades, and the Rocky Mountains may be on the verge of "chronically high acidity."

The report concluded that acid deposition is a complex and difficult problem to correct. The agency noted that further reductions in sulfur and nitrogen emissions will be needed. The agency also found, however, that the 1990 Clean Air Act Amendments have reduced sulfur emissions and acid deposition in much of the United States. In 1998 the EPA ordered 22 states in the East and Midwest to reduce nitrogen oxides, which, when accomplished, should lower acid levels further.

ACID MINE DRAINAGE. Acid mine drainage is wastewater resulting from various coal mining operations. It forms when the mineral pyrite (FeS_2) in coal is exposed to air and water. The resulting chemical reaction forms sulfu-

ric acid and iron hydroxide. Surface waters contaminated by these chemicals become extremely acidic and iron-rich. Rivers and streams develop a sickly yellowish-orange color due to coating of their bottom sediments with iron hydroxide. Acid mine drainage can also be high in metals content.

Too Many Nutrients

Agriculture and forestry have also played a role in surface water pollution. The use of fertilizers, pesticides, and herbicides soared during the 1960s and 1970s. Figure 5.3 shows that the use of fertilizers containing nitrogen, phosphorus, and potash tripled between 1961 and 1981. Runoff of rain and irrigation waters washed nutrients (like nitrogen) into streams, rivers, and lakes.

Excessive nutrients are a problem in surface waters because they cause conditions called eutrophication and hypoxia. Eutrophication occurs when nutrients stimulate the rapid growth of algae and aquatic plants. When these plants and algae die, bacteria in the water decompose them. This depletes the amount of dissolved oxygen in the water—a condition called hypoxia. Fish and other aquatic creatures require dissolved oxygen to live and thrive. Hypoxic areas become dead zones in the environment.

Nitrate (NO_3) is a common form of nitrogen found in water. The EPA has monitored the nitrate load in the

FIGURE 5.6

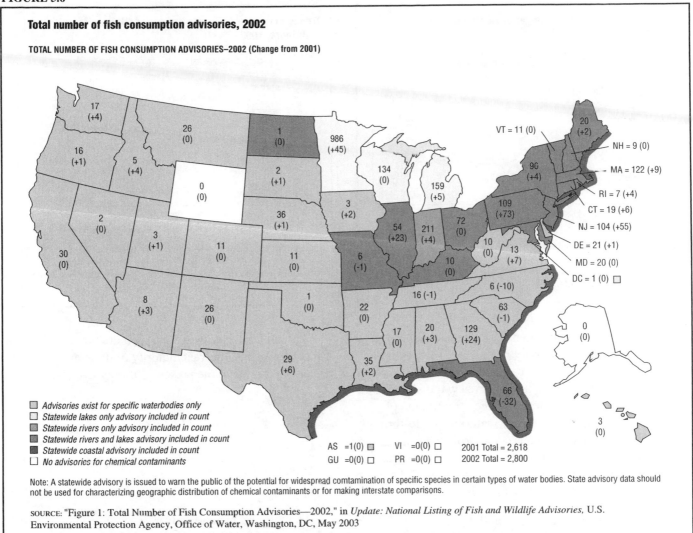

Total number of fish consumption advisories, 2002

TOTAL NUMBER OF FISH CONSUMPTION ADVISORIES—2002 (Change from 2001)

☐ Advisories exist for specific waterbodies only
☐ Statewide lakes only advisory included in count
☐ Statewide rivers only advisory included in count
☐ Statewide rivers and lakes advisory included in count
☐ Statewide coastal advisory included in count
☐ No advisories for chemical contaminants

AS = 1(0) ☐   VI = 0(0) ☐   2001 Total = 2,618
GU = 0(0) ☐   PR = 0(0) ☐   2002 Total = 2,800

Note: A statewide advisory is issued to warn the public of the potential for widespread comtamination of specific species in certain types of water bodies. State advisory data should not be used for characterizing geographic distribution of chemical contaminants or for making interstate comparisons.

SOURCE: "Figure 1: Total Number of Fish Consumption Advisories—2002," in *Update: National Listing of Fish and Wildlife Advisories*, U.S. Environmental Protection Agency, Office of Water, Washington, DC, May 2003

country's major rivers since the 1950s. The data show a disturbing trend, particularly in the Midwest, where fertilizer use and soil erosion rates are high. The nitrate load in the Mississippi River increased from approximately 250,000 tons per year in the early 1960s to approximately 1 million tons per year in 1999. The result has been the development of a massive hypoxic area near the mouth of the river in the Gulf of Mexico. Figure 5.4 shows how this area grew in size between 1985 and 2002. The data reflect midsummer measurements, because that is the time of year when hypoxia is at its worst.

Human Health

Polluted waters also pose a health hazard to humans. People can become ill from drinking contaminated water or consuming fish and shellfish taken from contaminated waters. Even swimming in contaminated waters can be a health hazard. Swimmers accidentally swallow tiny amounts of water during their activities. The presence of pathogens (disease-causing agents) in the water can lead to serious illnesses, as shown in Table 5.3.

CONTAMINATION OF FISH AND SHELLFISH. Fish and shellfish (such as oysters, clams, shrimp, and lobsters) that live in polluted waters can become very dangerous to eat because of a process called biomagnification. Biomagnification works like this: Many pollutants stick to aquatic vegetation and are readily stored in the fatty tissues of animals. As a result, as small fish and shellfish eat aquatic plants, and larger fish eat smaller fish and shellfish, and birds eat large fish, and humans eat birds and large fish, these pollutants accumulate in organisms in increasing concentrations as they move up the food chain. This effect is called bioaccumulation. Figure 5.5 shows the movement of water pollutants through the food chain.

In 1956 more than 600 people died in Minamata, Japan, from eating shellfish contaminated with methyl mercury. Many other people suffered neurological damage.

The consumption of fish and shellfish can also pass water-found pathogens to people. In the United States dozens of people contract cholera each year after eating contaminated shellfish. In fact, it is not unusual to have three or four cases of cholera in Louisiana during the summer months.

FIGURE 5.7

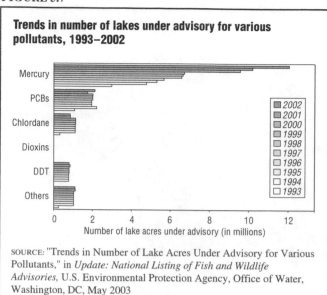

Trends in number of lakes under advisory for various pollutants, 1993–2002

SOURCE: "Trends in Number of Lake Acres Under Advisory for Various Pollutants," in *Update: National Listing of Fish and Wildlife Advisories,* U.S. Environmental Protection Agency, Office of Water, Washington, DC, May 2003

FIGURE 5.8

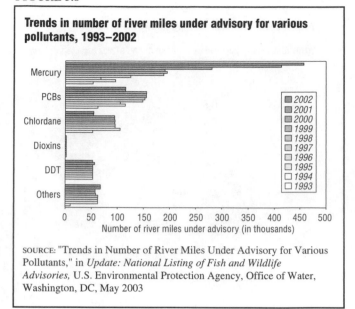

Trends in number of river miles under advisory for various pollutants, 1993–2002

SOURCE: "Trends in Number of River Miles Under Advisory for Various Pollutants," in *Update: National Listing of Fish and Wildlife Advisories,* U.S. Environmental Protection Agency, Office of Water, Washington, DC, May 2003

Although some pathogens are present naturally in marine waters, human activity has greatly increased their types and quantities. Human pathogens come mainly from discharges of raw sewage and from sewage sludge and wastewater outflow from sewage treatment plants, although they can enter marine waters directly through surface runoff. Viruses, bacteria, and protozoa can exist in marine environments for months or years. Concentrations of some intestinal viruses may be 10 to 10,000 times greater in coastal sediments than in other waters.

When states find dangerous pollutants in their fish or shellfish, they issue warnings for people to limit their consumption of or to stop eating fish or shellfish from particular water bodies. In May 2003 the EPA published *The 2002 National Listing of Fish and Wildlife Advisories.* Figure 5.6 shows the number of fish consumption advisories issued in each of the states in 2002. Only two states (Wyoming and Alaska) had no advisories that year. The total number of advisories issued during 2002 was 2,800. This was up from 2,618 advisories issued during 2001.

The report noted that the size of waters under advisory in the continental United States increased substantially from 2001 to 2002. The number of lake areas under advisory increased from 28 percent in 2001 to 33 percent in 2002. A total of 94,715 individual lakes were under advisory in 2002. The number of river miles under advisory increased from 14 percent in 2001 to 15 percent in 2002. A total of 544,036 river miles were under advisory in 2002. These increases were primarily due to issuances of statewide mercury advisories for all lakes and rivers in Florida, Illinois, and Rhode Island. The EPA reports that 100 percent of the Great Lakes and their connecting waters and 71 percent of all coastal waters of the continental United States were under advisory during 2002.

Although advisories were issued in 2002 for 39 chemical contaminants, the vast majority of these advisories (96 percent) were due to the presence of only five chemicals:

• Mercury

• PCBs

• Chlordane

• Dioxins

• DDT

Mercury is a metal. PCBs are organic compounds used in hundreds of industrial and commercial applications. Dioxins are also organic compounds. They are largely associated with pulp and paper plants that use particular bleaching processes, incineration facilities, and specific types of chemical manufacturing facilities. Chlordane and DDT are pesticides that have been banned in the United States for decades.

These chemicals are particularly toxic in water environments, because they are persistent and they bioaccumulate. The chemicals are considered persistent, because they endure without being degraded for relatively long periods of time in the sediments lying at the bottom of surface water bodies. This makes them readily accessible to the bottom-dwelling organisms that tend to be eaten by larger creatures in the water. These chemicals are also bioaccumulative, meaning that they become concentrated in tissues as they pass up through the food chain. For example, a largemouth bass can have concentrations of these chemicals that are millions of times higher than the concentrations found in the surrounding water.

Figure 5.7 and Figure 5.8 show the advisory trends from 1993 to 2002 for these chemicals in lakes and rivers, respectively. Mercury is by far responsible for the largest number of lake and river miles under advisory. Air pollution is believed to be the most significant source of mercury contamination in surface water. The mercury is deposited in the water via rain, snow, fog, or dust particles.

PATHOGENS IN BEACH WATERS. Each year hundreds (and maybe thousands) of American beaches are closed to protect the public from the presence of disease-carrying organisms in the water. Many coastal states do not regularly monitor surf pollution. This means that millions of tourists may be unaware of whether it is safe to swim, boat, or fish at any given time or place. Currently, the federal government does not monitor beach water or require the states to do so.

In 1997 the EPA created the BEACH Watch Program to promote greater consistency in beach health programs and provide information to the public about beach closings. Each year the EPA sends out questionnaires to hundreds of state, tribal, and local agencies that monitor and/or maintain swimming beaches. Participation in the program is voluntary.

In May 2003 the EPA released its findings for the 2002 swimming season. The survey results cover 2,823 beaches in 31 states plus Puerto Rico, Guam, the U.S. Virgin Islands, and the Northern Mariana Islands. The vast majority of the beaches (72 percent) are located along the ocean coast. The remainder are located on inland waterways. The EPA found that 709 beaches had at least one advisory or area closed during the 2002 swimming season. This represents 25 percent of the beaches included in the survey.

Most of the advisories and closings lasted from three to seven days. The presence of elevated bacterial levels in the water was cited as the primary cause for an advisory or closing in 75 percent of the cases. In nearly half the cases (43 percent) the agencies could not identify the source of the pollution that caused the advisory or closing. Stormwater runoff and/or wildlife were blamed as the cause in one-third of the cases. The remainder of the cases were attributed to contaminants from boat discharges, septic systems, and miscellaneous sewer problems.

The Natural Resources Defense Council (NRDC) is a not-for-profit environmental organization based in New York. Every year since 1971 it has performed its own nationwide survey of beach closings and beach water monitoring programs in coastal states. The NRDC survey for 2002 was published in August 2003. It reports that pollution caused more than 12,000 days of beach closings and advisories during 2002.

The major causes of beach closings and advisories were as follows:

- 87 percent were due to excessive bacteria levels measured in the water

- 10 percent were precautionary measures taken in response to heavy rainfall events carrying pollution into swimming waters

- 5 percent were precautionary measures taken in response to failures at nearby sewage treatment plants or breaks in sewage pipes

- 2 percent were due to other causes, including dredging and algal blooms

(Note that the figures do not add up to 100 percent due to rounding.)

Despite the threat of pollution, many states with popular beach areas still do not have regular beach-monitoring programs. The NRDC found that only 13 states—California, Connecticut, Delaware, Illinois, Indiana, Iowa, Massachusetts, New Hampshire (coastal beaches only), New Jersey, New York (coastal and state parks only), North Carolina, Ohio, and Pennsylvania—monitored recreational beaches regularly for swimmer safety during 2002 and notified the public of their findings.

Other states monitor infrequently or monitor only a portion of their recreational beaches. Legislation passed by Congress in 2000 requires that states adopt EPA standards or the equivalent by 2004 for beach closings and advisories.

The NRDC complains that the United States lacks uniform national standards for beach closings and advisories. However, the organization notes that the states are required under the federal BEACH Act to adopt EPA standards (or standards equally protective of public health) by April 2004.

THE *NATIONAL WATER QUALITY INVENTORY*

The CWA requires that each state prepare and submit to the EPA a report on

- the water quality of all navigable waters in the state,

- the extent to which the waters provided for the protection and propagation of marine animals and allowed recreation in and on the water,

- the extent to which pollution had been eliminated or was under control, and

- the sources and causes of pollutants.

The EPA requires the states to assess their water quality every two years and report their findings to the agency. The EPA summarizes the findings and issues them in a national water quality inventory. In August 2002, the EPA published the *National Water Quality Inventory: 2000 Report.*

The states use chemical and biological monitoring and other types of data, such as surveys of fisheries, water quality models, and information from citizens. The purpose of these evaluations is to determine what percent of each type of body of water is supporting its intended uses (such as drinking water supply, recreation, and warm and cold water fisheries) as part of the EPA-approved water quality standards.

Due to funding limitations, most states assess only a portion of their total water resources during each two-year

FIGURE 5.9

Summary of use support

For water bodies with more than one designated use, the states, tribes and other jurisdictions consolidate the individual use support information into a summary use support determination:

Good/Fully Supporting All Uses – Based on an assessment of available data, water quality supports all designated uses. Water quality meets narrative and/or numeric criteria adopted to protect and support a designated use.

Good/Threatened for One or More Uses – Although all the assessed uses are currently met, data show a declining trend in water quality. Projections based on this trend indicate water quality will be impaired in the future, unless action is taken to prevent further degradation.

Impaired for One or More Uses – Based on an assessment of available data, water quality does not support one or more designated uses.

Use Not Attainable – The state, tribe, or other jurisdiction performed a use-attainability analysis and demonstrated that one or more designated uses are not attainable due to one of six conditions specified in the *Code of Federal Regulations* (40CFR 131.10).

SOURCE: "Summary of Use Support," in *National Water Quality Inventory: 1998 Report to Congress,* U.S. Environmental Protection Agency, Washington, DC, 2000

---

ed. Under federal mandate, each state must designate uses for the rivers, streams, lakes, and estuaries within its boundaries. In general the EPA consolidates the various state uses into six major categories:

- Drinking Water Supply—meaning the water is of excellent quality and suitable for drinking after treatment with common standard methods
- Aquatic Life Support—meaning the water is of good enough quality to support a healthy, balanced population of aquatic organisms such as fish, insects, plants, and algae
- Fish Consumption—meaning that people can safely eat fish from the water body
- Primary Contact Recreation—meaning that people can safely swim in the water without risk to their health
- Secondary Contact Recreation—meaning that people can participate in recreational activities (such as boating) on the water surface without risk to their health
- Agricultural Use—meaning that the water is of sufficient quality for irrigating fields and watering livestock

Obviously some uses require higher quality than others. The requirements for suitable drinking water are much stricter than the requirements for secondary recreation use. It is not uncommon for a body of water to have more than one designated use. For example, a river can be designated for drinking water within one section, but for recreation in another.

Following EPA guidelines, the states determine whether their bodies of water meet the standards set for their designated use. Figure 5.9 lists and defines the "use support levels" reported by the states. They range from "fully supporting all uses" to "not attainable." As long as a water body meets the requirements for its designated use, it is considered fully supporting. For example, if agricultural use is the designated use for a particular water body, it is not considered polluted if it can be safely used for that purpose, even if it is unfit for other purposes, such as drinking water.

Point and Nonpoint Sources of Pollution

Pollution is the main reason that a body of water cannot support its designated uses. There are a vast number of pollutants that can make water use threatened, impaired, or not attainable, but to control pollution it is necessary to find out what the pollutant is, as well as its source. Although there are many ways in which pollutants can enter waterways, sources of pollution are generally categorized as point sources and nonpoint sources.

Point sources are localized sources of water pollution that disperse pollutants from a single point, such as a sewage drain or an industrial discharge pipe. Pollutants that are commonly discharged from point sources include bacteria discharged through sewer pipes and toxic chemicals and heavy metals discharged via pipes from industrial plants.

---

reporting cycle. Their goal is usually to assess all their waters over a five- to ten-year period. This means that each national inventory reports on only a portion of the nation's waters. Because of the sparse reporting by the states and differences in support criteria and measurement techniques between states, a complete assessment of the quality of the nation's surface waters is not possible. However, the reports are valuable for identifying the major sources and causes of water pollution.

Designated Uses and Use Support

Generally, the key measure of the quality of any body of surface water is the degree to which the water is able to support the uses for which it has been officially designat-

FIGURE 5.10

Quality of assessed rivers, lakes, and estuaries, 2000

Waterbody type	Total size	Amount assessed* (% of total)	Good (% of assessed)	Good but threatened (% of assessed)	Polluted (% of assessed)
Rivers (miles)	3,692,830	699,946 (19%)	007,109 (53%)	59,504 (8%)	269,258 (39%)
Lakes (acres)	40,603,893	17,339,080 (43%)	8,026,988 (47%)	1,348,903 (8%)	7,702,370 (45%)
Estuaries (sq. miles)	87,369	31,072 (36%)	13,850 (45%)	1,023 (<4%)	15,676 (51%)

*Includes waterbodies assessed as not attainable for one or more uses.

Note: percentages may not add up to 100% due to rounding.

SOURCE: "Figure 1. Summary of Quality of Assessed Rivers, Lakes, and Estuaries," in *Water Quality Conditions in the United States, A Profile from the 2000 National Water Quality Inventory,* U.S. Environmental Protection Agency, Office of Water, August 2002

Nonpoint sources are spread out over a large area and have no specific outlet or discharge point. Examples include runoff from farm fields and urban areas. Nonpoint source pollutants can include pesticides, fertilizers, toxic chemicals, and asbestos and salts from road construction. The EPA estimates that as much as 65 percent of surface water pollutants come from nonpoint sources.

THE QUALITY OF U.S. RIVERS, STREAMS, LAKES, AND ESTUARIES

Figure 5.10 shows that the *National Water Quality Inventory: 2000 Report* covered only 19 percent of the country's river miles, 43 percent of its lake acreage, and 36 percent of its estuary area (measured in square miles). The EPA reports that the area of surface waters included in the 2000 national inventory is actually less than it was in the 1998 inventory.

Rivers and Streams

The United States has about 3.7 million miles of rivers and streams. As shown in Figure 5.11 nearly 700,000 of these miles were assessed for the 2000 inventory. The results indicate that just over half (53 percent) of the river miles assessed fully supported all intended uses. (See Figure 5.12) Another 8 percent were considered in good condition, but threatened for one or more uses. The remaining 39 percent were considered impaired for one or more uses.

The leading pollutants and stressors on river and stream miles are shown in Figure 5.11. Note that more than one factor can be responsible for impairing a river segment. Pathogens and siltation were the two leading causes of river impairment during 2000. Pathogens are

FIGURE 5.11

Leading pollutants in impaired rivers and streams, 2000

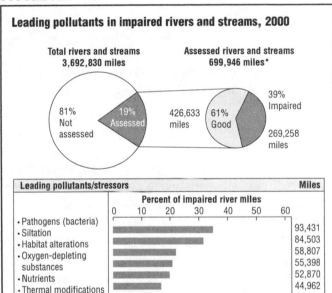

*Includes miles assessed as not attainable.

Note: Percentages do not add up to 100% because more than one pollutant or source may impair a river segment.

SOURCE: "Figure 2-4. Leading Pollutants in Impaired Rivers and Streams," in *National Water Quality Inventory 2000 Report,* EPA-841-R-02-001, U.S. Environmental Protection Agency, Office of Water, Washington, DC, August 2002

biological pollutants (such as harmful bacteria). Siltation is a condition in which too much soil and dust is present in a water body. As shown in Figure 5.13, the resulting sediment reduces the water area available to aquatic life

FIGURE 5.12

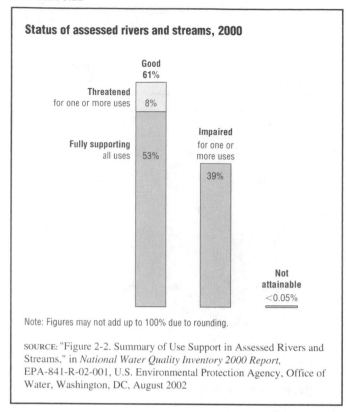

Status of assessed rivers and streams, 2000

Good
61%

Threatened
for one or more uses   8%

Fully supporting
all uses   53%

Impaired
for one or
more uses

39%

Not
attainable
<0.05%

Note: Figures may not add up to 100% due to rounding.

SOURCE: "Figure 2-2. Summary of Use Support in Assessed Rivers and Streams," in *National Water Quality Inventory 2000 Report*, EPA-841-R-02-001, U.S. Environmental Protection Agency, Office of Water, Washington, DC, August 2002

FIGURE 5.13

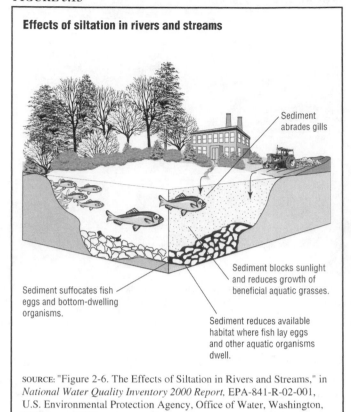

Effects of siltation in rivers and streams

Sediment
abrades gills

Sediment suffocates fish
eggs and bottom-dwelling
organisms.

Sediment blocks sunlight
and reduces growth of
beneficial aquatic grasses.

Sediment reduces available
habitat where fish lay eggs
and other aquatic organisms
dwell.

SOURCE: "Figure 2-6. The Effects of Siltation in Rivers and Streams," in *National Water Quality Inventory 2000 Report*, EPA-841-R-02-001, U.S. Environmental Protection Agency, Office of Water, Washington, DC, August 2002

and suffocates their eggs. It can also clog fish gills and block needed sunlight from reaching aquatic vegetation.

Siltation is caused by excessive erosion of river banks and surrounding land, windblown dust (particularly during dry weather), and runoff and other discharges of water carrying soil particles. These can be due to natural conditions in the environment or to human activities. Many human activities exaggerate the effects of these events. For example, clearing of vegetation along river banks removes protective vegetative cover and worsens bank erosion.

Besides pathogens and siltation, other major pollutants and stressors impairing rivers and streams during 2000 were habitat alterations, oxygen-depleting substances, nutrients, thermal modifications, metals, and flow alterations. Habitat alterations do not directly affect stream flow, but can adversely affect aquatic organisms living in the water. For example, removing submerged logs can endanger young fish that use the logs to hide from larger predators.

Oxygen-depleting substances are biodegradable materials (such as sewage or food waste) that are broken down by naturally occurring bacteria in the water. Many of these bacteria are aerobic, meaning that they need oxygen to survive. They utilize dissolved oxygen present in the water to break down carbon chains in organic compounds to simple inorganic molecules (mostly carbon dioxide and water). If a large amount of biodegradable waste is present in a water body, aerobic bacteria

use up much of the dissolved oxygen in the water. This harms larger aquatic life forms (such as fish) that need a minimum amount of dissolved oxygen in the water to survive and thrive.

Agriculture was, by far, the leading source of pollution responsible for impairing river miles during 2000. (See Figure 5.14.) Nearly half of all impaired river miles reported by the states were negatively impacted by agricultural activities such as crop production and animal feeding operations. Other major sources of pollution included hydrologic modifications (for example, dredging and dam construction), habitat modifications (such as removal of stream bank vegetation), storm water runoff and discharges from urban areas, commercial forestry activities, municipal point sources (sewage pipe discharges), and resource extraction (such as mining).

Lakes, Reservoirs, and Ponds

There are approximately 40.6 million acres of lakes, reservoirs, and ponds in the United States. More than 17.3 million acres were assessed as part of the *National Water Quality Inventory: 2000 Report*. The results indicate that 47 percent of the acres assessed fully supported all intended uses. (See Figure 5.15) An additional 8 percent were considered in good condition, but threatened for one or more uses. The remaining 45 percent were considered impaired for one or more uses.

FIGURE 5.14

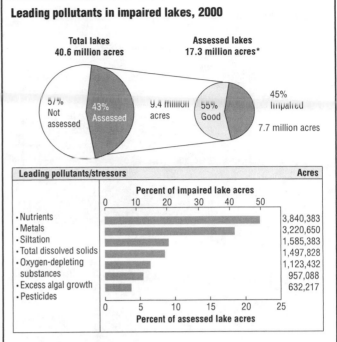

Leading sources of river and stream impairment, 2000

Leading sources	Miles
• Agriculture	120,050
• Hydrologic modification	53,850
• Habitat modification	37,654
• Urban runoff/storm sewers	34,871
• Forestry	28,156
• Municipal point sources	27,988
• Resource extraction	27,695

Percent of impaired river miles (0, 10, 20, 30, 40, 50)
Percent of assessed river miles (0, 5, 10, 15, 20)

Note: Percentages do not add up to 100% because more than one pollutant or source may impair a river segment. Figure excludes unknown and natural sources.

SOURCE: "Figure 2-5. Leading Sources of River and Stream Impairment," in *National Water Quality Inventory 2000 Report,* EPA-841-R-02-001, U.S. Environmental Protection Agency, Office of Water, Washington, DC, August 2002

FIGURE 5.15

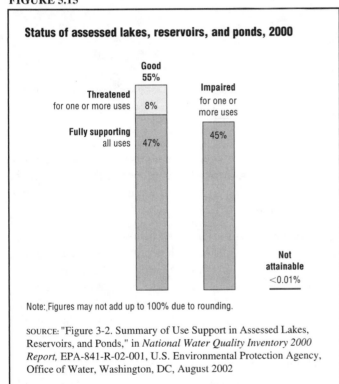

Status of assessed lakes, reservoirs, and ponds, 2000

- Good 55%
  - Threatened for one or more uses 8%
  - Fully supporting all uses 47%
- Impaired for one or more uses 45%
  - Not attainable <0.01%

Note: Figures may not add up to 100% due to rounding.

SOURCE: "Figure 3-2. Summary of Use Support in Assessed Lakes, Reservoirs, and Ponds," in *National Water Quality Inventory 2000 Report,* EPA-841-R-02-001, U.S. Environmental Protection Agency, Office of Water, Washington, DC, August 2002

The leading pollutants and stressors on lake acres are shown in Figure 5.16. Note that more than one factor can be responsible for impairing a particular lake acre. Excessive levels of nutrients were responsible for the majority of the impaired lake acres during 2000. Nutrients (such as nitrogen from fertilizers) are problematic because they lead to overgrowth of aquatic vegetation and algae. Figure 5.17 shows a lake impaired by excessive nutrients. Other major pollutants reported in 2000 were metals, siltation,

FIGURE 5.16

Leading pollutants in impaired lakes, 2000

Total lakes 40.6 million acres — 57% Not assessed, 43% Assessed
Assessed lakes 17.3 million acres* — 9.4 million acres, 55% Good, 45% Impaired, 7.7 million acres

Leading pollutants/stressors	Acres
• Nutrients	3,840,383
• Metals	3,220,650
• Siltation	1,585,383
• Total dissolved solids	1,497,828
• Oxygen-depleting substances	1,123,432
• Excess algal growth	957,088
• Pesticides	632,217

Percent of impaired lake acres (0, 10, 20, 30, 40, 50)
Percent of assessed lake acres (0, 5, 10, 15, 20, 25)

*Includes acres assessed as not attainable.

Note: Percentages do not add up to 100% because more than one pollutant or source may impair a river segment.

Eleven states did not include the effects of statewide fish consumption advisories when reporting the pollutants and sources responsible for impairment. Therefore, certain pollutants and sources, such as metals atmospheric deposition, may be underrepresented.

SOURCE: "Figure 3-4. Leading Pollutants in Impaired Lakes," in *National Water Quality Inventory 2000 Report,* EPA-841-R-02-001, U.S. Environmental Protection Agency, Office of Water, Washington, DC, August 2002

total dissolved solids, oxygen-depleting substances, excessive algal growth, and pesticides.

Agricultural activities were blamed as the leading source of pollution responsible for impairing lake areas during 2000. (See Figure 5.18) Other major sources of pollution were similar to those impairing rivers and streams, such as hydrologic modifications, urban runoff, etc.

Estuaries

An estuary is an inlet, bay, or other area where a river meets an ocean. Estuaries and the nearby coastal areas are among the biologically richest and most useful areas in the world. Fish and shellfish lay their eggs in estuaries, where the progeny hatch and develop into adult fish. About two-thirds of all fish caught are hatched in estuaries. Birds and many animals live in the wetlands that border estuaries.

There are more than 87,000 square miles of estuaries in the United States. More than 31,000 square miles were assessed as part of the *National Water Quality Inventory: 2000 Report.* The results indicate that 45 percent of the square miles assessed fully supported all intended uses.

FIGURE 5.17

Comparison of impaired and healthy lake ecosystems

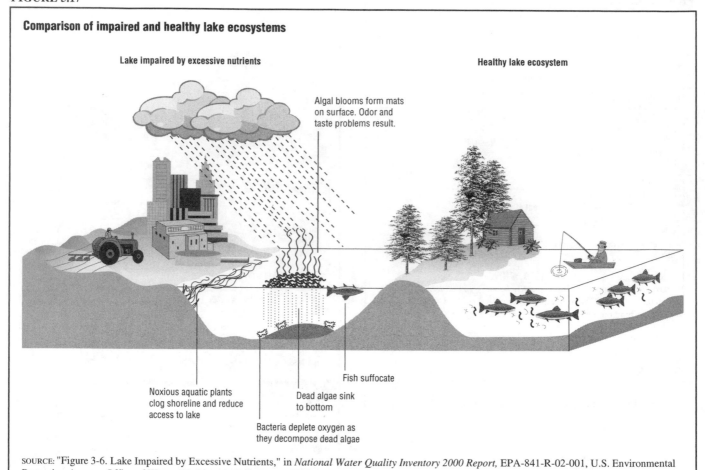

SOURCE: "Figure 3-6. Lake Impaired by Excessive Nutrients," in *National Water Quality Inventory 2000 Report,* EPA-841-R-02-001, U.S. Environmental Protection Agency, Office of Water, Washington, DC, August 2002

FIGURE 5.18

Leading sources of lake impairment, 2000

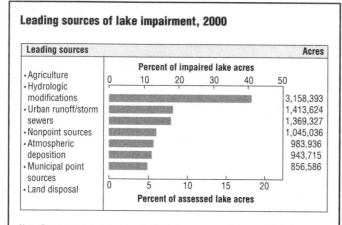

Note: Percentages do not add up to 100% because more than one pollutant or source may impair a lake.

Figure excludes unknown, natural, and other sources.

Eleven states did not include the effects of statewide fish consumption advisories when reporting the pollutants and sources responsible for impairment. Therefore, certain pollutants and sources, such as metals and atmospheric deposition, may be under represented.

SOURCE: "Figure 3-5. Leading Sources of Lake Impairment," in *National Water Quality Inventory 2000 Report,* EPA-841-R-02-001, U.S. Environmental Protection Agency, Office of Water, Washington, DC, August 2002

(See Figure 5.19.) Approximately 4 percent were considered in good condition, but threatened for one or more uses. The remaining 51 percent were considered impaired for one or more uses.

The leading pollutants and stressors on estuaries are shown in Figure 5.20. Note that more than one factor can be responsible for impairing a particular estuary area. Excessive levels of metals were responsible for the majority of the impaired estuary areas during 2000. Table 5.4 lists the metals that threaten marine environments, such as estuaries.

Other major pollutants reported as impairing estuaries during 2000 were pesticides, oxygen-depleting substances, pathogens (bacteria), priority toxic organic chemicals, PCBs, and total dissolved solids.

Municipal point sources (sewage discharges) were blamed as the leading source of pollution responsible for impairing estuary areas during 2000. (See Figure 5.21.) Other major sources of pollution included storm water runoff and discharges from urban areas, industrial discharges, atmospheric deposition, agriculture, hydrologic modifications, and resources extraction (such as in mining activities).

FIGURE 5.19

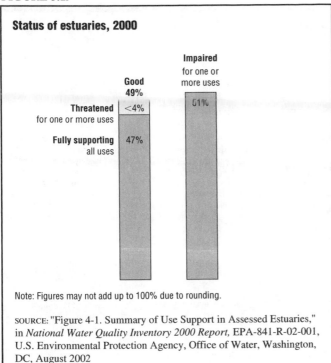

Status of estuaries, 2000

Note: Figures may not add up to 100% due to rounding.

SOURCE: "Figure 4-1. Summary of Use Support in Assessed Estuaries," in *National Water Quality Inventory 2000 Report,* EPA-841-R-02-001, U.S. Environmental Protection Agency, Office of Water, Washington, DC, August 2002

THE QUALITY OF U.S. WETLANDS

The EPA defines wetlands as "lands where saturation with water is the dominant factor determining the nature of soil development and the types of plant and animal communities living in the soil and on its surface" (*National Water Quality Inventory: 2000 Report,* August 2002). Wetlands are areas that retain shallow water depths at least part of the year. They are neither completely terrestrial nor completely aquatic, but include characteristics of both environments. This unique combination supports an incredible variety of plant, aquatic, and animal life. In 2003 the U.S. Fish and Wildlife Service estimated that approximately 43 percent of all federally threatened and endangered species rely directly or indirectly on wetlands for their survival.

Wetlands are found throughout the United States in coastal and inland areas. They are frequently referred to as marshes, mires, bogs, swamps, fens, or wet meadows. During the 1600s and 1700s, more than 200 million acres of wetlands existed in the area that now comprises the lower 48 states. As America developed, many wetlands were drained and filled for conversion to farmland and urban development. The EPA estimates that nearly half of the original acreage of wetlands was destroyed. The three states thought to have sustained the greatest percentage of wetland loss are California (91 percent), Ohio (90 percent), and Iowa (89 percent). The U.S. Fish and Wildlife Service estimates that wetland acreage decreased at a rate of 58,500 acres per year between 1986 and 1997.

According to the *National Water Quality Inventory: 2000 Report,* the United States has 105.5 million acres of

FIGURE 5.20

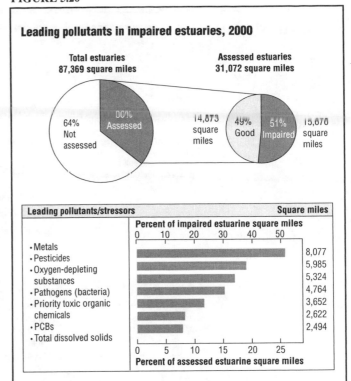

Leading pollutants in impaired estuaries, 2000

Note: Percentages do not add up to 100% because more than one pollutant or source may impair an estuary.

SOURCE: "Figure 4-3. Leading Pollutants in Impaired Estuaries," in *National Water Quality Inventory 2000 Report,* EPA-841-R-02-001, U.S. Environmental Protection Agency, Office of Water, Washington, DC, August 2002

FIGURE 5.21

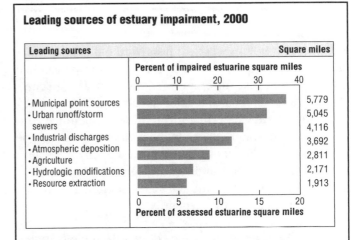

Leading sources of estuary impairment, 2000

Note: Percentages do not add up to 100% because more than one pollutant or source may impair an estuary.

Figure excludes unknown, natural, and other sources.

SOURCE: "Figure 4-4. Leading Sources of Estuary Impairment," in *National Water Quality Inventory 2000 Report,* EPA-841-R-02-001, U.S. Environmental Protection Agency, Office of Water, Washington, DC, August 2002

TABLE 5.4

Properties and effects of metals of primary concern in marine environments

	Arsenic	Cadmium	Lead	Mercury
Bioaccumulation	Low except in some fish species	Moderate	Low or none	Significant (methylated form)
Biomagnification	Low or none	Low or none	Low or none	Significant (methylated form)
Properties	Metallic form: insoluble Readily methylated by sediment bacteria to become highly soluble, but low in toxicity	Metalic form: relatively soluble Not subject to biomethylation Less bioavailable in marine than in fresh water Long biological residence time Synergistic effects with lead	Generally insoluble Adsorption rate age-dependent, 4 to 5 times higher in children than adults Synergistic effects with cadmium	Metallic form: relatively insoluble Readily methylated by sediment bacteria to become more soluble, bioavailable, persistent, and highly toxic
Major environmental sink	Sediments	Sediments	Sediments	Sediments
Major routes of human exposure:				
Marine environments	Seafood: very minor route, except for some fish species	Seafood contributes approximately 10% of total for general population	Seafood comparable to other food sources	Seafood is primary source of human exposure
Other environments	Inhalation: the major route	Food, primarily grains	Diet and drinking water	Terrestrial pathways are minor sources in comparison
Health effects	Acute: gastrointestinal hemorrhage; loss of blood pressure; coma and death in extreme cases Chronic: liver and peripheral nerve damage; possibly skin and lung cancer	Emphysema and other lung damage; anemia; kidney, pancreatic, and liver impairment; bone damage; animal (and suspected human) carcinogen and mutagen	Acute: gastrointestinal disorders Chronic: anemia; neurological and blood disorders; kidney dysfunction; joint impairments; male/female reproductive effects; teratogenic	Kidney dysfunction; neurological disease; skin lesions; respiratory impairment; eye damage; animal teratogen and carcinogen

SOURCE: Adapted from "Table 8. Properties and effects of metals of primary concern in marine environments," in *Wastes in Marine Environments,* U.S. Congress, Office of Technology Assessment, Washington, DC, 1987

wetlands. Only 8 percent of these wetland acres (or 8.3 million acres) were assessed by the states for the national inventory. Because different methods were used to complete the assessments, and since the acreage assessed was so small, the EPA feels that it can draw only limited conclusions about water quality in the nation's wetlands. The reason wetlands do not receive greater scrutiny is because they are not covered under water quality standards in many states. In 2000 only 11 states included wetlands under their water quality standards.

The conclusions that can be drawn from the *National Water Quality Inventory: 2000 Report* regarding wetlands are:

• The leading causes of wetland loss were filling and draining, agriculture, and residential and urban development.

• The primary causes of wetland degradation were sedimentation/siltation, flow alterations, and excessive nutrients.

• Major sources contributing to wetland degradation included agriculture, construction, and hydrologic modifications.

THE QUALITY OF U.S. OCEAN SHORELINE WATERS

Coastal water pollution has a significant economic impact on coastal states. Failing to invest in clean waters costs states economic growth—jobs, job productivity, tourism, and property tax dollars. Beaches are popular vacation destinations in the United States, generating over $100 billion in revenues.

The *National Water Quality Inventory: 2000 Report*

There are 58,618 miles of ocean shoreline in the United States. Just over 3,000 miles (or 6 percent) of the total shoreline were assessed as part of the *National Water Quality Inventory: 2000 Report*. The results indicate that 79 percent of the shoreline miles assessed fully supported all intended uses. (See Figure 5.22.) An additional 7 percent were considered in good condition, but threatened for

FIGURE 5.22

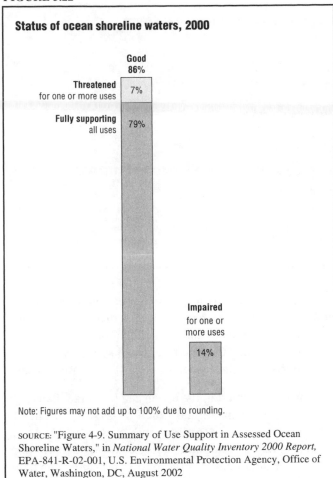

Status of ocean shoreline waters, 2000

Note: Figures may not add up to 100% due to rounding.

SOURCE: "Figure 4-9. Summary of Use Support in Assessed Ocean Shoreline Waters," in *National Water Quality Inventory 2000 Report*, EPA-841-R-02-001, U.S. Environmental Protection Agency, Office of Water, Washington, DC, August 2002

FIGURE 5.23

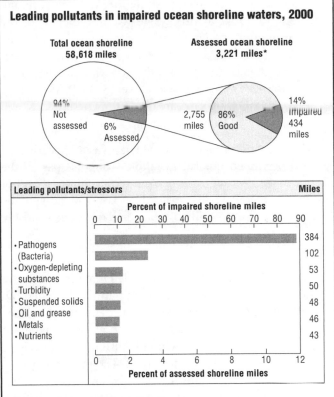

Leading pollutants in impaired ocean shoreline waters, 2000

*Includes miles assessed as not attainable.

Note: Percentages do not add up to 100% because more than one pollutant or source may impair a segment of ocean shoreline.

SOURCE: "Figure 4-11. Leading Pollutants in Impaired Ocean Shoreline Waters," in *National Water Quality Inventory 2000 Report*, EPA-841-R-02-001, U.S. Environmental Protection Agency, Office of Water, Washington, DC, August 2002

FIGURE 5.24

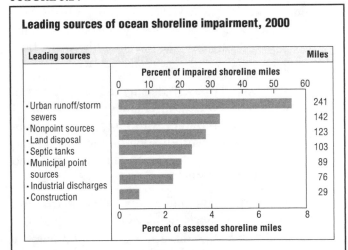

Leading sources of ocean shoreline impairment, 2000

Note: Percentages do not add up to 100% because more than one pollutant or source may impair a segment of ocean shoreline. Figure excludes natural sources.

SOURCE: "Figure 4-12. Leading Sources of Ocean Shoreline Impairment," in *National Water Quality Inventory 2000 Report*, EPA-841-R-02-001, U.S. Environmental Protection Agency, Office of Water, Washington, DC, August 2002

one or more uses. The remaining 14 percent were considered impaired for one or more uses.

The leading pollutants and stressors on ocean shoreline miles are shown in Figure 5.23. Note that more than one factor can be responsible for impairing a particular mile. Pathogens (such as bacteria) were by far the leading pollutant reported, accounting for nearly 90 percent of impaired ocean shoreline miles. Other major pollutants reported in 2000 were oxygen-depleting substances, turbidity (the presence of very fine suspended matter from clay, silt, or other matter in water), suspended solids, oil and grease, metals, and nutrients.

Rainfall runoff and storm sewer discharges from urban areas were blamed as the leading source of pollution responsible for impairing ocean shoreline miles during 2000. (See Figure 5.24.) Other major sources of pollution included nonpoint sources, land disposal of wastes, septic tanks, municipal point sources (sewage pipe discharges), industrial discharges, and construction activities.

Other Threats to Oceans and Shorelines

MEDICAL WASTE. During the summers of 1987 and 1988, medical wastes from hospitals, including containers of blood and syringes used to give injections, floated onto the shore along the East Coast, mainly in New York and New Jersey. Some of this waste was infected with the human immunodeficiency virus (HIV, the virus that causes AIDS) and a virus that causes a type of hepatitis (a serious liver disease). As a result, the government closed the beaches in these areas for several weeks. In 1988 medical waste also washed up onshore along the Great Lakes, and those beaches had to be shut down.

The sensational nature of medical waste appearing on beaches prompted quick legislation. Congress passed the 1988 Medical Waste Tracking Act, requiring producers of medical waste to be held accountable for safe disposal of the waste or face up to $1 million in fines and five years in prison.

In 1990 the Agency for Toxic Substances and Disease Registry (ATSDR), a division of the U.S. Department of Health and Human Services, concluded that medical waste presents little danger to the general public. Results of an ATSDR investigation revealed that the general public does not normally come in contact with medical waste unless it originates from homes in which health care is provided and the waste is carelessly discarded. The public may also be at risk when encountering needles and syringes disposed of by intravenous drug users. Furthermore, despite the furor raised by the public over medical waste, studies show that it accounts for only 0.01 percent of all waste collected and analyzed on the nation's beaches.

MARINE DEBRIS. The Ocean Conservancy (formerly the Center for Marine Conservation), located in Washington, D.C., defines marine debris as human-made items, such as those made of glass, plastic, metal, or paper, that have been lost or disposed of in the marine (ocean) environment. The items may have been intentionally discarded, accidentally dropped, or indirectly deposited from the land. The debris may sink to the bottom of the water, float on top of the water, or drift beneath the surface.

The International Coastal Cleanup (ICC) is a program coordinated by the Ocean Conservancy. The mission of the Coastal Cleanup program is to remove debris from U.S. shorelines, collect information on the amount and types of debris, educate people about marine debris, and use the information collected to effect positive change.

In 2002 data from the International Coastal Cleanup revealed the top 10 debris items found along the U.S. coastline. Table 5.5 lists these items, the total number reported, and the percentage each comprised of the total debris collected. Cigarette butts made up more than a quarter of shoreline debris. Food wrappers/containers (10.8 percent) and caps and lids (8 percent) were also a problem.

The Ocean Conservancy uses data from the Coastal Cleanup Program to identify sources of marine debris. The Conservancy has identified ocean-based sources as

TABLE 5.5

Most prevalent coastal debris items, 2002

	Debris items	Total number	Percent
1.	Cigarettes/cigarette filters	1,640,614	26.2%
2.	Food wrappers/containers	575,360	10.8%
3.	Caps, lids	498,566	8.0%
4.	Beverage bottles (plastic) 2 liters or less	423,829	6.8%
5.	Cups, plates, forks, knives, spoons	362,388	5.8%
6.	Beverage cans	360,104	5.7%
7.	Beverage bottles (glass)	347,137	5.5%
8.	Bags	335,070	5.4%
9.	Straws, stirrers	255,972	4.1%
10.	Cigar tips	148,658	2.4%
	Totals	**5,047,698**	**80.6%**

SOURCE: "Top Ten," in *2002 ICC Fast Facts,* The Ocean Conservancy, Washington, DC [Online] http://www.oceanconservancy.org/dynamic/press/kits/iccKit/icc_fastFacts.pdf [accessed November 10, 2003]

sea-going vessels (from small recreational vehicles to large ships), and offshore rigs and drilling platforms. Land-based sources include beach visitors and overflowing sewer systems. Creeks, rivers, and storm water drains carry debris from these sources downstream to the ocean.

The debris found in the ocean can be a great danger to ocean wildlife. An animal, such as a seal, might get trapped in a net, rope, or line, and drown. In fact, some scientists think this might be the reason why the seal population has declined over the past two decades. Whales and dolphins also get caught in old fishing nets. The New England Aquarium reported that 56 percent of endangered whales photographed by Aquarium personnel had scars from plastic gill nets or lobster gear entanglement.

Ocean debris can be a serious threat to seabirds and shorebirds. They become caught in fishing nets, fishing lines, or plastic beer and soda container rings and drown or choke to death. Sometimes pelicans get fishing lines or plastic beer container rings caught around their beaks so they cannot catch food. As a result, they starve to death. Pelicans and egrets may get fishing line caught around their wings and legs so they cannot fly. They, too, starve to death.

Plastic items are a particular hazard to marine organisms. Some birds and sea turtles eat little pieces of plastic, thinking it is food. Dead whales and dolphins have been found with their stomachs full of plastic bags. Adult birds eat small plastic pellets resembling fish eggs and feed them to their young. An estimated 2 million sea birds and 100,000 marine animals die each year as a result of ingesting or becoming entangled in plastic.

In 1988, 31 nations ratified an agreement making it illegal for their ships to dump plastic debris, including fishing nets, into the ocean. As part of that agreement, the United States enacted the Marine Plastics Pollution

Research and Control Act, which, among other things, imposed a $25,000 fine for each violation.

Diving and boating safety can be jeopardized by marine debris. Skin divers and scuba divers can be caught in old nets and fishing lines. Fishing nets can wrap around boat propellers, making it impossible for boats to operate. The junk washed up on shores fouls beaches and makes them less attractive to visitors. Fewer people will want to visit the beach if it is littered, which hurts the economy of beach areas.

DREDGING. Every year, millions of tons of materials are dredged from the bottoms of harbors and coastal areas to clear or enlarge navigational channels or for development purposes. This material ends up in U.S. marine waters, most of it in the Gulf of Mexico. Dredged materials may contain high concentrations of pesticides, metals, and toxic chemicals. During dredging or when the dredged material is dumped, pollutants that have settled into the sediment are stirred up and released into open water, giving them a greater potential to harm marine life.

COASTAL DEVELOPMENT AND RECREATION. Almost three-fourths of the U.S. population lives within 50 miles of a coastline, and more people move to coastal regions each year. Millions visit seaside areas, drawn by the mild climates, scenic beauty, and recreational activities. To accommodate an increasing number of residents and tourists, developers are building more houses, resorts, marinas, and boatyards. Commercial establishments built to accommodate the influx of new residents add to the population density.

Development often comes at the expense of ocean life. Destruction of marine habitats is common in populated areas. Many aquatic organisms and animals have little tolerance for disturbances such as light and temperature changes. When one species is eliminated from an ecosystem, the food chain is broken, and other species will often be destroyed or leave the area in search of a more suitable habitat. Other marine animals are sometimes harmed by collisions with recreational and fishing boats, causing extensive injuries or death.

OIL SPILLS. Oil spills are a dramatic form of water pollution. They are highly visible, and their impact is sometimes immediate and severe. While it is true that oil can have a devastating effect on marine life, the size of the spill itself is often not the determining factor in the amount of damage it causes. Other factors include the amount and type of marine life in the area and weather conditions that might disperse the oil.

In 1989 the *Exxon Valdez* ran into a reef in Prince William Sound, Alaska, spilling 11 million gallons of oil into one of the richest and most ecologically sensitive areas in North America. A slick the size of Rhode Island developed, threatening fish and wildlife. Despite the cleaning and rescue efforts of thousands of workers and volunteers, the oil slick had a terrible toll on local marine life. Otters died by the thousands, because they cannot tolerate even a small amount of oil on their fur. Oil-soaked birds lined the shores, only to be eaten by larger predator birds, which then died from the ingested oil.

In response to the *Exxon Valdez* disaster, Congress passed the Oil Pollution Act of 1990, which called for prompt reaction and a $1 billion cleanup-damage fund, early planning for response to spills, stricter crew standards, and double hulls on new tankers. (When equipped with two hulls, if the tanker's exterior hull is punctured, the interior hull holding the oil will still likely remain intact.) The law requires older tankers to be fitted with double hulls by the year 2015. The *Exxon Valdez* was not double-hulled. An Alaskan state commission estimated that if the *Valdez* had been equipped with a double-hull design, 20 to 60 percent of the spill might have been prevented.

In November 2002 another single-hulled oil tanker was responsible for a major oil spill in marine waters. The *Prestige* split apart during a storm at sea and spilt 17 million gallons of fuel oil into the Atlantic Ocean about 150 miles off the coast of northern Spain. Environmental groups estimate that hundreds of thousands of seabirds and other creatures were killed by the oil, as nearly 200 miles of coastline were soiled. The cleanup is predicted to last for years and cost nearly $3 billion. The tragedy renewed calls in Europe to enact a requirement for double-hulled tankers to take effect sooner than 2015.

The U.S. National Research Council estimates that approximately 8.4 billion gallons of oil enter marine waters each year, not from major oil spills, but from street runoff, industrial liquid wastes, and intentional discharge from ships flushing their oil tanks. The agency indicated concern for areas that are habitually exposed to oil pollution, since as little as one part of oil per million parts of water can be detrimental to the reproduction and growth of fish, crustaceans, and plankton.

CHAPTER 6
POLLUTION OF GROUNDWATER

Groundwater lies beneath the earth's surface. It is found in the pores, cracks, and other open spaces within subsurface rock formations and between rocks and grains of soil. The earth contains massive amounts of groundwater. It is the largest source of fresh (not saline) water on the planet. As shown in Figure 6.1, only a tiny fraction of all the water on earth is fresh water available for use.

Groundwater comprises 96 percent of this fresh water. This makes it an extremely vital resource and one that must be protected from contamination.

Groundwater can become polluted when contaminants seep down through the soil from the surface or are introduced under the ground. Because groundwater is hidden

FIGURE 6.1

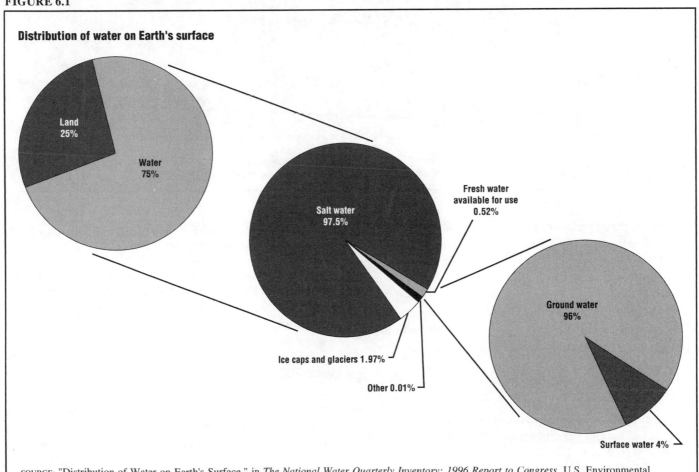

Distribution of water on Earth's surface

Land 25%

Water 75%

Salt water 97.5%

Fresh water available for use 0.52%

Ice caps and glaciers 1.97%

Other 0.01%

Ground water 96%

Surface water 4%

SOURCE: "Distribution of Water on Earth's Surface," in *The National Water Quarterly Inventory: 1996 Report to Congress,* U.S. Environmental Protection Agency, Washington, DC, 1998

FIGURE 6.2

Ground water in the hydrologic cycle

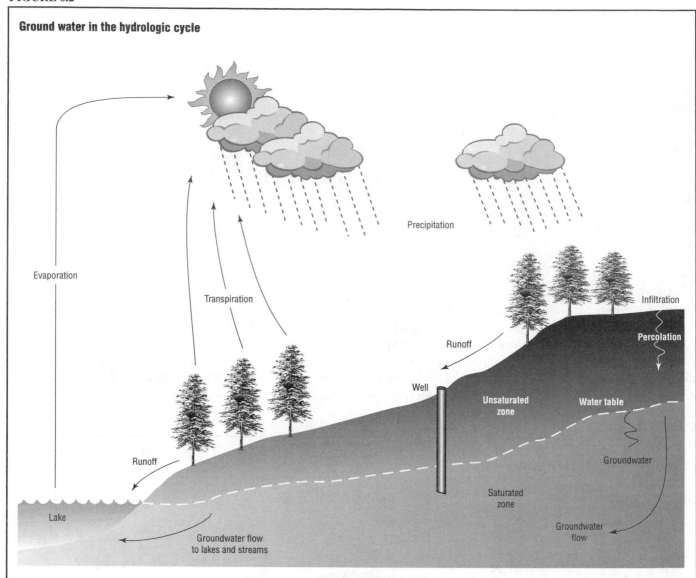

SOURCE: "Ground Water in the Hydrologic Cycle," in "Chapter 7 Section A: Assessing Risk," *Guide for Industrial Waste Management*, EPA530-C-03-002, U.S. Environmental Protection Agency, Office of Solid Waste and Emergency Response, Washington, DC, February 2003

from view, contamination is not readily obvious and can occur for many years before it is discovered. Groundwater quality is threatened by many human activities, particularly by improper storage and disposal of chemicals and wastes. Pollutants from these materials make their way into the groundwater and are very difficult to remove. Most groundwater is not stationary, but flows and moves around. This can spread contamination across large areas.

GROUNDWATER AND THE HYDROLOGIC CYCLE

Groundwater is part of the hydrologic cycle, along with surface water, as shown in Figure 6.2. Sometimes groundwater discharges into surface water, and sometimes, surface water replenishes (recharges) groundwater. Therefore, polluted groundwater can contaminate surface water and polluted surface water can contaminate ground-

water. Groundwater can become contaminated from the precipitation that recharges it as well.

Groundwater supplies are recharged by precipitation and surface waters that seep into the ground. The recharge process includes two steps: infiltration and percolation. Infiltration occurs when water is able to seep into the ground rather than running off the ground surface. Percolation occurs when the water seeps deeper into the ground. Infiltration is only possible through surface materials like soil, sand, rock, gravel, etc. These are called permeable materials, because they have spaces and voids that allow water to infiltrate. Materials like asphalt and concrete are said to be impermeable, because water runs off them.

Water that does seep underground resides in two zones: the unsaturated zone and the saturated zone. The unsaturated zone lies just beneath the surface of the land.

Here, both air and water fill the spaces between particles of soil and rock. The amount of water present depends on climate. During periods of heavy rain the unsaturated zone may temporarily become completely saturated with water. During dry periods the pockets in the unsaturated zone contain mostly air.

In most cases, the saturated zone lies within rocky formations beneath the unsaturated zone. In the saturated zone, water always fills all the voids, cracks, and other spaces within and between the rock particles. Typical types of rock found in the saturated zone include sandstone, gravel, fractured limestone, and fractured granite. These are considered permeable rocks. The water residing in the saturated zone is termed groundwater.

The topmost edge of the saturated zone is called the water table. This is where groundwater will be found when digging down from the surface. The water table is not fixed at a constant level. It moves up and down depending on how much water is present in the saturated zone. Heavy rains can cause the water table to move close to the ground surface. Droughts can cause the water table to drop to a deeper level.

Water in the unsaturated zone is at atmospheric pressure. Water in the saturated zone is under higher-than-atmospheric pressure due to geologic forces from the surrounding rock formations. That is why wells are drilled into the saturated zone. Pressure pushes water in this zone into the well shaft and up to the water table level.

An aquifer is a saturated zone that contains enough water to yield significant amounts when a well is tapped into it. Aquifers vary from a few feet thick to tens or hundreds of feet thick. They can be located just below the earth's surface or thousands of feet beneath it, and can cover a few acres or many thousands of square miles. Any one aquifer may be a part of a large system of aquifers that feed into one another.

GROUNDWATER USE

Water use in the United States is monitored and reported by the United States Geological Survey (USGS) in its *Estimated Use of Water in the United States,* published at five-year intervals since 1950. The report published in 1998 reflects data for 1995. As shown in Figure 6.3, irrigation accounted for 63 percent of all groundwater used in 1995. Another 20 percent were used for public water supplies. Minor uses include industrial, commercial and mining activities; domestic water supply; livestock watering; and generation of thermoelectric power.

Irrigation

The U.S. Department of Agriculture (USDA) tracks large-scale irrigation operations in the United States. These are irrigation projects that water at least 10,000 acres each.

FIGURE 6.3

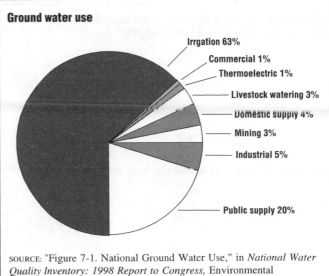

Ground water use

Irrigation 63%
Commercial 1%
Thermoelectric 1%
Livestock watering 3%
Domestic supply 4%
Mining 3%
Industrial 5%
Public supply 20%

SOURCE: "Figure 7-1. National Ground Water Use," in *National Water Quality Inventory: 1998 Report to Congress,* Environmental Protection Agency, Washington, DC, 2000

According to the USDA's 1997 *Census of Agriculture,* large-scale irrigation is concentrated in the Midwestern farm belt, southern Florida, the fertile valleys of California, and along the Mississippi River. More than 50 million acres were irrigated in 1997, primarily in western states.

Modern technological developments allow massive quantities of water to be pumped out of the ground. According to the U.S. Environmental Protection Agency (EPA), approximately 77.5 billion gallons per day of groundwater are withdrawn in the United States. When large amounts of water are removed from the ground, underground aquifers can become depleted much more quickly than they can naturally be replenished. In some areas this has led to the subsidence, or sinking, of the ground above major aquifers. Farmers in California's San Joaquin Valley began tapping the area's aquifer in the late nineteenth century. Since that time, dehydration of the aquifer has caused the soil to subside by as much as 29 feet, cracking foundations, canals, and roadways. Removal of groundwater also disturbs the natural filtering process that occurs as water travels through rocks and sand.

Public Supply

The USGS reports that in 1995 groundwater supplied drinking water for 46 percent of the nation's total population and for 99 percent of the nation's rural population.

The EPA and state health or environmental departments regulate public water supplies. Public suppliers are required to ensure that the water meets certain government-defined health standards. The Safe Drinking Water Act of 1974 (SDWA) governs this regulation. The law mandates that all public suppliers test their water on a regular basis to check for the existence of contaminants, and treat their water supplies constantly to take out or reduce

TABLE 6.1

Population served by community water systems with no reported violations of health-based standards, 1993–2002

Fiscal year	Population served by CWSs that had no reported violations	Percent of CWS-served population that was served by systems with no reported violations
2002	250,596,287	94
2001	239,927,650	91
2000	239,299,701	91
1999	229,805,285	91
1998	224,808,251	89
1997	215,351,842	87
1996	213,109,672	86
1995	208,700,100	84
1994	202,626,433	83
1993	196,229,162	79

CWS = Community water system

SOURCE: "Exhibit 2-7: Population Served by Community Water Systems with No Reported Violations of Health-Based Standards, 1993–2002," in "Chapter 2—Purer Water," *EPA's Draft Report on the Environment 2003*, U.S. Environmental Protection Agency, Washington, DC, 2003

certain pollutants to levels that will not harm human health. In 2002 about 94 percent of all people served by community water systems received water from systems that had no reported violations of the drinking water standards. (See Table 6.1.)

Private water supplies, usually wells, are not regulated under the SDWA. System owners are solely responsible for the quality of the water provided from private sources. However, many states have programs designed to help well owners protect their water supplies. Usually, these state-run programs are not regulatory but provide safety information. This type of information is vital because private wells often are shallower than those used by public suppliers. The shallower the well, the greater is the potential for contamination.

THE HISTORY OF GROUNDWATER PROTECTION

Waste was historically discarded in streets and waterways for centuries prior to the 1900s. By the 1920s, wastes were dumped into open pits or buried in containers that soon corroded. Although landfill practices are more sophisticated today and protect groundwater from pollutants, there is still some danger of chemicals leaching into the groundwater from old landfill areas. Additionally, many other practices place chemicals on the ground that can flow into surface waters or seep into groundwater. For example, cities spray icy roads with salts and chemicals. Farmers use pesticides and fertilizers to help grow their crops and feed our population.

While the threat to surface waters from these practices became evident in the 1960s, no one suspected at that time that many of these pollutants would eventually work their way into the groundwater, only to reappear in the drinking water, in the water used to raise food crops, or in fish and

shellfish. It was thought that the soil provided a barrier or protective filter that neutralized the downward migration of pollutants from the land surface and prevented the groundwater from becoming contaminated with them. The discovery of pesticides and other pollutants in groundwater, however, demonstrated that human activities do influence groundwater quality. Although the Clean Water Act of 1970 was considered the answer to many water problems, it did little to address groundwater pollution problems.

Once it became apparent in the late 1970s and early 1980s that groundwater was being contaminated, the questions of which waters were being polluted, the severity of contamination, and what should be done about it had to be addressed. Many government and private organizations are working to find the answers, but it is not an easy task. As with other types of pollution control, problems include lack of accurate data, inadequate reporting and measurement techniques, the determination of acceptable standards, illegal dumping, the designation of cleanup responsibilities, and, of course, funding.

From 1978 to 1995, the USGS assessed 25 of the most important regional aquifer systems in the United States as part of the Regional Aquifer-System Analysis (RASA) Program. After that time, Congress became concerned that efforts to evaluate these aquifers were declining, which led to a 1998 USGS report to Congress that outlined a strategy for addressing key issues about the nation's aquifers (*Strategic Directions for the U.S. Geological Survey Ground-Water Resources Program: A Report to Congress*, USGS, Washington, DC, November 1998).

The National Research Council (NRC) concurred, stating that there was little ongoing assessment of America's groundwater resources, and concluded that the regional groundwater assessment activity of the nature proposed by the USGS should be pursued (*Investigating Groundwater Systems on Regional and National Scales*, NRC, Washington, DC, 2000).

The U.S. General Accounting Office (GAO), in its 1997 report *Information on the Quality of Water Found at Community Water Systems and Private Wells*, surveyed the quality of water from 5,500 private wells in nine states. The survey measured coliform bacteria, *E. coli*, nitrate, and the herbicide atrazine. The wells that were studied ranged in age from 1 to 200 years and represented many different construction types. More than 41 percent of wells tested positive for coliform bacteria, 11.2 percent contained *E. coli* bacteria, and 13.4 percent contained nitrate levels above federal standards. Nearly 5,000 of the wells showed concentrations of atrazine above the federal standard.

Since 1991 the USGS has operated the National Water-Quality Assessment (NAWQA) program to collect water quality data at thousands of surface water sites and wells across the country. In October 2001 the agency

FIGURE 6.4

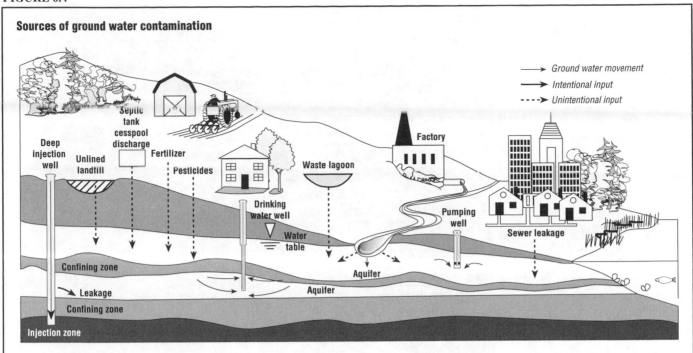

Sources of ground water contamination

SOURCE: "Figure 7-5. Sources of Ground Water Contamination," in *National Water Quality Inventory: 1998 Report to Congress,* U.S. Environmental Protection Agency, Washington, DC, 2000

reported that volatile organic compounds (VOCs) had been detected in approximately one-third of wells sampled, primarily in urban areas. VOCs are widely used in industrial manufacturing and cleaning processes. The most commonly detected VOCs were trihalomethanes, solvents, and oxygenates.

A gasoline oxygenate called methyl tertiary-butyl ether (MTBE) was detected in approximately 5 percent of the groundwater samples. Although the concentrations were generally well below EPA drinking-water advisory concentrations based on taste and odor thresholds, MTBE has been tentatively classified as a possible human carcinogen and its exact health effects are unknown. MTBE was commonly added to gasoline during the 1990s to decrease emissions of air pollutants from vehicles. Preliminary analysis by USGS and EPA of data from community water systems in 12 states showed that MTBE was detected in the groundwater sources used by nine percent of the systems. Again, concentrations were generally low.

FACTORS AFFECTING GROUNDWATER POLLUTION

The process by which groundwater becomes polluted depends on a variety of factors, such as:

• The mineral composition of the soil and rocks in the unsaturated zone. Heavy soil and organic materials lessen the potential for contamination. For example, clay is virtually impermeable. A thick layer of clay lying just beneath the ground surface can prevent percolation of contaminant-containing waters into the groundwater.

• The presence or absence of biodegrading microbes in the soil.

• The amount of rainfall. Less rainfall results in less water entering the saturated zone and, therefore, lower quantities of contaminants.

• The evapotranspiration rate. This is the rate at which water is discharged to the atmosphere via evaporation from the soil, surface water, and plants. High rates reduce the amount of contaminated water reaching the saturated zone.

• The distance between the land surface where pollution occurs and the depth of the water table. The greater the distance, the greater the chance that the pollutants will biodegrade (break down) or react with soil minerals before they reach the water table.

Groundwater can become polluted from activities occurring aboveground, within the ground above the water table, and within the ground below the water table. Figure 6.4 shows some of the types of activities that can cause groundwater contamination at each of these levels.

Typical surface activities include disposal of wastes in unlined landfills and lagoons and excessive application of fertilizers and pesticides onto the ground. Pollutants introduced at the ground surface are less likely to affect

FIGURE 6.5

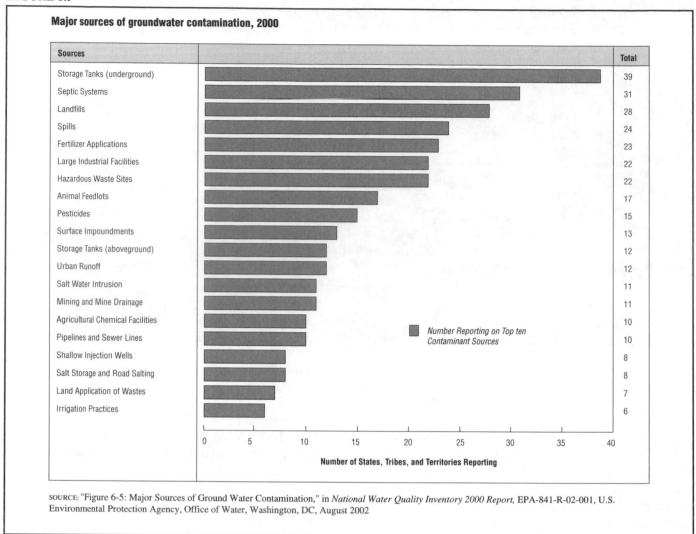

Major sources of groundwater contamination, 2000

Sources		Total
Storage Tanks (underground)		39
Septic Systems		31
Landfills		28
Spills		24
Fertilizer Applications		23
Large Industrial Facilities		22
Hazardous Waste Sites		22
Animal Feedlots		17
Pesticides		15
Surface Impoundments		13
Storage Tanks (aboveground)		12
Urban Runoff		12
Salt Water Intrusion		11
Mining and Mine Drainage		11
Agricultural Chemical Facilities		10
Pipelines and Sewer Lines		10
Shallow Injection Wells		8
Salt Storage and Road Salting		8
Land Application of Wastes		7
Irrigation Practices		6

Number Reporting on Top ten Contaminant Sources

Number of States, Tribes, and Territories Reporting

SOURCE: "Figure 6-5: Major Sources of Ground Water Contamination," in *National Water Quality Inventory 2000 Report,* EPA-841-R-02-001, U.S. Environmental Protection Agency, Office of Water, Washington, DC, August 2002

the groundwater than those pollutants introduced directly into the groundwater. This is because movement through layers of soil can filter out pollutants or give them time to decay or become diluted.

Typical activities that occur above the water table include leaks from septic tanks, underground storage tanks, and underground pipelines. Leaks from landfills, holding ponds, and lagoons also occur at this level.

Typical activities that occur below the water table include waste disposal in wells and mining and other drilling operations.

THE *NATIONAL WATER QUALITY INVENTORY: 2000 REPORT*

The EPA requires the states to assess their water quality every two years and report their findings to the agency. The EPA summarizes the findings and issues them in a national water quality inventory. In the report (*National Water Quality Inventory: 2000 Report*) published in August 2002, the EPA notes that groundwater data collection is

"still too immature to provide comprehensive national assessments." However the report does present general information and findings based on the data collected.

Figure 6.5 shows the major sources of groundwater contamination reported by state, tribal, and territorial agencies. Leaking underground storage tanks are the top potential source of pollution of groundwater, followed by septic systems and landfills.

In its report, the EPA identified four broad categories as the most important potential sources of groundwater contamination:

- Fuel Storage Practices
- Waste Disposal Practices
- Agricultural Practices
- Industrial Practices

Fuel Storage Practices

Improper storage of liquid fuels is a major source of groundwater contamination. In the United States liquid fuels are stored in aboveground and underground storage tanks. Underground storage tanks pose a particular risk to groundwater, because they are not readily accessible for inspection and maintenance. Leaks can go undetected for long periods of time.

LEAKING UNDERGROUND STORAGE TANKS. Leaking underground storage tanks (USTs) were the most frequently cited source of groundwater contamination in the *National Water Quality Inventory: 2000 Report*. Figure 6.6 shows a typical profile of a UST leaking gasoline. The liquid fraction forms a plume of contamination at the water table that is carried along by the groundwater flow. The soils above this level are contaminated with vapors from the plume. The saturated zone is contaminated with dissolved gasoline.

In 2003 the EPA estimated that there are in the United States approximately 700,000 USTs storing petroleum products or hazardous substances. The federal government classifies a storage tank system as a UST if at least 10 percent of its total volume lies underground. Thus an aboveground storage tank with extensive underground piping can be considered a UST under this definition.

The EPA's *RCRA Orientation Manual* reports that roughly 97 percent of the country's USTs contain petroleum products, such as gasoline, diesel fuel, crude oil, and heating oil. The vast majority of these USTs are located at retail establishments (mainly gas stations) and petroleum refining facilities. Less than 3 percent of all USTs contain hazardous chemicals.

In 1984 Congress amended the Resource Conservation and Recovery Act (RCRA) to deal with the construction, installation, and monitoring of underground tanks. In 1986 Congress established the Leaking Underground Storage Tank (LUST) program to enforce cleanups. It established a trust fund, derived primarily from a 0.1 cent-per-gallon motor fuel tax from 1987 to 1995, which generated approximately $150 million per year, and was reinstated in the Taxpayer Relief Act of 1997, effective through March 2005.

In 1988 the EPA issued new rules requiring installation of devices to detect leaks, modification of tanks to prevent corrosion, regular monitoring, and immediate cleanup of leaks and spills. Older tanks had to be upgraded, replaced, or closed by December 22, 1998. Many small UST owner/operators, "Mom and Pop" gasoline stations, could not afford the cost of replacements and the liability insurance for storage tanks, resulting in the closing of many smaller, independently-owned operations.

Currently, owners of USTs must determine at least every 30 days whether their USTs and piping are leaking by using proper release detection methods. Figure 6.7 shows an example of a tank with proper monitoring systems. Leaking petroleum products release vapors. The purpose of the vapor

FIGURE 6.6

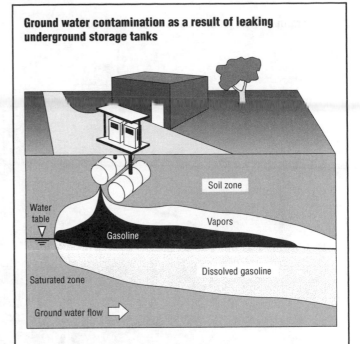

Ground water contamination as a result of leaking underground storage tanks

SOURCE: "Figure 7-7. Ground Water Contamination as a Result of Leaking Underground Storage Tanks," in *National Water Quality Inventory: 1998 Report to Congress*, U.S. Environmental Protection Agency, Washington, DC, 2000

monitoring well is to allow sampling of any vapors in the soil around the UST. Monitoring is also performed to detect leaks in the space between the UST and a second barrier. This is called interstitial monitoring. The groundwater monitoring well is used to check the water table near the UST for the presence of leaked petroleum.

The EPA reports that more than 418,000 confirmed UST releases occurred between 1984 and 2001. Approximately 6,500 releases were reported between September 2000 and September 2001. The agency estimates that approximately 60 percent of these releases have negatively affected the underlying groundwater. Most of the releases were blamed on corrosion of tank materials, faulty installation, spills, and overfills.

Waste Disposal Practices

The EPA's *National Water Quality Inventory: 2000 Report* identified several waste disposal practices and systems associated with groundwater contamination. Four types of disposal systems were among the top 10 causes of contamination: septic tanks, landfills, hazardous waste sites, and surface impoundments.

SEPTIC TANK SYSTEMS. Septic tank systems are backyard underground systems for handling sewage and other wastewaters from houses and small businesses. A septic tank system includes a large concrete or steel tank that discharges water through long perforated pipes into a drain field. Solids are held in the tank and are reduced

FIGURE 6.7

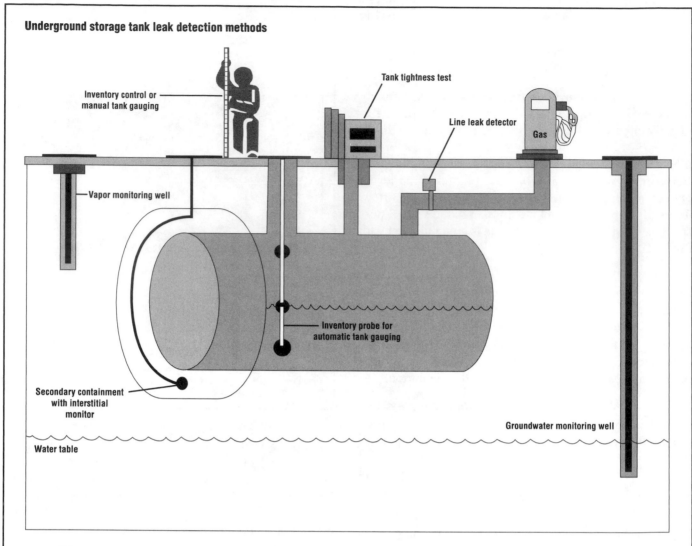

Underground storage tank leak detection methods

Inventory control or manual tank gauging

Tank tightness test

Line leak detector

Gas

Vapor monitoring well

Inventory probe for automatic tank gauging

Secondary containment with interstitial monitor

Groundwater monitoring well

Water table

SOURCE: "Underground Storage Tank leak detection methods," in *Operating and Maintaining Underground Storage Tank Systems: Practical Help and Checklists*, U.S. Environmental Protection Agency, Washington, DC, 2000

somewhat by ongoing organic degradation. Over time, the solids can build up so much in the tank that they must be pumped out. Wastewaters released into the soil are naturally degraded over time.

Septic systems that are poorly constructed, improperly used or maintained, or abandoned can allow groundwater contamination to occur. Typical contaminants from septic systems include bacteria, viruses, nitrates from human waste, phosphates from detergents, and chemicals from household cleaners.

The 1990 national census indicated that 24.7 million housing units in the United States used septic tanks. This represented 24 percent of all housing units in the country at the time. Septic tank systems are most common in rural areas and small communities where they are a leading cause of groundwater contaminated with pathogens and nitrates.

LANDFILLS. Landfills are areas where waste materials are placed into and onto the land. Different kinds of land-

fills receive different kinds of waste. Thousands of landfills in the United States handle municipal solid waste (MSW). As shown in Figure 6.8, landfilling has historically been the most common disposal method for MSW. Some landfills are specially designed to receive industrial hazardous and/or nonhazardous wastes.

Materials that are commonly discarded in landfills include plastics, metals, sludge, low-level radioactive waste, wood, brick, cellulose (plant matter), petroleum compounds, ceramics, synthetics, polypropylene, and ash. In the past, landfills were generally located on land considered to have no other use—abandoned sand and gravel pits, old strip mines, marshlands, and sinkholes. In many instances, the water table was at or very near the surface, and the potential for groundwater contamination was high.

Early environmental regulation aimed at reducing air and surface-water pollution called for disposing of solid wastes underground. Many of the disposal sites were nothing more than large holes in the ground, and chemicals and bacteria seeped through the earth into underground aquifers. The leachate (the liquid that percolates through the waste materials) from landfills contains contaminants that can easily pollute groundwater. Modern landfills have liner systems and other safeguards to prevent groundwater contamination. (See Figure 6.9.)

Although regulations have changed dramatically, past practices continue to cause a threat to groundwater. Some studies estimate that 75 percent of all active and inactive landfill sites are leaking contaminants into the groundwater.

HAZARDOUS WASTE SITES. Some materials that have been regularly deposited in landfills for many years are now known to be hazardous to human health. The majority of those sites considered dangerous contain industrial chemical wastes. Some are municipal dumps, where high concentrations of pesticides and hazardous household cleaning solvents are present. In many areas, the extent of the problem is only now becoming apparent. In remote areas, for example, dumping was often permitted. Today, as new suburban communities spread out from the cities, these sites have become serious contamination problems since people now live so close by.

FIGURE 6.8

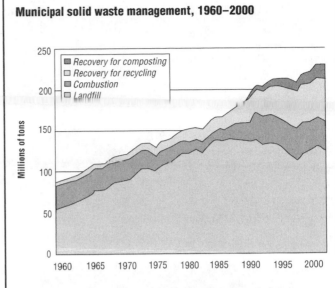

Municipal solid waste management, 1960–2000

*Composting of yard trimmings and food wastes. Does not include mixed municipal solid waste composting or backyard composting.

SOURCE: "Exhibit 3-9: Municipal Solid Waste Management, 1960–2000," "in "Chapter 3—Better Protected Land," *EPA's Draft Report on the Environment 2003,* U.S. Environmental Protection Agency, Washington, DC, 2003

FIGURE 6.9

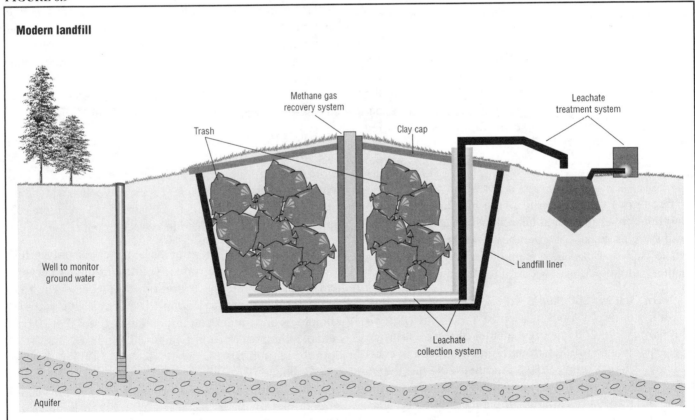

Modern landfill

SOURCE: "Modern Landfill," in *Landfilling,* U.S. Department of Energy, Energy Information Administration, Washington, DC, 2003 [Online] http://www.eia.doe.gov/kids/recycling/solidwaste/landfiller.html [accessed September 30, 2003]

FIGURE 6.10

Contaminated ground water migration at identified hazardous waste sites, 2002–03

a. Contaminated ground water migration under control at Superfund National Priorities List (NPL) hazardous waste sites

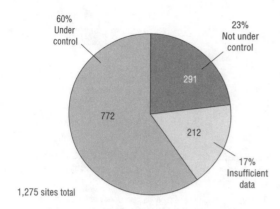

60% Under control

23% Not under control

291

772

212

17% Insufficient data

1,275 sites total

b. Contaminated ground water migration under control at Resource Conservation and Recovery Act (RCRA) Corrective Action hazardous waste sites

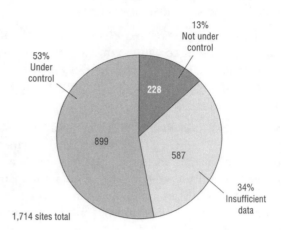

13% Not under control

53% Under control

228

899

587

34% Insufficient data

1,714 sites total

SOURCE: "Exhibit 3-12: Contaminated Ground Water Migration Under Control at Identified Hazardous Waste Sites," in "Chapter 3—Better Protected Land," *EPA's Draft Report on the Environment 2003*, U.S. Environmental Protection Agency, Washington, DC, 2003

When a site is found to be so badly contaminated with hazardous waste that it represents a serious threat to human health (for example, contamination of groundwater used for drinking), it is placed on the National Priorities List, commonly known as "Superfund," making it eligible for federal intervention and cleanup assistance.

The EPA reported in 1995 that approximately 73 million people lived fewer than four miles from at least one Superfund site, and much debate has occurred about the extent to which these sites pose health risks to those residents. The EPA found that one-third of the sites studied posed serious health risks to nearby residents, primarily through groundwater (*Superfund—Information on Current Health Risks*, 1995).

Groundwater monitoring is the primary method of detecting contamination at hazardous waste sites. Monitoring systems consist of a number of wells placed around a waste facility. Data taken from those wells can indicate whether contamination is occurring at the site.

As of October 2002 there were 1,275 Superfund sites. According to the EPA publication *EPA's Draft Report on the Environment: 2003* nearly a quarter of these sites were experiencing uncontrolled groundwater migration of contaminants. (See Figure 6.10.) Another 228 hazardous waste sites (13 percent) under the RCRA Corrective Action program were experiencing uncontrolled groundwater migration of contaminants.

SURFACE IMPOUNDMENTS. Surface impoundments are pits, lagoons, and ponds that receive treated or untreated wastes directly from a discharge point or are used to store chemicals for later use, to wash or treat ores, or to treat water for further use.

In March 2001 the EPA published the study *Industrial Surface Impoundments in the United States* describing the nature and variety of industrial surface impoundments and the wastewaters they manage. Data for the study were collected between 1996 and 2000. The study estimates that approximately 18,000 industrial surface impoundments are in use at 7,500 facilities around the country. Most are located east of the Mississippi River and in Pacific Coast states.

The EPA found that surface impoundments vary in size from less than one-third acre to hundreds of acres. More than half of all impoundments are used by facilities within the chemical, concrete, paper, and petroleum industries. The paper industry is responsible for the largest volume of wastewater managed in surface impoundments.

Most of the impoundments are located only a few meters above the water table, yet do not have liner systems to prevent releases to soil or groundwater. The EPA estimates that more than 20 million people live within 2 kilometers of an industrial impoundment, and that 10 percent of all impoundments are located within 150 meters of domestic drinking water wells. Nearly 2,000 of the surface impoundments were found to have the potential to generate contaminated groundwater plumes that could extend for 150 meters or more beyond their boundaries. Another 4,000 impoundments could not be adequately assessed due to incomplete data.

The EPA design standards for surface impoundments are illustrated in Figure 6.11. The system includes a

FIGURE 6.11

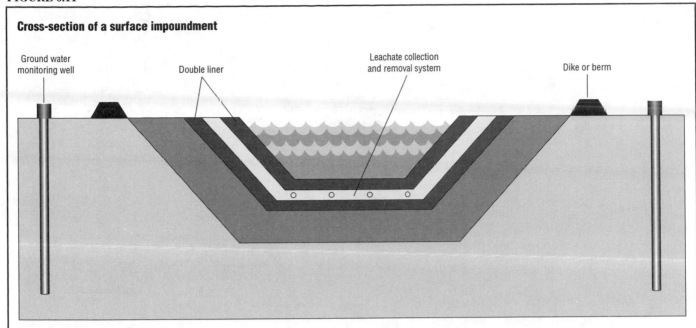

Cross-section of a surface impoundment

Ground water monitoring well

Double liner

Leachate collection and removal system

Dike or berm

SOURCE: "Figure III-12: Cross-Section of a Surface Impoundment," in *RCRA Orientation Manual*, EPA530-R-02-016, U.S. Environmental Protection Agency, Office of Solid Waste and Emergency Response, Washington, DC, January 2003

double liner with a leachate collection and removal system between the two liners. Leachate is pumped back into the surface impoundment. Monitoring wells surrounding the impoundment ensure that any leaks through the second liner will be detected.

Agricultural Practices

The EPA's *National Water Quality Inventory: 2000 Report* identified five agricultural practices that are associated with groundwater contamination. Excessive use of fertilizers and pesticides and discharges from animal feedlots were among the top 10 major sources of contamination.

FERTILIZERS. Fertilizers are substances that are spread on or through the soil to enrich it with nutrients for plant growth. Fertilizers include manure and synthetic chemical mixtures. Figure 5.3 shows that in the United States the use of fertilizers containing nitrogen, phosphorus, and potash tripled between 1961 and 1981.

Nitrogen is essential for plant photosynthesis and the chemical of most concern in fertilizers. It occurs in a variety of chemical forms as part of the nitrogen cycle. (See Figure 6.12). Nitrogen combines with oxygen to form nitrate (NO_3). Nitrate is readily taken up by plant roots. However, nitrate is also extremely mobile in water. Excessive application of fertilizer to crops or spills of liquid and solid fertilizers can lead to excess levels of nitrate in the soil that easily migrate to the groundwater table.

HERBICIDES. Herbicides are chemicals used to kill weeds. In *Distribution of Major Herbicides in Ground Water of the United States* (1999), the USGS reported on a study it conducted in the early to mid-1990s in which it measured the presence of seven herbicides in groundwater samples throughout the United States. The herbicides studied included seven high-use herbicides: atrazine, alachlor, cyanazine, simazine, prometon, acetochlor, and metolachlor. Figure 6.13 shows the use in pounds per year of the seven agricultural herbicides from 1964 to 1994. Six of these chemicals (all except acetochlor) were found in samples taken from shallow groundwater, which had been recharged within the past 10 years. Samples found atrazine, metolachlor, prometon, and simazine most frequently, with atrazine the most commonly reported chemical, especially in agricultural areas. (See Figure 6.14.)

However, results of the study revealed that more than 98 percent of the samples had concentrations of less than one microgram per liter of each herbicide. These data confirmed that fewer than 0.1 percent of the sites did not meet the standards necessary for safe drinking water; most did meet the standards. Although these results show that most aquifers were not contaminated with troublesome levels of herbicides, the USGS pointed out that the conclusions of the report do not fully reflect the overall health risks of herbicide use because data were collected on only seven herbicides. Additionally, the USGS noted that they did not know what the additive effects of mixtures of these chemicals were on human and aquatic health.

PESTICIDES. A pesticide is a chemical used to kill insects or other pests (such as fungi) harmful to cultivated plants. The ancient Greeks were the first documented users

FIGURE 6.12

The nitrogen cycle

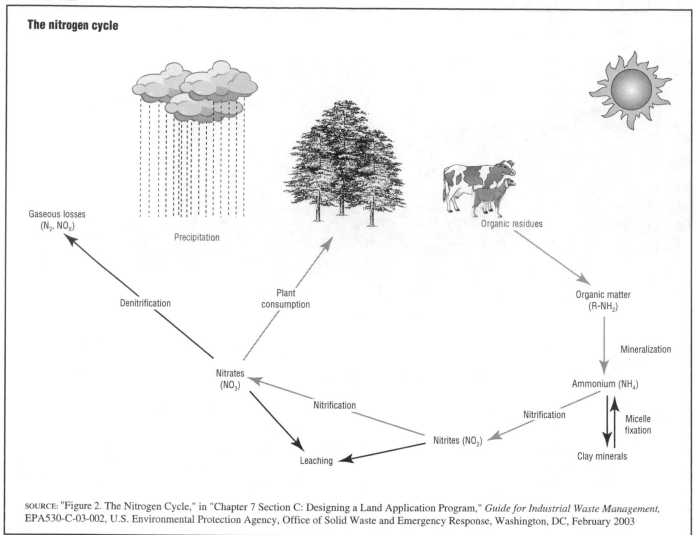

SOURCE: "Figure 2. The Nitrogen Cycle," in "Chapter 7 Section C: Designing a Land Application Program," *Guide for Industrial Waste Management*, EPA530-C-03-002, U.S. Environmental Protection Agency, Office of Solid Waste and Emergency Response, Washington, DC, February 2003

of pesticides. Pliny the Elder (C.E. 23–79) reported using common compounds such as arsenic, sulfur, caustic soda, and olive oil to protect crops. The Chinese later used similar substances to repel insects and retard the growth of fungi on plants. Such inorganic (non-carbon-based) pesticides were used until the 1900s. They were then banned because they persist in the environment for long periods, and they harm or kill many forms of life, including humans.

The invention of dichloro-diphenyl-trichloroethane (DDT), a powerful organic (carbon-based) insecticide, in 1939 marked a revolution in the war against pests. DDT was effective, relatively inexpensive, and apparently safe—a miracle chemical that promised a world without insects and with unprecedented crop yields. In 1948 Swiss researcher Paul Mueller received a Nobel Prize for its discovery. Convinced that chemicals were the modern wave of the future, farmers began using pesticides intensively and began to accept chemicals as essential to agriculture.

The use of organic pesticides came with problems, however. Like inorganic pesticides, they harmed or killed many forms of life and persisted in the environment.

Often, insects became immune to their effects. In 1947 Congress passed the Federal Insecticide, Fungicide, and Rodenticide Act (FIFRA), which requires all pesticides sold or distributed in the United States (including imported pesticides) to be registered by the EPA. Even if manufacture and use in the United States is permitted, each pesticide must be re-registered every five years and may be banned if information has emerged that it is exceptionally harmful. Many pesticides have been banned in the United States.

In 1972 the EPA banned all use of DDT in the United States. The ban was based on scientific research showing that DDT was harmful to birds and other wildlife and a possible carcinogen (cancer-causing agent) in humans. Scientists found that DDT was extremely persistent in the environment. A chemical is considered persistent if it is not easily and quickly broken down into less harmful forms. According to the EPA, the degradation of DDT in soil can take decades. DDT is also very mobile. It transfers easily from soil to air or water and can be carried far from its original source.

FIGURE 6.13

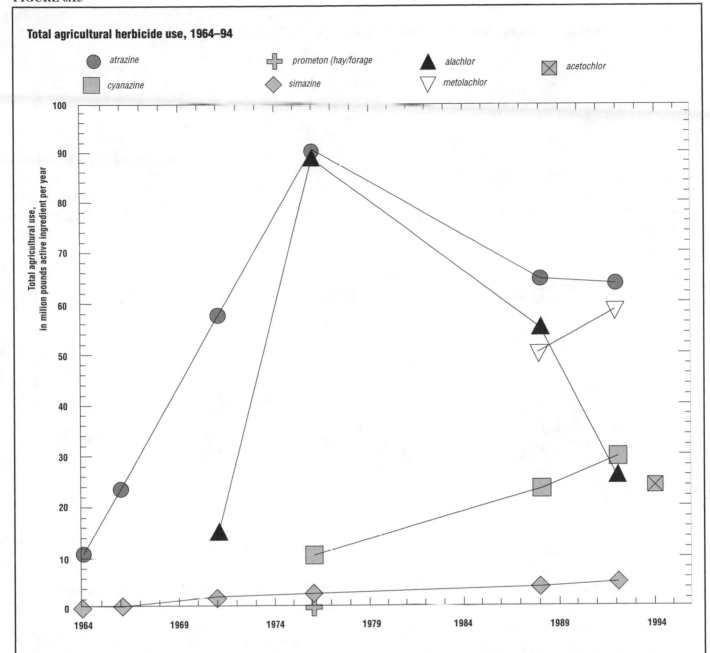

Total agricultural herbicide use, 1964–94

- atrazine
- cyanazine
- prometon (hay/forage
- simazine
- alachlor
- metolachlor
- acetochlor

Note: Total nationwide agricultural use of the seven herbicides of interest from 1964 to 1994. Use of prometon for hay and forage in 1976 was 20,000 pounds active ingredient per year.

SOURCE: Jack E. Barbash et al., *Distribution of Major Herbicides in Ground Water of the United States,* U.S. Geological Survey, prepared in cooperation with the U.S. Environmental Protection Agency, Sacramento, CA, 1999

Two by-products of DDT breakdown are toxic and persistent chemicals known as DDE and DDD. All three chemicals are bioaccumulative. They accumulate in living tissues. This allows them to work their way up the food chain—from water and soils to plants, fish, and birds and ultimately to animals and people.

Today, farmers apply about 1.1 billion pounds of pesticides per year to their crops. Seventy-five percent of pesticide use is in industrialized countries. In the United States, pesticide use in agriculture has approximately tripled since 1965.

In recent years, improved safety testing has prompted tougher standards for a new generation of pesticides. The best of the new pesticides can be used in minute quantities and cause few health problems. They are, however, more expensive than older types of pesticides. Many farmers continue to use the older pesticides, especially in developing countries. DDT is now banned in most industrialized

FIGURE 6.14

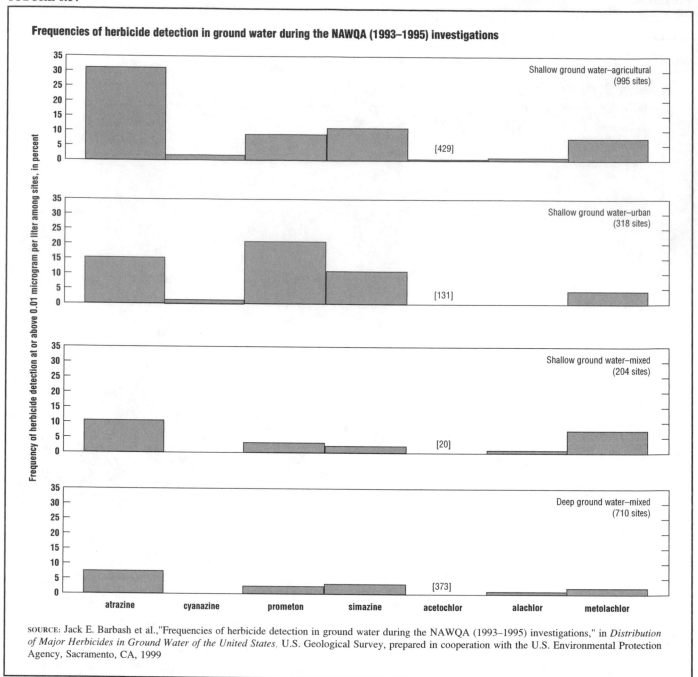

Frequencies of herbicide detection in ground water during the NAWQA (1993–1995) investigations

SOURCE: Jack E. Barbash et al.,"Frequencies of herbicide detection in ground water during the NAWQA (1993–1995) investigations," in *Distribution of Major Herbicides in Ground Water of the United States*, U.S. Geological Survey, prepared in cooperation with the U.S. Environmental Protection Agency, Sacramento, CA, 1999

countries, but it is still used in developing nations, where many farmers see it as an inexpensive way to control pests. Nonetheless, even the new formulations are not entirely safe, especially for wildlife.

As an alternative to pesticide use and abuse, many scientists and the federal government encourage the practice of Integrated Pest Management (IPM). This method combines biological controls (such as natural predators of pests), certain agricultural practices (such as planting rotation and diversification), and genetic manipulation (such as the use of pest-resistant crop varieties) with a modest use of chemicals. Rather than attempting the impossible task of eliminating pests, the goal is to strike a

sustainable, profitable balance with nature. IPM is becoming increasingly common in the United States and in many parts of the world.

ANIMAL FEEDLOTS. Animal feedlots are a product of modern agriculture. These are confined areas (pens, lots, barns, or other structures) in which large numbers of farm animals are concentrated for production purposes. So-called "factory farming" relies on feedlots to produce meat and related products in a highly efficient and cost-effective manner.

Because feedlots can contain hundreds or even thousands of animals in a confined space, they produce incredibly

TABLE 6.2

Federal laws administered by EPA affecting ground water

Clean Water Act (CWA)
Ground water protection is addressed in Section 102 of the CWA, providing for the development of federal, state, and local comprehensive programs for reducing, eliminating, and preventing ground water contamination.

Safe Drinking Water Act (SDWA)
Under the SDWA, EPA is authorized to ensure that water is safe for human consumption. To support this effort, SDWA gives EPA the authority to promulgate Maximum Contaminant Levels (MCLs) that define safe levels for some contaminants in public drinking water supplies. One of the most fundamental ways to ensure consistently safe drinking water is to protect the source of that water (i.e., ground water). Source water protection is achieved through four programs: the Wellhead Protection Program (WHP), the Sole Source Aquifer Program, the Underground Injection Control (UIC) Program, and, under the 1996 Amendments, the Source Water Assessment Program.

Resource Conservation and Recovery Act (RCRA)
The intent of RCRA is to protect human health and the environment by establishing a comprehensive regulatory framework for investigating and addressing past, present, and future environmental contamination or ground water and other environmental media. In addition, management of underground storage tanks is also addressed under RCRA.

Comprehensive Environmental, Response, Compensation, and Liability Act (CERCLA)
CERCLA provides a federal "Superfund" to clean-up soil and ground water contaminated by uncontrolled or abandoned hazardous waste sites as well as accidents, spill, and other emergency releases of pollutants and contaminants into the environment. Through the Act, EPA was given power to seek out those parties responsible for any release and assure their cooperation in the clean-up. The program is designed to recover costs, when possible, from financially viable individuals and companies when the clean-up is complete.

Federal Insecticide, Fungicide, and Rodenticide Act (FIFRA)
FIFRA protects human health and the environment from the risks of pesticide use by requiring the testing and registration of all chemicals used as active ingredients of pesticides and pesticide products. Under the Pesticide Management Program, states and tribes wishing to continue use of chemicals of concern are required to prepare a prevention plan that targets specific areas vulnerable to ground water contamination.

SOURCE: "Federal Laws Administered by EPA Affecting Ground Water," in *Safe Drinking Water Act, Section 1429 Ground Water Report to Congress*, U.S. Environmental Protection Agency, Office of Water, Washington, DC, 1999

huge amounts of manure and droppings. The government refers to feedlots as "animal feeding operations," or AFOs. There are many different kinds of AFOs. Concentrated animal feeding operations, or CAFOs, are AFOs that must obtain special permits because they use waste disposal methods that can impact local water sources.

The environmental organization the Sierra Club claims that AFOs produce 2.7 trillion pounds of waste each year. This waste is typically collected and stored in open lagoons or concrete cisterns. Rainfall runoff and leachate can contaminate the underlying groundwater with harmful pathogens, like bacteria, and hormones and antibiotics commonly fed to livestock.

Industrial Practices

The EPA's *National Water Quality Inventory: 2000 Report* identified large industrial facilities and spills as two of the top ten causes of groundwater contamination. Large industrial facilities often transport, handle, and store large quantities of chemicals. Improper handling and storage methods can lead to spills that endanger groundwater quality.

GROUNDWATER LEGISLATION

The States' Role

Since the 1980s, the individual states have conducted extensive activities to protect groundwater. Studies by the National Conference of State Legislatures indicated that all 50 states have enacted legislation with groundwater management provisions since that time. Additionally, under the Clean Water Act, the EPA has provided a total of nearly $80 million since 1987 to the states to develop statewide groundwater strategies. These programs are called Comprehensive State Groundwater Protection Programs (CSGW-PPs) and consist of a set of six strategic activities. The goal of these activities is to foster the protection of groundwater through a coordinated operation of all relevant federal, state, and local programs within a state.

The Federal Role

Many federal laws administered by the EPA help protect groundwater. Table 6.2 lists most of these laws and describes each. Additional laws include those described below.

The Superfund Amendments and Reauthorization Act of 1986 (SARA) amended CERCLA, the Comprehensive Environmental, Response, Compensation, and Liability Act. SARA made additions and changes to CERCLA based on the EPA's experience in administering the complex Superfund program during its first six years. SARA also required the cleanup of hazardous wastes that can seep into the groundwater. SARA included a provision that cities and industry build better-managed and better-constructed landfills for hazardous materials so that the groundwater will not be polluted in the future.

The Toxic Substances Control Act (TSCA) of 1976 was enacted by Congress to give the EPA the ability to track the 75,000 industrial chemicals currently produced or imported into the United States, including those with a potential to contaminate groundwater.

In August 1993 the Oil Pollution Act of 1990 went into effect. The law, which was passed in response to the 1989 *Exxon Valdez* oil spill in Alaska, requires companies involved in storing and transporting petroleum to have standby plans for cleaning up spills on land or in water. A result of the law has been a resurgence of interest in and a new market for innovative methods for oil-spill cleanup.

CHAPTER 7
HAZARDOUS WASTE

WHAT IS HAZARDOUS WASTE?

Hazardous waste is dangerous solid waste. The U.S. government's definition of solid waste includes materials we would ordinarily consider "solid," as well as sludges, semi-solids, liquids, and even containers of gases. The vast majority of hazardous waste is generated by industrial sources. Small amounts come from commercial and residential sources.

Officially hazardous waste is defined as a waste that is either listed as such in the U.S. Environmental Protection Agency (EPA) regulations or exhibits one or more of the following characteristics: ignitability, corrosivity, reactivity, or contains toxic constituents in excess of federal standards. (See Figure 7.1.) In 2003 the EPA had a list of more than 500 hazardous wastes.

Because of its dangerous characteristics, hazardous waste requires special care when being stored, transported, or discarded. Hazardous wastes are regulated under Subtitle C of the Resource Conservation and Recovery Act (RCRA). The EPA has the primary responsibility for permitting facilities that treat, store, and dispose of hazardous waste. The states can adopt more stringent regulations if they wish.

Contamination of the air, water, and soil with hazardous waste can frequently lead to serious health problems. Exposure to some hazardous wastes is believed to cause cancer, degenerative diseases, mental retardation, birth defects, and chromosomal changes. While most scientists agree that exposure to high doses of hazardous waste is dangerous, there is less agreement on the danger of exposure to low doses.

INDUSTRIAL HAZARDOUS WASTE

Industrial hazardous wastes are usually a combination of compounds, one or more of which may be hazardous. For example, used pickling solution from a metal processor may contain acid, a hazardous waste, along with water and other nonhazardous compounds. (Pickling is a chemical method of cleaning metal and removing rust during processing.) A mixture of wastes produced regularly as a result of industrial

processes generally consists of diluted rather than full-strength compounds. Often the hazardous components are suspended or dissolved in a mixture of dirt, oil, or water.

Every two years the EPA, in partnership with the states, publishes *The National Biennial RCRA Hazardous Waste Report*. The latest report available was published in 2003 and includes data from 2001.

FIGURE 7.1

Types of hazardous waste

- Corrosive — A corrosive material can wear away (corrode) or destroy a substance. For example, most acids are corrosives that can eat through metal, burn skin on contact, and give off vapors that burn the eyes.

- Ignitable — An ignitable material can burst into flames easily. It poses a fire hazard; can irritate the skin, eyes, and lungs; and may give off harmful vapors. Gasoline, paint, and furniture polish are ignitable.

- Reactive — A reactive material can explode or create poisonous gas when combined with other chemicals. For example, chlorine bleach and ammonia are reactive and create a poisonous gas when they come into contact with each other.

- Toxic — Toxic materials or substances can poison people and other life. Toxic substances can cause illness and even death if swallowed or absorbed through the skin. Pesticides, weed killers, and many household cleaners are toxic.

SOURCE: "What kinds of hazardous waste are there?" in *Fast Flash 1: Hazardous Substances and Hazardous Waste*, U.S. Environmental Protection Agency, Washington, DC [Online] http://www.epa.gov/superfund/students/clas_act/haz-cd/ff_01.htm [accessed November 6, 2003]

TABLE 7.1

Typical hazardous waste generated by small businesses

Type of business	How generated	Typical wastes	Waste codes
Drycleaning and laundry plants	Commercial drycleaning processes	Still residues from solvent distillation, spent filter cartridges, cooked powder residue, spent solvents, unused perchloroethylene	D001, D039, F002, F005, U210
Furniture/wood manufacturing and refinishing	Wood cleaning and wax removal, refinishing/stripping, staining, painting, finishing, brush cleaning and spray brush cleaning	Ignitable wastes, toxic wastes, solvent wastes, paint wastes	D001, F001-F005
Construction	Paint preparation and painting, carpentry and floor work, other specialty contracting activities, heavy construction, wrecking and demolition, vehicle and equipment maintenance for construction activities	Ignitable wastes, toxic wastes, solvent wastes, paint wastes, used oil, acids/bases	D001, D002, F001-F005
Laboratories	Diagnostic and other laboratory testing	Spent solvents, unused reagents, reaction products, testing samples, contaminated materials	D001, D002, D003, F001-F005, U211
Vehicle maintenance	Degreasing, rust removal, paint preparation, spray booth, spray guns, brush cleaning, paint removal, tank cleanout, installing lead-acid batteries, oil and fluid replacement	Acids/bases, solvents, ignitable wastes, toxic wastes, paint wastes, batteries, used oil, unused cleaning chemicals	D001, D002, D006, D007, D008, D035, F001-F005, U002, U080, U134, U154, U159, U161, U220, U228, U239
Printing and allied industries	Plate preparation, stencil preparation for screen printing, photoprocessing, printing, cleanup	Acids/bases, heavy metal wastes, solvents, toxic wastes, ink, unused chemicals	D002, D006, D008, D011, D019, D035, D039, D040, D043, F001-F005, U002, U019, U043, U055, U056, U069, U080, U112, U122, U154, U159, U161, U210, U211, U220, U223, U226, U228, U239, U259, U359
Equipment repair	Degreasing, equipment cleaning, rust removal, paint preparation, painting, paint removal, spray booth, spray guns, and brush cleaning.	Acids/bases, toxic wastes, ignitable wastes, paint wastes, solvents	D001, D002, D006, D008, F001-F005
Pesticide end-users/application services	Pesticide application and cleanup	Used/unused pesticides, solvent wastes, ignitable wastes, contaminated soil (from spills), contaminated rinsewater, empty containers	D001, F001-F005, U129, U136, P094, P123
Educational and vocational shops	Automobile engine and body repair, metalworking, graphic arts-plate preparation, woodworking	Ignitable wastes, solvent wastes, acids/bases, paint wastes	D001, D002, F001-F005
Photo processing	Processing and developing negatives/prints, stabilization system cleaning	Acid regenerants, cleaners, ignitable wastes, silver	D001, D002, D007, D011
Leather manufacturing	Hair removal, bating, soaking, tanning, buffing, and dyeing	Acids/bases, ignitables wastes, toxic wastes, solvent wastes, unused chemicals	D001, D002, D003, D007, D035, F001-F005, U159, U228, U220

SOURCE: "Typical Hazardous Waste Generated by Small Businesses," in *Managing Your Hazardous Waste, A Guide for Small Businesses,* EPA530-K-01-005, U.S. Environmental Protection Agency, Office of Solid Waste and Emergency Response, Washington, DC, December 2001

The EPA distinguishes between large-quantity generators and small-quantity generators of hazardous waste. A large-quantity generator is one that:

- generates at least 1,000 kilograms (2,200 pounds) of RCRA hazardous waste in any single month,

- generates in any single month or accumulates at any time at least 1 kilogram (2.2 pounds) of RCRA acute hazardous waste, or

- generates or accumulates at any time at least 100 kilograms (220 pounds) of spill cleanup material contaminated with RCRA acute hazardous waste.

In 2001 there were 18,135 large-quantity generators and 889 small-quantity generators. Together they generated 40.8 million tons of RCRA hazardous waste. The five states with the largest generation of hazardous waste were Texas (7.6 million tons), Louisiana (3.9 million tons), New York (3.5 million tons), Kentucky (2.7 million tons), and Mississippi (2.2 million tons). Together, these states accounted for 49 percent of the total quantity generated.

The chemical industry was by far the largest producer, responsible for 15.5 million tons of hazardous waste or 38 percent of the total. Petroleum and coal products manufacturers were responsible for 6.2 million tons (15 percent of the total), followed by the waste treatment and disposal industry with 2.5 million tons (6 percent of the total).

HAZARDOUS WASTE FROM SMALL BUSINESSES AND HOUSEHOLDS

A small percentage of hazardous waste comes from thousands of small-quantity generators—businesses that

FIGURE 7.2

Waste management hierarchy

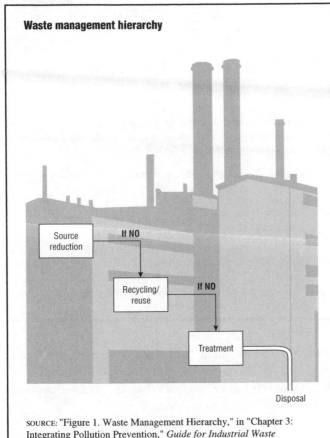

SOURCE: "Figure 1. Waste Management Hierarchy," in "Chapter 3: Integrating Pollution Prevention," *Guide for Industrial Waste Management*, EPA530-C-03-002, U.S. Environmental Protection Agency, Office of Solid Waste and Emergency Response, Washington, DC, February 2003

TABLE 7.2

Common household waste products

Cleaning products
- Oven cleaners
- Drain cleaners
- Wood and metal
  cleaners and polishes
- Toilet cleaners
- Tub, tile, shower cleaners
- Bleach (laundry)
- Pool chemicals

Automotive products
- Motor oil
- Fuel additives
- Carburetor and fuel
  injection cleaners
- Air conditioning refrigerants
- Starter fluids
- Automotive batteries
- Transmission and brake fluid
- Antifreeze

Lawn and garden products
- Herbicides
- Insecticides
- Fungicides/wood preservatives

Other flammable products
- Propane tanks and other
  compressed gas cylinders
- Kerosene
- Home heating oil
- Diesel fuel
- Gas/oil mix
- Lighter fluid

Indoor pesticides
- Ant sprays and baits
- Cockroach sprays and baits
- Flea repellents and shampoos
- Bug sprays
- Houseplant insecticides
- Moth repellents
- Mouse and rat poisons
  and baits

Workshop/painting supplies
- Adhesives and glues
- Furniture strippers
- Oil or enamel based paint
- Stains and finishes
- Paint thinners and turpentine
- Paint strippers and removers
- Photographic chemicals
- Fixatives and other solvents

Miscellaneous
- Batteries
- Mercury thermostats or
  thermometers
- Fluorescent light bulbs
- Driveway sealer

SOURCE: "List of Common HHW Products," in *Municipal Solid Waste*, U.S. Environmental Protection Agency, Office of Solid Waste and Emergency Response, Washington, DC, October 29, 2002 [Online] http://www.epa.gov/epaoswer/non-hw/muncpl/hhw-list.htm [accessed September 30, 2003]

produce less than 1,000 kilograms of hazardous waste per month. Table 7.1 shows a list of typical small-quantity generators and the types of hazardous waste they produce. Hazardous wastes from small-quantity generators and households are regulated under Subtitle D of RCRA.

Household hazardous waste (HHW) includes solvents, paints, cleaners, stains, varnishes, pesticides, motor oil, and car batteries. (See Table 7.2.) The EPA reports that Americans generate 1.6 million tons of household hazardous waste every year. The average home can have as much as 100 pounds of these wastes in basements, garages, and storage buildings. Because of the relatively low amount of hazardous substances in individual products, HHW is not regulated as a hazardous waste. Since the 1980s many communities have held special collection days for household hazardous waste to ensure that it is disposed of properly. More than 3,000 such programs have been held in the United States.

METHODS OF MANAGING HAZARDOUS WASTE

Hazardous waste management follows a hierarchy introduced by the EPA in the Pollution Prevention Act of 1990. (See Figure 7.2.) Source reduction is the preferred method for waste management. This is an activity that prevents the generation of waste in the first place, for example, a change in operating practices or raw materials. The second choice is recycling, followed by energy recovery. If none of these methods is feasible, then treatment prior to disposal is recommended.

A variety of techniques exist for safely managing hazardous wastes, including:

- Reduction—Waste generators change their manufacturing processes and materials in order to produce less hazardous waste. For example, a food packaging plant might replace solvent-based adhesives, which result in hazardous waste, with water-based adhesives, which result in nonhazardous waste.

- Recycling—Some waste materials become raw material for another process or can be recovered, reused, or sold.

- Treatment—A variety of chemical, biological, and thermal processes can be applied to neutralize or destroy toxic compounds in hazardous waste. (See Table 7.3.) For example, microorganisms or chemicals can remove hazardous hydrocarbons from contaminated water.

TABLE 7.3

Technology for land disposal of waste

Technology	Description
Biodegradation	Biodegradation uses microorganisms to break down organic compounds to make a waste less toxic.
Chemical reduction	Chemical reduction converts metal and inorganic constituents in wastewater into insoluble precipitates that are later settled out of the wastewater, leaving a lower concentration of metals and inorganics in the wastewater.
Combustion	Combustion destroys organic wastes or makes them less hazardous through burning in boilers, industrial furnaces, or incinerators.
Deactivation	Deactivation is treatment of a waste to remove the characteristic of ignitability, corrosivity, or reactivity. Deactivation can be achieved using many of the treatment technologies in 40 CFR §268.42, Table 1. Part 268, Appendix VI recommends technologies that can be used to deactivate specific wastestreams.
Macroencapsulation	Macroencapsulation is the application of a surface coating material to seal hazardous constituents in place and prevent them from leaching or escaping.
Neutralization	Neutralization makes certain wastes less acidic or certain substances less alkaline.
Precipitation	Precipitation removes metal and inorganic solids from liquid wastes to allow the safe disposal of the hazardous solid portion.
Recovery of metals	Recovery of organics uses direct physical removal methods to extract metal or inorganic constituents from a waste.
Recovery of organics	Recovery of organics uses direct physical removal methods (e.g., distillation, steam stripping) to extract organic constituents from a waste.
Stabilization	Stabilization (also referred to as solidification) involves the addition of stabilizing agents (e.g., Portland cement) to a waste to reduce the leachability of metal constituents.

SOURCE: Adapted from "Figure III-21: Excerpts from the 40 CFR 268.42 Technology-Based Standards Table," in *RCRA Orientation Manual*, EPA530-R-02-016, U.S. Environmental Protection Agency, Office of Solid Waste and Emergency Response, Washington, DC, January 2003

• Land disposal—State and federal regulations require the pre-treatment of most hazardous wastes before they can be discarded in landfills. These treated materials can only be placed in specially designed land disposal facilities.

• Injection wells—Hazardous waste may be injected deep underground under high pressure in wells thousands of feet deep. (See Figure 7.3.)

• Incineration—Hazardous waste can be burned in incinerators. Figure 7.4 shows a typical hazardous waste incinerator. However, as waste is burned, hot gases are released into the atmosphere, carrying toxic materials not consumed by the flames. In 1999 the Clinton Administration imposed a ban on new hazardous waste incinerators.

THE TOXICS RELEASE INVENTORY

The Toxics Release Inventory (TRI) was established under the Emergency Planning and Community Right-to-Know Act of 1986. Under the program, certain industrial facilities using specific toxic chemicals must report annually on their waste management activities and toxic chemical releases. These releases are to air, land, or water. Nearly 650 toxic chemicals are on the TRI list.

Manufacturing facilities (called "original" industries) have had to report under the TRI program since 1987. In 1998 the TRI requirements were extended to a second group of industries called the "new" industries. These include metal and coal mining, electric utilities burning coal or oil, chemical wholesale distributors, petroleum terminals, bulk storage facilities, Resource Conservation and Recovery Act (RCRA) Subtitle C hazardous water

treatment and disposal facilities, solvent recovery services, and federal facilities. However, only facilities with 10 or more full-time employees that use certain thresholds of toxic chemicals are included.

The *2001 Toxics Release Inventory (TRI) Public Data Release Report* was published in July 2003. The report states that 6.2 billion pounds (just over 3 million tons) of TRI chemicals were released during 2001. (See Table 7.4.) As shown in Figure 7.5, more than half of the releases were on-site land releases.

A breakdown by industry is provided in Figure 7.6. The metal mining industry was responsible for nearly half of the releases (46 percent), followed by electric utilities (17 percent), and chemical manufacturing facilities (9 percent). Table 7.5 lists the 20 chemicals with the largest releases. Copper compounds, zinc compounds, and hydrochloric acid were the most commonly released chemicals in the TRI.

GOVERNMENT REGULATION

The Resource Conservation and Recovery Act

The Resource Conservation and Recovery Act (RCRA), first enacted by Congress in 1976 and expanded by amendments in 1980, 1984, 1992, and 1996, was designed to manage the disposal, incineration, treatment, and storage of waste in landfills, surface impoundments, waste piles, tanks, and container storage areas. It regulates the production and disposal of hazardous waste, and provides guidelines and mandates to improve waste disposal practices. The EPA also has the authority under the RCRA to require businesses with hazardous waste operations to take corrective action to clean up the waste they have released into the environment.

FIGURE 7.3

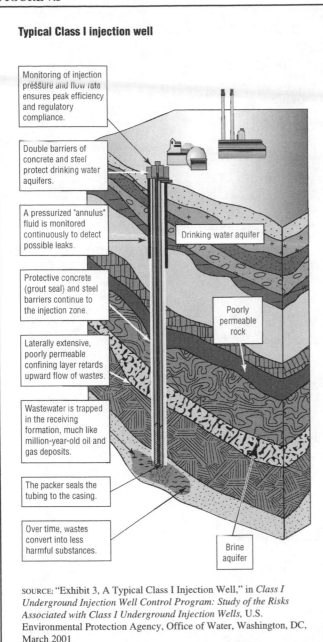

Typical Class I injection well

Monitoring of injection pressure and flow rate ensures peak efficiency and regulatory compliance.

Double barriers of concrete and steel protect drinking water aquifers.

A pressurized "annulus" fluid is monitored continuously to detect possible leaks.

Protective concrete (grout seal) and steel barriers continue to the injection zone.

Laterally extensive, poorly permeable confining layer retards upward flow of wastes.

Wastewater is trapped in the receiving formation, much like million-year-old oil and gas deposits.

The packer seals the tubing to the casing.

Over time, wastes convert into less harmful substances.

Drinking water aquifer

Poorly permeable rock

Brine aquifer

SOURCE: "Exhibit 3, A Typical Class I Injection Well," in *Class I Underground Injection Well Control Program: Study of the Risks Associated with Class I Underground Injection Wells*, U.S. Environmental Protection Agency, Office of Water, Washington, DC, March 2001

FIGURE 7.4

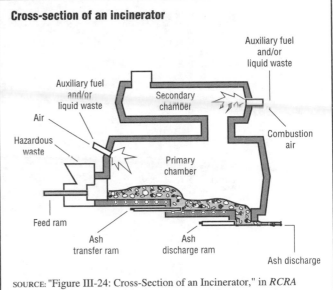

Cross-section of an incinerator

Auxiliary fuel and/or liquid waste

Secondary chamber

Auxiliary fuel and/or liquid waste

Air

Combustion air

Hazardous waste

Primary chamber

Feed ram

Ash transfer ram

Ash discharge ram

Ash discharge

SOURCE: "Figure III-24: Cross-Section of an Incinerator," in *RCRA Orientation Manual*, EPA530-R-02-016, U.S. Environmental Protection Agency, Office of Solid Waste and Emergency Response, Washington, DC, January 2003

FIGURE 7.5

Distribution of Toxics Release Inventory on-site and off-site releases, 2001

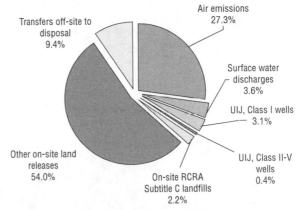

Transfers off-site to disposal 9.4%

Air emissions 27.3%

Surface water discharges 3.6%

UIJ, Class I wells 3.1%

UIJ, Class II-V wells 0.4%

Other on-site land releases 54.0%

On-site RCRA Subtitle C landfills 2.2%

Note: Off-site Releases include metals and metal category compounds transferred off-site for solidification/stabilization and for wastewater treatment, including to publicly owned treatment works. Off-site Releases do not include transfers to disposal sent to other Toxic Release Inventory facilities that reported the amount as on-site release.

UIJ = Underground injection

SOURCE: "Figure ES-1: Distribution of TRI On-Site and Off-Site Releases, 2001," in *2001 Toxics Release Inventory Executive Summary*, EPA 260-S-03-001, U.S. Environmental Protection Agency, Office of Environmental Information, Washington, DC, July 2003

The RCRA imposes design and maintenance standards for waste disposal facilities, such as the installation of liners to prevent waste from migrating into groundwater. Land disposal facilities in operation after November 1980 are regulated under the act, and are required to meet RCRA standards or close. Owners of facilities that ceased operation prior to November 1980 are required to clean up any hazardous waste threats their facilities still pose. Abandoned sites and those that owners cannot afford to clean up under the RCRA are usually referred to the national Superfund program.

CERCLA and the Superfund

The Comprehensive Environmental Response, Compensation, and Liability Act of 1980 (CERCLA) estab-lished the Superfund program to pay for cleaning up highly contaminated hazardous waste sites that had been abandoned or where a sole responsible party could not be identified. Originally a $1.6 billion five-year program, Superfund was focused initially on cleaning up leaking dumps that jeopardized groundwater.

TABLE 7.4

Toxics Release Inventory on-site and off-site releases by state, 2001

State	Total facilities/ Number	Total air emissions/ Pounds	Surface water discharges/ Pounds	Underground injection — Class I wells/ Pounds	Underground injection — Class II-V wells/ Pounds	On-site land releases — RCRA Subtitle C landfills/ Pounds	On-site land releases — Other on-site land releases/ Pounds	Total on-site releases/ Pounds	Off-site releases — Transfers off-site to disposal/ Pounds	Total on- and off-site releases/ Pounds	Rank
Alabama	566	75,567,809	4,713,394	0	92,912	7,161,905	34,615,126	122,151,146	12,294,431	134,445,577	13
Alaska	32	3,201,013	76,438	0	20,554,878	0	498,234,331	522,066,660	6,071	522,072,731	3
American Samoa	2	6,920	0	0	0	0	0	6,920	0	6,920	56
Arizona	275	4,600,105	6,376	0	0	4,886	601,481,177	606,092,545	721,776	606,814,321	2
Arkansas	385	20,036,562	3,190,528	1,492,971	93,263	227,275	6,416,583	31,457,181	12,585,384	44,042,566	31
California	1,612	20,020,008	4,924,819	0	55,902	23,436,456	4,644,856	53,082,041	5,467,403	58,549,443	27
Colorado	231	3,629,554	3,752,564	0	0	41,889	24,026,000	31,450,008	5,596,405	37,046,413	34
Connecticut	385	4,821,957	785,064	0	0	0	2,462	5,609,483	4,145,809	9,755,293	47
Delaware	79	6,651,525	573,937	0	0	0	965,666	8,191,129	3,883,235	12,074,363	44
District of Columbia	8	40,733	13,943	0	0	0	4,927	59,603	970	60,573	54
Florida	702	83,429,911	1,590,342	23,796,396	709	1,236,511	8,368,063	118,421,931	4,780,008	123,201,939	15
Georgia	795	91,834,154	8,391,937	0	0	17,986	13,615,623	113,859,700	2,659,943	116,519,643	17
Guam	8	192,898	17	0	0	26	5,519	198,460	23	198,483	53
Hawaii	38	2,379,957	29,770	5	2,066	0	224,400	2,636,198	430,339	3,066,537	49
Idaho	92	5,000,464	5,821,110	0	0	33,341,745	29,655,656	73,818,976	1,362,893	75,181,868	23
Illinois	1,376	59,411,352	8,087,041	327	2,172	24,623,694	20,127,859	112,252,445	25,496,565	137,749,010	12
Indiana	1,101	77,828,675	20,104,003	1,074,584	140	163,777	29,918,043	129,089,222	76,468,560	205,557,782	8
Iowa	433	24,332,303	3,145,360	0	0	17,600	5,504,922	33,000,185	4,873,295	37,873,480	32
Kansas	302	14,768,804	1,149,296	558,721	500	0	8,381,934	24,859,255	6,807,335	31,666,590	36
Kentucky	494	58,703,794	2,118,567	0	54,425	1,609	21,102,560	81,980,954	11,714,700	93,695,654	19
Louisiana	382	75,960,815	11,908,380	37,112,860	0	3,737,937	11,909,258	140,629,250	5,191,651	145,820,901	11
Maine	118	4,657,404	3,975,970	0	0	0	725,873	9,359,246	1,353,438	10,712,685	46
Maryland	211	36,076,213	3,839,690	0	56,057	0	2,806,914	42,778,874	2,645,338	45,424,212	29
Massachusetts	654	7,447,906	73,437	0	0	935	825,302	8,347,581	2,738,148	11,085,729	45
Michigan	939	56,656,492	1,043,401	2,509,470	100	12,843,205	9,419,827	82,472,496	49,444,297	131,916,793	14
Minnesota	505	14,252,131	1,571,683	0	0	250	9,696,375	25,520,439	7,874,871	33,395,310	35
Mississippi	356	37,063,726	12,964,677	11,046,901	0	176,756	7,943,087	69,195,147	1,891,154	71,086,301	24
Missouri	619	34,177,643	1,660,217	0	0	67,560	76,783,159	112,688,579	7,201,119	119,889,698	16
Montana	49	4,292,997	48,785	0	369,092	2,395	58,030,810	62,744,079	2,644,099	65,388,178	25
Nebraska	185	7,875,435	9,601,101	0	0	0	6,383,985	23,860,521	2,808,896	26,669,417	38
Nevada	103	2,728,933	82,849	0	785	3,988,273	774,255,862	781,056,702	2,437,928	783,494,630	1
New Hampshire	156	4,496,284	10,675	0	0	10,088		4,517,047	241,606	4,758,653	48
New Jersey	604	13,809,784	3,729,623	0	6	159,935	154,682	17,854,029	40,987,748	58,841,777	26
New Mexico	80	1,072,357	40,023	37,389	0	0	102,121,661	103,271,430	2,561,720	105,833,149	18
New York	775	29,629,649	6,733,053	1	0	7,677	3,398,501	39,768,882	5,062,168	44,831,050	30
North Carolina	914	115,130,332	9,887,436	0	0	765	12,415,324	137,433,858	10,234,240	147,668,098	10
North Dakota	47	4,328,230	110,470	0	0	0	12,303,643	16,742,343	8,534,710	25,277,053	39
Northern Marianas	3	7,953	0	0	0	0	2	7,955	0	7,955	55
Ohio	1,725	121,295,468	8,339,219	31,993,954	0	12,953,608	22,897,310	197,479,559	57,084,073	254,563,632	6
Oklahoma	343	17,377,943	2,391,127	4,828	0	2,518,028	2,976,818	25,268,743	3,618,278	28,887,021	37
Oregon	307	12,914,088	2,912,278	0	0	3,999,477	16,602,446	36,428,289	1,148,229	37,576,517	33
Pennsylvania	1,436	89,034,059	18,741,435	0	0	339,536	11,188,248	119,303,278	88,180,766	207,484,044	7
Puerto Rico	161	14,556,276	35,624	0	0	0	13,664	14,605,814	1,000,785	15,606,599	42
Rhode Island	160	824,582	10,171	0	0	250	108	835,111	262,989	1,098,100	50

TABLE 7.4

Toxics Release Inventory on-site and off-site releases by state, 2001 [CONTINUED]

State	Total facilities/ Number	Total air emissions/ Pounds	Surface water discharges/ Pounds	Underground injection Class I wells/ Pounds	Class II-V wells/ Pounds	On-site land releases RCRA Subtitle C landfills/ Pounds	Other on-site land releases/ Pounds	Total on-site releases/ Pounds	Off-site releases Transfers off-site to disposal/ Pounds	Total on- and off-site releases/ Pounds	Rank
South Carolina	561	54,977,393	2,778,925	0		16,281	5,300,147	63,072,746	18,188,165	81,260,912	20
South Dakota	91	1,799,135	2,413,621	0	704,700	12,380	8,520,378	13,450,214	77,038	13,527,252	43
Tennessee	692	79,573,558	3,067,358	0	5	341,993	58,960,603	141,943,517	7,017,705	148,961,221	9
Texas	1,556	102,748,862	26,007,896	77,648,758	0	1,454,403	28,396,993	236,256,913	34,278,163	270,535,075	5
Utah	179	19,220,667	1,215,070	0	0	5,266,999	740,512,297	766,215,034	982,691	767,197,725	2
Vermont	47	136,536	75,573	0	0	178	255	212,542	150,460	363,002	52
Virgin Islands	5	892,660	132,256	0	5	0	7,283	1,032,199	6,419	1,038,618	51
Virginia	507	57,216,768	6,963,083	0	5	1,076	6,434,629	70,615,561	9,168,292	79,783,853	22
Washington	347	14,295,076	2,123,223	0	6	6,109	5,096,793	21,521,207	2,371,067	23,892,274	40
West Virginia	188	59,430,131	3,788,537	14,397	0	5,484	11,485,102	74,723,651	5,416,357	80,140,007	21
Wisconsin	931	25,139,472	4,033,349	0	0	43,034	2,871,611	32,087,466	14,721,061	46,803,527	28
Wyoming	44	1,817,602	11,395	6,145,000	0	0	8,715,656	16,689,653	902,273	17,591,926	41
Total	**24,896**	**1,679,373,058**	**220,796,115**	**193,436,563**	**21,987,723**	**138,220,131**	**3,326,460,403**	**5,580,273,993**	**577,723,085**	**6,157,997,078**	

Note: **Off-site Releases** include metals and metal category compounds transferred off-site for solidification/stabilization and for wastewater treatment, including to publicly owned treatment works. **Off-site Releases** do not include transfers to disposal sent to other Toxics Release Inventory Facilities that reported the amount as an on-site release.
RCRA = Resource Conservation and Recovery Act.

SOURCE: "Table ES-2: TRI On-Site and Off-Site Releases by State, 2001," in *2001 Toxics Release Inventory Executive Summary*, EPA 260-S-03-001, U.S. Environmental Protection Agency, Office of Environmental Information, Washington, DC, July 2003

TABLE 7.5

Top twenty chemicals with the largest total releases, 2001

CAS number	Chemical	Total air emissions Pounds	Surface water discharges Pounds	Underground injection Class I wells Pounds	Underground injection Class II-V wells Pounds	On-site land releases RCRA Subtitle C landfills Pounds	On-site land releases Other on-site land releases Pounds	Total on-site releases Pounds	Off-site releases Transfers off-site to disposal Pounds	Total on- and off-site releases Pounds
—	Copper compounds	1,416,114	418,663	176,425	717,758	4,123,867	994,136,994	1,000,989,821	17,096,211	1,018,086,032
—	Zinc compounds	6,159,692	2,172,966	537,865	9,119,066	19,080,399	719,530,209	756,600,197	205,468,291	962,068,488
7647-01-0	Hydrochloric acid	587,134,079	2,445	46,398	2,172	0	188,608	587,373,702	746,442	588,120,144
—	Lead compounds	1,254,381	362,122	206,138	0	5,986,663	358,128,545	371,964,527	50,213,158	422,177,685
—	Manganese compounds	1,877,226	6,236,782	11,316,486	1,165,027	3,562,861	328,138,941	352,297,323	47,995,623	400,292,945
—	Arsenic compounds	177,832	141,172	65,713	1,466,028	3,130,653	373,104,273	378,085,671	3,000,912	381,086,583
—	Nitrate compounds	515,899	192,795,905	36,865,869	1,643	87,500	13,419,054	243,685,870	14,174,527	257,860,397
—	Barium compounds	2,163,853	1,475,918	15,514	1,965,433	2,351,397	198,668,435	206,640,550	45,504,419	252,144,968
67-56-1	Methanol	175,844,606	3,380,299	13,377,821	80,001	97,719	1,354,297	194,134,743	2,829,290	196,964,033
7664-41-7	Ammonia	122,057,546	6,621,166	22,930,936	43,301	15,065	3,605,984	155,273,998	3,247,048	158,521,046
7664-93-9	Sulfuric acid	146,397,844	694	679,045	0	66,810	481,965	147,626,358	129,606	147,755,964
—	Chromium compounds	671,106	178,352	2,188,916	51,250	2,676,859	94,041,777	99,808,260	16,725,832	116,534,092
—	Vanadium compounds	1,399,953	639,856	882,575	0	51,005	78,884,807	81,858,196	6,641,947	88,500,143
108-88-3	Toluene	71,539,704	75,909	264,765	365	82,903	44,754	72,008,400	1,780,473	73,788,873
7664-39-3	Hydrogen fluoride	67,248,474	21,549	4,400,000	0	30,407	249,168	71,949,598	136,470	72,086,068
—	Nickel compounds	1,004,693	244,846	710,080	270,609	5,600,859	45,383,246	53,214,334	13,753,100	66,967,433
7439-96-5	Manganese	904,434	165,392	0	0	3,796,840	12,535,661	17,402,327	31,582,035	48,984,362
100-42-5	Styrene	46,466,141	2,993	394,001	0	106,595	58,625	47,028,355	1,953,117	48,981,473
1330-20-7	Xylene (mixed isomers)	47,081,406	21,972	80,521	550	133,072	44,222	47,361,743	1,158,921	48,520,664
110-54-3	n-Hexane	47,644,345	10,531	69,663	0	343	9,600	47,734,482	427,958	48,162,440
	Subtotal (top 20 chemicals)	**1,328,959,329**	**214,969,533**	**95,208,731**	**20,909,880**	**50,981,817**	**3,222,009,165**	**4,933,038,455**	**464,565,380**	**5,397,603,835**
	Total (all chemicals)	**1,679,373,058**	**220,796,115**	**193,436,563**	**21,987,723**	**138,220,131**	**3,326,460,403**	**5,580,273,993**	**577,723,085**	**6,157,997,078**

Note: **Off-site Releases** include metals and metal category compounds transferred off-site for solidification/stabilization and for wastewater treatment, including to publicly owned treatment works. **Off-site Releases** do not include transfers to disposal sent to other Toxics Release Inventory facilities that reported the amount as an on-site release.
RCRA = Resource Conservation and Recovery Act.

SOURCE: "Table ES-4: Top 20 Chemicals with the Largest Total Releases, 2001," in *2001 Toxics Release Inventory Executive Summary*, EPA 260-S-03-001, U.S. Environmental Protection Agency, Office of Environmental Information, Washington, DC, July 2003

TABLE 7.6

Number of National Priorities List site actions and milestones, 1992–2004

Action	1992	1993	1994	1995	1996	1997	1998	1999	2000	2001	2002	2003	2004
Sites proposed to the NPL	30	52	36	9	27	20	34	37	40	45	9	14	0
Sites finalized on the NPL	0	33	43	31	17	18	17	43	39	29	19	20	0
Sites deleted from the NPL	2	12	13	25	34	32	20	23	10	30	17	9	2
Milestone	**1992**	**1993**	**1994**	**1995**	**1996**	**1997**	**1998**	**1999**	**2000**	**2001**	**2002**	**2003**	**2004**
Partial deletions*	-	-	-	-	0	6	7	3	5	4	7	7	1
Construction completions	88	68	61	68	64	88	87	85	87	47	42	40	4

A fiscal year is October 1 through September 30.
Partial deletion totals are not applicable until fiscal year 1996, when the policy was first implemented.
* These totals represent the total number of partial deletions by fiscal year and may include multiple partial deletions at a site. As of November 2003, there are 40 partial deletions at 36 sites.

SOURCE: "Number of NPL Site Actions and Milestones," in *National Priorities List*, U.S. Environmental Protection Agency, Washington, DC, October 14, 2003 [Online] http://www.epa.gov/superfund/sites/query/queryhtm/nplfy.htm [accessed December 16, 2003]

During the original mandate of Superfund, only six sites were cleaned up. When the program expired in 1985, many observers viewed it as a billion-dollar fiasco rampant with scandal and mismanagement. Nonetheless, the negative publicity surrounding the program increased public awareness of the magnitude of the cleanup job in America. Consequently, in 1986 and 1990, Superfund was reauthorized.

THE NATIONAL PRIORITIES LIST. CERCLA requires the government to maintain a list of hazardous waste sites that pose the highest potential threat to human health and the environment. This list is known as the National Priorities List (NPL) and is a published list of hazardous waste sites in the country that are being cleaned up under the Superfund program.

The NPL is constantly changing as new sites are officially added (finalized) and other sites are deleted. Table 7.6 shows NPL site actions and milestones achieved by fiscal year (October through September) for 1992 through 2004. These data were reported in October 2003, thus only data for one month are included for fiscal year 2004.

Table 7.7 shows the status of the 1,233 final sites on the NPL at the end of fiscal year 2002. At that time, 21 percent of the sites were in the preconstruction stage, which meant they were undergoing studies and design projects. Another 31 percent had construction activities underway. Nearly half (47 percent) were classified as "construction completed." The EPA determines construction completed when all physical construction of cleanup actions are completed, all immediate threats have been addressed, and all long-term threats are under control.

In 2002 the EPA proposed 62 new sites be added to the NPL based on preliminary investigations. Officials estimate that about one-fourth of these sites will actually be added to the NPL. As shown in Table 7.6 the number of sites proposed for the NPL is outpacing the number deleted.

FIGURE 7.6

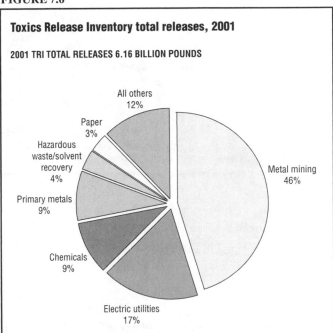

Toxics Release Inventory total releases, 2001

2001 TRI TOTAL RELEASES 6.16 BILLION POUNDS

- Metal mining 46%
- Electric utilities 17%
- Chemicals 9%
- Primary metals 9%
- Hazardous waste/solvent recovery 4%
- Paper 3%
- All others 12%

Note: Off-site Releases include metals and metal compounds transferred off-site for solidification/stabilization and for wastewater treatment, including to publicly owned treatment works. Off-site Releases do not include transfers to disposal sent to other TRI Facilities that reported the amount as an on-site release.

TRI = Toxics Release Inventory

SOURCE: "TRI Total Releases, 2001," in *2001 TRI Press Materials*, U.S. Environmental Protection Agency, Office of Environmental Information, Washington, DC, July 2003

According to the EPA, more than three times as many Superfund sites were cleaned up between 1993 and 2000 than in all of the prior years of the program combined. Figure 7.7 shows the cleanup status of NPL sites for the period 1993 to 2002. Many NPL sites are still years away from being cleaned up. The EPA estimates that 85 percent of the NPL sites will be cleaned up by 2008. Completion for the remaining 15 percent of the sites may take well beyond 2008.

TABLE 7.7

Cleanup status of proposed, final, and deleted National Priorities List sites, end of fiscal year 2002

NPL status	Study and design phase				Construction under way	Construction completed	Deferred to another authority	Total
	Awaiting study	Study under way	Remedy selected	Design under way				
Proposed	14	30	6		11		1	62
Final	19	155	29	58	387	585		1,233
Deleted						261	4	265
Total	**33**	**185**	**35**	**58**	**398**	**846**	**5**	**1,560**

SOURCE: "Table 2: Cleanup Status of Proposed, Final, and Deleted NPL Sites at the End of Fiscal Year 2002," in *Superfund Program: Current Status and Future Fiscal Challenges,* GAO-03-850, U.S. General Accounting Office, Washington, DC, July 31, 2003

TABLE 7.8

Revenue into the Superfund, fiscal years 1993–2002

CONSTANT 2002 DOLLARS IN MILLIONS

Revenue source	Fiscal year									
	1993	1994	1995	1996	1997	1998	1999	2000	2001	2002
Taxes	$2,019	$1,685	$1,672	$ 705	$ 82	$ 85	$ 22	$ 5	$ 6	$ 7
Cost recoveries	214	231	285	276	341	343	338	239	205	248
Interest on unexpended balance	165	202	359	388	359	313	233	245	223	111
Fines and penalties	4	3	3	4	3	5	4	1	2	1
Total	**$2,403**	**$2,121**	**$2,318**	**$1,372**	**$785**	**$745**	**$597**	**$490**	**$437**	**$368**

SOURCE: "Table 1: Revenue into the Superfund Trust Fund, Fiscal Years 1993 through 2002," in *Superfund Program: Current Status and Future Fiscal Challenges,* GAO-03-850, U.S. General Accounting Office, Washington, DC, July 31, 2003

FUNDING FOR SUPERFUND. Funding for the Superfund program is derived through two major sources: the Superfund Trust Fund and monies appropriated from the federal government's general fund.

The Superfund Trust Fund was set up as part of the original Superfund legislation of 1980. It was designed to help the EPA pay for cleanups and related program activities. Table 7.8 shows the revenue going into the Superfund Trust Fund each year between 1993 and 2002. Until 1995 the Superfund Trust Fund was financed primarily by dedicated taxes collected from companies in the chemical and crude oil industries. The system was extremely unpopular with many corporations arguing that environmentally responsible companies should not have to pay for the mistakes of others. In 1995 the tax was eliminated.

The Superfund Trust Fund is also financed through cost recoveries—money that the EPA recovers through legal settlements with responsible parties.

The EPA is authorized to compel parties responsible for creating hazardous pollution, such as waste generators, waste haulers, site owners, or site operators, to clean up the sites. If these parties cannot be found, or if a settlement cannot be reached, the Superfund program finances the cleanup. After completing a cleanup, the EPA can take

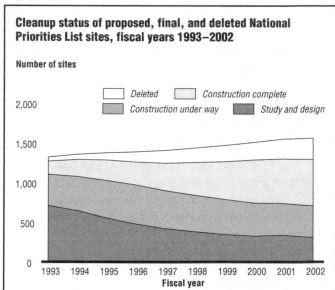

FIGURE 7.7

Cleanup status of proposed, final, and deleted National Priorities List sites, fiscal years 1993–2002

Number of sites

Notes: Data is verified and corrected only for fiscal year 2002. Deleted sites include sites deferred to another authority. Study and design sites include sites that are awaiting study, have study under way, have had a remedy selected, or have design under way.

SOURCE: "Figure 6: Cleanup Status of Proposed, Final, and Deleted NPL Sites, Fiscal Years 1993 through 2002," in *Superfund Program: Current Status and Future Fiscal Challenges,* GAO-03-850, U.S. General Accounting Office, Washington, DC, July 31, 2003

FIGURE 7.8

Environmental Protection Agency's Superfund program expenditures, fiscal years 1993–2002

CONSTANT 2002 DOLLARS IN MILLIONS

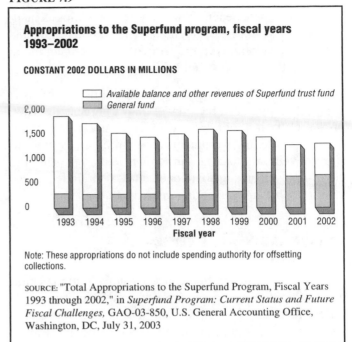

SOURCE: "Figure 4: EPA's Superfund Program Expenditures, Fiscal Years 1993 through 2002," in *Superfund Program: Current Status and Future Fiscal Challenges,* GAO-03-850, U.S. General Accounting Office, Washington, DC, July 31, 2003

FIGURE 7.9

Appropriations to the Superfund program, fiscal years 1993–2002

CONSTANT 2002 DOLLARS IN MILLIONS

☐ *Available balance and other revenues of Superfund trust fund*
▨ *General fund*

Note: These appropriations do not include spending authority for offsetting collections.

SOURCE: "Total Appropriations to the Superfund Program, Fiscal Years 1993 through 2002," in *Superfund Program: Current Status and Future Fiscal Challenges,* GAO-03-850, U.S. General Accounting Office, Washington, DC, July 31, 2003

action against the responsible parties to recover costs and replenish the fund. The average cost of cleanup is about $30 million, large enough to make it worthwhile for parties to pursue legal means to spread the costs among large numbers of responsible parties. Many cleanups involve dozens of parties.

Disputes have arisen between industries and cities over who is responsible for a cleanup, and numerous lawsuits have been filed by industries against cities over responsibility for what is usually a huge expense. Many businesses and municipalities may be unable to assume such expense. The EPA reports that the government currently collects only one-fifth of the cleanup costs that could be recovered from polluters under the Superfund law. According to the EPA, in many cases, the polluters have disappeared or are unable to pay. In other cases, the agency lacks the staff or evidence to proceed with lawsuits.

All of these factors have resulted in only modest amounts of money being collected for the Superfund Trust Fund through cost recoveries. Total revenue into the Fund dropped from $2.4 billion in 1993 to $368 million in 2002, as shown in Table 7.8. However, the EPA has continued to add sites to the NPL that require cleanup. According to a GAO analysis conducted in 2003, the EPA consistently spent between $1.3 and $1.7 billion each year between 1993 and 2002 to operate the Superfund Program. The GAO reports that the unexpended balance of the Superfund Trust Fund stood at only $3.4 billion at the end of fiscal year 2002. At current rates of spending, the Fund is expected to be depleted in a short amount of time. (See Figure 7.8.)

In recent years the EPA has increasingly relied on money appropriated from the federal government's general fund to pay for NPL cleanups. During the early 2000s, the general fund accounted for roughly half of all appropriations to the Superfund Program as shown in Figure 7.9. This means that all American taxpayers are increasingly paying to clean up hazardous waste sites under the Superfund Program. The GAO estimates that the general fund will supply about 80 percent of the monies needed for the Superfund Program in EPA's fiscal year 2004 budget.

Some critics have called for the federal government to reinstate dedicated taxes against petroleum and chemical corporations to fund the Superfund Program, instead of burdening tax-paying citizens. The GAO notes that Congress is reluctant to appropriate more general fund monies to the Superfund Program and fears the Program costs will continue to escalate as the EPA adds more sites to the NPL. A major complaint is that the Superfund Program lacks an effective system for indicating the progress that it is making toward cleaning up the nation's hazardous waste sites. Congress has asked the EPA to develop performance indicators that could help them make better funding decisions for the Superfund Program. An EPA advisory council is expected to make its recommendations during 2004.

BROWNFIELDS

Brownfields are former industrial sites that are moderately contaminated but can be redeveloped for commercial or residential use. The EPA defines Brownfields as abandoned, idled, or underused industrial or commercial sites where expansion or redevelopment is complicated by real or perceived environmental contamination. Real estate developers generally perceive Brownfields as inappropriate sites for redevelopment. There are an estimated 450,000 Brownfields in the United States, concentrated mostly in the Northeast and Midwest.

Most Brownfield sites are not as contaminated as is generally thought. In fact, fewer than 1 percent are listed on the NPL and will require federal Superfund action. State and federal governments have strong motivations to want developers to clean up Brownfields: restoring the environment; reusing abandoned sites; revitalizing cities; creating jobs; and generating municipal tax revenues.

ENVIRONMENTAL JUSTICE—AN EVOLVING ISSUE

Environmental justice concerns stem from the claim that racial minorities are disproportionately subject to pollution hazards. The environmental justice movement gained national attention in 1982 when a demonstration took place to protest the building of a hazardous waste landfill in Warren County, North Carolina, a county with a predominantly African American population. A resulting 1983 congressional study found that in three out of four landfill areas surveyed, African Americans made up the majority of the population living nearby. In addition, at least 26 percent of the population in those communities were living below the poverty level. In 1987 the United Church of Christ published a nationwide study, *Toxic Waste and Race in the United States,* and reported that race was the most significant factor among the variables tested in determining locations of hazardous waste facilities.

In 1990 an EPA report (*Environmental Equity: Reducing Risk for All Communities*) concluded that racial minorities and low-income people bear a disproportionate burden of environmental risk. These groups were exposed to lead, air pollutants, hazardous waste facilities, contaminated fish, and agricultural pesticides in far greater frequencies than the general population. In 1994 President Clinton issued Executive Order 12898 (*Federal Actions to Address Environmental Justice in Minority Populations and Low-Income Populations*), which requires federal agencies to develop a comprehensive strategy for including environmental justice factors in their decision-making.

The findings were different when it came to nonhazardous waste. A 1995 U.S. General Accounting Office report (*Hazardous and Nonhazardous Wastes: Demographics of People Living Near Waste Facilities*, Washington, DC) found that minorities and low-income people were not disproportionately represented near the majority of nonhazardous landfills. The data showed that people living near municipal landfills were likely to have poverty rates similar to or lower than rates in the rest of the country. In fact, median household income was as likely to be higher than the national average as it was to be lower than the national average. The study suggested that the results differed from prior studies because the various studies used differing methods.

Kennedy Heights Lawsuit

In 1997 residents of Kennedy Heights, a Houston, Texas, neighborhood of about 1,400 residents, complained about a variety of illnesses such as cancer, tumors, lupus (an autoimmune disease), and rashes. Their homes had been built three decades prior atop abandoned oil pits, and residents believed oil sludge from the pits had seeped into their water supply. Some tests of the municipal water found traces of crude oil. Kennedy Heights attracted ever-wider attention because of accusations of environmental racism. Homeowners, who were predominantly African American, were not told the property sat on an oil dump abandoned in the 1920s. Chevron Oil Company, which acquired the property from Gulf Oil, denied that contamination could have caused any illness. The homes lost virtually all their resale value because of the claims.

In 2000 Chevron and the Kennedy Heights homeowners reached a $12.7 million settlement. Of this settlement award, $7.6 million was to be divided among 2,000 homeowners and $5.1 million was to be paid to their attorney.

RADIOACTIVE WASTE

What Is Radioactivity?

Radioactivity is the spontaneous emission of energy and/or high-energy particles from the nucleus of an atom. One type of radioactivity is produced naturally and is emitted by radioactive isotopes (or radioisotopes), such as radioactive carbon (carbon-14) and radioactive hydrogen (H-3 or tritium). The energy and high-energy particles that radioactive isotopes emit include alpha rays, beta rays, and gamma rays.

Isotopes are atoms of an element that have the same number of protons but different numbers of neutrons in their nuclei. For example, the element carbon has 12 protons and 12 neutrons comprising its nucleus. One isotope of carbon, C-14, has 12 protons and 14 neutrons in its nucleus.

Radioisotopes (such as C-14) are unstable isotopes and their nuclei decay, or break apart, at a steady rate. Decaying radioisotopes produce other isotopes as they emit energy and/or high-energy particles. If the newly formed nuclei are radioactive too, they emit radiation and change into other nuclei. The final products in this chain are stable, nonradioactive nuclei.

Radioisotopes reach our bodies daily, emitted from sources in outer space, and from rocks and soil on earth. Radioisotopes are also used in medicine and provide useful diagnostic tools.

FIGURE 7.10

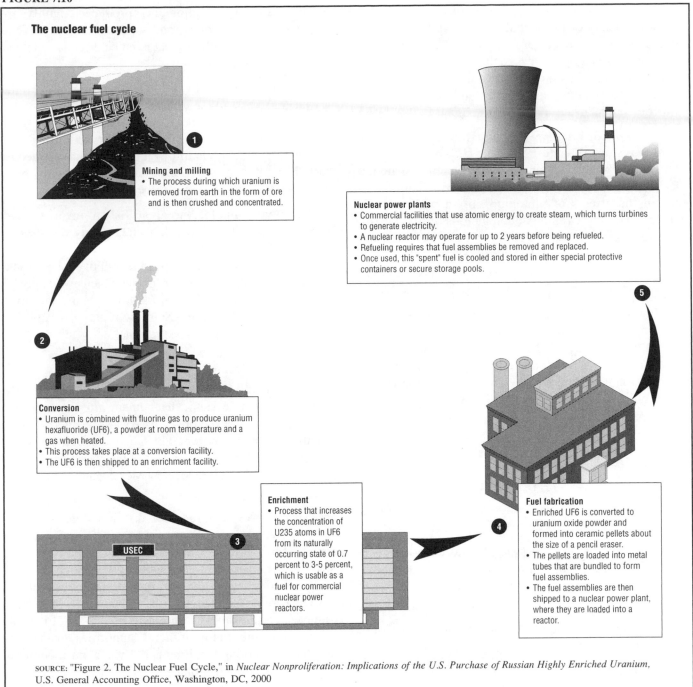

The nuclear fuel cycle

Mining and milling
• The process during which uranium is removed from earth in the form of ore and is then crushed and concentrated.

Nuclear power plants
• Commercial facilities that use atomic energy to create steam, which turns turbines to generate electricity.
• A nuclear reactor may operate for up to 2 years before being refueled.
• Refueling requires that fuel assemblies be removed and replaced.
• Once used, this "spent" fuel is cooled and stored in either special protective containers or secure storage pools.

Conversion
• Uranium is combined with fluorine gas to produce uranium hexafluoride (UF6), a powder at room temperature and a gas when heated.
• This process takes place at a conversion facility.
• The UF6 is then shipped to an enrichment facility.

Enrichment
• Process that increases the concentration of U235 atoms in UF6 from its naturally occurring state of 0.7 percent to 3-5 percent, which is usable as a fuel for commercial nuclear power reactors.

USEC

Fuel fabrication
• Enriched UF6 is converted to uranium oxide powder and formed into ceramic pellets about the size of a pencil eraser.
• The pellets are loaded into metal tubes that are bundled to form fuel assemblies.
• The fuel assemblies are then shipped to a nuclear power plant, where they are loaded into a reactor.

SOURCE: "Figure 2. The Nuclear Fuel Cycle," in *Nuclear Nonproliferation: Implications of the U.S. Purchase of Russian Highly Enriched Uranium*, U.S. General Accounting Office, Washington, DC, 2000

Energy can be released by "artificially" breaking apart atomic nuclei. Such a process is called nuclear fission. The fission of uranium 235 (U-235) releases several neutrons that can penetrate other U-235 nuclei. In this way, the fission of a single U-235 atom can begin a cascading chain of nuclear reactions. If this series of reactions is regulated to occur slowly, as it is in nuclear power plants, the energy emitted can be captured for a variety of uses, such as generating electricity. (See Figure 7.10.) If this series of reactions is allowed to occur all at once, as in a nuclear (atomic) bomb, the energy emitted is explosive. (Plutonium-239 can also be used to generate a chain reaction similar to that of U-235.)

A Culture of Secrecy

As scientists raced to develop an atomic bomb during World War II (1939–45), wartime concern for national security led to a "culture of secrecy" that became characteristic of agencies dealing with nuclear power. On July 16, 1945, the first bomb, "Trinity," was exploded above ground in Alamogordo, New Mexico. A few weeks later, two nuclear bombs were dropped on Japan. World War II ended and the nuclear age began.

In 1948 the Atomic Energy Commission warned that then-existing disposal practices for nuclear materials would result in contamination of the environment. The commission's advice was dismissed, in part because of the expense of improving disposal methods. By the 1950s, there was already evidence that the commission's advice should have been heeded. Officials at the Hanford, Washington, nuclear facility discovered that high-level waste had corroded the tanks in which it was contained, and radioactive waste was leaking into the soil and groundwater. A number of similar events occurred in subsequent years.

In 1993 U.S. Energy Secretary Hazel O'Leary disclosed that since the late 1940s, the U.S. nuclear establishment had conducted hundreds of unannounced atomic tests (from 1948 to 1952), experimented with human subjects on the effects of plutonium, often without their knowledge or approval, and dumped tons of toxic waste across the United States. Secretary O'Leary revealed that of 925 nuclear tests, 204 had been secret, and that the government was storing 33.5 metric tons of plutonium in six U.S. locations.

Although nuclear waste management received little attention from government policymakers for three decades after the development of the atomic bomb in 1945, considerably more attention has focused on nuclear waste as a national and worldwide issue since the 1970s. In fact, during the 1990s, the U.S. Department of Energy (DOE) spent hundreds of millions of dollars to treat, store, and dispose of radioactive wastes generated at over 50 of its nuclear facilities around the country.

RADIOACTIVE WASTE DISPOSAL

The nuclear energy process produces five basic types of radioactive waste.

- Uranium mill tailings are sand-like wastes produced in uranium refining operations that emit low levels of radiation.

- Low-level waste contains varying lesser levels of radioactivity, and includes trash, contaminated clothing, and hardware.

- Spent fuel is "used" reactor fuel that will be classified as waste if not reprocessed to recover usable uranium and plutonium, which can be used again as nuclear reactor fuel.

- High-level waste is the by-product of a reprocessing plant. These wastes contain highly toxic and extremely dangerous fission products that require great care in disposal.

- Transuranic wastes are 11 man-made radioactive elements with an atomic number (number of protons) greater than that of uranium (92) and therefore beyond ("trans-") uranium ("-uranic") on the periodic chart of the elements. Their half-lives, the time it takes for half the radioisotopes present in a sample to decay to non-radioactive elements, are thousands of years. They are

found in trash (such as protective clothing, tools, glassware, and equipment) produced mainly by nuclear weapons plants and are therefore a part of the nuclear waste problem that must be directly resolved by the government.

The end of the Cold War brought the problem of military nuclear waste to the forefront. Both the United States and Russia agreed to begin to destroy many of their nuclear weapons. In fact, in November 2001 President Bush and President Vladimir Putin of Russia pledged to slash the number of long-range nuclear weapons by two-thirds—to the lowest level in three decades.

Destroying nuclear weapons is an involved and lengthy process that will likely take many decades to complete. The highly toxic and extremely dangerous fission wastes produced by this process will likely have to be stored for extended periods of time and then eventually be moved to permanent storage facilities. Many facilities scattered across the United States will play a role in dismantling the American nuclear arsenal.

Uranium Mill Tailings

Uranium mill tailings are the earthen residues, usually in the form of fine sand, that remain after mining and extracting uranium from ores. These wastes emit low levels of radiation, mostly radon, which can contaminate water and air. Most tailing sites are west of the Mississippi River, primarily in Utah, Colorado, New Mexico, and Arizona.

Prior to the early 1970s, the tailings were believed to have such low levels of radiation that they were not harmful to humans. Miners, many of whom were Native Americans, received little protection from the radiation. Now, many of these workers are reporting very high rates of cancer. Tailings were also left in scattered piles without posted warnings or safeguards, exposing anyone who came near. Some tailings were deposited in landfills, and homes were built on top of them. Authorities now recognize that mill tailing handling and disposal must be properly managed to control radiation exposure.

Proper management of uranium mill tailings is particularly important because they are generated in relatively large volumes—about 10 to 15 million tons annually. About 15 percent of the radioactivity is removed during the milling process, while the remainder (85 percent) stays in the tailings. Radium-226, the major radioactive waste product, retains its radioactivity for thousands of years and produces two potentially hazardous radiation conditions—gamma radiation and the emission of gaseous radon. Results of research studies show a causal relationship between these radioactive elements and leukemia and lung cancer.

In response to growing concern, Congress passed the Uranium Mill Tailing Radiation Control Act of 1978 to regulate mill tailing operations. The law called for the cleanup of abandoned mill sites, primarily at federal expense, although owners of still-active mines were financially responsible for their own cleanup.

Low-Level Waste

Low-level radioactive waste decays in 10 to 100 years. Until the 1960s, the United States dumped low-level wastes into the ocean. The first commercial site to house such waste was opened in 1962, and by 1971 six sites were licensed for disposal. The volume of low-level waste increased during the initial years of commercially generated waste disposal (1963–1980) until the Low-Level Radioactive Waste Policy Act of 1980, and its amendments in 1985. At that time, approximately 3.25 million cubic feet of radioactive wastes were disposed per year. Since then, the volume has declined to under 1 million cubic feet per year.

By 1979 only three commercial low-level waste sites were still operating—Richland (Hanford), Washington; Beatty, Nevada; and Barnwell, South Carolina. The facility at Beatty, Nevada, closed permanently in 1982. In response to the threatened closing of the South Carolina site, Congress called for the establishment of a national system of such facilities under the Low-Level Radioactive Waste Policy Act. Every state became responsible for finding a low-level disposal site for wastes generated within its borders by 1986. It also gave states the right to bar low-level wastes if they were engaged in regional compacts for waste disposal. The disposal of high-level wastes remained a federal responsibility.

COMPACTS. The 1980 Low-Level Radioactive Waste Policy Act and its amendments encouraged states to organize themselves into compacts to develop new radioactive waste facilities. As of 2001, Congress had approved 10 such compacts serving 44 states. No compact or state has, however, successfully developed a new disposal facility for low-level wastes. Compacts and unaffiliated states have confronted significant barriers to developing disposal sites, including public health and environmental concerns, antinuclear sentiment, substantial financial requirements, political issues, and "not in my backyard" campaigns by citizen activists.

STORAGE AND TRANSPORT PROBLEMS. Developing storage areas for hazardous waste is difficult for many reasons. One reason is that regulatory requirements mandate a buffer zone of land surrounding each site, which, along with the storage area, requires constant monitoring and limited land-use applications for at least a century. Larger sites collectively reduce the total number of acres required because they only need one buffer zone, but smaller and more numerous local facilities reduce the probability of transportation accidents. Other storage problems include the degradation of the packages that contain stored waste. Depending on the environment, degradation can occur from temperature fluctuations, corrosion, and containers becoming brittle.

Spent Fuel and High-Level Waste

Spent fuel, the used uranium that has been removed from a nuclear reactor, is far from being completely "spent." It contains highly penetrating and toxic radioactivity and requires isolation from living things for thousands of years. It still contains significant amounts of uranium, as well as plutonium, created during the nuclear fission process. Spent fuel is a disposal problem for nuclear power plants that will be decommissioned before the projected availability of a long-term, high-level waste disposal repository for this waste. Unless a temporary site becomes available, commercial and government nuclear reactor facilities have the following options:

- Leave the fuel on site.

- Use on-site casks (large barrel-like containers) for storage. This is not an option for hot fuel—fuel that has been out of the core of the reactor for less than five years.

- Ship the spent fuel to France for reprocessing. France, which is heavily dependent on nuclear power, has developed the technology to reprocess spent fuel, something not available in the United States. In a controversial action, spent nuclear fuel from the defunct Shoreham plant was shipped to France in 1993 for reprocessing at a cost of $74 million to utility customers. Nuclear watchdog groups, including the Friends of the Earth and the Union of Concerned Scientists, oppose sending nuclear fuel abroad because they fear the possibility of theft or accidental spread of nuclear materials. The safe transport of spent fuel is primarily a federal responsibility. The U.S. Department of Transportation (DOT) and the Nuclear Regulatory Commission (NRC) are responsible for packaging regulations, container safety, regulations regarding sabotage, escorts, routing, and employee training.

- Continue to operate the unit. Some plants might not be decommissioned, as originally planned, but would continue to operate and keep any spent fuel on site.

- Ship the fuel to a monitored retrievable storage facility, if one is available.

DISPOSAL OF RADIOACTIVE WASTE

The Nuclear Energy Agency (NEA) of the Organization for Economic Cooperation and Development (OECD) is an international group established in 1958 and comprised of 27 countries, including the United States. Its purpose is to help member nations maintain and develop safe, environmentally friendly, and economical use of nuclear energy for peaceful purposes. One area of competence of the NEA is radioactive waste management.

In a 2000 publication, *Geologic Disposal of Radioactive Waste in Perspective,* the NEA notes that there has been little fundamental change in the basic technology of geologic (underground) repositories (waste disposal sites) in the past ten years. However, the book notes that there has been significant progress in the development of what is termed robust engineered barrier systems.

Robust engineered barrier systems combine multiple physical barriers with chemical controls and provide a high level of long-term containment for radioactive waste. An example of a robust engineered barrier system would place radioactive waste, which had been chemically treated for long-term storage, into steel drums. The drums would be placed in a concrete container. Many of these drum-filled concrete containers, surrounded with special chemically treated backfill material, would be placed in a larger concrete container deep in the ground. The rock surrounding this large concrete container would have low groundwater flow. The multiple barriers, chemical conditions, and geologic conditions under which the wastes are stored ensure that the wastes dissolve slowly and pose little danger to the groundwater.

Geologic Repositories in the United States

In the United States, the government is focusing on two locations as geologic repositories: the Waste Isolation Pilot Plant (WIPP) in southeastern New Mexico for transuranic (defense) waste and Nevada's Yucca Mountain for nuclear power plant waste.

THE WASTE ISOLATION PILOT PLANT. The Waste Isolation Pilot Plant (WIPP) became the world's first deep depository for nuclear waste when it received its first shipment on March 26, 1999. The large facility near Carlsbad, New Mexico, is restricted to defense or transuranic waste. WIPP is 655 meters (1,248 feet) below the surface, in the salt beds of the Salado Formation, and is intended to house up to 6.25 million cubic feet of transuranic waste for more than 10,000 years.

More than 99 percent of transuranic waste is temporarily stored in drums at nuclear defense sites around the country. As transuranic waste is transported to the WIPP, it is tracked by satellite and moved at night when traffic is light. It can be transported only in good weather and must be routed around major cities.

By the beginning of the twenty-first century, about 61 million Americans lived within 50 miles of a military nuclear waste storage site. By the time the WIPP has been in operation for 10 years that number should drop to 4 million. By 2035, barring court challenges, almost 40,000 truckloads of nuclear waste will have been transported across the country to the WIPP.

According to the Southwest Research and Information Center (SRIC), Carlsbad's political and economic leaders pursued the WIPP project during the early 1970s to bring jobs to the area. SRIC is a nonprofit public-interest organization based in Albuquerque, NM. SRIC's Web site says "federal officials always found support for WIPP in Carlsbad, and usually from the state's U.S. senators and representatives." A public opinion poll conducted of state residents in 2001 by the University of New Mexico's Institute of Public Policy found that 59 percent of respondents supported keeping the WIPP open, while only 31 percent thought it should be closed down.

YUCCA MOUNTAIN. The centerpiece of the federal government's geologic disposal plan for spent fuel and high-level waste is the Yucca Mountain site in Nevada. (See Figure 7.11.) The Nuclear Waste Policy Act of 1982 requires the Secretary of Energy to investigate the site and, if it is suitable, to recommend to the president that the site be established. In February 2002 President George W. Bush received such a recommendation and approved it. Despite opposition from New Mexico's governor, the project was subsequently approved by the U.S. House of Representatives and the U.S. Senate. In July 2002 President Bush signed the Yucca Mountain resolution into law. The next step for the project is licensing from the Nuclear Regulatory Commission (NRC).

In order for the Yucca Mountain Repository to be built, the DOE must satisfactorily demonstrate to the NRC that the combination of the site and the repository design complies with the standards set forth by the EPA. The EPA's standard is based on a new approach of using numerical probabilities to establish requirements for containing radioactivity within the repository. Their quantitative terms are:

- Cumulative releases of radioactivity from a repository must have a likelihood of less than one chance in ten of exceeding limits established in the standard and a likelihood of less than one chance in 1,000 of exceeding ten times the limits for a period of 10,000 years.

- Exposures of radiation to individual members of the public for 1,000 years must not exceed specified limits.

- Limits are placed on the concentration of radioactivity for 1,000 years after disposal from the repository to a nearby source of groundwater that (1) currently supplies drinking water for thousands of persons, and (2) is irreplaceable.

- Prescribed technical or institutional procedures or steps must provide confidence that the containment requirements are likely to be met.

Between 2001 and 2003 the State of New Mexico filed numerous lawsuits against the DOE, the EPA, the NRC, and President Bush, seeking to invalidate approval of the Yucca Mountain project. The cases are expected to be heard in federal court sometime in 2004. If the lawsuits

FIGURE 7.11

Sites storing spent nuclear fuel, high-level radioactive waste, and/or surplus plutonium, 2002

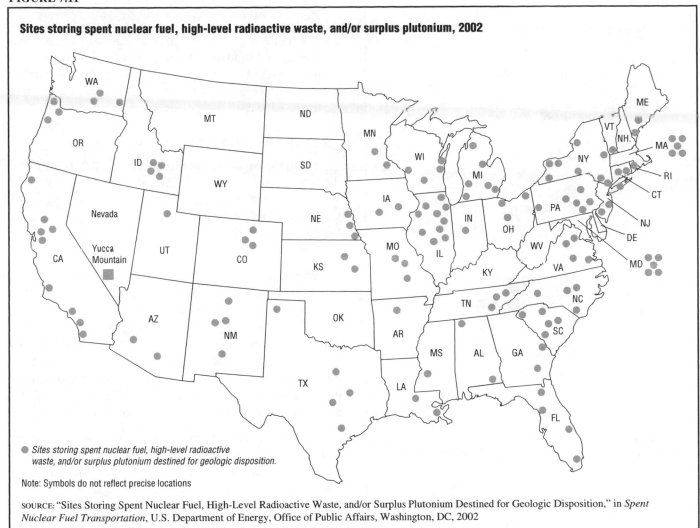

● *Sites storing spent nuclear fuel, high-level radioactive
waste, and/or surplus plutonium destined for geologic disposition.*

Note: Symbols do not reflect precise locations

SOURCE: "Sites Storing Spent Nuclear Fuel, High-Level Radioactive Waste, and/or Surplus Plutonium Destined for Geologic Disposition," in *Spent Nuclear Fuel Transportation*, U.S. Department of Energy, Office of Public Affairs, Washington, DC, 2002

are unsuccessful, the DOE plans to begin construction on the Yucca Mountain repository in 2008 and begin nuclear waste shipments in 2010.

Crisis in the Nuclear Power Industry

The long delay in providing a disposal site for nuclear wastes, coupled with the accelerated pace at which nuclear plants are being retired, has created a crisis in the nuclear power industry. Several aging plants are being maintained—at a cost of $20 million a year for each reactor—simply because there is no place to send the waste once the plants are decommissioned. Under the Nuclear Waste Policy Act of 1982, the DOE was scheduled to begin picking up waste on January 31, 1998. Nuclear power plants have been paying one cent per 10 kilowatt-hours produced by the reactors to finance a waste repository.

In February 1999 the DOE announced that because it was unable to receive nuclear waste for permanent storage, it would take ownership of the waste and pay temporary storage costs with money the utilities have paid to develop the permanent repository. The waste will stay where it currently is being stored. Figure 7.11 shows sites

around the country storing spent nuclear fuel, high-level radioactive waste, and/or surplus plutonium destined for geologic disposal.

Both the Senate and the House have passed legislation to build a temporary repository in Nevada. The Clinton Administration, however, opposed the temporary site, claiming that it had not been proven safe and would deflect funds and engineering talent needed to build the permanent facility. Even without the expense of temporary storage, the nuclear waste fund (from the one cent per 10 kilowatt-hours of nuclear power generated by the utilities) is many billions short of what Yucca Mountain is expected to cost.

According to the NRC, which licenses nuclear power plants, almost all nuclear plants will soon reach their capacity for storing their spent nuclear waste for several reasons.

• There is a backlog of nuclear waste. At least 35,000 metric tons of nuclear waste is sitting in what are called "spent fuel pools" at 70 nuclear energy plants around the country. By 2010, the earliest feasible date

FIGURE 7.12

A spent fuel dry storage container

At some nuclear reactors across the country, spent fuel is kept on site, above ground, in systems basically similar to the one shown here.

1 Once the spent fuel has cooled, it is loaded into special canisters, each of which is designed to hold about two dozen assemblies. Water and air are removed. The canister is filled with inert gas, welded shut, and rigorously tested for leaks. It may then be placed in a "cask" for storage or transportation.

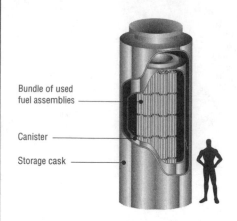

Bundle of used fuel assemblies —

Canister —

Storage cask —

2 The canisters can also be stored in above ground concrete bunkers, each of which is about the size of a one-car garage. Eventually they may be transported elsewhere for storage.

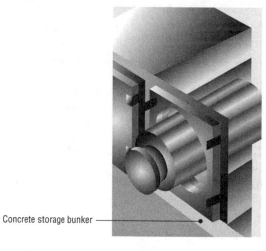

Concrete storage bunker —

SOURCE: "Figure 6: A Spent Fuel Dry Storage Container," in *Spent Nuclear Fuel: Options Exist to Further Enhance Security,* GAO-03-426, U.S. General Accounting Office, Washington, DC, July 15, 2003. Data from Nuclear Regulatory Commission

for opening the Yucca Mountain repository, the total waste is expected to reach 60,000 metric tons.

• Many nuclear plants are shutting down well ahead of schedule because of premature aging and high maintenance and repair costs. Although the NRC licenses power plants to operate for 40 years, they do not last

that long. The average life of the more than 20 reactors that have been shut down has been about 13 years.

• The nation's power system has been restructured from a regulated industry to one driven by competition. As many as 26 U.S. nuclear power plants are vulnerable to shutdown because production costs are higher than the projected market prices of electricity.

TRANSPORTING RADIOACTIVE WASTE

Since the beginning of this country's nuclear program, there have been more than 2,500 shipments of spent fuel and many more shipments of low-level waste. However, shipments of radioactive waste increased in 1999 when the Waste Isolation Pilot Plant (WIPP) began operation and will rise dramatically when Yucca Mountain opens.

Transportation of nuclear waste is of particular concern to states and Native American reservations along the main transportation routes to possible disposal sites. Several transportation organizations are actively preparing for potential shipments across country. Under the Hazardous Materials Transportation Act of 1975, the DOT and the NRC share responsibility for regulating standards of safety for packaging and transport of hazardous materials by any mode in interstate and foreign commerce.

Spent nuclear fuel and radioactive wastes are solid material shipped in large, heavy metal containers called casks, which are designed to shield radiation and withstand severe accidents without releasing their toxic contents. (See Figure 7.12.) Such fuel is usually transported by truck or rail. Casks, which are regulated by the NRC, have multiple layers of walls. Each container can hold fourteen 55-gallon drums. A satellite tracking system maintains constant contact with the trucks, and drivers are tested for safety and trained in emergency response.

INTERNATIONAL APPROACHES TO HIGH-LEVEL WASTE DISPOSAL

Governments, scientists, and engineers around the world generally believe that deep geologic disposal, such as that in operation at the WIPP and proposed for Yucca Mountain, offers the best option for isolating highly radioactive waste. According to the NEA of the OECD, in *Geologic Disposal of Radioactive Waste in Perspective* (2000), several countries have made significant progress toward implementation of geologic disposal, but the rate of progress has been slower than expected. Additionally, some countries have experienced serious setbacks in the implementation of their plans because of political, public, and regulatory issues.

A few countries have implemented geologic disposal of many types of radioactive waste. The United States opened the first (and only) deep geologic repository for long-lived nuclear wastes in the world at the WIPP in

1999. The only other geologic disposal sites are in Germany, Sweden, Finland, and Norway, but these sites accept only low- and medium-level radioactive wastes. Germany has operated a deep repository in a salt dome at Morsleben since 1981, although it is not accepting waste at this time. Sweden has operated a repository in caverns at the Forsmark nuclear site since 1988. Finland began operation of a repository in caverns at the Olkiluoto nuclear site in 1992 and at the Loviisa site in 1998. Norway began operation of a waste site in caverns at the Himdalen facility in 1999.

Other sites for deep geologic repositories for long-lived nuclear wastes are in the planning stages in Finland and Sweden. Planning in Belgium, France, and Japan is on track, but far from implementation. The Yucca Mountain site will likely be the second long-lived nuclear waste deep geologic repository in the world.

In 1993 the United Kingdom opened a nuclear fuel reprocessing plant, one of only two in the world (the other is in France) that reprocesses used fuel from nuclear power generators around the world.

CHAPTER 8

PUBLIC OPINION AND ENVIRONMENTAL POLICY

Although most Americans say they are concerned about the environment, their involvement in environmental causes appears to have dropped between the early 1990s and the early 2000s. In 1991 a Gallup Poll asked people whether they thought of themselves as environmentalists. Seventy-eight percent said they were environmentalists, while only 19 percent indicated they were not.

In 2003 the Gallup organization asked people about their involvement in the environmental movement. The results indicated that only 14 percent of the respondents considered themselves active participants in the movement. Another 47 percent claimed to be sympathetic toward the movement, but not active in it. Nearly a third of the respondents (32 percent) indicated they were neutral, while 6 percent were unsympathetic to the movement, and 1 percent had no opinion.

As shown in Figure 8.1, many people did report making changes in their shopping and living habits during the late 1990s and early 2000s to help protect the environment. In 2000 nearly 90 percent of the respondents to a Gallup poll indicated that they had made major or minor changes. In 2003 this number was down to 84 percent.

During 2000 and 2003 the Gallup Organization asked poll participants about their participation within the previous year in specific environmental-related activities. The results are shown in Figure 8.2. In both polls a large majority of respondents (around 90 percent) said that they had voluntarily recycled newspapers, glass, or other common items, though the number dropped slightly between 2000 and 2003. Between 80 and 90 percent had reduced their household's energy usage, also a figure that had decreased from 2000 to 2003. Nearly three-quarters of respondents to both polls had bought specific products they considered more environmentally friendly than competing products. Yet few people in either poll had contributed money or time to an environmental organization.

FIGURE 8.1

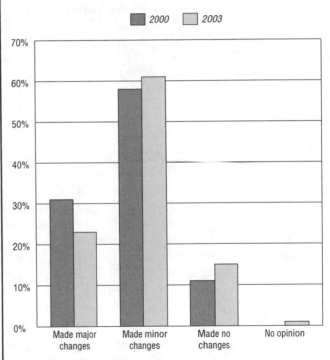

Public opinion on personal lifestyle and the environment, 2000 and 2003

Thinking about your own shopping and living habits over the last five years, would you say you have made major changes, minor changes or no changes to help protect the environment?

SOURCE: Adapted from "Thinking About Your Own Shopping And Living Habits Over The Last Five Years, Would You Say You Have Made Major Changes, Minor Changes Or No Changes To Help Protect The Environment?" in *Poll Topics and Trends: Environment*, © 2003 The Gallup Organization, Princeton, NJ, March 2003 [Online] http://www.gallup.com/ [accessed October 20, 2003]. Reproduced with permission.

The poll respondents also showed little active involvement in environmental issues from a political standpoint. Only around 30 percent of them had voted for or worked

FIGURE 8.2

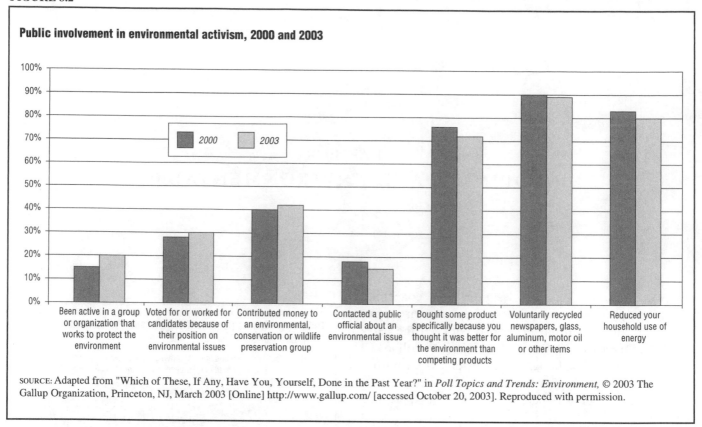

Public involvement in environmental activism, 2000 and 2003

SOURCE: Adapted from "Which of These, If Any, Have You, Yourself, Done in the Past Year?" in *Poll Topics and Trends: Environment,* © 2003 The Gallup Organization, Princeton, NJ, March 2003 [Online] http://www.gallup.com/ [accessed October 20, 2003]. Reproduced with permission.

for candidates because they approved of positions on environmental issues. In both polls fewer than 20 percent of respondents had contacted a public official regarding an environmental issue.

CONDITION OF THE ENVIRONMENT

Americans appear to have a fairly pessimistic attitude regarding the state of the environment. Gallup Poll results from 2001 through 2003 show that between 45 percent and 50 percent of the respondents ranked the overall quality of the nation's environment as "only fair" (See Figure 8.3.) Another 5–10 percent considered it "poor." The percentage of people ranking the environment in poor condition increased from 6 percent in 2001 to 10 percent in 2003. Although many respondents believe that the environment is in "good" condition, support for this position dropped during 2003. Few respondents in any of the polls gave the environment an "excellent" ranking.

This same pessimism is apparent in the Gallup Poll results shown in Figure 8.4. A majority of participants in the 2001, 2002, and 2003 polls expressed the opinion that the quality of the environment is getting worse. Between 30 and 40 percent believe that it is getting better. A small percentage believe that it is about the same.

According to Gallup analysts, the overall percentage of people holding a negative view of environmental conditions increased sharply between 2002 and 2003. In 2002

the percentage of respondents who rated environmental conditions as "poor" or "fair" in the first question and then indicated in the second question that they believe that the environment is staying the same or getting worse was 38 percent. In 2003 this value climbed to 47 percent.

SPECIFIC WORRIES ABOUT THE ENVIRONMENT

Gallup pollsters have been questioning Americans about their environmental concerns for more than a decade. Analysis of the results over time shows some profound changes in American attitudes regarding specific environmental problems. Table 8.1 shows the list of environmental problems presented to participants in polls conducted during various years between 1989 and 2003. The respondents were asked to indicate the degree to which they personally worry about each problem.

The results show that worries about water and air pollution, in general, declined sharply between 1989 and 2003. The percentage expressing a great deal of worry about these issues declined by 21 percent in each category over this time period. Declines between 10 and 20 percent are seen in the number of people expressing a great deal of worry about specific air and water pollution problems—contamination of soil and water by toxic waste, damage to the ozone layer, acid rain, and pollution of drinking water. Concerns about the greenhouse effect (or global warming) and the loss of tropical rain forests did not subside nearly as much over this period of time.

FIGURE 8.3

Public opinion on the overall quality of the environment, 2001–2003

How would you rate the overall quality of the environment in this country today: as excellent, good, only fair, or poor?

■ 2001   ■ 2002   ■ 2003

SOURCE: Adapted from "How Would You Rate the Overall Quality of the Environment in This Country Today—as Excellent, Good, Only Fair, or Poor?" in *Poll Topics and Trends: Environment*, © 2003 The Gallup Organization, Princeton, NJ, March 2003 [Online] http://www .gallup.com/ [accessed October 20, 2003]. Reproduced with permission.

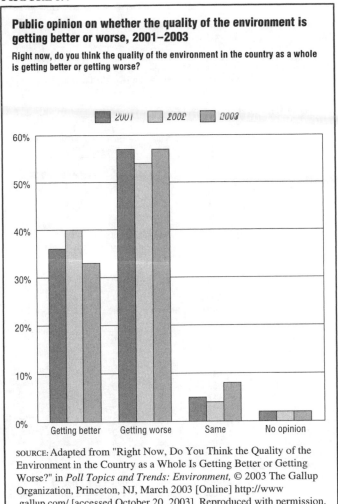

Public opinion on whether the quality of the environment is getting better or worse, 2001–2003

Right now, do you think the quality of the environment in the country as a whole is getting better or getting worse?

■ 2001   ■ 2002   ■ 2003

SOURCE: Adapted from "Right Now, Do You Think the Quality of the Environment in the Country as a Whole Is Getting Better or Getting Worse?" in *Poll Topics and Trends: Environment*, © 2003 The Gallup Organization, Princeton, NJ, March 2003 [Online] http://www .gallup.com/ [accessed October 20, 2003]. Reproduced with permission.

During the years from 2000 to 2003, declines in concern about various environmental issues declined by over 10 percent. Americans apparently felt less concerned about extinction of plant and animal species in 2003, with the percentage of respondents expressing a great deal of worry about this issue declining from 45 to 34 percent between 2000 and 2003. Concerns about the greenhouse effect (or global warming) and the loss of tropical rain forests also subsided by a similar percent (12 percent in each case).

Worry about the nation's fresh water supply actually increased over time. The percentage of respondents expressing a great deal of worry about this issue increased by 7 percent between 2000 and 2003.

Figure 8.5 ranks all ten environmental concerns discussed above in terms of the number of respondents in 2003 who indicated that they worry a great deal about these problems. The number one concern is drinking water pollution, followed by surface water pollution, and pollution due to toxic waste. More than half of all poll participants indicated that they worry a great deal about these three issues.

ENVIRONMENTAL LEGISLATION

Americans appear to feel the government is falling short in its role at protecting the environment. As shown in Figure 8.6, a majority of respondents in Gallup Polls conducted in 1992, 2000, and 2003 indicated that they believe the government does too little to protect the environment. The number expressing this opinion has fallen sharply over time from 68 percent in 1992 to 51 percent in 2003. Roughly one third of the respondents feel that the government is doing about the right amount of effort to protect the environment. Less than 10 percent of respondents in all three polls indicated that the government is doing too much.

Similar responses were recorded in polls conducted by the National Environmental Education and Training Foundation (NEETF). The NEETF is a private nonprofit organization that was chartered by Congress to facilitate public-private partnerships that support environmental education. Every year since 1992 the NEETF has commissioned Roper Starch Worldwide to conduct surveys of the American people on environmental issues.

TABLE 8.1

Public opinion on seriousness of environmental issues, 1989–2003

I'm going to read you a list of environmental problems. As I read each one, please tell me if you personally worry about this problem a great deal, a fair amount, only a little, or not at all. First, how much do you personally worry about — [RANDOM ORDER]?

Pollution of rivers, lakes, and reservoirs

	Great deal %	Fair amount %	Only a little %	Not at all %	No opinion %
2003 Mar 3-5	51	31	13	5	—
2002 Mar 4-7	53	32	12	3	*
2001 Mar 5-7	58	29	10	3	*
2000 Apr 3-9	66	24	8	2	*
1999 Apr 13-14	61	30	7	2	*
1999 Mar 12-14	55	30	12	3	*
1991 Apr 11-14	67	21	8	3	1
1990 Apr 5-8	64	23	9	4	—
1989 May 4-7	72	19	5	3	1

Air pollution

	Great deal %	Fair amount %	Only a little %	Not at all %	No opinion %
2003 Mar 3-5	42	32	20	6	*
2002 Mar 4-7	45	33	18	4	*
2001 Mar 5-7	48	34	14	4	*
2000 Apr 3-9	59	29	9	3	*
1999 Apr 13-14	52	35	10	3	*
1999 Mar 12-14	47	33	16	4	*
1997 Oct 27-28	42	34	18	5	1
1991 Apr 11-14	59	28	10	4	*
1990 Apr 5-8	58	29	9	4	*
1989 May 4-7	63	24	8	4	*

Damage to the earth's ozone layer

	Great deal %	Fair amount %	Only a little %	Not at all %	No opinion %
2003 Mar 3-5	35	31	21	12	1
2002 Mar 4-7	38	29	21	11	1
2001 Mar 5-7	47	28	16	8	1
2000 Apr 3-9	49	29	14	7	1
1999 Apr 13-14	44	32	15	8	1
1997 Oct 27-28	33	27	25	13	2
1991 Apr 11-14	49	24	16	8	4
1990 Apr 5-8	43	28	15	10	4
1989 May 4-7	51	26	13	8	2

The loss of tropical rain forests

	Great deal %	Fair amount %	Only a little %	Not at all %	No opinion %
2003 Mar 3-5	39	29	21	11	*
2002 Mar 4-7	38	27	21	12	2
2001 Mar 5-7	44	32	15	8	1
2000 Apr 3-9	51	25	14	9	1
1999 Apr 13-14	49	30	14	6	1
1991 Apr 11-14	42	25	21	10	2
1990 Apr 5-8	40	24	19	14	3
1989 May 4-7	42	25	18	12	3

TABLE 8.1

Public opinion on seriousness of environmental issues, 1989–2003 [CONTINUED]

I'm going to read you a list of environmental problems. As I read each one, please tell me if you personally worry about this problem a great deal, a fair amount, only a little, or not at all. First, how much do you personally worry about — [RANDOM ORDER]?

The "greenhouse effect" or global warming

	Great deal %	Fair amount %	Only a little %	Not at all %	No opinion %
2003 Mar 3-5	28	30	23	17	2
2002 Mar 4-7	29	29	23	17	2
2001 Mar 5-7	33	30	22	13	2
2000 Apr 3-9	40	32	15	12	1
1999 Apr 13-14	34	34	18	12	2
1999 Mar 12-14	28	31	23	16	2
1997 Oct 27-28	24	26	29	17	4
1991 Apr 11-14	35	27	22	12	5
1990 Apr 5-8	30	27	20	16	6
1989 May 4-7	35	28	18	12	7

Contamination of soil and water by toxic waste

	Great deal %	Fair amount %	Only a little %	Not at all %	No opinion %
2003 Mar 3-5	51	28	16	5	*
2002 Mar 4-7	53	29	15	3	*
2001 Mar 5-7	58	27	12	3	*
2000 Apr 3-9	64	25	7	4	*
1999 Apr 13-14	63	27	7	3	*
1999 Mar 12-14	55	29	11	5	*
1991 Apr 11-14	62	21	11	5	1
1990 Apr 5-8	63	22	10	5	*
1989 May 4-7	69	21	6	3	*

Acid rain

	Great deal %	Fair amount %	Only a little %	Not at all %	No opinion %
2003 Mar 3-5	24	26	27	21	2
2002 Mar 4-7	25	23	31	19	2
2001 Mar 5-7	28	28	26	16	2
2000 Apr 3-9	34	31	19	15	1
1999 Apr 13-14	29	35	23	11	2
1991 Apr 11-14	34	30	20	14	3
1990 Apr 5-8	34	30	18	14	4
1989 May 4-7	41	27	19	11	3

Pollution of drinking water

	Great deal %	Fair amount %	Only a little %	Not at all %	No opinion %
2003 Mar 3-5	54	25	15	6	—
2002 Mar 4-7	57	25	13	5	*
2001 Mar 5-7	64	24	9	3	*
2000 Apr 3-9	72	20	6	2	*
1999 Apr 13-14	68	22	7	3	*
1991 Apr 11-14	67	19	10	3	1
1990 Apr 5-8	65	22	9	4	*

Figure 8.7 shows the results of the NEETF survey published in August 2002 and based on polling done in 2001. Participants were asked their opinion regarding environmental protection laws and regulations. The survey showed that 44 percent felt that such laws have not gone far enough at protecting the environment. Another 30 percent felt that the laws have achieved about the right balance, 21 percent felt that the laws had gone too far, and 6 percent had no opinion.

The poll respondents were also asked their opinion regarding the extent of legislation affecting particular environmental concerns as shown in Figure 8.8. Water pollution received the highest percentage of people responding that laws had not gone far enough to protect it. This result is consistent with data from 1999, but is 10

TABLE 8.1

Public opinion on seriousness of environmental issues, 1989–2003 [CONTINUED]

I'm going to read you a list of environmental problems. As I read each one, please tell me if you personally worry about this problem a great deal, a fair amount, only a little, or not at all. First, how much do you personally worry about — [RANDOM ORDER]?

Extinction of plant and animal species

	Great deal %	Fair amount %	Only a little %	Not at all %	No opinion %
2003 Mar 3-5	34	32	21	12	1
2002 Mar 4-7	35	30	22	12	1
2001 Mar 5-7	43	30	19	7	1
2000 Apr 3-9	45	33	14	8	*

Maintenance of the nation's supply of fresh water for household needs

	Great deal %	Fair amount %	Only a little %	Not at all %	No opinion %
2003 Mar 3-5	49	28	15	8	*
2002 Mar 4-7	50	28	17	5	*
2001 Mar 5-7	35	34	19	10	2
2000 Apr 3-9	42	31	14	12	1

SOURCE: "I'm Going to Read You A List of Environmental Problems. As I Read Each One, Please Tell Me If You Personally Worry About This Problem a Great Deal, a Fair Amount, Only a Little, or Not at All," in *Poll Topics and Trends: Environment*, © 2003 The Gallup Organization, Princeton, NJ, March 2003 [Online] http://www.gallup.com/ [Accessed October 20, 2003]. Reproduced with permission.

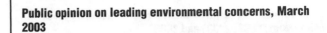

FIGURE 8.5

Public opinion on leading environmental concerns, March 2003

"I'm going to read you a list of environmental problems. As I read each one, please tell me if you personally worry about this problem a great deal, a fair amount, only a little, or not at all. First, how much do you personally worry about--"

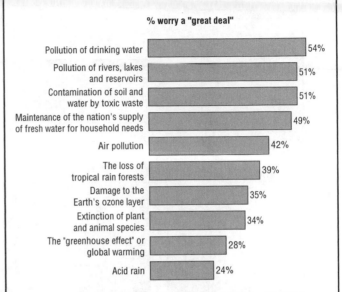

% worry a "great deal"

Pollution of drinking water — 54%
Pollution of rivers, lakes and reservoirs — 51%
Contamination of soil and water by toxic waste — 51%
Maintenance of the nation's supply of fresh water for household needs — 49%
Air pollution — 42%
The loss of tropical rain forests — 39%
Damage to the Earth's ozone layer — 35%
Extinction of plant and animal species — 34%
The "greenhouse effect" or global warming — 28%
Acid rain — 24%

SOURCE: Lydia Saad, "Americans' Environmental Worries," in *Giving Global Warming the Cold Shoulder*, © 2003 The Gallup Organization, Princeton, NJ, April 22, 2003 [Online] http://www.gallup.com/ [accessed September 30, 2003]. Reproduced with permission.

percent less than it was in 1992. Regarding air pollution, 63 percent of respondents felt that laws had not gone far enough compared to 60 percent for energy resource conservation, 45 percent for wetland, and 41 percent for endangered species.

Taken together, the Gallup and NEETF poll results indicate that roughly 40–50 percent of Americans believe that the government is not doing enough to protect the environment.

A MISINFORMED PUBLIC—THE NINTH ANNUAL NATIONAL REPORT CARD

The NEETF regularly surveys Americans about their knowledge of environmental issues. A comprehensive survey was performed in 2001 and published in *National Report Card on Environmental Attitudes, Knowledge, and Behaviors*.

Researchers conducted telephone interviews with 1,505 Americans, 18 years of age and older, asking them about their beliefs and knowledge regarding environmental issues.

The NEETF found that 67 percent of adults failed a simple test on environmental knowledge. For example, only one in three knew that the burning of fossil fuels—coal, natural gas, and oil—produces most of the country's electricity. Half the public thought electricity is produced mostly by waterpower (at the Hoover Dam, for example).

Actually waterpower produces less than 15 percent of America's energy.

Similar misunderstandings showed up throughout the test and may explain why lawmakers often find it difficult to engage the general public in issues such as global warming and the maintenance of air quality.

The *National Report Card* also revealed that the proportion of respondents saying they try to conserve water, reduce the amount of garbage they produce, purchase biodegradable or recyclable products, avoid using chemicals in their yard or garden, or use alternative transportation is lower than in past surveys.

In trying to explain this decline in environmentally conscious behaviors, the Roper researchers uncovered a relationship between environmental knowledge and engagement in environmental-related activities. Correlation studies showed that as overall environmental knowledge increased, the likelihood of participation in several environmental activities also increased. This trend was most evident for turning off lights when not in use, recycling newspapers, cans, and glass, and avoiding the use of chemicals in the yard. It is likely, then, that increasing the environmental knowledge of the U.S. populace would increase overall involvement in environmental activities.

FIGURE 8.6

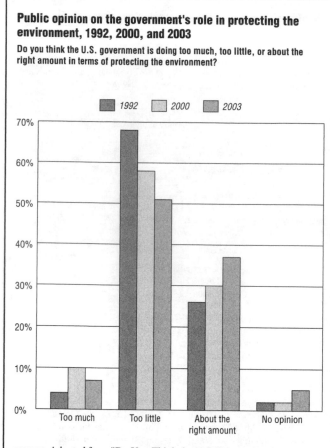

Public opinion on the government's role in protecting the environment, 1992, 2000, and 2003

Do you think the U.S. government is doing too much, too little, or about the right amount in terms of protecting the environment?

SOURCE: Adapted from "Do You Think the U.S. Government Is Doing Too Much, Too Little, or About the Right Amount in Terms of Protecting the Environment?" in *Poll Topics and Trends: Environment,* © 2003 The Gallup Organization, Princeton, NJ, March 2003 [Online] http://www.gallup.com/ [accessed October 20, 2003]. Reproduced with permission.

Respondents did support the idea of advancing environmental education. The survey found that 95 percent of the adults asked believe environmental education should be taught in schools.

ENVIRONMENT VERSUS ECONOMY AND ENERGY

In a 1998 report on the environmental attitudes of Americans, Wirthlin Worldwide concluded that environmental support in the United States generally moves in accord with the economy. Wirthlin compared U.S. unemployment rates to data they collected on environmental support among Americans. They found a statistically significant inverse relationship between the unemployment level and support for environmental protection—that is, when unemployment rises, environmental support falls. The report stated, "When consumer confidence reflects a good economy, public concern for social issues is heightened, and pro-environmental sentiments run high. But when the economy is bad, the environment tends to fall to the back burner." ("Environmental Support Systems Amid Economic Uncertainty," *The Wirthlin Report 8,* no. 9, September 1998, p. 1.)

NEETF/Roper survey results published between 1992 and 2001 in (*National Report Card*) reports support the conclusions of the 1998 Wirthlin Worldwide report. The NEETF found that the majority of Americans believe that environmental protection and economic development can go hand in hand. According to these reports, most Americans do not believe that they must choose between environmental protection and economic development, but feel they can find a balance between the two. If forced to choose, however, 71 percent of the public in the 2000 survey chose to make the environment a priority. This percentage was relatively unchanged from previous years.

In 2001 the Gallup Organization surveyed Americans regarding their approval or disapproval of President George W. Bush's rejection of the Kyoto Protocol. The Kyoto Protocol is an international treaty that sets voluntary limits on the production of carbon dioxide and other gases believed responsible for global warming. President Bush has stated that he believes adherence to the treaty would place an excessive burden on the American economy. Results indicated that 48 percent of those polled disapproved of Bush's actions in this matter, while 41 percent approved. This seems to indicate some willingness to put economic growth at risk for the sake of the environment.

Figure 8.9 shows Gallup Poll results from various years between 1984 and 2003. The participants were asked to choose between economic growth and the environment, assuming that choosing one could have negative consequences on the other. The results show that the environment was given priority over economic growth in every poll. However the gap between the two choices narrowed considerably in the early 2000s. In 2003 priority to the environment was supported by 47 percent of respondents, while priority to economic growth was supported by 42 percent of respondents.

Figure 8.10 shows the results of another Gallup Poll in which participants had to choose between the environment and energy supplies. Roughly 50 percent of those asked gave priority to the environment, while roughly 40 percent chose energy supplies.

ENVIRONMENTAL PROPOSALS FOR THE FUTURE

In 2003 the Gallup Organization asked Americans their general opinions regarding some specific proposals related to energy resources and environmental regulations. The results are shown in Table 8.2. The most popular proposals were those that set higher emissions standards on business, industry, and automobiles or imposed other pollution controls. These ideas were favored by 70–80 percent of those asked. Stronger enforcement of federal environmental regulations was

FIGURE 8.7

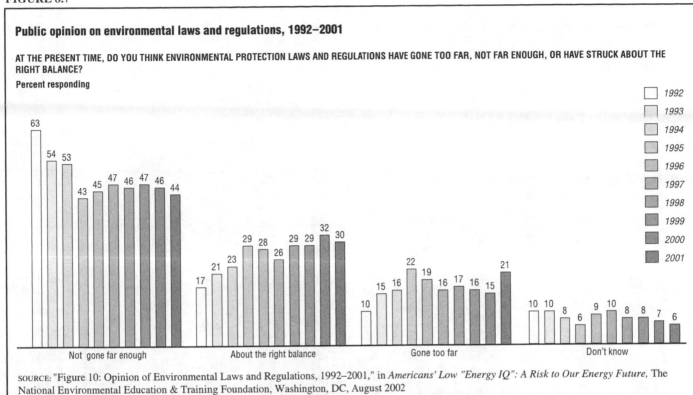

Public opinion on environmental laws and regulations, 1992–2001

AT THE PRESENT TIME, DO YOU THINK ENVIRONMENTAL PROTECTION LAWS AND REGULATIONS HAVE GONE TOO FAR, NOT FAR ENOUGH, OR HAVE STRUCK ABOUT THE RIGHT BALANCE?

Percent responding

Legend: 1992, 1993, 1994, 1995, 1996, 1997, 1998, 1999, 2000, 2001

Not gone far enough: 63, 54, 53, 43, 45, 47, 46, 47, 46, 44
About the right balance: 17, 21, 23, 29, 28, 26, 29, 29, 32, 30
Gone too far: 10, 15, 16, 22, 19, 16, 17, 16, 15, 21
Don't know: 10, 10, 8, 6, 9, 10, 8, 8, 7, 6

SOURCE: "Figure 10: Opinion of Environmental Laws and Regulations, 1992–2001," in *Americans' Low "Energy IQ": A Risk to Our Energy Future,* The National Environmental Education & Training Foundation, Washington, DC, August 2002

also favored by 75 percent of the respondents. The two least popular proposals were expanding the use of nuclear energy (favored by 41 percent of respondents) and opening up the Arctic National Wildlife Refuge in Alaska for oil exploration (favored by 41 percent). Comparison of the responses over time for all proposals show little difference between polls conducted in previous years.

THE ANTIREGULATORY MOVEMENT

Over the past decade and a half, dissatisfaction with government regulation has grown. In 1994 the newly elected Republican-controlled Congress attempted to strike down a wide variety of federal regulations, including environmental regulations they considered overly burdensome. Bills were introduced to relax regulations under the Clean Water Act, Endangered Species Act, the Superfund Toxic Waste Clean-up Program, the Safe Drinking Water Act, and other environmental statutes. Although much of that legislation ultimately failed to pass, budget cuts resulted in a lack of enforcement of many statutes.

Several factors contributed to this reaction to federal regulation. During the early days of the environmental era, the United States was experiencing a post-World War II (1939-1945) economic boom, leading Americans to regard regulatory costs as sustainable. But during the 1970s and 1980s, economic growth slowed, wages stagnated, and Americans became uncertain about the future. An increasing number of Americans started to question the costs of

FIGURE 8.8

Public opinion on regulation of specific environmental and energy laws, 2001

AT THE PRESENT TIME, DO YOU THINK LAWS AND REGULATIONS FOR (INSERT ISSUE) HAVE GONE TOO FAR, NOT FAR ENOUGH, OR HAVE STRUCK ABOUT THE RIGHT BALANCE?

Gone too far | About the right balance | Not gone far enough

Percent responding

	Gone too far	About the right balance	Not gone far enough	Not gone far enough 1999	Not gone far enough 1992
Water pollution	4	22	69	70%	79%
Air pollution	8	26	63	63	72
Conserving energy resources	7	26	60	n/a	n/a
Wetlands	14	28	45	44	53
Endangered species	21	32	41	39	51

SOURCE: "Figure 13: Current Regulation of Specific Environmental and Energy Issues," in *Americans' Low "Energy IQ": A Risk to Our Energy Future,* The National Environmental Education & Training Foundation, Washington, DC, August 2002

FIGURE 8.9

Public opinion on protecting the environment versus economic growth, 1984–2003

With which of the following statements about the environment and economy do you most agree?

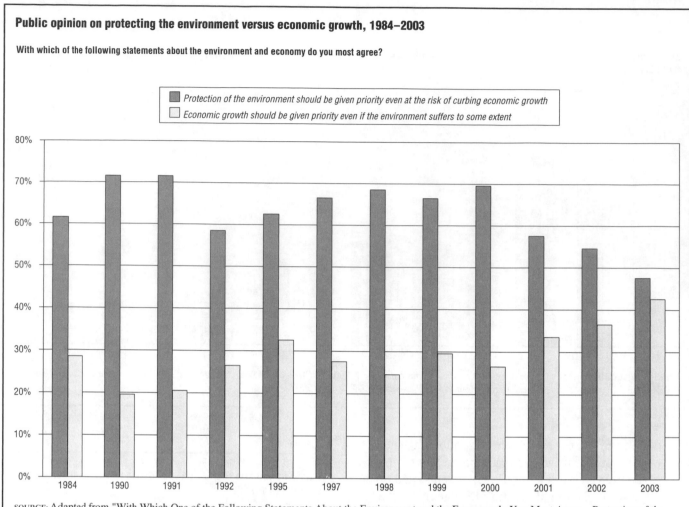

■ Protection of the environment should be given priority even at the risk of curbing economic growth
□ Economic growth should be given priority even if the environment suffers to some extent

SOURCE: Adapted from "With Which One of the Following Statements About the Environment and the Economy do You Most Agree—Protection of the Environment Should Be Given Priority, Even at the Risk of Curbing Economic Growth (or) Economic Growth Should Be Given Priority, Even if the Environment Suffers to Some Extent?" in *Poll Topics and Trends: Environment,* © 2003 The Gallup Organization, Princeton, NJ, March 2003 [Online] http://www.gallup.com/ [accessed October 20, 2003]. Reproduced with permission.

environmental protection. The return of a vigorous economy in recent years has revived the American commitment to environmental issues, but not to the levels that some environmentalists had hoped. Most recently, the economy has taken a downturn, which may cause Americans to place environmental issues on the back burner once again.

Private property use has also played a very important role in the antiregulatory movement. The Endangered Species Act and the wetlands provisions of the Clean Water Act spurred a grassroots "private property rights" movement. Many people became concerned about legislation that would allow the government to "take" or devalue properties without compensation. For example, if federal regulations prohibited a landowner from building a beach house on his own private property, which happened to be protected land, the owner wanted the government to compensate him for devaluing the land. In addition, some observers believe that regulation of the waste industry, among others, has accomplished its goals and that it is time to relax control in favor of economic growth.

COMPARATIVE RISK ASSESSMENT— HOW CLEAN IS CLEAN?

Some Americans believe that pollution control budgets are too high in comparison to threats to the environment. They also believe that when pollution occurs, governments overreact on the theory that the safest thing to do is clean up everything completely. This is no longer considered practical by many Americans, especially as regulatory agencies begin focusing on smaller and smaller pollution sources. Instead of responding immediately to every potential threat, many experts believe there needs to be a pause for evaluation. Such an approach is termed comparative risk assessment.

Comparative risk assessment differs from the scientific discipline of quantitative risk assessment and cost-benefit analysis that some congressmen advocate. Comparative risk assessment factors in more subjective criteria than does quantitative risk assessment. Comparative risk assessment works like this: A committee of citizens looks into potential pollution problems, reviewing pertinent scientific information—including risk assessments and cost-benefit

FIGURE 8.10

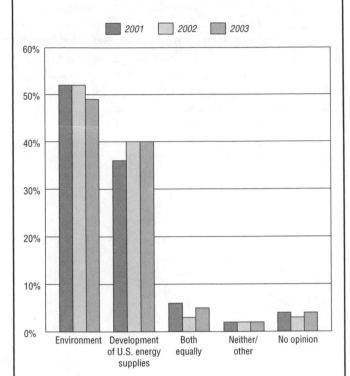

Public opinion on whether the environment or energy supplies should be given priority, 2001–2003

With which one of these statements about the environment and energy production do you most agree: protection of the environment should be given priority, even at the risk of limiting the amount of energy supplies which the U.S. produces, or development of U.S. energy supplies should be given priority, even if the environment suffers to some extent?

☐ 2001 ☐ 2002 ☐ 2003

Note: "Energy supplies" refers to items such as oil, gas, or coal.

SOURCE: Adapted from "With Which One of These Statements About the Environment and Energy Production Do You Most Agree—Protection of the Environment Should Be Given Priority, Even at the Risk of Limiting the Amount of Energy Supplies (such as Oil, Gas and Coal) which the United States Produces (or) Development of U.S. Energy Supplies (such as Oil, Gas and Coal) Should Be Given Priority, Even if the Environment Suffers to Some Extent?" in *Poll Topics and Trends: Environment,* © 2003 The Gallup Organization, Princeton, NJ, March 2003 [Online] http://www.gallup.com/ [accessed October 20, 2003]. Reproduced with permission.

TABLE 8.2

Public opinion on specific environmental proposals, 2001–03

NEXT I AM GOING TO READ SOME SPECIFIC ENVIRONMENTAL PROPOSALS. FOR EACH ONE, PLEASE SAY WHETHER YOU GENERALLY FAVOR OR OPPOSE IT. HOW ABOUT – [RANDOM ORDER]?

Expanding the use of nuclear energy

	Favor	Oppose	No opinion
2003 Mar 3–5	43%	51	6
2002 Mar 4–7	45%	51	4
2001 Mar 5–7	44%	51	5

Opening up the Arctic National Wildlife Refuge in Alaska for oil exploration

	Favor %	Oppose %	No opinion %
2003 Mar 3–5	41	55	4
2002 Mar 4–7	40	56	4
2001 Nov 8–11[a]	44	51	5
2001 May 7–9[a, b]	38	57	5
2001 Mar 5–7[b]	40	56	4

More strongly enforcing federal environmental regulations

	Favor	Oppose	No opinion
2003 Mar 3–5	75%	21	4
2002 Mar 4–7	78%	19	3
2001 Mar 5–7	77%	20	3

Setting higher auto emissions standards for automobiles

	Favor	Oppose	No opinion
2003 Mar 3–5	73%	24	3
2002 Mar 4–7	72%	26	2
2001 Mar 5–7	75%	23	2

Setting higher emissions and pollution standards for business and industry

	Favor	Oppose	No opinion
2003 Mar 3–5	80%	19	1
2002 Mar 4–7	83%	16	1
2001 Mar 5–7	81%	17	2

Imposing mandatory controls on carbon dioxide emissions and other greenhouse gases

	Favor	Oppose	No opinion
2003 Mar 3–5	75%	22	3

[a]Next, here are some things that can be done to deal with the energy situation. For each one, please say whether you generally favor or oppose it. How about — [RANDOM ORDER]?
[b]WORDING: Opening up the Alaskan Arctic Wildlife Refuge for oil exploration.

SOURCE: "Next I am going to read some specific environmental proposals. For each one, please say whether you generally favor or oppose it," in *Poll Topics and Trends: Environment,* © 2003 The Gallup Organization, Princeton, NJ, March 2003 [Online] http://www.gallup.com/ [accessed October 20, 2003]. Reproduced with permission.

analyses—about the hazards, and then ranks the perils to a city's health, natural surroundings, and general quality of life. In short, comparative risk assessment asks communities to decide for themselves what environmental problems to take most seriously by factoring in both scientific evidence and quality-of-life concerns that cannot be economically quantified. A number of states have launched comparative risk assessment projects. Critics of this approach fear it will be used as a way to cloud issues and hold up progress.

LITIGATION AND ENVIRONMENTAL POLICY

Courts have been an important forum for developing environmental policy because they allow citizens to challenge complex environmental laws and to affect the decision-making process. Individuals and groups can sue after a regulation has been enacted if an agency fails to enforce a policy, or if they feel the legislature is unsympathetic to their cause. Just the threat of litigation has changed policy within agencies enforcing environmental laws.

An environmental law can be challenged on grounds that it violates the Constitution of the United States.

Successful challenges can force the legislature to bring the law into constitutional compliance. A lawsuit can also be filed based on harm to a person, property, or an economic interest, such as major claims involving asbestos, lead, or loss of private property. Lawsuits have also prompted legislation, such as the federal Superfund law and the Toxic Substances Control Act, requiring agencies to control pollutants.

NORTH AMERICAN AGREEMENT ON ENVIRONMENTAL COOPERATION

In 1993 the United States, Canada, and Mexico signed the North American Agreement on Environmental Cooperation (NAAEC), the environmental side agreement to the North American Free Trade Agreement (NAFTA), to discourage countries from weakening environmental standards to encourage trade. Other countries may become members of the NAAEC, and a country may withdraw from the agreement and still remain a NAFTA member.

A member country can be challenged in two ways under the NAAEC if one of its states fails to enforce environmental laws. First, a nongovernmental agency, such as the Sierra Club or Audubon Society, may petition the commission. This alerts the public to the violation. Second, a member country can initiate proceedings against another member country showing a "persistent pattern of failure...to enforce its environmental law" that can be directly linked to goods and services traded between the parties. If the conflict is not resolved through initial consultations, arbitration may be required and fines levied for failure to cooperate. If fines are not paid, a complaining party may suspend NAFTA benefits in an amount not exceeding the assessment.

IMPORTANT NAMES AND ADDRESSES

BioCycle
419 State Ave.
Emmaus, PA 18049
(610) 967-4135
URL: http://www.biocycle.net/

Environmental Defense National Headquarters
257 Park Ave. South
New York, NY 10010
(212) 505-2100
FAX: (212) 505-2375
E-mail: members@environmentaldefense.org
URL: http://www.environmentaldefense.org

Environmental Industry Associations
4301 Connecticut Ave., NW, Suite 300
Washington, DC 20008
FAX: (202) 966-4818
(800) 424-2869
URL: http://www.envasns.org

Foodservice and Packaging Institute, Inc.
150 S. Washington St., Suite 204
Falls Church, VA 22046
(703) 538-2800
FAX: (703) 538-2187
E-mail: fpi@fpi.org
URL: http://www.fpi.org

Friends of the Earth
1717 Massachusetts Ave., NW, Suite 600
Washington, DC 20036-2002
FAX: (202) 783-0444
(877) 843-8687
E-mail: foe@foe.org
URL: http://www.foe.org

The Garbage Project
The University of Arizona
Tucson, AZ 85741
(520) 621-6299
FAX: (520) 621-9608
E-mail: twj@gas.uug.arizona.edu

URL: http://info-center.ccit.arizona.edu/~bara/gbg_in~1.htm

General Accounting Office
441 G St., NW
Washington, DC 20548
(202) 512-4800
E-mail: webmaster@gao.gov
URL: http://www.gao.gov

Glass Packaging Institute
515 King St., Suite 420
Alexandria, VA 22314
(703) 684-6359
FAX: (703) 684-6048
E-mail: abopp@gpi.org
URL: http://www.gpi.org

Greenpeace USA
702 H St., NW, Suite 300
Washington, DC 20001
(202) 462-1177
FAX: (202) 462-4507
(800) 326-0959
E-mail: greenpeace.usa@wdc.greenpeace.org
URL: http://www.greenpeaceusa.org

National Acid Precipitation Assessment Program
1315 East-West Highway
Silver Spring, MD 20910
(301) 713-0460
FAX: (301) 713-3515
E-mail: napap@noaa.gov
URL: http://www.oar.noaa.gov/organization/napap.html

National Consumers League
1701 K St., NW, Suite 1200
Washington, DC 20006
(202) 835-3323
FAX: (202) 835-0747
E-mail: info@nclnet.org
URL: http://www.nclnet.org

National Environmental Education and Training Foundation
1707 H St., NW, Suite 900
Washington, DC 20006-3915
(202) 833-2933
FAX: (202) 261-6464
E-mail: president@neetf.org
URL: http://www.neetf.org

Natural Resources Defense Council
40 W. 20th St.
New York, NY 10011
(212) 727-2700
FAX: (212) 727-1773
E-mail: nrdcinfo@nrdc.org
URL: http://www.nrdc.org

Sierra Club
85 Second St., Second Floor
San Francisco, CA 94105
(415) 977-5500
FAX: (415) 977-5799
E-mail: information@sierraclub.org
URL: http://www.sierraclub.org

Steel Recycling Institute
680 Andersen Dr.
Pittsburgh, PA 15220-2700
(800) 937-1226
E-mail: sri@recycle-steel.org
URL: http://www.recycle-steel.org

U.S. Department of Energy (DOE)
1000 Independence Ave., SW
Washington, DC 20585
FAX: (202) 586-4403
(800) DIAL-DOE
E-mail: the.secretary@hq.doe.gov
URL: http://www.energy.gov

U.S. Environmental Protection Agency Headquarters (EPA)
Ariel Rios Building
1200 Pennsylvania Ave., NW
Washington, DC 20460

(202) 272-0167
E-mail: public-access@epa.gov
URL: http://www.epa.gov

U.S. Fish and Wildlife Service
1849 C St., NW
Washington, DC 20240
(202) 208-5634
(800) 344-WILD
URL: http://www.fws.gov

U.S. Geological Survey National Center
12201 Sunrise Valley Dr.
Reston, VA 20192

(703) 648-4000
(888) 275-8747
URL: http://www.usgs.gov

U.S. Nuclear Regulatory Commission (NRC)
Office of Public Affairs
Mail Stop O-2A13
Washington, DC 20555
(301) 415-8200
(800) 368-5642
E-mail: opa@nrc.gov
URL: http://www.nrc.gov

Worldwatch Institute
1776 Massachusetts Ave., NW
Washington, DC 20036-1904
(202) 452-1999
FAX: (202) 296-7365
E-mail: worldwatch@worldwatch.org
URL: http://www.worldwatch.org

RESOURCES

The U.S. Environmental Protection Agency (EPA) is the most significant source of information on solid waste and pollution in America. The EPA is responsible for keeping statistics on pollution, educating the American people about pollution and environmental issues, and ensuring that environmental regulations are obeyed. The EPA report *Municipal Solid Waste in the United States: 2000 Facts and Figures* (2002) is an invaluable resource. It is part of a series of reports that characterizes municipal solid waste in the United States.

The EPA's *Let's Reduce and Recycle: Curriculum for Solid Waste Awareness* (1990) is a teaching guide for introducing students to recycling and environmental pollution awareness. *The Plain English Guide to the Clean Air Act* (1993) offers a basic introduction to the Clean Air Act and the problems of air pollution. It is available on the Internet on the EPA Web site at www.epa.gov.

Other useful EPA publications include *EPA's Draft Report on the Environment 2003, Ozone: Good Up High, Bad Nearby* (2003), *Latest Findings on National Air Quality: 2002 Status and Trends* (2003), *Guide for Industrial Waste Management* (2003), *National Water Quality Inventory: 2000 Report* (2002), *RCRA Orientation Manual* (2003), *25 Years of RCRA: Building on Our Past to Protect Our Future* (2002), and *2001 Toxics Release Inventory* (2003), which is a publicly available database containing information on toxic chemical releases and other waste management activities.

Helpful publications from the Department of Energy include *Annual Energy Review 2001* (2003), *Spent Nuclear Fuel Transportation* (2002), *Renewable Energy Trends 2002* (2003), *Yucca Mountain Science and Engineering Report* (2001), *The Waste Isolation Pilot Plant: Pioneering Nuclear Waste Disposal* (2000), and *Alternatives to Traditional Transportation Fuels* (1999).

The U.S. Geological Survey (USGS) provides scientific information to help describe and understand the earth; minimize loss of life and property from natural disasters; manage water, energy, and biological and mineral resources; and enhance and protect the quality of life. Its report *Distribution of Major Herbicides in Ground Water of the United States* (1999) was compiled in conjunction with the EPA and describes chemical contamination of American groundwater.

The now-defunct Office of Technology Assessment (OTA), a branch of the United States Congress, provided studies on scientific problems facing the United States. The OTA's *Wastes in Marine Environments* (1987), *Bioremediation for Marine Oil Spills* (1991), and *Acid Rain and Transported Air Pollutants: Implications for Public Policy* (1984) are useful resources. OTA publications are still available from the U.S. Government Printing Office.

The General Accounting Office (GAO) is the investigative arm of the United States Congress. GAO publications include *Climate Change: Information on Three Air Pollutants' Climate Effects and Emissions Trends* (GAO-03-25), *Superfund Program: Current Status and Future Fiscal Challenges* (GAO-03-850), *Spent Nuclear Fuel: Options Exist to Further Enhance Security* (GAO-03-426), and *Clean Air Act: EPA Should Use Available Data to Monitor the Effects of Its Revisions to the New Source Review Program* (GAO-03-947).

Other government publications concerning the study of garbage and pollution are *Federal Enforcement of Environmental Laws, 1997* (1999) from the Bureau of Justice Statistics of the U.S. Department of Justice, *Indoor Pollution—Status of Federal Research Activities* (1999), *Solid Waste: State and Federal Efforts to Manage Nonhazardous Waste* (1995), *Animal Agriculture—Waste Management Practices* (1999), and *Hazardous and Nonhazardous Wastes: Demographics of People Living Near Waste Facilities* (1995).

The Environmental Industry Associations, the waste management industry's trade association, provides brochures and booklets on waste management, including the timeline *Garbage Then and Now.*

The Natural Resources Defense Council (NRDC), a private environmental research organization, published *Testing the Waters: A Guide to Water Quality at Vacation Beaches* (2001), on the condition of the nation's recreational beaches.

In December 2001 *BioCycle,* a journal of composting and recycling, discusses waste disposal in its annual "State of Garbage in America" survey.

The National Conference of State Legislatures published "New Developments in Environmental Justice," a survey of state enforcement of environmental laws, in its 1999 *Legisbrief.*

Roper Starch conducts an annual study for the National Environmental Education and Training Founda-

tion. In 2002 he completed *Americans' Low "Energy IQ" : A Risk to Our Energy Future.*

John C. Ryan and Alan Thein Durning of Northwest Environmental Watch published *Stuff—The Secret Lives of Everyday Things* (1997), on consumption in the United States.

Susan Strasser's *Waste and Want—A Social History of Trash* (Henry Holt and Company, New York, 1999) explores the treatment and role of garbage through history. It also provides background on the history of solid waste.

The surveys of the Gallup Organization are resources that gauge public opinion on many different issues, including the environment.

Information Plus sincerely thanks all of the organizations listed above for the valuable information they provide.

INDEX

pH scale values and, 71
   quality of rivers, streams and, 78
Aquatic Life Support category, 76
Aquifer
   assessment of, 90
   defined, 89
   water removed from, 89
Arctic National Wildlife Refuge (AK), 129
Asthma
   outcomes in children, 1980-2001, 54
     (*f*4.13)
   ozone levels and, 53
Athens (Greece), 1
Atlantic Coast Demolition and Recycling
   Inc. v. Atlantic County, 33
Atomic bomb, 115–116
Atomic Energy Commission, 115–116
Atrazine, 90
ATSDR (Agency for Toxic Substances and
   Disease Registry), 84
Automobiles
   air pollution from, 57–59
   alternative transportation fuels, 59–62,
     59*t*, 60*t*
   comparison of growth areas and
     emissions, 1970-2002, 58*f*
   cutting emissions further and, 63
   obsolescence and, 13
   recycling, 45

B

Bacteria
   in beach waters, 75
   organic matter decomposition and, 21–22
   in private wells, 90
Batteries
   cadmium, lead, mercury from, 27
   Mercury-Containing and Rechargeable
     Battery Management Act, 44
BEACH Watch Program, 75
Beaches
   coastal debris items, most prevalent,
     2000, 84*t*
   ocean shoreline waters, quality of, 82–85
   pathogens in beach waters, 75
Beef industry packaging, 19–20
Ben Oehrleins, Inc. v. Hennepin County, 33
The Benefits and Costs of the Clean Air Act,
   1970 to 1990 (Environmental Protection
   Agency), 62–63
Benzene, 56
Beverage cans, 19
Bioaccumulation
   of chemicals in water environments, 74
   of pollutants in food chain, 72*f*
   process, 73
BioCycle (journal)
   MSW management methods data of,
     20–21, 20*t*–21*t*
   MSW survey by, 13–14
Biodiesel, 59*t*
Biomagnification
   bioaccumulation of pollutants in food
     chain, 72*f*
   process, 73
Biomass fuels, 29*t*
Birds, ocean debris threat to, 84

Blacks/African Americans, 114
Black carbon, 64*f*
Black Death, 1
Boats, air pollution and, 62
Brownfields, 113–114
Bush, George H.W., 116
Bush, George W.
   Kyoto Protocol and, 65, 128
   Yucca Mountain and, 118
Buy-back centers, 42

C

C & A Carbone v. Clarkstown, 32–33
CAA. *See* Clean Air Act (CAA)
   Amendments of 1990; Clean Air Act
   (CAA) of 1970
Cadmium in landfills, 27
CAFE (Corporate Average Fuel Efficiency)
   standards, 58–59
California
   acid precipitation in, 71–72
   boat rules in, 62
   curbside programs of, 41
   irrigation in, 89
   oil-drilling accident in, 69
   particulate matter concentrations in, 53
Canada, 132
Carbon dioxide (CO_2)
   CAFE standards and, 58–59
   emissions, 63–65
   sources/lifetime of, 64*f*
Carbon monoxide (CO)
   air quality, 1983-2002, 51 (*f*4.9)
   emissions, 1983-2002, 51 (*f*4.8)
   emissions/dangers of, 50
Carlsbad (NM), 118
Casks
   radioactive waste transported in, 120
   spent fuel dry storage container, 120*f*
Cassettes, 39
CD (compact disc), 39
Census of Agriculture (U.S. Department of
   Agriculture), 89
CERCLA. *See* Comprehensive
   Environmental, Response,
   Compensation, and Liability Act
Chemical industry, 104
Chemical Waste Management, Inc. v. Hunt,
   25, 31
Chemicals
   on Toxics Release Inventory, 106
   Toxics Release Inventory on-site/off-site
     releases by state, 2001, 108*t*–109*t*
   Toxics Release Inventory, top twenty
     chemicals with largest total releases,
     110*t*
   See also Hazardous waste
Chesapeake Bay, excess nitrogen in, 71
Chevron, 114
Children
   asthma outcomes in children, 1980-2001,
     54 (*f*4.13)
   ozone levels and, 53
China, fossil fuel use in, 65–66
Chlordane
   advisory trends for lakes, 74 (*f*5.7)
   advisory trends for river miles, 74 (*f*5.8)

in water, 74
Cholera, 73
Cigarette smoke, 66
Cities
   cleaning up ancient cities, 1
   early waste management, 6
Clarkstown, C & A Carbone v., 32–33
Class I injection well, 107 (*f*7.3)
Clean Air Act (CAA) Amendments of 1990
   Acid Rain Program under, 49
   motor vehicle emissions and, 58
   protection of, 8
   reduced sulfur emissions/acid deposition,
     72
   solid waste management regulations, 32
     (*t*2.9)
   success of, 62–63
Clean Air Act (CAA) of 1970
   air quality standards under, 47
   motor vehicle pollution and, 57
   success of, 62–63
Clean Water Act (CWA)
   goals of, 69–70
   groundwater protection with, 90, 101, 101*t*
   private property use and, 130
Climate, 64*f*
   See also Global warming
Clinton, Bill
   Executive Order 12898 issued by, 114
   Executive Order 13101 signed by, 42
   Kyoto Protocol and, 65
CNG (compressed natural gas), 59*t*, 60
CO. *See* Carbon monoxide
CO_2. *See* Carbon dioxide
Coal, 65–66
Coal products manufacturers, 104
Coastal debris
   marine debris, 84–85
   most prevalent items, 2000, 84*t*
Coastal development, 85
Coastal waters. *See* Ocean shoreline waters
Coliform bacteria, 90
Collection and sorting of products for
   recycling, 40–42
Colorado, 71–72
Combustion
   average heat content of selected biomass
     fuels, 29*t*
   energy consumption associated with fuel
     from waste, 1965-2002, 29*f*
   MSW management with, 20
   municipal solid waste handling methods,
     1960-2000, 21*f*
   process, 30 (*f*2.13)
   process for MSW, 27–29
   scrap tire combustion, 26–27
   waste combustion plant with pollution
     control system, 28*f*
Commercial recyclables collection, 41–42
Compact disc (CD), 39
Compacts, 117
Comparative risk assessment, 130–131
Composting, 44
Comprehensive Environmental, Response,
   Compensation, and Liability Act
   (CERCLA)
   groundwater protection with, 101, 101*t*

condition of, 124
lack of concern for, 5
landfills and, 27
See also Environmental policy, public opinion and
Environmental activism, 123–124, 124*f*
Environmental Equity: Reducing Risk for All Communities (Environmental Protection Agency), 114
Environmental justice, 114
Environmental legislation
public opinion on, 125–127
public opinion on environmental laws/regulations, 1992-2001, 129 (*f*8.7)
public opinion on regulation of specific environmental/energy laws, 2001, 129 (*f*8.8)
Environmental policy, public opinion and
antiregulatory movement, 129–130
comparative risk assessment, 130–131
environment, condition of, 124
environment *vs.* economy and energy, 128
environmental legislation, 125–127
environmental proposals for future, 128–129
litigation and, 131–132
National Report Card, 127–128
North American Agreement on Environmental Cooperation, 132
public involvement in environmental activism, 123–124
public involvement in environmental activism, 2000 and 2003, 124*f*
public opinion on environmental laws and regulations, 1992-2001, 129 (*f*8.7)
public opinion on government's role in protecting environment, 1992, 2000, 2003, 128*f*
public opinion on leading environmental concerns, March 2003, 127*f*
public opinion on overall quality of environment, 2001-2003, 125 (*f*8.3)
public opinion on personal lifestyle and environment, 2000 and 2003, 123*f*
public opinion on protecting environment *vs.* economic growth, 1984-2003, 130*f*
public opinion on regulation of specific environmental/energy laws, 2001, 129 (*f*8.8)
public opinion on seriousness of environmental issues, 1989-2003, 126*t*–127*t*
public opinion on specific environmental proposals, 2001-2003, 131*t*
public opinion on whether environment or energy supplies should be given priority, 2001-2003, 131*f*
public opinion on whether quality of environment is getting better/worse, 2001-2003, 125 (*f*8.4)
worries about environment, 124–125
Environmental proposals for future, 128–129, 131*t*
Environmental Protection Agency (EPA)
BEACH Watch Program of, 75
on Clean Air Act value, 62–63
Clean Water Act and, 69, 70

environmental justice and, 114
fish advisories report by, 73*f*, 74
groundwater pollution and, 92–93
hazardous waste and, 103–104
Landfill Methane Outreach Program, 27
MSW generation rates, 13, 14, 15–19, 15*f*
National Air Toxic Trend Site network, 56
National Priorities List and, 111
National Water Quality Inventory: 2000 Report, 75–83
ozone/particulates standards, 63
pesticides and, 98
responsibilities of, 7
Superfund program appropriations, fiscal years 1993-2002, 113 (*f*7.9)
Superfund program expenditures, fiscal years 1993-2002, 113 (*f*7.8)
Superfund program funding, 112–113
surface impoundments report by, 96
Toxics Release Inventory, distribution of on-site/off-site releases, 2001, 107 (*f*7.5)
Toxics Release Inventory, on-site/off-site releases by state, 2001, 108*t*–109*t*
Toxics Release Inventory, requirements/releases, 106
Toxics Release Inventory, top twenty chemicals with largest total releases, 110*t*
Toxics Release Inventory, total releases, 2001, 111*f*
tracks particulate matter emissions, 52–53
tracks primary air pollutants, 48
waste production estimate of, 8–9
Yucca Mountain and, 118
See also National Water Quality Inventory: 2000 Report (Environmental Protection Agency)
"Environmental Support Systems Amid Economic Uncertainty" (*The Wirthlin Report 8*, no. 9), 128
EPA. *See* Environmental Protection Agency
Estimated Use of Water in the United States (United States Geological Survey), 89
Estuaries
defined, 67
estuary impairment, leading sources of, 2000, 81 (*f*5.21)
leading pollutants in impaired estuaries, 2000, 81 (*f*5.20)
pollutants/stressors on, 79–80
quality of assessed, 2000, 77 (*f*5.10)
status of, 2000, 81 (*f*5.19)
Ethanol (E85), 59, 59*t*
Europe
garbage history, 1, 5
geologic disposal sites in, 121
recycling in, 45
European Union Parliament, 45
Eutrophication
excessive nutrients in water, 72
high nitrogen concentrations, 49
EV1 (electric vehicle), 61
Evapotranspiration rate, 91
EVs (electric vehicles), 61, 62
Executive Order 12759, 60–61

Executive Order 12898, 114
Executive Order 13101, 42
Exports of waste by states, 2000, 25, 25*t*
Extinction of plants/animals, 125
Exxon Valdez oil spill, 85, 102

F

Federal Actions to Address Environmental Justice in Minority Populations and Low-Income Populations (Executive Order 12898), 114
Federal government
nuclear power secrecy, 115–116
public opinion on government's role in protecting environment, 125–126
public opinion on government's role in protecting environment, 1992, 2000, 2003, 128*f*
reaction to federal environmental regulation, 129–130
regulation of hazardous waste, 106–107, 111–113
role in groundwater protection, 101–112, 101*t*
role in MSW management, 31–33
role in recycling, 42–43, 45
solid waste management regulations, 32 (*t*2.9)
See also specific government agencies
Federal Insecticide, Fungicide, and Rodenticide Act (FIFRA), 98, 101*t*
Federal Water Pollution Control Act, 8, 69
Ferrous metals
generated in municipal solid waste, 16–17
recovery rates of, 39
Fertilizers
groundwater pollution and, 91, 97
surface water pollution from, 72–73
use, 1960-98, 70 (*f*5.3)
FIFRA (Federal Insecticide, Fungicide, and Rodenticide Act), 98, 101*t*
Finland, 121
Fish
contamination of, 73–75
fish consumption advisories, 2002, 74
fish consumption advisories, 2002, total number of, 73*f*
pH scale values and, 71
Fish Consumption category, 76
Flow control laws, 31–33
Food chain
bioaccumulation of pollutants in, 72*f*
movement of water pollutants in, 73
Food scraps
composting, 44
generated in municipal solid waste, 15, 15 (*f*2.2)
historical trends in MSW composition, 17, 17*f*, 18*t*
Ford, Henry, 13
Ford Motor Company, 61
Forests
ozone levels and, 53, 53*t*
rain forests, concerns about, 124, 125
Fossil fuels
air pollution from burning of, 47

IPM (Integrated Pest Management), 100
Irrigation, 89
Isotopes, 114

J

Japan Economic Newswire, 45
Japan, MSW generation by, 45–46
Jarvik, Robert, 19
Jerusalem, 1

K

Kennedy Heights (Houston, TX) lawsuit, 114
Kyoto Protocol to the United Nations
   Framework Convention on Climate
   Change
   history of, 65
   public opinion on George W. Bush's
      rejection of, 128

L

Lakes
   under advisory, 74
   impaired/healthy lake ecosystems
      comparison, 80 (f5.17)
   lake impairment, leading pollutants in,
      2000, 79 (f5.16)
   lake impairment, leading sources of,
      2000, 80 (f5.18)
   lakes, reservoirs, ponds, status of
      assessed, 2000, 79 (f5.15)
   pollutants/stressors on, 78–79
   quality of assessed, 2000, 77 (f5.10)
   status of assessed, 2000, 79 (f5.15)
   trends in number of lakes under advisory
      for various pollutants, 1993-2002, 74
      (f5.7)
Land disposal
   hazardous waste, 106
   hazardous waste, technology for land
      disposal of, 106t
   MSW management, 20–21
   municipal solid waste handling methods,
      2000, 20f
   municipal solid waste tonnages,
      recycling, incineration, and landfilling
      rates by state, 20t–21t
   RCRA regulations for, 107
   See also Landfills
Landfill Methane Outreach Program, 27
Landfill Practice (American Society of Civil
   Engineers), 6
Landfills
   federal role in MSW management and,
      31
   groundwater pollution and, 91, 92, 94–95
   groundwater protection and, 90
   landfill methane recovery sites,
      actual/potential by state, 2003, 26f
   modern, 95 (f6.9)
   MSW management method, 20–21
   municipal (or sanitary) landfills, 21–23,
      25–27
   municipal solid waste handling methods,
      1960-2000, 21f

municipal solid waste handling methods,
   2000, 20f
municipal solid waste tonnages,
   recycling, incineration, and landfilling
   rates by state, 20t–21t
number of MSW landfills/incinerators,
   average tip fees, capacity by state,
   2000, 24t
number of municipal solid waste
   landfills, 2000, 23f
popular disposal method, 6
properly closed landfill example, 22f
scrap tire utilization, 2001, 25f
scrap tires sent to, 26
waste imports/exports by state, 25t
Large-quantity generator of hazardous
   waste, 104
*Latest Findings on National Air Quality:
   2002 Status and Trends* (Environmental
   Protection Agency), 48
LDPE (low-density polyethylene)/LLDPE
   (linear low-density polyethylene), 16
Leachate
   landfill design and, 95, 95 (f6.9)
   landfill design standards and, 23
   surface impoundment, 97, 97f
Lead (Pb)
   air quality, 1983-2002, 50 (f4.7)
   emissions, 1983-2002, 50 (f4.6)
   emissions/impact of, 49–50
   health problems from, 47
   in landfills/effects of, 27
Leaking Underground Storage Tank (LUST)
   program, 93
Leather recovery rates, 37t
Legislation and international treaties
   Clean Air Act, 8, 58, 62–63
   Clean Water Act, 69–70
   Clean Water Act, groundwater and, 90
   Clean Water Act, groundwater protection
      with, 101, 101t
   Clean Water Act, private property use
      and, 130
   Comprehensive Environmental,
      Response, Compensation, and Liability
      Act, 101, 101t, 107, 111–113
   Corporate Average Fuel Efficiency
      (CAFE) standards, 58–59
   Emergency Planning and Community
      Right-to-Know Act of 1986, 106
   Endangered Species Act, 130
   Energy Policy Act of 1992, 61
   environmental legislation, 125–127, 129f
   Federal Insecticide, Fungicide, and
      Rodenticide Act (FIFRA), 98, 101t
   federal regulations on solid waste
      management, 32 (t2.9)
   federal role in MSW management, 31–33
   Federal Water Pollution Control Act, 8,
      69
   groundwater legislation, 101–102, 101t
   Hazardous Materials Transportation Act
      of 1975, 120
   hazardous waste regulation, 106–107,
      111–113
   Intermodal Surface Transportation
      Efficiency Act of 1991, 42

Kyoto Protocol to the United Nations
   Framework Convention on Climate
   Change, 65, 128
litigation and environmental policy,
   131–132
Low-Level Radioactive Waste Policy Act
   of 1980, 117
Marine Plastics Pollution Research and
   Control Act, 84–85
Mercury-Containing and Rechargeable
   Battery Management Act, 27, 44
National Defense Authorization Act, 60
National Highway System Designation
   Act, 42
1988 Medical Waste Tracking Act, 84
1975 Automobile Fuel Efficiency Act, 58
North American Agreement on
   Environmental Cooperation (NAAEC),
   132
North American Free Trade Agreement
   (NAFTA), 132
Nuclear Waste Policy Act of 1982, 118,
   119
Oil Pollution Act of 1990, 85, 102
Oregon Recycling Opportunity Act, 42
Pollution Prevention Act of 1990, 105
recycling legislation, 42–43, 45
Resource Conservation and Recovery
   Act, 6–8, 7f, 22
Resource Conservation and Recovery
   Act, amendment, 93
Resource Conservation and Recovery
   Act, groundwater protection with, 101t
Resource Conservation and Recovery
   Act, hazardous waste regulation,
   106–107
Resource Conservation and Recovery
   Act, interrelated programs, 6 (t1.3)
Resource Conservation and Recovery
   Act, outline of, 6 (t1.2)
Resource Conservation and Recovery
   Act, recycling and, 42
Safe Drinking Water Act of 1974, 8,
   89–90, 101t
Solid Waste Disposal Act, 1965, 6
Superfund Amendments and
   Reauthorization Act of 1986, 101
Superfund Amendments and
   Reauthorization Act of 1986, Title IV
   of, 66
Taxpayer Relief Act of 1997, 93
Toxic Substances Control Act, 101
Uranium Mill Tailing Radiation Control
   Act of 1978, 116–117
Used Oil Recycling Act, 27
Water Pollution Control Act
   Amendments of 1956, 69
on yard trimmings, 15
Liquefied natural gas (LNG), 59t
Liquefied petroleum gas (LPG), 59t, 60
Litigation, environmental policy and,
   131–132
LNG (liquefied natural gas), 59t
Long-term exposure, 54 (f4.14)
Low-density polyethylene (LDPE)/Linear
   low-density polyethylene (LLDPE), 16

MENTAL HEALTH

HOW DO AMERICANS COPE?

ISSN 1548-8039

MENTAL HEALTH

HOW DO AMERICANS COPE?

Barbara Wexler

INFORMATION PLUS® REFERENCE SERIES
Formerly published by Information Plus, Wylie, Texas

Detroit • New York • San Francisco • San Diego • New Haven, Conn. • Waterville, Maine • London • Munich

THOMSON
™
GALE

Mental Health: How Do Americans Cope?

Barbara Wexler

Project Editor
Ellice Engdahl

Editorial
Beverly Baer, Paula Cutcher-Jackson, Pamela A. Dear, Kathleen Edgar, Debra Kirby, Prindle LaBarge, Elizabeth Manar, Kathleen Meek, Charles B. Montney, Heather Price

Permissions
Margaret Abendroth, William Sampson, Sheila Spencer

Imaging and Multimedia
Lezlie Light, Dan Newell

Composition and Electronic Prepress
Evi Seoud

Manufacturing
Keith Helmling

LIBRARY OF CONGRESS CATALOGING-IN-PUBLICATION DATA

ISBN 0-7876-5103-6 (set)
ISBN 0-7876-9107-0
ISSN 1548-8039

Printed in the United States of America
10 9 8 7 6 5 4 3 2 1

TABLE OF CONTENTS

Ideas about the causes and symptoms of mental illness have varied
throughout history. Over time, biological and psychological explanations replaced early beliefs about supernatural causation, and the
mentally ill were treated more humanely. A proponent of psychological causation, Sigmund Freud revolutionized early modern thinking
about mental health, while other theoreticians also contributed to current definitions of mental health and illness.

Due to the ongoing debate about possible causes (now including genetics) of mental disorders, estimates for the number of mentally ill people
in America differ. So do diagnostic criteria, despite their codification in
official publications. Interviews and several types of tests help medical
personnel diagnose abnormal conditions, including depression, anxiety,
eating problems, schizophrenia, and suicidal tendencies.

Treatments for mental illness have included techniques like electroconvulsive therapy (ECT) and lobotomy, as well as antipsychotic,
antidepressant, and anxiolytic drugs. Mild to moderate mental problems may be alleviated by psychotherapy (cognitive and behavioral,
marriage and family, group, or art). Treatment is not always successful and frequently not available to those who need it.

A combination of biological, psychological, environmental, and social
factors could increase the risk for pervasive developmental disorders,
attention-deficit hyperactivity disorder, depression, anxiety, or disruptive disorders in young people. To treat younger patients, modified
adult psychotherapy and psychoactive medications may be prescribed.
Gender differences and effectiveness are two aspects of mental health
treatments for children and adolescents that have been studied.

Access to mental health care is limited by lack of a single system
encompassing all programs needed by patients; shorter lengths of stay
in treatment facilities; disparities related to culture, race, ethnicity,
and age; social stigma; and financial barriers. People who obtain
treatment despite these obstacles may face various patients' rights
issues, including privacy and confidentiality, coercion and commitment, and satisfaction with the therapy they receive.

It is generally agreed that the indirect costs of untreated mental illness
are greater than the direct costs of treating it. Local, state, and federal
governments funded most mental health treatment until the 1960s,
when private sources began to provide more money. With the Mental
Health Parity Act of 1996, insurance benefits for mental health care
started to match those for other illnesses. Several studies have examined such aspects of this legislation as business costs, access to care,
quality of care, and compliance.

Over the past 75 years, landmark Supreme Court decisions concerning
mental health have attempted to balance state interests and individual
rights. Mental health research, community mental health centers, substance abuse treatment, protection for individuals with mental disabilities, mental health services for children, and insurance coverage for
mental health care have been subjects of federal legislation from 1946
to 2003. Policy-setting bodies range from the World Health Organization to the President's New Freedom Commission on Mental Health.

Mental health service delivery is provided by four sectors: specialty
(via psychiatrists, psychologists, psychiatric nurses, and clinical
social workers); general medical/primary care (in office-based practices, clinics, hospitals, nursing homes, etc.); human services (through
social services, schools, rehabilitation centers, correctional facilities,
churches, etc.); and voluntary support (self-help groups). Long-term
care in institutional facilities (the norm between 1890 and 1950) has
given way to more community-oriented treatment in recent years.

Heading off the development of diseases, diagnosing early those that
nevertheless occur, and treating mental illness effectively are the

goals of programs promoting early childhood and adolescent interventions, suicide prevention, worksite wellness, effective community-based services, and even online help via the Internet.

     Surveys and studies have produced data on serious psychological distress, disorders affecting children, happiness levels, correlation between financial status and mental health, impact of job dissatisfaction on employees' personal lives, and importance of social relationships to emotional wellness. Two controversial mental health issues currently in the public eye are so-called "recovered memories" and direct-to-consumer advertising.

PREFACE

Mental Health: How Do Americans Cope? is one of the latest volumes in the Information Plus Reference Series. The purpose of each volume of the series is to present the latest facts on a topic of pressing concern in modern American life. These topics include today's most controversial and most studied social issues: abortion, capital punishment, care for the elderly, crime, health care, the environment, immigration, minorities, social welfare, women, youth, and many more. Although written especially for the high school and undergraduate student, this series is an excellent resource for anyone in need of factual information on current affairs.

By presenting the facts, it is Thomson Gale's intention to provide its readers with everything they need to reach an informed opinion on current issues. To that end, there is a particular emphasis in this series on the presentation of scientific studies, surveys, and statistics. These data are generally presented in the form of tables, charts, and other graphics placed within the text of each book. Every graphic is directly referred to and carefully explained in the text. The source of each graphic is presented within the graphic itself. The data used in these graphics are drawn from the most reputable and reliable sources, in particular from the various branches of the U.S. government and from major independent polling organizations. Every effort has been made to secure the most recent information available. The reader should bear in mind that many major studies take years to conduct, and that additional years often pass before the data from these studies are made available to the public. Therefore, in many cases the most recent information available in 2004 dated from 2001 or 2002. Older statistics are sometimes presented as well if they are of particular interest and no more recent information exists.

Although statistics are a major focus of the Information Plus Reference Series, they are by no means its only content. Each book also presents the widely held positions and important ideas that shape how the book's subject is discussed in the United States. These positions are explained in detail and, where possible, in the words of their proponents. Some of the other material to be found in these books includes: historical background; descriptions of major events related to the subject; relevant laws and court cases; and examples of how these issues play out in American life. Some books also feature primary documents or have pro and con debate sections giving the words and opinions of prominent Americans on both sides of a controversial topic. All material is presented in an even-handed and unbiased manner; the reader will never be encouraged to accept one view of an issue over another.

HOW TO USE THIS BOOK

The concepts of mental health and mental illness have changed radically over time. Historically, mental illness was sometimes looked on as a supernatural punishment that only afflicted those who in some way deserved it. With the advent of the modern scientific era, much more is known about mental illness, but much still remains misunderstood as well. The field is filled with controversy over everything from how to define terminology to how many Americans currently suffer from mental problems, what the root causes of such problems are, and how best to provide, maintain, and fund appropriate treatments and preventive services.

Mental Health: How Do Americans Cope? consists of ten chapters and three appendices. Each of the chapters is devoted to a particular aspect of mental health in the United States. For a summary of the information covered in each chapter, please see the synopses provided in the Table of Contents at the front of the book. Chapters generally begin with an overview of the basic facts and background information on the chapter's topic, then proceed to examine subtopics of particular interest. For example, Chapter 8, Mental Health Professionals, Facilities, and

Service Delivery, begins with a listing of the four major components of the U.S. mental health system, then goes on to describe in detail the professionals who work in that system, including psychiatrists, psychologists, psychiatric nurses, clinical social workers, and counselors. The middle of the chapter presents the historical changes that have occurred in mental health services and then describes the different types of facilities where the mentally ill are treated today. The chapter concludes with the national goals for mental health service delivery. Readers can find their way through a chapter by looking for the section and subsection headings, which are clearly set off from the text. They can also refer to the book's extensive index if they already know what they are looking for.

Statistical Information

The tables and figures featured throughout *Mental Health: How Do Americans Cope?* will be of particular use to the reader in learning about this issue. These tables and figures represent an extensive collection of the most recent and important statistics on mental health and related issues—for example, graphics in the book cover the symptoms and triggers of depression, antidepressant drugs, the prevalence of mental and addictive disorders in children, U.S. mental health expenditures, the percentage of adults using various mental and addictive disorder services in a one-year period, the suicide rate for U.S. Air Force members, and survey results on how many Americans consider themselves happy. Thomson Gale believes that making this information available to the reader is the most important way in which we fulfill the goal of this book: to help readers to understand the issues and controversies surrounding mental health in the United States and to reach their own conclusions.

Each table or figure has a unique identifier appearing above it for ease of identification and reference. Titles for the tables and figures explain their purpose. At the end of each table or figure, the original source of the data is provided.

In order to help readers understand these often complicated statistics, all tables and figures are explained in the text. References in the text direct the reader to the relevant statistics. Furthermore, the contents of all tables and figures are fully indexed. Please see the opening section of the index at the back of this volume for a description of how to find tables and figures within it.

Appendices

In addition to the main body text and images, *Mental Health: How Do Americans Cope?* has three appendices.

The first is the Important Names and Addresses directory. Here the reader will find contact information for a number of government and private organizations that can provide further information on mental health. The second appendix is the Resources section, which can also assist the reader in conducting his or her own research. In this section, the author and editors of *Mental Health: How Do Americans Cope?* describe some of the sources that were most useful during the compilation of this book. The final appendix is the detailed Index, which facilitates reader access to specific topics in this book.

ADVISORY BOARD CONTRIBUTIONS

The staff of Information Plus would like to extend their heartfelt appreciation to the Information Plus Advisory Board. This dedicated group of media professionals provides feedback on the series on an ongoing basis. Their comments allow the editorial staff who work on the project to make the series better and more user-friendly. Our top priority is to produce the highest-quality and most useful books possible, and the Advisory Board's contributions to this process are invaluable.

The members of the Information Plus Advisory Board are:

- Kathleen R. Bonn, Librarian, Newbury Park High School, Newbury Park, California

- Madelyn Garner, Librarian, San Jacinto College— North Campus, Houston, Texas

- Anne Oxenrider, Media Specialist, Dundee High School, Dundee, Michigan

- Charles R. Rodgers, Director of Libraries, Pasco-Hernando Community College, Dade City, Florida

- James N. Zitzelsberger, Library Media Department Chairman, Oshkosh West High School, Oshkosh, Wisconsin

COMMENTS AND SUGGESTIONS

The editors of the Information Plus Reference Series welcome your feedback on *Mental Health: How Do Americans Cope?* Please direct all correspondence to:

Editors
Information Plus Reference Series
27500 Drake Rd.
Farmington Hills, MI 48331-3535

ACKNOWLEDGMENTS

The editors wish to thank the copyright holders of material included in this volume and the permissions managers of many book and magazine publishing companies for assisting us in securing reproduction rights. We are also grateful to the staffs of the Detroit Public Library, the Library of Congress, the University of Detroit Mercy Library, Wayne State University Purdy/Kresge Library Complex, and the University of Michigan Libraries for making their resources available to us.

Following is a list of the copyright holders who have granted us permission to reproduce material in Mental Health: How Do Americans Cope? Every effort has been made to trace copyright, but if omissions have been made, please let us know.

For more detailed source citations, please see the sources listed under each individual table and figure.

American Psychiatric Nurses Association: Table 8.4, Table 8.5, Table 8.6, Table 8.7, Table 8.8

AP/Wide World Photos: Figure 1.3, Figure 3.1

Archive Photos, Inc.: Figure 1.5

B. Bodine/Custom Medical Stock Photo: Figure 2.4

Centers for Disease Control and Prevention, National Center for Chronic Disease Prevention and Health Promotion: Table 10.1

Centers for Disease Control and Prevention, National Center for Health Statistics: Table 2.11, Table 5.2, Table 5.3, Table 5.4, Table 5.5, Table 5.8, Table 6.1, Figure 8.2, Figure 8.3, Table 8.14, Table 8.15, Table 8.16, Table 8.17, Table 8.18, Table 8.19, Table 8.20, Table 8.21, Figure 10.1, Figure 10.2, Figure 10.3, Table 10.2

Corbis-Bettmann: Figure 1.8

DIZ Munchen GmbH: Figure 1.6

EPD Photos. Gale Group: Figure 1.11

Farrell Grehan/Corbis: Figure 1.12

The Gallup Organization: Figure 10.4, Figure 10.5, Figure 10.6, Figure 10.7, Figure 10.8, Figure 10.9, Figure 10.10, Figure 10.11, Figure 10.12, Table 10.3, Table 10.4

The Library of Congress: Figure 1.2, Figure 1.7, Figure 1.9, Figure 1.13

NIH/Science Source, National Audubon Society Collection/ Photo Researchers, Inc.: Figure 2.3

Photo Researchers, Inc.: Figure 2.2, Figure 2.5

President's New Freedom Commission on Mental Health: Figure 2.6, Table 5.1, Figure 6.1, Table 9.2, Table 9.3

Public Domain: Figure 1.1

Stanley Publishing: Figure 3.2

Ted Streshinsky/Corbis: Figure 1.4

UPI/Corbis Bettmann: Figure 1.10

U.S. Department of Health and Human Services: Table 4.1, Figure 9.1

U.S. Department of Health and Human Services, Administration for Children and Families, Head Start Bureau: Table 9.1

U.S. Department of Health and Human Services, National Institutes of Health, National Institute of Mental Health: Figure 2.7, Table 2.5, Table 2.8, Table 4.3

U.S. Department of Health and Human Services, National Institutes of Health, National Institute on Drug Abuse: Figure 2.1

U.S. Department of Health and Human Services, Substance Abuse and Mental Health Services Administration: Figure 6.2, Figure 6.3, Figure 6.4, Figure 6.5, Figure 6.7, Table 8.11, Table 9.5

U.S. Department of Health and Human Services, Substance Abuse and Mental Health Services Administration, Center for Mental Health Services: Table 5.6, Table 5.7, Figure 8.1, Table 8.10, Table 8.12, Table 8.13

U.S. Department of Health and Human Services, Substance Abuse and Mental Health Services Administration, with National Institutes of Health: Table 2.2, Table 2.3, Table 3.1, Table 3.2, Figure 4.1, Figure 4.2, Table 4.2, Table 4.4, Table 8.1, Table 8.2, Table 9.4

U.S. Department of Labor, Bureau of Labor Statistics: Table 8.3, Table 8.9

U.S. General Accounting Office: Figure 6.6, Table 6.2, Table 6.3, Table 6.4, Table 6.5

Will & Deni McIntyre. Photo Researchers, Inc.: Figure 3.3

World Health Organization: Table 2.1, Table 2.4, Table 2.6, Table 2.7, Table 2.9, Table 2.10, Figure 7.1

CHAPTER 1
UNDERSTANDING MENTAL HEALTH AND MENTAL ILLNESS

Nothing defines the quality of life in a community more clearly than people who regard themselves, or whom the consensus chooses to regard, as mentally unwell.

—Renata Adler, *Toward a Radical Middle: Fourteen Pieces of Reporting and Criticism,* Random House, New York, 1969

Concepts and understanding of mental health and mental illness have changed throughout history and varied from one culture to another. For the most part mental health was not well described or defined; it was simply the absence of mental illness. Mental illness encompassed a wide range of problems but was generally understood as behavior that deviated from the majority of society.

The symptoms associated with mental illness varied considerably over time and across cultures. For example, some cultures revered people who claimed to speak directly with God and anointed them spiritual leaders in their communities. In contrast, other cultures might have interpreted such behavior as a sign or symptom of mental illness.

Similarly, ideas about the causes of mental illness changed during each era. There were varieties of beliefs about the causes of mental illness. Historically mental illness was alternately attributed to supernatural, biological, psychological, social, and political forces. By the 20th century the etiology (origin, source, or cause) of mental illness was understood to arise in response to many factors, including evolutionary biology, environment, and psychosocial experiences.

EARLY BELIEFS ABOUT THE ORIGINS OF MENTAL ILLNESS

Prehistoric and ancient cultures held mythical beliefs and ascribed mental illness to magical, supernatural forces. Since this era preceded the development of scientific technique, mental illness was attributed to evil minds, thoughts, and actions. Mental illness was thought to strike those who failed to perform ritual obligations, persons who violated taboos, and victims of demonic possession.

The Greeks also assumed that demonic possession caused mental illness, positing that the devil or another evil force resided in the mentally ill person and assumed complete control of the affected individual's thoughts and actions. The Greek physician Hippocrates (460–377 B.C.E.) was among the first to reject the view that mental illness was caused by possession of evil spirits and displeasure of the gods. He favored a somatic (of the body, with a physical cause), biological explanation. He was also the first physician to propose that thoughts, ideas, and feelings came from the brain and not the heart, as his contemporaries believed.

According to the Greeks, temperament or personality type was attributable to the relative balance of four body fluids called humors. An excess of yellow bile indicated a choleric type—angry and irritable. An overabundance of phlegm (thick mucus produced in the respiratory tract) produced the phlegmatic type—calm, unemotional, and sluggish. Too much black bile produced melancholy—persons consumed by sadness and gloom. A predominance of blood relative to the other humors characterized the sanguine type—cheerful, optimistic, and friendly.

While Hippocrates theorized about physical and biological sources of mental illness, Plato (428–348 B.C.) believed that mental illness was psychological—that it originated in the mind rather than the physical brain—in response to lack of self-awareness and self-deception. These two great thinkers of the time held opposing viewpoints about whether the mind or body was the origin of mental illness.

During the decline and fall of the Roman Empire, another exceptional thinker, politician, orator, and philosopher, Marcus Tullius Cicero (106–43 B.C.E.), furthered the psychological theory of mental illness. He observed that anxiety and excessive worry predisposed people to making mistakes and errors in judgment. Although many Romans persisted in the belief that supernatural forces caused mental and physical illness, Cicero maintained that mental health resulted from harmony of the rational, irrational, and lustful parts of the soul.

While supernatural beliefs continued through the Middle Ages, some biological explanations of mental illness emerged. For example, Constantinus Africanus (1010–87), a Benedictine monk and medical translator who is credited with translating the treatises of Hippocrates and Galen, elaborated on the Greek description of the humors as causes of mental illness. He was certain that an excess of bile (the liver secretion that aids in the digestion of fats) and other physiological imbalances produced mental disorders such as melancholia (depression).

During this era, a less punitive and judgmental, more humanistic view of mental illness also emerged, though it did not gain widespread acceptance. Asylums were opened to protect and care for afflicted persons, and some cultures chose to revere persons with mental illness. Sending persons with mental illness away to asylums was actually considered an enlightened and progressive approach to treatment, since asylums removed the affected individuals from society's view and provided custodial care.

Consistent with the explanation of mental illness offered by other major religions, traditional Islamic belief had held that mental illness was caused by a jinni (spirit or genie) entering the afflicted person. Many Muslims however, believed that mentally ill persons were chosen by God to tell the truth and viewed caring for such persons as meritorious acts for which God would reward them.

Yet many irrational beliefs about mental illness were deeply entrenched. From the 14th through the 17th centuries, witch hunts and inquisitions were staged to persecute persons believed to be possessed by the devil. The 1692 Salem witchcraft trials sentenced 19 people to hang. This seemingly consuming preoccupation with witchcraft not only abruptly ended the lives of many persons suffering from mental illnesses, but also extinguished some of the progressive thinking about biological and psychological causes of mental illness that began during the Renaissance.

CHANGING IDEAS ABOUT THE ORIGINS OF MENTAL ILLNESS

During the first half of the 17th century, mental illness was still thought to have demonic or Satanic origins. Native American shamans (healers or medicine men) invoked supernatural powers to treat the mentally ill, performing rituals of atonement and purification. Colonial American society called persons suffering from mental illness lunatics because they believed that mental illness was caused by a full moon at the time of birth or an infant

sleeping in the light of a full moon. The colonists considered lunatics to be possessed by the devil and chose to remove them from society and lock them in institutions that were crosses between hospitals and prisons. Lunatics were determined to be suffering from either melancholy or mania (crazed, excessive physical activity and emotional excitement) and were subjected to treatment intended to catalyze crisis or expel crisis from the affected individuals.

By modern-day standards, early treatment of mental illness and the remedies offered during this period were barbaric. Efforts were made to induce vomiting, and persons were immersed in ice water until they lost consciousness. Another ineffective and dangerous practice, since many did not survive it, was bleeding—draining the bad blood from the affected individual. These procedures aimed to redistribute the volume of blood to the brain. Early efforts to treat mental illness also sought to alter blood volume in the brain by trepanation—cutting one or two small holes in the skull using a surgical drill known as a trepan. There is some archeological evidence that Stone Age cave dwellers may have used trepanation to treat mental illness, and the medical practice of trepanation continued through the twentieth century. Ancient cultures considered it an effective way to relieve pressure on the brain or release the demons that possessed it. Later, the purpose of trepanation was described as offering the closed skull of the adult an expansion window to restore the blood flow that was diminished when, during the course of normal development, the skull sealed in infancy.

Despite lingering superstitions and dangerous therapies, the 17th century also saw the birth of the theories and philosophies that would supplant supernatural causation of mental illness. In 1602 the Swiss physician Felix Platter published the first textbook on psychiatry (the medical specialty devoted to the study, diagnosis, and treatment of mental illness) to offer physiological explanations of mental illness. Thomas Sydenham(1624–89), a London physician dubbed the "English Hippocrates," observed and documented the importance of physical and behavioral symptoms of mental illness. Other physicians and philosophers detailed the psychological and social causes of mental illness and named a variety of conditions such as jealousy, solitude, fear, poverty, and unrequited love as contributing factors.

By the 18th century, witchcraft and mystical explanations of mental illness had given way to clinical rationales. The celebrated New England Puritan clergyman Cotton Mather (1663–1728), formerly a true believer in witchcraft, publicly expressed his doubts about supernatural causation of mental illness. Mather advanced physical explanations for mental illnesses and exhorted physicians to study the states of mind of their patients as probable causes of illness.

In 1756, at the behest of Benjamin Franklin, the Pennsylvania Hospital was established as the first public institution in the United States to accept mentally ill patients. This milestone did not, however, resolve the debate between physicians who believed in the potential of mental health treatment and those who steadfastly held that mental illness was incurable. The early 18th century was a period of considerable scientific advancement, but the mentally ill were still deemed inhuman and their treatment often consisted of shackles, chains, and other forms of restraint.

Changing Views Prompt More Humane Treatment in Europe

During the latter part of the 18th century, growing acceptance of scientific and biological explanations of mental illness inspired more enlightened, humane understanding and treatment of sufferers. A new approach to the treatment of persons with mental illness, known as moral management, emerged in Europe. This approach was based on the belief that the environment played a vital role in the treatment of the mentally ill. In Italy, Vincenzo Chiarugi (1759–1820) was appointed by the Grand Duke Leopoldo I to design the new hospital of St. Bonifacio, which would become one of the first facilities devoted to the humane care of people with mental illness. Chiarugi contended that "it is a supreme moral duty and medical obligation to respect the insane individual as a person" and wrote a medical treatise on insanity in which he distinguished between types of mental illnesses, speculated about their causes, and provided humane approaches to treatment. With Chiarugi serving as its director, St. Bonifacio opened in 1788.

Around the same time, William Tuke (1732–1819), a Quaker merchant living in England, was appalled by the abusive treatment of patients in asylums and sought to end the reign of cruelty toward persons suffering from mental illness. Tuke opened the York Retreat in 1796. The Retreat was a country house in which patients were treated with kindness and understanding in a supportive environment, without any form of physical restraint. Comfortable beds, pictures, and curtains replaced shackles, chains, and barren cement cells. Consistent with the principles of moral management, Tuke believed that recovery would be more likely in sheltered, homelike surroundings. Patients were expected to work in the house and garden as part of their treatment. A prototype of the modern-day therapeutic community, the Retreat combined work with exercise, walks, conversations, reading, games, arts, and crafts. The Retreat pioneered another novel therapeutic approach—patients' privileges increased incrementally in response to their progress. This approach was the forerunner of using positive reinforcement to promote behavior modification.

Along with William Tuke, Philip Pinel (1745–1826), the leading French psychiatrist of his day, endorsed moral management, describing the "mentally deranged" as diseased rather than evil or sinful. Pinel literally freed the

FIGURE 1.1

Benjamin Rush.

mentally ill from their chains and restraints at the Bicêtre and Salpêtrière asylums. In addition to advocating understanding and compassionate treatment of mentally ill persons, Pinel contributed to the scientific advancement of mental health treatment by classifying types of mental illness based on categories of symptoms. He described four classes of mental illness: melancholia (feelings of severe depression), mania (excessive nervous excitement with or without delirium), dementia (disturbance in thought processes), and idiocy (defective intellectual functions). Pinel also introduced the practices of documenting individual case histories and systematic record keeping. Both Tuke and Pinel emphasized the importance of work and vocational skills in recovery. Structured work programs and organized recreation were key therapeutic activities in their facilities and served to ease the planned transition from institutionalization to reentry into the community.

A Celebrated American Physician Advocates Humane Treatment

Benjamin Rush (1745–1813) was a patriot, a signer of the Declaration of Independence, and the leading social reformer of his time. He also was a celebrated physician who helped to establish medicine and psychiatry as important ways of caring for people in the Colonies. (See Figure 1.1.) Rush contended that persons suffering from mental illness had the right to be treated with respect and protested the harsh, inhuman treatment of mentally ill patients at Pennsylvania Hospital. A champion of the mentally ill, in 1812 he published *Medical Inquiries and Observations Upon Diseases of the Mind,* the first American textbook of psychiatry. He is regarded by many as the father of American psychiatry.

Rush developed a taxonomy (classification system based on common characteristics) that strongly resembles the modern classification system of mental illness. He theorized that variables such as heredity, age, marital status, wealth, and environment might predispose people to mental illness. His approach to treatment of the mentally ill was rooted in his biological understanding of mental illness and his conviction that it involved impaired function of the blood vessels that supply the brain. As a result, his treatment philosophy relied on regimens consisting of bleeding, cold baths, dietary restriction, and purges as well as humane, compassionate care.

Rush's notion that improving patients' physical health would demonstrably improve their mental health contributed to growing acceptance of the medical model of mental illness. Rush also integrated psychological approaches to diagnosing and treating mental illness, inviting patients to confide in him, interpreting their dreams, and prescribing occupational therapy—the use of purposeful activity to help patients recover from mental illness and gain work and life skills. Along with his contributions to medicine and psychiatry, he was a founding member of the first American antislavery society, opposed capital punishment, advocated for women's education and free public schools, established a free medical dispensary for the poor in Philadelphia, served as a member of the first U.S. Congress, and helped to establish Dickinson College.

The Civil War Catalyzes Change in the United States

In the United States the Civil War was a turning point in the understanding of mental illness and the approach to its treatment. Many Civil War veterans suffered from postwar trauma (later known as post-traumatic stress disorder, or PTSD)—emotional and psychological war wounds that were often as or more disabling than their physical injuries. These veterans were treated in state mental hospitals and asylums, where treatment consisted of physical restraints such as straightjackets and arm and leg chains, along with the use of drugs such as opium, a narcotic derived from the juice of unripe pods of the poppy plant.

Public outcries about the dilapidated facilities and harsh care the veterans and other asylum patients were receiving, coupled with a growing need for institutional placement for persons suffering from mental illnesses, sparked the opening of asylums throughout the country. The homeless sought refuge in the asylums, and the elderly were sent to live in asylums when their families were unable to care for them. Worsening the problem of over-

crowding was the fact that most facilities lacked established criteria for admitting patients. Rapid growth in populations, coupled with inadequate staffing, caused a sharp decline in the quality of patient care. Many historians and first-person accounts decried the neglect and abuse of mentally ill persons, described the asylums as "snake pits," and termed this period "mental health care's darkest hours."

Thomas Story Kirkbride (1809–83), a Pennsylvania native originally trained to become a surgeon, instead became a prominent designer of asylums, known for architectural features that directly influenced patient care and treatment. His designs enabled the least disturbed patients to be housed close to the center building to facilitate interaction with the staff, and if the patients' conditions deteriorated they could be relocated through each wing toward the back of the facility. Kirkbride was a founding member and president of the Association of Medical Superintendents of American Institutions for the Insane, the predecessor of the American Psychiatric Association. The standardized method of construction, floor plans, and mental health treatment he championed became known as the Kirkbride Plan.

This period also saw the introduction of phrenology, the practice of studying the shape of the skull to assess character traits and diagnose illnesses. Though this practice is still used by a few practitioners today, its usefulness and scientific merit have been discredited. Hypnosis and relaxation techniques also were offered as treatment for mental illness during this time, and these techniques are still widely accepted and used today.

Biological Causes of Mental Illness Are Favored Over Psychological Explanations

Throughout the 19th century, both biological (body) and psychological (mind) explanations of mental illness were put forth by psychiatrists, philosophers, and scientists in Europe and the United States. The two schools of thought were mutually exclusive—adherents endorsed either somatic or psychological origins of mental illness. German psychiatry made the first attempts to combine elements of each in an effort to develop a more integrated philosophy that considered both body and mind as involved in the etiology of mental illness.

Although the seeds of the notion that both mind and body were involved in mental illness were planted, they were not cultivated during the 19th century. Instead, the theories espoused focused almost exclusively on biological origins of mental health and mental illness. German psychiatrist and neurologist Wilhelm Griesinger (1817–68) introduced the concept of pathological anatomy and physiology—structural and functional abnormalities of the brain—to psychiatry as the cause of mental illness. Biological origins of mental illness were further supported by Louis Pasteur's (1822–95) germ theory of disease, which held that most infectious diseases are caused by microorganisms. The emphasis on biological explanations effectively suppressed research and hypotheses about possible psychological origins of mental illness.

A RADICAL NEW CONCEPTUAL AND THERAPEUTIC FRAME OF REFERENCE EMERGES IN THE 20TH CENTURY

During the 20th century the psychoanalytic movement gained credibility as a model to explain mental illness and to treat it. Psychological causation was espoused by Sigmund Freud (1856–1939), the renowned physician and psychoanalyst who pronounced the mind a complex energy system and its structural research the appropriate domain of psychology. (See Figure 1.2.) Building on the work of his mentor Joseph Breuer, Freud became arguably the most influential thinker and practitioner of 20th-century mental health care and today is regarded as the father of psychoanalysis. He expressed, refined, and popularized the concepts of the unconscious and conscious mind as part of a new conceptual and therapeutic frame of reference for understanding the human psyche, the origins of mental illness, and its treatment.

Sigmund Freud's Theories

Freud distinguished the conscious mind as an individual's awareness at any particular moment—thoughts, memories, observations, fantasies, and emotions. He characterized the preconscious as ideas or feelings that can readily be made conscious, such as memories that are easily retrieved and revisited. The unconscious is the source and realm of the ideas, feelings, and memories that are not readily accessible, such as motivations and instincts or suppressed memories of pain or other trauma. Freud viewed the unconscious as the origin of motivations, compulsions, and ambitions that when denied or resisted were only accessible to the conscious mind in camouflaged forms.

Freudian theory holds that all organisms, including humans, are distinguished by their instinctive needs to survive and reproduce, and many of their actions are motivated by impulses such as hunger, thirst, and avoidance of pain. The id is the part of the psyche associated with satisfaction of these instinctual impulses, needs, and drives, which Freud termed wishes. The id may be viewed as the psychic representative of biological need, and the translation from need to wish is called the primary process. Applying Freud's theory, infants use nearly only id, since they act to satisfy impulses without understanding or considering the consequences of their actions.

Often unsatisfied needs, such as the need for water, begin to demand increasing amounts of attention, until they become all-consuming and enter into consciousness. The ego, the component part of the psyche that is conscious, is best attuned to external reality and generally

FIGURE 1.2

Sigmund Freud. *The Library of Congress*

controls behavior. The ego seeks to satisfy the wishes that originate in the id in response to the organism's needs. Unlike the id, however, the ego employs reason in its efforts to initiate action. This rational, problem-solving action is called the secondary process. Freud called the desires for food and water as well as the instinct to reproduce "life instincts," and he termed the psychic and emotional energy to pursue these biological drives or life instincts "libido," from the Latin word for desire.

Another component of the psyche is the superego, which identifies, catalogues, and incorporates prevailing moral standards. The superego begins by considering the greatest influences in its environment—in the case of a child, his or her parents. It internalizes socially accepted and socially unacceptable actions by associating the behaviors that elicit punishments and warnings as well as those that result in rewards and positive reinforcement. The superego is involved in the process that gives rise to feelings such as pride, shame, guilt, and remorse.

EXPLAINING ANXIETY. Freud described three types of anxiety—feeling threatened, intensely uneasy, or overwhelmed—as resulting from conflicting demands on the ego that threaten its survival. He distinguished between realistic anxiety, moral anxiety, and neurotic anxiety. An example of realistic anxiety is the fear that might reasonably be anticipated before a final examination or performing in a play. Moral anxiety is discomfort resulting from internal as opposed to societal or environmental causes. Guilt, shame, and fear of punishment are moral anxieties that originate in the superego. Moral anxiety might arise in response to cheating on a test or betraying a friend's confidence. Neurotic anxiety is fear of being overwhelmed by impulses from the id and "losing it" in an uncontrollable outburst of anger, rage, or inability to make rational decisions. The term "neurotic" comes from the Latin for nervous, and "neurotic anxiety" was Freud's term for the most common experience of anxiety.

When anxiety threatens the ego, the ego acts to protect itself by blocking the impulses or transforming anxiety-producing actions and events so they appear less threatening. These mechanisms are known as ego defense techniques. Examples of ego defense techniques include:

- Asceticism—denying specific or all desires. Anorexia, an eating disorder in which sufferers deny themselves food, is an example of asceticism.

- Denial—blocking actions and events from awareness in an effort to completely ignore reality.

- Displacement—redirecting an emotion, impulse, or desire. For example, a student who feels unwelcome and disliked by peers may misdirect anger and frustration toward his siblings. Turning against the self is a form of displacement in which self-hatred and anger result in depression and guilt.

- Introjection—also known as identification, involves assuming the characteristics of someone else to resolve an emotional problem. Identification with the aggressor is a form of introjection that entails assuming the negative characteristics of an individual in order to more closely resemble an oppressor. An example of this phenomenon is hostages who become sympathetic to their captors and victims of abuse who defend their abusers.

- Isolation—also known as intellectualization, this defense involves recalling a difficult memory or situation without emotion. An example of isolation occurs when moviegoers laugh in discomfort during graphically violent or extremely disturbing scenes.

- Projection—seeing one's own unacceptable qualities in others. An example of projection occurs when the individual who habitually lies and misleads others suspects and accuses friends and coworkers of dishonesty.

- Rationalization—making excuses and altering the facts of an event or situation so that it appears less threatening.

- Reaction formation—transforming an unacceptable impulse or emotion into its opposite. For example, victims

of domestic violence often misinterpret violence for affection and return to, rather than flee from, their abusers.

- Regression—responding to fear or stress by reverting to childlike behaviors. For example, school-aged children stressed by prolonged illness, loss of a parent, or moving to a new home may seek comfort in old habits such as carrying a toy or blanket, sleeping with stuffed animals, or sucking their thumbs.

- Repression—intentionally forgetting disagreeable actions or events.

- Sublimation—a positive form of rationalization that involves using unacceptable impulses in manners condoned or even praised by society. For example, an individual with violent tendencies may seek a career in the military or take up hunting, boxing, or football for recreation. Further, according to Freud, nearly all creative endeavors, such as art, playwriting, or performing, are examples of sublimation.

Psychosexual Stages of Development

Freud attributed many impulses, desires, and ambitions as well as fears and anxieties to aspects of sexuality and sexual development. He observed that during the course of a lifetime, humans derived sensual pleasure from different areas of the body, and he developed a stage theory to describe the maturation process. Freud described an oral stage that begins at birth and ends at about 18 months. Infants enjoy sucking not only to obtain nutrients from breast milk or bottles of formula but also to comfort themselves. Babies explore their environments with their mouths, putting toys, crayons, and their fingers into their mouths. The oral stage generally culminates in weaning, when the baby ceases to breast-feed or discards the bottle and pacifier in favor of drinking from cups. From 18 months to about three years, toddlers are in an anal stage, fascinated by bowel movements and their growing ability to control them. The developmental challenge during this stage is potty training, when toddlers acquire sufficient control and motor skills to use the toilet.

Children between three and seven are considered to be in the phallic stage, in which their attention centers on pleasure from their genitals. During this stage many children engage in masturbation. Freud believed that the challenge of the phallic stage was a phenomenon he termed the Oedipal complex, after the ancient Greek myth of Oedipus, a heroic king who unwittingly murdered his father and married his mother. The complex involves libidinal (psychological and emotional energy associated with sexual drives) feelings in a child, especially a male child, for the parent of the opposite gender. Freud asserted that an Oedipal crisis was an inevitable developmental phase because the male child's first love is his mother, and his father is a rival for her attention and affection. Around this time the male child also observes gender differences, particularly the fact that he has a penis and his mother, female siblings, and other girls do not. Since at this early age, gender differences are not well understood, the male child may wonder if the females somehow lost their penises. Freud called the internalization of this fear—the boy's worry that he too may be at risk of losing his penis—castration anxiety. (This term is not actually correct, because castration refers to removal of the testicles or ovaries and does not mean removal or loss of the penis.)

Since girls' early lives also naturally center on their relationships and love for their mothers, Freud proposed that young girls experienced the Oedipal crisis because they suffered from penis envy. Realizing that she lacks a penis, and the societal privileges afforded to men, the young girl wants to align with her father and feels competition with her mother for his love. Freud also characterized women's desires for children as at least partially motivated by penis envy, because in his view, the baby could serve as a surrogate for a penis.

The latent stage may begin as early as age five and ends just before the teen years. The term "latent" means present or potential but not evident or active. Based on his observation that children expressed fewer sexual interests or motivations at these ages, Freud contended that during this phase children's sexual interest and impulses were somewhat muted or suppressed by their involvement in organized activities such as school. Toward the end of the latent stage, the Oedipal crisis resolves and boys, in response to castration anxiety, engage the ego defense mechanism of identification with their fathers.

Puberty, the stage at which adolescents become capable of sexual reproduction, signaled the onset of the genital stage. Physiological readiness to reproduce rekindles the sex drive, and adolescents experience desires for sexual relationships.

Character Traits and Personality

Freud determined that persons who did not meet the challenges associated with any of the stages of development might suffer long-term consequences such as retaining characteristics from a particular stage. He called the retention of infantile or childlike traits fixation. In addition to problems stemming from difficulties traversing each stage of development, Freud believed that traumas or severe stress suffered during a particular stage could result in fixation.

For example, traumas associated with infancy such as premature weaning or even inability to satisfy the instinctual need to suck might produce an individual who seeks to compensate for early deprivation by pursuing oral pleasures such as eating, drinking, or smoking. Freud termed these tendencies emblematic of an oral-passive character. He described persons deprived of satisfying ways to soothe the discomforts of teething as likely to become oral-aggressive, preferring to chew gum and/or bite their fingernails or pencils. Oral-aggressive people also display biting personalities—they tend to be verbally aggressive, sarcastic, argumentative, and abrasive.

Similarly, Freud posited that children whose parents were overly permissive during toilet training were likely to develop anal aggressive personalities, displaying expansive generosity along with the inclination to be disorganized, messy, cruel, and destructive. In contrast, parents who were extremely strict or demanding during this stage of development, especially those who used negative reinforcement such as humiliation to toilet train, might encourage their offspring to become anal retentive. This personality is best described as literally and figuratively constipated. Preoccupied with cleanliness, rigid, dictatorial, and stingy, they display the opposite traits of anal aggressive personalities.

Difficulties during the phallic stage also were thought to give rise to phallic personalities. Boys who suffered rejection by their mothers were presumed to have poor self-esteem in terms of their sexual identities. As a result they might demonstrate behavior at either end of a continuum, opting to withdraw entirely from sexual interactions or becoming flamboyantly macho. Girls rejected by their fathers suffer comparable losses of self-esteem and react by either withdrawing or displaying extremely feminine behavior.

Freud's penchant for extreme characterization is underscored by his descriptions of the origins and attributes of phallic personalities. Boys whose mothers preferred them over their fathers were deemed likely to develop grandiose, overly inflated senses of self-worth and self-importance or, alternatively, adopt effeminate behaviors. Girls whose fathers treated them reverentially and favored them over the mothers might assume distinctly masculine behaviors or become vain and self-involved.

Implications for Treatment

Freud's groundbreaking work had its greatest impact on the therapeutic practices of the 20th century. It inspired efforts to harness the therapeutic potential of insight—awareness of stress or trauma that is the source of an emotion—and catharsis—the sudden burst of emotion that accompanies resurfaced memory and experience of trauma. It also intensified interest in hypnosis—an induced sleeplike state in which the client is especially responsive to the therapist's suggestions—and interpretation of dreams to reach and heal the unconscious mind by releasing forgotten emotions about specific traumatic events. Dream analysis enables the therapist and client to examine symbols and conflicts that more easily emerge in dreams when there is less resistance to unconscious desires. Freud placed special emphasis on dream analysis because it exemplified his overarching goal of therapy, to make the unconscious conscious.

Among the enduring contributions he made to psychoanalytic practice were his beliefs that clients must feel relaxed and able to communicate their innermost thoughts and feelings without fear of judgment or reprisal. Freudian therapists advocate interactions in quiet, serene settings with low lights and comfortable furniture. This relaxed atmosphere is thought to stimulate free association—openended, seemingly random discourse during which unconscious conflicts surface. The therapist may question or encourage the client but generally assumes a quiet, unobtrusive role. The classic image of the client reclining on a psychiatrist's sofa with the therapist sitting beside him and listening is typically Freudian.

Freud viewed resistance—the client's effort to avoid discussing certain topics, arriving late, or forgetting scheduled appointments—as indicative that the client and therapist were closing in on challenging material. Similarly, he found meaning in slips of the tongue, also known as parapraxes, deeming them indicators of unconscious, unresolved conflicts. Today parapraxes are more commonly known as Freudian slips. He also believed that transference—when clients project feelings toward their therapists that are actually intended for significant others in their lives—enabled deeply repressed emotions such as anger to surface in a safer, less potentially charged relationship.

His convictions about the therapeutic value of transference and man's tendency to project interpretations and emotions onto ambiguous stimuli also prompted him to popularize the use of projective testing such as inkblots and Rorschach tests in which clients' interpretations offered clues to their unconscious minds—the deepest recesses of their psyches. Named after the Swiss psychiatrist Hermann Rorschach (1884–1922), who developed the inkblots and claimed they enabled him to assess patients' perceptive abilities, intelligence, and emotional characteristics, the inkblots are intentionally unclear until described or interpreted by the client.

Enduring Contributions

While few would argue that Freud's work forever changed the understanding and treatment of mental illness, even his most ardent supporters and present-day practitioners of Freudian therapy do not necessarily agree with all of his theories. The enduring and most widely accepted tenets of his work were the observations that human behavior is largely influenced by biology and society—that societal norms, cultural values, and family dynamics played critical roles in shaping the individual's psyche. It is important to remember that not long before Freud demonstrated the effects of biology and society on mental health and illness, they were considered to be determined solely by God or dark, supernatural forces. Viewed in this historical context, the magnitude of his contribution to present-day understanding of mental health is readily apparent.

FIGURE 1.3

Anna Freud. *AP/Wide World Photos. Reproduced by permission.*

Freud also introduced the notion that psychological traumas experienced during childhood may have lasting effects and influence adult life. Today it is universally accepted that children who suffer from abuse or neglect as well as those who endure serious losses and tragedy are at greater risk of developing mental health problems as adults than those who had happy, uneventful early lives. Similarly, his descriptions of ego defense mechanisms are largely considered accurate representations of unconscious actions taken to protect deeply held beliefs. Perhaps, however, his greatest contribution was in the realm of treatment. Freud demonstrated and popularized talk therapy as a therapeutic practice and emphasized the quality of the therapist-client relationship as vital for effective treatment.

Freud's daughter Anna promoted and expanded Freud's legendary work. Her accomplishments may be viewed as another, albeit indirect, of Freud's contributions to the rapidly evolving fields of psychology and mental health treatment. Adopting his beliefs and practices, she became a psychotherapist. (See Figure 1.3.) Unlike her father, who worked exclusively with adults in his practice, Anna concentrated on children. She made pioneering contributions to the understanding of the relationship between the therapist and child and described developmental milestones such as eating, hygiene, and peer relationships to help determine whether children were progressing normally, without significant problems.

Support for Freud's Theories Is Not Universal

Many scholars, researchers, and mental health professionals consider Freud misguided and overly influenced by his own personal experiences. Others deem his views outdated, narrow-minded, and ethnocentric—too deeply tied to European cultural norms to be broadly applicable today.

Many mental health professionals and academicians take issue with Freud's assertion that the unconscious is the sole source of all human motivation, behavior, and emotion. Although few would completely discount the role of the unconscious in driving certain behaviors, it is generally viewed as much less predominant a force than Freud proposed. Today, the unconscious is viewed as a repository of needs, desires, and memories that are either unnecessary or unwanted, such as extremely painful memories or emotions resulting from traumatic events.

Detractors also cite Freud's seeming preoccupation with sex and death as the primary motivators in human existence as both narrow and outdated. They observe that human behavior is likely influenced by other factors, especially 21st-century human behavior. Likewise, his unwavering belief in the Oedipal complex and the inevitability of castration anxiety and penis envy have been challenged. Today, even staunch Freudians concede that these concepts are not universally applicable and are better understood as metaphors rather than actual feelings and motivations. In a society dominated by males, it may be that boys fear losing the very attribute that affords them supremacy, and that girls seeking power and privilege covet maleness; however, it seems unlikely that all boys literally fear the loss of their penises and all girls desire male genitalia.

Other Thinkers Influence 20th-Century Understanding of Mental Health and Mental Illness

In addition to Sigmund Freud and his daughter Anna, dozens of other thinkers—philosophers, sociologists, psychologists, physicians, and scholars from related disciplines—left their imprints on 20th-century understanding of mental health and mental illness. Erik Erickson (1902–94), a German-born Freudian psychotherapist, expanded and refined Freud's stage theory. (See Figure 1.4.) He theorized that human development is governed by the epigenetic principle, positing genetically determined progress through eight distinct stages of personality development. The three stages he added to Freud's original five stages assume that personality development does not abruptly end during adolescence but continues throughout adulthood and into old age.

The Viennese physician Alfred Adler (1870–1937) developed the theory of individual psychology, a holistic

FIGURE 1.4

Erik Erickson. © *Ted Streshinsky/Corbis. Reproduced by permission.*

approach to psychology that viewed people as wholes rather than the sum of their parts. (See Figure 1.5.) He believed that the sole force driving human behavior was the overwhelming desire to be perfect or ideal. He termed this motivation "striving for perfection," but he is better known for his descriptions of the effects of birth order and siblings on personality development. For example, Adler felt that only children were most likely to be pampered, second children tended toward competitiveness in an effort to outpace the older sibling, and that the youngest child, though also likely to be pampered, could feel inferior to older siblings.

While a prisoner in a Nazi concentration camp, the Viennese physician Viktor Frankl (1905–97) observed that prisoners who remained hopeful and those who were deeply religious had better chances of survival than those who were hopeless. (See Figure 1.6.) He developed a form of therapy that combined science and spirituality and called it "logotherapy." The name incorporated the Greek word *logos,* which has multiple meanings, including god, spirit, word, and meaning. His intent was to rehumanize psychotherapy and assist clients to discover meaning in their lives that is individual rather than dictated by societal values. Frankl also coined the term "anticipatory anxiety" to describe the cycle in which an individual so fears developing symptoms of anxiety that

FIGURE 1.5

Alfred Adler. *Archive Photos, Inc. Reproduced by permission.*

FIGURE 1.6

Victor Frankl. *DIZ Munchen GmbH. Reproduced by permission.*

experiencing the symptoms is practically guaranteed. For example, a student having difficulty sleeping during finals week may become so anxious about losing sleep that she is unable to sleep. He also described "hyperintention," trying so hard that the act of trying actually impedes success. The student using every conceivable strategy to fall asleep before an exam is an example of how trying too hard can itself perpetuate insomnia. Similarly, "hyperreflection," or overthinking, can create a self-fulfilling prophecy in which worst-case scenarios come to pass simply because the deeply held beliefs that they will happen encourage attitudes and actions to ensure their occurrence.

Another German psychotherapist, Erich Fromm (1900–80), drew upon the teachings of Freud and Karl Marx to develop a theory that considered biological, cultural, and economic origins of personality. (See Figure 1.7.) He contended that an all-consuming focus on materialism—acquiring possessions—predisposed people to favor "having" as opposed to "being." This led to people deriving their self-worth from consuming rather than from their actions, experiences, and relationships.

Physician Karen Horney (1885–1952) was one of very few women to make a significant contribution to mental health theory and practice, largely because so few women were involved in medicine or psychology during the first half of the 20th century. (See Figure 1.8.) Horney offered a novel perspective on neurosis (mental or emotional dysfunction with no apparent physical cause), choosing to view it as a coping strategy rather than a serious mental illness. She distinguished between three broad categories of coping strategies:

- Moving-toward strategy or compliance—used by those with neurotic needs for approval and the wholesale desire to please others, the neurotic need for a partner to completely manage one's life, or the neurotic need to lead a narrow, unassuming life with few aspirations or ambitions.

- Moving-against, also termed aggression—employed by those with neurotic needs for power and control, recognition, status or acclaim, personal achievement or admiration, as well as persons inclined to exploit others.

- Moving-away-from or withdrawal—strategies used by those with neurotic needs to lead sharply restricted lives, live entirely autonomously without reliance on other, and strive to be perfectionists.

FIGURE 1.7

Erich Fromm. *The Library of Congress*

FIGURE 1.8

Karen Horney. *Corbis-Bettmann. Reproduced by permission.*

Interestingly, Horney proposed an analogous condition to penis envy that might account for certain male behaviors. She termed it "womb envy" and offered that men's driving ambitions to succeed might be a compensatory mechanism, or a way to create legacies since they could not give birth to, and nurture, new life. Along with a feminist perspective that was ahead of its time, Horney also wrote one of the first self-help books. *Self-Analysis* (W.W. Norton & Company, New York, reissue edition 1994) was first published in 1942 and exhorted readers to use psychoanalytic techniques to solve their own personal problems.

Another colleague of Freud was Carl Jung (1875–1961), a psychiatrist best known for integrating psychoanalytic theory with mythical, religious, and spiritual philosophies such as alchemy, cabala, Buddhism, and Hinduism and his description of the collective unconscious—the sum total of all of mankind's unconscious. (See Figure 1.9.) Jung asserted that each individual was born with a kind of genetic legacy of psychic awareness. He cited phenomena such as deja vu (the illusion of having already experienced an event actually being experienced for the first time) and the simultaneous emergence of parallel themes in art, religion, and dreams across cultures and continents as evidence of the collective unconscious.

The American psychologist Abraham Maslow (1908–70) posited that in terms of survival some human needs were more compelling than others. (See Figure 1.10.)

He developed a hierarchy of needs that placed physiological needs such as the need for oxygen, water, and other nutrients at the base of a pyramid. Once these physiological needs are met, the next requirement is for safety and security—structure, stability, and order. The third tier of the pyramid is the need to belong, which includes the desire for friends, family, romantic relationships, and a sense of community. The fourth tier encompasses two levels of esteem needs—the first includes needs for respect, dignity, attention, appreciation, recognition, status, and reputation, while the second level refers to aspects of self-esteem such as self-respect, confidence, mastery, autonomy (independence), and freedom. The highest level is the need for self-actualization—the notion of fulfilling one's potential, becoming as full and complete as possible. (See Figure 1.11.)

Maslow hypothesized that a scant 2 percent of the world's population was truly self-actualized. In order to achieve self-actualization, Maslow not only concluded that all of the lower tier needs must first be met but also that persons who were self-actualized were distinguished by specific, shared characteristics. For example, self-actualized individuals relied on their own good judgment and were better able to resist pressures to conform than others. They were creative, spontaneous, appreciative, filled with awe and wonder, and open-minded—accepting of themselves and others. Maslow named Abraham Lincoln,

FIGURE 1.9

FIGURE 1.10

Carl Jung. *The Library of Congress*

Abraham Maslow. *UPI/Corbis Bettmann. Reproduced by permission.*

Thomas Jefferson, Mahatma Gandhi, and Albert Einstein as individuals who met his criteria for self-actualization.

Toward the end of his life, the American existential psychologist Rollo May (1909–94) published *The Cry for Myth* (W.W. Norton & Company, New York, 1991), in which he described the vital importance of mythology and how people use myths to make meaning of their lives. He proclaimed traditional American mythology obsolete. Depicting 20th-century Americans as anxious, rudderless, and at a loss for values, he called for the creation of new myths or narratives that support people's efforts at finding meaning in their lives rather than undermining them.

Swiss biologist and child psychologist Jean Piaget (1896–1980) studied the development of thinking, learning, intelligence, and knowledge, a field he dubbed genetic epistemology. (Epistemology is the study of theories of knowledge or ways of knowing.) (See Figure 1.12.) His theory centers on the idea of cognitive structures—patterns of physical or mental action that underlie specific intelligence and correspond to stages of child development.

According to Piaget, there are four primary cognitive structures or developmental stages: sensorimotor, preoperations, concrete operations, and formal operations. During the sensorimotor stage (0–2 years), the infant uses senses and motor skills to learn about the world. The preopera-tional stage (3–7 years) is marked by the child's ability to engage in creative play using symbols—words and objects stand in for one another. During this stage, younger children are able to focus on only a single aspect of any issue or communication. For example, complex verbal instructions to perform more than one task are poorly or incompletely understood. The concrete operational stage (8–11 years) is characterized by the child's ability to use symbols as representations and manipulate those symbols logically. Early in this stage children learn about reversibility. For example, they understand that a ball of yarn is no bigger when it is unraveled than it is when it is stretched end to end, and that once the strand is rewound into a ball, it would look as it did at the beginning of the experiment. In the final stage of formal operations (12–15 years), abstract or hypothetical thinking is mastered.

Piaget also distinguished between three types of knowledge that children acquire. He described physical knowledge as "knowledge about objects in the world, which can be gained through their perceptual properties," logical-mathematical knowledge as "abstract knowledge that must be invented," and social-arbitrary knowledge as "culture-specific knowledge learned from people within one's culture-group."

Carl Rogers (1902–87) was an American psychologist who contributed a detailed description of mental

FIGURE 1.11

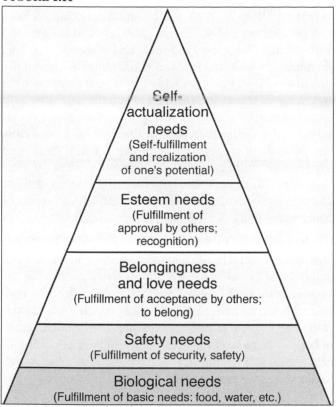

Maslow's hierarchy of needs. *EPD Photos. Gale Group*

FIGURE 1.12

Jean Piaget. *Farrell Grehan/Corbis. Reproduced by permission.*

health he termed the "fully functioning" individual. Rogers characterized the fully functioning person as:

- Open and accepting—receptive to new experiences, his or her own feelings, and objective reality. People described as defensive—continually guarding against attack—are not open and accepting.

- Creative—poised to generously contribute through personal relationships, social activism, or original work to improve the life of others.

- Living in the present—Rogers called this quality "existential living," by which he meant learning from the past and speculating about the future but living in the here and now.

- Experiential freedom—Rogers believed that self-actualized people experienced freedom when they were offered choices and that fully functioning people realize this freedom and assume responsibility for their choices.

- Organismic trusting—The self-actualized trust themselves and rely on their own inner guidance and direction.

Rogers championed the practice of non-directive or client-centered therapy, in which the client rather than the therapist directed the course and progress of therapy. Known today simply as Rogerian therapy, it also involves the practice of reflection—a technique in which the therapist mirrors the client's statement to clarify and confirm understanding

and to reassure the client that he or she has been heard. Rogers felt that the minimum requirements for effective therapists are the capacity to demonstrate empathy and respect for their clients as well as congruence—the ability and willingness to respond sincerely and honestly to client concerns.

American psychologist and academician Burrhus Frederic Skinner, known as B. F. Skinner (1904–90) developed explanations of human behavior based on operant conditioning—a type of conditioning in which an organism learns the behaviors that yield desirable outcomes or permit it to avoid undesirable outcomes. (See Figure 1.13.) Skinner taught rats to respond to specific situations in a predetermined manner by using "reinforcers" to stimulate and train them to repeat behaviors and failing to offer these reinforcers or delivering aversive stimuli—unpleasant or punishing actions—to extinguish or stop other behaviors.

The therapeutic method based on his theories is called behavior modification and involves extinguishing an undesirable behavior by removing the reinforcer and replacing it with a desirable behavior by reinforcement. Behavior modification has been successfully used to resolve a variety of mental health problems, including addictions, and is considered particularly effective in children. A kind of behavior

FIGURE 1.13

B. F. Skinner. *The Library of Congress*

modification known as systematic desensitization has been used to treat persons with phobias such as fear of flying in airplanes, fear of riding in elevators, and fears of spiders, snakes, and insects. This therapy involves learning to relax rather than feeling anxious or fearful in the face of progressively more threatening situations until exposure to the previously feared act or object no longer triggers anxiety.

MODERN DEFINITIONS OF MENTAL HEALTH AND MENTAL ILLNESS

[Mental health is] the successful performance of mental function, resulting in productive activities, fulfilling relationships with other people, and the ability to adapt to change and to cope with adversity; from early childhood until late life, mental health is the springboard of thinking and communication skills, learning, emotional growth, resilience, and self esteem.

—David Satcher, U.S. Surgeon General, 1999

Health is a state of complete physical, mental and social well-being and not merely the absence of disease or infirmity.

— Preamble to the Constitution of the World Health Organization as adopted by the International Health Conference, New York, 19–22 June 1946; signed on 22 July 1946 by the representatives of 61 States (Official Records of the World Health Organization, no. 2, p. 100) and entered into force on 7 April 1948. (The definition has not been amended since 1948.)

Mental health may be measured in terms of an individual's abilities to think and communicate clearly, learn and grow emotionally, deal productively and realistically with change and stress, and form and maintain fulfilling relationships with others. Mental health is fundamentally linked to physical health and is a principal component of wellness—self-esteem, resilience, and the ability to cope with adversity influence how people feel about themselves and whether they choose lifestyles and behaviors that promote or jeopardize their health. While there is no single, universally accepted definition of positive or ideal mental health, it is probably some combination of these characteristics and attributes coupled with a sense of coherence—unity of purpose—and optimism.

It is important to recognize that like physical health and well-being, mental health and mental illness are understood and defined in cultural contexts. In sharp contrast to the Western construct of mental health, Eastern philosophy considers health, including mental health, which is not considered to be separate or distinct from physical health, in terms of body systems working in harmony. Imbalances cause illness and result from physical or psychological stress as well as nutritional, environmental, or spiritual influences.

Mental illness refers to all identifiable mental health disorders and mental health problems. *Mental Health: A Report of the Surgeon General, 1999* defines mental disorders as "health conditions that are characterized by alterations in thinking, mood, or behavior (or some combination thereof) associated with distress and/or impaired functioning." The report distinguishes mental disorders from mental health problems, describing the signs and symptoms of mental health problems as less intense and of shorter duration than those of mental health disorders. However, it acknowledges that both mental health disorders and problems may be distressing and disabling.

The symptoms of mental disorders differentiate one type of disorder from another; however, the symptoms of mental illness vary far more widely in both type and intensity than do the symptoms of most physical illnesses. In general, people are usually considered mentally healthy if they are able to maintain their mental and emotional balance in times of crisis and stress and cope effectively with the problems of daily life. When coping ability is lost, then there is some degree of mental dysfunction. The goals of diagnosis and treatment of mental disorders are to recognize and understand the conditions, identify and reduce their underlying causes, and work toward restoring mental and emotional equilibrium.

Further, the Surgeon General's report posits that mental health and mental illness are not opposite states of being. Rather, they are points on a continuum. It confirms the interrelationship and inextricability of the mind-body connection and proposes that instead of viewing mental health and physical health as separate, or only tangentially related, a more useful distinction is between somatic health and mental health. Defined in this manner, mental disorders are those in which changes in mental function are predominant while somatic conditions are those in which nonmental functions are largely responsible for changes. Because this definition focuses on the types of changes produced by the disorder, it explains why all disorders of the brain are not necessarily mental disorders. For example, the presence of a tumor in the brain that produces blindness is not considered a mental disorder, whereas a neurological condition that produces changes in thinking or behavior would be termed a mental disorder.

The report also observes that the challenge to define mental health has impeded the development of programs to support and promote mental health in the community. Absent a uniformly applicable definition, and constrained by a variety of values and culturally determined interpretations, it is difficult to conceive of, let alone implement, a concerted set of actions or programs aimed at improving and maintaining mental health that would be effective in even a small, homogenous community. The diversity, in terms of race, age, ethnicity, religion, and socioeconomic status, present throughout the United States compounds this already formidable task.

CHAPTER 2
RECOGNIZING AND DIAGNOSING MENTAL ILLNESS

My world falls apart, crumbles, "The center cannot hold." There is no integrating force, only the naked fear, the urge of self-preservation. I am afraid. I am not solid, but hollow. I feel behind my eyes a numb, paralyzed cavern, a pit of hell, a mimicking nothingness. I never thought. I never wrote, I never suffered. I want to kill myself, to escape from responsibility, to crawl back abjectly into the womb. I do not know who I am, where I am going—and I am the one who has to decide the answers to these hideous questions. I long for a noble escape from freedom—I am weak, tired, in revolt from the strong constructive humanitarian faith which presupposes a healthy, active intellect and will. There is nowhere to go...

—Sylvia Plath, on her depression, *The Unabridged Journals of Sylvia Plath,* Anchor Books, New York, 2000

Although there are varying opinions about the personality traits and characteristics that taken together constitute optimal mental health, historically it has been somewhat easier to define and identify mental illness—deviations from, or the absence of, mental health. Within the broad diagnosis of mental illness, there is more consensus about the origins, nature, and symptoms of mental disorders—serious, and often long-term conditions in which changes in cognition, behavior, or mood impair functioning—than exists about mental health problems—shorter term, less intense conditions that often resolve spontaneously, without treatment.

HOW MANY PEOPLE ARE MENTALLY ILL?

It is challenging to determine how many people suffer from mental illness because of changing definitions of mental illness and difficulties classifying, diagnosing, and reporting mental disorders. There are social stigmas attached to being labeled crazy, preventing some sufferers of mental illness from seeking help. Many of those seeking help do not reveal it on surveys. Some people do not realize that their symptoms are caused by mental disor-

ders, and mental health professionals themselves often disagree about diagnoses.

A World Health Organization (WHO) study found that nearly one-quarter (24 percent) of patients who make visits to primary-care physicians (general practitioners, family practitioners, internists, and pediatricians) suffer from a mental disorder as defined by the ICD-10. The ICD-10 is the 10th revision of the International Statistical Classification of Diseases and Related Health Problems, a coding system used to track national morbidity (rates of illness or occurrence of a disease) and mortality (death rates) data. Table 2.1 is a list of categories of mental and

TABLE 2.1

Categories of mental and behavioral disorders, 1998

F00#	Dementia
F05	Delirium
FI0	Alcohol use disorders
F11#	Drug use disorders
F17.1	Tobacco use disorders
F20#	Chronic psychotic disorders
F23	Acute psychotic disorders
F31	Bipolar disorder
F32#	Depression
F40	Phobic disorders
F41.0	Panic disorder
F41.1	Generalized anxiety
F41.2	Mixed anxiety and depression
F43.2	Adjustment disorder
F44	Dissociative (conversion) disorder
F45	Unexplained somatic complaints
F48.0	Neurasthenia
F50	Eating disorders
F51	Sleep problems
F52	Sexual disorders
F70	Mental retardation
F90	Hyperkinetic (attention deficit) disorder
F91#	Conduct disorder
F98.0	Enuresis
Z63	Bereavement disorders

SOURCE: T. B. Ustun, "Categories of mental and behavioural disorders," in *Mental Disorders in Primary Care,* World Health Organization, Geneva, Switzerland, 1998. Reproduced with permission.

behavioral disorders from the ICD-10 that were included in the WHO study, as well as its guidelines for diagnosis. These categories were chosen on the basis of their:

- Frequency of occurrence, especially among patients seeking care from primary-care physicians.

- Significant impact on public health in terms of resource allocation and utilization as well as burdens to families and the community.

- Widespread agreement among primary care practitioners and psychiatrists about the diagnosis and management of the disorder.

- Availability and acceptability of management or treatment that is likely to benefit patients, their families, and the community.

- Applicability across cultures and treatment settings.

How Many Americans Suffer from Mental Disorders?

Psychiatric epidemiologists, mental health researchers, and other public health professionals assess the mental health of a population by determining the rates of mental disorders and resulting disability. Estimates of the frequency with which mental disorders occur and the number of persons affected are vital for mental health-service planning and resource allocation. Incidence is a measure of the rate at which people without a disorder develop the disorder during a specific period of time. Incidence describes the continuing occurrence of diseases over time. Prevalence describes a group or population at a specific interval in time. For example, one study found the one-year prevalence rate for addictive disorders, such as substance abuse, to be nearly 30 percent.

There have been several attempts to determine how many Americans suffer from mental disorders, but because of differences in definitions and diagnosis of mental illness and differences in data collection by those studying the issue, it is difficult to measure accurately and consistently. A 1999 report by the U.S. Surgeon General, *Mental Health: A Report of the Surgeon General, 1999* identified 20 percent of the U.S. population as affected by mental disorders and 15 percent as using some type of mental health service every year. Table 2.2 shows the estimated prevalence of mental health disorders among Americans aged 18–54 based on survey data from the National Institute of Mental Health Epidemiologic Catchment Area Program (ECA) and the National Comorbidity Survey (NCS). In 1998 the CDC estimated that 10 percent of adults suffered disability from a diagnosed mental illness such as phobia, depression, and/or an anxiety disorder, and as many as one-quarter of adults had experienced a mental disorder during the preceding year. The National Institute of Mental Health (NIMH) confirms that mental health disorders are common—estimating that more than

TABLE 2.2

Best-estimate one-year prevalence rates of anxiety and mood disorders based on Epidemiological Catchment Area Study (ECA) and National Comorbidity Survey (NCS), ages 18–54, 1999

	Epidemiological Catchment Area Study (ECA) Prevalence (%)	National Comorbidity Survey (NCS) Prevalence (%)	Best Estimate (%)
Any anxiety disorder	13.1	18.7	16.4
Simple phobia	8.3	8.6	8.3
Social phobia	2.0	7.4	2.0
Agoraphobia	4.9	3.7	4.9
Generalized anxiety disorder (GAD)	(1.5)	3.4	3.4
Panic disorder	1.6	2.2	1.6
Obsessive-compulsive disorder (OCD)	2.4	(0.9)	2.4
Post-traumatic stress disorder (PTSD)	(1.9)	3.6	3.6
Any mood disorder	7.1	11.1	7.1
Major depression (MD) episode	6.5	10.1	6.5
Unipolar MD	5.3	8.9	5.3
Dysthymia	1.6	2.5	1.6
Bipolar I	1.1	1.3	1.1
Bipolar II	0.6	0.2	0.6
Schizophrenia	1.3	–	1.3
Nonaffective psychosis	–	0.2	0.2
Somatization	0.2	–	0.2
Antisocial personality disorder (ASP)	2.1	–	2.1
Anorexia nervosa	0.1	–	0.1
Severe cognitive impairment	1.2	–	1.2
Any disorder	19.5	23.4	21.0

SOURCE: David Satcher, "Table 2-6. Best estimate 1-year prevalence rates based on ECA and NCA, ages 18–54," in *Mental Health: A Report of the Surgeon General,* U.S. Department of Health and Human Services, Substance Abuse and Mental Health Services Administration, with National Institutes of Health, Rockville, MD, 1999 [Online] http://www.mentalhealth.org/features/surgeongeneralreport/toc.asp [accessed December 18, 2003]

22 percent of persons aged 18 and older, or more than one in five adults, suffer from a mental disorder every year.

The statistics cited in the Surgeon General's report suggest to some that the United States is in the throes of an epidemic (the occurrence of a disease clearly in excess of the number of cases normally found in the population) of mental illness. About 20 percent of children have symptoms of mental disorders over the course of a year, and half of the U.S. population will develop mental disorders over the course of their lifetimes. Mental illness is the second leading cause of disability (as measured in years lived with a disability of specified severity and duration).

REVISED PREVALENCE ESTIMATES. Confused by discrepancies between rates, and aware of the need for more accurate projections to assist planners and policy makers involved in decisions about service delivery, William E. Narrow and his colleagues at the American Psychiatric Institute for Research and Education, Washington, D.C., and Department of Psychiatry, Washington University School of Medicine, St Louis, Missouri, presented modified estimates of the prevalence of mental disorders in the United States in "Revised Prevalence Estimates of Mental Disorders in the United States: Using a Clinical Significance Criterion to

Reconcile 2 Surveys' Estimates" (*Archives of General Psychiatry,* vol. 59, no. 2, February 2002). The investigators analyzed and correlated data from the two most frequently cited sources, the ECA and NCS, and produced revised national prevalence rates.

Although the ECA and NCS surveys differed in methodologies, the investigators' analyses produced lower rates of mental health disorders than previously reported in either survey. (The rates cited by the investigators differed from the prevalence estimates included in the Surgeon General's report. Such discrepancies often occur when investigators use different criteria, methods, and models to develop prevalence estimates.) According to the American Psychiatric Institute study, the overall prevalence of mental disorders fell from the ECA estimate of 29.6 percent and from the NCS estimate of 30.2 percent, to 20.9 percent, a decline that represents a decrease of about 13.3 million and 13.9 million Americans, respectively. For all adults older than 18 years, the revised estimate of 18.5 percent represents a decrease of about 19.2 million people from the ECA estimate of 28 percent. Similarly, the revised estimate for any mental health disorder was 18.5 percent, nearly 4 percent less than NIMH estimates. The investigators concluded that "the policy implications of epidemiologic survey results continue to resonate as mental health systems, both public and private, struggle to compete for shrinking health care dollars. Even relatively modest changes in the prevalence rate of mental disorders will have an impact on the planning of service systems."

CHANGING CRITERIA FOR MENTAL ILLNESS

There are many controversies in mental health diagnosis, beginning with the definitions and classification of mental illnesses. Which criteria distinguish conditions as mental illness rather than normal variations in thinking and behavior? Should conditions such as attention deficit hyperactivity disorder (ADHD) be classified as learning problems or mental disorders? Should practitioners distinguish between neurological conditions that cause brain dysfunction and cognitive impairment such as Alzheimer's disease and mental illness involving brain dysfunction such as depression that may result from an imbalance of chemicals in the brain?

The authoritative encyclopedia of diagnostic criteria for mental disorders is the *Diagnostic and Statistical Manual* (American Psychiatric Publishing, 4th edition, Arlington, Virginia, 2000). Known to practitioners as DSM-IV because it is presently in its fourth edition, this definitive guide, which expands upon the ICD-10, is the most widely used psychiatric reference in the world and catalogs more than 300 mental disorders. Table 2.3 lists the major classifications of mental disorders contained in the DSM-IV.

An examination of past versions of the DSM reveals that the definitions of mental illnesses have changed dramatically from one edition to another. Persons diagnosed with a specific mental disorder based on diagnostic criteria in one edition might no longer be considered mentally ill according to the next edition. Critics of the DSM, which has expanded more than tenfold since its inception, claim that diseases are added arbitrarily by the American Psychiatric Association (APA) and that while some entries represent changing ideas about mental health and illness, others are politically motivated. For example, homosexuality was once considered a mental illness, but today, largely in response to changing societal attitudes, it is no longer termed an illness.

Skeptics also question the sharp increase in the number of diagnoses and the number of Americans receiving these diagnoses. Does the increasing number of diagnoses reflect rapid advances in mental health diagnostic techniques? Have mental health professionals simply improved their diagnostic skills? Are the stresses of 21st-century life precipitating an epidemic of mental illness in the United States? Or are mental health professionals—psychiatrists, psychologists, clinical social workers, marriage and family therapists, and other mental health practitioners—simply labeling more behaviors and aspects of everyday life as pathological (diseased)?

Further, there is dissent even within the mental health field about diagnosis that is rooted in the ongoing debate about the origins of mental illness. After analyzing all of the relevant medical research, the Surgeon General's report concluded that for most mental illnesses there is no demonstrable physiological cause. This means there is no laboratory test, imaging study (X-ray, magnetic resonance imaging, or positron emission tomography), or abnormality in brain tissue that has been definitively identified as causing mental illness. The majority of persons suffering from

TABLE 2.3

Major diagnostic classes of mental disorders, 1999

Disorders usually first diagnosed in infancy, childhood, or adolescence
Delerium, dementia, and amnestic and other cognitive disorders
Mental disorders due to a general medical condition
Substance-related disorders
Schizophrenia and other psychotic disorders
Mood disorders
Anxiety disorders
Somatoform disorders
Factitious disorders
Dissociative disorders
Sexual and gender identity disorders
Eating disorders
Sleep disorders
Impulse-control disorders
Adjustment disorders
Personality disorders

SOURCE: David Satcher, "Table 2-5. Major Diagnostic Classes of Mental Disorders," in *Mental Health: A Report of the Surgeon General,* U.S. Department of Health and Human Services, Substance Abuse and Mental Health Services Administration, with National Institutes of Health, Rockville, MD, 1999 [Online] http://www.mentalhealth.org/features/surgeongeneralreport/toc.asp [accessed December 18, 2003]

mental illness apparently have normal brains, and those with abnormal brain structure or function are diagnosed with neurological disorders rather than mental illnesses.

Finally, there are those who view mental illness as a social condition rather than one requiring medical diagnosis. They observe that even the Surgeon General's report, which favors biological explanations of the origin, diagnosis, and treatment of mental illness, concedes that mental health is poorly understood and defined differently across cultures. If mental health and illness are rooted in cultural mores and values, then they are likely socioeconomic and political in origin. The proponents of societal causes of mental illness contend that if mental illness is in part defined as functional impairment, and during the course of their lives half the U.S. population will be impaired, then perhaps it is not the individual who is ailing but the society. This theory is supported by the fact that the WHO estimates that 25 percent of individuals will be diagnosed with mental illness in developed and developing countries, half of the percent of the American population estimated to be at risk.

GENETIC ORIGINS OF MENTAL DISORDERS

Genetic susceptibility maintains that the genes an individual inherits affect how likely he or she is to develop a particular condition or disease. When an individual is genetically susceptible to a particular disease, his or her risk of developing the disease is higher. Genetic susceptibility interacts with environmental factors to produce disease, but they do not necessarily make equal contributions to causation. Genes can cause a slight susceptibility or a strong susceptibility. When the genetic contribution is weak, the environmental influence must be strong to produce disease and vice versa.

In most instances a susceptibility gene strongly influences the risk of developing a disease only in response to a specific environmental exposure. A critical mix of nature and nurture is likely to determine individual traits and characteristics, including personality and behavior. Genetic factors may be considered as the foundation on which environmental agents exert their influence. Based on this premise, it is now widely accepted that while certain environmental factors alone and certain genetic factors alone may explain the origins of some traits and diseases, most of the time the interaction of both genetic and environmental factors will be required for their expression.

In recent years researchers have identified more and more genes that influence an individual's susceptibility to disease. Scientists have already linked specific DNA variations with increased risk of common diseases and conditions, including cancer, diabetes, hypertension, and Alzheimer's disease (a progressive neurological disease that causes impaired thinking, memory, and behavior). These findings lend credence to the heritability of mental illness reported by twin studies and family patterns of inheritance.

Researchers are scouring the humane genome because the complex interaction of multiple genes is likely to be the key to understanding dysfunction in the brain in mental illness. There is preliminary evidence that unaffected family members may share genes with their affected relatives that increase their chances of developing much less severe but similar behavioral traits and characteristics. For example, relatives of persons suffering from anxiety disorders or schizophrenia may manifest subtle cognitive problems or very mild expressions of the symptoms of these disorders. NIMH-supported researchers are scrutinizing such families to identify and fully describe these behavioral and physiological traits, in an effort to accurately trace them back to their genetic origins.

There is great excitement in the scientific community about the potential of genetic discoveries to catalyze rapid advances in the prevention, diagnosis, and treatment of mental illness. However, when the lay media translates the results of genetic research for the public, they are often misinterpreted or misleading. For example, an article with a headline trumpeting "Gene for Suicide Discovered" (*BBC News Online,* U.K., April 6, 2001) then explains that two studies of psychiatric hospital patients revealed that patients with alterations in one of two genes were more likely to attempt suicide. Since the altered genes disturbed the brain's production of serotonin, the chemical known to play an important role in regulating mood and anxiety levels, scientists hypothesized that it might be involved in depression and impulse control. Similarly, an article titled "Gene for Panic Attacks Found" (*BBC News Online,* U.K., August 22, 2001) reported that 90 percent of affected persons had a specific genetic abnormality—DUP25—and the article also observed that persons who carry the DUP25 mutation are more likely to suffer from anxiety disorders. But the article also observed that in families of affected persons, 20 percent of relatives with DUP25 were entirely free of anxiety. For this reason, media reports must be read cautiously and preliminary research results presented accurately. Science in the 21st century acknowledges genetic susceptibility, but there is no support for the notion of genetic inevitability—that all persons carrying a specific genetic mutation will be afflicted by mental illness.

How Do Genes Influence Behavior and Attitudes?

The question of interest is no longer whether human social behavior is genetically determined; it is to what extent.

—Edward O. Wilson, *On Human Nature.* Harvard University Press, Cambridge, MA, 1978

Studies of families and twins have strongly suggested genetic influences on the development and expression of specific behaviors, but there is no conclusive research demonstrating that genes determine behaviors. In "The

Interplay of Nature, Nurture, and Developmental Influences: The Challenge Ahead for Mental Health" (*Archives of General Psychiatry,* vol. 59, no. 11, November 2002) psychiatrist Michael Rutter observed that a range of mental health disorders from autism and schizophrenia to attention deficit hyperactivity disorder (ADHD) involve at least indirect genetic effects, with heritability ranging from 20 percent to 50 percent. He further asserted that genetically influenced behaviors also bring about gene-environment correlations.

Rutter explained the mechanism of genetic influence on behavior—genes affect proteins, and through the effects of these proteins on the functioning of the brain there are resultant effects on behavior. He views environmental influences as comparable to genetic influences in that they are strong and pervasive but do not determine behaviors, and studies of environmental effects have shown that there are individual differences in response. Some individuals are severely affected and others experience few repercussions from environmental factors. This has given rise to the idea of varying degrees of resiliency—that people vary in their relative resistance to the harmful effects of psychosocial adversity—as well as the premise that genetics may offer protective effects from certain environmental influences.

Jan Strelau, a widely published author and psychology faculty member at the University of Warsaw in Poland, contends that the proportion of phenotypic variance (visible characteristics and/or behaviors that result from the interaction of an organism's genotype and the environment) that may be attributed to genetic variance ranges from about 40 to about 60 percent, but it is primarily environmental influences that explain individual differences in personality traits, including temperament, as well as specific behaviors and intelligence. He also offers that genetics influence the environment experienced by individuals. These interactions explain how children growing up in the same family often experience and interpret their environments differently. This also explains why individuals who share the same genes, though living apart, show some concordance in selecting or creating similar experiences ("The Contribution of Genetics to Psychology Today and in the Decade to Follow," *European Psychologist,* vol. 6, no. 4, December 2001).

Traditional psychological theory holds that attitudes are learned and most strongly influenced by environment. In "The Heritability of Attitudes: A Study of Twins" (*Journal of Personality and Social Psychology,* vol. 80, no. 6, June 2001), James Olson and his colleagues examined whether there was a genetic basis to attitudes by reviewing earlier studies and conducting original research on identical and fraternal twins. The investigators felt that the premise that attitudes are learned was not incompatible with the idea that biological and genetic factors also influence attitudes. They hypothesized that genes probably influence predispositions or natural inclinations, which then shape environmental experiences in ways that increase the likelihood of the individual developing specific traits and attitudes. For example, children who are small for their age might be teased or taunted by other children more than their larger peers. As a result, these children might develop anxieties about social interaction, with consequences for their personality such as shyness or low self-esteem and their attitudes such as dislike of large groups.

In their twin study, nonshared environmental factors—unique experiences of each member of a twin pair—were the most powerful contributors to variability in 30 attitude factors, whereas shared environmental factors—experiences common to both members of a twin pair—contributed only slightly to variance in the 30 factors. There also was strong evidence that differences between respondents in many of their expressed attitudes were partly determined by genetic factors. Twenty-six of the 30 individual attitude items yielded significant genetic effects, and these effects were observed on a wide range of topics, from attitudes about organized religion and support for the death penalty to attitudes toward participating in organized sports and enjoyment of roller-coaster rides. The investigators concluded that attitudes are learned but also depend on biological factors.

In a study supported by the NIH, researchers Amy Abrahamson, Laura Baker, and Avshalom Caspi looked at genetic influences on attitudes of adolescents and reported their findings in an article, "Rebellious Teens? Genetic and Environmental Influences on the Social Attitudes of Adolescents [Personality Processes and Individual Differences]" (*Journal of Personality and Social Psychology,* vol. 83, no. 6, December 2002). The purpose of their study was to investigate sources of familial influence on adolescent social attitudes in an effort to understand whether and how families exert an influence on the attitudes of adolescents. They wanted to pinpoint the age when genetic influences actually emerge and determine the extent to which parents and siblings shape teens' views about controversial issues. The researchers explored genetic and environmental influences in social attitudes in 654 adopted and nonadopted children and their biological and adoptive relatives in the Colorado Adoption Project. Conservatism and religious attitudes were measured in the children annually from ages 12 to 15 and in the parents during the 12-year-old visit.

The study found that both conservatism and religious attitudes were strongly influenced by shared-family environmental factors throughout adolescence. It also detected significant genetic influence in conservatism as early as age 12 but found no evidence of genetic influence on religious attitudes during adolescence. Familial resemblance for conservative attitudes arose from both genetic and common environmental factors, but familial resemblance on religious attitudes was almost entirely in response to shared family environmental factors. These findings were different from previous findings from twin studies, which suggested that genetic influence on social attitudes did not emerge until adulthood. The researchers for the Colorado study concluded that genetic factors exert an influence on social attitudes much earlier than previously indicated. The study provided further evidence that shared environmental factors contribute significantly to individual differences in social attitudes during adolescence.

Psychologist David Cohen downplayed environmental influences—specifically discounting parents' responsibility for mental illness and emotional problems in their children. In *Stranger in the Nest: Do Parents Really Shape Their Child's Personality, Intelligence, or Character?* (John Wiley & Sons, New York, 1999) Cohen asserted that good parenting cannot overcome bad genes and that it is impossible to separate genetic background from environmental influence. Making a strong case for genetic influence, he wrote, "The truth of the matter is that, if sufficiently strong, inborn potentials can trump parental influence, no matter how positive or negative. Some traits manifest themselves in such unexpected and uncontrollable ways that, for better or for worse, one's child may indeed seem like a perfect stranger."

Twin Studies Shed Light on Substance Abuse

Twin studies have also been conducted to find out whether genes influence the risk for alcohol and drug abuse. Research supported by the National Institute on Drug Abuse (NIDA is part of the National Institutes of Health) have tried to pinpoint the role genes play in predisposing individuals to drug abuse. For example, researchers at the Medical College of Virginia in Richmond found that genetic factors played a major role in patterns of progression from marijuana and cocaine use to abuse by female twins. The study found that concordance rates—both twins using, abusing, or dependent on drugs—were higher for identical than fraternal twins. For cocaine use, concordance was 54 percent in identical twins and 42 percent in fraternal twins; for abuse, 47 percent in identical twins and 8 percent in fraternal twins; and for dependence, 35 percent in identical twins and zero for fraternal twins. (See Figure 2.1.) (Kenneth Kendler, and Carol Prescott, "Cocaine Use, Abuse, and Dependence in a Population-Based Sample of Female Twins," *British Journal of Psychiatry,* vol. 173, no. 10, 1998).

The research supported earlier studies that indicated family and social environmental factors are influential in determining whether an individual begins using drugs. The more significant finding was that progression from drug use to abuse or dependence (as defined in the *Diagnostic and Statistical Manual of Mental Disorders, Fourth*

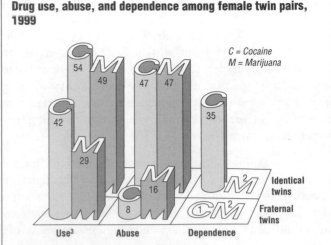

FIGURE 2.1

Drug use, abuse, and dependence among female twin pairs, 1999

C = Cocaine
M = Marijuana

[1]No instance in which both twins were dependent.
[2]Only 2 instances (1 identical pair, 1 fraternal pair) in which both twins were dependent.
[3]For marijuana, use more than 10 times in any month; for cocaine, any use.

SOURCE: Patrick Zickler, "Drug Use, Abuse, and Dependence Among Female Twin Pairs," in "Twin Studies Help Define the Role of Genes in Vulnerability to Drug Abuse," *NIDA Notes,* vol. 14, no. 4, November 1999

Edition (DSM-IV) American Psychiatric Association, Washington, D.C., 1994) was the result largely of genetic factors. For cocaine and marijuana, approximately 60 to 80 percent of the differences in abuse and dependence between fraternal and identical twin pairs were attributable to genetic factors.

Another NIDA supported study conducted by investigators at Harvard University looked at 1,874 pairs of identical male and 1,498 fraternal male twin pairs to see if genetic influences contributed to susceptibility for abusing drugs. The researchers found that genetic influences are stronger for abuse of some drugs than for others and that abusing any category of drugs, such as sedatives, stimulants, opiates, or heroin, was associated with a marked increase in the probability of abusing every other category of drugs. The study also revealed that each category of drug had unique genetic influences, and not surprisingly, heroin was the drug with the greatest genetic influence for abuse (Ming Tsuang, et al., "Co-occurrence of Abuse of Different Drugs in Men," *Archives of General Psychiatry,* vol. 55, 1998). Other NIDA-sponsored twin studies have suggested that genetic factors for drug abuse or dependence are stronger in males than in females.

ESTABLISHING A DIAGNOSIS OF MENTAL ILLNESS

Unlike physical health problems and medical conditions, there are no laboratory tests such as blood and urine analyses or X-rays to assist practitioners to definitively diagnose mental illnesses. Instead practitioners generally

TABLE 2.4

Mental disorders checklist, 1998

Depression		Anxiety		Alcohol use disorders	
	Yes		**Yes**		
I. Low mood / sadness	☐	I. Feeling tense or anxious?	☐	I. No. standard drinks in a typical day when drinking?___	
II. Loss of interest or pleasure	☐	II. Worrying a lot about things?	☐	II. No. of days/wk. having alcoholic drinks?_____	
III. Decreased energy and/or increased fatigue	☐				

Depression		Anxiety		Alcohol use disorders	
If YES to any of the above, continue below		**If YES to any of the above, continue below**		**If above limit, or if there is a regular/hazardous pattern, continue below**	
1. Sleep disturbance difficulty falling asleep early morning wakening	☐	1. Symptoms of arousal and anxiety? 2. Experienced intense or sudden fear unexpectedly or for no apparent reason?	☐	1. Have you been unable to stop, reduce or continue your drinking?	☐
2. Appetite disturbance appetite loss appetite increase	☐	Fear of dying ☐ Feeling dizzy, Fear of losing control ☐ lightheaded or faint ☐ Pounding heart ☐ Numbness or tingling		2. Have you ever felt such a strong desire or urge to drink that you could not resist it? 3. Did stopping or cutting down on your	☐
3. Concentration difficulty	☐	Sweating ☐ sensations ☐		drinking ever cause you problems such as:	
4. Psychomotor retardation or agitation	☐	Trembling, or shaking ☐ Feelings of unreality ☐		the shakes ☐ heart beating fast ☐	
5. Decreased libido	☐	Chest pains or Nausea ☐		being unable to sleep ☐ headaches ☐	
6. Loss of self-confidence or self esteem	☐	difficulty breathing ☐		feeling nervous or restless ☐ fits or seizures ☐	
7. Thought of death or suicide	☐	3. Experiences fear/anxiety in specific situations		sweating ☐	
8. Feelings of guilt	☐	leaving familiar places	☐	4. Have you ever continued to drink when you know that you had problems that can be made worse by drinking?	☐
		traveling alone, e.g. train, car, plane	☐		
		crowds confined places/public places	☐	5. Has anyone expressed concern about your drinking, for example:	
		4. Experienced fear/anxiety in social situations		your family, friends or your doctor?	☐
		speaking in front of others	☐		
		social events	☐		
		eating in front of others	☐		
		worry a lot about what others think or self-consciousness?	☐		

Summing up		**Summing up**		**Summing up**	
Positive to I, II, or III and at least 5 positive from 1 to 8 all occurring most of the time for 2 weeks or more. Indication of *depression*	☐ ☐	Positive to I or II and negative to 2, 3, and 4: Indication of *generalized anxiety* Positive to 1 and 2: indication of *panic disorder* Positive to 1 and 3: indication of *agoraphobia* Positive to 1 and 4: indication of *social phobia*	 ☐ ☐ ☐ ☐	If I × II is 21/wk or more for men or 14/wk or more for women, then possible *alcohol problem* Positive to 1 and any of 1-5 then likely *alcohol problem*	☐ ☐

Functioning & disablement

1. During the last month have you been limited in one or more of the following activities most of the time:

Self care: bathing, dressing, eating? ☐ Doing housework or household tasks? ☐
Family relations: spouse, children, relatives? ☐ Social activities, seeing friends? ☐
Going to work or school? ☐ Remembering things? ☐

II. Because of these problems during the last month

For how many days were you unable to fully carry out your usual daily activities?_____

How many days did you spend in bed in order to rest? _____

SOURCE: T. B. Ustun, "Mental Disorders Checklist," in *Mental Disorders in Primary Care*, World Health Organization, Geneva, Switzerland, 1998. Reproduced with permission.

rely on listening carefully to patients' complaints and observing their behavior to assess their moods, motivations, and thinking. Sometimes mental health disorders may accompany physical complaints or medical conditions. The presence of more than one disease or disorder is termed comorbidity.

Since many mental health disorders are identified by primary-care physicians (general practitioners, family practitioners, internists, pediatricians), the WHO developed educational materials and guidelines to assist practitioners in general medical, as opposed to psychiatric or other mental health settings, to assess and treat the mental health problems and disorders of patients in their care. The guidelines describe an assessment interview as a series of screening questions for which predominantly positive answers suggest the patient has an "identified mental disorder," as defined by the ICD-10, or a "subthreshold disorder"—the patient responds positively to

many questions but not enough to fulfill the diagnostic criteria for a disorder. Table 2.4 shows checklists of assessment interview questions used to screen patients for three common mental health disorders—depression, anxiety, and alcohol use. Practitioners are encouraged to ask open-ended questions that encourage patients to freely express their emotions, assure confidentiality, acknowledge patients' responses, and closely observe their body language and tones of voice.

Projective Testing Techniques

Although most diagnoses of mental illness are made on the basis of symptoms reported by the patient, the practitioner's observations, and the use of designated guidelines or criteria for distinguishing between disorders and establishing diagnoses, there are additional diagnostic tests practitioners may perform to confirm diagnoses. Projective tests, thought to provide insight into clients' unconscious minds, such as the Rorschach, Thematic

FIGURE 2.2

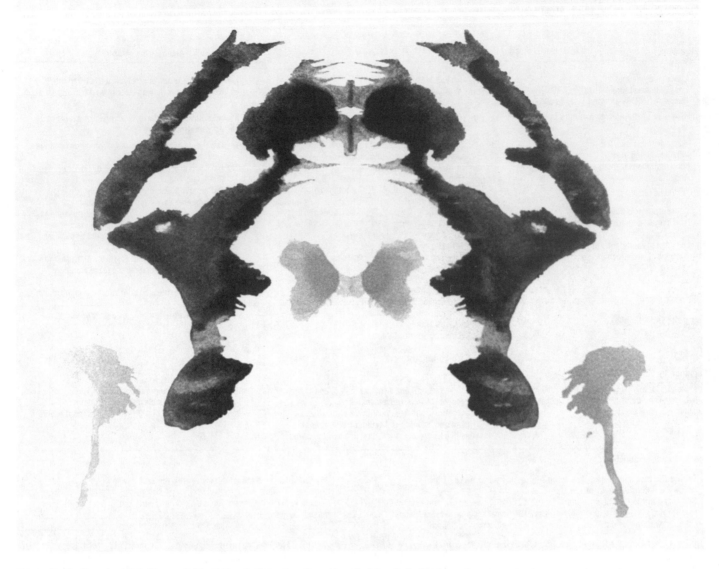

Example of a Rorschach ink blot test. *Photo Researchers, Inc. Reproduced with permission.*

Apperception Test (TAT), human figure drawings, and the Washington University Sentence Completion Test, have been used to characterize and describe symptoms, as well as to detect physical abuse, sexual abuse, and child abuse. (Figure 2.2 is an example of a Rorschach inkblot test.) There is widespread agreement that projective tests should be just one component of a comprehensive diagnostic study and that results from the tests should be integrated with history and interview information, since test results should be weighted only when they are consistent with other data.

There has been harsh criticism of projective tests during recent years, with detractors detailing their shortcomings, concluding that they lack a scientific underpinning and produce exaggerated estimates of pathology. In an effort to address this controversy, Howard Garb and his colleagues analyzed the efficacy of a variety of projective tests and reported their findings in "Effective Use of Pro-

jective Techniques in Clinical Practice: Let the Data Help With Selection and Interpretation [Assessment in Professional Practice]" (*Professional Psychology: Research and Practice,* vol. 35, no. 5, October 2002).

The investigators concluded that for making diagnoses, psychologists should rely primarily on interview and history information, but that results from psychological tests, including self-report personality inventories and projective techniques, may be helpful. They advised psychologists that they were likely to be "on safer ground when they use projective techniques as an aid for exploration in psychotherapy rather than as an assessment device."

Further, the investigators exhorted psychologists to rely heavily on history and interview data to predict behavior. They recommended that to evaluate psychiatric symptoms and personality traits, practitioners should depend on interview and history information, self-report personality inventories, and, in selected instances, projective tests. Although evaluation of symptoms and personality traits are ostensibly the ideal task for projective techniques, the investigators found that findings derived from Rorschach, TAT, and human figure drawings have not been independently and consistently replicated.

Automated and Online Diagnostic Testing

There are other diagnostic tests and case-finding instruments—tools practitioners may employ to screen for and identify persons suffering from mental illness. Jonathan Shedler and his colleagues from Harvard Medical School and the Clinical Research Unit of Kaiser Permanente in Colorado evaluated the utility and validity of Quick PsychoDiagnostics (QPD) Panel, an automated mental health test. They reported their findings in "Practical Mental Health Assessment in Primary Care: Validity and Utility of the Quick PsychoDiagnostics Panel" (*Journal of Family Practice,* vol. 49, no. 7, July 2000).

QPD was designed to meet the needs of primary-care physicians who do not have sufficient time to administer even brief diagnostic tests. The test combines features of an inventory and a structured interview and screens for nine frequently occurring psychiatric disorders and requires no physician time to administer or score. Patients respond to a core set of 59 questions and, when responses suggest a possible psychiatric disorder, the test offers pointed questions that, like a structured interview, probe in-depth. Although the test contains more than 200 diagnostic questions, patients see and respond to a customized, relevant subset of them. Scoring is performed electronically.

The investigators evaluated validity by correlating QPD Panel scores to the Structured Clinical Interview for DSM-IV (SCID) and established mental health measures. They assessed utility, in terms of acceptability to physicians and patients, by administering satisfaction surveys to both groups. The researchers concluded that the QPD Panel is a valid mental health assessment tool with the capacity to diagnose a range of common psychiatric disorders. They deemed it practical for routine use in busy primary-care practices and observed that "routine screening would benefit the many patients who currently go undiagnosed and untreated."

Even if computerized diagnostic capabilities are imperfect and unproved, University of Pittsburgh Department of Psychiatry researcher Howard Garb suggested that computer programs will become more prominent in mental health practice in "Computers Will Become Increasingly Important for Psychological Assessment: Not That There's Anything Wrong With That!" (*Psychological Assessment,* vol. 12, no. 1, March 2000). Garb contended that computers would be widely used for psychological assessment because mental health professionals are not good at some judgment tasks and that the use of computers to make judgments might prevent problems associated with clinicians' judgments. He concluded, "Using computers to make judgments and decisions in personality assessment can lead to dramatically improved reliability, a decrease in the occurrence of biases, and an overall increase in validity and utility."

Tom Buchanan, from the University of Westminster Department of Psychology, described the strengths and weaknesses of Internet-mediated, or online, psychological assessment in "Online Assessment: Desirable or Dangerous?" (*Professional Psychology: Research and Practice,* vol. 33, no. 2, April 2002). Buchanan cited the strengths of online personality testing as allowing more people to complete them than would otherwise be possible. It enables persons who were previously unable to do so, because of distance or time constraints, to access mental health services. (Those who favor online therapy or counseling make the same arguments.) There also is the possibility that people may be more candid when completing tests online and willing to disclose more information about themselves to computers than to other people.

Weaknesses of Web-based assessment include computer anxiety that may affect participants' responses and the observation that online respondents tend to report higher levels of negative affect than those who complete conventional paper questionnaires. Mental health researchers wonder whether online respondents are simply more inclined to self-disclosure or whether they are actually a more depressed group. There are also professional and ethical concerns such as the likelihood of well-meaning but untrained individuals who offer tests and opinions about a range of psychological conditions. One concern is the consequences of providing already troubled individuals with information that might be potentially distressing. Without appropriate follow-up or counseling, delivering such sensitive and potentially emotionally charged information is ethically and professionally unacceptable.

Other potential problems center on the technology itself. Interruptions in connectivity may interfere with the assessment process. This is especially true when assessment is performed live during a videoconferencing session. Further, without use of a secure server and encrypted communications, electronic communications may be intercepted by a third party. Buchanan concluded that "online clinical tests are both desirable and dangerous. There is clearly great potential, but a lot of work must be done before this potential is realized. Only time and extensive research can tell us whether these instruments will become a useful tool in behavioral telehealth contexts."

DEPRESSION

According to the NIMH, depressive disorders such as major depressive disorder and bipolar disorder (in which patients alternate between periods of manic behavior and depressive episodes) afflict about 18.8 million American

TABLE 2.5

Symptoms of depression and mania

Depression
- Persistent sad, anxious, or "empty" mood
- Feelings of hopelessness, pessimism
- Feelings of guilt, worthlessness, helplessness
- Loss of interest or pleasure in hobbies and activities that were once enjoyed, including sex
- Decreased energy, fatigue, being "slowed down"
- Difficulty concentrating, remembering, making decisions
- Insomnia, early-morning awakening, or oversleeping
- Appetite and/or weight loss or overeating and weight gain
- Thoughts of death or suicide; suicide attempts
- Restlessness, irritability
- Persistent physical symptoms that do not respond to treatment, such as headaches, digestive disorders, and chronic pain

Mania
- Abnormal or excessive elation
- Unusual irritability
- Decreased need for sleep
- Grandiose notions
- Increased talking
- Racing thoughts
- Increased sexual desire
- Markedly increased energy
- Poor judgment
- Inappropriate social behavior

SOURCE: Margaret Strock, "Symptoms of Depression and Mania," in *Depression,* U.S. Department of Health and Human Services, National Institute of Mental Health, Bethesda, MD, 2000

TABLE 2.6

Questionnaire for depressive disorder

During the *last month* have you had any of the following complaints most of the time for at least two weeks. If yes, please check or mark the relevant box.

I.	Have you been feeling sad, blue or depressed?	☐
II.	Have you lost interest or pleasure in things that you enjoyed previously?	☐
III.	Have you been feeling your energy decreased and/or you are tired all the time?	☐

If YES to any of the above, continue below

1.	Have you been experiencing any problems falling asleep or waking up much earlier than before?	☐
2.	Have you lost your appetite or have you been eating much more than usual?	☐
3.	Any difficulties concentrating; for example, listening to others, working, watching TV, listening to the radio?	☐
4.	Have you noticed any slowing down in your thinking or moving around?	☐
5.	Has your interest in sex decreased?	☐
6.	Have you felt negative about yourself or lost confidence?	☐
7.	Have you thought of death, wished that you were dead or tried to end your life?	☐
8.	Do you often feel guilty?	☐

I. **During the last month have you been limited in one or more of the following areas most of the time:**
- Self care: bathing, dressing, eating? ☐
- Family relations: spouse, children, relatives? ☐
- Going to work or school? ☐
- Doing housework or household tasks? ☐
- Social activities, seeing friends, hobbies? ☐
- Remembering things? ☐

II. **Because of these problems during the last month:**
How many days were you unable to fully carry out your usual daily activities? ___
How many days did you spend in bed in order to rest? ___

SOURCE: T. B. Ustun, "ICD-10 PC: Questionnaire for Depressive Disorder," in *Mental Disorders in Primary Care,* World Health Organization, Geneva, Switzerland, 1998. Reproduced with permission.

---

adults; nearly 10 percent of the U.S. population suffers a depressive disorder every year. Women are affected (12 percent) almost twice as often as men (6.6 percent).

Depression is a whole-body illness, involving physical, mental, and emotional problems. A depressive disorder is not a temporary sad mood, and it is not a sign of personal weakness or a condition that can simply be willed away. People with depressive illness cannot just pull themselves together and will themselves well. Without treatment, the symptoms can persist for months or even years. (See Table 2.5 for a list of symptoms that characterize depression.) Not everyone who is depressed experiences all of the symptoms. Some people have very few symptoms; some have many. Like other mental illnesses, the severity and duration of the symptoms of depression may vary.

The WHO diagnostic guidelines distinguish between physical and psychological symptoms as well as changes in mood and motivation. Physical symptoms may include fatigue, lack of energy, sleep disturbances, and changes in appetite that can result in weight loss or weight gain. Psychological symptoms include guilt, negative feelings about one's self, problems with memory or concentration, and pervasive thoughts about death or suicide. Along with unremitting low mood, depression also involves feelings of hopelessness, helplessness, and worthlessness. Table 2.6 is a self-administered questionnaire that assists practitioners and patients to determine the presence, duration, and severity of symptoms associated with depression. Table 2.7 shows how

alterations in mood and motivation combined with physical and psychological changes can impair functioning. People suffering from depression may be unable to work, attend school, or perform their responsibilities at home.

Types of Depressive Disorders

There are several types of depressive disorders. The most common form is dysthymic disorder (dysthymia), a less severe but chronic form of depression that, by definition, lasts at least two years in adults and one year in children. Dysthymic disorders commonly appear for the first time in children, teens, and young adults. While they may not disable people as severely as other forms of depression, these disorders can ruin lives by robbing them of joy, energy, and productivity. An estimated 5.4 percent (10.9 million) of Americans suffer from dysthymia, and many also suffer from major depression during the course of their lives.

Major depression (also called unipolar major depression) is a more severe and disabling form; nearly 10 million Americans are affected every year. Major depression

TABLE 2.7

Common symptoms and triggers of depression

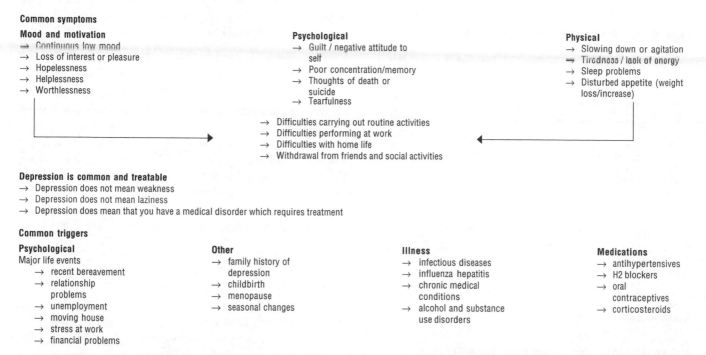

Common symptoms

Mood and motivation
→ Continuous low mood
→ Loss of interest or pleasure
→ Hopelessness
→ Helplessness
→ Worthlessness

Psychological
→ Guilt / negative attitude to self
→ Poor concentration/memory
→ Thoughts of death or suicide
→ Tearfulness

Physical
→ Slowing down or agitation
→ Tiredness / lack of energy
→ Sleep problems
→ Disturbed appetite (weight loss/increase)

→ Difficulties carrying out routine activities
→ Difficulties performing at work
→ Difficulties with home life
→ Withdrawal from friends and social activities

Depression is common and treatable
→ Depression does not mean weakness
→ Depression does not mean laziness
→ Depression does mean that you have a medical disorder which requires treatment

Common triggers

Psychological
Major life events
→ recent bereavement
→ relationship problems
→ unemployment
→ moving house
→ stress at work
→ financial problems

Other
→ family history of depression
→ childbirth
→ menopause
→ seasonal changes

Illness
→ infectious diseases
→ influenza hepatitis
→ chronic medical conditions
→ alcohol and substance use disorders

Medications
→ antihypertensives
→ H2 blockers
→ oral contraceptives
→ corticosteroids

SOURCE: T. B. Ustun, "Depression," in *Mental Disorders in Primary Care,* World Health Organization, Geneva, Switzerland, 1998. Reproduced with permission.

is second only to heart disease as a cause of disability when disability is measured in years of healthy life lost. (The measure is called DALY—disability adjusted life years.) Table 2.8 shows the causes of disease burden—disability from various diseases—measured in DALYs.

Major depression and bipolar disorder can strike at any age but usually begin during the second decade of life. Sufferers may lose the ability to work, eat, sleep, and enjoy the activities that once gave them pleasure. Bipolar disorder (also called manic depression) is characterized by wide mood swings from excessive elation and hyperactivity to the more common symptoms of depression. (See Table 2.5 for symptoms of manic depression.) About 10 percent of the population will experience at least one episode of major depression during the course their lifetime.

Causes of Depression

Combinations of genetic, psychological, and environmental factors are involved in the development of depressive disorders. Some types of depression run in families, and research studies of twins demonstrated that genetic factors determine susceptibility to depression. Major depression seems to recur in generation after generation of some families, but it also occurs in people with no family history of depression.

In July 2003 an international team of researchers led by scientists at the University of Wisconsin—Madison

proposed a genetic explanation of why some people escape emotional trauma relatively unscathed while others descend into deep depression. In "Behavioral Genetics: Getting the Short End of the Allele" (*Science,* vol. 301, July 2003), the researchers followed nearly 850 New Zealanders for five years during their early 20s, the age when depression frequently begins.

The researchers looked at the serotonin transporter 5-HTT gene, which helps regulate serotonin, a neurochemical messenger involved in mood, anxiety, and depression. A person can inherit long or short versions of this gene from their parents, yielding three possible combinations— two short, two long, or one short and one long.

They also considered the number of stressful life events the participants had experienced between ages 21 and 26 and whether they developed depression. The study defined depression as a period of at least two weeks in the past year in which the participant experienced an unremitting sadness, depressed mood, or loss of pleasure and interest in activities. The criteria for depression also required participants to report at least four of the following symptoms of depression—changes in weight or appetite, sleep, or activity level; decreased energy; feelings of worthlessness or guilt; difficulty thinking or concentrating; and persistent thoughts of death or suicide or suicide attempts.

Participants with two short versions of the gene were twice as likely to develop depression following stressful

TABLE 2.8

Disease burdens by leading source, selected illness categories, and mental illness in established market economies, 1990

The leading sources of disease burden (measured in DALYs*)

		Total (millions)	Percent of total
	All Causes	98.7	
1	Ischemic heart disease	8.9	9.0
2	**Unipolar major depression**	**6.7**	**6.8**
3	Cardiovascular disease	5.0	5.0
4	Alcohol use	4.7	4.7
5	Road traffic accidents	4.3	4.4
6	Lung & UR cancers	3.0	3.0
7	Dementia & degenerative CNS	2.9	2.9
8	Osteoarthritis	2.7	2.7
9	Diabetes	2.4	2.4
10	COPD	2.3	2.3

Disease burden by selected illness categories (measured in DALYs*)

	Percent of total
All cardiovascular conditions	18.6
All mental illness including suicide	**15.4**
All malignant disease (cancer)	15.0
All respiratory conditions	4.8
All alcohol use	4.7
All infectious and parasitic disease	2.8
All drug use	1.5

Mental illness as a source of disease burden (measured in DALYs*)

	Total (millions)	Percent of total
All Causes	98.7	6.8
Unipolar major depression	6.7	2.3
Schizophrenia	2.3	1.7
Bipolar disorder	1.7	1.5
Obsessive-compulsive disorder	1.5	1.5
Panic disorder	0.7	0.7
Post-traumatic stress disorder	0.3	0.3
Self-inflicted injuries (suicide)	2.2	2.2
All mental disorders	**15.3**	**15.4**

* DALYs measure lost years of healthy life regardless of whether the years were lost to premature death or disability.

SOURCE: "…the burden of psychiatric conditions has been underestimated," in *The Impact of Mental Illness on Society,* NIH Publication no. 01-4586, U.S. Department of Health and Human Services, National Institute of Mental Health, Bethesda, MD, 2001

leagues at Carnegie Mellon University wrote in "D2S2944 Identifies a Likely Susceptibility Locus for Recurrent, Early-Onset, Major Depression in Women" (*Molecular Psychiatry,* vol. 7, July 2002) that this genetic variation may explain why women are twice as likely as men to develop depression.

Zubenko asserted that "these findings confirm our earlier research suggesting the existence of susceptibility genes that have sex-limited effects on the vulnerability of women to developing severe depression." The study focused on CREB1, a gene that encodes a regulatory protein called CREB that influences the expression of large numbers of other genes with vital roles in the brain. More than 80 percent of women in the study with a specific variant of CREB1 developed depressive disorders. Interestingly, a second version of this gene appeared to have protective effects against depression.

Other studies of the brain support the premise that depression may have a biological and chemical basis. Figure 2.3 compares positron emission (PET) scans of the brain of a healthy person with the brain of a depressed person. Although there are clearly differences between the PET scans, it is not yet known if these differences cause the depression or result from it. Researchers speculate that the problem may be caused by the complex neurotransmission (chemical messaging) system of the brain and that persons suffering depression have either too much or too little of certain neurochemicals in the brain. Investigators believe that depressed patients with normal levels of neurotransmitters may suffer from an inability to regulate them. Most antidepressant drugs currently used to treat the disorder attempt to correct these chemical imbalances.

A person's psychological makeup is another factor in depressive disorders. People who are easily overwhelmed by stress or who suffer from low self-esteem or a pessimistic view of life, themselves, and the world tend to be prone to depression. Events outside the person's control can also trigger a depressive episode. A major change in the patterns of daily living, such as a serious loss, a chronic illness, a difficult relationship, or financial problems, can trigger the onset of depression. Table 2.7 lists some common life events, illnesses, and medications that may trigger depression.

ANXIETY DISORDERS

Everyone experiences some degree of anxiety almost every day. In today's world a certain amount of anxiety is unavoidable and in some cases may even be beneficial. For example, anxiety before an exam or a job interview can actually improve performance. Anxiety prior to a surgical operation, giving a speech, or driving in bad weather is normal.

Nevertheless, when anxiety becomes extreme or when an attack of anxiety strikes suddenly, without an apparent

events than the general population. In contrast, those with two long versions were half as likely to develop depression. About 17 percent of the population have the stress-sensitive version of the gene, and 32 percent carry the protective version. Among study participants, 43 percent of those with two short genes—the stress-sensitive version—developed depression after experiencing multiple stressful events. Just 17 percent of those with two long genes—the combination believed to protect against depression—became depressed.

One year before the University of Wisconsin—Madison investigators published their findings, University of Pittsburgh researchers reported the identification of variations of a single gene that, when inherited by women, may contribute to the development of depression. Men appear unaffected by this variation. George Zubenko and his col-

FIGURE 2.3

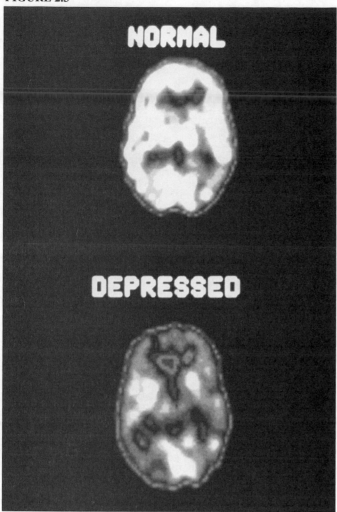

NORMAL

DEPRESSED

Two false-colored positron emission tomography (PET) scans of human brains. At the top is the brain of a healthy person, and below that is the brain of a depressed person. © NIH/Science Source, National Audubon Society Collection/ Photo Researchers, Inc. Reproduced with permission.

TABLE 2.9

Questionnaire for anxiety

During the *last month* have you had any of the following complaints most of the time? If yes, please check or mark the relevant box.

I. Have you been feeling tense or anxious? ☐
II. Have you been worrying a lot about things? ☐

If YES to any of the above, continue below

1. **Have you experienced in the last month:**
    → Fear of dying? ☐
    → Fear of losing control? ☐
    → Pounding heart? ☐
    → Sweating? ☐
    → Trembling or shaking? ☐
    → Chest pain / difficulty breathing? ☐
    → Nausea, feeling dizzy, lightheadedness or feeling faint? ☐
    → Numbness or tingling sensations? ☐
    → Feelings of unreality? ☐
    → Nausea? ☐

2. **Have you experienced these symptoms while:**
    → going to unfamiliar places ☐
    → travelling alone, e.g. train, car, plane ☐
    → crowds / confined places / public places ☐
    → taking lifts, elevators ☐

3. **Fear/anxiety in social situations?**
    → speaking in front of others ☐
    → social events ☐
    → eating in front of others ☐
    → worrying / tension / feelings of apprehension ☐

I. **During *the last month* have you been limited in one or more of the following areas most of the time:**
    • Self care: bathing, dressing, eating? ☐
    • Family relations: spouse, children, relatives? ☐
    • Going to work or school? ☐
    • Doing housework or household tasks? ☐
    • Social activities, seeing friends, hobbies? ☐
    • Remembering things? ☐

II. **Because of these problems during the *last month*:**
    How many days were you unable to fully carry out your usual daily activities? ___
    How many days did you spend in bed in order to rest? ___

SOURCE: T. B. Ustun, "ICD-10 PC: Questionnaire for Anxiety," in *Mental Disorders in Primary Care,* World Health Organization, Geneva, Switzerland, 1998. Reproduced with permission.

external cause, it can be both debilitating and destructive. Table 2.9 is a self-administered questionnaire to assist patients and practitioners to identify anxiety disorders and distinguish between generalized anxiety, panic disorders, and phobias. Anxiety's symptoms may include nervousness, fear, a knot in the stomach, sweating, or elevated blood pressure. If the anxiety is severe and long lasting, more serious problems may develop. People suffering from anxiety over an extended period may have headaches, ulcers, irritable bowel syndrome, insomnia, and depression. Because anxiety tends to create various other emotional and physical symptoms, a snowball effect can occur in which these problems produce even more anxiety. Table 2.10 depicts how common psychological and physical symptoms can disrupt the lives of sufferers and their families.

Chronic anxiety can interfere with an individual's ability to lead a normal life. Mental health professionals consider persons who suffer from prolonged anxiety as having anxiety disorders. The Surgeon General's report estimated that more than 16 percent of Americans suffered from anxiety disorders. See Table 2.2 for the estimated prevalence of anxiety disorders among persons 18–54 years old.

Unrelenting anxiety that appears unrelated to specific environments, events, or situations is called generalized anxiety disorder (GAD). Persons suffering from this disorder worry excessively about the events of daily life and the future. They are also more likely to experience physical symptoms such as shortness of breath, dizziness, rapid heart rate, nausea, stomach pains, and muscle tension than persons afflicted with other panic disorders, social phobias, or agoraphobia. See Table 2.10 for a complete list of physical symptoms linked to anxiety.

Causes and Triggers of Anxiety

Like most other physical and mental health problems, anxiety disorders probably occur in response to genetic susceptibility, the individual's innate capacity to cope

TABLE 2.10

Common symptoms and forms of anxiety

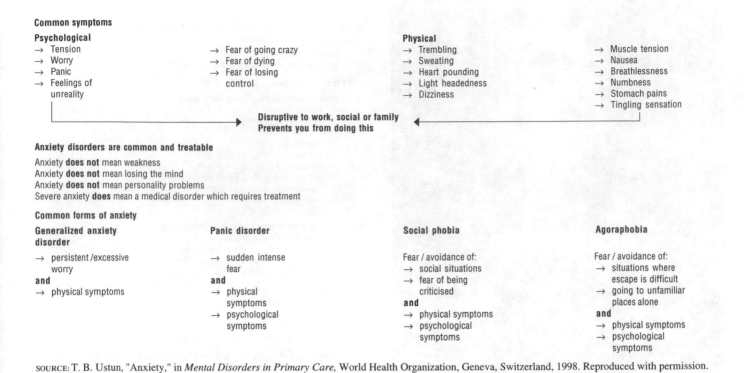

Common symptoms

Psychological
→ Tension
→ Worry
→ Panic
→ Feelings of unreality
→ Fear of going crazy
→ Fear of dying
→ Fear of losing control

Physical
→ Trembling
→ Sweating
→ Heart pounding
→ Light headedness
→ Dizziness
→ Muscle tension
→ Nausea
→ Breathlessness
→ Numbness
→ Stomach pains
→ Tingling sensation

Disruptive to work, social or family
Prevents you from doing this

Anxiety disorders are common and treatable

Anxiety **does not** mean weakness
Anxiety **does not** mean losing the mind
Anxiety **does not** mean personality problems
Severe anxiety **does** mean a medical disorder which requires treatment

Common forms of anxiety

Generalized anxiety disorder	Panic disorder	Social phobia	Agoraphobia
→ persistent /excessive worry	→ sudden intense fear	Fear / avoidance of:	Fear / avoidance of:
and	**and**	→ social situations	→ situations where escape is difficult
→ physical symptoms	→ physical symptoms	→ fear of being criticised	→ going to unfamiliar places alone
	→ psychological symptoms	**and**	**and**
		→ physical symptoms	→ physical symptoms
		→ psychological symptoms	→ psychological symptoms

SOURCE: T. B. Ustun, "Anxiety," in *Mental Disorders in Primary Care,* World Health Organization, Geneva, Switzerland, 1998. Reproduced with permission.

with stress, and the effectiveness of learned coping strategies in the presence of an external or environmental trigger. During 2002 a team of investigators from the NIMH identified variants of a gene called SLC6A4 they believe may be linked to increased susceptibility to anxiety. SLC6A4 has a central role in the transmission of the serotonin around the brain. Each parent passes either a short or a long version SLC6A4 to their offspring. The short version transports serotonin less efficiently, and people with one or two of these are more likely to experience abnormal levels of anxiety.

Additional support for biochemical causes of anxiety is the finding by British researchers that anxiety during pregnancy can double a mother's risk of having a child with emotional or behavioral problems. (Though the researchers found that 9 out of 10 children even of the most anxious mothers were entirely unaffected.) The researchers surveyed more than 7,000 women, focusing on those who were anxious during pregnancy but felt less anxious after delivery. By focusing on this subgroup, researchers were able to see the impact of anxiety during pregnancy on the baby's rather than their mother's mood during their first years of life. Anxious expectant mothers who had boys were twice as likely to have a child with problems with hyperactivity and inattention by the age of four. A link between anxiety and behavioral problems in girls was also established.

Among those susceptible to abnormal or excessive anxiety, and even among persons who are not prone to anxiety, certain biological and physiological actions may trigger or intensify symptoms of anxiety. For example, hyperventilation (rapid, deep breathing), which reduces the amount of carbon dioxide in the lungs, can precipitate anxiety. Similarly, excessive alcohol consumption and other drug abuse may, via biochemical pathways, generate symptoms of anxiety.

Examples of psychological stresses that may precipitate an anxiety disorder include:

• Death of a loved one
• Relationship problems, separations, divorce
• Work pressure, loss of a job, chronic unemployment
• Financial struggles
• Sleep deprivation
• Physical or sexual abuse

Interestingly, worry and negative thinking, considered common symptoms of anxiety, may also trigger it. It has been observed that persons who engage in certain kinds of thinking—unrealistic and overly pessimistic—are at greater risk for anxiety disorders.

Panic Disorder

Extremely high levels of anxiety may produce panic attacks that are both unpredicted and seemingly without cause. In one type of panic attack, termed "unexpected," the sufferer is unable to anticipate when an attack will occur. Other types of panic attacks are linked to a particular location, circumstance, or event and are called "situationally bound" or "situationally predisposed" panic attacks. These panic episodes can last as long as 30 minutes and are marked by an overwhelming sense of impending doom while the person's heart races and breathing quickens to the point of gasping for air. Sweating, nausea, weakness, dizziness, terror, and feelings of unreality are also typical. Individuals undergoing a panic attack fear they are going to die, go crazy, or, at the very least, lose control.

Repeated panic attacks may be termed a panic disorder. However, panic attacks do not necessarily indicate a mental disorder—up to 10 percent of people with no other problems experience a single panic attack each year. According to the American Psychiatric Association, panic disorder occurs twice as often among women than men, it can run in families, and most sufferers begin to experience attacks between the ages of 15 and 19. Research has revealed that persons who experience panic attacks tend to suppress their emotions. Investigators hypothesize that this tendency leads to an emotional buildup for which a panic attack is a form of release. Interestingly, most persons who suffer from panic attacks do not experience anxiety between attacks.

Researchers believe that panic attacks, like other mental disorders, may occur more frequently among persons with a specific genetic mutation. Studies of families in which multiple members suffer from panic attacks and phobias have found that 90 percent of the affected family members carried a genetic abnormality called DUP25. These studies observed that this abnormality was very rarely found in persons with no anxiety disorders. Nonetheless, environmental triggers are almost certainly involved as well, since research has revealed that in affected families 20 percent of persons with DUP25 had not experienced anxiety or panic attacks.

Many panic attack sufferers are convinced they are having heart attacks and end up in hospital emergency rooms. When they are found to be free of heart disease, they may turn to neurologists and other specialists to seek answers to their problems. Research has found that of all patients who make the most visits to doctors, spend the most time in the hospital, and use the most prescription medications, approximately 12 percent suffer from undiagnosed panic disorders.

Phobias

Phobias are defined as unreasonable fears associated with particular situations or objects. The most common of the many varieties of phobias center on things like bees, snakes, rodents, heights, odors, blood, injections, and thunderstorms. Selected phobias, especially animal phobias, are common in children, but they can occur at any age. About 8 percent of American adults suffer from simple phobias and an additional 7 percent suffer from specific phobias such as social phobia and agoraphobia (the fear of crowds and open spaces). (See Table 2.2.) Most phobics understand that their fears are unreasonable, but that awareness does not make them feel any less anxious.

Some phobias, such as a fear of heights, usually do not interfere with daily life or cause as much distress as other forms, such as agoraphobia. Persons suffering from severe specific phobias may rearrange their lives drastically to avoid the situations they fear will trigger panic attacks.

Since panic attacks and phobias are related disorders, investigators think that the genetic abnormality DUP25 also may be implicated in increasing susceptibility to phobias. The genetic variant GRP, identified in mice, may also play a role. GRP appears to inhibit the brain's capacity to learn fear—the process during which animals learn about specific fears and dangers, as opposed to innate, instinctive fear. Researchers have found that mice without the GRP gene had intensified and longer fear responses than those with GRP. This finding lends additional credence to the premise that chronic anxiety, or instinctive fear, has a different biological basis than learned, or acquired fear.

SOCIAL PHOBIAS. Social phobias (also called social anxiety disorders) can be more serious than other phobias. The person with a social phobia is intensely afraid of being judged by others. At social gatherings, the social phobic expects to be singled out, scrutinized, judged, and found lacking. People with social phobias are usually very anxious about feeling humiliated or embarrassed. They are often so crippled by their own fears that they may have a hard time thinking clearly, remembering facts, or carrying on normal conversations. The individual with social phobia may tremble, sweat, or blush, and often fears fainting or losing bladder or bowel control in social settings. In response to these overwhelming fears, the social phobic tries to avoid public situations and gatherings of people. Social phobias tend to start between the ages of 15 and 20 and if untreated can continue throughout life.

Since social phobics fear being the center of attention or subject of criticism, public speaking, asking questions, eating in front of others, or even attending social events create anxiety. Social phobias should not be confused with shyness, which is considered a normal variation in personality. Social phobias can be disabling, preventing sufferers from attending school, working, and having friends.

AGORAPHOBIA. Many people who experience panic attacks go on to develop agoraphobia. The term comes from the Greek word *agora,* which means marketplace. This type of phobia is a severely disabling disorder that often traps its victims, rendering them virtual prisoners in their own homes, unable to work, shop, or attend social activities.

Agoraphobia normally develops slowly, following an initial unexpected panic attack. For example, on an ordinary day, while shopping, driving to work, or doing errands, the individual is suddenly struck by a wave of terror characterized by symptoms such as trembling, a pounding heart, profuse sweating, and difficulty breathing normally. The person desperately seeks safety, reassurance from friends and family, or a physician. The panic subsides and all is well—until another panic attack occurs.

Subsequent attacks may occur when the individual is in an unfamiliar and potentially threatening environment, feels trapped or unable to leave or escape from a situation, or fears that it would be impossible to obtain help in an emergency. Examples of commonly feared circumstances are traveling alone, crowds and public places, and leaving home.

The agoraphobic begins to avoid all places and situations where an attack has occurred and then begins to avoid places where an attack could possibly occur. Gradually, the agoraphobic becomes more and more limited in the choice of places that are deemed safe. Eventually, the agoraphobic cannot venture outside the immediate neighborhood or leave the house. The fear ultimately expands to touch every aspect of life.

Agoraphobia usually begins during the late teens or 20s, and about 5 percent of the adult population suffers from agoraphobia. (See Table 2.2.) Women tend to be affected twice as often as men.

Obsessive-Compulsive Disorder

People with obsessive-compulsive disorder (OCD) cannot control their thoughts or behaviors. OCD is an anxiety disorder marked by unwanted, often unpleasant recurring thoughts (obsessions) and repetitive, often mechanical behaviors (compulsions). The repetitive behaviors such as continually checking to be certain windows and doors are locked or repeated handwashing, are intended to dispel the obsessive thoughts that trigger them—that an intruder will enter the house through an unlocked door or window, or that disease will be prevented by handwashing. Persons suffering from OCD may fear causing harm to others, making mistakes, or behaving in a socially unacceptable manner. Many also feel a compelling need for symmetry and precision, creating exacting systems to organize their possessions and experiencing severe distress when these systems are disturbed or disrupted. The vicious cycle of obsessions and compulsions only serves to heighten anxiety, and OCD can debilitate sufferers.

The NIMH estimates that between 2 and 3 percent of adults between the ages of 18 and 54 suffer from OCD annually. OCD strikes men and women equally, sometimes coexists with other disorders such as substance abuse, eating disorders, or depression, and symptoms generally appear during childhood or adolescence. Imaging studies using PET (positron emission tomography) reveal that people with OCD have different patterns of brain activity than those without the disorder. Further, the PET scans show that the part of the brain most affected by OCD (the striatum) changes and responds to both medication and behavioral therapy.

Investigators theorize that a genetic defect leads to a disruption of levels of serotonin by altering the functioning of receptors in the brain that govern the release of serotonin. Researchers at the University of Toronto published "5HT1DBETA Receptor Gene Implicated in the Pathogenesis of Obsessive-Compulsive Disorder: Further Evidence from a Family-Based Association Study" (E. Mundo, et al., *Molecular Psychiatry,* vol. 7, no. 7, 2002) in which they reported research supporting the role of the 5HT1DBETA receptor gene in the origin and expression of OCD.

Many of the medications used to treat other anxiety disorders appear effective for OCD patients. Also effective is a behavioral type of therapy called exposure and response prevention, during which OCD patients learn new ways to manage their obsessive thoughts without resorting to compulsive behaviors.

EATING DISORDERS

Society today is preoccupied with body image. Americans are constantly bombarded with images of very thin, beautiful young women and lean, muscular men in magazines, on television, on billboards, and in the movies. The advertisers of many products suggest that to be thin and beautiful is to be happy. Many prominent weight-loss programs reinforce this suggestion. A well-balanced, low-fat food plan, combined with exercise, can help most overweight people achieve a healthier weight and lifestyle. Dieting to achieve a healthy weight is quite different from dieting obsessively to become model-thin, which can have consequences ranging from mildly harmful to life-threatening.

According to NIMH, dieting plays a role in the onset of two serious eating disorders—anorexia nervosa and bulimia. Preteens, teens, and college-age women are at special risk. In fact, it is estimated by some that more than 90 percent of those who develop an eating disorder are young women, although researchers are beginning to report rising rates of anorexia and bulimia among men. No one knows exactly how many men and teenage boys are afflicted. Until recently, there has been a lack of awareness that eating disorders can be a problem for males, perhaps because men are more likely to mask the symptoms of eating disorders with excuses and rationales such as preventing heart disease or diabetes or trying to build a more muscular physique. Some studies suggest that for every 10 women with an eating disorder, 1 male is afflicted. Others estimate the numbers may be higher, with males comprising about 5–15 percent of those with anorexia or bulimia and 35 percent of those with binge-eating disorders.

Anorexia Nervosa

Anorexia nervosa involves severe weight loss—a minimum of 15 percent below normal body weight. Anorexic people literally starve themselves, even though they may be very hungry. For reasons that researchers do not yet fully understand, anorexics become terrified of gaining weight. Both food and weight become obsessions. They often develop strange eating habits, refuse to eat with other people, and exercise strenuously to burn calories and prevent weight gain. Anorexic individuals continue to believe they are overweight even when they are dangerously thin.

The medical complications of anorexia are similar to starvation. When the body attempts to protect its most vital organs, the heart and the brain, it goes into slow gear. Monthly menstrual periods stop, and breathing, pulse, blood pressure, and thyroid function slow down. The nails and hair become brittle, and the skin dries. Water imbalance causes constipation, and the lack of body fat produces an inability to withstand cold temperatures. Depression, weakness, and a constant obsession with food are also symptoms of the disease. In addition, personality changes may occur. The person suffering from anorexia may have outbursts of anger and hostility or may withdraw socially. In the most serious cases, death can result.

Bulimia

The person who has bulimia eats compulsively and then purges (gets rid of the food) through self-induced vomiting, use of laxatives, diuretics, strict diets, fasts, exercise, or a combination of several of these compensatory behaviors. In 2001 the NIMH reported that based on community surveys, between 2 percent and 5 percent of Americans engage in binge eating and about half of those with anorexia will turn to bulimia. Bulimia often begins when a young person is disgusted with the excessive amount of "bad" food consumed and vomits to rid the body of the calories.

Many bulimics are at a normal body weight or above because of their frequent binge-purge behavior, which can occur from once or twice a week to several times a day. Those bulimics who maintain normal weights may manage to keep their eating disorders secret for years. As with anorexia, binge-eating disorder usually begins during adolescence, but many bulimics do not seek help until they are in their 30s or 40s.

Binge eating and purging is dangerous. In rare cases, binge eating can cause esophageal ruptures, and purging

FIGURE 2.4

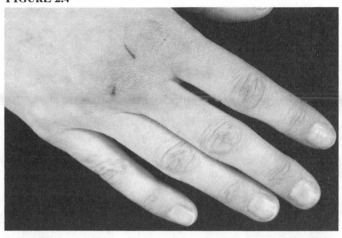

The cuts on the knuckles shown in this photograph are due to the teeth breaking the skin during self-induced vomiting. *B. Bodine/Custom Medical Stock Photo. Reproduced by permission.*

can result in life-threatening cardiac (heart) conditions because the body loses vital minerals. The acid in vomit wears down tooth enamel and the stomach lining, and teeth can cause scarring on the hands when fingers are pushed down the throat to induce vomiting. (See Figure 2.4.) The esophagus may become inflamed, and glands in the neck may become swollen.

Bulimics often talk of being hooked on certain foods and needing to feed their habits. This addictive behavior carries over into other areas of their lives, including substance (alcohol and drug) abuse. Many bulimic people suffer from comorbidities such as severe depression, which increases their risk for suicide.

Causes of Eating Disorders

There is evidence to suggest a genetic component to susceptibility to eating disorders. For example, in the general population the chance of developing anorexia is about one in 200, but when a family member has the disorder, the risk increases to one in 30. Twin studies demonstrate that when one twin is affected, there is a 50 percent chance the other will develop anorexia. In 2001 Dutch researchers examined the DNA (deoxyribonucleic acid, the material of heredity) of 145 anorexia patients and found that 11 percent carried the same genetic mutation. The mutation was of a gene that manufactures AgRP (Agouti Related Protein), which stimulates the desire to eat. The researchers hypothesized that a deficiency of AgRP may be involved in anorexia.

Bulimics and anorexics seem to have different personalities. Bulimics are likely to be impulsive (acting without thought of the consequences) and are more likely to abuse alcohol and drugs. Anorexics tend to be perfectionists, good students, and competitive athletes. They usually keep their feelings to themselves and rarely disobey their parents. Bulimics and anorexics share certain traits: they lack self-esteem, have feelings of helplessness, and fear gaining weight. In both disorders, the eating problems appear to develop as a way of handling stress and anxiety.

The bulimic consumes huge amounts of food (often junk food) in a search for comfort and stress relief. The bingeing, however, brings only guilt and depression. On the other hand, the anorexic restricts food to gain a sense of control and mastery over some aspect of her life. Controlling her weight seems to offer two advantages—she can take control of her body, and she can gain approval from others.

Demographics of Eating Disorders

Individuals with eating disorders usually come from white middle- or upper-class families. The NIMH noted that while eating disorders have increased substantially in industrialized countries during the past 20 years, they are almost unheard of in developing countries. Thinness is not necessarily admired among all people throughout the world, especially in countries where hunger is not a matter of choice.

SCHIZOPHRENIA

A person who hears voices, becomes violent, and sometimes ends up as a homeless person, muttering and shouting incomprehensibly, frequently suffers from schizophrenia. This disease generally presents in adolescence, causing hallucinations, paranoia, delusions, and social isolation. The effects begin slowly and, initially, are often considered the normal behavioral changes of adolescence. Gradually, voices take over in the schizophrenic's mind, obliterating reality and directing the person to all kinds of erratic behaviors. Suicide attempts and violent attacks are common in the lives of schizophrenics. Many schizophrenics turn to drugs in an attempt to escape the torment inflicted by their brains. NIMH estimated that as many as half of all schizophrenics are also drug abusers.

In 2001 the NIMH reported that 2.2 million Americans (about 1 percent of all persons over age 18) suffered from schizophrenia and similar disorders. Table 2.2 shows the estimated prevalence of schizophrenia among Americans aged 18–54. Although the precise causes of schizophrenia are unknown, for years researchers have hypothesized that genetic susceptibility is a risk factor for schizophrenia and bipolar disorder. The disease affects an estimated 2 percent of persons worldwide, but an individual with a parent or sibling who has schizophrenia has a 10 percent chance of developing the disease compared to the 1 percent chance of an individual with no family history. A prenatal developmental problem, or a combination of genetic, developmental, and environmental factors, may also be causative factors. Although physical and emotional stress can aggravate symptoms of schizophrenia, they do not cause the disease.

In the fall of 2003, Sabine Bahn and her colleagues at the Babraham Institute in Cambridge, England, found that sufferers of schizophrenia and bipolar disorder have abnormalities in genes responsible for proteins in the central nervous system related to myelin, a compound that insulates brain cells and peripheral nerves ("Oligodendrocyte Dysfunction in Schizophrenia and Bipolar Disorder," *The Lancet,* vol. 362, no. 9386, September 2003). This finding confirms earlier research that revealed that patients with both disorders have fewer oligodendrocytes—brain cells that make myelin. The investigators concluded that their results provide strong evidence for oligodendrocyte and myelin dysfunction in schizophrenia and bipolar disorder.

Other researchers, performing imaging studies of the brain, have revealed abnormal brain development in children who have schizophrenia, and imaging studies of adults with the disease have found enlargement of the brain's ventricles (the fluid-filled spaces in the center of the brain). Figure 2.5 compares PET scans of a normal brain and the brain of a person suffering from schizophrenia. Some research suggests that the brain of a schizophrenic manufactures too much dopamine, a chemical vital to normal nerve activity.

SUICIDE

Suicide may be the ultimate expression or consequence of depression or other serious mental disorders. Not all people who suffer from depression contemplate suicide, nor do all those who attempt suicide suffer from depressive or other mental illnesses. However, with the exception of certain desperate medical situations, suicide in the United States is generally considered an unacceptable act, the product of irrationality. Often referred to as a "permanent solution to a short-term problem," it is the leading cause of violent deaths throughout the world. (See Figure 2.6.)

In spite of this generally held philosophy, suicide was the 11th leading cause of death in the United States in 2001. Slightly more than 1 percent of all deaths were attributable to suicide—a total of 29,350 lives were lost. It was the third leading cause of death among young people ages 15–24; the fourth leading cause among persons 25–44; the fifth leading cause of death of American children ages 5–14; and the eighth leading cause among Americans ages 45–64. (See Table 2.11.)

Who Commits Suicide?

Suicide occurs among all age, sex, racial, occupational, religious, and social groups. While the overall rate of suicide has remained fairly stable, the rate nearly tripled from 1950 to 1999 among adolescents and young adults.

According to the American Association of Suicidology, the rate of suicide among young people increased 200 percent between the 1950s and 1990s and more teens and

FIGURE 2.5

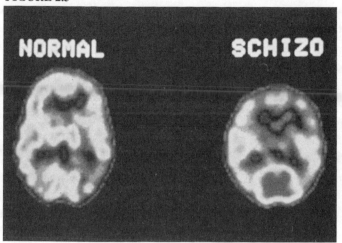

Colored positron emission tomography (PET) scans of human brains comparing normal brain (left) with the brain of a person with schizophrenia (right). © *Photo Researchers. Reproduced by permission.*

FIGURE 2.6

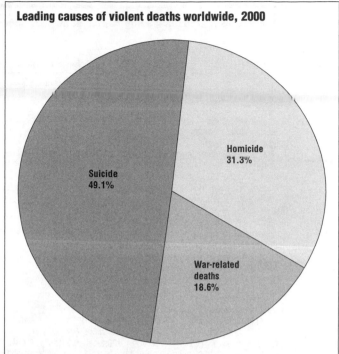

Leading causes of violent deaths worldwide, 2000

SOURCE: "Figure 1.2. Suicide Is the Leading Cause of Violent Deaths Worldwide," in *Achieving the Promise: Transforming Mental Health Care in America,* President's New Freedom Commission On Mental Health, Rockville, MD, 2001

FIGURE 2.7

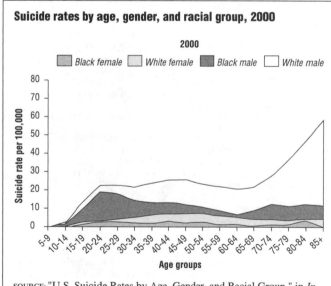

Suicide rates by age, gender, and racial group, 2000

SOURCE: "U.S. Suicide Rates by Age, Gender, and Racial Group," in *In Harm's Way: Suicide in America,* U.S. Department of Health and Human Services, National Institute of Mental Health, Bethesda, MD, May 2003

young adults died from suicide than from HIV/AIDS, birth defects, cancer, chronic lung disease, heart disease, pneumonia and influenza, and stroke combined.

Usually suicide attempts outnumber completed suicides by about eight to one. Among teens, however, the ratio is 25 to 30 attempts for every successful suicide. According to NIMH, approximately 1 million teens go through suicide crises each year. Depression, substance abuse, and physical and sexual abuse are risk factors for attempted suicide by adolescents.

While more than four times as many men die by suicide, women attempt suicide two to three times as often as men. Men make up about three-fourths of total suicides, and white males account for about 70 percent of that number. (See Figure 2.7.) In 2000 suicide was the 8th leading cause of death for males and the 19th leading cause of death for females.

Why Do People Commit Suicide?

There are many reasons for committing suicide. Notes left by people who have killed themselves usually tell of unbearable life crises. Many describe enduring chronic pain, losing loved ones, inability to pay bills, or finding themselves incapable of living independently. Other commonly cited reasons are:

- To punish loved ones
- To gain attention
- To join a deceased loved one
- To avoid punishment
- To express love

Some suicides are committed on an irrational, impulsive whim. Researchers observe that even among those most determined to commit suicide, the desire is not as much to die as it is to escape the lives they are leading and

the pain they are suffering. Whatever the cause of their despair, they are desperately crying for help.

Follow-up studies of suicide survivors reveal their intense ambivalence about actually dying. Not all survivors are glad to be alive, but for most, the attempted

TABLE 2.11

Deaths and death rates for the ten leading causes of death in specified age groups, preliminary 2000

Rank [1]	Cause of death and age (Based on the Tenth Revision, International Classification of Diseases, 1992)	Number	Rate
	All ages [2]		
...	All causes	2,404,624	873.6
1	Diseases of heart (I00-I09,I11,I13,I20-I51)	709,894	257.9
2	Malignant neoplasms (C00-C97)	551,833	200.5
3	Cerebrovascular diseases (I60-I69)	166,028	60.3
4	Chronic lower respiratory diseases (J40-J47)	123,550	44.9
5	Accidents (unintentional injuries) (V01-X59,Y85-Y86)	93,592	34.0
...	Motor vehicle accidents (V02-V04,V09.0,V09.2,V12-V14,V19.0-V19.2,V19.4-V19.6,V20-V79,V80.3-V80.5, V81.0-V81.1, V82.0-V82.1,V83-V86,V87.0-V87.8,V88.0-V88.8,V89.0,V89.2)	41,804	15.2
...	All other accidents (V01,V05-V06,V09.1,V09.3-V09.9,V10-V11,V15-V18,V19.3,V19.8-V19.9,V80.0-V80.2, V80.6-V80.9, V81.2-V81.9,V82.2-V82.9,V87.9,V88.9,V89.1,V89.3,V89.9,V90-V99,W00-X59,Y85,Y86)	51,788	18.8
6	Diabetes mellitus (E10-E14)	68,662	24.9
7	Influenza and pneumonia (J10-J18)	67,024	24.3
8	Alzheimer's disease (G30)	49,044	17.8
9	Nephritis, nephrotic syndrome and nephrosis (N00-N07,N17-N19,N25-N27)	37,672	13.7
10	Septicemia (A40-A41)	31,613	11.5
...	All other causes (Residual)	505,712	183.7
	1-4 years		
...	All causes	4,942	32.6
1	Accidents (unintentional injuries) (V01-X59,Y85-Y86)	1,780	11.7
...	Motor vehicle accidents (V02-V04,V09.0,V09.2,V12-V14,V19.0-V19.2,V19.4-V19.6,V20-V79,V80.3-V80.5,V81.0-V81.1, V82.0-V82.1,V83-V86,V87.0-V87.8,V88.0-V88.8,V89.0,V89.2)	630	4.2
...	All other accidents (V01,V05-V06,V09.1,V09.3-V09.9,V10-V11,V15-V18,V19.3,V19.8-V19.9,V80.0-V80.2, V80.6-V80.9, V81.2-V81.9,V82.2-V82.9,V87.9,V88.9,V89.1,V89.3,V89.9,V90-V99,W00-X59,Y85,Y86)	1,150	7.6
2	Congenital malformations, deformations and chromosomal abnormalities (Q00-Q99)	471	3.1
3	Malignant neoplasms (C00-C97)	393	2.6
4	Assault (homicide) (X85-Y09,Y87.1)	318	2.1
5	Diseases of heart (I00-I09,I11,I13,I20-I51)	169	1.1
6	Influenza and pneumonia (J10-J18)	96	0.6
7	Septicemia (A40-A41)	91	0.6
8	Certain conditions originating in the perinatal period (P00-P96)	84	0.6
9	In situ neoplasms, benign neoplasms and neoplasms of uncertain or unknown behavior (D00-D48)	56	0.4
10	Cerebrovascular diseases (I60-I69)	45	0.3
...	All other causes (Residual)	1,439	9.5
	5-14 years		
...	All causes	7,340	18.5
1	Accidents (unintentional injuries) (V01-X59,Y85-Y86)	2,878	7.3
...	Motor vehicle accidents (V02-V04,V09.0,V09.2,V12-V14,V19.0-V19.2,V19.4-V19.6,V20-V79,V80.3-V80.5, V81.0-V81.1, V82.0-V82.1,V83-V86,V87.0-V87.8,V88.0-V88.8,V89.0,V89.2)	1,716	4.3
...	All other accidents (V01,V05-V06,V09.1,V09.3-V09.9,V10-V11,V15-V18,V19.3,V19.8-V19.9,V80.0-V80.2, V80.6-V80.9, V81.2-V81.9,V82.2-V82.9,V87.9,V88.9,V89.1,V89.3,V89.9,V90-V99,W00-X59,Y85,Y86)	1,163	2.9
2	Malignant neoplasms (C00-C97)	1,017	2.6
3	Congenital malformations, deformations and chromosomal abnormalities (Q00-Q99)	387	1.0
4	Assault (homicide) (X85-Y09,Y87.1)	364	0.9
5	Intentional self-harm (suicide) (X60-X84,Y87.0)	297	0.7
6	Diseases of heart (I00-I09,I11,I13,I20-I51)	236	0.6
7	Chronic lower respiratory diseases (J40-J47)	130	0.3
8	In situ neoplasms, benign neoplasms and neoplasms of uncertain or unknown behavior (D00-D48)	106	0.3
9	Influenza and pneumonia (J10-J18)	83	0.2
10	Cerebrovascular diseases (I60-I69)	78	0.2
...	All other causes (Residual)	1,764	4.4
	15-24 years		
...	All causes	30,959	80.7
1	Accidents (unintentional injuries) (V01-X59,Y85-Y86)	13,616	35.5
...	Motor vehicle accidents (V02-V04,V09.0,V09.2,V12-V14,V19.0-V19.2,V19.4-V19.6,V20-V79,V80.3-V80.5, V81.0-V81.1, V82.0-V82.1,V83-V86,V87.0-V87.8,V88.0-V88.8,V89.0,V89.2)	10,357	27.0
...	All other accidents (V01,V05-V06,V09.1,V09.3-V09.9,V10-V11,V15-V18,V19.3,V19.8-V19.9,V80.0-V80.2, V80.6-V80.9, V81.2-V81.9,V82.2-V82.9,V87.9,V88.9,V89.1,V89.3,V89.9,V90-V99,W00-X59,Y85,Y86)	3,259	8.5
2	Assault (homicide) (X85-Y09,Y87.1)	4,796	12.5
3	Intentional self-harm (suicide) (X60-X84,Y87.0)	3,877	10.1
4	Malignant neoplasms (C00-C97)	1,668	4.3
5	Diseases of heart (I00-I09,I11,I13,I20-I51)	931	2.4
6	Congenital malformations, deformations and chromosomal abnormalities (Q00-Q99)	425	1.1
7	Cerebrovascular diseases (I60-I69)	193	0.5
8	Influenza and pneumonia (J10-J18)	188	0.5
9	Chronic lower respiratory diseases (J40-J47)	180	0.5
10	Human immunodeficiency virus (HIV) disease (B20-B24)	178	0.5
...	All other causes (Residual)	4,907	12.8

TABLE 2.11

Deaths and death rates for the ten leading causes of death in specified age groups, preliminary 2000 [CONTINUED]

Rank [1]	Cause of death and age (Based on the Tenth Revision, International Classification of Diseases, 1992)	Number	Rate
	25-44 years		
...	All causes	128,779	156.4
1	Accidents (unintentional injuries) (V01-X59,Y85-Y86)	24,017	30.1
...	Motor vehicle accidents (V02-V04,V09.0,V09.2,V12-V14,V19.0-V19.2,V19.4-V19.6,V20-V79,V80.3-V80.5, V81.0-V81.1, V82.0-V82.1,V83-V86,V87.0-V87.8,V88.0-V88.8,V89.0,V89.2)	13,261	16.1
...	All other accidents (V01,V05-V06,V09.1,V09.3-V09.9,V10-V11,V15-V18,V19.3,V19.8-V19.9,V80.0-V80.2, V80.6-V80.9, V81.2-V81.9,V82.2-V82.9,V87.9,V88.9,V89.1,V89.3,V89.9,V90-V99,W00-X59,Y85,Y86)	11,556	14.0
2	Malignant neoplasms (C00-C97)	20,200	24.5
3	Diseases of heart (I00-I09,I11,I13,I20-I51)	15,267	18.5
4	Intentional self-harm (suicide) (X60-X84,Y87.0)	10,884	13.2
5	Human immunodeficiency virus (HIV) disease (B20-B24)	8,302	10.1
6	Assault (homicide) (X85-Y09,Y87.1)	7,156	8.7
7	Chronic liver disease and cirrhosis (K70,K73-K74)	3,644	4.4
8	Cerebrovascular diseases (I60-I69)	3,122	3.8
9	Diabetes mellitus (E10-E14)	2,416	2.9
10	Influenza and pneumonia (J10-J18)	1,437	1.7
...	All other causes (Residual)	31,534	38.3
	45-64 years		
...	All causes	399,008	652.8
1	Malignant neoplasms (C00-C97)	136,363	223.1
2	Diseases of heart (I00-I09,I11,I13,I20-I51)	97,334	159.2
3	Accidents (unintentional injuries) (V01-X59,Y85-Y86)	18,252	29.9
...	Motor vehicle accidents (V02-V04,V09.0,V09.2,V12-V14,V19.0-V19.2,V19.4-V19.6,V20-V79,V80.3-V80.5, V81.0-V81.1, V82.0-V82.1,V83-V86,V87.0-V87.8,V88.0-V88.8,V89.0,V89.2)	8,483	13.9
...	All other accidents (V01,V05-V06,V09.1,V09.3-V09.9,V10-V11,V15-V18,V19.3,V19.8-V19.9,V80.0-V80.2, V80.6-V80.9, V81.2-V81.9,V82.2-V82.9,V87.9,V88.9,V89.1,V89.3,V89.9,V90-V99,W00-X59,Y85,Y86)	9,769	16.0
4	Cerebrovascular diseases (I60-I69)	15,735	25.7
5	Chronic lower respiratory diseases (J40-J47)	14,086	23.0
6	Diabetes mellitus (E10-E14)	13,958	22.8
7	Chronic liver disease and cirrhosis (K70,K73-K74)	12,206	20.0
8	Intentional self-harm (suicide) (X60-X84,Y87.0)	8,052	13.2
9	Human immunodeficiency virus (HIV) disease (B20-B24)	5,336	8.7
10	Nephritis, nephrotic syndrome and nephrosis (N00-N07,N17-N19,N25-N27)	4,821	7.9
...	All other causes (Residual)	72,865	119.2
	65 years and over		
...	All causes	1,805,187	5,190.8
1	Diseases of heart (I00-I09,I11,I13,I20-I51)	595,440	1,712.2
2	Malignant neoplasms (C00-C97)	392,082	1,127.4
3	Cerebrovascular diseases (I60-I69)	146,725	421.9
4	Chronic lower respiratory diseases (J40-J47)	107,888	310.2
5	Influenza and pneumonia (J10-J18)	60,261	173.3
6	Diabetes mellitus (E10-E14)	52,102	149.8
7	Alzheimer's disease (G30)	48,492	139.4
8	Nephritis, nephrotic syndrome and nephrosis (N00-N07,N17-N19,N25-N27)	31,588	90.8
9	Accidents (unintentional injuries) (V01-X59,Y85-Y86)	31,332	90.1
...	Motor vehicle accidents (V02-V04,V09.0,V09.2,V12-V14,V19.0-V19.2,V19.4-V19.6,V20-V79,V80.3-V80.5, V81.0-V81.1, V82.0-V82.1,V83-V86,V87.0-V87.8,V88.0-V88.8,V89.0,V89.2)	7,165	20.6
...	All other accidents (V01,V05-V06,V09.1,V09.3-V09.9,V10-V11,V15-V18,V19.3,V19.8-V19.9,V80.0-V80.2, V80.6-V80.9, V81.2-V81.9,V82.2-V82.9,V87.9,V88.9,V89.1,V89.3,V89.9,V90-V99,W00-X59,Y85,Y86)	24,167	69.5
10	Septicemia (A40-A41)	25,143	72.3
...	All other causes (Residual)	314,134	903.3

Note: . . .Category not applicable.
[1]Rank based on number of deaths.
[2]Includes deaths under 1 year of age.

SOURCE: Arialdi M. Minino and Betty L. Smith, "Table. 7. Deaths and death rates for the 10 leading causes of death in specified age groups: United States, preliminary 2000," in "Deaths: Preliminary Data for 2000," *National Vital Statistics Reports,* vol. 49, no. 12, October 9, 2001

---

suicide marked a definite turning point. It was an urgent and dramatic signal that their problems demanded serious and immediate attention. Most of the survivors said that what they really wanted was to change their lives.

The Biology of Suicide

According to the NIMH, depression and suicide both involve altered function of the neurotransmitter serotonin, a diminished number of serotonin transporter sites (tiny nerve cell components that assist in regulating the amount of serotonin in the synapse), and changes in both cerebrospinal fluid, the fluid that surrounds the brain and spinal cord, and platelets (a blood component involved in coagulation). Investigators hypothesize that the inclination toward impulsive aggression and suicide is related to brain dysfunction in a specific area of the prefrontal cortex. In contrast, depression is not localized to one region of the brain; it involves more widely dispersed brain circuitry. These findings suggest that suicide and major depression may be separate brain disorders, each with a distinct mechanism, although there is probably some overlap between the disorders because major depression is a significant risk factor for suicide.

In 2001 two separate studies of patients in psychiatric hospitals found that patients with alterations in one of two genes were more likely to attempt suicide. The altered genes disrupted the brain's natural mechanism for producing the chemical serotonin, which is known to regulate mood and anxiety levels. Other researchers speculate that genes that govern impulse control are involved in determining whether an individual is likely to attempt suicide.

Suicide Among the Terminally Ill

Not all suicides are categorized as the acts of mentally ill persons. Some people consider suicides committed by terminally ill people as rational choices. Many people believe that a terminally ill person has a right to choose his or her own death. Until a few years ago, persons with cancer and AIDS were, of the terminally ill, the most likely to commit suicide. Patients with terminal diseases often worry that they will suffer long and painful deaths, and that they stand a good chance of losing everything—health, independence, jobs, insurance, homes, and contact with loved ones and friends.

Researchers have found that factors with significant impact on the quality of life include security, family, love, pleasurable activity, and freedom from pain and suffering. Sufferers of debilitating disease may lose all of these. For some, suicide is an apparently attractive alternative that relieves pain and suffering, insecurity, self-pity, dependence, and hopelessness.

Suicide's Warning Signs

Researchers believe that most suicidal people convey their intentions to someone among their friends and family—either openly or indirectly prior to attempting suicide. The people they signal are those who know them well and are in the best position to recognize the signs and give help. Comments such as "You'd be better off without me," "No one will have to worry about me much longer," or even a casual "I've had it" may be signals of upcoming attempts. Some suicidal persons put their affairs in order. They draw up wills, give away prized possessions, or act as if they are preparing for a long trip. They may even talk about going away.

Often the indicator is a distinct change in personality or behavior. A normally happy person may become increasingly depressed. A regular churchgoer may stop attending services, or an avid runner may quit exercising. These types of changes, if added to expressions of worthlessness or hopelessness, can indicate not only that the person is seriously depressed but also that he or she may have decided on a suicide attempt. While the vast majority of depressed people are not suicidal, most of the suicide-prone are depressed. Researchers and health care practitioners caution that suicide threats and attempts should not be discounted as harmless bids for attention. Anyone thinking, talking about, or planning suicide should receive immediate professional evaluation and treatment.

People who have a record of previous suicide attempts are at the highest risk of actually killing themselves—over 600 times higher than the rate for the general population. Between 20 to 50 percent of those who complete suicide have tried it before. The prevalence rates of both suicide and suicide attempts are likely to be underestimated because of the social stigmatization associated with these acts.

CHAPTER 3
MENTAL HEALTH TREATMENT

The ideas of mental health and mental illness have replaced the idea of God and the Devil, and the institutionally legitimized explanations, justifications, and interventions of psychiatry have replaced those of organized religion.... Today, no clear line separates the psychiatric from the nonpsychiatric: the explanations, justifications, and interventions of psychiatry permeate the world and blend with it.

—Thomas Szasz, *The Myth of Mental Illness: Foundations of a Theory of Personal Conduct*, Quill, New York, revised edition, 1994

Historically, mental health treatment in the United States, including both attitudes about and care for persons suffering from mental illness, has undergone revolutionary changes. Colonial American society locked up those considered lunatics and subjected them to treatments that by today's standards were cruel, barbaric, and largely ineffective. Warehoused in barren, prison-like facilities, persons with mental illnesses were shackled and chained and forced to endure inhumane treatments. Bleedings, physical blows to the head, or immersions in icy water left them unconscious, further disabled, dead, or perhaps wishing for death as an escape from persecution. Since few colonists ventured inside these treatment facilities, most were unaware of the harsh treatment practices and were satisfied that persons with mental illnesses were out of sight.

By the early 19th century, the European concept of moral management, which advocated more humane treatment of persons suffering from mental illness, was attracting followers in the United States. Existing asylums were filled with persons suffering from a variety of mental disorders, including the dementia (cognitive impairment and emotional disturbances resulting from organic brain disease) that afflicts persons with tertiary, or late-stage syphilis (a sexually transmitted disease). At the close of the Civil War, the swelling ranks of returning servicemen with emotional wounds and their bereaved, disturbed relatives both urgently needed treatment, prompting the proliferation of asylums to care for them. Unlike colonial Americans con-

tent as long as the mentally ill were invisible, Americans during Reconstruction were deeply concerned about the plight of Civil War veterans. Public scrutiny was not however, sufficient to compensate for the combined effects of overcrowding, too few facilities, and the dearth of effective therapies. Absent new modes of treatment, the old ones resurfaced—patients were restrained, ice baths were reintroduced, and many of the afflicted were heavily sedated with narcotic drugs such as opium. Although there were a few notable exceptions—institutions where persons with mental illness received compassionate care in comfortable settings—the overcrowding and inhumane conditions that prompted critics to describe asylums as "snakepits" persisted until the middle of the 20th century.

20TH-CENTURY TREATMENT OF MENTAL ILLNESS

In 1908 Yale University graduate Clifford W. Beers (1876–1943) recounted the cruelty and atrocities he witnessed and endured as an institutionalized mental patient in *A Mind That Found Itself: An Autobiography* (University of Pittsburgh Press, Pittsburgh, 5th edition, 1981). (See Figure 3.1.) Beers contended that his experiences were not extraordinary but rather were the norm of institutional care of persons with mental illness. In 1909 his frustration with the shameful state of mental health care inspired Beers to create the National Committee for Mental Hygiene, which would become a powerful advocacy organization and the predecessor of the present-day the National Mental Health Association. The organization aimed to improve attitudes toward mental illness and the mentally ill, upgrade services and facilities, and intensify efforts to prevent mental illness and promote mental health. The National Committee for Mental Hygiene was responsible for enacting reforms in many states and conducting groundbreaking research about mental health, mental illness, and the efficacy of various forms of treatment. Beer's fearless determination and unwavering devotion to advocacy on behalf of persons with mental illness and creation of an organization that successfully changed attitudes about mental illness earned him recognition as the founder of the modern mental health movement.

Even as critics of asylums were agitating to improve the environments and treatment of institutionalized patients, the increasing acceptance of the biological origins of mental illness spurred a race to develop medical and biological therapies such as electroconvulsive therapy (ECT, commonly known as electroshock therapy) and lobotomies (surgery that separated the neural passages in the front of the brain from those in the back). Introduced in the United States during the 1930s, lobotomies were considered effective because patients who had undergone the surgical procedures apparently forgot about their depressions and their aggressive or antisocial behaviors were eliminated. Dull, detached, docile, and with diminished mental capacities, lobotomized patients were no longer threatening and displayed far fewer abnormal behaviors, and many could be released from asylums and returned to the community. Those without families, or unready for release into the community, were so much easier for asylum personnel to care for that some asylums moved to have the procedure performed on as many of their patients as possible.

Apart from the most obvious risks of this procedure—permanent disability or death—the delicate operation was time-consuming and required the skills of a highly trained surgeon. As a result, it was not applied to all the patients for whom it was considered curative until the 1940s. During those years Walter Freeman, an enterprising physician and professor of neurology (the medical specialty that focuses on disease of the brain and the central and peripheral nervous system) at George Washington University pioneered a quicker, easier approach that became known as the transorbital lobotomy. Although he was not trained as a surgeon, Freeman gained proficiency in performing the procedure. He delivered a shock to the patient's head, pushed an ice pick into the corner of the patient's ocular socket, and piercing the bone behind the eye, cut apart the brain tissue in the frontal lobe, severing the nerves at the base of the frontal lobe. Although many lobotomized patients gained relief from severe depression or agitation, most also became apathetic, with sharply diminished desire and impaired memory and ability to concentrate.

Although there was some dissension in the psychotherapeutic community about the practice of lobotomy, the debut, acceptance, and increasing use of other medical therapies such as drugs—metrazol, sodium amytal, and insulin—to induce convulsions and coma (treatments intended to jolt the individual out of mental illness) created a climate in which surgical treatment such as lobotomy seemed an acceptable treatment option. In fact to many it seemed the more humane option compared to drugs or electroshock therapies, since both were administered to patients while they were fully awake and could induce such violent seizures that patients routinely sustained broken bones or other injuries.

FIGURE 3.1

Clifford W. Beers. *AP/Wide World Photos. Reproduced by permission.*

tered to patients while they were fully awake and could induce such violent seizures that patients routinely sustained broken bones or other injuries.

Traditionally, neurologists held that mental illness originated in the body, and as such required medical or biological treatment, while psychologists and psychiatrists contended that mental disorders originated in the mind and required psychological treatment. The two groups engaged in a sort of turf war that persisted into the 21st century, hotly debating the origins of mental illness and who should rule the province of mental health treatment. As the debate raged, asylum and mental hospital populations soared. Shell-shocked veterans of World War II flooded the already overtaxed facilities, and the failure of either camp to produce a universally safe, effective cure for mental disorders coupled with the economic argument that a lobotomy could be performed for a fraction of the cost of inpatient care boosted the popularity of the procedure.

Freeman himself also rallied support by tirelessly promoting the psychosurgery he had popularized. He touted the procedure as an effective approach for controlling deviants—homosexuals, communists, schizophrenics, and any others society deemed outcasts. He savored the wealth, media attention, and celebrity it afforded him, and he traveled and lectured throughout the United States and Europe. In 1948 he was elected president of the

American Board of Psychiatry and Neurology and performed his most newsworthy transorbital lobotomy when he hammered his ice pick into the head of the outspoken movie star and communist sympathizer Frances Farmer. After the surgery Farmer never made another movie or uttered another rebellious word, and while she eventually was employed as a hotel clerk and was again able to work in the entertainment industry, she died in obscurity in 1970. In February 1967 Freeman performed his last lobotomy. During the procedure he tore a blood vessel in the patient's brain and the hospital where he operated revoked his surgical privileges.

Even more noteworthy, and more unfortunate than Farmer's experience with lobotomy, was the fate of Rosemary Kennedy, the sister of American president John Kennedy. Born in 1918, Rosemary was a mildly retarded child who became an aggressive, uncontrollable adolescent prone to tantrums, rages, and violent behavior. Her wealthy father, Joseph Kennedy, was deeply disturbed with Rosemary's behavior and arranged for her to undergo a lobotomy at St. Elizabeth's Hospital in Washington, D.C., in 1941. The failed surgery left her permanently disabled, paralyzed on one side, incontinent, and unable to speak coherently. Completely incapable of living a normal life, she was sent to live at St. Coletta's Convent in Wisconsin, where she lives today.

Lobotomies and other types of psychosurgery were performed during the 1940s through the mid-1950s until psychopharmacology—the use of drugs to treat symptoms of mental illness—gained widespread acceptance. Antipsychotics, antidepressants, and other drugs proved more effective in subduing mentally disturbed patients, and few patients suffered the irreversible or life-threatening consequences associated with drug-induced shock treatments or lobotomy. Talk therapies also gained credibility during this period because even though they had not been proven effective, they appeared benign compared to the alternatives. By the 1960s lobotomies fell out of favor for two reasons. First, they were potentially life-threatening and caused irreversible physical damage in the brain. Second, society came to disapprove of markedly altering, or in many instances completely obliterating, patients' personalities in the course of treatment.

Societal disapproval of lobotomy and other practices, such as electroconvulsive shock therapy (ECT), was underscored in the 1975 release of *One Flew Over the Cuckoo's Nest*, a film based on a novel written by Ken Kesey. Directed by Milos Foreman, it is the story of a prison inmate who pretends to be insane in order to be transferred from prison to a mental hospital. His plan to take advantage of what he believes will be a less restrictive setting backfires when the head nurse at the mental hospital takes an immediate dislike to him. After a series of incidents that lead to an awful episode of ECT, the head

TABLE 3.1

Selected types of pharmacotherapies

Category and class	Example(s) of clinical use
Antipsychotics (neuroleptics) Typical antipsychotics Atypical antipsychotics	Schizophrenia, psychosis
Antidepressants Selective serotonin reuptake inhibitors Tricyclic and heterocyclic antidepressants Monoamine oxidase inhibitors	Depression, anxiety
Stimulants	Attention-deficit/ hyperactivity disorder
Antimanic Lithium Anticonvulsants Thyroid supplementation	Mania
Antianxiety (anxiolytics) Benzodiazepines Antidepressants B-Adrenergic-blocking drugs	Anxiety
Cholinesterase inhibitors	Alzheimer's disease

SOURCE: David Satcher, "Table 2-9. Selected types of pharmacotherapies," in *Mental Health: A Report of the Surgeon General*, U.S. Department of Health and Human Services, Substance Abuse and Mental Health Services Administration, with National Institutes of Health, Rockville, MD, 1999 [Online] http://www.mentalhealth.org/features/surgeongeneralreport/toc.asp [accessed December 18, 2003]

nurse triumphs by convincing hospital authorities to perform a lobotomy on him. The film portrays the mental hospital, and its use of drugs, ECT, and lobotomy, as devices of repression of human free will. Viewers are encouraged to side with the patients rather than with the hospital personnel. Awarded five Oscars, the film gave voice to the growing sentiment that lobotomy was more than simply undesirable, it was a cruel punishment used to oppress and eliminate behavior deemed undesirable by unenlightened members of the medical profession.

PSYCHOPHARMACOLOGY

Psychopharmacology is the study of the effects of drugs on behavior, and drugs that affect behavior are known as psychoactive drugs, or psychopharmaceuticals. Drugs that act to alter behavior, mood, and consciousness are termed stimulants, depressants, and hallucinogens. Drugs used to treat psychopathologies (mental disorders) are called anxiolytics (anti-anxiety drugs), antidepressants, and antipsychotic drugs. Table 3.1 lists selected types of pharmacotherapies used to treat mental disorders.

To have an effect, psychoactive drugs must come into contact with neurons (nerve cells). Drugs may be administered orally, subcutaneously (immediately below the skin) via injection, transdermally (through the skin via a patch), intramuscularly (injected into a muscle), via inhalation, or directly injected into the bloodstream (via IV—intravenously) or very rarely, into the spinal cord (intrathecal administration). The choice of the route of administration usually considers the patient's preferences, including the cost of treatment, and capabilities such as the patient's ability to adhere to treatment. It depends as well on the characteristics of the drug, such as its solubility or effect on local tissue. The duration of drug action—the length of time it may be considered effective—depends on the rate at which it is metabolized (inactivated by enzymes). The drug's metabolites (breakdown products) are excreted as waste in the bowel, urine, through the skin or respiration.

Like other drugs, the effects of psychoactive agents depend on the dose—the level of the drug in the body. Most psychoactive drugs have a predictable dose-response relationship in which low doses are ineffective, moderate doses are effective, and high doses impair rather than improve symptoms, produce new symptoms, or have untoward side effects. The effects of a drug, especially a psychoactive drug, are also greatly influenced by the patient's psychological state at the time the drug is administered. This finding, known as the rate-dependency effect, has been observed when, for example, persons who are not anxious are given anxiolytic drugs and report that the drugs have no perceptible effect.

History of Psychoactive Drugs

Alcohol was used medicinally by the ancient Greeks and Romans. Later plant extracts such as opium from the poppy, atropine from nightshade, and digitalis from the foxglove plant were used to relieve pain and other somatic ailments as well as to improve mood. By the 17th century, coffee and tea, which both contain caffeine, were considered therapeutic, and coffee was promoted as a healthful alternative to alcohol. During the same period, tobacco seeds from America were transported to Europe because it was considered powerful medicine for pulmonary and other ailments. The mildly stimulating effects of nicotine also were noted. Ether was discovered during the 18th century, but it was not until the 1840s that its anesthetic (ability to produce numbness or loss of sensation) properties were used for medicinal purposes. Around the same time, ether's psychoactive properties were favored by American youth as an alternative to the recreational use of alcohol. Toward the end of the 19th century, heroin compounded from opium was promoted as a safe alternative to opium or morphine (an opium derivative), although all three substances influenced cognition (thinking) and mood.

The 1800s saw the introduction of cocaine, derived from coca leaves. Sigmund Freud, the famed father of psychoanalysis, endorsed cocaine as an effective medicine to combat fatigue and depression. In 1887 amphetamines, known for their potent stimulant properties, were synthesized. In 1896 the Bayer Company began to manufacture heroin. Although hallucinogens, also known as psychedelic drugs, had long been known for their psychoactive properties, it was not until the middle of the

20th century—the 1960s and 1970s—that drugs such as peyote, mescaline, and psilocybin became well known. Peyote and mescaline are derived from mescal cactus plants, and psilocybin from mushrooms. All were used ritually by Native Americans. In 1938 lysergic acid diethylamide (LSD), derived from ergot (a rye fungus), became one of the best-known hallucinogens. A generation of hippies and musicians sang its praises as a "mind-expanding" drug. Nearly two decades later, a powerful psychedelic anesthetic, phencyclidine (PCP, also known as "angel dust") was discovered and abused by a generation of adolescents and young adults.

The drugs used during the first half of the 20th century to treat mental illness aimed largely at subduing symptoms by inducing catharsis to alter brain function and behavior. Many drugs used to treat mental illnesses were reapplications of remedies used throughout the ages; a few were used in response to emerging knowledge of the relationship between the brain and behavior; and others were discovered purely by accident. The development of nearly all early somatic treatments was largely based on speculation and a process of trial and error. For example, metrazol shock treatment was based on the erroneous notion that epilepsy, a neurological disorder characterized by seizures, and schizophrenia were antagonistic and that inducing seizures would somehow eliminate schizophrenia.

By some accounts, many patients did find relief from their agitated mental states following these early somatic treatments. Most, however, also emerged confused, weak, and in need of continuing institutional care because they were unable to return to the community. While these early drug therapies may have muted the symptoms of patients suffering from mental illness, they carried considerable risk, and some patients did not survive them. For example, insulin shock therapy, used to treat psychoses, involved inducing a state of hypoglycemia (precariously low blood sugar levels) in the patient by administering successive injections of insulin. Patients remained comatose (unconscious) for several hours, and then a sugar solution was introduced through a nasal gastric tube to reverse the hypoglycemia. Patients were treated as often as daily and in the entire course of treatment might endure 50 insulin-induced comas. These patients required close nursing supervision, and fatal complications were not uncommon. Some comas proved irreversible, and unattended patients could easily suffocate in their own vomit or other secretions.

ANTIPSYCHOTIC AGENTS

Until the middle of the 20th century, treatment of psychoses—a broad range of complex and severe mental disorders that includes schizophrenia and other bizarre and socially unacceptable behavior—was imperfect at best and fatal at worst. It relied on extreme measures such as physical restraints, psychosurgery, and sedation using drugs.

The 1954 introduction of chlorpromazine (better known by its trade name Thorazine), quickly dubbed the "chemical lobotomy," because of its dramatic ability to calm severely psychotic patients, was heralded as a medical miracle and the dawn of a new age in mental health treatment.

The results of treatment with chlorpromazine and other drugs in the same class that became known as neuroleptic (repressing excess activity in the nervous system) or antipsychotics were nothing short of miraculous. Patients who had been agitated and uncontrollable or impassive and unresponsive and patients who hallucinated could be freed from restraints, communicate with others, and perform activities without direct supervision. The drugs' ability to calm patients without debilitating sedation enabled persons previously deemed hopeless to reclaim their lives and reenter society. A decade after its introduction in the United States, more than 50 million people worldwide had used the drug.

The antipsychotic qualities of chlorpromazine were discovered by chance when a French surgeon was looking for a drug to reduce the amount of anesthesia necessary for surgery. Because of the way it was discovered, during its first decade of use there was little understanding of how this class of drugs acted on the brain to affect behavior. As researchers attempted to uncover their modes of action, they also began to document evidence that extended use of the drugs occasionally produced severe, troubling side effects. Some patients who had taken the drug for several years experienced neurological or neuromuscular symptoms such as uncontrollable, spastic muscular contractions and tremors, as well as involuntary movements of the face, lips, and tongue (known as tardive dyskinesia). Although they were certainly not life-threatening side effects, for some patients these uncontrollable movements were embarrassing and proved to be obstacles to reintegrating patients into the community.

According to the NIMH, at first investigators could not identify the mechanism of action of antipsychotic agents because understanding of the relationship between neurotransmitters (chemicals in the brain that enable messages to pass from one neuron to another) and receptors on the cell walls (the sites where neurotransmitters and drugs influence cellular actions) of neurons was incomplete. In the early 1990s just 2 receptors had been identified for the neurotransmitter serotonin, but by 2000, researchers had identified 12 additional serotonin receptors and 5 receptors for dopamine. These discoveries, along with imaging studies of the brain, such as positron emission tomography (PET scans) helped researchers to decipher the therapeutic action of antipsychotic drugs and determine how each acted to block specific neurotransmitter receptors. As researchers sought to modify the drugs to reduce side effects, mental health professionals developed psychosocial (the psychological and social factors that influence mental health) strategies and other community treatment programs to assist patients to adhere to drug treatment despite adverse drug side effects.

Conventional antipsychotic drug treatment focuses on blocking dopamine receptors in the brain, but not all schizophrenics responded to this treatment. Identification of the additional receptor sites and the need to improve treatment for schizophrenia spurred development of a second generation of newer antipsychotic medications. In 1990 the U.S. Food and Drug Administration (FDA) approved a new type of antipsychotic agent, clozapine (Clozaril), which did not produce the disturbing neuromuscular side effects of the first generation of antipsychotic drugs. Clozapine, however, required close medical monitoring and weekly blood tests, because in approximately 1 percent of patients it was found to cause agranulocytosis, a potentially life-threatening condition in which there is a sharp decrease in the number of neutrophils (white blood cells that combat infection) in the blood. Despite this side effect, second-generation antipsychotics like clozapine, risperidone (Risperidol), olanzapine (Zyprexa), and quetiapine (Serquel) still have fewer side effects than previously used medications.

The Actions of Antipsychotic Drugs Offer Clues About the Origins of Mental Illness

Antipsychotic drugs influence neurochemistry by selectively blocking transmission of impulses from neuron to neuron in four major dopamine pathways. Investigators theorize that schizophrenia may be caused by too much activity in some dopamine pathways. This theory was in part based on observations that drugs that reduce dopamine activity (dopamine antagonists) relieve many symptoms of schizophrenia. In addition, the prolonged use of drugs that increase dopamine activity (dopamine agonists), such as amphetamines and cocaine, produces schizophrenic symptoms in otherwise normal persons.

Some researchers believe that there is too much dopamine in the brains of persons with schizophrenia. Another theory arose in response to postmortem examinations of the brains of persons with schizophrenia, which have found increased receptors in schizophrenics compared to persons who did not have schizophrenia. Persons with schizophrenia also have been found to have lower-than-average levels of monoamine oxidase, which allows dopamine to remain active longer.

Another theory to explain the biological origins of psychosis is that the serotonin system is overly active. This hypothesis is supported by two factors. First, many hallucinogenic drugs are similar in structure to serotonin. Second, elevated levels of serotonin metabolites (breakdown products) are found in the urine of hallucinating schizophrenics but that these levels return to normal when patients are in remission.

FIGURE 3.2

ANTIDEPRESSANT DRUGS

Brand Name (Generic Name)	Possible Common Side Effects Include:
Desyrel (trazodone hydrochloride)	Allergic skin reactions, blurred vision, decreased appetite, fluid retention, headache
Effexor (venlafaxine hydrochloride)	Diarrhea, dizziness, gas, headache, insommia, rash, vomiting
Elavil (amitriptyline hydrochloride)	Constipation, dizziness, high blood pressure, fever, nausea, rash, weight gain or loss
Nardil (phenelzine sulfate)	Dry mouth, fatigue, headache, muscle spasms, tremors
Norpramin (desipramine hydrochloride)	Blurred vision, cramps, hallucinations, hair loss, vomiting
Pamelor (nortriptyline hydrochloride)	Diarrhea, fatigue, headache, decreased coordination
Paxil (paroxetine hydrochloride)	Cold symptoms, drowsiness, nervousness, stomach pain
Prozac (fluoxetine hydrochloride)	Bronchitis, drowsiness, fatigue, nausea, tremors
Sinequan (doxepin hydrochloride)	Bruising, constipation, fluid retention, itching, increased heartbeat
Surmontil (trimipramine maleate)	Disorientation, flushing, headache, nausea, vomiting
Tofranil (imipramine hydrochloride)	Bleeding sores, fever, hives, decreased coordination
Travil	Asthma, diarrhea, dizziness, fatigue, seizures
Wellbutrin (bupropion hydrochloride)	Agitation, dry mouth, headache, nausea, rash
Zoloft (sertraline)	Diarrhea, fainting, gas, headache, nervousness

Antidepressant drugs. *Stanley Publishing. Reproduced by permission.*

ANTIDEPRESSANT DRUGS

Antidepressant medications that alter brain chemistry have been used to effectively treat depressive disorders. Figure 3.2 lists antidepressant medications by their brand names and generic names. Monoamine oxidase inhibitors (MAOIs) such as Nardil influence the function of neurotransmitters such as dopamine or norepinephrine. Selective serotonin reuptake inhibitors (SSRIs) include drugs such as Prozac, Desyrel, Paxil, and Zoloft. Lithium and tricyclic antidepressants (such as Elavil, Norpramin, Pamelor, Sinequan, Surmontil, and Tofranil) are the other major classes of drugs used to treat depression. Drugs that do not belong to these broad classes of antidepressant agents include Effexor, which is known as an SNRI (serotonin and norepinephrine reuptake inhibitor). It is believed to act by affecting the level of two chemicals in the brain—serotonin and norepinephrine. In addition, there is Wellbutrin, which is chemically unrelated to tricyclic, tetracyclic, SSRIs, or other known antidepressant agents. Wellbutrin's mechanism of action to treat depression is not yet known.

Monoamine oxidase (MAO) is an enzyme that enhances the breakdown of monoamines, and as a result, the regulation of the availability neurotransmitters. For example, MAO usually breaks down dopamine. MAO inhibitors increase levels of monoamine neurotransmitters by preventing their breakdown, which acts to increase their release. These drugs (such as phenelzine, tranylcypromine, and iproniazid) act by binding to the MAO molecule and rendering it inactive. This action is possible because the drugs are very similar in structure to the monoamine neurotransmitters and take their places. But unlike the neurotransmitters they are replacing, they are not broken down by the enzyme. While they have demonstrated efficacy as potent antidepressants, MAOIs may cause serious side effects such as hypertension and hypotension (dangerously elevated or decreased blood pressure) and liver damage. Figure 3.2 lists the more common side effects associated with some of the most frequently prescribed antidepressant drugs, including MAOIs.

As their name suggests, selective serotonin reuptake inhibitors (SSRIs) inhibit the reuptake of serotonin and their overall effect is to enhance serotinergic activity. They do not affect norepinephrine or dopamine, nor do they increase the activity of serotonin by preventing its breakdown by MAO. SSRIs are considered the first-line drugs of choice in terms of pharmacological depression treatment today. Prozac is probably the best-known brand name SSRI, but variations exist, each with a unique chemical identity and pattern of clinical effects and side effects. Table 3.2 shows the efficacy of SSRIs by comparing their ability to effectively relieve symptoms of major depression and dysthymia (minor depression) with treatment with a placebo (an inactive substance used as a control in an experiment). Although SSRIs have some reported side effects such as sedation, headache, weight gain or loss, and nausea, they generally produce fewer and less severe side effects than MAOIs and tricyclic antidepressants. (See Figure 3.2.)

Tricyclic antidepressants are named for their three-ring molecular structure. This class of drugs inhibits the reuptake of catecholamines, which results in an increase in the activity of norepinephrine, dopamine, and serotonin. Each tricyclic has a specific, measurable effect on each neurotransmitter. Imipramine acts equally on norepinephrine and serotonin. Amitryptiline is more specific to serotonin, and desipramine is more specific to norepinephrine. All have demonstrated efficacy as antidepressants, but choosing the best one for individual patients is largely a process of trial and error, with patients frequently trying more than one tricyclic in an effort to optimally relieve depressive symptoms. Figure 3.2 shows some of the side effects associated with tricyclic antidepressant therapy.

Inorganic salts of the metal element lithium are used to treat bipolar disorder. Although the mechanism of action of lithium is not yet known, investigators speculate that lithium may substitute for the metal ions of chemically similar sodium, potassium, magnesium, and calcium at various sites in neurons. This causes changes in the rate of transport of ions and the rate of neurotransmitter release. Patients taking lithium are closely monitored for serious side effects such as impaired kidney function.

In addition to serving as an effective treatment for bipolar disorder, lithium also may reduce the risk of suicide in this population. This finding is important, since as many as one in five bipolar patients attempts suicide at some point in their lives. Frederick Goodwin and his colleagues reported the results of a study comparing suicide risk during treatment with lithium and a newer drug, divalproex (Depakote) in "Suicide Risk in Bipolar Disorder During Treatment with Lithium and Divalproex" (*Journal*

TABLE 3.2

Treatment of depression—newer pharmacotherapies

- Newer antidepressant drugs are effective treatments for major depression and dysthymia.
  - They are efficacious in primary care and specialty mental health care settings:
    – Major depression:
      50 percent response to active agent
      32 percent response to placebo
    – Dysthymia (fluoxetine, sertraline, and amisulpride):
      59 percent response to active agent
      37 percent response to placebo
- Both older and newer antidepressants demonstrate similar efficacy.
- Drop-out rates due to all causes combined are similar for newer and older agents:
  - Drop-out rates due to adverse effects are slightly higher for older agents.
  - Newer agents are often easier to use because of single daily dosing and less titration.

SOURCE: David Satcher, "Figure 4-2. Treatment of depression—newer pharmacotherapies: Summary findings," in *Mental Health: A Report of the Surgeon General*, U.S. Department of Health and Human Services, Substance Abuse and Mental Health Services Administration, with National Institutes of Health, Rockville, MD, 1999 [Online] http://www.mentalhealth.org/features/surgeongeneralreport/toc.asp [accessed December 18, 2003]

of the American Medical Association, vol. 290, no. 11, September 2003). The investigators reviewed the medical records of more than 20,000 bipolar patients in California and Washington and compared rates of hospital admission and death resulting from suicide attempts. They found 31.3 suicide attempts per 1,000 patients per year taking divalproex compared with 10.8 per 1,000 among patients taking lithium. Although the investigators could not explain the significantly different rates, other researchers theorize that lithium's proven ability to reduce aggressive and impulsive behavior may explain its ability to prevent suicide, which is often an aggressive, impulsive act.

Antidepressants do not offer immediate relief from symptoms; most take full effect in about four weeks, and some take up to eight weeks to achieve optimal therapeutic effects. Antidepressant drugs are not physically addictive, but patients must be closely monitored by health professionals to monitor side effects, dosage, and effectiveness. In some cases of chronic depression, medication may be needed continuously, on a long-term basis, to prevent recurrence of symptoms of the disorder.

Some people obtain relief from the symptoms of depression using drugs alone, while other respond well to psychotherapy and do not require antidepressants. Many do best with a combination of treatment—drugs for relatively quick relief of symptoms and therapy to learn how to cope with life's problems more effectively.

ECT As Treatment for Depression

After falling out of favor during the 1970s, when talk therapies and psychopharmacology predominated, electroconvulsive therapy (ECT)—electrical stimulation of the brain—reemerged during the 1990s as treatment for severe or life-threatening depression that has not responded to medication. Performed under brief anesthesia, modern ECT requires multiple sessions to achieve results, and patients usually receive three sessions per week over the course of several weeks. It is generally used for patients with the most serious depressions, such as those who are suicidal or may harm others, persons unable to take medication, and patients for whom medication and psychotherapy have proven ineffective.

ANXIOLYTIC AGENTS

Some antidepressants are effective for treatment of anxiety disorders. According to the NIMH, the first medication specifically approved for use in the treatment of obsessive-compulsive disorder (OCD) was the tricyclic antidepressant clomipramine (Anafranil). However SSRIs, including fluoxetine (Prozac), fluvoxamine (Luvox), paroxetine (Paxil), and sertraline (Zoloft) also have been approved to treat OCD. Paroxetine has also been approved for social anxiety disorder (social phobia), generalized anxiety disorder (GAD), and panic disorder. Sertraline is approved for panic disorder and post-traumatic stress disorder (PTSD), and venlafaxine (Effexor) has been approved for GAD.

Other anti-anxiety medications include the benzodiazepines, which can relieve symptoms more quickly than antidepressants. Commonly used benzodiazepines are clonazepam (Klonopin), alprazolam (Xanax), diazepam (Valium), and lorazepam (Ativan). Benzodiazepines have relatively few side effects—the most commonly reported are drowsiness and loss of coordination—but fatigue, mental slowing, and confusion also may occur. For this reason, persons taking these drugs are advised not to drive or operate machinery. Similarly, they are counseled to abstain from using alcohol when taking benzodiazepines because the interaction between benzodiazepines and alcohol can lead to serious and possibly life-threatening complications.

Individual reactions to benzodiazepines vary. Some people achieve lasting symptom relief from a single daily dose; others have better results with two or three smaller doses per day; and still others use the drugs only occasionally, as needed. Patients are usually prescribed low doses that are gradually increased until symptoms diminish or disappear. The choice of drug, dosage, and frequency of administration depend on the symptoms and the individual's response to the medication. Benzodiazepines are generally prescribed for brief periods of time—days or weeks—or to help an individual cope with a stressful event or circumstance.

With prolonged use—weeks or months—patients may develop tolerance for, and dependence on, these drugs. If treatment stops abruptly, a withdrawal reaction may occur, marked by symptoms such as anxiety, shakiness, headache, dizziness, sleeplessness, loss of appetite, or in extreme cases, seizures. Following prolonged use of benzodiazepines, the dosage is gradually reduced before it is stopped completely.

Another drug specifically developed to relieve symptoms of anxiety disorders is buspirone (BuSpar). Unlike benzodiazepines, buspirone must be taken consistently for at least two weeks to achieve an anti-anxiety effect and therefore cannot be used periodically or on an as-needed basis. Beta blockers such as propranolol (Inderal, Inderide, drugs also used to treat heart conditions and high blood pressure) are sometimes used to help individuals cope with "stage fright"—a specific stressful situation such as a speech, oral presentation in class, or other performance.

PSYCHOTHERAPY

Psychotherapy has also been demonstrated as effective therapy for mild to moderate depression and anxiety. Talking about problems with mental health professionals can help many patients better understand their feelings. The success of the client—therapist relationship relies on mutual trust and the shared goal of modifying destructive, unhealthy, or negative thoughts, attitudes, emotions, and behaviors. Psychotherapy aims to identify and resolve unconscious conflicts, increase insight, improve problem-solving and communication skills, and enhance understanding and effectiveness of interpersonal relationships.

Psychoanalysis, the first modern form of psychotherapy, employs a psychodynamic approach that involves the application of certain Freudian concepts such as free association, dream interpretation, the unconscious, resistance, and transference as a method of treatment. Freudian psychoanalysis seeks to expose unconscious conflicts and break down defenses. Another school of psychoanalysis is Adlerian psychoanalysis (named for Viennese physician Alfred Adler), which emphasizes the importance of birth order and sibling rivalry. Jungian psychoanalysis, developed by psychiatrist Carl Jung, emphasizes symbols, spirituality, and the collective unconscious (the sum total of all of mankind's unconscious as well as repressed masculine and feminine identities). Generally, psychoanalysis is a long-term process in which client and therapist meet once or twice weekly over the course of several years. It is considered effective for persons struggling to resolve inner conflicts that significantly impair their mental health and well-being, but it is costly in time and dollars, and results—therapeutic gains—are realized slowly and incrementally over time.

Two types of short-term therapy, lasting 10 to 20 weeks, that appear to improve symptoms of depression are interpersonal therapy and cognitive/behavioral therapy. Interpersonal therapy concentrates on helping patients improve personal relationships with family and friends. Behavioral/cognitive therapy attempts to help patients replace negative thoughts and feelings with more positive, optimistic approaches and actions.

Interpersonal Psychotherapy

Interpersonal psychotherapy (IPT) is short-term therapy that has demonstrated efficacy for the treatment of depression. According to the International Society for Interpersonal Psychotherapy, IPT does not assume that mental illness arises exclusively from problematical interpersonal relationships. It does emphasize, however, that mental health and emotional problems occur within an interpersonal context. For this reason, the therapy aims to intervene specifically in social functioning to relieve symptoms.

Generally, therapists and clients meet weekly for hour-long sessions for as many as 20 weeks. Because it is a short-term, highly structured psychodynamic therapy, it focuses on the one or two key issues that appear to be most closely related to the depression. As its name implies, ITP emphasizes the quality of interactions with others and instructs clients about how better to relate to others. The therapy concentrates on interpersonal relationships and events such as marital, family, or work-related disputes and conflicts. It also assists clients undergoing interpersonal role transitions, such as bereavement, separation, divorce, job loss, or retirement.

The first sessions are devoted to assessment and identification, information gathering, and clarifying the specific interpersonal issues that will be the focus of the therapy. The metal health problem or disorder is described in interpersonal terms, and an interpersonal inventory of the key relationships in the client's life is prepared. During sessions 3 through 14 the problematic relationships are addressed and symptom severity and responses to treatment are monitored and assessed. The final sessions concentrate on termination, which is viewed as a loss experience. During these sessions clients can learn about their own responses to loss and determine the extent to which the objectives of the therapeutic process have been achieved.

ITP employs methods and techniques adapted from other types of therapy, including crisis intervention and cognitive-behavior therapy. These techniques include:

- clarification—this line of questioning aims to anticipate and identify the client's biases when describing interpersonal relationships and issues

- supportive listening—the therapist may offer supportive words, but does not interrupt; instead she or he listens attentively and nonjudgmentally

- role playing—to enable clients to enact problematic relationships from the vantage point of others and to practice new behaviors

- communication analysis—behavioral intervention to assist clients to listen and communicate in a manner conducive to resolving interpersonal disputes

- encouragement of affect (affect is the psychological term for an observable expression of emotion)—allows clients to experience unpleasant or unwanted emotions in a safe, therapeutic environment. This process enables clients to acknowledge the affective component of an interpersonal issue to accept it as a part of their experience

Like other forms of psychotherapy, IPT may be used in conjunction with medications. Since depression may be a recurrent illness, it is recommended that successful short-term treatment be combined with ongoing, maintenance therapy, such as monthly sessions following completion of the short-term phase.

Cognitive and Behavioral Therapy

Cognitive-behavioral therapy (CBT) is based on the premise that thinking influences emotions and behavior—that feelings and actions originate with thoughts. Therefore, if clients experience unwanted feelings and behaviors, it is important for them to identify the thinking that is causing the feelings and behaviors and learn how to replace it with thoughts that produce more desirable reactions. CBT posits that it is possible to change the way people feel and act even if their circumstances do not change. It teaches the advantages of feeling, at worst, calm when faced with undesirable situations. CBT clients learn that they will confront undesirable events and circumstances whether they become troubled about them or not. When they are troubled about events or circumstances, they have two problems—the troubling event or circumstance, and the troubling feelings about the event or circumstance. Clients learn that when they do not become troubled about trying events and circumstance, they can reduce the number of problems they face by half.

CBT is a relatively fast-acting, structured, and directed treatment modality. It is short term, with clients receiving an average of just 16 sessions. In contrast to other forms of therapy, CB therapists tend to offer more instruction than practitioners of other forms of therapy and usually assign "homework" in the form of reading assignments and practicing the techniques learned.

Unlike other therapies in which the therapist-client relationship is central to the process, CBT emphasizes an active, collaborative, client-directed process in which clients learn rational self-counseling skills. Cognitive-behavioral therapists aim to understand what their clients want out of life and then help their clients achieve those objectives. Since CBT is based on an educational model and the assumption that most emotional and behavioral reactions are learned, therapists serve as teachers—they question, listen, instruct, encourage their clients to question themselves, and support clients' progress. In turn clients become "students of life" as they speak, learn, and implement the action, behaviors, and strategies they have learned.

The National Association of Cognitive-Behavioral Therapists (NACBT) asserts that CBT is much more than just talking and that the educational emphasis and reliance on rational thinking as opposed to assumptions enable clients to achieve lasting, long-term results. The professional association claims that "when people understand how and why they are doing well, they can continue doing what they are doing to make themselves well."

Marriage and Family Therapy

Although most psychotherapy is conducted in one-on-one sessions with therapist and client, marriage and family counseling involves the married couple (or established partners in a relationship) or family who attend counseling to resolve specific problems in their relationships. Instead of singling out individuals for treatment, marriage and family counseling considers the couple or family as a whole. Marriage and family therapists and counselors are trained in psychotherapy and family systems and concentrate on understanding how interactions contribute to problems in family relationships.

Marriage counseling is generally short-term therapy that aims to identify and resolve problems in relationships. Therapy begins with inquiries about the couple's roles, patterns, rules, goals, and beliefs and an analysis of the positive and negative aspects of the relationship. The therapist helps the couple to understand how in most cases both partners contribute to problems in the relationship. Equipped with this awareness, the partners can learn to change how they interact with one another and develop effective approaches for problem solving. In some instances, it is helpful for partners to draw up a contract in which each partner commits to changing a particular behavior or using a newly learned problem-solving technique to resolve differences rather than resorting to old, dysfunctional patterns of interaction.

Many therapists also offer premarital counseling for couples before they get married to help them identify and anticipate potential problems and sources of stress in their relationships. Postmarital therapy, in which separating or divorcing couples seek help in working out their differences, can help to minimize stress and discomfort during negotiation of emotionally charged interpersonal issues such as child custody.

Family therapy involves all the members of a nuclear or extended family and may be conducted by a single mental health practitioner, pair, or team of therapists. Cotherapists or teams often include male and female therapists to address gender-related issues or serve as role models through their interactions with one another during sessions for family members. The therapists analyze family interactions and communication, and while they do not focus on or align themselves with individual family members, they try to enhance awareness and understanding of dysfunctional patterns.

The advent of family therapy occurred just after World War II, when physicians caring for schizophrenic patients observed that the patients' families had markedly disturbed patterns of communication and that the patients' symptoms flared or subsided in response to the level of tension between their parents. These observations prompted mental health practitioners to develop a therapeutic framework that viewed the family as an organism or system with its own internal organization, patterns of functioning, and tendency to resist change. When therapists treated the families of schizophrenic patients rather than simply the patients, they found greater, more lasting improvement. The success of this treatment for patients with schizophrenia inspired therapists to apply it to families with members suffering from a wide range of mental health problems and disorders.

Today family therapy is applied to treat a variety of problems such as eating disorders, substance abuse, and adjustment problems stemming from new jobs, schools, or geographic relocation. It is short-term therapy, intended to help families effectively overcome challenges. Example of these include:

- Multigenerational families—problems arising from parents sharing housing with grandparents, or homes in which children are reared by grandparents.

- Families that depart from social norms—blended families involving children from multiple marriages, gay couples, and racially mixed families may not experience interfamilial problems but may require support and assistance to cope with unfavorable or judgmental attitudes expressed by others.

- Families that are not supportive of a member suffering from a mental disorder or those that actively undermine the treatment of a family member in individual therapy.

- Families in which the identified patient's problems seem attributable to, or associated with, other family members' problems. The identified patient is the family member with the problem that caused the family to enter treatment.

While some of family therapy is based on cognitive-behavioral or psychodynamic principles, the most common approach relies on family systems theory. This theory considers the family as the unit of treatment and focuses on relationships and communication patterns within the family rather than on the personality traits or symptoms displayed by individual family members. Problems are addressed by modifying the system rather than trying to change an individual family member.

One important premise of family systems theory is homeostasis—the notion that families work to maintain their traditional organization and functioning and resist change. Family systems theory proposes that triangular emotional relationships in families serve to maintain homeostasis. When any two family members have problems with

FIGURE 3.3

Group therapy sessions often take place in a home-like environment to make members feel more comfortable. *Will & Deni McIntyre. Photo Researchers, Inc. Reproduced by permission.*

one another, they draw in a third member to stabilize their own relationship. Another key concept is differentiation—the ability of each family member to maintain a sense of self while remaining emotionally connected to the family. Family systems theory asserts that healthy families allow and even encourage members to differentiate, while troubled families may act to impede individuals from differentiating or try to punish or expel those who attempt it.

The objectives and desired outcomes of family systems therapy include enhanced insight, increased differentiation of individual family members, improved communication, awareness and modification of dysfunctional behavior patterns, and successful resolution of the problems that prompted the family to enter treatment. The changing definitions and composition of American families has contributed to the increasing popularity of this treatment modality.

Group Therapy

Group therapy gathers a small group—usually 6 to 12 persons—to meet regularly to talk, interact, and discuss problems with each other and the therapist, who serves as facilitator and group leader. In some groups, two therapists shepherd group members' processes of self-discovery. Group therapy offers a safe, comfortable setting where members may identify and address problems and emotional issues. (See Figure 3.3.) This treatment modality is distinguished from individual therapy by the opportunity it offers for members to counsel and support others. Group therapy provides social acceptance and powerful reassurance that members are not alone—others face comparable challenges—and may effectively reduce feelings of isolation and stigmatization. It also provides opportunities to display empathy and practice communication and other relationship skills in a supportive environment, under the watchful eye of a mental health professional. Finally, through the act of helping group members identify, address, and resolve their problems, group therapy members may gain more self-esteem.

Groups may be homogeneous or heterogeneous. Homogeneous groups have members with similar diagnoses or circumstances. Examples of these are support groups for teenagers, women with breast cancer, and bereavement groups for persons recovering from the loss of a loved one. Heterogeneous groups are composed of individuals with varying concerns and circumstances. The therapeutic philosophy used in group therapy depends on the group and the psychological training of the therapist. Most groups use psychodynamic, cognitive-behavioral, or Gestalt therapy techniques. Gestalt therapy focuses on the experiential present moment—an awareness of the here and now, and the notion of the interactive field—the belief that it is possible for people to truly know themselves only in relation to the world around them. Gestalt therapists feel their approach is uniquely suited to responding to the difficulties and challenges of daily life, both in its ability to relieve distress and by paving a path toward self-actualization.

Depending on the philosophical and treatment orientations of the therapist, she or he may lead the group through a structured program or allow it to set its own course. Therapists may gently redirect the group when it veers off course while allowing members to raise and explore relevant issues. Along with offering positive reinforcement for desirable behaviors, such as displays of empathy, the therapist models effective communication and interpersonal skills and identifies the concerns and traits group members share to foster a sense of group identity

Short-term groups are time limited, with a predetermined number of meetings. While long-term or continuing groups may gain and lose members, most short-term groups have a fixed membership throughout their duration. Therapeutic groups operate based on rules governing confidentiality—members may not share the details of therapy sessions with anyone outside of the group. They may also be asked to agree not to socialize with other group members outside of therapy because it might adversely effect the dynamics of the group.

Art Therapy

Unlike talk therapies, art therapy relies on the use of art-making and art interpretation rather than solely on verbal communication to uncover and explore feelings, emotions, and ideas. The use of art, creation, action, and myth to access preverbal, nonsemantic, and intrapsychic material first emerged as a therapeutic modality during the late 1960s and early 1970s. From its inception, art therapy strove to free clients and therapists from the ironclad, indelible belief that what is experienced through the linear lens of language is reality itself—that thought is experience, that it is language, and that it is truth. With its roots in psychotherapy, art therapy first became a tool for releasing hidden emotions in the unconscious through spontaneous art and that the creative process of art-making could foster rehabilitation, change, and growth. It demonstrated utility with clients unable, unwilling, or unlikely to articulate their feelings in conventional problem-oriented and solution-focused psychotherapy. Art therapy became widely used, with great success, by mental health practitioners working with children and persons who had suffered physical or sexual abuse. More recently, interest in the connection of mind, body, and spirit has lead to explorations through the art process of emotional conflicts, physical symptoms, and personal growth.

Nearly all philosophical differences, variations, and approaches to art therapy share the common belief that therapeutic change ultimately results from bringing forward deeply hidden and repressed materials within the client's psyche so they can be balanced through insight and awareness. Inner conflict surfaces and is reexperienced, resolved, and reintegrated. Within some approaches, art-making became a symbolic moment in which personal change was tried and tested, and gains were deepened and cemented.

Early art therapists made meaning of the client's art and formulated strategies to help distressed individuals uncover and face the cause of their symptoms and pathologies. Gradually the focus of art therapy began to shift from the therapist to the client. There was greater recognition of the value of client insight and the importance of the client assuming personal responsibility for analysis and change. This shift actually acted to increase the dynamic potential of art therapy by favoring the importance of client involvement, action, and understanding in the therapeutic process. Although at first it appeared counterintuitive, the freer, open-ended, and more fluid approach to art therapy appeared better suited for uncovering and communicating possibilities and opportunities for change. Further, since it was not strictly outcome oriented, modern art therapy enabled clients to derive therapeutic benefits from the process of art-making as well as the collaborative efforts with the therapist to interpret the artwork.

Art therapists may be more readily able to relinquish the construct of therapist-defined problems and hypotheses in favor of client-defined problems and perspectives because artists are more attuned to the ebb and flow of creative process and the benefit of multiple perspectives when viewing the whole. The openness and receptivity inherent to the creative process may enable art therapists to accept the dynamic process of revealing truths and enhance their capacity to envision opportunities for change.

How Effective Is Psychotherapy?

The 1999 U.S. Surgeon General's comprehensive report on mental illness confirmed that there is no one-size-fits-all treatment for mental disorders. The relative merits of one form of therapy versus another and the effectiveness of different types of psychotherapy have been debated during the past decade.

An article in the November 1995 issue of *Consumer Reports* reported the results of a large-scale survey about psychotherapy in which 4,000 of the magazine's subscribers participated. Nearly 9 out of 10 respondents who had received mental health care indicated that their conditions improved significantly following psychotherapy. This benchmark study was commended by the mental health community because it concluded that patients benefited greatly from psychotherapy, that long-term treatment did considerably better than short-term treatment, and that psychotherapy alone was just as effective as the combination of medication and psychotherapy.

Surprisingly, no specific type of psychotherapy was deemed better than any other for any disorder. Similarly, there were no reported differences in treatment process or outcomes between psychologists, psychiatrists, and social workers, although they received higher praise than marriage counselors and long-term therapy received from primary care physicians. The advantages of long-term treatment by a mental health professional held not only for the specific problems that led to treatment but also for general measures of mental health and well-being. The survey participants reported improvement in the ability to relate to others, cope with everyday stress, and enjoy life more, as well as personal growth and understanding, self-esteem, and confidence. Persons whose choice of therapist or duration of treatment was limited by their insurance coverage fared worse than those who chose their therapists, determined how often they would meet, and determined how long they would remain in therapy.

Critics of the study observed that it was not applicable to the general population because all the survey participants chose their treatment and results were gathered via self-report and not verified by a third party. This fact introduces significant bias—each participant sought treatment and believed that both the treatment modality and practitioner he or she had selected would be effective. The unanswered question remains: Would people who denied they needed help, and had not chosen their treatment or therapist, have experienced the same level of satisfaction with their care? Another study limitation was the absence of a control group. This raises the question of whether study participants would have recovered without any treatment at all or would have received comparable relief from talking with sympathetic friends.

OTHER ASPECTS OF TREATMENT

The Surgeon General's report asserted that to be optimally effective, treatment must be tailored to the individual's age, gender, race, and culture. It also concluded that "care and treatment in the real world of practice do not conform to what research determines as best. For many reasons, at times care is inadequate but there are models for improving treatment." Further, a follow-up to the Surgeon General's report documented serious disparities in access to, and the quality of, mental health care for members of racial and ethnic minorities and acknowledged that "all Americans do not share equally in the hope for recovery from mental illness" (*Mental Health: Culture, Race and Ethnicity A Supplement to Mental Health: A Report of the Surgeon General,* U.S. Department of Health and Human Services, Rockville, MD, 2001).

The following section presents the example of eating disorders to illustrate the interdisciplinary, multifaceted approach used to treat specific mental disorders. It also summarizes the results of research intended to estimate the patterns of mental health treatments received by persons with three common mental disorders—depression, panic disorder, and generalized anxiety disorder (GAD). It concludes with the observation that while part of the U.S. population suffers from untreated and poorly treated mental disorders, not all persons with mental health problems require professional treatment.

Treatment of Eating Disorders

Many anorexics deny their illness, and getting and keeping anorexic patients in treatment can be difficult. Treating bulimia is also not easy. Many bulimics are easily frustrated and want to leave treatment if their symptoms are not quickly relieved.

Generally a physician treats the medical complications of the disease, while a nutritionist advises on specific diet and eating plans. To help the patient face his or her underlying problems and emotional issues, psychotherapy is usually necessary. Group therapy has been found helpful for bulimics, who are relieved to find that they are not unique in their binge-eating behaviors. A combination of behavioral therapy and family systems therapy is often the most effective with anorexics. Patients suffering from depression may benefit from antidepressants such as SSRIs to help relieve the anxiety associated with anorexia.

A long-term study (approximately 11.5 years) of 173 young women diagnosed with bulimia reiterated the strong hold eating disorders have on their victims (P. K. Keel, et al., "Long-Term Outcome of Bulimia Nervosa," *Archives of General Psychiatry,* vol. 56, January 1999). At the final follow-up, 30 percent of the patients still showed symptoms of eating disorders. Eighteen percent were diagnosed with "eating disorder not otherwise specified," 11 percent with bulimia, and 1 percent with anorexia nervosa.

Of the 70 percent in remission, one-third had achieved only partial remission. Patients who had longer periods of symptoms before beginning treatment and those who had a history of substance abuse were less likely to be successful. The results of this study underscore the observation that the earlier the eating disorder is diagnosed and treated, the more likely the patient will recover to a healthy weight.

Too Few Seek or Receive Quality Treatment

Philip Wang and his colleagues at Harvard Medical School sought to determine whether persons with three specific diagnoses—depression, panic disorder, and generalized anxiety disorder—received mental health treatment and the extent to which the treatment they received was consistent with existing guidelines and standards of care. They published the methods, measures, and results of their study in "Recent Care of Common Mental Disorders in the United States: Prevalence and Conformance with Evidence-Based Recommendations" (*Journal of General Internal Medicine,* vol. 15, no. 5, May 2000).

Previous studies found that only a minority of people with active depression and anxiety disorders in the United States had been treated in the year prior to the study, and only a fraction of those treated received care that was deemed adequate. The investigators reviewed the medical records of more than 3,000 patients diagnosed with these mental disorders. Their goal was to assess if they received treatment and, among those who were treated, whether treatment could be considered consistent with evidence-based treatment recommendations. They considered it vitally important to identify the reasons persons with mental disorders receive no care or substandard mental health care.

The investigators reported that while nearly two-thirds of those with depression and anxiety disorders received at least some mental health care in the year prior to the survey, only one-fourth received treatments that could be considered consistent with evidence-based recommendations, even among those with the most serious and impairing mental illness. The factors associated with receiving no mental health care included having less severe mental illness, fewer comorbid physical illnesses, and lacking insurance coverage for mental health visits. Factors associated with receiving treatment that was not consistent with evidence-based recommendations were race and gender—African Americans and males were less likely to receive treatment consistent with established guidelines, as were persons with less serious mental disorders and those without health insurance.

Not All People Need Treatment

The NIMH observes that not all mental health problems require treatment because many people experience relatively brief, self-limiting illnesses that are not disabling enough to warrant treatment. As much as 70 percent of mental illness goes untreated, and many cases are believed to resolve spontaneously. Despite mounting evidence documenting the effectiveness of various forms of mental health treatment, there are those who contend that Americans with minor mental health problems are already too quick to seek pharmaceutical and other treatment to relieve emotional distress. These social commentators believe that reliance on prescription medication prevents people from learning and honing coping, interpersonal, and stress-management skills. Worse, they contend that this overdependence on treatment ultimately renders people less resilient. There is also the concern that too many Americans seek treatment for minor mental health problems because mental health professionals arbitrarily classify behavior that is unusual, but not impaired or dysfunctional, as pathological.

CHAPTER 4
DIAGNOSIS AND MENTAL HEALTH TREATMENT
OF CHILDREN AND ADOLESCENTS

No other illnesses damage so many children so seriously.

—*Blueprint for Change: Research on Child and Adolescent Mental Health*, National Advisory Mental Health Council Workgroup on Child and Adolescent Mental Health Intervention Development and Deployment, National Institute of Mental Health, Washington, D.C., 2001

The 1999 U.S. Surgeon General's comprehensive report on mental health and illness defined mental health in childhood and adolescence as "the achievement of expected developmental cognitive, social, and emotional milestones and by secure attachments, satisfying social relationships, and effective coping skills." The report described mentally healthy children and adolescents as those who function well at home, in school, and in their communities, and are not impaired by symptoms of psychopathology (*Mental Health: A Report of the Surgeon General,* U.S. Department of Health and Human Services, Rockville, MD, 1999).

According to the National Institute of Mental Health (NIMH), more than one-fifth of American children do not enjoy positive mental health—they suffer from mental problems and disorders that interfere with normal development and impair their functioning. Studies of prevalence (occurrence of a condition during a specific period of time) of mental illness, which included mental disorders and addictive disorders, estimate that more than one-fifth (nearly 21 percent) of U.S. children ages 9–17 suffer some degree of impaired functioning resulting from a mental or addictive disorder. (See Figure 4.1 and Table 4.1.) Although the same research found that just 11 percent of this group suffers from significant impairment, this prevalence estimate translates into a staggering 4 million children and teens for whom difficulties at school and with their families and friends are attributable to mental illness.

In any given year, the NIMH estimates that about one in five children suffering from mental illness receives needed treatment. The Surgeon General's report found that about 21 percent of the child and adolescent population

FIGURE 4.1

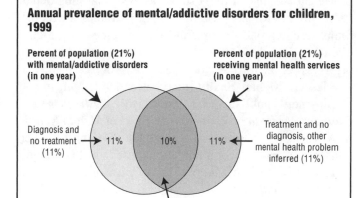

Annual prevalence of mental/addictive disorders for children, 1999

Percent of population (21%) with mental/addictive disorders (in one year)

Percent of population (21%) receiving mental health services (in one year)

Diagnosis and no treatment (11%)

11% 10% 11%

Treatment and no diagnosis, other mental health problem inferred (11%)

Diagnosis and treatment (10%)

SOURCE: David Satcher, "Figure 2-6a. Annual prevalence of mental/addictive disorders for children," in *Mental Health: A Report of the Surgeon General,* U.S. Department of Health and Human Services, Substance Abuse and Mental Health Services Administration, with National Institutes of Health, Rockville, MD, 1999 [Online] http://www.mentalhealth.org/features/surgeongeneralreport/toc.asp [accessed December 18, 2003]

TABLE 4.1

Children and adolescents age 9–17 with mental or addictive disorders, 1999

	%
Anxiety disorders	13.0
Mood disorders	6.2
Disruptive disorders	10.3
Substance use disorders	2.0
Any disorder	20.9

*Disorders include diagnosis-specific impairment and CGAS < or = 70 (mild global impairment)
Note: MECA = Methodology for Epidemiology of Mental Disorders in Children and Adolescents

SOURCE: David Satcher, "Table 3-1. Children and adolescents age 9–17 with mental or addictive disorders, combined MECA sample, 6-month (current) prevalence*," in *Mental Health: A Report of the Surgeon General,* U.S. Department of Health and Human Services, Rockville, MD, 1999

that actually needed care used mental health services annually. Nine percent receive care from the health care sector, and 17 percent receive treatment from the human services sector, chiefly in the school system. (See Figure 4.2.) The magnitude of the problem is daunting enough today, and the World Health Organization (WHO) projects that by the year 2020, the prevalence of mental illness among children will increase by more than 50 percent. The WHO estimates that in less than two decades, neuropsychiatric (mental) disorders will be one of the five most common causes of morbidity (illness), mortality (death), and disability among children throughout the world.

The size and scope of this problem, its potential to have long-term and far-reaching intergenerational consequences, and public attention to childhood mental health prompted several recent research initiatives and reports intended to identify problems and recommend strategies, programs, and services to address them. During 2000 the National Institute of Mental Health (NIMH) established a special subgroup of its National Advisory Mental Health Council to review major research findings on child and adolescent psychiatric disorders over the past decade and to recommend research priorities for the next decade. This Workgroup on Child and Adolescent Mental Health Intervention Development and Deployment published its report, titled *Blueprint for Change: Research on Child and Adolescent Mental Health,* in August 2001, and many of the data, research findings, conclusions, and recommendations cited in this chapter were drawn from this report. The *Report of the Surgeon General's Conference on Children's Mental Health: A National Action Agenda* (Department of Health and Human Services, Department of Justice, and Department of Education, Washington, D.C., 2001) also provided scientific rationales for mental health treatment program planning.

DEVELOPMENT OF PSYCHOPATHOLOGY

The brain shapes behavior, and learning shapes the brain.

—*Mental Health: A Report of the Surgeon General,* Substance Abuse and Mental Health Services Administration and National Institue of Mental Health, 1999

Psychologists and other mental health professionals have long recognized that irregularities in the process of growth, maturation, and development may increase the risk of developing mental illnesses or precipitate mental disorders. The origin of mental illness in children is thought to arise from the interaction of biological, psychological, environmental, and social factors. These factors include genetic susceptibility or predisposition to specific mental disorders, physical development, psychological and emotional maturation, relationships with family and peers, characteristics of the school environment, and immediate community as well as broader societal and cultural considerations. While all of these factors are considered to contribute to mental health and illness, external,

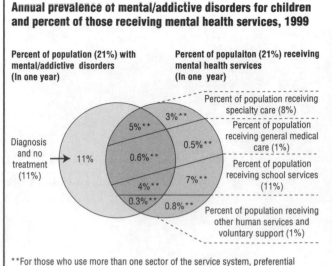

FIGURE 4.2

Annual prevalence of mental/addictive disorders for children and percent of those receiving mental health services, 1999

Percent of population (21%) with mental/addictive disorders (in one year)

Percent of populaiton (21%) receiving mental health services (in one year)

Diagnosis and no treatment (11%) → 11%

5%** | 3%**
0.6%** | 0.5%**
4%** | 7%**
0.3%** | 0.8%**

Percent of population receiving specialty care (8%)

Percent of population receiving general medical care (1%)

Percent of population receiving school services (11%)

Percent of population receiving other human services and voluntary support (1%)

**For those who use more than one sector of the service system, preferential assignment is to the most specialized level of mental health treatment in the system.

SOURCE: David Satcher, "Table 2-6b. Annual prevalence of mental/addictive disorders for children," in *Mental Health: A Report of the Surgeon General,* U.S. Department of Health and Human Services, Substance Abuse and Mental Health Services Administration, with National Institutes of Health, Rockville, MD, 1999 [Online] http://www.mentalhealth.org/features/surgeongeneralreport/toc.asp [accessed December 18, 2003]

environmental factors may make greater contributions to the development of some mental disorders when the disorders represent children's efforts to adapt to unfavorable or severely disturbed environments.

One challenge in identifying behaviors that may be symptoms of mental illness or evaluating the influence of various factors on the development of mental illness in children is the fact that although growth and change occur throughout life, they are occurring most rapidly during childhood and adolescence. Determining age-appropriate behavior or the potential impact of environmental stressors requires close attention to the timing of their appearance. For example, a toddler's temper tantrum might be viewed as normal behavior, whereas similar behavior displayed by an older child might indicate incipient mental illness. Similarly, external factors such as geographic relocation may have greater impact on mental health at various ages. Moving to a new town may have little effect on the preschooler's life, while an adolescent may suffer from the separation from close friends and anxiety about entering a new school. In addition to the ages at which external stressors occur, the broader context in which they occur acts to determine their effect. Disruption across multiple aspects of a child's life, such as simultaneous adjustment to divorce, relocation, and a new school, will naturally have a more profound impact than simply moving to a new home.

Finally, family, societal, and cultural contexts play important roles in distinguishing children's mental health and illness. Psychologists concur that the quality of early relationships with caregivers, usually but not necessarily parents, exerts a powerful influence on the child's development, maturation, and physical and emotional health. Changing social mores and cultural contexts also determine whether behaviors are considered normal or abnormal. For example, until the second half of the 20th century, many Americans believed that ideal children were docile, quiet, obedient, and unquestioning, speaking only when they were addressed. Today children are encouraged and expected to be active, curious, and assertive. In fact, a child displaying the behaviors valued in the early part of the 20th century might even risk being diagnosed as suffering from pathological shyness or social anxiety disorder.

Risk Factors

According to the U.S. Surgeon General's report, identifying the risk factors that increase a child's vulnerability to, or likelihood of developing a specific mental disorder enables researchers and practitioners to understand their origin and helps policy makers and planners develop effective prevention and treatment programs. Most children are flexible and resilient enough to successfully cope with some degree of stress and adverse environmental influences. Others, however, perhaps children with inherited susceptibility to a disorder, may be traumatized by environmental stressors.

Biological influences are thought to contribute to the development of specific mental disorders such as autism (developmental disorders characterized by severely impaired communication and social skills as well as repetitive behaviors), obsessive-compulsive disorder, social phobia, and schizophrenia. Prenatal and postnatal exposures to specific environmental factors may influence the development of the neural systems involved in attention, impulsivity, and disruptive behavior. Biological factors that may impede a child's emotional development or increase the risk of developing a mental disorder include:

- Malnutrition during pregnancy

- Prenatal exposure to drugs, alcohol, and tobacco

- Low birth weight

- Inherited genetic susceptibility to a specific mental disorder

- Inherited temperament—traits such as timidity, anxiety, or distractibility that might predispose to mental illness

- Environmental exposures to toxins such as lead

- Perinatal trauma or traumatic brain injury—physical injury around the time of birth or brain injury sustained early in life

Some investigators theorize that infections that occur in the womb or during infancy may increase risk for, or lead to,

mental illness. Researchers at the Columbia University School of Public Health, the University of California, Irvine, and the University of California, Los Angeles, examined tissue specimens from more than 2,000 patients diagnosed with schizophrenia and bipolar disorder to detect the presence of the Borna virus—a virus that had previously been isolated from human brain tissue. They believe that there may be a link between viral infection and subsequent mental illness, since viruses are known to infect the central nervous system. For example, West Nile virus can cause encephalitis (inflammation of the brain), and the bacterial infection toxoplasmosis has been linked to schizophrenia. Another hypothesis is that it is not the pathogen that precipitates mental illness; rather, it is the pregnant mother's immune response to combat the pathogens that leads to development of mental disorders. These hypotheses are controversial because the presence of the virus does not mean that it is the cause of mental illness (Linda Marsa, "In the Lab Mental Illness Clues," *Los Angeles Times*, September 29, 2003).

Similarly, a variety of psychosocial factors may increase the likelihood of a child developing an antisocial personality disorder, conduct disorder, or behavioral problem. For example, children who suffer physical abuse may be more prone to develop conduct disorders, posttraumatic stress disorders, attention-deficit hyperactivity disorders, and problematic social relationships. In contrast, children who are victims of psychological abuse tend to develop depression, conduct disorders, and problems functioning in school and with peers. Examples of psychosocial risk factors include:

- Troubled or dysfunctional family relationships, including marital discord

- Parents involved in criminal or other antisocial activities

- Overcrowded housing and large family size

- Economic hardship and insecurity

- Exposure to acts of violence or other abuse

- Maltreatment, inadequate care, and inconsistent discipline

- Parents who model behaviors associated with mental illness, such as excessive irritability, depression, anxiety, or suicide attempts

MENTAL DISORDERS IN CHILDREN

Table 4.2 lists the broad categories of mental disorders that begin during childhood and adolescence. Children and teens with mood and anxiety disorders suffer from unfounded fears, prolonged sadness or tearfulness, withdrawal, low self-esteem, and feelings of worthlessness and hopelessness. These youth often display comorbidity—for example, symptoms of depression and anxiety together.

Children who repeatedly get into trouble at school, on the playground, and in other environments with peers may

TABLE 4.2

Selected mental disorders of childhood and adolescence

- Anxiety disorders
- Attention-deficit and disruptive behavior disorders
- Autism and other pervasive developmental disorders
- Eating disorders
- Elimination disorders
- Learning and communication disorders
- Mood disorders (e.g., depressive disorders)
- Schizophrenia
- Tic disorders

SOURCE: David Satcher, "Table 3-2. Selected mental disorders of childhood and adolescence from the DSM-IV," in *Mental Health: A Report of the Surgeon General*, U.S. Department of Health and Human Services, Substance Abuse and Mental Health Services Administration, with National Institutes of Health, Rockville, MD, 1999 [Online] http://www.mentalhealth.org/features/surgeongeneralreport/toc.asp [accessed December 18, 2003]

suffer from behavior disorders. They demonstrate hyperactivity, aggression, defiance, or inattention and may be diagnosed with oppositional defiant disorder, disruptive disorder, or attention-deficit hyperactivity disorder (ADHD). These children also may have comorbid conditions of depression or anxiety, substance abuse, or learning problems.

Children with disorganized thinking and difficulty communicating verbally, and those who have trouble understanding and navigating the world around them may be diagnosed with autism or another pervasive developmental disorder. These disorders may be among the most disabling because they are associated with serious learning difficulties and impaired intelligence. Examples of pervasive developmental disorders include autism, Asperger's disorder, and Rett's disorder.

Detection and understanding of signs and symptoms of mental illness and early intervention with children suffering from mental disorders are associated with improved prognoses. There also is research suggesting that certain disorders predispose or lead to others. Examples of such gateway conditions are oppositional defiant disorder (ODD) as a gateway to conduct disorders, trauma as a gateway to post-traumatic stress disorder (PSTD), and ADHD as a gateway to conduct disorders or substance abuse.

Pervasive Developmental Disorders

Autism is a condition that results from a neurological disorder that typically appears during the first three years of childhood and continues throughout life. It was first described by Dr. Leo Kanner in 1943, who reported on 11 children who displayed an unusual lack of interest in other people but were extremely interested in unusual aspects of the inanimate environment. Autistic children

appear unattached to parents or caregivers, assume rigid or limp body postures when held, suffer impaired language, and exhibit bizarre behavior such as head banging, violent tantrums, and screaming. They are often self-destructive and uncooperative and experience delayed mental and social skills. Autism is associated with a variety of neurological symptoms such as seizures and persistence of reflexes that usually disappear during normal child development. Autism is the most common of the pervasive developmental disorders, and the CDC (Centers for Disease Control and Prevention) estimate that it occurs in as many as 10 to 12 in 10,000 individuals. Its prevalence is four times more frequent in boys than girls. About 75 percent of autistic children also have some degree of mental retardation.

While it was once thought to have psychological origins or occur as the result of bad parenting, both of these hypotheses have been discarded in favor of a biological explanation of causality. Although the cause of autism remains unknown, the disorder has been associated with maternal rubella infection, phenylketonuria (an inherited disorder of metabolism), tuberous sclerosis (an inherited disease of the nervous system and skin), lack of oxygen at birth, and encephalitis. There is evidence of the heritability of autism, since it affects approximately 0.2 percent of children in the general population, but the risk of bearing a second child with autism rises to between 10 and 20 percent. Studies have found that concordance for autism in identical twins is more likely than in fraternal twins or other siblings.

Autism varies from quite mild to quite severe, and the prognosis depends on the extent of the individual's disabilities and whether he or she receives the early, intensive interventions associated with improved outcomes. A diagnosis of "atypical autism" or "pervasive developmental disorder not otherwise specified" (PDD-NOS) is generally used to refer to mild cases of autism or children with impaired social interaction and verbal and nonverbal communication who are not asocial enough to be considered autistic. Treatment of autism is individualized and may include applied behavior analysis, medications (the antipsychotic drug, haloperidol; the tricyclic antidepressant, clomipramine; and the SSRI, fluoxetine), dietary management and supplements, music therapy, occupational therapy, physical therapy, speech and language therapy, and vision therapy.

Asperger's disorder is a milder form of autism and sufferers are sometimes called "high functioning children with autism." Affected children tend to be socially isolated and behave oddly. They have impaired social interactions, are unable to express pleasure in others' happiness, and lack social and emotional reciprocity. They are below average in nonverbal communication, and their speech is marked by peculiar abnormalities of inflection and a repetitive pattern. Unlike in autism, however, cognitive and communicative development is normal or near-normal during the first years of life, and verbal skills are usually relatively strong. Sufferers also have impaired gross motor skills, tend to be clumsy, and may engage in repetitive finger flapping, twisting, or awkward whole-body movements. They usually have very narrow areas of interest that are highly specific, idiosyncratic, and so consuming that they do not pursue age-appropriate activities. Examples of such interests include train schedules, spiders, or telegraph pole insulators.

The disorder is named for the Austrian physician Hans Asperger, who first described it in 1944. About 3 per 1,000 children have Asperger's disorder, and it appears to be more common in boys. The Australian Scale for Asperger's Syndrome is a questionnaire designed to identify behaviors and abilities suggestive of Asperger's syndrome in children during their primary-school years when their unusual behaviors may be most obvious. Affected individuals with higher IQ and high-level social skills have better prognoses. Treatment for those with severe impairments is comparable to therapies prescribed for children with autism.

While it is sometimes mistaken for autism when diagnosed in very young children (and is linked to autism, Asperger's syndrome, ADHD, and schizophrenia), Rett's disorder, also known as Rett's syndrome, is much less prevalent and has a distinctive onset and course. The condition occurs primarily in girls who, after early normal development, experience slower-than-expected head growth in the first months of life and a loss of purposeful hand motions between ages 5 and 30 months. Affected children are usually profoundly mentally retarded and exhibit stereotypical repetitive behaviors such as hand wringing or handwashing. Interest in socialization diminishes during the first few years of the disorder but may resume later in life, despite severe impairment in expressive and receptive language development. Affected individuals experience problems in the coordination of gait or trunk movements, and walking may become difficult.

Rett's disorder is caused by a mutation of the MECP2 gene on the long leg of the X chromosome. Rett's disorder familial studies have found that persons with autism also test positive for the MECP2 mutation. Rett's disorder is the leading cause of severe mental retardation in females, surpassing even Down syndrome. Male fetuses that have the disorder are more severely affected and miscarry or die shortly after birth, usually before the second year. Newborns can be evaluated for the disorder using a genetic test, and researchers are optimistic that when an effective treatment is developed and instituted before the child is six months of age, they will be able to prevent regression from occurring. Absent this promising but as yet undiscovered effective treatment, recovery is limited, although some very modest developmental gains may be made and interest in social interaction may be observed as affected children enter adolescence. Communication and behavioral difficulties usually persist throughout life.

Childhood disintegrative disorder is a rarely occurring and frightening condition that strikes children between the ages of 2 and 10 who have been developing and functioning normally. Over a period of months, affected children regress in many areas, losing previously acquired intellectual, social, and language skills. There may also be loss of bladder and bowel control, loss of motor skills, lack of play, and inability to sustain peer relationships. To date the cause of childhood disintegrative disorder remains unknown, but it has been linked to neurological conditions such as seizures and tuberous sclerosis, a rare disorder primarily characterized by seizures, mental retardation, and skin and eye lesions. Treatment for this disorder is the same as that used for autism, but treatment generally aims only to modify specific behaviors since the loss of functioning is irreversible.

Attention-Deficit Hyperactivity Disorder

The NIMH asserts that attention-deficit hyperactivity disorder is very likely the most studied, diagnosed, and treated childhood-onset (condition that begins or becomes apparent before age 18) mental disorder. There are three subcategories of attention deficit disorder—attention-deficit/hyperactivity disorder: combined type; attention-deficit/hyperactivity disorder: predominantly inattentive; and attention-deficit/hyperactivity disorder: predominantly hyperactive or impulsive.

Attention-deficit hyperactivity disorder (ADHD) is a relatively new name for a psychiatric disorder that usually begins or becomes apparent in preschool and elementary school-aged children. Children with ADHD cannot sit still, have difficulty controlling their impulsive actions, and are unable to focus on projects long enough to complete them. Though teachers originally dubbed ADHD a learning problem, the disorder affects more than simply schoolwork. Children with ADHD have trouble socializing, are often unable to make friends, and suffer from low self-esteem. Left untreated, ADHD can leave children unable to cope academically or socially, and the disorder may progress to depression, conduct disorder, or substance abuse.

The NIMH estimates that more than 4 percent of children aged 9–17 suffer from ADHD, and boys are affected two to three times more frequently than girls. ADHD is frequently comorbid (coexists) with other mental health problems such as substance abuse, anxiety disorders, depression, or antisocial behavior. Children diagnosed with ADHD are usually affected into their teen years, but for most, symptoms subside in adulthood and adults become more adept at controlling their behavior.

Vigilance is warranted, however, because research reveals an increased incidence in juvenile delinquency and subsequent encounters with the criminal justice system among adults who were diagnosed with ADHD in their youth.

The reported incidence of ADHD has increased over the past 20 years, possibly because of better diagnosis, changing expectations, or insufficient supportive social structures. In the absence of clear criteria for ADHD or guidelines by which to diagnose it, researchers fear that the disorder may be underdiagnosed or overdiagnosed. The cause of ADHD is as yet unknown. Factors thought to contribute increase risk of developing the disorder include prenatal toxic exposures and premature birth as well as a family history of school problems, behavioral disorders, or other psychosocial problems. A biological explanation of ADHD arose because its symptoms respond to treatment with stimulants such as methylphenidate, which increase the availability of dopamine—the neurotransmitter that is vital for purposeful movement, motivation, and alertness. This led researchers to theorize that ADHD may be caused by unavailability of dopamine in the central nervous system.

The evidence of a genetic component is inconclusive. There is an increased incidence of ADHD in children with a first-degree relative with ADHD, conduct disorders, antisocial personality, substance abuse, and others, but this observation does not resolve the question of whether nature (genetics) or nurture (family and environmental influences) contributes more strongly to the origins of ADHD. Twin studies have found that when ADHD is present in one twin, it is significantly more likely also to be present in an identical twin than in a fraternal twin. These findings support inheritance as an important risk in a proportion of children with ADHD.

Although imaging studies have revealed differences in the brains of children with ADHD, and scientists have found a link between inability to pay attention and diminished utilization of glucose in parts of the brain, some researchers question whether these changes cause the disorder. They argue that the observed changes may result from the disorder, or simply coexist with it. Today, there are mental health professionals and educators who concede that while some children are legitimately diagnosed with ADHD, others are mislabeled. They speculate that maybe the latter group may be simply high-spirited, undisciplined, or misbehaving.

TREATMENT FOR ADHD. Further controversy about ADHD has focused on its treatment. Prescription stimulants, such as methylphenidate (Ritalin), dextromethamphetamine (Dexedrine), and amphetamine (Adderall), have proven safe and effective for short-term treatment of ADHD. Despite the results of a study of 600 children reported by the NIMH in December 1999 confirming the safety of this treatment, some researchers still question

the wisdom of treatment with potentially addicting, powerful stimulants. Although many health care practitioners offer behavioral therapy along with medication to treat children with ADHD, the NIMH study found that in terms of reducing their levels of inattention, hyperactivity, impulsiveness, and aggression, the children fared better on medication alone than with the combination of medication and behavioral therapy.

Alternatives to drug treatment include therapy techniques such as behavior modification and parent counseling along with modifying the environment to minimize distractions and offering opportunities for one-to-one instruction with teachers. Parental concern about drug treatment of ADHD and intensifying interest in alternative therapies were reported in an article by Benedict Carey, "Focusing on the Mind: Interest Rises in Non-Drug Therapies for Attention Deficit in Children" (*Los Angeles Times*, September 15, 2003). The article cited increased interest in using restrictive diets and nutritional supplements, such as vitamins, iron, zinc, and fatty acids, as well as use of biofeedback to treat children and teens with ADHD.

Use of restrictive or eliminatio diets is based on the notion that food dyes, preservatives, and other additives found in processed foods may cause allergic reactions in susceptible children. Ohio University emeritus professor of psychiatry L. Eugene Arnold estimated that between 5 and 10 percent of children with ADHD might benefit from restrictive diets. Other investigators feel there is no harm experimenting with this alternative therapy provided that parents consider other strategies if the diet fails to improve symptoms. They caution, however, that effective treatment should be actively pursued so that children do not suffer life-altering consequences of the disorder, such as dropping out of school or progressing to an even more disabling mental disorder.

Using electroencephalogram (EEG) technology, researchers have found that persons with ADHD have distinctive patterns of lower frequency wave patterns emanating from the frontal cortexes of their brains. Biofeedback uses EEG technology to teach affected individuals to sharpen their focus and enhance their concentration. Several small studies comparing the use of biofeedback to treatment with methylphenidate (Ritalin) revealed that weekly biofeedback improved symptoms of participants receiving drug treatment as well as those who were not taking drugs, but the results are not conclusive. Detractors question the variable and subjective measures used to assess the effectiveness of biofeedback and wonder whether study participants are simply benefiting from the placebo effect—responding favorably to the attention given them during the biofeedback sessions.

Finally, a 19-year-old college student who was interviewed for the *Los Angeles Times* article offered an entirely different approach to managing her ADHD. Forgoing treatment, she opted to eliminate any free time from her daily schedule by pursuing a variety of school, extracurricular, and volunteer service activities. Setting objectives, using lists, maintaining a strict schedule, and focusing on organization to help her accomplish an ambitious program of activities proved to be a successful behavioral approach to the disorder, one she characterized as working with the ADHD, as opposed to attempting to "change her personality." Therapists grant that this type of intensive, scheduled activity may be beneficial but observe that it requires tremendous discipline as well as family and school support to sustain it.

Depression

The most frequently diagnosed mood disorders in children and adolescents are major depressive disorder, dysthymic disorder, and bipolar disorder. Major depressive disorder is defined as one or more major depressive episodes that in children and adolescents last an average of seven to nine months. Children who are depressed are not unlike their adult counterparts. They may be teary and sad, lose interest in friends and activities, and become listless, self-critical, and hypersensitive to criticism from others. They feel unloved, helpless, and hopeless about the future, and they may think about suicide. Depressed children and adolescents also may be irritable, aggressive, and indecisive. They may have problems concentrating and sleeping and often become careless about their appearance and hygiene. The Surgeon General's report distinguishes childhood depression from adult depression, noting that children display fewer psychotic symptoms, such as hallucinations and delusions, and more anxiety symptoms, such as clinging to parents or unwillingness to go to school. Depressed children also experience more somatic symptoms, such as general aches and pains, stomachaches, and headaches, than adults with depression.

Dysthymic disorder usually begins in childhood or early adolescence and is a chronic but milder depressive disorder with fewer symptoms. The child or adolescent is continuously depressed for months to years. Since the average duration of the disorder is about four years, some children become so accustomed to feeling depressed that they may not identify themselves as depressed or complain about symptoms. Nearly three-quarters of children and adolescents with dysthymic disorder experience at least one major depressive episode in the course of their lives.

Adults and adolescents with bipolar disorder alternate between episodes of mania and episodes of depression. The onset of bipolar illness is usually a depressive episode during adolescence. Manic episodes may not appear for months or even years. During manic episodes adolescents are tireless, overly confident, and tend to have rapid-fire or pressured speech. They may perform tasks and schoolwork quickly and energetically but in a wildly disorganized manner. Manic adolescents may seriously overestimate their capabilities, and the combination of bravado and loosened inhibitions may prompt them to participate in high-risk behaviors, such as vandalism, drug abuse, or unsafe sex.

Reactive depression (formerly termed adjustment disorder with depressed mood) is the most common mental health problem in children and adolescents. It is not considered a mental disorder, and many health professionals consider occasional bouts of reactive depression as entirely consistent with normal adolescent development. It is characterized by transient depressed feelings in response to some negative experience, such as a rejection from a boyfriend or girlfriend or a failing grade. Sadness or listlessness spontaneously resolves in a few hours or may last as long as two weeks. Generally distraction, in the form of a change of activity or setting, helps to improve the mood of affected individuals.

According to the NIMH, until recently, physicians and family members did not recognize depression in children and often attributed mood changes in children and adolescents to a normal process of development. During the past 10 years, there has been increasing recognition that clinical depression occurs in children and adolescents. Recent epidemiological studies suggest that up to 1 percent of preschoolers, 2 percent of schoolchildren, and 8 percent of adolescents may have major depressive disorder. The lifetime risk of major depressive disorder and dysthymia among adolescents has been estimated at about 15 percent, which is comparable to the adult lifetime risk.

Prepubescent girls and boys are equally likely to experience major depression and dysthymic disorder, but from 10 to 14 years of age, girls outpace boys, soon reaching the two-to-one ratio observed among adults. Depression in young people often is comorbid with anxiety and behavioral problems and predicts continued and possibly more severe depression in adulthood. Depression also increases the risk for substance abuse and is a major risk factor for suicide. The incidence of suicide attempts peaks during adolescence. Mortality from suicide increases through the teens and is the third leading cause of death among adolescents and young adults.

Anxiety Disorders

Taken together, the different types of anxiety disorders—separation anxiety disorder, generalized anxiety disorder (GAD), social phobia, and obsessive-compulsive disorder—constitute the mental disorders most prevalent among children and adolescents. According to the Surgeon General's report, 13 percent of children ages 9 to 17 suffer from some form of anxiety disorder. (See Table 4.1.)

Separation anxiety is normal among infants, toddlers, and very young children. For example, nearly every child experiences at least a momentary pang of separation anxiety on the first day of preschool or kindergarten. When this condition occurs in older children or adolescents and it is severe enough to impair social, academic, or job functioning for at least one month, it is considered separation anxiety disorder. The risk factors associated with social anxiety disorder include stress, such as the illness or death of a family member, geographic relocation, and physical or sexual assault.

Children with separation anxiety may be clingy, and often they harbor fears that accidents or natural disasters will forever separate them from their parents. Since they fear being apart from their parents, they may resist attending school or going anywhere without a parent. Separation anxiety can produce physical symptoms such as dizziness, nausea, or palpitations. It is often associated with symptoms of depression. Young children may have difficulties falling asleep alone in their rooms and may have recurrent nightmares.

Children suffering from social anxiety disorder (also known as social phobia) worry excessively about being embarrassed in social situations. Although the degree to which social anxiety disorder debilitates affected children and teens varies, many are unable to speak in class, enter into conversation with peers, or eat, drink, or write in public. The anxiety produces symptoms such as blushing, palpitations, sweating, and diarrhea. Young children may not be able to verbally express their fears but may cry, cling, or avoid contact with others. Reluctant to attend school and unable to socialize with peers, affected children may suffer from low self-esteem, viewing themselves as academic and social failures. The disorder affects more girls than boys. While it may become less severe or completely resolve over time, most sufferers are affected to some degree throughout their lives.

Obsessive-compulsive disorder (OCD) often begins during childhood or adolescence. It is an anxiety disorder marked by recurrent obsessive or compulsive behaviors that are distressing and may impair functioning. Obsessions may be repetitive disturbing images, thoughts, or impulses and compulsions such as handwashing or ritualistically checking and rechecking doors and windows. These behaviors are attempts to dislodge the obsessive thoughts. There is evidence from twin studies of both genetic susceptibility and environmental influences. When one twin has OCD, the other twin is more likely to have OCD if the children are identical twins rather than fraternal twins. There is also increased incidence of the disorder among first-degree relatives of children with OCD. Researchers do not think that OCD is a learned behavior—that the affected child is mimicking the family member's behavior—because children with OCD tend to display different symptoms from those of relatives with the disease.

According to the Surgeon General's report, research suggests that some children develop OCD following an infection with a specific type of streptococcus. This condition is known as Pediatric Autoimmune Neuropsychiatric Disorders Associated with Streptococcal infections (PANDAS). It is believed that antibodies intended to combat the strep infection mistakenly attack a region of the brain and trigger an inflammatory reaction, which in turn leads to development of OCD. Selective serotonin reuptake inhibitors (SSRIs) are effective in reducing or even eliminating the symptoms of OCD in many affected children and adolescents. However, side effects such as dry mouth, sleepiness, dizziness, fatigue, tremors, and constipation are common and may themselves impair functioning.

Disruptive Disorders

Children and adolescents with disruptive disorders, which include oppositional defiant disorder and conduct disorder, display antisocial behaviors. Like separation anxiety, the diagnosis of a disruptive disorder largely depends on assessing whether behavior is age appropriate. For example, just as clinging may be considered normal for a toddler but abnormal behavior in an older child, toddlers and very young children often behave aggressively—grabbing toys and even biting one another. When, however, an child older than five displays such aggressive behavior, it may indicate an emerging oppositional defiant or conduct disorder.

It is important to distinguish isolated acts of aggression or the normal childhood and adolescent phases of testing limits from the pattern of ongoing, persistent defiance, hostility, and disobedience that is the hallmark of oppositional defiant disorder (ODD). Children with ODD are argumentative, lose their tempers, refuse to adhere to rules, blame others for their own mistakes, and are spiteful and vindictive. Their behaviors often alienate them from family and peers and cause problems at school.

Family strife, volatile marital relationships, frequently changing caregivers, and inconsistent child-rearing practices may increase risk for the disorder. Some practitioners consider oppositional defiant disorder a gateway condition to conduct disorder. According to the Surgeon General's report, estimates of the prevalence of ODD range from 1 to 6 percent, depending on the population and the way the disorder was evaluated. Rates are lower when impairment criteria are stricter and information is obtained from teachers and parents rather than from the children alone. Prepubescent boys are diagnosed more often with ODD than girls of the same age, but after puberty the rates in both genders are equal.

Children or adolescents with conduct disorder are aggressive. They may fight, sexually assault, or behave cruelly to people or animals. Since lying, stealing, vandalism, truancy, and substance abuse are common behaviors, adults, social service agencies, and the criminal justice system often view affected young people as "bad" rather than mentally ill. The American Academy of Child and Adolescent Psychiatry describes an array of generally antisocial behaviors that when exhibited by children or adolescents suggest a diagnosis of conduct disorder. These actions and behaviors include:

- bullies, threatens, or intimidates others

- often initiates physical fights

- uses a weapon such as a bat, brick, knife, or gun that could cause serious physical harm

- physically cruel to people or animals

- steals from a victim while confronting them

- engages in coercive or forced sexual activity

- deliberately sets fires with the intention to cause damage

- deliberately destroys others' property

- breaks into a building, house, or car

- lies to obtain goods, or favors or to avoid obligations

- steals items without confronting a victim

- often stays out at night despite parental objections

- runs away from home

- often truant from school

Conduct disorder severely compromises the lives of affected children and adolescents. Their schoolwork suffers, as do their relationships with adults and peers. The Surgeon General's report found that youths with conduct disorders have higher rates of injury and sexually transmitted diseases (STDs) and are likely to be expelled from school and have problems with the law. Rates of depression, suicidal thoughts, suicide attempts, and suicide are all higher in children and teens diagnosed with conduct disorders. Children in whom the disorder presents before age 10 are predominantly male. Early onset places them at greater risk for adult antisocial personality disorder. More than one-quarter of severely antisocial children become antisocial adults.

The origins of conduct disorder have not been pinpointed, but, like other mental disorders, it is probably caused by some combination of biological and psychosocial factors. Psychosocial risk factors for conduct disorder include maternal rejection, separation from parents with no surrogate caregiver, early institutionalization, family neglect, abuse or violence, parental marital conflict, large family size, overcrowding, and poverty. In these circumstances children may lack feelings of attachment to their parents or families, and later, to the community. Eventually they express these feelings of alienation by behaving with disregard for societal rules and values. Some mental health practitioners describe affected individuals as appearing to lack a moral compass.

Since one risk factor for conduct disorder is a family history of mental illness, especially parents with serious mental disorders, some researchers believe the etiology (the origin or cause of a problem, disorder, or disease)of the disorder is largely genetic. Other biological and physical factors also increase risk, including neurological damage caused by birth complications or low birth weight, ADHD, fearlessness and stimulation-seeking behavior, learning impairments, and insensitivity to physical pain and punishment. Investigators endeavoring to identify the causes of disruptive disorders and other mental disorders theorize that abuse and neglect may affect brain cell survival, neuron density, and neurochemical aspects of brain development, as well as the way people react to stress in childhood and later life. Because risk factors for conduct disorder surface during the first years of life, early screening to identify risk factors and signs of conduct disorder in young children is imperative to ensure prompt intervention.

To date there are no medications that have proven effective in treating conduct disorder. While psychosocial interventions can reduce their antisocial behavior, living with a child or teen with a conduct disorder stresses the entire family. Support programs train parents how to positively reinforce appropriate behaviors and how to strengthen the emotional bonds between parent and child. Identifying and intervening with high-risk children to enhance their social interaction and prevent academic failure can mitigate some of the potentially harmful long-term consequences of conduct disorder.

TREATMENT AND SERVICES

Children and adolescents suffering from mental illness receive many of the same treatments, such as psychotherapy and psychotropic medications, that are prescribed for adults. There are, however, treatments such as play therapy that are used almost exclusively with young children. Play is widely acknowledged as being beneficial to children's emotional development and well-being, and it also has demonstrated therapeutic value. Play therapy uses a variety of play and creative arts techniques to address chronic, mild, and moderate psychological and emotional conditions in children that are causing behavioral problems. Play therapists form short- to medium-term therapeutic relationships and often work holistically and systemically, evaluating and often assisting children to interact more effectively with their social environments—peers, siblings, family, and school.

The kinds of psychotherapy originally intended for adults—supportive, psychodynamic, cognitive-behavioral, interpersonal, and family systems therapy—have been modified for use with children and adolescents. According to the Surgeon General's report, most psychotherapies are considered effective for children and adolescents because those who receive them show more improvement than those who do not. However, there has been little research to determine which therapies are best applied to specific conditions or disorders. The report decried the lack of well-controlled studies of each type of psychotherapy for each disorder, but concluded that psychotherapy is valuable. This is especially true for children unable to tolerate medication, for conditions for which there are no medications with demonstrated efficacy, and to relieve family stress resulting from a child's mental disorder.

Prescribing Psychoactive Medication to Children

In a publication aimed at parents of children with a range of mental disorders (*Questions & Answers: Treatment of Children with Mental Disorders,* Department of Health and Human Services, National Institute of Mental Health, Bethesda, MD, 2000), the NIMH acknowledged public concern that psychotropic medication is being prescribed to very young children and that the safety and efficacy of most psychotropic medications have not yet been established. Several widely used drugs have not received FDA (U.S. Food and Drug Administration) approval for use in young children simply because there are not enough data to support their use.

The data are lacking because historically there were ethical concerns about involving children in clinical trials to determine not only the most effective treatments but also proper dosage, potential side effects, and the long-term effects of drug use on learning and development. Policies about research involving children affect the FDA approval process and recommendations for use. For example, methylphenidate (Ritalin) is approved for use in children age six and older, but its use was not evaluated in children younger than age six. In contrast, dextromethamphetamine (Dexedrine) received approval for use in children as young as three because by the time approval was sought, study guidelines permitted participation of younger children. Table 4.3 lists the brand and generic names of medications in four major classes of drugs used to treat mental disorders in children and adolescents and indicates the ages at which drug use is approved.

Since the FDA approval process often requires years of research to demonstrate safety and efficacy, and practitioners are eager to provide symptom relief for severely troubled children, many recommend off-label use of medications. Off-label treatment may involve use of a medication that has not yet received official FDA approval for use in children or the use of a drug the FDA has approved for children to treat a specific condition for which its use has not been approved. The NIMH *Blueprint for Change: Research on Child and Adolescent Mental Health* (Washington, D.C., 2001) found that three-quarters of all drugs approved by the FDA for adult use have not been approved for use in children. As such, they are prescribed off-label when used in pediatric and adolescent medicine. The NIMH observes that some off-label use is supported

TABLE 4.3

Medications chart for children with mental disorders, 2000

Brand name	Generic name	Approved age
Stimulant medications		
Adderall	amphetamines	3 and older
Concerta	methylphenidate	6 and older
Cylert*	pemoline	6 and older
Dexedrine	dextroamphetamine	3 and older
Dextrostat	dextroamphetamine	3 and older
Ritalin	methylphenidate	6 and older
Antidepressant and antianxiety medications		
Anafranil	clomipramine (for OCD)	10 and older
BuSpar	buspirone	18 and older
Effexor	venlafaxine	18 and older
Luvox (SSRI)	fluvoxamine (for OCD)	8 and older
Paxil (SSRI)	paroxetine	18 and older
Prozac (SSRI)	fluoxetine	18 and older
Serzone (SSRI)	nefazodone	18 and older
Sinequan	doxepin	12 and older
Tofranil	imipramine (for bed-wetting)	6 and older
Wellbutrin	bupropion	18 and older
Zoloft (SSRI)	sertraline (for OCD)	6 and older
Antipsychotic medications		
Clozaril (atypical)	clozapine	18 and older
Haldol	haloperidol	3 and older
Risperdal (atypical)	risperidone	18 and older
Seroquel (atypical)	quetiapine	18 and older
(generic only)	thioridazine	2 and older
Zyprexa (atypical)	olanzapine	18 and older
Orap	pimozide	12 and older (for Tourette's syndrome). Data for age 2 and older indicate similar safety profile.
Mood stabilizing medications		
Cibalith-S	lithium citrate	12 and older
Depakote	divalproex sodium (for seizures)	2 and older
Eskalith	lithium carbonate	12 and older
Lithobid	lithium carbonate	12 and older
Tegretol	carbamazepine (for seizures)	any age

*Due to its potential for serious side effects affecting the liver, Cylert should not ordinarily be considered as first line drug therapy for ADHD (Attention Deficit Hyperactivity Disorder).
Note: OCD = Obsessive-compulsive disorder

SOURCE: "Medications Chart," in *Questions & Answers: Treatment of Children with Mental Disorders,* U.S. Department of Health and Human Services, National Institute of Mental Health, Bethesda, MD, September 2000

by data from well-controlled studies, but cautions that other off-label prescribing, particularly to very young children whose responses to these drugs have not been scrutinized, should be performed prudently.

The Surgeon General's report found strong support for the safety and efficacy of several classes of agents for several conditions, specifically, SSRIs for childhood/adolescent obsessive-compulsive disorder, and psychostimulants for ADHD. The report lamented the lack of information about the safety and efficacy of other psychotropics and urged researchers to produce data for SSRIs, mood stabilizers, and new antipsychotics, since

TABLE 4.4

Grading the level of evidence for efficacy of psychotropic drugs in children, 1999

Category	Indication	Short-term efficacy	Long-term efficacy	Short-term safety	Long-term safety	Estimated frequency of use — Rank
Stimulants	Attention deficit/hyperactivity disorder (ADHD)	A	B	A	A	1
Selective Serotonin Reuptake Inhibitors	Major depression	B	C	A	C	
	Obsessive-compulsive disorder (OCD)	A	C	A	C	2
	Anxiety disorders	C	C	C	C	
Central Adrenergic Agonists	Tourette syndrome	B	C	B	C	
	Attention deficit/hyperactivity disorder (ADHD)	C	C	C	C	3
Valporoate and Carbamazepine	Bipolar disorders	C	C	A	A	
	Aggressive conduct	C	C	A	A	4
Tricyclic Antidepressants	Major depression	C	C	B	B	
	Attention deficit/hyperactivity disorder (ADHD)	B	C	B	B	5
Benzodiazepines	Anxiety disorders	C	C	C	C	6
Antipsychotics	Childhood schizophrenia and psychoses	B	C	C	B	
	Tourette syndrome	A	C	B	B	7
Lithium	Bipolar disorders	B	C	B	C	
	Aggressive conduct	B	C	C	C	8

Key: A = ≥ 2 randomized controlled trials (RCTs).
B = At least 1 RCT.
C = Clinical opinion, case reports, and uncontrolled trials.

SOURCE: David Satcher, "Figure 3-2. Grading the Level of Evidence for Efficacy of Psychotropic Drugs in Children," in *Mental Health: A Report of the Surgeon General*, U.S. Department of Health and Human Services, Substance Abuse and Mental Health Services Administration, with National Institutes of Health, Rockville, MD, 1999 [Online] http://www.mentalhealth.org/features/surgeongeneralreport/toc.asp [accessed December 18, 2003]

these medications appear to be high on the growing list of psychotropic medications used to treat children and adolescents. Table 4.4 offers letter grades that rate the short- and long-term safety and efficacy of eight classes of drugs used to treat specific mental disorders in children.

The NIMH publication advises parents that medication should be prescribed when the potential benefits of treatment outweigh the risks. When children are prescribed psychotropic medication, it is imperative that caregivers—parents, teachers, coaches, and others who regularly interact the child—actively monitor behavior and overall health. Children should be observed and questioned about the appearance, duration, and severity of side effects, because many children, especially younger ones, do not readily volunteer information. Caregivers also must monitor children to ensure that medication is taken as prescribed—the proper dosage on the correct schedule. Finally, the NIMH reiterates that in some instances, delaying drug treatment may compromise its efficacy and warns that untreated, some problems may be so severe and have such potentially damaging consequences that medication, even with its known risks, is warranted.

Does Gender Influence Treatment?

There are documented differences in the medical and mental health care and treatment of adults based on gender. Generally studies have found that women are less likely to be diagnosed with medical conditions such as cardiovascular disease but more likely to be diagnosed with anxiety and depressive disorders. In contrast, research has revealed that among children and adolescents, boys are more likely than girls to be diagnosed with a mental disorder in primary-care settings such as physicians' offices and clinics. They also are more likely to receive specialized mental health services.

William Gardener and his colleagues from the University of Pittsburgh and the University of Vermont Departments of Pediatrics were interested in finding out whether a child's gender influenced the diagnosis and treatment of mental health problems by primary-care practitioners—family practitioners, pediatricians, and nurse practitioners. The investigators also wondered whether boys and girls with similar profiles of mental health symptoms were equally likely to receive mental health treatment, regardless of whether primary-care practitioners had identified them as having a problem. They collected and analyzed data from more than 21,000 child visits in 204 primary-care practices and reported their findings in "Child Sex Differences in Primary Care Clinicians' Mental Health Care of Children and Adolescents" (*Archives of Pediatrics & Adolescent Medicine,* vol. 156, no. 5, May 2002).

The investigators found significant differences in primary-care practitioners' identification of boys and girls with similar parent-reported symptoms. These disparities in the identification of mental health problems produced differences in their treatment. Specifically, primary-care clinicians were more likely to find behavior or conduct problems and attention-deficit/hyperactivity problems in boys than girls. Boys were more likely to receive counseling, medication, or a referral to a specialist than girls, and practitioners were more likely to prescribe medication for boys than for girls. The medication difference was almost entirely attributable to the more frequent diagnosis of ADHD among boys, because stimulants were the only psychotropic medications prescribed by the primary-care practitioners.

While the research did not address whether either gender was under- or overdiagnosed or treated, it did reveal some gender bias in the identification of mental health problems in children. The investigators suggested that the higher rates of ADHD or behavior or conduct problems in boys might be due to the widespread understanding that these are stereotypically boys' problems. The bias also may have resulted from how parents described these children in terms of the severity of their symptoms or the urgency for treatment. The investigators concluded that "to remedy the disparities in the finding and treatment of children's mental health problems, we need to consider how to improve both the screening and identification processes used and communication between parents and clinicians about these issues."

Determining the Efficacy of Treatment

In the past decade there has been a move toward ensuring that medical care and mental health treatment are evidence-based—grounded in the best scientific knowledge available. Outpatient treatment using psychosocial interventions has been identified as efficacious for conditions such as ADHD, anxiety, oppositional-defiant disorder, conduct disorder, and depression. There also is growing evidence of the benefits of specific community-based, as opposed to institutional, interventions. Examples include case management, which involves close attention, coordination, and supervision of the affected child's treatment, academic progress, and living situation; intensive home-based services aimed at preventing unnecessary out-of-home placement (inpatient treatment, residential care, or foster care); and therapeutic foster care, which entails relocating the child to an environment more conducive to recovery.

Barbara Burns and her colleagues conducted an exhaustive review of the literature assessing the effectiveness of mental health treatment for children and their families in the United States and published the results in "Effective Treatment for Mental Disorders in Children and Adolescents" (*Clinical Child and Family Psychology Review,* vol. 2, no. 4, December 1999). The authors report that "the strongest evidence base supportive of positive outcomes for children and families exists for five forms of

services and treatments: home-based services, therapeutic foster care, some forms of case management, and both pharmaceutical and psychosocial treatments for specific syndromes." They also cited family involvement as a vital component and predictor of treatment efficacy.

Intensive home-based services, also known as family preservation services because they are intended to support families to reunite and remain intact, are provided by mental health, child welfare, and juvenile justice systems. The specific home-based services provided may include evaluation, assessment, counseling, skills training, and case management—coordination of services. According to the Surgeon General's report, family preservation services succeed because services are delivered in the community setting; family members collaborate to define the services; backup services are available 24 hours a day; and training provided is in response to the needs of individual family members. In addition, family preservation programs offer marital and family interventions and case management to ensure efficient coordination of care. Many programs also offer tangible assistance such as food, housing, and clothing.

Elizabeth Farmer and her colleagues assessed the outcomes and overall effectiveness of treatment for disruptive disorders and ADHD in "Review of the Evidence Base for Treatment of Childhood Psychopathology: Externalizing Disorders" (*Journal of Consulting and Clinical Psychology,* vol. 70, no. 6, December 2002). The investigators reported positive outcomes for a variety of interventions, particularly parent training and community-based interventions for disruptive behavior disorders and medication for treatment of ADHD.

A review of available research in the National Advisory Mental Health Council Workgroup on Child and Adolescent Mental Health Intervention Development and Deployment publication *Blueprint for Change: Research on Child and Adolescent Mental Health* (National Institute of Mental Health, Washington, D.C., 2001) concluded that some treatments are ineffective and some may even be harmful. For example, the gains made in some forms of residential treatment are not sustained once the child or adolescent returns to the community. Boot camps, some of which promise to rescue struggling teens from self-destructive behaviors using military-style discipline, and residential services for delinquent juveniles are considered largely ineffective. In fact, peer-group-based interventions actually may increase behavioral problems in high-risk adolescents.

The NIMH blueprint called for more psychosocial treatment programs to address potentially life-threatening conditions, such as suicide and eating disorders, along with research on treating serious mental illness with psychopharmacology. It also exhorted scientists and mental health practitioners to recognize the lack of connection between basic science (neurobiology and behavioral science) and the design of clinical interventions. It urged investigators to undertake research about relatively understudied conditions, such as bipolar disorder, autism, neglect, physical and sexual abuse, and early-onset schizophrenia.

Today, mental health researchers, policy makers, and practitioners observe that mental health treatment of children and teens is shifting from clinic-based models toward patient-centered family care delivered in the community-based systems of care such as home- and school-based services. Investigators and practitioners concur that interventions must be developed and deployed that combine and respond to scientific, social, cultural, and community perspectives. In view of the urgent need to disseminate information, educate, and provide timely intervention, researchers should consider the potential benefits of providing treatment and support services using new technology—via telephone and the Internet—to reach children and adolescents along with their parents, caregivers, and teachers.

CHAPTER 5
ACCESS TO MENTAL HEALTH TREATMENT AND PATIENT ISSUES

All Americans do not share equally in the hope for recovery from mental illness.

—*Mental Health: Culture, Race, and Ethnicity—A Supplement to Mental Health: A Report of the Surgeon General*, U.S. Department of Health and Human Services, Rockville, MD, 2001

One of the fundamental challenges of mental health service delivery is access to timely, appropriate care and treatment. There is no single, organized mental health system in the United States, and care of persons with mental illness often involves a wide range of institutional, community, and social support services. Therefore, access is more than simply the availability of medical or psychiatric diagnosis, medication, therapy, and case management. In the context of mental health, access to care also involves the availability of education, housing, transportation, employment, and peer and family support services.

Another challenge is accurately assessing the extent of unmet needs for mental health treatment and the barriers to access. On April 29, 2002, President George W. Bush launched the President's New Freedom Commission on Mental Health to research and recommend ways to improve access to effective mental health treatment for Americans. After only six months, the commission submitted an interim report on October 29, 2002, detailing some of the problems it uncovered. In a letter to President Bush, Michael F. Hogan, the commission's chairman, decried the present fragmented mental health delivery system:

> Our review for this interim report leads us to the united belief that America's mental health service delivery system is in shambles. We have found that the system needs dramatic reform because it is incapable of efficiently delivering and financing effective treatments—such as medications, psychotherapies, and other services—that have taken decades to develop. Responsibility for these services is scattered among agencies, programs, and levels of government. There are so many programs operating under such different rules that it is often impossible for families and consumers to find the care

that they urgently need. The efforts of countless skilled and caring professionals are frustrated by the system's fragmentation. As a result, too many Americans suffer needless disability, and millions of dollars are spent unproductively in a dysfunctional service system that cannot deliver the treatments that work so well.

On July 22, 2003, the commission presented its final report, *Achieving the Promise: Transforming Mental Health Care in America,* with a letter to the President that concluded:

> The time has long passed for yet another piecemeal approach to mental health reform. Instead, the Commission recommends a fundamental transformation of the Nation's approach to mental health care. This transformation must ensure that mental health services and supports actively facilitate recovery, and build resilience to face life's challenges. Too often, today's system simply manages symptoms and accepts long-term disability. Building on the principles of the New Freedom Initiative, the recommendations we propose can improve the lives of millions of our fellow citizens now living with mental illnesses. The benefits will be felt across America in families, communities, schools, and workplaces.

The final report contained six overarching goals and the commission's proposed strategies and recommendations about how to realize these goals in order to effectively transform mental health care in the United States. Broadly speaking, the goals relate to access to mental health services and patient issues such as the acceptability, quality, and effectiveness of mental health care. For example, achievement of the first goal, to improve Americans' understanding that mental health is vital for overall health, would doubtless improve access by reducing the stigma associated with seeking treatment for mental illness. The second goal, of delivering consumer and family-driven care, would also act to improve access by offering care that is more acceptable to consumers and less likely to infringe on the rights of persons with mental illnesses. Goals 3 and 6—eliminating disparities in mental health services and using technology to reach underserved populations—are clear moves to improve access. Goals 4 and 5 address the quality and effectiveness of mental health care; however, they too directly affect access by improving screening and detection of mental illness and expanding the workforce that provides mental health and support services. (See Table 5.1.)

MENTAL HEALTH SERVICE UTILIZATION

Access to care relies in part on the availability of institutional and organizational resources. The overall number of mental health organizations increased between 1986 and 1998, from 4,747 to 5,722. However, also during this period the number of state and county mental hospitals declined from 285 to 229. This resulted in a commensurate decline in the number of beds, from 111.7 per 100,000 persons in 1986 to 99.1 per 100,000 in 1998. (See Table 5.2.)

As the number of state and mental hospital beds declined, nonfederal general hospital psychiatric services increased, as did residential treatment services for emotionally disturbed children and other mental health organizations providing ambulatory (less than 24-hour care) services. (See Table 5.3.)

Rates of discharge from nonfederal short-stay hospitals for diagnoses of serious mental illness rose from 1990 to 2000. The greatest increases were among young men and women. The discharge rate for men aged 18 to 44 rose from 3.4 per 1,000 in 1990 to 5.4 per 1,000 in 2000. For women aged 18 to 44 it increased from 3.7 per 1,000 to 5.4 per 1,000. (See Table 5.4.)

As nonfederal short-stay hospital discharges for serious mental illness among men aged 18 to 44 increased by more than 60 percent from 1990 to 2000, the average length of stay (ALOS) for these admissions declined from 13.8 days in 1990 to 8.2 in 2000. The increase was even greater among men aged 45 to 64—more than twice as many persons with a serious mental illness diagnosis were discharged in 2000 than had been in 1990, as this group also experienced reduced ALOS. Less dramatic increases in rates of hospitalization for serious mental illness were observed among older men, although men aged 65 to 74 and those 75 and older had the longest ALOS—more than 11 days. (See Table 5.5.)

Women aged 18 to 44 had the most hospitalizations for serious mental illness throughout the decade, though their ALOS declined sharply from 14.8 days in 1990 to 7.6 days in 2000. Fewer women in the 65–74 age range were hospitalized with serious mental illness as the first-listed diagnosis, but those who were had the longest ALOS— 16.3 days in 1990 and 11.7 in 2000. This even surpassed those older than 75, whose length of stay dropped dramatically, from 18.7 to 10.5 days. (See Table 5.5.)

TABLE 5.1

Goals and recommendations for a transformed mental health system

GOAL 1 **Americans understand that mental health is essential to overall health.**

| Recommendations | 1.1 | Advance and implement a national campaign to reduce the stigma of seeking care and a national strategy for suicide prevention. |
| | 1.2 | Address mental health with the same urgency as physical health. |

GOAL 2 **Mental health care is consumer and family driven.**

Recommendations	2.1	Develop an individualized plan of care for every adult with a serious mental illness and child with a serious emotional disturbance.
	2.2	Involve consumers and families fully in orienting the mental health system toward recovery.
	2.3	Align relevant federal programs to improve access and accountability for mental health services.
	2.4	Create a Comprehensive State Mental Health Plan.
	2.5	Protect and enhance the rights of people with mental illnesses.

GOAL 3 **Disparities in mental health services are eliminated.**

| Recommendations | 3.1 | Improve access to quality care that is culturally competent. |
| | 3.2 | Improve access to quality care in rural and geographically remote areas. |

GOAL 4 **Early mental health screening, assessment, and referral to services are common practice.**

Recommendations	4.1	Promote the mental health of young children.
	4.2	Improve and expand school mental health programs.
	4.3	Screen for co-occurring mental and substance use disorders and link with integrated treatment strategies.
	4.4	Screen for mental disorders in primary health care, across the life span, and connect to treatment and supports.

GOAL 5 **Excellent mental health care is delivered and research is accelerated.**

Recommendations	5.1	Accelerate research to promote recovery and resilience, and ultimately to cure and prevent mental illnesses.
	5.2	Advance evidence-based practices using dissemination and demonstration projects and create a public-private partnership to guide their implementation.
	5.3	Improve and expand the workforce providing evidence-based mental health services and supports.
	5.4	Develop the knowledge base in four understudied areas: mental health disparities, long-term effects of medications, trauma, and acute care.

GOAL 6 **Technology is used to access mental health care and information.**

| Recommendations | 6.1 | Use health technology and telehealth to improve access and coordination of mental health care, especially for Americans in remote areas or in underserved populations. |
| | 6.2 | Develop and implement integrated electronic health record and personal health information systems. |

SOURCE: "Goals and Recommendations in a Transformed Mental Health System," in *Achieving the Promise: Transforming Mental Health Care in America*, President's New Freedom Commission On Mental Health, Rockville, MD, 2003

TABLE 5.2

Mental health organizations and beds for 24-hour hospital and residential treatment according to type of organization, selected years 1986–98

Type of organization	1986	1990	1992	1994[1]	1998[1]
	Number of mental health organizations				
All organizations	4,747	5,284	5,498	5,392	5,722
State and county mental hospitals	285	273	273	256	229
Private psychiatric hospitals	314	462	475	430	348
Non-Federal general hospital psychiatric services	1,351	1,674	1,616	1,612	1,707
Department of Veterans Affairs medical centers[2]	139	141	162	161	145
Residential treatment centers for emotionally disturbed children	437	501	497	459	461
All other organizations[3]	2,221	2,233	2,475	2,474	2,832
	Number of beds				
All organizations	267,613	272,253	270,867	290,604	266,729
State and county mental hospitals	119,033	98,789	93,058	81,911	63,769
Private psychiatric hospitals	30,201	44,871	43,684	42,399	34,154
Non-federal general hospital psychiatric services	45,808	53,479	52,059	52,984	55,145
Department of Veterans Affairs medical centers[2]	26,874	21,712	22,466	21,146	13,742
Residential treatment centers for emotionally disturbed children	24,547	29,756	30,089	32,110	33,997
All other organizations[3]	21,150	23,646	29,511	60,054	65,922
	Beds per 100,000 civilian population				
All organizations	111.7	111.6	107.5	112.1	99.1
State and county mental hospitals	49.7	40.5	36.9	31.6	23.7
Private psychiatric hospitals	12.6	18.4	17.3	16.4	12.7
Non-federal general hospital psychiatric services	19.1	21.9	20.7	20.4	20.5
Department of Veterans Affairs medical centers[2]	11.2	8.9	8.9	8.2	5.1
Residential treatment centers for emotionally disturbed children	10.3	12.2	11.9	12.4	12.6
All other organizations[3]	8.8	9.7	11.7	23.2	24.6

[1]Beginning in 1994 data for supportive residential clients (moderately staffed housing arrangements such as supervised apartments, group homes, and halfway houses) are included in the totals and all other organizations.
[2]Includes Department of Veterans Affairs (VA) neuropsychiatric hospitals, VA general hospital psychiatric services, and VA psychiatric outpatient clinics.
[3]Includes freestanding psychiatric outpatient clinics, partial care organizations, and multiservice mental health organizations.

SOURCE: P. N. Pastor, D. M. Makuc, C. Reuben, and H. Xia, "Table 108. Mental health organizations and beds for 24-hour hospital and residential treatment according to type of organization: United States, selected years 1986–98," in *Health United States, 2002 with Chartbook on Trends in the Health of Americans*, Centers for Disease Control and Prevention, National Center for Health Statistics, Hyattsville, MD, 2002

Of the six diagnoses that accounted for more than 1 million hospital discharges in 2000, the 1.4 million hospitalizations for psychoses (among the most serious mental disorders) had the longest ALOS, exceeding hospital stays for malignant neoplasms (cancer). (See Table 5.5.)

Among men ages 18–44, hospital admission for alcohol and drug treatment was more frequent than hospitalization for serious mental illness. For all other persons rates of hospital discharge were higher for serious mental illness than substance abuse, and ALOS for alcohol and drug treatment was shorter by as much as 50 percent. (See Table 5.5.)

Unmet Needs

The final report of the President's New Freedom Commission cited estimates that between 5 and 7 percent of adults and a similar percentage of children suffer from serious mental illness. These rates translate into millions of affected Americans, about half of whom receive needed mental health treatment. Even those who seek mental health treatment may find it is unavailable, especially in rural areas; is inadequate in terms of quality or scope of available services; or is unaffordable.

BARRIERS TO ACCESS

The report of the President's New Freedom Commission identified five barriers to care within the mental health system:

- Fragmentation and gaps in care for children—Programs to meet the needs of children are uneven, and vary in terms of eligibility, setting, and treatment philosophy. Lack of coordination and follow-through often result in children slipping through the cracks. Such children are at risk for school failure, substance abuse, juvenile delinquency, and suicide.

- Fragmentation and gaps in care for adults with serious mental illness—Services vary by program type and geography and may deliver or pay for treatment ranging from medication to counseling, supported housing, or employment. The variety of treatment settings, philosophies, providers, and payers compromises the coordination and continuity of care that has been demonstrated to be vital for effective treatment of serious mental illness.

- High unemployment and disability for people with serious mental illness—Many persons who do not

TABLE 5.3

Additions to mental health organizations according to type of service and organization, selected years 1986–98

Service and organization	1986	1990	1992	1994[1]	1998[1]	1986	1990	1992	1994[1]	1998[1]
24-hour hospital and residential treatment[2]	Additions in thousands					Additions per 100,000 civilian population				
All organizations	1,819	2,035	2,092	2,267	2,314	759.9	833.7	830.1	874.6	860.0
State and county mental hospitals	333	276	275	238	206	139.1	113.2	109.3	92.0	76.4
Private psychiatric hospitals	235	407	470	485	481	98.0	166.5	186.4	187.1	179.0
Non-federal general hospital psychiatric services	849	960	951	1,067	1,145	354.8	393.2	377.4	411.5	425.8
Department of Veterans Affairs psychiatric services[3]	180	198	181	173	144	75.1	81.2	71.6	66.9	53.7
Residential treatment centers for emotionally disturbed children	25	42	36	47	49	10.2	17.0	14.4	18.0	18.2
All other organizations[4]	198	153	179	257	288	82.7	62.6	70.9	99.0	106.9
Less than 24-hour care[5]										
All organizations	2,955	3,298	3,164	3,516	3,967	1,233.4	1,352.4	1,255.2	1,356.8	1,474.6
State and county mental hospitals	68	48	50	42	42	28.4	19.8	19.7	16.1	15.5
Private psychiatric hospitals	132	163	206	214	226	55.2	66.9	81.8	82.4	84.1
Non-federal general hospital psychiatric services	533	659	480	498	615	222.4	270.0	190.2	192.0	228.6
Department of Veterans Affairs psychiatric services[3]	133	184	159	132	143	55.3	75.3	63.1	51.1	53.3
Residential treatment centers for emotionally disturbed children	67	100	121	167	153	28.1	40.8	48.0	64.6	56.9
All other organizations[4]	2,022	2,145	2,149	2,464	2,788	844.0	879.6	852.4	950.7	1,036.2

[1]Beginning in 1994 data for supportive residential clients (moderately staffed housing arrangements such as supervised apartments, group homes, and halfway houses) are included in the totals and all other organizations.
[2]These data exclude mental health care provided in non-psychiatric units of hospitals such as general medical units.
[3]Includes Department of Veterans Affairs (VA) neuropsychiatric hospitals, VA general hospital psychiatric services, and VA psychiatric outpatient clinics.
[4]Includes freestanding psychiatric outpatient clinics, partial care organizations, and multiservice mental health organizations.
[5]These data exclude office-based mental health care (psychiatrists, psychologists, licensed clinical social workers, and psychiatric nurses).

SOURCE: P. N. Pastor, D. M. Makuc, C. Reuben, and H. Xia, "Table 87. Additions to mental health organizations according to type of service and organization: United States, selected years 1986–98," in *Health United States, 2002 with Chartbook on Trends in the Health of Americans*, Centers for Disease Control and Prevention, National Center for Health Statistics, Hyattsville, MD, 2002

obtain needed treatment join the ranks of the impoverished, homeless, or incarcerated.

• Older adults with mental illness are not receiving care— Among the most vulnerable of all populations of persons with mental illness, older adults are often least able to navigate the fragmented mental health service delivery system to gain access to care. Depression is underdiagnosed among persons aged 65 and older and older men have the highest rates of suicide in the United States.

• Mental health and suicide prevention are not yet national priorities—About half of the 30,000 people who commit suicide each year are believed to suffer from serious mental illness, and public health professionals view at least a portion of these deaths as preventable.

The report concluded that these barriers impede the system from achieving its single most important goal: offering the people it serves the hope of recovery. The commission found that in many communities, access to quality care was poor, resulting in wasted resources and missed opportunities for recovery. It contended that more Americans could recover from even the most serious mental illnesses if they had local access to evidence-based treatment and support services tailored to their needs.

The commission attributed the deficiencies of the existing mental health care system to the ways in which the U.S. community-based mental health system has evolved over the past 50 years. It called upon government policy makers, payors, and mental health agencies to replace institutional care with efficient, effective community services and to fully integrate programs that are presently fragmented across levels of government and providers of care and services.

Disparities in Access Related to Culture, Race, and Ethnicity

According to the research findings cited in *Mental Health: A Report of the Surgeon General* (U.S. Department of Health and Human Services, Rockville, MD, 1999), rates of treatment for racial and ethnic minorities are lower than for the general population and fewer quality services are available. These findings prompted closer scrutiny of the unmet needs of members of minority groups and publication of *Mental Health: Culture, Race, and Ethnicity—A Supplement to Mental Health: A Report of the Surgeon General* (U.S. Department of Health and Human Services, Rockville, MD, 2001). This supplemental report elaborated on and conclusively confirmed the findings of the 1999 report that minority populations suffer not only from more unmet mental health needs but also endure greater losses to their overall health, productivity, and quality of life.

In the supplemental report, the leaders of the Substance Abuse and Mental Health Services Administration

TABLE 5.4

Rates of discharges and days of care in non-federal short-stay hospitals, according to sex, age, and selected first-listed diagnoses, selected years 1990–2000

Sex, age, and first-listed diagnosis	Discharges				Days of care			
	1990	1995	1999	2000	1990	1995	1999	2000
Both sexes	Number per 1,000 population							
Total[1,2]	125.2	118.0	117.8	114.9	818.9	638.6	588.8	566.1
Male								
All ages[1,2]	113.0	104.8	103.4	99.9	805.8	623.9	565.4	539.9
Under 18 years[2]	46.3	43.1	43.0	40.8	233.6	199.8	197.7	195.0
Pneumonia	5.3	6.4	6.3	5.4	22.6	23.3	22.0	17.3
Asthma	3.3	3.8	3.3	3.5	9.3	10.1	7.7	7.4
Injuries and poisoning	6.8	5.4	4.9	5.0	30.1	22.1	*22.4	21.3
Fracture, all sites	2.2	1.8	1.6	1.8	9.3	8.4	5.3	7.2
18–44 years[2]	57.9	50.7	46.0	45.5	351.7	273.0	223.2	220.1
Alcohol and drug[3]	3.7	4.7	3.6	4.1	33.1	29.7	17.4	19.3
Serious mental illness[4]	3.4	*4.8	5.0	*5.4	47.1	*48.4	42.9	*44.1
Diseases of heart	3.0	2.9	3.0	2.7	16.3	12.1	10.9	9.5
Intervertebral disc disorders	2.6	1.7	1.5	1.5	10.7	4.3	*4.6	3.2
Injuries and poisoning	13.1	9.7	8.2	7.4	65.7	47.9	37.8	33.6
Fracture, all sites	4.0	3.2	2.8	2.6	22.7	17.8	12.3	13.0
45–64 years[2]	140.3	121.2	118.5	115.8	943.4	682.3	603.4	585.9
Malignant neoplasms	10.6	7.6	6.4	6.3	99.1	53.4	43.9	43.3
Trachea, bronchus, lung	2.7	1.5	1.0	0.9	19.1	10.2	6.3	5.3
Diabetes	2.9	3.4	3.3	3.8	21.2	22.3	20.0	23.1
Alcohol and drug[3]	3.5	4.0	4.0	3.6	29.7	*25.7	20.0	16.2
Serious mental illness[4]	2.5	3.0	4.0	*4.1	34.8	*38.0	40.4	*35.6
Diseases of heart	31.7	29.7	28.5	27.1	185.0	143.8	111.3	104.3
Ischemic heart disease	22.6	21.3	19.6	18.2	128.2	99.1	72.3	65.5
Acute myocardial infarction	7.4	7.5	6.7	6.0	55.8	42.5	30.9	28.6
Congestive heart failure	3.0	2.9	3.1	3.4	19.7	16.3	17.0	17.7
Cerebrovascular diseases	4.1	3.8	3.9	3.9	40.7	25.7	21.7	20.3
Pneumonia	3.5	3.0	4.0	3.5	27.4	20.6	24.5	21.1
Injuries and poisoning	11.6	10.2	9.5	9.0	82.6	56.2	51.0	51.1
Fracture, all sites	3.3	3.0	2.8	2.6	24.2	18.4	14.9	16.6
65–74 years[2]	287.8	276.2	283.5	269.7	2,251.5	1,769.7	1,639.7	1,516.6
Malignant neoplasms	27.9	24.5	22.7	17.9	277.6	191.9	152.3	123.4
Large intestine and rectum	3.0	2.6	2.9	3.0	34.2	27.9	25.9	27.8
Trachea, bronchus, lung	6.4	5.2	3.9	2.9	55.7	40.0	29.0	19.5
Prostate	5.1	5.0	4.7	3.8	33.1	26.7	14.6	14.2
Diabetes	4.4	5.4	5.1	4.8	39.8	47.1	28.7	29.5
Serious mental illness[4]	2.5	2.4	2.9	*3.5	43.8	*37.2	36.6	40.6
Diseases of heart	69.4	74.5	75.6	71.9	487.2	419.3	354.4	337.9
Ischemic heart disease	42.0	44.0	44.0	40.4	285.2	246.1	208.1	174.2
Acute myocardial infarction	14.0	15.5	15.2	12.7	122.4	102.3	92.1	67.7
Congestive heart failure	11.4	14.9	13.7	13.7	90.2	87.5	70.1	78.2
Cerebrovascular diseases	13.8	17.1	14.3	13.4	114.8	112.6	70.3	60.1
Pneumonia	11.4	12.7	14.9	13.0	107.8	87.3	89.1	83.5
Hyperplasia of prostate	14.4	7.5	4.8	5.5	65.0	22.5	*	15.2
Osteoarthritis	5.0	5.9	7.5	9.8	44.9	33.6	36.5	47.6
Injuries and poisoning	17.6	16.1	17.8	18.3	139.0	107.0	107.1	107.7
Fracture, all sites	4.5	4.4	4.9	4.8	45.9	32.3	30.0	30.5
Fracture of neck of femur (hip)	1.5	1.8	1.6	*2.0	*18.1	14.7	*11.7	*16.1
75 years and over[2]	478.5	474.7	481.8	461.5	4,231.6	3,261.7	3,045.7	2,851.7
Malignant neoplasms	41.0	30.2	28.2	21.6	408.3	251.2	215.9	163.1
Large intestine and rectum	5.4	4.9	4.3	4.1	80.7	53.1	44.6	43.5
Trachea, bronchus, lung	5.4	3.5	4.8	3.0	53.4	31.3	33.8	18.1
Prostate	9.7	4.3	3.7	3.1	65.6	17.6	*16.6	*19.1
Diabetes	4.6	6.9	6.9	6.4	51.2	42.0	52.5	42.7
Serious mental illness[4]	*2.6	2.5	2.8	2.9	*40.5	*29.6	26.6	*32.2
Diseases of heart	106.2	113.9	113.9	111.8	855.7	677.2	583.5	593.3
Ischemic heart disease	49.1	51.8	50.5	52.3	398.1	321.9	246.4	272.6
Acute myocardial infarction	23.1	22.3	21.3	22.7	227.5	169.3	127.3	134.8
Congestive heart failure	31.0	31.3	34.5	30.2	242.3	193.4	191.5	173.2

(SAMHSA) and Center for Mental Health Services (CMHS) write that their agencies "envision a Nation where all persons, regardless of their culture, race, or ethnicity, enjoy the benefits of effective mental health preventive and treatment services." The supplemental report, however, found that the United States has not yet realized this goal and described the nature and extent of striking disparities in the accessibility, availability, and quality of

TABLE 5.4

Rates of discharges and days of care in non-federal short-stay hospitals, according to sex, age, and selected first-listed diagnoses, selected years 1990–2000 [CONTINUED]

Sex, age, and first-listed diagnosis	Discharges				Days of care			
	1990	1995	1999	2000	1990	1995	1999	2000
Male				Number per 1,000 population				
Cerebrovascular diseases	30.2	32.0	30.7	29.9	298.3	215.3	169.0	169.2
Pneumonia	38.6	40.4	41.0	36.7	393.6	325.1	281.1	230.4
Hyperplasia of prostate	17.9	9.4	7.5	6.7	109.2	32.9	*30.2	21.3
Osteoarthritis	5.8	6.5	8.0	6.1	60.7	*	37.7	28.4
Injuries and poisoning	31.2	32.7	32.9	33.2	341.3	223.5	233.5	254.5
Fracture, all sites	13.7	16.1	13.7	14.2	145.1	115.0	108.5	*117.7
Fracture of neck of femur (hip)	8.5	9.0	8.0	8.3	97.8	68.9	61.1	62.5
Female								
All ages[1,2]	139.0	131.7	132.2	129.8	840.5	654.9	613.6	591.8
Under 18 years[2]	46.4	41.6	41.3	39.4	218.7	168.8	172.7	160.8
Pneumonia	4.0	4.5	4.9	4.7	17.4	16.9	17.7	17.1
Asthma	2.2	2.6	2.3	2.4	6.8	7.2	5.6	5.5
Injuries and poisoning	4.3	3.9	3.5	3.1	16.7	13.1	*14.1	*11.9
Fracture, all sites	1.3	1.1	0.8	0.9	6.4	4.5	2.4	2.3
18–44 years[2]	146.8	131.8	126.4	125.7	582.0	429.8	409.8	403.9
Delivery	69.9	65.1	66.1	65.0	195.0	138.7	163.4	161.4
Alcohol and drug[3]	1.6	2.0	1.9	*2.1	14.1	12.9	*8.9	*10.9
Serious mental illness[4]	3.7	5.3	5.1	*5.4	54.3	50.8	38.4	*41.4
Diseases of heart	1.3	2.0	1.7	1.7	7.2	9.7	7.1	6.3
Intervertebral disc disorders	1.5	1.1	1.1	1.0	7.3	3.1	2.6	2.5
Injuries and poisoning	6.7	5.6	4.7	4.3	36.6	24.7	19.6	18.2
Fracture, all sites	1.6	1.3	1.2	1.0	10.7	5.6	5.6	4.6
45–64 years[2]	131.0	116.0	115.4	112.6	886.5	634.2	570.1	545.6
Malignant neoplasms	12.7	9.6	6.9	6.2	107.4	60.8	46.9	35.5
Trachea, bronchus, lung	1.7	1.5	0.9	0.5	14.8	8.0	*6.7	3.4
Breast	2.8	2.1	1.4	1.3	12.1	7.6	3.6	2.7
Diabetes	2.9	3.2	3.0	3.0	25.8	19.4	15.8	15.3
Alcohol and drug[3]	1.0	1.1	1.2	1.5	8.0	*7.5	*6.3	*7.2
Serious mental illness[4]	4.0	4.4	4.6	4.7	60.5	48.9	40.6	43.6
Diseases of heart	16.6	15.0	15.9	15.0	101.1	70.9	68.3	60.8
Ischemic heart disease	9.9	8.4	8.9	8.0	57.4	37.9	34.9	30.1
Acute myocardial infarction	2.8	2.5	2.7	2.0	21.6	15.1	12.8	10.2
Congestive heart failure	2.1	2.6	2.7	3.0	15.8	14.5	13.5	13.9
Cerebrovascular diseases	3.0	3.2	3.4	3.6	32.1	21.4	18.7	19.9
Pneumonia	3.4	3.3	3.8	3.7	26.5	22.0	20.5	21.2
Injuries and poisoning	9.4	8.4	8.4	7.9	63.3	45.4	46.2	42.2
Fracture, all sites	3.1	2.7	2.7	2.8	25.0	14.0	13.5	13.6
65–74 years[2]	241.1	246.9	260.0	251.9	1,959.3	1,616.2	1,527.3	1,430.1
Malignant neoplasms	20.9	20.3	15.5	14.4	189.8	148.6	106.3	103.4
Large intestine and rectum	2.4	2.3	2.0	1.7	34.9	19.9	18.2	15.6
Trachea, bronchus, lung	2.6	2.8	2.1	2.5	26.9	25.3	*17.5	*17.9
Breast	3.9	3.2	2.6	2.9	17.6	10.0	8.1	*
Diabetes	5.8	4.7	5.9	4.7	46.8	36.2	39.2	26.7
Serious mental illness[4]	3.9	5.8	4.2	4.1	62.8	82.9	49.7	47.4
Diseases of heart	45.1	48.3	54.3	53.3	316.9	276.9	268.3	262.1
Ischemic heart disease	24.4	24.3	25.8	23.9	153.8	135.4	125.1	116.6
Acute myocardial infarction	7.5	7.9	8.2	8.2	58.1	58.6	50.0	54.0
Congestive heart failure	9.2	10.3	11.1	13.0	81.8	67.6	59.5	70.0
Cerebrovascular diseases	11.3	10.6	13.0	12.6	96.0	72.0	67.7	60.8
Pneumonia	8.7	10.6	12.1	11.9	81.8	80.1	73.1	75.2
Osteoarthritis	6.9	8.6	10.1	9.5	68.9	49.0	48.2	44.6
Injuries and poisoning	17.8	18.1	17.8	18.8	166.2	113.8	108.6	112.5
Fracture, all sites	8.4	7.0	7.8	7.9	97.3	43.9	44.7	44.8
Fracture of neck of femur (hip)	3.6	2.9	3.1	3.2	*59.6	21.5	19.7	21.6

mental health care for racial and ethnic minorities. It also offered a groundbreaking examination of the role of culture as a factor with the potential to impede access to mental health care. For example, it described idioms of distress, or culturally influenced differences in how people experience, communicate, and cope with distress, and culture-bound syndromes, symptoms observed more frequently in some cultures than others. (See Table 5.6.)

The supplement documented the disparities in the mental health care of racial and ethnic minorities compared with whites. It reported that members of minorities have less access to mental health services; are less likely to receive needed mental health services; often fail to receive quality mental health treatment; and are underrepresented in mental health research. It observed that along with access issues that exist for all Americans—cost,

TABLE 5.4

Rates of discharges and days of care in non-federal short-stay hospitals, according to sex, age, and selected first-listed diagnoses, selected years 1990–2000 [CONTINUED]

Sex, age, and first-listed diagnosis	Discharges				Days of care			
	1990	1995	1999	2000	1990	1995	1999	2000
Female				Number per 1,000 population				
75 years and over[2]	409.6	450.1	481.4	472.3	3,887.1	3,239.9	2,993.1	2,914.5
Malignant neoplasms	22.1	20.5	20.6	18.1	257.3	175.2	168.2	129.4
Large intestine and rectum	4.6	3.7	4.5	3.5	69.8	48.5	46.7	29.2
Trachea, bronchus, lung	2.1	1.9	2.2	2.0	20.6	16.2	17.1	14.4
Breast	3.9	3.1	2.5	2.6	22.0	9.0	6.5	*9.2
Diabetes	4.6	6.2	5.7	6.5	55.3	44.0	30.8	35.0
Serious mental illness[4]	4.2	5.0	4.3	4.8	78.4	72.7	58.1	50.7
Diseases of heart	84.6	96.1	103.0	102.0	672.8	601.3	541.5	538.9
Ischemic heart disease	33.7	37.3	38.2	36.6	253.2	220.9	194.5	190.9
Acute myocardial infarction	13.1	15.2	17.3	16.9	125.9	116.0	112.9	113.9
Congestive heart failure	28.0	32.3	32.2	33.1	236.6	224.0	186.8	187.1
Cerebrovascular diseases	29.6	30.4	26.9	28.4	302.0	207.5	150.5	161.4
Pneumonia	23.9	28.0	32.2	31.4	260.1	227.3	222.9	215.9
Osteoarthritis	5.3	8.8	9.2	8.9	54.1	58.5	41.5	41.6
Injuries and poisoning	46.3	48.2	49.7	46.0	489.2	372.8	308.4	283.6
Fracture, all sites	31.5	31.5	32.7	30.9	352.7	251.5	200.2	195.7
Fracture of neck of femur (hip)	18.8	19.5	19.7	18.4	236.3	171.4	126.3	129.0

*Estimates are considered unreliable. Data preceded by an asterisk have a relative standard error of 20–30 percent. Data not shown have a relative standard error of greater than 30 percent.
[1]Estimates are age adjusted to the year 2000 standard population using six age groups: under 18 years, 18–44 years, 45–54 years, 55–64 years, 65–74 years, and 75 years and over.
[2]Includes discharges with first-listed diagnoses not shown in table.
[3]Includes abuse, dependence, and withdrawal. These estimates are for non-federal short-stay hospitals and do not include alcohol and drug discharges from other types of facilities or programs such as the Department of Veterans Affairs or day treatment programs.
[4]These estimates are for non-federal short-stay hospitals and do not include serious mental illness discharges from other types of facilities or programs such as the Department of Veterans Affairs or long-term hospitals.
Note: Excludes newborn infants.

SOURCE: P. N. Pastor, D. M. Makuc, C. Reuben, and H. Xia, "Table 93. Rates of discharges and days of care in non-Federal short-stay hospitals, according to sex, age, and selected first-listed diagnoses: United States, selected years 1986–98," in *Health United States, 2002 with Chartbook on Trends in the Health of Americans*, Centers for Disease Control and Prevention, National Center for Health Statistics, Hyattsville, MD, 2002

fragmentation of services, lack of availability of services, and societal stigma—racial and ethnic minorities face additional barriers. These include mistrust and fear of treatment, racism and discrimination, and differences in language and communication. The issue of communication is significant in all health care delivery, but it is especially important in mental health because mental disorders affect thoughts, moods, and communication and mental health diagnosis and treatment rely on effective communication.

Another disturbing finding was that racial and ethnic minorities experience a greater disability burden from mental illness than do whites. This greater disability burden is not because mental illness is more severe or more prevalent among these populations; instead, it is because minorities receive less care and less quality care. Another troubling finding was that this preventable disability from mental illness, and its burden for minorities, is growing. The report attributed this growth to persisting inequalities and the fact that minorities face greater exposure to racism, discrimination, violence, and poverty. It concluded that "culture counts"—patients' cultures influences their mental health and services utilization.

The supplement found that while discrimination, violence, and poverty adversely influence mental health,

poverty makes the strongest contribution to rates of mental illness. Similarly, an array of cultural issues deters many minorities from seeking mental health care, but the biggest single impediment to access to care is their mistrust of mental health services.

Access to Care and Treatment of Minorities

Though barriers to access to mental health exist for all Americans, some are compounded by language barriers, ethnic and cultural compatibility of practitioners, and geographic availability of services for racial and ethnic minorities.

AFRICAN AMERICANS. The supplement noted that the following problems occurred among African Americans:

• Among African Americans living in the community (as opposed to those who are institutionalized), rates of mental illness are comparable to those for whites. The reason African Americans are disproportionately represented in occurrence rates of mental illness is that they are overrepresented in vulnerable, at-risk populations such as the homeless, persons incarcerated, and children living in foster care.

• African Americans have less access to care than whites at least in part because they lack health

TABLE 5.5

Discharges and average length of stay in non-federal short-stay hospitals, according to sex, age, and selected first-listed diagnoses, selected years 1990–2000

Sex, age, and first-listed diagnosis	Discharges				Average length of stay			
	1990	1995	1999	2000	1990	1995	1999	2000
Both sexes	Number in thousands				Number of days			
Total[1,2]	30,788	30,722	32,132	31,706	6.5	5.4	5.0	4.9
Male								
All ages[1,2]	12,280	12,198	12,748	12,514	7.1	6.0	5.5	5.4
Under 18 years[2]	1,572	1,565	1,592	1,515	5.0	4.6	4.6	4.8
Pneumonia	178	234	233	199	4.3	3.6	3.5	3.2
Asthma	111	137	121	129	2.8	2.7	2.4	2.1
Injuries and poisoning	232	196	182	185	4.4	4.1	*4.5	4.3
Fracture, all sites	76	66	60	68	4.2	4.6	3.2	3.9
18–44 years[2]	3,120	2,761	2,521	2,498	6.1	5.4	4.8	4.8
Alcohol and drug[3]	201	258	197	224	8.9	6.3	4.8	4.7
Serious mental illness[4]	184	*262	275	*296	13.8	*10.0	8.6	*8.2
Diseases of heart	163	157	164	148	5.4	4.2	3.6	3.5
Intervertebral disc disorders	138	94	84	81	4.2	2.5	*3.0	2.2
Injuries and poisoning	704	529	449	408	5.0	4.9	4.6	4.5
Fracture, all sites	217	176	155	141	5.6	5.5	4.4	5.0
45–64 years[2]	3,115	3,053	3,390	3,424	6.7	5.6	5.1	5.1
Malignant neoplasms	235	191	183	188	9.4	7.0	6.8	6.8
Trachea, bronchus, lung	60	37	28	26	7.1	6.9	6.5	6.0
Diabetes	65	86	96	114	7.3	6.5	6.0	6.0
Alcohol and drug[3]	77	102	115	106	8.5	*6.4	5.0	4.5
Serious mental illness[4]	56	75	115	*120	13.7	*12.7	10.0	*8.8
Diseases of heart	704	749	815	802	5.8	4.8	3.9	3.8
Ischemic heart disease	502	537	561	539	5.7	4.6	3.7	3.6
Acute myocardial infarction	165	188	191	178	7.5	5.7	4.6	4.7
Congestive heart failure	66	73	90	101	6.7	5.6	5.4	5.2
Cerebrovascular diseases	91	96	111	116	10.0	6.8	5.6	5.2
Pneumonia	77	75	113	104	7.9	6.9	6.2	6.0
Injuries and poisoning	257	257	271	266	7.2	5.5	5.4	5.7
Fracture, all sites	74	74	81	77	7.2	6.3	5.3	6.4
65–74 years[2]	2,268	2,290	2,310	2,199	7.8	6.4	5.8	5.6
Malignant neoplasms	220	203	185	146	9.9	7.8	6.7	6.9
Large intestine and rectum	24	22	24	24	11.4	10.7	8.8	9.2
Trachea, bronchus, lung	50	44	32	23	8.7	7.6	7.5	6.8
Prostate	40	41	38	31	6.5	5.3	3.1	3.8
Diabetes	34	44	41	39	9.1	8.8	5.6	6.2
Serious mental illness[4]	20	20	23	*28	17.4	*15.7	12.8	*11.7
Diseases of heart	547	618	616	586	7.0	5.6	4.7	4.7
Ischemic heart disease	331	365	358	329	6.8	5.6	4.7	4.3
Acute myocardial infarction	110	129	124	104	8.8	6.6	6.1	5.3
Congestive heart failure	90	123	111	112	7.9	5.9	5.1	5.7
Cerebrovascular diseases	108	141	116	109	8.3	6.6	4.9	4.5
Pneumonia	90	105	122	106	9.5	6.9	6.0	6.4
Hyperplasia of prostate	113	62	39	45	4.5	3.0	*	2.8
Osteoarthritis	39	49	61	80	9.0	5.7	4.9	4.9
Injuries and poisoning	139	133	145	149	7.9	6.7	6.0	5.9
Fracture, all sites	36	36	40	39	10.2	7.4	6.2	6.4
Fracture of neck of femur (hip)	12	15	13	*17	*11.8	8.1	*7.1	*7.9
75 years and over[2]	2,203	2,528	2,935	2,878	8.8	6.9	6.3	6.2
Malignant neoplasms	189	161	172	135	10.0	8.3	7.7	7.6
Large intestine and rectum	25	26	26	26	15.0	10.8	10.5	10.6
Trachea, bronchus, lung	25	19	29	18	10.0	8.9	7.0	6.1
Prostate	45	23	23	20	6.8	4.1	*4.4	*6.1
Diabetes	21	37	42	40	11.0	6.1	7.6	6.6
Serious mental illness[4]	*12	13	17	18	*15.5	*11.9	9.6	*11.2
Diseases of heart	489	606	694	697	8.1	5.9	5.1	5.3
Ischemic heart disease	226	276	308	326	8.1	6.2	4.9	5.2
Acute myocardial infarction	106	119	130	141	9.9	7.6	6.0	5.9
Congestive heart failure	143	167	210	188	7.8	6.2	5.5	5.7

insurance. However, even African Americans with private health insurance are less likely to seek and obtain mental health care.

• African Americans are more likely than whites to seek mental health care from primary-care practitioners, hospital emergency departments, and psychiatric hospitals

TABLE 5.5

Discharges and average length of stay in non-federal short-stay hospitals, according to sex, age, and selected first-listed diagnoses, selected years 1990–2000 [CONTINUED]

Sex, age, and first-listed diagnosis	Discharges				Average length of stay			
	1990	1995	1999	2000	1990	1995	1999	2000
Male	Number in thousands				Number of days			
Cerebrovascular diseases	139	171	187	186	9.9	6.7	5.5	5.7
Pneumonia	178	215	250	229	10.2	8.0	6.9	6.3
Hyperplasia of prostate	82	50	46	42	6.1	3.5	*4.0	3.2
Osteoarthritis	27	35	49	38	10.5	*	4.7	4.6
Injuries and poisoning	144	174	201	207	10.9	6.8	7.1	7.7
Fracture, all sites	63	86	84	89	10.6	7.1	7.9	*8.3
Fracture of neck of femur (hip)	39	48	49	52	11.5	7.7	7.6	7.5
Female								
All ages[1,2]	18,508	18,525	19,384	19,192	6.0	5.0	4.6	4.6
Under 18 years[2]	1,500	1,437	1,458	1,397	4.7	4.1	4.2	4.1
Pneumonia	129	155	174	168	4.4	3.8	3.6	3.6
Asthma	71	90	82	85	3.1	2.8	2.4	2.3
Injuries and poisoning	138	136	122	111	3.9	3.3	*4.1	*3.8
Fracture, all sites	42	36	29	32	5.0	4.2	2.9	2.5
18–44 years[2]	8,018	7,235	6,980	6,941	4.0	3.3	3.2	3.2
Delivery	3,815	3,574	3,650	3,588	2.8	2.1	2.5	2.5
Alcohol and drug[3]	85	108	102	*116	9.1	6.6	*4.8	*5.2
Serious mental illness[4]	200	289	283	*300	14.8	9.7	7.5	*7.6
Diseases of heart	73	108	94	95	5.4	4.9	4.2	3.7
Intervertebral disc disorders	84	62	59	58	4.7	2.7	2.4	2.3
Injuries and poisoning	366	305	261	237	5.5	4.4	4.2	4.2
Fracture, all sites	85	74	65	57	6.9	4.2	4.8	4.4
45–64 years[2]	3,129	3,115	3,508	3,534	6.8	5.5	4.9	4.8
Malignant neoplasms	303	258	211	195	8.5	6.3	6.8	5.7
Trachea, bronchus, lung	41	39	27	17	8.6	5.5	*7.6	6.4
Breast	67	56	42	40	4.3	3.6	2.7	2.1
Diabetes	70	86	91	93	8.9	6.0	5.3	5.2
Alcohol and drug[3]	23	30	38	47	8.2	*6.8	*5.0	*4.8
Serious mental illness[4]	95	118	140	146	15.2	11.1	8.8	9.4
Diseases of heart	397	403	484	470	6.1	4.7	4.3	4.1
Ischemic heart disease	237	225	272	251	5.8	4.5	3.9	3.8
Acute myocardial infarction	68	68	83	64	7.6	6.0	4.7	5.0
Congestive heart failure	51	68	83	94	7.4	5.7	4.9	4.6
Cerebrovascular diseases	72	86	104	113	10.7	6.7	5.5	5.5
Pneumonia	80	88	117	117	7.9	6.7	5.3	5.7
Injuries and poisoning	225	225	255	248	6.7	5.4	5.5	5.3
Fracture, all sites	75	72	81	87	7.9	5.2	5.1	4.9
65–74 years[2]	2,421	2,542	2,573	2,479	8.1	6.5	5.9	5.7
Malignant neoplasms	210	209	154	142	9.1	7.3	6.8	7.2
Large intestine and rectum	24	23	20	17	14.5	8.8	8.9	9.0
Trachea, bronchus, lung	26	29	21	25	10.2	8.9	*8.4	*7.1
Breast	40	33	26	29	4.5	3.1	*3.1	*
Diabetes	59	49	58	47	8.0	7.7	6.7	5.6
Serious mental illness[4]	39	60	42	40	16.3	14.2	11.7	11.7
Diseases of heart	453	497	537	525	7.0	5.7	4.9	4.9
Ischemic heart disease	245	250	255	235	6.3	5.6	4.8	4.9
Acute myocardial infarction	75	82	81	81	7.8	7.4	6.1	6.6
Congestive heart failure	92	106	110	128	8.9	6.5	5.4	5.4
Cerebrovascular diseases	114	109	128	124	8.5	6.8	5.2	4.8
Pneumonia	87	109	120	117	9.4	7.6	6.0	6.3
Osteoarthritis	69	89	100	94	10.0	5.7	4.8	4.7
Injuries and poisoning	179	187	176	185	9.3	6.3	6.1	6.0
Fracture, all sites	85	72	77	77	11.5	6.2	5.7	5.7
Fracture of neck of femur (hip)	36	29	30	32	*16.7	7.5	6.4	6.7

as opposed to mental health specialty care. Table 5.7 shows that almost twice as many African Americans seek mental health care from providers other than mental health specialists. Increased use of institutional treatment reflects delays in seeking treatment until symptoms are so severe that emergency intervention is required.

• Specific mental disorders such as mood disorders and schizophrenia are under- and overdiagnosed more often in African Americans than whites.

• African Americans are less likely than whites to receive care consistent with evidence-based practice guidelines.

NATIVE AMERICANS/ALASKA NATIVES. Supplement findings specific to Native Americans and Alaska Natives included the following:

• Native Americans and Alaska Natives suffer higher than expected rates of mental illness.

TABLE 5.5

Discharges and average length of stay in non-federal short-stay hospitals, according to sex, age, and selected first-listed diagnoses, selected years 1990–2000 [CONTINUED]

Sex, age, and first-listed diagnosis	Discharges				Average length of stay			
	1990	1995	1999	2000	1990	1995	1999	2000
Female	Number in thousands				Number of days			
75 years and over[2]	3,440	4,196	4,865	4,840	9.5	7.2	6.2	6.2
Malignant neoplasms	185	191	209	186	11.7	8.5	8.1	7.1
Large intestine and rectum	39	34	45	36	15.1	13.3	10.4	8.4
Trachea, bronchus, lung	18	17	23	20	9.9	8.7	7.7	7.3
Breast	33	29	26	27	5.7	2.9	2.6	*3.5
Diabetes	39	58	57	67	11.9	7.1	5.5	5.4
Serious mental illness[4]	35	47	43	49	18.7	14.5	13.5	10.5
Diseases of heart	711	896	1,041	1,045	8.0	6.3	5.3	5.3
Ischemic heart disease	283	347	386	375	7.5	5.9	5.1	5.2
Acute myocardial infarction	110	142	175	174	9.6	7.6	6.5	6.7
Congestive heart failure	235	301	325	339	8.5	6.9	5.8	5.6
Cerebrovascular diseases	249	283	272	292	10.2	6.8	5.6	5.7
Pneumonia	201	261	326	322	10.9	8.1	6.9	6.9
Osteoarthritis	45	82	93	91	10.2	6.6	4.5	4.7
Injuries and poisoning	389	449	502	472	10.6	7.7	6.2	6.2
Fracture, all sites	265	294	331	316	11.2	8.0	6.1	6.3
Fracture of neck of femur (hip)	158	182	199	189	12.5	8.8	6.4	7.0

*Estimates are considered unreliable. Data preceded by an asterisk have a relative standard error of 20–30 percent. Data not shown have a relative standard error of greater than 30 percent.
[1]Average length of stay estimates are age adjusted to the year 2000 standard population using six age groups: under 18 years, 18–44 years, 45–54 years, 55–64 years, 65–74 years, and 75 years and over.
[2]Includes discharges with first-listed diagnoses not shown in table.
[3]Includes abuse, dependence, and withdrawal. These estimates are for non-federal short-stay hospitals and do not include alcohol and drug discharges from other types of facilities or programs such as the Department of Veterans Affairs or day treatment programs.
[4]These estimates are for non-federal short-stay hospitals and do not include serious mental illness discharges from other types of facilities or programs such as the Department of Veterans Affairs or long-term hospitals.
Note: Excludes newborn infants.

SOURCE: P. N. Pastor, D. M. Makuc, C. Reuben, and H. Xia, "Table 94. Discharges and average length of stay in non-Federal short-stay hospitals, according to sex, age, and selected first-listed diagnoses: United States, selected years 1990–2000," in *Health United States, 2002 with Chartbook on Trends in the Health of Americans,* Centers for Disease Control and Prevention, National Center for Health Statistics, Hyattsville, MD, 2002

TABLE 5.6

Idioms of distress and culture-bound syndromes

Idioms of distress are ways in which different cultures express, experience, and cope with feelings of distress. One example is *somatization*, or the expression of distress through physical symptoms. Stomach disturbances, excessive gas, palpitations, and chest pain are common forms of *somatization* in Puerto Ricans, Mexican Americans, and whites. Some Asian groups express more cardiopulmonary and vestibular symptoms, such as dizziness, vertigo, and blurred vision. In Africa and South Asia, *somatization* sometimes takes the form of burning hands and feet, or the experience of worms in the head or ants crawling under the skin.

Culture-bound syndromes are clusters of symptoms much more common in some cultures than in others. For example, some Latino patients, especially women from the Caribbean, display *ataque de nervios*, a condition that includes screaming uncontrollably, attacks of crying, trembling, and verbal or physical aggression. Fainting or seizure-like episodes and suicidal gestures may sometimes accompany these symptoms. A culture-bound syndrome from Japan is *taijin kyofusho*, an intense fear that one's body or bodily functions give offense to others. This syndrome is listed as a diagnosis in the Japanese clinical modification of the World Health Organization (WHO) International Classification of Diseases, 10th edition.

Numerous other culture-bound syndromes are given in the DSM–IV "Glossary of Culture-Bound Syndromes." Researchers have taken initial steps to examine the interrelationships between culture-bound syndromes and the diagnostic classifications of DSM–IV. For example, in a sample of Latinos seeking care for anxiety disorders, 70 percent reported having at least one *ataque*. Of those, over 40 percent met DSM–IV criteria for panic disorder, and nearly 25 percent met criteria for major depression. In past research, there has been an effort to fit culture-bound syndromes into variants of DSM diagnoses. Rather than assume that DSM diagnostic entities or culture-bound syndromes are the basic patterns of illness, current investigators are interested in examining how the social, cultural, and biological contexts interact to shape illnesses and reactions to them. This is an important area of research in a field known as cultural psychiatry or ethnopsychiatry.

SOURCE: "Box 1-3. Idioms of Distress and Culture-Bound Syndromes," in *Mental Health: Culture, Race, and Ethnicity—A Supplement to Mental Health: A Report of the Surgeon General*, U.S. Department of Health and Human Services, Substance Abuse and Mental Health Services Administration, Center for Mental Health Services, Rockville, MD, 2001

• Geography, especially rural and isolated communities, limits access to mental health care.

• Access may also be limited by preference for traditional native healing techniques as opposed to Western medicine.

ASIAN AMERICANS/PACIFIC ISLANDERS. Racial trends for Asian Americans and Pacific Islanders included:

• Asian Americans and Pacific Islanders have comparable rates of mental illness to whites; however, they are more at risk for post-traumatic stress disorder

TABLE 5.7

Use of mental health services by African Americans, 1994

12-month disorder	Mental health specialist[1] % (se)[3]	Any provider[2] % (se)[3]
Mood disorder	15.6 (3.5)	28.7 (4.5)
Anxiety disorder	12.6 (2.4)	25.6 (5.3)

[1]Psychologist, psychiatrist, or social worker
[2]Mental health specialist, general medical provider, other professional (nurse, occupational therapist, other health professional, minister, priest, rabbi, counselor), spiritualist, herbalist, natural therapist, or faith healer
[3]The SE (Standard Error) is the average dispersion around the percentage.

SOURCE: "Table 3-2. Use of Mental Health Services by African Americans," in *Mental Health: Culture, Race, and Ethnicity—A Supplement to Mental Health: A Report of the Surgeon General*, U.S. Department of Health and Human Services, Substance Abuse and Mental Health Services Administration, Center for Mental Health Services, Rockville, MD, 2001

(PTSD) as a result of harsh conditions endured prior to immigration.

- Language is a significant barrier to access, and there are relatively few mental health practitioners with language proficiency sufficient to deliver mental health treatment to this population. Understandably, when therapists and clients share the same ethnicity, service utilization is higher.

- Stigmatization and shame are significant deterrents to seeking and obtaining needed mental health treatment.

HISPANIC AMERICANS. The supplement found that Hispanics as an ethnic group face these issues:

- Hispanic Americans' rates of mental illness are generally comparable to those of whites, but Hispanic youth suffer higher rates of depression, anxiety, suicidal thinking, and suicide attempts than white youth.

- Language and ethnicity are barriers to access. There is a shortage of ethnically similar mental health practitioners with language proficiency to deliver treatment to persons who speak only Spanish.

- Hispanic Americans are the least likely of all minorities to have public or private health insurance.

- Hispanic American adults and children are less likely than whites to receive needed mental health care. When they seek care, it is more likely to be in primary-care settings than from mental health specialists.

- Research indicates that Hispanic Americans are less likely than whites to receive evidence-based treatment consistent with established practice guidelines.

ACCESS TO CARE AND TREATMENT OF CHILDREN. Sheryl Kataoka and her colleagues at the Department of Psychiatry and Biobehavioral Sciences, Child and Adolescent Psychiatry Division, and the Research Center on Managed Care for Psychiatric Disorders, University of California, Los Angeles; and RAND, Santa Monica, California, considered three national data sets to examine ethnic disparities in unmet mental health needs of children and adolescents. The results of their analyses appeared in "Unmet Need for Mental Health Care Among U.S. Children: Variation by Ethnicity and Insurance Status" (*American Journal of Psychiatry*, vol. 159, no. 9, September 2002).

The investigators analyzed data from three nationally representative household surveys—the National Health Interview Survey, the National Survey of American Families, and the Community Tracking Survey. They determined rates of mental health services used by children and adolescents 3–17 years of age and differences by ethnicity and insurance status, and examined the association of unmet need with ethnicity and insurance status. They found that during a 12-month period, 2 to 3 percent of children 3–5 years old and 6 to 9 percent of children and adolescents 6–17 years old used mental health services. Of those defined as needing mental health services, nearly 80 percent did not receive mental health care. The investigators determined that the rate of unmet need was greater among Latino than white children and greater among uninsured than publicly insured children.

They also observed that utilization of mental health services was extremely low among preschool children. The investigators concluded that their research supported the findings reported in the Surgeon General's report—that there is substantial unmet need for child mental health care, which is particularly acute for some minority and uninsured groups.

The *Report of the Surgeon General's Conference on Children's Mental Health: A National Action Agenda* (Department of Health and Human Services, Washington, D.C., 2000) enumerated eight goals to improve mental health care for children. Nearly all the goals relate to improving access to care by promoting public awareness, improving identification and detection, and eliminating racial, ethnic, and socioeconomic disparities in access to mental health care. Goal 6—"Increase access to and coordination of quality mental healthcare services"—states this intent most directly. Goal 8—"Monitor the access to and coordination of quality mental healthcare services,"—advises development of national quality improvement protocols, use of process and outcome measures to evaluate aspects of service delivery, and ongoing assessment of efforts to coordinate services and reduce mental health access disparities through public health surveillance and evaluation research.

The report recommended the following actions to achieve the goal of increased access:

- Development and use of a common language, sensitive to ecological, cultural and familial concerns, to describe children's mental health

- Development of a universal measurement system that is age-appropriate, culturally competent, and gender-sensitive to identify children in need of mental health services, track their progress, and assess outcomes of treatment

- Refine definition and evaluation procedures that identify children and adolescents in need of mental health care so that they are more inclusive—facilitating rather than impeding access to care

- Provide services in locations where youth and families gather, such as schools, churches, and recreation centers

- Enhance the skills and capabilities of emergency medical personnel so that children in need of mental health treatment or referral are identified in hospital emergency departments

- Encourage coordination and collaboration among mental health service providers without compromising patient and family confidentiality

- Urge agencies and organizations to promote family education so families may make informed choices and decisions about treatment

- Include youth in treatment decision-making and provide information about service options

- Deploy family advocates to assist families to navigate the complex mental health service delivery system, as well as healthcare, education, juvenile justice, child welfare, and substance abuse treatment services

- Solicit youth and family involvement in establishing a national mental health agenda to assess policies and programs and promote mental health services delivery

PILOT PROJECT TARGETS ACCESS TO CARE AND TREATMENT FOR RURAL YOUTH. In July 2003 the National Institute of Mental Health (NIMH) announced the implementation of a new program aimed at improving access to, and treatment of, emotional and behavioral problems of rural youth in eight of the poorest Appalachian counties in eastern Tennessee. (The NIMH is part of the National Institutes of Health, the federal government's primary agency for biomedical and behavioral research. NIH is a component of the U.S. Department of Health and Human Services.) The program involves collaboration between University of Tennessee researchers, judges, school administrators, and community leaders to surmount barriers to access to mental health services. The *Rural Appalachia Project* is a pilot program that is hoped will serve as a model for reducing the social and economic consequences of juvenile delinquency in rural communities.

According to the NIMH, research demonstrates that home-based, family-oriented mental health services for children referred to juvenile court can improve their behavior and prevent further involvement with the juvenile courts and criminal justice system. This pilot program

not only will improve access to quality treatment but also provide intensive education to inform community leaders about how timely, effective intervention can improve lives and reduce the costs of incarceration and residential care.

The five-year study, funded by a $4 million grant to the University of Tennessee from the NIMH, will involve 720 children with serious conduct and other mental health disorders, ages 9 to 17 years old, who were referred to juvenile courts. Half of the children participating in the study will receive evidence-based practice multisystemic therapy (MST), which is typically four to five months in duration and aims to assist youth in modifying their behaviors in a normal environment rather than a clinical setting. The other half of the study participants will receive the usual care for children referred to juvenile court. Investigators believe that the pilot program will provide immediate intervention and help for at-risk youth in these rural communities and may promote attitudinal change among state policy makers, providers of mental health, social support services, and community opinion leaders.

Barriers to Access to Treatment of Social Anxiety

Research reveals that most adults in the United States who suffer from social phobia do not receive mental health care for their symptoms, despite the availability of effective treatments for this disorder. Mark Olfson and his colleagues from the New York State Psychiatric Institute, Department of Psychiatry, College of Physicians and Surgeons, Columbia University, sought to determine the specific barriers to treatment that impede affected persons from receiving care. The investigators reported the results of their research in "Barriers to the Treatment of Social Anxiety" (*American journal of Psychiatry,* vol. 157, no. 4, April 2000).

The investigators reviewed data collected from persons who participated during a National Anxiety Disorders Screening Day, a nonprofit program to help participants determine if they have symptoms of common anxiety disorders and assist persons seeking information about anxiety disorders. Conducted every year during the first week of May, the program is sponsored by professional associations such as the American Psychiatric Association, the American Psychological Association, the Anxiety Disorders Association of America, the National Institute of Mental Health, and the National Mental Health Association. Using data from this program enabled the researchers to analyze self-reported barriers to treatment in a large adult population with symptoms of social anxiety. The analysis aimed to describe screening-day participants with symptoms of social anxiety, the barriers that prevented them from seeking prompt treatment prior to the screening day, and factors that influenced professional recognition and referral for further evaluation of their symptoms.

The screening questionnaire contained two social anxiety questions—"Were you afraid to do things in front of people, such as public speaking, eating, performing, teaching, or other things?," and "Did you either avoid or feel very uncomfortable in situations involving people, such as parties, weddings, dating, dances, and other social events?" Participants who answered yes to both of these screening questions were considered to suffer from symptoms of social anxiety. Participants who responded negatively to both queries were thought to have no social anxiety. The screening questionnaire also gathered sociodemographic data (age, sex, race, ethnicity, education, employment status, and geographic location) and specific psychiatric symptoms (thoughts of suicide, depressed mood, hopelessness, panic attack, persistent worry, and feelings of social isolation) in the month prior to the screening. In addition, it asked about mental health treatment history and measures of functional impairment. It also contained eight common barriers to treatment and asked participants if these issues or concerns had prevented them from seeking care.

The data analysis revealed that 42.4 percent of the 14,462 program participants answered yes to both questions and were deemed to have symptoms of social anxiety. Social anxiety was associated with other psychiatric symptoms, such as feelings of social isolation and functional impairment, as well as past and current mental health treatment. Nearly one in four adults with social anxiety said they had thought about suicide in the month preceding the screening. Participants with social anxiety also often reported feelings of social isolation and pervasive anxiety-related interference in daily activities.

Among participants with social anxiety on screening day, not knowing where to seek help was the most frequently reported barrier to mental health treatment. Many participants chose not to seek treatment earlier because they hoped they could manage their symptoms by themselves. Lack of insurance and inability to afford treatment were also common barriers to treatment.

Ironically, the symptoms that prompt socially anxious persons to seek care may actually interfere with their ability to obtain treatment. Socially anxious people are often ashamed of their symptoms and embarrassed to discuss them with friends or health care professionals. Among participants with social anxiety, the fear of what others might think or say frequently inhibited treatment seeking. The investigators concluded that social anxiety is associated with a distinct pattern of treatment barriers. They expressed the opinions that access to care may be improved by building public awareness of available services, alleviating the psychological and financial burden of entering treatment, and increasing health professionals' awareness of the disorder.

Stigma

Stigma leads to isolation, and discourages people from seeking the treatment they need.

—President George W. Bush, April 28, 2002

Stigma refers to a cluster of negative attitudes and beliefs that motivate the general public to fear, reject, avoid, and discriminate against people with mental illnesses. Stigma is widespread in the United States and other Western nations. Stigma leads others to avoid living, socializing, or working with, renting to, or employing people with mental disorders—especially severe disorders, such as schizophrenia. It leads to low self-esteem, isolation, and hopelessness. It deters the public from seeking and wanting to pay for care. Responding to stigma, people with mental health problems internalize public attitudes and become so embarrassed or ashamed that they often conceal symptoms and fail to seek treatment.

—Achieving the Promise: Transforming Mental Health Care in America, The President's New Freedom Commission on Mental Health, July 2003

The social stigmas attached to being labeled "crazy" prevent some sufferers of mental illness from seeking and obtaining needed care. Myths about mental illness persist, especially the mistaken beliefs that mental illness is a sign of moral weakness or that an affected individual can simply choose to wish or will away the symptoms of mental illness. People with mental illness cannot just pull themselves together and will themselves well. Without treatment, symptoms can worsen or persist for months or even years.

In addition to reluctance to seek care, social stigma can have far-reaching consequences for persons with mental illnesses. They may face discrimination at the workplace, in school, and in efforts to find housing. Thwarted in their efforts to maintain independence, they may become trapped in a cycle characterized by feelings of worthlessness and hopelessness and become further isolated from the social and community supports and treatments most able to help them to recover.

Among the President's Commission's many ambitious goals is to reduce or eliminate stigma as a barrier to seeking care for mental illness. The commission foresees public-education initiatives as forces able to shatter myths about mental illness and increase Americans' willingness to seek care. To encourage Americans to seek care for mental illness as readily as they do care for other health problems, the commission advised national education campaigns. It also called for education initiatives aimed at reaching specific target populations. These include rural Americans who have not historically had exposure or access to mental health services, racial and ethnic minority groups, and persons for whom English is a second language.

Financial Barriers

Many persons in need of mental health treatment are unable to pay for it. Mental health insurance benefits are quickly exhausted; reimbursement rates that do not keep pace with costs discourage providers from expanding or even continuing to offer services; state mental hospitals have closed; and community hospitals that offer inpatient psychiatric services often have waiting lists. Community mental health centers are underfunded and overutilized.

In "Nowhere Else to Turn: As the Ax Falls on Mental Health Funding, Hospital EDs Fill the Gap—Reluctantly" (*Hospitals & Health Networks,* vol. 76, no. 4, April 2002), Richard Haugh asserted that homeless shelters, prisons, and hospital emergency departments (EDs) have become stopgap measures for persons suffering from mental illness. Haugh said that EDs throughout the country are seeing increasing numbers of psychiatric patients who are uninsured and unable to pay for care. By law these patients must be held until the hospital can locate available beds in psychiatric facilities, so many EDs end up holding patients for hours or even days in arguably one of the most expensive treatment settings possible. By occupying ED beds, psychiatric patients delay treatment of other patients for whom ED care is more appropriate.

Haugh reported that at least one ED had experimented with placing a social worker in the ED to perform triage (immediate assessment, evaluation, and referral) and case management for persons with mental illness. The pilot program reduced emergency department visits and inpatient hospital costs in the study group, most of whom were uninsured and suffered from mental illness and/or substance abuse.

Education, Partnerships, Cooperation, and Personalized Care

The commission cited knowledge as pivotal for the transformation of the mental health care system. All participants in the system—clients, families, and practitioners—need timely, reliable, easy access to information about effective mental health treatment and services. The commission envisions the transformed system as one in which consumers and family members will have access to relevant research findings. Also, it will provide accurate information that promotes learning, self-monitoring, and accountability. In addition, mental health providers will use the most current evidence-based treatment to provide optimal care and outcomes.

Further, the commission believes that informed consumers and professionals will be better able to establish therapeutic alliances—partnerships that enable them to collaborate to develop individualized care plans. Specifically, the partnership of personalized care should involve shared decision making about which mental health professionals will be providing care, the type of care and treatment to be provided, the setting in which it will be provided, and the option to agree or disagree with a proposed treatment plan. Such consumer- and family-centered services and treatments should aim to offer consumers meaningful choices about preferred treatment and providers. It should also be seamless and convenient,

and focus on clients' and families' needs rather than the organizational and administrative requirements of the many agencies and providers that constitute the current bureaucratic delivery system.

Equally important, the commission recommended a philosophical shift in service delivery—away from simply focusing on reducing or managing the symptoms of mental illness and moving toward facilitating as complete recovery as possible. Moreover, the commission exhorted providers to emphasize treatment and services to build resilience—personal and community qualities that enable people to rebound from adversity, trauma, tragedy, threats, or other stresses and to live with a sense of mastery, competence, and hope. Research reveals that resilience is nurtured by positive child rearing along with cultivation of positive individual traits, such as optimism and effective problem-solving skills. Closely knit communities also foster resiliency by supporting individuals and families.

System Problems Impede Access

Even persons with health insurance may experience access problems. In an article entitled "Behavioral Health Matters" in *Drug Benefit Trends* (vol. 114, no. 9, October 2002), Dr. Jay Pomerantz, a clinical professor of psychiatry at Harvard Medical School in Boston, Massachusetts, stated that the behavioral health marketplace is complicated and confusing and requires patients to navigate a complex system.

Dr. Pomerantz explained that a patient seeking care from a behavioral health "carveout" (a program that organizes delivery of mental health treatment for a managed care organization by contracting with a network of mental health professionals) may find a scarce network of participating providers or even that all network practitioners are too busy to accept new patients. Further, he contended that left on their own to select a practitioner from a list of network providers, many patients might not select the most appropriate provider. For example, a patient in need of prescription medication receiving care from a psychiatric social worker might then also have to schedule an appointment with a psychiatrist to obtain prescription medication.

Further, Dr. Pomerantz suggested that behavioral health carveouts had little incentive to improve access. This is because they are separately purchased services that are typically part of managed care packages and often involve a specialized vendor or group of providers to supply services. As such, they benefit financially when potential patients never successfully access covered treatment. He speculated that in frustration some patients resort to seeking mental health help from their primary-care practitioners, forgo treatment altogether, or opt to pay out of pocket to gain access to care.

The President's Commission also cited system problems as barriers to access and stated, "Improving services for individuals with mental illnesses will require paying close attention to how mental health care and general medical care systems work together. While mental health and physical health are clearly connected, the transformed system will provide collaborative care to bridge the gap that now exists." One example of collaboration to bridge the gap between medical care and mental health care is increasing the availability and quality of mental health diagnosis and treatment in primary-care settings. When effective mental health care is available in the physician's office or clinic, and primary-care practitioners are better trained to detect and treat mental illness, then consumer access to recovery-oriented care will be enhanced.

Improving Access to Mental Health Care

Healthy People 2010, the prevention agenda for the United States, lists leading health indicators and objectives related to each. (See Table 5.8.) One objective, shown under Mental Health, is to more than double the 1997 proportion of depressed adults in treatment by 2010. Other objectives, shown under "Access to Health Care," would also affect access to mental health care. Healthy People 2010 also enumerates other objectives not shown in the graphic that are related to improved access, calling for increases in:

- The proportion of local health departments that have established culturally appropriate and linguistically competent community health promotion and disease prevention programs.

- The number of persons seen in primary health care who receive mental health screening and assessment.

- The proportion of children with mental health problems who receive treatment.

- The proportion of juvenile justice facilities that screen new admissions for mental health problems.

- The proportion of adults with mental disorders who receive treatment.

- The proportion of local governments with community-based jail diversion programs for adults with serious mental illness (SMI).

- The number of States, Territories, and the District of Columbia with an operational mental health plan that addresses cultural competence.

- The number of States, Territories, and the District of Columbia with operational mental health plans that address mental health crisis interventions, ongoing screening, and treatment services for elderly persons.

In an effort to support the attainment of the objectives outlined in Healthy People 2010, the President's Commission recommended offering the states financial and other incentives for coordinating and integrating existing resources—agencies and providers—into an organized mental health care delivery system. For example, in exchange for a state's establishment of successful, working alliances between the health care delivery system, the criminal justice system, social support services, and clients and families, it would be given the flexibility and authority to combine federal, state, and local resources to administer the redesigned system.

MENTAL HEALTH PATIENT CARE ISSUES

Arguably, persons suffering from mental illness may be among the most vulnerable members of the population. It is a sad irony that these individuals often face additional obstacles when seeking safe, effective treatment than persons with physical health problems.

Barriers to access to treatment include patient or client-related issues such as ability to pay for needed care and willingness to risk stigmatization and discrimination when seeking care. Access problems also may occur as a result of an inadequate supply of effective treatment options, practitioners, and community support services. Another issue that may deter access to care is the acceptability of treatment. If treatment is not culturally sensitive or available in the affected individual's language and community, or if it produces side effects nearly as debilitating as the illness itself, persons with mental illnesses may be reluctant to adhere to it.

Persons who gain access to mental health care remain at risk for other types of abuses, including violations of their rights, coercion, ineffective or otherwise inappropriate treatment, loss of privacy and independence, and in some instances neglect or even physical abuse from caregivers.

Those who fail to gain access to appropriate, effective treatment may endure needless anguish, unemployment, homelessness, victimization, or incarceration. Untreated mental illness exacts a tremendous toll on the affected individuals, their families, business and industry, the health care and criminal justice systems, and the community at large.

PATIENTS' RIGHTS

In 1997 the leadership of nine major mental health professional societies, including the American Psychological Association, the American Psychiatric Association, and the National Association of Social Workers, developed and presented a *Mental Health Bill of Rights*. The professional organizations united to produce this document in response to their common concern that many persons with mental disorders were not receiving quality care, and the observation that some were being harmed by inappropriate treatment or lack of access to care.

The protections sought for consumers of mental health care services included the rights to:

- Equitable insurance—health care coverage regardless of health status, reasonable deductible and co-payment provisions

TABLE 5.8

Leading health indicators with 22 measures, 1990–2000 and projected 2010

Leading health indicators, measures, and Healthy People 2010 objective numbers	1990	1995	1996	1997	1998	1999	2000	2010 target
Physical activity								
1. Adolescents in grades 9–12: percent who engaged in 20 minutes or more of vigorous activity 3 or more days per week (obj 22-07)	—	64	—	64	—	65	—	85
2. Adults age 18 years and over: age-adjusted percent who engaged in moderate activity (at least 30 minutes, 5 days per week) or vigorous activity (at least 20 minutes, 3 days per week) (obj 22-02)[1]	—	—	—	32	30	30	32	50
Overweight and obesity[2]								
3. Overweight or obese children and adolescents, age 6–19 years: percent who are at or above the sex- and age-specific 95th percentile of Body Mass Index (BMI) based on CDC Growth Charts: United States (obj 19-03c)	11	—	—	—	—	—	—	5
4. Obese adults age 20 years and over: age-adjusted percent with BMI of 30 kg/m² or more (obj 19-02)	23	—	—	—	—	26	—	15
Tobacco use								
5. Adolescents in grades 9–12: percent who smoked cigarettes one or more days in the past 30 days (obj 27-02b)	—	35	—	36	—	35	—	16
6. Adults age 18 years and over: age-adjusted percent who smoked more than 100 cigarettes in their lifetime and now report smoking on some days or every day (obj 27-01a)[1]	25	25	—	25	24	23	23	12
Substance abuse[3]								
7. Adolescents age 12–17 years: percent who reported no use of alcohol or illicit drugs in the past 30 days (obj 26-10a)	—	—	—	—	—	80	80	89
8. Adults age 18 years and over: percent who reported illicit drug use in the past 30 days (obj 26-10c)	—	—	—	—	—	6	6	2
9. Adults age 18 years and over: percent who reported binge drinking in the past 30 days (obj 26-11c)	—	—	—	—	—	21	22	6
Responsible sexual behavior								
10. Adolescents in grades 9–12: percent who are not sexually active or sexually active and used condoms (obj 25-11)	—	83	—	85	—	85	—	95
11. Sexually active unmarried women age 18–44 years: percent who reported condom use by partners (obj 13-06a)	—	23	—	—	—	—	—	50
Mental health								
12. Adults age 18 years and over: percent with recognized depression who received treatment (obj 18-09b)	—	—	—	23	—	—	—	50
Injury and violence								
13. Age-adjusted death rate for motor vehicle traffic-related injuries per 100,000 standard population (obj 15-15a)[4]	18.0	16.1	16.0	15.8	15.6	15.0	—	9.2
14. Age-adjusted death rate for homicide per 100,000 standard population (obj 15-32)	9.4	8.4	7.6	7.2	6.5	6.2	—	3.0
Environmental quality								
15. Percent of population exposed to ozone above EPA standard (obj 08-01a)	—	—	—	43	43	43	43	0
16. Persons age 4 years and over: age-adjusted percent of nonsmokers exposed to environmental tobacco smoke (obj 27-10)[2]	65	—	—	—	—	—	—	45
Immunization								
17. Children age 19–35 months: percent who received all DTaP, polio, MMR, Hib, and HepB vaccines (obj 14-24a)	—	—	—	—	73	73	73	80
18. Adults age 65 years and over: age-adjusted percent who received influenza vaccine in the past 12 months (obj 14-29a)[1]	—	59	—	63	64	66	65	90
19. Adults age 65 years and over: age-adjusted percent who ever received pneumococcal vaccine (obj 14-29b)[1]	—	35	—	43	46	50	53	90

• Choice—the ability to choose a qualified provider (mental health practitioner), and treatment option, such as cognitive-behavioral therapy without medication, in a convenient location

• Privacy and Confidentiality—the ability to control the release of personal medical and other health-related information to any third party

• Information—clear, accurate information about treatment options as well as health plan terms, conditions,

benefits, premiums, and other financial or administrative decisions that affect care and full disclosure of the reasons care is authorized or denied

• Quality—timely authorization, delivery, and continuity of care as well as treatment decision-making by qualified professionals using evidence-based, ethical criteria

• Accountability—health plans and managed care organizations must be responsible for their actions and

TABLE 5.8

Leading health indicators with 22 measures, 1990–2000 and projected 2010 [CONTINUED]

Leading health indicators, measures, and Healthy People 2010 objective numbers	1990	1995	1996	1997	1998	1999	2000	2010 target
Access to health care								
20. Persons under age 65 years: age-adjusted percent with health insurance (obj 01-01)[1]		84	83	83	83	84	83	100
21. Persons of all ages: age-adjusted percent with a specific source of ongoing primary care (obj 01-04a)[1]	—	87	88	86	87	86	87	96
22. Pregnant women: percent who received prenatal care in the first trimester (obj 16-06a)	76	81	82	83	83	83	83	90

Note: —Data not available.
[1]Data for 1997 and later years are not strictly comparable with data for earlier years due to the 1997 questionnaire redesign. Data for 2000 are provisional.
[2]NHANES data for 1990 are for the period 1988–94. NHANES data for 1999 are preliminary estimates, limited in sample size and geographic coverage and, therefore, subject to more sampling error than multi-year NHANES. As a result, annual prevalence estimates may fluctuate more than those from multi-year NHANES.
[3]In a major redesign of the survey in 1999, the sample size, mode of administration, and survey content changed. Data are not shown for 1998 and earlier years because only limited comparisons can be made between data from the redesigned surveys (1999 onward) and data obtained from surveys prior to 1999.
[4]Motor vehicle traffic-related injuries
NHANES = National Health and Nutrition Examination Survey

SOURCE: P. N. Pastor, D. M. Makuc, C. Reuben, and H. Xia, "Table 52. Healthy People 2010 Leading Health Indicators with 22 measures: United States, 1990–2000 and 2010 target," in *Health United States, 2002 with Chartbook on Trends in the Health of Americans*, Centers for Disease Control and Prevention, National Center for Health Statistics, Hyattsville, MD, 2002

maintain effective procedures for responding to consumers' appeals and grievances

Privacy and Confidentiality

The 1996 Health Insurance Portability and Accountability Act (HIPAA) was intended to provide better portability of employer-sponsored insurance so that workers would not be forced to remain in the same position to retain health care coverage. HIPAA also served to improve medical confidentiality by making it illegal for health insurance companies to bar consumers from obtaining coverage because of preexisting medical conditions, and it contained provisions that allowed consumers greater access to their medical records.

In 2001, the U.S. Department of Health and Human Services (DHHS) strengthened the medical privacy protections offered by HIPAA. The DHHS regulations required health care providers to comply with the following stipulations by 2003:

- Consumers must be given the right to examine, copy, and retain their medical records, except for selected information such as medical records of psychotherapy

- Health care providers are required to obtain consumers' written consent before disclosing their medical records for purposes of treatment, billing or health plan administration

- Strict limits are applied to the use of medical record information for purposes of research or marketing

- Violations of medical confidentiality are subject to civil and criminal sanctions

In March 2002 the Bush administration proposed revisions to the existing regulation that may compromise medical privacy. According to the National Mental Health Association (NMHA), one of the most worrisome modifications is the proposal to eliminate the requirement for consumer consent prior to disclosing medical record data. The proposed change asks only that health care providers make good-faith efforts to obtain a consumer's written consent before disclosing his or her medical record.

The NMHA opposed the proposed revisions, asserting that were these revisions to be incorporated, they would too readily allow disclosure of personal information. The NMHA stated that the revisions might erode consumer confidence in the health care system and even impede consumers from seeking care because they fear that the personal information they share with their providers might become known to insurers, employers, schools, and other third parties.

In October 2002 several Democrats from the House of Representatives introduced legislation aimed at restoring the specific privacy and consent provisions that had been eliminated. Although the bill, HR 5646, had nearly no chance of passage, many industry observers believe that it sent a clear signal that the issues of patient confidentiality and privacy will be revisited by policy makers and legislators.

Coercion and Commitment

Involuntary treatment, coercion, and commitment are human rights issues of vital importance to persons suffering from serious mental illness, their families, and caregivers. Involuntary commitment to mental hospitals or outpatient treatment and voluntary entry to treatment to prevent involuntary commitment are among the most hotly debated ethical issues in mental health care.

In February 2001 the John D. and Catherine T. MacArthur Foundation, a private, independent organization "dedicated to helping groups and individuals foster lasting improvements in the human condition," released a research report, *The MacArthur Coercion Study,* about mental health patients' moral rights to independent decision making and human dignity. The research looked at perceptions of coercion—the circumstances and actions that make patients and their families feel they have been coerced into treatment—and the effects of coerced treatment.

The researchers found that the official documented hospital admission status did not offer a complete, or entirely accurate, assessment of whether patients were admitted entirely voluntarily or subjected to coercion. Among the study participants, a significant minority of "legally voluntary" patients experienced coercion, and a comparable portion of those involuntarily admitted believed they had freely chosen hospitalization.

The study found that the kinds of pressures applied to gain hospital admission strongly influence patient perceptions of coercion. Threats, force, and other such negative pressures generated feelings of coercion, whereas persuasion and incentives did not. Patients who felt they had a role in the hospitalization decision felt less coerced than those who said they had no voice in the process. Further, patients who reported being treated with respect, concern, and good faith throughout the admission process were significantly less likely to feel they had been coerced than those who felt they had not been treated with dignity and concern. Finally, the researchers observed that some patients' perceptions change over time—about half of the patients who at first denied the need for hospitalization were later able to admit the need for inpatient care.

In 1972 the U.S. Supreme Court ruled that involuntary civil commitment to a psychiatric institution is a deprivation of liberty that the state cannot effect without due process of law. The courts have since reiterated that unless an individual cannot live safely in freedom—poses a risk to self or others—the diagnosis of mental illness is not a sufficient basis for involuntary confinement.

The Judge David L. Bazelon Center for Mental Health Law, a nonprofit legal advocacy organization based in Washington, D.C., opposes involuntary inpatient commitment except "in response to an emergency, and then only when based on a standard of imminent danger of significant harm to self or others and when there is no less restrictive alternative."

The Bazelon Center also opposes involuntary outpatient commitment—mandated treatment with which the patient must comply or risk legal sanctions—deeming it an infringement of an individual's constitutional rights and a strategy that makes coercion appear reasonable within the mental health care delivery system. In addition to compromising consumer confidence and deterring persons from seeking needed care, the center contends that enforcing outpatient commitment diverts resources from treatment and community support services.

Many other patient advocacy organizations agree with the Bazelon Center position that patients should be able to participate in, approve, and decide which treatments to use. They view outpatient commitment as an approach that unfairly punishes patients for mental health system failings, namely an inadequate supply of mental health treatment programs and appropriate community support services.

Mental Health Treatment Issues

There are many raging controversies in mental health treatment, beginning with the definitions and classification of mental illnesses. Which criteria distinguish conditions as mental illness rather than normal variations in thinking and behavior? Should conditions such as attention deficit hyperactivity disorder (ADHD) be classified as learning disorders or mental illnesses? Should neurological conditions that cause brain dysfunction such as Alzheimer's disease be distinguished from mental illness involving brain dysfunction such as depression that may result from (or produce) an imbalance of chemicals in the brain?

Other philosophical questions about mental illness focus on the extent to which persons with mental illness are responsible for their behavior. One such question, for example, is whether certain disorders like substance abuse (alcoholism and other addictions) are entirely outside of the affected individuals' ability to control and whether diagnoses of mental illness are used as excuses for immoral or illegal actions. These questions give rise to the kinds of interventions health professionals, policy makers, and legislators favor—strategies that range from reliance on medical pharmacological therapies (prescription drugs), to social programs offering opportunities for education, housing, and supported employment, to incarceration.

Few People Seek Treatment from Mental Health Professionals

The National Institute of Mental Health (NIMH) observes that not all mental disorders require treatment, because many people with mental disorders have relatively brief, self-limiting illnesses that are not disabling enough to warrant treatment. As much as 70 percent of mental illness goes untreated, and many cases are believed to resolve without any intervention. Among persons seeking help, about half see their primary-care physicians. The remainder visit psychiatrists, clinical psychologists, clinical social workers, or other trained mental health professionals.

Primary-care physicians are often the first professionals to encounter people with mental health disorders. For this reason, the NIMH encourages all primary-care practitioners, who often lack special training to recognize these disorders, to send patients who seek help to mental health professionals for screening to ensure that mental disorders are properly diagnosed and treated. Further, the NIMH recommends that general practice (GPs) physicians receive more training to improve recognition and treatment of psychiatric disorders.

One likely explanation for the relatively small number of persons seeking help from psychiatrists, clinical psychologists, or other trained mental health professionals is the high cost of these services, and the reluctance of insurance companies to cover treatment of mental health disorders or problems. Many private insurance policies offer only limited coverage for mental health services. In addition, mental health practitioners and facilities covered by insurance are unevenly distributed throughout the country. In January 1998, however, Congress made significant progress toward more equitable access to mental health treatment when the Mental Health Parity Act of 1996 (PL 104-204) took effect. The act requires that mental health benefits be comparable to medical/surgical benefits in health plans that cover groups of 50 or more employees.

Satisfaction with Mental Health Treatment?

Increasingly, consumer (patient, client, or family) satisfaction with care received is becoming an important measure of the quality of general medical and mental health care. Satisfaction with mental health services is known to influence both the process and outcomes of treatment, but it is difficult to measure. Consumer satisfaction may be entirely unrelated to actual treatment received; instead it may depend largely on prior experiences with mental health services, the setting in which care is delivered, expectations of services, and whether the services were sought by the client or enforced by court order or some form of coercion.

Although it is challenging to assess client and family satisfaction with mental health treatment, it is imperative for both ethical and pragmatic reasons. There is an ethical imperative that the client and family experience the process as respectful, participatory, and helpful. The client and family are ultimately the persons whose lives are most affected by the outcomes. Pragmatically, mental health treatment cannot be optimally effective unless clients trust their therapists or other practitioners, share actual concerns, continue to attend and actively participate, adhere to prescribed treatment, and implement suggested changes.

The Pennsylvania Department of Public Welfare Office of Mental Health and Substance Abuse Services offers guidelines intended to emphasize and promote client and family satisfaction with treatment. These include:

- Mental health treatment is respectful, recognizing the knowledge and the capabilities of the clients and families

- Identified concerns are clarified and addressed, with the mental health professional listening and asking questions, not just informing and directing

- There is clear commitment to build on identified capabilities and strengths

- Treatment decisions such as the plan to broaden the therapeutic agenda and to address other relevant issues are made jointly by the client, family, and the mental health professional, based on a shared exploration and negotiation, with the client's desired outcomes in mind

- The mental health professional is alert to therapeutic process—how the client may be experiencing the immediate event—so that access, voice, and ownership are all valued and promoted

Ann Garland and her colleagues examined factors linked to youths' satisfaction with mental health care and reported their findings in "Correlates of Adolescents' Satisfaction with Mental Health Services" (*Mental Health Services Research,* vol. 2, no. 3, 2000). The investigators administered the Multidimensional Adolescent Satisfaction Scale (MASS), a relatively new 21-item self-administered questionnaire, to 180 randomly selected adolescents currently or previously receiving mental health services in San Diego County, California. The MASS measures satisfaction with four aspects of services—the perceived quality of the relationship between the counselor and clients; the client's perception of whether his or her needs are being met; the client's perception of the effectiveness of the treatment; and whether there is conflict between the client and counselor.

The investigators found that satisfaction was related to various factors: the type of site where treatment was received, with highest reported satisfaction among participants treated in a specialty clinic for mistreated adolescents; client attitudinal variables such as the adolescent's motivation to seek or remain in treatment; the reason for seeking treatment; and the duration of treatment, with those in treatment longer reporting greater satisfaction. Factors that were not linked to high satisfaction ratings were age, gender, race, ethnicity, single-parent versus two-parent families, type of treatment received, total number of lifetime visits, prior history of receiving care, role of parent, courts, or school system in seeking services, and the type of behavior or emotional problems treated.

Does Everyone Benefit from Mental Health Treatment?

Even the staunchest advocates of psychotherapy, psychopharmacology, and other mental health treatment concur that not everyone needs or will benefit from mental health care. Persons suffering from mental health problems, as opposed to the more serious mental health disorders, usually do not require professional intervention. Minor mental health problems often resolve spontaneously, and traditional sources of community support—family, friends, and clergy members—may be as effective, more accessible, and certainly less costly than professional mental health treatment.

Although most health professionals acknowledge the need for, and role of, mental health treatment for persons with severe, persistent mental health disorders, there are those who decry mental health treatment as useless, or even potentially harmful. Thomas Szasz, M.D., an emeritus professor of psychiatry, has published many books, including his well-known *The Myth of Mental Illness: Foundations of a Theory of Personal Conduct* (Quill, New York, Revised edition, 1994) and articles espousing his belief that mental illness is simply thinking and behavior that are unacceptable in society. Dr. Szasz contends that the only conditions that should be termed mental illnesses are those that have been conclusively demonstrated to result from anatomical (structural) changes or physiological processes. Examples of conditions that are currently termed mental health problems that Szasz would consider behaviors include mild depression, hyperactivity, and shyness.

Szasz and others assert that the mental illness label may become a self-fulfilling prophecy for some; in other instances it is used as a way to control people who are threats to society but not necessarily criminals. Many industry observers are especially uneasy about labeling children with psychiatric diagnoses. Some diagnoses, they argue, prompt placing children on powerful prescription drugs to alter their moods and behavior. Further, these psychiatric labels may follow them for life, subjecting them to stigmatization and discrimination.

An outspoken critic of his own profession, Szasz believes not only that the incidence and prevalence of mental illness have been fabricated but also that the safety and benefits of mental health treatment have been exaggerated. Further, he feels that the myth of mental illness and efficacy of treatment are promoted by psychiatrists, psychologists, drug companies, and other mental health professionals, who profit financially from the view that mental illness is a medical problem amenable to professional intervention.

CHAPTER 6
THE MENTAL HEALTH ECONOMY

Mental Health: Better Benefits Won't Break the Bank

—Paul Raeburn, headline in *BusinessWeek online,* December 17, 2001

The Center for Mental Health Services (CMHS) is the agency within the Substance Abuse and Mental Health Services Administration (SAMHSA) of the U.S. Department of Health and Human Services (DHHS) that gathers national mental health statistics. CMHS uses these statistics to project the mental health economy. Every two years CMHS prepares a report, *Mental Health: United States,* that considers psychiatric epidemiology (the study of the causes, extent, and types of illness in populations), the status of mental health service delivery, and mental health policy. Other sources of information about mental health spending include the U.S. General Accounting Office (GAO), the Centers for Disease Control and Prevention (CDC) (which tracks mental health service utilization), and the comprehensive review *Mental Health: A Report of the Surgeon General, 1999.*

MENTAL HEALTH COSTS

The total cost of mental health is measured in terms of direct costs—expenses incurred for medical resources such as hospitalization, treatment, and rehabilitation—and the indirect costs of mental illness—costs not related to treatment. Direct costs are generally easier to quantify, because they reflect services provided by facilities, organizations, and specialty providers (psychiatrists, clinical psychologists, social workers, marriage and family counselors, psychiatric nurses, and other mental health workers). However, even these estimates vary, depending on the diagnoses included in the classification "mental disorders." For example, of the $99 billion spent on direct treatment of mental disorders in 1996, $69 billion was devoted to mental health services, $13 billion to substance abuse treatment, and $18 billion for treatment of persons with Alzheimer's disease and other dementias. When dis-

eases traditionally viewed as having both mental and physical health components, such as Alzheimer's disease and other dementias, are included for the purpose of cost accounting, the direct and indirect costs of mental health disorders increase.

An international study conducted by the World Bank and World Health Organization (WHO) found that indirect costs of mental illness contribute to more than 15 percent of the global burden of disease in the United States. The WHO estimated that in 2002, the U.S. economy suffered an excess of $63 billion in productivity losses, including the time employees took off from work to care for their mentally ill family members. The WHO also factors into its cost estimates the inability of disabled people to obtain an education or to find jobs when their illnesses go untreated. Figure 6.1 shows that during 2002 mental illness was the leading cause of disability in the United States, Canada, and western Europe.

Indirect Costs Far Exceed Costs of Treatment

Measures of indirect costs vary considerably because some include only lost wages and productivity, while others calculate the costs of increased absenteeism, short- and long-term disability, and workers' compensation. The U.S. Surgeon General's report observed that the indirect costs of mental illness totaled almost $79 billion in 1990 and that 80 percent of the indirect costs were due to morbidity (illness-related losses of productivity) as opposed to mortality (death). Of the total, $63 billion was attributable to lost productivity, $12 billion resulted from premature death, and $4 billion was lost on criminal justice system involvement with incarcerated persons and the time family members devoted to providing custodial care.

The most comprehensive measures of indirect costs also may contain estimates of losses such as those sustained as a result of criminal activity, property damage, and motor vehicle accidents. Some calculations of

FIGURE 6.1

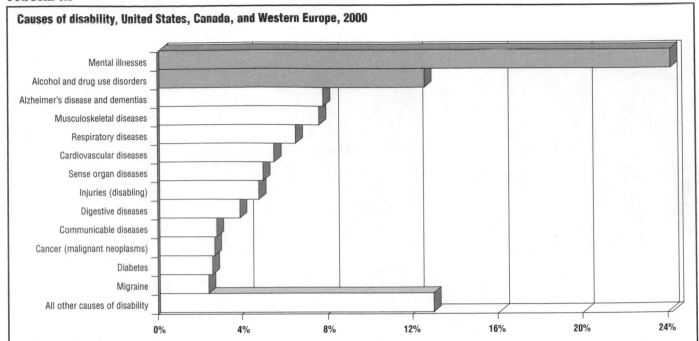

Causes of disability, United States, Canada, and Western Europe, 2000

Note: Causes of disability for all ages combined. Measures of disability are based on the number of years of "healthy" life lost with less than full health (i.e., YLD: years lost due to disability) for each incidence of disease, illness, or condition. All data shown add up to 100%.

SOURCE: "Figure 1.1. Causes of disability—United States, Canada, and Western Europe, 2000," in *Achieving the Promise: Transforming Mental Health Care in America,* President's New Freedom Commission On Mental Health, Rockville, MD, 2001

indirect costs attempt to include the effects of mental illness on socioeconomic status, since men who develop mental health disorders before age 16 are less likely to complete their education and more likely to be unemployed. According to American Psychiatric Association estimates published in 1997, the indirect costs of mental illness are in excess of $273 billion per year, more than four times the amount spent on direct costs. The SAMHSA's estimate of indirect costs came close to $300 billion when it included social welfare and medical costs related to treatment of diseases resulting from substance abuse, such as HIV (human immunodeficiency virus) infection acquired through intravenous drug use or cirrhosis of the liver from abuse of alcohol. This was about 4 times more than was spent on mental health treatment and 25 times more than was spent on treatment of substance abuse alone (*National Expenditures for Mental Health, and Substance Abuse Treatment, 1997*).

MENTAL HEALTH SPENDING

Figure 6.2 shows that Americans spent more on mental health treatment in 1997 than they did on software, movies and records, and home furnishings.

According to the Surgeon General's report, between 1987 and 1997, spending for mental health rose more slowly (3.7 percent annually) than overall health care spending, which grew by 5 percent annually during the same period. (See Figure 6.3.) The slower growth and the

FIGURE 6.2

Mental health/substance abuse (MH/SA) expenditures and other major economic expenditures, 1997

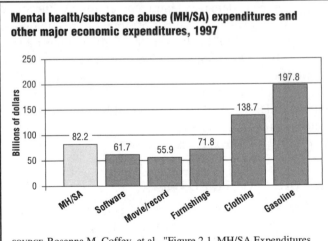

SOURCE: Rosanna M. Coffey, et al., "Figure 2.1. MH/SA Expenditures Were a Major Component of U.S. Economy in 1997," in *National Estimates of Expenditures for Mental Health and Substance Abuse Treatment, 1997,* U.S. Department of Health and Human Services, Substance Abuse and Mental Health Services Administration, Rockville, MD, July 2000

fact that spending on mental health care declined as a percentage of total health care spending were primarily the result of less spending on hospitals. During the period, inpatient hospital volume sharply declined in favor of outpatient and less restrictive treatment settings.

Further, enrollment in managed care organizations (MCOs) such as health maintenance organizations

FIGURE 6.3

Mental health/substance abuse (MH/SA) expenditure growth rates, 1987–97

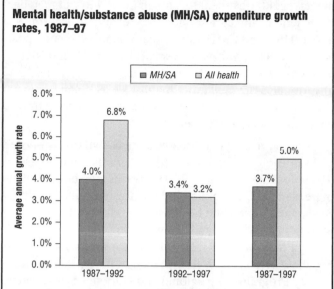

SOURCE: Rosanna M. Coffey, et al., "Figure 3.1. MH/SA Expenditures Grew More Slowly than All Health between 1987 and 1997," in *National Estimates of Expenditures for Mental Health and Substance Abuse Treatment, 1997*, U.S. Department of Health and Human Services, Substance Abuse and Mental Health Services Administration, Rockville, MD, July 2000

FIGURE 6.4

Mental health prescription drug spending, 1997

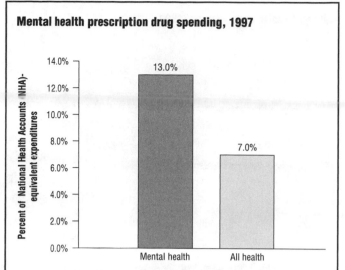

SOURCE: Rosanna M. Coffey, et al., "Figure 4.3. Retail Drugs Were a Much Larger Share of MH Spending Than of All Health in 1997," in *National Estimates of Expenditures for Mental Health and Substance Abuse Treatment, 1997*, U.S. Department of Health and Human Services, Substance Abuse and Mental Health Services Administration, Rockville, MD, July 2000

(HMOs), preferred provider organizations (PPOs), and behavioral medicine plans grew rapidly during the early 1990s. MCOs have demonstrated the capacity to control expenditures by shifting inpatient services to outpatient settings and decreasing volume by reducing both the average lengths of hospital stay (ALOS) and the average number of outpatient visits. Managed behavioral health care plans contain costs by applying stringent case management to prevent costly inpatient hospitalizations or reduce lengths of stay. Case management activities include attentive follow-up to ensure continuity of care, adherence to prescribed treatment, and effective use of community, as opposed to institutional, resources.

In contrast, the fastest growing sector of mental health spending was for newly available prescription medications, particularly antidepressants—tricyclics and the newer selective serotonin reuptake inhibitors (such as Prozac, Paxil, and Zoloft)—and, to a lesser extent, antipsychotic drugs to treat mental health disorders. Prescription drugs accounted for only 7 percent of all health care costs in 1987, but in 1997, they represented 13 percent of all mental health spending. (See Figure 6.4.) Despite the higher spending for psychoactive prescription drugs, some industry observers feel that the increased availability of effective drug therapy actually served to contain mental health spending by enabling providers to offer drug therapy instead of more costly inpatient treatment. Office-based physician services for mental health and substance abuse treatment also rose 5.5 percent from 1987–97, more than the 4.5 percent increase observed for

all of health care. The growth of both of these components of care was more rapid during the second half of the decade—from 1992 to 1997.

Sources of Mental Health Funding

In 1996 more than half (53 percent) of the funds for mental health treatment were from public payors, and federal spending grew at more than twice the rate of state and local spending. Of the public monies spent on mental health in 1996, 19 percent came from Medicaid, 18 percent from state and local programs, 14 percent from Medicare, and 2 percent from other federal funds. Although the Medicaid program covered just 12 percent of the U.S. population, it paid 19 percent of the costs for mental health treatment.

By 1997, national expenditures for mental health and substance abuse treatment were 7.8 percent of the $1 trillion health care economy and totaled $82.2 billion. (When social service expenditures were added, there was a higher total of $85.3 billion for 1997.) Public sources provided 58 percent of funds, up 5 percent from the previous year. Of this total, 86 percent was for mental health treatment and 14 percent was for substance abuse treatment. (See Figure 6.5.)

The public sector bore a disproportionate and increasing share of the direct costs for mental health treatment. Figure 6.6 compares 1987 and 1997 funding sources and shows the slight declines in state, local, and private funds and increased reliance on federal funds. From 1987 to 1997 Medicaid's combined state and federal proportion of mental health spending rose from just over 15 percent ($5.7 billion)

FIGURE 6.5

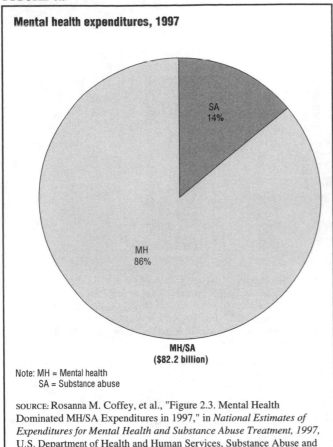

Mental health expenditures, 1997

SA
14%

MH
86%

MH/SA
($82.2 billion)

Note: MH = Mental health
SA = Substance abuse

SOURCE: Rosanna M. Coffey, et al., "Figure 2.3. Mental Health Dominated MH/SA Expenditures in 1997," in *National Estimates of Expenditures for Mental Health and Substance Abuse Treatment, 1997,* U.S. Department of Health and Human Services, Substance Abuse and Mental Health Services Administration, Rockville, MD, July 2000

Similarly, state and local government funds pay for mental health treatment to a much greater extent than they do general health care services. For example, according to a SAMHSA and CMHS study released in 1997 and updated in July 2000, *National Expenditures for Mental Health, and Substance Abuse Treatment,* in 1997 state and local governments devoted more than twice as much to mental health and substance abuse treatment (28 percent) than to health care services (13 percent).

For the fiscal year 2004 budget, SAMHSA proposed $834 million for mental health programs, an increase of $11.9 million over the 2003 President's budget. This increased budget acknowledged the priority President Bush placed on mental health services issues. Of the $11.9 million increase, $10 million was earmarked for the Children's Program and $3.2 million is for programs to assist homeless persons with serious mental illness. (The discretionary Programs of Regional and National Significance, aimed at improving services, expanding capacity, and enhancing effectiveness, will be reduced by $1.3 million.)

State Mental Health Agency Expenditures

A number of court rulings during the 1970s and an evolution in professional thinking prompted the release of many persons with serious mental illness from institutions to community treatment programs. The census (number of patients or occupants, which is frequently referred to as a rate) of public mental hospitals sharply declined, and there was increasing pressure on the states to deliver community-based treatment.

State mental health agencies (SMHAs) operate the public mental health system that acts as a safety net for poor, uninsured, and otherwise indigent persons suffering from mental illness. In a report comparing SMHA expenditures for mental health services throughout the nation between 1981 and 1997, researchers Ted Lutterman and Michael Hogan also characterized these public mental health systems as "safety valves for inadequate private sector response to mental illness" ("Key Elements of the National Statistical Picture," *Chapter 16, State Mental Health Agency Controlled Expenditures and Revenues for Mental Health Services, FY 1981 to FY 1997,* United States Department of Health and Human Services, Substance Abuse and Mental Health Services Administration, Center for Mental Health Services, Rockville, MD, 2000). SMHAs vary from state to state—some purchase, regulate, administer, manage, and provide care and treatment; others simply purchase care, using public funds that include general state revenues and federal funds. Generally, the federal funds are Medicare and Medicaid payments made to state-owned or operated facilities, although SMHAs also administer additional Medicaid payments when the state Medicaid agency grants the SHMA control of all Medicaid mental health expenditures.

Similar to the movement of privately insured persons into managed care, during the 1990s state Medicaid

to almost 20 percent ($14.4 billion), and Medicare's contribution increased from 8 percent to over 12 percent, which translates into an increase from $3 billion to $9 billion.

A report prepared for the U.S. Senate Committee on Finance, *Mental Health Community-Based Care Increases for People With Serious Mental Illness* (U.S. General Accounting Office, Washington, D.C., December 2000), attributed the Medicaid increase to higher costs for psychiatric prescription medications, the states' increased use of Medicaid to pay for community-based care, and a change in the location of inpatient service delivery. Instead of obtaining inpatient care in psychiatric hospitals, which is not covered by Medicaid, Medicaid beneficiaries received inpatient mental health care in the psychiatric units of general acute-care hospitals, where such services are covered. The rise in Medicare spending is believed to have occurred in response to 1990 legislation that expanded coverage of care from nonphysician mental health practitioners, also known as "specialty providers," such as psychologists, clinical social workers, and nurse practitioners. Specialty providers deliver the majority of mental health treatment—specialty providers received 71 percent of total mental health expenditures in 1997, compared to 14.3 percent received by general providers. (See Figure 6.7.)

FIGURE 6.6

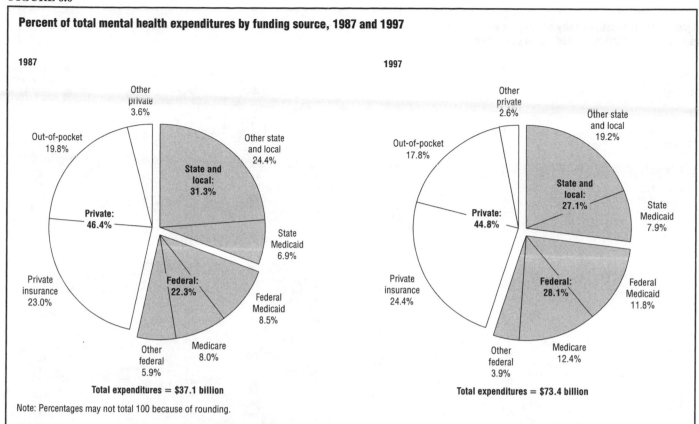

Percent of total mental health expenditures by funding source, 1987 and 1997

1987

Other private 3.6%
Out-of-pocket 19.8%
Other state and local 24.4%
State and local: 31.3%
Private: 46.4%
State Medicaid 6.9%
Private insurance 23.0%
Federal: 22.3%
Federal Medicaid 8.5%
Other federal 5.9%
Medicare 8.0%

Total expenditures = $37.1 billion

1997

Other private 2.6%
Out-of-pocket 17.8%
Other state and local 19.2%
State and local: 27.1%
Private: 44.8%
State Medicaid 7.9%
Private insurance 24.4%
Federal: 28.1%
Federal Medicaid 11.8%
Other federal 3.9%
Medicare 12.4%

Total expenditures = $73.4 billion

Note: Percentages may not total 100 because of rounding.

SOURCE: "Figure 1. Percentage of Total Mental Health Expenditures by Funding Source, 1987 and 1997," in "Community-Based Care Increases for People with Serious Mental Illness," *Mental Health,* GAO-01-224, December 2000

programs turned to MCOs and behavioral health services in an effort to contain costs. About half the states have separated the administration and financing of physical health and mental health in their MCO contracts.

Lutterman and Hogan reported that throughout the 1990s, SHMA spending for inpatient psychiatric care decreased from 53 percent to 41 percent of all SHMA spending in 1997, cutting state hospital expenditures by 29 percent between 1990 and 1997. Simultaneously, SMHAs increased community mental health funding, including residential services such as supported housing and group homes, by 86 percent. The researchers found considerable regional variation in SMHA spending. States with the highest expenditures were in the Northeast and Northwest, while southern states spent the least. They also observed that although total SMHA expenditures for mental health had increased, spending had not kept up with inflation or other government spending such as funds for state corrections programs and other health and welfare programs since the early 1990s. Table 6.1 shows changes in spending by SHMAs from 1981 to 1997 and the geographic variations in per capita spending.

SMHAs manage funds from the SAMHSA (Substance Abuse and Mental Health Services Administration) Community Mental Health Block Grant Program

FIGURE 6.7

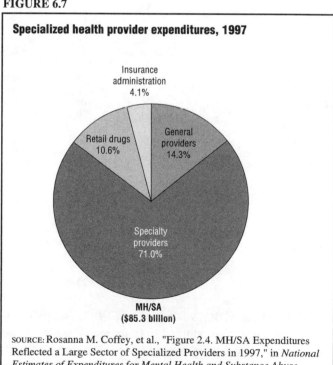

Specialized health provider expenditures, 1997

Insurance administration 4.1%
Retail drugs 10.6%
General providers 14.3%
Specialty providers 71.0%

MH/SA ($85.3 billion)

SOURCE: Rosanna M. Coffey, et al., "Figure 2.4. MH/SA Expenditures Reflected a Large Sector of Specialized Providers in 1997," in *National Estimates of Expenditures for Mental Health and Substance Abuse Treatment, 1997,* U.S. Department of Health and Human Services, Substance Abuse and Mental Health Services Administration, Rockville, MD, July 2000

TABLE 6.1

State mental health agency per capita expenditures for mental health services and average annual percent change by geographic division and state, selected fiscal years 1981–97

Geographic division and state	1981	1983	1985	1987	1990[1]	1993[1,2]	1997[1,2]	Average annual percent change 1981–97
				Amount per capita				
United States	$ 27	$ 31	$ 35	$ 38	$ 48	$ 54	$ 64	5.5
New England:								
Maine	25	32	36	42	67	70	88	8.2
New Hampshire	35	39	42	36	63	78	99	6.8
Vermont	32	40	44	44	54	74	92	6.8
Massachusetts	32	36	46	62	84	83	90	6.7
Rhode Island	36	32	35	41	50	61	63	3.6
Connecticut	32	39	44	56	73	82	99	7.4
Middle Atlantic:								
New York	67	74	90	99	118	131	113	3.3
New Jersey	26	31	36	43	57	68	69	6.2
Pennsylvania	41	47	52	50	57	68	68	3.3
East North Central:								
Ohio	25	29	30	34	41	47	52	4.8
Indiana	19	23	27	31	47	39	40	4.8
Illinois	18	21	24	25	34	36	51	6.8
Michigan	33	39	49	61	74	75	87	6.3
Wisconsin	22	27	28	31	37	35	44	4.3
West North Central:								
Minnesota[3]	17	30	32	42	54	69	87	10.8
Iowa	8	10	11	12	17	13	29	8.5
Missouri	24	25	28	32	35	41	56	5.5
North Dakota	39	42	36	42	40	43	48	1.4
South Dakota	17	21	22	27	25	47	54	7.5
Nebraska	17	19	21	21	29	34	39	5.5
Kansas	18	22	27	28	35	48	59	7.9
South Atlantic:								
Delaware	44	51	46	41	55	56	73	3.2
Maryland	33	37	40	49	61	64	76	5.4
District of Columbia[4]	—	23	28	130	268	315	337	—
Virginia	23	29	32	35	45	40	49	4.9
West Virginia	20	20	22	23	24	22	23	1.0
North Carolina	24	29	38	41	46	50	62	6.2
South Carolina	31	33	33	45	51	56	64	4.7
Georgia	25	26	23	32	51	49	47	4.0
Florida	20	23	26	25	37	31	44	5.1
East South Central:								
Kentucky	15	17	19	23	23	25	35	5.5
Tennessee	18	20	23	24	29	37	23	1.6
Alabama	20	24	28	29	38	43	47	5.5
Mississippi	14	16	24	22	34	41	56	9.2
West South Central:								
Arkansas	17	20	24	24	26	30	30	3.7
Louisiana	19	23	26	25	28	39	43	5.3
Oklahoma	22	33	31	30	36	38	41	3.9
Texas	13	16	17	19	23	31	39	7.1
Mountain:								
Montana	25	28	29	28	28	34	93	8.7
Idaho	13	15	15	17	20	26	29	4.9
Wyoming	23	28	31	30	35	42	43	4.0
Colorado	24	25	28	30	34	41	57	5.6
New Mexico	24	25	25	24	23	24	31	1.7
Arizona	10	10	12	16	27	60	68	12.7
Utah	13	16	17	19	21	25	28	4.8
Nevada	22	25	26	28	33	32	45	4.6

(MHBG). The MHBG was created in 1982, and its flexible funding enables states to innovate, develop, and expand successful community-based programs. Block grants are awarded based on a formula that considers each state's population, service costs, income, and taxable resources. The funds enable the states to finance community mental health treatment programs. Since its start, MHBG expenditures dropped by 49 percent in inflation-adjusted dollars during the 1990s, but in 1999 Congress appropriated an additional $13.4 million to the MHBG. SAMHSA provided $356 million in block grant funding during fiscal year 2000. Of this total, each state received an average of $5.7 million and SAMHSA allocated $18 million for system development, technical assistance, data collection, and evaluation. In fiscal year 2002 mental health block grant funding had risen to $433 million, with

TABLE 6.1

State mental health agency per capita expenditures for mental health services and average annual percent change by geographic division and state, selected fiscal years 1981–97 [CONTINUED]

Geographic division and state	1981	1983	1985	1987	1990[1]	1993[1,2]	1997[1,2]	Average annual percent change 1981–97
				Amount per capita				
United States	$ 27	$ 31	$ 35	$ 38	$ 48	$ 54	$ 64	5.5
Pacific:								
Washington	18	24	30	37	43	66	79	9.8
Oregon	21	21	25	28	41	60	68	7.8
California	28	29	34	30	42	50	58	4.6
Alaska	38	41	45	50	72	86	79	4.7
Hawaii	19	22	23	26	38	71	85	9.9

—Data not available.
[1]Puerto Rico is included in U.S. total.
[2]Guam is included in U.S. total.
[3]Data for 1981 not comparable with 1983–93 data for Minnesota. Average annual percent change is for 1983–97.
[4]Transfer of St. Elizabeth's Hospital from the National Institute of Mental Health to the District of Columbia Office of Mental Health took place over the years 1985–93.
Note: Expenditures for mental illness, excluding mental retardation and substance abuse.

SOURCE: P. N. Pastor, D. M. Makuc, C. Reuben, and H. Xia, "Table 143. State mental health agency per capita expenditures for mental health services and average annual percent change by geographic division and State: United States, selected fiscal years 1981–97," in *Health United States, 2002 with Chartbook on Trends in the Health of Americans*, Centers for Disease Control and Prevention, National Center for Health Statistics, Hyattsville, MD, 2002

the same dollar amount included in the 2003 budget and 2004 budget estimate.

Is Mental Health Spending Adequate?

In view of the 1999 Surgeon General's report documenting a wide gap between those in need of mental health treatment and those receiving care, many observers question whether present levels of mental health spending are sufficient. They wonder if inadequate funding delays or impedes access to care and whether an additional investment in direct expenditures could prevent even greater indirect losses associated with mental illness.

Timely, appropriate mental health treatment not only reduces the morbidity and mortality associated with mental illness but also has been demonstrated to increase productivity among persons with mental illness and generate cost savings in areas unrelated to mental health. Preliminary findings from the RAND *Partners in Care* (PIC) program support the premise that a modest investment of resources to treat mental illness produces substantial returns in terms of health outcomes, quality of life, and employment. PIC is a study involving quality improvement initiatives among more than 27,000 patients, 125 providers, and 46 primary-care clinics within six nonacademic managed care practices in various locations throughout the United States.

Not unexpectedly, the PIC program significantly increased the rates of counseling and appropriate use of antidepressant medications. More surprising was the program's ability to promote and support continued employment among participants. Compared to the control group that received traditional care, 5 percent more PIC participants remained in the workforce 12 months after treatment began. Although remaining employed is just one measure of productivity, it has far-reaching economic and policy implications because it prevents a range of indirect losses, including loss of health insurance coverage, reliance on health care entitlement programs and financial assistance, and use of social services.

Researchers from the Yale University Departments of Psychiatry and Public Health compared the health and disability costs associated with depression and four other chronic health conditions among employees and reported their results in "Health and Disability Costs of Depressive Illness in a Major U.S. Corporation" (*American Journal of Psychiatry*, vol. 157, no. 8, August 2000). They found that employees treated for depression cost more, in terms of health and disability-related expenses, particularly absenteeism, than employees with other chronic health problems. Depressed employees took an average of nearly 10 sick days, significantly more than employees suffering from other medical problems. Further, the combination of depression with any other medical condition was found to be greater than the total costs associated with either condition alone.

Despite mounting evidence of the health, social, and economic benefits of appropriate treatment, other policy makers assert that spending is adequate to meet existing need and that the slower rate of mental health spending in comparison to general health care spending reflects successful efforts to contain costs as well as the advent of effective drug therapies to treat mental illness without costly inpatient hospitalization.

MENTAL HEALTH PARITY

In the discussion of mental health care, parity refers to the premise that the same range and scope of insurance benefits available for other illnesses should be provided for persons with mental illness. Until the 1960s mental health care was financed primarily by the government. As mental health services expanded, support programs and treatment were funded by a variety of public and private sources. Public funding sources for support programs included Supplemental Security Income (SSI), housing voucher programs, and state vocational rehabilitation services.

Historically, private health insurance plans have provided less coverage for mental illness than for the diagnosis and treatment of other medical conditions. Coverage for mental health was more restricted and often involved more cost sharing—higher co-payments and deductibles—than coverage for medical care. As a result, many patients with severe mental illness, who frequently required multiple hospitalizations and other treatment, quickly depleted their mental health coverage.

During the 1990s there was growing interest in parity of mental health with other health services such as medical and surgical care. The *Mental Health Parity Act of 1996* sought to bring mental health benefits closer to other health benefits. The act amended the *Employee Retirement Income Security Act* of 1974 (ERISA) and the *1944 Public Health Service Act,* which required parity for annual and lifetime dollar limits but did not place restrictions on other plan features such as hospital and office visit limits. It also imposed federal standards on the mental health coverage offered by employers through group health plans.

The federal law became effective for group health plans on January 1, 1998. Selected employers were exempt from the law, such as those with 50 or fewer employees, group plans that experienced increased claims costs of 1 percent or more as a result of compliance with the law, and plans that offered individual, nongroup coverage. By 2003 more than half of the state laws governing mental health parity were more comprehensive in scope than the federal legislation, and nearly one-third of the states required full parity.

COSTS OF PARITY

Critics of the parity legislation and many employers expressed concern that the law would sharply increase costs; however, several studies, including those performed by the Congressional Budget Office and projections made by private actuarial and accounting firms, forecast cost increases of about 1 percent for parity in terms of dollar limits. Full parity for mental health and substance abuse was estimated by most studies to increase costs by 2.5 to 4 percent. (See Table 6.2.)

Some studies conducted before the implementation of parity legislation estimated that the cost of providing the same level of outpatient mental health care is about twice as

TABLE 6.2

Estimated cost increases for full parity in mental health and substance abuse benefits

Study	Scope	Increase[1]
Coopers and Lybrand	National	3.2%
Milliman and Robertson	National	3.9
Congressional Budget Office	National	4.0
Mathematica Policy Research	National	3.6
Department of Banking, Insurance, Securities, and Health Care Administration	Vermont	0–3
North Carolina Psychological Association	North Carolina	[2]
Price Waterhouse Coopers[3]	16 states[4]	2.5–3.9

[1]The national figures are estimates of premium increases. The figures for the individual states represent an expected increase in claims costs. The percentages are a composite of the estimated cost increases for fee-for-service, preferred provider organization, point of service, and health maintenance organization (HMO) plans. Typically, cost estimates assume that HMO and other managed care plans have lower cost increases.
[2]Between 1992 and June 1998, mental health payments as a percentage of total health payments for the N.C. Comprehensive Major Medical Plan for Teachers and State Employees decreased from 6.4 to 3.1 percent, representing a cumulative cost reduction of 52 percent. In this health plan, the mental health benefits are managed by a managed behavioral health care organization.
[3]Price Waterhouse Coopers is the result of a merger between Price Waterhouse and Coopers and Lybrand.
[4]Price Waterhouse Coopers estimated the claims costs increases of parity for mental health and substance abuse benefits in Arizona, California, Delaware, Kentucky, Massachusetts, Michigan, Missouri, Nebraska, New Jersey, New Mexico, Nevada, North Carolina, Ohio, Oregon, South Carolina, and Vermont.

SOURCE: "Table 6. Estimated Cost Increases for Full Parity in Mental Health and Substance Abuse Benefits," in "Despite New Federal Standards, Mental Health Benefits Remain Limited," *Mental Health Parity Act,* vol. GAO/HEHS-00-95, May 2000

much as for general medical care. As a result of these estimates, traditional fee-for-service indemnity insurers projected that providing insurance protection against the risks of mental illness would be substantially more costly than for other medical problems. Insurers also feared adverse selection—that plans with comprehensive mental health benefits would attract a disproportionate number of persons with severe mental illness who would be costly to treat. Similarly, in the absence of mandated minimum mental health benefits, insurers could offer poor mental health benefits to deter persons in need of treatment from enrolling in their plans.

Managed care plans may be as compelled as indemnity insurers to discourage persons with potentially costly illnesses from enrolling in their plans; however, they have different utilization and cost controls than indemnity insurers. Rather than reducing demand for services by increasing cost sharing, such as consumers' out-of-pocket expenses like co-payments and deductibles, managed care regulates treatment decision making. For example, managed care plans may direct consumers to outpatient as opposed to inpatient services or to peer counseling programs instead of mental health professionals. By controlling treatment and related services, managed care plans are able to extend coverage and benefits to more people at little or no additional cost.

An interim report to Congress from the National Advisory Mental Health Council (NAMHC), *Parity in*

Financing Mental Health Services: Managed Care Effects On Cost, Access, and Quality (Department of Health and Human Services, National Institutes of Health, National Institute of Mental Health, May 1998), found that in health systems already using managed care, instituting parity resulted in less than a 1 percent increase in total health care costs during a one-year period. Further, as the proportion of the population enrolled in managed care increased, the projected cost of parity decreased. Health care delivery systems that did not use managed care actually experienced significant reductions—between 30 and 50 percent—in total mental health costs. (Unmanaged systems had more savings because their costs were so much higher than managed care costs before parity was instituted.)

A more recent analysis performed during 2000 for the NAMHC considered the effects of parity on costs, utilization, and access for an employer with more than 150,000 employees. The four-year study that began one year before parity went into effect found that by the third year of parity the proportion of persons receiving mental health services grew from less than 5 percent to more than 7 percent and costs were reduced by half. The cost reductions were attributed to substantial declines in inpatient utilization, reduced lengths of stay, lower per diem costs, and lower costs for mental health care for children and adolescents.

ACCESS TO CARE UNDER PARITY

The NAMHC report asserted that parity does not necessarily improve access to mental health care, because managed care and behavioral health plans serve to control access and counter some of the gains made as a result of parity. Managed behavioral health "carveout" arrangements appear to influence access by offering more people access to basic mental health care than was available through traditional fee-for-service practice. To offset the costs of this increased access, these plans generally reduce the intensity of more costly services, primarily inpatient treatment and long-term psychotherapy.

Parity May Not Solve All Access Problems

According to researchers from the Harvard Medical School and University of Maryland School of Medicine, parity alone will not eliminate all obstacles to gaining access to mental health care. In "Will Parity Coverage Result in Better Mental Health Care?" (*New England Journal of Medicine*, vol. 345, no. 23, December 6, 2001), Drs. Richard Frank, Howard Goldman, and Thomas McGuire stated that most private insurance does not cover vital components of effective mental health services. For example, private insurance does not usually cover day-hospital programs, case management, psychosocial rehabilitation, or residential treatment. Nor does it cover services such as supervised housing or supported employment. The researchers contended that true parity would

require an expanded concept of health insurance and would necessitate coverage of all services deemed necessary for optimally effective mental health care.

THE RELATIONSHIP BETWEEN QUALITY OF CARE AND PARITY

Questions about the impact of parity on the quality of care have focused on access to mental health services and whether managed care or behavioral health plans will unduly limit access to needed services for persons with severe mental illness—an especially vulnerable group. Since quality of mental health care has historically been measured in terms of process rather than outcome measures, and the process of mental health care delivery varies considerably across managed care plans, there has not been a conclusive determination of the effect of parity on the quality of mental health treatment.

Researcher and academician David Mechanic observed that the application of parity poses quality concerns because definitions of medical necessity—the requirement that managed care plans provide all necessary services—and standards of mental health care are not as well defined as those for medical and surgical care. Consequently, Mechanic contended that mental health care might be managed more rigorously with larger reductions in treatment and services. He cited evidence that while managed care may provide more people with access to nominal mental health care, it also may provide less intensive services than needed to those with severe mental illness (*Mental Health Policy at the Millennium: Challenges and Opportunities, Mental Health United States, 2000, Chapter 7*, U.S. Department of Health and Human Services, Substance Abuse and Mental Health Services Administration, The Center for Mental Health Services, Washington, D.C., 2000).

THE EFFECTS OF FEDERAL MENTAL HEALTH PARITY LEGISLATION ON EMPLOYERS

In 2000 the U.S. General Accounting Office (GAO) completed a study to determine the extent to which employers had complied with the requirements of the *Mental Health Parity Act of 1996*; the act's effect on the cost of health insurance claims; and the actions federal agencies had taken to assure compliance with the act. The study involved analyzing the results of a questionnaire mailed to a representative sample of employers that offered mental health benefits and interviewing officials from the federal agencies charged with ensuring compliance.

The GAO employer survey found that 86 percent of the employers that responded said their health plans were consistent with federal parity requirements that annual and lifetime dollar limits for mental health benefits were comparable to medical and surgical benefits. Just four years earlier, before the parity legislation was enacted, a

TABLE 6.3

Compliant employer plans reporting more restrictive limits on mental health benefits than medical and surgical benefits, 1999

Mental health plan design feature	Percent
Lower outpatient office visit limits	66
Lower hospital day limits[1]	65
Higher outpatient office visit copayments[1]	27
Higher outpatient office visit coinsurance[1]	25
Higher cap on enrollee out-of-pocket costs	12
Higher hospital stay coinsurance	10
Higher hospital stay copayments[1]	5

[1]The differences between compliant and noncompliant plans placing more restrictive limits on mental health services for these plan design features were not statistically significant.

SOURCE: "Table 3. Compliant Employer Plans Reporting More Restrictive Limits on Mental Health Benefits Than Medical and Surgical Benefits, 1999," in "Despite New Federal Standards, Mental Health Benefits Remain Limited," *Mental Health Parity Act*, vol. GAO/HEHS-00-95, May 2000

TABLE 6.4

Employee opinion poll on access to mental health services, 1999

IN YOUR VIEW, HAVE THE CHANGES MADE TO YOUR MENTAL HEALTH BENEFITS SINCE DECEMBER 1996 AFFECTED EMPLOYEES' ACCESS TO MENTAL HEALTH SERVICES?

Type of access	Number of responses	Greatly or somewhat increased	Neither increased nor decreased	Greatly or somewhat decreased
Access to inpatient services	501	13%	84%	2%
Access to outpatient services	500	16	80	4
Access to preventive services	496	13	86	1
Access to mental health services overall	501	17	81	3

SOURCE: "Table 24. Employees' Access to Benefits," in "Despite New Federal Standards, Mental Health Benefits Remain Limited," *Mental Health Parity Act*, vol. GAO/HEHS-00-95, May 2000

TABLE 6.5

Employee opinion poll eligibility for mental health benefits, 1999

IN CONSIDERING ALL OF THE HEALTH PLANS OFFERED BY YOUR ORGANIZATION SINCE DECEMBER 1996, WOULD YOU SAY THAT THE PROPORTION OF YOUR EMPLOYEES WHO ARE ELIGIBLE TO ENROLL IN A HEALTH PLAN THAT CONTAINS MENTAL HEALTH BENEFITS HAS CHANGED?

	Number of responses	Greatly or somewhat increased	Neither increased nor decreased	Greatly or somewhat decreased
Employees eligible to enroll	522	8%	91%	2%

SOURCE: "Table 25. Employees' Eligibility for Coverage," in "Despite New Federal Standards, Mental Health Benefits Remain Limited," *Mental Health Parity Act*, GAO/HEHS-00-95, May 2000

claims costs had changed since they had complied with the terms of the act, and less than 1 percent opted to drop their health coverage altogether or cease to offer mental health coverage since the law was enacted.

The majority of employers felt that changes they had made to comply with the parity legislation had not affected their employees' access to mental health services, nor had it affected employee eligibility for coverage. (See Table 6.4 and Table 6.5.)

Federal agency management of the parity law was discovered to vary from a relatively lax complaint-oriented approach to oversight to the more stringent use of random employer investigations to assess compliance with the parity law. Failure to comply may be costly—health plans may be fined as much as $100 per day per violation for each individual affected by the insurance carrier's noncompliance.

ARGUMENTS AGAINST ENACTING MENTAL HEALTH PARITY LEGISLATION

The National Center of Policy Analysis (NCPA), a nonprofit, nonpartisan organization that develops private alternatives to government regulation, is a widely cited opponent of mental health parity legislation. The NCPA insists that parity legislation fails to improve access or quality of care and argues that it will not only cost businesses but also individuals. It maintains that faced with skyrocketing premiums, individuals will voluntarily drop their health insurance coverage.

Another argument offered by opponents of parity is that mental health care is ineffective and does not merit any allocation of resources at all, let alone parity funding. Writing for the NCPA in August 2002, John C. Goodman and Wess Mitchell took issue with the conclusions of *Mental Health: A Report of the Surgeon General, 1999,* that described quality mental health care as safe, effective, and socially useful. Goodman and Mitchell conceded that some scientific breakthroughs have advanced mental health treatment. They cited the schizophrenia

survey found that about 55 percent of employers reported mental health benefit parity in terms of dollar limits.

Although the survey found that most employers' plans offered parity in dollar limits for mental health coverage, 87 percent continued to restrict mental health benefits more than medical and surgical benefits. To compensate for the increased dollar limits offered as a result of the legislative requirement, many employers chose to limit at least one other mental health benefit. For example, Table 6.3 shows that some employers reduced the numbers of covered hospital days or outpatient visits or instituted greater cost sharing for mental health benefits, increasing patients' deductibles or co-payments.

Contrary to employers' fears that compliance with the act would sharply increase their plans' claims costs, the survey found that only 3 percent of employers reported increased costs in response to compliance with the parity requirement. Interestingly, about 60 percent of the employers surveyed said they did not know if their plans'

that afflicted Nobel Prize–winning economist John Nash and was depicted in the film *A Beautiful Mind* as an example of the efficacy of some drug therapy. Despite such advances in diagnosis and treatment, they questioned the U.S. expenditure of more than $100 billion per year for mental health services.

Goodman and Mitchell decried the lack of objective criteria for mental health diagnoses, the seemingly politically motivated inclusion or exclusion of diagnoses in the *Diagnostic and Statistical Manual of Mental Disorders (DSM-IV)*, and the uncertainty about the effectiveness and outcomes of treatment. They contended that mental health professionals' credentials were unrelated to the efficacy of therapy and questioned the effectiveness of pharmacological therapy. They cited studies in which placebos (inactive substances usually used as controls in experiments) were as effective as prescription psychotropic drugs. Their conclusion was even more drastic than simply refuting the wisdom of parity funding; they offered that the United States could sharply reduce its current mental health budget with no resulting loss of benefits or harm to consumers.

Still other critics of parity legislation assert that patients with mental illnesses would be better served by consumer-driven health plans that enable patients and their families to assume more direct control over treatment and services than programs offering federally mandated benefits. Unlike the NCPA, these opponents of legislation do not disagree about the extent to which mental health care should be funded; they simply advocate for local consumer administration and control of service delivery rather than oversight by the state.

CHAPTER 7

MENTAL HEALTH LAW, LEGISLATION, AND POLICY

The focus of mental health law in the United States has changed throughout the history of the discipline. It has variously emphasized the law's relation to psychiatry and forensic psychiatry (the subspecialty of psychiatry in which scientific and clinical expertise is applied to legal issues); protecting the legal rights of persons with disabilities, or depriving such persons of their rights; consideration of legal regulation of mental health service delivery; and the extent to which the law has a protective and beneficial effect on individuals, institutions, and society.

Mental health law addresses regulations and policies that disproportionately affect persons with mental illnesses, laws directly aimed at governing care and treatment of persons with mental illness, and modifications of existing law to accommodate the individual differences of persons challenged by mental disorders. Along with rights and protections of individuals, mental health law defines the patient-psychotherapist privilege and the role of expert testimony in special defenses that lead to such verdicts as "not guilty by reason of insanity" and "guilty but mentally ill."

One key issue facing the field of mental health law at the beginning of the 21st century is the competence of persons with mental disorders to make autonomous (independent) decisions in civil law (treatment competence) and in criminal law (adjudicative competence). Other issues include the risk of violence that may accompany mental disorder and the coercion that may be involved in interventions to redress incompetence or reduce risk. Questions about competence and coercion persist, even though modern society acknowledges that mental disorders do not necessarily lead to incompetence. When they do, the capacity to make some decisions about one's own treatment under civil law or in the criminal process may remain intact. Controversies arise when decisions must be made that specify the kinds of decisions that mentally disordered individuals are competent to make. The state's use of coercive power to hospitalize and treat persons with mental

disorders has long been controversial in mental health law. Examples of issues are the use of force or persuasion in involuntary hospitalization and the decision-making process, including the importance of the prospective patient's role in the process.

According to the World Health Organization (WHO), about one-quarter of the 160 countries that reported information about mental health legislation had not enacted any legislation. Figure 7.1 displays the percentages of WHO member states in six regions that have enacted mental health policies and legislation. About 20 percent of existing legislation was enacted more than 40 years ago, before the advent of modern treatment. About half of existing legislation is more recent—dating just to the early 1990s. The WHO exhorts governments of its member states to reconsider existing legislation and institute up-to-date legislation to reflect their aim to provide quality care to persons with mental disorders, prevent discrimination, and safeguard human rights.

FEDERAL JUDICIAL DECISIONS

U.S. legal standards serve to determine the treatment of persons with mental illness. They establish competence, the legal determination that an individual is able to participate in legal proceedings, enter into contracts, transfer assets, refuse confinement and involuntary treatment, and assume responsibility for his or her actions.

Section 1 of the Fourteenth Amendment of the U.S. Constitution states, "All persons born or naturalized in the United States, and subject to the jurisdiction thereof, are citizens of the United States and of the state wherein they reside. No state shall make or enforce any law which shall abridge the privileges or immunities of citizens of the United States; nor shall any state deprive any person of life, liberty, or property, without due process of law; nor deny to any person within its jurisdiction the equal protection of the laws." As such, this section of the Fourteenth

FIGURE 7.1

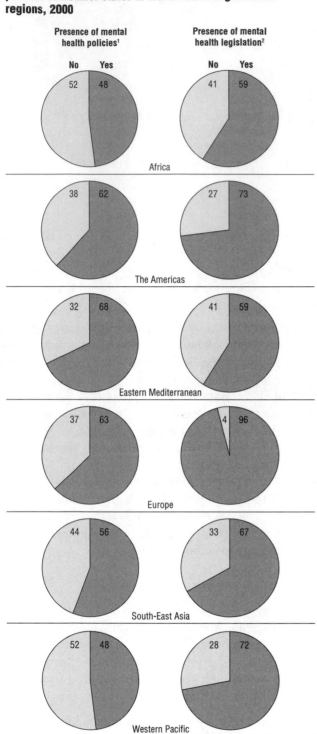

Presence of mental health policies and legislation and percent of member states in World Health Organization regions, 2000

¹Based on information from 181 member states.
²Based on information from 160 member states.

SOURCE: Rangaswamy Srinivasa Murthy, José Manoel Bertolote, JoAnne Epping-Jordan, Michelle Funk, Thomson Prentice, Benedetto Saraceno, and Shekhar Saxena, "Figure 4.1. Presence of mental health policies and legislation, percentage of Member States in WHO Regions, 2000," in *The World Health Report 2001, Mental Health: New Understanding, New Hope,* World Health Organization, Geneva, Switzerland, 2001. Reproduced with permission.

Amendment governs many of the legal decisions about the circumstances in which persons with mental illness may be forced to receive treatment against their will or involuntarily committed to treatment facilities. Such decisions involve due process because they trespass on an individual's right to be free of unnecessary confinement and free of governmental restraint.

The federal government determines the conditions that permit defendants to use insanity defenses, and the states decide when insanity pleas may be used in the state court system. Passage of the 1984 *Insanity Defense Reform Act* required the defendant to prove insanity and reduced the use of this defense strategy. According to the Legal Information Institute of Cornell Law School, insanity pleas are used infrequently today, and when they are invoked, less than one-quarter are successful.

Landmark U.S. Supreme Court Decisions Concerning Mental Health

During the 1970s and 1980s, mental health law was primarily concerned with issues such as the role of psychiatry in civil commitment proceedings and the legality of voluntarily and involuntarily administering various types of treatment, such as prescription medication and electroconvulsive therapy (ECT). Over the past 25 years, mental health law has expanded its scope to encompass policy initiatives outside of psychiatry and forensic applications to criminal proceedings.

Recent Supreme Court decisions have addressed social as well as legal issues, including justifications for involuntary commitment of persons with mental illness, coercion, determinations of mental competence, discrimination on the basis of mental disability, as well as individual civil rights, autonomy, and human dignity. Decisions also have considered assessment of risk—the danger that a person with a mental disorder will harm others and the liability for mental health professionals who negligently assess risk or fail to disclose risk to those who might be endangered.

Buck v. Bell, 274 U.S. 200 (1927)

The state of Virginia performed a sterilization procedure on the plaintiff, Carrie Buck, when she was an 18-year-old resident of the State Colony for Epileptics and Feeble Minded. Justice Holmes delivered an opinion of the court that favored state interests when he declared:

> ...[T]he Commonwealth is supporting in various institutions many defective persons who, if now discharged, would become a menace, but, if incapable of procreating, might be discharged with safety and become self-supporting with benefit to themselves and to society... [E]xperience has shown that heredity plays an important part in the transmission of insanity, imbecility, &c....

The court affirmed that the Virginia statute providing for sterilization of inmates of institutions supported by the state found to be "afflicted with a hereditary form of insanity or imbecility" was within the power of the state under the Fourteenth Amendment.

Powell v. Texas, 392 U.S. 514 (1968)

In this appeal from a county court decision, the appellant, Leroy Powell, had been arrested and charged with a violation of Article 477 of the Texas Penal Code, which prohibits being intoxicated in a public place. His appeal was based on the contention that he suffered from chronic alcoholism, a disease that compelled him to continue drinking and appear in public drunk. A psychiatrist testified that while Powell was a chronic alcoholic and subject to compulsions, the compulsions, though not overpowering, might be considered to strongly influence his behavior.

In upholding the conviction, Justices Marshall, Black, and Harlan observed that there was no consensus that alcoholism was a disease, or even that it produced a compulsion. They argued that the appellant had not been arrested for being a chronic alcoholic but rather for public drunkenness on a particular occasion. They also concluded that the conviction did not violate the cruel and unusual punishment clause of the Eighth Amendment.

Pennhurst State School and Hospital v. Halderman, 451 U.S. 1 (1984)

Pennsylvania owned the Pennhurst State School and Hospital, a facility that provided custodial care for persons who are mentally retarded. Terri Lee Halderman, a retarded resident of Pennhurst, brought a class action suit against Pennhurst, alleging that its conditions were "unsanitary, inhumane, and dangerous" and requesting that the facility be closed and community living situations be provided for its residents. The suit alleged that Pennhurst had violated various federal constitutional and statutory rights of the residents under the Fourteenth Amendment.

The district court found that certain of the residents' rights had been violated and granted the remedies they sought, including community living arrangements and closure of the institution. The court of appeals affirmed the decision and used the Developmentally Disabled Assistance and Bill of Rights Act of 1975 to support its affirmation. This act established a federal-state grant program whereby the federal government provides financial assistance to participating states to help them create programs to care for and treat the developmentally disabled. The states could choose to comply with the conditions set forth in the act or forgo the benefits of federal funding. The "bill of rights" provision of the act states that mentally retarded persons "have a right to appropriate treatment, services, and habilitation" in "the setting that is least restrictive of ... personal liberty." The district court concluded that Pennhurst violated federal and state statutory rights and that "deinstitutionalization is the favored approach to

habilitation." Accordingly, the school was required to provide the least restrictive treatment setting feasible.

The Supreme Court reversed and remanded the case, ruling that neither the Fourteenth Amendment nor the act obligated the state to assume financial obligations for providing appropriate treatment in the least restrictive environment. The Court stated, "we find nothing in the Act or its legislative history to suggest that Congress intended to require States to assume the high cost of providing 'appropriate treatment' in the 'least restrictive environment' to their mentally retarded citizens." The Court ruled that the act was meant as an incentive for the states to improve services, "not as a device for the Federal Government to compel a state to provide services that Congress itself is unwilling to fund."

Youngberg v. Romeo, 457 U.S. 307 (1982)

Concerned about injuries her son, Nicholas Romeo, sustained during an involuntary commitment to a Pennsylvania state institution, Mrs. Romeo filed a suit in federal district court against the institution. She claimed that her son had "constitutional rights to safe conditions of confinement, freedom from bodily restraint, and training or 'habilitation.' She stated that petitioners knew, or should have known, about his injuries, but failed to take appropriate preventive procedures, thus violating his rights under the Eighth and the Fourteenth Amendments." She believed that the cruel and unusual punishment clause of the Eighth Amendment, as well as the Fourteenth Amendment, had been violated because he had not been free of bodily restraints.

The trial judge instructed the jury on the assumption that the Eighth Amendment applied. The jury returned a verdict for the defendant under the Eighth Amendment, and the plaintiff appealed. The Third Circuit Court of Appeals reversed and remanded for a new trial, holding that the Eighth Amendment did not apply to the facts of the case but that the Fourteenth Amendment involved liberty interests in freedom of movement and personal security that involuntarily committed individuals retained.

The Supreme Court agreed that the Eighth Amendment issues did not apply, but held that under the due process clause of the Fourteenth Amendment the young man had the right to safe conditions of confinement, freedom from unreasonable bodily restraints, and minimal training. The Court acknowledged that the determination of whether the state had adequately protected the young man's rights benefited from the judgment of a qualified professional, and further decreed that courts must show deference to the professional's judgment in such cases.

City of Cleburne, Texas v. Cleburne Living Center, Inc., 473 U.S. 432 (1985)

The Cleburne Living Center (CLC) was denied a conditional use permit by the city council for a group home for persons who were mentally retarded. The city contended that the facility was a hospital, so the CLC reapplied for a special use permit. Following a public hearing, this application was also denied. CLC filed suit against the city, alleging that the city's application of the zoning ordinance violated the equal protection rights of CLC and its potential residents.

The district court found that "[i]f the potential residents of the Featherston Street home were not mentally retarded, but the home was the same in all other respects, its use would be permitted under the city's zoning ordinance," and that the City Council's decision "was motivated primarily by the fact that the residents of the home would be persons who are mentally retarded." Nonetheless, it held the ordinance and its application constitutional. The court of appeals reversed this decision, citing mental retardation as a "quasi-suspect classification" and rendering the ordinance invalid. The Supreme Court concurred with the court of appeals that the ordinance was invalid, but for different reasons. The Supreme Court determined that the court of appeals erred in deeming mental retardation a "quasi-suspect classification," but still held for the CLC.

The judgment observed that:

The record does not reveal any rational basis for believing that the proposed group home would pose any special threat to the city's legitimate interests. Requiring the permit in this case appears to rest on an irrational prejudice against the mentally retarded, including those who would occupy the proposed group home and who would live under the closely supervised and highly regulated conditions expressly provided for by state and federal law.

Ford v. Wainwright, 477 U.S. 399 (1986)

In 1974 Alvin Bernard Ford was convicted of murder in a Florida state court and sentenced to death. By all accounts, he appeared competent to stand trial; however, he later began to exhibit behavior suggestive of mental illness. Two psychiatrists examined him, but disagreed about his competency—only one concluded that the defendant was not competent and should not be executed. The governor received both psychiatrists' reports and decided to sign a death warrant without issuing an explanation or statement.

The defendant's counsel sought and failed to obtain a new hearing in state court. The federal district court and the court of appeals affirmed the governor's decision. A five-member majority of the Supreme Court, however, reversed the decision, concluding that the Eighth Amendment's cruel and unusual punishment clause prohibited the state from inflicting the death penalty on an insane prisoner.

Penry v. Lynaugh, 492 U.S. 302 (1989)

John Paul Penry, a defendant charged with murder in Texas state court, was found competent to stand trial despite a psychologist's finding that the defendant was moderately retarded and functioned with the mental capacity of someone six and one-half years old. The insanity defense relied on psychiatric testimony concluding that Penry suffered from a combination of organic brain damage and moderate retardation that resulted in poor impulse control and an inability to learn from experience. There was also evidence presented about abuses Penry had suffered as a child.

The state held that Penry was sane but antisocial, and a jury found him guilty of capital murder and sentenced him to death. The Texas Court of Criminal Appeals, the federal district court, and the court of appeals all upheld the death sentence.

The Supreme Court affirmed part of the judgment, reversed part of it, and remanded (sent back) the case. (When a case is remanded, it is sent to another court or agency for further proceedings.) The Court stated that Texas juries must be given instructions about mitigating evidence, such as the defendant's mental retardation and history of abuse, that would influence sentencing—in this instance evidence that might lead to a sentence of life imprisonment rather than the death penalty. The Court did not, however, agree with the defense counsel's interpretation of the Eighth Amendment to prevent imposition of the death penalty. The Court asserted that "the Eighth Amendment does not categorically prohibit the execution of mentally retarded capital murderers of petitioner's reasoning ability."

Foucha v. Louisiana, No. 90-5844 (1992)

The petitioner, Terry Foucha, had been found not guilty by reason of insanity and committed to a mental hospital. Upon a trial to consider his release from the hospital the state court ordered Foucha returned to the mental hospital in response to a physician's testimony that while medication effectively controlled his psychosis, he suffered from an antisocial personality, an untreatable condition that is not considered a mental disease. The physician stated that Foucha had been in several altercations in the facility and that he would not "feel comfortable in certifying that he would not be a danger to himself or to other people."

The state court of appeals and state supreme courts affirmed that denying Foucha's release did not violate the due process clause of the Fourteenth Amendment. The Supreme Court reversed the decision. It determined that the Louisiana statute allowing an individual acquitted by virtue of insanity to be committed to an institution until he can demonstrate that he is not a danger to himself or others, even when he does not suffer from mental illness, was a violation of the due process clause.

The opinion of the Court was that the state was not entitled to hold Foucha in the hospital if it had determined that he was not mentally ill but merely antisocial. The

Court also said that due process required that the nature of commitment bear some relationship to the purpose of commitment. As such, if Foucha was not mentally ill, he could not be confined in a mental hospital. Further, the Court observed that while the state may imprison convicted criminals, Louisiana had no reason to do this, since Foucha was not convicted and could not be punished.

Medina v. California, No. 90-8370 (1992)

Before Teofilo Medina's trial for first-degree murder, the California court granted him a competency hearing, since state law forbids a mentally incompetent person to be tried or punished. The competency hearing found him competent to stand trial, and he was convicted and sentenced to death. The state supreme court affirmed this judgment, rejecting Medina's contention that the statute's presumption of competence and requirement that the petitioner prove incompetence by a preponderance of evidence violated his right to due process.

The Supreme Court upheld the lower court decision, confirming that the due process clause allows a state to require a defendant claiming incompetence to produce a preponderance of evidence to support the claim.

Riggins v. Nevada, No. 90-8466 (1992)

David Riggins, a defendant awaiting trial on murder and robbery charges in Nevada, was prescribed Mellaril, an antipsychotic medication, after he complained to a psychiatrist about hearing voices and having sleep disorders. After he was found competent to stand trial, Riggins moved to suspend his use of the medication, contending that its effects on his mental state during trial would deny him due process as well as the opportunity to show jurors his true mental state when he offered an insanity defense.

The court denied the request, and Riggins was tried, convicted, and sentenced to death. In affirming the lower court decision, the state supreme court stated that expert testimony presented at trial was sufficient to explain to jurors the effects of the medication on Riggins's demeanor and testimony.

The Supreme Court disagreed, reversing and remanding the case. It contended that Riggins's rights under the Sixth and Fourteenth amendments had been violated by the forced administration of the antipsychotic drug. The Court stated that:

> There is a strong possibility that the trial court's error impaired Riggins' constitutionally protected trial rights. Efforts to prove or disprove actual prejudice from the record before this Court would be futile, and guesses as to the trial's outcome had Riggins' motion been granted would be speculative. While the precise consequences of forcing Mellaril upon him cannot be shown from a trial transcript, the testimony of doctors who examined Riggins establishes the strong possibility that his

defense was impaired. Mellaril's side effects not only may have impacted his outward appearance, but also his testimony's content, his ability to follow the proceedings, or the substance of his communication with counsel. Thus, even if the expert testimony presented at trial allowed jurors to assess Riggins' demeanor fairly, an unacceptable risk remained that forced medication compromised his trial rights.

Sawyer v. Whitley, No. 91-6382 (1992)

The defendant, Robert Wayne Sawyer, was convicted by a Louisiana jury for a murder in which the victim was beaten, scalded with boiling water, and set afire. In postconviction appeals, Sawyer's trial lawyer's failure to introduce Sawyer's mental health history during the sentencing phase was presented as ineffective counsel. The court of appeals affirmed the conviction, and it was upheld by the Supreme Court. The Supreme Court stated:

> Sawyer has failed to show that he is actually innocent of the death penalty to which he has been sentenced. The psychological evidence allegedly kept from the jury does not relate to his guilt or innocence of the crime or to the aggravating factors found by the jury—that the murder was committed in the course of an aggravated arson, and that it was especially cruel, atrocious, or heinous—which made him eligible for the death penalty.

Heller v. Doe, No. 92-351 (1993)

Kentucky allows the involuntary commitment of mentally retarded or mentally ill persons who "present a threat of danger to themselves, family, or others, who can reasonably benefit from the available treatment, and for whom the least restrictive alternative is placement in the relevant facility." Mental retardation commitment procedures require "clear and convincing evidence," while for mental illness commitments the burden of proof is "beyond a reasonable doubt."

In this case the respondents were an involuntarily committed group of mentally retarded persons who contended that differing standards for confinement violated the Fourteenth Amendment's equal protection clause. The district court granted them summary judgment, and the court of appeals affirmed.

The Supreme Court reversed the lower courts' decisions and held for the state of Kentucky, explaining that the Equal Protection Clause was not violated if there was a reasonable rationale for the differing treatment and a legitimate government purpose. Further, the Court contended that:

> Kentucky has proffered more than adequate justifications for its burden of proof scheme. Mental retardation, which is a developmental disability usually well documented throughout childhood, is easier to diagnose than is mental illness, which may have a sudden onset in adulthood. Thus, it could have assigned a higher burden of proof to mental illness to equalize the risk of erroneous determination that the subject of a commitment

proceeding has the condition in question. Ease of diagnosis could also result in a more accurate dangerousness determination for the mentally retarded, who have a relatively static condition and a well-documented record of previous behavior. In contrast, since manifestations of mental illness may be sudden, past behavior may not be an adequate predictor of future actions. A higher standard for the mentally ill is also justified on the ground that in general their treatment is much more intrusive than that received by the mentally retarded.

Shannon v. United States, No. 92-8346 (1994)

The Insanity Defense Reform Act of 1984 created the verdict "not guilty by reason of insanity" and established procedures for civil commitment. Terry Lee Shannon, a petitioner on trial for federal criminal charges, asked the district court to inform the jury that a not guilty by reason of insanity verdict would result in his involuntary commitment. The court refused his request and he was found guilty. The court of appeals affirmed the decision, asserting that juries were not required to be informed of the consequences of an insanity acquittal and that the 1984 act had contained no directive to do so.

The Supreme Court held that a federal district court is not required to instruct juries about the consequences of a not guilty by reason of insanity verdict to the defendant.

Jafee, Special Administrator for Allen, Deceased v. Redmond, et al., No. 95-266 (1996)

This case reconfirmed the acceptance of psychotherapist-patient privilege under Federal Rule of Evidence 501. Petitioner Carrie Jaffee was an administrator for the estate of Ricky Allen, Sr., an individual who had been killed by a police officer, Mary Lu Redmond. Jaffee argued that Allen's constitutional rights were violated when he was killed. The court ordered that notes made by a licensed clinical social worker that counseled the officer after the shooting be given to the respondent. At trial, the jury awarded the petitioner damages after being instructed that refusal to disclose the notes was without legal justification and that the jury could decide that the notes would have been unfavorable to the officer's case.

The court of appeals reversed and remanded, recognizing therapist-patient privilege, though it found that privilege would not apply if the need for disclosure outweighed the patient's privacy interests. The Supreme Court held that the counseling session notes were protected from compelled disclosure and wrote:

> Significant private interests support recognition of a psychotherapist privilege. Effective psychotherapy depends upon an atmosphere of confidence and trust, and therefore the mere possibility of disclosure of confidential communications may impede development of the relationship necessary for successful treatment. The privilege also serves the public interest, since the mental health of the Nation's citizenry, no less than its physical health, is a

public good of transcendent importance. In contrast, the likely evidentiary benefit that would result from the denial of the privilege is modest. That it is appropriate for the federal courts to recognize a psychotherapist privilege is confirmed by the fact that all 50 States and the District of Columbia have enacted into law some form of the privilege. The federal privilege, which clearly applies to psychiatrists and psychologists, also extends to confidential communications made to licensed clinical social workers in the course of psychotherapy. The reasons for recognizing the privilege for treatment by psychiatrists and psychologists apply with equal force to clinical social workers, and the vast majority of States explicitly extend a testimonial privilege to them.

Kansas v. Hendricks, No. 95-1649 (1997)

The Kansas Sexually Violent Predator Act includes procedures to commit persons who, as a result of a "mental abnormality" or "personality disorder," are likely to engage in future sexual violence. The state moved to commit Leroy Hendricks, a petitioner with a long history of sexual molestation of children.

At a jury trial, Hendricks conceded that he continues to harbor uncontrollable sexual desires for children, and the jury decided he was a sexually violent predator. Determining that this characteristic qualified as a mental abnormality under the Sexually Violent Predator Act, the court ordered him committed. The state supreme court invalidated the act on the basis that the precommitment finding of mental abnormality did not meet the requirement of mental illness as the diagnosis prompting involuntary civil commitment.

The Supreme Court reversed the lower court decisions and held for the state, observing that the act did not establish criminal proceedings and that involuntary confinement under the act was not punishment. Since the act was civil, its proceedings could not be considered a second prosecution of Hendricks, even though confinement followed a prison term.

Lindh v. Murphy, Warden, No. 96-6298 (1997)

Petitioner Aaron Lindh was convicted in Wisconsin of murder and attempted murder and offered an insanity defense. Shortly after his appeal was heard, the Antiterrorism and Effective Death Penalty Act of 1996 amended the federal habeas corpus statute (a writ to bring a party before a court to prevent unlawful restraint). The Court of Appeals for the Seventh Circuit determined that the new standards could not be applied retroactively to Lindh's case.

The Supreme Court reversed and remanded the case, stating that Wisconsin erred in its decision not to permit retroactive application of the new standards.

Washington v. Glucksberg, No. 96-110 (1997)

Historically, it has been a crime to assist a suicide in the state of Washington, and present law considers promoting a suicide attempt a felony. In this case, four Washington physicians (Harold Glucksberg, Abigail Halperin, Thomas A. Preston, and Peter Shalit) who treat terminally ill patients declared that they would assist patients to end their lives if not for the state's ban. They asserted that the ban was unconstitutional because the Fourteenth Amendment's due process clause protects a liberty interest that includes the personal choice by a mentally competent person to commit physician-assisted suicide.

The federal district court agreed, and the Ninth Circuit Court affirmed that the ban was unconstitutional. The Supreme Court disagreed with the lower courts and found that Washington's ban against causing or aiding suicide did not violate due process. The Supreme Court concluded that in view of the nation's history and traditions, to hold for the physician respondents the Court "would have to reverse centuries of legal doctrine and practice, and strike down the considered policy choice of almost every State."

Bell v. Cone, No. 01-400 (2002)

A Tennessee court found the defendant, Gary Bradford Cone, guilty of the brutal murder of an elderly couple. In view of four aggravating factors and no mitigating circumstances, he was sentenced to death. The double murder occurred at the conclusion of a two-day crime spree during which the defendant also committed a robbery and shot a police officer and another citizen. The defense had argued that the respondent was not guilty by reason of insanity because of substance abuse and post-traumatic stress disorders following military service in Vietnam.

The Sixth Circuit reversed with respect to the sentence and remanded the case, finding that the respondent's rights had been violated because his legal counsel had not adequately countered the state's call for the death penalty. The Supreme Court overturned this ruling, dismissing the claim that counsel had been ineffective by arguing that the attorney had exercised his best professional judgment in a difficult case. It concluded that the Sixth Circuit had erred and affirmed that lower court rulings for the death penalty did not constitute unreasonable application of the law.

Other Federal and State Litigation Focuses on Preserving Rights

Recent federal and state court cases have focused on defending and protecting the rights of individuals suffering from mental illness by eliminating segregated housing, disparities in insurance coverage for mental illness, and criminalization arising from institutional failings. Similarly, legal initiatives such as those undertaken by the Judge David L. Bazelon Center for Mental Health Law, a nonprofit legal advocacy organization based in Washington, D.C., aim to protect privacy of medical records, ensure educational opportunities, and improve access to recovery-oriented mental health treatment. The Bazelon Center and other legal advocates for persons with mental illness also seek to expand entitlement programs such as the *Americans with Disabilities Act,* Medicaid, and mental health block grant funding.

THE BAZELON CENTER'S MODEL LAW. In 2002 the Bazelon Center drafted and disseminated a model law, *An Act Providing a Right to Mental Health Services and Supports,* to provide states with a template for enacting statutes to provide "entitlement to recovery-oriented mental health services and supports, in sufficient amount, duration, scope and quality to support recovery, community integration and economic self-sufficiency." Under a statute based on this model law, states are able to define eligibility for services broadly or narrowly, but they may not exclude any eligible individual.

Intended to assist states to discuss and implement mental health reforms, the model law contains sections detailing:

- Findings and Purpose—documenting need, inadequate resources, costs, and expenditures, as well as the intent of the law to make services and supports accessible and available

- Definitions—the terms used in the model law such as "potentially eligible person," "recovery-oriented," and "service matrix" are defined

- Rights to Recovery-Oriented Services and Supports—delineates the individual's legal entitlement and describes how individuals will partner with professionals to plan their treatment

- Petition Procedure for Securing Services and Supports—how an individual establishes eligibility for mental health services and supports under the model law

- Service-Planning Process—describes key components of the planning process

- Outreach—encourages public education and efforts to reach persons most likely to benefit from recovery-oriented services

- Advocates—the model law strongly advises use of peer advocates who have personal experience with mental illness

- Appeals—how an individual contests actions such as omissions or denials of services

- Emergency Hearings—describes circumstances in which denial of services places an individual at risk of serious harm such as hospitalization, incarceration, or homelessness

- Quality Improvement and Evaluation—mandates development of ongoing systems to track, monitor, measure, and improve services and supports

- Administration of Model Law—addresses development of regulations, authorizations, and medical record confidentiality

- Authorization of Appropriations—allocates funds to conduct the programs described in the model law

Federal Government Funds Services for Mental Health Court Program

In 2002 Congress allocated $4 million to the U.S. Department of Justice to develop a pilot mental health program. The program offers treatment instead of jail sentences to nonviolent offenders with mental illness and provides ongoing supervision for offenders redirected to treatment. It also trains law enforcement workers and judges. Many industry observers, including the National Mental Health Organization, an advocacy group, consider diversion programs such as mental health court as useful alternatives to criminal sanctions.

The program was funded under legislation enacted during 2000, America's Law Enforcement and Mental Health Project Act, which gives Congress the option to spend up to $10 million per year for five years to operate the pilot program. Among the champions of this legislation and a strong advocate for its funding were U.S. Representative Ted Strickland, a Democrat from Ohio who is also a psychologist; Senator Pete Domenici; a Republican from New Mexico; Republican Senator Mike DeWine of Ohio; and the late Senator Paul Wellstone of Minnesota.

Rep. Strickland observed that:

After years of effort, America is finally ready to begin treating people with mental illness instead of punishing them. These courts are just the first step in easing the burden on law enforcement officials who are forced to serve as surrogate caretakers for mentally ill offenders, and give mentally ill individuals the help they need to avoid future run-ins with the law.

MENTAL HEALTH LEGISLATION

The delivery, financing, and regulation of mental health services are all governed by legislation. Legislation directs issues of vital importance to persons with mental illness, mental health professionals, and service providers. It also affects aspects of mental health care such as Medicare coverage of prescription drugs, access to housing, medical privacy provisions, and mental health parity—insurance that offers comparable coverage and benefits for mental and physical health care rather than requiring consumers to pay more out of pocket for mental health treatment than any other medical care.

Landmark Legislation

On July 3, 1946, President Harry Truman signed the National Mental Health Act (P.L. 76-19), which authorized the surgeon general to improve the mental health of Americans through research, improved diagnosis, and treatment of psychiatric disorders. This legislation paved the way for the establishment of the National Institute of Mental Health (NIMH) on April 15, 1949.

The 1955 Mental Health Study Act (P.L. 84-183) called for the creation of the Joint Commission on Mental Illness and Health and authorized NIMH to research mental health and illness in the United States.

THE MENTAL RETARDATION FACILITIES AND COMMUNITY MENTAL HEALTH CENTERS CONSTRUCTION ACT OF 1963. In one of his final acts, President John F. Kennedy signed P.L. 88-164, the Mental Retardation Facilities and Community Mental Health Centers Construction Act, which funded grants to enable construction of community mental health centers throughout the nation. The money for state planning was handed directly from NIMH to the states, which were required to "include details on how information would be secured, and the methods to be used to insure active and continuing participation by all relevant state and community groups."

The community mental health centers were intended to focus on community-wide improvement of mental health and quality of life. This goal was to be accomplished by mental health professionals' efforts to better understand community needs, dynamics, and resources and to develop effective strategies for making them more favorable to the emotional well-being of individuals.

In 1965, P.L. 89-105, amendments to P.L. 88-164, provided grants to staff the newly established community mental health centers. Among the qualifications for mental health professionals staffing community mental health centers was a proviso to remain true to Kennedy's intent—"his vision of what the institution's potentialities are for the job of helping individuals achieve more effective skills of living."

In 1970, P.L. 92-2111, Community Mental Health Centers Amendments, authorized building and staffing the centers for an additional three years, and in 1975, 1978, and 1980 amendments strengthened and extended the Community Mental Health Centers (CMHC) Act. Centers were required to offer key service components—outpatient treatment, inpatient care, consultation and education, partial hospitalization, and emergency/crisis intervention. The act also mandated partnerships and affiliations with other community agencies in an attempt to encourage greater responsiveness to the needs of the centers' constituents. In 1981 the Omnibus Budget Reconciliation Act (OBRA) made states the primary funding source for the centers by federal block grants.

MEDICARE AND MEDICAID. Although they do not relate exclusively to mental health care and treatment, the Medicaid and Medicare entitlement programs significantly influence the financing and delivery of mental health services. Since the 1965 enactment of these entitlements, the public sector has borne a disproportionate share of the direct costs of mental health treatment.

Medicaid is operated by the state and federal government to provide health care insurance for persons younger than 65 years who cannot afford to pay for private insurance. The federal government matches the states' contribution on a certain minimal level of available coverage, and the states may elect to cover additional services at their own expense.

Medicare is the federal health insurance program run by the Centers for Medicare and Medicaid Services for persons 65 years of age and older, selected younger persons with disabilities, and persons with end-stage renal disease (permanent kidney failure necessitating dialysis or transplant, also known as ESRD). Medicare part A covers hospitalization and is a compulsory benefit. Medicare part B covers outpatient services, and enrollment in it is voluntary.

LEGISLATION ABOUT SUBSTANCE ABUSE TREATMENT. The 1972 Drug Abuse Office and Treatment Act created a National Institute on Drug Abuse within the National Institutes of Health (NIH). In 1974 President Richard Nixon signed P.L. 93-282, establishing the Alcohol, Drug Abuse and Mental Health Administration (ADAMHA).

When President Ronald Reagan signed the Omnibus Budget Reconciliation Act of 1981, he repealed the Mental Health Systems Act and consolidated ADAMHA's programs into a single block grant that allowed each state to administer its allocated funds.

P.L. 98-24, Alcohol Abuse Amendments of 1983, established Title V of the Public Health Service Act of 1944 and reauthorized the ADAMHA, the agency that governed NIMH. In 1992 ADAMHA was abolished by the ADAMHA Reorganization Act that also created the Substance Abuse and Mental Health Services Administration (SAMHSA) and transferred NIMH research activities to the NIH.

THE AMERICANS WITH DISABILITIES ACT. The Americans with Disabilities Act (ADA) is a federal civil rights law that was enacted on July 26, 1990. The act was intended to protect qualified persons with disabilities from discrimination in employment, government services and programs, transportation, public accommodations, and telecommunications. The ADA supplements, complements, and strengthens other federal and state laws that protect persons with disabilities.

In terms of mental illness, the ADA defines disability as "mental impairment that substantially limits one or more major life activities. A person is considered disabled if the person has such a physical or mental impairment, has a record of such an impairment, or is regarded as having such an impairment." The ADA covers a wide range of conditions and includes learning disabilities, emotional illnesses, and a history of alcoholism or prior substance abuse.

On July 26, 2002, the 12th anniversary of the ADA, President George W. Bush proclaimed the ADA:

... one of the most compassionate and successful civil rights laws in American history. In the 12 years since President George H. W. Bush signed the ADA into law, more people with disabilities are participating fully in our society than ever before. As we mark this important anniversary, we celebrate the positive effect this landmark legislation has had upon our Nation, and we recognize the important influence it has had in improving employment opportunities, government services, public accommodations, transportation, and telecommunications for those with disabilities.

Today, Americans with disabilities enjoy greatly improved access to countless facets of life; but more work needs to be done. We must continue to build on the important foundations established by the ADA. Too many Americans with disabilities remain isolated, dependent, and deprived of the tools they need to enjoy all that our Nation has to offer.

Mental Health Legislation Passed by the 106th Congress

On December 14, 1999, the Foster Care Independence Act became P.L. 106-169. An amendment to the Social Security Act, P.L. 106-169, provides states with more funding and greater flexibility to manage and administer programs aimed at assisting children to transition from foster care to self-sufficiency. By financing and supporting the acquisition of skills necessary for independent living by teens aged 16 to 18, it aims to prevent institutionalization of teens and young adults with emotional and mental health problems.

Three days later, on December 17, 1999, the Ticket to Work and Work Incentives Improvement Act of 1999 became P.L. 106-70. An amendment to the Social Security Act, P.L. 106-70 expands the availability of health care coverage for working persons with disabilities and offers such persons increased opportunities for meaningful employment.

On October 17, 2000, the Children's Health Act of 2000 became P.L. 106-310. An amendment to the Public Health Service Act of 1944, P.L. 106-310 incorporated provisions from many bills advocating for children's health services, youth drug services, and mental health services. Its alternative titles—Ecstasy Anti-Proliferation Act of 2000, Methamphetamine Anti-Proliferation Act of 2000, Drug Addiction Treatment Act of 2000, and Youth Drug and Mental Health Services Act—directly address the substance abuse and mental health problems named in each act.

America's Law Enforcement and Mental Health Project became P.L. 106-15 on November 13, 2000. It provides grants to establish model demonstration mental health courts intended to reduce criminalization of persons with serious mental illnesses.

THE MENTAL HEALTH PARITY ACT OF 1996. Enacted in 1996, the Mental Health Parity Act (MHPA) stipulates that insurance or group health plans that provide medical and surgical benefits as well as mental health benefits may not designate annual dollar limits or aggregate lifetime dollar limits on mental health benefits that are lower than the limits placed on medical/surgical benefits. MHPA did not, however, require group health plans to provide mental health benefits, nor did the law mandate the amount, scope, duration, or limits of mental health benefits. The MHPA allowed two exemptions from these parity requirements—small businesses with between 2 and 50 employees and employers that would incur a cost increase of 1 percent or greater were they to offer mental health parity. The act was set to expire after six years.

Federal Mental Health Parity Legislation

Since the Mental Health Parity Act was only to remain in effect for six years, Congress tried to pass a new law, the Mental Health Equitable Treatment Act, by the 1996 law's deadline at the end of 2002. The Mental Health Equitable Treatment Act of 2001 (S. 543) would have required employers with 50 or more employees to provide the same level of insurance coverage for mental health care as they do for medical or surgical care. All mental health conditions listed in the *Diagnostic and Statistical Manual of Mental Disorders* (DSM) would be covered, but employers would not be required to provide coverage for substance abuse problems.

Although industry observers believed that S. 543 was an improvement over the 1996 law, the Mental Health and Substance Abuse Parity Act of 2001 (H.R. 162) offered more aggressive action to end discrimination in health coverage for more affected individuals. It required that all limits on coverage for "severe biologically-based mental illnesses" be equal to those for medical and surgical benefits. The most significant difference between the House and Senate parity bills was that H.R. 162 applied to persons with mental illness or substance abuse disorders.

The nonpartisan Congressional Budget Office estimated that either bill would increase the cost of insurance by about 1 percent. Federal legislation would bring parity to residents of the 20 states currently lacking these laws and could expand the coverage offered in states with more limited laws. Senate support for parity was strong, and the Senate passed the Mental Health Equitable Treatment Act as an amendment to the FY2002 Labor-HHS-Education Appropriations bill (H.R. 3061). Despite support in Congress, from President Bush, and from national organizations, Congress did not pass either law.

Mental Health Parity Legislation Reintroduced in the 108th Congress

On February 27, 2003, Senators Pete Domenici (R-N.M.) and Edward Kennedy, (D-Mass.) and Representatives Patrick Kennedy (D-R.I.) and Jim Ramstad (R-Minn.) reintroduced the Mental Health Equitable Treatment Act into the Senate and House. Renamed the Senator Paul Wellstone Mental Health Equitable Treatment Act of 2003 (S. 486 and H.R. 953) in honor of the late senator from Minnesota who championed mental health parity, the bill also aims to eliminate loopholes in the 1996 legislation that allowed employers to substitute new benefit restrictions for those the bill outlawed. The new law would require full parity for all categories of mental health conditions listed in the DSM.

Once again, despite overwhelming support in Congress and from more than 250 national organizations, and the stated support of President Bush, Congress had not passed the new law as of early 2004. Instead, Congress voted each year to extend the 1996 law for an additional year. President George W. Bush signed an extension to the MHPA each year, including signing the Reauthorization Act of 2003 on December 19, 2003 (P.L. 108-197, 117 Stat. 2998), keeping the MHPA to December 31, 2004.

State Mental Health Legislative Initiatives

Since the mid-1990s, many states have introduced legislation to achieve mental health parity, reduce criminalization of persons with mental illnesses, expand health insurance coverage of mental disorders, safeguard patients' rights, and deliver coordinated, effective community-based mental health services. According to the Bazelon Center for Mental Health Law, by mid-2003, 33 states had enacted parity legislation. Several states have chosen to stage parity implementation, which incrementally increases the scope and extent of the legislation.

A COMPREHENSIVE MODEL FOR STATE MENTAL HEALTH LEGISLATION. The National Alliance for the Mentally Ill (NAMI) has prepared the Omnibus Mental Illness Recovery Act (OMIRA) as model legislation the states may use as templates to improve mental health services. According to NAMI, the bill may be used by state legislatures as a comprehensive package to attain a baseline of adequate mental health services or as individual initiatives, depending on the needs of each state.

The model legislation addresses eight distinct aspects of mental health care and services:

- Increased Consumer and Family Participation in Services Planning—Calls for more consumer and family involvement on state mental health planning and medical advisory councils

- Equitable Health Care Coverage—Requires public and private health insurance plans to provide mental health parity—coverage and benefits commensurate with those provided for other physical illnesses

- Access to Newer Medications—Obligates health plans to provide all effective and medically necessary prescription medications

- Programs for Assertive Community Treatment (PACT)—Makes it possible for states to finance assertive community treatment programs using Medicaid and Community Mental Health Service funds

- Work Incentives for Persons With Severe Mental Illness—Enables persons with severe mental illnesses to purchase Medicaid coverage if their income is not more than 250 percent of the federal poverty level

- Reduction of Life-Threatening and Harmful Care (Restraints and Seclusion)—Stipulates that physical restraints be used exclusively in emergencies to ensure safety

- Reduction of Criminalization of Persons with Severe Mental Illness—Trains police and probation officers and authorizes mental health courts to redirect nonviolent offenders with severe mental illness into treatment rather than incarceration

- Increased Access to Permanent, Safe, Affordable Housing with Appropriate Community-Based Services—Creates a Mental Illness Housing Assistance Program to not only help persons with severe mental illness to secure housing but also to develop appropriate, affordable housing in communities where it is lacking or nonexistent

NAMI describes this model legislation as a blueprint for recovery and contends that upon implementation, such initiatives "will close the gap between what this country knows about treating mental illnesses and the discriminatory policies that dismiss individuals with such disorders as second class citizens and abandon them to cruel and unnecessary suffering."

MENTAL HEALTH POLICY

Mental health has been shaped as much by cultural changes and major social policies designed with other populations in mind as by the efforts of persons working in the mental health field itself.

—David Mechanic, *Mental Health, United States, 2000,* Chapter 7, Center for Mental Health Services, 2001

The World Health Organization (WHO) defines mental health policies as "statements by governments or health authorities that aim to formulate clear and relevant objectives for the prevention, treatment, care and rehabilitation related to mental disorders." The WHO contends that mental health policies are vital in order to ensure coordinated service delivery with continuity. They are also essential to creating overarching principles about the types of services to be provided and deciding how funds should be spent.

Mental health policies enable nations to act with unity of purpose to secure access and equity. They stipulate equitable allocation of resources and institute procedures to ensure efficacy—that mental health treatment achieves measurable health benefits and efficiency—and create the optimal distribution of resources to ensure health gains. According to the WHO, the key objectives of mental health policy are to:

- Reduce the number of persons who develop mental health problems

- Help persons with mental illness to improve the quality of their lives

- Offer effective mental health treatment and social service interventions to all persons who would benefit from these services

- Eliminate the stigmas associated with mental illness to encourage access to care and prevent discrimination and human rights violations

- Encourage research to determine the causes and effective treatment of mental disorders

Despite the enormous global economic and social toll of mental illness, a survey of 185 countries published in 2001 by the WHO, *Atlas of Mental Health Resources in the World 2001,* revealed that nearly 40 percent lack both national mental health policies and community-based care programs for persons with mental illness. Nearly one-third did not have programs in place to improve mental health conditions; one-quarter had not enacted any mental health legislation; and the majority of countries' budgets devoted less than 1 percent of total health expenditures to mental health.

GLOBAL INITIATIVE TO IMPROVE MENTAL HEALTH CARE

On December 17, 1991, the United Nations General Assembly adopted a resolution presented by the U.N. Office of the High Commissioner for Human Rights intended to safeguard the rights of persons suffering from mental illness, *Principles for the Protection of Persons with Mental Illness and the Improvement of Mental Health Care.* The resolution outlined the following principles and practices of ethical and humane mental health treatment:

- Fundamental freedoms and human rights—guarantees that persons with mental disorders, including criminal offenders, have access to the best available treatment, are treated with dignity, and are protected from discrimination and abuse

- Protection of minors

- Life in the community—the assurance that persons with mental illness have the right to live and work in the community and to receive treatment appropriate to their cultural backgrounds

- Determination of mental illness—the promise that diagnoses will be made in accordance with internationally accepted medical definitions, rather than on the basis of race, religion, political affiliation, or socioeconomic status

- Medical examination and confidentiality—to ensure than no one must undergo medical examination to determine the presence of mental illness except when authorized by domestic law

- Standards of care—persons with mental illness have the right to health and social services best able to meet their needs, care and treatment comparable to that offered to persons suffering from other illnesses, and protection from discomfort and abuse such as unjustified medication or harassment from other patients

- Treatment—patients are entitled to treatment for which they have expressed fully informed consent, in the least restrictive settings, from qualified staff who perform ongoing review to ensure timely, appropriate, and effective care aimed at preserving patient autonomy (independence)

- Medication—medication should be administered by mental health practitioners with legal prescribing authority and only for diagnostic and therapeutic purposes—never as punishment or for the convenience of caregivers

- Rights and conditions in mental health facilities—patients must be afforded respect, recognition, privacy, freedom of communication, and freedom of religion, as well as living conditions as comparable as possible to those offered to persons of similar age

- Resources for mental health facilities—facilities should provide comprehensive treatment, be appropriately staffed and equipped, and regularly inspected to ensure quality conditions and care

- Admission—access to mental health facilities should be comparable to that of other health facilities and every effort should be made to avoid involuntary admission

- Impartial review and safeguards—periodic review of involuntary admissions should be performed and patients should be provided counsel and representation to protect their rights and interests

- Access to information—patients and former patients are entitled to access to medical records maintained by mental health facilities unless disclosure presents risk of harm to patients or others

U.S. INITIATIVE TO IMPROVE MENTAL HEALTH CARE

On June 18, 2001, President George W. Bush issued an executive order supporting community-based services and programs for individuals with disabilities. One element of the President's plan to promote full access to community life was the April 29, 2002, establishment of the President's New Freedom Commission on Mental Health. As he announced the creation of the commission, President Bush reiterated his aim to improve mental health care

in the United States, asserting, "Our country must make a commitment. Americans with mental illness deserve our understanding and they deserve excellent care."

The commission studied the U.S. mental health service delivery system, including both the private- and public-sector providers, and was charged with advising the President about ways to improve the system. Specifically, the commission was to recommend programs and strategies aimed at fully integrating adults with serious mental illness and children with serious emotional disturbances in their communities. To realize this overarching goal, the commission was tasked with the following responsibilities:

- Review the current quality and effectiveness of public and private providers and federal, state, and local government involvement in the delivery of services to individuals with serious mental illnesses and children with serious emotional disturbances, and identify unmet needs and barriers to services.

- Identify innovative mental health treatments, services, and technologies that are demonstratively effective and can be widely replicated in different settings.

- Formulate policy options that could be implemented by public and private providers and federal, state, and local governments to integrate the use of effective treatments and services, improve coordination among service providers, and improve community integration for adults with serious mental illnesses and children with serious emotional disturbances.

The commission was advised to use the following principles to guide both its research and recommendations:

- To emphasize the desired outcomes of mental health care, which are to attain each individual's maximum level of employment, self-care, interpersonal relationships, and community participation.

- Concentrate on community-based models of care that efficiently coordinate the multiple health and human service providers and public and private payers involved in mental health service delivery.

- Focus on those policies that maximize the utility of existing resources by increasing cost effectiveness and reducing unnecessary and burdensome regulatory barriers.

- Consider how mental health research findings may be used to enhance service delivery.

- Adhere to the principles of federalism, and ensure that recommendations promote innovation, flexibility, and accountability at all levels of government and respect the constitutional role of states.

On July 22, 2003, the President's Commission issued a report, *Achieving the Promise: Transforming Mental*

Health Care in America, that provided the first comprehensive study of the nation's public and private mental health service delivery systems in nearly 25 years. The commission confirmed that there are unmet needs and barriers that sharply restrict access to care for persons suffering from mental illness and proposed that the existing mental health system be entirely transformed to improve access. It outlined goals and objectives of such a transformation and presented model programs for prevention and treatment of mental illness.

CHAPTER 8

MENTAL HEALTH PROFESSIONALS, FACILITIES, AND SERVICE DELIVERY

A wide range of services, therapies, and practitioners are available to help persons suffering from mental illness in the United States. Mental disorders and mental health problems may be treated by highly trained medical and mental health professionals, or by a variety of skilled practitioners from other disciplines, such as pastoral counselors, school guidance counselors, child welfare specialists, and peer counselors. Mental health professionals and other practitioners work in public and privately owned and operated facilities and agencies that, taken together, are optimistically described by some as a loosely coordinated and by others as a hopelessly fragmented mental health service delivery system.

SECTORS OF MENTAL HEALTH SERVICE DELIVERY

Mental Health: A Report of the Surgeon General (U.S. Department of Health and Human Services, Rockville, MD, 1999) described the U.S. mental health system as containing four major components or domains:

- The specialty mental health sector is composed of mental health professionals such as psychiatrists, psychologists, psychiatric nurses, and psychiatric social workers who are trained to diagnose and treat persons with mental disorders. Most specialty treatment is delivered in ambulatory-care (outpatient) settings, such as office-based practices or clinics. Nearly all hospital care is provided in the psychiatric units of general acute-care hospitals, although private psychiatric hospitals and residential treatment centers for children and adolescents also provide acute care in the private sector. Public-sector specialty mental health care providers include state and county mental hospitals and mental health facilities, which often coordinate a comprehensive array of inpatient and outpatient treatment, case management, partial hospitalization (day programs that do not have inpatient overnight

TABLE 8.1

Proportion of adult population using mental/addictive disorder services in one year

Total health sector	11%*
Specialty mental health	6%
General medical	6%
Human services professionals	5%
Voluntary support network	3%
Any of above services	15%

*Subtotals do not add to total due to overlap.

SOURCE: David Satcher, "Table 6–1. Proportion of adult population using mental/addictive disorder services in one year," in *Mental Health: A Report of the Surgeon General*, U.S. Department of Health and Human Services, Substance Abuse and Mental Health Services Administration, with National Institutes of Health, Rockville, MD, 1999 [Online] http://www.mentalhealth.org/features/surgeongeneralreport/toc.asp [accessed December 18, 2003]

stays), and social services. Approximately 6 percent of the adult population and about 8 percent of children and adolescents (ages 9 to 17) use specialty mental health services each year. (See Table 8.1 and Table 8.2 for annual projections estimated using data from research performed in 1996.)

- The general medical/primary-care sector consists of health care professionals such as general and family-practice physicians, internists, pediatricians, and nurse practitioners in office-based practices, clinics, hospitals, and nursing homes. The general medical/primary-care sector practitioners are often the first professionals to encounter adults with mental health disorders. Research reveals that among adults seeking mental health help, about half see their primary-care physicians first, and for some, these practitioners may be their only source of mental health services. (Table 8.1 shows that 6 percent of the adult population using mental health services see general medical practitioners.) For this reason, the National Institute of Mental Health (NIMH) encourages all primary-care

TABLE 8.2

Proportion of child/adolescent populations using mental/addictive disorder services in one year, ages 9–17

Total health sector	9%*
Specialty mental health	8%
General medical	3%
Human services professionals	17%*
School services	16%
Other human services	3%
Any of above services	21%

*Subtotals do not add to total due to overlap.

SOURCE: David Satcher, "Figure 3–2. Grading the Level of Evidence for Efficacy of Psychotropic Drugs in Children," in *Mental Health: A Report of the Surgeon General,* U.S. Department of Health and Human Services, Substance Abuse and Mental Health Services Administration, with National Institutes of Health, Rockville, MD, 1999 [Online] http://www.mentalhealth .org/features/surgeongeneralreport/toc.asp [accessed December 18, 2003]

practitioners, who often lack special training, to recognize these disorders and send patients who seek help to mental health professionals for screening to ensure that mental disorders are properly diagnosed and treated. Further, NIMH recommends that general physicians receive more training to improve recognition and treatment of psychiatric disorders. Of children and adolescents seeking mental health care, just 3 percent visit general medical/primary-care physicians for mental health services. (See Table 8.2.)

• The human services sector comprises social services, school-based counseling services, residential rehabilitation services, vocational rehabilitation, criminal justice/prison-based services, and professional pastoral counselors (specially trained members of the clergy). While just 5 percent of adults use these services, 16 percent of children receive mental health services in school, and other human services sector providers (such as services in the child welfare and juvenile justice systems) serve about 3 percent of the child/adolescent population. (See Table 8.1 and Table 8.2.)

• The voluntary support network sector, which includes self-help groups such as 12-step programs and peer counselors, is an increasingly popular and growing component of the mental health system. During the early 1980s, a scant 1 percent of adults participated in self-help groups. A decade later, 3 percent sought care from this sector. (See Table 8.1.)

MENTAL HEALTH PROFESSIONALS

The specialty mental health sector includes a range of professionals—psychiatrists, psychologists, psychiatric nurses, psychiatric social workers, and marriage and family therapists. Within this group, the training, orientation, philosophy, and practice styles differ, even within a single discipline. For example, clinical psychologists may endorse and offer dramatically different forms of therapy, ranging from long-term psychoanalytic psychotherapy to short-term cognitive-behavioral therapy. Psychiatric social workers (also known as licensed clinical social workers) may see clients individually or in groups, and some mental health practitioners specialize in the diagnosis and treatment of specific problems such as eating disorders, post-traumatic stress disorder (PSTD), or phobias. Others specialize in selected populations such as adolescents, children with learning problems, older adults, or persons with disabilities. In addition to varying philosophies and practice styles, mental health professionals differ in terms of their training, licensure, certification, and scopes of practice.

Psychiatrists

Psychiatrists are physicians who have earned the M.D. or D.O. (medical doctor or doctor of osteopathy) degree and have completed psychiatric residency training in the prevention, diagnosis, and treatment of mental illness, mental retardation, and substance abuse disorders. Since they are trained physicians, they are often especially well equipped to care for persons who have co-existing medical diseases and mental health problems. They are able to prescribe medication, including psychoactive drugs. Psychiatrists also may obtain additional training that prepares them to treat selected populations such as children and adolescents or older adults (this subspecialty is termed geriatric psychiatry or geropsychiatry) or they may specialize in a specific treatment modality.

The U.S. Department of Labor Bureau of Labor Statistics observes that physicians' formal education and training requirements are among the most demanding of any occupation, and their earnings are among the highest. Of all mental health practitioners, psychiatrists generally have the highest earning potential. According to the American Medical Association, in 1998 psychiatrists' median income after expenses was $130,000 per year.

The American Psychiatric Association (APA) is a medical specialty professional society that boasts 37,000 U.S. and international members. The APA collects and projects data about the profession, as does the U.S. Department of Labor Bureau of Labor Statistics. In 2002, in terms of numbers, psychiatry was the fourth largest medical specialty, with approximately 45,000 psychiatrists practicing in the United States; about 6,000 of this total are devoted to child psychiatry. In the United States there are about 14 adult psychiatrists per 100,000 persons. However, they are not evenly distributed throughout the country. New York has the largest number of psychiatrists (6,119), followed by California, Massachusetts, Pennsylvania, and Texas. Wyoming has the fewest psychiatrists (35), followed in ascending order by South Dakota, Alaska, Idaho, and North Dakota. Washington, D.C., has the highest number of psychiatrists per capita, while Alaska has the lowest.

It is difficult to assess whether the current ratio of psychiatrists is adequate to provide the treatment needed by the U.S. population. Compared to other countries, the United States has an ample supply of psychiatrists. When child psychiatrists are included, in 2000 it was estimated that there were 16 psychiatrists per 100,000 U.S. residents, compared to 4 per 100,000 in Great Britain, 4.3 per 100,000 in New Zealand, 10.6 per 100,000 in Australia, and 12 per 100,000 in Canada and Holland.

SPECIALLY TRAINED PSYCHIATRISTS. According to the U.S. Bureau of Health Professions projections, the number of child and adolescent psychiatrists will increase to 8,312 (about 30 percent) by 2020—far less than the estimated 12,624 needed to meet demand. The American Academy of Child and Adolescent Psychiatry (AACAP) attributes the shortfall to recruitment and funding programs. The AACAP reports that:

- The number of child and adolescent psychiatry residents has decreased in the past decade—from 712 in 1990 to 657 in 2001—and the number of child and adolescent psychiatry training programs decreased by seven during the same period.

- More than 20 percent of child and adolescent psychiatry residency positions were unfilled in 1999; 718 residents filled 874 approved positions.

- Escalating educational debt, pressure to pursue a primary-care career, a long training period, and reduced reimbursement from managed care plans discourage medical students from choosing a career in child and adolescent psychiatry.

- Federal mandates to decrease the overall physician workforce and efforts to remedy the perceived oversupply of specialists has served to exacerbate the continuing critical shortage of child and adolescent psychiatrists.

Similarly, the American Association for Geriatric Psychiatry (AAGP) asserts that the existing 2,300 geriatric psychiatrists constitute less than half the projected need for such specialists by 2010. To meet the need for psychiatric care for the aging population in the United States, workforce projections made by the National Institute on Aging estimated that about 5,000 to 7,000 clinical geropsychiatrists would be required during the first years of the 21st century. It seems unlikely that there will be sufficient specialists to meet the needs of the aging population, since the AAGP reports that while there is an increasing number of training slots for geriatric psychiatrists, many go unfilled.

Psychologists

During their education and throughout their careers, psychologists study the human mind and human behav-

ior. Research psychologists investigate the physical, cognitive, emotional, or social aspects of human behavior. They work in academic and private research centers and in business, nonprofit, and governmental organizations. They study behavior processes of human beings and animals to learn more about aspects of human behavior such as motivation, thinking, attention, learning and memory, and genetic and neurological factors affecting behavior. Like their clinician counterparts, most research psychologists specialize in a specific disorder or population. For example, developmental psychologists study the physiological, cognitive, and social development that occurs throughout life. Some specialize in behavior during infancy, childhood, and adolescence; others consider aspects of aging.

Clinical psychologists are practitioners who provide mental health care in publicly funded hospitals, counseling centers, clinics, schools, or private settings such as independent or group practices, proprietary hospitals, or clinics. They help mentally and emotionally disturbed clients better manage their symptoms and behaviors and assist hospitalized patients to recover from illnesses or injuries. Some work in rehabilitation, treating patients with spinal cord injuries, chronic pain or illness, strokes, arthritis, and neurologic conditions. Others help people cope during times of personal crisis, such as divorce or the loss of a loved one. Psychologists also are called upon to help communities recover from the trauma of manmade or natural disasters, for example, students who have witnessed school violence or persons who have lost their homes to earthquakes, fires, or floods.

Along with assessment and treatment of children and adolescents, clinical psychologists frequently specialize in health psychology, neuropsychology, and geropsychology. Health psychologists actively promote healthy lifestyles and behaviors and provide counseling such as smoking cessation, weight reduction, and stress management to assist people to reduce their health risks. Neuropsychologists often work in stroke rehabilitation and head-injury programs and geropsychologists work with older adults in institutional and community settings. Counseling psychologists focus on helping people manage the stresses and challenges of everyday living. They work in voluntary health and social service agencies, university counseling centers, hospitals, and individual or group practices.

School psychologists endeavor to identify, diagnose, and address students' learning and behavior problems. They work with teachers, parents, and school personnel to improve classroom management strategies or parenting skills, and design educational programs to meet the needs of students with disabilities or gifted and talented students. They may evaluate the effectiveness of academic programs, behavior management procedures, and other services provided in the school setting.

Industrial-organizational psychologists aim to improve productivity and the quality of life in the workplace. They screen prospective employees and conduct training and development, counseling, and organizational development and analysis. While industrial-organizational psychologists examine aspects of work-life, social psychologists consider interpersonal relationships and interactions with the social environment. They work in organizational consultation, market research, systems design, or other applied psychology fields. For example, both industrial and social psychologists may be involved in efforts to understand and influence consumer purchasing behaviors.

EDUCATION, TRAINING, LICENSURE, AND EARNINGS. Most psychologists hold a doctoral degree in psychology, which entails five to seven years of graduate study. Clinical psychologists usually must have earned a Ph.D. or Psy.D. degree and completed an internship of at least one year. An Educational Specialist degree (Ed.S.) qualifies an individual to work as a school psychologist, though most school psychologists complete a master's degree followed by a one-year internship. Persons with a master's degree in psychology may work as industrial-organizational psychologists, as psychological assistants, or under the supervision of doctoral-level psychologists. They may also conduct research or psychological evaluations. Vocational and guidance counselors usually need two years of graduate education in counseling and one year of counseling experience. A master's degree in psychology requires at least two years of full-time graduate study. Persons with undergraduate degrees in psychology assist psychologists and other professionals in community mental health centers, vocational rehabilitation offices, and correctional programs. They also may work in research or administrative capacities.

Psychologists in clinical practice must be certified or licensed in all states and the District of Columbia. Licensing laws and requirements for certification vary by state and type of position, but all states require that applicants pass an examination. Most state boards administer a standardized test, and many supplement that with additional oral or essay questions. Most states certify those with a master's degree as school psychologists after completion of an internship, and some states require continuing education for license renewal.

According to the U.S. Department Of Labor, Bureau of Labor Statistics, the average annual salary for psychologists employed by the federal government was $72,830 in 2001, and median annual earnings of salaried psychologists were $48,596 in 2000. Median annual earnings were $48,320 for clinical, counseling, and school psychologists and $66,880 for industrial-organizational psychologists. Table 8.3 shows the median annual earning of psychologists working in a variety of other settings in 2000.

TABLE 8.3

Median annual earnings in the industries employing the largest numbers of psychologists, 2000

Hospitals	$52,460
Elementary and secondary schools	51,310
Offices of other health practitioners	50,990
Offices and clinics of medical doctors	47,890
Individual and family services	35,720

SOURCE: "Median annual earnings in the industries employing the largest numbers of psychologists in 2000 were as follows:," in *Occupational Outlook Handbook 2002–03*, U.S. Department of Labor, Bureau of Labor Statistics, Washington, DC, 2003

The American Psychological Association (APA) is the largest scientific and professional association of psychologists in the United States and worldwide, with more than 150,000 members. The APA describes the discipline of psychology as an all-encompassing "understanding of behavior" that addresses every aspect of human experience from the conduct of individuals to the course of action of nations.

Psychiatric Nurses

Psychiatric nurses have earned a degree in nursing, are licensed as registered nurses (RNs), and have obtained additional experience in psychiatry. Advanced-practice psychiatric nurses are registered nurses prepared at the master's level as nurse practitioners or certified nurse specialists in psychiatric-mental health care. Advanced-practice psychiatric nurses may prescribe psychotropic medications and conduct individual, group, and family psychotherapy, as well as perform crisis intervention and case management functions. Along with primary-care physicians, they often are the first points of contact for persons seeking mental health help.

The American Psychiatric Nurses Association (APNA) is the professional society that represents psychiatric nurses and examines the changing profile of the profession. The APNA characterizes its membership as over age 40 with significant experience in the field. In addition, about 65 percent of APNA members hold master's or doctoral degrees, and they are about evenly divided in inpatient and outpatient treatment settings. (See Table 8.4.) Slightly less than half of APNA members responding to a salary survey (49 percent) reported earnings in excess of $50,000 a year. (See Table 8.5.)

Table 8.6 shows that nearly half of APNA members are employed in private, nonprofit or public/federal hospitals (42 percent). More than 40 percent specialize in the treatment of adults, 16 percent care for older adults, and 13 percent provide mental health services to adolescents. (See Table 8.7.) More than half of APNA members provide direct services. Just 27 percent describe their primary

TABLE 8.4

Level of care provided by psychiatric nurses, 2003

Inpatient	42%
Outpatient/ambulatory	38%
Partial program	8%
Home care	7%
Residential	6%

SOURCE: "Level of Care Provided," in *APNA Membership Profile*, American Psychiatric Nurses Association, Arlington, VA, 2003 [Online] http://www.apna.org/membership/profile.html [accessed November 19, 2003]. Reproduced with permission.

TABLE 8.6

Primary work setting for psychiatric nurses, 2003

Private/non-profit hospital	24%
Public/federal hospital	18%
School/college of nursing	15%
Private practice	14%
Community agency	13%
Private, investor-owned hospital	4%
Behavioral care company/HMO	4%
Home health agency	3%
Military	2%
Primary care office	1%
Prison/jail	1%
Industry	1%

SOURCE: "Primary Work Setting," in *APNA Membership Profile*, American Psychiatric Nurses Association, Arlington, VA, 2003 [Online] http://www.apna.org/membership/profile.html [accessed November 19, 2003]. Reproduced with permission.

TABLE 8.8

Primary roles for psychiatric nurses, 2003

Clinical Nurse Specialist	19%
Staff Nurse	15%
Head Nurse/Manager/Asst. Head Nurse	10%
Therapist	9%
Educator-Clinical	8%
Nurse Practitioner	8%
Faculty-Academic	7%
Administrator/Director/VP of Nursing	6%
Consultant	6%
Case Manager	5%
Researcher	3%

SOURCE: "Primary Role," in *APNA Membership Profile*, American Psychiatric Nurses Association, Arlington, VA, 2003 [Online] http://www.apna.org/membership/profile.html [accessed November 19, 2003]. Reproduced with permission.

role as faculty, administrator, consultant, case manager, or researcher. (See Table 8.8.)

Clinical Social Workers

Clinical social workers are the largest group of professionally trained mental health care providers in the United States. According to U.S. Department of Labor Bureau of Labor Statistics, in 2000 about 468,000 social workers were employed in the United States. Of this

TABLE 8.5

Annual income of psychiatric nurses, 2003

<$39,000	15%
$40,000–$49,000	16%
$50,000–$59,000	20%
$60,000–$69,000	15%
$70,000–$70,000	11%
>$80,000	3%

SOURCE: "Annual Income," in *APNA Membership Profile*, American Psychiatric Nurses Association, Arlington, VA, 2003 [Online] http://www.apna.org/membership/profile.html [accessed November 19, 2003]. Reproduced with permission.

TABLE 8.7

Subspecialties of psychiatric nursing

Adult	41%
Geriatric	16%
Adolescent	13%
Substance abuse	11%
Child	8%
Consult/liaison	7%
Forensic	3%

SOURCE: "Subspecialty," in *APNA Membership Profile*, American Psychiatric Nurses Association, Arlington, VA, 2003 [Online] http://www.apna.org/membership/profile.html [accessed November 19, 2003]. Reproduced with permission.

total, 281,000 were child, family, and school social workers, 104,000 worked in medical and public health settings, and 83,000 worked in mental health and substance abuse treatment. In 2000 the median annual earnings of child, family, and school social workers were $31,470. The median annual earnings of medical and public health social workers were $34,790. For mental health and substance abuse social workers, the median earnings were $30,170.

Clinical social workers offer psychotherapy or counseling and a range of diagnostic services in public agencies, clinics, and private practice. They assist people to improve their interpersonal relationships and solve personal and family problems, and advise them about how to function effectively in their communities. Not all social workers in mental health services practice psychotherapy. Some work as case managers, coordinating a comprehensive range of needed services for clients, such as housing, psychiatric, medical, legal, education, or financial services. Social workers specialize in many fields and are employed in a variety of settings, including gerontology, mental health, hospital administration, child welfare agencies, criminal justice, and child or adult protective services.

EDUCATION, CERTIFICATION, AND LICENSURE. A bachelor's degree in social work (BSW) degree is usually the minimum requirement for employment as a social worker, and an advanced degree has become the standard for many positions. A master's degree in social work (MSW) is necessary for positions in health and mental health settings and typically is required for certification for clinical work. Licensed Clinical Social Workers (LCSW) hold a master's degree in social work (MSW), along with additional clinical training. Supervisory, administrative, and staff training positions usually require an advanced degree. University teaching positions and research appointments normally require a doctorate in social work (DSW or Ph.D.).

All the states and the District of Columbia have licensing, certification, or registration requirements that delineate the scope of social work practice and the use of professional titles, but standards for licensing vary by state. The National Association of Social Workers (NASW) is the largest membership organization of professional social workers in the world, with nearly 150,000 members. The NASW offers voluntary credentials. The Academy of Certified Social Workers (ACSW) credential is granted to social workers who have met established eligibility criteria. Clinical social workers may earn either the Qualified Clinical Social Worker (QCSW) credential or the advanced credential—Diplomate in Clinical Social Work (DCSW). Credentials are vitally important for social workers in private practice because many health insurance plans will not reimburse social workers without credentials.

Counselors

Counselors assist people with personal, family, educational, mental health, and job-related challenges and problems. Their roles and responsibilities depend on the clients they serve and on the settings in which they work. According to the U.S. Department of Labor Bureau of Labor Statistics, more than half of all counselors have earned a master's degree. In 2001, 46 states and the District of Columbia had some form of counselor credentialing, licensure, certification, or registry legislation governing counselors who practice outside schools, but requirements vary from state to state. Some states mandate credentialing, while in others it is voluntary. The American Counseling Association (ACA) is the world's largest counseling association, exclusively representing more than 52,000 professional counselors in various practice settings. The ACA has taken an active role in advocating for certification, licensure, and registry of counselors.

Of the 465,000 counselors employed in the United States during 2000, about 205,000 worked as educational, vocational, and school counselors in elementary, secondary, and postsecondary schools. (See Table 8.9.) These counselors work with students to evaluate their aptitudes, interests, talents, and ambitions and help them to develop academic and career goals. Counselors may use interviews, counseling sessions, tests, or other methods to eval-

TABLE 8.9

Employment distribution among counseling specialities, 2000

Educational, vocational, and school counselors	205,000
Rehabilitation counselors	110,000
Mental health counselors	67,000
Substance abuse and behavioral disorder counselors	61,000
Marriage and family therapists	21,000

SOURCE: "Counselors held about 465,000 jobs in 2000. Employment was distributed among the counseling specialities as follows:," in *Occupational Outlook Handbook 2002–03*, U.S. Department of Labor, Bureau of Labor Statistics, Washington, DC, 2003

uate and advise students. They create and staff career information centers and career education programs. High school counselors help students with the many aspects of the college application and admission processes, including admission requirements, entrance exams, and financial aid. They also assist students seeking vocational training at trade or technical schools or through apprenticeship programs. In addition, they teach students job-search skills such as resume-writing and interviewing skills.

Elementary school counselors evaluate younger children after observing them during classroom and recreational activities and collaborate with teachers and parents to resolve problems or meet special needs. They also help students cultivate good study habits. School counselors help students with social, behavioral, and personal problems. They may also offer prevention programs such as alcohol and drug prevention programs and classes that teach students to resolve conflicts without resorting to violence. Counselors identify and intervene in cases of domestic violence, neglect, and other family problems that may adversely affect a student's life. All states require school counselors to hold state school counseling certification, but certification requirements vary. Some states require public school counselors to have both counseling and teaching certificates. For example, in some states, a master's degree in counseling and two to five years of teaching experience may be required to obtain a school counseling certificate.

Vocational counselors (also called employment counselors when working outside an academic setting) help people evaluate career options. They explore and evaluate the client's education, training, work history, interests, skills, and preferences, and coordinate aptitude and achievement tests. They also perform job development—working with clients to refine job search skills and assisting them to find and apply for jobs. Some job developers specialize in assisting clients with special needs, such as welfare recipients, persons with disabilities, or those with histories of involvement with the criminal justice system.

Rehabilitation counselors work with persons with disabilities to help them surmount the personal, social, and vocational effects of disabilities. They advise people with disabilities resulting from birth defects, illness or disease, accidents, or the stress of daily life. They assess the capabilities and limitations of clients, offer personal and vocational counseling, and arrange for medical care, vocational training, and job placement. Working with the client and other health and social service professionals, they develop a rehabilitation program, which often includes training to help the client acquire job skills. The goal of rehabilitation counselors is to enhance the client's capacity to live independently. In 2000 about 110,000 rehabilitation counselors were employed in the United States. (See Table 8.9.)

In 2000 approximately 67,000 mental health counselors worked in prevention programs to promote optimum mental health and provided a wide range of counseling services. (See Table 8.9.) For example, some mental health counselors teach stress management to help people learn to cope with the pressures of modern life. They help individuals manage a variety of mental health problems and mental disorders, including substance abuse, suicidal impulses, low self-esteem, issues associated with aging, job and career concerns, educational decisions, and family, parenting, and marital problems. Mental health counselors work closely with other mental health professionals, including psychiatrists, psychologists, clinical social workers, psychiatric nurses, and school counselors.

Substance abuse and behavioral disorder counselors help people overcome addictions to alcohol, drugs, gambling, and eating disorders. They counsel individuals, families, or groups in clinics, hospital-based outpatient treatment programs, community mental health centers, and inpatient chemical dependency treatment programs. In 2000 about 61,000 substance abuse and behavioral disorder counselors were employed in the United States. (See Table 8.9.)

Marriage and family therapists use varying techniques to intervene with individuals, families, and couples or to help them to resolve emotional conflicts. They aim to modify perceptions and behavior, enhance communication and understanding among family members, and prevent family and individual crises. Individual marriage and family therapists also may offer psychotherapy intended to assist individuals, couples, and families to improve their interpersonal relationships. During 2000, 21,000 marriage and family therapists were working in the United States. (See Table 8.9.)

Pastoral counselors offer a type of psychotherapy that combines spiritual resources as well as psychological understanding for healing and growth. According to the American Association of Pastoral Counselors (AAPC), this therapeutic modality is more than simply the comfort, support, and encouragement a religious community can offer; instead it provides "psychologically sound therapy that weaves in the religious and spiritual dimension." Typically, an AAPC-certified counselor has obtained a bachelor's degree from a college or university, a three-year professional degree from a seminary, and a specialized master's or doctoral degree in the mental health field. Postgraduate training involves completion of at least 1,375 hours of supervised clinical experience and 250 hours of direct approved supervision of the therapist's work in both crisis and long-term counseling situations. Candidates seeking AAPC certification are tested and evaluated to assure that AAPC certifies only the most competent individuals who not only have the requisite education and clinical training but also who possess the highest personal standards.

The AAPC asserts that demand for spiritually based counseling is on the rise, in part because interest in spirituality is on the rise in the United States. The organization also believes that despite increased interest in psychotherapy and increasing numbers of therapists, the advent of managed mental health care has reduced the availability of, and payment for, counseling services for many people. As a result, more people are turning to clergy for help with personal, marital, and family issues as well as faith issues. For many working-poor Americans without health insurance benefits, free or low-cost counseling from pastoral counselors is the most accessible, available, affordable, and acceptable form of mental health care.

CHANGING ATTITUDES ABOUT MENTAL ILLNESS

Until the 20th century, persons with mental illness were often treated with suspicion, fear, contempt, and scorn. Mental illness was viewed by many as the result of demonic possession or moral weakness, and early treatment consisted of banishing persons with mental illness to asylums. Sending persons with mental illness away to asylums was actually considered an enlightened and progressive approach to treatment, since asylums removed the affected individuals from society's view and provided custodial care.

Before the emphasis on institutional care and the growth of long-term care facilities between 1890 and 1950, many persons suffering from mental illness were cared for by their families in the community. Others were cared for in almshouses supported by local governments or in state hospitals. Gradually, the states assumed increasing responsibility for long-term care of persons with mental illness. Local jurisdictions, pleased to be relieved of the financial burden of housing persons with mental illness, relocated them, as well as senile older adults, to state mental hospitals.

During the 1900s the population of mental hospitals was a diverse mix—many suffered from medical conditions that produced their cognitive, behavioral, or emotional problems. Some of the conditions included syphilis (a sexually transmitted disease that can produce neurological and cognitive impairment), brain tumors, stroke, and Huntington's chorea (an inherited, degenerative disorder of the central nervous system, caused by a dominant gene, that progressively leads to dementia). Lengths of stay increased, and patients became long-term or even lifetime residents of the mental hospitals.

By the 1940s public sentiment began to shift and state mental hospitals were criticized as overcrowded, uncaring, and largely ineffective facilities that served as little more than warehouses for the mentally ill. Concurrently, psychiatry began to emphasize treatment that considered life experiences and social problems as potential causes of mental illness. Psychiatrists began to assume therapeutic, as opposed to purely custodial, relationships with their patients. Changing public opinion, new philosophies about treatment, optimism about the potential for persons with mental disorders to function in the community, and financially depleted state governments combined to promote the shift from inpatient residential treatment to community-based policies and programs.

CHANGING SERVICE DELIVERY SYSTEMS

During the 1950s support for community-based policies grew. In 1954 New York enacted its Community Mental Health Services Act to fund outpatient clinics. By 1959 more than a half million persons were receiving care in more than 1,400 clinics. Schools, courts, and social service agencies also launched community treatment programs. But according to researcher Gerald Grob, in "Looking Ahead and Reflecting Upon the Past" (*Mental Health United States, 2000,* Chapter 2, U.S. Department of Health and Human Services, Substance Abuse and Mental Health Services Administration, The Center for Mental Health Services, Rockville, MD, 2001), the claims about the effectiveness of community-based care were largely unsupported.

Grob explained that the efficacy of community care was based on several assumptions—that patients had homes, sympathetic families, or other caregivers, and that the patients' homes were supportive of, as opposed to contributing factors to, the illness. Community care relied on the presence of stable, supportive families, but a 1960 study found that nearly half of inpatients in mental hospitals had never married, 12 percent were widowed, and 13 percent were divorced or separated. For those without families or homes, community care was not feasible.

Community-oriented treatment received a resounding vote of confidence with passage of the Community Mental Health Centers Act of 1963, which further elevated the status of outpatient clinics and community treatment programs. During this same period, mental hospital census began a slow decline. The decline was in part a response to growing enthusiasm for outpatient treatment, but it also arose in response to condemnation of mental hospitals, which were assailed as "snake pits," repressive, and dehumanizing institutions that systematically denied patients civil rights. Enactment of public entitlement programs—Medicare and Medicaid—and third-party payors' preference for less costly outpatient treatment also encouraged the exodus from inpatient facilities.

According to Grob, more than simply the location of service delivery had changed. The National Institute of Mental Health (NIMH) documented 1,028 patient episodes for mental health treatment per 100,000 population in 1955; by 1968 the rate had risen to 1,713 per 100,000. During this time, the population of inpatient facilities not only declined but also changed—by the late 1960s hospitals offered short and intermediate-term care for persons with serious mental illness and less chronic, long-term care. Public hospitals continued to care for more severe and long-term mental illness than general acute hospitals, while community mental health centers focused on persons with less serious mental health disorders.

During the 1970s legislation passed that expanded community mental health center funding and services, but disagreement about the financing and delivery of mental health treatment persisted. The deinstitutionalization from public mental hospitals that began during the 1960s accelerated during the 1970s as states began to make use of federal funds such as Medicare, Medicaid, Social Security Disability Insurance (SSDI), and Supplemental Security Income for the Aged, the Disabled and the Blind (SSI). These funds enable states to support persons with serious mental illness in the community. Older adults were among the first to be relocated from mental hospitals to nursing homes, many of which were entirely unprepared to treat mental illnesses. Others were young adults who had grown up in mental institutions. With few coping skills, they were unable to manage in the community. These young adults often suffered from substance abuse and mental illness, and some were homeless or became fixtures in hospital emergency departments, shelters, and correctional facilities.

Although state hospitals experienced declining numbers—from 560,000 inpatients in 1955 to less than 60,000 in 1998—and shorter lengths of stay, they remained the single largest provider of inpatient mental health care. The number of state psychiatric hospitals dropped from 277 in 1970 to 230 in 1998. The populations of these public hospitals changed dramatically, with a sharp rise in violent, aggressive, severely mentally ill patients who had often "failed" other types of treatment in other less restrictive settings.

Still, most observers believe that deinstitutionalization was a sound policy choice. Research has demonstrated that with a comprehensive range of community support services, including day treatment and residential settings for persons in crisis, job training, employment opportunities, and housing, persons with serious and persistent mental illness can live in the community. Managed care (plans and payors that exert a significant influence over service delivery so that they may better control health care costs) has supported the deinstitutionalization movement and has further reduced inpatient lengths of stay. Health maintenance organizations (HMOs) and preferred provider organizations (PPOs) are examples of managed care plans. Further, a rising consumer movement and coalitions to advocate for persons with mental illness, such as the National Alliance for the Mentally Ill (NAMI), confirmed that the majority of affected individuals preferred and benefited from community life.

Advances in Treatment Favor Community-Based Care

Research and advances in neuroscience, genetics, behavioral science, and neuroimaging—imaging studies of the brain such as computer tomography (CT) scans, magnetic resonance imaging (MRI), and positron emission tomography (PET) scans—have made strides in understanding the origins and triggers of mental illness. Although newer psychotropic drugs such as selective serotonin reuptake inhibitors (SSRIs) do not appear to be more effective in terms of symptom control than older medications, they have fewer side effects and are more readily tolerated, so patients are more likely to adhere to long-term treatment. The increasing variety of available pharmacological agents also increases the likelihood that patients and practitioners will arrive at an optimal therapeutic regimen—medication that provides excellent relief of symptoms with minimal untoward side effects. Adherence to drug treatment is vital for many persons with mental illnesses, and lapses can result in acute episodes of illness, hospitalization, or serious declines in functioning.

Similarly, new approaches to therapy, such as the program of assertive community treatment (PACT) used to manage serious mental illness in the community, have gained recognition for their effectiveness. Studies of PACT programs have documented reduced rates of hospitalizations, shorter lengths of stay, less emergency department utilization, improved adherence to medication regimens, and high levels of patient satisfaction. Cost savings resulting from PACT programs are the result of fewer hospitalizations and shorter hospital stays.

Another innovation believed to have favorably influenced mental health treatment are policies and programs incorporating consumer and peer counseling. Peer support programs may improve adherence and offer clients practical information and real-life strategies for coping with employment, housing, as well as social challenges and situations.

Similarly, adoption and widespread use of evidence-based clinical practice guidelines not only recognize that the outcomes of mental health treatment are measurable but also aim to ensure consistent delivery of quality diagnostic and treatment services. Mental health practice guidelines have been developed by federal organizations such as

the Agency for Healthcare Research and Quality and Veteran's Health Administration as well as professional organizations such as the American Psychological Association.

David Mechanic, a renowned health policy researcher, observed that views of mental illness and policy are cyclical, and though currently there is a strong preference for medication instead of psychotherapy, counseling and interpersonal therapy are important additions to drug treatment. Mechanic contends that individual and group therapy and rehabilitation improve comfort, social functioning, and quality of life for persons with mental disorders (*Mental Health United States, 2000,* Chapter 7, Mental Health Policy at the Millennium: Challenges and Opportunities, U.S. Department of Health and Human Services, Substance Abuse and Mental Health Services Administration, the Center for Mental Health Services, Rockville, MD, 2001).

MENTAL HEALTH FACILITIES

In earlier centuries, mental illness was often considered a sign of possession by the devil or, at best, moral weakness. A change in these attitudes began in the late 18th century, when mental illness began to be perceived as a treatable condition. It was then that the concept of asylums was developed, not simply to lock the mentally ill away but also to care for affected individuals and provide them with relief from the conditions they found troubling.

Today mental health care is provided in a variety of treatment settings by different types of organizations. The U.S. Department of Health and Human Services Substance Abuse and Mental Health Services Administration, Center for Mental Health Services, describes the following mental health organizations:

- A psychiatric hospital (public or private) provides 24-hour inpatient care to persons with mental illnesses in a hospital setting. It also may offer 24-hour residential care and less-than-24-hour care, but these are not requirements. Psychiatric hospitals are operated under state, county, private for-profit, and private not-for-profit auspices.

- General hospitals with separate psychiatric services, units, or designated beds are under government or nongovernment auspices and maintain assigned staff for 24-hour inpatient care, 24-hour residential care, and less-than-24-hour care (outpatient care or partial hospitalization) to provide mental health diagnosis, evaluation, and treatment.

- VA hospitals are operated by the Department of Veterans Affairs and include VA general hospital psychiatric services and VA psychiatric outpatient clinics that exclusively serve persons entitled to VA benefits.

- An outpatient mental health clinic provides only ambulatory mental health services. Generally a psychiatrist has overall medical responsibility for clients

TABLE 8.10

Number of mental health organizations by type of organization, selected years, 1970–98[1]

Type of organization	1970	1976	1980	1986	1990	1992	1994	1998
	Number of mental health organizations							
All organizations	3,005	3,480	3,727	4,747	5,284	5,498	5,392	5,722
State and county mental hospitals	310	303	280	285	273	273	256	229
Private psychiatric hospitals	150	182	184	314	462	475	430	348
Non-federal general hospitals with separate psychiatric services	797	870	923	1,351	1,674	1,616	1,612	1,707
VA medical centers[2]	115	126	136	139	141	162	161	145
Federally funded community mental health centers	196	517	691	–	–	–	–	–
Residential treatment centers for emotionally disturbed children	261	331	368	437	501	497	459	461
All other mental health organizations[3]	1,176	1,151	1,145	2,221	2,233	2,457	2,474	2,832
	Number with 24-hour hospital and residential treatment service							
All organizations	1,734	2,273	2,526	3,039	3,430	3,415	3,827	3,729
State and county mental hospitals	310	303	280	285	273	273	256	229
Private psychiatric hospitals	150	182	184	314	462	475	430	348
Non-federal general hospitals with separate psychiatric services	664	791	843	1,287	1,571	1,517	1,531	1,593
VA medical centers[2]	110	112	121	124	130	133	135	123
Federally funded community mental health centers	196	517	691	–	–	–	–	–
Residential treatment centers for emotionally disturbed children	261	331	368	437	501	497	459	461
All other mental health organizations[3]	43	37	39	592	493	520	1,016	975
	Number with less than 24-hour care[4]							
All organizations	2,156	2,318	2,431	3,146	3,189	3,390	4,087	4,387
State and county mental hospitals	195	147	100	83	84	75	70	60
Private psychiatric hospitals	100	60	54	114	176	198	347	263
Non-federal general hospitals with separate psychiatric services	376	303	299	497	633	618	875	965
VA medical centers[2]	100	113	127	137	141	161	148	129
Federally funded community mental health centers	196	517	691	–	–	–	–	–
Residential treatment centers for emotionally disturbed children	48	57	68	99	163	167	227	210
All other mental health organizations[3]	1,141	1,121	1,092	2,016	1,992	2,171	2,420	2,760

[1] Some organizations were reclassified as a result of changes in reporting procedures and definitions. For 1979–80, comparable data were not available for certain organization types and data for either an earlier or a later period were substituted. These factors influence the comparability of 1980, 1986, 1990, 1992, and 1994 data with those of earlier years.
[2] Includes Department of Veterans Affairs (formerly Veterans Administration) (VA) neuropsychiatric hospitals, VA general hospital psychiatric services, and VA psychiatric outpatient clinics.
[3] Includes freestanding psychiatric outpatient clinics, partial care organizations, and multiservice mental health organizations. Multiservice mental health organizations were redefined in 1984.
[4] The 1994 survey format was changed and partial care is now included with outpatient, and together are called "less than 24-hour care."

SOURCE: Ronald W. Manderscheid, Joanne E. Atay, Maria del R. Hernandez-Cartagena, Pamela Y. Edmond, Alisa Male, Albert C.E. Parker, and Hongwei Zhang, "Table 1. Number of mental health organizations by type of organization: United States, selected years, 1970–98[1]," in chap. 14, *Mental Health, United States, 2000*, edited by Ronald W. Manderscheid and Marilyn J. Henderson, U.S. Department of Health and Human Services, Substance Abuse and Mental Health Services Administration, Center for Mental Health Services, Rockville, MD, 2001

and the philosophy and orientation of the mental health program. In 1986 the definition of an outpatient mental health clinic was modified such that to be classified as an outpatient clinic, it must provide only outpatient services. In surveys taken in 1994 and 1998, no distinction was made between clinics providing outpatient and partial care (a combination of hospital and outpatient) services. Any organization previously termed a freestanding psychiatric outpatient clinic, freestanding partial care organization, or multiservice mental health organization with neither 24-hour inpatient nor residential care is now classified as an organization with less-than-24-hour care services.

• Community mental health centers were funded under the Federal Community Mental Health Centers Act of 1963 and subsequent amendments to the act. During the early 1980s, when the federal government reverted to funding mental health services through block grants to the states rather than funding them directly, the federal government stopped tracking these mental health organizations (MHOs) individually. Statistical reports now include them in the category termed "all other mental health organizations." This term also includes freestanding psychiatric outpatient clinics, freestanding partial care organizations, and multiservice mental health organizations such as residential treatment centers.

• Residential treatment centers (RTCs) for emotionally disturbed children must serve children and youth primarily under the age of 18, provide 24-hour residential services, and offer a clinical program that is directed by a psychiatrist, psychologist, social worker, or psychiatric nurse who holds a master's or a doctorate degree.

According to researchers Ronald W. Manderscheid and his colleagues (Chapter 14, "Highlights of Organized Mental Health Services in 1998 and Major National and State Trends," *Mental Health United States, 2000,* U.S. Department of Health and Human Services, Substance Abuse and Mental Health Services Administration, The Center for Mental Health Services, Rockville, MD, 2001), the total number of MHOs in the United States increased

FIGURE 8.1

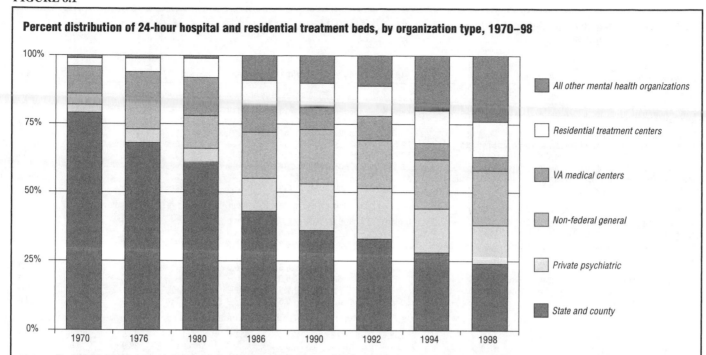

Percent distribution of 24-hour hospital and residential treatment beds, by organization type, 1970–98

Legend:
- All other mental health organizations
- Residential treatment centers
- VA medical centers
- Non-federal general
- Private psychiatric
- State and county

SOURCE: Ronald W. Manderscheid, Joanne E. Atay, Maria del R. Hernandez-Cartagena, Pamela Y. Edmond, Alisa Male, Albert C.E. Parker, and Hongwei Zhang, "Figure 1. Percent distribution of 24-hour hospital and residential treatment beds, by organization type, 1970–98," in chap. 14, *Mental Health, United States, 2000,* edited by Ronald W. Manderscheid and Marilyn J. Henderson, U.S. Department of Health and Human Services, Substance Abuse and Mental Health Services Administration, Center for Mental Health Services, Rockville, MD, 2001

from 3,005 to 5,722 from 1970 to 1998. (See Table 8.10.) Nearly all of this increase occurred as a result of gains in the number of private psychiatric hospitals, separate psychiatric services of nonfederal general hospitals, RTCs, and "all other organizations," since the number of state and county mental hospitals and freestanding outpatient clinics (included in the designation "all other mental health organizations") decreased, while the number of VA medical centers with psychiatric services remained relatively unchanged.

Along with the overall increase in MHOs, the number of organizations providing services in multiple treatment settings increased. For example, from 1970 to 1994, the number providing 24-hour service more than doubled, then declined slightly from 1994 to 1998, to 3,729. The number of MHOs offering less-than-24-hour care rose steadily from 1970 to 1998, from 2,156 to 4,387. (See Table 8.10.)

As the number of MHOs providing hospital inpatient and residential treatment more than doubled over the 28-year period, the number of available psychiatric beds was reduced by half, from 524,878 in 1970 to 261,903 in 1998. (See Table 8.11.) Most of the decrease was attributable to the sharp reduction of state mental hospital beds, which represented nearly 80 percent of all psychiatric beds in 1970, compared to just 24 percent in 1998. Figure 8.1 shows that private psychiatric hospitals and nonfederal general hospital psychiatric inpatient services increased considerably between 1970 and 1990.

There was an overall increase in the availability of 24-hour hospital and residential treatment from 1970 to 1998. The decline of state mental hospitals from 1970 to 1998, along with increases in 24-hour services at nonfederal general hospitals and private psychiatric hospitals after 1979, favored a shift of patients into nonfederal and private hospitals. In 1998 nonfederal general hospital inpatient psychiatric services accounted for about half, and private psychiatric hospitals for about 21 percent, of all inpatient services, while the proportion of state mental hospital inpatient services plummeted. RTCs made steady gains from 1970 to 1990, dipped in 1992, and then rebounded to surpass the 1990 level in 1994–98.

From 1969 to 1998 the number of less-than-24-hour service additions to MHOs skyrocketed from 1,202,098 to 3,967,019. (See Table 8.12.) Much of this increase occurred during the 1970s, when the number and rate of outpatient services spiked in the freestanding psychiatric outpatient clinics and in the "all other organizations" category (which contained federally funded CMHCs and other multiservice MHOs). Less-than-24-hour services declined slightly during the early 1990s, largely because there were fewer outpatient additions to nonfederal hospital psychiatric services. However, additions to nonfederal hospitals bounced back and increased from 1994 to 1998.

Not unexpectedly, the number of 24-hour hospital and residential patients showed an overall decrease from 1969 to 1998. (See Table 8.13.) In 1969 there were 471,451

TABLE 8.11

Number, percent distribution, and rate[1] of 24-hour hospital and residential treatment beds, by type of mental health organization, selected years, 1970–98[2]

Type of organization	1970	1976	1980	1986	1990	1992	1994[5]	1998
	Number of 24-hour hospital and residential treatment beds							
All organizations	524,878	338,963	274,713	267,613	272,253	270,867	290,604	261,903
State and county mental hospitals	413,066	222,202	156,482	119,033	98,789	93,058	81,911	63,525
Private psychiatric hospitals	14,295	16,091	17,157	30,201	44,871	43,684	42,399	33,635
Non-federal general hospitals with separate psychiatric services	22,394	28,706	29,384	45,808	53,479	52,059	52,984	54,266
VA medical centers[3]	50,688	35,913	33,796	26,874	21,712	22,466	21,146	13,301
Federally funded community mental health centers	8,108	17,029	16,264	–	–	–	–	–
Residential treatment centers for emotionally disturbed children	15,129	18,029	20,197	24,547	29,756	30,089	32,110	33,483
All other organizations[4]	1,198	993	1,433	21,150	23,646	29,511	60,054	63,693
	Percent distribution of 24-hour hospital and residential treatment beds							
All organizations	100.0	100.0	100.0	100.0	100.0	100.0	100.0	100.0
State and county mental hospitals	78.7	65.6	57.0	44.5	36.3	34.4	28.2	24.3
Private psychiatric hospitals	2.7	4.7	6.2	11.3	16.5	16.1	14.6	12.8
Non-federal general hospitals with separate psychiatric services	4.3	8.5	10.7	17.1	19.6	19.2	18.2	20.7
VA medical centers[3]	9.7	10.6	12.3	10.0	8.0	8.3	7.3	5.1
Federally funded community mental health centers	1.5	5.0	5.9	–	–	–	–	–
Residential treatment centers for emotionally disturbed children	2.9	5.3	7.4	9.2	10.9	11.1	11.0	12.8
All other organizations[4]	0.2	0.3	0.5	7.9	8.7	10.9	20.7	24.3
	24-hour hospital and residential treatment beds per 100,000 civilian population							
All organizations	263.6	160.3	124.3	111.7	111.6	107.5	112.1	97.4
State and county mental hospitals	207.4	105.1	70.2	49.7	40.5	36.9	31.6	23.6
Private psychiatric hospitals	7.2	7.6	7.7	12.6	18.4	17.3	16.4	12.5
Non-federal general hospitals with separate psychiatric services	11.2	13.6	13.7	19.1	21.9	20.7	20.4	20.2
VA medical centers[3]	25.5	17.0	15.7	11.2	8.9	8.9	8.2	4.9
Federally funded community mental health centers	4.1	8.0	7.3	–	–	–	–	–
Residential treatment centers for emotionally disturbed children	7.6	8.5	9.1	10.3	12.2	11.9	12.4	12.4
All other organizations[4]	0.6	0.5	0.6	8.8	9.7	11.7	23.2	23.7

[1] The population used in the calculation of these rates is the July 1 civilian population of the United States for the respective years.
[2] Some organizations were reclassified as a result of changes in reporting procedures and definitions. For 1979–80, comparable data were not available for certain organization types and data for either an earlier or a later period were substituted. These factors influence the comparability of 1980, 1986, 1990, 1992, and 1994 data with those of earlier years.
[3] Includes Department of Veterans Affairs (formerly Veterans Administration) (VA) neuropsychiatric hospitals, VA general hospital psychiatric services, and VA psychiatric outpatient clinics.
[4] Includes freestanding psychiatric outpatient clinics, partial care organizations, and multiservice mental health organizations. Multiservice mental health organizations were redefined in 1984.
[5] The data for 1994 include residential supportive additions that were excluded in previous years. This is not new material except for the category "all other organizations."

SOURCE: Ronald W. Manderscheid, Joanne E. Atay, Maria del R. Hernandez-Cartagena, Pamela Y. Edmond, Alisa Male, Albert C.E. Parker, and Hongwei Zhang, "Table 2. Number, percent distribution, and rate[1] of 24-hour hospital and residential treatment beds, by type of mental health organization: United States, selected years, 1970–98[2]," in chap. 14, *Mental Health, United States, 2000,* U.S. Department of Health and Human Services, Substance Abuse and Mental Health Services Administration, Washington, DC, 2001

patients, but by 1998 there were just 215,798. The rate per 100,000 civilian population declined from 236.8 in 1969 to 80.2 in 1998. From 1986 to 1998 state and county mental hospitals saw their beds reduced by more than one-half, from 49.7 to 23.7 beds per 100,000 persons. (See Table 5.2 in Chapter 5.) The decrease was attributed to dramatic reductions in the numbers of residents in state mental hospitals and in VA medical center psychiatric inpatient services. This was not necessarily the result of more or better outpatient treatment for the mentally ill but rather a consequence of reduced funding for those institutions and individuals. Unfortunately, many patients who were once housed in mental institutions were released to fend for themselves on the streets, shelters, or in prisons. The total resident patient count continued to decline as inpatient numbers in state mental hospitals, VA medical centers, and private psychiatric hospitals were not offset by increases in nonfederal general hospital psychiatric services, RTCs, and other MHOs.

Where Are the Mentally Ill Today?

Providers of mental health care distinguish between people who are severely mentally ill (defined by diagnosis), those who are mentally disabled (defined by level of disability), and those who are chronic mental patients (defined by duration of hospitalization). These three dimensions—diagnosis, disability, and duration—are the models used to describe the mentally ill population in the United States.

The chronically mentally ill reside either in mental hospitals or in community settings, such as with families, in boarding homes and shelters, in single-room-occupancy hotels (usually cheap hotels or boardinghouses), in jail, or even on the streets as part of the homeless population. The institutionalized mentally ill are those persons with psychiatric diagnoses who have lived in mental hospitals for more than one year, or those with diagnosed mental disorders who are living in nursing homes.

TABLE 8.12

Number, percent distribution, and rate[1] of additions to less than 24-hour care services, by type of mental health organization, selected years, 1969–98[2]

Type of organization	1969	1975	1979	1986	1990	1992	1994	1998
	Number of less than 24-hour care additions							
All organizations	1,202,098	2,453,105	2,807,058	2,955,337	3,298,473	3,164,437	3,516,403	3,987,019
State and county mental hospitals	174,737	160,283	91,727	67,986	48,211	49,609	41,759	41,692
Private psychiatric hospitals	28,412	36,044	33,471	132,175	163,164	206,169	213,566	226,325
Non-federal general hospitals with separate psychiatric services	188,652	268,881	237,008	532,960	658,567	479,596	497,523	614,866
VA medical centers[3]	20,290	101,723	127,221	132,589	183,621	158,982	132,417	143,338
Federally funded community mental health centers	189,670	878,730	1,320,637	–	–	–	–	–
Residential treatment centers for emotionally disturbed children	8,591	23,215	22,172	67,344	99,503	121,131	167,344	153,051
All other mental health organizations[4]	591,746	984,229	974,822	2,022,283	2,145,407	2,148,950	2,463,794	2,787,747
	Percent distribution of less than 24-hour care additions							
All organizations	100.0	100.0	100.0	100.0	100.0	100.0	100.0	100.0
State and county mental hospitals	14.5	6.5	3.3	2.3	1.5	1.6	1.2	1.1
Private psychiatric hospitals	2.4	1.5	1.2	4.5	4.9	6.5	6.1	5.7
Non-federal general hospitals with separate psychiatric services	15.7	11.0	8.4	18.0	20.0	15.2	14.1	15.5
VA medical centers[3]	1.7	4.1	4.5	4.5	5.6	5.0	3.8	3.6
Federally funded community mental health centers	15.8	35.8	47.0	–	–	–	–	–
Residential treatment centers for emotionally disturbed children	0.7	0.9	0.8	2.3	3.0	3.8	4.8	3.9
All other mental health organizations[4]	49.2	40.1	34.7	68.4	65.0	67.9	70.1	70.3
	Less than 24-hour care additions per 100,000 civilian population							
All organizations	603.8	1,142.7	1,236.6	1,233.4	1,352.4	1,255.2	1,356.8	1,474.6
State and county mental hospitals	87.8	74.7	40.4	28.4	19.8	19.7	16.1	15.5
Private psychiatric hospitals	14.3	16.8	14.7	55.2	66.9	81.8	82.4	84.1
Non-federal general hospitals with separate psychiatric services	94.8	125.3	104.4	222.4	270.0	190.2	192.0	228.6
VA medical centers[3]	10.2	47.4	56.0	55.3	75.3	63.1	51.1	53.3
Federally funded community mental health centers	95.3	409.3	581.8	–	–	–	–	–
Residential treatment centers for emotionally disturbed children	4.3	10.8	9.8	28.1	40.8	48.0	64.6	56.9
All other mental health organizations[4]	297.2	458.5	429.4	844.0	879.6	852.4	950.7	1,036.2

[1] The population used in the calculation of these rates is the July 1 civilian population of the United States for the respective years. Data for 1969–92 are the summation of partial care and outpatient care additions. The 1994 survey format was changed and partial care is now included with outpatient, and together are called "less than 24-hour care."
[2] Some organizations were reclassified as a result of changes in reporting procedures and definitions. For 1979–80, comparable data were not available for certain organization types and data for either an earlier or a later period were substituted. These factors influence the comparability of 1980, 1986, 1990, 1992, and 1994 data with those of earlier years.
[3] Includes Department of Veterans Affairs (formerly Veterans Administration) (VA) neuropsychiatric hospitals, VA general hospital psychiatric services, and VA psychiatric outpatient clinics.
[4] Includes freestanding psychiatric outpatient clinics, partial care organizations, and multiservice mental health organizations. Multiservice mental health organizations were redefined in 1984.

SOURCE: Ronald W. Manderscheid, Joanne E. Atay, Maria del R. Hernandez-Cartagena, Pamela Y. Edmond, Alisa Male, Albert C.E. Parker, and Hongwei Zhang, "Table 4. Number, percent distribution, and rate[1] of less than 24-hour care additions, by type of mental health organization: United States, selected years, 1969–98[2]," in chap. 14, *Mental Health, United States, 2000*, edited by Ronald W. Manderscheid and Marilyn J. Henderson, U.S. Department of Health and Human Services, Substance Abuse and Mental Health Services Administration, Center for Mental Health Services, Rockville, MD, 2001

Data from the 2000 National Hospital Discharge Survey (NHDS), which provides annual estimates of hospital use, revealed that six diagnostic categories each accounted for more than a million hospital discharges, and one of the six was psychoses, which was responsible for 1.4 million discharges. (See Figure 8.2.) The average length of stay for psychoses—8.1 days—was longer than any of the other selected diagnostic categories, even longer than for malignant neoplasms (cancer). (See Figure 8.3.)

Mental Health Care Is Provided in Physicians' Offices

The 2000 National Ambulatory Medical Care Survey (NAMCS), the ambulatory care component of the National Health Care Survey that measures utilization across various types of providers, found that 28,854 visits were made to psychiatrists in 2000. This translates into 10.5 visits per 100 persons per year and accounted for 3.5 percent of all physician office visits. (See Table 8.14.) About 29.6 percent of patients were referred to psychiatry by another physician or health plan. (See Table 8.15.) Presumably the latter group includes persons referred by schools, health and social service agencies, the juvenile and criminal justice systems, and other community agencies as well as persons who self-referred to psychiatrists.

The NAMCS also collected data about patients' reasons for seeking office-based care. Table 8.16 shows that nearly 30,000 visits, which represents 3.6 percent of ambulatory visits, were made for "symptoms referable to psychological/mental disorders."

Of the 823,542 physician office visits in 2000, physicians named mental disorders as their primary diagnosis for 5.3 percent, or 43,893 of patient office visits. (See Table 8.17.) During 2000, 18,403 physician office visits included orders for, or provision of, counseling about stress management and 18,221 visits involved mental health counseling. (See Table 8.18.) Nearly 20,000 visits resulted in a prescription for psycho-pharmacotherapy,

TABLE 8.13

Number, percent distribution, and rate[1] of patients in 24-hour hospital and residential treatment, by type of mental health organization, selected years, 1969–98[2]

Type of organization	1969	1975	1979	1986	1990	1992	1994	1998
	Number of hospital and residential treatment residents at end of year							
All organizations	471,451	284,158	230,186	237,845	226,953	214,714	236,110	215,798
State and county mental hospitals	369,969	193,436	140,355	111,135	90,572	83,180	72,096	56,955
Private psychiatric hospitals	10,963	11,576	12,921	24,591	32,268	24,053	26,519	21,478
Non-federal general hospitals with psychiatric services	17,808	18,851	18,753	34,474	38,327	35,611	35,841	37,002
VA medical centers[3]	51,696	31,850	28,693	24,322	17,233	18,531	18,019	10,882
Federally funded community mental health centers	5,270	10,818	10,112	–	–	–	–	–
Residential treatment centers for emotionally disturbed children	13,489	16,307	18,276	23,171	27,785	27,751	29,493	30,370
All other organizations[4]	2,256	1,320	1,076	20,152	20,768	25,588	54,142	59,111
	Percent distributions of hospital and residential treatment residents							
All organizations	100.0	100.0	100.0	100.0	100.0	100.0	100.0	100.0
State and county mental hospitals	78.5	68.1	61.0	46.7	39.9	38.7	30.5	26.4
Private psychiatric hospitals	2.3	4.1	5.6	10.3	14.2	11.2	11.2	10.0
Non-federal general hospitals with psychiatric services	3.8	6.6	8.1	14.5	16.9	16.6	15.2	17.1
VA medical centers[3]	11.0	11.2	12.5	10.2	7.6	8.6	7.6	5.0
Federally funded community mental health centers	1.1	3.8	4.4	–	–	–	–	–
Residential treatment centers for emotionally disturbed children	2.9	5.7	7.9	9.7	12.2	12.9	12.5	14.1
All other organizations[4]	0.5	0.5	0.5	8.5	9.2	11.9	22.9	27.4
	Hospital and residential treatment residents per 100,000 civilian population							
All organizations	236.8	134.4	103.9	99.6	93.0	85.2	91.1	80.2
State and county mental hospitals	185.8	91.5	63.0	46.5	37.1	33.0	27.8	21.2
Private psychiatric hospitals	5.5	5.5	5.8	10.3	13.2	9.5	10.2	8.0
Non-federal general hospitals with psychiatric services	8.9	8.9	8.6	14.4	15.7	14.1	13.8	13.8
VA medical centers[3]	26.0	15.1	13.3	10.2	7.1	7.4	7.0	4.0
Federally funded community mental health centers	2.7	5.1	4.5	–	–	–	–	–
Residential treatment centers for emotionally disturbed children	6.8	7.7	8.2	9.7	11.4	11.0	11.4	11.3
All other organizations[4]	1.1	0.6	0.5	8.5	8.5	10.2	20.9	22.0

[1] The population used in the calculation of these rates is the July 1 civilian popluation of the United States for the respective years.

[2] Some organizations were reclassified as a result of changes in reporting procedures and definitions. For 1979–80, comparable data were not available for certain organization types and data for either an earlier or a later period were substituted. These factors influence the comparability of 1980, 1986, 1990, 1992, and 1994 data with those of earlier years.

[3] Includes Department of Veterans Affairs (formerly Veterans Administration) (VA) neuropsychiatric hospitals, VA general hospital psychiatric services, and VA psychiatric outpatient clinics.

[4] Includes freestanding psychiatric outpatient clinics, partial care organizations, and multiservice mental health organizations. Multiservice mental health organizations were redefined in 1984.

[5] The number of residents increased because all residential treatment residents were combined with 24-hour care hospital residents; previously, residential supportive patients were excluded.

SOURCE: Ronald W. Manderscheid, Joanne E. Atay, Maria del R. Hernandez-Cartagena, Pamela Y. Edmond, Alisa Male, Albert C.E. Parker, and Hongwei Zhang, "Table 5. Number, percent distribution, and rate[1] of 24-hour hospital and residential treatment residents, by type of mental health organization: United States, selected years, 1969–98[2]," in chap. 14, *Mental Health, United States, 2000*, edited by Ronald W. Manderscheid and Marilyn J. Henderson, U.S. Department of Health and Human Services, Substance Abuse and Mental Health Services Administration, Center for Mental Health Services, Rockville, MD, 2001

and 18,669 included referral to or provision of psychotherapy services. More women were offered stress management services than men (2.5 percent compared with 1.8 percent), but slightly fewer women were offered psycho-pharmacotherapy and psychotherapy services.

The NAMCS terms visits with one or more drug mentions "drug visits." During visits with psychiatrists, drugs were mentioned in more than three-quarters of office visits (78.1 percent) deeming them, in NAMCS terminology, "drug visits." Psychiatrists reported the second highest percent of drug visits, vying with specialists in internal medicine, who reported the highest percent (78.8 percent) of drug visits. (See Table 8.19.) Zoloft, a selective serotonin reuptake inhibitor (SSRI) used to treat depression and other mental disorders, was among the 20 drugs most frequently prescribed during office visits. (See Table 8.20.)

Psychiatrists spent more time in office visits with their patients than any other physician specialists. Visits with psychiatrists had a mean length of 36 minutes, nearly twice the mean time (18.9 minutes) spent with physicians during all visits. This finding is not surprising, since psychiatrists often provide time-consuming talk-therapy along with information about medication. (See Table 8.21.)

Mental Health Care Is Provided in Other Ambulatory Care Settings

In addition to mental health units or beds in acute care medical/surgical hospitals and physicians' offices, mental health care and treatment is offered in offices of other mental health clinicians such as psychologists, clinical social workers, and marriage and family

FIGURE 8.2

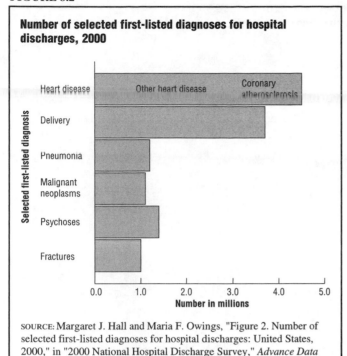

Number of selected first-listed diagnoses for hospital discharges, 2000

SOURCE: Margaret J. Hall and Maria F. Owings, "Figure 2. Number of selected first-listed diagnoses for hospital discharges: United States, 2000," in "2000 National Hospital Discharge Survey," *Advance Data From Vital and Health Statistics,* no. 329, June 19, 2002

FIGURE 8.3

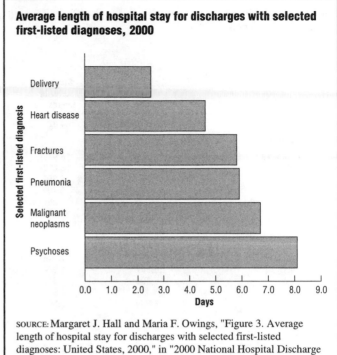

Average length of hospital stay for discharges with selected first-listed diagnoses, 2000

SOURCE: Margaret J. Hall and Maria F. Owings, "Figure 3. Average length of hospital stay for discharges with selected first-listed diagnoses: United States, 2000," in "2000 National Hospital Discharge Survey," *Advance Data From Vital and Health Statistics,* no. 329, June 19, 2002

therapists as well as other settings. Private psychiatric hospitals provide mental health evaluation and treatment in day treatment programs as well as inpatient programs. Like acute-care hospitals, these facilities are accredited by the Joint Commission on Accreditation of Health Care Organizations (JCAHCO) and may offer outpatient services via referral to a local network of qualified mental health providers.

Community mental health centers are public organizations that receive state and local funding to provide mental health services to individuals in designated geographic areas. They have sliding-scale fees and accept Medicaid, Medicare, private health insurance, and private fee-for-service payment. Mental health care also is available from not-for-profit mental health or counseling services offered by health and social service agencies such as Catholic Social Services, family and children's service agencies, Jewish Family Services, and Lutheran Social Services that are staffed by qualified mental health professionals to provide counseling services.

Because community mental health centers and agencies that provide mental health prevention, diagnosis, and screening are, for the purposes of national data collection, considered along with other related service providers as "all other organizations," it is difficult to determine whether the number of each type of facility or organization has increased or decreased during the past decade. Some states continue to report the mental health service providers they fund by type, but others classify MHOs based on services provided.

NATIONAL GOALS FOR MENTAL HEALTH SERVICE DELIVERY

Healthy People 2010 (U.S. Department of Health and Human Services, Washington, D.C., U.S. Government Printing Office, 2000) is a set of health objectives for the nation to achieve during the first decade of the new century. Practitioners, states, communities, professional organizations, and others use these objectives to assist them to develop programs to improve health. Twenty-one of the 467 health objectives enumerated in *Healthy People 2010* relate to mental health and mental disorders. While nearly all of the objectives intend to reduce the incidence and prevalence of mental illness in the United States and to improve access to care and treatment, several specifically address issues related to mental health professionals and treatment facilities.

For example, objective 7-11 is to "Increase the proportion of local health departments that have established culturally appropriate and linguistically competent community health promotion and disease prevention programs," and 18-13 is to "Increase the number of States, Territories, and the District of Columbia with an operational mental health plan that addresses cultural competence." Although there is an overall objective to increase the proportion of persons with mental disorders who receive treatment, objective 18-6 aims to "Increase the number of persons seen in primary health care who receive mental health screening and assessment," and 18-8 is to "Increase the proportion of juvenile justice facilities that screen new admissions for mental health

TABLE 8.14

Number, percent distribution, and annual rate of office visits with corresponding standard errors, by selected physician practice characteristics, 2000

Physician practice characteristic	Number of visits in thousands	Standard error in thousands	Percent distribution	Standard error of percent	Number of visits per 100 persons per year	Standard error of rate
All visits	823,542	34,820	100.0	—	300.4	12.7
Physician specialty						
General and family practice	198,578	18,965	24.1	1.8	72.4	6.9
Internal medicine	125,556	13,823	15.2	1.5	45.8	5.0
Pediatrics	103,734	9,859	12.6	1.2	37.8	3.6
Obstetrics and gynecology	65,135	5,706	7.9	0.7	23.8[1]	2.1
Orthopedic surgery	46,155	4,251	5.6	0.5	16.8	1.6
Ophthalmology	42,735	4,919	5.2	0.6	15.6	1.8
Dermatology	34,509	3,382	4.2	0.4	12.6	1.2
Psychiatry	28,864	3,824	3.5	0.4	10.5	1.4
Cardiovascular diseases	21,598	2,255	2.6	0.3	7.9	0.8
Urology	18,703	2,316	2.3	0.3	6.8	0.8
General surgery	16,897	1,904	2.1	0.2	6.2	0.7
Otolaryngology	16,399	1,698	2.0	0.2	6.0	0.6
Neurology	8,411	818	1.0	0.1	3.1	0.3
All other specialties	96,269	10,391	11.7	1.1	35.1	3.8
Professional identity						
Doctor of medicine	756,813	32,812	91.9	0.9	276.1	12.0
Doctor of osteopathy	66,729	8,224	8.1	0.9	24.3	3.0
Geographic region						
Northeast	183,029	11,558	22.2	1.4	350.6	22.1
Midwest	206,727	20,776	25.1	2.1	305.9	30.7
South	251,300	20,799	30.5	2.0	259.3	21.5
West	182,485	14,692	22.2	1.6	318.4	25.6
Metropolitan status						
MSA[2]	645,299	27,968	78.4	2.4	294.6	12.8
Non-MSA[2]	178,243	23,612	21.6	2.4	324.0	42.9

[1]The visit rate is 46.4 per 100 females.
[2]MSA is metropolitan statistical area.
Note: — Category not applicable. Numbers may not add to totals because of rounding.

SOURCE: Donald K. Cherry and David A. Woodwell, "Table 1. Number, percent distribution, and annual rate of office visits with corresponding standard errors, by selected physician practice characteristics: United States, 2000," in "National Ambulatory Medical Care Survey: 2000 Summary," *Advance Data from Vital and Health Statistics*, no. 328, June 5, 2002

problems." Objective 18-11 is to "Increase the proportion of local governments with community-based jail diversion programs for adults with serious mental illness."

The *Healthy People 2010* objectives also call for systemwide improvements in mental health service delivery. Number 18-14 is to "Increase the number of States, Territories, and the District of Columbia with an operational mental health plan that addresses mental health crisis interventions, ongoing screening, and treatment services for elderly persons," and 18-12 calls upon the nation to "Increase the number of States and the District of Columbia that track consumers' satisfaction with the mental health services they receive."

TABLE 8.15

Percent distribution of office visits with corresponding standard errors by physician specialty, according to referral status and prior-visit status, 2000

Physician specialty	Total	Referred by another physician or health plan for this visit		Not referred by another physician or health plan for this visit		Unknown/blank referral for for this visit	
		New patient	Old patient	New patient	Old patient	New patient	Old patient
		Percent distribution[1]					
All visits	100.0	5.4	11.4	5.6	72.1	1.0	4.4
General and family practice	100.0	*	*2.1	5.8	87.0	*1.5	2.8
Internal medicine	100.0	*	3.2	*5.4	86.5	*	*3.6
Pediatrics	100.0	*	*2.8	4.7	87.7	*	*3.6
Obstetrics and gynecology	100.0	4.2	8.2	7.3	73.4	*	5.6
Orthopedic surgery	100.0	15.0	30.8	5.4	39.4	*1.9	*7.5
Ophthalmology	100.0	5.9	17.6	7.4	62.8	*	*5.5
Dermatology	100.0	8.5	16.6	9.8	57.9	*	5.9
Psychiatry	100.0	4.4	25.2	4.2	59.4	*	*4.5
Cardiovascular diseases	100.0	9.3	24.0	3.2	60.8	*	*2.2
Urology	100.0	14.7	33.3	2.8	45.2	*	3.4
General surgery	100.0	18.3	31.7	3.1	45.1	*	*
Otolaryngology	100.0	17.8	23.0	10.9	45.3	*	*2.5
Neurology	100.0	25.6	30.9	4.1	36.6	*	*2.2
All other specialties	100.0	12.5	20.8	4.3	53.5	*	*8.3
		Standard error of percent					
All visits	—	0.4	0.8	0.4	1.2	0.1	0.7
General and family practice	—	—	0.6	0.6	1.5	0.5	0.8
Internal medicine	—	—	0.8	1.8	2.5	—	1.8
Pediatrics	—	—	1.3	0.6	2.3	—	1.6
Obstetrics and gynecology	—	0.9	1.6	1.0	2.9	—	1.7
Orthopedic surgery	—	1.5	3.0	0.8	3.5	0.7	2.8
Ophthalmology	—	0.8	4.1	1.3	3.8	—	3.0
Dermatology	—	1.4	3.5	1.2	4.5	—	1.6
Psychiatry	—	0.9	4.2	0.9	4.8	—	1.9
Cardiovascular diseases	—	1.3	4.1	0.6	4.7	—	1.1
Urology	—	1.1	5.7	0.6	5.3	—	1.0
General surgery	—	2.1	4.0	0.7	4.5	—	—
Otolaryngology	—	1.9	2.4	1.4	3.5	—	1.1
Neurology	—	2.3	3.7	1.1	3.8	—	0.8
All other specialties	—	2.0	3.5	0.9	4.8	—	4.1

[1]Nonresponses (blanks) for prior-visit status have been removed before analysis, accounting for 16.5 million visits or 2.0 percent, overall.
Note: — Category not applicable. Numbers may not add to totals because of rounding.
*Figure does not meet standard of reliability or precision.

SOURCE: Donald K. Cherry and David A. Woodwell, "Table 5. Percent distribution of office visits with corresponding standard errors by physician specialty, according to referral status and prior-visit status: United States, 2000," in "National Ambulatory Medical Care Survey: 2000 Summary," *Advance Data From Vital and Health Statistics*, no. 328, June 5, 2002

TABLE 8.16

Number and percent distribution of office visits with corresponding standard errors, by patient's principal reason for visit, 2000

Principal reason for visit	Number of visits in thousands	Standard error in thousands	Percent distribution	Standard error of percent
All visits	823,542	34,820	100.0	—
Symptom module	427,994	19,916	52.0	1.0
General symptoms	48,666	3,247	5.9	0.3
Symptoms referable to psychological/mental disorders	29,939	2,936	3.6	0.3
Symptoms referable to the nervous system (excluding sense organs)	24,156	1,695	2.9	0.2
Symptoms referable to the cardiovascular/lymphatic system	4,118	617	0.5	0.1
Symptoms referable to the eyes and ears	44,210	2,949	5.4	0.3
Symptoms referable to the respiratory system	79,422	5,553	9.6	0.5
Symptoms referable to the digestive system	37,770	3,876	4.6	0.4
Symptoms referable to the genitourinary system	32,279	2,095	3.9	0.2
Symptoms referable to the skin, hair, and nails	47,877	3,483	5.8	0.3
Symptoms referable to the musculoskeletal system	79,557	5,436	9.7	0.5
Disease module	82,952	6,316	10.1	0.7
Diagnostic, screening, and preventive module	149,854	9,357	18.2	0.8
Treatment module	96,958	6,656	11.8	0.7
Injuries and adverse effects module	20,734	1,785	2.5	0.2
Test results module	17,394	1,750	2.1	0.2
Administrative module	8,886	1,881	1.1	0.2
Other*	18,771	2,998	2.3	0.4

*Includes problems and complaints not elsewhere classified, entries of "none," blanks, and illegible entries.
Note: — Category not applicable. Numbers may not add to totals because of rounding.

SOURCE: Donald K. Cherry and David A. Woodwell, "Table 8. Number and percent distribution of office visits with corresponding standard errors, by patient's principal reason for visit: United States, 2000," in "National Ambulatory Medical Care Survey: 2000 Summary," *Advance Data From Vital and Health Statistics*, no. 328, June 5, 2002

TABLE 8.17

Number and percent distribution of office visits with corresponding standard errors, by physician's diagnosis, 2000

Major disease category	Number of visits in thousands	Standard error in thousands	Percent distribution	Standard error of percent
All visits	823,542	34,820	100.0	–
Infectious and parasitic diseases	25,298	2,146	3.1	0.2
Neoplasms	31,189	4,454	3.8	0.5
Endocrine, nutritional and metabolic diseases, and immunity disorders	42,183	4,351	5.1	0.5
Mental disorders	43,893	4,214	5.3	0.5
Diseases of the nervous system and sense organs	69,297	4,283	8.4	0.5
Diseases of the circulatory system	65,843	5,506	8.0	0.6
Diseases of the respiratory system	90,803	6,993	11.0	0.6
Diseases of the digestive system	29,401	3,258	3.6	0.4
Diseases of the genitourinary system	42,674	3,360	5.2	0.4
Diseases of the skin and subcutaneous tissue	43,650	3,316	5.3	0.3
Diseases of the musculoskeletal system and connective tissue	59,270	5,451	7.2	0.6
Symptoms, signs, and ill-defined conditions	50,940	3,651	6.2	0.3
Injury and poisoning	45,295	4,290	5.5	0.4
Supplementary classification	149,189	8,549	18.1	0.8
All other diagnoses[1]	21,424	2,166	2.6	0.3
Unknown[2]	13,193	3,689	1.6	0.4

[1]Includes diseases of the blood and blood-forming organs; complications of pregnancy, childbirth, and the puerperium; congenital anomalies; and certain conditions originating in the perinatal period.
[2]Includes blank diagnoses, uncodable diagnoses, and illegible diagnoses.
Note: – Category not applicable. Numbers may not add to totals because of rounding.

SOURCE: Donald K. Cherry and David A. Woodwell, "Table 11. Number and percent distribution of office visits with corresponding standard errors, by physician's primary diagnosis: United States, 2000," in "National Ambulatory Medical Care Survey: 2000 Summary," *Advance Data From Vital and Health Statistics*, no. 328, June 5, 2002

TABLE 8.18

Number and percent of office visits with corresponding standard errors, by therapeutic and preventive services ordered or provided and patient's sex, 2000

| Therapeutic and preventive services ordered or provided | Number of visits in thousands[1] | Standard error in thousands | Percent of visits | Standard error of percent | Patient's sex | | | |
| | | | | | Female[2] | | Male[3] | |
					Percent of visits	Standard error of percent	Percent of visits	Standard error of percent
All visits	823,542	34,820	–	–	–	–	–	–
None	515,550	23,198	62.6	1.2	61.6	1.3	64.0	1.5
Counseling/education								
Diet	126,988	9,441	15.4	0.9	15.4	0.9	15.5	1.0
Exercise	80,839	7,250	9.8	0.7	9.8	0.7	9.8	0.9
Injury prevention	24,610	3,193	3.0	0.4	2.5	0.3	3.6	0.5
Growth/development	21,460	2,657	2.6	0.3	2.2	0.3	3.2	0.4
Stress management	18,403	2,768	2.2	0.3	2.5	0.4	1.8	0.3
Prenatal instructions	18,396	2,117	2.2	0.2	3.8	0.4	*	–
Mental health	18,221	3,109	2.2	0.4	2.2	0.4	2.2	0.4
Tobacco use/exposure	18,213	2,265	2.2	0.3	2.0	0.3	2.5	0.3
Breast self-examination	17,827	3,052	2.2	0.4	3.6	0.6	*	–
Skin cancer prevention	14,311	2,486	1.7	0.3	1.4	0.2	2.2	0.4
Family planning/contraception	9,564	1,155	1.2	0.1	1.9	0.2	*	–
HIV/STD transmission[4,5]	5,190	716	0.6	0.1	0.9	0.1	0.3	0.1
Other therapy								
Complementary and alternative medicine	31,589	3,481	3.8	0.4	3.8	0.4	3.9	0.4
Physiotherapy	22,273	2,221	2.7	0.2	2.5	0.3	2.9	0.3
Psycho-pharmacotherapy	19,947	2,828	2.4	0.3	2.3	0.3	2.6	0.4
Psychotherapy	18,669	2,992	2.3	0.4	2.2	0.4	2.4	0.4
Other	36,839	3,569	4.5	0.4	4.3	0.4	4.7	0.4
Blank	21,356	3,146	2.6	0.4	2.3	0.3	3.0	0.5

Note: – Category not applicable.
*Figure does not meet standard of reliability or precision.
[1]Total exceeds "All visits" because more than one service may be reported per visit.
[2]Based on 488,199,000 visits made by females.
[3]Based on 335,343,000 visits made by males.
[4]HIV is human immunodeficiency virus.
[5]STD is sexually transmitted disease.

SOURCE: Donald K. Cherry and David A. Woodwell, "Table 16. Number and percent of office visits with corresponding standard errors, by therapeutic and preventive services ordered or provided and patient's sex: United States, 2000," in "National Ambulatory Medical Care Survey: 2000 Summary," *Advance Data From Vital and Health Statistics*, no. 328, June 5, 2002

TABLE 8.19

Number and percent distribution of drug visits, drug mentions, and drug mention rates per 100 visits with corresponding standard errors, by physician specialty, 2000

Physician specialty	Drug visits				Drug mentions				Percent drug visits		Drug mention rates	
	Number in thousands[1]	Standard error in thousands	Percent distribution	Standard error of percent	Number in thousands	Standard error in thousands	Percent distribution	Standard error of percent	Percent drug visits[2]	Standard error of percent	Number of drug mentions per 100 visits	Standard error of rate
All specialties	544,772	26,997	100.0	...	1,263,503	74,006	100.0	...	66.1	1.2	153.4	5.0
General and family practice	151,458	15,367	27.8	2.1	358,118	40,492	28.3	2.4	76.3	2.3	180.3	8.9
Internal medicine	98,906	11,241	18.2	1.8	255,962	29,801	20.3	2.1	78.8	2.3	203.9	11.9
Pediatrics	69,666	7,097	12.8	1.3	124,186	13,914	9.8	1.1	67.2	1.7	119.7	5.3
Obstetrics and gynecology	29,928	3,527	5.5	0.6	42,345	5,084	3.4	0.4	45.9	3.1	65.0	4.9
Dermatology	23,055	2,469	4.2	0.4	43,138	5,121	3.4	0.4	66.8	2.9	125.0	7.1
Psychiatry	22,554	3,279	4.1	0.6	46,274	7,065	3.7	0.6	78.1	4.3	160.3	12.2
Ophthalmology	22,287	3,047	4.1	0.6	45,062	7,157	3.6	0.6	52.2	4.0	105.4	13.9
Cardiovascular diseases	16,700	2,047	3.1	0.4	63,513	8,967	5.0	0.7	77.3	3.7	294.1	21.5
Orthopedic surgery	15,184	1,574	2.8	0.3	23,206	2,895	1.8	0.2	32.9	2.2	50.3	4.8
Urology	9,378	1,417	1.7	0.3	14,249	2,139	1.1	0.2	50.1	2.9	76.2	6.8
Otolaryngology	8,372	986	1.5	0.2	15,272	2,012	1.2	0.2	51.1	2.8	93.1	7.6
Neurology	5,508	548	1.0	0.1	10,713	1,332	0.8	0.1	65.5	2.7	127.4	10.4
General surgery	5,054	883	0.9	0.2	10,936	2,344	0.9	0.2	29.9	4.0	64.7	12.0
All other specialties	66,723	9,240	12.2	1.4	210,529	35,150	16.7	2.2	69.3	5.2	218.7	24.6

[1]Visits at which one or more drugs were provided or prescribed by the physician.
[2]Percent of visits to specialist that included one or more drug mentions (number of drug visits divided by number of office visits multiplied by 100).
[3]Average number of drugs that were mentioned per 100 visits to each specialty (number of drug mentions divided by total number of visits multiplied by 100).
Note: ... Category not applicable. Numbers may not add to totals because of rounding.

SOURCE: Donald K. Cherry and David A. Woodwell, "Table 19. Number and percent distribution of drug visits, drug mentions, and drug mention rates per 100 visits with corresponding standard errors, by physician specialty: United States, 2000," in "National Ambulatory Medical Care Survey: 2000 Summary," *Advance Data From Vital and Health Statistics*, no. 328, June 5, 2002

TABLE 8.20

Number, percent distribution, and therapeutic classification for the 20 drugs most frequently prescribed at office visits, with corresponding standard errors, by entry name of drug, 2000

Entry name of drug[1]	Number of drug mentions in thousands	Standard error in thousands	Percent distribution	Standard error of percent	Therapeutic classification
All drug mentions	1,263,503	74,006	100.0	...	...
Claritin	17,145	2,398	1.4	0.1	Antihistamines
Lipitor	16,267	1,638	1.3	0.1	Hyperlipidemia
Synthroid	15,999	2,512	1.3	0.2	Thyroid agents
Premarin	14,775	1,648	1.2	0.1	Estrogens/progestins
Amoxicillin	13,068	1,723	1.0	0.1	Penicillins
Tylenol	12,789	1,514	1.0	0.1	Nonnarcotic analgesics
Lasix	12,577	1,400	1.0	0.1	Diuretics
Celebrex	12,161	1,353	1.0	0.1	NSAIDs[2]
Glucophage	11,468	1,361	0.9	0.1	Blood glucose regulators
Albuterol sulfate	10,862	1,228	0.9	0.1	Antiasthmatics/bronchodilators
Vioxx	10,801	1,212	0.9	0.1	NSAIDs[2]
Prilosec	10,751	1,205	0.9	0.1	Gastric antisecretory agents
Norvasc	10,635	1,305	0.8	0.1	Calcium channel blockers
Atenolol	10,372	1,332	0.8	0.1	Beta blockers
Influenza virus vaccine	10,197	1,409	0.8	0.1	Vaccines/antisera
Prednisone	10,049	1,482	0.8	0.1	Adrenal corticosteroids
Amoxil	9,719	1,505	0.8	0.1	Penicillins
Prevacid	9,268	1,222	0.7	0.1	Gastric antisecretory agents
Zocor	9,202	1,133	0.7	0.1	Hyperlipidemia
Zoloft	9,183	1,277	0.7	0.1	Antidepressants
All other	1,026,216	59,032	81.2	0.4	...

[1]The entry made by the physician on the prescription or other medical records. This may be a trade name, generic name, or desired therapeutic effect.
[2]NSAIDs are nonsteroidal anti-inflammatory drugs.
Note: ... Category not applicable. Numbers may not add to totals because of rounding.

SOURCE: Donald K. Cherry and David A. Woodwell, "Table 22. Number, percent distribution, and therapeutic classification for the 20 drugs most frequently prescribed at office visits with corresponding standard errors, by entry name of drug: United States, 2000," in "National Ambulatory Medical Care Survey: 2000 Summary," *Advance Data From Vital and Health Statistics*, no. 328, June 5, 2002

TABLE 8.21

Mean time spent with physician, with corresponding standard errors, by physician specialty, 2000

Physician specialty	Mean time spent with physician*	Standard error of mean	25th percentile	50th percentile	75th percentile
All visits	18.9	0.3	13.9	14.7	19.8
Psychiatry	36.0	1.7	19.2	29.9	49.0
Neurology	28.0	0.8	14.0	24.4	29.8
Cardiovascular diseases	21.5	0.7	13.1	18.3	28.3
Internal medicine	19.7	0.7	14.2	14.8	19.7
General surgery	19.0	0.9	13.4	14.8	24.5
Obstetrics and gynecology	18.2	0.6	10.0	14.8	20.0
Orthopedic surgery	17.1	0.7	9.9	14.6	19.1
General and family practice	17.0	0.5	10.0	14.6	18.8
Ophthalmology	16.9	1.0	9.8	14.5	19.2
Otolaryngology	16.8	0.7	9.8	14.5	19.3
Urology	16.2	0.9	9.6	14.5	19.4
Dermatology	15.8	0.7	9.6	14.4	19.3
Pediatrics	15.4	0.5	9.7	14.4	18.1
All other specialties	23.5	1.3	14.3	19.2	27.2

*Only visits where a physician was seen are included.

SOURCE: Donald K. Cherry and David A. Woodwell, "Table 26. Mean time spent with physician with corresponding standard errors, by physician specialty: United States, 2000," in "National Ambulatory Medical Care Survey: 2000 Summary," *Advance Data From Vital and Health Statistics*, no. 328, June 5, 2002

CHAPTER 9
PREVENTING MENTAL ILLNESS AND PROMOTING MENTAL HEALTH

Life is complex. Each one of us must make his own path through life. There are no self-help manuals, no formulas, no easy answers. The right road for one is the wrong road for another.... The journey of life is not paved in blacktop; it is not brightly lit, and it has no road signs. It is a rocky path through the wilderness.

—M. Scott Peck, *The Road Less Traveled, 25th Anniversary Edition : A New Psychology of Love, Traditional Values and Spiritual Growth,* Touchstone Books, Carmichael, California, 2003

The World Health Organization (WHO) definition of health affirms that mental and emotional well-being are vital for overall health. The 191 member states of the WHO accept the premise that "health is a state of complete physical, mental and social well-being and not merely the absence of disease or infirmity." The WHO describes mental health promotion as "an umbrella term that covers a variety of strategies, all aimed at having a positive effect on mental health. The encouragement of individual resources and skills and improvements in the socio-economic environment are among them." The WHO also asserts that effective mental health promotion requires "multi-sectoral action, involving a number of government sectors such as health, employment/industry, education, environment, transport, and social and community services as well as non-governmental or community-based organizations such as health support groups, churches, clubs and other bodies."

DEFINING MENTAL HEALTH PREVENTION AND PROMOTION

Mental Health: A Report of the Surgeon General (U.S. Department of Health and Human Services, Rockville, MD, 1999) emphasized the importance of primary prevention of mental illness. Primary prevention measures fall into two categories. The first includes actions to protect against disease and disability, such as measures to strengthen family and community support systems. The second includes actions to promote mental

health, such as teaching children communication and interpersonal skills, conflict management, and other relationship and life skills that foster emotional resiliency. Health promotion also includes education about other interdependent dimensions of health known as wellness. Examples of health promotion programs aimed at mental health and wellness include stress management, parenting education classes, and programs to assist older adults to make the transition from the workforce to retirement.

Secondary prevention programs are intended to identify and detect disease in its earliest stages, when it is most likely to be successfully treated. With early detection and diagnosis, it may be possible to cure the disease, slow its progression, prevent or minimize complications, and limit disability. An example of mental health secondary prevention is the effort to identify young children with behavior problems in order to intervene early and prevent development of, or progression to, more serious mental disorders.

Tertiary prevention programs aim to improve the quality of life for persons with various diseases by limiting complications and disabilities, reducing the severity and progression of the disease, and providing rehabilitation (therapy to restore function and self-sufficiency). Unlike primary and secondary prevention, tertiary prevention involves actual treatment for the disease. In the case of mental illness it is conducted primarily by medical and mental health care practitioners rather than public health agencies. An example of tertiary prevention is outreach programs that monitor persons with mental disorders who live in the community to ensure that they adhere to their prescribed medication regimens. Such tertiary prevention programs have demonstrated efficacy in reducing acute psychiatric hospital admissions and long-term institutionalization and enabling persons with mental disorders to live independently.

Mental Health: A Report of the Surgeon General advocated initiating primary prevention efforts even before children are born by teaching prospective parents crucial child-rearing skills. The report also suggested intensifying prevention programs targeting young children, since many adult mental disorders have related or latent problems in childhood. It also observed that human service and law enforcement agencies have established prevention of mental illness as a priority. Along with medical and mental health professionals, policy makers and frontline workers in education, social services, and juvenile justice believe in early intervention in children's lives. These professionals understand that mental health is closely linked with physical health, child care, and academic success, and that robust mental health protects against involvement in the juvenile justice system.

In 1998 the National Institute of Mental Health (NIMH) established an Advisory Council Workgroup on Mental Disorders Prevention Research (subsequently called the National Advisory Mental Health Council, NAMHC). The first set of recommendations issued by the group called upon NIMH to expand its definition of prevention research and to launch several new prevention initiatives aimed at improving the nation's mental health. Among the workgroup's subsequent recommendations, which proposed to increase the knowledge base for primary prevention, were the following:

- The NIMH definition of prevention research should be broader and should include studies of risk factors for mental illness, co-morbidity of mental illnesses, and relapse and disability caused by mental illness.

- Prevention research should include not only individuals but also larger social units such as families, communities, and other social systems. It should also include public policy and laws that may influence the effectiveness of prevention interventions.

- More research should be conducted to determine how best to decrease relapse and disability in persons with major mental disabilities such as schizophrenia.

- More studies should be done to determine and quantify the cost-effectiveness of prevention programs.

- The NIMH fund should fund more research that integrates social, behavioral, and genetic risk factors into prevention interventions.

- More research should be conducted on strategies, programs, and community interventions to prevent depression and aggression.

- The NIMH should fund more research on common sets of risk factors that occur early in life and lead to a variety of adolescent and adult disorders. Specifically, the workgroup advised research about these early risk factors and about interventions to modify these early risk factors in order to eliminate or at least reduce their impact and resultant negative outcomes.

- There should be increased emphasis on theory and research on the adoption, implementation, and dissemination of prevention research findings.

The 1999 and 2001 NAMHC reports were considered milestones in the evolution of prevention research at federal agencies. The reports detailed a number of critically needed new areas for research that are essential for expanding prevention efforts in the field of mental health. Although most mental health professionals concurred with the reports' findings and conclusions, some objected to their expanded definition of prevention research, which included treatment. Mark Greenberg and Roger Weissberg expressed this concern in their critique "Commentary on 'Priorities for Prevention Research at NIMH'" (*Prevention and Treatment,* vol. 4, June 2001). The Pennsylvania State University researchers argued that the NAMHC erred when it advised that treatment be considered a component of prevention and that the NAMHC neglected to emphasize the importance of wellness and competence as crucial prevention activities.

Finally, Rex Cowdry of the National Alliance for the Mentally Ill (NAMI), a well-known advocacy group, weighed in on prevention research priorities in "An Advocate for Individuals with Severe and Persistent Mental Illness Looks at Prevention Research" (*Prevention and Treatment,* vol. 4, June 2001), Cowdry asserted that many advocates for persons with mental illness view past prevention programs as vague, unscientific efforts at mental health promotion and considered them wasteful because they diverted scarce resources from those most in need. Advocates also contend that some prevention initiatives blame the victims—affected individuals or their families—for mental disorders. Agencies such as NAMI that provide advocacy services favor well-defined, cost-effective interventions focusing on the biological, experiential, and environmental risk factors for mental illnesses. They are optimistic that advances in the genetics and biology of mental illness will help researchers use appropriate tools to target prevention efforts to carefully defined at-risk populations. They would also like to see research aimed at preventing relapse, recurrence, and disability. Cowdry also called for attention to the ethics of preventive interventions and recommended programs to formulate and address the ethical issues posed by specific facets of prevention research.

EXEMPLARY MENTAL HEALTH PREVENTION AND PROMOTION PROGRAMS

Prevention will require both selected specific programs directed especially at known causes, and the general strengthening of our fundamental community, social welfare, and educational programs which can do much to eliminate or correct the harsh environmental conditions which are often associated with mental retardation and mental illness.

—President John F. Kennedy, 1963

Some investigators and mental health professionals advocate that the United States adopt an expansive concept of health promotion, like the definition presented by the WHO, that incorporates models for reducing risk and enhancing protective factors. They contend that the broad goal of health promotion involves enhancing competence across social, psychological, physical, and spiritual domains and that the most effective prevention programs acknowledge and address these human needs and values. Interventions such as family involvement programs, peer leadership training, school-based life skills and social-competency curricula, community-wide activities, health-enhancing mass media, and public-policy initiatives to enhance health would all be included in this encompassing definition of mental health promotion.

Mental Health: A Report of the Surgeon General (U.S. Department of Health and Human Services, Rockville, MD, 1999) described several "exemplary interventions" programs that simultaneously aim to promote and enhance mental health and prevent behavior problems and mental disorders. These programs targeted populations considered at risk—young children, adolescents, and their parents or caregivers. *Achieving the Promise: Transforming Mental Health Care in America* (President's New Freedom Commission on Mental Health, Rockville, MD, 2003) also described successful interventions to prevent mental health problems. This section presents two programs named in the Surgeon General's report—Project Head Start and The Carolina Abecedarian Project—and two programs described in the final report issued by the President's New Freedom Commission—a model nurse-family partnership program and a model screening program for youth. It also offers recommendations and descriptions of interventions deemed effective at preventing suicide from *Reducing Suicide: A National Imperative (2002)* (Committee on Pathophysiology and Prevention of Adolescent and Adult Suicide, Board of Neuroscience and Behavioral Health, Institute of Medicine [IOM], National Academies Press, Washington, D.C., 2002).

The IOM *Reducing Suicide* report characterizes current prevention programs as rooted in the "universal, selective, and indicated (USI) prevention model." This model considers three defined populations—the entire population is included in universal programs, specific high-risk groups are targeted by selective programs, and indicated programs address specific high-risk individuals. Universal programming assumes a basically healthy population and generally aims at protection against developing a disorder by offering, for example, enhanced coping skills and resiliency training. Examples of universal programs are educational programs to heighten awareness of a problem and mass-media campaigns intended to increase understanding of and attitudes about a particular issue. The WHO model promotes universal prevention, advocating for mental health education for all students, and efforts to reduce environmental threats to mental health.

Population-based programs often produce greater gains than programs targeting individuals because there are higher rates of program participation. For example, all the students in a given grade will be exposed to school-based drug prevention programs. Selective programs target subsets of populations that have been identified as at-risk but are not yet diagnosed with a specific problem or disorder—persons who have a greater-than-average likelihood of developing mental disorders, such as adolescents with truancy or suspected substance abuse problems. Indicated programs are aimed at specific high-risk individuals—persons who have evidenced early signs or symptoms of mental disorders, such as children diagnosed with attention deficit hyperactivity disorder (ADHD) who may be at greater risk of developing conduct disorders, or students who have engaged in disruptive or other disturbed behavior at school.

By recounting the histories, benefits, and scientific evaluation of mental health prevention and promotion programs, these three reports offer a framework for developing and implementing mental health promotion programs and policies in a wide range of settings, including primary medical care practices and clinics, maternal and infant health and mental health programs, child care centers, school-based health centers, vocational training programs, social service agencies, parent education programs, and the media. Further, these recently issued reports make good on the promise to disseminate the methods and results of effective programs, enabling mental health service providers and other stakeholders throughout the country to replicate these results in their local communities.

Early Childhood Interventions

Project Head Start is a well-known national prevention program. In 1965, the Office of Economic Opportunity (OEO) launched Head Start in 2,500 communities as an eight-week summer program. Head Start was on the frontlines of the War on Poverty, and its aim was to educate economically disadvantaged preschool children to help break the "cycle of poverty" by providing them and their parents or caregivers with a flexible, comprehensive program to meet their emotional, social, health, nutritional, and psychological needs. Education and child development specialists, community leaders, and parents throughout the nation embraced Head Start and recruited children age three to school entry age. The eight-week demonstration project was expanded to include full-day, year-round services and many program options.

In 1969 Head Start was transferred from OEO to the Office of Child Development in the U.S. Department of Health, Education, and Welfare. Today it is under the auspices of the Administration for Children, Youth and Families (ACFY), Administration for Children and Families (ACF) in the U.S. Department of Health and Human

Services, and is locally administered by community-based nonprofit organizations and school systems.

To expand participation, families with children from birth to age three were included and have been served in Head Start. The 1994 reauthorization of the Head Start Act established a new Early Head Start program for low-income families with infants and toddlers. During fiscal year 2002, $653.7 million funded nearly 650 programs to provide Early Head Start child development and family support services in all 50 states, the District of Columbia, and Puerto Rico. Early Head Start programs promote healthy prenatal outcomes, enhance the development of infants and toddlers, and promote healthy family functioning. These programs served more than 62,000 children under the age of three in 2002.

The Head Start program has enrolled 21,214,295 children since its inception in 1965. During 2002 more than 47,000 children participated in home-based Head Start program services; 29 percent of Head Start program staff members were parents of current or former Head Start children; and more than 867,000 parents volunteered in Head Start programs. Table 9.1 shows information about Head Start participants and centers as well as the numbers of paid staff and volunteers and average cost per child in 2002.

Although some studies of Head Start have shown that early education improves test scores, the advantage gained by Head Start graduates is short-lived. The test scores of children who do not receive early childhood education quickly catch up with those who have been in Head Start programs, but there are other enduring academic benefits. There is now considerable evidence that offering preschoolers a suitably stimulating environment promotes significant advances in knowledge and reasoning ability. Research has shown that graduates of Head Start and other early childhood programs are less likely to be placed in special education classes and more likely to graduate from high school. Head Start and other forms of early education aim to produce lifelong learners and bestow additional benefits, including enhanced social and interpersonal skills, less truancy, and less antisocial behavior. It is not known, however, whether these important social benefits, which may effectively inoculate children against mental illness, result from the child's or parent's participation in Head Start programs.

The Carolina Abecedarian Project is an early educational intervention for high-risk children. The project was started by Dr. Craig Ramey with 57 infants from low-income families who were randomly assigned to enriched, quality child care. Another 54 infants in a control group did not receive the same intervention, although some did attend other child care centers. The project included small class sizes, well-trained and well-compensated teachers, and a strong curriculum. It was groundbreaking because it was among the first carefully controlled scientific studies

TABLE 9.1

Head Start program statistics, fiscal year 2002

Fiscal year–2002 data	
Enrollment	912,345
Ages:	
Number of 5 year olds and older	5%
Number of 4 year olds	52%
Number of 3 year olds	36%
Number under 3 years of age	7%
Racial/ethnic composition:	
American Indian	2.9%
Hispanic	29.8%
Black	32.6%
White	28.4%
Asian	2.0%
Hawaiian/Pacific Islander	1.0%
Number of grantees	1,570
Number of classrooms	49,800
Number of centers	18,865
Average cost per child	$6,934
Paid staff	198,000
Volunteers	1,450,000

SOURCE: "FY–2002 Program Statistics," in *Research/Statistics*, U.S. Department of Health and Human Services, Administration for Children & Families, Head Start Bureau, Washington, DC, 2003 [Online] http://www2 .acf.dhhs.gov/programs/hsb/research/2003.htm [accessed December 15, 2003]

of the potential benefits of early childhood education for children from low-income families. The project enrolled children who had been identified as high risk based on socioeconomic variables in a prevention-oriented day care setting from infancy to age five. The preschool featured an infant curriculum to enhance development and activities for parents. When the children entered elementary school, a second intervention was provided—15 home visits per year for three years from a teacher who designed an individualized program of educational activities to supplement the school curriculum. Activities focused on social, emotional, and cognitive development with special emphasis on language. The two-phase intervention had a positive impact on intellectual development and academic achievement, and these effects were maintained through age 12, a full four years after the intervention ended.

The North Carolina project was designed to evaluate the long-term impact of quality early care and learning programs that begin shortly after birth and continue until school entry. Research at the University of North Carolina at Chapel Hill followed the children through age 21 and found significant long-term positive impacts on educational achievement and a variety of factors associated with sound social and emotional development. Selected findings from the analysis of the Carolina Abecedarian Project included:

• Participants in the early intervention program had higher cognitive test scores from the toddler years to age 21.

• Academic achievement in both reading and math was higher from the primary grades through young adulthood.

TABLE 9.2

Nurse-Family Partnership program to prevent mental health problems in mothers and children

Program	Nurse-Family Partnership
Goal	To improve pregnancy outcomes by helping mothers adopt healthy behavior, improve child health and development, reduce child abuse and neglect, and improve families' economic self-sufficiency
Features	A nurse visits the homes of high-risk women when pregnancy begins and continues for the first year of the child's life. The nurse adheres to visit-by-visit protocols to help women adopt healthy behaviors and to responsibly care for their children. In many states, Nurse-Family Partnership programs are funded as special projects or through state appropriations.
Outcomes	*For mothers:* 80% reduction in abuse of their children, 25% reduction in maternal substance abuse, and 83% increase in employment. *For children (15 years later):* 54% to 69% reduction in arrests and convictions, less risky behavior, and fewer school suspensions and destructive behaviors This is the only prevention trial in the field with a randomized, controlled design and 15 years of follow-up. The program began in rural New York 20 years ago and its benefits have been replicated in Denver and in minority populations in Memphis.
Biggest challenge	To preserve the program's core features as it grows nationwide. The key feature is a trained nurse, rather than a paraprofessional, who visits homes. A randomized, controlled trial found paraprofessionals to be ineffective.
How other organizations can adopt	Modify requirements of federal programs, where indicated, to facilitate adopting this successful, cost-effective model.
Sites	270 communities in 23 states.

SOURCE: "Figure 4.1. Model Program: Intervening Early to Prevent Mental Health Problems," in *Achieving the Promise: Transforming Mental Health Care in America*, President's New Freedom Commission On Mental Health, Rockville, MD, 2003

- Participants completed more years of education and were more likely to attend a four-year college.

- Participants postponed having their own children and were older on average, when their first child was born.

- The cognitive and academic benefits from this program were stronger than for many other early childhood programs.

- Higher cognitive test scores may be attributable to enhanced language development.

- Mothers whose children participated in the program achieved higher educational and employment status than mothers whose children were not in the program. These results were especially pronounced for teen mothers.

A cost-benefit analysis of the project conducted in 2002 revealed that in addition to enduring academic benefits, the project conferred greater earning potential for participants and their mothers. Researchers Steven Barnett and Leonard Massey found that children in quality programs are likely to earn about $143,000 more over their lifetimes than those who do not participate in such programs. Similarly, mothers of participants can also anticipate greater earnings—about $133,000 more over their lifetimes—and children of participants are projected to earn nearly $48,000 more throughout their lifetimes.

School districts can save more than $11,000 per child because participants are less likely to require special or remedial education. Further, the study also suggested a possible impact on cigarette smoking. Participants were less likely to smoke (39 percent versus 55 percent in the control group), resulting in improved health and longer lives, for a total benefit of $164,000 per person. The researchers concluded that the average annual cost of the Abecedarian intervention would be about $13,000 per

child in 2002 dollars—about twice the cost of the average Head Start program. They asserted that "even at that, the benefits outweigh the costs by a factor of four dollars for every dollar spent."

The President's New Freedom Commission on Mental Health also cited accessible quality screening and early interventions such as the "Nurse-Family Partnership" as strategies able to help the United States achieve one of the commission's goals—to "promote the mental health of young children." This rigorously evaluated model program intervenes before birth—a specially trained nurse makes home visits to expectant mothers considered high-risk to help them maintain healthy pregnancies. Along with assisting expectant mothers to adopt healthy lifestyles, the nurses teach new baby care and parenting skills. Table 9.2 outlines the features, outcomes, and challenges faced during implementation of the "Nurse-Family Partnership" program.

Adolescent Intervention Programs

Another recommendation from the report of the President's New Freedom Commission on Mental Health was to "improve and expand school mental health programs." It cited research demonstrating that about 42 percent of students with serious emotional disturbances graduate from high school compared with 57 percent of students with other disabilities. The commission believed this could be changed, since it found ample evidence that school mental health programs improved academic achievement—improved test scores, fewer absences, and less discipline problems—by detecting mental health problems early and providing timely referral to appropriate treatment.

The commission observed that the concerted effort needed to deliver quality mental health services in schools

TABLE 9.3

Columbia University teen mental health screening program

Program	Columbia University TeenScreen® Program
Goal	To ensure that all youth are offered a mental health check-up before graduating from high school. TeenScreen® identifies and refers for treatment those who are at risk for suicide or suffer from an untreated mental illness.
Features	All youngsters in a school, with parental consent, are given a computer-based questionnaire that screens them for mental illnesses and suicide risk. At no charge, the Columbia University TeenScreen® Program provides consultation, screening materials, software, training, and technical assistance to qualifying schools and communities. In return, TeenScreen® partners are expected to screen at least 200 youth per year and ensure that a licensed mental health professional is on-site to give immediate counseling and referral services for youth at greatest risk. The Columbia TeenScreen® Program is a not-for-profit organization funded solely by foundations. When the program identifies youth needing treatment, their care is paid for depending on the family's health coverage.
Outcomes	The computer-based questionnaire used by TeenScreen® is a valid and reliable screening instrument. The vast majority of youth identified through the program as having already made a suicide attempt, or at risk for depression or suicidal thinking, are not in treatment. A follow-up study found that screening in high school identified more than 60% of students who, four to six years later, continued to have long-term, recurrent problems with depression and suicidal attempts.
Biggest challenge	To bridge the gap between schools and local providers of mental health services. Another challenge is to ensure, in times of fiscal austerity, that schools devote a health professional to screening and referral.
How other organizations can adopt	The Columbia University TeenScreen® Program is pilot-testing a shorter questionnaire, which will be less costly and time-consuming for the school to administer. It is also trying to adapt the program to primary care settings.

SOURCE: "Figure 4.2. Model Program: Screening Program for Youth," in *Achieving the Promise: Transforming Mental Health Care in America*, President's New Freedom Commission On Mental Health, Rockville, MD, 2003

entailed collaboration with parents and local providers of mental health care to support screening, assessment, and early intervention. It also asserted that mental health services must be integral parts of school health centers and that federal funds must be available to support the programs.

The report lauded the Columbia University Teen-Screen program as a model program of screening and early intervention. The program ensures mental health screening of all students before they leave high school and early identification of students at risk for suicide or those with symptoms of depression or other mental illness. Evaluation of the program found it to be remarkably effective—identifying more than 60 percent of students later found to have recurrent mental health problems or mental disorders. Table 9.3 summarizes the goals, features, outcomes, and principal challenges faced during implementation of the TeenScreen program. Funding a dedicated health professional to perform screening and referral proved to be a significant obstacle to program implementation.

PREVENTING SUICIDE

The 1999 surgeon general's report that termed suicide a serious public health problem recommended a three-pronged national strategy to prevent suicide, which included programs to educate, heighten understanding, intervene, and advance the science of suicide prevention. Table 9.4 shows the components of AIM (awareness, intervention, and methodology)—the national strategy for suicide prevention—as well as risk factors and protective factors for suicide.

The Institute of Medicine (IOM) report *Reducing Suicide: A National Imperative (2002)* (Committee on Pathophysiology and Prevention of Adolescent and Adult

TABLE 9.4

Suicide risk factors, protective factors, and national prevention strategy

- National Strategy for Suicide Prevention: AIM
  - Awareness: promote public awareness of suicide as a public health problem
  - Intervention: enhance services and programs
  - Methodology: advance the science of suicide prevention

- Risk factors
  - Male gender
  - Mental disorders, particularly depression and substance abuse
  - Prior suicide attempts
  - Unwillingness to seek help because of stigma
  - Barriers to accessing mental health treatment
  - Stressful life event/loss
  - Easy access to lethal methods such as guns

- Protective factors
  - Effective and appropriate clinical care for underlying disorders
  - Easy access to care
  - Support from family, community, and health and mental health care staff

SOURCE: Adapted from "Figure 4.1. Surgeon General's Call to Action to Prevent Suicide—1999," in *Mental Health: A Report of the Surgeon General*, U.S. Department of Health and Human Services, Substance Abuse and Mental Health Services Administration, with National Institutes of Health, Rockville, MD, 1999 [Online] http://www.mentalhealth.org/features/surgeongeneralreport/toc.asp [accessed December 18, 2003]

Suicide, Board of Neuroscience and Behavioral Health, Institute of Medicine, National Academies Press, Washington, D.C., 2002) described suicide as "a major national and international public health problem with about 30,000 deaths in the United States and 1,000,000 deaths in the world each year and every year."

In view of the magnitude of the problem, the IOM report called for development, testing, expansion, and implementation of programs for suicide prevention funded by appropriate agencies, including the NIMH, the Department of Veterans' Affairs (DVA), the Centers for Disease Control and Prevention (CDC), and the

FIGURE 9.1

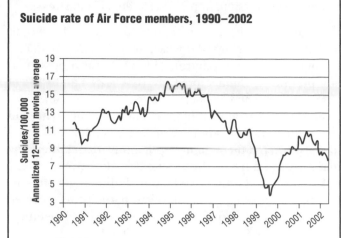

Suicide rate of Air Force members, 1990–2002

SOURCE: "Suicide Rate—US Air Force Members 1990–2002," in "Air Force Suicide Prevention Program, a Population-based, Community Approach: The United States Air Force Medical Service (2002)," *Best Practice Initiative,* U.S. Department of Health and Human Services, Washington, DC, 2002 [Online] http://phs.os.dhhs.gov/ophs/BestPractice/usaf.htm [accessed November 19, 2003]

Substance Abuse Mental Health Services Administration (SAMHSA). Specific recommendations about prevention programs included:

- Creating partnerships among federal, state, and local agencies to implement effective suicide prevention programs.

- Collaborating with professional societies, including the American Psychiatric Association and the American Psychological Association, and nonprofit organizations dedicated to the prevention of suicide, such as the American Association of Suicidology.

- Expanding programs that have demonstrated success in select populations. For example, the Air Force program (see below) should be adopted by comparable organizations that experience increased suicide rates such as police and emergency rescue workers. There should be a systematic identification of high suicide risk groups for targeted intervention.

- Including coping and resiliency training in the curricula for school-aged children and intensifying or expanding these when feasible. In view of the link between cumulative life stresses and suicide and the existing data supporting the efficacy of these programs, it is expected that this training will act to reduce the frequency of suicidal behavior as well as other mental health disorders.

- Restricting access to common means of suicide by enacting or strengthening legislation to ensure gun safety, building barriers on bridges, modifying contents of cooking gas, reinforcing packaging of commonly used pills, and poison control.

- Evaluating public education campaigns to determine and quantify their effectiveness to change knowledge and attitudes and to reduce suicide and suicidal behaviors.

The Air Force Suicide Prevention Program

The IOM report considered a variety of prevention programs that address risk factors and aim to enhance protective factors in order to reduce the incidence of suicide and suicidal behaviors. It observed that programs that appear effective, such as one initiated by the U.S. Air Force, are comprehensive and simultaneously act to increase knowledge and change attitudes within a community, dispel barriers to treatment, and improve access to support and intervention.

The Air Force Suicide Prevention Program is a population-based, community approach to suicide risk prevention and behavioral health promotion that was named a "best practice initiative" by the assistant secretary for health of the U.S. Department of Health and Human Services. It integrated human, medical, and mental health services, uniting a coalition of community agencies from within and outside of the health care delivery system to significantly reduce suicide among air force personnel, which had risen to an all-time high during the mid-1990s. Figure 9.1 shows suicide rates among air force personnel from 1990 to 2002.

The program attempted to reduce risk factors, such as problems with the law, finances, intimate relationships, mental health, job performance, substance abuse, social isolation, and poor coping skills. It simultaneously sought to strengthen protective factors such as effective coping skills, a sense of social connectedness, support, and policies and norms that encourage effective help-seeking behaviors. To stimulate help-seeking behaviors the air force chief of staff forcefully communicated the urgent need for air force leaders, supervisors, and frontline workers to support one another during times of heightened life stress. He exhorted airmen to seek help from mental health clinics and observed that seeking help early was likely to enhance careers rather than hinder them. The chief of staff instructed commanders and supervisors to support and protect those who sought mental health care and eliminated policies that served as barriers to seeking and obtaining mental health care.

To improve surveillance, a Web-based database was established to capture demographic, risk factor, and protective factor information about individuals who attempted or completed suicide. This extremely secure tool protected privacy and permitted timely detection of changes in patterns in suicidal behavior that could be used to strengthen policies and enhance practices throughout the air force community. To improve crisis management, critical incident stress management teams were assembled and poised for deployment to installations hard hit by potentially traumatizing events such as combat deployments, serious aircraft accidents, and natural disasters, as well as suicides within the units.

When the program commenced in 1995, suicide was the second leading cause of death among air force personnel. After its inception, the suicide rate declined significantly for three consecutive years. During the first six months in 1999, the rate dropped to less than 3.5/100,000—more than 50 percent less than the lowest rate on record prior to 1995 and an 80 percent drop from the peak rates in the mid-1990s. Although the suicide rates increased in 2000 and early 2001, they declined again and remained much lower than rates prior to 1995. (See Figure 9.1.)

The air force experience is not necessarily applicable to the general population because the air force is a tightly controlled and relatively homogenous community with identifiable leaders readily able to influence community norms and priorities. It can still serve as a model for comparable hierarchical organizations and offers insight into prevention program planning. The program's overarching principles, such as engaging community leaders to change cultural norms, improving coordination of diverse human and health services, and providing educational programs to community members, can inform national efforts and may be replicable in other populations.

School-Based Prevention Programs

After reviewing 11 universal prevention strategies targeting high school students and more than 15 programs aimed at younger students, the IOM report confirmed that school-based programs have demonstrated success in reducing suicidal behavior, but it also observed that effective school-based interventions were far more than simply awareness or education programs. Successful programs offer services such as screening, support and skills training groups, and establish school-based crisis response plans and teams of professionals to enact the plans. They emphasize the importance of telling adults about emotional distress and seeking help for oneself or friends, as well as cultivation of the competence and skills that offer protection from the adverse effects of stress.

The IOM cited *Reconnecting Youth,* a personal competency training program piloted in five urban high schools as a model selective prevention program that uses a combination of support and skills training. Between 35 and 40 percent of youth at risk for academic failure are also at risk for suicide, so the program targeted potential high school dropouts. The program was offered as a single-semester, daily, 55-minute elective class with one facilitator or teacher and about 10 students. Participants completed a comprehensive suicide-risk assessment and learned a variety of skills that produced measurable gains in increasing personal control—self-efficacy, self-esteem,

and reliance on social supports. Participants also reported decreased depression, hopelessness, anger, and stress.

The school-based prevention programs for youth identified as being at risk focused on enhancing students' feelings of personal control. The IOM report presented two programs, Counselors Care (C-CARE) and Project CAST (Coping and Support Training). C-CARE interventions targeted potential high school dropouts who had shown specific early signs of suicide and related risk factors and offered them an in-depth motivational interview that assessed a list of direct suicide risk factors, related risk factors, and protective factors. Following a one-on-one, two-hour assessment interview, participants received an additional two-hour counseling session and meetings with parents and school personnel, intended to strengthen social connections. A booster session, consisting of further assessment and counseling, was provided between six and eight weeks following the initial intervention.

Project CAST provided 12 sessions of small-group-skills training and case management along with the initial and booster sessions provided by C-CARE for a comparable target population. The 12 sessions emphasized building personal resources such as self-esteem, personal control of moods, school performance, drug use, positive coping strategies, staying on track, and monitoring and setting goals. The sessions also concentrated on empathy and motivation as well as identifying support needs and resources, and how to access help and support.

Participants from both programs were followed and assessed on four different occasions, including nine months after completion of either program. Both programs were found to enhance self-esteem and reduce depression, anxiety, hopelessness, and anger. Each also decreased use of "hard" drugs, but CAST was more effective at reducing alcohol and marijuana use and produced more enduring increases in problem-solving, coping, and personal control. There were no measurable changes in suicide rates, but this finding is not surprising in view of the low risk of suicide during the limited follow-up period and the relatively small sample sizes of the populations.

Do Telephone Hotlines and Crisis Centers Prevent Suicide?

Although crisis centers and telephone hotlines that aim to prevent suicide attempts are ubiquitous, the IOM report observed that their effectiveness is unknown. The institute recommended research to determine not only whether such services are effective preventive measures or deterrents but also which model of crisis counseling or telephone service is most effective. Is anonymous telephone counseling preferable to telephone counseling in which the caller must disclose his or her identity? Is face-to-face counseling a better intervention than telephone counseling in terms of connecting persons in crisis to mental health services they might otherwise fail to seek or obtain? Should crisis centers and telephone hotlines be staffed by professional mental health workers or trained volunteers? Finally, the IOM report encouraged researchers to consider whether provision of crisis intervention services via the Internet is a workable alternative, especially for youths who may be more comfortable seeking help online than in person or by telephone.

MENTAL HEALTH PROMOTION

On the Job

Work is at the very core of contemporary life for most people, providing financial security, personal identity, and an opportunity to make a meaningful contribution to community life.

—*Mental Health in the Workplace: United States,* Situation Analyses, International Labour Office, Geneva, 2000

During the last 20 years, there has been increasing acknowledgment of the role of work and the quality of life in the workplace in promoting mental wellness and protecting against mental illness. Many employers actively promote mental health in the workplace. In 1996, 89 percent of employers had offered on-site health promotion programs, up from 64 percent in 1992.

The Substance Abuse and Mental Health Services Administration (SAMHSA) defines worksite health promotion and wellness as

the systematic approach endorsed by an organization designed to enhance the health of the company and its most important asset: its employees. In order to reach the greatest health improvement and cost containment potential, programs may include initiatives based in the worksite as well as in the employee's community, clinic, and home. These efforts may take the shape of awareness education, behavior and lifestyle change, and the creation of supportive environments. The ultimate goal of worksite health promotion is to create a culture that values and meets both individual and organizational needs for health improvement.

One strategy for worksite wellness is to offer employee assistance programs (EAPs)—company-sponsored programs designed to relieve and assist to resolve workplace problems caused by family or personal challenges. EAPs typically offer a range of diagnostic, support, information and referral, and counseling or treatment services. Although EAPs began as worksite substance abuse treatment programs, over time they have expanded to address a broad range of issues with the potential to adversely affect job performance. EAP services aimed at improving employees' mental health may include on-site and telephone counseling; referral for psychological symptoms or mental health disorders such as depression, stress, and anxiety; marital or family-related issues; legal and financial problems; eating disorders; preretirement planning

needs; child care and elder care services (in-home care and facilities that provide full- or part-time supervision of children or older adults); and bereavement counseling.

A MODEL WORKSITE WELLNESS PROGRAM. The SAMSHA describes evidence-based prevention programs as conceptually sound and internally consistent with activities grounded in the concepts of the programs that are reasonably well implemented and evaluated. It distinguishes between evidence-based programs, rating them as promising—having some positive outcomes; effective—demonstrating consistently positive outcomes and characterized by strong implementation and evaluation; or model—well-implemented, well-evaluated programs reviewed by the National Registry of Effective Programs (NREP) using rigorous standards of research. Model Programs score at least 4.0 on a 5-point scale that measures program integrity and utility.

The Healthy Workplace program is an example of a model worksite prevention program that simultaneously aims to reduce unsafe drinking, illegal drug use, and prescription drug abuse while improving the health practices of workers. Rooted in a health promotion framework, the program uses a social-cognitive approach to induce behavioral change. It consists of five interventions that are delivered in small group sessions using specially developed videos and print materials. Along with powerful education about the health risks of substance abuse, the program emphasizes stress management, weight management/nutrition, and fitness. For example, it shows participants how healthful stress management techniques such as relaxation exercises are preferable to using alcohol or drugs for stress relief.

By effectively integrating substance abuse prevention concepts and activities into health promotion programs, the program lessens the stigma associated with substance abuse so that affected individuals are not deterred from seeking help. The success of the Healthy Workplace program is attributed to its capacity to:

- Engage workers through the positive vehicle of health promotion

- Motivate workers by demonstrating that others have successfully overcome substance abuse

- Heighten awareness of the benefits of healthful practices and the hazards of substance abuse

- Teach workers specific techniques for improving health and reducing use of alcohol, tobacco, and illegal drugs, such as how to monitor and pace alcohol consumption and refuse illegal drugs

- Use media, including videos, to raise self-efficacy and provide true-to-life models of how healthful practices can be adopted

The Healthy Workplace program interventions were field-tested in five worksites, using research methods to

TABLE 9.5

Healthy Workplace Program participants' use of alcohol and drugs, compared to control group

- 47% reduction in the number of drinks consumed in past 30 days
- 67% reduction in the number of days of heavy drinking in past 30 days
- Improved motivation to reduce drinking
- Reduced use of alcohol or illegal drugs to relieve stress
- Increased perceived risks of alcohol and illegal drug use
- Improved health practices and beliefs, such as confidence in abilty to improve health

SOURCE: "Proven Results," in "Healthy Workplace," *SAMHSA Model Programs*, U.S. Department of Health and Human Services, Substance Abuse and Mental Health Services Administration, Washington, DC, October 20, 2002 [Online] http://www.modelprograms.samhsa.gov/template_cf.cfm?page=model&pkProgramID=239 [accessed November 19, 2001]

assess attitude and behavioral change before and after the program was completed. Outcomes were evaluated using a Health Behavior Questionnaire, which contained multiple measures of health and substance use practices and attitudes. Evaluative research of the Healthy Workplace program has shown significant reductions in alcohol and drug use among participants, along with improvements in other health measures such as stress-coping abilities and dietary practices. Table 9.5 lists some of the measurable results of the Healthy Workplace program.

Promoting Mental Health in the Community

Most health and social service agencies name mental health promotion as among their many goals, but it is the mission and overarching goal of the Institute for Mental Health Initiatives (IMHI) at the George Washington University School of Public Health & Health Services. The IMHI works with the media, communities, academia, and policy makers to translate mental health research into concepts that assist people to lead lives characterized by productivity, resilience, and emotional fitness.

To fulfill its mission, the IMHI operates in three arenas—media, community education, and mental health policy. To deliver reliable information about mental health and mental illness to writers, producers, directors, and other members of the media, the IMHI publishes *Dialogue: Insights into Human Emotions for Creative Professionals* and produces critically acclaimed interactive forums called *Dialogues: Insights into Human Emotion and Perspectives*. The publication has addressed an array of mental health topics, including children's first day of school, prevention of violence, risk taking, loss, fear, stereotyping, hate, drug abuse, family secrets, and the stresses faced by working women. Forum topics have included programs describing risks and challenges faced by teens; the changing images, expectations, and roles of fathers; and issues related to aging women such as television and news portrayals of mature women's creativity, strength, courage, value, and accomplishments. They also have addressed how to overcome trauma and have created

customized programs to meet the needs of specific populations, such as how to help Oklahoma City children cope with their fears after the April 19, 1995, bombing of the Murrah Federal Building. The forums emphasize the value of emotional reserves and resiliency, such as authenticity of character, independence, strength, overall sense of personal control, and the ability to welcome challenges that accompany growth and aging.

The IMHI community programs have focused on violence prevention and anger management programs targeting families, parents, teens, and children. The intent of creating these programs was to produce anger management programs based on the most current research and to create information on anger management that would be readily accessible to the public.

The IMHI asserts that creating and sustaining peaceful communities promotes mental health and wellness and that empowering individuals, families, and communities with skills to manage conflict and angry feelings in constructive, nonviolent ways is an important way to nurture peaceful communities.

Since IMHI's mission is mental health promotion, its focus is on positive qualities and skills rather than on negative or pathological behavior. In 1987 IMHI began to examine the literature describing how people succeed against the odds. IMHI researched the science of hope, optimism, competency, emotional regulation, happiness, and creativity, in an attempt to answer the question "what facilitates personal growth and builds societies that flourish?" For more than a decade, IMHI has conducted conferences, seminars, brainstorming sessions, and workshops, with leading researchers in the field of resilience trying to pinpoint the predictors and prerequisite qualities for resilience and developing a paradigm for fostering resilience.

The success of IMHI research and programming to encourage resilience was acknowledged by the Center for Mental Health Services (CMHS), and IMHI was funded in 1998 and 1999 by CMHS to convene leading researchers in the field of resilience to review the status of the research and existing effective programs. Today, IMHI researchers continue to refine and evaluate various conceptual models and frameworks for resilience program development, measurement, and further research.

Online

The newest venue for mental health promotion programs is online via the Internet. Many health and social service agencies provide a wealth of mental health self-care resources online. The Veteran's Health Administration (VHA), Center for Health Promotion and Disease Prevention Web site offers information about mental health and emotional well-being for medical and mental health practitioners and consumers. For example, the

VHA provides consumers with definitions of stress and examples of ways to minimize their experience of stress. It advises visitors to its Web site that negative thinking and attitudes exacerbate stress, telling them to "Get the Stinking Out of Your Thinking!" and exhorts them to "stand up for themselves with others, socialize and maintain close relationships with others, and include fun, enjoyable, and pleasurable experiences in their daily lives."

The Web site also offers examples of sensible, realistic, and positive thoughts such as:

- If I allow myself to get stressed out, I'm the one who suffers.

- Why should I waste my energy getting upset, what difference will it make?

- I don't have to like everything that happens, I just have to get through it.

- I am going to keep my dignity right now instead of making a fool of myself by letting myself get upset.

- Nobody promised that life would be fair. That's not realistic.

- One little thing like this isn't going to make any difference in my life as a whole.

- I just have to deal with today, tomorrow can wait.

- I choose to live each day to its fullest and enjoy that day.

- I cannot control other people's behavior. I only have to worry about my own.

Along with these examples and affirmations, Web site visitors are informed about the relationship between physical health, mental health, and mood. They are advised to engage in aerobic exercise four to six times each week, adopt a healthy diet that is low in fat and high in fiber, and limit salt and sugar intake. Other strategies for helping the body better manage stress include getting enough rest to avoid feeling tired and using massage or a hot bath or shower to relieve physical tension. To counteract or transiently escape stressful situations, the VHA advises daydreaming, deep breathing, listening to music, and practicing the relaxation response; it even provides an online relaxation tape to help people learn to relax.

Finally, the Web site suggests lifestyle changes to reduce stress, such as breaking big tasks into smaller ones, tackling one problem at a time, scheduling some quiet time each day, avoiding procrastination, and planning ahead to avoid rushing to complete tasks. It also recommends assertiveness, standing up for one's beliefs and rights, talking about troubles with trusted friends, and prayer or meditation.

CHAPTER 10

PUBLIC OPINION ABOUT MENTAL HEALTH AND MENTAL ILLNESS

For too long mental health problems have been treated as dirty secrets instead of challenges like any others, to be faced and dealt with by individuals, families, and communities.... I have seen first-hand the ravaging effects of large-scale psychological distress, especially as it is left untreated and even untouched as a topic of discussion. That is why I am glad to unite my voice with those of the World Health Organization and other far-sighted individuals who have recognized that care and treatment, rather than exclusion and disregard, are what is needed to confront mental illness in the world.

— Oscar Arias, former president of Costa Rica and 1987 Nobel Peace Laureate, in a letter to Dr. Gro Harlem Brundtland, General Director, World Health Organization, dated March 26, 2001

COLLECTING AND ANALYZING INFORMATION ABOUT MENTAL HEALTH

There are several ongoing measures that consider Americans' self-reported assessments of their mental health and well-being. The Division of Adult and Community Health and the Mental Health Work Group of the National Center for Chronic Disease Prevention and Health Promotion (part of the Centers for Disease Control and Prevention, or CDC) collaborate with state health departments to analyze data about mental health. The Behavioral Risk Factor Surveillance System (BRFSS) tracks adults' perceptions of the days they experienced as "mentally unhealthy," and the U.S. National Health Interview Survey (NHIS) also poses questions about mental health. The BRFSS is an ongoing, state-based, random-digit-dialed telephone survey of the noninstitutionalized U.S. population aged 18 or older that assesses the prevalence of key health-related behaviors and characteristics. Since January 1993 more than 1.2 million survey participants have responded to four health-related quality-of-life (HRQOL) questions, including the following general mental health question: "Now, thinking about your mental health, which includes stress, depression and problems with emotions, for how many days during the past 30 days

TABLE 10.1

Perceived mentally unhealthy days of the past 30 reported by adults responding to the Behavioral Risk Factor Surveillance System telephone survey, 1993–2001

NOW, THINKING ABOUT YOUR MENTAL HEALTH, WHICH INCLUDES STRESS, DEPRESSION, AND PROBLEMS WITH EMOTIONS, FOR HOW MANY DAYS DURING THE PAST 30 WAS YOUR MENTAL HEALTH NOT GOOD?

Year	Mean	Lower CI	Upper CI	Number of nationwide respondents for the year
1993	2.9	2.8	3.0	102,263
1994	2.9	2.8	3.0	105,853
1995	3.0	2.8	3.1	113,934
1996	2.9	2.8	3.0	122,268
1997	3.0	2.9	3.1	133,321
1998	3.0	2.9	3.1	146,993
1999	3.0	2.9	3.1	156,937
2000	3.2	3.1	3.3	180,244
2001	3.4	3.3	3.5	204,802

Total number of nationwide respondents for all years = 1,266,615

Note: CI stands for Confidence Interval

SOURCE: "Mean mentally unhealthy days," in "Mental Health Prevalence Data," *Mental Health Work Group*, Centers for Disease Control and Prevention, National Center for Chronic Disease Prevention and Health Promotion, Atlanta, GA, February 25, 2003 [Online] http://www.cdc.gov/mentalhealth/prevalence_data.htm [accessed November 21, 2003]

was your mental health not good?" Table 10.1 shows the mean number of days respondents considered themselves mentally unhealthy from 1993 through 2001. With the exception of 1996, each year saw the mean days unchanged or incrementally increased, with a mean increase of one-half day since 1993.

BRFSS survey participants who report that their mental health was not good for 14 days or more during the 30 days preceding the survey are defined as having self-reported frequent mental distress (FMD). The 14-day minimum period was selected because a similar period is often used by mental health clinicians and researchers as a threshold or marker to distinguish transient mood changes from clinical depression and anxiety disorders.

FIGURE 10.1

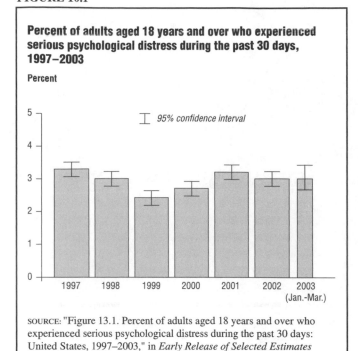

Percent of adults aged 18 years and over who experienced serious psychological distress during the past 30 days, 1997–2003

Percent

SOURCE: "Figure 13.1. Percent of adults aged 18 years and over who experienced serious psychological distress during the past 30 days: United States, 1997–2003," in *Early Release of Selected Estimates Based on Data From the January to March 2003 National Health Interview Survey,* Centers for Disease Control and Prevention, National Center for Health Statistics, Hyattsville, MD, September 30, 2003

FIGURE 10.2

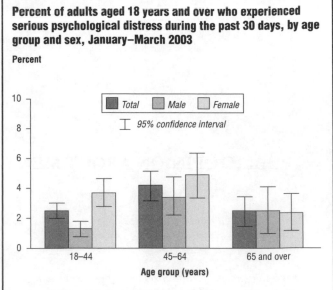

Percent of adults aged 18 years and over who experienced serious psychological distress during the past 30 days, by age group and sex, January–March 2003

Percent

SOURCE: "Figure 13.2. Percent of adults aged 18 years and over who experienced serious psychological distress during the past 30 days, by age group and sex: United States, January–March 2003," in *Early Release of Selected Estimates Based on Data From the January–March 2003 National Health Interview Survey,* Centers for Disease Control and Prevention, National Center for Health Statistics, Hyattsville, MD, September 30, 2003

The NHIS contains data on adults experiencing feelings of depression, despondency, inadequacy, nervousness, or uneasiness. The NHIS questions are derived from the Kessler Psychological Distress Scale, a 10-question screening scale and shorter 6-question scale of psychological distress developed for the redesigned NHIS. The 6-question measure of serious psychological distress asks how often a survey respondent experienced specific symptoms of psychological distress such as sadness, hopelessness, restlessness, nervousness, worthlessness, and the feeling that everything was an effort during the 30 days preceding the survey. The NHIS estimates of the mental health of the U.S. adult population are stratified by age, sex, and race/ethnicity.

Demographic Data about Mental Health

Figure 10.1 shows NHIS data about the percent of adults who reported serious psychological distress during the 30 days preceding the survey from 1997 through the first quarter of 2003. Although the annual percent of adults who experienced serious psychological distress declined from 3.3 percent in 1997 to 2.4 percent in 1999, by 2002 it had returned to 3 percent. In 2003 for both genders combined, adults aged 45 to 64 were more likely to have experienced serious psychological distress (4.2 percent) than younger adults aged 18 to 44 (2.5 percent) and adults aged 65 and older (2.5 percent). Among persons aged 18 to 44, women were more likely than men to have experienced serious psychological distress during the 30

days preceding the survey. (See Figure 10.2.) Some researchers contend that women do not actually experience more serious psychological distress than their male counterparts; rather, they are simply more likely to report such distress.

The prevalence of serious psychological distress was higher among Hispanic persons than among non-Hispanic white persons and non-Hispanic black persons. Adjusting for age and gender, the prevalence of serious psychological distress was 4.8 percent for Hispanic persons, compared to 2.8 percent for both non-Hispanic white persons and non-Hispanic black persons. (See Figure 10.3.)

Gallup Organization polls conducted from 2000 through 2002 found that whites and nonwhites were equally likely to rate their mental/emotional health as excellent (43 percent and 44 percent, respectively), but nonwhites were significantly more likely (24 percent) than whites (15 percent) to consider their mental/emotional health as fair or poor. Rick Blizzard, a health care consultant with the Gallup Organization, asserted that "nonwhites are more likely than whites to be economically and socially disadvantaged, and perhaps more likely to feel alienated from the broader society—two possible factors in their greater likelihood to suffer from emotional and mental stress."

The most recent NHIS data about children's mental health estimated that 4.5 million children ages 3 to 17 (7.5 percent) were afflicted with learning disabilities, and an

FIGURE 10.3

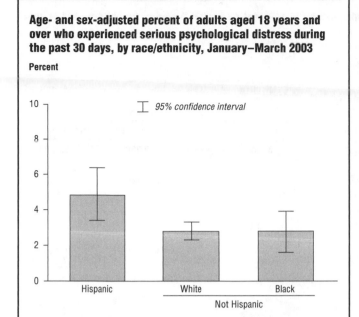

Age- and sex-adjusted percent of adults aged 18 years and over who experienced serious psychological distress during the past 30 days, by race/ethnicity, January–March 2003

SOURCE: "Figure 13.3. Age- and sex-adjusted percent of adults aged 18 years and over who experienced serious psychological distress during the past 30 days, by race/ethnicity: United States, January–March 2003," in *Early Release of Selected Estimates Based on Data From the January–March 2003 National Health Interview Survey,* Centers for Disease Control and Prevention, National Center for Health Statistics, Hyattsville, MD, September 30, 2003

FIGURE 10.4

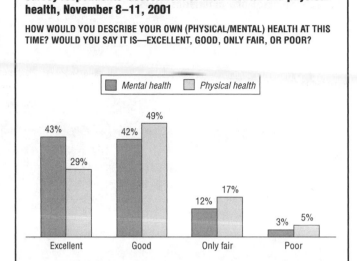

Survey respondents' assessment of their mental and physical health, November 8–11, 2001

HOW WOULD YOU DESCRIBE YOUR OWN (PHYSICAL/MENTAL) HEALTH AT THIS TIME? WOULD YOU SAY IT IS—EXCELLENT, GOOD, ONLY FAIR, OR POOR?

SOURCE: David W. Moore and Joseph Carroll, "How would you describe your own (physical/mental) health at this time? Would you say it is—excellent, good, only fair, or poor?," in *Most Americans Call Their Physical and Mental Health "Good" or "Excellent,"* The Gallup Organization, Princeton, NJ, November 28, 2001. Reproduced with permission.

estimated 3.6 million children (5.9 percent) suffered from attention deficit disorder (ADD). (See Table 10.2.) Almost twice as many boys (9.5 percent) as girls (5.4 percent) had learning disorders, and 8.5 percent of boys were diagnosed with ADD compared to just 3.2 percent of girls. Compared to children from the highest income group, nearly twice as many children in the lowest income group had learning disorders. Children with fair or poor overall health status were more than four times as likely to have a learning disability and three times as likely to suffer from ADD as children with good, very good, or excellent health status.

AMERICANS SAY THEIR MENTAL HEALTH IS FINE

According to a November 2001 Gallup Organization poll, most Americans rate their physical and mental health as excellent or good, and more Americans give high marks to their mental health than to their physical health. More than 8 in 10 Americans (85 percent) rate their mental health as excellent (43 percent) or good (42 percent), while 12 percent said their mental health was only fair and just 3 percent said it was poor. (See Figure 10.4.) Slightly more men rate their mental health as excellent or good (89 percent) than do women (82 percent). (See Figure 10.5.)

When the excellent and good ratings are combined, there is little difference in self-assessed mental health ratings by age. Figure 10.6 shows that more than three-quarters of par-

ticipants in every age group said their mental health was excellent or good, although the percentage of excellent ratings declined among older participants. More than half (56 percent) of people under age 30 rate their mental health as excellent, compared with just 30 percent of people 65 and older.

When the Gallup Organization asked "During the past month, for about how many days did poor mental health or emotional well-being keep you from doing your usual activities, such as self-care, work or recreation?" the majority (85 percent) of respondents claimed that mental health problems did not deter them from their usual activities. (See Table 10.3.) The mean number of days lost because of poor mental health was just 1.3, less than half the mean number of days respondents reported that their mental health or emotional well-being was not good. (See Table 10.4.) The Gallup Poll analysis conceded that the average days lost due to poor mental health it reported may be misleading because it is the result of a small number of people who miss large numbers of days of activity.

Americans Gave Their Mental Health High Marks During 2003

The results of the November 2003 Gallup Health and Healthcare poll were consistent with results of 2001 and 2002 polls that posed questions about Americans' perceptions of their physical and mental health. The 2003 poll revealed that most Americans continue to report favorable mental health. Nearly 9 in 10 respondents (87 percent) rated their mental health or emotional well-being as either excellent (43 percent) or good (44

TABLE 10.2

Frequencies and percents (with standard errors) of ever having a learning disability or Attention Deficit Disorder, for children 3–17 years of age, by selected characteristics, 1998

Selected characteristic	All children 3–17 years	Ever told had		Ever told had	
		Learning disability	Attention Deficit Disorder	Learning disability	Attention Deficit Disorder
		Number in thousands		Percent (standard error)	
Total	59,948	4,481	3,551	7.5 (0.30)	5.9 (0.27)
Sex					
Male	30,735	2,915	2,611	9.5 (0.44)	8.5 (0.45)
Female	29,212	1,566	940	5.4 (0.43)	3.2 (0.28)
Age					
3–4 years	7,930	210	*55	2.7 (0.63)	*0.7 (0.25)
5–17 years	52,018	4,270	3,496	8.2 (0.33)	6.7 (0.31)
5–11 years	28,463	1,879	1,725	6.6 (0.38)	6.1 (0.39)
12–17 years	23,555	2,391	1,771	10.2 (0.55)	7.5 (0.49)
Race/ethnicity[1]					
Non-Hispanic white	39,395	2,954	2,746	7.5 (0.40)	7.0 (0.35)
Non-Hispanic black	9,111	880	441	9.7 (0.85)	4.9 (0.55)
Non-Hispanic other	2,546	*103	*57	*4.0 (1.23)	*2.2 (0.72)
Hispanic	8,896	544	307	6.1 (0.64)	3.5 (0.49)
Mexican American	4,810	242	105	5.0 (0.87)	2.2 (0.47)
Family structure[2]					
Mother and father	43,388	2,877	2,332	6.6 (0.34)	5.4 (0.32)
Mother, no father	12,865	1,191	925	9.3 (0.69)	7.2 (0.60)
Father, no mother	1,898	138	98	7.3 (1.54)	5.2 (1.24)
Neither mother nor father	1,738	268	179	15.4 (2.49)	10.5 (1.86)
Parent's education[3]					
Less than high school diploma	7,504	770	364	10.3 (0.97)	4.9 (0.68)
High school diploma or GED[4]	14,827	1,160	976	7.8 (0.63)	6.6 (0.57)
More than high school	35,344	2,270	2,015	6.4 (0.36)	5.7 (0.35)
Family income[5]					
Less than $20,000	11,882	1,311	837	11.1 (0.84)	7.1 (0.59)
$20,000 or more	45,460	2,934	2,574	6.5 (0.32)	5.7 (0.32)
$20,000–$34,999	9,392	830	625	8.8 (0.93)	6.7 (0.76)
$35,000–$54,999	11,136	754	537	6.8 (0.59)	4.8 (0.56)
$55,000–$74,999	7,895	416	455	5.3 (0.77)	5.8 (0.80)
$75,000 or more	10,882	618	671	5.7 (0.63)	6.2 (0.66)
Poverty status[6]					
Poor	8,461	962	565	11.4 (1.10)	6.7 (0.73)
Near poor	10,467	989	727	9.5 (0.88)	7.0 (0.74)
Not poor	29,969	1,789	1,703	6.0 (0.33)	5.7 (0.38)
Health insurance coverage[7]					
Private	41,696	2,522	2,169	6.1 (0.34)	5.2 (0.31)
Medicaid/other public	8,957	1,413	879	15.8 (1.22)	9.9 (0.91)
Other	1,548	78	133	5.0 (1.44)	8.6 (2.02)
Uninsured	7,543	456	368	6.0 (0.76)	4.9 (0.77)
Place of residence					
Large MSA[8]	28,303	2,003	1,561	7.1 (0.43)	5.5 (0.39)
Small MSA[8]	18,810	1,395	1,124	7.4 (0.53)	6.0 (0.45)
Not in MSA[8]	12,834	1,083	866	8.4 (0.73)	6.8 (0.61)
Region					
Northeast	11,378	908	634	8.0 (0.79)	5.6 (0.53)
Midwest	15,210	1,292	1,029	8.5 (0.66)	6.8 (0.52)
South	20,504	1,515	1,259	7.4 (0.50)	6.2 (0.47)
West	12,856	765	629	6.0 (0.46)	4.9 (0.62)

percent). Just 11 percent considered their mental health as fair and 2 percent said their mental health and emotional state were poor.

Further, 85 percent of Americans said that poor mental or emotional health did not prevent them from performing their usual activities for even a single day.

Nearly two-thirds (64 percent) of survey respondents claimed that they had not experienced a single day in the past month preceding the poll when their mental or emotional health was not good. Another 15 percent said they had suffered 5 or more days of poor mental or emotional health.

TABLE 10.2

Frequencies and percents (with standard errors) of ever having a learning disability or Attention Deficit Disorder, for children 3–17 years of age, by selected characteristics, 1998 [CONTINUED]

Selected characteristic	All children 3–17 years	Ever told had Learning disability	Ever told had Attention Deficit Disorder	Ever told had Learning disability	Ever told had Attention Deficit Disorder
		Number in thousands		Percent (standard error)	
Current health status					
Excellent/very good/good	58,927	4,158	3,341	7.1 (0.30)	5.7 (0.27)
Fair/poor	1,006	323	210	32.1 (3.66)	21.0 (2.89)
Sex and age					
Male:					
3–4 years	4,098	151	*55	3.7 (0.91)	*1.4 (0.49)
5–17 years	26,638	2,764	2,556	10.4 (0.48)	9.6 (0.52)
5–11 years	14,597	1,192	1,237	8.2 (0.58)	8.5 (0.63)
12–17 years	12,041	1,572	1,319	13.1 (0.85)	11.0 (0.83)
Female:					
3–4 years	3,832	*59	*–	*1.5 (0.91)	*–
5–17 years	25,380	1,507	940	5.9 (0.46)	3.7 (0.33)
5–11 years	13,866	687	488	5.0 (0.53)	3.5 (0.46)
12–17 years	11,514	819	452	7.1 (0.72)	3.9 (0.50)

Note: * Figure does not meet standard of reliability or precision.
– Quantity zero.
[1]"Non-Hispanic other" includes non-Hispanic children whose race was identified as American Indian, Alaska Native, Asian, or Pacific Islander. Children of Hispanic origin may be of any race.
[2]Mother and father can include biological, adoptive, step, in-law, or foster relationships. Legal guardians are classified in "Neither mother nor father."
[3]Parent's education is the education level of the parent with the higher level of education, regardless of that parent's age.
[4]GED is General Educational Development high school equivalency diploma.
[5]"Less than $20,000" and "$20,000 or more" include both respondents reporting specific dollar amounts and respondents reporting that their incomes were within those categories. The indented categories include only those respondents who reported specific dollar amounts. Children with unknown family income are not shown.
[6]Poverty status is based on family income and family size using the Census Bureau's poverty thresholds. "Poor" children are in families defined as below the poverty threshold. "Near poor" children are in families with incomes of 100% to less than 200% of the poverty threshold. "Not poor" children are in families with incomes that are 200% of the poverty threshold or greater.
[7]Private health insurance may be obtained through the workplace or purchased directly. Among children under 18 years of age, "Medicaid/other public" includes those with Medicaid or other public health insurance coverage (e.g., most state-sponsored coverage). "Other coverage" includes Medicare, military health insurance coverage, and/or another form of government-sponsored health insurance coverage. Children with only Indian Health Service coverage are considered uninsured.
[8]"MSA" is metropolitan statistical area. Large MSAs have a population size of 1,000,000 or more; small MSAs have a population size of less than 1,000,000. "Not in MSA" consists of persons not living in a metropolitan statistical area.

SOURCE: Debra Blackwell and Luong Tonthat, "Table 3. Frequencies and percents (with standard errors) of ever having a learning disability or Attention Deficit Disorder, for children 3–17 years of age, by selected characteristics: United States, 1998," in "Summary Health Statistics for U.S. Children: National Health Interview Survey, 1998," *Vital and Health Statistics,* series 10, no. 208, October 2002

Consistent with the findings of the earlier surveys, the 2003 poll concluded that Americans lose an average of one day per month because of poor mental health. This lost day of activity results from the observation that the 12 percent of Americans who suffered poor mental or emotional health experienced an average of 3 days when they were unable to perform their normal activities of daily living.

Many Americans Are Happy

The landmark study *Mental Health: A Report of the Surgeon General* (U.S. Department of Health and Human Services, Rockville, MD, 1999) reported an epidemic of mental illness in the United States. It found that one in five Americans had a diagnosable mental disorder and projected that half of the U.S. population will develop mental disorders over the course of their lifetimes. The findings of an October 2002 Gallup Poll, that Americans are a reasonably happy people, are seemingly at odds with the dire predictions in the surgeon general's report.

The Gallup Poll found that 37 percent of Americans said they were "very happy" while 52 percent considered themselves "fairly happy," and just 11 percent reported that they were "not too happy." (See Figure 10.7.) Gallup researcher Deborah Jordan Brooks noted, however, that this poll recorded the lowest reported rates of happiness Gallup has found in 11 polls dating back to 1956.

Slightly more women (40 percent) than men (34 percent) said they were very happy; however, slightly more women (12 percent) than men (9 percent) said they were not too happy. The biggest difference by gender is among persons who consider themselves midway on the road to happiness—more men (57 percent) than women (48 percent) report being fairly happy. (See Figure 10.7.)

Many well-designed research studies have found that regular, vigorous exercise is associated with improved mood and emotional well-being, and the Gallup data confirmed this premise. More than half of survey participants said they exercised strenuously at least three times per week, and these highly active people were more likely to be very happy (42 percent) than less active persons. Roughly the same percent of people who exercise 1 or 2

FIGURE 10.5

Survey respondents' assessment of their mental and physical health, by gender, November 8–11, 2001

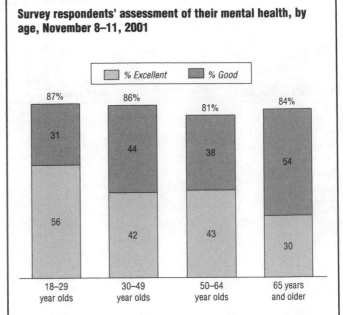

SOURCE: David W. Moore and Joseph Carroll, "Mental/Physical Health Rating by Gender," in *Most Americans Call Their Physical and Mental Health "Good" or "Excellent,"* The Gallup Organization, Princeton, NJ, November 28, 2001. Reproduced with permission.

FIGURE 10.6

Survey respondents' assessment of their mental health, by age, November 8–11, 2001

SOURCE: David W. Moore and Joseph Carroll, "Mental Health Rating by Age," in *Most Americans Call Their Physical and Mental Health "Good" or "Excellent,"* The Gallup Organization, Princeton, NJ, November 28, 2001. Reproduced with permission.

TABLE 10.3

Days lost due to mental and physical health problems reported by survey respondents, November 8–11, 2001

	All adults	
	Physical health	Mental health
	%	%
None	73	85
Less than one day	–	–
One	5	3
Two	4	2
Three	3	1
Four	2	1
Five to ten	6	4
Eleven or more	7	4
No opinion	–	–
Mean	2.3	1.3

SOURCE: David W. Moore and Joseph Carroll, "During the past month, for about how many days did poor physical health/mental health or emotional well-being keep you from doing your usual activities, such as self-care, work, or recreation?," in *Most Americans Call Their Physical and Mental Health Good" or "Excellent,"* The Gallup Organization, Princeton, NJ, November 28, 2001. Reproduced with permission.

TABLE 10.4

Number of days during the past month that survey respondents assessed their mental health or emotional well-being as not good, November 8–11, 2001

NOW, THINKING ABOUT YOUR MENTAL HEALTH OR EMOTIONAL WELL-BEING, FOR HOW MANY DAYS DURING THE PAST MONTH WAS EITHER OF THESE NOT GOOD?

	%
None	62
Less than one day	–
One	5
Two	8
Three	4
Four	2
Five to ten	9
Eleven or more	8
No opinion	2
Mean	2.7
Median	0

SOURCE: David W. Moore and Joseph Carroll, "Now, thinking about your mental health or emotional well-being, for how many days during the past month was either of these not good?," in *Most Americans Call Their Physical and Mental Health "Good" or "Excellent,"* The Gallup Organization, Princeton, NJ, November 28, 2001. Reproduced with permission.

times per week (31 percent) and people who do not exercise (30 percent) said they were very happy. On the other hand, participants who said they did not exercise at all were twice as likely to describe themselves as not too happy (19 percent) as those who said they exercise 1 or 2 times a week (8 percent) or strenuously several times per week (10 percent). (See Figure 10.8.)

Church attendance is also associated with happiness. Participants who had attended church within the 7 days

prior to the poll were considerably more likely to describe themselves as very happy (44 percent) than those who had not attended church during that time (32 percent). (See Figure 10.8.) Although exercise and religious involvement are linked to happiness, it is difficult to determine whether these activities cause or contribute to happiness and well-being. It may be the case that unhappy people are simply less motivated to participate in these activities, and as a result less likely to reap the potential rewards of enhanced well-being.

FIGURE 10.7

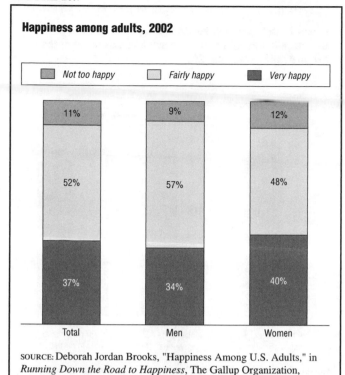

Happiness among adults, 2002

SOURCE: Deborah Jordan Brooks, "Happiness Among U.S. Adults," in *Running Down the Road to Happiness*, The Gallup Organization, Princeton, NJ, October 8, 2002. Reproduced with permission.

FIGURE 10.9

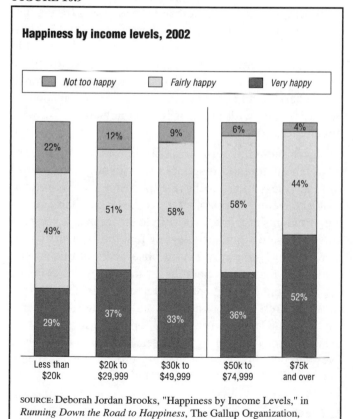

Happiness by income levels, 2002

SOURCE: Deborah Jordan Brooks, "Happiness by Income Levels," in *Running Down the Road to Happiness*, The Gallup Organization, Princeton, NJ, October 8, 2002. Reproduced with permission.

FIGURE 10.8

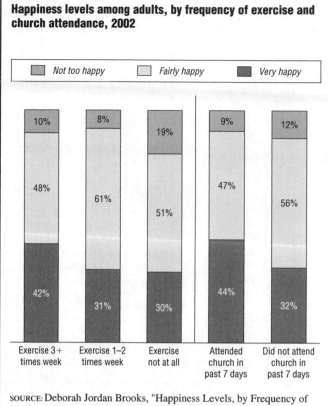

Happiness levels among adults, by frequency of exercise and church attendance, 2002

SOURCE: Deborah Jordan Brooks, "Happiness Levels, by Frequency of Exercise and Church Attendance," in *Running Down the Road to Happiness*, The Gallup Organization, Princeton, NJ, October 8, 2002. Reproduced with permission.

Does Money Buy Mental Health?

Although money does not necessarily buy happiness, the 2002 Gallup data revealed that participants with higher household incomes were much more likely to consider themselves to be very happy than were those with lower incomes. Among participants from households earning $75,000 or more annually, more than half (52 percent) said they were very happy, compared to just 29 percent of persons earning less than $20,000 per year. Similarly, the percentage of not too happy people increases steadily with decreasing income. (See Figure 10.9.)

The November 2001 Gallup Poll found that 85 percent of people considered their mental health and emotional well-being as good or excellent. While money may not purchase peace of mind or optimal mental health, the Gallup Poll found that 25 percent of persons with household incomes of less than $30,000 per year reported fair or poor mental health. In contrast, just 6 percent of persons from households earning $50,000 or more per year said they were in fair or poor mental health. (See Figure 10.10.)

Those who reported fair (12 percent) or poor (3 percent) mental health are likely to benefit from mental health screening, but Gallup data revealed that persons in need may be the least likely to have the financial resources

FIGURE 10.10

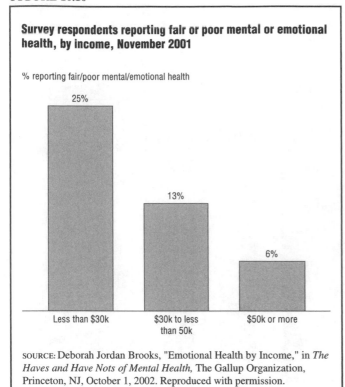

Survey respondents reporting fair or poor mental or emotional health, by income, November 2001

% reporting fair/poor mental/emotional health

SOURCE: Deborah Jordan Brooks, "Emotional Health by Income," in *The Haves and Have Nots of Mental Health,* The Gallup Organization, Princeton, NJ, October 1, 2002. Reproduced with permission.

FIGURE 10.11

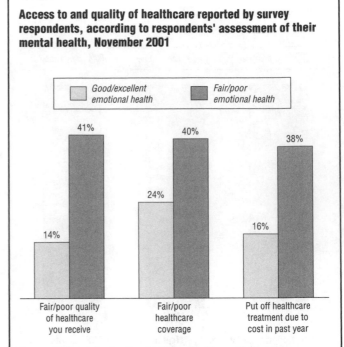

Access to and quality of healthcare reported by survey respondents, according to respondents' assessment of their mental health, November 2001

SOURCE: Deborah Jordan Brooks, "Low Healthcare Ratings More Common Among Those Reporting Poorer Emotional Health," in *The Haves and Have Nots of Mental Health,* The Gallup Organization, Princeton, NJ, October 1, 2002. Reproduced with permission.

to gain access to screening, diagnostic, and treatment services. Unfortunately, people with mental health problems are disproportionately more likely to lack access to quality health services. Among persons who considered themselves as having fair or poor emotional health in 2001, 41 percent felt the quality of health care they received was fair or poor while just 14 percent of persons who rated their emotional well-being as excellent or good said that they received fair or poor health care. (See Figure 10.11.)

Further, persons with minimal health insurance coverage and benefits are unlikely to be covered for mental health services. Of Gallup Poll respondents who reported that their emotional health was fair or poor, 2 out of 5 also rated their health insurance coverage as fair or poor, while nearly 1 out of 4 persons in better emotional health gave their health insurance low marks. Nearly 40 percent of Americans coping with mental and emotional challenges have delayed seeking treatment because of cost. In comparison, fewer than half as many persons not facing mental health challenges (16 percent) have put off medical treatment during the past year because of cost. (See Figure 10.11.)

A Harris Poll conducted by Harris Interactive in November 2002 found that poor people suffer more stress in their daily lives than do those in the higher income brackets. Similarly, younger adults and women tend to experience more stress than older adults, and men and African Americans experience more stress in daily living than whites or Hispanics. These stressors include financial concerns, exposure to noise, threats to privacy, and

loneliness. Using 13 measures of stress drawn from a battery of questions called a "daily hassle scale" that included stressors such as too many things to do, trouble relaxing, concerns about health and money for basic necessities, and problems with children or aging parents, researchers found significant differences in the responses of participants with more or less money and those with more or less education.

Even though the greatest differences related to concerns about money, respondents with higher incomes were also less likely to have experienced stress-related health concerns, illness of a family member, trouble relaxing, problems at work, exposure to frequent or excessive noise, abuse of their privacy, or loneliness. Harris Poll investigator Humphrey Taylor observed that this survey confirmed that while persons in the upper echelons of education and earnings may lead hectic lives, they experience less stress than less affluent and educated Americans. Taylor posited that persons at the top of the socioeconomic ladder probably feel a greater sense of control over their lives and that this sense of mastery protects against negative experiences of stress in their daily lives.

The Gallup and Harris polls revealed that age, gender, race, ethnicity, and socioeconomic status influence experiences of stress in daily life; timely access to prevention, diagnosis, and treatment; and perceptions about the quality of mental health care received. The 2001 *Mental Health: Culture, Race, Ethnicity,* a supplement to *Mental*

Health: A Report of the Surgeon General, found mental health care lacking for minorities in America. Along with barriers to care experienced by all Americans, members of racial and ethnic minority groups face additional obstacles such as language barriers and mental health professionals' reliance on stereotypes that contribute to inadequate prevention and treatment of mental illness. For example, few mental health practitioners identify themselves as Spanish speaking, and about 4 in 10 Hispanics do not have strong enough English skills to interact with mental health professionals in English. Native Americans living in geographically isolated communities have severely limited mental health treatment options, and though Asian Americans are no more likely than whites to suffer from mental disorders, they often do not seek or obtain the help they need. Finally, for those who do seek mental health care, treatment may be substandard, unacceptable because it is culturally insensitive, or too late to be optimally effective.

Work Woes Contribute to Unhappiness

An article entitled "Gallup Study Finds That Misery at Work Is Likely to Cause Unhappiness at Home" in the June 23, 2003, issue of the *Gallup Management Journal* asserted that while Americans are generally satisfied with their personal lives, those who are decidedly unhappy at work, or actively disengaged, are more likely to be unhappy in their personal lives than those who are engaged in their jobs. Engaged employees are those who identify with their work, derive satisfaction from it, and actively promote company objectives.

Gallup researchers asked employees if there were three or more days in the month preceding the survey when the stress of work caused them to behave poorly with their families or friends. More than half (51 percent) of actively disengaged workers responded affirmatively to this question, compared to 29 percent of those who were not engaged (persons who were not engaged with their work but were not actively disenchanted). Just 18 percent of engaged workers said they had behaved badly with family or friends.

Gallup analysts posited that a lack of connection with work diminished respondents' enthusiasm for other aspects of their lives. The finding that employees who were not engaged on the job were more likely to report discontent with their lives in general and their personal lives in particular may simply reflect their inability to form satisfying relationships—professionally or personally. However, since Gallup data revealed that different family conditions, such as marital and parental status and number of wage earners per household, were unrelated to employee engagement or disengagement, researchers speculated that it is more likely that work life influences home life rather than vice versa. This finding, that home life circumstances made little difference in work engagement status, underscores the pivotal role of work in promoting mental health and overall emotional well-being.

SATISFYING WORK, SOCIAL ACTIVITIES, AND PERSONAL RELATIONSHIPS ARE KEY TO HEALTH AND WELLNESS

Family, friends, active interests, and community involvement may do more than simply help people enjoy their lives. Social activities and relationships may actually enable people to live longer by preventing or delaying development of many diseases, including mental illnesses such as dementia. During the past two decades, research has demonstrated that social experiences, activities, relationships, and work stress are related to health, well-being, and longevity. The kind of work stress that causes the greatest harm to physical and mental health is effort-reward imbalance—when great effort is made and the effort is neither recognized nor rewarded. Studies have found that women appear more vulnerable to job stress, while men's health seems more dependent on the availability of social relationships and emotional support.

Several studies have shown that marriage or living with a partner has greater health benefits for men than women, because traditionally women are caregivers. Newer findings question whether the nurturing qualities of women are solely responsible for married men's improved health. Recent research reveals that men and women living alone have better health than those with unsatisfactory relationships with their partners. An alternative explanation of these findings may be that healthier people are more likely to marry than those with physical or mental health problems.

Laura Fratiglioni and her colleagues found that among older Swedish adults, the risk of developing dementia rose with increased social isolation but that the quality rather than frequency of social contacts was more important in staving off impairment. People who had infrequent but satisfying interactions with families and friends fared better than those with unhappy or stressful relationships. The Swedish project also suggested that a variety of strong relationships is important—a single bond is insufficient to reduce risk. Older adults with several kinds of enduring interpersonal relationships, such as marriage, children, friends, and relatives, were at lowest risk.

A promising finding from the study, published in the April 2000 issue of *The Lancet,* is the observation that one tie may substitute for another. This is a key concern, since death of a spouse or close friend may increase the survivor's risk for social isolation. The observation that strong connections with children, relatives, and friends can substitute for relationships with spouses or partners is especially significant for widowed, divorced, or never-married older adults.

Along with personal relationships, social activities and mental stimulation also seem to protect against disease and increase longevity, even when the activities do not involve physical exercise. A study conducted by Thomas A. Glass, Carlos Mendes de Leon, Richard A. Marottoli, and Lisa F. Berkman beginning in 1982 tracked the health and longevity of 2,761 older adults living in New Haven, Connecticut. After 13 years, the researchers determined that "social and productive activities that involve little or no enhancement of fitness lower the risk of all cause mortality as much as fitness activities do." Some mental health professionals caution older adults that the adage "use it or lose it" not only applies to muscles but also to cognitive abilities. They advise older adults to seek opportunities to maintain their mental fitness using techniques such as memorizing shopping lists, taking classes, reading, playing word games, joining discussion groups, and keeping abreast of world events.

Mental Health, Aging, and Longevity

Mental health research has demonstrated that strong emotional and mental health in early life promotes emotional resiliency and quality of mental health in later life. In "Can Aging Boomers Stay Mentally Fit?" (*Gallup Poll Tuesday Briefing,* July 22, 2003) health care consultant Rick Blizzard reported about the mental health and psychological well-being of the baby boom generation. Baby boomers are the cohort of Americans born between 1946 and 1964 that will soon become the nation's largest generation of older adults and retirees.

Far-reaching societal change is practically inevitable when a population includes an unusually large number of people in a single birth cohort. During the 1960s, youthful baby boomers spurred changes in social values, from sexual freedom to antiwar sentiments. In the early decades of the 21st century, retirement-aged boomers will likely drive changes in housing, health care, and retirement funding.

Gallup Organization researchers analyzed data from their health and health care surveys conducted during 2000, 2001, 2002, and 2003 and found that fewer baby boomers (ages 39 to 57) and older adults (age 58 and older) rated their mental and emotional health as excellent, compared to younger adults, aged 18 to 38. In 2003, 42 percent of baby boomers rated their mental health as excellent, compared to 50 percent of adults between the ages of 18 and 38, and 35 percent of adults aged 58 and older. (See Figure 10.12.)

Analysis of Gallup data indicates that mental health problems are more likely to compromise the ability of older adults to perform the activities of daily living, such as self-care, work, and recreation, than they are to affect younger adults. Gallup researchers asked, "During the past month, for about how many days did poor mental health or emotional well-being keep you from doing your usual activities, such as self-care, work, or recreation?" Among respondents who reported at least one poor mental health day in the month prior to the survey, those

FIGURE 10.12

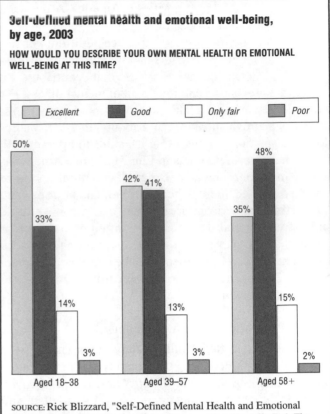

Self-defined mental health and emotional well-being, by age, 2003

HOW WOULD YOU DESCRIBE YOUR OWN MENTAL HEALTH OR EMOTIONAL WELL-BEING AT THIS TIME?

SOURCE: Rick Blizzard, "Self-Defined Mental Health and Emotional Well-Being, by Age," in *Can Aging Boomers Stay Mentally Fit?*, The Gallup Organization, Princeton, NJ, July 22, 2003. Reproduced with permission.

between ages 18 and 38 said they were prevented from participating in normal activities an average of 2.7 days. In contrast, baby boomers were kept from performing normal activities for 4.1 days, and persons aged 58 and older lost 5.5 days of normal activities.

Rick Blizzard suggested that along with agitating for improved diagnosis and treatment of mental disorders, baby boomers themselves should take measures to enhance their mental health and emotional well-being. Blizzard cited social connectedness through concerted efforts to avoid isolation and remain active socially, regular participation in community or religious activities, and successful marriages as an important strategy for preventing mental illness and promoting mental health.

CONTROVERSIES IN MENTAL HEALTH

Mental health research, diagnosis, treatment, financing, and policy are fraught with disagreement, uncertainty, and controversy. There is even debate about the causes and definitions of mental health and illness and the prevalence of mental disorders in the United States. Among the most hotly debated topics are:

- Parity funding for mental health—whether mental health should be funded to the same level and extent as medical care for physical and medical ailments

- The use of mental illness as an explanation, rationale, or excuse for inappropriate, antisocial, or illegal behavior or actions

- The most effective therapies and treatment settings for persons suffering from mental disorders

The following sections consider two other hotly debated topics in mental health research and practice: the reliability and validity of recovered memories of past abuse and the value or harm of direct-to-consumer advertising of psychoactive prescription medication.

Recovered Memories

In recent years the media have detailed the controversies surrounding the existence, nature, and accuracy of recovered memories of child abuse and the responsibility of psychotherapists who may unwittingly create false memories of such abuse. Psychologists Samuel Knapp and Leon VandeCreek described current professional consensus about child abuse, the nature of human memory, diagnosis and treatment of adults who have or may have lost memories of sexual or other physical abuse, and the role of the psychotherapist in considering these issues in "Recovered Memories of Childhood Abuse: Is There an Underlying Professional Consensus?" (*Professional Psychology: Research and Practice,* vol. 31, no. 4, August 2000).

Knapp and VandeCreek observed that despite the debate about recovered memory, there is professional consensus about the prevalence of child abuse and the harm caused by it, including the fact that it is a risk factor for psychological problems later in life. The controversy about recovered memories centers on adults who claim to have lost and later regained memories of abuse. There is professional accord about the ways in which memories are created, which includes agreement that:

- Continuous memories of abuse are likely to be accurate.

- Some persons may lose and later recall memories of abuse.

- Memories from early infancy are highly unreliable.

- False memories of abuse can be created.

- Magnification and minimization may be better ways to understand memory recall with some patients, since memory tends to be a mixture of accurate and inaccurate reconstruction, as opposed to simply completely true or completely false characterizations of events or circumstances.

- It is difficult to separate accurate from inaccurate memories if memory recovery techniques such as hypnosis or interviews with patients under the influence of drugs have been used.

Agreement about professional diagnostic and treatment techniques is rooted in the premise that psychotherapists should question patients about childhood abuse when it is clinically indicated. There is consensus that child abuse is not a diagnosis, cannot be inferred retroactively from a set of symptoms, and that mental distress can have many causes: mental disorders may be linked to other factors, such as unhealthy and unproductive thoughts, conflicts, or anxieties. Further, mental health professionals concur that effective therapy can occur without memory recall of abuse. Recovery of a memory of childhood abuse may be necessary, but is not sufficient to cure the patient. Even if abuse occurred and is confirmed, there is no evidence that identifying, reliving, or disclosing it is requisite for successful treatment. The emphasis of therapy should be on the current functioning of the patient, with treatments customized to meet individual patients' needs. Finally, in some instances, patients may have to learn to live with uncertainty about whether abuse occurred.

The appropriate role of the psychotherapist is to respect and promote patient autonomy, unerringly maintain boundaries with patients, and maintain neutrality on important life decisions. Psychotherapists can help patients make their own decisions about the appropriate course of action but should not direct patients or make these decisions for them.

Knapp and VandeCreek identified the following areas of uncertainty and disagreement:

- The precise contribution of child abuse to psychopathology in later life is unknown and is limited by knowledge about the relationship of specific types of child abuse to specific mental disorders. For example, it is not yet known why similar events produce post-traumatic stress disorder in one person, a generalized anxiety disorder in another, and no sign of mental distress in a third person.

- There is uncertainty about the mechanisms whereby traumatic memories are lost. It may be through simply forgetting, denial, repression, suppression, dissociation, or some other process or processes as yet unidentified. It is not known whether memories of trauma are processed, stored, encoded, and retrieved in the same way as memories of ordinary events or the extent to which they may be altered by postevent discussions.

- There are unsettled issues about the optimal treatment procedures for persons with a history of abuse or suspected abuse who are suffering from mental disorders.

In "More Questions about Recovered Memories" (*American Journal of Psychiatry,* vol. 157, no. 8, August 2000), psychiatrist James Chu attempted to reconcile the beliefs of psychotherapists who entirely reject any evidence of traumatic amnesia and recovered memory and those who uncritically accept and validate all patient accounts of childhood abuse. Chu and his colleagues sought to corroborate patient accounts of abuse using relatively stringent criteria, requiring that other individuals report that they knew (rather than believed) that the remembered abuse had occurred. The researchers found high rates of corroboration—13 of 14 cases for physical abuse and 17 of 19 cases for sexual abuse. They did, however, acknowledge the limitations of their study, including its reliance on patients' self-reports about possible abuse and corroboration and the difficulties of determining whether subtle suggestion had been a part of the patients' psychotherapy. Still, Chu disputed the premise that recovered memories are entirely the result of the therapist's suggestion. He contends that "there is no evidence to suggest that a brief series of direct questions about the possibility of abuse can lead to the immediate creation of complex pseudomemories [false memories] of such abuse."

"Position Statement on Therapies Focused on Memories of Childhood Physical and Sexual Abuse" (*American Journal of Psychiatry,* vol. 157, no. 10, October 2000) from the Commission on Psychotherapy by Psychiatrists of the American Psychiatric Association (APA) addressed the use of specific techniques intended to elicit memories of childhood as a principal technique for relieving emotional distress. The commission observed that memory does not always record events accurately, and under severe or prolonged stress, people may suffer significant impairment of the retention, recall, and accuracy of memories. It acknowledged that memories may be revised in response to suggestions from a trusted person or authority figure. The statement also acknowledged that discrediting true accounts of past events and accepting false accounts has the potential to seriously harm patients and others.

The APA commission recommended that independent of concerns or allegations of childhood abuse, all patients should receive a complete psychiatric evaluation, and that psychiatrists should maintain an "empathic, nonjudgmental, neutral stance toward reported memories of sexual abuse." Absent evidence to confirm or refute the accuracy of new memories of childhood abuse, treatment should concentrate on assisting patients to draw their own conclusions about the accuracy of their memories or to accept uncertainty about the events or actions that may have occurred. The goal of therapy is to help patients to understand and assuage the impact of the memories and abuse experiences on their lives. The commission advised psychiatrists to refrain from issuing public statements about the historical accuracy of uncorroborated individual patient reports of new memories based on observations made during psychotherapy.

Is Direct-to-Consumer Advertising Helpful or Harmful?

At what point does an understandable response to distressing life events become an indication for drug treatment—and a market opportunity?

— Barbara Mintzes, University of British Columbia health policy researcher

The 1999 U.S. surgeon general's report on mental illness estimated that about 20 percent of Americans experience mental health problems and that nearly half of all Americans with severe mental illness do not seek treatment, often because they fear the social stigma and potential loss of employment or health insurance that might result from a diagnosis of mental illness. Gallup Organization research confirmed that a substantial percentage of Americans are routinely affected by mental health problems. A 2001 Gallup survey that asked respondents "how many days during the past month was your mental health not good?" found that nearly half (48 percent) of respondents said they had at least one day when their mental health was not good.

Although these studies rely primarily on self-reports, they do suggest that the United States is in the throes of an epidemic of mental illness. Some researchers, however, argue that Americans' mental health is no worse than it was in past decades. They contend that the availability and aggressive marketing of psychopharmacological agents—prescription drugs aimed at mental health problems such as nervousness, anxiety, panic, and shyness— has prompted overdiagnosis of mental health problems and conditions motivated primarily by the desire to increase drug sales.

There have been advocates and opponents of direct-to-consumer prescription drug advertising since its inception. Consumer surveys support the contention that advertising exerts a significant influence on consumer preferences and behavior. Two such surveys, one conducted by researchers from Massachusetts General Hospital/Harvard University and another by Harris Interactive, found that 35 percent of respondents discussed an advertised drug with their physicians as a result of direct-to-consumer advertising. Among patients prompted by consumer drug advertising to discuss a health problem with their physicians, one-quarter received a new diagnosis and a new prescription. About 4 out of 5 patients who received a prescription drug and took it as prescribed reported that they felt much better or somewhat better overall after taking the prescription medication. These findings were interpreted as supporting the premise that direct-to-consumer drug advertising increases awareness of specific health problems, provides reliable information, and encourages affected individuals to seek treatment.

Opponents usually contend that direct-to-consumer advertising is primarily intended to drive sales and that it:

- Increases prescription drug costs.

- Does not provide the impartial, objective information that would enable consumers to make informed health choices.

- Increases risk because, unlike other consumer goods, prescription drugs even when administered properly may cause serious adverse reactions.

- Takes unfair advantage of vulnerable persons, especially persons who suffer from mental illness, facing difficult treatment choices.

- Aims to increase awareness and utilization of newer products to gain market share and recoup development costs. (New drugs are not necessarily safer or more effective, but are usually costlier, and often little is known about long-term risks.)

- Does not enhance consumer awareness or public health, since there is no evidence that advertising helps patients to make better choices about prescription drug use.

- May unduly influence physician prescribing practices. Physicians often rely on manufacturers for information about drugs, rather than independent sources, and numerous studies have shown that the physicians most influenced by pharmaceutical advertising tend to prescribe less judiciously.

In an article, "High Anxiety," that originally appeared in the September 20, 2003, edition of *The Globe and Mail*, a Canadian newspaper, Anne McIlroy asserts that "nervousness, panic, and shyness are now part of the most-diagnosed group of mental illnesses—and drug companies just happen to have an array of products to treat them." McIlroy observes that 20 years ago, social anxiety was a new and rare mental illness, characterized by debilitating shyness and fear of public humiliation. Today, it is considered the third most frequently occurring mental health problem in the world, and one of half a dozen anxiety disorders that are the most frequently diagnosed mental illnesses.

McIlroy claims that depression was the fashionable disease of the 1990s and that anxiety has taken its place in the first decade of the 21st century, but she does not think that there has been a surge of anxiety disorders or that anxiety disorders constitute a "hidden epidemic." Instead, she believes that marketing has played a role in the rise of social anxiety and other anxiety disorders and worries that antidepressants such as Paxil, Prozac, Zoloft, and Celexa have been "repurposed" by their manufacturers as anti-anxiety drugs to penetrate a new market and reap additional profits. McIlroy also fears that some pharmaceutical marketing blurs the distinction between normal levels of anxiety and pathological anxiety. Its goal is to "medicalize" normal human conditions and convince consumers that nearly all anxiety is evidence of mental disorders that may be readily resolved with prescription medication.

Other skeptics agree with McIlroy's assertion that drug companies market mental illness as well as its treatment. In 1999, after GlaxoSmithKline received U.S. Food and Drug Administration (FDA) approval to market Paxil for social-anxiety disorder, the company engaged a public-relations firm, which created the slogan, "Imagine Being Allergic to People." The advertising campaign did not include the drug company name. Instead, it directed consumers to contact the Social Anxiety Disorder Coalition, a drug industry-funded group. In 2001, Paxil was approved for yet another anxiety disorder—generalized anxiety disorder (or excessive worrying)—and the drug company's public-relations firm promoted what was formerly considered a problematic personality trait as another disorder that could be effectively treated with Paxil. The campaigns were extremely successful; during the first quarter of 2002, Paxil sales in the United States rose by 25 percent.

Still, many mental health professionals favor direct-to-consumer advertising, crediting it with informing consumers that there is effective treatment for potentially debilitating mental disorders and helping them to overcome reluctance to seek needed treatment. Jacques Bradwejn, chief of psychiatry at the Royal Ottawa Hospital in Ottawa, Canada, believes that anxiety disorders remain underdiagnosed and claims he has never had a patient ask to be treated for an anxiety disorder who was not suffering from one.

IMPORTANT NAMES AND ADDRESSES

American Academy of Child and Adolescent Psychiatry
3615 Wisconsin Avenue NW
Washington, DC 20016-3007
(202) 966-7300
FAX: (202) 966-2891
Toll-free: (800) 272-3900
E-mail: info@alz.org
URL: http://www.aacap.org

American Academy of Psychoanalysis and Dynamic Psychiatry
One Regency Drive
P.O. Box 30
Bloomfield, CT 06002
FAX: (860) 286-0787
Toll-free: (888) 691-8281
E-mail: info@AASPA.org
URL: http://www.aapsa.org

American Association for Geriatric Psychiatry
7910 Woodmont Avenue, Suite 1050
Bethesda, MD 20814-3004
(301) 654-7850
FAX: (301) 654-4137
E-mail: main@aagponline.org
URL: http://www.aagpgpa.org

American Association for Marriage and Family Therapy
112 South Alfred Street
Alexandria, VA 22314-3061
(703) 838-9808
FAX: (703) 838-9805
E-mail: MemberService@aamft.org
URL: http://www.aamft.org

American Association of Pastoral Counselors
9504A Lee Highway
Fairfax, VA 22031-2303
(703) 385-6967
FAX: (703) 352-7725
E-mail: info@aapc.org
URL: http://www.aapc.org

American Association of Suicidology
4201 Connecticut Avenue NW, Suite 408
Washington, DC 20008
(202) 237-2280
FAX: (202) 237-2282
Toll-free: (800) SUI-CIDE
URL: http://www.suicidology.org

American Counseling Association
5999 Stevenson Avenue
Alexandria, VA 22304
FAX: (800) 473-2329
Toll-free: (800) 347-6647
URL: http://www.counseling.org

American Psychiatric Association
1000 Wilson Boulevard, Suite 1825
Arlington, VA 22209-3901
(703) 907-7300
Toll-free: (888) 35-PSYCH
E-mail: apa@psych.org
URL: http://www.psych.org

American Psychiatric Nurses Association
1555 Wilson Boulevard, Suite 515
Arlington, VA 22209
(703) 243-2443
FAX: (703) 243-3390
E-mail: inform@apna.org
URL: http://www.apna.org

American Psychological Association
750 First Street NE
Washington, DC 20002-4242
(202) 336-5500
Toll-free: (800) 374-2721
E-mail: public.affairs@apa.org
URL: http://www.apa.org

American Psychological Society
1010 Vermont Avenue NW, Suite 1100
Washington, DC 20002-4907
(202) 783-2077
FAX: (202) 783-2083
E-mail: aps@psychologicalscience.org
URL: http://www.psychologicalscience.org

Association for the Advancement of Behavior Therapy
305 7th Avenue, 16th Floor
New York, NY 10001
(212) 647-1890
FAX: (212) 647-1865
URL: http://www.aabt.org

Association for the Advancement of Gestalt Therapy
37 Brunswick Road
Montclair, NJ 07042
(973) 783-0740
FAX: (586) 314-2490
E-mail: bfeder@comcast.net
URL: http://www.aagt.org

Association for Humanistic Psychology
1516 Oak Street, #320A
Alameda, CA 94501-2947
(510) 769-6495
E-mail: ahpoffice@aol.com
URL: http://www.ahpweb.org

Autism Society of America
7910 Woodmont Avenue, Suite 300
Bethesda, MD 20814-3067
(301) 657-0881
Toll-free: (800) 3AUTISM
E-mail: info@autism-society.org
URL: http://www.autism-society.org

Center for Mental Health Services of the U.S. Department of Health and Human Services Substance Abuse and Mental Health Services Administration
P.O. Box 42557
Washington, DC 20015
FAX: (301) 984-8796
Toll-free: (800) 789-2647
URL: http://www.mentalhealth.samhsa.gov

Centers for Disease Control and Prevention
Public Inquiries/MASO, Mailstop F07
1600 Clifton Road

Atlanta, GA 30333
(404) 639-3534
Toll-free: (800) 311-3435
URL: http://www.cdc.gov

Institute for Mental Health Initiatives
2175 K Street NW, Suite 700
Washington, DC 20037
(202) 467-2285
FAX: (202) 467-2289
E-mail: info@imhi.org
URL: http://www.imhi.org

**International Society for Interpersonal
Psychotherapy (ISIPT)**
Manning Valley Medical Center
P.O. Box 480
Taree NSW 2430
Australia
FAX: 61 2 6552 0059
E-mail: reay@netspeed.com.au
URL: http://www.interpersonalpsychotherapy.
org

Mental Research Institute
555 Middlefield Road
Palo Alto, CA 94301
(650) 321-3055

FAX: (650) 321-3785
E-mail: mri@mri.org
URL: http://www.mri.org

National Association of School Psychologists
4340 East West Highway, Suite 402
Bethesda, MD 20814
(301) 657-0270
FAX: (301) 657-0275
E-mail: center@naspweb.org
URL: http://www.nasponline.org/index2.html

National Association of Social Workers
750 First Street NE, Suite 700
Washington, DC 20002-4241
(202) 336-8228
E-mail: media@naswdc.org
URL: http://www.naswdc.org

**National Center for Health
Workforce Analysis**
5600 Fishers Lane, Room 8-47
Rockville, MD 20857
(301) 443-6921
FAX: (301) 443-8003
Toll-free: (800) 400-0816
URL: http://bhpr.hrsa.gov/healthworkforce/

**National Institute of Mental Health
(NIMH)**
6001 Executive Boulevard, Room 8184,
MSC 9663
Bethesda, MD 20892-9663
(301) 443-4513
FAX: (301) 443-4279
Toll-free: (866) 615-6464
E-mail: nimhinfo@nih.org
URL: http://www.nimh.nih.gov/

National Mental Health Association
2001 N. Beauregard Street, 12th Floor
Alexandria, VA 22311
(703) 684-7722
FAX: (703) 684-5968
Toll-free: (800) 969-6642
URL: http://www.nmha.org

World Health Organization
Avenue Appia 20
1211 Geneva 27
Switzerland
(+41 22) 791-2111
FAX: (+41 22) 791-3111
E-mail: inf@who.int
URL: http://www.who.int

RESOURCES

There are many published accounts of the history of mental illness and the practitioners who shaped modern thinking about its causes and treatment. Some of the most vivid descriptions, however, were written by the researchers and mental patients themselves. Yale University graduate Clifford W. Beers (1876–1943) recounted the cruelty and atrocities he witnessed and endured as an institutionalized mental patient in *A Mind That Found Itself: An Autobiography,* 5th edition (Pittsburgh: University of Pittsburgh Press, 1981). Benjamin Rush, a physician who helped to establish medicine and psychiatry as important ways of caring for people in the Colonies, published the first American textbook of psychiatry, *Medical Inquiries and Observations Upon Diseases of the Mind,* in 1812. Philip Bean and Patricia Mounser recounted the plight of deinstitutionalized mental patients in *Discharged from Mental Hospitals* (Palgrave MacMillan, United Kingdom, 1992).

The World Health Organization (WHO) issues periodic reports describing the incidence and prevalence of mental illness throughout the world and tracks the efforts of member nations to prevent mental illness and promote mental health. The WHO definitions of mental health and illness are cited in this text. In collaboration with the World Bank, the WHO examines the costs of mental illness and the global burden of mental disorders.

Mental health and illness in the United States were detailed in the landmark report by the U.S. Surgeon General, *Mental Health: A Report of the Surgeon General, 1999,* and follow-up reports including *Mental Health: Culture, Race and Ethnicity: A Supplement to Mental Health: A Report of the Surgeon General* (U.S. Department of Health and Human Services, Rockville, MD, 2001) and the *Report of the Surgeon General's Conference on Children's Mental Health: A National Action Agenda* (Department of Health and Human Services, Department of Justice, and Department of Education, Washington, DC, 2001). Issued in 2003, *Achieving the Promise: Transforming Mental Health Care in America,* a report from the President's New Freedom Commission on Mental Health, recommended ways to improve access to effective mental health treatment for Americans.

The Centers for Disease Control and Prevention (CDC) in Atlanta, Georgia, tracks mental health nationwide. The National Center for Health Statistics (NCHS) provides a complete statistical overview of the nation's health in its annual *Health, United States.* Data about mental illness are collected and reported by the National Institute of Mental Health Epidemiologic Catchment Area Program (ECA) and the National Comorbidity Survey (NCS). Data from the National Hospital Discharge Survey and National Ambulatory Medical Care Survey provide estimates of hospital and outpatient utilization. The National Health Interview Surveys offer information about the lifestyles, health behaviors, and health risks of Americans. Working with other agencies and professional organizations, the CDC produced *Healthy People 2010,* the source document that serves as a blueprint for improving the health status, including mental health, of Americans.

The Center for Mental Health Services (CMHS) is the agency within the Substance Abuse and Mental Health Services Administration (SAMHSA) of the U.S. Department of Health and Human Services (DHHS) that gathers national mental health statistics. CMHS uses these statistics to project the mental health economy. CMHS prepares a report, *Mental Health: United States,* every two years that considers psychiatric epidemiology, the status of mental health service delivery, and mental health policy. Other sources of information about mental health spending include the U.S. General Accounting Office (GAO) and the CDC, which tracks mental health service utilization. Data from *Mental Health Community-Based Care Increases for People with Serious Mental Illness* (U.S. General Accounting Office, Washington, DC, December 2000) are referenced in this text. The U.S. Department of Labor's Bureau of Labor Statistics and U.S. Bureau of Health Professions describe the roles, responsibilities, compensation, and projected need for mental health professionals.

The National Institute of Mental Health (NIMH) publishes data and periodic studies on a range of mental health issues. NIMH is part of the National Institutes of Health (NIH), the federal government's primary agency for biomedical and behavioral research. The NIMH describes mental disorders and problems in an online publication called *Science on Our Minds* and recommends modifications to existing mental health services and policy in publications such as *Blueprint for Change: Research on Child and Adolescent Mental Health* (National Advisory Mental Health Council Workgroup on Child and Adolescent Mental Health Intervention Development and Deployment, National Institute of Mental Health, Washington, DC, 2001). The U.S. Food and Drug Administration (FDA) publishes research about prescription drugs, including those approved to treat mental disorders.

The authoritative encyclopedia of diagnostic criteria for mental disorders is the fourth edition of the *Diagnostic and Statistical Manual (DSM)* (Arlington, VA: American Psychiatric Publishing, 2000). Recommendations and descriptions of interventions deemed effective at preventing suicide are described in *Reducing Suicide: A National Imperative (2002)* (Committee on Pathophysiology and Prevention of Adolescent and Adult Suicide Board of Neuroscience and Behavioral Health, Institute of Medicine (IOM), National Academies Press, Washington, DC, 2002).

Medical, public health, psychology, social work, and consumer journals and publications offer a wealth of disorder-specific information and research findings. The studies cited in this edition are drawn from a range of professional publications, including the *Annals of Internal Medicine, Archives of General Psychiatry, Archives of Pediatrics & Adolescent Medicine, British Journal of Psychiatry, Clinical Child and Family Psychology Review, Consumer Reports, Drug Benefit Trends, European Psychologist, Hospitals & Health Networks, Journal of Consulting and Clinical Psychology, Journal of Personality and Social Psychology, Journal of the American Medical Association, Journal of General Internal Medicine, Los Angeles Times, Mental Health Services Research, Molecular Psychiatry, New England Journal of Medicine, Prevention and Treatment, The Journal of Family Practice, Professional Psychology: Research and Practice, Psychological Assessment, Science, The American Journal of Psychiatry*, and *The Lancet.*

The Gallup Organization provides survey and poll data as well as insights and information from the *Gallup Management Journal* and *Gallup Poll Tuesday Briefing* about Americans' self-reported mental health. Harris Interactive gives data about stressors in Americans' lives. In addition, there are many professional associations, voluntary mental health and social service organizations, and charitable foundations dedicated to research, education, and advocacy about specific mental disorders that provided timely information included in this edition.

INDEX

Electroconvulsive shock therapy (ECT), 41, 45–46
Electroencephalogram (EEG) technology, 58
Elementary school counselors, 118
Emergency departments (EDs), 80
Emotions, 50
Employee assistance programs (EAPs), 143
Employee Retirement Income Security Act of 1974, 94
Employees
    employee opinion poll eligibility for mental health benefits, 1999, 96 (t6.5)
    employee opinion poll on access to mental health services, 1999, 96 (t6.4)
    mental health parity legislation and, 95–96
    work and unhappiness, 155
Employers
    compliant employer plans reporting more restrictive limits on mental health benefits than medical and surgical benefits, 1999, 96 (t6.3)
    costs of parity, 95
    effects of federal mental health parity legislation on, 95–96
    employee opinion poll eligibility for mental health benefits, 1999, 96 (t6.5)
    employee opinion poll on access to mental health services, 1999, 96 (t6.4)
    Mental Health Parity Act of 1996 and, 94
    mental health promotion in workplace, 143–144
Employment counselors, 118
Encouragement of affect, 47
Environmental factors
    influence on behavior, 21
    mental illness in children, 54, 55
Epidemiologic Catchment Area Program (ECA), 18, 18t, 19
Epilepsy, 42
Equal Protection Clause, 103–104
Erickson, Erik, 9, 9f
Ether, 42
Ethnicity. See Race/ethnicity
Exercise
    happiness and, 151–152
    happiness levels among adults, by frequency of exercise and church attendance, 2002, 153 (f10.8)
Expenditures, mental health. See Mental health spending

F

Facilities. See Mental health facilities
Family
    early childhood intervention prevention programs, 137–139, 138t, 139t
    health/wellness and, 155–156
    satisfaction with mental health treatment, 85
    treatment of children with mental disorders, 64
Family preservation services, 64
Family systems theory, 48–49
Family therapy, 48–49
Farmer, Elizabeth, 64
Farmer, Frances, 41

Federal Community Mental Health Centers Act of 1963, 122
Federal government
    mental health court program funds, 106
    sources of mental health funding, 89–90
Federal judicial decisions, 99–106
Federal mental health parity legislation, 108
Financial barriers to mental health treatment access, 79–80
5-HTT gene, 27–28
"Focusing on the Mind: Interest Rises in Non-Drug Therapies for Attention Deficit in Children" (Carey), 58
Ford, Alvin Bernard, 102
Ford v. Wainwright, 102
Foreman, Milos, 41
Foster Care Independent Act, 107
Foucha, Terry, 102–103
Foucha v. Louisiana, 102–103
Fourteenth Amendment
    mental health court cases and, 103–105
    mental health law and, 99–100, 101
Frank, Richard, 95
Frankl, Viktor, 9–10, 10 (f1.6)
Fratiglioni, Laura, 155
Free association, 8
Freeman, Walter, 40–41
Freud, Anna
    contributions of, 8–9
    photograph of, 8f
Freud, Sigmund
    character traits and personality, 7
    cocaine and, 42
    detractors, 9
    enduring contributions of, 8–9
    Freudian psychoanalysis, 46
    photograph of, 5f
    psychosexual stages of development, 6–7
    theories of, 5–6
    treatment and, 7–8
Freudian psychoanalysis, 46
Freudian slips, 8
Fromm, Erich, 10, 11 (f1.7)
Funding
    for mental health court program, 106
    mental health funding sources, 89–90
    percent of total mental health expenditures by funding source, 1987 and 1997, 91 (f6.6)

G

GAO (U.S. General Accounting Office), 95–96
GAD. See Generalized anxiety disorder
Gallup Management Journal, 155
Gallup Organization polls
    Americans' happiness, 151, 153–155
    American's mental health, 149
    mental health, 148, 158
"Gallup Study Finds That Misery at Work Is Likely to Cause Unhappiness at Home" (Gallup Management Journal), 155
Garb, Howard
    on computerized diagnostic tests, 25
    evaluation of projective tests, 24
Gardener, William, 63–64
Garland, Ann, 85

Gender
    survey respondents' assessment of their mental and physical health, by gender, November 8–11, 2001, 152 (f10.5)
    treatment of mental illness in children and, 63–64
"Gene for Panic Attacks Found" (BBC News Online), 20
"Gene for Suicide Discovered" (BBC News Online), 20
General hospitals, 121
General medical/primary-care sector, 113–114
Generalized anxiety disorder (GAD)
    Paxil for, 159
    symptoms of, 29
    treatment for, 52
Genes
    anxiety and, 30
    genetic origins of mental disorders, 20–22
    suicide and, 38
Genetic epistemology, 12
Genetics
    ADHD and, 59
    conduct disorder and, 61
    depression and, 27–28
    eating disorders and, 33
    obsessive-compulsive disorder and, 32, 60
    origins of mental disorders, 20–22
    panic disorder/phobias and, 31
    Rett's disorder and, 57
    schizophrenia and, 34
Genital stage, 7
Geriatric psychiatrists, 115
Gestalt therapy, 50
Girls
    depression and, 59
    oppositional defiant disorder and, 60
    treatment of mental illness in, 63–64
Glass, Thomas A., 156
GlaxoSmithKline, 159
Glucksberg, Harold, 104–105
Glucksberg, Washington v., 104–105
Goldman, Howard, 95
Goodman, John C., 96–97
Goodwin, Frederick, 45
Greeks, 1
Greenberg, Mark, 136
Griesinger, Wilhelm, 4
Grob, Gerald, 120
Group therapy
    for bulimics, 51
    described, 49–50
    environment for, 59f
GRp genetic variant, 31

H

Halderman, Pennhurst State School and Hospital v., 101
Halderman, Terri Lee, 101
Hallucinogens, 42
Halperin, Abigail, 104–105
Happiness
    access/quality of health care reported by survey respondents, according to

Jung, Carl
    collective unconscious, 11
    Jungian Psychoanalysis, 46
    photograph of, 12 (f1.9)
Jungian Psychoanalysis, 46

K

Kanner, Leo, 56
Kansas Sexually Violent Predator Act, 104
Kansas v. Hendricks, 104
Kataoka, Sheryl, 77
Keel, P.K., 51
Kennedy, John F., 106, 136
Kennedy, Joseph, 41
Kennedy, Rosemary, 41
Kentucky, 103–104
Kesey, Ken, 41
Kessler Psychological Distress Scale, 148
"Key Elements of the National Statistical
    Picture" (Lutterman and Hogan), 90–91
Kirkbride Plan, 4
Kirkbride, Thomas Story, 4
Knapp, Samuel, 157
Knowledge, 12

L

The Lancet, 155
Language, 77
Latent stage, 7
Law, mental health
    federal judicial decisions, 99–106
    issues, 99
    presence of mental health
        policies/legislation and percent of
        member states in World Health
        Organization regions, 2000, 100f
Learning disorder
    children with, 149
    frequencies and percents (with standard
        errors) of ever having a learning
        disability or ADD, for children 3-17
        years of age, by selected characteristics,
        1998, 150t–151t
Legislation and international treaties
    ADAMHA Reorganization Act, 107
    Alcohol Abuse Amendments of 1983,
        107
    Americans with Disabilities Act, 107
    America's Law Enforcement and Mental
        Health Project Act, 106, 107
    Antiterrorism and Effective Death
        Penalty Act of 1996, 104
    Children's Health Act of 2000, 107
    Community Mental Health Centers Act
        of 1963, 120
    Community Mental Health Services Act,
        120
    Developmentally Disabled Assistance
        and Bill of Rights Act of 1975, 101
    Drug Abuse Office and Treatment Act,
        1972, 107
    Employee Retirement Income Security
        Act of 1974, 94
    Federal Community Mental Health
        Centers Act of 1963, 122
    federal mental health parity legislation,
        108

Foster Care Independent Act, 107
    Insanity Defense Reform Act of 1984,
        100, 104
    Kansas Sexually Violent Predator Act,
        104
    Mental Health Equitable Treatment Act,
        108
    mental health legislation, 106–109
    Mental Health Parity Act of 1996, 83, 94
    Mental Health Parity Act of 1996, effects
        on employers, 95–96, 96t
    Mental Health Parity Act of 1996,
        requirements of, 108
    mental health parity legislation,
        arguments against, 96–97
    Mental Health Study Act, 1955, 106
    Mental Retardation Facilities and
        Community Mental Health Centers
        Construction Act of 1963, 106
    National Mental Health Act, 106
    Omnibus Budget Reconciliation Act, 106
    Omnibus Mental Illness Recovery Act,
        108–109
    Public Health Service Act, 94
    state mental health legislative initiatives,
        108–109
    Ticket to Work and Work Incentives
        Improvement Act of 1999, 107
Leopoldo I, Grand Duke, 3
Licensure, 116, 118
Lindh, Aaron, 104
Lindh v. Murphy, Warden, 104
Lithium, 45
Lobotomy, 40–41
Local government, 90
Logotherapy, 9
"Long-Term Outcome of Bulimia Nervosa"
    (Keel et al.), 51
"Looking Ahead and Reflecting Upon the
    Past" (Grob), 120
Los Angeles Times, 58–59
Louisiana, Foucha v., 102–103
LSD (lysergic acid diethylamide), 42
Lunatics
    in colonial America, 2
    treatment of, 39
Lutterman, Ted, 90–91
Lynaugh, Penry v., 102
Lysergic acid diethylamide (LSD), 42

M

The MacArthur Coercion Study (John D. and
    Catherine T. MacArthur Foundation), 84
Major depression
    described, 26–27
    suicide and, 37–38
Major depressive disorder, 59
Managed care organizations (MCOs)
    deinstitutionalization movement and, 121
    mental health spending and, 88–89
    SMHA expenditures and, 90–91
Managed care plans, 94, 95
Manderscheid, Ronald W., 122–123
Mania
    in children/adolescents, 59
    defined, 3
    symptoms of, 26 (t2.5)

MAO (monoamine oxidase), 44–45
MAOIs (monoamine oxidase inhibitors), 44
Marijuana, 22
Marottoli, Richard A., 156
Marriage, health and, 155
Marriage therapy
    counselors, 119
    described, 48
Maslow, Abraham
    hierarchy of needs, 11–12, 13 (f1.11)
    photograph of, 12 (f1.10)
MASS (Multidimensional Adolescent
    Satisfaction Scale), 85
Massey, Leonard, 139
Mather, Cotton, 2
May, Rollo, 12
McGuire, Thomas, 95
McIlroy, Anne, 159
MCOs. *See* Managed care organizations
Mechanic, David
    mental health, 109
    parity and, 95
    views of mental illness, 121
MECP2 gene, 57
Media, 144
Medicaid
    mental health funding from, 89–90
    mental health services and, 106–107
    SMHA expenditures and, 90–91
*Medical Inquiries and Observations Upon
    Diseases of the Mind* (Rush), 4
Medical record, privacy, 83
Medicare
    mental health funding from, 89, 90
    mental health services and, 106–107
    SMHA expenditures and, 90
Medina, Teofilo, 103
Medina v. California, 103
Melancholia, 3
Mellaril, 103
Men
    eating disorders and, 32–33
    happiness of, 151
    mental health service utilization, 68, 69
    psychological distress of, 148, 148
        (f10.2)
    suicide and, 35
    survey respondents' assessment of their
        mental and physical health, by gender,
        November 8-11, 2001, 152 (f10.5)
Mendes de Leon, Carlos, 156
Mental disorders
    checklist, 1998, 23t
    definition of, 14–15
    diagnostic classes of, 1999, 19t
    genetic origins of, 20–22, 22f
    number of Americans with, 18–19
    prevalence of mental/addictive disorders
        for children, 53–54, 53f, 53t, 54f
    prevalence rates of anxiety/mood
        disorders based on ECA and NCS, ages
        18–54, best-estimate one-year, 1999,
        18t
    psychopathology, 54–55
    treatment for, 51–52
Mental disorders in children
    anxiety disorders, 59–60

presence of mental health
policies/legislation and percent of
member states in World Health
Organization regions, 2000, 100*f*
U.S. initiative to improve mental health
care, 110–111
*"Mental Health Policy at the Millennium:
Challenges and Opportunities, Mental
Health United States, 2000, Chapter 7*
(Mechanic), 95
Mental health prevention and promotion
Columbia University teen mental health
screening program, 140 (*t*9.3)
defining, 135–136
Head Start program statistics, fiscal year
2002, 138*t*
mental health promotion, 143–145, 144*t*
Nurse-Family Partnership program to
prevent mental health problems in
mothers and children, 139*t*
programs, 135–136
suicide prevention, 140–143
suicide rate of Air Force members,
1990–2002, 141*f*
suicide risk factors, protective factors,
and national prevention strategy, 140
(*t*9.4)
Mental health problems
defined, 14
diagnosis of, 17
do not always require mental health
treatment, 85–86
Mental health professionals
clinical social workers, 117–118
counseling specialties, employment
distribution among, 2000, 118*t*
counselors, 118–119
drug visits, drug mentions, and drug
mention rates per 100 visits with
corresponding standard errors, by
physician specialty, number and percent
distribution of, 2000, 132*t*
in general, 114
mean time spent with physician, with
corresponding standard errors, by
physician specialty, 2000, 133 (*t*8.21)
office visits with corresponding standard
errors, by patient's principal reason for
visit, number and percent distribution
of, 2000, 123 (*t*8.16)
office visits with corresponding standard
errors by physician specialty, according
to referral status and prior-visit status,
percent distribution of, 2000, 129*t*
office visits with corresponding standard
errors, by physician's diagnosis,
number and percent distribution of
2000, 123 (*t*8.17)
office visits with corresponding standard
errors, by therapeutic and preventive
services ordered or provided and
patient's sex, number and percent of,
2000, 131*t*
office visits with corresponding standard
errors, number, percent distribution,
and annual rate of, by selected

physician practice characteristics, 2000,
128*t*
psychiatric nurses, 116–117, 117*t*
psychiatrists, 114–115
psychologists, 115–116
psychologists, median annual earnings in
the industries employing the largest
numbers of, 2000, 116*t*
20 drugs most frequently prescribed at
office visits, with corresponding
standard errors, by entry name of drug,
number, percent distribution, and
therapeutic classification for, 2000, 133
(*t*8.20)
Mental health service delivery
changing systems, 120–121
drug visits, drug mentions, and drug
mention rates per 100 visits with
corresponding standard errors, by
physician specialty, number and percent
distribution of, 2000, 132*t*
mean time spent with physician, with
corresponding standard errors, by
physician specialty, 2000, 133 (*t*8.21)
national goals for, 127–128
office visits with corresponding standard
errors, by patient's principal reason for
visit, number and percent distribution
of, 2000, 123 (*t*8.16)
office visits with corresponding standard
errors by physician specialty, according
to referral status and prior-visit status,
percent distribution of, 2000, 129*t*
office visits with corresponding standard
errors, by physician's diagnosis,
number and percent distribution of
2000, 123 (*t*8.17)
office visits with corresponding standard
errors, by therapeutic and preventive
services ordered or provided and
patient's sex, number and percent of,
2000, 131*t*
office visits with corresponding standard
errors, number, percent distribution,
and annual rate of, by selected
physician practice characteristics, 2000,
128*t*
proportion of adult population using
mental/addictive disorder services in
one year, 113*t*
proportion of child/adolescent
populations using mental/addictive
disorder services in one year, ages 9-17,
114*t*
sectors of, 113–114
20 drugs most frequently prescribed at
office visits, with corresponding
standard errors, by entry name of drug,
number, percent distribution, and
therapeutic classification for, 2000, 133
(*t*8.20)
Mental health spending
adequacy of, 93
growth of, 88–89
mental health expenditures, 1997, 90*f*
mental health prescription drug spending,
1997, 89 (*f*6.4)

mental health/substance abuse (MH/SA)
expenditure growth rates, 1987–97, 89
(*f*6.3)
mental health/substance abuse (MH/SA)
expenditures and other major economic
expenditures, 1997, 88 (*f*6.2)
percent of total mental health
expenditures by funding source, 1987
and 1997, 91 (*f*6.6)
sources of mental health funding, 89–90
specialized health provider expenditures,
1997, 91 (*f*6.7)
state mental health agency expenditures,
90–93
state mental health agency per capita
expenditures for mental health services
and average annual percent change by
geographic division and state, selected
fiscal years 1981–97, 92*t*–93*t*
Mental Health Study Act, 1955, 106
Mental health/substance abuse (MH/SA)
expenditure growth rates, 1987–97, 89
(*f*6.3)
expenditures and other major economic
expenditures, 1997, 88 (*f*6.2)
mental health expenditures, 1997, 90*f*
Mental health treatment
advances favor community-based care,
121
antidepressant drugs, 44–46, 44*f*
antipsychotic agents, 42–43
anxiolytic agents, 46
Civil War and, 4
Clifford W. Beers, 40*f*
eating disorders, 51
history of, 39
not all people need treatment, 52
pharmacotherapies, selected types of, 41*t*
psychopharmacology, 41–42
psychotherapy, 46–51, 49*f*
Sigmund Freud's impact on, 7–8
too few seek /receive quality treatment,
51–52
treatment of depression, newer
pharmacotherapies, 45*t*
20th-century treatment of mental illness,
39–41
See also Mental health facilities;
Treatment
Mental health treatment, access to
African Americans use of mental health
services, 1994, 77*t*
barriers to access, 69–81
challenges of, 67
discharges and average length of stay in
non-federal short-stay hospitals,
according to sex, age, and selected first-
listed diagnoses, selected years
1990–2000, 74*t*–76*t*
goals for, 67–68, 68*t*
idioms of distress and culture-bound
syndrome, 76 (*t*5.6)
leading health indicators with 22
measures, 1990–2000 and projected
2010, 82*t*–83*t*
mental health organizations and beds for
24-hour hospital and residential

Mental Health   Index   173

organization, selected years 1986–98, 69t

mental health prescription drug spending, 1997, 89 (f6.4)

mental health/substance abuse expenditure growth rates, 1987–97, 89 (f6.3)

mental health/substance abuse expenditures and other major economic expenditures, 1997, 88 (f6.2)

number of days during the past month that survey respondents assessed their mental health or emotional well-being as not good, November 8-11, 2001, 152 (t10.4)

number of mental health organizations by type of organization, selected years, 1970–98, 122t

number of selected first-listed diagnoses for hospital discharges, 2000, 127 (f8.2)

number, percent distribution, and rate of 24-hour hospital and residential treatment beds, by type of mental health organization, selected years 1970–98, 124t

number, percent distribution, and rate of additions to less than 24-hour care services, by type of mental health organization, selected years 1969–98, 125t

number, percent distribution, and rate of patients in 24-hour hospital and residential treatment, by type of mental health organization, selected years, 1969–98, 126t

Nurse-Family Partnership program to prevent mental health problems in mothers and children, 139t

office visits with corresponding standard errors, by patient's principal reason for visit, number and percent distribution of, 2000, 123 (t8.16)

office visits with corresponding standard errors by physician specialty, according to referral status and prior-visit status, percent distribution of, 2000, 129t

office visits with corresponding standard errors, by physician's diagnosis, number and percent distribution of 2000, 123 (t8.17)

office visits with corresponding standard errors, by therapeutic and preventive services ordered or provided and patient's sex, number and percent of, 2000, 131t

office visits with corresponding standard errors, number, percent distribution, and annual rate of, by selected physician practice characteristics, 2000, 128t

perceived mentally unhealthy days of the past 30 reported by adults responding to the Behavioral Risk Factor Surveillance System telephone survey, 1993–2001, 147t

percent distribution of 24-hour hospital and residential treatment beds, by organization types, 1970–98, 123f

percent of adults aged 18 years and over who experienced serious psychological distress during the past 30 days, 1997–2003, 148 (f10.1)

percent of adults aged 18 years and over who experienced serious psychological distress during the past 30 days, by age group and sex, January-March 2003, 148 (f10.2)

percent of total mental health expenditures by funding source, 1987 and 1997, 91 (f6.6)

presence of mental health policies/legislation and percent of member states in World Health Organization regions, 2000, 100f

prevalence of mental/addictive disorders for children, annual, 1999, 53f

prevalence rates of anxiety/mood disorders based on ECA and NCS, ages 18–54, 1999, 18t

proportion of adult population using mental/addictive disorder services in one year, 113t

proportion of child/adolescent populations using mental/addictive disorder services in one year, ages 9-17, 114t

psychiatric nurses, annual income of, 2003, 117 (t8.5)

psychiatric nurses, level of care provided by, 2003, 117 (t8.4)

psychiatric nurses, primary roles for, 2003, 117 (t8.8)

psychiatric nurses, primary work setting for, 2003, 117 (t8.6)

psychiatric nursing, subspecialties of, 117 (t8.7)

psychologists, median annual earnings in the industries employing the largest numbers of, 2000, 116t

rates of discharges and days of care in non-federal short-stay hospitals, according to sex, age, and selected first-listed diagnoses, selected years 1990–2000, 71t–73t

self-defined mental health and emotional well-being, by age, 2003, 156f

specialized health provider expenditures, 1997, 91 (f6.7)

state mental health agency per capita expenditures for mental health services and average annual percent change by geographic division and state, selected fiscal years 1981–97, 92t–93t

suicide rate of Air Force members, 1990–2002, 141f

suicide rates by age, gender, racial group, 2000, 35 (f2.7)

survey respondents' assessment of their mental and physical health, by gender, November 8-11, 2001, 152 (f10.5)

survey respondents' assessment of their mental and physical health, November 8-11, 2001, 149 (f10.4)

survey respondents' assessment of their mental health, by age, November 8-11, 2001, 152 (f10.6)

survey respondents reporting fair or poor mental or emotional health, by income, November 2001, 154 (f10.10)

20 drugs most frequently prescribed at office visits, with corresponding standard errors, by entry name of drug, number, percent distribution, and therapeutic classification for, 2000, 133 (t8.20)

violent deaths worldwide, leading causes of, 2000, 35 (f2.6)

Sterilization, 100–101

Stigma, 79

Stranger in the Nest: Do Parents Really Shape Their Child's Personality, Intelligence, or Character? (Cohen), 22

Strelau, Jan, 21

Streptococcus, 60

Stress, 154

Stressors, 54–55

Strickland, Ted, 106

Sublimation, 6

Substance abuse
   MH/SA expenditure growth rates, 1987–97, 89 (f6.3)
   MH/SA expenditures and other major economic expenditures, 1997, 88 (f6.2)
   MH/SA mental health expenditures, 1997, 90f
   schizophrenia and, 34
   treatment legislation, 107
   twin studies on genetic influence on, 22, 22f
   worksite wellness program and, 143, 144t

Substance abuse and behavioral disorder counselors, 119

Substance Abuse and Mental Health Services Administration (SAMHSA)
   on mental health spending, 90
   on mental health treatment, 70–71
   SMHAs manage funds from, 91–92
   worksite health promotion definition by, 143

Suicide
   among terminally ill, 37
   biology of, 36–37
   deaths/death rates for ten leading causes of death in specified age groups, preliminary 2000, 36t–37t
   demographics, 34–35
   depression in children/adolescents and, 59
   genes and, 20
   Hispanic Americans and, 77
   mental health treatment access barriers, 70
   prevention programs, 137, 140–143
   rates by age, gender, racial group, 2000, 35 (f2.7)
   reasons for committing, 35, 36

risk during treatment, 45
risk factors, protective factors, and
national prevention strategy, 140(*t*9.4)
social anxiety and, 79
suicide rate of Air Force members,
1990–2002, 141*f*
violent deaths worldwide, leading causes
of, 2000, 35 (*f*2.6)
warning signs, 37
Washington v. Glucksberg, 104–105
"Suicide Risk in Bipolar Disorder During
Treatment with Lithium and Divalproex"
(Goodwin), 45
Superego, 5
Supportive listening, 47
Sydenham, Thomas, 2
System problems, 80–81
Systematic desensitization, 14
Szasz, Thomas
mental illness and treatment, 86
mental illness myths, 39

T

Taylor, Humphrey, 154
Tea, 42
Telephone hotlines, 142–143
Tennessee, 78
Terminally ill, 38
Tertiary prevention programs, 135
Texas, Powell v., 101
Therapeutic practices, 7–8
Therapist-patient privilege, 104
Therapy
for ADHD, 58–59
new approaches to, 121
Rogerian therapy, 13
See also Psychotherapy
Thinking, 47
Thorazine (chlorpromazine), 43
Ticket to Work and Work Incentives
Improvement Act of 1999, 107
Tobacco, 42
*Toward a Radical Middle: Fourteen Pieces
of Reporting and Criticism* (Adler), 1
Traits fixation, 7
Transference, 8
Treatment
ADHD, 58–59
children with mental illness, 53–54, 54*f*,
61–65
community-based care, 121
conduct disorder, 61
efficacy of psychotropic drugs in
children, 1999, 63*t*
medications chart for children with
mental disorders, 2000, 62*t*
mental health prevention, 136
mental illness in 17th century, 2
mental illness in 18th century, 3–7
OCD in children/adolescents, 60
pervasive developmental disorders, 56,
57
See also Mental health treatment
Trepanation, 2
Tricyclic antidepressants, 45

Truman, Harry, 106
Tuke, William, 3
Twins
ADHD and, 59
drug use, abuse, and dependence among
female twin pairs, 1999, 22*f*
eating disorders and, 33
genetic origins of mental disorders and,
21
obsessive-compulsive disorder and, 60
studies on substance abuse, 22

U

The Unabridged Journals of Sylvia Plath
(Plath), 17
Unconscious
Freud's theory about, 5
modern view of, 9
Unemployment, 69–70
Unhappiness, 155
United Nations General Assembly, 109–110
United States, initiative to improve mental
health care, 110–111
United States, Shannon v., 104
Universal programs, 137
Universal, selective, and indicated (USI)
prevention model, 137
University of Wisconsin—Madison, 27–28
"Unmet Need for Mental Health Care
Among U.S. Children: Variation by
Ethnicity and Insurance Status"
(Kataoka), 77
U.S. Air Force, Suicide Prevention Program,
141–142, 141*f*
U.S. Congress, 106
U.S. Department of Health and Human
Services (DHHS)
on mental health organizations, 121–122
privacy regulations, 83
U.S. General Accounting Office (GAO),
95–96
U.S. National Health Interview Survey
(NHISS)
adults with psychological distress, 148*f*
children's mental health, 148–149,
150*t*–151*t*
mental health information and, 147
U.S. Senate Committee on Finance, 90
U.S. Supreme Court
decisions concerning mental health,
100–106
on involuntary commitment, 84
USI (universal, selective, and indicated)
prevention model, 137

V

VA hospitals, 121
VandeCreek, Leon, 157
Veteran's Health Administration (VHA)
Center for Health Promotion and Disease
Prevention Web site, 144–145
Violent deaths
leading causes of violent deaths
worldwide, 2000, 35 (*f*2.6)
from suicide, 34

Vocational counselors, 118
Voluntary support network sector, 114

W

Wainwright, Ford v., 102
Wang, Philip, 51–52
Washington v. Glucksberg, 104–105
Web sites, online mental health promotion,
144–145
Weissberg, Roger, 136
Wellbutrin, 44
Wellstone, Paul, 106
West Nile virus, 55
White Americans, psychological distress of,
148, 149 (*f*10.3)
Whitley, Sawyer v., 103
WHO. *See* World Health Organization
"Will Parity Coverage Result in Better
Mental Health Care?" (Frank, Goldman
and McGuire), 95
Wilson, Edward O., 20
Witchcraft, 2
"womb envy," 11
Women
eating disorders and, 32, 33
happiness of, 151
mental health service utilization, 68
psychological distress of, 148, 148
(*f*10.2)
suicide and, 35
survey respondents' assessment of their
mental and physical health, by gender,
November 8-11, 2001, 152 (*f*10.5)
Work, 155–156
Workgroup on Child and Adolescent Mental
Health Intervention Development and
Deployment, 54
Workplace, mental health promotion in,
143–144, 144*t*
World Bank, 87
World Health Organization (WHO)
definition of health, 135
mental and behavioral disorders,
categories of, 1998, 17*t*
mental health costs, 87
mental health legislation, 99, 100*f*
mental health policy and, 109
prevalence of mental illness in children
projection, 54
study on mental disorder, 17–18
Worldwide initiative to improve mental
health care, 109–110

Y

Yale University Departments of Psychiatry
and Public Health, 93
York Retreat, 3
Youngberg v. Romeo, 101
Youth Drug and Mental Health Services Act,
107

Z

Zoloft, 126
Zubenko, George, 28